AUDIT GUIDE

Government Auditing Standards and Single Audits

FEBRUARY 1, 2015

Copyright © 2015 by
American Institute of Certified Public Accountants, Inc.
New York, NY 10036-8775

All rights reserved. For information about the procedure for requesting permission to make copies of any part of this work, please e-mail copyright@aicpa.org with your request. Otherwise, requests should be written and mailed to the Permissions Department, AICPA, 220 Leigh Farm Road, Durham, NC 27707-8110.

1 2 3 4 5 6 7 8 9 0 AAP 1 9 8 7 6 5

ˉBN 978-1-94165-197-1

Preface

(Updated as of February 1, 2015)

About AICPA Audit Guides

This AICPA Audit Guide presents guidance for the audits of financial statements conducted in accordance with *Government Auditing Standards, December 2011 Revision* (also referred to as the Yellow Book), issued by the Comptroller General of the United States of the U.S. Government Accountability Office. It also presents the recommendations of the AICPA Single Audit Working Group for the conduct of audits in accordance with the Single Audit Act and Office of Management and Budget (OMB) Circular A-133, *Audits of States, Local Governments, and Non-Profit Organizations* (Circular A-133). This edition of the guide has been updated to include guidance regarding performing a compliance audit under the audit requirements of Title 2 U.S. *Code of Federal Regulations* (CFR) Part 200, *Uniform Administrative Requirements, Cost Principles, and Audit Requirements for Federal Awards* (Uniform Guidance).

Auditing guidance included in an AICPA Audit Guide is recognized as an interpretive publication pursuant to AU-C section 200, *Overall Objectives of the Independent Auditor and the Conduct of an Audit in Accordance With Generally Accepted Auditing Standards* (AICPA, *Professional Standards*). Interpretive publications are recommendations on the application of generally accepted auditing standards (GAAS) in specific circumstances, including engagements for entities in specialized industries. An interpretive publication is issued under the authority of the AICPA Auditing Standards Board (ASB) after all ASB members have been provided an opportunity to consider and comment on whether the proposed interpretive publication is consistent with GAAS. The members of the ASB have found the auditing guidance in this guide to be consistent with existing GAAS.

Although interpretive publications are not auditing standards, AU-C section 200 requires the auditor to consider applicable interpretive publications in planning and performing the audit because interpretive publications are relevant to the proper application of GAAS in specific circumstances. If the auditor does not apply the auditing guidance in an applicable interpretive publication, the auditor should document how the requirements of GAAS were complied with in the circumstances addressed by such auditing guidance.

The ASB is the designated senior committee of the AICPA authorized to speak for the AICPA on all matters related to auditing. Conforming changes made to the auditing guidance contained in this guide are approved by the ASB chair (or his or her designee) and the Director of the AICPA Audit and Attest Standards staff. Updates made to the auditing guidance in this guide that exceed that of conforming changes are issued after all ASB members have been provided an opportunity to consider and comment on whether the guide is consistent with the Statements on Auditing Standards (SASs).

An appendix to a guide or a guide chapter has no authoritative status. However, any auditing guidance in an appendix is considered other auditing guidance. In applying other auditing guidance, the auditor should, exercising professional judgment, assess the relevance and appropriateness of such guidance to the circumstances of the audit. Although the auditor determines the relevance of other auditing guidance, auditing guidance in an appendix to a guide or a guide chapter has been reviewed by the AICPA Audit and Attest Standards staff and the auditor may presume that it is appropriate.

Attestation guidance included in an AICPA Audit Guide is recognized as an attestation interpretation as defined in AT section 50, *SSAE Hierarchy* (AICPA, *Professional Standards*). Attestation interpretations are recommendations on the application of the Statements on Standards for Attestation Engagements (SSAEs) in specific circumstances, including engagements for entities in specialized industries. Attestation interpretations are issued under the authority of the ASB. The members of the ASB have found the attestation guidance in this guide to be consistent with existing SSAEs.

A practitioner should be aware of and consider attestation interpretations applicable to his or her attestation engagement. If the practitioner does not apply the guidance included in an applicable AICPA Audit Guide, the practitioner should be prepared to explain how he or she complied with the SSAE provisions addressed by such attestation guidance.

The ASB is the designated senior committee of the AICPA authorized to speak for the AICPA on all matters related to attestation. Conforming changes made to the attestation guidance contained in this guide are approved by the ASB chair (or his or her designee) and the Director of the AICPA Audit and Attest Standards staff. Updates made to the attestation guidance in this guide that exceed that of conforming changes are issued after all ASB members have been provided an opportunity to consider and comment on whether the guide is consistent with the SSAEs.

Purpose and Applicability

This guide provides guidance (chapters 1–4) on the auditor's responsibilities when conducting an audit of financial statements in accordance with *Government Auditing Standards*. This guide has been prepared using the *Government Auditing Standards, December 2011 Revision*.

Financial statement audits of state and local governments are often required to be performed in accordance with *Government Auditing Standards* because they are subject to Circular A-133 or the Uniform Guidance, or because state and local laws and regulations require it. Because an audit of a government's financial statements under the provisions of AICPA Audit and Accounting Guide *State and Local Governments* is based on opinion units, the auditor's consideration of items, such as materiality and internal control over financial reporting in planning, performing, evaluating the results of, and reporting on the audit of a government's basic financial statements, should address each opinion unit. This guide does not provide specific guidance related to auditing state and local governmental entities in accordance with GAAS; however, the concept of opinion units should be considered when applying the guidance in chapters 1–4 of this guide to the financial statement audit of an entity subject to the provisions of Audit and Accounting Guide *State and Local Governments*. See that guide for information on performing a GAAS audit of a governmental entity.

Concerning an audit of financial statements in accordance with *Government Auditing Standards*, this guide

- describes the applicability of *Government Auditing Standards*.

- discusses the relationship between GAAS and *Government Auditing Standards*.
- discusses the standards and guidance found in chapters 1–4 of *Government Auditing Standards*, with an emphasis on the standards for financial audits.
- describes the auditor's responsibility for considering internal control over financial reporting, compliance with applicable laws, regulations, and provisions of contracts and grants agreements, fraud, and abuse.
- describes the auditor's responsibility for reporting and other communications and provides examples of the required auditor's reports.

It also provides guidance (chapters 1 and 5–14) on the auditor's responsibilities when conducting a single audit or program-specific audit in accordance with the Single Audit Act and Circular A-133. This guide was originally issued as Statement of Position (SOP) 98-3, *Audits of States, Local Governments, and Not-for-Profit Organizations Receiving Federal Awards*, in March 1998 and updated annually for conforming changes for relevant guidance contained in authoritative auditing standards and other requirements. The AICPA converted SOP 98-3 into an audit guide in 2003. That conversion did not supersede the guidance that appeared in SOP 98-3 but only changed its format.

It also provides guidance (chapters 1 and 15–24) on the auditor's responsibilities when conducting a single audit or program-specific audit in accordance with the Single Audit Act and the Uniform Guidance for federal awards.

Concerning an audit of federal awards in accordance with either Circular A-133 or the Uniform Guidance,[1] this guide

- describes the applicability of and provides an overview of the requirements of the Single Audit Act and Circular A-133 and the Single Audit Act and the Uniform Guidance.
- discusses the relationship between *Government Auditing Standards* and Circular A-133 and, in addition, *Government Auditing Standards* and the Uniform Guidance.
- describes the auditor's additional responsibilities for considering internal control over compliance with applicable laws, regulations, and program compliance requirements; performing tests of compliance with those requirements; and performing procedures on the schedule of expenditures of federal awards.
- discusses considerations in designing an audit approach that includes audit sampling to achieve both compliance and internal

---

[1] In this guide, the use of the phrases *single audit* or *audit in accordance with Circular A-133* includes both the financial statement audit and the compliance audit that is performed under Office of Management and Budget Circular A-133, *Audits of States, Local Governments, and Non-Profit Organizations*. The use of the term *Circular A-133 compliance audit* includes only the compliance audit that is performed under Circular A-133. In addition, in part III, *Uniform Guidance Audits*, of this guide, the use of the phrases *single audit* or *audit in accordance with the Uniform Guidance* includes both the financial statement audit and the compliance audit that is performed under Title 2 U.S. *Code of Federal Regulations* (CFR) Part 200, *Uniform Administrative Requirements, Cost Principles, and Audit Requirements for Federal Awards* (Uniform Guidance). The use of the term *Uniform Guidance compliance audit* includes only the compliance audit that is performed under the Uniform Guidance audit requirements.

control over compliance related audit objectives in a compliance audit performed under Circular A-133 or the Uniform Guidance.
- describes the auditor's responsibilities in a program-specific audit.
- describes the auditor's responsibility for reporting and provides examples of the required auditor's reports.
- provides guidance on applying GAAS in a Circular A-133 or Uniform Guidance compliance audit and adapts that guidance, as appropriate, to the objectives of that compliance audit.[2]

Recognition

2015 Guide Edition
AICPA Senior Committee
Auditing Standards Board

Gerry Boaz, *Member*
Bruce P. Webb, *Chair*

The AICPA gratefully acknowledges those members of the AICPA Governmental Audit Quality Center (GAQC) Executive Committee, who reviewed or otherwise contributed to the development of this edition of the guide: Heather Acker, Erica Forhan, Michael Fritz, Amanda Nelson, and the chair of the executive committee, Brian Schebler. In addition, the AICPA gratefully acknowledges others who have contributed to the development of this edition: Ralph DeAcetis, John Good, Terry Ramsey, and George A. Rippey.

AICPA Staff

Susan Reed
Technical Manager
Accounting and Auditing—Member Learning and Competency

Teresa Bordeaux
Technical Manager
Governmental Auditing and Accounting

Guidance Considered in This Edition

This edition of the guide has been modified by AICPA staff to include certain changes necessary due to the issuance of authoritative guidance since the guide was originally issued and other revisions as deemed appropriate. Authoritative

---

[2] AU-C section 935, *Compliance Audits* (AICPA, *Professional Standards*), states that when performing a compliance audit, the auditor, using professional judgment, should adapt and apply the AU-C sections to the objectives of a compliance audit, except for the AU-C sections listed in the appendix, "AU-C Sections That Are Not Applicable to Compliance Audits," of AU-C section 935. This appendix notes that the AU-C sections identified as not applicable to a compliance audit are identified as such either because (*a*) they are not relevant to a compliance audit environment, (*b*) the procedures and guidance would not contribute to meeting the objectives of a compliance audit, or (*c*) the subject matter is specifically covered in paragraph .12 of AU-C section 935. Part II, *Circular A-133 Audits*, of this audit guide includes the appropriate AU-C sections as adapted for a Circular A-133 compliance audit. Part III of this audit guide includes the appropriate AU-C sections as adapted for a Uniform Guidance compliance audit.

guidance issued through February 1, 2015, has been considered in the development of this edition of the guide. However, this guide does not include all audit, reporting, and other requirements applicable to an entity or a particular engagement. This guide is intended to be used in conjunction with all applicable sources of authoritative guidance.

Authoritative guidance that is issued and effective for entities with fiscal years ending on or before February 1, 2015, is incorporated directly in the text of this guide.

This guide includes relevant guidance issued up to and including the following:

- SAS No. 128, *Using the Work of Internal Auditors* (AICPA, *Professional Standards*, AU-C sec. 610)
- Interpretations issued (or reissued) through February 1, 2015
- The Single Audit Act Amendments of 1996[3]
- OMB Circular A-133, as revised on June 26, 2007
- OMB *Uniform Administrative Requirements, Cost Principles, and Audit Requirements for Federal Awards*, as issued on December 26, 2013[4]
- *Government Auditing Standards, December 2011 Revision*

Users of this guide should consider guidance issued subsequent to those items listed previously to determine their effect on entities covered by this guide. In determining the applicability of recently issued guidance, its effective date should also be considered.

The changes made to this edition of the guide are identified in the Schedule of Changes appendix. The changes do not include all those that might be considered necessary if the guide was subjected to a comprehensive review and revision.

Terms Used to Define Professional Requirements in This AICPA Audit Guide

Any requirements described in this guide are normally referenced to the applicable standards or regulations from which they are derived. Generally the terms used in this guide describing the professional requirements of the referenced standard setter (for example, the ASB) are the same as those used in the applicable standards or regulations (for example, *must* or *should*).

It is important to note that the Uniform Guidance use of the terms to define professional requirements is somewhat different than the use of these terms in GAAS and *Government Auditing Standards*. The use of the term *must* in the Uniform Guidance indicates a requirement. This is consistent with the use of the term *must* in GAAS and *Government Auditing Standards*. The use of the term *should* in the Uniform Guidance indicates a best practice or recommended approach. However, GAAS and *Government Auditing Standards* use the term *should* to indicate a presumptively mandatory requirement. An auditor must comply with a presumptively mandatory requirement in all cases in which such

---

[3] This guide uses the term *Single Audit Act* when referencing this legislation.

[4] Part III has been added to this edition of the guide and contains information on performing a compliance audit of federal awards under the Uniform Guidance. Part II should be used for performing a compliance audit of federal awards under Circular A-133.

a requirement is relevant, except in rare circumstances. In this guide, the term ***should***, when italicized and bolded, indicates a best practice or recommended approach in the Uniform Guidance. This is intended to differentiate it from the term *should* used throughout the guide to refer to presumptively mandatory requirements in GAAS and *Government Auditing Standards*.

Readers should refer to the applicable standards and regulations for more information on the requirements imposed by the use of the various terms used to define professional requirements in the context of the standards and regulations in which they appear.

Certain exceptions apply to these general rules, particularly in those circumstances when the guide describes prevailing or preferred industry practices for the application of a standard or regulation. In these circumstances, the applicable senior committee responsible for reviewing the guide's content believes the guidance contained herein is appropriate for the circumstances.

References to Professional Standards

In citing GAAS and their related interpretations, references use section numbers within *Professional Standards* and not the original statement number.

Applicability of Quality Control Standards

QC section 10, *A Firm's System of Quality Control* (AICPA, *Professional Standards*), addresses a CPA firm's responsibilities for its system of quality control for its accounting and auditing practice. A system of quality control consists of policies that a firm establishes and maintains to provide it with reasonable assurance that the firm and its personnel comply with professional standards, as well as applicable legal and regulatory requirements. The policies also ensure reports issued by the firm are appropriate in the circumstances. This section applies to all CPA firms with respect to engagements in their accounting and auditing practice.

AU-C section 220, *Quality Control for an Engagement Conducted in Accordance With Generally Accepted Auditing Standards* (AICPA, *Professional Standards*), addresses the auditor's specific responsibilities regarding quality control procedures for an audit of financial statements. When applicable, it also addresses the responsibilities of the engagement quality control reviewer.

Because of the importance of audit quality, a new appendix, appendix A, "Overview of Statements on Quality Control Standards," has been added to this guide. Appendix A summarizes key aspects of the quality control standard. This summarization should be read in conjunction with QC section 10 and AU-C section 220, as applicable.

AICPA.org Website

The AICPA encourages you to visit its website at www.aicpa.org and the Financial Reporting Center at www.aicpa.org/frc. The Financial Reporting Center supports members in the execution of high quality financial reporting. Whether you are a financial statement preparer or a member in public practice, this center provides exclusive member only resources for the entire financial reporting process and provides timely and relevant news, guidance, and examples supporting the financial reporting process, including accounting, preparing financial statements, and performing compilation, review, audit, attest or assurance, and advisory engagements. Certain content on the AICPA's website referenced in this guide may be restricted to AICPA members only.

Government Audit Quality Center

The GAQC is a voluntary membership center for CPA firms and state audit organizations designed to improve the quality and value of governmental audits. For the purposes of the GAQC, governmental audits are performed under *Government Auditing Standards* and are audits and attestation engagements of federal, state, or local governments; not-for-profit entities; and certain for-profit organizations, such as housing projects and colleges and universities that participate in governmental programs or receive governmental financial assistance. The GAQC keeps members informed about the latest developments and provides them with tools and information to help them better manage their audit practice. Certain content on the GAQC's website referenced in this guide may be restricted to GAQC members only.

An Auditee Resource Center, open to the public, is also available on the GAQC website and provides information, practice aids, tools, and other resources that is of interest and benefit to auditees undergoing an audit performed under *Government Auditing Standards*.

For more information about the GAQC, visit the GAQC website at www.aicpa.org/gaqc.

Select Recent Developments Significant to This Guide

Uniform Guidance for Federal Awards

In December 2013, the OMB issued 2 CFR 200 (Uniform Guidance)[5] that establishes uniform cost principles and audit requirements for federal awards to nonfederal entities and administrative requirements for all federal grants and cooperative agreements. This guidance consolidates the requirements from OMB Circulars A-21, A-87, A-89, A-102, A-110, A-122, and A-133, as well as the guidance in Circular A-50 on Single Audit Act follow-up. Once the audit requirements of the Uniform Guidance are effective and the cost principles and administrative requirements of the Uniform Guidance are effective for all federal awards to nonfederal entities, the circulars will be superseded. Note that the cost principles for hospitals have not yet been incorporated into the Uniform Guidance.

The Uniform Guidance is effective for nonfederal entities for all federal awards and certain funding increments provided on or after December 26, 2014. The effective date provisions mean that an auditor will be required to use the cost principles and administrative requirements found in the circulars for awards

---

[5] Some content in this guide refers to a specific section (or paragraph number) in the Uniform Guidance. An example of such section reference is 2 CFR 200.518.

and funding increments awarded prior to December 26, 2014, and the Uniform Guidance cost principles and administrative requirements for federal awards and certain funding increments[6] awarded on or after December 26, 2014. Going forward, depending upon the award dates of the nonfederal entity's federal awards, an auditor may be required to use both of these sources of guidance when performing the compliance audit of federal awards because some federal awards (those awarded prior to December 26, 2014) are subject to the pre-Uniform Guidance requirements (for example, Circular A-122, *Cost Principles for Non-Profit Organizations*), while other federal awards (those awarded on or after December 26, 2014) are subject to the cost principles and administrative requirements of the Uniform Guidance. These effective date provisions of the Uniform Guidance cost principles and administrative requirements are not affected by whether the audit is performed under Circular A-133 or the Uniform Guidance audit requirements.

The requirements in Subpart F, "Audit Requirements," of the Uniform Guidance are effective for audits of fiscal years beginning on or after December 26, 2014. Therefore, auditees subject to a single audit with December 25, 2015, and later year ends will be required to undergo the audit under the Uniform Guidance audit requirements.

The audit requirements applicable to an auditee that undergoes biennial audits is dependent on the beginning date of the biennial audit period. (For example, for a nonfederal entity that has a biennial audit period of July 1, 2014 to June 30, 2016, the audit will be performed under Circular A-133.) See the section "Transition Considerations Related to the Uniform Guidance" in chapter 15, "Overview of the Single Audit Act, the Uniform Guidance Audit Requirements, and the Compliance Supplement," of this guide for more information. Similarly, the audit requirements for the audit of a short fiscal period is determined by the beginning date of the short fiscal period.

On December 19, 2014, a joint interim final rule was issued containing the implementing regulations of all federal awarding agencies. Those regulations were effective on December 26, 2014. That document notes that some agencies received OMB approval for exceptions to the Uniform Guidance. The exception language is included throughout the joint interim final rule. OMB states that it has approved exceptions only when they are consistent with existing policies of the agency. Therefore, all regulatory language included in the joint interim final rule should be consistent with either the Uniform Guidance or the agencies' existing policies and procedures. See the Chief Financial Officers Council document, "Uniform Guidance Crosswalk for Federal Agency Exceptions and Additions," available at https://cfo.gov/wp-content/uploads/2014/12/Agency-Exceptions.pdf, which isolates the exceptions made by the agency to determine how any agency exceptions and additions to the federal agency implementation of the Uniform Guidance will affect a particular audit.

---

[6] The "Frequently Asked Questions" document issued by the Council on Financial Assistance Reform (COFAR) clarifies that federal awards made with modified award terms and conditions at the time of the incremental funding action are subject to the Uniform Guidance if that action occurred on or after December 26, 2014. Funding increments with no change to award terms and conditions continue to be subject to pre-Uniform Guidance cost principles and administrative requirements (for example, those found in Circular A-122, *Cost Principles for Non-Profit Organizations*) if the related award was made prior to December 26, 2014.

The Uniform Guidance and related resources are available on the Council on Financial Assistance Reform (COFAR) website at https://cfo.gov/cofar/. Documents included on that site are as follows:

- 2 CFR 200, as issued on December 26, 2013
- "Uniform Guidance Crosswalk for Federal Agency Exceptions and Additions"
- Frequently Asked Questions
- Other related resources

Note that some documents on the COFAR website are based on the original guidance issued, and do not reflect the most current guidance. However, they may provide information to assist in understanding what revisions were made and the source of those revisions.

It is important that auditors access the most current document to ensure that any technical corrections and other revisions to the Uniform Guidance are being used in the audit. The Uniform Guidance, as updated for the joint interim final rule implementing the Uniform Guidance, is available on e-CFR (link labeled "PART 200, UNIFORM ADMINISTRATIVE REQUIREMENTS, COST PRINCIPLES, AND AUDIT REQUIREMENTS FOR FEDERAL AWARDS").

The 2015 edition of this guide has been fully updated for the Uniform Guidance. The update includes technical corrections issued up through the date of this guide, that is, February 1, 2015. The updated chapters are located in part III of this guide. Many chapters in parts II and III of this guide contain a section titled "Transition Considerations Related to the Uniform Guidance," that provides information regarding significant areas of change, or things to consider, as it relates to that chapter's content.

The 2015 *OMB Compliance Supplement (Compliance Supplement)* was not finalized at the publication date of this guide. Therefore, information regarding revisions to the *Compliance Supplement* in this guide are based on the draft version. Users of the guide should refer to the final 2015 *Compliance Supplement* for the relevant information needed in performing the compliance audit.

AICPA's Ethics Codification Project

AICPA's Professional Ethics Executive Committee (PEEC) restructured and codified the AICPA Code of Professional Conduct (code) so that members and other users of the code can apply the rules and reach appropriate conclusions more easily and intuitively. This is referred to as the AICPA Ethics Codification Project.

Although PEEC believes it was able to maintain the substance of the existing AICPA ethics standards through this process and limited substantive changes to certain specific areas that were in need of revision, the numeric citations and titles of interpretations have all changed. In addition, the ethics rulings are no longer in a question and answer format but, rather, have been drafted as interpretations, incorporated into interpretations as examples, or deleted where deemed appropriate. For example,

- Rule 101, *Independence* [ET sec. 101.01], is referred to as the "Independence Rule" [ET sec. 1.200.001] in the revised code.
- the content from the ethics ruling entitled "Financial Services Company Client has Custody of a Member's Assets" [ET sec. 191.081–.082] is incorporated into the "Brokerage and Other

Accounts" interpretation [ET sec. 1.255.020] found under the subtopic "Depository, Brokerage, and Other Accounts" [ET sec. 1.255] of the "Independence" topic [ET sec. 1.200].

The revised code was effective December 15, 2014 and is available at http://pub.aicpa.org/codeofconduct. References to the code in this guide are to the codified Code of Professional Conduct. To assist users in locating in the revised code content from the prior code, PEEC created a mapping document. The mapping document is available in Excel format in appendix D in the revised code.

ASB's Clarity Project

To address concerns over the clarity, length, and complexity of its standards, the ASB redrafted standards for clarity and also converged the standards with the International Standards on Auditing, issued by the International Auditing and Assurance Standards Board. As part of redrafting the standards, they now specify more clearly the objectives of the auditor and the requirements with which the auditor has to comply when conducting an audit in accordance with GAAS. The clarified auditing standards are now fully effective.

As part of the clarity project, the "AU-C" identifier was established to avoid confusion with references to existing "AU" sections. The AU-C identifier had been scheduled to revert back to the AU identifier at the end of 2013, by which time the previous AU sections would be superseded for all engagements. However, in response to user requests, the AU-C identifier will be retained indefinitely. The superseded AU sections were removed from *Professional Standards* at the end of 2013, as scheduled.

The ASB has completed the Clarity Project with the issuance of SAS No. 128 in February 2014. This guidance is effective for audits of financial statements for periods ending on or after December 15, 2014.

TABLE OF CONTENTS

Chapter		Paragraph
1	Introduction and Overview of *Government Auditing Standards*	.01-.19
	Purpose and Applicability of This Guide	.01-.11
	Overview of *Government Auditing Standards*	.12-.19
	Applicability of *Government Auditing Standards*	.12-.13
	Additional Requirements of *Government Auditing Standards*	.14-.15
	Use of Terminology to Define *Government Auditing Standards* Requirements	.16-.19

Part I   *Government Auditing Standards* Audits

2	*Government Auditing Standards*—Ethical Principles and General Standards	.01-.51
	Introduction	.01
	Government Auditing Standards—Ethical Principles	.02-.05
	Government Auditing Standards—General Standards	.06-.50
	Independence	.07-.30
	Professional Judgment	.31-.33
	Competence	.34-.42
	Quality Control and Assurance	.43-.45
	External Peer Review	.46-.50
	Appendix—*Government Auditing Standards* Conceptual Framework for Independence	.51
3	Planning and Performing a Financial Statement Audit in Accordance With *Government Auditing Standards*	.01-.71
	Introduction	.01-.03
	Agreeing Upon the Terms of the Engagement With Management	.04-.07
	Planning the Audit	.08-.15
	Communications With Other Entities	.15
	Group Audits	.16
	Materiality	.17-.18
	Audit Documentation	.19-.22
	Understanding the Entity and Its Environment and Assessing the Risks of Material Misstatement	.23-.31
	The Entity's Internal Control	.25-.28
	Identifying and Assessing the Risks of Material Misstatement	.29-.31
	Performing Audit Procedures and Evaluating Audit Evidence Obtained	.32-.35
	Tests of Controls	.34-.35

Chapter		Paragraph
3	**Planning and Performing a Financial Statement Audit in Accordance With *Government Auditing Standards*—continued**	
	Consideration of Fraud	.36-.42
	Assessing the Risk of Material Misstatements Resulting From Fraud	.40-.42
	Consideration of Laws and Regulations in an Audit of Financial Statements	.43-.52
	Consideration of Abuse	.53-.58
	Evaluating Identified Misstatements	.59
	Developing Elements of a Finding	.60
	The Auditor's Communication With Those Charged With Governance	.61-.65
	Communicating Internal Control Matters Identified in an Audit	.66
	Written Representations From Management	.67-.68
	Other Considerations	.69-.70
	Exit Conference	.69-.70
	Appendix—Examples of Deficiencies in Internal Control	.71
4	**Auditor Reporting Requirements and Other Communication Considerations of *Government Auditing Standards***	.01-.88
	Introduction	.01
	Report on the Financial Statements—GAAS Requirements	.02-.04
	Additional Reporting Requirements of Government Auditing Standards	.05-.06
	Reporting on Internal Control Over Financial Reporting and on Compliance	.07-.12
	Internal Control Over Financial Reporting	.13-.23
	Fraud, Noncompliance With Provisions of Laws, Regulations, Contracts, and Grant Agreements, and Abuse	.24-.45
	Fraud	.25-.30
	Noncompliance With Laws and Regulations	.31-.34
	Noncompliance With Provisions of Contracts and Grant Agreements and Abuse	.35-.38
	Other Considerations	.39
	Additional Considerations Related to Fraud, Noncompliance With Provisions of Laws, Regulations, Contracts, and Grant Agreements, and Abuse	.40-.42
	Government Auditing Standards—Reporting Findings Directly to Parties Outside the Entity	.43-.45
	Report on Audited Financial Statements	.46-.52
	Other Considerations—Citing Compliance With *Government Auditing Standards* in the Auditor's Report	.49-.51
	Other Reporting Responsibilities in an Audit of Financial Statements	.52

Chapter		Paragraph
4	Auditor Reporting Requirements and Other Communication Considerations of *Government Auditing Standards*—continued	
	Report on Internal Control Over Financial Reporting and on Compliance and Other Matters Based on an Audit of Financial Statements Performed in Accordance With *Government Auditing Standards*	.53-.54
	Other Reporting and Communication Considerations	.54-.83
	Findings—Deficiencies in Internal Control, Noncompliance With Provisions of Laws, Regulations, Contracts and Grant Agreements, Fraud, and Abuse	.55-.62
	Reporting Views of Responsible Officials and Planned Corrective Action	.63-.66
	Distributing Reports	.67
	Reporting Confidential and Sensitive Information	.68-.71
	Other Written Communications	.72-.73
	Portions of the Entity Not Audited in Accordance With *Government Auditing Standards*	.74-.76
	Referring to the Work of a Component Auditor	.77-.83
	Freedom of Information Act and Similar Laws and Regulations	.84-.85
	Assurance to Regulators and Oversight Agencies	.86-.87
	Appendix—Illustrative Auditor's Reports Under *Government Auditing Standards*	.88

Part II   Circular A-133 Audits

Chapter		Paragraph
5	Overview of the Single Audit Act, Circular A-133, and the *Compliance Supplement*	.01-.49
	Introduction	.01-.02
	Single Audit Act and Circular A-133 Requirements	.03-.46
	Objectives of a Single Audit	.03-.07
	General Audit Requirements	.08-.20
	Reporting Matters	.21-.23
	Auditor Selection and Audit Costs	.24-.25
	Basis for Determining When Federal Awards Are Expended	.26-.27
	Subrecipient and Vendor Determinations	.28
	Major Program Determination	.29-.32
	Auditee Responsibilities	.33-.39
	Federal Awarding Agency Responsibilities	.40
	Pass-Through Entity Responsibilities	.41
	Cognizant Agency for Audit	.42-.43
	Oversight Agency for Audit	.44-.45
	Program-Specific Audits	.46
	OMB Compliance Supplement	.47-.48
	Transition Considerations Related to the Uniform Guidance	.49

Chapter		Paragraph
6	Planning Considerations of Circular A-133	.01-.78
	Introduction	.01-.02
	Adapting and Applying Applicable Auditing Standards to a Circular A-133 Compliance Audit	.03-.06
	Identifying Supplementary Audit Requirements	.07
	Agreeing Upon the Terms of the Engagement With Management	.08-.09
	Audit Documentation	.10
	Additional Audit Requirements of the Single Audit Act and Circular A-133 Regarding Audit Documentation Access and Audit Follow-Up	.11-.13
	Audit Documentation Access and Retention	.11-.12
	Audit Follow-Up	.13
	Financial Statement Audit Considerations	.14-.17
	Defining the Entity to Be Audited	.18
	Determining the Audit Period	.19-.20
	Fiscal Year and Program Period May Differ	.19
	Stub Periods	.20
	Initial-Year Audit Considerations	.21-.22
	Preceding Period Audited by Another Auditor	.21
	Factors to Consider Under the Risk-Based Approach	.22
	Timing of the Completion of the Audit and Report Submission Deadlines	.23
	Determining the Major Programs to Be Audited	.24
	Identifying Direct and Material Compliance Requirements	.25-.27
	Audit Risk of Noncompliance Considerations	.28-.38
	Components of Audit Risk of Noncompliance	.30-.32
	Performing Risk Assessment Procedures	.33-.38
	Assessing the Risks of Material Noncompliance	.39-.49
	Assessing the Risks of Material Noncompliance Due to Fraud	.44-.49
	Audit Materiality Considerations	.50-.55
	Materiality Differences Between the Financial Statement Audit and the Circular A-133 Compliance Audit	.51-.52
	Materiality for Purposes of Reporting Audit Findings	.53-.55
	Developing an Efficient Audit Approach	.56
	Group Audit Considerations in a Circular A-133 Compliance Audit	.57-.59
	Existence of an Internal Audit Function	.60-.69
	Considerations Related to the Internal Audit Function	.62-.69
	Communications With the Cognizant or Oversight Agency for Audit and Others	.70
	State and Local Compliance Requirements	.71
	Desk Reviews and On-Site Reviews	.72-.73

Chapter		Paragraph
6	Planning Considerations of Circular A-133—continued	
	Restriction on the Auditor's Preparation of Indirect Cost Proposals	.74
	Transition Considerations Related to the Uniform Guidance	.75-.78
7	**Schedule of Expenditures of Federal Awards (Circular A-133)**	**.01-.36**
	Introduction	.01-.02
	Identification of Federal Awards	.03-.04
	Federal Agency and Pass-Through Entity Requirements	.03
	Auditee Requirements	.04
	Audit Considerations Related to the Schedule of Expenditures of Federal Awards	.05-.18
	Conditions for and Procedures Related to Issuing the In-Relation-To Opinion	.05-.11
	Additional Auditor Requirements Relating to Compliance Audit Objectives and Internal Control Over Compliance	.12-.15
	Management Representations Relating to the Schedule of Expenditures of Federal Awards	.16
	Subsequent Events	.17
	Reporting on the Schedule of Expenditures of Federal Awards	.18
	General Presentation Requirements	.19-.25
	Basis of Accounting	.19
	Required Content for the Schedule of Expenditures of Federal Awards	.20
	Providing Additional Information	.21
	Schedule May Not Agree With Other Federal Award Reporting	.22
	Inclusion of Nonfederal Awards	.23
	Considerations Relating to State Awards	.24
	CFDA Number Not Available	.25
	Pass-Through Awards	.26-.27
	Treatment of Pass-Through Awards	.26
	Commingled Assistance	.27
	Noncash Awards	.28-.31
	Treatment of Noncash Awards	.28
	Determining the Value of the Noncash Awards Expended	.29
	Loan and Loan Guarantee Continuing Compliance Requirements	.30
	Documentation Requirements	.31
	Issuing an Opinion on the Schedule of Expenditures of Federal Awards Under AU-C Section 805 When the Auditor Is Engaged to Perform Only the Compliance Audit Under Circular A-133	.32-.34

Chapter		Paragraph
7	**Schedule of Expenditures of Federal Awards (Circular A-133)**—*continued*	
	Transition Considerations Related to the Uniform Guidance	.35
	Appendix—Illustrative Schedules of Expenditures of Federal Awards	.36
8	**Determination of Major Programs (Circular A-133)**	.01-.39
	Introduction	.01-.02
	Applying the Risk-Based Approach	.03-.23
	Step 1—Determination of Type A and Type B Programs	.04-.10
	Step 2—Identification of Low-Risk Type A Programs	.11-.14
	Step 3—Identification of High-Risk Type B Programs	.15-.17
	Step 4—Determination of Programs to Be Audited as Major	.18-.20
	Percentage-of-Coverage Rule	.21
	Documentation of Risk Assessment	.22
	Auditor Judgment in the Risk Assessment Process	.23
	Other Considerations Regarding the Risk-Based Approach	.24-.27
	Deviation From Use of Risk Criteria	.24
	Federal Agency and Pass-Through Entity Requests for Additional Major Programs	.25
	Low-Risk Auditee Criteria	.26-.27
	Criteria for Federal Program Risk	.28-.38
	Current and Prior Audit Experience	.29-.35
	Oversight Exercised by Federal Agencies and Pass-Through Entities	.36-.37
	Inherent Risk of Noncompliance of the Federal Programs	.38
	Transition Considerations Related to the Uniform Guidance	.39
9	**Consideration of Internal Control Over Compliance for Major Programs (Circular A-133)**	.01-.60
	Summary of Circular A-133 Requirements Related to Internal Control Over Compliance for Federal Programs	.02-.04
	Auditee Responsibilities	.02
	Auditor Responsibilities	.03-.04
	Circular A-133 Definition of *Internal Control Over Federal Programs*	.05
	Control Objectives and the Elements of Internal Control	.06-.07
	Auditor's Consideration of Internal Control Over Compliance for Each Major Program	.08-.11
	Obtaining an Understanding of Internal Control Over Direct and Material Compliance Requirements for Major Programs	.12-.20
	Understanding Direct and Material Compliance Requirements and Identifying Relevant Controls	.12-.17
	Compliance Supplement Internal Control Guidance	.18

Chapter		Paragraph
9	Consideration of Internal Control Over Compliance for Major Programs (Circular A-133)—continued	
	Multiple Organizational Unit Considerations	.19
	Subrecipient Considerations	.20
	Planning and Performing the Test of Operating Effectiveness of Internal Control Over Direct and Material Compliance Requirements for Each Major Program	.21-.54
	Assessing Control Risk of Noncompliance	.21-.22
	Planning the Test of Operating Effectiveness of Internal Control Over Compliance for Each Major Program to Support a Low Assessed Level of Control Risk of Noncompliance	.23-.26
	Existence of Ineffective Internal Control in Preventing ory Detecting Noncompliance	.27-.29
	Performing Tests to Evaluate the Effectiveness of Controls	.30-.33
	Evaluating the Results of Tests of Controls	.34-.40
	Significant Deficiencies and Material Weaknesses in Internal Control Over Compliance Related to Federal Programs	.41-.54
	Documentation Requirements	.55-.58
	Transition Considerations Related to the Uniform Guidance	.59-.60
10	Compliance Auditing Applicable to Major Programs (Circular A-133)	.1-.79
	Compliance Objectives in a Circular A-133 Compliance Audit	.02-.03
	Responsibilities of Auditee	.04-.05
	Use of Professional Judgment	.06
	Audit Risk of Noncompliance Considerations	.07-.09
	Performing Further Audit Procedures in Response to Assessed Risks	.08-.09
	Materiality Considerations	.10-.13
	Materiality Judgments About Compliance Applied to Each Major Program	.11-.12
	Effect of Material Noncompliance on the Financial Statements	.13
	Performing a Circular A-133 Compliance Audit	.14-.69
	Identifying Major Programs to Be Tested	.16
	Identifying Direct and Material Compliance Requirements	.17-.28
	Planning the Engagement	.29-.32
	Consideration of Internal Control Over Compliance for Major Programs	.33
	Performing Compliance Testing	.34-.44
	Consideration of Abuse	.45
	Consideration of Subsequent Events	.46-.48
	Evaluation and Reporting of Noncompliance	.49-.62
	Performing Follow-Up Procedures	.63-.69

Chapter		Paragraph
10	**Compliance Auditing Applicable to Major Programs (Circular A-133)**—continued	
	Documentation Requirements	.70-.71
	Management Representations Related to Federal Awards	.72-.74
	Suggested Representations	.73
	Refusal to Furnish Written Representations	.74
	State and Local Government Compliance Auditing Considerations	.75
	Transition Considerations Related to the Uniform Guidance	.76-.79
11	**Audit Sampling Considerations of Circular A-133 Compliance Audits**	.01-.137
	Introduction	.01-.04
	Audit Sampling in a Circular A-133 Compliance Audit	.05-.11
	Purpose and Nature of Audit Sampling in a Circular A-133 Compliance Audit	.06-.09
	Audit Sampling in the Context of Other Audit Procedures	.10-.11
	Procedures That May Not Involve Audit Sampling	.12-.30
	Inquiry and Observation	.13
	Analytical Procedures	.14-.17
	Procedures Applied to Every Item in a Population or Subpopulation in Compliance Testing	.18-.20
	Individually Important Items in Compliance Testing	.21-.28
	Understanding and Testing the Operating Effectiveness of Controls Over Compliance	.29-.30
	Planning Considerations for Sampling Related to Tests of Controls Over Compliance and Compliance Testing	.31-.89
	Determining Audit Objectives	.31-.32
	Defining the Population and Considering Completeness	.33-.48
	Considering the Effect of Population Size	.49
	Defining Control Deviation and Compliance Exception Conditions	.50-.51
	Dual Purpose Samples Considerations	.52-.57
	Determining the Sample Size	.58-.89
	Selecting Sample Items for Testing	.90-.98
	Random Selection	.94
	Haphazard Selection	.95-.96
	Systematic Selection With a Random Start	.97-.98
	Performing the Test Procedures	.99-.105
	Investigate and Understand the Nature and Cause of Control Deviations and Compliance Exceptions	.100-.101
	Determine If Additional Testing Is Warranted in Response to an Observed Deviation or Exception	.102-.105
	Evaluating Sample Results	.106-.130
	Evaluating Control Deviations	.106-.113
	Reaching an Overall Conclusion on Tests of Controls	.114-.115

Chapter		Paragraph
11	**Audit Sampling Considerations of Circular A-133 Compliance Audits—continued**	
	Evaluating Compliance Exceptions	.116-.127
	Reaching an Overall Conclusion on Tests of Compliance	.128-.130
	Documenting the Sampling Procedure	.131-.135
	Transition Considerations Related to the Uniform Guidance	.136-.137
12	**Audit Considerations of Federal Pass-Through Awards (Circular A-133)**	.01-.49
	Introduction	.01
	Definitions	.02
	Applicability of Circular A-133	.03-.07
	Pass-Through Entities, Subrecipients, and Vendors	.08-.17
	Subrecipient Status Versus Vendor Status	.08-.11
	Description of Relationships	.12-.14
	Vendor Compliance Considerations	.15-.17
	Single Audit Considerations of Pass-Through Entities	.18-.43
	Pass-Through Entity Responsibilities	.19-.20
	Audit Planning Considerations	.21-.23
	Consideration of Internal Control Over Compliance	.24
	Subrecipient Monitoring	.25-.36
	Reporting Considerations	.37-.40
	For-Profit Subrecipients	.41
	Non-U.S.-Based Entities	.42
	State Designation of a Cluster of Programs	.43
	Circular A-133 Audit Considerations of Subrecipients	.44-.48
	Additional Compliance Requirements Established by Pass-Through Entities	.45
	Information Included in the Schedule of Expenditures of Federal Awards	.46
	Audit Findings	.47
	Submission of the Report	.48
	Transition Considerations Related to the Uniform Guidance	.49
13	**Auditor Reporting Requirements and Other Communication Considerations in a Single Audit (Circular A-133)**	.01-.58
	Overview	.01-.08
	Circular A-133 Requirements	.03-.04
	Reporting Package	.05
	Recommended Auditor's Reports	.06-.08
	Reporting on the Financial Statements and Supplementary Schedule of Expenditures of Federal Awards in Accordance With GAAS and *Government Auditing Standards* in a Single Audit	.09-.20
	Basis of Accounting	.09

Chapter		Paragraph
13	Auditor Reporting Requirements and Other Communication Considerations in a Single Audit (Circular A-133)—continued	
	Implementing Regulations of Federal Awarding Agencies May Define the Entity to Be Audited Differently Than Does GAAP	.10
	Elements of the In-Relation-To Report on the Supplementary Schedule of Expenditures of Federal Awards	.11-.13
	Potential Report Modifications When Reporting on the Schedule of Expenditures of Federal Awards	.14-.15
	Considerations When Dating the Report on the Schedule of Expenditures of Federal Awards	.16-.19
	Issuing an Opinion on the Schedule of Expenditures of Federal Awards Under AU-C Section 805 When the Auditor Is Engaged to Perform Only the Compliance Audit Under Circular A-133	.20
	Reporting on Compliance and Internal Control Over Compliance Applicable to Each Major Program	.21-.28
	Material Instances of Noncompliance	.22
	Scope Limitations	.23-.25
	Report on Compliance for Each Major Program, Report on Internal Control Over Compliance, and Report on the Schedule of Expenditures of Federal Awards Required by Circular A-133	.26-.27
	Dating the Report on Compliance With Requirements That Could Have a Direct and Material Effect on Each Major Federal Program and on Internal Control Over Compliance	.28
	Other Reporting Considerations	.29-.32
	Reissuance of the Circular A-133 Report	.29-.30
	Other Auditors	.31
	When the Audit of Federal Awards Does Not Encompass the Entirety of the Auditee's Operations	.32
	Schedule of Findings and Questioned Costs	.33-.43
	What Should Be Reported	.34-.35
	Findings Related to the Financial Statements	.36-.37
	Findings Related to Federal Awards	.38
	Findings of Abuse	.39
	Detail of Audit Findings—Federal Awards	.40-.41
	Other Preparation Guidance	.42-.43
	Communicating Other Findings to Management	.44
	Summary Schedule of Prior Audit Findings and Corrective Action Plan	.45-.47
	Data Collection Form	.48-.50
	Submission of Reporting Package and Data Collection Form	.51-.54
	Submission by Subrecipients	.52
	Distribution of Reporting Package to Federal Agencies	.53-.54

Chapter		Paragraph
13	Auditor Reporting Requirements and Other Communication Considerations in a Single Audit (Circular A-133)—continued	
	Freedom of Information Act and Similar Laws and Regulations	.55
	Transition Considerations Related to the Uniform Guidance	.56-.57
	Appendix—Illustrative Auditor's Reports Under Circular A-133	.58
14	Program-Specific Audits (Circular A-133)	.01-.17
	Use of a Program-Specific Audit to Satisfy Circular A-133 Audit Requirements	.02
	Program-Specific Audit Requirements	.03
	Availability of Program-Specific Audit Guides	.04-.05
	Auditee's Responsibilities When a Program-Specific Audit Guide Is Not Available	.06
	Auditor's Responsibilities When a Program-Specific Audit Guide Is Not Available	.07-.11
	Audit Scope and Requirements	.07
	Auditor Procedures	.08
	Auditor's Reports	.09-.11
	Evaluating and Reporting Abuse	.12
	Submission of Report	.13-.16
	Timing of Submission	.13
	Submission When a Program-Specific Audit Guide Is Available	.14
	Submission When a Program-Specific Audit Guide Is Not Available	.15-.16
	Appendix—Illustrative Auditor's Reports for Program-Specific Audits (Circular A-133)	.17

Part III Uniform Guidance Audits

15	Overview of the Single Audit Act, the Uniform Guidance Audit Requirements, and the Compliance Supplement	.01-.57
	Introduction	.01-.02
	Uniform Guidance	.03
	Single Audit Act and Uniform Guidance Audit Requirements	.04-.47
	Objectives of a Single Audit	.04-.08
	General Audit Requirements	.09-.20
	Reporting Matters	.21-.23
	Auditor Selection and Audit Costs	.24-.25
	Basis for Determining When Federal Awards Are Expended	.26-.27
	Subrecipient and Contractor Determinations	.28

Chapter		Paragraph
15	Overview of the Single Audit Act, the Uniform Guidance Audit Requirements, and the Compliance Supplement—continued	
	Major Program Determination	.29-.32
	Auditee Responsibilities	.33-.39
	Federal Awarding Agency Responsibilities	.40
	Pass-Through Entity Responsibilities	.41
	Cognizant Agency for Audit	.42-.43
	Oversight Agency for Audit	.44-.45
	Program-Specific Audits	.46
	Required Government-wide Evaluation of Single Audit Quality	.47
	OMB Compliance Supplement	.48-.49
	Transition Considerations Related to the Uniform Guidance	.50-.57
	Frequently Asked Questions	.56
	Reference Materials	.57
16	Auditor Planning Considerations Under the Uniform Guidance	.01-.78
	Introduction	.01-.02
	Adapting and Applying Applicable Auditing Standards to a Uniform Guidance Compliance Audit	.03-.06
	Identifying Supplementary Audit Requirements	.07
	Agreeing Upon the Terms of the Engagement With Management	.08-.09
	Financial Statement Audit Considerations	.10-.13
	Developing an Efficient Audit Approach	.14
	Defining the Entity to Be Audited	.15
	Determining the Audit Period	.16-.17
	Fiscal Year and Program Period May Differ	.16
	Stub Periods	.17
	Initial-Year Audit Considerations	.18-.19
	Preceding Period Audited by Another Auditor	.18
	Factors to Consider Under the Risk-Based Approach	.19
	Timing of the Completion of the Audit and Report Submission Deadlines	.20
	Determining the Major Programs to Be Audited	.21
	Identifying Direct and Material Compliance Requirements	.22-.24
	Audit Risk of Noncompliance Considerations	.25-.35
	Components of Audit Risk of Noncompliance	.27-.29
	Performing Risk Assessment Procedures	.30-.35
	Assessing the Risks of Material Noncompliance	.36-.46
	Assessing the Risks of Material Noncompliance Due to Fraud	.41-.46
	Audit Materiality Considerations	.47-.52
	Materiality Differences Between the Financial Statement Audit and the Uniform Guidance Compliance Audit	.48-.49

Chapter		Paragraph
16	Auditor Planning Considerations Under the Uniform Guidance—continued	
	Materiality for Purposes of Reporting Audit Findings	.50-.52
	Audit Documentation	.53
	Audit Documentation Access and Audit Follow-Up	.54-.56
	Audit Documentation Access and Retention	.54-.55
	Audit Follow-Up	.56
	Group Audit Considerations in a Uniform Guidance Compliance Audit	.57-.59
	Existence of an Internal Audit Function	.60-.69
	Considerations Related to the Internal Audit Function	.62-.69
	Communications With the Cognizant or Oversight Agency for Audit and Others	.70
	State and Local Compliance Requirements	.71
	Desk Reviews and On-Site Reviews	.72-.73
	Restriction on the Auditor's Preparation of Indirect Cost Proposals	.74
	Transition Considerations Related to the Uniform Guidance	.75-.78
17	Schedule of Expenditures of Federal Awards (Uniform Guidance)	.01-.43
	Introduction	.01-.02
	Identification of Federal Awards	.03-.05
	Federal Agency and Pass-Through Entity Requirements	.03-.04
	Auditee Requirements	.05
	Audit Considerations Related to the Schedule of Expenditures of Federal Awards	.06-.19
	Conditions for and Procedures Related to Issuing the In-Relation-To Opinion	.06-.12
	Additional Auditor Requirements Relating to Compliance Audit Objectives and Internal Control Over Compliance	.13-.16
	Management Representations Relating to the Schedule of Expenditures of Federal Awards	.17
	Subsequent Events	.18
	Reporting on the Schedule of Expenditures of Federal Awards	.19
	General Presentation Requirements	.20-.28
	Basis of Accounting	.20
	Required Content for the Schedule of Expenditures of Federal Awards	.21-.23
	Providing Additional Information	.24
	Schedule May Not Agree With Other Federal Award Reporting	.25
	Inclusion of Nonfederal Awards	.26
	Considerations Relating to State Awards	.27
	CFDA Number Not Available	.28

Chapter		Paragraph
17	**Schedule of Expenditures of Federal Awards (Uniform Guidance)**—continued	
	Pass-Through Awards	.29-.30
	Treatment of Pass-Through Awards	.29
	Commingled Assistance	.30
	Noncash Awards	.31-.35
	Treatment of Noncash Awards	.31-.32
	Determining the Value of the Noncash Awards Expended	.33
	Loan and Loan Guarantee Continuing Compliance Requirements	.34
	Documentation Requirements	.35
	Issuing an Opinion on the Schedule of Expenditures of Federal Awards Under AU-C Section 805 When the Auditor Is Engaged to Perform Only the Compliance Audit Under the Uniform Guidance	.36-.38
	Transition Considerations Related to the Uniform Guidance	.39-.42
	Appendix—Illustrative Schedules of Expenditures of Federal Awards	.43
18	**Determination of Major Programs (Uniform Guidance)**	.01-.39
	Introduction	.01
	Determining Major Programs Under the Uniform Guidance	.02-.19
	Step 1—Determination of Type A and Type B Programs	.03-.08
	Step 2—Identification of Low-Risk Type A Programs	.09-.13
	Step 3—Identification of High-Risk Type B Programs	.14-.15
	Step 4—Determination of Programs to Be Audited as Major	.16
	Percentage of Coverage Rule	.17
	Documentation of Risk Assessment	.18
	Auditor Judgment in the Risk Assessment Process	.19
	Other Considerations Regarding the Determination of Major Programs	.20-.21
	Federal Agency and Pass-Through Entity Requests for Additional Major Programs	.20
	Low-Risk Auditee Criteria	.21
	Assessing Risk When Determining Major Programs	.22
	Criteria for Federal Program Risk	.23-.32
	Current and Prior Audit Experience	.24-.29
	Oversight Exercised by Federal Agencies and Pass-Through Entities	.30-.31
	Inherent Risk of Noncompliance of the Federal Programs	.32
	Transition Considerations Related to the Uniform Guidance	.33-.39

Chapter		Paragraph
19	**Consideration of Internal Control Over Compliance for Major Programs (Uniform Guidance)**	.01-.65
	Uniform Guidance-Definitions	.02-.03
	Internal Control Over Compliance for Federal Awards	.04-.06
	Auditee Responsibilities	.04-.06
	Requirements Related to Internal Control in the Uniform Guidance Compliance Audit	.07-.08
	Auditor Responsibilities	.07-.08
	Control Objectives and the Components of Internal Control	.09-.10
	Auditor's Consideration of Internal Control Over Compliance for Each Major Program	.11-.14
	Obtaining an Understanding of Internal Control Over Direct and Material Compliance Requirements for Major Programs	.15-.23
	Understanding Direct and Material Compliance Requirements and Identifying Relevant Controls	.15-.20
	Compliance Supplement Internal Control Guidance	.21
	Multiple Organizational Unit Considerations	.22
	Subrecipient Considerations	.23
	Planning and Performing the Test of Operating Effectiveness of Internal Control Over Direct and Material Compliance Requirements for Each Major Program	.24-.57
	Assessing Control Risk of Noncompliance	.24-.25
	Planning the Test of Operating Effectiveness of Internal Control Over Compliance for Each Major Program to Support a Low Assessed Level of Control Risk of Noncompliance	.26-.29
	Existence of Ineffective Internal Control in Preventing or Detecting Noncompliance	.30-.32
	Performing Tests to Evaluate the Effectiveness of Controls	.33-.36
	Evaluating the Results of Tests of Controls	.37-.43
	Significant Deficiencies and Material Weaknesses in Internal Control Over Compliance Related to Federal Programs	.44-.57
	Documentation Requirements	.58-.61
	Transition Considerations Related to the Uniform Guidance	.62-.65
20	**Compliance Auditing Applicable to Major Programs (Uniform Guidance)**	.01-.78
	Compliance Objectives in a Uniform Guidance Compliance Audit	.02-.03
	Responsibilities of Auditee	.04-.05
	Use of Professional Judgment	.06
	Audit Risk of Noncompliance Considerations	.07-.09
	Performing Further Audit Procedures in Response to Assessed Risks	.08-.09

Chapter		Paragraph
20	**Compliance Auditing Applicable to Major Programs (Uniform Guidance)**—continued	
	Materiality Considerations	.10-.13
	Materiality Judgments About Compliance Applied to Each Major Program	.11-.12
	Effect of Material Noncompliance on the Financial Statements	.13
	Performing a Uniform Guidance Compliance Audit	.14-.68
	Identifying Major Programs to Be Tested	.16
	Identifying Direct and Material Compliance Requirements	.17-.28
	Planning the Engagement	.29-.32
	Consideration of Internal Control Over Compliance for Major Programs	.33
	Performing Compliance Testing	.34-.43
	Consideration of Abuse	.44
	Consideration of Subsequent Events	.45-.47
	Evaluation and Reporting of Noncompliance	.48-.61
	Performing Follow-Up Procedures	.62-.68
	Documentation Requirements	.69-.70
	Management Representations Related to Federal Awards	.71-.73
	Suggested Representations	.72
	Refusal to Furnish Written Representations	.73
	State and Local Government Compliance Auditing Considerations	.74
	Transition Considerations Related to the Uniform Guidance	.75-.78
21	**Audit Sampling Considerations of Uniform Guidance Compliance Audits**	.01-.137
	Introduction	.01-.04
	Audit Sampling in a Uniform Guidance Compliance Audit	.05-.11
	Purpose and Nature of Audit Sampling in a Uniform Guidance Compliance Audit	.06-.09
	Audit Sampling in the Context of Other Audit Procedures	.10-.11
	Procedures That May Not Involve Audit Sampling	.12-.30
	Inquiry and Observation	.13
	Analytical Procedures	.14-.17
	Procedures Applied to Every Item in a Population or Subpopulation in Compliance Testing	.18-.20
	Individually Important Items in Compliance Testing	.21-.28
	Understanding and Testing the Operating Effectiveness of Controls Over Compliance	.29-.30
	Planning Considerations for Sampling Related to Tests of Controls Over Compliance and Compliance Testing	.31-.89
	Determining Audit Objectives	.31-.32
	Defining the Population and Considering Completeness	.33-.48
	Considering the Effect of Population Size	.49

Chapter		Paragraph
21	Audit Sampling Considerations of Uniform Guidance Compliance Audits—continued	
	Defining Control Deviation and Compliance Exception Conditions	.50-.51
	Dual Purpose Sample Considerations	.52-.57
	Determining the Sample Size	.58-.89
	Selecting Sample Items for Testing	.90-.98
	Random Selection	.94
	Haphazard Selection	.95-.96
	Systematic Selection With a Random Start	.97-.98
	Performing the Test Procedures	.99-.105
	Investigate and Understand the Nature and Cause of Control Deviations and Compliance Exceptions	.100-.101
	Determine If Additional Testing Is Warranted in Response to an Observed Deviation or Exception	.102-.105
	Evaluating Sample Results	.106-.130
	Evaluating Control Deviations	.106-.113
	Reaching an Overall Conclusion on Tests of Controls	.114-.115
	Evaluating Compliance Exceptions	.116-.127
	Reaching an Overall Conclusion on Tests of Compliance	.128-.130
	Documenting the Sampling Procedure	.131-.135
	Transition Considerations Related to the Uniform Guidance	.136-.137
22	Audit Considerations of Federal Pass-Through Awards (Uniform Guidance)	.01-.55
	Introduction	.01
	Definitions	.02
	Applicability of the Uniform Guidance for Federal Awards	.03-.07
	Pass-Through Entities, Subrecipients, and Contractors	.08-.18
	Subrecipient Status Versus Contractor Status	.08-.11
	Description of Relationships	.12-.14
	Contractor Compliance Considerations	.15-.18
	Single Audit Considerations of Pass-Through Entities	.19-.45
	Pass-Through Entity Responsibilities	.20
	Audit Planning Considerations	.21-.24
	Auditor Consideration of Internal Control Over Compliance	.25
	Subrecipient Monitoring	.26-.38
	Reporting Considerations	.39-.42
	For-Profit Subrecipients	.43
	Foreign Public Entities and Foreign Organizations	.44
	State Designation of a Cluster of Programs	.45
	Audit Considerations of Subrecipients	.46-.49
	Additional Compliance Requirements Established by Pass-Through Entities	.47

Chapter		Paragraph
22	Audit Considerations of Federal Pass-Through Awards (Uniform Guidance)—continued	
	Information Related to the Schedule of Expenditures of Federal Awards	.48
	Audit Findings	.49
	Transition Considerations Related to the Uniform Guidance	.50-.55
23	Auditor Reporting Requirements and Other Communication Considerations in a Single Audit (Uniform Guidance)	.01-.67
	Overview	.01-.08
	Requirements Under the Uniform Guidance for Federal Awards	.03-.04
	Reporting Package	.05
	Illustrative Auditor's Reports	.06-.08
	Reporting on the Financial Statements and Supplementary Schedule of Expenditures of Federal Awards in Accordance With GAAS and *Government Auditing Standards* in a Single Audit	.09-.20
	Basis of Accounting	.09
	Implementing Regulations of Federal Awarding Agencies May Define the Entity to Be Audited Differently Than Does GAAP	.10
	Elements of the In-Relation-To Report on the Supplementary Schedule of Expenditures of Federal Awards	.11-.13
	Potential Report Modifications When Reporting on the Schedule of Expenditures of Federal Awards	.14-.15
	Considerations When Dating the Report on the Schedule of Expenditures of Federal Awards	.16-.19
	Issuing an Opinion on the Schedule of Expenditures of Federal Awards Under AU-C Section 805 When the Auditor Is Engaged to Perform Only the Compliance Audit Under the Uniform Guidance	.20
	Reporting on Compliance and Internal Control Over Compliance Applicable to Each Major Program	.21-.28
	Material Instances of Noncompliance	.22
	Scope Limitations	.23-.25
	Report on Compliance for Each Major Program, Report on Internal Control Over Compliance and Report on the Schedule of Expenditures of Federal Awards Required by the Uniform Guidance for Federal Awards	.26-.27
	Dating the Report on Compliance With Requirements That Could Have a Direct and Material Effect on Each Major Program and on Internal Control Over Compliance	.28
	Other Reporting Considerations	.29-.32
	Reissuance of the Uniform Guidance Compliance Report	.29-.30
	Other Auditors	.31
	When the Audit of Federal Awards Does Not Encompass the Entirety of the Auditee's Operations	.32

Chapter		Paragraph
23	**Auditor Reporting Requirements and Other Communication Considerations in a Single Audit (Uniform Guidance)—continued**	
	Schedule of Findings and Questioned Costs	.33-.44
	What Is Required to Be Reported	.34-.35
	Findings Related to the Financial Statements	.36-.37
	Audit Findings Related to Federal Awards	.38-.39
	Findings of Abuse	.40
	Detail of Audit Findings–Federal Awards	.41-.42
	Other Preparation Guidance	.43-.44
	Communicating Other Findings to Management	.45
	Summary Schedule of Prior Audit Findings and Corrective Action Plan	.46-.50
	Data Collection Form	.51-.58
	Submission of Reporting Package and Data Collection Form	.55
	Federal Audit Clearinghouse Responsibilities	.56-.58
	Freedom of Information Act and Similar Laws and Regulations	.59
	Transition Considerations Related to the Uniform Guidance	.60-.66
	Appendix—Illustrative Auditor's Reports Under the Uniform Guidance for Federal Awards	.67
24	**Program-Specific Audits (Uniform Guidance)**	.01-.16
	Use of a Program-Specific Audit to Satisfy Uniform Guidance Audit Requirements	.02
	Program-Specific Audit Requirements	.03
	Availability of Program-Specific Audit Guide	.04-.05
	Auditee's Responsibilities When a Program-Specific Audit Guide Is Not Available	.06
	Auditor's Responsibilities When a Program-Specific Audit Guide Is Not Available	.07-.11
	Audit Scope and Requirements	.07
	Auditor Procedures	.08
	Auditor's Reports	.09-.11
	Submission of Report	.12-.15
	Timing of Submission	.12
	Submission When a Program-Specific Audit Guide Is Available	.13
	Submission When a Program-Specific Audit Guide Is Not Available	.14-.15
	Appendix—Illustrative Auditor's Reports for Program-Specific Audits (Uniform Guidance)	.16

Supplement

A   Single Audit Act Amendments of 1996

B   OMB Circular A-133, Audits of States, Local Governments, and Non-Profit Organizations

Appendix

A   Overview of Statements on Quality Control Standards

B   Schedule of Changes Made to the Text From the Previous Edition

Index of Pronouncements and Other Technical Guidance

Subject Index

Chapter 1

Introduction and Overview of Government Auditing Standards

> **Update 1-1: Uniform Guidanc for Federal Awards**
>
> In December 2013, the Office of Management and Budget (OMB) issued Title 2 U.S. *Code of Federal Regulations* Part 200, *Uniform Administrative Requirements, Cost Principles, and Audit Requirements for Federal Awards* (Uniform Guidance), that establishes uniform cost principles and audit requirements for federal awards to nonfederal entities and administrative requirements for all federal grants and cooperative agreements. The Uniform Guidance is effective for nonfederal entities for all federal awards and certain funding increments provided on or after December 26, 2014. The standards in Subpart F, "Audit Requirements," are effective for audits of fiscal years beginning on or after December 26, 2014, with no early implementation permitted. Therefore, auditees subject to a single audit with December 25, 2015, and later year ends will be required to undergo the audit under Subpart F of the Uniform Guidance. Note that audits of fiscal years ending prior to the effective date of the Uniform Guidance audit requirements are subject to an audit under OMB Circular A-133, *Audits of States, Local Governments, and Non-Profit Organizations* (Circular A-133). See the preface for more information.
>
> **Important Note**
>
> *Government Auditing Standards* are applicable to a single audit, whether performed under Circular A-133 or the Uniform Guidance. This edition of the guide includes guidance for performing a compliance audit under both Circular A-133 and the Uniform Guidance. See part II, *Circular A-133 Audits*, or part III, *Uniform Guidance Audits*, as applicable to the compliance audit being performed.

Purpose and Applicability of This Guide

1.01 This guide[1] has a two-fold purpose:

    a. The first purpose is to provide auditors with a basic understanding of the procedures to be performed and of the reports that should be issued for audits of financial statements conducted in accordance with *Government Auditing Standards* (also referred to as the Yellow Book), issued by the Comptroller General of the United States of the Government Accountability Office (GAO).[2]

    b. The second purpose is to provide auditors of states, local governments, and not-for-profit entities (NFPs) that receive federal awards with a basic understanding of the procedures to be performed and of the reports that should be issued for single audits

---

[1] References to specific paragraph numbers throughout the guide are to paragraphs contained in the guide unless otherwise specified.

[2] *Government Auditing Standards* is available on the Yellow Book page of the U.S. Government Accountability Office (GAO) website at www.gao.gov/yellowbook.

and program-specific audits conducted in accordance with the Single Audit Act Amendments of 1996,[3] Circular A-133,[4] the Uniform Guidance, and the related *OMB Compliance Supplement*.[5]

1.02 *Government Auditing Standards* contains requirements and guidance for financial audits, attestation engagements, and performance audits. This guide addresses the *Government Auditing Standards* requirements and guidance for financial audits, generally only as they relate to audits of financial statements prepared in accordance with generally accepted accounting principles or a special purpose framework, and compliance audits conducted in accordance with the Single Audit Act and Circular A-133 or the Uniform Guidance.

1.03 *Government Auditing Standards* states that auditors may use *Government Auditing Standards* in conjunction with professional standards issued by the PCAOB and the International Auditing and Assurance Standards Board. Audits performed in accordance with *Government Auditing Standards* using either PCAOB auditing standards or International Standards on Auditing are not addressed in this guide.

1.04 *Government Auditing Standards* incorporates by reference AICPA Statements on Auditing Standards.[6] Therefore, auditors performing financial statement audits in accordance with *Government Auditing Standards* should comply with generally accepted auditing standards (GAAS), the requirements found in chapters 1–3 of *Government Auditing Standards,* and the additional requirements for financial audits found in chapter 4, "Standards for Financial Audits," of *Government Auditing Standards.* This guide does not contain all the GAAS requirements and guidance that an auditor will need to know and understand in order to perform an audit in accordance with *Government Auditing Standards.* The guide discusses GAAS requirements and guidance only to the extent necessary to provide the reader with an understanding of the additional requirements of *Government Auditing Standards* and also provides information on other GAAS guidance with particular relevance to an audit performed in accordance with *Government Auditing Standards.* Included in this guide's discussion of GAAS is information found in relevant AU-C section paragraphs titled "Considerations Specific to Governmental Entities" that highlight considerations specific to governmental entities, entities receiving government funding, and entities being audited in accordance with *Government Auditing Standards.* Additional information on GAAS requirements for financial statement audits can be found in the relevant professional standards

---

[3] The Single Audit Act Amendments of 1996 (Public Law 104-156) were enacted into law in July 1996 and replaced the Single Audit Act of 1984. Supplement A, "Single Audit Act Amendments of 1996," of this guide is a reprint of the act. Hereafter, this guide uses the term *Single Audit Act* to refer to this legislation.

[4] Supplement B, "OMB Circular A-133, *Audits of States, Local Governments, and Non-Profit Organizations*," of this guide reprints Circular A-133 as revised on June 26, 2007. The circular can be obtained at the Office of Management and Budget (OMB)'s website on the Circulars page at www.whitehouse.gov/omb/circulars default. The audit requirements in the Uniform Guidance are effective for audits of fiscal years beginning on or after December 26, 2014. The Uniform Guidance and related resources are available on the Council on Financial Assistance Reform website at https://cfo.gov/cofar/.

[5] The *Compliance Supplement* is updated at least annually. The *Compliance Supplement* is available on the OMB website at www.whitehouse.gov/omb/circulars default.

[6] Paragraph 4.01 of *Government Auditing Standards* notes that all sections of the Statements on Auditing Standards are incorporated into *Government Auditing Standards*, including the introduction, objectives, definitions, requirements, and application and other explanatory material.

Introduction and Overview of *Government Auditing Standards*

and applicable Audit and Accounting Guides, such as *Not-for-Profit Entities*; *State and Local Governments*; *Health Care Entities*; *Gaming*; *Employee Benefit Plans*; and *Depository and Lending Institutions: Banks and Savings Institutions, Credit Unions, Finance Companies, and Mortgage Companies*.

1.05 As further discussed in the preface to this guide, auditing guidance included in an AICPA Audit Guide is recognized as an interpretive publication pursuant to AU-C section 200, *Overall Objectives of the Independent Auditor and the Conduct of an Audit in Accordance With Generally Accepted Auditing Standards* (AICPA, *Professional Standards*). Interpretive publications are not auditing standards. Interpretive publications are recommendations on the application of GAAS in specific circumstances, in this case to audits performed in accordance with *Government Auditing Standards* and to single and program-specific audits under Circular A-133 or the Uniform Guidance. The GAO, OMB, and AICPA promulgate applicable standards and requirements. Refer to those organizations' websites[7] for the full text of the organizations' original standards and requirements.

1.06 When covering certain topics, *Government Auditing Standards* contains information specific to internal audit organizations. This guide discusses the *Government Auditing Standards* guidance relevant to independent auditors and does not highlight guidance that is specific to internal audit organizations. Refer to *Government Auditing Standards* for information on, and requirements for, internal audit organizations.

1.07 This guide is organized into three parts that discuss important considerations for audits performed under *Government Auditing Standards* (part I), single audits and program-specific audits performed under Circular A-133 (part II), and single audits and program-specific audits performed under the Uniform Guidance (part III).[8] Each part presents chapters with topics relating to planning, performing, evaluating the results of, and reporting on those audits. See the table of contents for the specific topics addressed in each part and chapter.

1.08 This guide is not a complete manual of procedures, and *Government Auditing Standards* states that the auditor must use professional judgment in planning and performing audit engagements and in reporting the results. Because of the variety and complexity of the laws and regulations that govern audits performed under *Government Auditing Standards*, Circular A-133, and the Uniform Guidance, the procedures included in this guide cannot cover all the circumstances or conditions that may be encountered in an audit.

1.09 This guide does not address requirements when conducting a compliance audit of for-profit entities that participate in federal programs subject to an audit in accordance with a federal agency audit guide (for example, the U.S. Department of Housing and Urban Development [HUD] *Consolidated Audit Guide for Audits of HUD Programs*, the U.S. Department of Energy *Audit Guidance for For-Profit Recipients*, and the U.S. Department of Education audit

---

[7] See footnotes 2, 4, and 5 in paragraph 1.01 for links to applicable guidance. Also see the AICPA's website at www.aicpa.org and the Governmental Audit Quality Center's website at www.aicpa.org/GAQC.

[8] The standards in Subpart F, "Audit Requirements" of Title 2 U.S. Code of Federal Regulations Part 200, *Uniform Administrative Requirements, Cost Principles, and Audit Requirements for Federal Awards* (Uniform Guidance), are effective for audits of fiscal years beginning on or after December 26, 2014. Circular A-133 should be used when performing single audits prior to that effective date.

guides, among others). Refer to AU-C section 935, *Compliance Audits* (AICPA, *Professional Standards*), and the specific federal agency audit guide for related requirements and guidance when performing such audits.

1.10 Certain states have imposed additional audit requirements related to state or local financial assistance and may require additional audit procedures and reporting. Furthermore, pass-through entities may impose additional audit requirements on their subrecipients related to the financial assistance passed through. The guidance in this guide generally does not discuss or extend to those requirements.

1.11 The terminology found in *Government Auditing Standards* is consistent with the terminology found in the auditing sections of AICPA *Professional Standards*. Additionally, the terms used in this guide are intended to be consistent with the definitions in *Government Auditing Standards*, the Single Audit Act, Circular A-133, the Uniform Guidance, and AU-C section 935. Note that the term *not-for-profit entity* as used in this guide is consistent with the definition of the term *nonprofit organization* as found in Circular A-133 and the Uniform Guidance[9] and includes not-for-profit institutions of higher education, hospitals, and other health care providers.

Overview of *Government Auditing Standards*

Applicability of *Government Auditing Standards*

1.12 The professional standards and guidance for financial audits contained in *Government Auditing Standards* provide a framework for conducting high quality audits with competence, integrity, objectivity, and independence. Those requirements and guidance apply to audits of governmental entities, programs, activities, and functions. Those requirements and guidance also apply to audits of government assistance administered by contractors, NFPs, and other nongovernmental entities, including foreign entities, when the use of *Government Auditing Standards* is required or is voluntarily followed. Appendix I section A1.04 of *Government Auditing Standards* states that even if not required to do so, auditors may find it useful to follow *Government Auditing Standards* in performing audits of federal, state, and local government programs as well as audits of government awards administered by contractors, NFPs, and other nongovernmental entities.

1.13 Entities for which an auditor may need to apply *Government Auditing Standards* when auditing financial statements include federal, state, and local governments; NFPs; health care entities; entities with mortgage banking, real estate, or student lending and servicing activities; Indian Tribes; and other entities receiving federal awards. As discussed in chapter 5, "Overview of the Single Audit Act, Circular A-133, and the *Compliance Supplement*," and chapter 15, "Overview of the Single Audit Act, the Uniform Guidance Audit Requirements, and the *Compliance Supplement*," of this guide, audits required by the Single Audit Act and performed under Circular A-133 or the Uniform Guidance require the use of *Government Auditing Standards*. Other laws, regulations, agreements, contracts, or other authoritative sources may require the

---

[9] The term *nonfederal entity* is used throughout the Uniform Guidance. Subpart A, "Acronyms and Definitions, of the Uniform Guidance defines a *nonfederal entity* as a state, local government, Indian tribe, institution of higher education, or nonprofit organization that carries out a federal award as a recipient or subrecipient.

Introduction and Overview of *Government Auditing Standards*

use of *Government Auditing Standards*. Federal audit guidelines pertaining to program requirements, such as those issued for HUD programs and Student Financial Assistance programs, also may require the use of *Government Auditing Standards*. In addition, state and local laws and regulations may require auditors of state and local governments to follow *Government Auditing Standards*. Therefore, reading an entity's grant agreements and contracts and relevant state and local laws may provide important information to the auditor about the type of audit the entity is required to undergo.

Additional Requirements of *Government Auditing Standards*

1.14 In conducting audits of financial statements in accordance with *Government Auditing Standards*, the auditor assumes certain responsibilities beyond those of audits performed in accordance with GAAS. The standards and guidance applicable to financial audits, including audits of financial statements, are contained in chapters 1–4 of *Government Auditing Standards* and include ethical principles, general standards, and additional standards for performing and reporting on financial audits. For example, in addition to an auditor's report that expresses an opinion or disclaimer of opinion on the financial statements as required by GAAS,[10] a written report on internal control over financial reporting and on compliance and other matters is required under *Government Auditing Standards*.

1.15 It is important that both the auditor and management understand the type of engagement that is required to be performed. Chapter 3, "Planning and Performing a Financial Statement Audit in Accordance With *Government Auditing Standards*," of this guide further discusses GAAS and *Government Auditing Standards* requirements for agreeing upon the terms of the audit engagement with the auditee, which includes communicating with the auditee, through a written communication, the auditor's understanding of the services to be performed.

Use of Terminology to Define *Government Auditing Standards* Requirements

1.16 Auditors have a responsibility to consider the entire text of *Government Auditing Standards* when carrying out their work and in understanding and applying the requirements in those standards. Not every paragraph of the standard carries a requirement; rather, the requirements are identified through the use of specific language.

1.17 Chapter 2, "Standards for Use and Application of GAGAS," of *Government Auditing Standards* uses two categories of professional requirements, identified by specific terms, to describe the degree of responsibility they impose on auditors and audit organizations.[11] Unconditional requirements are

---

[10] As explained in the AICPA Audit and Accounting Guide *State and Local Governments*, the auditor generally expresses or disclaims an opinion on a government's basic financial statements by providing an opinion or disclaimer of opinion on each opinion unit required to be presented in those financial statements. In addition, the auditor may provide opinions or disclaimers of opinions on additional opinion units if engaged to set the scope of the audit and assess materiality at a more detailed level than by the opinion units required for the basic financial statements. Throughout this guide, the use of the singular terms *opinion* and *disclaimer of opinion* encompasses the multiple opinions and disclaimers of opinion that generally will be provided on a government's basic financial statements.

[11] The terminology is consistent with the terminology defined in the auditing sections of AICPA *Professional Standards*.

those requirements that the auditor and audit organization must comply with in all cases where such requirement is relevant. The word *must* is used to indicate an unconditional requirement. Presumptively mandatory requirements are indicated by the use of the word *should*. Presumptively mandatory requirements also must be complied with in all cases where such a requirement is relevant. However, in rare circumstances an auditor or audit organization may determine it necessary to depart from a relevant presumptively mandatory requirement. This is expected to arise only when the requirement is for a specific procedure to be performed and, in the specific circumstances of the audit, that procedure would be ineffective in achieving the intent of the requirement. In this rare circumstance the auditor should perform alternative procedures to achieve the audit objective. Furthermore, auditors must document their justification for the departure and how the alternative procedures performed were sufficient to achieve the intent of the requirement.

1.18 In addition to requirements discussed in the preceding paragraph, *Government Auditing Standards* contains related guidance in the form of application and other explanatory material that provides further explanation of the requirements and guidance for carrying out those requirements. In particular, it may explain more precisely what a requirement means or is intended to cover or include examples of procedures that may be appropriate in the circumstances. Although such guidance does not in itself impose a requirement, it is relevant to the proper application of the requirements. Auditors should have an understanding of the application and other explanatory material; how auditors apply the guidance in the audit depends on the exercise of professional judgment in the circumstances consistent with the objectives of the requirement. The words *may*, *might*, and *could* are used to describe these actions and procedures. Note that the application and other explanatory material may also provide background information on matters addressed in *Government Auditing Standards*.

1.19 *Government Auditing Standards* states that in planning and performing audits of financial statements in accordance with *Government Auditing Standards*, auditors also use interpretative publications which are issued under the authority of GAO and provide recommendations on the application of *Government Auditing Standards* in specific circumstances. Interpretive publications, such as related *Government Auditing Standards* guidance documents and interpretations, are found on the GAO website.[12] Interpretive publications are not auditing standards, but have the same level of authority as application and other materials in *Government Auditing Standards*.

---

[12] An example is the document "*Government Auditing Standards*: Guidance on GAGAS Requirements for Continuing Professional Education," that is found on the GAO website at www.gao.gov/yellowbook.

Part I

Government Auditing Standards *Audits*

Chapter 2

Government Auditing Standards—Ethical Principles and General Standards

> **© Update 2-1: Uniform Guidance for Federal Awards**
>
> In December 2013, the Office of Management and Budget (OMB) issued Title 2 U.S. *Code of Federal Regulations* Part 200, *Uniform Administrative Requirements, Cost Principles, and Audit Requirements for Federal Awards* (Uniform Guidance), that establishes uniform cost principles and audit requirements for federal awards to nonfederal entities and administrative requirements for all federal grants and cooperative agreements. The Uniform Guidance is effective for nonfederal entities for all federal awards and certain funding increments provided on or after December 26, 2014. The standards in Subpart F, "Audit Requirements," are effective for audits of fiscal years beginning on or after December 26, 2014, with no early implementation permitted. Therefore, auditees subject to a single audit with December 25, 2015, and later year ends will be required to undergo the audit under Subpart F of the Uniform Guidance. Note that audits of fiscal years ending prior to the effective date of the Uniform Guidance audit requirements are subject to an audit under OMB Circular A-133, *Audits of States, Local Governments, and Non-Profit Organizations* (Circular A-133). See the preface for more information.
>
> **Important Note**
>
> *Government Auditing Standards* are applicable to a single audit, whether performed under Circular A-133 or the Uniform Guidance. This edition of the guide includes guidance for performing a compliance audit under both Circular A-133 and the Uniform Guidance. See part II, *Circular A-133 Audits*, or part III, *Uniform Guidance Audits*, as applicable to the compliance audit being performed.

Introduction

2.01 This chapter discusses the ethical principles and general standards found in chapter 1, "Government Auditing: Foundation and Ethical Principles," and chapter 3, "General Standards," of *Government Auditing Standards* (also referred to as the Yellow Book), issued by the Comptroller General of the United States, who heads the Government Accountability Office (GAO). Chapter 1, "Introduction and Overview of *Government Auditing Standards*," of this guide contains an overview of *Government Auditing Standards* as well as a discussion of certain requirements in chapter 2, "Standards for Use and Application of GAGAS" of *Government Auditing Standards*. Chapter 3, "Planning and Performing a Financial Statement Audit in Accordance With *Government Auditing Standards*," of this guide provides information to be considered when planning and performing a financial audit under *Government Auditing Standards*, whereas chapter 4, "Auditor Reporting Requirements and Other Communication Considerations of *Government Auditing Standards*," of this guide provides information related to reporting on a financial audit performed in accordance with *Government Auditing Standards*. Refer to the full text of

Government Auditing Standards for a complete discussion of the relevant requirements.

Government Auditing Standards—Ethical Principles

2.02 Although the ethical principles presented in chapter 1 of *Government Auditing Standards* do not establish specific standards or requirements, the ethical principles are important in that they provide the foundation, discipline, structure, and climate that influence the application of *Government Auditing Standards*. *Government Auditing Standards* states that ethical principles apply in preserving auditor independence, taking on only work that the audit organization is competent to perform, performing high quality work, and following the applicable standards cited in the auditor's report. Integrity and objectivity are maintained when auditors perform their work and make decisions that are consistent with the broader interest of those relying on the auditor's report, including the public.

2.03 *Government Auditing Standards* states that management of the audit organization sets the tone for ethical behavior throughout the organization by maintaining an ethical culture, clearly communicating acceptable behavior and expectations to each employee, and creating an environment that reinforces and encourages ethical behavior throughout all levels of the organization. The ethical tone maintained and demonstrated by management and staff of the audit organization is an essential element of a positive ethical environment. Further, it states that conducting audit work in accordance with ethical principles is a matter of personal and organizational responsibility.

2.04 The five ethical principles that guide the work of auditors who conduct audits in accordance with *Government Auditing Standards* are

   a. the public interest;
   b. integrity;
   c. objectivity;
   d. proper use of government information, resources, and positions; and
   e. professional behavior.

Refer to chapter 1 of *Government Auditing Standards* for a full discussion of these principles.

2.05 *Government Auditing Standards* states that other ethical requirements or codes of professional conduct may also be applicable to auditors who conduct an audit in accordance with *Government Auditing Standards*. For example, individual auditors who are members of professional organizations or are licensed or certified professionals may also be subject to ethical requirements of those professional organizations or licensing bodies. Auditors employed by governmental entities may also be subject to government ethics laws and regulations.

Government Auditing Standards—General Standards

2.06 Chapter 3 of *Government Auditing Standards* contains general standards that, along with the overarching ethical principles found in chapter 1 of *Government Auditing Standards*, establish a foundation for the credibility of an auditor's work. The general standards are as follows:

Government Auditing Standards—Ethical Principles and General Standards **11**

- *Independence.* In all matters relating to the audit work, the audit organization and the individual auditor, whether government or public, must be independent.
- *Professional judgment.* Auditors must use professional judgment in planning and performing audits and in reporting the results.
- *Competence.* The staff assigned to perform the audit must collectively possess adequate professional competence needed to address the audit objectives and perform the work in accordance with *Government Auditing Standards.*
- *Quality control and assurance.* Each audit organization performing audits in accordance with *Government Auditing Standards* must (*a*) establish and maintain a system of quality control that is designed to provide the audit organization with reasonable assurance that the organization and its personnel comply with professional standards and applicable legal and regulatory requirements, and (*b*) have an external peer review performed by reviewers independent of the audit organization being reviewed at least once every three years.

Independence

2.07 AU-C section 200, *Overall Objectives of the Independent Auditor and the Conduct of an Audit in Accordance With Generally Accepted Auditing Standards* (AICPA, *Professional Standards*), states that auditors should comply with relevant ethical requirements relating to financial statement audit engagements. Therefore, in an audit performed in accordance with generally accepted auditing standards, members are required to comply with the "Independence Rule" (AICPA, *Professional Standards*, ET sec. 1.200.001) of the AICPA Code of Professional Conduct. Furthermore, when an audit is performed in accordance with *Government Auditing Standards*, members are subject to the AICPA Code of Professional Conduct as well as the additional independence requirements found in chapter 3 of *Government Auditing Standards*. Paragraphs 2.07–.27 of this guide describe the independence requirements contained in *Government Auditing Standards*.

2.08 *Government Auditing Standards* states that in all matters relating to the audit work, the audit organization and individual auditor, whether government or public, must be independent. If independence is impaired, auditors should decline to perform a prospective audit or terminate an audit in progress.[1] Except under the limited circumstances discussed in paragraphs 3.47–.48 of *Government Auditing Standards*, auditors should be independent from an auditee during

    a. any period of time that falls within the period covered by the financial statements or subject matter of the audit, and

    b. the period of the professional engagement, which begins when the auditors either sign an initial engagement letter or other agreement to perform an audit or begin to perform an audit, whichever is earlier. The period lasts for the entire duration of the professional

---

[1] See paragraph 2.26 for a discussion of conditions under which a government auditor may be required by law or regulation to perform both an audit and a nonaudit service that could impair the auditor's independence and who cannot decline to perform or terminate the service due to requirements over which the auditor has no control.

relationship (which, for recurring audits, could cover many periods) and ends with the formal or informal notification, either by the auditors or the auditee, of the termination of the professional relationship or by the issuance of a report, whichever is later. Accordingly, the period of professional engagement does not necessarily end with the issuance of a report and recommence with the beginning of the following year's audit or a subsequent audit with a similar objective.

2.09 *Government Auditing Standards* establishes a conceptual framework that auditors use to identify, evaluate, and apply safeguards to address threats to independence. The conceptual framework assists auditors in maintaining both independence of mind and independence in appearance. The framework can be applied to many variations in circumstances that create threats to independence and allows auditors to address threats to independence that result from activities that are not specifically prohibited by *Government Auditing Standards*.[2] Auditors should apply the conceptual framework at the audit organization, audit, and individual auditor levels to

- identify threats to independence;
- evaluate the significance of the threats identified, both individually and in the aggregate; and
- apply safeguards as necessary to eliminate the threats or reduce them to an acceptable level.

If no safeguards are available to eliminate an unacceptable threat or reduce it to an acceptable level, independence would be considered impaired. As noted previously, if independence is impaired, the auditor should decline to perform a prospective audit or terminate an audit in progress.

2.10 Threats to independence are circumstances that could impair independence and are conditions to be evaluated using the conceptual framework. Threats do not necessarily impair independence. Whether independence is impaired depends on the nature of the threat, whether the threat is of such significance that it would compromise an auditor's professional judgment or create the appearance that the auditor's professional judgment may be compromised, and on the specific safeguards applied to eliminate the threat or reduce it to an acceptable level. Broad categories of threats (and a brief explanation of the threat) are identified in paragraph 3.14 of *Government Auditing Standards*. They are

- self-interest threat,
- self-review threat,
- bias threat,
- familiarity threat,
- undue influence threat,
- management participation threat, and
- structural threat.

---

[2] The appendix, "*Government Auditing Standards* Conceptual Framework for Independence," of this chapter (paragraph 2.51) reprints *Government Auditing Standards* Appendix II, "GAGAS Conceptual Framework for Independence," which is a flowchart to assist auditors in the application of the conceptual framework for independence. For more information, visit the Yellow Book page of the Government Accountability Office (GAO) website at www.gao.gov/yellowbook.

Circumstances that result in a threat to independence may involve more than one of the broad categories of threats. Appendix I sections A3.02–.09 of *Government Auditing Standards* provides examples of circumstances that create various types of threats for auditors.

2.11 Safeguards are controls designed to eliminate or reduce to an acceptable level threats to independence. Under the conceptual framework, the auditor applies safeguards that address the specific facts and circumstances under which significant threats to independence exist. In some cases, multiple safeguards may be necessary to address a significant threat. The independence section in chapter 3 of *Government Auditing Standards* provides examples of safeguards that may be effective, either individually or in combination, in addressing threats for a number of situations that may be encountered. Although the examples presented do not provide safeguards for all circumstances, the content provides a starting point for auditors who have identified significant threats to independence and are considering what safeguards could eliminate those threats or reduce them to an acceptable level. See paragraphs 3.17–.19 of *Government Auditing Standards* for examples of safeguards.

Applying the Conceptual Framework

2.12 Auditors should evaluate threats to independence using the conceptual framework when the facts and circumstances under which auditors perform their work may create or augment threats to independence. Auditors should evaluate threats both individually and in the aggregate because threats can have a cumulative effect on an auditor's independence. Whenever relevant new information about a threat to independence comes to the attention of the auditor during the audit, the auditor should evaluate the significance of the threat in accordance with the conceptual framework.

2.13 Auditors should determine whether identified threats to independence are at an acceptable level or have been eliminated or reduced to an acceptable level. A threat to independence is not acceptable if it could

- impact the auditor's ability to perform an audit without being affected by influences that compromise professional judgment, or
- expose the auditor or audit organization to circumstances that would cause a reasonable and informed third party to conclude that the integrity, objectivity, or professional skepticism of the audit organization, or a member of the audit team, had been compromised.

2.14 When an auditor identifies threats to independence and, based on an evaluation of those threats, determines that they are not at an acceptable level, the auditor should determine whether appropriate safeguards are available and can be applied to eliminate the threats or reduce them to an acceptable level. The auditor should exercise professional judgment in making that determination and should take into account whether both independence of mind and independence in appearance are maintained. Both qualitative and quantitative factors should be evaluated when determining the significance of a threat.

2.15 In cases where threats to independence are not at an acceptable level, and therefore require the application of safeguards, the auditor should document the threats identified and the safeguards applied to eliminate the threats or reduce them to an acceptable level. Certain conditions may lead to threats that are so significant that they cannot be eliminated or reduced to an acceptable level through the application of safeguards. This situation results in impaired independence, and under such conditions auditors should decline to perform a prospective audit or terminate an audit in progress. Paragraph 3.26 of *Government Auditing Standards* explains what action should be taken in the case where a threat to independence is initially identified after the audit report is issued and, after evaluation, it is determined that the newly identified threat had an impact on the audit that would have resulted in the auditor's report being different than the report issued.

2.16 The independence standard applies to auditors in governmental entities whether they report to third parties externally, to senior management within the auditee, or both. Paragraphs 3.27–.32 of *Government Auditing Standards* contain information for government auditors, including safeguards that may mitigate the effects of structural threats (the threat that an audit organization's placement within a governmental entity will impact the audit organization's ability to perform work and report the results objectively).

Nonaudit Services[3]

2.17 Auditors have traditionally provided a range of nonaudit services for entities for which they also perform audits. Providing nonaudit services may create threats to an auditor's independence. Paragraphs 3.33–.58 of *Government Auditing Standards* provide information and guidance related to the performance of nonaudit services, including the evaluation of threats to independence and examples of safeguards in response to those threats. That content also enumerates specific nonaudit services that always impair independence with respect to audited entities.

2.18 Routine activities performed by auditors that relate directly to the performance of an audit are not considered to be nonaudit services. Paragraphs 3.40–.41 of *Government Auditing Standards* provide information as to what is considered to be a routine service. It is important to note that activities such as financial statement preparation, cash to accrual conversions, and reconciliations[4] are considered nonaudit services under *Government Auditing Standards* and not routine activities related to the performance of an audit. Such services are evaluated using the conceptual framework.

2.19 Before an auditor agrees to provide a nonaudit service to an auditee, the auditor should determine whether providing that service would create a threat to independence, either by itself or in the aggregate with other nonaudit

---

[3] In response to practice concerns, a practice aid, "2011 Yellow Book Independence—Non-Audit Services Documentation Practice Aid," has been developed to assist an auditor in evaluating nonaudit services and the effect of performing such services on auditor independence under *Government Auditing Standards, December 2011 Revision*. The practice aid was developed through a coordinated effort of the Government Audit Quality Center (GAQC) and AICPA ethics and peer review teams. In addition, practitioners and federal agencies provided input into its content. This practice aid contains numerous explanations and illustrations that will help auditors in applying the *Government Auditing Standard*'s conceptual framework for independence as it relates to nonaudit services and in documenting such consideration. The practice aid highlights nonaudit services that are frequently performed for smaller entities, such as preparation of financial statements, preparing journal entries and other proposed audit entries, and preparing reconciliations. The practice aid is available as a PDF file at no cost to AICPA and GAQC members, accessible from the GAQC website at www.aicpa.org/GAQC. An electronic version can be purchased and used by the auditor to document the consideration of nonaudit services and serve as part of the audit documentation regarding independence. The electronic version is available at www.cpa2biz.com (product no. APAYBI12D).

[4] These activities are considered nonaudit services under the revised AICPA Code of Professional Conduct, which was effective for periods beginning on or after December 15, 2014.

services provided. A critical component of the determination is consideration of management's ability to effectively oversee the nonaudit service to be performed. The auditor should determine whether the auditee has designated an individual who possesses suitable skill, knowledge, or experience, and that the individual understands the services to be performed sufficiently to oversee them. However, the individual is not required to possess the expertise to perform or reperform the services. The auditor should document consideration of management's ability to effectively oversee nonaudit services to be performed, regardless of whether the threats to independence are determined to be significant. As noted in the following paragraphs, if an auditee does not have suitable skill, knowledge, or experience as it relates to the service, then independence would be impaired if the nonaudit service were performed.

2.20 If an auditor were to assume management responsibilities for an auditee, the management participation threats created would be so significant that no safeguards could reduce them to an acceptable level. Management responsibilities involve leading and directing an entity, including making decisions regarding the acquisition; deployment; and control of human, financial, physical and intangible resources. Whether an activity is a management responsibility depends on the facts and circumstances, and auditors exercise professional judgment in identifying these activities. Paragraph 3.36 of *Government Auditing Standards* provides examples of activities that are considered to be management responsibilities and would therefore impair independence if performed for an auditee.

2.21 Auditors performing nonaudit services for entities for which they perform audits should obtain assurance that auditee management performs the following functions in connection with the nonaudit services:

    a. Assumes all management responsibilities

    b. Oversees the services by designating an individual, preferably within senior management, who possesses suitable skill, knowledge, or experience

    c. Evaluates the adequacy and results of the services performed

    d. Accepts responsibility for the results of the services

2.22 In the case where the auditee is unable or unwilling to assume these responsibilities, the auditor's provision of the nonaudit services would impair independence. Examples of this would be when the auditee does not have an individual with suitable skill, knowledge, or experience to oversee the nonaudit services provided, or is unwilling to perform those functions due to lack of time or desire.

2.23 In connection with the nonaudit services performed, auditors should establish and document their understanding with the auditee's management and those charged with governance, as appropriate, regarding

- objectives of the nonaudit service;
- services to be performed;
- auditee's acceptance of its responsibilities (as described in paragraph 2.19);
- the auditor's responsibilities; and
- any limitations of the nonaudit service.

2.24 Auditors may be able to provide nonaudit services in the broad areas discussed in paragraphs 3.45–.58 of *Government Auditing Standards* without impairing independence if

- the nonaudit services are not expressly prohibited in *Government Auditing Standards*;
- the auditor has determined that the requirements in paragraphs 3.34–.44 of *Government Auditing Standards* for performing nonaudit services are met; and
- any significant threats to independence have been eliminated or reduced to an acceptable level through the use of safeguards.

Auditors should use the conceptual framework to evaluate independence given the facts and circumstances of individual services not specifically prohibited in the standard.

2.25 An auditor who previously performed nonaudit services for an entity that is the prospective subject of an audit should evaluate the impact of those nonaudit services on independence before accepting an audit. Nonaudit services provided by auditors can impact independence of mind and in appearance in periods subsequent to the period in which the nonaudit service was provided. See paragraphs 3.42–.43 of *Government Auditing Standards* for additional considerations related to these circumstances.

2.26 *Government Auditing Standards* allows government auditors who may be required by law or regulation to perform both an audit and a nonaudit service that could impair the auditor's independence and who cannot decline to perform or terminate the service due to requirements over which the auditor has no control. In this situation, government auditors should disclose the nature of the threat that could not be eliminated or reduced to an acceptable level, and modify the compliance statement in the auditors' report. See chapter 4 of this guide for information regarding modifying the compliance statement in the auditor's report.

Documentation of Independence

2.27 Documentation of independence considerations provides evidence of the auditor's judgment in forming conclusions regarding compliance with independence requirements. *Government Auditing Standards* require the auditor to

- document threats to independence that require the application of safeguards, along with safeguards applied, in accordance with the conceptual framework for independence,
- document the safeguards required if an audit organization is structurally located within a governmental entity and is considered independent based on those safeguards,
- document consideration of auditee management's ability to effectively oversee a nonaudit service to be provided by the auditor. (The auditor should determine that the auditee has designated an individual who possesses suitable skills, knowledge, or experience, and that the individual understands the services to be performed sufficiently to oversee them.)
- document the auditor's understanding with an auditee for which the auditor will perform a nonaudit service.

Government Auditing Standards—Ethical Principles and General Standards **17**

> **Emphasis Point**
>
> Auditor independence is first considered very early in the planning stages of the audit process. Auditors are cautioned that circumstances often change during the performance of an audit, which may require the auditor to reevaluate conclusions reached regarding the significance of threats to independence. For example, the significance of threats in the aggregate and the necessity for the application and types of safeguards to be applied to eliminate or reduce those threats to an acceptable level may need to be reevaluated if the auditor is engaged to perform additional nonaudit services.

AICPA—Government Auditing Standards *Rules Comparison*[5]

2.28 Because the independence rules of both *Government Auditing Standards* and the AICPA apply to a financial audit performed in accordance with *Government Auditing Standards*, this section provides a discussion of the main areas of difference between *Government Auditing Standards* and the AICPA Code of Professional Conduct. Such differences relate to

- when the conceptual framework is used and
- documentation of the assessment of management's skills, knowledge, or experience.

2.29 *When the conceptual framework is used.* Both *Government Auditing Standards* and the AICPA Code of Professional Conduct contain conceptual frameworks for independence with similar characteristics. Under *Government Auditing Standards*, the conceptual framework is used to evaluate threats to independence when making decisions on conditions or activities that are not specifically prohibited by *Government Auditing Standards*. The AICPA conceptual framework should be used when making decisions on independence matters that are not explicitly addressed by the Code of Professional Conduct. Consequently, the *Government Auditing Standards* conceptual framework will be used more often than the AICPA conceptual framework.

2.30 *Documentation regarding the assessment of management's skills, knowledge, or experience.* Government Auditing Standards requires the auditor to document the consideration of management's ability to effectively oversee nonaudit services to be performed. Although the requirement to assess management's skills, knowledge, or experience is found in AICPA rules related to nonaudit services, the AICPA rules do not contain a requirement to document this assessment. See paragraph 2.27 for additional documentation requirements of *Government Auditing Standards*.

Professional Judgment

2.31 *Government Auditing Standards* states that auditors must use professional judgment in planning and performing audits and in reporting the

---

[5] See the preface section titled "AICPA's Ethics Codification Project," for information on the codification of the AICPA Code of Professional Conduct. The revised code was effective December 15, 2014, and the content in this guide has been updated to reflect that effective date.

results. Although this standard is similar to the discussion of due professional care in AU-C section 200, *Government Auditing Standards* provides its own discussion on this topic which is summarized in the following paragraphs.

2.32 Professional judgment includes exercising reasonable care and professional skepticism. Reasonable care includes acting diligently in accordance with applicable professional standards and ethical principles. Professional skepticism is an attitude that includes a questioning mind and a critical assessment of evidence. Professional skepticism includes a mindset in which auditors assume that management is neither dishonest nor of unquestioned honesty.

2.33 Chapter 3 of *Government Auditing Standards* provides guidance regarding the use of professional judgment in the audit process. The following are considerations when exercising professional judgment:

- A critical component of an audit is the use of the auditor's professional knowledge, skills, and experience to diligently perform, in good faith and with integrity, the gathering of information and the objective evaluation of the sufficiency and appropriateness of evidence. Professional judgment and competence are interrelated because judgments made are dependent upon the auditor's competence.

- Professional judgment represents the application of the collective knowledge, skills, and experiences of all the personnel involved with an audit, as well as the professional judgment of individual auditors. In addition to personnel directly involved in the audit, professional judgment may involve collaboration with other stakeholders, external specialists, and management in the audit organization.

- Using professional judgment is important to auditors in carrying out all aspects of their professional responsibilities, including following the independence standards and related conceptual framework; maintaining objectivity and credibility; assigning competent staff to the audit; defining the scope of work; evaluating, documenting, and reporting the results of the work; and maintaining appropriate quality control over the audit process.

- Using professional judgment is important to auditors in applying the conceptual framework to determine independence in a given situation. This includes the consideration of any threats to the auditor's independence and related safeguards that may mitigate the identified threats. Auditors use professional judgment in identifying and evaluating any threats to independence, including threats to the appearance of independence.

- Using professional judgment is important to auditors in determining the required level of understanding of the audit subject matter and related circumstances. This includes consideration about whether the audit team's collective experience, training, knowledge, skills, abilities, and overall understanding are sufficient to assess the risks that the subject matter of the audit may contain a significant inaccuracy or could be misinterpreted.

- An auditor's consideration of the risk level of each audit, including the risk of arriving at improper conclusions, is also important. Within the context of audit risk, exercising professional judgment in determining the sufficiency and appropriateness of evidence to be used to support the findings and conclusions based on the audit objectives and any recommendations reported is an integral part of the audit process.

Although *Government Auditing Standards* places responsibility on each auditor and the audit organization to exercise professional judgment in planning and performing an audit, it does not imply unlimited responsibility or infallibility on the part of either the individual auditor or the audit organization. Absolute assurance is not attainable due to factors such as the nature of evidence and characteristics of fraud. Professional judgment does not mean eliminating all possible limitations or weaknesses associated with a specific audit, but rather identifying, assessing, mitigating, and explaining them.

Competence

2.34 AU-C section 200 requires the auditor to have an understanding of the entire text of an AU-C section, including its application and other explanatory material, to understand its objectives and to apply it properly. *Government Auditing Standards* includes its own requirements and guidance in the area of competence, technical knowledge, and continuing professional education (CPE) as further discussed in the following paragraphs.

2.35 *Government Auditing Standards* states that the staff assigned to perform the audit must collectively possess adequate professional competence needed to address the audit objectives and perform the work in accordance with *Government Auditing Standards*. The audit organization's management should assess skill needs to consider whether its workforce has the essential skills that match those necessary to perform the particular audit. Accordingly, audit organizations should have a process for recruitment, hiring, continuous development, assignment, and evaluation of staff to maintain a competent workforce. The nature, extent, and formality of the process will depend on various factors such as the size of the audit organization, its structure, and its work.

2.36 Staff assigned to conduct an audit in accordance with *Government Auditing Standards* also should collectively possess the technical knowledge, skills, and experience necessary to be competent for the type of work being performed before beginning work on that audit. Paragraph 3.72 of *Government Auditing Standards* provides a listing of the technical knowledge, skills, and experience that staff should collectively possess. In addition, auditors performing financial audits should be knowledgeable in U.S generally accepted accounting principles, or with the applicable financial reporting framework being used, and the AICPA Statements on Auditing Standards (SASs); auditors should be competent in applying AICPA SASs to the audit work.

2.37 Auditors engaged to perform financial audits in accordance with *Government Auditing Standards* should be licensed CPAs, persons working for a licensed CPA firm or for a government auditing organization, or licensed accountants in states that have multiclass licensing systems that recognize licensed accountants other than CPAs.

Continuing Professional Education

2.38 Auditors performing work in accordance with *Government Auditing Standards*, including planning, directing, performing audit procedures, or reporting on an audit, should maintain their professional competence through CPE. Each auditor performing work under *Government Auditing Standards* should complete, every 2 years, at least 24 hours of CPE that directly relates to government auditing, the government environment, or the specific or unique environment in which the auditee operates. Those auditors who are involved in any amount of planning, directing, or reporting on *Government Auditing Standards* audits and auditors who are not involved in those activities but charge 20 percent or more of their time annually to *Government Auditing Standards* audits should also obtain at least an additional 56 hours of CPE (for a total of 80 hours of CPE in every 2-year period) that enhances the auditor's professional proficiency to perform audits. At least 20 of those 80 hours should be completed in each year of the 2-year period. Auditors hired or initially assigned to audits performed in accordance with *Government Auditing Standards* after the beginning of an audit organization's 2-year CPE period should complete a prorated number of CPE hours.[6]

2.39 Determining what subjects are appropriate for individual auditors is a matter of professional judgment to be exercised by auditors in consultation with appropriate officials in the audit organization. Considerations in exercising that judgment are the auditor's experience, the responsibilities they assume in performing audits under *Government Auditing Standards*, and the operating environment of the auditee. Although meeting the CPE requirements is primarily the responsibility of individual auditors, the audit organization should have quality control procedures to help ensure that auditors meet the CPE requirements, including documentation of the CPE completed.

2.40 The GAO has issued Government Auditing Standards: *Guidance on GAGAS Requirements for Continuing Professional Education,*[7] which provides additional guidance to auditors and audit organizations in implementing the CPE requirements prescribed by *Government Auditing Standards*. Among other things, the guidance discusses who is subject to the CPE requirements; the programs, activities, subjects, and topics that qualify as acceptable CPE; how compliance with CPE requirements is measured; how to measure CPE hours; and how CPE requirements are to be administered. The guidance states that the CPE requirements found in *Government Auditing Standards* apply to external auditors and internal auditors, both government and nongovernment, who perform audits or attestation engagements that are conducted in accordance with *Government Auditing Standards*. (Note that the CPE requirements apply to public accountants both certified and noncertified.)

2.41 *Government Auditing Standards* does not require external specialists to meet its CPE requirements; however, the audit team should determine that the external specialists are qualified and competent in their areas of specialization. Internal specialists consulting on an audit performed under *Government Auditing Standards* who are not involved in directing, performing audit procedures, or reporting on the audit are not required to meet the *Government*

---

[6] The document, Government Auditing Standards: *Guidance on GAGAS Requirements for Continuing Professional Education*, provides an explanation of how to calculate the prorated number of hours required in this situation. GAO-05-568G can be found on the Yellow Book page of the GAO's website at www.gao.gov/govaud/ybcpe2005.pdf. See paragraph 2.40 for additional information regarding the publication.

[7] Although this is a 2005 publication, because CPE requirements have not changed, the guidance in this document is still in effect. However, paragraph references to *Government Auditing Standards* as found within the document are not correct since they are based on a previous revision of the Yellow Book.

Auditing Standards CPE requirements. Nevertheless, the audit team should determine that they are qualified and competent in their areas of specialization.

2.42 The audit team should determine that internal specialists who are performing work in accordance with *Government Auditing Standards* as part of the audit team, including directing, performing audit procedures, or reporting on the audit, comply with *Government Auditing Standards*, including the CPE requirements. Training in their areas of specialization qualifies under the requirement for 24 hours of CPE directly relating to government auditing, the government environment, or the specific or unique environment in which the auditee operates. The *Government Auditing Standards* CPE requirements become effective for internal specialists when an audit organization first assigns an internal specialist to an audit performed in accordance with *Government Auditing Standards*.

Emphasis Point

Auditors subject to *Government Auditing Standards* CPE requirements have the additional responsibility to obtain qualifying CPE. Determining what subjects are appropriate to satisfy this CPE requirement is a matter of professional judgment, and includes the consideration of certain factors related to the individual auditor. See paragraphs 2.40–.41 for more information.

Quality Control and Assurance

2.43 The Auditing Standards Board of the AICPA issues Statements on Quality Control Standards that must be adhered to by CPA firms that are enrolled in an AICPA approved practice monitoring program.[8] See QC section 10, *A Firm's System of Quality Control* (AICPA, *Professional Standards*), for the applicable requirements and guidance.[9] Furthermore, *Government Auditing Standards* states that each audit organization performing audits in accordance with *Government Auditing Standards* must (*a*) establish and maintain a system of quality control that is designed to provide the audit organization with reasonable assurance that the organization and its personnel comply with professional standards and applicable legal and regulatory requirements, and (*b*) have an external peer review performed by reviewers independent of the audit organization being reviewed at least once every three years.[10]

2.44 The nature, extent, and formality of an audit organization's quality control system will vary based on the organization's circumstances, such as the organization's size, number of offices and locations, knowledge and experience of its personnel, nature and complexity of its audit work, and cost-benefit considerations. Each audit organization should document its quality control policies and procedures and communicate those policies and procedures to its personnel. The audit organization should document compliance with its quality

---

[8] See appendix A, "Overview of Statements on Quality Control Standards," of this guide for additional information on AICPA quality control standards.

[9] When performing audits under *Government Auditing Standards*, firms that are enrolled in an AICPA approved practice monitoring program must adhere to both the Statements on Quality Control Standards and the quality control and assurance requirements in *Government Auditing Standards*.

[10] See the discussion beginning at paragraph 2.46 for information on external peer review.

control policies and procedures and maintain the documentation for a period of time sufficient to enable those performing monitoring procedures and peer reviews to evaluate the extent of the audit organization's compliance with its quality control policies and procedures. The form and content of the documentation are a matter of professional judgment and will vary based on the audit organization's circumstances.

2.45 An audit organization should establish policies and procedures in its system of quality control that collectively address

- leadership responsibilities for quality within the audit organization;
- independence, legal, and ethical requirements;
- initiation, acceptance, and continuance of audits;
- human resources;
- audit performance, documentation, and reporting; and
- monitoring of quality.

Paragraphs 3.86–.95 of *Government Auditing Standards* address the requirements for a system of quality control that should be collectively addressed in an audit organization's policies and procedures. Appendix I section A3.10 of *Government Auditing Standards* provides supplemental guidance to assist auditors and audit organizations in establishing policies and procedures in a system of quality control.

External Peer Review

2.46 As noted previously, *Government Auditing Standards* requires audit organizations to have an external peer review performed by reviewers independent of the audit organization being reviewed at least once every three years. *Government Auditing Standards* provides that the first peer review for an audit organization not already subject to a peer review requirement covers a review period ending no later than three years from the date an audit organization begins its first audit in accordance with *Government Auditing Standards*. The period under review generally covers one year, although peer review programs may choose a longer review period. Generally, the deadlines for peer review reports are established by the entity that administers the peer review program. Extensions of the deadlines for submitting the peer review report exceeding three months beyond the due date are granted by the entity that administers the peer review program and GAO.

2.47 The external peer review should be sufficient in scope to provide a reasonable basis for determining whether, for the period under review, the reviewed audit organization's system of quality control was suitably designed and whether the audit organization is complying with its quality control system in order to provide the audit organization with reasonable assurance of conforming with applicable professional standards. Paragraphs 3.97–.104 of *Government Auditing Standards* contain requirements and guidance relating to the overall criteria for the peer review team, required elements in the scope of the peer review, assessing peer review risk, selecting individual audits for review, and preparing written reports to communicate the results of the peer review. Peer review report types identified under *Government Auditing*

Standards are *Pass, Pass with Deficiencies,* and *Fail,* all of which are consistent with AICPA peer review report categories.[11]

2.48 An external audit organization should make its most recent peer review report publicly available (for example, on a publicly available website or to a publicly available file designed for public transparency of peer review results). If these options are not available to the audit organization, it should use the same transparency mechanism it uses to make other information public. The audit organization should provide the peer review report to others upon request. If a separate communication detailing findings, conclusions, and recommendations is issued, public availability of that communication is not required. Appendix I section A3.12 of *Government Auditing Standards* provides additional information related to achieving transparency of the peer review report, including information that may be included with the publicly available report to help users understand the meaning of the peer review report.

2.49 Audit organizations seeking to enter into a contract to perform an audit in accordance with *Government Auditing Standards* should provide the following to the party contracting for the services when requested:

- The audit organization's most recent peer review report
- Any subsequent peer review reports received during the period of the contract

2.50 Auditors who are using another audit organization's work should request a copy of that organization's latest peer review report and any other written communication issued, and the audit organization should provide these documents when requested.

---

[11] The document Government Auditing Standards: *Guidance for Understanding the New Peer Review Ratings*, published January 13, 2014, is available on the Yellow Book page of the GAO's website.

2.51

Appendix—*Government Auditing Standards* Conceptual Framework for Independence

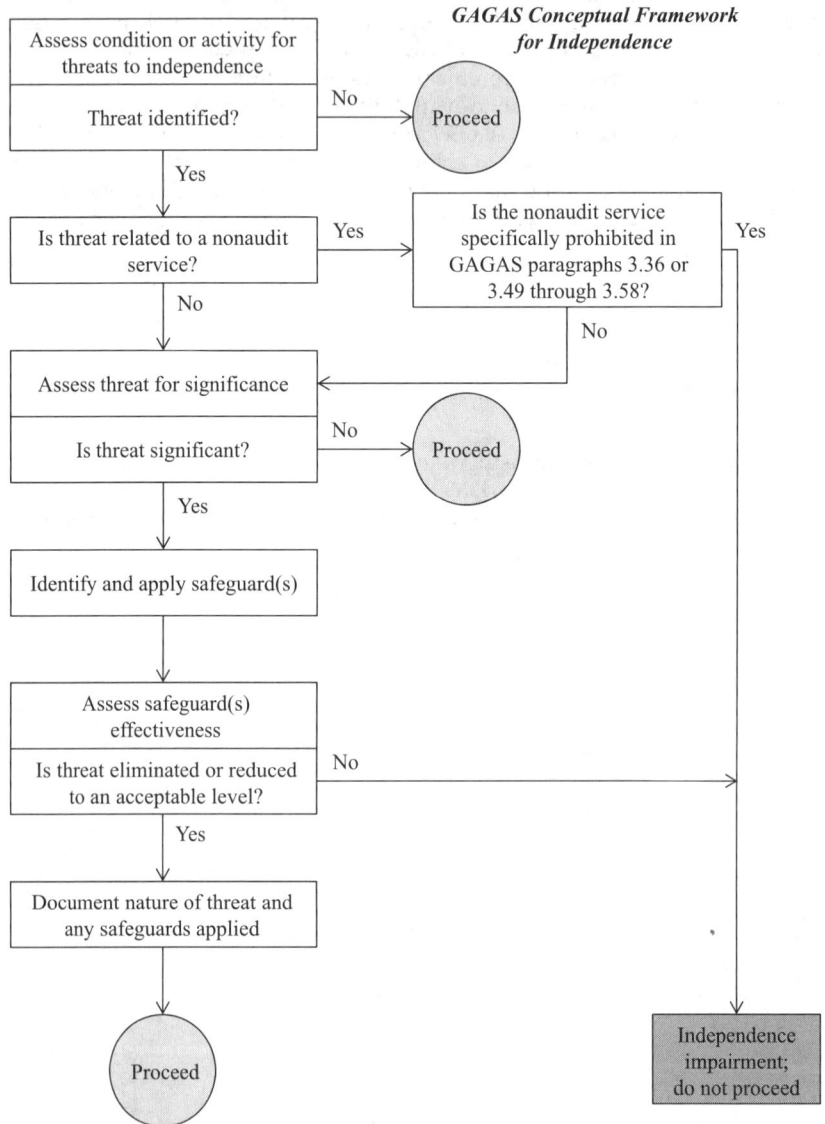

Source: Appendix II of *Government Auditing Standards*, December 2011 Revision.

Chapter 3

Planning and Performing a Financial Statement Audit in Accordance With Government Auditing Standards

> **۞ Update 3-1: Uniform Guidance for Federal Awards**
>
> In December 2013, the Office of Management and Budget (OMB) issued Title 2 U.S. *Code of Federal Regulations* (CFR) Part 200, *Uniform Administrative Requirements, Cost Principles, and Audit Requirements for Federal Awards* (Uniform Guidance), that establishes uniform cost principles and audit requirements for federal awards to nonfederal entities and administrative requirements for all federal grants and cooperative agreements. The Uniform Guidance is effective for nonfederal entities for all federal awards and certain funding increments provided on or after December 26, 2014. The standards in Subpart F, "Audit Requirements," are effective for audits of fiscal years beginning on or after December 26, 2014, with no early implementation permitted. Therefore, auditees subject to a single audit with December 25, 2015, and later year ends will be required to undergo the audit under Subpart F of the Uniform Guidance. Note that audits of fiscal years ending prior to the effective date of the Uniform Guidance audit requirements are subject to an audit under OMB Circular A-133, *Audits of States, Local Governments, and Non-Profit Organizations* (Circular A-133). See the preface for more information.
>
> **Important Note**
>
> *Government Auditing Standards* are applicable to a single audit, whether performed under Circular A-133 or the Uniform Guidance. This edition of the guide includes guidance for performing a compliance audit under both Circular A-133 and the Uniform Guidance. See part II, *Circular A-133 Audits*, or part III, *Uniform Guidance Audits*, as applicable to the compliance audit being performed.

Introduction

3.01 *Government Auditing Standards* incorporates by reference AICPA Statements on Auditing Standards.[1] Therefore, auditors performing financial statement audits in accordance with *Government Auditing Standards* should comply with generally accepted auditing standards (GAAS), the requirements found in chapters 1–3 of *Government Auditing Standards*, and the additional requirements for financial audits found in chapter 4, "Standards for Financial Audits," of *Government Auditing Standards*. This chapter focuses on the considerations for planning and performing a financial statement audit in accordance with *Government Auditing Standards*. It provides a description of

---

[1] *Government Auditing Standards* provides that the auditor may elect to use auditing standards established by the PCAOB or the International Auditing and Assurance Standards Board in conjunction with *Government Auditing Standards*. See chapter 1, "Introduction and Overview of *Government Auditing Standards*," of this guide for additional information.

relevant GAAS requirements and guidance[2] only to the extent necessary to assist auditors in understanding the requirements of *Government Auditing Standards* and how they relate to GAAS. This chapter also includes information on relevant guidance found in the AU-C section paragraphs titled "Considerations Specific to Audits of Governmental Entities."[3]

3.02 Financial audits performed in accordance with *Government Auditing Standards* include financial statement audits and other related financial audits. *Government Auditing Standards* notes that reporting on a financial statement audit performed under *Government Auditing Standards* includes reports on internal control over financial reporting and on compliance with provisions of laws, regulations, contracts, and grant agreements that have a material effect on the financial statements.[4] Other types of financial audits include those auditing compliance with applicable compliance requirements relating to one or more government programs. Examples of this type of financial audit are the compliance audits required by Circular A-133, the Uniform Guidance, and U.S. Department of Housing and Urban Development's *Consolidated Audit Guide for Audits of HUD Programs*, all of which are performed using the requirements and guidance in *Government Auditing Standards* and AU-C section 935, *Compliance Audits* (AICPA, *Professional Standards*).[5]

3.03 Management is responsible for complying with applicable laws and regulations, including identifying and obtaining audits that satisfy relevant legal, regulatory, or contractual requirements. This may include audit requirements in addition to an audit in accordance with GAAS. For example, requirements could include the need to have an audit performed in accordance with *Government Auditing Standards* or the Single Audit Act and Circular A-133. See paragraph 3.61 for additional information when an audit under *Government Auditing Standards*, or a single audit, is required but not performed.

---

[2] Additional information for planning and performing a financial statement audit in accordance with generally accepted auditing standards can be found in the relevant AICPA professional standards and applicable Audit and Accounting Guides, such as *Not-for-Profit Entities*; *State and Local Governments*; *Health Care Entities*; *Gaming*; *Employee Benefit Plans*; and *Depository and Lending Institutions: Banks and Savings Institutions, Credit Unions, Finance Companies, and Mortgage Companies*.

[3] The guidance found in the AU-C section paragraphs titled "Considerations Specific to Governmental Entities" highlights considerations specific to governmental entities, entities receiving government funding, and entities being audited in accordance with *Government Auditing Standards*. Relevant guidance related to entities receiving government funding and those being audited in accordance with *Government Auditing Standards* has been incorporated into this chapter.

[4] As explained in the AICPA Audit and Accounting Guide *State and Local Governments*, the auditor generally expresses or disclaims an opinion on a government's basic financial statements by providing an opinion or disclaimer of opinion on each opinion unit required to be presented in those financial statements. In addition, the auditor may provide opinions or disclaimers of opinions on additional opinion units if engaged to set the scope of the audit and assess materiality at a more detailed level than by the opinion units required for the basic financial statements. Throughout this guide, the use of the singular terms *opinion* and *disclaimer of opinion* encompasses the multiple opinions and disclaimers of opinion that generally will be provided on a government's basic financial statements.

[5] Other types of financial audits may require an audit performed under *Government Auditing Standards*. This guide addresses financial statement audits performed in accordance with *Government Auditing Standards* (part I) and compliance audits performed under both Office of Management and Budget (OMB) Circular A-133, *Audits of States, Local Governments, and Non-Profit Organizations (Circular A-133)* (part II), and Title 2 U.S. *Code of Federal Regulations* Part 200, *Uniform Administrative Requirements, Cost Principles, and Audit Requirements for Federal Awards* (Uniform Guidance) (part III).

Agreeing Upon the Terms of the Engagement With Management

3.04 Agreeing upon the terms of the audit engagement with management of the auditee reduces the risk of misunderstanding about the respective responsibilities of management and the auditor. Therefore, the auditor should agree upon the terms of the engagement with management or those charged with governance, as appropriate. AU-C section 210, *Terms of Engagement* (AICPA, *Professional Standards*), states that the objective of the auditor is to accept an audit engagement for a new or existing audit client only when the basis upon which it is to be performed has been agreed upon through

   a. establishing whether the preconditions for an audit are present, and
   b. confirming that a common understanding of the terms of the audit engagement exists between the auditor and management and, when appropriate, those charged with governance.

3.05 AU-C section 210 notes that in order to establish that the preconditions for an audit are present, the auditor should determine whether the financial reporting framework to be applied in the preparation of the financial statements is acceptable. In addition, the auditor should obtain the agreement of management that it acknowledges and understands its responsibility

- for the preparation and fair presentation of the financial statements in accordance with the applicable reporting framework;
- for the design, implementation, and maintenance of internal control relevant to the preparation and fair presentation of financial statements that are free from material misstatement whether due to fraud or error; and
- to provide the auditor access to all information relevant to the preparation and fair presentation of the financial statements, additional information that the auditor may request, and unrestricted access to persons within the entity from whom the auditor determines it necessary to obtain audit evidence.

3.06 If the preconditions for an audit are not present the auditor should discuss the matter with management. Unless the auditor is required by law or regulation to do so, the auditor should not accept the proposed engagement if (*a*) the auditor has determined the financial reporting framework to be applied in the preparation of the financial statements to be unacceptable, or (*b*) the agreement with management has not been obtained. See AU-C section 210 for more information related to preconditions for an audit.

3.07 The agreed upon terms of the audit engagement should be documented in an engagement letter or other suitable form of written agreement.[6] AU-C section 210 describes the general requirements for this communication. In addition to those items noted in paragraphs .A24–.26 of AU-C section 210,

---

[6] Paragraph .A42 of AU-C section 210, *Terms of Engagement* (AICPA, *Professional Standards*), provides an illustrative audit engagement letter for an audit of general purpose financial statements prepared in accordance with generally accepted accounting principles as promulgated by FASB. The communication will vary according to individual requirements and circumstances. For example, the illustration would have to be modified when the audit is also performed under *Government Auditing Standards* as further discussed in this paragraph.

examples of items the auditor may consider including, as applicable, in the communication when he or she is engaged to perform an audit of financial statements in accordance with *Government Auditing Standards* follow:

- A description of the financial statements to be audited and of the reports the auditor is expecting to prepare and issue
- The reporting period
- The auditing standards and requirements that will be followed (that is, GAAS and *Government Auditing Standards*)
- A description of management's responsibility[7] for the following:
  — The preparation and fair presentation of the financial statements in accordance with the applicable financial reporting framework[8]
  — Complying with applicable laws and regulations
  — Implementing systems designed to achieve compliance with applicable laws and regulations
  — Establishing and maintaining effective internal control to help ensure that appropriate goals and objectives are met, following laws and regulations, and ensuring that management and financial information is reliable and properly reported
  — Identifying and providing report copies of previous audits, attestation engagements, or other studies that directly relate to the objectives of the audit, including whether related recommendations have been implemented
  — Addressing the findings and recommendations of auditors, and for establishing and maintaining a process to track the status of such findings and recommendations
  — Taking timely and appropriate steps to remedy fraud and noncompliance with provisions of laws, regulations, contracts, and grant agreements or abuse that the auditor reports
- A description of management and auditor responsibilities for additional information that accompanies the basic financial statements—for example supplementary information[9] and required supplementary information

---

[7] Appendix I, "Supplemental Guidance," section A1.08 of *Government Auditing Standards* contains an expanded list of management responsibilities.

[8] Auditor independence will be impaired if the auditor takes on the role of management or performs management functions on behalf of the audited entity. An auditor's performance of certain nonaudit and other services may also have an impact on auditor independence. See chapter 2, "*Government Auditing Standards*—Ethical Principles and General Standards," of this guide for information regarding auditor independence when the auditor performs nonaudit and certain other services for the auditee.

[9] See chapter 7, "Schedule of Expenditures of Federal Awards (Circular A-133)," of this guide for more information as it relates to a Circular A-133 audit. See chapter 17, "Schedule of Expenditures of Federal Awards (Uniform Guidance)," of this guide for more information as it relates to a Uniform Guidance compliance audit.

Planning and Performing a Financial Statement Audit

- A statement that because the determination of abuse is subjective, *Government Auditing Standards* does not require auditors to detect abuse
- The following items when nonaudit services are to be performed:
  — Objectives of the nonaudit service
  — Nonaudit services to be performed
  — Auditee's acceptance of its responsibilities, including a statement that it assumes all management responsibilities; that it oversees the nonaudit services by designating an individual, preferably within senior management, who possesses suitable skill, knowledge, or experience; that it evaluates the adequacy and results of the nonaudit services performed; and that it accepts responsibility for the results of the nonaudit services
  — The auditor's responsibilities
  — Any limitations of the nonaudit service
- Pertinent information that, in the auditor's professional judgment, needs to be communicated to individuals contracting for or requesting the audit, and to cognizant legislative committees when auditors perform the audit pursuant to a law or regulation, or they conduct the work for the legislative committee that has oversight of the audited entity[10]
- Report distribution responsibilities, including which officials or organizations will receive the report and the steps to be taken to make the report available to the public when the audit organization is responsible for report distribution[11]
- A statement that, subject to applicable laws and regulations, appropriate individuals, as well as audit documentation, will be made available upon request and in a timely manner to appropriate auditors and reviewers
- A statement that receipt of written representations related to management's responsibilities[12] will be expected, along with written representations required by other AU-C sections

Planning the Audit

3.08 AU-C section 300, *Planning an Audit* (AICPA, *Professional Standards*), addresses the auditor's responsibility to plan a financial statement audit. The auditor should establish an overall audit strategy that sets the scope, timing, and direction of the audit and that guides the development of an audit

---

[10] As noted in paragraph 4.03 of *Government Auditing Standards*, this requirement does not apply if the law or regulation requiring an audit of the financial statements does not specifically identify the entities to be audited, such as audits required under the Single Audit Act.

[11] Special considerations may apply to reports that contain confidential or sensitive information. See paragraphs 4.40–.44 of *Government Auditing Standards*.

[12] Paragraphs .10–.11 of AU-C section 580, *Written Representations* (AICPA, *Professional Standards*), provide requirements and guidance related to written representations regarding management's responsibilities. See paragraphs 3.67–.68 for further discussion of written representations from management.

plan.¹³ The nature and extent of planning activities will vary according to the size and complexity of the entity, the key engagement team members' previous experience with the entity, and changes in circumstances that occur during the audit engagement.

3.09 Paragraph .08 of AU-C section 300 sets forth the auditor requirements for establishing the audit strategy. The auditor's responsibilities include identifying characteristics of the engagement that define its scope and ascertaining the reporting objectives of the engagement in order to plan the timing of the audit and the nature of the communications required. Paragraph .09 of AU-C section 300 sets forth the auditor requirements for the audit plan. The audit plan is more detailed than the overall audit strategy in that it includes the nature, timing, and extent of audit procedures to be performed by engagement team members.

3.10 When the financial statement audit is performed under *Government Auditing Standards*, there are additional audit planning considerations. For example, one additional consideration is ensuring that appropriate personnel are assigned to the audit team and that such personnel meet the *Government Auditing Standards* competency requirements, including the continuing professional education (CPE) requirements. See chapter 2, "Government Auditing Standards—Ethical Principles and General Standards," of this guide for more information.

3.11 In planning the consideration of the internal control and compliance aspects of the audit, the auditor should obtain an understanding of the possible effects of provisions of laws, regulations, contracts, and grant agreements that will have a material effect on the financial statements. The auditor should also assess whether management has identified the laws, regulations, and provisions of contracts and grant agreements that are relevant to the audit. See the discussion beginning at paragraph 3.23 for information regarding understanding the entity and its environment.

3.12 *Government Auditing Standards* states that auditors should evaluate whether the auditee has taken appropriate corrective action to address findings and recommendations from previous engagements that could have a material effect on the financial statements or other financial data significant to the audit objectives.¹⁴ When planning the audit, auditors should ask management of the auditee to identify previous audits, attestation engagements, and other studies that directly relate to the audit objectives, including whether related recommendations have been implemented. This information should be used in assessing risk and determining the nature, timing, and extent of current audit work, including determining the extent to which testing the implementation of the corrective actions is applicable to the current audit objectives.¹⁵

---

¹³ This discussion is written in the context of recurring audits. See paragraph .13 of AU-C section 300, *Planning an Audit* (AICPA, *Professional Standards*), for additional considerations in initial audit engagements.

¹⁴ Throughout part I of this guide, "material effect on the financial statements or other financial data significant to the audit objectives" is referred to as "material effect on the financial statements."

¹⁵ There are additional requirements for follow up on prior audit findings in a single audit. See chapter 10, "Compliance Auditing Applicable to Major Programs (Circular A-133)," and chapter 13, "Auditor Reporting Requirements and Other Communication Considerations in a Single Audit

(continued)

Planning and Performing a Financial Statement Audit

3.13 During planning, the auditor may need to give consideration to an auditee's internal audit function, including the availability of work of the internal auditors and the extent of the auditor's potential use of that work. AU-C section 610, *Using the Work of Internal Auditors* (AICPA, *Professional Standards*), addresses the external auditor's responsibilities if using the work of internal auditors. This includes using the work of the internal audit function in obtaining audit evidence and using internal auditors to provide direct assistance under the direction, supervision, and review of the external auditor. See paragraphs 3.31–.32 of *Government Auditing Standards* for a discussion of independence as it related to internal audit functions. See chapter 2 of this guide for information related to CPE requirements for internal auditors.

3.14 As noted in paragraph .11 of AU-C section 260, *The Auditor's Communication With Those Charged With Governance* (AICPA, *Professional Standards*), the auditor should communicate with those charged with governance an overview of the planned scope and timing of the audit. This communication may be either oral or written. The auditor should document any communications made with those charged with governance or others, as well as any decisions reached as a result of those communications. Professional judgment is required when communicating with those charged with governance about the planned scope and timing of the audit so as not to compromise the effectiveness of the audit, particularly when some or all of those charged with governance are involved in managing the entity. For example, communicating the nature and timing of detailed audit procedures may reduce the effectiveness of those procedures by making them too predictable. See paragraph 3.65 for additional communication considerations regarding communicating pertinent information to certain parties, as found in paragraph 4.03 of *Government Auditing Standards*.

Communications With Other Entities

3.15 When professional judgment indicates it is appropriate, the auditor may communicate with grantor agencies (including pass-through entities), federal or state auditors, or other oversight entities to aid in planning the audit. As part of establishing the overall audit strategy, the auditor should document such communications, as well as any decisions reached as a result. If a planning meeting is held matters such as the following may be discussed:

- The audit plan

- The scope of the review and testing of internal control over financial reporting and of compliance

- The identification of grant awards and compliance requirements, including current year changes to those requirements

---

(footnote continued)

(Circular A-133)," of this guide for this information as it relates to a Circular A-133 compliance audit. See chapter 20, "Compliance Auditing Applicable to Major Programs (Uniform Guidance)," and chapter 23, "Auditor Reporting Requirements and Other Communication Considerations in a Single Audit (Uniform Guidance)," of this guide for this information as it relates to a Uniform Guidance compliance audit.

- The form and content of required supplemental reporting
- The status of prior-year findings and recommendations
- Recent audits or other reviews conducted by federal or state auditors or other oversight entities

Group Audits

3.16 AU-C section 600, *Special Considerations—Audits of Group Financial Statements (Including the Work of Component Auditors)* (AICPA, *Professional Standards*), provides requirements and guidance for audits of group financial statements (including the work of component auditors). This guidance applies when the audited entity has components, as defined by AU-C section 600, regardless of whether there is only one or more than one auditor involved. Note that paragraph .02 of AU-C section 600 states that the guidance in AU-C section 600, adapted as necessary, may be useful to an auditor when the audit involves other auditors in the audit of financial statements that are not group financial statements.[16] Additional information on audits of group financial statements can be found in the relevant professional standards and applicable Audit and Accounting Guides, such as *Not-for-Profit Entities*, *State and Local Governments*, and *Health Care Entities*. See chapter 6, "Planning Considerations of Circular A-133," of this guide for group audit considerations related to a Circular A-133 compliance audit and chapter 16, "Auditor Planning Considerations Under the Uniform Guidance," for group audit considerations related to a Uniform Guidance compliance audit.

Materiality

3.17 AU-C section 320, *Materiality in Planning and Performing an Audit* (AICPA, *Professional Standards*), notes that the concept of materiality is applied by the auditor in both planning and performing an audit; in evaluating the effect of identified misstatements on the audit and the effect of uncorrected misstatements, if any, on the financial statements; and in forming the opinion in the auditor's report. The auditor's determination of materiality is a matter of professional judgment and is affected by the auditor's perception of the financial information needs of users of the financial statements. Detailed concepts surrounding materiality in a financial statement audit can be found in the relevant professional standards and applicable Audit and Accounting Guides, such as *Not-for-Profit Entities*, *State and Local Governments*, and *Health Care Entities*.

3.18 *Government Auditing Standards* acknowledges that the AICPA's standards require the auditor to apply the concept of materiality appropriately in planning and performing the audit, but states that additional considerations may apply to audits of government entities or entities that receive government awards. For example, auditors may find it appropriate to use lower materiality levels as compared with the materiality levels used in non-*Government Auditing Standards* audits because of the public accountability of

---

[16] The AICPA's Audit Risk Alert *Understanding the Responsibilities of Auditors for Audits of Group Financial Statements* provides information on implementing the guidance found in AU-C section 600, *Special Considerations—Audits of Group Financial Statements (Including the Work of Component Auditors)* (AICPA, *Professional Standards*).

Planning and Performing a Financial Statement Audit

government entities and entities receiving government funding, various legal and regulatory requirements, and the visibility and sensitivity of government programs.

Audit Documentation

3.19 Audit documentation is the record of audit procedures performed, relevant audit evidence obtained, and conclusions reached. AU-C section 230, *Audit Documentation* (AICPA, *Professional Standards*), states that the objective of the auditor is to provide documentation that provides both a sufficient and appropriate record of the basis for the auditor's report and evidence that the audit was planned and performed in accordance with GAAS and applicable legal and regulatory requirements. The auditor should prepare audit documentation that is sufficient to enable an experienced auditor, having no previous connection to the audit, to understand the nature, timing, and extent of the audit procedures performed; the results of audit procedures performed and the audit evidence obtained; and significant findings or issues arising during the audit, the conclusions reached, and significant professional judgments made in reaching those conclusions.

3.20 AU-C section 230 provides guidance related to identifying the preparer, reviewer, and timing of audit documentation; documenting specific items tested; documenting departures from relevant presumptively mandatory requirements; revising audit documentation after the date of the auditor's report; and ownership and confidentiality of audit documentation.[17] Documentation requirements for specific audit areas are found in the applicable AU-C sections. Paragraph .A30 of AU-C section 230 lists the main paragraphs in other AU-C sections that contain specific documentation requirements. Documentation requirements with particular relevance to an audit performed in accordance with *Government Auditing Standards* are included in the discussion of those topics located throughout this guide.

3.21 In addition to the requirements found in GAAS related to audit documentation, auditors should comply with the following additional requirements when performing an audit in accordance with *Government Auditing Standards*. The auditor should

- document supervisory review, before the report release date, of the evidence that supports the findings, conclusions, and recommendations contained in the auditor's report.

- document any departures from the *Government Auditing Standards* requirements and the impact on the audit and on the auditor's conclusions when the audit report is not in compliance with applicable *Government Auditing Standards* requirements due to law, regulation, scope limitations, restrictions on access to records, or other issues impacting the audit. This applies to

---

[17] Interpretation No. 1, "Providing Access to or Copies of Audit Documentation to a Regulator," of AU-C section 230, *Audit Documentation* (AICPA, *Professional Standards*, AU-C sec. 9230 par. .01–.15), provides guidance related to client confidentiality when the auditor provides audit documentation to a regulator. The guidance addresses situations where the auditor is required by law, regulation, or audit contract to provide the audit documentation and when the auditor provides audit documentation to a regulator when not required.

departures from unconditional and presumptively mandatory requirements when alternative procedures performed in the circumstances were not sufficient to achieve the objectives of the requirements.

3.22 When performing *Government Auditing Standards* financial audits and subject to applicable provisions of laws and regulations, auditors should make appropriate individuals, as well as audit documentation, available upon request and in a timely manner to other auditors or reviewers. Underlying *Government Auditing Standards* audits is the premise that audit organizations cooperate in auditing programs of common interest so that auditors may use others' work and avoid duplication of efforts. The use of the auditor's work by other auditors may be facilitated by contractual arrangements for *Government Auditing Standards* audits that provide for full and timely access to appropriate individuals, as well as audit documentation.

Understanding the Entity and Its Environment and Assessing the Risks of Material Misstatement [18]

3.23 AU-C section 315, *Understanding the Entity and Its Environment and Assessing the Risks of Material Misstatement* (AICPA, *Professional Standards*), states that the objective of the auditor is to identify and assess the risks of material misstatement, whether due to fraud or error, at the financial statement and relevant assertion levels through understanding the entity and its environment, including the entity's internal control, thereby providing a basis for designing and implementing responses to the assessed risks of material misstatements. Obtaining an understanding of an entity and its environment is a continuous, dynamic process of gathering, updating, and analyzing information throughout the audit. The understanding of the entity establishes a frame of reference within which an auditor plans the audit and exercises professional judgment throughout the audit.

3.24 Risk assessment procedures provide the auditor with a basis for the identification and assessment of risks of material misstatement at the financial statement and relevant assertions levels. Risk assessment procedures should include inquiry of management, appropriate individuals within the internal audit function (if such function exists), and others within the entity who may have information that is likely to assist in identifying risks of material misstatement due to fraud or error, analytical procedures, and observation and inspection.[19]

---

[18] This guide focuses on the additional auditing requirements of *Government Auditing Standards*. Therefore, it does not present full coverage of the risk assessment standards. Refer to relevant professional standards and applicable Audit and Accounting Guides, such as *Not-for-Profit Entities*; *State and Local Governments*; *Health Care Entities*; *Gaming*; *Employee Benefit Plans*; and *Depository and Lending Institutions: Banks and Savings Institutions, Credit Unions, Finance Companies, and Mortgage Companies*, and the Audit Guide *Assessing and Responding to Audit Risk in a Financial Statement Audit* for more detailed coverage.

[19] AU-C section 315, *Understanding the Entity and Its Environment and Assessing the Risks of Material Misstatement* (AICPA, *Professional Standards*), notes that inquiries of appropriate individuals in the internal audit function can assist the external auditor in identifying the risk of material noncompliance with applicable laws and regulations and the risk of deficiencies in internal control over financial reporting.

The Entity's Internal Control[20, 21]

3.25 As part of understanding the entity and its environment the auditor should obtain an understanding of internal control relevant to the audit.[22] An understanding of internal control assists the auditor in identifying the types of potential misstatements and factors that affect the risks of material misstatement and in designing the nature, timing, and extent of further audit procedures.

3.26 Paragraph .04 of AU-C section 315 defines internal control as follows:

> *Internal control* is a process effected by those charged with governance, management, and other personnel that is designed to provide reasonable assurance about the achievement of the entity's objectives with regards to the reliability of financial reporting, effectiveness and efficiency of operations, and compliance with applicable laws and regulations.

Controls Relevant to the Audit

3.27 A direct relationship exists between an entity's objectives and the controls it implements to provide reasonable assurance about their achievement. The entity's objectives and, therefore, controls relate to financial reporting, operations, and compliance; however, not all of these objectives and controls are relevant to the auditor's risk assessment. Paragraph .A61 of AU-C section 315 provides an illustration showing the five components of internal control that may be considered as it relates to financial reporting, operations, and compliance. They are

- control environment;
- risk assessment;
- information and communications;
- control activities; and
- monitoring.

The division of internal control into the five components, for purposes of GAAS, provides a useful framework for auditors when considering how different aspects of an entity's internal control may affect the audit.

3.28 When obtaining an understanding of controls that are relevant to the audit, the auditor should evaluate the design of the controls and determine whether they have been implemented by performing procedures in addition to

---

[20] Paragraph .04 of AU-C section 315 notes that the section recognizes the definition and description of internal control contained in *Internal Control—Integrated Framework*, published by the Committee of Sponsoring Organizations of the Treadway Commission (COSO). Appendix I section A.04 of *Government Auditing Standards* notes that the COSO document may be useful to an auditor in assessing the internal control structure of an organization.

[21] In September 2014 the Government Accountability Office issued its revision of *Standards for Internal Control in the Federal Government* (known as the Green Book). It is effective for an entity's 2016 fiscal year, however, early adoption may be elected. Although the Green Book is the source of internal control standards for federal agencies, it may also be adopted by state, local, and quasi-governmental entities, as well as not-for-profit entities.

[22] Because an audit of a government's financial statements under the provisions of AICPA Audit and Accounting Guide *State and Local Governments* is based on opinion units, the auditor's consideration of internal control over financial reporting in planning, performing, evaluating the results of, and reporting on the audit of a government's basic financial statements should address each opinion unit. See that guide for further guidance.

inquiry of the entity's personnel. An improperly designed control may represent a significant deficiency or material weakness in the entity's internal control. The understanding of internal control incorporates knowledge about the design of controls relevant to compliance with laws, regulations, contracts, and grant agreements that have a material effect on the financial statements, as well as knowledge about whether they have been placed in operation. Appendix I, "Supplemental Guidance," section A.06 of *Government Auditing Standards* provides examples of control deficiencies.

Identifying and Assessing the Risks of Material Misstatement

3.29 To provide a basis for designing and performing further audit procedures, the auditor should identify and assess the risks of material misstatement at the financial statement level and the relevant assertion level. Risks of material misstatement at the financial statement level refer to risks that relate pervasively to the financial statements as a whole and potentially affect many assertions.

3.30 Appendix C, "Conditions and Events That May Indicate Risks of Material Misstatement," of AU-C section 315 provides examples of conditions and events that may indicate the existence of risks of material misstatement. The examples cover a broad range of conditions and events that may be relevant to an audit. One example of a condition or event that may indicate a risk of material misstatement that may be relevant in an audit performed in accordance with *Government Auditing Standards* is the situation where there have been inquiries into the entity's operations or financial results by regulatory or government bodies.

3.31 Note that as part of risk assessment, the auditor should determine whether any of the risks identified are, in the auditor's professional judgment, a significant risk. In exercising this judgment, the auditor should exclude the effects of identified controls related to the risk. As noted in paragraph .29 of AU-C section 315, there are several considerations related to identifying significant risks, including whether the risk is a risk of fraud. If the auditor determines that a significant risk exists, the auditor should obtain an understanding of the entity's controls, including control activities, relevant to the risk. Based on that understanding the auditor should evaluate whether such controls have been suitably designed and implemented to mitigate the significant risk identified.

Performing Audit Procedures and Evaluating Audit Evidence Obtained

3.32 AU-C section 330, *Performing Audit Procedures in Response to Assessed Risks and Evaluating the Audit Evidence Obtained* (AICPA, *Professional Standards*), addresses the auditor's responsibility to design and implement responses to the risks of material misstatement identified and assessed by the auditor in accordance with AU-C section 315, and to evaluate the audit evidence obtained in an audit of financial statements. This guidance provides that the auditor should design and perform further audit procedures whose nature, timing, and extent are based on, and are responsive to, the assessed risks of material misstatement at the relevant assertion level. The auditor should obtain more persuasive audit evidence the higher the auditor's assessment of risk.

3.33 The auditor should conclude whether sufficient appropriate audit evidence has been obtained. In forming a conclusion, the auditor should consider all relevant audit evidence, regardless of whether it appears to corroborate or contradict the assertions in the financial statements. If the auditor has not obtained sufficient appropriate audit evidence about a relevant assertion, the auditor should attempt to obtain further audit evidence. If the auditor is unable to obtain sufficient appropriate audit evidence, the auditor should express a qualified opinion or disclaim an opinion on the financial statements.

Tests of Controls

3.34 The auditor should design and perform tests of controls to obtain sufficient appropriate audit evidence about the operating effectiveness of relevant controls if

   a. the auditor's assessment of risks of material misstatement at the relevant assertion level includes an expectation that the controls are operating effectively (that is, the auditor intends to rely on the operating effectiveness of controls in determining the nature, timing, and extent of substantive procedures), or

   b. substantive procedures alone cannot provide sufficient appropriate audit evidence at the relevant assertion level.

In designing and performing tests of controls, the auditor should obtain more persuasive audit evidence the greater the reliance the auditor places on the effectiveness of a control.

3.35 When evaluating the operating effectiveness of relevant controls, the auditor should evaluate whether misstatements that have been detected by substantive procedures indicate that controls are not operating effectively. The absence of misstatements detected by substantive procedures, however, does not provide audit evidence that controls related to the relevant assertion being tested are effective. See AU-C section 330 for further guidance related to testing internal control and performing substantive procedures performed in response to assessed risks. Chapter 4, "Auditor Reporting Requirements and Other Communication Considerations of *Government Auditing Standards*," of this guide provides information regarding the auditor's responsibilities for reporting on internal control, including the applicable requirements under *Government Auditing Standards*.

Consideration of Fraud

3.36 In a GAAS audit, the auditor is responsible for obtaining reasonable assurance that the financial statements as a whole are free from material misstatement, whether due to fraud or error. AU-C section 240, *Consideration of Fraud in a Financial Statement Audit* (AICPA, *Professional Standards*), addresses the auditor's responsibilities relating to fraud in an audit of financial statements. The distinguishing factor between fraud and error is whether the underlying action that results in the misstatement of financial statements is intentional or unintentional.

3.37 The risk of not detecting a material misstatement resulting from fraud is higher than the risk of not detecting one resulting from error. Paragraph .06 of AU-C section 240 notes that this is because fraud may involve sophisticated and carefully organized schemes designed to conceal it, such as forgery, deliberate failure to record transactions, or intentional misrepresentations being made to the auditor. Collusion may also affect the ability of the auditor to detect fraud. The auditor's ability to detect fraud depends on factors such as the skillfulness of the perpetrator, the frequency and extent of manipulation, the degree of collusion involved, the relative size of individual amounts manipulated, and the seniority of those individuals involved. Furthermore, the risk of the auditor not detecting a material misstatement resulting from management fraud is greater than for employee fraud because management is frequently in a position to directly or indirectly manipulate accounting records, present fraudulent financial information, or override control procedures designed to prevent similar frauds by other employees.

3.38 The auditor should maintain professional skepticism throughout the audit, recognizing the possibility that a material misstatement due to fraud may exist, notwithstanding the auditor's past experience of the honesty and integrity of management and those charged with governance. When obtaining reasonable assurance, the auditor is responsible for considering the potential for management override of controls and recognizing the fact that audit procedures that are effective for detecting error may not be effective in detecting fraud. See appendix A, "Examples of Fraud Risk Factors," and appendix C, "Examples of Circumstances That Indicate the Possibility of Fraud," of AU-C section 240. In addition, Appendix I section A.09–.10 of *Government Auditing Standards* contains information related to indicators of fraud risk. Applicable AICPA Audit and Accounting Guides, such as *Not-for-Profit Entities*; *State and Local Governments*; *Health Care Entities*; *Gaming*; *Employee Benefit Plans*; and *Depository and Lending Institutions: Banks and Savings Institutions, Credit Unions, Finance Companies, and Mortgage Companies* provide additional industry-specific guidance on fulfilling the requirements of AU-C section 240.

3.39 A unique aspect of fraud is that whenever the auditor has identified fraud, or has obtained information that indicates that fraud may exist, that matter should be brought to the attention of an appropriate level of management, even if the matter is considered inconsequential. Chapter 4 of this guide provides information regarding communicating instances of fraud, including the applicable requirements under *Government Auditing Standards*.

Assessing the Risk of Material Misstatements Resulting From Fraud

3.40 Paragraph .15 of AU-C section 240 notes that, as part of planning the audit, there should be a discussion among the audit team members to consider how and where the entity's financial statements might be susceptible to material misstatement due to fraud, how management could perpetrate fraud, and how assets of the entity could be misappropriated. See paragraphs .17–.33 of AU-C section 240 for auditor requirements regarding obtaining information related to the risk of fraud, identifying such risks, assessing risks identified, responding to the assessment of identified risks, and addressing the risk of management override.

3.41 Paragraphs .43–.46 of AU-C section 240 provide guidance related to items and events that the auditor should document regarding their consideration of fraud. Among other things, the auditor should document the discussion among engagement personnel in planning the audit regarding the susceptibility of the entity's financial statements to material misstatement due to fraud, procedures performed to obtain information necessary to identify and assess the risks of material misstatement due to fraud, the specific risks of material misstatement due to fraud that were identified, and a description of the auditor's response to those risks.

3.42 AU-C section 240 also addresses the evaluation of audit evidence and communications about possible fraud to management, those charged with governance, and others. Refer to paragraphs .39–.42 of AU-C section 240 for more information. Chapter 4 of this guide discusses the auditor's responsibilities under AU-C section 240 for communications about fraud.

Consideration of Laws and Regulations in an Audit of Financial Statements

3.43 The guidance and requirements in AU-C section 250, *Consideration of Laws and Regulations in an Audit of Financial Statements* (AICPA, *Professional Standards*), address the auditor's responsibility to consider laws and regulations in an audit of financial statements and are designed to assist the auditor in identifying material misstatements of the financial statements due to noncompliance with laws and regulations.[23]

3.44 AU-C section 250 discusses two categories of laws and regulations, and the auditor's responsibilities related to each category. For those provisions of laws and regulations generally recognized to have a direct effect on the determination of material amounts and disclosures in the financial statements, paragraph .07 of AU-C section 250 states that the auditor's responsibility is to obtain sufficient appropriate audit evidence regarding material amounts and disclosures in the financial statements that are determined by the provisions of those laws and regulations. For the second category, (those provisions of other laws and regulations that do not have a direct effect on the determination of the amounts and disclosures in the financial statements but compliance with which may be fundamental to the operating aspects of the entity, the entity's ability to continue operating, or necessary for the entity to avoid material penalties), the auditor's responsibility is limited to performing the procedures specified in paragraph .14 of AU-C section 250 that may identify instances of noncompliance with other laws and regulations that may have a material effect on the financial statements.

3.45 *Government Auditing Standards* states that auditors should extend the AICPA requirements pertaining to the auditor's responsibilities for laws and regulations to also apply to the consideration of compliance with the provisions of contracts and grant agreements. Therefore, in an audit performed under *Government Auditing Standards*, the following guidance should be applied when considering the auditee's compliance with the provisions of contracts and grant agreements.

3.46 Management is responsible for ensuring compliance with laws and regulations, and the provisions of contracts and grant agreements. That

---

[23] AU-C section 250, *Consideration of Laws and Regulations in an Audit of Financial Statements* (AICPA, *Professional Standards*), applies only to audits of financial statements and not to compliance audits performed under AU-C section 935, *Compliance Audits* (AICPA, *Professional Standards*). See part II of this guide for information related to this topic when performing a Circular A-133 compliance audit, and part III of this guide for information related to this topic when performing a Uniform Guidance compliance audit.

responsibility encompasses the identification of relevant provisions of laws, regulations, contracts, and grant agreements, and the establishment of internal control designed to provide reasonable assurance that the auditee complies with those provisions of laws, regulations, contracts, and grant agreements.[24]

3.47 In an audit performed in accordance with *Government Auditing Standards* the auditor should obtain an understanding of the provisions of laws, regulations, contracts, and grant agreements relevant to the entity, and how the entity is complying with them. The auditor should perform procedures that may identify instances of noncompliance with provisions of laws, regulations, contracts, and grant agreements that may have a material effect on the financial statements. The following procedures are among those that may assist the auditor in assessing management's identification of these compliance requirements and in obtaining an understanding of their possible effects on the financial statements:

   a. Consider knowledge about these compliance requirements that has been obtained from prior years' audits.
   b. Discuss these compliance requirements with the auditee's CFO, legal counsel, or grant administrators.
   c. Review the relevant portions of any directly related agreements, such as those related to grants and debt agreements.
   d. Obtain an understanding from management of the sources of revenue, review any related agreements (for example, debt agreements or grant agreements), and inquire about the applicability of any overall governmental regulations to the accounting for the revenue.
   e. Obtain copies of, and review pertinent sections of, laws and regulations—including federal and state constitutions, articles of incorporation, charters, and bylaws—concerning the auditee. The sections of these documents pertaining, as applicable, to financial reporting, investments, debt, taxation, budget, and appropriation and procurement matters may be especially relevant.
   f. Review the minutes of meetings of the governing body of the auditee for the enactment of laws and regulations or information about contracts and grant agreements that have a material effect on the determination of financial statement amounts.
   g. Inquire of the office of the federal, state, or local auditor or other appropriate audit oversight organization about the compliance requirements applicable to entities within their jurisdiction, including statutes and uniform reporting requirements.
   h. Review information about applicable federal and state program compliance requirements, such as the information included in the *OMB Compliance Supplement*, the *Catalog of Federal Domestic Assistance*, federal audit guides, and state and local policies and procedures.
   i. Review the guidance contained in the applicable AICPA Audit and Accounting Guides and the materials available from other professional organizations, such as state societies of CPAs or industry associations.

---

[24] This guide sometimes collectively refers to provisions of laws, regulations, contracts, and grant agreements as *compliance requirements*.

j. Inquire of finance personnel or program administrators from which the auditee receives grants about the restrictions, limitations, terms, and conditions under which such grants were provided. Those administrators usually can be helpful in identifying compliance requirements, which they may identify separately or publish in an audit guide.

The auditor should remain alert to the possibility that other audit procedures applied may bring instances of noncompliance to the auditor's attention.

3.48 If the auditor becomes aware of information concerning an instance of noncompliance or suspected noncompliance with provisions of laws, regulations, contracts, and grant agreements, the auditor should obtain

- *a.* an understanding of the nature of the act and the circumstances in which it has occurred, and
- *b.* further information to evaluate the possible effect on the financial statements.

3.49 If the auditor suspects noncompliance may exist, the auditor should discuss the matter with management (at a level above those involved with the suspected noncompliance, if possible) and, when appropriate, those charged with governance. If sufficient evidence supporting the entity's compliance with the matter at issue cannot be obtained, the auditor should consider the need to obtain legal advice. In addition, the auditor should evaluate the effect of the lack of sufficient appropriate audit evidence on the auditor's opinion.

3.50 It is important to note that obtaining a written representation from management regarding the auditee's compliance with laws and regulations is required under the provisions of AU-C section 580, *Written Representations* (AICPA, *Professional Standards*). That guidance states that the auditor should request management to provide written representations that all instances of identified or suspected noncompliance with laws and regulations whose effects should be considered by management when preparing financial statements have been disclosed to the auditor. See the discussion beginning at paragraph 3.67 for more information on obtaining written representations from management.

3.51 Auditees may be affected by many other laws and regulations, including those related to occupational safety and health, environmental protection, equal employment, food and drug administration, and price fixing or other antitrust violations. Those laws and regulations generally concern an auditee's operations more than financial reporting and accounting. Their effect on an auditee's financial statements is indirect and normally takes the form of the disclosure of a contingent liability that follows from the allegation or determination of illegality. The auditor ordinarily does not have a sufficient basis to recognize possible noncompliance with these laws and regulations. Even when noncompliance with such laws and regulations can have consequences that are material to the financial statements, the auditor may not become aware of the existence of the noncompliance with laws or regulations unless he or she is informed by the auditee, or unless there is evidence of an investigation or enforcement proceeding in the records, documents, or other information normally inspected in an audit of financial statements.

3.52 Because of the inherent limitations described in paragraph .05 of AU-C section 250, an audit conducted in accordance with GAAS or *Government Auditing Standards* provides no assurance that all noncompliance with laws and regulations (including the provisions of contracts and grant agreements) will be detected or that any contingent liabilities that may result will be disclosed.

Consideration of Abuse

3.53 Abuse is a concept that is not addressed in GAAS. However, *Government Auditing Standards* contain requirements and guidance related to abuse, including a requirement to communicate abuse that is, either quantitatively or qualitatively material to the financial statements. *Government Auditing Standards* state that abuse involves behavior that is deficient or improper when compared with behavior that a prudent person would consider reasonable and necessary business practice given the facts and circumstances. Abuse also includes misuse of authority or position for personal financial interests or those of an immediate or close family member or business associate. Abuse does not necessarily involve fraud, or noncompliance with provisions of laws, regulations, contracts, and grant agreements.

3.54 The determination of abuse is subjective, and auditor judgment is a factor. Section A.08 of Appendix I of *Government Auditing Standards* provides the following examples that, depending on the facts and circumstances, may constitute abuse:

- Creating unneeded overtime,
- Requesting staff to perform personal errands or work tasks for a supervisor or manager,
- Misusing the official's position for personal gain,
- Making travel choices that are contrary to existing travel policies or are unnecessarily extravagant or expensive, and
- Making procurement or vendor selections that are contrary to existing policies or are unnecessarily extravagant or expensive.

3.55 Because the determination of abuse is subjective, auditors are not required to detect abuse in financial audits. However, as part of an audit in accordance with *Government Auditing Standards*, if an auditor becomes aware of abuse that could be quantitatively or qualitatively material to the financial statements, the auditor should apply audit procedures specifically directed to determining the potential effect on the financial statements. Examples of such procedures may be extending sample sizes by selectively choosing items for test work, and making inquiries of auditee officials about the nature of and reasons for the situation or transaction.

3.56 After performing additional work, the auditor may discover that the abuse represents potential fraud or noncompliance with provisions of laws, regulations, contracts, or grant agreements. Distinguishing whether a situation or transaction constitutes abuse or, instead, fraud or noncompliance with the provisions of laws and regulations is important because *Government Auditing Standards*[25] has different reporting standards for abuse (and noncompliance

---

[25] In a Circular A-133 audit, as discussed in chapter 9, "Consideration of Internal Control Over Compliance for Major Programs (Circular A-133)," and chapter 10 of this guide, because the OMB cost principles circulars require that costs charged to federal awards be reasonable and necessary for the

(continued)

with contracts or grant agreements) as compared to fraud and noncompliance with provisions of laws and regulations, as discussed in chapter 4 of this guide.

3.57 If the auditor concludes that a situation or transaction is abuse, the auditor should evaluate whether the situation or transaction that constitutes abuse is material to financial statement amounts based on both quantitative and qualitative factors. Qualitative factors that the auditor may consider relevant to that evaluation include the following:

- Whether the abuse is the result of a significant deficiency or material weakness in internal control
- The potential effect of the abuse on the entity's ability to raise resources (for example, through taxes, grants, contributions, or debt or loan financings) in the future
- The potential effect of the abuse on the continuation of existing relationships with vendors, employees, and elected and appointed officials
- Whether the abuse involves collusion or concealment
- Whether the abuse involves an activity that often is scrutinized by elected or appointed officials, citizens, the press, creditors, or rating agencies
- Whether the fact of the abuse is unambiguous rather than a matter of judgment
- Whether the abuse is an isolated event or instead has occurred with some frequency
- Whether the abuse results from management's continued unwillingness to correct internal control deficiencies
- The likelihood that similar abuse will continue in the future
- The cost-benefit of establishing internal control to prevent similar abuse in the future
- The risk that possible undetected abuse would affect the auditor's evaluation

3.58 Exhibit 3-1 summarizes the evaluation and reporting of abuse under *Government Auditing Standards*. See chapter 4 of this guide for further discussion of reporting or otherwise communicating instances of abuse.

(footnote continued)

performance and administration of the awards, situations or transactions involving federal awards that might otherwise appear to constitute abuse instead generally are instances of noncompliance. This concept is discussed in chapter 19, "Consideration of Internal Control Over Compliance for Major Programs (Uniform Guidance)," and chapter 20 of this guide as it relates to a Uniform Guidance compliance audit.

Exhibit 3-1

Evaluation and Reporting of Findings of Possible Abuse

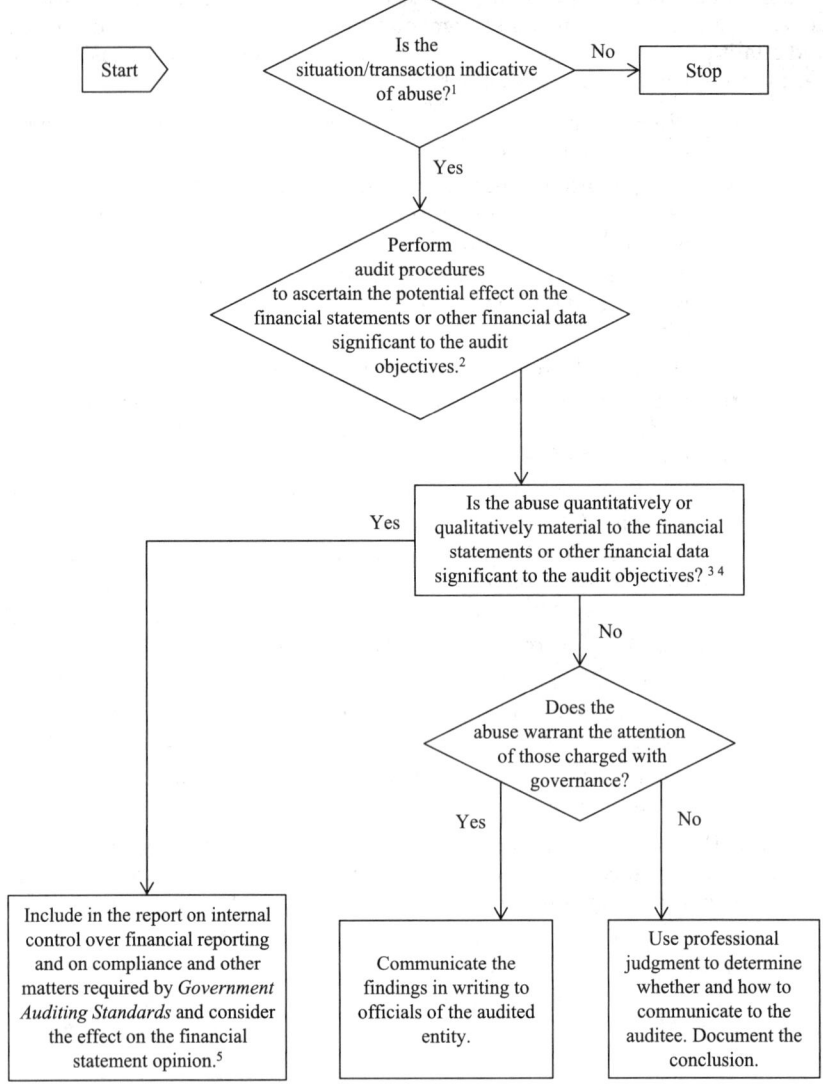

---

[1] Auditors have no responsibility to design the audit to detect abuse. The steps in this flowchart may be used when the auditor becomes aware of indications of abuse.

[2] Chapter 9, "Consideration of Internal Control Over Compliance for Major Programs (Circular A-133)," and chapter 10, "Compliance Auditing Applicable to Major Programs (Circular A-133)," of this guide discuss additional considerations in evaluating abuse related to federal awards in an audit conducted in accordance with Office of Management and Budget Circular

A-133, *Audits of States, Local Governments, and Non-Profit Organizations*. Chapter 19, "Consideration of Internal Control Over Compliance for Major Programs (Uniform Guidance)," and chapter 20, "Compliance Auditing Applicable to Major Programs (Uniform Guidance)," of this guide discuss additional considerations in evaluating abuse related to federal awards in a compliance audit performed under Title 2 U.S. CFR Part 200, *Uniform Administrative Requirements, Cost Principles, and Audit Requirements for Federal Awards* (Uniform Guidance). Of note in those discussions is that situations or transactions involving federal awards that might otherwise appear to constitute abuse instead generally are instances of noncompliance.

[3] Chapter 4, "Auditor Reporting Requirements and Other Communication Considerations of *Government Auditing Standards*," of this guide discusses paragraphs 4.30–.32 of *Government Auditing Standards*, which state that auditors should report abuse directly to parties outside of the auditee in certain circumstances.

[4] Generally, *Government Auditing Standards* instructs the auditor to evaluate findings based on their consequence to the financial statements.

[5] The auditor should report material abuse findings related to a financial statement audit in the report on internal control over financial reporting and on compliance and other matters required by *Government Auditing Standards*. Chapter 4 of this guide discusses when to report those abuse findings in the internal control section of that report or instead in the section on compliance and other matters. Chapter 13, "Auditor Reporting Requirements and Other Communication Considerations in a Single Audit (Circular A-133)," of this guide discusses the reporting of abuse findings related to federal awards in a Circular A-133 audit. Chapter 23, "Auditor Reporting Requirements and Other Communication Considerations in a Single Audit (Uniform Guidance)," of this guide discusses the reporting of abuse findings related to federal awards in a Uniform Guidance compliance audit.

Evaluating Identified Misstatements [26]

3.59 AU-C section 450, *Evaluation of Misstatements Identified During the Audit* (AICPA, *Professional Standards*), provides requirements and guidance regarding the auditor's responsibility to evaluate the effect of identified misstatements on the audit and the effect of uncorrected misstatements, if any, on the financial statements. Paragraph .05 of AU-C section 450 notes that the auditor should accumulate misstatements identified during the audit, other than those that are clearly trivial. The auditor should determine whether the overall audit plan and strategy need to be revised if the aggregate of the misstatements accumulated during the audit approaches materiality determined in accordance with AU-C section 320, or if the nature of the identified misstatements and circumstances of their occurrence indicate that other misstatements

---

[26] Because an audit of a government's financial statements under the provisions of AICPA Audit and Accounting Guide *State and Local Governments* is based on opinion units, the auditor's consideration of financial statement misstatements due to noncompliance with provisions of laws, regulations, contracts, and grant agreements, fraud, or error in evaluating the results of and reporting on the audit of a government's basic financial statements should address each opinion unit. See that guide for further guidance.

may exist that, when aggregated with other misstatements accumulated during the audit, could be material.

Developing Elements of a Finding

3.60 In a financial audit, findings may involve deficiencies in internal control; noncompliance with provisions of laws, regulations, contracts, and grant agreements; fraud; or abuse. *Government Auditing Standards* provides that when auditors identify findings they should plan and perform procedures to develop the elements of the findings that are relevant and necessary to achieve the audit objectives. The four elements of a finding are criteria, condition, cause, and effect (or potential effect). See paragraphs 4.11–.14 of *Government Auditing Standards* for information on the elements of a finding. Chapter 4 of this guide further discusses findings and the *Government Auditing Standards* requirement to obtain and report the views of management concerning the findings, conclusions, and recommendations as well as any planned corrective actions. (Chapter 13, "Auditor Reporting Requirements and Other Communication Considerations in a Single Audit (Circular A-133)," and chapter 23, "Auditor Reporting Requirements and Other Communication Considerations in a Single Audit (Uniform Guidance)," of this guide, as applicable, discuss applying the elements of a finding in reporting the results of a single audit.)

The Auditor's Communication With Those Charged With Governance

3.61 AU-C section 260 addresses the auditor's responsibility to communicate to those charged with governance and provides an overarching framework for that communication. A communication with those charged with governance may be necessary when the auditor becomes aware that the entity is subject to an audit requirement that is not encompassed in the terms of the engagement. The communication would be appropriate when the auditor determines that an audit conducted in accordance with GAAS may not satisfy the relevant legal, regulatory, or contractual requirements—for example, when an entity engages an auditor to perform an audit of its financial statements in accordance with GAAS and the auditor becomes aware the entity also is required to have an audit performed in accordance with one or more of the following:

   a. *Government Auditing Standards*

   b. Circular A-133 or the Uniform Guidance

   c. Other compliance audit requirements, such as state or local laws or program-specific audits under federal audit guides

3.62 When the auditor communicates matters in writing in accordance with AU-C section 260 the communication is considered a by-product report. Therefore, the auditor should include an alert using the guidance in AU-C section 905, *Alert That Restricts the Use of the Auditor's Written Communication* (AICPA, *Professional Standards*). See chapter 4 of this guide for more information.

3.63 An entity requiring an audit under *Government Auditing Standards* may be a not-for-profit entity, a governmental entity, a corporation, or some other form of organization. As noted in Appendix I section A1.06 of *Government Auditing Standards*, those charged with governance are responsible for overseeing the strategic direction of the entity and obligations related to the accountability of the entity. This includes overseeing the financial reporting process, subject matter, or program under audit including related internal controls. In certain entities, those charged with governance may also be part of the entity's management. In some instances, multiple parties may be charged with governance, including oversight bodies, members or staff of legislative committees, boards of directors, audit committees, or parties contracting for the audit.

3.64 Because the governance structures of government entities and organizations receiving government funding can vary widely, it may not always be clearly evident who is charged with key governance functions. In these situations, auditors evaluate the organizational structure for directing and controlling operations to achieve the auditee's objectives. This evaluation also includes how the auditee delegates authority and establishes accountability for its management personnel. In situations where the appropriate person(s) is not clearly identifiable, the auditor and engaging party may need to discuss and agree on the relevant person(s) within the governance structure with whom the auditor will communicate. *Government Auditing Standards* provides that, in those situations where there is not a single individual or group that both oversees the strategic direction of the auditee and the fulfillment of its accountability obligations or in other situations where the identity of those charged with governance is not clearly evident, auditors should document the process followed and conclusions reached for identifying the appropriate individuals to receive the required auditor communications.

3.65 *Government Auditing Standards* provides that, in addition to the requirements under GAAS for auditor communication, auditors should communicate pertinent information that in the auditor's professional judgment needs to be communicated to individuals contracting for or requesting the audit, and to cognizant legislative committees when auditors perform the audit pursuant to a law or regulation or they conduct the work for the legislative committee that has oversight of the auditee.[27]

Communicating Internal Control Matters Identified in an Audit

3.66 AU-C section 265, *Communicating Internal Control Related Matters Identified in an Audit* (AICPA, *Professional Standards*), contains requirements and provides guidance when the auditor identifies deficiencies in internal control in the audit of financial statements. When significant deficiencies or material weaknesses in internal control are identified, the auditor is required to communicate them to those charged with governance and management. In an audit performed in accordance with *Government Auditing Standards* the issuance of the internal control report described in chapter 4 of this guide meets the AU-C section 265 communication requirements. Therefore, a separate communication to meet AU-C section 265 requirements is not necessary when the auditor is issuing a report on internal control over financial reporting and on compliance and other matters that is required by *Government Auditing*

---

[27] Paragraph 4.03 of *Government Auditing Standards* notes that this does not apply if the law or regulation requiring an audit of the financial statements does not specifically identify the entities to be audited, such as audits required by the Single Audit Act. See also paragraph 3.07.

Standards. See chapter 4 of this guide for more information related to the reporting of internal control matters.

Written Representations From Management

3.67 AU-C section 580 states that the auditor should obtain written representations from management as part of an audit conducted in accordance with GAAS. It also includes an illustrative management representation letter and an appendix containing additional representations that may be appropriate to be included in a management representation letter in certain circumstances. With respect to a financial statement audit conducted in accordance with GAAS and *Government Auditing Standards*, representations ordinarily should be tailored to include additional appropriate representations from management relating to matters specific to the auditee.[28] The subsequent examples contain representations that may be relevant to an audit performed in accordance with *Government Auditing Standards* acknowledging that management[29]

    a. is responsible for the preparation and fair presentation of the financial statements in accordance with the applicable financial reporting framework.

    b. is responsible for compliance with the laws, regulations, and provisions of contracts and grant agreements applicable to the auditee.

    c. has identified and disclosed to the auditor all instances, that have occurred or are likely to have occurred, of fraud and noncompliance with provisions of laws and regulations that have a material effect on the financial statements, and any other instances that warrant the attention of those charged with governance.

    d. has identified and disclosed to the auditor all instances, that have occurred or are likely to have occurred, of noncompliance with provisions of contracts and grant agreements that has a material effect on the determination of financial statement amounts.

    e. has identified and disclosed to the auditor all instances that have occurred or are likely to have occurred of abuse that could be quantitatively or qualitatively material to the financial statements.

    f. is responsible for the design, implementation, and maintenance of internal control relevant to the preparation and fair presentation of financial statements that are free from material misstatement, whether due to fraud or error.

    g. acknowledges its responsibility for the design, implementation, and maintenance of internal controls to prevent and detect fraud.

    h. has taken timely and appropriate steps to remedy fraud, noncompliance with provisions of laws, regulations, contracts, and grant agreements, or abuse that the auditor reports.

---

[28] See chapter 7 of this guide for representations the auditor should obtain when issuing an in-relation-to-opinion on the schedule of expenditures of federal awards in a Circular A-133 audit. See chapter 17 of this guide for representations the auditor should obtain when issuing an in-relation-to-opinion on the schedule of expenditures of federal awards in a Uniform Guidance compliance audit. Note that two separate management representation letters may be necessary when the required procedures on the schedule of expenditures of federal awards are completed after the date of the auditor's report on the financial statements.

[29] The auditor may modify these representations, as appropriate, for different conditions, such as if management does not have a process to track the status of audit findings and recommendations.

i. has a process to track the status of audit findings and recommendations.

j. has identified for the auditor previous audits, attestation engagements, and other studies related to the audit objectives and whether related recommendations have been implemented.

k. has provided views on the auditor's reported findings, conclusions, and recommendations, as well as management's planned corrective actions, for the report.

l. acknowledges its responsibilities as it relates to nonaudit services performed by the auditor, including a statement that it assumes all management responsibilities; that it oversees the services by designating an individual preferably within senior management who possesses suitable skill, knowledge, or experience; that it evaluates the adequacy and results of the services performed; and that it accepts responsibility for the results of the services.

3.68 An auditor should obtain representations from those members of management with overall responsibility for financial and operating matters that the auditor believes are responsible for, and knowledgeable about, directly or through others in the organization, the matters covered by the representations. Those individuals may vary depending on the governance structure of the entity. Such members of management may include the CEO and CFO or others in equivalent positions (such as the management of significant components). It often is desirable to obtain representation letters from other auditee officials. The written representations should be dated as of the date of the auditor's report. This is to ensure that the auditor's report is not dated prior to the date on which the auditor has obtained sufficient appropriate audit evidence.

Other Considerations

Exit Conference

3.69 Upon completion of audit work, the auditor may hold a closing or exit conference with senior officials of the auditee. The exit conference assists the auditor in obtaining the views of responsible officials concerning the findings, conclusions, and recommendations, as well as planned corrective action, as required by *Government Auditing Standards*. (Chapter 4 of this guide discusses that *Government Auditing Standards* requirement and its guidance.) That conference also provides the auditee with an advance opportunity to discuss whether planned corrective actions adequately address the auditor's recommendations and to initiate corrective action without waiting for a final audit report. In the case of decentralized operations, auditors may consider having preliminary exit meetings with directors, department heads, and other operating personnel who have direct responsibility for financial management systems and the administration of federal awards.

3.70 The auditor may also consider documenting the names of the auditors who conducted the exit conference, the names and positions of the representatives with whom exit conferences were held and any comments that they had, and other details of the discussions.

3.71

Appendix—Examples of Deficiencies in Internal Control

This appendix contains the listing of examples of control deficiencies found in Appendix I, "Supplemental Guidance," of *Government Auditing Standards*. Although the appendix does not list all circumstances that would constitute a control deficiency, it does provide the auditor with a frame of reference for determining what might be a control deficiency. The following are examples of control deficiencies:

   a. Insufficient control consciousness within the organization. For example, the tone at the top and the control environment. Control deficiencies in other components of internal control could lead the auditor to conclude that weaknesses exist in the control environment.

   b. Ineffective oversight by those charged with governance of the entity's financial reporting, performance reporting, or internal control, or an ineffective overall governance structure.

   c. Control systems that did not prevent, or detect and correct, material misstatements so that it was necessary to restate previously issued financial statements or operational results. Control systems that did not prevent or detect material misstatements in performance or operational results so that it was later necessary to make significant corrections to those results.

   d. Control systems that did not prevent, or detect and correct, material misstatements identified by the auditor. This includes misstatements involving estimation and judgment for which the auditor identifies potential material adjustments and corrections of the recorded amounts.

   e. An ineffective internal audit function or risk assessment function at an entity for which such functions are important to the monitoring or risk assessment component of internal control, such as for a large or complex entity.

   f. Identification of fraud of any magnitude on the part of senior management.

   g. Failure by management or those charged with governance to assess the effect of a significant deficiency (or material weakness) previously communicated to them and either to correct it or to conclude that it does not need to be corrected.

   h. Inadequate controls for the safeguarding of assets.

   i. Evidence of intentional override of internal control by those in authority to the detriment of the overall objectives of the system.

   j. Deficiencies in the design or operation of internal control that could fail to prevent, or detect and correct, fraud, noncompliance with provisions of laws, regulations, contracts or grant agreements, or abuse having a material effect on the financial statements or the audit objective.

   k. Inadequate design of information systems general, application, and user controls that prevent the information system from providing

Planning and Performing a Financial Statement Audit

complete and accurate information consistent with financial, compliance, or performance reporting objectives or other current needs.

l. Failure of an application control caused by a deficiency in the design or operation of an information systems general control.

m. Employees or management who lack the qualifications and training to fulfill their assigned functions.

Chapter 4

Auditor Reporting Requirements and Other Communication Considerations of Government Auditing Standards

> **© Update 4-1: Uniform Guidance for Federal Awards**
>
> In December 2013, the Office of Management and Budget (OMB) issued Title 2 U.S. *Code of Federal Regulations* Part 200, *Uniform Administrative Requirements, Cost Principles, and Audit Requirements for Federal Awards* (Uniform Guidance), that establishes uniform cost principles and audit requirements for federal awards to nonfederal entities and administrative requirements for all federal grants and cooperative agreements. The Uniform Guidance is effective for nonfederal entities for all federal awards and certain funding increments provided on or after December 26, 2014. The standards in Subpart F, "Audit Requirements," are effective for audits of fiscal years beginning on or after December 26, 2014, with no early implementation permitted. Therefore, auditees subject to a single audit with December 25, 2015, and later year ends will be required to undergo the audit under Subpart F of the Uniform Guidance. Note that audits of fiscal years ending prior to the effective date of the Uniform Guidance audit requirements are subject to an audit under OMB Circular A-133, *Audits of States, Local Governments, and Non-Profit Organizations* (Circular A-133). See the preface for more information.
>
> **Important Note**
>
> *Government Auditing Standards* are applicable to a single audit, whether performed under Circular A-133 or the Uniform Guidance. This edition of the guide includes guidance for performing a compliance audit under both Circular A-133 and the Uniform Guidance. See part II, *Circular A-133 Audits*, or part III, *Uniform Guidance Audits*, as applicable to the compliance audit being performed.

Introduction

4.01 *Government Auditing Standards* incorporates by reference AICPA Statements on Auditing Standards (SASs).[1] Therefore, auditors performing financial statement audits in accordance with *Government Auditing Standards* should comply with generally accepted auditing standards (GAAS), the requirements found in chapters 1–3 of *Government Auditing Standards*, and the additional requirements for financial audits found in chapter 4, "Standards for Financial Audits," of *Government Auditing Standards*. This chapter discusses the auditor's reporting requirements and other communication considerations in an audit of financial statements conducted in accordance with *Government*

---

[1] *Government Auditing Standards* provides that the auditor may elect to use auditing standards established by the PCAOB or the International Auditing and Assurance Standards Board in conjunction with *Government Auditing Standards*. See chapter 1, "Introduction and Overview of *Government Auditing Standards*," of this guide for additional information.

Auditing Standards. It provides a description of relevant GAAS requirements and guidance[2] only to the extent necessary to assist auditors in understanding the requirements of *Government Auditing Standards* and how they relate to GAAS. This chapter also emphasizes explanatory material found in the AU-C section paragraphs titled "Considerations Specific to Audits of Governmental Entities."[3] The appendix, "Illustrative Auditor's Reports Under *Government Auditing Standards*," of this chapter (paragraph 4.88) presents illustrative auditor's reports for those audits.

Report on the Financial Statements—GAAS Requirements

4.02 AU-C section 700, *Forming an Opinion and Reporting on Financial Statements* (AICPA, *Professional Standards*), addresses the auditor's responsibility to form an opinion on the financial statements[4] and the form and content of the auditor's report issued as a result of an audit of financial statements. As noted in paragraph .A2 of AU-C section 700, for audits of governmental entities, the objectives of a financial statement audit are often broader than forming and expressing an opinion on the financial statements. These additional objectives include audit and reporting responsibilities beyond those found in GAAS. An example is the *Government Auditing Standards* requirement to report on internal control over financial reporting and on compliance with provisions of laws, regulations, contracts, and grant agreements. Such reporting on internal control and compliance is an integral part of an audit performed under *Government Auditing Standards*. See the discussion beginning at paragraph 4.05 for additional information.

4.03 A number of AU-C sections establish requirements and provide guidance related to opining and reporting on audits of financial statements in addition to AU-C section 700. Those that are particularly relevant to an audit performed in accordance with *Government Auditing Standards* address how the form and content of the auditor's report are affected in certain circumstances, such as when the auditor expresses a modified opinion (a qualified opinion, an adverse opinion, or a disclaimer of opinion), or includes an emphasis-of-matter paragraph or other-matter paragraph in the auditor's report.[5] AU-C

---

[2] Additional information for planning and performing a financial statement audit in accordance with generally accepted auditing standards (GAAS) can be found in the relevant AICPA professional standards and applicable Audit and Accounting Guides, such as *Not-for-Profit Entities*; *State and Local Governments*; *Health Care Entities*; *Gaming*; *Employee Benefit Plans*; and *Depository and Lending Institutions: Banks and Savings Institutions, Credit Unions, Finance Companies, and Mortgage Companies*.

[3] The guidance found in the AU-C section paragraphs titled "Considerations Specific to Governmental Entities" highlights considerations specific to governmental entities, entities receiving government funding, and entities being audited in accordance with *Government Auditing Standards*. Relevant guidance related to entities receiving government funding and those being audited in accordance with *Government Auditing Standards* has been incorporated into this chapter.

[4] As explained in the AICPA Audit and Accounting Guide *State and Local Governments*, the auditor generally expresses or disclaims an opinion on a government's basic financial statements by providing an opinion or disclaimer of opinion on each opinion unit required to be presented in those financial statements. In addition, the auditor may provide opinions or disclaimers of opinions on additional opinion units if engaged to set the scope of the audit and assess materiality at a more detailed level than by the opinion units required for the basic financial statements. Throughout this guide, the use of the singular terms *opinion* and *disclaimer of opinion* encompasses the multiple opinions and disclaimers of opinion that generally will be provided on a government's basic financial statements.

[5] The AU-C sections that are particularly relevant include: AU-C section 705, *Modifications to the Opinion in the Independent Auditor's Report* and AU-C section 706, *Emphasis-of-Matter Paragraphs and Other-Matter Paragraphs in the Independent Auditor's Report* (AICPA, *Professional Standards*).

section 720, *Other Information in Documents Containing Audited Financial Statements*; AU-C section 725, *Supplementary Information in Relation to the Financial Statements as a Whole*; and AU-C section 730, *Required Supplementary Information* (AICPA, *Professional Standards*), provide guidance on the auditor's responsibility with respect to certain information that may be, or may be required to be, presented with the financial statements.[6] Auditors may also refer to applicable AICPA Audit and Accounting Guides, such as *Not-for-Profit Entities*; *State and Local Governments*; *Health Care Entities*; *Gaming*; *Employee Benefit Plans*; and *Depository and Lending Institutions: Banks and Savings Institutions, Credit Unions, Finance Companies, and Mortgage Companies* for additional guidance on reporting on the financial statements of specific industries and for additional GAAS only illustrative auditor's reports.

4.04 Paragraph .31 of AU-C section 700 states that the auditor's report should state that the audit was performed in accordance with GAAS and identify the United States of America as the source of those standards. Furthermore, paragraph .42 of AU-C section 700 notes that the auditor may indicate that the audit was also conducted in accordance with another set of auditing standards. However, the auditor should not refer to having conducted an audit in accordance with another set of standards unless the audit was conducted in accordance with both sets of standards.

Additional Reporting Requirements of *Government Auditing Standards*

4.05 In addition to the AICPA requirements for reporting, the auditor should comply with certain additional requirements when citing *Government Auditing Standards* in their reports. The additional requirements relate to

    a. reporting auditors' compliance with *Government Auditing Standards*;

    b. reporting on internal control and compliance with provisions of laws, regulations, contracts, and grant agreements;

    c. communicating deficiencies in internal control, fraud, noncompliance with provisions of laws, regulations, contracts, and grant agreements, and abuse;

    d. reporting views of responsible officials;

    e. reporting confidential or sensitive information; and

    f. distributing reports.

---

[6] See chapter 7, "Schedule of Expenditures of Federal Awards (Circular A-133)," and chapter 13, "Auditor Reporting Requirements and Other Communication Considerations in a Single Audit (Circular A-133)," of this guide for information related to applying AU-C section 725, *Supplementary Information in Relation to the Financial Statements as a Whole* (AICPA, *Professional Standards*), in a compliance audit performed under Office of Management and Budget Circular A-133, *Audits of States, Local Governments, and Non-Profit Organizations* (Circular A-133). See chapter 17, "Schedule of Expenditures of Federal Awards (Uniform Guidance)," and chapter 23, "Auditor Reporting Requirements and Other Communication Considerations in a Single Audit (Uniform Guidance)," of this guide for information related to applying AU-C section 725 in a compliance audit performed under Title 2 U.S. *Code of Federal Regulations* (CFR) Part 200, *Uniform Administrative Requirements, Cost Principles, and Audit Requirements for Federal Awards* (Uniform Guidance).

The remainder of this chapter discusses the additional requirements for reporting on financial audits as found in paragraphs 4.18–.45 of *Government Auditing Standards*.

4.06 When auditors comply with all applicable *Government Auditing Standards* for a financial statement audit, those standards require the auditor to include a statement in the auditor's report that the audit was performed in accordance with *Government Auditing Standards*. Although *Government Auditing Standards* do not require auditors to cite compliance with AICPA standards when citing compliance with *Government Auditing Standards*, GAAS requires the auditor's report to state that the audit was performed in accordance with GAAS. Furthermore, *Government Auditing Standards* acknowledge that an auditee may need a financial statement audit for purposes other than to comply with a requirement calling for an audit in accordance with *Government Auditing Standards*. For example, the auditee may need a financial statement audit to issue bonds or for other financing purposes. *Government Auditing Standards* do not prohibit auditors from issuing a separate report conforming only to AICPA or other standards.[7]

Reporting on Internal Control Over Financial Reporting and on Compliance

4.07 Auditors should communicate in the report on internal control over financial reporting and compliance, based upon the work performed, (*a*) significant deficiencies and material weaknesses in internal control; (*b*) instances of fraud and noncompliance with provisions of laws or regulations that have a material effect on the financial statements or other financial data significant to the audit objectives[8] and any other instances that warrant the attention of those charged with governance; (*c*) noncompliance with provisions of contracts or grant agreements that has a material effect on the financial statements; and (*d*) abuse that has a material effect, either qualitatively or quantitatively. Auditors report on internal control and compliance regardless of whether or not they identify internal control deficiencies or instances of noncompliance.

4.08 Auditors should include either in the same or in separate report(s) a description of the scope of the auditors' testing of internal control over financial reporting and of compliance with provisions of laws, regulations, contracts, and grant agreements. Auditors should also state in the reports whether the tests they performed provided sufficient, appropriate evidence to support opinions on the effectiveness of internal control and on compliance with provisions of laws, regulations, contracts, and grant agreements.

4.09 The objective of the reporting on internal control over financial reporting in an audit under *Government Auditing Standards* differs from the objective of an examination of internal control in accordance with AICPA Statements on Standards for Attestation Engagements, which is to express an

---

[7] The AICPA Audit and Accounting Guide *State and Local Governments* contains examples and information when financial statements are being issued for such other purpose and cite only GAAS.

[8] Throughout part I of this guide, "material effect on the financial statements or other financial data significant to the audit objectives" is referred to as "material effect on the financial statements."

Auditor Reporting and Other Communication Considerations

opinion on the design or the design and operating effectiveness of an entity's internal control, as applicable. To form a basis for expressing such an opinion, the auditor would need to plan and perform the examination to provide a high level of assurance about whether the entity maintained, in all material respects, effective internal control over financial reporting as of a point in time or for a specified period of time. Although not required, if auditors issue an opinion on internal control, the opinion would satisfy the *Government Auditing Standards* requirement for reporting on internal control. However, in an audit performed under *Government Auditing Standards* the auditor would be required to communicate deficiencies in internal control, fraud, noncompliance with provisions of laws, regulations, contracts, and grant agreements, and abuse as detailed in paragraph 4.07.

4.10 When auditors report separately (including separate reports bound in the same document) on internal control over financial reporting and on compliance with provisions of laws, regulations, contracts, and grant agreements, they should state in the auditor's report on the financial statements that they are issuing those additional reports. They should include a reference to the separate reports and also state that the reports on internal control over financial reporting and on compliance with provisions of laws, regulations, contracts, and grant agreements are an integral part of a *Government Auditing Standards* audit in considering the auditee's internal control over financial reporting and compliance.

4.11 This guide recommends a separate report on internal control over financial reporting and on compliance and other matters,[9] which is referred to in this guide as the "Report on Internal Control over Financial Reporting and on Compliance and Other Matters." This guide also recommends that the reference to the separate report indicate that the separate report does not provide an opinion on internal control over financial reporting or on compliance.[10] See the illustrative reports in examples 4-3–4-9 in the appendix of this chapter (paragraph 4.88).[11] Paragraphs 4.53–.54 further discuss the report on internal control over financial reporting and on compliance.

4.12 Table 4-1 summarizes the *Government Auditing Standards* requirements for reporting matters relating to internal control over financial reporting, fraud, noncompliance with provisions of laws, regulations, contracts, and grant agreements, and abuse, as discussed in this chapter.

---

[9] "Other matters" in the context of reporting under *Government Auditing Standards* is referring to certain fraud and abuse that is required to be reported in the auditor's report.

[10] This guide makes this recommendation so that report users who are accustomed to an opinion on internal control over financial reporting in the auditor's reports for *issuers*, as that term is defined by the Sarbanes-Oxley Act of 2002, or whose audit is prescribed by the rules of the SEC, do not assume that the separate report provides opinions on internal control over financial reporting or compliance. If the auditor provides an opinion on internal control over financial reporting or on compliance, this guide recommends that the reference to the separate report be modified to indicate that there is such an opinion.

[11] These illustrative reports provide example wording based on an audit of a governmental entity, that is, with regards to using titles of governmental financial statements and references to opinions units. However, footnotes are provided to indicate the revisions that would be made to the reports if the entity being audited is a nongovernmental entity, such as a not-for-profit entity.

Table 4-1
Government Auditing Standards Requirements for Reporting Findings

	Report on Internal Control Over Financial Reporting and on Compliance and Other Matters	Communicate in Writing[1]	Auditors Use Professional Judgment to Determine Reporting
Deficiencies in internal control over financial reporting:			
Significant deficiencies	X		
Material weaknesses	X		
Other deficiencies in internal control that are not significant deficiencies or material weaknesses			X
Fraud and noncompliance with provisions of laws or regulations:			
Has a material effect on the financial statements and any other instances that warrant the attention of those charged with governance.	X		
Does not warrant the attention of those charged with governance			X
Noncompliance with provisions of contracts and grant agreements:			

AAG-GAS 4.12   ©2015, AICPA

	Report on Internal Control Over Financial Reporting and on Compliance and Other Matters	Communicate in Writing[1]	Auditors Use Professional Judgment to Determine Reporting
Has a material effect on the determination of financial statement amounts or other financial data significant to the audit objectives	X		
Has an effect on the financial statements that is less than material but warrants the attention of those charged with governance		X	
Does not warrant the attention of those charged with governance			X
Abuse:			
That is material, either quantitatively or qualitatively	X		
Has an effect on the financial statements that is less than material but warrants the attention of those charged with governance		X	
Does not warrant the attention of those charged with governance			X

[1] See paragraphs 4.72–.73.

Internal Control Over Financial Reporting[12]

4.13 *Government Auditing Standards* states that the AICPA requirements to communicate significant deficiencies and material weaknesses identified during an audit form the basis for the reporting required under *Government Auditing Standards*. Therefore, it is important to understand the AICPA guidance and requirements, keeping in mind that the form of communication of significant deficiencies and material weaknesses in internal control in an audit performed in accordance with *Government Auditing Standards* will be the report on internal control over financial reporting and on compliance and other matters. The following paragraphs provide information on the guidance found in GAAS.

4.14 AU-C section 265, *Communicating Internal Control Related Matters Identified in an Audit* (AICPA, *Professional Standards*), provides guidance on communicating deficiencies in an auditee's internal control over financial reporting identified in an audit of financial statements. It states that the auditor should communicate to those charged with governance, in writing and on a timely basis, deficiencies identified during the audit that are considered to be significant deficiencies or material weaknesses, including those that were remediated during the audit. Paragraph .14 of AU-C section 265 provides requirements regarding the content of that communication.

4.15 Paragraph .12 of AU-C section 265 states that the auditor should communicate to management at an appropriate level of responsibility, on a timely basis

- in writing, significant deficiencies and material weaknesses that the auditor has communicated or intends to communicate to those charged with governance, unless it would be inappropriate to communicate directly to management in the circumstances.

- in writing or orally, other deficiencies in internal control identified during the audit that have not been communicated to management by other parties and that, in the auditor's professional judgment, are of sufficient importance to merit management's attention. If other deficiencies in internal control are communicated orally, the auditor should document the communication.

Although AU-C section 265 states that the written communication should be made no later than 60 days following the report release date, the written communication is best made by the report release date because the receipt of the communication may be an important factor in enabling those charged with governance to discharge their oversight responsibilities.

4.16 Paragraphs .11–.16 of AU-C section 265 provide guidance on what should be included in the auditor's written communication of significant deficiencies and material weaknesses in various circumstances. Paragraph .07 of AU-C section 265 defines the terms *material weakness* and *significant deficiency* and paragraphs .09–.10 of AU-C section 265 provide a discussion

---

[12] Chapter 3, "Planning and Performing a Financial Statement Audit in Accordance With *Government Auditing Standards*," of this guide discusses the auditor's consideration of internal control over financial reporting. Because an audit of a government's financial statements under the provisions of the AICPA Audit and Accounting Guide *State and Local Governments* is based on opinion units (see footnote 4 in paragraph 4.02), the auditor's consideration of internal control over financial reporting in planning, performing, evaluating the results of, and reporting on the audit should address each opinion unit.

of the factors affecting the evaluation of deficiencies to determine if they are significant deficiencies or material weaknesses.

4.17 When performing an audit in accordance with *Government Auditing Standards*, the issuance of the required internal control reporting described in paragraphs 4.53–.54 meets the AU-C section 265 communication requirements. Therefore, a separate communication to meet AU-C section 265 requirements is not necessary when the auditor is issuing a *Government Auditing Standards* report, "Report on Internal Control over Financial Reporting and on Compliance and Other Matters," that describes the scope of the auditor's testing of internal control over financial reporting and presents the results of those tests, and that report is distributed to management and those charged with governance within 60 days following the financial statement report release date. If that report is not issued within 60 days, a communication under AU-C section 265 is required.

> **Emphasis Point**
>
> When the compliance work in a single audit is performed at a later date, the "single audit reporting package" may be issued later than 60 days after the financial statement report release date. In this case a separate communication would be required. Paragraph .14 of AU-C section 265 provides information about what should be included in the auditor's written communication in this situation.

4.18 Law or regulation may require the auditor to communicate to those charged with governance or other relevant parties (such as regulators) deficiencies in internal control that the auditor has identified during the audit using specific terms and definitions that differ from those in AU-C section 265. In such circumstances, the auditor uses such terms and definitions when communicating deficiencies in internal control in accordance with the requirements of the law or regulation and in accordance with AU-C section 265. Furthermore, paragraph .A13 of AU-C section 265 provides that when law or regulation requires the auditor to communicate deficiencies in internal control that the auditor has identified during the audit using specific terms, but such terms have not been defined, the auditor may use the definitions, requirements, and guidance in AU-C section 265 to comply with the law or regulation. The requirements of AU-C section 265 remain applicable, notwithstanding that law or regulation may require the auditor to use specific terms or definitions.

4.19 AU-C section 265 notes that early communication of some matters may be important because of their relative significance and the urgency for corrective follow up action. Regardless of the timing of the written communication of significant deficiencies and material weaknesses, the auditor may communicate certain matters orally during the course of the audit to those charged with governance or management. Note, however, that oral communication does not relieve the auditor of the responsibility to communicate the significant deficiencies and material weaknesses in writing. *Government Auditing Standards* notes that when a control deficiency results in noncompliance with provisions of laws, regulations, contracts, and grant agreements, or abuse, early communication is important to allow management to take prompt corrective action to prevent further noncompliance. In addition, *Government Auditing Standards* states that when a deficiency is communicated early, the reporting requirements in paragraphs 4.19–.23 of *Government Auditing Standards* still apply.

4.20 Paragraph .A28 of AU-C section 265 notes that auditors performing audits of entities receiving government funding may have additional responsibilities to communicate deficiencies in internal control identified during the audit, in a different format, at a level of detail, or to parties not envisioned in AU-C section 265. For example, significant deficiencies and material weaknesses may have to be communicated to a governmental authority, and such communications may be required to be made publicly available. Law or regulation also may require auditors to report deficiencies in internal control, irrespective of their severity. Further, law or regulation may require auditors to report on broader internal control related matters (for example, controls related to compliance with law, regulation, or provisions of contracts and grant agreements).

4.21 As noted in paragraph .14 of AU-C section 265, the auditor's written communication of significant deficiencies and material weaknesses in internal control should contain an appropriate alert in accordance with AU-C section 905, *Alert That Restricts the Use of the Auditor's Written Communication* (AICPA, *Professional Standards*). Paragraph .11 of AU-C section 905 states that the general alert language found in paragraph .07 of that standard should not be used when the engagement is performed in accordance with *Government Auditing Standards* and the auditor's written communication pursuant to that engagement is issued in accordance with AU-C section 265. Instead the required alert should describe the purpose of the auditor's written communication and state that the auditor's written communication is not suitable for any other purpose. Different alert language is used in an audit performed in accordance with *Government Auditing Standards* because those standards regard the auditor's written communication issued in the report on internal control over financial reporting and on compliance and other matters to be an integral part of the audit engagement for purposes of assessing the results of the engagement. For an illustration of this alert, see the illustrative reports in examples 4-3–4-9 in the appendix of this chapter (paragraph 4.88).

4.22 Table 4-2 summarizes the differences between AU-C section 265 and *Government Auditing Standards* with respect to reporting on internal control over financial reporting.

Table 4-2

Reporting on Internal Control Over Financial Reporting

	Government Auditing Standards	AU-C Section 265
How are significant deficiencies and material weaknesses reported?	In a written report on internal control over financial reporting	In a written communication to management and those charged with governance
When is reporting required?	For every financial statement audit	When significant deficiencies or material weaknesses are identified

Auditor Reporting and Other Communication Considerations

4.23 As noted previously, in an audit performed in accordance with *Government Auditing Standards*, a report on internal control over financial reporting and on compliance and other matters is issued, and this report will provide information on whether material weaknesses have been identified. There may be situations where management or those charged with governance may request a written communication indicating that no material weaknesses were identified during the audit. A communication indicating that no material weaknesses were identified during the audit does not provide any assurance about the effectiveness of an entity's internal control over financial reporting. However, the auditor is not precluded from issuing such a communication provided that it includes the matters required by paragraph .15 of AU-C section 265. It is important to note that paragraph .16 of AU-C section 265 prohibits the auditor from issuing a written communication stating that no significant deficiencies were identified during an audit because such a communication has the potential to be misunderstood or misused.

Fraud, Noncompliance With Provisions of Laws, Regulations, Contracts, and Grant Agreements, and Abuse [13]

4.24 The consideration of fraud and noncompliance with provisions of laws, regulations, contracts, and grant agreements in an audit performed in accordance with *Government Auditing Standards* is based on the guidance found in GAAS. Although the guidance in GAAS is presented in separate AU-C sections, the additional reporting requirements found in *Government Auditing Standards* are generally presented based on how the fraud and noncompliance is reported in the audit. Note that the concept of abuse found in *Government Auditing Standards* is not found in GAAS. Table 4-1 in paragraph 4.12 provides a summary of reporting requirements for fraud, noncompliance with provisions of laws, regulations, contracts, and grant agreements, and abuse.

Fraud

4.25 AU-C section 240, *Consideration of Fraud in a Financial Statement Audit* (AICPA, *Professional Standards*), addresses the auditor's responsibility regarding fraud, including reporting instances of fraud. This guidance provides a basis for the auditor's reporting of fraud in the report "Internal Control over Financial Reporting and on Compliance and Other Matters" that is required in an audit performed under *Government Auditing Standards*.

4.26 As noted in paragraph .39 of AU-C section 240, if the auditor has identified a fraud or has obtained information that indicates that a fraud may exist, the auditor should communicate these matters on a timely basis to the appropriate level of management. It is important that the matter be brought to the attention of the appropriate level of management as soon as practicable. This is true even if the matter might be considered inconsequential (for

---

[13] Chapter 3 of this guide discusses the auditor's consideration of fraud, noncompliance with the provisions of laws, regulations, contracts, and grant agreements, and abuse. Because an audit of a government's financial statements under the provisions of the AICPA Audit and Accounting Guide *State and Local Governments* is based on opinion units (see footnote 4 in paragraph 4.02), the auditor's consideration of fraud, provisions of laws, regulations, contracts, and grant agreements, and abuse in planning, performing, evaluating the results of, and reporting on the audit should address each opinion unit.

example, a minor defalcation by an employee at a low level in the entity's organization). The level of management with whom to communicate is a matter of professional judgment and is affected by such factors as the likelihood of collusion and the nature and magnitude of the suspected fraud. Ordinarily, the appropriate level of management is at least one level above the persons who appear to be involved with the suspected fraud.

4.27 Unless all of those charged with governance are involved in managing the entity, if the auditor has identified or suspects fraud involving (*a*) management; (*b*) employees who have significant roles in internal control; or (*c*) others, when the fraud results in a material misstatement in the financial statements, the auditor should communicate these matters to those charged with governance on a timely basis. The auditor's communication with those charged with governance may be made orally or in writing. Due to the nature and sensitivity of fraud involving senior management, or fraud that results in a material misstatement in the financial statements, in order to make the communication on a timely basis, the auditor may decide to make the communication orally and follow up with a communication in writing. If the auditor suspects fraud involving management, the auditor should communicate these suspicions to those charged with governance and discuss with them the nature, timing, and extent of audit procedures necessary to complete the audit.

4.28 Paragraph .41 of AU-C section 240 notes that the auditor should communicate with those charged with governance any other matters related to fraud that are, in the auditor's professional judgment, relevant to their responsibilities. In some cases the auditor may consider it appropriate to communicate with those charged with governance fraud involving employees other than management that does not result in a material misstatement. The communication process is assisted if the auditor and those charged with governance agree at an early stage of the audit the nature and extent of this type of communication.

4.29 If the auditor has identified or suspects a fraud, the auditor should determine whether the auditor has a responsibility to report the occurrence or suspicion to a party outside the entity. As noted in paragraph .42 of AU-C section 240, although the auditor's professional duty to maintain the confidentiality of client information may preclude such reporting, the auditor's legal responsibilities may override the duty of confidentiality in some circumstances. See the discussion beginning at paragraph 4.43 for information on the additional requirements and guidance found in *Government Auditing Standards* related to reporting findings directly to parties outside the entity.

Reporting Fraud Under Government Auditing Standards

4.30 In an audit performed in accordance with *Government Auditing Standards* the auditor has additional responsibilities related to reporting fraud. When the auditor concludes that fraud has occurred or is likely to have occurred, he or she should include in the report on internal control over financial reporting and on compliance and other matters the relevant information about fraud that has a material effect on the financial statements and any other instances that warrant the attention of those charged with governance. When instances of fraud are detected that do not warrant the attention of those charged with governance, the auditor's determination of whether and how to

Auditor Reporting and Other Communication Considerations

communicate such instances to auditee officials is a matter of professional judgment.

Noncompliance With Laws and Regulations

4.31 AU-C section 250, *Consideration of Laws and Regulations in an Audit of Financial Statements* (AICPA, *Professional Standards*), addresses the auditor's responsibility to consider laws and regulations in an audit of financial statements. The auditor's consideration of laws and regulations under AU-C section 250 provides a basis for the auditor's reporting of noncompliance with laws and regulations in the report "Internal Control over Financial Reporting and on Compliance and Other Matters" that is required in an audit performed under *Government Auditing Standards*.

4.32 AU-C section 250 provides that the auditor should communicate with those charged with governance matters involving noncompliance with laws and regulations that come to the auditor's attention during the course of the audit, other than when the matters are clearly inconsequential. In addition, if the auditor suspects that management or those charged with governance are involved in noncompliance, the auditor should communicate the matter to the next higher level of authority at the entity, if it exists. When no higher authority exists, or if the auditor believes that the communication may not be acted upon or is unsure about the person to whom to report, the auditor should consider the need to obtain legal advice.

4.33 If the auditor has identified or suspects noncompliance with laws and regulations, the auditor should determine whether the auditor has a responsibility to report the identified or suspected noncompliance to parties outside the entity. The auditor may be required to communicate instances of noncompliance to appropriate oversight bodies and funding agencies. See the discussion beginning at paragraph 4.43 for the *Government Auditing Standards* requirements and guidance related to reporting findings directly to parties outside of the auditee.

Reporting Noncompliance With Provisions of Laws and Regulations Under Government Auditing Standards

4.34 The responsibilities related to reporting noncompliance with provisions of laws and regulations in an audit performed in accordance with *Government Auditing Standards* are identical to the requirements related to fraud. Therefore, when the auditor concludes that noncompliance with laws and regulations has occurred or is likely to have occurred, he or she should include in the report on internal control over financial reporting and on compliance and other matters the relevant information about noncompliance with laws and regulations that have a material effect on the financial statements and any other instances that warrant the attention of those charged with governance. When instances of noncompliance with laws and regulations are detected that do not warrant the attention of those charged with governance, the auditor's determination of whether and how to communicate such instances to auditee officials is a matter of professional judgment.

Noncompliance With Provisions of Contracts and Grant Agreements and Abuse

4.35 *Government Auditing Standards* states that when performing an audit in accordance with *Government Auditing Standards* the auditor should extend the AICPA requirements pertaining to the auditor's responsibilities for laws and regulations to also apply to the consideration of compliance with provisions of contracts and grant agreements. Therefore, in an audit performed in accordance with *Government Auditing Standards*, the requirements and guidance found in AU-C section 250 should be used when considering both the provisions of laws and regulations and the provisions of contracts and grant agreements.

4.36 Furthermore, *Government Auditing Standards* contains requirements and guidance regarding abuse—a concept that is not found in GAAS. The additional reporting requirements under *Government Auditing Standards* for abuse are the same as those for noncompliance with provisions of grants and contract agreements. Therefore, the reporting requirements for both are presented together in the following paragraphs. See chapter 3, "Planning and Performing a Financial Statement Audit in Accordance With *Government Auditing Standards*," of this guide for more information on the consideration of abuse in an audit performed under *Government Auditing Standards*.

Reporting Noncompliance With Provisions of Contract and Grant Agreements and Abuse Under Government Auditing Standards

4.37 It is important to note that the reporting requirements found in *Government Auditing Standards* differ with respect to the reporting of noncompliance with provisions of laws and regulations and the reporting of noncompliance with provisions of contracts and grant agreements. (See paragraph 4.07 for additional information.) Furthermore, although the determination of reportable instances of abuse differs from the determination of reportable instances of noncompliance with provisions of contracts and grant agreements, reportable abuse that is identified is reported in the same manner as noncompliance with provisions of contracts and grant agreements.

4.38 Relevant information regarding noncompliance with provisions of contracts and grant agreements that has a material effect on the determination of financial statement amounts and abuse that is material, either quantitatively or qualitatively, should be included in the report "Internal Control over Financial Reporting and on Compliance and Other Matters." When auditors detect instances of noncompliance with provisions of contracts or grant agreements or abuse that have an effect on the financial statements that are less than material but warrant the attention of those charged with governance, they should communicate those findings in writing to audited entity officials. When instances of noncompliance with provisions of contracts or grant agreements or abuse are identified that do not warrant the attention of those charged with governance, the auditor's determination of whether and how to communication such instances to auditee entity officials is a matter of professional judgment.

Other Considerations

4.39 As noted previously, *Government Auditing Standards* requires the auditor to issue a report that describes the scope of the auditor's testing of compliance with provisions of laws, regulations, contracts, and grant agreements and present the results of those tests. As part of that audit the auditor should report in writing instances of fraud and noncompliance with provisions of laws or regulations that have a material effect on the financial statements and any other instances that warrant the attention of those charged with governance, and noncompliance with provisions of contracts and grant agreements, and abuse that could have a material effect on the determination of financial statement amounts. (Paragraphs 4.55–.62 contain the *Government Auditing Standards* requirements for presenting audit findings.) Exhibit 4-1 is a flowchart that illustrates the evaluation and reporting of findings of fraud and noncompliance under *Government Auditing Standards*. Chapter 3 of this guide includes a flowchart that illustrates its discussion of the evaluation and reporting of findings of abuse.

Exhibit 4-1

Evaluation and Reporting of Findings of Fraud and Noncompliance Under *Government Auditing Standards*[1]

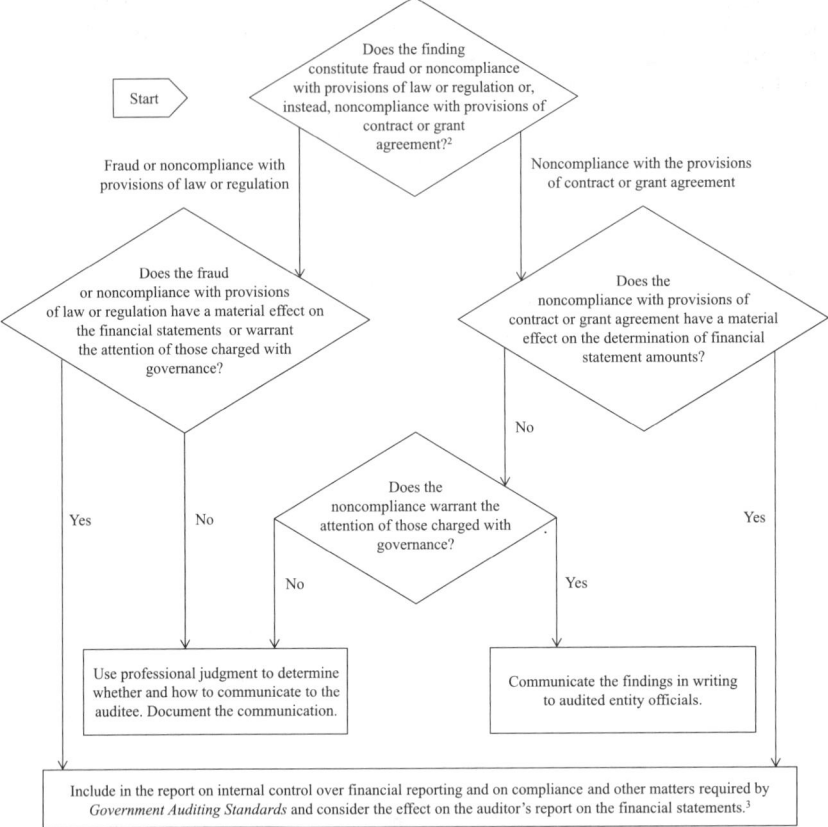

---

[1] This flowchart represents the evaluation and reporting of findings of fraud and noncompliance with provisions of laws, regulations, contracts, and grant agreements under *Government Auditing Standards*.

[2] The auditor should consider the direct reporting requirement of *Government Auditing Standards*. Paragraphs 4.43–.45 of this guide discuss the requirements in paragraphs 4.30–.32 of *Government Auditing Standards* that auditors report fraud and noncompliance directly to parties outside of the auditee in certain circumstances.

[3] Paragraph 4.58 discusses how to report noncompliance findings that relate to both internal control over financial reporting and to compliance. Paragraph 4.59 discusses when to report fraud findings in the internal control section of the report or instead in the section on compliance and other matters.

Additional Considerations Related to Fraud, Noncompliance With Provisions of Laws, Regulations, Contracts, and Grant Agreements, and Abuse

4.40 As indicated in exhibit 4-1, *Government Auditing Standards* has differing standards for including in the report on internal control over financial reporting and on compliance and other matters (*a*) noncompliance with provisions of laws or regulations as compared to (*b*) noncompliance with provisions of contracts and grant agreements. The reporting for (*a*) is a threshold of noncompliance that has a material effect on the financial statements and any other instances that warrant the attention of those charged with governance, whereas the reporting for (*b*) is a higher threshold of a material effect on the determination of financial statement amounts. Consequently, it is important that auditors carefully evaluate whether compliance requirements arise from laws or regulations or, instead, from provisions of contracts and grant agreements. Often, contracts and grant agreements have compliance requirements that are based in law or regulation but those contracts or agreements do not indicate that laws or regulations are the source of the provisions. Further, it may not be apparent whether a document that provides guidance on the provisions of contracts and grant agreements (such as a program management or procedures manual) has the standing of a regulation. The auditor may want to consult with program administrators, grantors, pass-through entities, oversight agencies, legal counsel, or others about the source and standing of compliance requirements.

4.41 When fraud, noncompliance with provisions of laws, regulations, contracts, and grant agreements, or abuse either have occurred or are likely to have occurred, auditors may consult with authorities or legal counsel about whether publicly reporting such information would compromise investigative or legal proceedings. Auditors may limit their public reporting to matters that would not compromise those proceedings and, for example, report only on information that is already a part of the public record.

4.42 *Government Auditing Standards* states that avoiding interference with investigations or legal proceedings is important in pursuing indications of fraud, noncompliance with provisions of laws, regulations, contracts, and grant agreements, or abuse. Laws, regulations, or policies may require auditors to report indications of certain types of fraud, noncompliance with provisions of laws, regulations, contracts, and grant agreements, or abuse to law enforcement or investigatory authorities before performing additional audit procedures. When investigations or legal proceedings are initiated or in process, auditors should evaluate the impact on the current audit. In some cases, it may be appropriate for the auditors to work with investigators or legal authorities, or withdraw from or defer further work on the audit engagement or a portion of the engagement to avoid interfering with an ongoing investigation or legal proceeding. See the discussion beginning at paragraph 4.43 for information related to the *Government Auditing Standards* requirement to report findings directly to outside parties in certain circumstances.

Government Auditing Standards—Reporting Findings Directly to Parties Outside the Entity

4.43 *Government Auditing Standards* states that auditors should report known or likely fraud, noncompliance with provisions of laws, regulations, contracts, and grant agreements, or abuse directly to parties outside the audited entity in the following two circumstances:

    a. When entity management fails to satisfy legal or regulatory requirements to report such information to external parties specified in law or regulation, auditors should first communicate the failure to report such information to those charged with governance. If the audited entity still does not report this information to the specified external parties as soon as practicable after the auditors' communication with those charged with governance, then the auditors should report the information directly to the specified external parties.

    b. When entity management fails to take timely and appropriate steps to respond to known or likely fraud, noncompliance with provisions of laws, regulations, contracts, and grant agreements, or abuse that (i) is likely to have a material effect on the financial statements and (ii) involves funding received directly or indirectly from a government agency, auditors should first report management's failure to take timely and appropriate steps to those charged with governance. If the audited entity still does not take timely and appropriate steps as soon as practicable after the auditors' communication with those charged with governance, then the auditors should report the entity's failure to take timely and appropriate steps directly to the funding agency.

4.44 The reporting required under *Government Auditing Standards* is in addition to any legal requirements to report such information directly to parties outside the audited entity. Auditors should comply with these requirements even if they have resigned or been dismissed from the audit prior to its completion.

4.45 Auditors should obtain sufficient, appropriate evidence (for example, by confirmation from outside parties), to corroborate assertions by management of the audited entity that it has reported such findings in accordance with laws, regulations, or funding agreements. When auditors are unable to do so, they should report such information directly set forth in the preceding paragraphs.

Report on Audited Financial Statements

4.46 As noted in paragraph .13 of AU-C section 700, the auditor should form an opinion on whether the financial statements are presented fairly, in all material respects, in accordance with the applicable reporting framework. In order to form that opinion, the auditor should conclude whether the auditor has obtained reasonable assurance about whether the financial statements as a whole are free from material misstatement, whether due to error or fraud.

4.47 The auditor's report on the financial statements expresses the opinion on the financial statements through a written report[14] that also describes the basis for that opinion.[15] The AICPA Audit and Accounting Guides, such

---

[14] A written report may be issued in hard copy format or using an electronic medium.

[15] Because an audit of a government's financial statements under the provisions of the AICPA Audit and Accounting Guide *State and Local Governments* is based on opinion units (see footnote 4 in paragraph 4.02), the auditor's report on those financial statements may include more than one opinion paragraph.

Auditor Reporting and Other Communication Considerations 71

as *Not-for-Profit Entities*; *State and Local Governments*; *Health Care Entities*; *Gaming*; *Employee Benefit Plans*; and *Depository and Lending Institutions: Banks and Savings Institutions, Credit Unions, Finance Companies, and Mortgage Companies*, are the primary source of guidance for the nuances of GAAS reporting on the financial statements of entities in certain industries. AU-C section 700 provides requirements and guidance related to the content of the auditor's report on financial statements. AU-C section 705, *Modifications to the Opinion in the Independent Auditor's Report*, and AU-C section 706, *Emphasis-of-Matter Paragraphs and Other-Matter Paragraphs in the Independent Auditor's Report* (AICPA, *Professional Standards*), provides requirements and guidance when the auditor concludes that a modification to the auditor's opinion on the financial statements is necessary.[16] AU-C section 706 provides requirements and guidance when the auditor considers it necessary to draw users' attention to certain matters that are fundamentally important to users' understanding of the audit, the auditor's responsibility, or the auditor's report. This may be done through the use of an emphasis-of-matter or other-matter paragraph. Other AU-C sections provide reporting requirements and guidance if the basic financial statements are accompanied by or required to be accompanied by information presented outside the basic financial statements.[17] Those standards may require additional language in the auditor's report on the financial statements.

> **Emphasis Point**
>
> *Government Auditing Standards* contains a requirement for the auditor to provide certain information about the auditor's reporting on internal control over financial reporting and on compliance with provisions of laws, regulations, contracts, and grant agreements when the reporting is done separately from the financial statement reporting. This includes separate reports bound in the same document. See paragraph 4.48*u*–*w* for the content required to be in the financial statement report in this situation. See also paragraph 4.52 for additional information.

4.48 The following includes a listing of basic elements of an auditor's report on the financial statement that is intended to provide a more generic list of elements, along with the additional elements that are appropriate when the financial statement audit is also performed under *Government Auditing Standards*. See the illustrative report examples 4-1–4-2 in the appendix of this chapter (paragraph 4.88) for examples of reports containing these elements for

---

[16] As noted in paragraph .A16 of AU-C section 705, in an audit performed under *Government Auditing Standards*, in certain circumstances withdrawal from the audit may not be possible if the auditor is required by law or regulation to continue the audit engagement. This may be the case for an auditor who is appointed to audit the financial statements of governmental entities. It may also be the case in circumstances when the auditor is appointed to audit the financial statements covering a specific period, or appointed for a specific period, and is prohibited from withdrawing before the completion of the audit of those financial statements or before the end of that period, respectively. In these circumstances, the auditor may also consider it necessary to include an other-matter paragraph in the auditor's report.

[17] AU-C section 720, *Other Information in Documents Containing Audited Financial Statements*, AU-C section 725, and AU-C section 730, *Required Supplementary Information* (AICPA, *Professional Standards*), provide guidance on the auditor's responsibility with respect to certain information that may be, or may be required to be, presented with the financial statements.

a governmental entity and a not-for-profit entity. The basic elements of the auditor's report on the financial statements (as applicable) include[18]

a. a title that includes the word *independent*.
b. an addressee as required by the circumstances of the engagement.
c. when applicable, a section with the heading "Report on the Financial Statements" (this heading should be used when the report contains a separate section on other reporting responsibilities).
d. an introductory paragraph that should
   i. identify the entity whose financial statements have been audited;
   ii. state that the financial statements have been audited;
   iii. identify the title of each statement that the financial statements comprise;[19] and
   iv. specify the date or period covered by each financial statement that the financial statements comprise.
e. a section with the heading "Management's Responsibility for the Financial Statements."
f. a statement that management is responsible for the preparation and fair presentation of the financial statements in accordance with accounting principles generally accepted in the United States of America; this includes the design, implementation, and maintenance of internal control relevant to the preparation and fair presentation of financial statements that are free from material misstatement, whether due to fraud or error.
g. a section with the heading "Auditor's Responsibility."
h. a statement that the responsibility of the auditor is to express an opinion on the financial statements based on the audit.
i. a statement that the audit was conducted in accordance with auditing standards generally accepted in the United States of America and the standards applicable to financial audits contained in *Government Auditing Standards*, issued by the Comptroller General of the United States.
j. a statement that those standards require that the auditor plan and perform the audit to obtain reasonable assurance about whether the financial statements are free from material misstatement.
k. a statement that
   i. an audit involves performing procedures to obtain audit evidence about the amounts and disclosures in the financial statements.
   ii. the procedures selected depend on the auditor's judgment, including the assessment of the risks of material misstatement of the financial statements, whether due to fraud or error. In making those risk assessments, the auditor considers internal control relevant to the entity's preparation

---

[18] The report elements presented in this section may not be applicable for all reporting circumstances and adjustments to elements to be included in the report may be needed.

[19] Identification of the title of each statement that the financial statements comprise may be done by referencing the table of contents.

Auditor Reporting and Other Communication Considerations

and fair presentation of the financial statements in order to design audit procedures that are appropriate in the circumstances, but not for the purpose of expressing an opinion on the effectiveness of the entity's internal control. Accordingly, the auditor expresses no such opinion.

    iii. an audit also includes evaluating the appropriateness of accounting policies used and the reasonableness of significant accounting estimates made by management, as well as evaluating the overall presentation of the financial statements.

l. a statement regarding whether the auditor believes that the audit evidence obtained is sufficient and appropriate to provide a basis for the auditor's opinion.

m. a section with the heading "Opinion."

n. an opinion statement regarding whether the financial statements are fairly presented, in all material respects, in accordance with the applicable reporting framework.

o. the titles of the financial statements identified in the introductory paragraph of the auditor's report.

p. identification of the applicable financial reporting framework and its origin (for example, accounting principles generally accepted in the United States of America).

q. a section with the heading "Other Matters."[20]

r. a section with a subheading "Supplementary Information."[21]

s. a description of the other reporting responsibilities, one example of which is reporting on supplementary information.[22]

t. a section with the heading "Other Reporting Required by *Government Auditing Standards*."

u. a statement that the auditor has issued a report dated [*date of report*] on the consideration of the entity's internal control over financial reporting and on the tests of its compliance with certain provisions of laws, regulations, contracts, and grant agreements, and other matters.

---

[20] In some circumstances, the auditor may have additional responsibilities to report on other matters that are supplementary to the auditor's responsibility under GAAS to report on the financial statements. An example is the reporting on supplementary information (SI) when the auditor is engaged to provide an "in-relation-to" opinion on SI and also when explanatory language will be provided relating to other information (OI) when the auditor is disclaiming an opinion on the OI. The form and content of the "Other Matters" section of the auditor's report will vary depending on the nature of the auditor's other reporting responsibilities. Note that AU-C section 700, *Forming an Opinion and Reporting on Financial Statements* (AICPA, *Professional Standards*), states that the subtitle of this section of the report should be titled as appropriate to the content of the section.

[21] The caption provided in this list is one way an auditor could title the section. Among other alternatives are "Supplementary and Other Information" and "Accompanying Information." Note that AU-C section 706 states that when relevant, one or more subheadings may be used that describe the content of the other-matter paragraph.

[22] The content of this section will vary depending on the nature of the other reporting requirements. See examples 4-1–4-2 for example language for reporting on required supplementary information, supplementary information, and other information.

v. a statement that the purpose of that report is to describe the scope of the testing of internal control over financial reporting and compliance and the results of that testing, and not to provide an opinion on internal control over financial reporting or on compliance.

w. a statement that the report is an integral part of an audit performed in accordance with *Government Auditing Standards* in considering the entity's internal control over financial reporting and compliance.

x. the signature of the auditor (manual or printed).

y. the auditor's city and state.[23]

z. the date of the auditor's report.

Emphasis Point

Paragraph .41 of AU-C section 700 states that the date of the auditor's report should be "no earlier than the date on which the auditor has obtained sufficient appropriate audit evidence on which to base the auditor's opinion on the financial statements." In the situation where final approval of the financial statements by a governmental legislative body is required before the financial statements can be issued, that approval is not necessary in order for the auditor to conclude that sufficient appropriate audit evidence has been obtained. Note that *Government Auditing Standards* requires documentation, before the report release date, of supervisory review of the evidence that supports the findings, conclusions, and recommendations contained in the auditor's report.

Other Considerations—Citing Compliance With *Government Auditing Standards* in the Auditor's Report

4.49 As discussed in paragraphs 4.06, when the report on the financial statements is submitted to comply with a requirement for an audit in accordance with *Government Auditing Standards*, or when those standards are voluntarily followed, the report should include a *Government Auditing Standards* compliance statement. An unmodified compliance statement should be used when the auditor has (*a*) followed all applicable unconditional and presumptively mandatory *Government Auditing Standards* requirements or (*b*) followed unconditional requirements and documented justification for any departure from applicable presumptively mandatory requirements and have achieved the objectives of those requirements through other means. This guide recommends the following language be included in the auditor's report to meet this requirement:

> We conducted our audit in accordance with auditing standards generally accepted in the United States of America and the standards

---

[23] Technical Questions and Answers (Q&A) section 9100.07, "Naming the City and State Where the Auditor Practices," and Q&A section 9100.08, "Audit Firm With Multiple Offices on Their Company Letterhead and Effect on Report" (AICPA, *Technical Questions and Answers*), provide guidance related to naming the city and state in the auditor's report. The city and state where the auditor practices is not required to be placed under the auditor's signature and may be named in the firm's letterhead on which the report is issued. However, if the firm's letterhead includes multiple offices it will not be clear which location is the issuing office and, in that case, the auditor would need to indicate the city and state where the auditor practices in the auditor's report.

Auditor Reporting and Other Communication Considerations 75

applicable to financial audits contained in *Government Auditing Standards*, issued by the Comptroller General of the United States.

4.50 A modified compliance statement should be used when the requirements for the unmodified compliance statement are not met. One situation the auditor should consider using a modified compliance statement is in the case of a scope limitation, such as restrictions on access to records, government officials, or other individuals needed to conduct the audit. When a modified compliance statement is used, the auditor should disclose in the report the applicable requirement(s) not followed, the reasons for not following the requirement(s), and how not following the requirement(s) affected, or could have affected, the audit and the assurance provided. A modified compliance statement is made by stating that (*a*) the auditor performed the audit in accordance with *Government Auditing Standards*, except for specific applicable requirements that were not followed, or (*b*) because of the significance of the departure(s) from the requirements, the auditor was unable to and did not perform the audit in accordance with *Government Auditing Standards*. When the auditors do not comply with any applicable requirements, they should (*a*) assess the significance of the noncompliance to the audit objectives; (*b*) document the assessment, along with their reasons for not following the requirement; and (*c*) determine the type of *Government Auditing Standards* compliance statement. The auditor's determination is a matter of professional judgment, which is affected by the significance of the requirements not followed in relation to the audit objectives.

4.51 Appendix I section A2.06 of *Government Auditing Standards* provides guidance related to the determination of the type of compliance statement to be included in the auditor's report. That guidance notes that the determination of whether an unmodified or modified *Government Auditing Standards* compliance statement is appropriate is based on the consideration of the individual and aggregate effect of exceptions to *Government Auditing Standards* requirements. Quantitative and qualitative factors that the auditor may consider include

   a. the likelihood that the exception(s) will affect the perceptions of report users about the audit findings, conclusions, and recommendations;

   b. the magnitude of the effect of the exception(s) on the perceptions of report users about the audit findings, conclusions, and recommendations;

   c. the pervasiveness of the exception(s);

   d. the potential effect of the exception(s) on the sufficiency and appropriateness of evidence supporting the audit findings, conclusions, and recommendations; and

   e. whether report users could be misled if the *Government Auditing Standards* compliance statement were not modified.

Other Reporting Responsibilities in an Audit of Financial Statements

4.52 In an audit in accordance with *Government Auditing Standards*, the auditor's report on the financial statements should report on or reference a separate report on internal control over financial reporting and on compliance with provisions of laws, regulations, contracts, and grant agreements, and other matters. This guide recommends a separate report on internal control over financial reporting and on compliance and other matters. Referencing this separate report is done in a separate section of the report following the "Report on the Financial Statements" section that this guide recommends be titled "Other Reporting Required by *Government Auditing Standards*." This section should include a statement that the purpose of the report is to describe the scope of testing of internal control over financial reporting and compliance and the results of that testing. As noted in paragraph 4.11, this guide recommends that the reference to the separate report indicate that the separate report does not provide an opinion on internal control over financial reporting or on compliance.[24] The reference to the separate report also should include a statement that the separate report is an integral part of an audit performed in accordance with *Government Auditing Standards* in considering the entity's internal control over financial reporting and compliance. See the discussion beginning at paragraph 4.05 for information on the reporting requirements under *Government Auditing Standards*. The illustrative reports in the appendix of this chapter (paragraph 4.88), examples 4-1–4-2 provide example wording regarding referencing the separate report on internal control over financial reporting and on compliance and other matters.

Report on Internal Control Over Financial Reporting and on Compliance and Other Matters Based on an Audit of Financial Statements Performed in Accordance With *Government Auditing Standards*

4.53 This guide recommends combining into one report the reporting required by *Government Auditing Standards* on the scope and results of testing of the auditee's internal control over financial reporting and compliance with laws, regulations, and provisions of contracts and grant agreements, and other matters, which concern certain fraud and abuse. (Paragraph 4.59 discusses the placement of findings relating to "other matters.")

4.54 The following list provides the basic elements of the auditor's standard report on internal control over financial reporting and on compliance and other matters based on an audit of the financial statements in accordance with *Government Auditing Standards*. See the illustrative reports in the appendix of this chapter (paragraph 4.88), and the discussion of the presentation of findings (paragraphs 4.55–.62) and the views of responsible officials and their planned corrective actions (paragraphs 4.63–.66):

    a. A title that includes the word *independent*.

    b. An appropriate addressee.

    c. A statement that the auditor has audited the financial statements of the auditee and a reference to the auditor's report on the financial statements (including the title of each statement the financial statements comprise) and a description of the nature of any opinion modification. The period covered by the report and the date of the auditor's report should be stated.

    d. A statement that the audit was conducted in accordance with GAAS and an identification of the United States of America as the country of origin of those standards (for example, auditing standards

---

[24] See footnote 10.

generally accepted in the United States of America or U.S. generally accepted auditing standards) and with the standards applicable to financial audits contained in *Government Auditing Standards* issued by the Comptroller General of the United States.

e. A section with the heading "Internal Control Over Financial Reporting."

f. A statement that in planning and performing the audit of the financial statements, the auditor considered the entity's internal control over financial reporting (internal control) to determine the audit procedures that are appropriate in the circumstances for the purpose of expressing an opinion on the financial statements, but not for the purpose of expressing an opinion on the effectiveness of the entity's internal control. Accordingly, the auditor does not express an opinion on the effectiveness of the entity's internal control.[25]

g. The definitions of *deficiency in internal control*, *significant deficiency*, and *material weakness*.[26]

h. If no significant deficiencies or material weaknesses have been identified

- a statement that the auditor's consideration of internal control was for the limited purpose described in the first paragraph of this section and was not designed to identify all deficiencies in internal control that might be material weaknesses or significant deficiencies.

- a statement that, given the limitations, during the audit the auditor did not identify any deficiencies in internal control that are considered to be material weaknesses.[27] However, material weaknesses may exist that have not been identified.

i. If significant deficiencies have been identified

- a statement that the auditor's consideration of internal control was for the limited purpose described in the first paragraph of this section and was not designed to identify all deficiencies in internal control that might be material weaknesses or significant deficiencies, and therefore material weaknesses or significant deficiencies may exist that were not identified.

- a statement that given these limitations, during the audit the auditor did not identify any deficiencies in internal control that were considered to be material weaknesses.[28]

---

[25] If the auditor provides an opinion on internal control over financial reporting or on compliance (see footnote 10 in paragraph 4.11), this guide recommends that the reference to the separate report be modified to indicate that there is such an opinion.

[26] The definitions included in this report are based on the definitions found in AU-C section 265, *Communicating Internal Control Related Matters Identified in an Audit* (AICPA, *Professional Standards*).

[27] This wording is based on the requirement in paragraph .16 of AU-C section 265, which states that the auditor should not issue a written communication stating that no significant deficiencies were identified during the audit.

[28] See footnote 26.

- a statement that certain deficiencies in internal control over financial reporting were identified that the auditor considers to be significant deficiencies.
- a description of the significant deficiencies identified, including the title of the schedule in which the findings are reported. (Alternatively the findings may be listed in this report.)

j. If material weaknesses and significant deficiencies have been identified

- a statement that the auditor's consideration of internal control was for the limited purpose described in the first paragraph of this section and was not designed to identify all deficiencies in internal control that might be material weaknesses or significant deficiencies and therefore, material weaknesses or significant deficiencies may exist that were not identified.
- a statement that certain deficiencies in internal control over financial reporting were identified that the auditor considers to be material weaknesses and significant deficiencies.
- a description of the material weaknesses, including the title of the schedule in which the findings are reported. (Alternatively the findings may be listed in this report.)
- a description of the significant deficiencies identified, including the title of the schedule in which the findings are reported. (Alternatively the findings may be listed in this report.)

k. A section with the heading "Compliance and Other Matters."

l. A statement that as part of obtaining reasonable assurance about whether the entity's financial statements are free from material misstatement, the auditor performed tests of its compliance with certain provisions of laws, regulations, contracts, and grant agreements, noncompliance with which could have a direct and material effect on the determination of financial statement amounts. However, providing an opinion on compliance with those provisions was not an objective of the audit, and accordingly, the auditor does not express such an opinion.

m. If no instances of noncompliance or other matters have been identified that are required to be reported, a statement that the results of tests disclosed no instances of noncompliance or other matters that are required to be reported under *Government Auditing Standards.*

n. If instances of noncompliance or other matters have been identified that are required to be reported, a statement that the results of the tests disclosed instances of noncompliance or other matters that are required to be reported under *Government Auditing Standards* and which are described in the accompanying [*include the title of the schedule in which the findings are reported*].[29]

o. If applicable, a statement that additional matters were communicated to the auditee in a written communication.[30]

p. If material weaknesses, significant deficiencies, or reportable instance of noncompliance or other matters are identified, a section with the heading "[*Name of entity*]'s Response to Findings."

q. A statement that the audited entity's response to the findings identified in the audit are described in the accompanying [*include the title of the schedule in which the findings are reported* or "*previously*" *if findings and responses are included in the body of the report*].

r. A statement that [*Name of Entity*]'s response was not subjected to the auditing procedures applied in the audit of the financial statements and, accordingly, the auditor does not express an opinion on it.

s. A section with the heading "Purpose of this Report."[31]

t. A statement that the purpose of the report is solely to describe the scope of the testing of internal control and compliance and the result of that testing, and not to provide an opinion on the effectiveness of the entity's internal control or on compliance. This report is an integral part of an audit performed in accordance with *Government Auditing Standards* in considering the entity's internal control and compliance. Accordingly, this communication is not suitable for any other purpose.

u. The manual or printed signature of the auditor's firm.

v. The auditor's city and state.[32]

w. The date of the auditor's report.[33]

Emphasis Point

Because *Government Auditing Standards* incorporates the AICPA SASs into those standards, the definitions in the auditor's report should be based on the definitions found in the SASs. See the report illustrations found in paragraph 4.88 for example wording.

---

[29] Paragraph 4.07 discusses noncompliance and other matters—certain fraud and abuse—for which *Government Auditing Standards* requires reporting in the auditor's report. Paragraph 4.59 discusses where to report findings of fraud and abuse in the report on internal control over financial reporting and on compliance and other matters.

[30] Paragraph 4.72 discusses the *Government Auditing Standards* requirements for communicating in writing immaterial violations of provisions of contracts and grant agreements and immaterial abuse to officials of the audited entity.

[31] See paragraph 4.21 for information related to the alert required by AU-C section 905, *Alert That Restricts the Use of the Auditor's Written Communication* (AICPA, *Professional Standards*).

[32] See footnote 23.

[33] Because this report relates to the audit of the financial statements, and is based on the GAAS audit procedures performed, it is subject to the provisions of AU-C section 700. Therefore, it should be dated the same date as the auditor's report on the financial statements, which per paragraph .41 of AU-C section 700 is "no earlier than the date on which the auditor has obtained sufficient appropriate audit evidence on which to base the auditor's opinion on the financial statements."

Other Reporting and Communication Considerations

Findings—Deficiencies in Internal Control, Noncompliance With Provisions of Laws, Regulations, Contracts and Grant Agreements, Fraud, and Abuse[34, 35]

4.55 In an audit performed in accordance with *Government Auditing Standards* the auditor has certain responsibilities related to findings, including developing the elements of a finding, communicating the findings to entity officials, and presenting the findings in the auditor's report.

4.56 Findings may involve deficiencies in internal control; noncompliance with provisions of laws, regulations, contracts, and grant agreements; fraud; or abuse. As part of a *Government Auditing Standards* audit, when auditors identify findings, auditors should plan and perform procedures to develop the elements of the findings that are relevant and necessary to achieve the audit objectives.

4.57 The elements of a finding are

a. criteria (the required or desired state);

b. condition (the situation that exists);

c. cause (why it happened); and

d. effect or potential effect (the difference between the situation that exists and the required or desired state).

Paragraphs 4.11–.14 and 4.28 of *Government Auditing Standards* further describe the elements of a finding.

4.58 *Government Auditing Standards* provides that the report on internal control over financial reporting and on compliance and other matters should either describe the findings required to be included in the report or refer to a separate schedule that describes them. (As discussed in paragraphs 4.63–.66, the auditor also should include the reporting of the auditee's views and planned corrective action.) Findings that relate to both internal control over financial reporting and to compliance are generally reported in both the section of the report concerning internal control over financial reporting and the section of the report concerning compliance and other matters. However, the reporting in one section of the report or schedule may be in summary form with a reference to a detailed reporting in the other section.

4.59 This guide recommends that the auditor present or refer to findings of fraud and abuse in the compliance and other matters section of the report,

---

[34] For an audit in accordance with Circular A-133 or the Uniform Guidance, all findings, including those required to be reported under *Government Auditing Standards*, should be included in the schedule of findings and questioned costs. See the further discussion in chapters 13 and 23 of this guide, as applicable to the guidance being used.

[35] There is no option for the auditor to report in a management letter, or other written communication, findings that *Government Auditing Standards*, Circular A-133, or the Uniform Guidance requires to be reported in the auditor's report or Schedule of Findings and Questioned Costs.

Auditor Reporting and Other Communication Considerations 81

unless the primary nature of the finding is a significant deficiency or material weakness in internal control. In that case, it is recommended that findings of fraud and abuse that represent significant deficiencies or material weakness in internal control be presented in the internal control section. *Government Auditing Standards* does not require the auditor's report to use the terms *fraud* or *abuse* in presenting or referring to such findings. The illustrative reports in the appendix of this chapter (paragraph 4.88) illustrate language in the compliance and other matters section of the report to refer to findings that do or may include fraud and abuse. This guide recommends that this language appear in all reports, even if the report does not describe or refer to findings of fraud or abuse or even if the only findings of fraud or abuse are described in or referred to from the section on internal control over financial reporting.

4.60 *Government Auditing Standards* provides that when presenting findings such as deficiencies in internal control, fraud, noncompliance with provisions of laws, regulations, contracts, and grant agreements, or abuse, auditors should develop the elements of the findings to the extent necessary, including findings related to deficiencies from the previous year that have not been remediated. Clearly developed findings assist management or oversight officials of the auditee in understanding the need for taking corrective action and assist auditors in making recommendations for corrective action. If auditors sufficiently develop the elements of a finding, they may provide recommendations for corrective action.

4.61 Auditors should place their findings in perspective by describing the nature and extent of the issues being reported and the extent of the work performed that resulted in the finding. To give the reader a basis for judging the prevalence and consequences of these findings, auditors should, as appropriate, relate the instances identified to the population or the number of cases examined and quantify the results in terms of dollar value or other measures. If the results cannot be projected, auditors should limit their conclusions appropriately.

4.62 This guide recommends that each audit finding reported in accordance with *Government Auditing Standards* explicitly address each of the elements referred to previously to the extent necessary to achieve the audit objective and that each finding be assigned a reference number.[36] One option for assigning reference numbers is to use the fiscal year being audited as the beginning digits of each reference number, followed by a three digit numeric sequence. For example, findings identified and reported in the audit of fiscal year 20X1 would be assigned reference numbers 20X1-001, 20X1-002, and so forth.

---

[36] As discussed in chapter 13 of this guide, when performing a Circular A-133 compliance audit, Circular A-133 requires all findings (including findings related to the audit of the financial statements for which *Government Auditing Standards* requires reporting) to have a reference number. This is also the case for an audit performed under the Uniform Guidance. This paragraph illustrates the standardized audit finding reference number format for audit findings required for data collection form submissions to the Federal Audit Clearinghouse. Under the Uniform Guidance the auditor is required to use this format when reporting findings in the compliance audit.

Reporting Views of Responsible Officials and Planned Corrective Action[37]

4.63 When performing an audit in accordance with *Government Auditing Standards*, if the auditor's report discloses deficiencies in internal control, fraud, noncompliance with provisions of laws, regulations, contracts, and grant agreements, or abuse, the auditor should obtain and report the views of responsible officials of the auditee concerning the findings, conclusions, and recommendations, as well as any planned corrective actions. *Government Auditing Standards* states that obtaining the comments in writing is preferred, but oral comments are acceptable.

4.64 When auditors receive written comments from the responsible officials, they should include in their report a copy of the officials' written comments or a summary of the comments received. When the responsible officials provide oral comments only, auditors should prepare a summary of the oral comments and provide a copy of the summary to the responsible officials to verify that the comments are accurately stated. Auditors should also include in the report an evaluation of the comments, as appropriate.

4.65 When the auditee's comments are inconsistent or in conflict with the findings, conclusions, or recommendations in the draft report, or when planned corrective actions do not adequately address the auditor's recommendations, the auditors should evaluate the validity of the auditee's comments. If the auditors disagree with the comments, they should explain in the report their reasons for disagreement. Conversely, the auditors should modify their report as necessary if they find the comments valid and supported with sufficient, appropriate evidence.

4.66 If the auditee refuses to provide comments or is unable to provide comments within a reasonable period of time, the auditors may issue the report without receiving comments from the audited entity. In such cases, the auditors should indicate in the report that the audited entity did not provide comments.

Distributing Reports

4.67 The distribution of reports completed in accordance with *Government Auditing Standards* depends on the relationship of the auditors to the audited organization and the nature of the information contained in the report. Audit organizations in government entities should distribute auditors' reports to those charged with governance, to the appropriate audited entity officials, and to the appropriate oversight bodies or organizations requiring or arranging for the audits. As appropriate, auditors should also distribute copies of the reports to other officials who have legal oversight authority or who may be responsible for acting on audit findings and recommendations, and to others authorized to receive such reports. Public accounting firms contracted to perform an audit in accordance with *Government Auditing Standards* should clarify report distribution responsibilities with the engaging organization. If

---

[37] In an audit in accordance with Circular A-133 and the Uniform Guidance, the auditee is required to submit a corrective action plan. For those audits, depending on the status of the development of the corrective action plan at the time the auditor's reports are released and the information provided by the auditee regarding corrective action, the auditor may be able to refer to the corrective action plan to satisfy the required presentation of the auditee's views and planned corrective actions. For further discussion, see chapter 13 and chapter 23 of this guide.

Auditor Reporting and Other Communication Considerations

the auditor is responsible for the distribution, an agreement should be reached with the auditee about which officials or organizations will receive the report and the steps being taken to make the report available to the public. Auditors should document any limitation on report distribution.

Reporting Confidential and Sensitive Information

4.68 *Government Auditing Standards* contains requirements and guidance related to reporting confidential or sensitive information in an audit performed under *Government Auditing Standards*. In a financial audit, if certain pertinent information is prohibited from public disclosure or is excluded from a report due to the confidential or sensitive nature of the information, auditors should disclose in the report that certain information has been omitted and the reason or other circumstances that make the omission necessary.

4.69 Certain information may be classified or may otherwise be prohibited from general disclosure by federal, state, or local laws or regulations. In such circumstances, auditors may issue a separate, classified, or limited use report containing such information and distribute the report only to persons authorized by law or regulation to receive it.

4.70 Additional circumstances associated with public safety, privacy, or security concerns could also justify the exclusion of certain information from a publicly available or widely distributed report. For example, detailed information related to computer security for a particular program may be excluded from publicly available reports because of the potential damage that could be caused by the misuse of this information. In such circumstances, auditors may issue a limited use report containing such information and distribute the report only to those parties responsible for acting on the auditor's recommendations. In some instances, it may be appropriate to issue both a publicly available report with the sensitive information excluded and a limited use report. The auditors may consult with legal counsel regarding any requirements or other circumstances that may necessitate the omission of certain information.

4.71 Considering the broad public interest in the program or activity under audit assists auditors when deciding whether to exclude certain information from publicly available reports. When circumstances call for omission of certain information, auditors should evaluate whether this omission could distort the audit results or conceal improper or illegal practices.

Other Written Communications

4.72 *Government Auditing Standards* states that auditors should communicate in writing instances of noncompliance with provisions of contracts and grant agreements and abuse that have an effect on the financial statements that are less than material but warrant the attention of those charged with governance (see table 4-1).[38] This written communication may be done in what is commonly called a management letter. See the preceding discussion for considerations regarding reporting confidential and sensitive information. When auditors detect instances of fraud, noncompliance with provisions of laws, regulations, contracts and grant agreements, and abuse that do not warrant the attention of those charged with governance, the auditor's determination of

---

[38] See footnote 35 to the heading before paragraph 4.55.

whether and how to communicate such instances to audited entity officials is a matter of professional judgment.

4.73 Auditors often communicate information to the auditee about ways to improve operational efficiency and effectiveness or otherwise improve internal control or other policies or procedures (other than those for which communication is required by GAAS or *Government Auditing Standards*). In communicating such information, auditors may consider wording the discussions so that readers can distinguish those matters that are required to be included by GAAS or *Government Auditing Standards* from matters that are recommendations for improvements or information about "best practices."

Portions of the Entity Not Audited in Accordance With Government Auditing Standards

4.74 Because of the provisions of GAAP, entities that are required to have an audit in accordance with *Government Auditing Standards* sometimes include in their financial statements organizational units that are not required to have such an audit. For example, Governmental Accounting Standards Board Statement No. 14, *The Financial Reporting Entity*, as amended, requires reporting entity financial statements to include component units. Similarly, Financial Accounting Standards Board *Accounting Standards Codification* 958-810-25 requires presentation of consolidated financial statements when one not-for-profit entity (NFP) (the parent) controls the voting majority of the board of directors and has an economic interest in another NFP. When included organizational units do not have an audit in accordance with *Government Auditing Standards*, the auditor should consider modifying his or her reports on the financial statements and on internal control over financial reporting and on compliance and other matters, as discussed in the following paragraphs.

4.75 With regard to the report on the financial statements of a governmental reporting entity, consolidated NFP, or other consolidated entity, if a material portion of the entity (such as a component unit or fund)[39] is not required to have an audit in accordance with *Government Auditing Standards*, the auditor should modify the auditor's responsibility section of the report on the financial statements to indicate the portion of the entity that was not audited in accordance with *Government Auditing Standards*. Example wording follows:

> We conducted our audit in accordance with auditing standards generally accepted in the United States of America and the standards applicable to financial audits contained in *Government Auditing Standards*, issued by the Comptroller General of the United States. Those standards require that we plan and perform the audit to obtain reasonable assurance about whether the financial statements are free from material misstatement. The financial statements of [*name of the portion of the entity, such as the name of the component unit or fund*][40]

---

[39] Because an audit of a government's financial statements under the provisions of the AICPA Audit and Accounting Guide *State and Local Governments* is based on opinion units (see footnote 4 in paragraph 4.02), the auditor's consideration of materiality in this instance should be considered in terms of the materiality of the component unit or fund to its related opinion unit. See that guide for further guidance.

[40] For audits of a state or local government's financial statements, if it is not evident from the financial statements to which opinion unit the component unit or fund relates, the auditor should consider identifying the opinion unit in addition to the name of the component unit or fund.

were not audited in accordance with *Government Auditing Standards*. An audit includes examining...

4.76 With regard to the report on the internal control over financial reporting and on compliance and other matters, the auditor should modify the opening auditor's responsibility paragraph to indicate the portion of the entity that was not audited in accordance with *Government Auditing Standards*. Example wording for a state or local government follows:

> We have audited the financial statements of the governmental activities, the business-type activities, the aggregate discretely presented component units, each major fund, and the aggregate remaining fund information of Example Entity as of and for the year ended June 30, 20X1, and the related notes to the financial statements, which collectively comprise Example Entity's basic financial statements and have issued our report thereon dated August 15, 20X1. We conducted our audit in accordance with auditing standards generally accepted in the United States of America and the standards applicable to financial audits contained in *Government Auditing Standards*, issued by the Comptroller General of the United States. The financial statements of [*name of component unit or fund*] were not audited in accordance with *Government Auditing Standards*, and accordingly, this report does not include reporting on internal control over financial reporting or instances of reportable noncompliance associated with [*name of component unit or fund*].

Referring to the Work of a Component Auditor

4.77 AU-C section 600, *Special Considerations—Audits of Group Financial Statements (Including the Work of Component Auditors)* (AICPA, *Professional Standards*), addresses special considerations that apply to group audits, in particular those that involve component auditors. See chapter 6, "Planning Considerations of Circular A-133," and chapter 16, "Auditor Planning Considerations Under the Uniform Guidance," for a high level discussion of group audits. Additional information on audits of group financial statements can be found in AU-C section 600 and applicable Audit and Accounting Guides, such as *Not-for-Profit Entities*, *State and Local Governments*, and *Health Care Entities*.

4.78 When a group auditor refers to the work of a component auditor in the report on an entity's financial statements, the group auditor also should acknowledge the involvement of the component auditor in the report on internal control over financial reporting and compliance and other matters issued as part of the financial statement audit performed in accordance with *Government Auditing Standards*. The group auditor has two options for making such an acknowledgement:

1. Referring to the component auditor's involvement in the group auditor's report and indicating that the results of the component audit is not included—*the reference option*.

2. Referring to the component auditor's involvement in the group auditor's report and including the results of the component audit (for

example, material weaknesses, material instances of noncompliance, significant deficiencies, and abuse)—*the inclusion option*.

Regardless of which of the preceding options is chosen by the auditor, the group auditor is not responsible for the specific findings of component auditors.

4.79 When planning the engagement, the group auditor should consider discussing with the auditee how component auditors' results will be addressed in the group auditor's report on internal control over financial reporting and compliance and other matters required under *Government Auditing Standards*. The group auditor also may want to discuss with both the auditee and component auditors the timing of reports from component auditors to ensure an understanding of expectations. This guide recommends that, if possible, the group auditor use only one option in a report (that is, not referencing the results of some component auditors' work and including the results of others).[41] Paragraphs 4.80–.83 describe considerations relating to the inclusion option. Example 4-4 in the appendix of this chapter (paragraph 4.88) provides illustrative report wording for the reference option, and example 4-6 provides illustrative wording for the inclusion option.

4.80 When relying on the reports of component auditors for the fair presentation of basic financial statements, the group auditor often has to take steps to ensure the component auditors' reports are issued timely so that the group auditor's report on the fair presentation of the reporting entity's financial statements can be issued timely. The same effort also is necessary for the report on internal control over financial reporting and on compliance and other matters required by *Government Auditing Standards* when the group auditor chooses to use the inclusion option and include component auditors' results. Communication, planning, establishing deadlines, and monitoring are important to ensure that the issuance of the group auditor's report is not delayed because one or more component auditors have not issued their reports. Establishing and successfully implementing this approach calls for coordination with both the auditee and the component auditors.

4.81 The use of the inclusion option may not be possible in certain situations due to challenges associated with the gathering and assessment of component auditors' work. For example, large governments may have many component units audited by component auditors and the group auditor may need to obtain, analyze, and include numerous results from component auditors' reports. Further, the component auditors' reports on internal control over financial reporting and compliance and other matters may not be issued in final form when the group auditor's report is issued. Finally, the audits performed by component auditors may not be performed under *Government Auditing Standards*, which may also affect whether the inclusion option can be used.[42]

---

[41] Although this guide recommends that the group auditor use only one option in a report (that is, not referencing the results of some component auditors' work and including the results of others), this may not always be possible. For example, the auditor may be precluded from using the inclusion option for certain components. See footnote 42 in paragraph 4.81 for more information.

[42] When a component auditor did not perform the audit under *Government Auditing Standards* the component auditor will not issue the reporting required by *Government Auditing Standards* (that is, the report on internal control over financial reporting and on compliance and other matters). Instead, the component auditor will issue the communication required by AU-C section 265 if there

(continued)

4.82 With both options, the group auditor's report on internal control over financial reporting and compliance and other matters should identify the organizations, functions, or activities audited by component auditors and whether any of those audits were not performed under *Government Auditing Standards*[43] in the opening paragraph as well as refer to the group auditor's report on the financial statements:

    a. With the reference option, ordinarily the opening paragraph also states that the report on internal control over financial reporting and compliance and other matters does not include the results of the audits performed by component auditors.

    b. With the inclusion option, the group auditor analyzes the results of the component audits to determine which findings, if any, may be included in the group auditor's report on internal control over financial reporting and compliance and other matters. The group auditor exercises professional judgment in evaluating those results for inclusion using the materiality levels appropriate for the scope of the group auditor's audit. For example, a control deficiency that is a significant deficiency or material weakness at the organizational unit level when it is separately audited may not rise to the level of a significant deficiency or material weakness when considered in the context of materiality for the entity covered by the group auditor's audit. Because an audit of a government's financial statements under the provisions of the AICPA Audit and Accounting Guide *State and Local Governments* is based on opinion units (see footnote 4 in paragraph 4.02), the auditor's consideration of the results of the component audits should address each opinion unit. Table 4-3 provides guidance to assist the group auditor in exercising judgment in this analysis process for an audit of a government taking into consideration the opinion unit concept.

(footnote continued)

are significant deficiencies or material weaknesses that were identified. In this circumstance, if the component auditor did not name the group auditor as a specified party in the AU-C section 265 communication, the group auditor is precluded from including the component auditor's significant deficiencies and material weaknesses in the report on internal control over financial reporting and on compliance and other matters. However, if the group auditor is named as a specified party in the AU-C section 265 communication, and the group auditor includes in the report on internal control over financial reporting and on compliance and other matters the significant deficiencies and material weaknesses of the component auditor, this guide recommends that the opening paragraph of example 4-6 in the appendix, "Illustrative Auditor's Reports Under *Government Auditing Standards*," of this chapter (paragraph 4.88) be modified to explain that, although certain of the audits were not performed under *Government Auditing Standards*, the deficiencies in internal control from those audits are included in the reporting.

[43] See example 4-4, footnotes 46–47, and example 4-6 in the appendix of this chapter (paragraph 4.88) for illustrations of the report wording in situations in which some or all of the component auditor's audits were not performed under *Government Auditing Standards*.

Table 4-3
Inclusion Option: Guidance for Determining Whether to Include the Component Auditors' Findings in the Group Auditor's Report on Internal Control Over Financial Reporting and Compliance and Other Matters for an Audit of a Government

The Component Auditors Perform the Audit of	The Component Auditors' Reports Include Material Weakness(es), Material Non-compliance, or Material Abuse	The Component Auditors' Reports Include Significant Deficiencies	The Component Auditors' Reported Matters Required by Government Auditing Standards to Be Communicated in Writing
One or more complete opinion units (for example, the component auditors' report on the financial statements of a major fund or of the aggregate discretely presented component unit opinion unit in its entirety)	Include the component auditors' findings in the group auditor's report[1]	Include the component auditors' findings in the group auditor's report	Exclude the component auditors' findings from the group auditor's report
Material portion of an opinion unit (for example, the component auditors' report on the financial statements of a department that is a material portion of the financial statements of a major fund or the component auditor audits a discretely presented	Include the component auditors' findings in the group auditor's report	Use professional judgment in considering whether to include the component auditors' findings in the group auditor's report	Exclude the component auditors' findings from the group auditor's report

Auditor Reporting and Other Communication Considerations

The Component Auditors Perform the Audit of	The Component Auditors' Reports Include Material Weakness(es), Material Non-compliance, or Material Abuse	The Component Auditors' Reports Include Significant Deficiencies	The Component Auditors' Reported Matters Required by Government Auditing Standards to Be Communicated in Writing
component unit that is material to the aggregate discretely presented component unit opinion unit)			
Immaterial portion of an opinion unit (for example, the component auditors' report on the financial statements of component units that are an immaterial portion of the aggregate discretely presented component unit opinion unit)	Use professional judgment in considering whether to include the component auditors' findings in the group auditor's report[2]	Use professional judgment in considering whether to include the component auditors' findings in the group auditor's report	Exclude the component auditors' findings from the group auditor's report

[1] For example, if the component auditor reports a material weakness or material noncompliance for a major enterprise fund's stand-alone financial statements, the group auditor would include that material weakness or material noncompliance in the group auditor's report.

[2] For example, if the component auditor reports a material weakness for a nonmajor enterprise fund's stand-alone financial statements, the group auditor would consider the nature and significance of the material weakness in relation to the aggregate remaining fund information opinion unit in its entirety to determine whether to include that material weakness in the group auditor's report.

4.83 For those material weaknesses, material instances of noncompliance, significant deficiencies, and abuse the group auditor decides to include in the report, the auditor normally would include the description of the component auditors' results exactly as reported by the component auditors. However, in some circumstances the group auditor may make minor changes to the descriptions of material weaknesses, material instances of noncompliance, significant deficiencies, and abuse (for example, to add clarity and perspective). Before making any changes to such descriptions in the group auditor's report, the auditor may consider discussing the proposed changes with the component auditors and document the results of that discussion. The group auditor uses professional judgment in determining how best to organize the reporting of results of component auditors. For example, the group auditor might organize the results by who identified them, describing the group auditor's results first followed by the results of component auditors. If the group auditor decides to organize all of the findings by subject matter or level of importance, the group auditor could add appropriate language to each of the component auditors' results to make it clear which matters were identified by component auditors.

Freedom of Information Act and Similar Laws and Regulations

4.84 Often, federal, state, and local laws and regulations, such as the Freedom of Information Act (Title 5 U.S. *Code of Federal Regulations* Section 552), require governments to release certain documents, including audit reports and other required written communications of entities for which the government has oversight responsibilities, to members of the press and the general public. Other laws and regulations require that audit reports of governments be made publicly available. Accordingly, auditors should not include names, Social Security numbers, other personal identification, or other potentially sensitive matters in either the body of audit reports or any attached or referenced schedules or letters.

4.85 *Government Auditing Standards* states that when audit organizations are subject to public records laws, auditors should determine whether public records laws could impact the availability of classified or limited use reports and determine whether other means of communicating with management and those charged with governance would be more appropriate. For example, the auditors may communicate general information in a written report and communicate detailed information orally. The auditors may consult with legal counsel regarding applicable public records laws.

Assurance to Regulators and Oversight Agencies

4.86 Federal and state regulators and other oversight agencies sometimes request or require that independent auditors sign a document, such as a standardized form or questionnaire, to provide some level of assurance about an auditee's financial or other data or systems. Auditors may only provide assurance about such data and systems when an engagement that complies with applicable professional standards has been performed. As an alternative to signing such a document, the auditor could suggest that the entity send the most recent financial statement audit report to the requesting party.

4.87 In particular, an auditor may be asked to report on the suitability of the design of an entity's internal control over financial reporting for preventing or detecting and correcting material misstatements of the entity's financial statements on a timely basis. For guidance related to pre-award survey requests see Interpretation No. 7, "Reporting on the Design of Internal Control," of AT section 101, *Attest Engagements* (AICPA, *Professional Standards*, AT sec. 9101 par. .59–.69), which provides useful guidance for such situations.

4.88

Appendix—Illustrative Auditor's Reports Under *Government Auditing Standards*

This appendix contains examples of the reports issued under generally accepted auditing standards (GAAS) and *Government Auditing Standards* in various circumstances, based primarily on the guidance found in *Government Auditing Standards*; AU-C section 700, *Forming an Opinion and Reporting on Financial Statements* (AICPA, *Professional Standards*); and AU-C section 265, *Communicating Internal Control Related Matters Identified in an Audit* (AICPA, *Professional Standards*). *Government Auditing Standards* requires that in addition to providing an opinion or a disclaimer of opinion on the financial statements,[1] auditors should report on the scope and results of testing of the auditee's internal control over financial reporting and compliance with laws, regulations, and provisions of contracts or grant agreements. They also should report certain fraud or abuse.

Auditors should exercise professional judgment in any situation not specifically addressed in this guide. For additional GAAS reporting guidance for those industries where *Government Auditing Standards* reporting is often required, refer to applicable AICPA Audit and Accounting Guides, such as *Not-for-Profit Entities*; *State and Local Governments*; *Health Care Entities*; *Gaming*; *Employee Benefit Plans*; and *Depository and Lending Institutions: Banks and Savings Institutions, Credit Unions, Finance Companies, and Mortgage Companies*.

Examples 4-3–4-9 provide example wording for the reporting required under *Government Auditing Standards* based on an audit of a governmental entity. Footnotes are provided to indicate the revisions that would be made if the entity is a nongovernmental entity, such as a not-for-profit entity.[2]

Example No.	Title
4-1	Unmodified Opinions on Basic Financial Statements Accompanied by Required Supplementary Information and Other Information—State or Local Governmental Entity
4-2	Unmodified Opinion on Consolidated Financial Statements Accompanied by Other Information—Not-for-Profit Entity

(continued)

---

[1] As explained in the AICPA Audit and Accounting Guide *State and Local Governments*, the auditor generally expresses or disclaims an opinion on a government's basic financial statements by providing an opinion or disclaimer of opinion on each opinion unit required to be presented in those financial statements. In addition, the auditor may provide opinions or disclaimers of opinions on additional opinion units if engaged to set the scope of the audit and assess materiality at a more detailed level than by the opinion units required for the basic financial statements. Throughout this guide, the use of the singular terms *opinion* and *disclaimer of opinion* encompasses the multiple opinions and disclaimers of opinion that generally will be provided on a government's basic financial statements. See example 4-1 for an example of reporting on state and local government financial statements.

[2] Because of the unique wording required in reporting for a governmental entity, report examples 4-3–4-9 provide wording for a governmental entity. Report wording for a not-for-profit entity is provided in footnotes.

Example No.	Title
4-3	Report on Internal Control Over Financial Reporting and on Compliance and Other Matters Based on an Audit of Financial Statements Performed in Accordance With *Government Auditing Standards* (for a Governmental Entity) (No Material Weaknesses Identified; No Significant Deficiencies Identified; No Reportable Instances of Noncompliance or Other Matters Identified)
4-4	Report on Internal Control Over Financial Reporting and on Compliance and Other Matters Based on an Audit of Financial Statements Performed in Accordance With *Government Auditing Standards* (for a Governmental Entity and With Reference to Audits by Other Auditors Using the Reference Option) (No Material Weaknesses Identified; No Significant Deficiencies Identified; No Reportable Instances of Noncompliance or Other Matters Identified)
4-5	Report on Internal Control Over Financial Reporting and on Compliance and Other Matters Based on an Audit of Financial Statements Performed in Accordance With *Government Auditing Standards* (for a Governmental Entity) (No Material Weaknesses Identified; Significant Deficiencies Identified; Reportable Instances of Noncompliance and Other Matters Identified)
4-6	Report on Internal Control Over Financial Reporting and on Compliance and Other Matters Based on an Audit of Financial Statements Performed in Accordance With *Government Auditing Standards* (for a Governmental Entity and With Reference to Audits by Other Auditors Using the Inclusion Option) (No Material Weaknesses Identified; Significant Deficiencies Identified; Reportable Instances of Noncompliance and Other Matters Identified)
4-7	Report on Internal Control Over Financial Reporting and on Compliance and Other Matters Based on an Audit of Financial Statements Performed in Accordance With *Government Auditing Standards* (for a Governmental Entity) (Material Weaknesses Identified; No Significant Deficiencies Identified; Reportable Instances of Noncompliance and Other Matters Identified)
4-8	Report on Internal Control Over Financial Reporting and on Compliance and Other Matters Based on an Audit of Financial Statements Performed in Accordance With *Government Auditing Standards* (for a Governmental Entity) (Material Weaknesses and Significant Deficiencies Identified; Reportable Instances of Noncompliance and Other Matters Identified)
4-9	Report on Internal Control Over Financial Reporting and on Compliance and Other Matters Based on an Audit of Financial Statements Performed in Accordance With *Government Auditing Standards* (for a Governmental Entity) (Opinion on the Financial Statements as a Whole Disclaimed; Material Weaknesses and Significant Deficiencies Identified; Reportable Instances of Noncompliance and Other Matters Identified)

Example 4-1

Unmodified Opinions on Basic Financial Statements Accompanied by Required Supplementary Information and Other Information—State or Local Governmental Entity[3,4]

Independent Auditor's Report

[*Appropriate Addressee*]

Report on the Financial Statements

We have audited the accompanying financial statements of the governmental activities, the business-type activities, the aggregate discretely presented component units, each major fund, and the aggregate remaining fund information of the City of Example, Any State, as of and for the year ended June 30, 20X1, and the related notes to the financial statements, which collectively comprise the City of Example's basic financial statements as listed in the table of contents.

Management's Responsibility for the Financial Statements

Management is responsible for the preparation and fair presentation of these financial statements in accordance with accounting principles generally accepted in the United States of America; this includes the design, implementation, and maintenance of internal control relevant to the preparation and fair presentation of financial statements that are free from material misstatement, whether due to fraud or error.

Auditor's Responsibility

Our responsibility is to express opinions on these financial statements based on our audit. We conducted our audit in accordance with auditing standards generally accepted in the United States of America and the standards applicable to financial audits contained in *Government Auditing Standards*,[5] issued by the Comptroller General of the United States. Those standards require that we plan and perform the audit to obtain reasonable assurance about whether the financial statements are free from material misstatement.

An audit involves performing procedures to obtain audit evidence about the amounts and disclosures in the financial statements. The procedures selected depend on the auditor's judgment, including the assessment of the risks of material misstatement of the financial statements, whether due to fraud or error. In making those risk assessments, the auditor considers internal control relevant to the entity's preparation and fair presentation of the financial statements in order to design audit procedures that are appropriate in the

---

[3] Refer to the AICPA Audit and Accounting Guide *State and Local Governments* for additional guidance on reporting on a government's basic financial statements. In particular, appendix A to chapter 15 of that guide describes conditions that may make modifications of the standard report necessary and illustrates several of those modifications, such as reference to the work of other auditors.

[4] This illustration is based on a similar example in the Audit and Accounting Guide *State and Local Governments*. However, unlike the example in *State and Local Governments*, which assumes that the financial statement audit is performed only under generally accepted auditing standards (GAAS), this illustration reflects the additional reporting when the financial statement audit is also performed in accordance with *Government Auditing Standards*. The supplementary information reporting in this illustration also presents the in-relation-to reporting on the schedule of expenditures of federal awards.

[5] For financial audits performed in accordance with *Government Auditing Standards*, chapters 1–4 of *Government Auditing Standards* apply.

circumstances, but not for the purpose of expressing an opinion on the effectiveness of the entity's internal control.[6] Accordingly, we express no such opinion. An audit also includes evaluating the appropriateness of accounting policies used and the reasonableness of significant accounting estimates made by management, as well as evaluating the overall presentation of the financial statements.

We believe that the audit evidence we have obtained is sufficient and appropriate to provide a basis for our audit opinions.

Opinions

In our opinion, the financial statements referred to above present fairly, in all material respects, the respective financial position of the governmental activities, the business-type activities, the aggregate discretely presented component units, each major fund, and the aggregate remaining fund information of the City of Example, Any State, as of June 30, 20X1, and the respective changes in financial position and, where applicable, cash flows thereof for the year then ended in accordance with accounting principles generally accepted in the United States of America.

Other Matters

Required Supplementary Information[7]

Accounting principles generally accepted in the United States of America require that the [*identify the required supplementary information, such as management's discussion and analysis and budgetary comparison information*] on pages XX–XX and XX–XX be presented to supplement the basic financial statements. Such information, although not a part of the basic financial statements, is required by the Governmental Accounting Standards Board who considers it to be an essential part of financial reporting for placing the basic financial statements in an appropriate operational, economic, or historical context.

---

[6] In circumstances when the auditor also has responsibility to express an opinion on the effectiveness of internal control in conjunction with the audit of the financial statements, this sentence would be worded as follows:

> In making those risk assessments, the auditor considers internal control relevant to the organization's preparation and fair presentation of the financial statements in order to design audit procedures that are appropriate in the circumstances.

In addition, the next sentence, "Accordingly, we express no such opinion," would not be included.

[7] Generally accepted accounting principles for state and local government entities often require that the financial statements be accompanied by certain required supplementary information (RSI). This RSI paragraph, within the "Other Matters" section of the report, illustrates a situation where RSI is included, the auditor has applied the specified procedures, and no material departures from prescribed guidelines have been identified.

If all of the RSI is omitted, the paragraph on RSI would be replaced with the following:

> Management has omitted [*identify the missing RSI, such as management's discussion and analysis and budgetary comparison information*] that accounting principles generally accepted in the United States of America require to be presented to supplement the basic financial statements. Such missing information, although not a part of the basic financial statements, is required by the Governmental Accounting Standards Board who considers it to be an essential part of financial reporting for placing the basic financial statements in an appropriate operational, economic, or historical context. Our opinion on the basic financial statements is not affected by this missing information.

For other situations in which some RSI is omitted and some is presented in accordance with prescribed guidelines, there are material departures from prescribed guidelines, specified procedures not completed, or there are unresolved doubts about whether the RSI is in accordance with prescribed guidelines, refer to the guidance in AU-C section 730, *Required Supplementary Information* (AICPA, *Professional Standards*), and the AICPA Audit and Accounting Guide *State and Local Governments.*

We have applied certain limited procedures to the required supplementary information in accordance with auditing standards generally accepted in the United States of America, which consisted of inquiries of management about the methods of preparing the information and comparing the information for consistency with management's responses to our inquiries, the basic financial statements, and other knowledge we obtained during our audit of the basic financial statements. We do not express an opinion or provide any assurance on the information because the limited procedures do not provide us with sufficient evidence to express an opinion or provide any assurance.

Other Information[8,9]

Our audit was conducted for the purpose of forming opinions on the financial statements that collectively comprise the City of Example's basic financial statements. The [*identify accompanying supplementary information such as the combining and individual nonmajor fund financial statements and schedule of expenditures of federal awards,*[10] *as required by (Office of Management and Budget Circular A-133,* Audits of States, Local Governments, and Non-Profit

---

[8] This section, within the "Other Matters" section of the report, is intended to include the reporting on supplementary information (SI) when the auditor is engaged to provide an "in-relation-to" opinion on SI and also when explanatory language will be provided relating to other information (OI) when the auditor is disclaiming an opinion on the OI. This illustration provides example language for both SI and OI reporting. The caption provided in this illustration is one way an auditor could title the section. Alternatively, the auditor could title it "Supplementary and Other Information," "Supplementary Information," or "Accompanying Information."

[9] This illustration assumes that the auditor has been engaged to provide an "in-relation-to" opinion on SI, the auditor is issuing an unmodified opinion on the financial statements, and the auditor has concluded that the SI is fairly stated, in all material respects, in relation to the financial statements as a whole. If there is no SI on which to report, the references to SI in these paragraphs would be deleted. If the auditor has issued an opinion other than unmodified on the financial statements, see the guidance in AU-C section 725, *Supplementary Information in Relation to the Financial Statements as a Whole* (AICPA, *Professional Standards*), and the AICPA Audit and Accounting Guide *State and Local Governments*. Additionally, the OI reporting contained within this section provides an example of explanatory language that the auditor may use to disclaim an opinion on OI. Note there is no required reporting on OI under AU-C section 720, *Other Information in Documents Containing Audited Financial Statements* (AICPA, *Professional Standards*). If there is no OI contained in the document containing the audited financial statements or if the auditor chooses not to include the disclaimer, the references to OI in this section would be deleted. See AU-C section 720 and the AICPA Audit and Accounting Guide *State and Local Governments* for more information.

[10] As noted in AU-C section 725, the date of the auditor's report on supplementary information in relation to the financial statements as a whole should not be earlier than the date on which the auditor completed the required procedures required by AU-C section 725. When a compliance audit performed in accordance with Office of Management and Budget Circular A-133, *Audits of States, Local Governments, and Non-Profit Organizations* (Circular A-133), or Title 2 U.S. *Code of Federal Regulations* (CFR) Part 200, *Uniform Administrative Requirements, Cost Principles, and Audit Requirements for Federal Awards* (Uniform Guidance), is performed after the financial statement audit, the required procedures on the schedule of expenditures of federal awards may not be completed until after the date of the auditor's report on the financial statements. In this case, if the in-relation-to reporting on the schedule of expenditures of federal awards is included in the financial statement report, the auditor would dual-date the financial statement report. The auditor may also consider including the in-relation-to reporting on the schedule of expenditures of federal awards in a separate report or in the auditor's reporting issued to meet the requirements of Circular A-133 or the Uniform Guidance. The illustrations contained in chapter 13, "Auditor Reporting Requirements and Other Communication Considerations in a Single Audit (Circular A-133)," provide examples of reporting on the schedule in the Circular A-133 report. The illustrations contained in chapter 23, "Auditor Reporting Requirements and Other Communication Considerations in a Single Audit (Uniform Guidance)," provide examples of reporting on the schedule in the Uniform Guidance compliance audit report. Additionally, see chapter 13 (for a Circular A-133 compliance audit) or chapter 23 (for a Uniform Guidance compliance audit) for further discussion of dating the in-relation-to reporting on the schedule of expenditures of federal awards.

Organizations) *or (Title 2 U.S. Code of Federal Regulations (CFR) Part 200, Uniform Administrative Requirements, Cost Principles, and Audit Requirements for Federal Awards) and the other information, such as the introductory and statistical section]* are presented for purposes of additional analysis and are not a required part of the basic financial statements.

[***Note:*** *If the schedule of expenditures of federal awards is presented and the auditor is performing the audit under OMB Circular A-133, the auditor would use the words "schedule of expenditures of federal awards, as required by Office of Management and Budget Circular A-133,* Audits of States, Local Governments, and Non-Profit Organizations." *If the schedule of expenditures of federal awards is presented and the auditor is performing the audit under the Uniform Guidance, the auditor would use the words "schedule of expenditures of federal awards, as required by Title 2 U.S. Code of Federal Regulations (CFR) Part 200,* Uniform Administrative Requirements, Cost Principles, and Audit Requirements for Federal Awards."]

The *[identify accompanying supplementary information]* is the responsibility of management and was derived from and relates directly to the underlying accounting and other records used to prepare the basic financial statements. Such information has been subjected to the auditing procedures applied in the audit of the basic financial statements and certain additional procedures, including comparing and reconciling such information directly to the underlying accounting and other records used to prepare the basic financial statements or to the basic financial statements themselves, and other additional procedures in accordance with auditing standards generally accepted in the United States of America. In our opinion, the *[identify accompanying supplementary information]* is fairly stated, in all material respects, in relation to the basic financial statements as a whole.

The *[identify accompanying other information]* has not been subjected to the auditing procedures applied in the audit of the basic financial statements, and accordingly, we do not express an opinion or provide any assurance on it.

Other Reporting Required by *Government Auditing Standards*[11]

In accordance with *Government Auditing Standards*, we have also issued our report dated *[date of report]* on our consideration of the City of Example's internal control over financial reporting and on our tests of its compliance with certain provisions of laws, regulations, contracts, and grant agreements and other matters.[12] The purpose of that report is to describe the scope of our testing of internal control over financial reporting and compliance and the results of that testing, and not to provide an opinion on internal control over financial reporting or on compliance.[13] That report is an integral part

---

[11] Paragraph .37 of AU-C section 700, *Forming an Opinion and Reporting on Financial Statements* (AICPA, *Professional Standards*), provides that the section related to an auditor's other reporting responsibilities should be subtitled "Report on Other Legal and Regulatory Requirements" or otherwise, as appropriate to the contents of the section. An example of an alternative title describing the reporting required by *Government Auditing Standards* is illustrated here.

[12] Paragraph 4.07 discusses noncompliance and other matters—that is, certain fraud and abuse—for which *Government Auditing Standards* requires reporting in the auditor's report.

[13] This sentence should be modified if the auditor is providing an opinion on internal control over financial reporting or on compliance in the *Government Auditing Standards* report. See footnote 10 at paragraph 4.11.

Auditor Reporting and Other Communication Considerations

of an audit performed in accordance with *Government Auditing Standards* in considering City of Example's internal control over financial reporting and compliance.

[*Auditor's signature*]

[*Auditor's city and state*][14]

[*Date of the auditor's report*]

Example 4-2

Unmodified Opinion on Consolidated Financial Statements Accompanied by Other Information—Not-for-Profit Entity[15,16]

Independent Auditor's Report

[*Appropriate Addressee*]

Report on the Financial Statements

We have audited the accompanying consolidated financial statements of Example NFP, which comprise the consolidated statement of financial position as of June 30, 20X1, and the related consolidated statements of activities, and cash flows[17] for the year then ended, and the related notes to the financial statements.

Management's Responsibility for the Financial Statements

Management is responsible for the preparation and fair presentation of these consolidated financial statements in accordance with accounting principles generally accepted in the United States of America; this includes the design, implementation, and maintenance of internal control relevant to the preparation and fair presentation of consolidated financial statements that are free from material misstatement, whether due to fraud or error.

---

[14] Technical Questions and Answers (Q&A) section 9100.07, "Naming the City and State Where the Auditor Practices," and Q&A section 9100.08, "Audit Firm With Multiple Offices on Their Company Letterhead and Effect on Report" (AICPA, *Technical Questions and Answers*), provide guidance related to naming the city and state in the auditor's report. The city and state where the auditor practices is not required to be placed under the auditor's signature and may be named in the firm's letterhead on which the report is issued. However, if the firm's letterhead includes multiple offices it will not be clear which location is the issuing office and, in that case, the auditor would need to indicate the city and state where the auditor practices in the auditor's report.

[15] Refer to the AICPA Audit and Accounting Guide *Not-for-Profit Entities* for additional guidance on reporting on the financial statements of a not-for-profit entity. In addition to the situations discussed in that guide, auditors may need to modify the report on the financial statements to refer to the work of other auditors, using the guidance in AU-C section 600, *Special Considerations—Audits of Group Financial Statements (Including the Work of Component Auditors)* (AICPA, *Professional Standards*).

[16] This illustration is based on a similar example in the Audit and Accounting Guide *Not-for-Profit Entities*. However, unlike the example in *Not-for-Profit Entities*, which assumes that the financial statement audit is performed only under GAAS, this illustration reflects the additional reporting when the financial statement audit is also performed in accordance with *Government Auditing Standards*. Additionally, the supplementary information reporting in this illustration reflects the in-relation-to reporting on the schedule of expenditures of federal awards.

[17] Each of the statements presented, which may include a statement of functional expenses, should be identified in the introductory paragraph. Paragraph .A23 of AU-C section 700 notes that the identification of the title for each statement that the financial statements comprise may be achieved by referencing the table of contents.

Auditor's Responsibility

Our responsibility is to express an opinion on these consolidated financial statements based on our audits. We conducted our audits in accordance with auditing standards generally accepted in the United States of America and the standards applicable to financial audits contained in *Government Auditing Standards*,[18] issued by the Comptroller General of the United States. Those standards require that we plan and perform the audit to obtain reasonable assurance about whether the consolidated financial statements are free from material misstatement.

An audit involves performing procedures to obtain audit evidence about the amounts and disclosures in the consolidated financial statements. The procedures selected depend on the auditor's judgment, including the assessment of the risks of material misstatement of the consolidated financial statements, whether due to fraud or error. In making those risk assessments, the auditor considers internal control relevant to the entity's preparation and fair presentation of the consolidated financial statements in order to design audit procedures that are appropriate in the circumstances, but not for the purpose of expressing an opinion on the effectiveness of the entity's internal control.[19] Accordingly, we express no such opinion. An audit also includes evaluating the appropriateness of accounting policies used and the reasonableness of significant accounting estimates made by management, as well as evaluating the overall presentation of the consolidated financial statements.

We believe that the audit evidence we have obtained is sufficient and appropriate to provide a basis for our audit opinion.

Opinion

In our opinion, the consolidated financial statements referred to above present fairly, in all material respects, the consolidated financial position of Example NFP as of June 30, 20X1, and the changes in its net assets and its cash flows for the year then ended in accordance with accounting principles generally accepted in the United States of America.

Other Matters

Other Information[20,21]

Our audit was conducted for the purpose of forming an opinion on the consolidated financial statements as a whole. The [*identify accompanying supplementary information such as the schedule of expenditures of federal awards,*[22] *as required by (Office of Management and Budget Circular A-133,* Audits of

---

[18] See footnote 5.

[19] See footnote 6.

[20] This section, within the "Other Matters" section of the report, is intended to include the reporting on SI when the auditor is engaged to provide an "in-relation-to" opinion on SI and also when explanatory language will be provided relating to OI when the auditor is disclaiming an opinion on the OI. This illustration assumes that the only information that accompanies the financial statements is the schedule of expenditures of federal award and that the auditor is providing an "in-relation-to" opinion on it. Example 4-1 provides illustrative wording that can be incorporated into this illustration when other information also accompanies the financial statements. The caption provided in this illustration is one way an auditor could title the section. Alternatively, the auditor could title it "Supplementary and Other Information," "Supplementary Information," or "Accompanying Information."

[21] If there is no SI on which to report, these paragraphs would be deleted. If the auditor has issued an opinion other than unmodified on the financial statements, see the guidance in AU-C section 725.

[22] See footnote 10.

Auditor Reporting and Other Communication Considerations

States, Local Governments, and Non-Profit Organizations, *or Title 2 U.S. Code of Federal Regulations (CFR) Part 200,* Uniform Administrative Requirements, Cost Principles, and Audit Requirements for Federal Awards*)*] is presented for purposes of additional analysis and is not a required part of the consolidated financial statements. Such information is the responsibility of management and was derived from and relates directly to the underlying accounting and other records used to prepare the consolidated financial statements. The information has been subjected to the auditing procedures applied in the audit of the consolidated financial statements and certain additional procedures, including comparing and reconciling such information directly to the underlying accounting and other records used to prepare the consolidated financial statements or to the consolidated financial statements themselves, and other additional procedures in accordance with auditing standards generally accepted in the United States of America. In our opinion, the information is fairly stated, in all material respects, in relation to the consolidated financial statements as a whole.

[***Note:*** *If the schedule of expenditures of federal awards is presented and the auditor is performing the audit under OMB Circular A-133, the auditor would use the words "schedule of expenditures of federal awards, as required by Office of Management and Budget Circular A-133,* Audits of States, Local Governments, and Non-Profit Organizations.*" If the schedule of expenditures of federal awards is presented and the auditor is performing the audit under the Uniform Guidance, the auditor would use the words "schedule of expenditures of federal awards, as required by Title 2 U.S. Code of Federal Regulations (CFR) Part 200,* Uniform Administrative Requirements, Cost Principles, and Audit Requirements for Federal Awards.*"*]

Other Reporting Required by *Government Auditing Standards*[23]

In accordance with *Government Auditing Standards,* we have also issued our report dated [*date of report*] on our consideration of Example NFP's internal control over financial reporting and on our tests of its compliance with certain provisions of laws, regulations, contracts, and grant agreements and other matters.[24] The purpose of that report is to describe the scope of our testing of internal control over financial reporting and compliance and the results of that testing, and not to provide an opinion on internal control over financial reporting or on compliance.[25] That report is an integral part of an audit performed in accordance with *Government Auditing Standards* in considering Example NFP's internal control over financial reporting and compliance.

[*Auditor's signature*]

[*Auditor's city and state*][26]

[*Date of the Auditor's Report*]

---

[23] See footnote 11.
[24] See footnote 12.
[25] See footnote 13.
[26] See footnote 14.

Example 4-3

Report on Internal Control Over Financial Reporting and on Compliance and Other Matters[27] Based on an Audit of Financial Statements Performed in Accordance With *Government Auditing Standards* (for a Governmental Entity)[28]

(No Material Weaknesses Identified; No Significant Deficiencies Identified; No Reportable Instances of Noncompliance or Other Matters Identified)[29]

Independent Auditor's Report

[*Appropriate Addressee*]

We have audited, in accordance with the auditing standards generally accepted in the United States of America and the standards applicable to financial audits contained in *Government Auditing Standards* issued by the Comptroller General of the United States,[30] the financial statements of the governmental activities, the business-type activities, the aggregate discretely presented component units, each major fund, and the aggregate remaining fund information of Example Entity, as of and for the year ended June 30, 20X1, and the related notes to the financial statements, which collectively comprise Example Entity's basic financial statements, and have issued our report thereon dated August 15, 20X1.[31]

---

[27] Chapter 2, "*Government Auditing Standards*—Ethical Principles and General Standards," and chapter 3, "Planning and Performing a Financial Statement Audit in Accordance With *Government Auditing Standards*," of this guide discuss the auditor's consideration of internal control over financial reporting and of fraud, noncompliance with provisions of laws, regulations, contracts, and grant agreements, and abuse.

[28] This illustration assumes that Example Entity is a governmental entity. If Example Entity is a not-for-profit entity, the wording in the first paragraph of this report should be modified using the following wording. Additionally, the first sentence under the heading "Internal Control over Financial Reporting" would be revised to refer to "our opinion" instead of "our opinions."

We have audited, in accordance with the auditing standards generally accepted in the United States of America and the standards applicable to financial audits contained in *Government Auditing Standards* issued by the Comptroller General of the United States, the financial statements of Example Entity, which comprise the consolidated statement of financial position as of June 30, 20X1, and the related consolidated statements of activities, and cash flows for the year then ended, and the related notes to the financial statements, and have issued our report thereon dated August 15, 20X1.

[29] Auditors may use portions of various illustrations included in this appendix to draft reports that apply to a specific auditee situation. For example, if the auditor has identified significant deficiencies but has not identified instances of noncompliance or other matters that are required to be reported under *Government Auditing Standards*, the internal control section of example 4-5 may be used along with the compliance and other matters section of example 4-3. Alternatively if the auditor has not identified significant deficiencies but has identified instances of noncompliance or other matters that are required to be reported under *Government Auditing Standards*, the internal control section of example 4-3 may be used along with the compliance section of example 4-5. See examples 4-7–4-9 for illustrative reporting for situations in which the auditor has identified material weaknesses.

[30] See footnote 5. Additionally, if the financial statements include organizational units that are not required to have a *Government Auditing Standards* audit, the auditor should consider modifying this paragraph. See paragraph 4.76.

[31] If the auditor expressed a modified opinion on the financial statements (that is, a qualified opinion, an adverse opinion, or a disclaimer of opinion), the auditor should include a statement describing the nature of the modification. The auditor may include certain additional communications when the auditor included such additional communications in the auditor's report on the financial statements that are not modifications to the auditor's opinion. For example, if the auditor included an emphasis-of-matter paragraph in the auditor's report on the financial statements because of an uncertainty about the entity's ability to continue as a going concern for a reasonable period of time, the auditor may also include mention of the additional communication here.

Auditor Reporting and Other Communication Considerations

Internal Control Over Financial Reporting[32,33]

In planning and performing our audit of the financial statements, we considered Example Entity's internal control over financial reporting (internal control) to determine the audit procedures that are appropriate in the circumstances for the purpose of expressing our opinions[34] on the financial statements, but not for the purpose of expressing an opinion on the effectiveness of Example Entity's internal control. Accordingly, we do not express an opinion on the effectiveness of Example Entity's internal control.

A *deficiency in internal control* exists when the design or operation of a control does not allow management or employees, in the normal course of performing their assigned functions, to prevent, or detect and correct, misstatements on a timely basis. A *material weakness* is a deficiency, or a combination of deficiencies, in internal control, such that there is a reasonable possibility that a material misstatement of the entity's financial statements will not be prevented, or detected and corrected on a timely basis. A *significant deficiency* is a deficiency, or a combination of deficiencies, in internal control that is less severe than a material weakness, yet important enough to merit attention by those charged with governance.

Our consideration of internal control was for the limited purpose described in the first paragraph of this section and was not designed to identify all deficiencies in internal control that might be material weaknesses or significant deficiencies. Given these limitations, during our audit we did not identify any deficiencies in internal control that we consider to be material weaknesses. However, material weaknesses may exist that have not been identified.

Compliance and Other Matters[35,36]

As part of obtaining reasonable assurance about whether Example Entity's financial statements are free from material misstatement, we performed tests of its compliance with certain provisions of laws, regulations, contracts, and grant agreements, noncompliance with which could have a direct and material effect on the determination of financial statement amounts. However, providing an opinion on compliance with those provisions was not an objective of our

---

[32] *Government Auditing Standards* permits, but does not require, auditors to express an opinion on internal control over financial reporting or on compliance if sufficient work was performed. See also footnote 13.

[33] This report sequences the reporting on internal control over financial reporting before the reporting on compliance and other matters. However, the Circular A-133 reports in the appendix in chapter 13 and the appendix in chapter 14, "Program-Specific Audits (Circular A-133)," of this guide sequence the reporting on compliance before the reporting on internal control over compliance. Similarly, the Uniform Guidance reports in the appendix in chapter 23 and the appendix in chapter 24, "Program-Specific Audits (Uniform Guidance)," of this guide sequence the reporting on compliance before the reporting on internal control over compliance. Auditors may present the internal control and compliance sections of the *Government Auditing Standards* and compliance audit reports in whichever sequence better meets their needs.

[34] See footnote 28.

[35] *Other matters* are certain findings of fraud or abuse. As per industry practice, the reference to "other matters" in both the heading and the following paragraph typically appears in all reports, even if the report does not present or refer to findings of fraud or abuse or even if the only findings of fraud or abuse are presented in or referred to from the section on internal control over financial reporting. See paragraph 4.59.

[36] Paragraph 4.26 of *Government Auditing Standards* notes that when auditors detect instances of noncompliance with provisions of contracts and grant agreements or abuse that have an effect on the financial statements that are less than material but warrant the attention of those charged with governance, they should communicate those findings in writing to audited entity officials. See paragraph 4.72.

audit, and accordingly, we do not express such an opinion. The results of our tests disclosed no instances of noncompliance or other matters that are required to be reported under *Government Auditing Standards*.

Purpose of this Report

The purpose of this report is solely to describe the scope of our testing of internal control and compliance and the results of that testing, and not to provide an opinion on the effectiveness of the entity's internal control or on compliance. This report is an integral part of an audit performed in accordance with *Government Auditing Standards* in considering the entity's internal control and compliance. Accordingly, this communication is not suitable for any other purpose.[37]

[*Auditor's signature*]

[*Auditor's city and state*][38]

[*Date of the auditor's report*][39]

Example 4-4

Report on Internal Control Over Financial Reporting and on Compliance and Other Matters[40] Based on an Audit of Financial Statements Performed in Accordance With *Government Auditing Standards* (for a Governmental Entity[41] and With Reference to Audits by Other Auditors Using the Reference Option)[42]

(No Material Weaknesses Identified; No Significant Deficiencies Identified; No Reportable Instances of Noncompliance or Other Matters Identified)[43]

Independent Auditor's Report

[*Appropriate Addressee*]

We have audited, in accordance with the auditing standards generally accepted in the United States of America and the standards applicable to financial audits contained in *Government Auditing Standards* issued by the Comptroller General of the United States,[44] the financial statements of the governmental activities, the business-type activities, the aggregate discretely presented component units, each major fund, and the aggregate remaining fund information of Example Entity as of and for the year ended June 30, 20X1, and the related

---

[37] This paragraph conforms to paragraph .11 of AU-C section 905, *Alert That Restricts the Use of the Auditor's Written Communication* (AICPA *Professional Standards*), which provides for a "purpose" alert in lieu of a "restricted use" alert for certain communications issued under *Government Auditing Standards*. See AU-C section 905 for additional guidance.

[38] See footnote 14.

[39] Because this report relates to the audit of the financial statements, and is based on the GAAS audit procedures performed, it is subject to the provisions of AU-C section 700. Therefore, it should be dated the same date as the auditor's report on the financial statements, which according to paragraph .41 of AU-C section 700, is "no earlier than the date on which the auditor has obtained sufficient appropriate audit evidence on which to base the auditor's opinion on the financial statements."

[40] See footnote 27.

[41] See footnote 28.

[42] See paragraphs 4.77–.83 for discussion of the reference option for acknowledging the involvement of other auditors (that is, component auditors) in the report on internal control over financial reporting and compliance and other matters.

[43] See footnote 29.

[44] See footnote 30.

notes to the financial statements, which collectively comprise Example Entity's basic financial statements, and have issued our report thereon dated August 15, 20X1.[45] Our report includes a reference to other auditors who audited the financial statements of [*identify organization, function, or activity*], as described in our report on Example Entity's financial statements. This report does not include the results of the other auditors' testing of internal control over financial reporting or compliance and other matters that are reported on separately by those auditors.[46,47]

Internal Control Over Financial Reporting[48,49]

In planning and performing our audit of the financial statements, we considered Example Entity's internal control over financial reporting (internal control) to determine the audit procedures that are appropriate in the circumstances for the purpose of expressing our opinions[50] on the financial statements, but not for the purpose of expressing an opinion on the effectiveness of Example Entity's internal control. Accordingly, we do not express an opinion on the effectiveness of Example Entity's internal control.

A *deficiency in internal control* exists when the design or operation of a control does not allow management or employees, in the normal course of performing their assigned functions, to prevent, or detect and correct, misstatements on a timely basis. A *material weakness* is a deficiency, or a combination of deficiencies, in internal control such that there is a reasonable possibility that a material misstatement of the entity's financial statements will not be prevented, or detected and corrected on a timely basis. A *significant deficiency* is a deficiency, or a combination of deficiencies, in internal control that is less severe than a material weakness, yet important enough to merit attention by those charged with governance.

Our consideration of internal control was for the limited purpose described in the first paragraph of this section and was not designed to identify all deficiencies in internal control that might be material weaknesses or significant deficiencies. Given these limitations, during our audit we did not identify any

---

[45] See footnote 31.

[46] There may be circumstances in which none of the other auditors' audits referred to in the financial statement report were performed under *Government Auditing Standards*. To clarify the portion that was not audited in accordance with *Government Auditing Standards*, this paragraph should be modified. The last sentence in this paragraph may be replaced with the following: The financial statements of [*identify organization, function, or activity*] were not audited in accordance with *Government Auditing Standards*.

See also paragraph 4.76 for additional guidance on modifying this paragraph when the financial statements include organizational units that are not required to have a *Government Auditing Standards* audit. Paragraph 4.75 provides guidance on similar modifications to the report on the financial statements.

[47] There may be circumstances in which some other auditors' audits were not performed under *Government Auditing Standards*, whereas some other auditors' audits were performed under those standards. In that situation, this paragraph should be modified. An additional sentence may be added as follows: The financial statements of [*identify organizations, functions, or activities audited by other auditors that were not performed under Government Auditing Standards*] were not audited in accordance with *Government Auditing Standards*.

See also paragraph 4.76 for additional guidance on modifying the auditor's responsibility paragraph when the financial statements include organizational units that are not required to have a *Government Auditing Standards* audit. Paragraph 4.75 provides guidance on similar modifications to the report on the financial statements.

[48] See footnote 32.

[49] See footnote 33.

[50] See footnote 28.

deficiencies in internal control that we consider to be material weaknesses. However, material weaknesses may exist that have not been identified.

Compliance and Other Matters[51,52]

As part of obtaining reasonable assurance about whether Example Entity's financial statements are free from material misstatement, we performed tests of its compliance with certain provisions of laws, regulations, contracts, and grant agreements, noncompliance with which could have a direct and material effect on the determination of financial statement amounts. However, providing an opinion on compliance with those provisions was not an objective of our audit, and accordingly, we do not express such an opinion. The results of our tests disclosed no instances of noncompliance or other matters that are required to be reported under *Government Auditing Standards*.

Purpose of this Report

The purpose of this report is solely to describe the scope of our testing of internal control and compliance and the result of that testing, and not to provide an opinion on the effectiveness of the entity's internal control or on compliance. This report is an integral part of an audit performed in accordance with *Government Auditing Standards* in considering the entity's internal control and compliance. Accordingly, this communication is not suitable for any other purpose.[53]

[*Auditor's signature*]

[*Auditor's city and state*][54]

[*Date of the auditor's report*][55]

Example 4-5

Report on Internal Control Over Financial Reporting and on Compliance and Other Matters[56] Based on an Audit of Financial Statements Performed in Accordance With *Government Auditing Standards (for a Governmental Entity)*[57]

(No Material Weaknesses Identified; Significant Deficiencies Identified; Reportable Instances of Noncompliance and Other Matters Identified)[58]

Independent Auditor's Report

[*Appropriate Addressee*]

We have audited, in accordance with the auditing standards generally accepted in the United States of America and the standards applicable to financial audits contained in *Government Auditing Standards* issued by the Comptroller General of the United States,[59] the financial statements of the governmental

---

[51] See footnote 35.
[52] See footnote 36.
[53] See footnote 37.
[54] See footnote 14.
[55] See footnote 39.
[56] See footnote 27.
[57] See footnote 28.
[58] See footnote 29.
[59] See footnote 30.

activities, the business-type activities, the aggregate discretely presented component units, each major fund, and the aggregate remaining fund information of Example Entity as of and for the year ended June 30, 20X1, and the related notes to the financial statements, which collectively comprise Example Entity's basic financial statements, and have issued our report thereon dated August 15, 20X1.[60]

Internal Control Over Financial Reporting[61,62]

In planning and performing our audit of the financial statements, we considered Example Entity's internal control over financial reporting (internal control) to determine the audit procedures that are appropriate in the circumstances for the purpose of expressing our opinions[63] on the financial statements, but not for the purpose of expressing an opinion on the effectiveness of Example Entity's internal control. Accordingly, we do not express an opinion on the effectiveness of Example Entity's internal control.

A *deficiency in internal control* exists when the design or operation of a control does not allow management or employees, in the normal course of performing their assigned functions, to prevent, or detect and correct, misstatements on a timely basis. A *material weakness* is a deficiency, or a combination of deficiencies, in internal control such that there is a reasonable possibility that a material misstatement of the entity's financial statements will not be prevented, or detected and corrected on a timely basis. A *significant deficiency* is a deficiency, or a combination of deficiencies, in internal control that is less severe than a material weakness, yet important enough to merit attention by those charged with governance.

Our consideration of internal control was for the limited purpose described in the first paragraph of this section and was not designed to identify all deficiencies in internal control that might be material weaknesses or significant deficiencies and therefore, material weaknesses or significant deficiencies may exist that were not identified. Given these limitations, during our audit we did not identify any deficiencies in internal control that we consider to be material weaknesses. We did identify certain deficiencies in internal control, described in the accompanying [*include the title of the schedule in which the findings are reported (e.g., schedule of findings and responses or schedule of findings and questioned costs)*] that we consider to be significant deficiencies. [*List the reference numbers of the related findings, for example, 20X1-001, 20X1-003, and 20X1-004*].[64]

[**Note:** *As discussed in paragraph 4.62, this guide recommends identifying each finding with a reference number. As discussed in paragraph 4.58, this report can, as an alternative, describe findings rather than refer to a separate schedule. Paragraph 4.58 also discusses how to report findings that relate to both internal control and to compliance; paragraph 4.59 discusses when findings*

---

[60] See footnote 31.
[61] See footnote 32.
[62] See footnote 33.
[63] See footnote 28.
[64] As discussed in chapters 13 and 23 of this guide, when performing the compliance audit, both Circular A-133 and the Uniform Guidance require all findings (including findings related to the audit of the financial statements for which *Government Auditing Standards* requires reporting) to have a reference number. This report illustrates the reference number format for audit findings required for data collection form submissions to the Federal Audit Clearinghouse.

of fraud and abuse may be reported in the section on internal control; paragraphs 4.61–.62 discuss the detail to use to present each finding; and paragraphs 4.63–.66 discuss the presentation of the views of responsible officials and their planned corrective actions. Further, in an audit in accordance with Office of Management and Budget Circular A-133, Audits of States, Local Governments, and Non-Profit Organizations (Circular A-133) *or Title 2 U.S. Code of Federal Regulations (CFR) Part 200,* Uniform Administrative Requirements, Cost Principles, and Audit Requirements for Federal Awards (Uniform Guidance), *findings related to the financial statements that are required to be reported in accordance with Government Auditing Standards should be reported in the schedule of findings and questioned costs. The schedule of findings and questioned costs shown in example 13-7 in the appendix in chapter 13, "Auditor Reporting Requirements and Other Communication Considerations in a Single Audit (Circular A-133)," and in example 23-7 in the appendix in chapter 23, "Auditor Reporting Requirements and Other Communication Considerations in a Single Audit (Uniform Guidance)," of this guide further describes the presentation of financial statement findings.]*

Compliance and Other Matters[65,66]

As part of obtaining reasonable assurance about whether Example Entity's financial statements are free from material misstatement, we performed tests of its compliance with certain provisions of laws, regulations, contracts, and grant agreements, noncompliance with which could have a direct and material effect on the determination of financial statement amounts. However, providing an opinion on compliance with those provisions was not an objective of our audit, and accordingly, we do not express such an opinion. The results of our tests disclosed instances of noncompliance or other matters that are required to be reported under *Government Auditing Standards*[67] and which are described in the accompanying [*include the title of the schedule in which the findings are reported (e.g., schedule of findings and responses or schedule of findings and questioned costs)*] as items [*list the reference numbers of the related findings, for example, 20X1-002 and 20X1-005*].

[***Note:*** *The referenced findings in this section include those that are instances of noncompliance and those that are fraud or abuse that are not material weaknesses or significant deficiencies reported in the internal control over financial reporting section of this report. (See paragraphs 4.39 and 4.59.) The "Note" in the internal control section of this example report further discusses the presentation of findings and auditee responses.*]

Example Entity's Response to Findings

Example Entity's response to the findings identified in our audit are described in the accompanying [*include the title of the schedule in which the findings are reported (e.g., schedule of findings and responses or schedule of findings and questioned costs)* "*or previously*" *if findings and responses are included in the body of the report*]. Example Entity's response was not subjected to the auditing

---

[65] See footnote 35.

[66] See footnote 36.

[67] See the discussion beginning at paragraph 4.24 for a discussion of the *Government Auditing Standards* criteria for reporting fraud, noncompliance with provisions of laws, regulations, contracts, and grant agreements, and abuse.

procedures applied in the audit of the financial statements and, accordingly, we express no opinion on it.[68]

Purpose of this Report

The purpose of this report is solely to describe the scope of our testing of internal control and compliance and the result of that testing, and not to provide an opinion on the effectiveness of the entity's internal control or on compliance. This report is an integral part of an audit performed in accordance with *Government Auditing Standards* in considering the entity's internal control and compliance. Accordingly, this communication is not suitable for any other purpose.[69]

[*Auditor's signature*]

[*Auditor's city and state*][70]

[*Date of the auditor's report*][71]

Example 4-6

Report on Internal Control Over Financial Reporting and on Compliance and Other Matters[72] Based on an Audit of Financial Statements Performed in Accordance With *Government Auditing Standards* (for a Governmental Entity[73] and With Reference to Audits by Other Auditors Using the Inclusion Option)[74]

(No Material Weaknesses Identified; Significant Deficiencies Identified; Reportable Instances of Noncompliance and Other Matters Identified)[75]

Independent Auditor's Report

[*Appropriate Addressee*]

We have audited, in accordance with the auditing standards generally accepted in the United States of America and the standards applicable to financial audits contained in *Government Auditing Standards* issued by the Comptroller General of the United States,[76] the financial statements of the governmental activities, the business-type activities, the aggregate discretely presented component units, each major fund, and the aggregate remaining fund information of Example Entity as of and for the year ended June 30, 20X1, and the related notes to the financial statements, which collectively comprise Example Entity's basic financial statements, and have issued our report thereon dated August

---

[68] Although the auditor does not audit management's responses to identified findings, the auditor does have certain responsibilities related to reporting the views of responsible officials under *Government Auditing Standards*. As noted in paragraph 4.33 of *Government Auditing Standards*, auditors should obtain and report the views of responsible officials concerning the findings, conclusions, and recommendations, as well as planned corrective actions. See paragraphs 4.63–.66.

[69] See footnote 37.

[70] See footnote 14.

[71] See footnote 39.

[72] See footnote 27.

[73] See footnote 28.

[74] See paragraphs 4.77–.83 for discussion of the inclusion option for acknowledging the involvement of other auditors (that is, component auditors) in the report on internal control over financial reporting and compliance and other matters.

[75] See footnote 29.

[76] See footnote 30.

15, 20X1.[77] Our report includes a reference to other auditors who audited the financial statements of [*identify organization, function, or activity*], as described in our report on Example Entity's financial statements. This report includes our consideration of the results of the other auditors' testing of internal control over financial reporting and compliance and other matters that are reported on separately by those other auditors. However, this report, insofar as it relates to the results of the other auditors, is based solely on the reports of the other auditors.[78]

Internal Control Over Financial Reporting[79,80]

In planning and performing our audit of the financial statements, we considered Example Entity's internal control over financial reporting (internal control) to determine the audit procedures that are appropriate in the circumstances for the purpose of expressing our opinions[81] on the financial statements, but not for the purpose of expressing an opinion on the effectiveness of Example Entity's internal control. Accordingly, we do not express an opinion on the effectiveness of Example Entity's internal control.

A *deficiency in internal control* exists when the design or operation of a control does not allow management or employees, in the normal course of performing their assigned functions, to prevent, or detect and correct, misstatements on a timely basis. A *material weakness* is a deficiency, or a combination of deficiencies, in internal control such that there is a reasonable possibility that a material misstatement of the entity's financial statements will not be prevented, or detected and corrected on a timely basis. A *significant deficiency* is a deficiency, or a combination of deficiencies, in internal control that is less severe than a material weakness, yet important enough to merit attention by those charged with governance.

Our consideration of internal control was for the limited purpose described in the first paragraph of this section and was not designed to identify all deficiencies in internal control that might be material weaknesses or significant deficiencies and therefore, material weaknesses or significant deficiencies may exist that were not identified. Given these limitations, during our audit we and the other auditors did not identify any deficiencies in internal control that we consider to be material weaknesses. We and the other auditors did identify certain deficiencies in internal control, described in the accompanying [*include the title of the schedule in which the findings are reported (e.g., schedule of findings and responses or schedule of findings and questioned costs)*] that we consider to be significant deficiencies. [*List the reference numbers of the related findings, for example, 20X1-001, 20X1-003, and 20X1-004*].[82]

[**Note:** *As discussed in paragraph 4.62, this guide recommends identifying each finding with a reference number. As discussed in paragraph 4.58, this report can, as an alternative, describe findings rather than refer to a separate schedule. Paragraph 4.58 also discusses how to report findings that relate to both internal control and to compliance; paragraph 4.59 discusses when findings of fraud and abuse may be reported in the section on internal control; paragraph*

---

[77] See footnote 31.
[78] See footnote 47.
[79] See footnote 32.
[80] See footnote 33.
[81] See footnote 28.
[82] See footnote 64.

Auditor Reporting and Other Communication Considerations

4.81 discusses considerations relating to including other auditors' results; paragraphs 4.61–.62 discuss the detail to use to present each finding; and paragraphs 4.63–.66 discuss the presentation of the views of responsible officials and their planned corrective actions. Further, in an audit in accordance with Circular A-133 or the Uniform Guidance, findings related to the financial statements which are required to be reported in accordance with *Government Auditing Standards* should be reported in the schedule of findings and questioned costs. The schedule of findings and questioned costs shown in example 13-7 in the appendix in chapter 13 and in example 23-7 in the appendix in chapter 23 of this guide further describes the presentation of financial statement findings.]

Compliance and Other Matters[83,84]

As part of obtaining reasonable assurance about whether Example Entity's financial statements are free from material misstatement, we performed tests of its compliance with certain provisions of laws, regulations, contracts, and grant agreements, noncompliance with which could have a direct and material effect on the determination of financial statement amounts. However, providing an opinion on compliance with those provisions was not an objective of our audit, and accordingly, we do not express such an opinion. The results of our tests and those of the other auditors disclosed instances of noncompliance or other matters that are required to be reported under *Government Auditing Standards*[85] and which are described in the accompanying [*include the title of the schedule in which the findings are reported (e.g., schedule of findings and responses* or *schedule of findings and questioned costs)*] as items [*list the reference numbers of the related findings, for example, 20X1-002 and 20X1-005*].

[***Note:*** *The referenced findings in this section include those that are instances of noncompliance and those that are fraud or abuse that are not material weaknesses or significant deficiencies reported in the internal control over financial reporting section of this report. (See paragraphs 4.39 and 4.59.) The "Note" in the internal control section of this example report further discusses the presentation of findings and auditee responses.*]

Example Entity's Response to Findings

Example Entity's response to the findings identified in our audit are described in the accompanying [*include the title of the schedule in which the findings are reported (e.g., schedule of findings and responses* or *schedule of findings and questioned costs) or "previously" if findings and responses are included in the body of the report*]. Example Entity's response was not subjected to the auditing procedures applied in the audit of the financial statements and, accordingly, we express no opinion on it.[86]

Purpose of this Report

The purpose of this report is solely to describe the scope of our testing of internal control and compliance and the result of that testing, and not to provide an opinion on the effectiveness of the entity's internal control or on compliance. This report is an integral part of an audit performed in accordance with *Government Auditing Standards* in considering the entity's internal control

---

[83] See footnote 35.
[84] See footnote 36.
[85] See footnote 67.
[86] See footnote 68.

and compliance. Accordingly, this communication is not suitable for any other purpose.[87]

[*Auditor's signature*]

[*Auditor's city and state*][88]

[*Date of the auditor's report*][89]

Example 4-7

Report on Internal Control Over Financial Reporting and on Compliance and Other Matters[90] Based on an Audit of Financial Statements Performed in Accordance With *Government Auditing Standards* (for a Governmental Entity)[91]

(Material Weaknesses Identified; No Significant Deficiencies Identified; Reportable Instances of Noncompliance and Other Matters Identified)[92]

Independent Auditor's Report

[*Appropriate Addressee*]

We have audited, in accordance with auditing standards generally accepted in the United States of America and the standards applicable to financial audits contained in *Government Auditing Standards* issued by the Comptroller General of the United States,[93] the financial statements of the governmental activities, the business-type activities, the aggregate discretely presented component units, each major fund, and the aggregate remaining fund information of Example Entity as of and for the year ended June 30, 20X1, and the related notes to the financial statements, which collectively comprise Example Entity's basic financial statements, and have issued our report thereon dated August 15, 20X1.[94]

Internal Control Over Financial Reporting[95,96]

In planning and performing our audit of the financial statements, we considered Example Entity's internal control over financial reporting (internal control) to determine the audit procedures that are appropriate in the circumstances for the purpose of expressing our opinions[97] on the financial statements, but not for the purpose of expressing an opinion on the effectiveness of Example Entity's internal control. Accordingly, we do not express an opinion on the effectiveness of Example Entity's internal control.

A *deficiency in internal control* exists when the design or operation of a control does not allow management or employees, in the normal course of performing

---

[87] See footnote 37.
[88] See footnote 14.
[89] See footnote 39.
[90] See footnote 27.
[91] See footnote 28.
[92] See footnote 29.
[93] See footnote 30.
[94] See footnote 31.
[95] See footnote 32.
[96] See footnote 33.
[97] See footnote 28.

Auditor Reporting and Other Communication Considerations

their assigned functions, to prevent, or detect and correct, misstatements on a timely basis. A *material weakness* is a deficiency, or a combination of deficiencies, in internal control such that there is a reasonable possibility that a material misstatement of the entity's financial statements will not be prevented, or detected and corrected on a timely basis. A *significant deficiency* is a deficiency, or a combination of deficiencies, in internal control that is less severe than a material weakness, yet important enough to merit attention by those charged with governance.

Our consideration of internal control was for the limited purpose described in the first paragraph of this section and was not designed to identify all deficiencies in internal control that might be material weaknesses or significant deficiencies and therefore, material weaknesses or significant deficiencies may exist that were not identified. We did identify certain deficiencies in internal control, described in the accompanying [*include the title of the schedule in which the findings are reported (e.g., schedule of findings and responses or schedule of findings and questioned costs)*] that we consider to be material weaknesses. [*List the reference numbers of the related findings, for example, 20X1-001, 20X1-003, and 20X1-004.*][98]

[***Note:*** *As discussed in paragraph 4.62, this guide recommends identifying each finding with a reference number. As discussed in paragraph 4.58, this report can, as an alternative, describe findings rather than refer to a separate schedule. Paragraph 4.58 also discusses how to report findings that relate to both internal control and to compliance; paragraph 4.59 discusses when findings of fraud and abuse may be reported in the section on internal control; paragraphs 4.61–.62 discuss the detail to use to present each finding; and paragraphs 4.63–.66 discuss the presentation of the views of responsible officials and their planned corrective actions. Further, in an audit in accordance with Circular A-133 or the Uniform Guidance, findings related to the financial statements which are required to be reported in accordance with* Government Auditing Standards *should be reported in the schedule of findings and questioned costs. The schedule of findings and questioned costs shown in example 13-7 in the appendix in chapter 13 and in example 23-7 in the appendix in chapter 23 of this guide further describes the presentation of financial statement findings.*]

Compliance and Other Matters [99,100]

As part of obtaining reasonable assurance about whether Example Entity's financial statements are free from material misstatement, we performed tests of its compliance with certain provisions of laws, regulations, contracts, and grant agreements, noncompliance with which could have a direct and material effect on the determination of financial statement amounts. However, providing an opinion on compliance with those provisions was not an objective of our audit, and accordingly, we do not express such an opinion. The results of our tests disclosed instances of noncompliance or other matters that are required to be reported under *Government Auditing Standards*[101] and which are described in the accompanying [*include the title of the schedule in which the findings are reported (e.g., schedule of findings and responses or schedule of findings and questioned costs)*] as items [*list the reference numbers of the related findings, for example, 20X1-002 and 20X1-005*].

---

[98] See footnote 64.
[99] See footnote 35.
[100] See footnote 36.
[101] See footnote 67.

[*Note:* *The referenced findings in this section include those that are instances of noncompliance and those that are fraud or abuse that are not material weaknesses or significant deficiencies reported in the internal control over financial reporting section of this report. (See paragraphs 4.39 and 4.59.) The "Note" in the internal control section of this example report further discusses the presentation of findings and auditee responses.*]

Example Entity's Response to Findings

Example Entity's response to the findings identified in our audit are described in the accompanying [*include the title of the schedule in which the findings are reported (e.g., schedule of findings and responses or schedule of findings and questioned costs) or "previously" if findings and responses are included in the body of the report*]. Example Entity's response was not subjected to the auditing procedures applied in the audit of the financial statements and, accordingly, we express no opinion on it.[102]

Purpose of this Report

The purpose of this report is solely to describe the scope of our testing of internal control and compliance and the result of that testing, and not to provide an opinion on the effectiveness of the entity's internal control or on compliance. This report is an integral part of an audit performed in accordance with *Government Auditing Standards* in considering the entity's internal control and compliance. Accordingly, this communication is not suitable for any other purpose.[103]

[*Auditor's signature*]

[*Auditor's city and state*][104]

[*Date of the auditor's report*][105]

Example 4-8

Report on Internal Control Over Financial Reporting and on Compliance and Other Matters[106] Based on an Audit of Financial Statements Performed in Accordance With *Government Auditing Standards* (for a Governmental Entity)[107]

(Material Weaknesses and Significant Deficiencies Identified; Reportable Instances of Noncompliance and Other Matters Identified)[108]

Independent Auditor's Report

[*Appropriate Addressee*]

We have audited, in accordance with auditing standards generally accepted in the United States of America and the standards applicable to financial audits contained in *Government Auditing Standards* issued by the Comptroller

---

[102] See footnote 68.
[103] See footnote 37.
[104] See footnote 14.
[105] See footnote 39.
[106] See footnote 27.
[107] See footnote 28.
[108] See footnote 29.

Auditor Reporting and Other Communication Considerations

General of the United States,[109] the financial statements of the governmental activities, the business-type activities, the aggregate discretely presented component units, each major fund, and the aggregate remaining fund information of Example Entity as of and for the year ended June 30, 20X1, and the related notes to the financial statements, which collectively comprise Example Entity's basic financial statements, and have issued our report thereon dated August 15, 20X1.[110]

Internal Control Over Financial Reporting[111,112]

In planning and performing our audit of the financial statements, we considered Example Entity's internal control over financial reporting (internal control) to determine the audit procedures that are appropriate in the circumstances for the purpose of expressing our opinions[113] on the financial statements, but not for the purpose of expressing an opinion on the effectiveness of Example Entity's internal control. Accordingly, we do not express an opinion on the effectiveness of Example Entity's internal control.

Our consideration of internal control was for the limited purpose described in the preceding paragraph and was not designed to identify all deficiencies in internal control that might be material weaknesses or significant deficiencies and therefore, material weaknesses or significant deficiencies may exist that were not identified. However, as described in the accompanying [*include the title of the schedule in which the findings are reported (e.g., schedule of findings and responses or schedule of findings and questioned costs*)], we identified certain deficiencies in internal control that we consider to be material weaknesses and significant deficiencies.

A *deficiency in internal control* exists when the design or operation of a control does not allow management or employees, in the normal course of performing their assigned functions, to prevent, or detect and correct, misstatements on a timely basis. A *material weakness* is a deficiency, or a combination of deficiencies, in internal control such that there is a reasonable possibility that a material misstatement of the entity's financial statements will not be prevented, or detected and corrected on a timely basis. We consider the deficiencies described in the accompanying [*include the title of the schedule in which the findings are reported (e.g., schedule of findings and responses or schedule of findings and questioned costs)*] to be material weaknesses. [*List the reference numbers of the related findings, for example, 20X1-001, 20X1-003, and 20X1-004*].[114]

A *significant deficiency* is a deficiency, or a combination of deficiencies, in internal control that is less severe than a material weakness, yet important enough to merit attention by those charged with governance. We consider the deficiencies described in the accompanying [*include the title of the schedule in which the findings are reported (e.g. schedule of findings and responses or schedule of findings and questioned costs)*] to be significant deficiencies. (*List the reference numbers of the related findings, for example, 20X1-002 and 20X1-005.*)]

[**Note:** *As discussed in* paragraph 4.62, *this guide recommends identifying each finding with a reference number. As discussed in* paragraph 4.58, *this report*

---

[109] See footnote 30.
[110] See footnote 31.
[111] See footnote 32.
[112] See footnote 33.
[113] See footnote 28.
[114] See footnote 64.

can, as an alternative, describe findings rather than refer to a separate schedule. Paragraph 4.58 *also discusses how to report findings that relate to both internal control and to compliance;* paragraph 4.59 *discusses when findings of fraud and abuse may be reported in the section on internal control;* paragraphs 4.61–.62 *discuss the detail to use to present each finding; and* paragraphs 4.63–.66 *discuss the presentation of the views of responsible officials and their planned corrective actions. Further, in an audit in accordance with Circular A-133 or the Uniform Guidance, findings related to the financial statements which are required to be reported in accordance with* Government Auditing Standards *should be reported in the schedule of findings and questioned costs. The schedule of findings and questioned costs shown in example 13-7 in the appendix in chapter 13 and in example 23-7 in the appendix in chapter 23 of this guide further describes the presentation of financial statement findings.]*

Compliance and Other Matters[115,116]

As part of obtaining reasonable assurance about whether Example Entity's financial statements are free from material misstatement, we performed tests of its compliance with certain provisions of laws, regulations, contracts, and grant agreements, noncompliance with which could have a direct and material effect on the determination of financial statement amounts. However, providing an opinion on compliance with those provisions was not an objective of our audit, and accordingly, we do not express such an opinion. The results of our tests disclosed instances of noncompliance or other matters that are required to be reported under *Government Auditing Standards*[117] and which are described in the accompanying [*include the title of the schedule in which the findings are reported (e.g., schedule of findings and responses or schedule of findings and questioned costs)*] as items [*list the reference numbers of the related findings, for example, 20X1-002 and 20X1-005*].

[**Note:** *The referenced findings in this section include those that are instances of noncompliance and those that are fraud or abuse that are not material weaknesses or significant deficiencies reported in the internal control over financial reporting section of this report. (See paragraphs 4.39 and 4.59.) The "Note" in the internal control section of this example report further discusses the presentation of findings and auditee responses.*]

Example Entity's Response to Findings

Example Entity's response to the findings identified in our audit are described in the accompanying [*include the title of the schedule in which the findings are reported (e.g., schedule of findings and responses or schedule of findings and questioned costs) or "previously" if findings and responses are included in the body of the report*]. Example Entity's response was not subjected to the auditing procedures applied in the audit of the financial statements and, accordingly, we express no opinion on it.[118]

Purpose of this Report

The purpose of this report is solely to describe the scope of our testing of internal control and compliance and the result of that testing, and not to provide

---

[115] See footnote 35.
[116] See footnote 36.
[117] See footnote 67.
[118] See footnote 68.

an opinion on the effectiveness of the entity's internal control or on compliance. This report is an integral part of an audit performed in accordance with *Government Auditing Standards* in considering the entity's internal control and compliance. Accordingly, this communication is not suitable for any other purpose.[119]

[*Auditor's signature*]

[*Auditor's city and state*][120]

[*Date of the auditor's report*][121]

Example 4-9

Report on Internal Control Over Financial Reporting and on Compliance and Other Matters[122] Based on an Audit of Financial Statements Performed in Accordance With *Government Auditing Standards (for a Governmental Entity)*[123]

(Opinion on the Financial Statements as a Whole Disclaimed;[124] Material Weaknesses and Significant Deficiencies Identified; Reportable Instances of Noncompliance and Other Matters Identified)[125]

<u>Independent Auditor's Report</u>

[*Appropriate Addressee*]

We were engaged to audit, in accordance with auditing standards generally accepted in the United States of America and the standards applicable to financial

---

[119] See footnote 37.
[120] See footnote 14.
[121] See footnote 39.
[122] See footnote 27.

[123] This illustration assumes that Example Entity is a governmental entity. If Example Entity is a not-for-profit entity, the wording in the first paragraph of this report should be modified using the following wording. Additionally, the use of the term "our opinions" would be changed to "our opinion" throughout the report. Finally, the term "basic" would be removed when describing the financial statements.

> We were engaged to audit, in accordance with auditing standards generally accepted in the United States of America and the standards applicable to financial audits contained in *Government Auditing Standards* issued by the Comptroller General of the United States, the financial statements of Example Entity, which comprise the consolidated statement of financial position as of June 30, 20X1, and the related consolidated statements of activities, and cash flows for the year then ended, and the related notes to the financial statements, and have issued our report thereon dated August 15, 20X1. Our report disclaims an opinion on such consolidated financial statements because of [*describe the scope limitation or matter causing the disclaimer*].

[124] This illustration assumes the disclaimer of opinion was expressed on the financial statements as a whole. As explained in the AICPA Audit and Accounting Guide *State and Local Governments*, the auditor should express a disclaimer of opinion on the financial statements as a whole when disclaimers of opinion are appropriate for both the governmental activities and business-type activities opinion units (or for only the governmental activities opinion unit if that is the only required presentation for the primary government in the reporting entity's government-wide financial statements). Other situations occur in which disclaimers of opinion on one or more opinion units are appropriate.

[125] Auditors may use portions of the illustrations included in this appendix to draft reports that apply to a specific auditee situation. Although a material weakness(es) may be the reason for a disclaimer, there may be other reasons a disclaimer is issued. Auditors, using professional judgment, may adapt the examples in this appendix to other situations not specifically addressed within the illustrations. For example, the compliance section of one example may be used along with the internal control section of another, as warranted by the particular situation.

audits contained in *Government Auditing Standards* issued by the Comptroller General of the United States,[126] the financial statements of the governmental activities, the business-type activities, the aggregate discretely presented component units, each major fund, and the aggregate remaining fund information of Example Entity as of and for the year ended June 30, 20X1, and the related notes to the financial statements, which collectively comprise Example Entity's basic financial statements and have issued our report thereon dated August 15, 20X1. Our report disclaims an opinion on such financial statements because of [*describe the scope limitation or other matter causing the disclaimer.*][127]

Internal Control Over Financial Reporting[128,129]

In connection with our engagement to audit the financial statements of Example Entity, we considered Example Entity's internal control over financial reporting (internal control) to determine the audit procedures that are appropriate in the circumstances for the purpose of expressing our opinions[130] on the financial statements, but not for the purpose of expressing an opinion on the effectiveness of Example Entity's internal control. Accordingly, we do not express an opinion on the effectiveness of Example Entity's internal control.

Our consideration of internal control was for the limited purpose described in the preceding paragraph and was not designed to identify all deficiencies in internal control that might be material weaknesses or significant deficiencies and therefore, material weaknesses or significant deficiencies may exist that were not identified. However, as described in the accompanying [*include the title of the schedule in which the findings are reported (e.g., schedule of findings and responses or schedule of findings and questioned costs)*], we identified certain deficiencies in internal control that we consider to be material weaknesses and significant deficiencies.

A *deficiency in internal control* exists when the design or operation of a control does not allow management or employees, in the normal course of performing their assigned functions, to prevent, or detect and correct, misstatements on a timely basis. A *material weakness* is a deficiency, or a combination of deficiencies, in internal control such that there is a reasonable possibility that a material misstatement of the entity's financial statements will not be prevented, or detected and corrected on a timely basis. We consider the deficiencies described in the accompanying [*include the title of the schedule in which the findings are reported (e.g., schedule of findings and responses or schedule of findings and questioned costs)*] to be material weaknesses. [*List the reference numbers of the related findings, for example, 20X1-001, 20X1-003, and 20X1-004*].[131]

A *significant deficiency* is a deficiency, or a combination of deficiencies, in internal control that is less severe than a material weakness, yet important enough to merit attention by those charged with governance. We consider the deficiencies described in the accompanying [*include the title of the schedule in which the findings are reported (e.g. schedule of findings and responses or schedule of findings and questioned costs) to be significant deficiencies. (List the reference numbers of the related findings, for example, 20X1-002 and 20X1-005.)*]

---

[126] See footnote 30.
[127] See footnote 31.
[128] See footnote 32.
[129] See footnote 33.
[130] See footnote 123.
[131] See footnote 64.

Auditor Reporting and Other Communication Considerations

[*Note:* As discussed in paragraph 4.62, this guide recommends identifying each finding with a reference number. As discussed in paragraph 4.58, this report can, as an alternative, describe findings rather than refer to a separate schedule. Paragraph 4.58 also discusses how to report findings that relate to both internal control and to compliance; paragraph 4.59 discusses when findings of fraud and abuse may be reported in the section on internal control; paragraphs 4.61–.62 discuss the detail to use to present each finding; and paragraphs 4.63–.66 discuss the presentation of the views of responsible officials and their planned corrective actions. Further, in an audit in accordance with Circular A-133 or the Uniform Guidance, findings related to the financial statements which are required to be reported in accordance with Government Auditing Standards should be reported in the schedule of findings and questioned costs. The schedule of findings and questioned costs shown in example 13-7 in the appendix in chapter 13 and in example 23-7 in the appendix in chapter 23 of this guide further describes the presentation of financial statement findings.]

Compliance and Other Matters[132,133]

In connection with our engagement to audit the financial statements of Example Entity, we performed tests of its compliance with certain provisions of laws, regulations, contracts, and grant agreements, noncompliance with which could have a direct and material effect on the determination of financial statement amounts. However, providing an opinion on compliance with those provisions was not an objective of our engagement, and accordingly, we do not express such an opinion. The results of our tests disclosed instances of noncompliance or other matters that are required to be reported under *Government Auditing Standards*[134] and which are described in the accompanying [*include the title of the schedule in which the findings are reported (e.g., schedule of findings and responses or schedule of findings and questioned costs)*] as items [*list the reference numbers of the related findings, for example, 20X1-006 and 20X1-007*]. Additionally, if the scope of our work had been sufficient to enable us to express opinions on the basic financial statements, other instances of noncompliance or other matters may have been identified and reported herein.[135]

[*Note:* The referenced findings in this section include those that are instances of noncompliance and those that are fraud or abuse that are not material weaknesses or significant deficiencies reported in the internal control over financial reporting section of this report. (See paragraphs 4.39 and 4.59.) The "Note" in the internal control section of this example report further discusses the presentation of findings and auditee responses.]

Example Entity's Response to Findings

Example Entity's response to the findings identified in our engagement is described in the accompanying [*include the title of the schedule in which the findings are reported (e.g., schedule of findings and responses or schedule of*

---

[132] See footnote 35.

[133] See footnote 36.

[134] See footnote 67.

[135] If no instances of noncompliance or other matters were identified, the last two sentences would be replaced with the following:

> The results of our tests disclosed no instances of noncompliance or other matters that are required to be reported under *Government Auditing Standards*. However, if the scope of our work had been sufficient to enable us to express opinions on the basic financial statements, instances of noncompliance or other matters may have been identified and reported herein.

findings and questioned costs) "or previously" if findings and responses are included in the body of the report]. Example Entity's response was not subjected to the auditing procedures applied in the engagement to audit the financial statements and, accordingly, we express no opinion on it.[136]

Purpose of this Report

The purpose of this report is solely to describe the scope of our testing of internal control and compliance and the results of that testing, and not to provide an opinion on the effectiveness of the entity's internal control or on compliance. This report is an integral part of an engagement to perform an audit in accordance with *Government Auditing Standards* in considering the entity's internal control and compliance. Accordingly, this communication is not suitable for any other purpose.[137]

[*Auditor's signature*]

[*Auditor's city and state*][138]

[*Date of the auditor's report*][139]

---

[136] See footnote 68.

[137] See footnote 37.

[138] See footnote 14.

[139] Because this report relates to an engagement to audit the financial statements, and is based on the GAAS audit procedures performed, it is subject to the provisions of AU-C section 700. Therefore, it should be dated the same date as the auditor's report on the financial statements.

Part II

Circular A-133 Audits

Chapter 5

Overview of the Single Audit Act, Circular A-133, and the Compliance Supplement

> **Update 5-1: Audits of Federal Awards**
>
> This chapter, and the remaining chapters of part II, *Circular A-133 Audits*, of this guide should be used for performing a compliance audit of federal awards under Office of Management and Budget (OMB) Circular A-133, *Audits of States, Local Governments, and Non-Profit Organizations* (Circular A-133). Part III, *Uniform Guidance Audits*, of this guide should be used when performing a compliance audit under Title 2 U.S. *Code of Federal Regulations* Part 200, *Uniform Administrative Requirements, Cost Principles, and Audit Requirements for Federal Awards* (Uniform Guidance). See the transitional guidance sections at the end of each chapter that highlight important matters for consideration.[1] Refer to the preface for additional information.
>
> **Important Uniform Guidance Effective Date Information**
>
> In December 2013, the OMB issued the Uniform Guidance, which is effective for nonfederal entities for all federal awards and certain funding increments provided on or after December 26, 2014. The requirements in Subpart F, "Audit Requirements," are effective for audits of fiscal years beginning on or after December 26, 2014, with no early implementation permitted. Therefore, auditees subject to a single audit with December 25, 2015, and later year ends (for example, December 31, 2015) will be required to undergo the audit under Subpart F of the Uniform Guidance. Note that audits of fiscal years ending prior to the effective date of the Uniform Guidance audit requirements are subject to an audit under Circular A-133.

Introduction[2]

5.01 This chapter provides an overview of the significant requirements and guidance in the Single Audit Act; OMB Circular A-133;[3] and the *OMB Compliance Supplement (Compliance Supplement)*. As discussed in paragraph 5.08, the Single Audit Act and Circular A-133 require nonfederal entities that expend $500,000 or more of federal awards in a fiscal year to have a single

---

[1] See the information found at the end of certain chapters in part II, *Circular A-133 Audits*, of this guide for transition considerations when performing an audit under Office of Management and Budget (OMB) Circular A-133, *Audits of States, Local Governments, and Non-Profit Organizations* (Circular A-133), as it relates to the applicability of certain aspects of Title 2 U.S. *Code of Federal Regulations* Part 200, *Uniform Administrative Requirements, Cost Principles, and Audit Requirements for Federal Awards* (Uniform Guidance), to audits performed under Circular A-133. Transition considerations related to an audit performed under the Uniform Guidance can be found at the end of chapters in part III, *Uniform Guidance Audits*, of this guide in sections titled "Transition Considerations Related to the Uniform Guidance."

[2] In chapters 5–14, the use of the terms *single audit* or *audit in accordance with Circular A-133* includes both the financial statement audit and the compliance audit that is performed under Circular A-133. The use of the term *Circular A-133 compliance audit* includes only the compliance audit that is performed under Circular A-133.

[3] Because Circular A-133 incorporates the requirements of the Single Audit Act, the requirements of Circular A-133 and the act often are discussed together as one in this guide. Accordingly, references to Circular A-133 also include the requirements of the Single Audit Act.

or program-specific audit. Refer to the Single Audit Act, Circular A-133, and the *Compliance Supplement* for a complete understanding of the requirements. Supplement B, "OMB Circular A-133, Audits of States, Local Governments, and Non-Profit Organizations," and supplement A, "Single Audit Act Amendments of 1996," of this guide reprint the Single Audit Act and Circular A-133. Footnote 22 in paragraph 5.48 provides instructions for obtaining the *Compliance Supplement*.

5.02 The Single Audit Act was enacted to streamline and improve the effectiveness of audits of federal awards and to reduce the audit burden on states, local governments, and not-for-profit entities (NFPs). The Single Audit Act and Circular A-133 require auditors to perform single and program-specific audits of federal awards in accordance with *Government Auditing Standards*, which incorporates by reference the AICPA Statements on Auditing Standards (SASs).[4] The Single Audit Act requires the audits to be conducted by an independent auditor.[5] The Single Audit Act gives the Director of OMB the authority to develop government-wide guidelines and policy on performing audits to comply with the act. The OMB issued Circular A-133 to establish audit guidelines and policy for a uniform system of auditing states, local governments, and NFPs that expend federal awards.[6] Individual federal departments and agencies have adopted Circular A-133 in regulation.

Single Audit Act and Circular A-133 Requirements

Objectives of a Single Audit

5.03 In a single audit, the auditor has the following objectives, each of which results in the issuance of certain auditor reports (as discussed in chapter 13, "Auditor Reporting Requirements and Other Communication Considerations in a Single Audit (Circular A-133)," and chapter 14, "Program-Specific Audits (Circular A-133)," of this guide):

- Audit of the entity's financial statements and reporting on the schedule of expenditures of federal awards
  — determine whether the financial statements of the auditee are presented fairly in all material respects in accordance with the applicable financial reporting framework (for example, generally accepted accounting principles

---

[4] *Government Auditing Standards* incorporates by reference AICPA Statements on Auditing Standards (SASs). Therefore, auditors performing financial statement audits and Circular A-133 compliance audits in accordance with *Government Auditing Standards* should comply with generally accepted auditing standards (GAAS), the requirements found in chapters 1–3 of *Government Auditing Standards*, and the additional standards and related requirements for financial audits found in chapter 4, "Standards for Financial Audits," of *Government Auditing Standards*.

[5] The Single Audit Act defines *independent auditor* as (a) an external state or local government auditor who meets the independence standards included in *Government Auditing Standards* or (b) a public accountant who meets such independence standards. Chapter 2, "*Government Auditing Standards*—Ethical Principles and General Standards," of this guide discusses the independence requirements of *Government Auditing Standards*.

[6] Circular A-133 was first revised and issued on June 30, 1997. That revision superseded OMB Circular A-128, *Audits of State and Local Governments,* and all previous versions of Circular A-133. The June 30, 1997, revision was subsequently revised by changes published in the *Federal Register* on June 27, 2003 and again by changes published in the *Federal Register* on June 26, 2007. Circular A-133, as revised on June 26, 2007, is available at www.whitehouse.gov/omb/grants circulars/. See also update 5-1 of this guide.

Overview of the Single Audit Act and the *Compliance Supplement*

[GAAP] or special purpose framework). (Note that Circular A-133 does not prescribe the basis of accounting for financial statement preparation.) (See the further discussion in chapter 6, "Planning Considerations of Circular A-133," of this guide.)

— determine whether the schedule of expenditures of federal awards is presented fairly in all material respects in relation to the auditee's financial statements as a whole. (See also chapter 7, "Schedule of Expenditures of Federal Awards (Circular A-133).")

- Compliance audit of federal awards[7]

— obtain an understanding of the internal control over compliance for each major program, assess the control risk of noncompliance,[8] and perform tests of those controls unless the controls are deemed to be ineffective. (The auditor should perform procedures to obtain an understanding of internal control over federal programs that is sufficient to plan the audit to support a low assessed level of control risk of noncompliance for each major program.) (See also chapter 9, "Consideration of Internal Control Over Compliance for Major Programs (Circular A-133).")

— determine whether the auditee has complied with laws, regulations, and the provisions of contracts or grant agreements pertaining to federal awards that may have a direct and material effect on each of its major programs (hereinafter referred to as *compliance requirements*). (See also chapter 10, "Compliance Auditing Applicable to Major Programs (Circular A-133).")

Audit of an Entity's Financial Statements and Reporting on the Schedule of Expenditures of Federal Awards

5.04 The financial statement audit required by Circular A-133 is performed in accordance with generally accepted auditing standards (GAAS) and the standards applicable to financial audits contained in *Government Auditing Standards*.[9] That audit results in the auditor reporting on the entity's financial

---

[7] AU-C section 935, *Compliance Audits* (AICPA, *Professional Standards*), defines *applicable compliance requirements* as the compliance requirements that are subject to the compliance audit. Paragraph .500(d) of Circular A-133 states that the auditor should determine whether the auditee has complied with laws, regulations, and the provisions of contracts or grant agreements that may have a direct and material effect on each of its major programs. Therefore, in a Circular A-133 compliance audit, the direct and material compliance requirements are those that are subject to audit. Accordingly, for the purpose of adapting AU-C section 935 to a Circular A-133 compliance audit, the term *applicable compliance requirements* has been replaced by *direct and material compliance requirements* in this guide except when directly citing content from AU-C section 935.

[8] Although Circular A-133 uses the term *control risk*, this guide uses the term *control risk of noncompliance* in order to be consistent with the term as used and defined in AU-C section 935.

[9] In performing audits in accordance with the standards applicable to financial audits contained in *Government Auditing Standards,* the auditor assumes certain responsibilities beyond those of audits performed in accordance with GAAS. Chapters 2, 3, "Planning and Performing a Financial Statement Audit in Accordance With *Government Auditing Standards*," and 4, "Auditor Reporting Requirements and Other Communication Considerations of *Government Auditing Standards*," of this guide discuss those responsibilities.

statements and on the scope of the auditor's testing of compliance and internal control over financial reporting and the results of those tests. The auditor also should report certain fraud and abuse. The primary sources of guidance and standards regarding financial statement audits are the AICPA SASs;[10] *Government Auditing Standards*; and the AICPA Audit and Accounting Guides, including *Not-for-Profit Entities, State and Local Governments*, and *Health Care Entities*. Chapter 6 of this guide discusses financial statement audit considerations under Circular A-133.

5.05 In an audit in accordance with Circular A-133, the auditee is responsible for the preparation of the schedule of expenditures of federal awards. The auditor is then required to determine and report on whether the schedule of expenditures of federal awards is presented fairly in all material respects in relation to the financial statements as a whole. AU-C section 725, *Supplementary Information in Relation to the Financial Statements as a Whole* (AICPA, *Professional Standards*), provides guidance on such reporting. Chapter 7 of this guide discusses the schedule of expenditures of federal awards and chapter 13 of this guide discusses the auditor's reporting on the schedule.

Circular A-133 Compliance Audit of Federal Awards

5.06 Under the Single Audit Act and Circular A-133, the auditor has additional testing and reporting responsibilities for compliance, as well as internal control over compliance, beyond a financial statement audit performed in accordance with GAAS and *Government Auditing Standards*. AU-C section 935, *Compliance Audits* (AICPA, *Professional Standards*), applies when an auditor is engaged, or required by law or regulation, to perform a compliance audit in accordance with all of the following: (*a*) GAAS, (*b*) the standards for financial audits under *Government Auditing Standards*, and (*c*) a governmental audit requirement[11] that requires an auditor to express an opinion on compliance. It is the primary source of guidance and standards regarding compliance audits. The guidance clarifies that AU-C section 935 does not apply to the financial statement audit component of a compliance audit. The Circular A-133 compliance audit of federal awards expended during the fiscal year provides a basis for issuing an additional report on compliance and on internal control over compliance related to major programs. Table 5-1 in paragraph 5.07 presents the additional compliance testing and internal control requirements relating to the Circular A-133 compliance audit of federal awards expended. Circular A-133 defines *major programs*; chapter 8, "Determination of Major Programs (Circular A-133)," of this guide discusses that definition. Chapters 9–11 of this guide discuss auditing considerations applicable to compliance and internal control over compliance related to major programs.

5.07 The additional compliance testing and internal control responsibilities related to a Circular A-133 compliance audit are presented in the following table.

---

[10] SASs are codified in AICPA *Professional Standards*. See the section in the preface "References to Professional Standards" for further explanation.

[11] AU-C section 935 defines a *governmental audit requirement* as a government requirement established by law, regulation, rule, or provision of contracts or grant agreements requiring that an entity undergo an audit of its compliance with applicable compliance requirements related to one or more government programs that the entity administers. An example of a governmental audit requirement is Circular A-133.

Table 5-1
Additional Compliance Testing and Internal Control Responsibilities

	Obtaining Sufficient Appropriate Audit Evidence	Reporting Responsibilities
Compliance Testing Responsibilities	The auditor should determine whether the entity complied with laws, regulations, and the provisions of contracts or grant agreements pertaining to federal awards that may have a direct and material effect on each major program.	The auditor should express an opinion on whether the entity complied with laws, regulations, and with the provisions of contracts or grant agreements that could have a direct and material effect on each major program and, where applicable, refer to a separate schedule of findings and questioned costs.
Internal Control Responsibilities	With regard to internal control over compliance, the auditor should (1) perform procedures to obtain an understanding of internal control over federal programs that is sufficient to plan the audit to support a low assessed level of control risk of noncompliance for major programs, (2) plan the testing of internal control over major programs to support a low assessed level of control risk of noncompliance for the assertions relevant to the compliance requirements for each major program,[1] and (3) perform tests of internal control (unless the internal control is likely to be ineffective in preventing or detecting noncompliance). The auditor may use evidence gained from the tests of controls relevant to compliance requirements to determine the nature, timing, and extent of the testing required to express an opinion on compliance with requirements that have a direct and material effect on major federal programs.	The auditor should provide a written report on internal control over major programs describing the scope of testing internal control and the results of the tests, and, where applicable, refer to a separate schedule of findings and questioned costs.

[1] Office of Management and Budget Circular A-133, *Audits of States, Local Governments, and Non-Profit Organizations* (Circular A-133), requires the auditor to plan the audit to support a low assessed level of control risk of noncompliance for major programs; however, it does not actually require the auditor to achieve a low assessed level of control risk of noncompliance. Chapter 9, "Consideration of Internal Control Over Compliance for Major Programs (Circular A-133)," of this guide further discusses that Circular A-133 provision.

General Audit Requirements

Audit Threshold

5.08 Circular A-133 states that nonfederal entities that expend $500,000 or more of federal awards (as discussed in paragraphs 5.09–.15) in a fiscal year should have a single or program-specific audit. Entities expending awards under only 1 program (excluding research and development [R&D]) may elect to have a program-specific audit if the program's laws, regulations, or grant agreements do not require a financial statement audit. A program-specific audit may not be elected for R&D unless (*a*) all expenditures are for awards received from the same federal agency or from the same federal agency and the same pass-through entity and (*b*) advance approval is obtained from the federal agency. (Chapter 14 provides additional guidance on program-specific audits.) Entities that expend less than $500,000 in a fiscal year in federal awards are exempt from audit requirements in the Single Audit Act and Circular A-133. However, those entities are not exempt from other federal requirements (including those to maintain records) concerning federal awards provided to the entity. Further, Section 200(d) of Circular A-133 states that records must be available for review or audit by appropriate officials of a federal agency, pass-through entity, and the U.S. Government Accountability Office (GAO). The Single Audit Act provides that, every 2 years, the OMB may review the amount for requiring audits and may adjust the dollar threshold amount to no less than $300,000.

Types of Federal Awards and Payment Methods

Definition of Federal Awards

5.09 Circular A-133 defines federal awards as *federal financial assistance* and *federal cost-reimbursement contracts* that auditees receive directly from federal awarding agencies or indirectly from pass-through entities. It does not include procurement contracts (under grants or contracts) used to buy goods or services from vendors. Paragraph 5.28 discusses subrecipient and vendor determinations.

Federal Financial Assistance—Classification and Types

5.10 Federal financial assistance is classified into program categories in the *Catalog of Federal Domestic Assistance* (CFDA), published by the Government Printing Office. (An electronic searchable version of the CFDA is available at www.cfda.gov.) Circular A-133 defines a federal program as all federal awards under the same CFDA number. Federal awards under the same CFDA number and federal programs that have been designated as a cluster should be treated as one program when determining major programs. R&D, student financial assistance (SFA), and certain other programs are defined as a cluster in the *Compliance Supplement* because they are closely related and share common compliance requirements. (Paragraphs 5.47–.48 discuss the *Compliance Supplement*. See paragraph 5.31 for a discussion of clusters of programs.)

5.11 Sometimes state governments combine funding from different federal awards in providing assistance to their subrecipients when the awards are closely related programs and share common compliance requirements. In this case, Circular A-133 states that the state may require the subrecipient to treat the combined federal awards as a cluster of programs, as discussed in paragraph 5.31.

5.12 There are more than 1,000 individual grant programs. Many of these programs are described in the CFDA; however, certain programs may not be included. For example, contracts may not be listed in the CFDA. Circular A-133 states that when a CFDA number is not assigned, all federal awards from the same agency that are made for the same purpose should be combined and considered 1 program. This results in those programs being treated as one program for major program determination purposes.

5.13 Programs in the CFDA are classified into 15 types of assistance. Benefits and services are provided through 7 financial and 8 nonfinancial types of assistance.[12] The following list describes the 8 principal types of assistance that are available:

- *Formula grants.* For activities of a continuing nature not confined to a specific project, allocations of money to nonfederal entities are made in accordance with a distribution formula prescribed by law or administrative regulation. One example is the Department of Agriculture's award to land-grant universities for cooperative extension services. Another example is the Department of Justice's award to state and local governments for drug control and systems improvement.

- *Project grants.* These involve the funding, for fixed or known periods, of specific projects. Project grants can include fellowships, scholarships, research grants, training grants, traineeships, experimental and demonstration grants, evaluation grants, planning grants, technical assistance grants, survey grants, and construction grants.

- *Direct payments for specific use.* Financial assistance is provided by the federal government directly to individuals, private firms, and other private institutions to encourage or subsidize a particular activity by conditioning the receipt of the assistance on a particular performance by the recipient. This does not include solicited contracts for the procurement of goods and services for the federal government.

- *Direct payments with unrestricted use.* Financial assistance is provided by the federal government directly to beneficiaries who satisfy federal eligibility requirements with no restrictions imposed on how the money is spent. Included are payments under retirement, pension, and compensation programs.

- *Direct loans.* Financial assistance is provided through the lending of federal monies for a specific period of time, with a reasonable expectation of repayment. Such loans may or may not require the payment of interest.

- *Guaranteed/insured loans.* Programs that the federal government makes an arrangement to indemnify a lender against part or all of any defaults by those responsible for the repayment of loans.

---

[12] The Catalog of Federal Domestic Assistance website at www.cfda.gov provides information on all types of assistance.

- *Insurance.* Financial assistance is provided to assure reimbursement for losses sustained under specified conditions. Coverage may be provided directly by the federal government or through a private carrier, and may or may not involve the payment of premiums.

- *Sale, exchange, or donation of property and goods.* These programs provide for the sale, exchange, or donation of federal real property, personal property, commodities, and other goods, including land, buildings, equipment, food, and drugs. This does not include the loan of, use of, or access to federal facilities or property.

Federal Cost-Reimbursement Contracts

5.14 The definition of federal awards also includes federal cost-reimbursement contracts. These are contracts with nonfederal entities to provide goods or services to the federal government. These contracts generally are governed by the Federal Acquisition Regulations (found in Title 48 U.S. *Code of Federal Regulations* Chapter 1) and the terms of the contracts.

Payment Methods

5.15 There are several distinct types of federal award payment methods. Awards may be provided to entities through reimbursement arrangements in which recipients bill grantors for costs as incurred. Some programs provide for advance payments or installment payments. Other programs permit entities to draw cash as grant expenditures are incurred.

Defining the Entity to Be Audited

5.16 As discussed in chapter 6 of this guide, the single audit should cover the entire operations of the auditee or, at the option of the auditee, the audit may include a series of audits that cover departments, agencies, and other organizational units that expended or otherwise administered federal awards during the fiscal year, provided that each audit encompasses the financial statements and the schedule of expenditures of federal awards for each such department, agency, and organizational unit.

Relationship to Other Audit Requirements

5.17 An audit in accordance with Circular A-133 is deemed to be in lieu of any financial audit of federal awards that an entity is required to undergo under any other federal law or regulation. However, notwithstanding an audit in accordance with Circular A-133, federal agencies (including their Inspectors General or GAO) may conduct or arrange for additional audits (for example, financial audits, performance audits, evaluations, inspections, or reviews) that are necessary to carry out their responsibilities under federal law or regulation. Any additional audits should be planned and performed in such a way that builds upon work performed by auditors. Circular A-133 requires a federal agency that conducts or contracts for additional audits to arrange for funding the full cost of such additional audits. Paragraph 5.32 discusses the federal agency option to request certain programs to be audited as major programs.

5.18 Circular A-133 states that the audit should be performed in accordance with *Government Auditing Standards*. Consequently, *Government*

Overview of the Single Audit Act and the *Compliance Supplement* **129**

Auditing Standards applies not only to the audit of the financial statements but also to the Circular A-133 compliance audit. Therefore, the requirements and guidance found in chapters 1–4 of *Government Auditing Standards* are applicable to a Circular A-133 compliance audit. Those standards are discussed in chapters 1–4 of this guide. Areas that may require particular attention in the Circular A-133 compliance audit are auditor communication; procedures and reporting on abuse; the reporting of findings and related management views and planned corrective actions; and the reporting of certain matters in writing to officials of the auditee. For example,

- auditors should communicate pertinent information that in the auditor's professional judgment needs to be communicated to individuals contracting for or requesting the audit, and to cognizant legislative committees when auditors perform the audit pursuant to a law or regulation, or they conduct the work for the legislative committee that has oversight of the auditee. (This requirement does not apply if the law or regulation requiring an audit of the financial statements does not specifically identify the entities to be audited, such as audits required by the Single Audit Act Amendments of 1996.)

- auditors have no responsibility to design the audit to detect abuse.[13] However, if auditors become aware of abuse that could be quantitatively or qualitatively material to the financial statements or other financial data significant to the audit objectives (for example, one or more major programs), auditors should apply audit procedures specifically directed to ascertain the potential effect on the financial statements or other financial data significant to audit objectives. Chapter 3, "Planning and Performing a Financial Statement Audit in Accordance With *Government Auditing Standards*," of this guide discusses procedures relating to the evaluation of indications of abuse and chapters 9–10 of this guide discusses the nature of abuse as it relates to federal awards. Chapter 13 of this guide discusses the reporting of abuse involving federal awards.

- auditors should obtain and report the views of responsible officials concerning findings, conclusions, and recommendations, as well as their planned corrective actions. As discussed in chapter 13 of this guide, the auditor may be able to refer to the auditee's corrective action plan required by Circular A-133 to satisfy that requirement for federal award-related findings. In addition, all audit findings, including federal award-related findings, are subject to the presentation requirements of *Government Auditing Standards*, as discussed in chapters 4, "Auditor Reporting Requirements and Other Communication Considerations of *Government Auditing Standards*," and 13 of this guide.

- *Government Auditing Standards* states that the auditor should communicate to officials of the auditee in writing instances of

---

[13] *Government Auditing Standards* describes *abuse* by stating that it does not necessarily involve fraud or noncompliance with provisions of laws, regulations, contracts, or grant agreements. Abuse, it states, "involves behavior that is deficient or improper when compared with behavior that a prudent person would consider reasonable and necessary business practice given the facts and circumstances."

©2015, AICPA   AAG-GAS 5.18

noncompliance with provisions of contracts or grant agreements or abuse that have an effect on the financial statements or other financial data significant to the audit objectives that are less than material but warrant the attention of those charged with governance. As discussed in chapter 13 of this guide, in an audit in accordance with Circular A-133, the auditor should evaluate such matters involving federal awards for the purpose of that communication based only on their consequence to the financial statements.

Frequency of Audits

5.19 Circular A-133 states that audits should be performed annually unless an auditee meets one of the following criteria that would allow it to have biennial audits (biennial audits should cover both years within the biennial period):

- State or local governments that are required by constitution or statute (in effect on January 1, 1987) to undergo audits less frequently than annually are permitted to have an audit in accordance with Circular A-133 performed biennially. This requirement should still be in effect for the biennial period under audit.

- NFPs that had biennial audits for all biennial periods ending between July 1, 1992, and January 1, 1995, are permitted to have an audit in accordance with Circular A-133 performed biennially.

Non-U.S.-Based Entities

5.20 Circular A-133 does not apply to non-U.S.-based entities expending federal awards received either directly as a recipient or indirectly as a subrecipient. For example, if a federal agency provides financial assistance to an orphanage operated by a foreign government, Circular A-133 would not apply. However, Circular A-133 does apply to expenditures made by U.S.-based entities outside of the United States and by foreign branches of U.S.-based entities. For example, if a university based in the United States receives a federal award for travel and a three-month residence in a foreign country to conduct research, Circular A-133 would apply to the travel and the related research costs incurred in the foreign country. Another example would be a hospital that receives a federal award to perform medical research in a foreign country. If the research is conducted in the hospital's research laboratory based in the foreign country, the federal award would be subject to an audit in accordance with Circular A-133.

Reporting Matters

Audit Reports

5.21 Section 505 of Circular A-133 includes specific auditor reporting requirements. It states that the auditor's reports should include (*a*) an opinion (or disclaimer of opinion) concerning whether the financial statements are presented fairly in all material respects in accordance with GAAP and an opinion (or disclaimer of opinion) concerning whether the schedule of expenditures of federal awards is presented fairly in all material respects in relation to the financial statements as a whole; (*b*) a report on internal control related to the financial statements and major programs; (*c*) a report on compliance with laws, regulations, and the provisions of contracts or grant agreements, which includes an opinion (or disclaimer of opinion) concerning whether the auditee complied with laws, regulations, and the provisions of contracts or grant agreements which could have a direct and material effect on each major program; and (*d*) a schedule of findings and questioned costs.[14] Chapters 13–14 of this guide discuss auditor reporting requirements for single and program-specific audits and include appendixes that illustrate schedules of findings and questioned costs and auditor's reports.

Timing of the Submission of the Report

5.22 Upon the completion of the single audit, the reporting package (described in paragraph 5.38), including the auditor's reports, and the data collection form (described in paragraph 5.39) should be electronically submitted by the auditee to the Federal Audit Clearinghouse (FAC). That submission should be completed within the earlier of 30 days after receipt of the auditor's reports or nine months after the end of the audit period.[15] Paragraphs 5.42–.45 discuss the definitions and responsibilities of cognizant and oversight agencies for audit. Chapter 13 of this guide further describes the report submission requirements of Circular A-133.

Audit Follow-Up

5.23 Circular A-133 states that the auditor should follow up on prior audit findings, perform procedures to assess the reasonableness of the summary schedule of prior audit findings prepared by the auditee, and report a current-year audit finding when the auditor concludes that the summary schedule of prior audit findings materially misrepresents the status of any prior audit finding. Chapter 6 of this guide further discusses the auditor's responsibility for audit follow-up.

Auditor Selection and Audit Costs

Procurement of Audit Services and Restriction on Auditors Who Prepare Indirect Cost Proposals

5.24 Circular A-133 establishes guidance on the procurement of audit services, as well as guidance on the restrictions on the selection of auditors who also prepare the indirect cost proposal or cost allocation plan. As further discussed in chapter 6 of this guide, auditors who prepare the indirect cost proposal or cost allocation plan may not also perform an audit in accordance with Circular A-133 if the indirect costs recovered by the auditee during the prior year exceeded $1 million.

---

[14] Chapter 4 of this guide further discusses the auditor's reports under GAAS and *Government Auditing Standards* (that is, an opinion [or disclaimer of opinion] concerning whether the financial statements are presented fairly in all material respects in accordance with the applicable financial reporting framework [for example, generally accepted accounting principles] and a report on internal control over financial reporting and compliance with laws, regulations, and provisions of contracts or grant agreements) and includes an appendix that illustrates those reports.

[15] If the auditee or auditor wishes to inform the federal government that the required submission will be late, the suggested way to do so is to contact the federal oversight or cognizant agency for the audit (contact information is available on the "Resources" tab at http://harvester.census.gov/fac/APPX3.htm).

Audit Costs

5.25 Circular A-133 provides guidance on whether the charging of audit costs to federal awards may be allowed. Unless prohibited by law, the costs of an audit in accordance with Circular A-133 are allowable charges to federal awards. The charges may be considered a direct cost or an allocated indirect cost, as determined in accordance with the provisions of applicable OMB Cost Principles Circulars, the Federal Acquisition Regulation, or other applicable cost principles or regulations. The costs of audits that are not conducted in accordance with Circular A-133 are unallowable. Furthermore, audit costs associated with an audit in accordance with Circular A-133 of entities that expend less than $500,000 per year in federal awards are unallowable. However, this provision does not prohibit pass-through entities from charging federal awards for the costs of agreed-upon procedures engagements[16] to monitor its subrecipients. Chapter 12, "Audit Considerations of Federal Pass-Through Awards (Circular A-133)," of this guide further discusses the allowability of audit costs associated with agreed-upon procedures engagements. With regard to the amount of audit cost that can be charged to a federal award, the Single Audit Act states that in the absence of documentation demonstrating a higher actual cost, the percentage of the cost of single audits charged to federal awards by an entity may not exceed the ratio of total federal awards expended to the entity's total expenditures for the fiscal year.

Basis for Determining When Federal Awards Are Expended

5.26 The determination of when an award is expended is based on when the activity related to the award occurs. In general, the activity pertains to events that require the auditee to comply with laws, regulations, and the provisions of contracts or grant agreements. Such events include the following:

- Expenditure or expense transactions associated with grants, cost reimbursement contracts, cooperative agreements, and direct appropriations
- The disbursement of funds passed through to subrecipients
- The use of loan proceeds under loan and loan-guarantee programs
- The receipt of property, including surplus property
- The receipt or use of program income
- The distribution or consumption of food commodities
- The disbursement of amounts entitling the auditee to an interest subsidy
- The period when insurance is in force

5.27 As further discussed in chapter 7 of this guide, Circular A-133 provides specific guidance on the basis for determining federal awards expended or the valuation for the following noncash items:

- Loans and loan guarantees, including those at institutions of higher education
- Prior loans and loan guarantees
- Endowment funds

---

[16] Circular A-133 uses the phrase "cost of limited-scope audits" but goes on to indicate that limited-scope audits only include agreed-upon procedure engagements.

Overview of the Single Audit Act and the *Compliance Supplement* **133**

- Free rent
- Noncash assistance, such as free rent, food stamps, food commodities, and donated property, including donated surplus property

Circular A-133 does not consider Medicare payments made to a nonfederal entity for patient care services to individuals to be federal awards. It also does not consider a state's Medicaid payments to a nonfederal entity for such services to be federal awards for purposes of the patient care service provider's audit unless the state requires it because the payments are on a cost-reimbursement basis. However, Circular A-133 considers the Medicaid payments made by a state to patient care service providers to be federal awards for purposes of the state's audit and reporting. In addition, loans made from the National Credit Union Share Insurance Fund and the Central Liquidity Facility that are funded by contributions from insured institutions are not considered federal awards expended.

Subrecipient and Vendor Determinations

5.28 An auditee may be a recipient, a subrecipient, and a vendor. Federal awards expended as a recipient or a subrecipient are subject to audit under Circular A-133. Section 210 of Circular A-133 states that payments that vendors receive from a federal program for goods and services are not considered to be federal awards to the vendors and therefore not subject to an audit in accordance with Circular A-133. Circular A-133 provides specific guidance on determining whether payments constitute a federal award or a payment for goods and services. Chapter 12 of this guide further discusses that guidance.

Major Program Determination

Risk-Based Approach

5.29 Circular A-133 states that the auditor should use a risk-based approach to determine which federal programs are major programs, which affects the scope of the audit. Circular A-133 places the responsibility for identifying major programs on the auditor, and provides criteria for the auditor to use in applying a risk-based approach. The auditor's determination of the programs to audit is based on an overall evaluation of the risks of noncompliance occurring that could be material to the individual federal programs. In evaluating risk, the auditor considers, among other things, the current and prior audit experience with the auditee, oversight by the federal agencies and pass-through entities, and the inherent risk of noncompliance of the federal programs, using a specific process established in the circular. Chapter 8 of this guide discusses that risk-based approach and the determination of major programs.

Low-Risk Auditee

5.30 Circular A-133 contains certain criteria for considering an auditee to be a low-risk auditee. A low-risk auditee is eligible for reduced audit coverage. *Low-risk auditee* is a term defined in Circular A-133 for the purpose of applying the percentage-of-coverage rule in the risk-based approach. (Chapter 8 of this guide discusses the low-risk auditee criteria and the percentage-of-coverage rule.) The term *low-risk auditee* does not imply or require the auditor to assess audit risk of noncompliance or any of its components as low for an entity that meets the Circular A-133 definition of a low-risk auditee.

©2015, AICPA　　　　　　　　　　　　　　　　　　　　　　　　AAG-GAS 5.30

Cluster of Programs

5.31 Circular A-133 defines a *cluster of programs* as a grouping of closely related federal programs that share common compliance requirements. The types of clusters of programs are R&D, SFA, and other clusters. *Other clusters* are defined by the OMB in the *Compliance Supplement* or are designated as such by a state for the federal awards the state provides to its subrecipients that meet the definition of a cluster of programs. An auditee or auditor may not create their own cluster of programs based on programs that share common compliance requirements. Similarly, an auditee or auditor may not de-cluster a cluster of programs that is defined by OMB or designated by a state. When a state designates federal awards as an other cluster, it also should identify the federal awards included in the cluster and advise the subrecipients of the compliance requirements applicable to the cluster. A cluster of programs should be considered as one program for determining major programs and (with the exception of R&D) whether a program-specific audit may be elected.

Federal Agency Selection of Additional Major Programs

5.32 Section 215(c) of Circular A-133 permits a federal agency to request an auditee to have a particular federal program audited as a major program in lieu of the federal agency conducting or arranging for additional audits. To allow for planning, such requests should be made at least 180 days before the end of the fiscal year to be audited. After consultation with its auditor, the auditee should promptly respond to such a request by informing the federal agency whether the program would otherwise be audited as a major program using the risk-based approach and, if not, the estimated incremental cost. The federal agency should then promptly confirm to the auditee whether it wants the program audited as a major program. If the program is to be audited as a major program based upon the federal agency's request, and the federal agency agrees to pay the full incremental costs, then the auditee should have the program audited as a major program. This approach also may be used by pass-through entities for a subrecipient.[17]

Auditee Responsibilities

Financial Statements and Schedule of Expenditures of Federal Awards

5.33 As discussed in chapter 6 of this guide, Circular A-133 states that auditees should prepare financial statements that reflect their financial position, the results of operations or changes in net assets, and, where appropriate, cash flows for the fiscal year audited. The financial statements should be for the same organizational unit and fiscal year that is chosen to meet the requirements of Circular A-133. However, organization-wide financial statements also may include departments, agencies, and other organizational units that have separate audits in accordance with Circular A-133 and prepare separate financial statements. As discussed in chapter 7 of this guide, Circular A-133

---

[17] In addition, Section 520(c)(2) of Circular A-133 permits a federal awarding agency to request that a type A program for certain recipients not be considered low risk so that it would be audited as a major program. Further, Section 525(c)(2) of Circular A-133 states that federal agencies, with the concurrence of the OMB, may identify federal programs that are higher risk. That identification is provided in the *OMB Compliance Supplement (Compliance Supplement)*. See the further discussion of those provisions and the definition of type A programs in chapter 8, "Determination of Major Programs (Circular A-133)," of this guide.

also states that auditees should prepare a schedule of expenditures of federal awards for the period covered by the financial statements.

Summary Schedule of Prior Audit Findings

5.34 In accordance with Circular A-133, the auditee should prepare a summary schedule of prior audit findings. The schedule should report the status of all audit findings included in the prior audit's schedule of findings and questioned costs relative to federal awards. It also should include audit findings reported in the prior audit's summary schedule of prior audit findings, except audit findings that have been corrected or are no longer valid. Prior audit findings that remain valid and uncorrected should be included in the schedule regardless of the year they were first reported. Chapter 13 of this guide further discusses that schedule.

Other Responsibilities

5.35 Circular A-133 establishes certain other responsibilities for auditees, including the following:

- Identifying in its accounts all federal awards received and expended and the federal programs under which they were received, including, as applicable, the CFDA title and number, the award number and year, the name of the federal agency, and the name of the pass-through entity

- Establishing and maintaining effective internal control over compliance for federal programs that provides reasonable assurance that the auditee is managing federal awards in compliance with laws, regulations, and the provisions of contracts or grant agreements that could have a material effect on each of its federal programs

- Complying with laws, regulations, and the provisions of contracts or grant agreements related to each of its federal programs

- Ensuring that the audits required by Circular A-133 are properly performed and submitted when due

- Following up and taking corrective action on audit findings (including the preparation of the previously discussed summary schedule of prior audit findings and a corrective action plan as discussed in paragraph 5.37); this guide recommends that corrective action be initiated within six months after the receipt of the audit report and proceed as rapidly as possible

Responsibility for Compliance at the Financial Statement Level and for Internal Control Over Financial Reporting

5.36 Although not specifically stated in Circular A-133, the auditee also is responsible for complying with the requirements of laws, regulations, and the provisions of contracts or grant agreements that could have a material effect on the financial statements and for establishing and maintaining effective internal control over financial reporting. *Government Auditing Standards* (which is required to be followed in a single audit) Appendix I, section A1.08 provides supplemental guidance stating that management of the audited entity is responsible for complying with applicable laws and regulations and implementing systems designed to achieve compliance with applicable laws and regulations.

Corrective Action Plan

5.37 At the completion of the audit, the auditee should prepare a corrective action plan to address each audit finding included in the current year's auditor's reports. Chapter 13 of this guide further discusses the corrective action plan.

Reporting Package

5.38 The auditee should submit to the FAC a reporting package that comprises the previously discussed financial statements and schedule of expenditures of federal awards, summary schedule of prior audit findings, auditor's reports, and corrective action plan. The auditee should submit the reporting package with the data collection form described in paragraph 5.39. These items are submitted electronically via the FAC's Internet Data Entry System. Chapter 13 of this guide describes the report submission process and related requirements of Circular A-133.

Data Collection Form

5.39 The auditee is required to submit a data collection form (SF-SAC) that provides information about the auditee, its federal programs, and the results of the audit. The auditor also is required to complete certain sections of the form and electronically sign an auditor statement provided on the form. Chapter 13 of this guide further discusses the data collection form and the submission process.

Federal Awarding Agency Responsibilities

5.40 Circular A-133 establishes certain responsibilities for federal agencies that provide federal awards to recipients, including the following:

- Identifying the federal awards made by informing each recipient of the CFDA title and number, the award name and number, the award year, and if the award is for R&D. When some of this information is not available, the federal agency should provide information necessary to clearly describe the federal award.
- Advising recipients of the requirements imposed on them by federal laws, regulations, and the provisions of contracts or grant agreements.
- Ensuring that audits are completed and reports are received in a timely manner and in accordance with the requirements of Circular A-133.
- Providing technical advice and counsel to auditees and auditors as requested.
- Issuing a management decision on audit findings within six months after receipt of the audit report and ensuring that the recipient takes appropriate and timely corrective action.
- Assigning a person to provide annual updates of the *Compliance Supplement* to the OMB.

Overview of the Single Audit Act and the *Compliance Supplement*

Pass-Through Entity Responsibilities[18]

5.41 Pass-through entities have many responsibilities that are similar to those of federal awarding agencies. Chapter 12 of this guide describes the responsibilities of pass-through entities.

Cognizant Agency for Audit

Definition

5.42 Circular A-133 defines the *cognizant agency for audit* as a federal agency designated to carry out the federal responsibilities with regard to a single audit. For recipients expending more than $50 million a year in federal awards, the cognizant agency for audit will be the federal awarding agency that provides the predominant amount of direct funding to the recipient unless the OMB makes a specific cognizant agency for audit assignment. The determination of the predominant amount of direct funding is based on the direct federal awards expended by a recipient during its fiscal year ending in 2004, 2009, 2014, and every fifth year thereafter.[19] For example, audit cognizance for periods ending in 2011–2015 will be determined based on the federal awards expended in 2009. Audit cognizance can be reassigned if both the old and the new federal agencies notify the auditee (and, if known, the auditor) of the change within 30 days of the reassignment. A recipient may have one federal agency responsible for audit cognizance and another federal agency responsible for the negotiation of indirect costs.

Responsibilities

5.43 Circular A-133 provides that a cognizant agency for audit is responsible for

- providing technical audit advice and liaison to auditees and auditors.
- obtaining or conducting quality control reviews[20] of selected audits made by nonfederal auditors and providing the results, when appropriate, to other interested organizations.
- promptly informing other affected federal agencies and appropriate federal law enforcement officials of any direct reporting by the

---

[18] See chapter 12, "Audit Considerations of Federal Pass-Through Awards (Circular A-133)," for information on the reporting responsibilities of pass-through entities under the Federal Funding Accountability and Transparency Act of 2006.

[19] A current listing of cognizant agency for audit assignments is available at the Federal Audit Clearinghouse website at https://harvester.census.gov/fac/dissem/reports.html. At this link select the option titled "Cognizant Agency Reports," "view reports," then select the appropriate cognizant agency report.

[20] Among the tools that cognizant and oversight agencies for audit use to perform quality control reviews of Circular A-133 audits and desk reviews of Circular A-133 audit reports are two guides, *Guide for Quality Control Reviews of OMB Circular A-133 Audits (2015 Edition)* and *Guide for Desk Reviews of OMB Circular A-133 Audit Reports (2015 Edition)*. These guides, published by the Council of the Inspectors General on Integrity and Efficiency (CIGIE), are to be used by federal agencies when reviewing Circular A-133 audits for the purpose of determining if such audits are conducted in accordance with applicable auditing standards and Circular A-133. In addition, the checklists are used to identify any follow-up work needed by the auditor to support the opinion contained in the audit report and to identify issues that may require federal program management attention. Auditors may want to consider utilizing these tools as part of an inspection and quality control program. They are available at www.ignet.gov/content/manuals-guides.

auditee or its auditor of irregularities or illegal acts, as required by *Government Auditing Standards* or laws and regulations.[21]

- advising the auditor and, where appropriate, the auditee of any deficiencies found in the audits when the deficiencies require corrective action by the auditor. When advised of deficiencies, the auditee should work with the auditor to take corrective action. If corrective action is not taken, the cognizant agency for audit should notify the auditor, the auditee, and the applicable federal awarding agencies and pass-through entities of the facts and make recommendations for follow-up action. Major inadequacies or repeated substandard performance by auditors will be referred to appropriate state licensing agencies and professional bodies for disciplinary action.
- coordinating, to the extent practicable, the audits or reviews made by or for federal agencies that are in addition to audits under Circular A-133, so that the additional audits or reviews build upon the audits performed in accordance with Circular A-133.
- coordinating a management decision for audit findings that affect the federal programs of more than one federal agency.
- coordinating the audit work and reporting responsibilities among auditors, to achieve the most cost-effective audit.

For biennial audits, the cognizant agency for audit also is responsible for considering auditee requests to qualify as a low-risk auditee.

Oversight Agency for Audit

Definition

5.44 An auditee that does not have a designated cognizant agency for audit (that is, one that expends $50 million or less in federal awards) will have an oversight agency for audit. Circular A-133 defines the oversight agency for audit as a federal awarding agency that provides the predominant amount of direct funding to a recipient not assigned a cognizant agency for audit as previously discussed. When there is no direct funding, the federal agency with the predominant indirect funding should assume the oversight responsibilities. An oversight agency for audit may reassign oversight to another federal agency that provides substantial funding and agrees to be the oversight agency for audit. Within 30 days after reassignment, both the old and the new oversight agency for audit should notify the auditee (and, if known, the auditor) of the reassignment.

Responsibilities

5.45 Circular A-133 describes the duties of oversight agencies for audit. The responsibilities of an oversight agency for audit are not as broad as those of a cognizant agency for audit. An oversight agency's primary responsibility is to provide technical advice to auditees and auditors when it is requested. However, an oversight agency may assume all or some of the responsibilities normally performed by a cognizant agency for audit.

---

[21] The term *illegal acts* is now referred to as *noncompliance with laws and regulations* in both GAAS and *Government Auditing Standards*.

Overview of the Single Audit Act and the *Compliance Supplement* **139**

Program-Specific Audits

5.46 Circular A-133 provides general guidance on performing program-specific audits. In some cases, a program-specific audit guide will be available from the federal agency's Office of Inspector General. The audit guide will provide specific guidance to the auditor with respect to internal control, compliance requirements, suggested audit procedures, and audit reporting requirements. When a program-specific audit guide is not available, the auditee and auditor have basically the same responsibilities for the federal program as they would have for an audit of a major program in a single audit. Chapter 14 of this guide further discusses program-specific audits.

OMB Compliance Supplement[22]

5.47 Circular A-133 states that the auditor should determine whether the auditee has complied with laws, regulations, and the provisions of contracts or grant agreements (compliance requirements) that may have a direct and material effect on each of its major programs. The principal tool for this purpose is the *Compliance Supplement*. Chapter 10 of this guide further discusses compliance requirements and the *Compliance Supplement*.

5.48 The *Compliance Supplement* is based on the requirements of the Single Audit Act and Circular A-133, which provide for the issuance of a compliance supplement to assist auditors in performing the required audits. The requirements and guidance found in the separate parts of the *Compliance Supplement* are interrelated, and should be used in conjunction with each other. One purpose of the *Compliance Supplement*, which is updated annually,[23] is to identify existing compliance requirements that the federal government expects to be considered as part of an audit in accordance with the Single Audit Act and Circular A-133:

- For the programs it includes, the *Compliance Supplement* provides a source of information for auditors to understand the federal program's objectives, procedures, and types of compliance requirements relevant to the audit, as well as the audit objectives and suggested audit procedures for determining compliance with these requirements.

- For programs not listed in the *Compliance Supplement*, the auditor should follow *Compliance Supplement* Part 7, "Guidance for Auditing Programs Not Included in This Compliance Supplement," which instructs the auditor to use the types of compliance requirements (for example, cash management, reporting, allowable costs/cost principles, activities allowed or unallowed, eligibility, and matching, level of effort, and earmarking) contained in the *Compliance Supplement* as guidance for identifying the types of compliance requirements to test, and to determine the requirements governing the federal program by reviewing the provisions

---

[22] See the section titled "Transition Considerations Related to the Uniform Guidance," in chapter 10, "Compliance Auditing Applicable to Major Programs (Circular A-133)," of this guide for important information regarding the 2015 *Compliance Supplement*.

[23] The *Compliance Supplement* is available on the OMB's website at www.whitehouse.gov/omb/grants circulars or for sale from the Government Printing Office by calling 202.512.1800.

©2015, AICPA AAG-GAS 5.48

of contracts and grant agreements and the laws and regulations referred to in such contracts and grant agreements.

Transition Considerations Related to the Uniform Guidance

5.49 The requirements in Subpart F, "Audit Requirements," of the Uniform Guidance are effective for audits of fiscal years beginning on or after December 26, 2014, with no early implementation permitted. For example, consider a nonfederal entity with a June 30, 2015, fiscal year end that has $600,000 in federal expenditures. In this situation, the auditor may not early adopt the Uniform Guidance or its updated audit threshold of $750,000. Therefore, the nonfederal entity in the example provided would be subject to an audit under Circular A-133 for its June 30, 2015, year-end because its federal expenditures exceed the Circular A-133 audit threshold of $500,000.

Chapter 6

Planning Considerations of Circular A-133

> **⊙ Update 6-1: Audits of Federal Awards**
>
> This chapter, and the remaining chapters of part II, *Circular A-133 Audits*, of this guide should be used for performing a compliance audit of federal awards under Office of Management and Budget (OMB) Circular A-133, *Audits of States, Local Governments, and Non-Profit Organizations* (Circular A-133). Part III, *Uniform Guidance Audits*, of this guide should be used when performing a compliance audit under Title 2 U.S. *Code of Federal Regulations* Part 200, *Uniform Administrative Requirements, Cost Principles, and Audit Requirements for Federal Awards* (Uniform Guidance). See the transitional guidance sections at the end of each chapter that highlight important matters for consideration.[1] Refer to the preface for additional information.
>
> **Important Uniform Guidance Effective Date Information**
>
> In December 2013, the OMB issued the Uniform Guidance, which is effective for nonfederal entities for all federal awards and certain funding increments provided on or after December 26, 2014. The requirements in Subpart F, "Audit Requirements," are effective for audits of fiscal years beginning on or after December 26, 2014, with no early implementation permitted. Therefore, auditees subject to a single audit with December 25, 2015, and later year ends (for example, December 31, 2015) will be required to undergo the audit under Subpart F of the Uniform Guidance. Note that audits of fiscal years ending prior to the effective date of the Uniform Guidance audit requirements are subject to an audit under Circular A-133.

Introduction

6.01 In planning an audit to meet the requirements of OMB Circular A-133 the auditor needs to consider a number of matters in addition to those ordinarily associated with an audit of financial statements in accordance with generally accepted auditing standards (GAAS) and *Government Auditing Standards*. This chapter discusses additional planning considerations in a single audit conducted in accordance with Circular A-133. Many of these planning considerations also are applicable in program-specific audits, which are discussed in chapter 14, "Program-Specific Audits (Circular A-133)," of this guide.

6.02 Chapter 3, "Planning and Performing a Financial Statement Audit in Accordance With *Government Auditing Standards*," of this guide discusses matters that are relevant to the planning of a financial statement audit. The

---

[1] See the information found at the end of certain chapters in part II, *Circular A-133 Audits*, of this guide for transition considerations when performing an audit under Office of Management and Budget (OMB) Circular A-133, *Audits of States, Local Governments, and Non-Profit Organizations* (Circular A-133), as it relates to the applicability of certain aspects of Title 2 U.S. *Code of Federal Regulations* Part 200, *Uniform Administrative Requirements, Cost Principles, and Audit Requirements for Federal Awards* (Uniform Guidance), to audits performed under Circular A-133. Transition considerations related to an audit performed under the Uniform Guidance can be found at the end of chapters in part III, *Uniform Guidance Audits*, of this guide in sections titled "Transition Considerations Related to the Uniform Guidance."

rest of this chapter discusses the following additional or expanded matters relevant to the planning of a single audit:

- Adapting and applying applicable auditing standards to a Circular A-133 compliance audit
- Identifying supplementary audit requirements
- Agreeing upon the terms of the engagement with management
- Audit documentation
- Supplementary audit requirements of the Single Audit Act and Circular A-133 regarding audit documentation access and audit follow-up
- Financial statement audit considerations
- Defining the entity to be audited
- Determining the audit period
- Initial-year audit considerations
- Timing of the completion of the audit and report submission deadlines
- Determining the major programs to be audited
- Identifying direct and material compliance requirements
- Audit risk of noncompliance considerations
- Assessing the risks of material noncompliance
- Audit materiality considerations
- Developing an efficient audit approach
- Group audit considerations in a Circular A-133 compliance audit
- Existence of an internal audit function
- Communications with the cognizant or oversight agency for audit and others
- State and local compliance and reporting requirements
- Desk reviews and on-site reviews
- Restriction on the auditor's preparation of indirect cost proposals

Adapting and Applying Applicable Auditing Standards to a Circular A-133 Compliance Audit

6.03 Single audits are required to be performed in accordance with *Government Auditing Standards*, which incorporates by reference the AICPA Statements on Auditing Standards. AU-C section 935, *Compliance Audits* (AICPA, *Professional Standards*), addresses a compliance audit, which is a component of a single audit. It is applicable when an auditor is engaged, or required by law or regulation, to perform a compliance audit in accordance with all of the following:

- GAAS
- The standards for financial audits under *Government Auditing Standards*
- A governmental audit requirement that requires the auditor to express an opinion on compliance

Planning Considerations of Circular A-133

6.04 AU-C section 935 defines a *governmental audit requirement* as a government requirement established by law, regulation, rule, or provision of contracts or grant agreements requiring that an entity undergo an audit of its compliance with applicable compliance requirements[2] related to one or more government programs that the entity administers. AU-C section 935 identifies Circular A-133 as an example of a governmental audit requirement that meets the preceding criteria. Therefore, AU-C section 935 is applicable to and provides requirements and guidance for auditors conducting an audit in accordance with Circular A-133. Chapters 9, "Consideration of Internal Control Over Compliance for Major Programs (Circular A-133)," and 10, "Compliance Auditing Applicable to Major Programs (Circular A-133)," of this guide provide additional information and guidance related to AU-C section 935. Part I of this guide provides information and guidance for an audit performed under *Government Auditing Standards*.

6.05 AU-C sections 200–800 address audits of financial statements, as well as other kinds of engagements. AU-C section 935 notes that when performing a compliance audit, the auditor, using professional judgment, should adapt and apply the AU-C sections to the objectives of a compliance audit except for those AU-C sections, or portions thereof, that are identified in the appendix, "AU-C Sections That Are Not Applicable to Compliance Audits," to AU-C section 935 as not applicable to a compliance audit.[3] For those AU-C sections that are applicable to a compliance audit, AU-C section 935 states that the auditor is not required, in planning and performing a compliance audit, to make a literal translation of each procedure that might be performed in a financial statement audit but rather to obtain sufficient appropriate audit evidence to support the auditor's opinion on compliance.

6.06 Paragraph .06 of AU-C section 935 notes that some AU-C sections can be adapted and applied to a compliance audit with relative ease, for example, by replacing the word *misstatement* with *noncompliance*. However, other AU-C sections are more difficult to adapt and apply without additional modification. For that reason, AU-C section 935 provides more specific guidance on how to adapt certain AU-C sections to a compliance audit. This guide also provides information on how an auditor may adapt certain AU-C sections to a Circular A-133 compliance audit.

Identifying Supplementary Audit Requirements

6.07 In a Circular A-133 compliance audit, the auditor should determine the additional audit requirements that are supplementary to GAAS and *Government Auditing Standards* and perform procedures to address those

---

[2] AU-C section 935, *Compliance Audits* (AICPA, *Professional Standards*), defines *applicable compliance requirements* as the compliance requirements that are subject to the compliance audit. Paragraph .500(d) of OMB Circular A-133 states that the auditor should determine whether the auditee has complied with laws, regulations, and the provisions of contracts or grant agreements that may have a direct and material effect on each of its major programs. Therefore, in a Circular A-133 compliance audit, the direct and material compliance requirements are those that are subject to audit. Accordingly, for the purpose of adapting AU-C section 935 to a Circular A-133 compliance audit, the term *applicable compliance requirements* has been replaced by *direct and material compliance requirements* in this guide except when directly citing content from AU-C section 935.

[3] The appendix, "AU-C Sections That Are Not Applicable to Compliance Audits," of AU-C section 935 provides a list of AU-C section requirements that are not applicable to a compliance audit. All other AU-C sections not identified in the appendix should be adapted and applied to a compliance audit.

requirements. Part II of this guide provides information to assist the auditor in addressing the supplementary audit requirements of Circular A-133. In instances in which the audit guidance provided by a governmental agency for the performance of a compliance audit has not been updated, or otherwise conflicts with current guidance, the auditor should comply with the most current applicable GAAS and *Government Auditing Standards* instead of the outdated guidance.

Agreeing Upon the Terms of the Engagement With Management

6.08 As discussed in chapter 3 of this guide, AU-C section 210, *Terms of Engagement* (AICPA, *Professional Standards*), provides guidance related to the auditor's responsibilities in agreeing upon the terms of an audit engagement with management or, when appropriate, those charged with governance. AU-C section 210 introduces certain preconditions that should be present before the auditor accepts the engagement. See chapter 3 of this guide for more information.

6.09 The terms of the engagement generally include the information found in paragraph .10 of AU-C section 210 and should be documented in an audit engagement letter or other suitable form of written agreement. In addition to the matters communicated as part of the financial statement audit performed in accordance with *Government Auditing Standards* (as further described in chapter 3), the communication should include the planned work and level of assurance related to internal control over compliance and compliance with provisions of laws, regulations, contracts, and grant agreements necessary for an audit in accordance with Circular A-133. Examples of the type of information that might be included in the communication when performing an audit in accordance with Circular A-133 are as follows:

- A statement that the supplementary schedule(s) to be considered in the audit include the schedule of expenditures of federal awards
- The objective of an audit in accordance with Circular A-133
- A description of the additional reports required by Circular A-133 that the auditor is expected to prepare and issue, including any limitation on their use
- A description of management's responsibility for (*a*) identifying all federal awards received; (*b*) preparing the schedule of expenditures of federal awards (including notes and noncash assistance received) in accordance with Circular A-133 requirements;[4] (*c*) internal control over compliance; (*d*) compliance with the provisions of laws, regulations, contracts, and grant agreements; (*e*) following up and taking corrective action on audit findings, including the preparation of a summary schedule of prior audit findings and a corrective action plan; and (*f*) submitting the reporting package and data collection form

---

[4] AU-C section 725, *Supplementary Information in Relation to the Financial Statements as a Whole* (AICPA, *Professional Standards*), sets forth specific requirements related to management's responsibility when the auditor is engaged to report on whether supplementary information (for example, the schedule of expenditures of federal awards) is fairly stated, in all material respects, in relation to the financial statements as a whole. See chapter 7, "Schedule of Expenditures of Federal Awards (Circular A-133)," for more information.

Planning Considerations of Circular A-133 **145**

- A statement that management will make the auditor aware of significant vendor relationships where the vendor is responsible for program compliance (so that the auditor can determine if additional procedures on vendor records will be necessary—see chapter 12, "Audit Considerations of Federal Pass-Through Awards (Circular A-133)," of this guide)
- A description of the auditor's responsibility in a compliance audit of major programs under Circular A-133, including the determination of major programs, the consideration of internal control over compliance, and reporting responsibilities
- A statement that the parties to whom audit documentation will be made available upon request include federal agencies and the U.S. Government Accountability Office (GAO)

In addition, paragraph .37 of AU-C section 935 states that the auditor should communicate to those charged with governance the auditor's responsibilities under GAAS, *Government Auditing Standards*, and the governmental audit requirement (for example, Circular A-133), an overview of the planned scope and timing of the compliance audit, and significant findings from the compliance audit.

Audit Documentation

6.10 As discussed in chapter 3 of this guide, audit documentation requirements and guidance are found in AU-C section 230, *Audit Documentation* (AICPA, *Professional Standards*). Audit documentation is important because it provides the principal support that the audit was performed in accordance with GAAS, *Government Auditing Standards*, and Circular A-133, and provides the principal support for each of the opinions issued. Furthermore, *Government Auditing Standards* contains additional documentation requirements that are applicable to a Circular A-133 compliance audit. See chapter 10 for more information regarding documentation requirements in a Circular A-133 compliance audit.

Additional Audit Requirements of the Single Audit Act and Circular A-133 Regarding Audit Documentation Access and Audit Follow-Up[5]

Audit Documentation Access and Retention

6.11 Based on language in the Single Audit Act, Section 515(b) of Circular A-133 states that audit working papers (referred to in this guide as *audit documentation*) "shall be made available upon request to the cognizant or oversight agency for audit or its designee, a federal agency providing direct or indirect funding, or GAO at the completion of the audit, as part of a quality review, to resolve audit findings, or to carry out oversight responsibilities...." It also states that access to the audit documentation includes the right to obtain copies. The

---

[5] Chapter 3, "Planning and Performing a Financial Statement Audit in Accordance With *Government Auditing Standards*," of this guide discusses the *Government Auditing Standards* audit documentation access and follow-up requirements.

©2015, AICPA AAG-GAS 6.11

Senate Committee report that accompanied the Single Audit Act Amendments of 1996 stated that federal agencies should be judicious in the exercise of this authority and that it was the committee's intent that the federal agencies recognize that audit documentation may contain trade secrets and confidential commercial and financial information and should treat such information as confidential under the Freedom of Information Act (*Government Organization and Employees*, *U.S. Code* Title 5, Section 552). Interpretation No. 1, "Providing Access to or Copies of Audit Documentation to a Regulator," of AU-C section 230 (AICPA, *Professional Standards*, AU-C sec. 9230 par. .01–.15), contains guidance for when a regulator requests access to audit documentation pursuant to law, regulation, or audit contract.

6.12 Circular A-133 states that auditors should retain audit documentation and reports for a minimum of three years after the date of issuance of the auditor's report to the auditee, unless the auditor is notified in writing by the cognizant agency for audit, oversight agency for audit, or pass-through entity to extend the retention period. Paragraph .17 of AU-C section 230 states that the audit documentation retention period should not be shorter than five years from the report release date; statutes, regulations, or an audit firm's quality control policies may dictate a longer period.[6] The AU-C section 230 documentation retention guidance should be followed for a Circular A-133 compliance audit because the five year retention period is longer than the three year period defined in Circular A-133. When the auditor is aware that the federal awarding agency, pass-through entity, or auditee is contesting an audit finding, the auditor should contact the parties contesting the audit finding for guidance before the destruction of the audit documentation and reports.

Audit Follow-Up

6.13 Circular A-133 states that the auditor should follow up on prior audit findings, perform procedures to assess the reasonableness of the summary schedule of prior audit findings prepared by the auditee, and report, as a current-year audit finding, when the auditor concludes that the summary schedule of prior audit findings materially misrepresents the status of any prior audit finding. Chapters 10 and 13, "Auditor Reporting Requirements and Other Communication Considerations in a Single Audit (Circular A-133)," of this guide further discuss the auditor's responsibility for audit follow-up.

Financial Statement Audit Considerations

6.14 Circular A-133 states that auditees should prepare financial statements that reflect their financial position, results of operations or changes in net assets, and, where appropriate, cash flows for the fiscal year audited. The financial statements should be for the same organizational unit and fiscal year that is chosen to meet the requirements of Circular A-133. However, organization-wide financial statements also may include departments, agencies, and other organizational units that have separate audits and prepare separate financial statements (see paragraph 6.18). Circular A-133 also states that auditees should prepare a schedule of expenditures of federal awards for the period covered by the financial statements. Chapter 7, "Schedule of

---

[6] Some state boards of accountancy prescribe longer document retention periods. Documents should be retained for the longest retention period of any required documentation retention periods that may apply.

Planning Considerations of Circular A-133

Expenditures of Federal Awards (Circular A-133)," of this guide discusses the schedule of expenditures of federal awards.

6.15 Circular A-133 does not prescribe the basis of accounting that auditees use to prepare their financial statements. However, auditees should disclose the basis of accounting and significant accounting policies used in preparing the financial statements. Circular A-133 states that auditees should be able to identify in their accounts all federal awards expended and the federal programs under which they were received. Generally, auditees evidence the ability to identify federal awards expended by preparing a reconciliation of amounts presented in the financial statements to the amounts and programs in the schedule of expenditures of federal awards.

6.16 Circular A-133 states that the auditor should issue an opinion (or a disclaimer of opinion) as to whether the financial statements are presented fairly in all material respects in accordance with generally accepted accounting principles (GAAP).[7] (Chapters 4, "Auditor Reporting Requirements and Other Communication Considerations of *Government Auditing Standards*," and 13 of this guide provide guidance on reporting on the auditee's financial statements.)

6.17 If the auditee prepares its financial statements in accordance with a special purpose framework,[8] the auditor still is required to express or disclaim an opinion on the special purpose financial statements. The auditor's report on special purpose financial statements should include an emphasis-of-matter paragraph that, among other things, states that the special purpose framework is a basis of accounting other than GAAP. However, if the special purpose financial statements are prepared in accordance with a regulatory basis of accounting and the special purpose financial statements together with the auditor's report are intended for general use, the auditor's report should not include such an emphasis-of-matter paragraph. Instead, the auditor should express an opinion about whether the financial statements are presented fairly, in all material respects, in accordance with GAAP and include in a separate paragraph an opinion about whether the financial statements are prepared in accordance with the special purpose framework. AU-C section 800, *Special*

---

[7] As explained in the AICPA Audit and Accounting Guide *State and Local Governments*, the auditor generally expresses or disclaims an opinion on a government's basic financial statements by providing an opinion or disclaimer of opinion on each opinion unit required to be presented in those financial statements. In addition, the auditor may provide opinions or disclaimers of opinion on additional opinion units if engaged to set the scope of the audit and assess materiality at a more detailed level than by the opinion units required for the basic financial statements. Throughout this guide, the use of the singular terms *opinion* and *disclaimer of opinion* encompasses the multiple opinions and disclaimers of opinion that generally will be provided on a government's basic financial statements.

[8] AU-C section 800, *Special Considerations—Audits of Financial Statements Prepared in Accordance With Special Purpose Frameworks* (AICPA, Professional Standards), defines a *special purpose framework* as a financial reporting framework other than generally accepted accounting principles and establishes requirements for reporting on those frameworks. Special purpose frameworks, such as the cash, tax, regulatory, and other bases of accounting, are sometimes referred to as an *other comprehensive bases of accounting* (OCBOA). The term *OCBOA* is sometimes used when referring to this guidance in this guide.

The AICPA Audit and Accounting Guide *State and Local Governments* discusses the application of AU-C section 800 to state and local governmental financial statements and also provides illustrative auditor's reports for financial statements prepared in accordance with a special purpose framework. In addition, the AICPA practice aid *Applying OCBOA in State and Local Governmental Financial Statements* (APAOCBO12P) provides nonauthoritative guidance on preparing and reporting on OCBOA financial statements of governmental entities. A second practice aid, *Accounting and Financial Reporting Guidelines for Cash- and Tax-Basis Financial Statements* (APACTB12P), provides nonauthoritative guidance for preparers regarding guidelines and best practices for the preparation of cash and tax basis financial statements. These publications are available at www.cpa2biz.com.

Considerations—Audits of Financial Statements Prepared in Accordance With Special Purpose Frameworks (AICPA, *Professional Standards*), contains relevant requirements and guidance.

> **Emphasis Point**
>
> As per paragraph .A5 of AU-C section 800, if a regulator permits, but not requires, a cash basis of accounting, it would not be considered a regulatory basis of accounting, but rather a cash basis of accounting. Therefore, in this situation, an emphasis-of-matter paragraph would be used in the auditor's report to indicate that the special purpose framework is a basis of accounting other than GAAP (versus the regulatory basis of accounting reporting which would include an opinion on whether the financial statements are prepared fairly, in all material respects, in accordance with GAAP).

Defining the Entity to Be Audited

6.18 One of the initial tasks during the planning process of a single audit is determining whether management has properly defined the entity to be audited. Circular A-133 states that single audits should cover the entire operations of the auditee. However, Circular A-133 provides auditees the option to meet the audit requirements of the circular through a series of audits that cover an auditee's departments, agencies, and other organizational units that expended or otherwise administered federal awards during a fiscal year. If an auditee elects this option, separate financial statements and a schedule of expenditures of federal awards should be prepared for each such department, agency, or other organizational unit. In these circumstances, an auditee's organization-wide financial statements also may include departments, agencies, or other organizational units that have separate audits and prepare separate financial statements. For example, if a local government has its school districts audited separately, it would be acceptable for the local government's financial statements to include the school districts, even though the school districts were not included in the local government's Circular A-133 audit (and consequently the schedule of expenditures of federal awards for the local government did not include the school districts' federal awards), because a separate Circular A-133 audit was conducted on the school districts. However, if separate financial statements were not prepared for the school districts, it would be unacceptable for a separate Circular A-133 audit to be conducted on the school districts (that is, the local government's organization-wide financial statements could not be used as a substitute for separate financial statements for the school districts). Chapter 13 of this guide discusses auditor reporting in situations in which (*a*) the implementation regulations of federal awarding agencies[9] define the entity to be audited differently than does GAAP and (*b*) the audit of federal awards does not encompass the entirety of the auditee's operations expending federal awards.

---

[9] Certain federal agencies, such as the U.S. Department of Housing and Urban Development, have specifically defined the level of the entity subject to audit.

Determining the Audit Period

Fiscal Year and Program Period May Differ

6.19 An audit performed in accordance with Circular A-133 should cover the auditee's financial transactions (including transactions related to federal awards) for its fiscal year (or a two-year period, if allowed by Circular A-133), which is not necessarily the same as the period of the program being funded. (Chapter 5, "Overview of the Single Audit Act, Circular A-133, and the *Compliance Supplement*," of this guide discusses the allowability of biennial audits). Thus, the audit might include only a part of the transactions of a federal award, because some transactions may not occur within the period covered by the audit.

Stub Periods

6.20 Stub periods may occur when an auditee converts from a program-specific audit to a single audit or changes audit periods. An example would be a community college with a September 30 year end that previously had a program-specific audit and is now converting to a single audit. The prior program-specific audits were performed based on a June 30 award year. The first single audit will be for the year ending September 30. This would leave the community college with an unaudited stub period of July 1 to September 30. The audit requirements of Circular A-133 still apply to federal expenditures during the stub period and are generally met through a separate audit of the stub period or by including the expenditures of the stub period in the scope of the following period's single audit. Either way, the threshold for audit requirement is still $500,000 in federal expenditures for the period. Auditees or their auditors can contact the cognizant or oversight agency for audit or the pass-through entity for advice on how stub periods can be addressed.

Initial-Year Audit Considerations

Preceding Period Audited by Another Auditor

6.21 AU-C section 210 provides guidance when an auditor is considering accepting an engagement in which the federal awards of the preceding period were audited by another auditor. Paragraph .11 of AU-C section 210 notes that before accepting an engagement for an initial audit, including a reaudit engagement, the auditor should request management to authorize the predecessor auditor to respond fully to the auditor's inquiries regarding matters that will assist the auditor in determining whether to accept the engagement.[10] If management refuses to authorize the predecessor auditor to respond, or limits the response, the auditor should inquire about the reasons and consider the implications of that refusal in deciding whether to accept the engagement.

Factors to Consider Under the Risk-Based Approach[11]

6.22 When the engagement includes the selection of major programs using the risk-based approach defined in Circular A-133, an auditor accepting,

---

[10] As noted in chapter 3 of this guide, an auditor may be required by law or regulation to audit the entity. However, inquiries of the predecessor auditor may still be relevant for the purpose of obtaining information that is used by the auditor in planning and performing the audit.

[11] See the discussion in chapter 8, "Determination of Major Programs (Circular A-133)," for more information on the risk-based approach to selecting major programs.

or contemplating accepting, an engagement might consider gathering certain information to assist in the major program determination process. Information that will assist the auditor includes the following:

- Federal awards expended by federal programs
- Prior-period findings and questioned costs (including the corrective action plan and management decision related to the findings and summary schedule of prior audit findings)
- Whether a predecessor auditor used the exception that allows deviation from the risk-based approach during the last three years, as discussed in chapter 8, "Determination of Major Programs (Circular A-133)," of this guide
- Correspondence from program officials indicating potential problems
- New programs
- Changes to programs
- Amount of funding passed through to subrecipients by individual federal programs
- Extent to which computer processing is used to administer federal programs
- Federal programs audited as a major program for the last two years

Timing of the Completion of the Audit and Report Submission Deadlines

6.23 When planning the timing of the single audit, an important consideration is the Circular A-133 requirement that the audit be completed and the data collection form and reporting package be submitted to the Federal Audit Clearinghouse within a certain time period.[12] Chapters 5 and 13 of this guide discuss the reporting package and the timing requirements for submission.

Determining the Major Programs to Be Audited

6.24 As discussed in chapter 5 of this guide, Circular A-133 includes a supplementary audit requirement that states that the auditor should use a risk-based approach to determine which federal programs are major programs. This determination will affect the scope of the Circular A-133 compliance audit and the compliance requirements to be tested. Chapter 8 of this guide discusses the determination of major programs and an exception available for certain first

---

[12] If the auditee or auditor wishes to inform the federal government that the required submission will be late, the suggested way to do so is to contact the federal oversight or cognizant agency for the audit (contact information is available on the "Resources" tab at http://harvester.census.gov/fac/APPX3.htm).

Additionally, Appendix 7, "Other OMB Circular A-133 Advisories," of the *OMB Compliance Supplement* (*Compliance Supplement*) clarifies that in order for an entity to meet the criteria for low-risk auditee status in the current year, the prior 2 years' audits must have met the requirements of Circular A-133, including report submission to the Federal Audit Clearinghouse (FAC) by the due date. As stated in the *Compliance Supplement*, a report submission is considered late if the entity is not in compliance with the 9 month due date rule or other revised due date in the case of a properly approved extension. Appendix 7 of the *Compliance Supplement* also includes suggested procedures to identify FAC submissions that do not meet the due date.

year audits that allows deviation from the use of risk criteria in determining major programs.

Identifying Direct and Material Compliance Requirements [13]

6.25 As noted in AU-C section 935, a compliance audit is based on the premise that management is responsible for identifying the entity's government programs and understanding and complying with the compliance requirements. As part of the compliance audit, the auditor should determine which of those government programs and compliance requirements to test in accordance with Circular A-133.

6.26 AU-C section 935 defines *applicable compliance requirements* as compliance requirements that are subject to a compliance audit. Some governmental audit requirements specifically identify the applicable compliance requirements. Paragraph .A9 of AU-C section 935 notes that other governmental audit requirements provide a framework for the auditor to determine the applicable compliance requirements and cites the *OMB Compliance Supplement* (*Compliance Supplement*) as such a framework in a Circular A-133 compliance audit. In a Circular A-133 compliance audit, the applicable compliance requirements are those that may have a direct and material effect on each major program (direct and material compliance requirements).

6.27 The *Compliance Supplement* is the primary source for identifying compliance requirements for federal programs in a Circular A-133 compliance audit, and the auditor, using professional judgment, determines which of the 12 types of compliance requirements may have a direct and material effect on each major program. These direct and material compliance requirements are tested as part of the compliance audit. A program specific audit guide issued by a grantor agency may be another source for identifying applicable compliance requirements. For programs not included in the *Compliance Supplement*, Part 7 of that document instructs auditors to, among other things, review the federal award document and referenced laws and regulations applicable to the program and the Catalog of Federal Domestic Assistance. Chapter 10 of this guide further discusses the use of the *Compliance Supplement* to identify direct and material compliance requirements.

Audit Risk of Noncompliance Considerations

6.28 The requirements and guidance related to the auditor's consideration of audit risk of noncompliance and materiality when planning and performing a single audit is found in AU-C section 935 and AU-C section 320, *Materiality in Planning and Performing an Audit* (AICPA, *Professional Standards*). Audit risk of noncompliance and materiality, among other matters, need to be considered together for each major program being audited as well as for each direct and material compliance requirement in determining the nature, timing, and extent of audit procedures and in evaluating the results of those procedures.

6.29 Furthermore, Circular A-133 states that the auditor should determine whether the auditee has complied with laws, regulations, and the

---

[13] See footnote 2.

provisions of contracts or grant agreements that may have a direct and material effect on each of its major programs. Therefore, in developing an audit plan for a single audit, the auditor should assess not only the risk that noncompliance may have a material effect on the financial statements, but also the risk that noncompliance may have a material effect on each major program.

Components of Audit Risk of Noncompliance

6.30 *Audit risk of noncompliance* is the risk that the auditor expresses an inappropriate audit opinion on the entity's compliance when material noncompliance exists. It is a function of the risks of material noncompliance and detection risk of noncompliance.

Risk of Material Noncompliance

6.31 The risk of material noncompliance is the risk that material noncompliance exists before the audit. It consists of inherent risk of noncompliance and control risk of noncompliance.[14] For the purposes of a single audit and the auditor's opinion on compliance, these risk components are defined as follows:[15]

> **inherent risk of noncompliance.** The susceptibility of a major program's compliance requirement to noncompliance that could be material, either individually or when aggregated with other instances of noncompliance, before consideration of any related controls over compliance.
>
> **control risk of noncompliance.** The risk that noncompliance with a compliance requirement that could occur and that could be material to a major program, either individually or when aggregated with other instances of noncompliance, will not be prevented, or detected and corrected, on a timely basis by the entity's internal control over compliance.

Detection Risk of Noncompliance

6.32 Detection risk of noncompliance is managed by the auditor's response to the risks of material noncompliance. It is defined as follows:

> **detection risk of noncompliance.** The risk that the procedures performed by the auditor to reduce audit risk of noncompliance to an acceptably low level will not detect noncompliance that exists and that could be material to a major program, either individually or when aggregated with other instances of noncompliance.

Performing Risk Assessment Procedures

6.33 For each of the major programs and direct and material compliance requirements selected for testing, the auditor should perform risk assessment procedures to obtain a sufficient understanding of the direct and material compliance requirements and the entity's internal control over compliance with those compliance requirements. Obtaining an understanding of the major program, the direct and material compliance requirements, and the entity's internal control over compliance establishes a frame of reference within which

---

[14] Although Circular A-133 uses the term *control risk*, this guide uses the term *control risk of noncompliance* in order to be consistent with the term as used and defined in AU-C section 935.

[15] The definitions of *inherent risk of noncompliance*, *control risk of noncompliance*, and *detection risk of noncompliance* have been modified from the definition found in AU-C section 935 to reflect terminology used in a Circular A-133 compliance audit.

the auditor plans the compliance audit and exercises professional judgment about assessing risks of material noncompliance and responding to those risks throughout the compliance audit.

6.34 The nature and extent of the risk assessment procedures performed may vary from entity to entity and are influenced by the following factors:

- The newness and complexity of the direct and material compliance requirements
- The auditor's knowledge of the entity's internal control over compliance with the direct and material compliance requirements obtained in previous audits or other professional engagements
- The nature of the compliance requirement
- The services provided by the entity and how they are affected by external factors
- The level of oversight by the grantor or pass-through entity
- How management addresses findings

6.35 As noted in paragraph .A14 of AU-C section 935, performing risk assessment procedures to obtain an understanding of the entity's internal control over compliance includes an evaluation of the design of controls and whether the controls have been implemented. Internal control consists of the following five interrelated components: control environment, the entity's risk assessment, information and communication systems, control activities, and monitoring. Circular A-133 requires the auditor to plan the testing of internal control over compliance for major programs to support a low assessed level of control risk of noncompliance for the assertions relevant to the compliance requirements for each major program. Circular A-133 does not, however, actually require the auditor to achieve a low assessed level of control risk of noncompliance. The assessment of control risk of noncompliance contributes to the auditor's evaluation of the risk that material noncompliance exists in a major program. See chapter 9 for more information.

6.36 The process of assessing inherent risk of noncompliance and control risk of noncompliance provides audit evidence about the risk that material noncompliance may exist. The auditor uses this audit evidence as part of the basis for his or her opinion on compliance. It is important to note that paragraph .19 of AU-C section 935 states that risk assessment procedures, tests of controls, and analytical procedures alone are not sufficient to address a risk of material noncompliance. Chapter 9 of this guide discusses the auditor's consideration of internal control over compliance for major programs, including a further discussion of the assessment of control risk of noncompliance.

6.37 In determining an acceptable level of detection risk of noncompliance, the auditor considers his or her assessments of inherent risk of noncompliance and control risk of noncompliance and the extent to which he or she seeks to restrict the audit risk of noncompliance related to the major program. As assessed inherent risk of noncompliance or control risk of noncompliance decreases, the acceptable level of detection risk of noncompliance increases. Accordingly, the auditor may alter the nature, timing, and extent of the compliance tests performed based on the assessments of inherent risk of noncompliance and control risk of noncompliance. Circular A-133 requires compliance testing to include tests of transactions and such other auditing procedures necessary to provide the auditor with sufficient evidence to support an opinion on compliance. Such compliance testing serves to limit detection risk of noncompliance. Chapter 11, "Audit Sampling Considerations of Circular A-133 Compliance Audits," of this guide discusses audit sampling as it relates to a compliance audit.

6.38 In performing risk assessment procedures, the auditor should inquire of management about whether there are findings and recommendations in reports or other written communications resulting from previous audits, attestation engagements, and internal or external monitoring[16] that directly relate to the objectives of the compliance audit. The auditor should gain an understanding of management's response to findings and recommendations that could have a material effect on the entity's compliance with direct and material compliance requirements (for example, taking corrective action). This information should be used to assess risk and determine the nature, timing, and extent of the audit procedures for the compliance audit, including determining the extent to which testing the implementation of any corrective actions is applicable to the audit objectives. These procedures are performed to assist the auditor in understanding whether management responded appropriately to such findings.

Assessing the Risks of Material Noncompliance

6.39 AU-C section 935 states that the auditor should assess the risks of material noncompliance whether due to fraud or error for each applicable compliance requirement[17] and should consider whether any of those risks are pervasive to the entity's compliance. If the risks are pervasive, they may affect the entity's compliance with many compliance requirements. Examples of situations in which there may be a risk of material noncompliance that is pervasive to the entity's noncompliance are (a) an entity that is experiencing financial difficulty and for which there is an increased risk that grant funds will be diverted for unauthorized purposes and (b) an entity that has a history of poor recordkeeping for its federal programs.

6.40 As part of the audit of the financial statements, members of the audit team, including the auditor with final responsibility for the audit, should discuss the susceptibility of the entity's financial statements to material misstatement as part of the risk assessment process. Similarly, the auditor should hold a discussion of the susceptibility of the entity's major programs to material noncompliance with compliance requirements in the planning meeting of the financial statement audit. This discussion may also be held separately from the general planning meeting if the planning of the Circular A-133 compliance audit is done at a later date.

6.41 In assessing the risks of material noncompliance, the auditor may evaluate inherent risk of noncompliance and control risk of noncompliance individually or in combination. See chapter 10 for information on performing further audit procedures in response to assessed risks.

6.42 In a Circular A-133 compliance audit, the factors an auditor may consider in assessing the risks of material noncompliance are as follows:

- The complexity of the direct and material compliance requirements

---

[16] Examples of external monitoring include regulatory reviews and program reviews by government agencies or pass-through entities. Examples of internal monitoring include reports prepared by the internal audit function and internal quality assessments.

[17] See footnote 2.

Planning Considerations of Circular A-133

- The susceptibility of the direct and material compliance requirements to noncompliance
- The length of time the entity has been subject to the direct and material compliance requirements
- The auditor's observations about how the entity has complied with the direct and material compliance requirements in prior years
- The potential effect on the entity of noncompliance with the direct and material compliance requirements
- The degree of judgment involved in adhering to the direct and material compliance requirements
- The auditor's assessment of the risks of material misstatement in the financial statement audit

6.43 In assessing the risks of material noncompliance, the auditor should

- identify risks throughout the process of obtaining an understanding of the entity and its environment, including relevant controls that relate to the risks;
- relate the identified risks to what can go wrong at the relevant compliance level;
- consider whether the risks are of a magnitude that could result in noncompliance with requirements that have a direct and material effect on one or more of the entity's major programs; and
- consider the likelihood that the risks could result in noncompliance with requirements that have a direct and material effect on one or more of the entity's major programs.

Assessing the Risks of Material Noncompliance Due to Fraud

6.44 As part of the risk assessment process, the auditor should specifically assess the risks of material noncompliance with a major program's compliance requirements occurring due to fraud (fraud risk). The auditor should consider that assessment in designing the audit procedures to be performed. The assessment of fraud risk should be ongoing throughout the audit.

6.45 AU-C section 240, *Consideration of Fraud in a Financial Statement Audit* (AICPA, *Professional Standards*), addresses the auditor's responsibility to plan and perform the audit to obtain reasonable assurance about whether the financial statements are free of material misstatement due to fraud. AU-C section 240 also applies to a compliance audit. In a Circular A-133 compliance audit, the assessment of fraud risk relates to fraudulent acts[18] that may result in material noncompliance with a major federal program's compliance requirements or the misappropriation of federal funds.

6.46 When performing the Circular A-133 compliance audit, the auditor, using professional judgment, should adapt AU-C section 240 to the objectives of a compliance audit. As part of that adaptation, the auditor may consider performing the following procedures for each major program. Auditor judgment regarding specific situations found with respect to the auditee may indicate alternative procedures. This list of procedures is not intended to be an all-inclusive list of procedures. These procedures include

---

[18] The auditor's assessment of fraud risk focuses on fraud that originates within the entity. It does not include fraud perpetrated by persons outside the entity.

- conducting a meeting of audit team members to discuss the risks of material noncompliance due to fraud. Depending on the number of major programs and the size of the overall audit team, it may be most effective to hold a separate meeting for each major program or groups of major programs audited by an individual segment of the overall audit team. For smaller engagements, holding one meeting covering all major programs may be sufficient.

- gathering information necessary to assess fraud risk factors for major programs prior to the audit team meeting. This may include considering the results of the financial statement fraud risk assessment to determine the applicability to the compliance audit's fraud risk assessment procedures. When identifying fraud risk factors, the auditor assesses whether those risk factors, individually or in combination, present a risk of material noncompliance with compliance requirements that could have a direct and material effect on a major federal program.

- documenting entity-wide programs and controls in place to prevent, detect, and deter fraud; auditor identification and evaluation of the suitability of the design; and whether such programs and controls have been implemented. Many of these programs and controls may have been considered and documented as part of the fraud risk assessment related to the financial statement audit.

- inquiring of management (including those involved with grants management), those charged with governance, internal audit, and others about the risks of fraud related to major programs. The auditor inquires about instances of possible or actual noncompliance or abuses of broad programs and controls that have come to their attention occurring during the period under audit or the period subsequent to that date. The inquiries may cover more than one major program.

6.47 Based on the information gathered, analyses, and communication among the audit team members, the auditor identifies and documents specific fraud risks, including the risk of management override of controls, that may result in material noncompliance with a major program's compliance requirements due to fraud. Consideration of any programs and controls in place to mitigate the risk of such fraud assists the auditor in the assessment of control risk of noncompliance of the related direct and material compliance requirement. Based on the specific fraud risks identified, and the results of tests of design and implementation of controls, the auditor determines the planned audit response (including consideration of testing major program journal entries).

6.48 Upon the completion of Circular A-133 compliance audit procedures, the auditor considers whether the results of audit procedures performed and other conditions affect the assessment of fraud risk made when planning the audit. This evaluation may provide further insight about the risks of material noncompliance due to fraud and whether there is a need to perform additional or alternative audit procedures.

6.49 Table 6-1 contains examples of fraud risk factors specific to a compliance audit. The risk factors are classified based on the three conditions generally present when material noncompliance due to fraud occurs:

1. Incentives or pressures
2. Opportunities
3. Attitudes or rationalizations

Although the risk factors cover a broad range of situations, they are examples only; accordingly, the auditor may consider additional or different risk factors. Also, the order of the examples of risk factors provided is not intended to reflect their relative importance or frequency of occurrence.

Table 6-1

Fraud Risk Factors

Incentives or Pressures

- Substantial political pressure on management creates an undue concern about federal award program accomplishments.
- Imminent or anticipated adverse changes in program legislation or regulations that could impair the financial stability or profitability of the entity.
- High degree of competition for federal awards, especially when accompanied by declining availability of federal awards nationally or regionally.
- A stagnant tax or revenue base or declining federal funding, enrollments, or eligible participants.
- Complex or frequently revised compliance requirements or participant requirements (such as cost sharing or matching requirements) that create incentives to shift costs or incorrectly value transactions.
- A significant portion of program management's compensation or performance appraisal is linked to federal award budgetary or program accomplishments or other incentives, the value or results of which are contingent upon the entity achieving unduly aggressive targets for budgetary or programmatic results.
- Unrealistically aggressive budget or program goals.
- A mix of fixed price and cost reimbursable program types that create incentives to shift costs or otherwise manipulate accounting transactions.
- Financial pressure due to declining revenues or increasing expenses, creating incentive to apply nonprogram costs to federal awards.
- Significant pressure to obtain additional funding necessary to stay viable and maintain levels of service considering the financial or budgetary position of the entity or of specific federal award programs, including need for funds to finance major research and development or capital expenditures.
- Threat of imminent program termination or significant reduction in scope, the effect of which could have a material financial impact on the entity.

Opportunities

- The nature of the entity's operations provide opportunities to engage in fraud.
- An organizational structure that is unstable or unnecessarily complex.
- Rapid growth due to significant increases in funds without the organizational structure to support it.

(continued)

Fraud Risk Factors—*continued*

- Inadequate internal controls due to outdated or ineffective accounting or information systems.
- Inadequate oversight by those charged with governance over the financial reporting process and management activities.
- Inadequate monitoring by management for compliance with policies, laws, and regulations.
- Lack of appropriate segregation of duties or independent checks, especially in areas such as eligibility determination and benefit awards.
- Lack of appropriate system of authorization and approval of transactions, such as purchasing, contracting, benefit determinations, and eligibility, due to either poorly designed or outdated controls.
- Lack of timely and appropriate documentation for transactions, such as eligibility and benefit determinations.
- Lack of asset accountability or safeguarding procedures.
- Rapid changes in federal award programs, such as significant centralization or decentralization initiatives, funding shifts from federal to state or local levels, increases or decreases in participant populations, high vulnerability to significant changes in compliance requirements, or pending program elimination.
- High turnover rates or employment of accounting, internal audit, or IT staff who are not effective.

Attitudes or Rationalizations

- An ineffective or nonexistent means of communicating and supporting the entity's values or ethics, especially regarding such matters as acceptable business practices, conflicts of interests, and codes of conduct.
- Significant subrecipient or subcontract relationships for which there appears to be no clear programmatic or business justification (for example, a subrecipient providing services it does not appear qualified to provide or a vendor geographically distant from the entity when nearby vendors are available).
- Management displaying or conveying an attitude of disinterest regarding strict adherence to federal award rules and regulations such as those related to participant eligibility, benefit determinations, or eligibility.
- An individual or individuals with no apparent executive position(s) within the entity appearing to exercise substantial influence over its affairs or over individual federal award programs (for example, a major donor, fund-raiser, or politician).
- An attitude among program personnel that given their position they, or parties related to them, are due benefits from the program, such as expenses reimbursed by the federal award or participation in the program, to which they would otherwise not be entitled, resulting in questioned costs.

Audit Materiality Considerations

6.50 Paragraph .13 of AU-C section 935 states that the auditor should establish and apply materiality levels for the compliance audit based on the governmental audit requirement. In a Circular A-133 compliance audit, there are multiple materiality considerations as discussed in the following paragraphs. As noted in paragraph .A8 of AU-C section 935, in a compliance audit, the auditor's judgment about matters that are material to users of the auditor's report is based on consideration of the needs of users as a group, including grantors.

Materiality Differences Between the Financial Statement Audit and the Circular A-133 Compliance Audit

6.51 In auditing compliance with requirements governing major programs in a Circular A-133 compliance audit, the auditor's consideration of materiality differs from that in an audit of financial statements in accordance with GAAS and *Government Auditing Standards*. In an audit of financial statements, materiality is considered in relation to the financial statements being audited.[19] However, in designing audit tests and developing an opinion on an auditee's compliance with requirements having a direct and material effect on each major program, paragraph .A7 of AU-C section 935 states that the auditor generally considers materiality in relation to each major program. Chapter 10 of this guide further discusses materiality considerations in a Circular A-133 compliance audit. Chapter 11 of this guide further discusses audit sampling in a compliance audit.

6.52 In a compliance audit, the auditor's purpose for establishing materiality levels is to

- determine the nature and extent of risk assessment procedures.
- identify and assess the risks of material noncompliance.
- determine the nature, timing, and extent of further audit procedures.
- evaluate whether the entity complied with the direct and material compliance requirements.
- report findings of noncompliance and other matters required to be reported by the governmental audit requirement.

Although the auditor's consideration of materiality for the purposes identified in this paragraph is generally in relation to the government program as a whole, the governmental audit requirement may specify a different level of materiality for one or more of these purposes. For example, for purposes of reporting findings, Circular A-133 establishes a specific materiality requirement as discussed in paragraph 6.53.

Materiality for Purposes of Reporting Audit Findings

6.53 Circular A-133 requires the auditor to consider a lower level of materiality for purposes of reporting audit findings in the schedule of findings and questioned costs than for other purposes. The Circular A-133 "audit finding" materiality is different (and generally lower) than (*a*) the materiality used for planning and performing the single audit, (*b*) the materiality used for planning, performing, evaluating the results of, and reporting on the financial statement

---

[19] Because an audit of a government's financial statements under the provisions of the AICPA Audit and Accounting Guide *State and Local Governments* is based on opinion units (see footnote 7), auditors make separate materiality determinations for purposes of planning, performing, evaluating the results of, and reporting for each opinion unit.

audit, or (c) expressing an opinion on the auditee's compliance with requirements having a direct and material effect on each major program.

6.54 Among other findings to be reported, Circular A-133 states that the auditor should report in the schedule of findings and questioned costs material noncompliance with the provisions of laws, regulations, contracts, or grant agreements related to each major program. (Chapter 13 of this guide describes other findings that Circular A-133 requires to be reported.) The auditor's determination of whether an instance of noncompliance with the provisions of laws, regulations, contracts, or grant agreements is material for the purpose of reporting an audit finding is in relation to 1 of the 12 types of compliance requirements (for example, activities allowed or unallowed, cash management, eligibility, or reporting) for a major program or an audit objective identified in the *Compliance Supplement*.

6.55 If, for example, when the auditor discovers one or more instances of noncompliance involving the reporting type of compliance requirement for a particular major program, certain materiality determinations should be made using professional judgment. First, the auditor should decide whether the noncompliance is material to the reporting type of compliance requirement for the particular major program. If the auditor determines the noncompliance is material to the reporting type of compliance requirement, the noncompliance would be reported as a finding in the schedule of findings and questioned costs. Second, the auditor should decide whether the discovered noncompliance is material, either individually or when aggregated with other noncompliance findings, in relation to the particular major program as a whole. If the auditor determines the noncompliance is material to the major program as a whole, the auditor would express a qualified or adverse opinion on compliance with respect to the particular major program.

Developing an Efficient Audit Approach

6.56 Consideration of ways to achieve maximum audit efficiency may be useful in the planning stage of the audit. Examples of ways to achieve audit efficiency follow:

- The financial statement audit and the Circular A-133 compliance audit could be planned at the same time.
- If the auditee's internal control for a compliance requirement is common to more than one major program, the transactions of those programs could be combined into one population for selecting sample sizes for internal control tests.[20] (See chapter 11 of this guide for information related to audit sampling in a compliance audit.)
- Because Circular A-133 requires the planning and performance of internal control over compliance work to assess control risk of noncompliance as low (unless control deficiencies are found), the auditor could take advantage of the low assessed level of control

---

[20] Although this approach may be efficient for internal control tests, experience has shown that it is preferable to select separate samples for compliance testing from each major program because the separate samples provide clear evidence of the compliance tests performed, the results of those tests, and the conclusions reached. See chapter 11, "Audit Sampling Considerations of Circular A-133 Compliance Audits," for more information.

risk of noncompliance when he or she performs the substantive testing of compliance.

- Helpful quality control materials (such as planning checklists and reporting checklists) could be used.[21]

Group Audit Considerations in a Circular A-133 Compliance Audit

6.57 The requirements of AU-C section 600, *Special Considerations—Audits of Group Financial Statements (Including the Work of Component Auditors)* (AICPA, *Professional Standards*), address special considerations that apply to group audits of financial statements that include the financial information of more than one component (that is, group financial statements). AU-C section 600 is, in part, intended to address the audit risk that results from the aggregation of component financial information (referred to here as aggregation risk). It also establishes requirements for when it is appropriate to make reference to a component auditor in the auditor's report on the financial statements. In accordance with AU-C section 935, the auditor should use professional judgment to adapt and apply the provisions in the AU-C sections to meet the objective of a compliance audit. Therefore, it will be necessary for the auditor to use professional judgment in adapting and applying the provisions of AU-C section 600 to a Circular A-133 compliance audit because of the differing nature and objectives of such an engagement. The following paragraphs are intended to provide guidance to auditors in adapting and applying the provisions of AU-C section 600 to a Circular A-133 audit.

6.58 The concept of aggregation risk in AU-C section 600 is not directly applicable to Circular A-133 compliance audits as each major program is being opined on separately. Unlike a financial statement audit, there is no entity-wide opinion on compliance in a Circular A-133 compliance audit. Additionally, even when a major program is administered by multiple organizational units, locations, or branches within a major program, because the focus of the Circular A-133 compliance audit is attribute based (that is, there is either compliance or noncompliance), the concepts of aggregation risk and component materiality as contemplated in AU-C section 600 would not be relevant. Instead, the auditor may have additional sampling considerations in such situations. See the guidance in chapter 11 of this guide for guidance on the effect of such a structure on the sampling considerations for the major program. Therefore, as a result of the unique nature of a Circular A-133 compliance audit, the concept of a component in AU-C section 600 generally should only be applied when other auditors have been separately engaged to perform a portion of a Circular A-133 compliance audit. In those cases, the auditor should follow the guidance in AU-C section 600 as it relates to other auditors (that is, component auditors), including considerations of whether to make reference to the other auditors in the auditor's report on compliance and on internal control over compliance. See chapter 13 of this guide for more information on referring to other auditors.

---

[21] See footnote 22 in paragraph 6.72. In addition, auditors may want to consider using AICPA peer review checklists for a similar purpose. These checklists are available at www.aicpa.org and a number of the checklists related to single audits can also be accessed via the Governmental Audit Quality Center website. To access these checklists go to the "Resources" page of the GAQC website at www.aicpa.org/gaqc.

6.59 Governmental entities and entities that receive governmental assistance may engage independent accounting firms on a joint venture or subcontract basis. This sometimes occurs due to legal or contractual requirements to make positive efforts to use small business, minority-owned firms, and women-owned business enterprises. Making reference to other auditors in these circumstances is usually not appropriate. In the case of a joint audit, each of the auditors participating in the audit will sign the audit reports. The guidance in AU-C section 600 is appropriate only when each auditor or firm has complied with GAAS and *Government Auditing Standards* and is in a position that would justify being the only signatory of the report. In the case of a subcontract relationship, the subcontracting auditor often does not issue a separate report. Therefore, without a separate report, it would also not be appropriate to make reference to the subcontracting auditor.

Existence of an Internal Audit Function

6.60 Internal auditors may monitor not only compliance requirements that affect the financial statement audit, but also those that affect major programs. AU-C section 610, *Using the Work of Internal Auditors* (AICPA, *Professional Standards*), provides requirements and guidance related to the external auditor's (auditor) responsibilities if using the work of internal auditors. Using the work of internal auditors includes both (*a*) using the work of the internal audit function in obtaining audit evidence and (*b*) using internal auditors to provide direct assistance under the direction, supervision, and review of the external auditor. AU-C section 610 does not apply when the activities of the internal audit function are not relevant to the audit, the external auditor does not expect to use the work of the internal audit function, or the external auditor does not plan to use an entity's internal auditors to provide direct assistance in the audit.

6.61 Paragraph .09 of AU-C section 610 states that the external auditor has sole responsibility for the audit opinion expressed and that responsibility is not reduced by the external auditor's use of the work of the internal audit function. The objectives of the external auditor, when the entity has an internal audit function and the auditor expects to use the work of internal auditors to modify the nature or timing, or reduce the extent, of audit procedures to be performed directly by the external auditor are

- to determine whether to use the work of the internal audit function in obtaining audit evidence or to use internal auditors to provide direct assistance, and if so, in which areas and to what extent.
- if using the work of the internal audit function in obtaining audit evidence, to determine whether that work is adequate for purposes of the audit.
- if using internal auditors to provide direct assistance, to appropriately direct, supervise, and review their work.

Considerations Related to the Internal Audit Function

6.62 When gaining an understanding of internal control, the auditor should obtain an understanding of the internal audit function sufficient to identify internal audit activities that are relevant to planning the audit. The work of internal auditors may affect the nature, timing, and extent of the procedures the auditor performs (*a*) to obtain an understanding of the entity and its environment, including its internal control over compliance, (*b*) to assess risk, and (*c*) in response to the assessed risk. In obtaining an understanding of the internal audit function as it relates to compliance requirements in a Uniform Guidance compliance audit, the following procedures may be helpful in assessing the relevance of internal audit activities:

- Consideration of knowledge from prior year audits
- Reviewing how the internal auditors allocate their audit resources to compliance activities
- Reading internal audit reports to obtain detailed information about the scope of internal audit activities as it relates to compliance with direct and material compliance requirements

Using the Work of the Internal Auditor in Obtaining Audit Evidence

6.63 The external auditor may be able to use the work of the internal audit function in obtaining audit evidence depending on

- the level of competency of the internal audit function,
- whether the internal audit function's organizational status and relevant policies and procedures adequately support the objectivity of the internal auditors, and
- whether the function applies a systematic and disciplined approach, including quality control.

6.64 In making judgments about the extent of the effect of the internal auditor's work on the auditor's procedures over direct and material compliance requirements, the auditor considers both the risks of material noncompliance (consisting of both inherent risk of noncompliance and control risk of noncompliance) and the degree of subjectivity involved in the evaluation of the audit evidence gathered in support of compliance with direct and material compliance requirements. As either the degree of risk of material noncompliance rises or the degree of subjectivity increases, the need for the auditor to perform his or her own tests increase.

6.65 In the case in which the work of internal auditors significantly affects the nature, timing, and extent of the auditor's procedures, the auditor should perform procedures to evaluate the quality and effectiveness of the internal auditor's work. In making the evaluation, the auditor should test some of the internal auditor's work relating to each direct and material compliance requirement. These tests may be accomplished by either (*a*) examining some of the controls or transactions examined or compliance requirements tested by the internal auditor or (*b*) examining similar controls or transactions not actually examined or compliance requirements not actually tested by the internal auditor. Such testing will assist the auditor in determining the nature, timing, and extent of further audit procedures. In reaching conclusions about the internal auditor's work, the results of the auditor's tests should be compared with the results of the internal auditor's work.

6.66 As noted in paragraph .A35 of AU-C section 610, and as it relates to a compliance audit, the more judgment involved, the higher the assessed risk of material noncompliance, the less the internal audit function's organization status and relevant policies and procedures adequately support the objectivity of the internal auditors, or the lower the level of competence of the internal audit function, the more audit procedures are needed to be performed by the external auditor on the overall body of work of the internal audit function to support the decision to use the work of the function in obtaining sufficient appropriate audit evidence on which to base the opinion.

6.67 When using the work of the internal audit function, the external auditor should make all significant judgments in the audit engagement. The auditor should evaluate whether, in aggregate, using the work of the internal audit function in obtaining audit evidence to the extent planned, together with any planned use of internal auditors to provide direct assistance, would result in the auditor still being sufficiently involved in the audit, given the auditor's sole responsibility for the audit opinion expressed.

Using Internal Auditors to Provide Direct Assistance to the Auditor

6.68 In performing the single audit, the auditor may request direct assistance from the internal auditors. Direct assistance relates to the use of internal auditors to perform procedures under the direction, supervision, and review of the external auditor. For example, internal auditors may assist the auditor in obtaining an understanding of internal control over compliance or performing tests of controls or tests of compliance. Prior to using internal auditors to provide direct assistance, the auditor should obtain written acknowledgment from management or those charged with governance, as appropriate, that internal auditors providing direct assistance will be allowed to follow the auditor's instructions and that the entity will not intervene in the work the internal auditors are providing to the auditor. The auditor should direct, supervise, and review the work performed by internal auditors on the engagement in accordance with AU-C section 220, *Quality Control for an Engagements Conducted in Accordance With Generally Accepted Auditing Standards* (AICPA, *Professional Standards*). Paragraphs .33–.35 of AU-C section 610 provide requirements regarding documentation when using the work of the internal audit function or using internal auditors to provide direct assistance on the audit.

6.69 Paragraphs .A42–.A43 of AU-C section 610 provide information on determining the nature and extent of work that can be assigned to internal auditors providing direct assistance. When direct assistance is provided, the auditor should assess the internal auditor's competence and objectivity and supervise, review, evaluate, and test the work performed by internal auditors to the extent appropriate in the circumstances. The auditor should inform the internal auditors of their responsibilities, the objectives of the procedures they are to perform, and matters that may affect the nature, timing, and extent of audit procedures, such as possible compliance and auditing issues. The auditor should also inform the internal auditors that all significant compliance and auditing issues identified during the audit should be brought to the auditor's attention.

Communications With the Cognizant or Oversight Agency for Audit and Others

6.70 Chapter 3 of this guide discusses planning the financial statement audit, and the areas that may be considered. In a single audit, the auditor may communicate with the cognizant agency for audit or the oversight agency for audit. If a planning meeting is held with that agency, the following matters may be discussed:

- The scope of the compliance testing of federal programs
- The intended use of the *Compliance Supplement*
- The identification of federal awards, including those that are considered to be major programs
- The form and content of the supplementary schedule of expenditures of federal awards
- The testing of the monitoring of subrecipients
- The scope of the review and testing of internal control over compliance
- The testing of compliance requirements
- The status of prior audit findings and questioned costs
- Federal agency or pass-through entity management decisions on prior audit findings
- Compliance requirements and any changes to those requirements

State and Local Compliance Requirements

6.71 In addition to testing and reporting on the compliance requirements as provided by *Government Auditing Standards* and Circular A-133, there may be state-imposed requirements on state funds provided to political subdivisions or not-for-profit entities (in this example, the state is not a pass-through entity). Even though such nonfederal awards are not considered part of the total federal awards expended by the auditee and are not subject to audit in accordance with Circular A-133, auditors would still need to consider such laws and regulations under GAAS and *Government Auditing Standards*. Therefore, in connection with the financial statement audit, auditors should obtain an understanding of applicable state and local compliance and reporting requirements that have a direct and material effect on the financial statements being audited. Chapter 3 of this guide discusses possible audit procedures to assess the completeness of management's identification of compliance requirements in connection with the financial statement audit. Chapter 7 of this guide discusses auditee reporting considerations.

Desk Reviews and On-Site Reviews

6.72 In addition to the quality control requirements set forth in *Government Auditing Standards* as discussed in chapter 2, "*Government Auditing Standards*—Ethical Principles and General Standards," of this guide, cognizant agencies for audit have implemented procedures for evaluating the quality of audits. These procedures include both desk reviews and on-site reviews (note that the oversight agencies for audit also may perform these reviews).[22] As a part of the cognizant agencies' evaluation of the completed reports of such engagements, and, as required by Circular A-133, the supporting audit

---

[22] Cognizant and oversight agencies use various checklists and tools to perform quality control reviews and desk reviews. One source of information regarding these reviews is the Council of Inspectors General on Integrity and Efficiency (CIGIE) website at https://www.ignet.gov/. Guides and manuals published by CIGIE that are used in quality control reviews and desk reviews of Circular A-133 compliance audits are available at www.ignet.gov/content/manuals-guides. While these resources are applicable for a Circular A-133 compliance audit, they have not yet been updated for the Uniform Guidance, and therefore should not be used for a review of a Uniform Guidance compliance audit.

documentation should be made available upon request by the representative of the federal agency. Audit documentation typically is reviewed at a location agreed upon by the cognizant agency for audit and the independent auditor. (Paragraph 6.11 and chapter 3 of this guide further discuss access to audit documentation.)

6.73 Whenever a review of the audit report or audit documentation discloses an inadequacy, the audit firm is contacted for corrective action. Where major inadequacies are identified and the representative of the cognizant agency for audit determines that the audit report and the audit documentation are substandard, cognizant agencies may take further steps. In those instances in which the audit is determined to be substandard by the federal agency, the matter may be submitted to state boards of public accountancy or the AICPA's Professional Ethics Division.

Restriction on the Auditor's Preparation of Indirect Cost Proposals

6.74 Circular A-133 precludes the auditor who prepares the indirect cost proposal or cost allocation plan from performing the single audit when indirect costs recovered by the auditee during the prior year exceeded $1 million.[23] This restriction applies to the base year used in the preparation of the indirect proposal or cost allocation plan and to any subsequent years in which the resulting indirect cost agreement or cost allocation plan is used to recover costs. For example, an auditor who prepares an indirect cost proposal or cost allocation plan that is used as the basis for charging indirect costs in the fiscal year ending June 30, 20X1, is not permitted to perform the 20X1 single audit (assuming that the indirect costs recovered during the prior year exceeded $1 million).

Transition Considerations Related to the Uniform Guidance

6.75 Auditors should consider the effective date provisions of the Uniform Guidance in a compliance audit performed under Circular A-133. This is because the administrative requirements and cost principles included in the Uniform Guidance are required to be implemented by nonfederal entities beginning December 26, 2014, for all new federal awards and funding increments (additional funding to existing federal awards) with modified award terms and conditions that are awarded on or after that date. Typically, the terms and conditions of the federal award should identify whether the funding increment is subject to the Uniform Guidance requirements or whether it will continue to be governed by the original terms and conditions of the federal award (that is, subject to the pre-Uniform Guidance requirements).

---

[23] The preparation of an entity's indirect cost proposal or cost allocation plan is considered to be a nonaudit service under *Government Auditing Standards*. Nonaudit services may create threats to an auditor's independence. When an auditor has prepared the entity's indirect cost proposal or cost allocation plan, and is not otherwise precluded from performing the audit under the guidance in Circular A-133, evaluation is needed as to whether independence is impaired. This evaluation is done using the conceptual framework in chapter 3, "General Standards," of *Government Auditing Standards*. See chapter 2, "*Government Auditing Standards*—Ethical Principles and General Standards," of this guide for more information on the requirements related to independence found in *Government Auditing Standards*.

6.76 In light of the Uniform Guidance effective date provisions, for a Circular A-133 compliance audit covering periods including December 26, 2014 and later, auditors should determine the applicable criteria that will be used to perform the compliance audit (that is, whether an award is subject to pre-Uniform Guidance requirements versus post-Uniform Guidance requirements) as part of the audit planning process. Federal awarding documents will be important tools for making this determination. Nonfederal entities and auditors that have questions regarding the applicable criteria for federal awards may consult with agency single audit coordinators or program officials. Contact information for these agency representatives can be found in Appendix III, "Federal Agency Single Audit and Program Contacts for A-133 Audits," of the *Compliance Supplement*.

6.77 One of the challenges that auditors may face is that a major program may include expenditures from both federal awards subject to the pre-Uniform Guidance requirements, as well as federal awards subject to the post-Uniform Guidance requirements. This situation could exist for several years until the pre-Uniform Guidance awards have been completely expended. When testing major program transactions, identification of the date of a federal award related to a particular expenditure is needed in order to determine the applicable criteria to use for the transaction being tested. It should be noted that a separate sample for pre-Uniform Guidance award transactions and post-Uniform Guidance award transactions within a major program would not typically be needed in this situation. However, this guide recommends that when testing major program transactions that the audit documentation for testing compliance and internal control over compliance include an identification of the transactions tested that were subject to post-Uniform Guidance requirements.

6.78 It is important to note that some federal agencies received OMB approval to make exceptions to the Uniform Guidance regulations as part of the agency implementing regulations. It may be challenging, particularly in the first year of implementation, for nonfederal entities and their auditors to determine such agency exceptions and the effect of any such exceptions on the audit. Appendix VII, "Other Audit Advisories," of the *Compliance Supplement* includes a summary, by federal agency, of the sections of the Uniform Guidance where agencies have made exceptions. Appendix VII refers to a document titled, "Uniform Guidance Crosswalk for Federal Agency Exceptions and Additions," posted on COFAR's website (https://cfo.gov/cofar/) for a complete listing and text of the exceptions. Nonfederal entities and auditors that have questions about the nature of agency exceptions and the effect of such exceptions on the audit, may consult with agency single audit coordinators or programs officials using the contact information in Appendix III of the *Compliance Supplement*.

Chapter 7

Schedule of Expenditures of Federal Awards (Circular A-133)

> **Ⓞ Update 7-1: Audits of Federal Awards**
>
> This chapter, and the remaining chapters of part II, *Circular A-133 Audits*, of this guide, should be used for performing a compliance audit of federal awards under Office of Management and Budget (OMB) Circular A-133, *Audits of States, Local Governments, and Non-Profit Organizations* (Circular A-133). Part III, *Uniform Guidance Audits*, of this guide should be used when performing a compliance audit under Title 2 U.S. *Code of Federal Regulations* Part 200, *Uniform Administrative Requirements, Cost Principles, and Audit Requirements for Federal Awards* (Uniform Guidance). See the transitional guidance sections at the end of each chapter that highlight important matters for consideration.[1] Refer to the preface for additional information.
>
> **Important Uniform Guidance Effective Date Information**
>
> In December 2013, the OMB issued the Uniform Guidance, which is effective for nonfederal entities for all federal awards and certain funding increments provided on or after December 26, 2014. The requirements in Subpart F, "Audit Requirements," are effective for audits of fiscal years beginning on or after December 26, 2014, with no early implementation permitted. Therefore, auditees subject to a single audit with December 25, 2015, and later year ends (for example, December 31, 2015) will be required to undergo the audit under Subpart F of the Uniform Guidance. Note that audits of fiscal years ending prior to the effective date of the Uniform Guidance audit requirements are subject to an audit under Circular A-133.

Introduction

7.01 OMB Circular A-133 requires the auditee to prepare a schedule of expenditures of federal awards that includes certain required elements (as described further in paragraph 7.20), including total federal expenditures for each individual federal program for the period covered by its financial statements. Circular A-133 requires the auditor to determine, and provide an opinion on, whether the auditee's schedule of expenditures of federal awards is presented fairly, in all material respects, in relation to the auditee's financial statements as a whole. In addition, Circular A-133 places the responsibility for identifying major programs on the auditor (see chapter 8, "Determination of Major Programs (Circular A-133)," of this guide), and the schedule of expenditures of federal awards serves as the primary basis for the auditor's major program

---

[1] See the information found at the end of certain chapters in part II, *Circular A-133 Audits*, of this guide for transition considerations when performing an audit under Office of Management and Budget (OMB) Circular A-133, *Audits of States, Local Governments, and Non-Profit Organizations* (Circular A-133), as it relates to the applicability of certain aspects of Title 2 U.S. *Code of Federal Regulations* Part 200, *Uniform Administrative Requirements, Cost Principles, and Audit Requirements for Federal Awards* (Uniform Guidance), to audits performed under Circular A-133. Transition considerations related to an audit performed under the Uniform Guidance can be found at the end of chapters in part III, *Uniform Guidance Audits*, of this guide in sections titled "Transition Considerations Related to the Uniform Guidance."

determination. Therefore, appropriate major program determination by the auditor is dependent on the accuracy and completeness of the information in the schedule of expenditures of federal awards.

7.02 This chapter describes the federal agency, pass-through entity, and auditee requirements relating to the identification of federal awards, and the general presentation requirements governing the schedule of expenditures of federal awards, pass-through awards, and noncash awards. This chapter also discusses the auditor's responsibilities related to issuing an in-relation-to opinion and the additional auditor considerations for the schedule of expenditures of federal awards relating to compliance audit objectives. Chapter 13, "Auditor Reporting Requirements and Other Communication Considerations in a Single Audit (Circular A-133)," of this guide discusses the auditor's reporting on the schedule of expenditures of federal awards. The appendix, "Illustrative Schedules of Expenditures of Federal Awards" of this chapter (paragraph 7.36), presents illustrative schedules of expenditures of federal awards.

Identification of Federal Awards

Federal Agency and Pass-Through Entity Requirements

7.03 According to Circular A-133, federal awarding agencies and pass-through entities have certain responsibilities related to the federal awards they make. Each recipient or subrecipient should be informed of the *Catalog of Federal Domestic Assistance* (CFDA) title and number, the award's name and number, the award year, and whether the award is for research and development (R&D). When some of this information is not available, the federal agency or pass-through entity should provide the auditee with information necessary to clearly describe the federal award.

Auditee Requirements

7.04 Circular A-133 states that the auditee should identify in its accounts all federal awards received and expended, as well as the federal programs under which they were received. Federal program and award identification includes, as applicable, the CFDA title and number, the award number and year, the name of the federal granting agency, and the name of the pass-through entity. Using this information, the auditee should be able to reconcile amounts presented in the financial statements to related amounts in the schedule of expenditures of federal awards.

Audit Considerations Related to the Schedule of Expenditures of Federal Awards[2]

Conditions for and Procedures Related to Issuing the In-Relation-To Opinion

7.05 AU-C section 725, *Supplementary Information in Relation to the Financial Statements as a Whole* (AICPA, *Professional Standards*), includes requirements and guidance on reporting on supplementary information, such

---

[2] *Government Auditing Standards* incorporates by reference AICPA Statements on Auditing Standards. Therefore, auditors performing financial statement audits and OMB Circular A-133

(*continued*)

Schedule of Expenditures of Federal Awards (Circular A-133)

as the schedule of expenditures of federal awards, when engaged to report on whether supplementary information[3] is fairly stated, in all material respects, in relation to the financial statements as a whole.[4] When issuing an in-relation-to opinion on the schedule of expenditures of federal awards, the auditor need not apply procedures as extensive as would be necessary to express an opinion on the schedule of expenditures of federal awards on a stand-alone basis. The following paragraphs describe the requirements and guidance in AU-C section 725 as they apply to the schedule of expenditures of federal awards.

7.06 In order to opine on whether the schedule of expenditures of federal awards is fairly stated, in all material respects, in relation to the financial statements as a whole, the auditor should determine that all of the following conditions are met:

- The information contained in the schedule of expenditures of federal awards was derived from, and relates directly to, the underlying accounting and other records used to prepare the financial statements.
- The information contained in the schedule of expenditures of federal awards relates to the same period as the financial statements.
- The financial statements were audited, and the auditor reporting on the schedule of expenditures of federal awards audited those financial statements.
- Neither an adverse opinion nor a disclaimer of opinion was issued on the financial statements (see chapter 13).
- The schedule of expenditures of federal awards will accompany the entity's audited financial statements, or such financial statements will be made readily available.[5]

7.07 The auditor should obtain the agreement of management that it acknowledges and understands its responsibility related to the schedule of expenditures of federal awards:

- For the preparation of the schedule of expenditures of federal awards in accordance with Circular A-133

(footnote continued)

compliance audits in accordance with *Government Auditing Standards* should comply with generally accepted auditing standards, the requirements found in chapters 1–3 of *Government Auditing Standards*, and the additional standards and related requirements for financial audits found in chapter 4, "Standards for Financial Audits," of *Government Auditing Standards*.

[3] Paragraph .04 of AU-C section 725, *Supplementary Information in Relation to the Financial Statements as a Whole* (AICPA, *Professional Standards*), defines *supplementary information* as information presented outside the basic financial statements, excluding required supplementary information, that is not considered necessary for the financial statements to be fairly presented in accordance with the applicable financial reporting framework. The reporting related to the schedule of expenditures of federal awards required by Circular A-133 is supplementary information subject to the requirements of AU-C section 725. In this chapter the terms *supplementary information* and *schedule of expenditures of federal awards* are both used to indicate supplementary information when discussing the guidance in AU-C section 725.

[4] In certain circumstances the auditor may not meet the requirements to issue an in-relation-to opinion on the schedule of expenditures of federal awards. See the discussion beginning at paragraph 7.32 for more information.

[5] Paragraph .A9 of AU-C section 725 notes that audited financial statements are deemed to be readily available if a third party user can obtain the financial statements without any further action by the audited entity. Financial statements posted on an entity's website may be considered readily available. However, being available by request is not considered readily available.

- To provide the auditor with certain written representations (see paragraph 7.16)
- To include the auditor's report on the schedule of expenditures of federal awards in any document that contains the schedule and that indicates that the auditor has reported on such information
- To present the schedule of expenditures of federal awards with the audited financial statements, or if the schedule will not be presented with the audited financial statements, to make the audited financial statements readily available[6] to the intended users of the schedule no later than the date of issuance of the schedule and the auditor's report thereon

Management's acknowledgement and understanding related to the schedule of expenditures of federal awards may be obtained as part of the engagement letter.

7.08 In order to opine on whether the schedule of expenditures of federal awards is fairly stated, in all material respects, in relation to the financial statements as a whole, the auditor should perform certain procedures that are in addition to the procedures performed during the audit of the financial statements. Using the same materiality level used in the audit of the financial statements the auditor should[7]

- inquire of management about the criteria used by management to prepare the schedule of expenditures of federal awards.
- determine whether the form and content of the schedule of expenditures of federal awards complies with Circular A-133.
- obtain an understanding about the methods of preparing the schedule of expenditures of federal awards and determine whether the methods have changed from those used in the prior period and, if those methods of preparing the schedule have changed, the reasons for such changes.
- compare and reconcile the schedule of expenditures of federal awards to the underlying accounting and other records used in preparing the financial statements or to the financial statements themselves.
- inquire of management about any significant assumptions or interpretations underlying the measurement or presentation of the schedule of expenditures of federal awards.
- evaluate the appropriateness and completeness of the information contained in the schedule of expenditures of federal awards, considering the results of the procedures performed and other knowledge obtained during the audit of the financial statements.
- obtain certain written representations from management (see paragraph 7.16).

---

[6] See footnote 5.
[7] As noted in paragraph .A15 of AU-C section 725, for most state and local governments, the auditor's report on the financial statements includes multiple opinions to address individual reporting units or aggregation of reporting units of the governmental entity. Accordingly, materiality is considered by the auditor for each opinion unit. However, in the context of AU-C section 725, the auditor's opinion on the schedule of expenditures of federal awards is in relation to the financial statements as a whole. Accordingly, in this situation, materiality is considered at a level that represents the entire governmental entity.

Schedule of Expenditures of Federal Awards (Circular A-133)

7.09 Materiality[8] may be considered when determining which information to compare and reconcile to the underlying accounting and other records, or to the financial statements. In addition, when evaluating the appropriateness and completeness of supplementary information the auditor may consider testing accounting or other records through observation or examination of source documents or other procedures ordinarily performed in an audit of the financial statements.

7.10 As noted in paragraph 7.19, Circular A-133 does not specifically prescribe the basis of accounting to be used by the auditee to prepare the schedule of expenditures of federal awards. Therefore, it is not unusual for the schedule of expenditures of federal awards to be prepared on a basis of accounting that is different from that of the financial statements. For example, the schedule of expenditures of federal awards may be prepared on the cash basis whereas the financial statements are prepared on an accrual basis in conformity with generally accepted accounting principles. AICPA Technical Questions & Answers section 9160.27, "Providing Opinion on a Schedule of Expenditures of Federal Awards in Relation to an Entity's Financial Statements as a Whole When the Schedule of Expenditures of Federal Awards Is on a Different Basis of Accounting Than the Financial Statements" (AICPA, *Technical Questions and Answers*), clarifies that the auditor may provide an in-relation-to opinion on the schedule of expenditures of federal awards in this situation as long as the schedule can be reconciled back to the underlying accounting and other records used in preparing the financial statements or to the financial statements themselves and as long as the other conditions and requirements of AU-C section 725 are met.

7.11 If the auditor concludes, on the basis of the procedures performed, that the schedule of expenditures of federal awards is materially misstated in relation to the financial statements as a whole, the auditor should discuss the matter with management and propose appropriate revision of the schedule. Chapter 13 discusses the effect on the auditor's report on the schedule of expenditures of federal awards when management does not revise the schedule in this circumstance.

Additional Auditor Requirements Relating to Compliance Audit Objectives and Internal Control Over Compliance

7.12 As noted previously, it is important to note that the schedule of expenditures of federal awards is unlike other types of supplementary information included in documents containing audited financial statements in that it serves as the primary basis for the auditor's major program determination. Therefore, compliance audit procedures should be performed to obtain sufficient appropriate audit evidence supporting the accuracy and completeness of the schedule of expenditures of federal awards, including the identification of federal programs in the schedule. In testing accuracy and completeness of the schedule of expenditures of federal awards, the auditor may use evidence obtained from audit procedures performed during the audit of the financial statements and the Circular A-133 compliance audit regarding the accuracy, completeness, and classification of recorded revenues and expenditures. Additionally, the auditor may consider reviewing an auditee prepared reconciliation of amounts reported in the schedule of expenditures of federal awards and the

---

[8] See footnote 7.

related notes to corresponding amounts reported in the financial statements or other underlying records used to prepare the schedule (for example, the general ledger, reimbursement requests, loan agreements, or other supporting documentation). The auditor may also consider sending confirmations to granting federal agencies or pass-through entities in an audit of a subrecipient. Finally, because Circular A-133 requires the auditee to include certain elements in the schedule of expenditures of federal awards, the procedures should also include a review of the auditee's schedule for the required elements set forth in Circular A-133 and described in paragraph 7.20.

7.13 AU-C section 725 does not require the auditor to obtain a separate understanding of the entity's internal control or to assess fraud risk. Although this provision is relevant in the context of the auditor reporting on the schedule of expenditures of federal awards under AU-C section 725, in order to satisfy Circular A-133 audit requirements, the auditor does have additional responsibilities related to the schedule concerning internal control. For example, as part of the Circular A-133 compliance audit, the auditor has a responsibility to consider internal control over compliance, including a consideration of internal control over the accuracy and completeness of the expenditure amounts reported on the schedule of expenditures of federal awards.

7.14 Chapter 9, "Consideration of Internal Control Over Compliance for Major Programs (Circular A-133)," of this guide further discusses the auditor's responsibility for considering internal control over compliance, including obtaining an understanding of the five components of internal control over compliance sufficient to assess the risks of material noncompliance. This understanding, coupled with the auditor's understanding of internal control over financial reporting required for the financial statement audit, should include the auditee's controls over the accuracy and completeness of the program information and expenditure amounts reported on the schedule of expenditures of federal awards, including controls over the accuracy of the CFDA numbers. Procedures may include inquiring of entity personnel, observing the application of specific controls, and inspecting documents and reports used in the preparation of the schedule of expenditures of federal awards. The understanding obtained should be sufficient for the auditor to assess the risks of material misstatement of the schedule of expenditures of federal awards and to design the nature, timing, and extent of further compliance audit procedures to test the accuracy and completeness of the schedule.[9]

7.15 When the auditor identifies deficiencies in internal control that relate to the auditee's preparation of a complete and accurate schedule of expenditures of federal awards, the auditor should evaluate the severity of each deficiency in internal control identified to determine whether the deficiency, individually or in combination, is a significant deficiency or material weakness in internal control over financial reporting, internal control over compliance, or both. Chapters 3, "Planning and Performing a Financial Statement Audit in Accordance With *Government Auditing Standards*," and 9 of this guide include a discussion of internal control and provide guidance to assist auditors in making an assessment of deficiencies in internal control. If a deficiency in internal control is determined to be a significant deficiency or material weakness, the auditor should report a finding in the schedule of findings and questioned

---

[9] The auditor's risk assessment may also be used in deciding what additional procedures, if any, should be performed in order to render an in-relation-to opinion.

costs. Chapter 13 of this guide further discusses the reporting of findings and the schedule of findings and questioned costs.

Management Representations Relating to the Schedule of Expenditures of Federal Awards

7.16 In addition to the written representations typically obtained in the financial statement audit and the Circular A-133 compliance audit, auditors should obtain certain additional representations related to the schedule of expenditures of federal awards. Representations should be obtained from management with regard to the schedule of expenditures of federal awards

- that management acknowledges and understands its responsibility for the presentation of the schedule of expenditures of federal awards in accordance with Circular A-133;
- that management believes the schedule of expenditures of federal awards, including its form and content, is fairly presented in accordance with Circular A-133;
- that the methods of measurement or presentation have not changed from those used in the prior period, or if the methods of measurement or presentation have changed, the reasons for such changes;
- about any significant assumptions or interpretations underlying the measurement or presentation of the schedule of expenditures of federal awards; and
- that when the schedule of expenditures of federal awards is not presented with the audited financial statements, management will make the audited financial statements readily available to the intended users of the schedule no later than the issuance date by the entity of the schedule of expenditures of federal awards and the auditor's report thereon.[10]

Paragraph .20 of AU-C section 580, *Written Representations* (AICPA, *Professional Standards*), notes that representations should be made as of the date of the auditor's report on the financial statements. Therefore, two separate management representation letters may be necessary when the financial statement opinion and schedule of expenditures of federal awards in-relation-to opinion contain different dates. This would occur when the audit procedures related to the schedule of expenditures of federal awards are completed subsequent to the financial statement report date. See chapter 13 for more information.

Subsequent Events

7.17 AU-C section 725 states that the auditor has no responsibility for the consideration of subsequent events with respect to the supplementary information. However, the relevant requirements of AU-C section 560, *Subsequent Events and Subsequently Discovered Facts* (AICPA, *Professional Standards*), should be applied if information comes to the auditor's attention

- prior to the release of the auditor's report on the financial statements regarding subsequent events that affect the financial statements, or

---

[10] See footnote 5.

176   *Government Auditing Standards* and Single Audits

- subsequent to the release of the auditor's report on the financial statements regarding facts that, had they been known to the auditor at the date of the auditor's report, may have caused the auditor to revise the auditor's report.

Although AU-C section 725 does not impose a subsequent event requirement with respect to supplementary information, there are additional subsequent event considerations relating to the compliance audit. See chapter 10, "Compliance Auditing Applicable to Major Programs (Circular A-133)," of this guide for further information.

Reporting on the Schedule of Expenditures of Federal Awards

7.18 The auditor should include the required AU-C section 725 in-relation-to reporting on the schedule of expenditures of federal awards in either (*a*) an other-matter paragraph in accordance with AU-C section 706, *Emphasis-of-Matter Paragraphs and Other-Matter Paragraphs in the Independent Auditor's Report* (AICPA, *Professional Standards*), or (*b*) in a separate report on the schedule of expenditures of federal awards. Chapter 13 provides additional information on the auditor's reporting on the schedule of expenditures of federal awards and other considerations such as dating the report and certain modifications to the report that are needed if the schedule of expenditures of federal awards is materially misstated.

General Presentation Requirements

Basis of Accounting

7.19 Circular A-133 does not specifically prescribe the basis of accounting to be used by the auditee to prepare the schedule of expenditures of federal awards. For example, the basis of accounting used may be an other comprehensive basis of accounting.[11] However, it does state that the determination of when an award is expended should be based on when the activity related to the award occurs. Circular A-133 provides the guidance shown in table 7-1. (Circular A-133 also specifies the values that should be presented for certain

---

[11] AU-C section 800, *Special Considerations—Audits of Financial Statements Prepared in Accordance With Special Purpose Frameworks* (AICPA, *Professional Standards*), provides requirements and guidance for auditor reporting when the auditee prepares financial statements in conformity with a special purpose framework. AU-C section 800 defines a *special purpose framework* as a financial reporting framework other than generally accepted accounting principles and establishes requirements for reporting on those frameworks. Special purpose frameworks, such as the cash, tax, regulatory, and other bases of accounting, are sometimes referred to as *other comprehensive bases of accounting* (OCBOA). The term *OCBOA* is sometimes used when referring to this guidance in this guide.

The AICPA Audit and Accounting Guide *State and Local Governments* discusses the application of AU-C section 800 to state and local governmental financial statements and also provides illustrative auditor's reports for financial statements prepared in accordance with a special purpose framework. In addition, the AICPA practice aid *Applying OCBOA in State and Local Governmental Financial Statements* (APAOCBO12P) provides nonauthoritative guidance on preparing and reporting on OCBOA financial statements of governmental entities. A second practice aid, *Accounting and Financial Reporting Guidelines for Cash- and Tax-Basis Financial Statements* (APACTB12P), provides nonauthoritative guidance for preparers regarding guidelines and best practices for the preparation of cash and tax basis financial statements. These publications are available at www.cpa2biz.com.

types of awards; see table 7-2 in paragraph 7.29). A schedule of expenditures of federal awards, or certain awards in the schedule, may be presented on a basis of accounting that differs from that used in the financial statements. In any case, the auditee should clearly disclose the basis of accounting and the significant accounting policies used in preparing the schedule of expenditures of federal awards in the notes to the schedule. As noted previously, the auditee should also be able to reconcile amounts presented in the financial statements to related amounts in the schedule of expenditures of federal awards.

Table 7-1

Basis for Determining When Federal Awards Are Expended

Federal Awards	Basis for Determining When Expended
Grants, cost reimbursement contracts, cooperative agreements, and direct appropriations	When the expenditure or expense transactions occur
Amounts passed through to subrecipients	When the disbursement is made to the subrecipient
Loan and loan guarantees	When the loan proceeds are used (See the further discussion on loans and loan guarantees in table 7-2 and paragraph 7.30.)
Donated property, including donated surplus property	When the property is received
Food commodities	When the food commodities are distributed or consumed
Interest subsidies	When amounts are disbursed entitling the entity to the subsidy
Insurance	When the insurance is in force
Endowments	When federally restricted amounts are held
Program income	When received or used

Required Content for the Schedule of Expenditures of Federal Awards

7.20 Circular A-133 states that the auditee should prepare a schedule of expenditures of federal awards for the period covered by the auditee's financial statements. At a minimum, the schedule of expenditures of federal awards should

- list individual federal programs by federal agency. For federal programs included in a cluster of programs, list individual federal programs within a cluster of programs. (Chapter 5, "Overview of the Single Audit Act, Circular A-133, and the *Compliance Supplement*," of this guide discusses clusters of programs.) For R&D, the total federal awards expended should be shown either by individual award or by federal agency and major subdivision within the federal agency. For example, the National Institutes of Health is a major subdivision in the Department of Health and Human Services (the federal agency).

- for federal awards received as a subrecipient, include the name of the pass-through entity and the identifying number assigned by the pass-through entity.

- provide the total federal awards expended for each individual federal program and the CFDA number or other identifying number when the CFDA information is not available.

- include notes that describe the significant accounting policies used in preparing the schedule.

- for federal awards received as a pass-through entity, identify, to the extent practical, the total amount provided to subrecipients from each federal program. This information may be presented on the face of the schedule or included in the notes to the schedule. (Chapter 12, "Audit Considerations of Federal Pass-Through Awards (Circular A-133)," of this guide further discusses the audit considerations of federal pass-through awards.)

- include, in either the schedule or a note to the schedule, the value of federal awards expended in the form of noncash assistance, the amount of insurance in effect during the year, and loans or loan guarantees outstanding at year end (see paragraph 7.30 and table 7-2).

Note that the auditor's opinion on the schedule of expenditures of federal awards is significantly impacted when required information is not included in the schedule. See paragraph 7.08 for more information. The appendix (paragraph 7.36) of this chapter presents example schedules of expenditures of federal awards.

Emphasis Point

The auditee should clearly disclose the basis of accounting and the significant accounting policies used in preparing the schedule of expenditures of federal awards in the notes to the schedule.

Providing Additional Information

7.21 Although not required, the auditee may choose to provide other information (in addition to the foregoing requirements) that is requested by federal awarding agencies and pass-through entities to make the schedule of expenditures of federal awards easier to use. For example, when a federal program has multiple award years, the auditee may choose to list the amount of federal awards expended for each award year separately.

Schedule May Not Agree With Other Federal Award Reporting

7.22 The information included in the schedule of expenditures of federal awards may not fully agree with other federal award reports that the auditee submits directly to federal granting agencies. AU-C section 725 requires the information in the schedule of expenditures of federal awards to relate to the same period as the financial statements. However, federal award reports submitted directly to a granting agency (*a*) may be prepared for a different fiscal period and, (*b*) may include cumulative (from prior years) data rather than data for the current year only.

Inclusion of Nonfederal Awards

7.23 Circular A-133 does not require nonfederal awards (for example, state awards) to be presented in the schedule of expenditures of federal awards. However, to meet state or other requirements, auditees may decide to include such awards in the schedule. See paragraph 7.24 for information on modifications to the schedule of expenditures of federal awards when including nonfederal awards in that schedule.

Considerations Relating to State Awards

7.24 Several state governments have auditing and reporting requirements for state awards that are similar to those for federal awards under Circular A-133. In these states, auditors may be engaged to test and report on compliance with the state compliance requirements as provided in the state award(s) and under applicable state laws or regulation. Some states require a separate compliance audit with a separate schedule of expenditures of state awards. However, others accept a combined schedule of federal and state awards along with additional testing of the state expenditures. If state (or other nonfederal) awards are included in the schedule of expenditures of federal awards they should be segregated and clearly designated as nonfederal. The title of the schedule should also be modified to indicate that nonfederal awards are included, and the reference to the schedule in the auditor's reporting on the schedule should reference the correct title.

CFDA Number Not Available

7.25 The auditee may be unable to obtain the CFDA number, which is sometimes the case for new federal programs and R&D programs. In addition, cost-type contracts normally will not have a CFDA number. When the CFDA number is not available, the auditee has alternatives for presenting that information. The auditee could indicate that the CFDA number is not available and include, if available, another identifying number, such as a contract or grant number. The auditee also could apply the guidance presented in the Federal Audit Clearinghouse's data collection form instructions for when a federal program does not have a CFDA number. Specifically, if the program has a contract or grant number, the number shown as the CFDA number could be the awarding agency's 2-digit prefix listed for the agency in an appendix to the form's instructions (or 99 if the agency is not listed) followed by the contract or grant number. If the program does not have a contract or grant number, the number shown as the CFDA number could be the awarding agency's 2-digit prefix (or 99) followed by "UNKNOWN."

Pass-Through Awards

Treatment of Pass-Through Awards

7.26 Circular A-133 defines a *subrecipient* as an entity that expends federal awards that are received from a pass-through entity to carry out a federal program. State or local government redistributions of federal awards to subrecipients, known as "pass-through awards," should be treated by the subrecipient as though they were received directly from the federal government. That is, pass-through awards should be included in the scope of the single audit on the same basis as that of federal awards that are received directly. Chapter 12 of this guide further discusses the audit considerations of federal pass-through awards. As noted in paragraph 7.20, in addition to the other general presentation requirements, Circular A-133 states that the schedule of expenditures of federal awards should include the name of the pass-through entity and the identifying number assigned by the pass-through entity for federal awards received as a subrecipient.

Commingled Assistance

7.27 The individual sources (that is, federal, state, and local) of federal awards may not be separately identifiable because of commingled assistance from different levels of government. If the commingled portion cannot be separated to specifically identify the individual funding sources, the total amount should be included in the schedule of expenditures of federal awards, with a note to the schedule describing the commingled nature of the funds.

Noncash Awards

Treatment of Noncash Awards

7.28 Most federal awards are in the form of cash awards. However, a number of federal programs do not involve cash transactions. These programs may include loans and loan guarantees (including interest subsidies), insurance, endowments, free rent, food stamps, food commodities, and donated property (including donated surplus property). Circular A-133 states that the value of federal awards expended in the form of noncash assistance should be reported either on the face of the schedule of expenditures of federal awards or disclosed in the notes to the schedule. However, Circular A-133 also states that although it is not required, it is preferable to present this information in the schedule rather than in the notes to the schedule. Paragraph 7.19, table 7-1, and chapter 5 of this guide discuss the determination of when awards, including noncash awards, are considered to be expended.

Determining the Value of the Noncash Awards Expended

7.29 Table 7-2 shows the bases generally used to determine the value of noncash awards expended. (See section 205 of Circular A-133 for additional details.)

Table 7-2
Determining the Value of Noncash Awards Expended

Types of Noncash Awards	Basis Used to Determine the Value of Noncash Awards Expended
Loans and loan guarantees (loans), including interest subsidies	Value equals amount of new loans made or received during the fiscal year plus the balance of loans from previous years for which the federal government imposes continuing compliance requirements (see paragraph 7.30), plus any interest subsidy, cash, or administrative cost allowance received. The proceeds of loans that were received and expended in prior years are not considered federal awards expended when the laws, regulations, and the provisions of contracts or grant agreements pertaining to such loans impose no continuing compliance requirements other than to repay the loans.
Loans at institutions of higher education	Value the same as for loans and loan guarantees (loans), including interest subsidies, mentioned previously, except that when loans are made to students but the institution of higher education does not make the loans, the value equals only the amount of new loans made during the year. The balance of loans for previous years is not considered federal awards expended because the lender accounts for the prior balances.
Insurance	Value equals the fair value of the insurance contract at the time of receipt, or the assessed value provided by the federal agency.
Endowments	Value equals the cumulative balances of federally restricted amounts.
Free rent	Value equals the fair value at the time of receipt, or the assessed value provided by the federal agency. Free rent is not considered an award expended unless it is received as part of an award to carry out a federal program.
Food stamps, food commodities, and donated property (including donated surplus property)	Value equals the fair value at the time of receipt, or the assessed value provided by the federal agency.

Loan and Loan Guarantee Continuing Compliance Requirements

7.30 As noted previously, in determining the value of total noncash awards expended for loans and loan guarantees, auditees should include the balances of loans from previous years in the schedule of expenditures of federal awards if the federal government imposes continuing compliance requirements.[12] Circular A-133 does not specifically define the term *continuing compliance requirements*, although some federal agencies indicate that their loans have continuing compliance requirements, such as the U.S. Department of Housing and Urban Development (HUD) with regard to their insured, direct, and HUD-held loans. Auditors may use professional judgment in evaluating the auditee's determination of whether continuing compliance requirements are significant enough to require inclusion of prior-year loan or loan guarantee balances. For example, if in a prior year an auditee expended the proceeds of a federal loan to construct a building, and the current-year activity consists only of loan repayments and a requirement by the federal lender for the auditee to submit a report that details only loan payment information, it may not be necessary to include the prior year's loan balance in determining the total amount of loans expended. However, if the federal lender requires the auditee to ensure on an ongoing basis that a certain percentage of the building is rented to low-income residents, it would likely be necessary to include the prior year's loan balance in determining the total amount of loans expended. Communication with the federal agency's Office of Inspector General may be appropriate if there is any question about an auditee's determination of whether continuing compliance requirements are significant enough to require inclusion of the balances of prior loans or loan guarantees.

Documentation Requirements

7.31 The audit procedures performed on the schedule of expenditures of federal awards supports the basis for the auditor's major program determination, as well as the auditor's in-relation-to opinion on the schedule. The audit work performed on the schedule to support these engagement objectives should be documented in accordance with AU-C section 230, *Audit Documentation* (AICPA, *Professional Standards*). Documenting the audit work performed on the schedule in an audit plan is an effective way to record the audit procedures performed, relevant audit evidence obtained, conclusions reached, and significant findings relating to the schedule, if any.

Issuing an Opinion on the Schedule of Expenditures of Federal Awards Under AU-C Section 805 When the Auditor Is Engaged to Perform Only the Compliance Audit Under Circular A-133

7.32 One of the required conditions in AU-C section 725 for an auditor to provide an in-relation-to opinion on supplementary information is that the financial statements were audited by the auditor. When this is not the case, the auditor is precluded from issuing an in-relation-to opinion on the supplementary information. See paragraph 7.08 and chapter 13 for additional information.

---

[12] See paragraph 7.28 for a discussion of the presentation options for noncash assistance.

7.33 Sometimes, an auditor is engaged to perform only the compliance audit required under Circular A-133 and not the financial statement audit.[13] When this occurs, the auditor is precluded from issuing an in-relation-to opinion on the schedule of expenditures of federal awards. Instead, to meet the reporting requirements of Circular A-133, the auditee may consider engaging the auditor to issue an opinion on the schedule of expenditures of federal awards under AU-C section 805, *Special Considerations—Audits of Single Financial Statements and Specific Elements, Accounts, or Items of a Financial Statement* (AICPA, *Professional Standards*).[14] See the appendix to chapter 13 for an illustration of reporting on the schedule of expenditures of federal awards under AU-C section 805.

7.34 When performing the audit of the schedule of expenditures of federal awards under AU-C section 805, the objective of the auditor is to obtain sufficient appropriate audit evidence to enable the auditor to express an opinion on the schedule. Such an audit is designed to provide the auditor with reasonable assurance that the schedule is not misstated by an amount that would be material to the information contained in the schedule.

Transition Considerations Related to the Uniform Guidance

7.35 The administrative requirements and cost principles included in the Uniform Guidance are required to be implemented by nonfederal entities beginning December 26, 2014, for all new federal awards and funding increments (additional funding to existing federal awards) with modified award terms and conditions that are awarded on or after that date. See the "Transition Considerations Related to the Uniform Guidance" section in chapter 6, "Planning Considerations of Circular A-133," of this guide for more information on the effective date and funding increments. As a result, in any Circular A-133 compliance audit covering periods including December 26, 2014, and later, a nonfederal entity may present both federal awards subject to the pre-Uniform Guidance requirements, as well as other federal awards subject to the Uniform Guidance requirements, in the schedule of expenditures of federal awards. When this occurs, the illustrative note to the schedule of expenditures of federal awards related to significant accounting policies may be revised to also reflect that expenditures subject to the Uniform Guidance requirements are recognized following the cost principles contained in the Uniform Guidance. See footnote 7 in the appendix of this chapter (paragraph 7.36) for more information.

---

[13] An auditee may use a separate auditor to perform the compliance audit under Circular A-133 for various reasons. For example, a common reason is for an auditee to make positive efforts to use small business, minority-owned firms, and women's business enterprises in conjunction with the Circular A-133 audit.

[14] An auditee may also consider engaging the auditor to examine the schedule of expenditures of federal awards or an assertion related to the schedule of expenditures of federal awards in accordance with AT section 101, *Attest Engagements* (AICPA, *Professional Standards*).

7.36

Appendix—Illustrative Schedules of Expenditures of Federal Awards

Example Entity
Schedule of Expenditures of Federal Awards[1]
For the Year Ended June 30, 20X1

Federal Grantor / Pass-Through Grantor / Program or Cluster Title	Federal CFDA Number[2]	Pass-Through Entity Identifying Number[3]	Federal Expenditures[4]
Department of Agriculture Direct Programs			
Summer Food Service Program for Children—Commodities	10.559		$ 46,000
Total Department of Agriculture Direct Programs			$ 46,000
Department of Housing and Urban Development Direct Programs			
Community Development Block Grant—Entitlement Grants (note 3)	14.218		$1,235,632
Section 8 Housing Choice Vouchers	14.871		800,534
Total Department of Housing and Urban Development Direct Programs			$2,036,166
Department of Education Direct Programs			
Impact Aid	84.041		$ 372,555
Arts in Education	84.351		28,655
Subtotal Department of Education Direct Programs			$ 401,210
Department of Education Pass-Through Programs From:			
State Department of Education—Title I Grants to Local Educational Agencies	84.010	23-8345-7612	$1,239,398
Total Department of Education			$1,640,608
Total Expenditures of Federal Awards			$3,722,774

The accompanying notes are an integral part of this schedule.

---

[1] To meet state or other requirements, auditees may decide to include certain nonfederal awards (for example, state awards) in this schedule. If such nonfederal awards are presented, they should be segregated and clearly designated as nonfederal. The title of the schedule also should be modified to indicate that nonfederal awards are included. See paragraphs 7.23–.24.

[2] When the Catalog of Federal Domestic Assistance number is not available, the auditee has alternatives for presenting that information. See paragraph 7.25.

[3] When awards are received as a subrecipient, the schedule should include the identifying number assigned by the pass-through entity.

[4] Office of Management and Budget Circular A-133, *Audits of States, Local Governments, and Non-Profit Organizations* (Circular A-133), states that the value of federal awards expended in the form of noncash assistance, the amount of insurance in effect during the year, and loans or loan guarantees outstanding at year end should be included in either the schedule or a note to the schedule. Although it is not required, Circular A-133 states that it is preferable to present this information in the schedule (versus the notes to the schedule). If the auditee presents noncash assistance in the notes to the schedule, such amounts are still required to be included in Part III of the data collection form.

Schedule of Expenditures of Federal Awards (Circular A-133)

Example Entity
Notes to the Schedule of Expenditures of Federal Awards
For the Year Ended June 30, 20X1

Note 1. Basis of Presentation[5]

The accompanying schedule of expenditures of federal awards (the "Schedule") includes the federal grant activity of Example Entity under programs of the federal government for the year ended June 30, 20X1. The information in this Schedule is presented in accordance with the requirements of the Office of Management and Budget (OMB) Circular A-133, *Audits of States, Local Governments, and Non-Profit Organizations*. Because the Schedule presents only a selected portion of the operations of Example Entity, it is not intended to and does not present the financial position, changes in net assets or cash flows of Example Entity.

Note 2. Summary of Significant Accounting Policies[6]

Expenditures reported on the Schedule are reported on the (identify basis of accounting) basis of accounting. Such expenditures are recognized following the cost principles contained in OMB Circular A-122, *Cost Principles for Non-profit Organizations*,[7] wherein certain types of expenditures are not allowable or are limited as to reimbursement. Negative amounts shown on the Schedule represent adjustments or credits made in the normal course of business to amounts reported as expenditures in prior years. Pass-through entity identifying numbers are presented where available.

Note 3. Subrecipients[8]

Of the federal expenditures presented in the Schedule, Example Entity provided federal awards to subrecipients as follows:

CFDA Number	Program Name	Amount Provided to Subrecipients
14.218	Community Development Block Grant—Entitlement Grants	$423,965

---

[5] This note is included to meet the Circular A-133 requirement that the schedule include notes that describe the significant accounting policies used in preparing the schedule.

[6] See footnote 5.

[7] As noted in paragraph 7.35, there may be situations when federal expenditures presented in the schedule of expenditures of federal awards also include expenditures subject to the Uniform Guidance requirements. In this situation, the second sentence of this illustrative note may be modified as follows:
> Such expenditures are recognized following, as applicable, either the cost principles in OMB Circular A-122, *Cost Principles for Non-Profit Organizations*, or the cost principles contained in Title 2 U.S. *Code of Federal Regulations* Part 200, *Uniform Administrative Requirements, Cost Principles, and Audit Requirements for Federal Awards*, wherein certain types of expenditures are not allowable or are limited as to reimbursement.

[8] Circular A-133 states that the schedule of expenditures of federal awards should include, to the extent practical, an identification of the total amount provided to subrecipients from each federal program. Although this example includes the required subrecipient information in the notes to the schedule, the information may be included on the face of the schedule as a separate column or section, if the auditee prefers.

Example Entity University
Schedule of Expenditures of Federal Awards[9]
For the Year Ended June 30, 20X1

Federal Grantor/Pass-Through Grantor/Program or Cluster Title	Federal CFDA Number[10]	Pass-Through Entity Identifying Number[11]	Federal Expenditures[12,13]
Student Financial Assistance—Cluster			
Department of Education Direct Programs[14]			
Federal Pell Grant Program	84.063		$ 4,757,853
Federal Direct Student Loans	84.268		2,143,587
Federal Supplemental Educational Opportunity Grants	84.007		974,873
Federal Work-Study Program	84.033		575,417
Teacher Education Assistance for College and Higher Education Grants (TEACH)	84.379		230,584
Postsecondary Education Scholarships for Veteran's Dependents	84.408		239,438
Federal Perkins Loan Program (note 3)	84.038		1,548,343
Total Department of Education Direct Programs			$10,470,095
Department of Health and Human Services Direct Programs			
Nursing Student Loans (note 3)	93.364		$ 823,582
Health Professions Student Loans (note 3)	93.342		689,021
Total Department of Health and Human Services Direct Programs			$1,512,603
Total Student Financial Assistance Cluster			$11,982,698

---

[9] See footnote 1.

[10] See footnote 2.

[11] See footnote 3.

[12] See footnote 4.

[13] Material construction projects funded by a federal program are often capitalized in the financial statements of an auditee. However, for purposes of the schedule of expenditures of federal awards they would be considered an expenditure. Such expenditures may be reported either on the face of the schedule of expenditures of federal awards or disclosed in the notes to the schedule. Accordingly, these amounts should be reported in Part III of the data collection form.

[14] Institutions of higher education often participate in certain loan and loan guarantee programs (for example, the Federal Family Education Loan Program and the Federal Direct Loan Program), as shown here. Circular A-133 requires that when loans are made to students but the institution of higher education does not make the loans, the value of the loans made during the year is considered federal awards expended. Those loans and loan guarantees should be reported either on the face of the schedule or disclosed in the notes to the schedule, as discussed in paragraph 7.30. Accordingly, these amounts should be reported in part III of the data collection form.

Schedule of Expenditures of Federal Awards (Circular A-133)

Federal Grantor/Pass-Through Grantor/Program or Cluster Title	Federal CFDA Number	Pass-Through Entity Identifying Number	Federal Expenditures
Research and Development—Cluster (note 4)[15]			
Department of Defense Direct Programs			
Department of Army			
Collaborative Research and Development	12.114		$87,403
Military Medical Research and Development	12.420		73,107
Subtotal Department of Defense Direct Programs			$160,510
Department of Defense Pass-Through Programs From:			
XYZ Labs—Effects of Ice on Radar Images	12.UNKNOWN	4532	$11,987
Total Department of Defense			$172,497
National Science Foundation Direct Programs			
Geosciences	47.050		$ 358.245
Biological Sciences	47.074		96,543
Subtotal National Science Foundation Direct Programs			$ 454,788
National Science Foundation Pass-Through Programs From:			
ABC University—Atmospheric Effects of Volcano Eruptions	47.ABC-852	ABC-852	25,987
Total National Science Foundation			$ 480,775
Department of Health and Human Services:			
National Institutes of Health Direct Programs			
Mental Health Research Grants	93.242		$110,499
Drug Abuse and Addiction Research Programs	93.279		89,075
National Institutes of Health Pass-Through Programs From:			
ABC Hospital—Heart Research	93.UNKNOWN	5489-5	230,433
Centers for Disease Control and Prevention Direct Programs			
Chronic Diseases: Research, Control, and Prevention	93.068		112,446
Total Department of Health and Human Services			$542,453

---

[15] For research and development, Circular A-133 states that total federal awards expended should be shown either by individual award or by federal agency and major subdivision within the federal agency. This example illustrates the individual award option.

Federal Grantor / Pass-Through Grantor / Program or Cluster Title	Federal CFDA Number	Pass-Through Entity Identifying Number	Federal Expenditures
Total Research and Development Cluster			$1,195,725
Trio Cluster			
Department of Education Direct Programs			
TRIO—Talent Search	84.044		$308,465
TRIO—Upward Bound	84.047		78,654
Total TRIO Cluster			$387,119
Other Programs			
Department of State Direct Programs			
Academic Exchange Programs—Scholars (note 4)	19.401		$17,823
Total Department of State Direct Programs			$17,823
Department of Education Direct Programs			
Safe and Drug-Free Schools and Communities—National Programs	84.184		$59,723
Undergraduate International Studies and Foreign Language Programs	84.016		34,688
Subtotal Department of Education Direct Programs			$94,411
Department of Education Pass-Through Programs From:			
State Department of Education—Career and Technical Education—Basic Grants to States	84.048	874-90-5473	$176,885
State Department of Education—Funds for the Improvement of Education	84.215	25-8594-2167	3,115
Subtotal Department of Education Pass-Through Programs			$180,000
Total Department of Education			$274,411
Total Expenditures of Federal Awards			$13,857,776

The accompanying notes are an integral part of this schedule.

Example Entity University
Notes to the Schedule of Expenditures of Federal Awards
For the Year Ended June 30, 20X1

Note 1. Basis of Presentation[16]

The accompanying schedule of expenditures of federal awards (the "Schedule") includes the federal grant activity of Example Entity University under programs of the federal government for the year ended June 30, 20X1. The information in this Schedule is presented in accordance with the requirements of the Office of Management and Budget (OMB) Circular A-133, *Audits of States, Local Governments, and Non-Profit Organizations*. Because the Schedule presents only a selected portion of the operations of Example Entity University, it is not intended to and does not present the financial position, changes in net assets or cash flows of Example Entity University.

Note 2. Summary of Significant Accounting Policies[17]

Expenditures reported on the Schedule are reported on the (identify basis of accounting) basis of accounting. Such expenditures are recognized following the cost principles contained in OMB Circular A-21, *Cost Principles for Education Institutions*,[18] wherein certain types of expenditures are not allowable or are limited as to reimbursement. Negative amounts shown on the Schedule represent adjustments or credits made in the normal course of business to amounts reported as expenditures in prior years. Pass-through entity identifying numbers are presented where available.

Note 3. Federal Student Loan Programs[19]

The federal student loan programs listed subsequently are administered directly by Example Entity University and balances and transactions relating to these programs are included in Example Entity University's basic financial statements. Loans made during the year are included in the federal expenditures presented in the Schedule. The balance of loans outstanding at June 30, 20X1 consists of:

CFDA Number	Program Name	Outstanding Balance at June 30, 20X1
84.038	Federal Perkins Loan	$6,341,180
93.364	Nursing Student Loans	$3,815,635
93.342	Health Professions Student Loans	$4,353,248

---

[16] See footnote 5.
[17] See footnote 6.
[18] See footnote 7.

[19] This note is intended to meet the Circular A-133 requirement that loans or loan guarantees outstanding at year end be included in the schedule. The basis used to determine loans or loan guarantees expended is the amount of new loans made or received during the fiscal year plus the balance of loans from previous years for which the federal government imposes continuing compliance requirements, plus any interest subsidy, cash, or administrative cost allowance received. See table 7-2 and paragraph 7.30 for more discussion of loans and loan guarantees.

Note 4. Subrecipients[20]

Of the federal expenditures presented in the Schedule, Example Entity University provided federal awards to subrecipients as follows:

CFDA Number	Program Name	Amounts Provided to Subrecipients
Various	Research & Development Cluster Academic Exchange Programs—Scholars	$985,465
19.401	Educational Exchange University Lecturers and Research Scholars	$5,104

---

[20] See footnote 8.

Chapter 8

Determination of Major Programs (Circular A-133)

> **© Update 8-1: Audits of Federal Awards**
>
> This chapter, and the remaining chapters of part II, *Circular A-133 Audits*, of this guide, should be used for performing a compliance audit of federal awards under Office of Management and Budget (OMB) Circular A-133, *Audits of States, Local Governments, and Non-Profit Organizations* (Circular A-133). Part III, *Uniform Guidance Audits*, of this guide should be used when performing a compliance audit under Title 2 U.S. *Code of Federal Regulations* Part 200, *Uniform Administrative Requirements, Cost Principles, and Audit Requirements for Federal Awards* (Uniform Guidance). See the transitional guidance sections at the end of each chapter that highlight important matters for consideration.[1] Refer to the preface for additional information.
>
> **Important Uniform Guidance Effective Date Information**
>
> In December 2013, the OMB issued the Uniform Guidance, which is effective for nonfederal entities for all federal awards and certain funding increments provided on or after December 26, 2014. The requirements in Subpart F, "Audit Requirements," are effective for audits of fiscal years beginning on or after December 26, 2014, with no early implementation permitted. Therefore, auditees subject to a single audit with December 25, 2015, and later year ends (for example, December 31, 2015) will be required to undergo the audit under Subpart F of the Uniform Guidance. Note that audits of fiscal years ending prior to the effective date of the Uniform Guidance audit requirements are subject to an audit under Circular A-133.

Introduction [2,3]

8.01 OMB Circular A-133 states that the auditee should identify in its accounts all federal awards received and expended and the federal programs

---

[1] See the information found at the end of certain chapters in part II, *Circular A-133 Audits*, of this guide for transition considerations when performing an audit under Office of Management and Budget (OMB) Circular A-133, *Audits of States, Local Governments, and Non-Profit Organizations* (Circular A-133), as it relates to the applicability of certain aspects of Title 2 U.S. *Code of Federal Regulations* Part 200, *Uniform Administrative Requirements, Cost Principles, and Audit Requirements for Federal Awards* (Uniform Guidance), to audits performed under Circular A-133. Transition considerations related to an audit performed under the Uniform Guidance can be found at the end of chapters in part III, *Uniform Guidance Audits*, of this guide in sections titled "Transition Considerations Related to the Uniform Guidance."

[2] *Government Auditing Standards* incorporates by reference AICPA Statements on Auditing Standards. Therefore, auditors performing financial statement audits and OMB Circular A-133 compliance audits in accordance with *Government Auditing Standards* should comply with generally accepted auditing standards (GAAS), the requirements found in chapters 1–3 of *Government Auditing Standards*, and the additional standards and related requirements for financial audits found in chapter 4, "Standards for Financial Audits," of *Government Auditing Standards*.

[3] As noted in AU-C section 935, *Compliance Audits* (AICPA, *Professional Standards*), the auditor should determine whether audit requirements are specified in a governmental audit requirement that are supplementary to GAAS and *Government Auditing Standards* and perform procedures to address those requirements, if any. In providing examples of supplementary audit requirements, AU-C section 935 identifies procedures performed to identify major programs in a Circular A-133 audit.

under which they were received. The auditee should also prepare a schedule of expenditures of federal awards for the period covered by its financial statements. (Chapter 7, "Schedule of Expenditures of Federal Awards (Circular A-133)," of this guide discusses the requirements related to that schedule.) However, Circular A-133 places the responsibility for identifying major programs on the auditor, and it provides the criteria to be used in applying a risk-based approach to determining major programs. The risk-based approach is designed to focus the Circular A-133 compliance audit on higher-risk programs. Paragraph 8.24 discusses when the auditor can deviate from the use of risk criteria.

8.02 The auditor's determination of the programs to be audited is based on an evaluation of the risks of noncompliance occurring that could be material to an individual major federal program. In evaluating such risks, the auditor considers, among other things, the current and prior audit experience with the auditee, the oversight exercised by federal agencies and pass-through entities, and the inherent risk of noncompliance of the federal programs. The auditor should use professional judgment and the guidance in Sections 520, 525, and 530 of Circular A-133 in the risk assessment process. In addition, the auditor may find it helpful to discuss the nature of federal programs with the management of the auditee and the federal or state agency that provided the funds to the auditee. (See chapter 6, "Planning Considerations of Circular A-133," of this guide for a related discussion.)

Applying the Risk-Based Approach

8.03 The guidance on the risk-based approach is organized here as provided in Circular A-133 and consists of the steps in the following listing. Exhibit 8-1 is a flowchart illustrating the application of the risk-based approach for determining major programs:

- Step 1—Determination of type A and type B programs (paragraphs 8.04–.10)
- Step 2—Identification of low-risk type A programs (paragraphs 8.11–.14)
- Step 3—Identification of high-risk type B programs (paragraphs 8.15–.17)
- Step 4—Determination of programs to be audited as major (paragraphs 8.18–.20)

Exhibit 8-1

Flowchart Illustration of Applying the Risk-Based Approach for Determining Major Programs

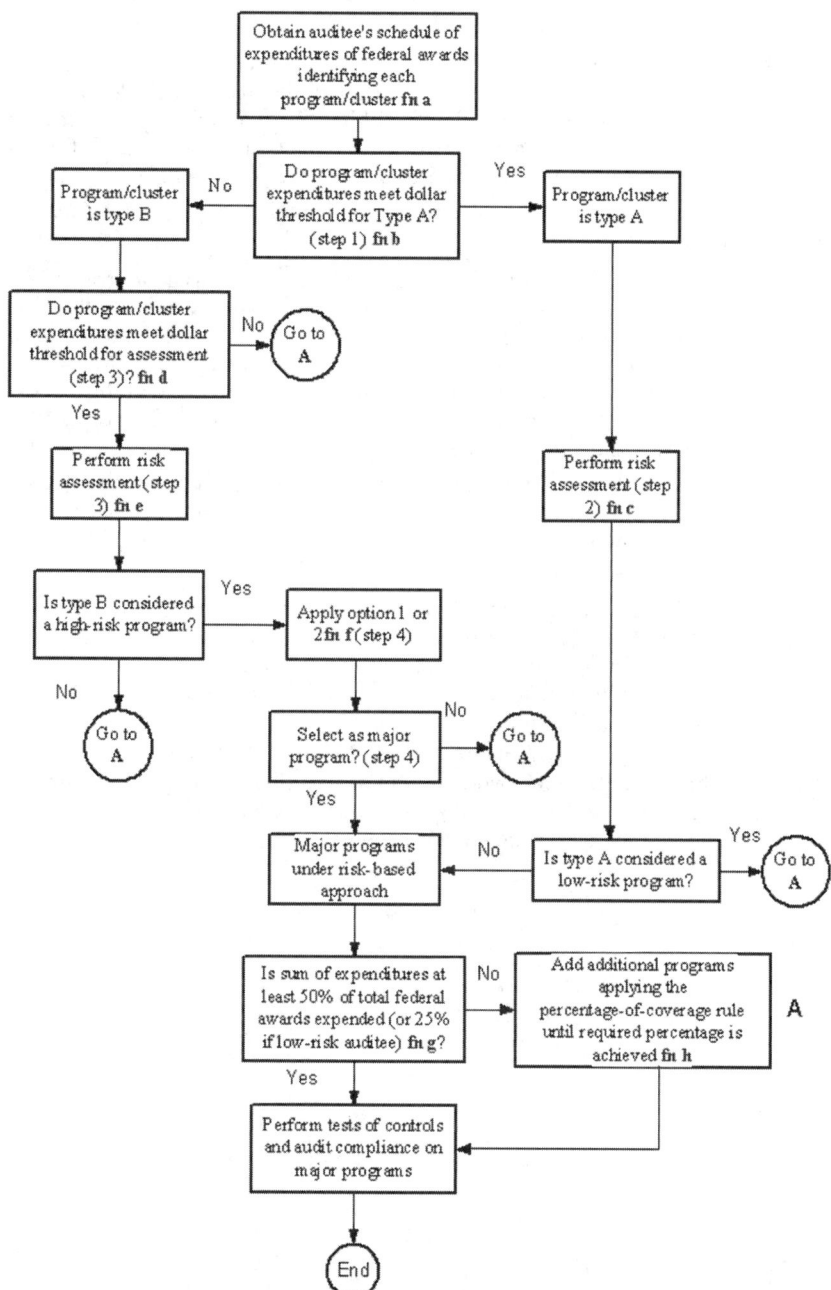

^a Chapter 5, "Overview of the Single Audit Act, Circular A-133, and the *Compliance Supplement*," of this guide defines federal programs, including clusters.

^b Paragraphs 8.04–.10 discuss step 1.

^c Paragraphs 8.11–.14 discuss step 2.

^d Paragraphs 8.15–.17 discuss step 3.

^e Before performing the risk assessment, this guide recommends the auditor consider whether option 1 or option 2 will be selected under step 4 because it will affect whether risk assessments need to be performed on all type B programs or only some type B programs. See paragraph 8.16.

^f The number of type B high-risk programs identified as major programs is either of the following:

- *Option 1.* One-half of the number of type B high-risk programs, unless this number exceeds the number of low-risk type A programs identified in step 2. In this case, the auditor would be required to audit as major the same number of high-risk type B programs as low-risk type A programs. Under this option, the auditor is expected to perform risk assessments on all type B programs that exceed the threshold for type B.
- *Option 2.* One high-risk type B program for each low-risk type A program. This option does not require the auditor to perform risk assessments on all type B programs. Paragraphs 8.18–.20 discuss step 4, including option 1 and option 2.

^g There may be instances when the auditee includes certain noncash assistance (such as loan guarantees or loans) in the notes to the schedule of expenditures of federal awards. (See chapter 7 of this guide.) Federal noncash assistance is included as part of total federal awards expended when performing this calculation.

^h The additional programs/clusters selected (marked "A" on the flowchart) to meet the percentage-of-coverage rule are audited as major programs in addition to type A and type B programs identified in steps 1–4. Paragraph 8.21 discusses the percentage-of-coverage rule.

> **Emphasis Point**
>
> The minimum $300,000 threshold noted in table 8-1, "Criteria for Identifying Type A Programs," is established by OMB and is used as part of the criteria for identifying type A programs. This threshold is different than the $500,000 threshold used in determining whether a single audit is required, which is sometimes a point of confusion for auditors. That is, Circular A-133 requires that a single audit be performed when nonfederal entities expend $500,000 or more of federal awards in a year, which is unrelated to the criteria to be used for identifying type A programs.

Step 1—Determination of Type A and Type B Programs

8.04 To determine which federal programs are to be audited as major, the auditor should obtain the schedule of expenditures of federal awards from the auditee and identify each federal program and cluster. The auditor should then identify federal programs as being either type A or type B as defined in Circular A-133. In general, type A programs are larger federal programs and type B programs are smaller federal programs. The schedule of expenditures of federal awards, prepared by the auditee, provides important program information and assists the auditor with the identification of type A and type B programs. Federal awards expended for purposes of determining type A and type B programs are the amount of cash and noncash awards, after all adjustments are made, in the *final* current-year schedule of expenditures of federal awards, including the notes thereto. An auditor who uses the prior-year schedule or preliminary current-year estimates to plan the audit should recalculate the threshold for type A programs based on the final amounts to ensure that federal awards are properly classified as type A or B. (For purposes of determining major programs, federal programs with the same Catalog of Federal Domestic Assistance [CFDA] number are considered as one program. In addition, a cluster of programs should be considered as one program. Chapter 5 of this guide discusses clusters of programs.)

Type A Program Criteria

8.05 The larger federal programs are labeled as type A. Table 8-1 presents the criteria that Circular A-133 establishes for identifying type A programs.

Table 8-1

Criteria for Identifying Type A Programs

When Total Federal Awards Expended[1] Are	A Type A Program Is Any Program With Federal Awards Expended That Exceed the Larger of—
More than or equal to $300,000 and less than or equal to $100 million	$300,000 or 3% (0.03) of federal awards expended
More than $100 million and less than or equal to $10 billion	$3 million or 0.3% (0.003) of federal awards expended
More than $10 billion	$30 million or 0.15% (0.0015) of federal awards expended

[1] Includes both cash and noncash awards.

Type B Program Criteria

8.06 Federal programs that do not meet the type A criteria are labeled type B programs.

Effect of Large Loans and Loan Guarantees on Identification of Type A Programs

8.07 Chapter 7 of this guide discusses the various types of noncash awards, including loans and loan guarantees, and when they are recognized as expended and how they are valued for purposes of the Circular A-133 audit. Circular A-133 states that when the auditor applies the dollar criteria shown in table 8-1 to identify type A programs, the inclusion of large loans and loan guarantees should not result in the exclusion of other federal programs as type A programs. (This requirement relates only to loans and loan guarantees and not to any other large noncash federal awards.) When a federal program providing loans or loan guarantees significantly affects the number or size of type A programs, Circular A-133 also states that the auditor should consider the federal program as a type A program and exclude its value in determining other type A programs.

8.08 The OMB has issued clarifying guidance related to this issue in the *OMB Compliance Supplement (Compliance Supplement)* as found in appendix 7, "Other OMB Circular A-133 Advisories," in the section "Safe Harbor for Treatment of a Large Loan and Loan Guarantee Programs in Type A Program Determination." This guidance states that in order to promote consistency of practice, auditors may consider the following as a "safe harbor" for treatment of large loan and loan guarantee programs in determining type A programs when planning audits:

    a. Each individual loan and loan guarantee program (the program consists of the loans and other program expenditures as described in .205[b] of Circular A-133) that does not exceed four times the largest nonloan program (a cluster of programs is treated as one program) is not considered to be large. The presumption is that only changes in the number or size of type A programs that result from the exclusion of individual loan and loan guarantee programs

Determination of Major Programs (Circular A-133)   **197**

      that are in excess of four times that of the largest nonloan program are significant.

    b. Auditors are only required to perform the recalculation of the type A threshold described in .520(b)(3) of Circular A-133 when the expenditures for a loan or loan guarantee program are more than four times that of the largest nonloan program (a cluster of programs is treated as one program).

    c. The recalculation is performed after removing the total of all large loan and loan guarantee programs.

The appendix 7 guidance referred to in the preceding items also includes a number of detailed examples to illustrate how it would be operationalized in various circumstances. These illustrations are useful to assist auditors in understanding how to address loan and loan guarantee programs in the major program determination process, especially when loan or loan guarantee programs are part of a cluster. Further, auditors with auditees that participate in the U.S. Department of Education's Student Financial Assistance (SFA) program may find the illustrations particularly helpful in understanding the complexities of how the safe harbor is applied when the SFA cluster is involved.

8.09 Paragraph 8.10 demonstrates the effect of loans and loan guarantees on major program determination using the example programs in table 8-2 and after applying the safe harbor provisions for large loan and loan guarantee programs found in the *Compliance Supplement*.

Table 8-2

Identification of Type A Programs and the Effect of Loans and Loan Guarantees[1]

Program / Federal Grantor	Federal Awards Expended
Cash program A—U.S. Department of Labor	$1,335,000
Cash program B—U.S. Department of Health and Human Services	8,000,000
Cash program C-1—U.S. Department of Education	175,000
Cash program C-2—U.S. Department of Education	280,000
Cash program D—U.S. Department of Housing and Urban Development (a pass-through grant from a local government)	310,000
Subtotal—Cash federal awards expended	$10,100,000
Commodities program E—U.S. Department of Agriculture (a pass-through grant from a state)	2,000,000
Subtotal—Cash and commodities federal awards expended (nonloan programs)	$12,100,000
Loan program F—U.S. Department of Housing and Urban Development	30,500,000[2]
Subtotal—federal awards expended— nonloan programs and a loan program that does not exceed the safe harbor threshold (see paragraph 8.10)	$42,600,000
Loan guarantee program G—U.S. Department of Agriculture	55,000,000[3]
Total federal awards expended	$97,600,000

---

[1] In accordance with Office of Management and Budget Circular A-133, *Audits of States, Local Governments, and Non-Profit Organizations*, loans and loan guarantees include new loans made during the year, plus prior-year loans for which the federal government imposes continuing compliance requirements, plus any interest subsidy, cash, or administrative cost allowance received. Chapter 7, "Schedule of Expenditures of Federal Awards (Circular A-133)," of this guide provides additional information.

[2] This loan guarantee program does not meet the criteria to be designated as a large loan or loan guarantee program because it does not exceed the safe harbor threshold of $32,000,000 [4 times the amount of the largest nonloan program (4 × $8,000,000 = $32,000,000)].

[3] This loan guarantee program meets the criteria to be designated as a large loan or loan guarantee program because it exceeds the safe harbor threshold of $32,000,000 [4 times the amount of the largest nonloan program (4 × $8,000,000 = $32,000,000)].

8.10 Table 8-2 shows that the auditee has $97,600,000 in total federal awards expended, including both loan and nonloan programs. However, using the safe harbor guidance in appendix 7 of the *Compliance Supplement*, before calculating the type A threshold for major program determination purposes there is one large loan guarantee program that needs to be excluded from the base of $97,600,000, that is, the $55,000,000 loan guarantee program G (see note 3 at table 8-2). After removing loan guarantee program G, the revised base becomes $42,600,000 ($97,600,000–$55,000,000), which results in a type A threshold of $1,278,000 (3 percent of $42,600,000). Therefore, in addition to the loan guarantee program G, programs A, B, E, and F would also be type A programs.

Step 2—Identification of Low-Risk Type A Programs

8.11 After completing step 1, the auditor should perform a risk assessment of each type A program to identify those that are low risk. Circular A-133 includes certain conditions that, when met, indicate that a type A program may be low risk.

General Conditions for Low-Risk Type A Programs

8.12 Type A programs generally may be considered low risk if both of the following conditions are met: (*a*) the program has been audited as a major program in at least one of the two most recent audit periods (in the most recent audit period in the case of a biennial audit) and (*b*) in the most recent audit period, the program had no audit findings. (Chapter 13, "Auditor Reporting Requirements and Other Communication Considerations in a Single Audit (Circular A-133)," of this guide discusses the situations that Circular A-133 requires the auditor to report as audit findings.) It is important for auditors to note that every type A program that was not audited in one of the two prior years should be audited as a major program. If a type A program is new to an entity in the current year (for example, because the entity did not previously participate in the program or because it is a new federal program, or because a new program was added to an other cluster as defined in Part 5 of the *Compliance Supplement*), it should be audited as a major program in the current year because it was not audited in one of the prior two years. If a program that previously was a type B program is a type A program in the current year (for example, because the funding level increased), and the program was not audited as a major program in one of the two prior years, it should be audited as a major program in the current year. Auditor judgment, as discussed in paragraph 8.13, cannot override the requirement that major programs should include every type A program that (*a*) was not audited in one of the two prior years or (*b*) had audit findings other than those indicated in paragraph 8.13.

Auditor Judgment in Determination of Low-Risk Type A Programs

8.13 Circular A-133 permits the auditor to conclude, based on professional judgment, that a type A program is low risk even though in the prior audit period (*a*) it may have had known or likely questioned costs greater than $10,000 for a type of compliance requirement, (*b*) known fraud has been identified, or (*c*) the summary schedule of prior audit findings materially misrepresents the status of a prior audit finding. (The auditor cannot conclude, based on professional judgment, that a type A program is low risk if there were other types of audit findings, such as significant deficiencies or material weaknesses in internal control over compliance or material noncompliance.) For example, consider a situation in which the funds expended under a federal program in the prior year totaled $10 million, there were known questioned costs of $11,000 that related to one isolated instance, and there were no additional likely questioned costs. In this example, the auditor, based on professional judgment, could decide that the program is low risk in the current year. In making the final determination of whether a type A program is low risk, the auditor should also consider the risk criteria in paragraphs 8.28–.38, the results of audit followup, and whether any changes in the personnel or systems affecting a type A program have significantly increased its risk. Based on all of this information, the auditor would apply professional judgment in determining whether a type A program is low risk.

Type A Program Not Considered Low Risk at Request of Federal Awarding Agency

8.14 Section 520(c)(2) of Circular A-133 permits a federal awarding agency to request that a type A program for certain recipients not be considered low risk so that it would be audited as a major program. For example, it may be necessary for a large type A program to be audited as major each year for particular recipients to allow the federal agency to comply with the Government Management Reform Act of 1994. In this instance, Circular A-133 requires the federal awarding agency to obtain approval from the OMB. (The OMB has not yet made any such approvals.) Furthermore, the federal awarding agency should notify the recipient and, if known, the auditor at least 180 days before the end of the fiscal year end to be audited. (Paragraph 8.37 discusses the federal agency option to identify federal programs as higher risk in the *Compliance Supplement*.)

Step 3—Identification of High-Risk Type B Programs

8.15 After completing steps 1–2, the auditor should identify type B programs that are high risk, using professional judgment and the risk criteria discussed in paragraphs 8.28–.38. Except for known significant deficiencies or material weaknesses in internal control over compliance or instances of noncompliance, a single risk criterion would, in general, seldom cause a type B program to be considered high risk.

8.16 Before beginning step 3, this guide recommends the auditor

- consider whether there are low-risk type A programs. When there are no type A programs identified as low risk (either because there are no type A programs or because none of the type A programs are low risk), the auditor is not required to perform step 3. If there are no type A programs, the auditor would audit as major enough type B programs to meet the percentage-of-coverage rule (see paragraph 8.21). When there are type A programs, but none are low risk, the auditor would audit as major all type A programs plus any additional type B programs needed to meet the percentage-of-coverage rule. In either case, any programs requested to be audited by a federal agency or pass-through entity should be audited as a major program and would be included in determining whether the percentage-of-coverage rule has been met (see paragraph 8.25).

- consider whether option 1 or option 2 will be used in step 4. (Paragraphs 8.19–.20 describe each option.) The auditor's decision of which option to choose will likely be based on audit efficiency and will affect how many type B programs are subject to risk assessment. This guide recommends that the auditor consider the following discussion before deciding whether to use option 1 or option 2:

    — Under option 1, the auditor should perform a risk assessment on all type B programs (excluding small type B programs as discussed in paragraph 8.17). In comparison with option 2, option 1 will likely require the auditor to perform more type B program risk assessments, but may also result in the auditor having to audit fewer major programs. For example, assume that an auditee has 4 low-risk type A programs and 10 type B programs that exceed the amount specified in table 8-3. Also assume that the auditor chooses option 1. In this scenario, the auditor would be required to perform a risk assessment on all type B programs. If the auditor finds that only four type B programs are high risk, the auditor would be required to audit only two of the four high-risk type B programs as major (one-half of the number of high-risk type B programs).

    — Under option 2, the auditor should identify high-risk type B programs up to the number of low-risk type A programs. In comparison with option 1, option 2 will likely require the auditor to perform fewer type B risk assessments, but may also result in the auditor having to audit more major programs. For example, assume that an auditee has 4 low-risk type A programs and 10 type B programs that exceed the amount specified in table 8-3. Assume also that the first 4 type B programs subject to risk assessment are determined by the auditor to be high risk. In this scenario, the auditor may choose option 2, identify the 4 high-risk type B programs as major, and not perform risk assessments on the remaining 6 type B programs. Using the same example but assuming that the auditee only has 1 low-risk type A program (instead of four), the auditor would be required to audit one type B program as major under either option 1 or 2. In this scenario, option 2 would likely be the most efficient choice for the auditor because the auditor would only need to perform type B program risk assessments until one high-risk type B program was identified (under option 1 the auditor would be required to perform a risk assessment on all type B programs).

Criteria for Performing Risk Assessments on Type B Programs

8.17 An auditor is not expected to perform risk assessments on relatively small federal programs. Therefore, Circular A-133 only requires the auditor to perform risk assessments on type B programs that exceed the larger of the criteria shown in table 8-3.

Table 8-3
Criteria for Performing Risk Assessments on Type B Programs

When Total Federal Awards Expended[1] Are—	Perform Risk Assessment for Type B Programs That Exceed the Larger of—
More than or equal to $300,000 and less than or equal to $100 million	$100,000 or 0.3% (0.003) of federal awards expended
More than $100 million	$300,000 or 0.03% (0.0003) of federal awards expended

[1] Includes both cash and noncash awards.

Step 4—Determination of Programs to Be Audited as Major

Criteria for Major Programs

8.18 After completing steps 1–3, the auditor identifies the major programs. At a minimum, Circular A-133 states that the auditor should audit all of the following as major programs:

- All type A programs, except those identified as low risk under step 2 (see paragraphs 8.11–.14)
- High-risk type B programs as identified under either of the two options described in paragraphs 8.19–.20
- Programs to be audited as major based on a federal agency request (in lieu of the federal agency conducting or arranging for additional audits; paragraph 8.25 provides further information)
- Additional programs, if any, that are necessary to meet the percentage-of-coverage rule described in paragraph 8.21

Two Options Available for Identifying High-Risk Type B Programs

8.19 Section 520(e)(2) of Circular A-133 provides two options for identifying high-risk type B programs:

- *Option 1.* Under option 1, the auditor should perform risk assessments of all type B programs that exceed the amount specified in table 8-3, and to audit at least one-half of the high-risk type B programs as major, unless this number exceeds the number of low-risk type A programs identified in step 2 (that is, the cap). In this case, the auditor would be required to audit as major the same number of high-risk type B programs as the cap. For example, consider an auditee that has 10 low-risk type A programs, and 50 type B programs above the amount specified in table 8-3. Under this option, the auditor would be required to perform risk assessments of the 50 type B programs. Assume that based on that assessment, the auditor determines that there are 25 high-risk type B programs. One-half of the 25 high-risk type B programs is 12.5, which rounds up to 13 programs. Under this option, the auditor would audit 13 of the high-risk type B programs as major; however, because the cap in this example is 10 (that is, the number of low-risk type A programs), the auditor is required to audit only 10 high-risk type B programs as major.

- *Option 2.* Under option 2, the auditor should audit as major only 1 high-risk type B program for each type A program identified as low risk in step 2. Under this option the auditor would not be required to perform risk assessments for any type B program when there are no low-risk type A programs (that is, the cap is zero). Continuing with the previous example, under option 2 the auditor would perform risk assessments of type B programs until 10 high-risk programs are identified (that is, 10 is the number of low-risk type A programs). The auditor would then audit as major the 10 type B programs identified as high risk. Depending on the order in which risk assessments on type B programs are performed, the auditor might only need to perform risk assessments of 10 type B programs determined to be high risk, or the auditor may need to perform risk assessments on additional type B programs until 10 high-risk programs are identified.

8.20 The auditor may choose option 1 or option 2. There is no requirement to justify the reasons for selecting either option. The results under options 1 and 2 may vary significantly, depending on the number of low-risk type A programs and high-risk type B programs (see paragraph 8.16). Circular A-133 encourages the auditor to use an approach that provides an opportunity for different high-risk type B programs to be audited as major over a period of time.

Percentage-of-Coverage Rule

8.21 Circular A-133 states that the auditor should audit, as major programs, federal programs with federal awards expended that, in the aggregate, encompass at least 50 percent of the total federal awards expended. However, if the auditee meets the criteria for a low-risk auditee (see paragraph 8.26), the auditor is required to audit as major programs federal programs with federal awards expended that, in the aggregate, encompass at least 25 percent of the total federal awards expended. A computation of the total federal awards expended for the major programs audited, determined under step 4, as a percentage of the total federal awards expended will indicate the percentage of coverage. If the total does not equal or exceed 50 percent (or 25 percent in the case of a low-risk auditee) of the total federal awards expended, the auditor should select additional programs (either type A or type B) to equal or exceed 50 percent (or 25 percent in the case of a low-risk auditee) and test them as major programs. The selection of additional programs to meet the percentage-of-coverage is based on the auditor's professional judgment. When selecting additional programs to meet the percentage-of-coverage rule, the auditor may select programs without regard to risk assessment. If loans or loan guarantees are major programs, these programs may be used for purposes of meeting the percentage-of-coverage rule. Furthermore, when a federal agency or pass-through entity requests and pays for a program to be audited as major (see paragraph 8.25), that program may also be used for purposes of meeting the percentage-of-coverage rule.

> **Emphasis Point**
>
> It is important to note that the percentage of coverage rule represents the minimum coverage to be achieved, and is calculated after the determination of programs to be audited is made in step 4 (described in paragraphs 8.18–.20). Once the initial determination of programs to be audited is made, the percentage of coverage rules determine if additional programs are required to be audited to meet the percentage of coverage required for the auditee.
>
> Note that the percentage of coverage calculation is based on final total federal expenditures. In some cases auditors begin the audit prior to the date the final year-end expenditure amounts are available. In this case, once final total federal expenditures are determined, both the type A major program threshold and the dollar amount required to meet the percentage of coverage will need to be rechecked to ensure that the appropriate federal programs are audited.

Documentation of Risk Assessment

8.22 Circular A-133 states that the auditor should document the risk assessment process used in determining major programs. It is therefore necessary for the auditor to develop adequate audit documentation, as required by generally accepted auditing standards (GAAS) and *Government Auditing Standards*, and which includes documentation supporting the determination of major programs. (Chapter 3, "Planning and Performing a Financial Statement Audit in Accordance With *Government Auditing Standards*," and chapter 6 of this guide discuss the audit documentation requirements of GAAS and *Government Auditing Standards*.)

Auditor Judgment in the Risk Assessment Process

8.23 Circular A-133 states that when the determination of major programs is performed and documented by the auditor in accordance with the circular, the auditor's judgment in applying the risk-based approach to determine major programs is presumed correct. Challenges by federal agencies and pass-through entities should be made only for clearly improper use of the guidance in Circular A-133. However, federal agencies and pass-through entities may provide the auditor with guidance about the risk of a particular federal program, which the auditor should consider when determining major programs.

Other Considerations Regarding the Risk-Based Approach

Deviation From Use of Risk Criteria

8.24 For first-year audits, Circular A-133 Section 520(h)(i) allows auditors to deviate from the previously described risk assessment process. A *first-year audit* is defined as the first year an entity is audited under Circular A-133 or as the first year of a change in auditors. This exception allows the auditor to elect to determine major programs as all type A programs plus any type B programs as are necessary to meet the percentage-of-coverage rule described in paragraph 8.21. Under this option, the auditor is not required to perform steps 2–4 as described in paragraphs 8.11–.20. However, to ensure that a frequent change of auditors would not preclude the audit of high-risk type B programs, this election for first-year audits may not be used more than once every three years. This guide recommends that auditors consider whether this exception is an option during the planning phase of the single audit. (Chapter 6 of this guide discusses other initial-year audit considerations).

Federal Agency and Pass-Through Entity Requests for Additional Major Programs

8.25 Section 215(c) of Circular A-133 permits a federal agency to request an auditee to have a particular federal program audited as a major program in lieu of the federal agency conducting or arranging for additional audits. To allow for planning, such requests should be made at least 180 days before the end of the fiscal year to be audited. After consultation with its auditor, the auditee should promptly respond to such a request by informing the federal agency whether the program would otherwise be audited as a major program using the risk-based approach and, if not, the estimated incremental cost. The federal agency should then promptly confirm to the auditee whether it wants the program audited as a major program. If the program is to be audited as a major program based on the federal agency's request, and the federal agency agrees to pay the full incremental costs, then the auditee should have the program audited as a major program. This approach also may be used by pass-through entities for a subrecipient.

Low-Risk Auditee Criteria

8.26 Circular A-133 establishes certain conditions for determining whether an auditee is low risk. An auditee that meets all of the following conditions for each of the preceding two years (or in the case of biennial audits, the preceding two audit periods)[4] qualifies as a low-risk auditee and is eligible for the reduced audit coverage discussed in paragraph 8.21:

- Single audits were performed on an annual basis in accordance with Circular A-133. An auditee that has biennial audits does not qualify as a low-risk auditee, unless agreed to in advance by the cognizant or oversight agency for audit. (See also paragraph 8.27.)
- The auditor's opinions on the financial statements[5] and the schedule of expenditures of federal awards were unmodified.[6] However, the cognizant or oversight agency for audit may judge that an

---

[4] An auditor may not use professional judgment to override these required conditions for low-risk auditee status. For example, it would not be appropriate for an auditor to make a determination that a material weakness under the requirements of *Government Auditing Standards* that was reported in one of the preceding two audit periods would not be important enough to cause an entity to lose its low-risk auditee status. Such a determination may only be made by the cognizant or oversight agency for audit.

[5] As explained in the AICPA Audit and Accounting Guide *State and Local Governments*, the auditor generally expresses or disclaims an opinion on a government's basic financial statements by providing an opinion or disclaimer of opinion on each opinion unit required to be presented in those financial statements. For purposes of determining low-risk auditee status for governmental entities, the auditor's opinion on each opinion unit should be unmodified.

[6] AU-C section 700, *Forming an Opinion and Reporting on Financial Statements* (AICPA, *Professional Standards*), uses the term *unmodified opinion* to refer to an opinion expressed by the auditor when the auditor concludes that the financial statements are presented fairly, in all material respects, in accordance with the applicable financial reporting framework. Although Circular A-133 refers to this type of opinion as an "unqualified opinion," this guide uses the term *unmodified opinion* when referring to such an opinion.

opinion modification does not affect the management of federal awards and may provide a waiver.

- There were no deficiencies in internal control over financial reporting that were identified as material weaknesses under the requirements of *Government Auditing Standards*. However, the cognizant or oversight agency for audit may judge that any identified material weaknesses do not affect the management of federal awards and may provide a waiver.

- None of the federal programs had audit findings from any of the following in either of the preceding two years (or in the case of biennial audits, the preceding two audit periods) in which they were classified as type A programs:

    — Material weaknesses in internal control over compliance

    — Noncompliance with the provisions of laws, regulations, contracts, or grant agreements that have a material effect on the type A program

    — Known or likely questioned costs that exceed five percent of the total federal awards expended for a type A program during the year

8.27 The *Compliance Supplement* provides guidance applicable to all auditees regarding low-risk auditee status. Appendix 7 clarifies that in order for an entity to meet the criteria for low-risk auditee status in the current year, the prior two years' audits must have met the requirements of Circular A-133, including report submission to the Federal Audit Clearinghouse (FAC) by the due date.[7] Per the *Compliance Supplement*, a report submission is considered late if the entity is not in compliance with the nine-month due date rule. Appendix 7 of the *Compliance Supplement* also includes suggested audit procedures to identify FAC submissions that do not meet the due date.

Emphasis Point

In order to meet the criteria for low-risk auditee status in the current year, the prior two year's audits must have met the requirements of OMB Circular A-133, including submission of the data collection form to the FAC by the due date. See appendix 7 of the *Compliance Supplement* for additional information and instructions for how to determine when previous data collection form submissions were made.

Criteria for Federal Program Risk

8.28 Circular A-133 includes certain conditions that, when met, indicate that a type A program may be low risk (see paragraphs 8.11–.12). As noted in paragraphs 8.13 and 8.15, in making the final determination of whether a

---

[7] If the auditee or auditor wishes to inform the federal government that the required submission will be late, the suggested way to do so is to contact the federal oversight or cognizant agency for the audit (contact information is available on the "Resources" tab at http://harvester.census.gov/fac/APPX3.htm).

type A program is low risk or a type B program is high risk, the auditor should use professional judgment and also consider the risk criteria discussed in paragraphs 8.29–.38. The auditor's risk assessment should be based on an overall evaluation of the risks of noncompliance occurring, which could be material to the federal program being evaluated. As a part of the risk assessment, the auditor may also wish to discuss a particular federal program with auditee management and with the federal agency or pass-through entity. The rest of this chapter discusses the criteria for federal program risk that are identified in Circular A-133 for the auditor's consideration.

Current and Prior Audit Experience

8.29 The auditor should consider his or her current and prior experience with the auditee and the results of audits performed in the past. The auditor should consider the following specific factors, as discussed in paragraphs 8.30–.35:

- Effectiveness of internal control over compliance for federal programs
- Federal programs administered under multiple internal control structures
- The system for monitoring subrecipients when significant parts of federal programs are passed through to subrecipients
- The extent to which computer processing is used
- Prior audit findings
- Federal programs not recently audited as major

Effectiveness of Internal Control Over Federal Programs

8.30 In assessing program risk, the auditor should consider internal control over compliance for federal programs. (See chapter 9, "Consideration of Internal Control Over Compliance for Major Programs (Circular A-133)," of this guide.) Weak internal control over compliance for federal programs is an indication of higher risk. Consideration also should be given to the control environment over federal programs and to such factors as the expectation of management's adherence to applicable laws and regulations and the provisions of contracts or grant agreements. The auditor may also consider the competence and experience of the personnel who administer federal programs. An indication of higher risk would exist in instances in which the staff are new or do not have experience with a program.

Federal Programs Administered Under Multiple Internal Control Structures

8.31 Federal programs administered by multiple internal control structures may have a higher risk. This often occurs when multiple organizational units (for example, locations or branches) are involved in the administration of federal programs. An example of this would be a university that has several campuses administering a federal program. When assessing risk, the auditor should consider whether any control deficiencies are isolated in a single operating unit (that is, one college campus) or are pervasive throughout the entity. If the identified control deficiencies are isolated, and absent other control deficiencies, the auditor could still potentially reach the conclusion that the program is low risk. The final determination would be based on the auditor's judgment.

System for Monitoring Subrecipients

8.32 Consideration should be given to the extent that federal programs are passed through to subrecipients. Circular A-133 states that when significant parts of a federal program are passed through to subrecipients, a weak system for monitoring subrecipients would indicate higher risk. Alternatively, if the auditee passes a significant portion of programs to subrecipients and the auditee has an effective system in place to monitor the subrecipients, this might be indicative of a lower level of risk to the program.

Extent to Which Computer Processing Is Used

8.33 When assessing risk, Circular A-133 states that the auditor should consider the extent to which computer processing is used to administer federal programs, as well as the complexity of that processing. A complex system does not always indicate higher risk. On the other hand, a newly installed system that has not been tested in the past, or a recently modified system, may indicate higher risk. AU-C section 500, *Audit Evidence*, and AU-C section 315, *Understanding the Entity and Its Environment and Assessing the Risks of Material Misstatement* (AICPA, *Professional Standards*), contain requirements and guidance when auditee information is transmitted, processed, maintained, or accessed electronically.

Prior Audit Findings

8.34 As a part of the risk assessment, Circular A-133 states that the auditor should consider prior audit findings. This information should be used in assessing risk and determining the nature, timing, and extent of current audit work. An indication of higher risk would exist for prior audit findings that could have a significant impact on a federal program or for which no corrective action has been implemented since the findings were identified. These findings may be the result, for example, of previous single audits by independent auditors or of compliance or financial audits performed by internal auditors or government auditors in conjunction with the federal awarding agency's monitoring activities.

Federal Programs Not Recently Audited as Major

8.35 Federal programs that have not recently been audited as major programs may be of higher risk than federal programs recently audited as major. For example, many type B programs may never have been audited as major programs in the past. A higher level of risk would likely be assessed on such programs than on those programs that have been consistently audited as major programs without audit findings.

Oversight Exercised by Federal Agencies and Pass-Through Entities

8.36 The oversight exercised by federal agencies or pass-through entities could indicate risk. An important factor in assessing risk is the results of recent audits performed by federal agencies or pass-through entities. For example, recent monitoring or other reviews that were performed by an oversight entity and that disclosed no audit findings may indicate lower risk, whereas monitoring that disclosed significant findings could indicate higher risk. However, reviews performed by federal agencies or pass-through entities vary widely with coverage and intensity. Therefore, consideration of the scope of reviews performed may assist the auditor in evaluating whether the reviews increase, decrease, or have no impact on risk.

8.37 Section 525(c)(2) of Circular A-133 states that federal agencies, with the concurrence of the OMB, may identify federal programs that are higher-risk. That identification is provided by the OMB in the *Compliance Supplement*. For example, the U.S. Department of Health and Human Services has identified the Medicaid Assistance Program as a program of higher risk in the *Compliance Supplement*. Although such an identification by a federal agency does not preclude an auditor from determining that a program is low risk (for example, because prior audits have shown strong internal control and compliance), the consideration of this identification of higher risk is part of the risk assessment process.

Inherent Risk of Noncompliance of the Federal Programs

8.38 As part of the risk assessment, the auditor should consider the inherent risk of noncompliance of federal programs. The nature of some programs may indicate higher inherent risk of noncompliance. Programs with higher inherent risk of noncompliance may be of a higher risk for the purpose of determining major programs. Circular A-133 provides the following examples of program characteristics with potentially higher inherent risk of noncompliance:

- Complex programs, and the extent to which a program contracts for goods and services, have the potential for higher risk. For example, federal programs that disburse funds through third-party contracts or have eligibility criteria may be of higher risk. Federal programs primarily involving staff payroll costs may have a high risk for time-and-effort reporting but may otherwise be at low risk.

- The phase of a federal program's life cycle at the federal agency may indicate risk. For example, a new program with new or interim regulations may have a higher risk than an established program with time-tested regulations. In addition, significant changes in federal programs, laws, or regulations or in the provisions of contracts or grant agreements may increase risk.

- The phase of a program's life cycle at the auditee may indicate risk. For example, during the first and last years in which an auditee participates in a program, the risk may be higher because of the start-up or closeout of the program's activities and staff.

- Type B programs with larger federal awards expended would be of higher risk than would programs with substantially smaller federal awards expended.

Transition Considerations Related to the Uniform Guidance

8.39 The requirements in Subpart F, "Audit Requirements," of the Uniform Guidance are effective for audits of fiscal years beginning on or after

December 26, 2014, with no early implementation permitted. For example, consider a nonfederal entity with a June 30, 2015, fiscal year end that has $600,000 in federal expenditures. In this situation, the auditor may not early adopt the Uniform Guidance or its updated audit threshold of $750,000. Therefore, the nonfederal entity in the example provided would be subject to an audit under Circular A-133 for its June 30, 2015, year-end because its federal expenditures exceed the Circular A-133 audit threshold of $500,000.

Chapter 9

Consideration of Internal Control Over Compliance for Major Programs (Circular A-133)

> **Update 9-1: Audits of Federal Awards**
>
> This chapter, and the remaining chapters of part II, *Circular A-133 Audits*, of this guide, should be used for performing a compliance audit of federal awards under Office of Management and Budget (OMB) Circular A-133, *Audits of States, Local Governments, and Non-Profit Organizations* (Circular A-133). Part III, *Uniform Guidance Audits*, of this guide should be used when performing a compliance audit under Title 2 U.S. *Code of Federal Regulations* (CFR) Part 200, *Uniform Administrative Requirements, Cost Principles, and Audit Requirements for Federal Awards* (Uniform Guidance). See the transitional guidance sections at the end of each chapter that highlight important matters for consideration.[1] Refer to the preface for additional information.
>
> **Important Uniform Guidance Effective Date Information**
>
> In December 2013, the OMB issued the Uniform Guidance, which is effective for nonfederal entities for all federal awards and certain funding increments provided on or after December 26, 2014. The requirements in Subpart F, "Audit Requirements," are effective for audits of fiscal years beginning on or after December 26, 2014, with no early implementation permitted. Therefore, auditees subject to a single audit with December 25, 2015, and later year ends (for example, December 31, 2015) will be required to undergo the audit under Subpart F of the Uniform Guidance. Note that audits of fiscal years ending prior to the effective date of the Uniform Guidance audit requirements are subject to an audit under Circular A-133.

    9.01 OMB Circular A-133 (Circular A-133) establishes requirements for additional audit procedures and reporting relative to the auditor's consideration of internal control over compliance for major programs. The requirements are beyond those of a financial statement audit conducted in accordance with generally accepted auditing standards (GAAS) and *Government Auditing Standards*.[2] Chapter 3, "Planning and Performing a Financial Statement

---

[1] See the information found at the end of certain chapters in part II, *Circular A-133 Audits*, of this guide for transition considerations when performing an audit under Office of Management and Budget (OMB) Circular A-133, *Audits of States, Local Governments, and Non-Profit Organizations* (Circular A-133), as it relates to the applicability of certain aspects of Title 2 U.S. *Code of Federal Regulations* Part 200, *Uniform Administrative Requirements, Cost Principles, and Audit Requirements for Federal Awards* (Uniform Guidance), to audits performed under Circular A-133. Transition considerations related to an audit performed under the Uniform Guidance can be found at the end of chapters in part III, *Uniform Guidance Audits*, of this guide in sections titled "Transition Considerations Related to the Uniform Guidance."

[2] *Government Auditing Standards* incorporates by reference AICPA Statements on Auditing Standards. Therefore, auditors performing financial statement audits and OMB Circular A-133 compliance audits in accordance with *Government Auditing Standards* should comply with generally accepted auditing standards, the requirements found in chapters 1–3 of *Government Auditing Standards*, and the additional standards and related requirements for financial audits found in chapter 4, "Standards for Financial Audits," of *Government Auditing Standards*.

Audit in Accordance With *Government Auditing Standards*," of this guide discusses the auditor's consideration of internal control over financial reporting in a financial statement audit. (As discussed in chapter 6, "Planning Considerations of Circular A-133," of this guide, Circular A-133 does not impose on the financial statement audit any additional audit requirements beyond *Government Auditing Standards*.) This chapter discusses the additional considerations of internal control over compliance for major programs, and adapts GAAS guidance to a Circular A-133 compliance audit as applicable. Paragraph 9.03 and chapter 13, "Auditor Reporting Requirements and Other Communication Considerations in a Single Audit (Circular A-133)," of this guide discuss the reporting on internal control over compliance for major programs.

Summary of Circular A-133 Requirements Related to Internal Control Over Compliance for Federal Programs

Auditee Responsibilities

9.02 Circular A-133 states that the auditee should maintain internal control over compliance for federal programs that provides reasonable assurance that the auditee is managing federal awards in compliance with laws, regulations, and provisions of contracts or grant agreements that could have a material effect on each of its federal programs (*compliance requirements*).

Auditor Responsibilities

9.03 In addition to the requirements of GAAS and *Government Auditing Standards*, Circular A-133 provides that the auditor should

- perform procedures to obtain an understanding of internal control over compliance for federal programs that is sufficient to plan the audit to support a low assessed level of control risk of noncompliance for major programs.[3]

- plan the testing of internal control over compliance for major programs to support a low assessed level of control risk of noncompliance for the assertions relevant to the compliance requirements for each major program.[4]

- perform testing of internal control over compliance as planned.

- report on internal control over compliance describing the scope of the testing of internal control and the results of the tests and, where applicable, referring to the separate schedule of findings and questioned costs. This schedule includes, where applicable, a statement that significant deficiencies and material weaknesses in internal control over compliance for major programs were identified in the audit.

---

[3] Although Circular A-133 uses the term *control risk*, this guide uses the term *control risk of noncompliance* in order to be consistent with the term as used and defined in AU-C section 935, *Compliance Audits* (AICPA, *Professional Standards*).

[4] See paragraphs 9.23–.26 for a discussion of planning tests of internal control over compliance to support a low assessed level of control risk of noncompliance. See paragraphs 9.27–.29 for situations where internal control over some or all of the compliance requirements for a major program is likely to be ineffective.

Consideration of Internal Control Over Compliance for Major Programs **213**

Auditor Responsibility for Internal Control Over Compliance for Programs That Are Not Major

9.04 The auditor has no responsibility under Circular A-133 to obtain an understanding of internal control over compliance for programs that are not considered major, or to plan or perform any related testing of internal control over compliance for those programs except for any procedures the auditor may choose to perform as part of the risk assessment process in determining major programs. (Chapter 8, "Determination of Major Programs (Circular A-133)," of this guide discusses the risk assessment process.) However, a program that is not considered major could still be material to the financial statements.[5] In that situation, in conjunction with the financial statement audit, the auditor may need to obtain an understanding of that program's internal control over financial reporting.

Circular A-133 Definition of *Internal Control Over Federal Programs*

9.05 Circular A-133 defines *internal control over federal programs* as follows:

> Internal control pertaining to the compliance requirements for federal programs (*internal control over federal programs*) means a process—effected by an entity's management and other personnel—designed to provide reasonable assurance regarding the achievement of the following objectives for federal programs:
>
> 1. Transactions are properly recorded and accounted for to:
>   a. Permit the preparation of reliable financial statements and federal reports;
>   b. Maintain accountability over assets; and
>   c. Demonstrate compliance with laws, regulations, and other compliance requirements;
> 2. Transactions are executed in compliance with:
>   a. Laws, regulations, and the provisions of contracts or grant agreements that could have a direct and material effect on a federal program; and
>   b. Any other laws and regulations that are identified in the compliance supplement; and
> 3. Funds, property, and other assets are safeguarded against loss from unauthorized use or disposition.

Control Objectives and the Elements of Internal Control

9.06 AU-C section 315, *Understanding the Entity and Its Environment and Assessing the Risks of Material Misstatement* (AICPA, *Professional Standards*), states that there are three objectives of internal control: reliability of

---

[5] As discussed in the AICPA Audit and Accounting Guide *State and Local Governments,* the auditor's consideration of materiality for purposes of planning, performing, evaluating the results of, and reporting on the audit of the financial statements of a state or local government is based on opinion units. See that guide for further guidance.

the entity's financial reporting, effectiveness and efficiency of its operations, and compliance with applicable laws and regulations. There is a direct relationship between an entity's objectives and the controls it implements to provide reasonable assurance about their achievement. For purposes of this guide, controls relevant to the audit of the financial statements are referred to as "internal control over financial reporting" and are encompassed in the report on internal control over financial reporting that is required by *Government Auditing Standards*. (See chapters 3–4 of this guide.) Controls relevant to an audit of compliance with requirements applicable to major federal programs are referred to collectively in this guide as "internal control over compliance" and are encompassed in the report on internal control over compliance required by Circular A-133. In a particular single audit engagement, some controls may be relevant to both the audit of the financial statements and the audit of compliance. When this occurs, those controls would be encompassed in both internal control reports. Chapter 13 of this guide provides guidance on reporting findings involving significant deficiencies and material weaknesses in internal control in such a circumstance.

9.07 Paragraph .A50 of AU-C section 315 states that the division of internal control into five interrelated components, for purposes of GAAS, provides a useful framework for auditors when considering how different aspects of an entity's internal control may affect the audit. The five components, as adapted to a Circular A-133 compliance audit, follow.

> **control environment.** Sets the tone of the entity, influencing the control consciousness of its people. It is the foundation for all other components of internal control over compliance, providing discipline and structure.
>
> **risk assessment.** The entity's identification, analysis, and management of risks relevant to the objectives of the Circular A-133 compliance audit. If the risk assessment process is appropriate to the circumstances, including the nature, size, and complexity of the entity, it assists the auditor in identifying risks of material noncompliance.
>
> **information and communication systems.** Includes the business processes relevant to compliance with the applicable compliance requirements. It consists of procedures and records designed and established to support the identification, capture, and exchange of information related to compliance in a form and time-frame that enable people to carry out their responsibilities.
>
> **control activities.** The policies and procedures that help ensure that management directives are carried out.
>
> **monitoring.** A process to assess the effectiveness of internal control over compliance performance over time.

These components assist the auditor in considering how the different aspects of an entity's internal control over compliance may affect the audit. When considering internal control over compliance for major programs the auditor's focus is on the internal control objective related to compliance with laws, regulations, and the provisions of contracts or grant agreements.

Auditor's Consideration of Internal Control Over Compliance for Each Major Program

9.08 The auditor's consideration of internal control over compliance for each major program is similar to the consideration of internal control over financial reporting in a financial statement audit as described in AU-C section 315. The same concepts apply for understanding internal control over compliance, assessing risk, and the testing of controls. However, as noted in paragraph 9.03, Circular A-133 adds requirements to plan the audit to support a low assessed level of control risk of noncompliance, to perform related procedures and testing, and to report on internal control over compliance. An important aspect of the consideration of internal control over compliance in an audit under Circular A-133 is that instead of the objective being reliability of financial reporting, it is compliance with laws, regulations, and the provisions of contracts or grant agreements.

9.09 When considering internal control over compliance, the auditor should obtain an understanding of the five elements of internal control sufficient to assess the risks of material noncompliance with each direct and material compliance requirement[6] for each major program. The auditor should obtain a sufficient understanding by performing risk assessment procedures to evaluate the design of controls relevant to the compliance audit and to determine whether they have been implemented. The auditor should use the information gathered by performing the risk assessment procedures, including the audit evidence obtained in evaluating the design of controls and determining whether they have been implemented, as audit evidence to support the risk assessment. The risk assessment should be used to determine the nature, timing, and extent of further audit procedures to be performed.

9.10 As noted in paragraph .20 of AU-C section 935, *Compliance Audits* (AICPA, *Professional Standards*), the auditor should design and perform further audit procedures in response to the assessed risks of material noncompliance. These procedures should include performing tests of controls over compliance if

- the auditor's risk assessment includes an expectation of the operating effectiveness of controls over compliance related to the direct and material compliance requirements;
- substantive procedures alone do not provide sufficient appropriate audit evidence; or
- such tests of controls over compliance are required by the governmental audit requirement.

As further described in paragraph 9.03, Circular A-133 requires testing of internal control over compliance, therefore, there are additional considerations related to testing controls in a Circular A-133 compliance audit.

---

[6] AU-C section 935 defines *applicable compliance requirements* as the compliance requirements that are subject to the compliance audit. Paragraph .500(d) of Circular A-133 states that the auditor should determine whether the auditee has complied with laws, regulations, and the provisions of contracts or grant agreements that may have a direct and material effect on each of its major programs. Therefore, in a Circular A-133 compliance audit, the direct and material compliance requirements are those that are subject to audit. Accordingly, for the purpose of adapting AU-C section 935 to a Circular A-133 compliance audit, the term *applicable compliance requirements* has been replaced by *direct and material compliance requirements* in this guide except when directly citing content from AU-C section 935.

9.11 Procedures for gaining an understanding of internal control over compliance and an assessment of the risks of noncompliance may be performed concurrently in an audit. Similarly, based on the assessed level of control risk of noncompliance that the auditor expects to support and on audit efficiency considerations, the auditor may perform some tests of controls concurrently with obtaining an understanding of controls. See the discussion beginning at paragraph 9.30 for information on the testing of controls.

Obtaining an Understanding of Internal Control Over Direct and Material Compliance Requirements for Major Programs

Understanding Direct and Material Compliance Requirements and Identifying Relevant Controls

9.12 As noted in paragraph 9.03, the auditor should perform procedures to obtain an understanding of internal control over compliance for federal programs that is sufficient to plan the audit to support a low assessed level of control risk of noncompliance for major programs. (Chapter 8 of this guide discusses the determination of major programs.) In order to do this, an understanding is needed of which of the 12 types of compliance requirements identified in the *OMB Compliance Supplement* (*Compliance Supplement*) have a direct and material effect on each major program.[7] Once the auditor has identified the compliance requirements that have a direct and material effect on each major program, an understanding of the direct and material compliance requirements will determine the types of controls the auditor needs to consider in a Circular A-133 compliance audit.

9.13 In order to identify the controls relevant to the direct and material compliance requirements, the auditor should obtain an understanding of the five components of internal control in relation to the direct and material compliance requirements for each major program. In obtaining an understanding of internal control, paragraphs .13–.25 of AU-C section 315 provide requirements and guidance. Obtaining an understanding of internal control involves evaluating the design of a control and determining whether it has been implemented. Evaluating the design of a control involves consideration of whether the control, individually or in combination with other controls, is capable of effectively preventing or detecting and correcting instances of noncompliance. Implementation of a control means that the control exists and that the entity is using it. The auditor should consider the design of the control in determining whether to consider its implementation. (See paragraph 9.27 for a discussion of ineffective internal control.)

9.14 For each of the programs and direct and material compliance requirements selected for testing, the auditor should perform risk assessment procedures to obtain a sufficient understanding of the direct and material compliance requirements and the entity's internal control over compliance with those compliance requirements. The objective of these procedures is to obtain audit evidence about the design and implementation of relevant controls over

---

[7] See chapter 10, "Compliance Auditing Applicable to Major Programs (Circular A-133)," for information on identifying the types of compliance requirements applicable to the program and related documentation requirements.

compliance, and may include procedures such as inquiry of entity personnel, observing the application of a specific control, and inspecting documents and reports. Paragraph .A69 of AU-C section 315 states that inquiry alone is not sufficient to evaluate the design of a control and to determine whether it has been implemented. (See chapter 6 for a discussion of risk assessment.)

9.15 In understanding the entity's control activities as it relates to a Circular A-133 compliance audit, the auditor should obtain an understanding of how the entity has responded to risks arising from IT, particularly in that the information systems and programs may include controls related to direct and material compliance requirements. An entity's use of IT may affect any of the five components of internal control relevant to the achievement of the entity's financial reporting, operations, or compliance objectives and its operating units or business functions. For example, an entity may use IT as part of discrete systems that support only particular business activities. Alternatively, an entity may have complex, highly integrated systems that share data and that are used to support all aspects of the entity's financial reporting, operations, and compliance objectives. As noted in paragraph .A98 of AU-C section 315, the use of IT affects the way that control activities are implemented. From the auditor's perspective, controls over the IT system(s) are effective when they maintain the integrity of information and the security of the data such systems process and when they include effective general IT controls and application controls. (See paragraphs .A98–.A101 of AU-C section 315 for more guidance on the effect IT has on the auditor's risk assessment process.)

9.16 Obtaining an understanding of an entity's controls ordinarily does not provide sufficient evidence about their operating effectiveness. Further, simply testing compliance in accordance with Circular A-133 does not provide evidence that controls are appropriately designed or operating effectively. Testing compliance gives indirect evidence on the effectiveness of controls, but cannot serve as the basis for assessing controls as operating effectively. Generally, testing controls assists the auditor in determining the nature, timing, and extent of substantive audit procedures to perform in order to gather evidence related to the opinion on compliance.

9.17 Entities may use the same controls for more than one federal program and for similar transactions (for example, cash disbursements). Accordingly, those controls will often provide assurance regarding the achievement of the compliance objectives related to some or all federal program transactions and assets. However, the use of the same controls does not negate the need to gain an understanding of internal control over compliance for each major program.

Compliance Supplement Internal Control Guidance

9.18 Part 6, "Internal Control," was removed from the 2015 *Compliance Supplement*. It is scheduled to be updated for the 2016 *Compliance Supplement*. See paragraph 9.59 for more information.

Multiple Organizational Unit Considerations

9.19 Federal programs often are administered by multiple organizational units (for example, operating units, locations, or branches) within an auditee. Each organizational unit may maintain separate internal control over compliance that is relevant to the programs, or parts of the programs, that the unit administers. In these situations, the auditor should perform procedures to obtain an understanding of internal control over compliance that is separately maintained by organizational units and that is relevant to each material part of a major program, and should plan and perform testing of those controls as discussed in this guide. (Chapters 8 and 10–11 of this guide discuss other multiple organizational unit considerations.)

Subrecipient Considerations

9.20 Many entities that are pass-through entities for federal awards make subcontract or subgrant awards and disburse their own funds, as well as federal funds, to subrecipients. The auditor of the pass-through entity has certain responsibilities related to the entity's internal control over the monitoring of subrecipients. If significant pass-through funds are awarded, subrecipient considerations could have a major impact on the risk assessment and internal control procedures performed. Chapter 12, "Audit Considerations of Federal Pass-Through Awards (Circular A-133)," of this guide discusses the audit considerations of federal pass-through awards.

Planning and Performing the Test of Operating Effectiveness of Internal Control Over Direct and Material Compliance Requirements for Each Major Program[8]

Assessing Control Risk of Noncompliance

9.21 *Control risk of noncompliance* is the risk that noncompliance with a compliance requirement that could occur and that could be material, either individually or when aggregated with other instances of noncompliance, will not be prevented, or detected and corrected, on a timely basis by the entity's internal control over compliance. After obtaining an understanding of internal control over compliance for major programs, the auditor makes a preliminary assessment of control risk of noncompliance related to the direct and material compliance requirements for each major program. This information is used to determine whether the auditor can support a low assessed level of control risk of noncompliance. When the auditor believes, based on the understanding of internal control, that controls are capable of effectively preventing or detecting and correcting material noncompliance, the auditor may initially assess control risk of noncompliance at less than the maximum during the risk assessment phase of the audit. (See also chapter 6 of this guide, which discusses audit risk of noncompliance considerations in a Circular A-133 compliance audit, including control risk of noncompliance.)

9.22 The assessment of control risk of noncompliance is the process of evaluating preliminarily the effectiveness of an entity's internal control over compliance in preventing or detecting and correcting material noncompliance with the compliance requirements for each major program. Paragraphs 9.23–.26 discuss the Circular A-133 requirement to plan the testing of internal control over compliance to support a low assessed level of control risk of noncompliance. Paragraphs 9.27–.29 discuss the auditor's responsibilities when internal control over compliance is ineffective in preventing or detecting and correcting noncompliance. The auditor's basis for judgment of the assessed level

---

[8] See also chapter 11, "Audit Sampling Considerations of Circular A-133 Compliance Audits," for more information related to understanding, planning, and performing tests related to internal control over compliance.

of control risk of noncompliance should be documented to support the decisions made. See paragraph 9.55 for a further discussion of audit documentation as it relates to internal control over compliance. The auditor should consider the results of his or her assessment of control risk of noncompliance, and any additional controls or tests of operating effectiveness in designing the nature, extent, and timing of substantive tests of compliance.

Planning the Test of Operating Effectiveness of Internal Control Over Compliance for Each Major Program to Support a Low Assessed Level of Control Risk of Noncompliance

9.23 Circular A-133 states that the auditor should plan the test of internal control over compliance for major programs to support a low assessed level of control risk for the assertions relevant to the compliance requirements for each major program. Professional standards do not define or quantify a low assessed level of control risk of noncompliance. Therefore, professional judgment is needed in determining the extent of control testing necessary to obtain a low level of control risk of noncompliance. In exercising professional judgment, one factor to consider is that this requirement is intended to address federal agencies' desire to know if conditions indicate that auditees have not implemented adequate internal control over compliance for federal programs to ensure compliance with applicable laws and regulations.

9.24 The auditor should obtain sufficient appropriate audit evidence to support that assessed level of control risk of noncompliance. The type of audit evidence, its source, its timeliness, and the existence of other audit evidence related to the conclusions to which it leads all bear on the degree of assurance the audit evidence provides.

9.25 The guidance in AU-C section 330, *Performing Audit Procedures in Response to Assessed Risks and Evaluating the Audit Evidence Obtained* (AICPA, *Professional Standards*), addresses the auditor's responsibility to design and implement responses to the risks of material misstatement identified and assessed by the auditor. In a compliance audit this responsibility relates to the risk of material noncompliance identified and assessed by the auditor. Paragraph .11 of AU-C section 330 states that the auditor should test controls for the particular time or throughout the period, for which the auditor intends to rely on those controls in order to provide an appropriate basis for the auditor's intended reliance. If the auditor intends to rely on a control over a period, audit evidence pertaining only to a point in time may be insufficient, and the auditor should supplement those tests with other tests of controls that are capable of providing audit evidence that the control operated effectively at relevant times during the period under audit. This guidance, along with the Circular A-133 requirement to perform the testing of internal control to support a low assessed level of control risk of noncompliance, supports the testing of internal control over compliance every year. (See paragraph 9.32 for related information.)

9.26 Paragraphs .08–.10 of AU-C section 330 contain guidance related to the extent of tests of controls. As it relates to a Circular A-133 compliance audit, and assuming an understanding that controls are effective, the auditor should design and perform tests of controls to obtain sufficient appropriate audit evidence that the controls are operating effectively for each direct and material compliance requirement for each major program throughout the period of reliance. Several factors are listed that auditors may consider in determining the extent of the tests of controls:

- The frequency of the performance of the control by the entity during the period
- The length of time during the audit period that the auditor is relying on the operating effectiveness of the control
- The expected deviation from the control
- The relevance and reliability of the audit evidence to be obtained in supporting that the control prevents, or detects and corrects, material noncompliance with respect to the type of compliance requirement being considered
- The extent to which audit evidence is obtained from tests of other controls related to the type of compliance requirement

In designing and performing tests of controls, the auditor should obtain more persuasive audit evidence when the auditor plans to place greater reliance on the effectiveness of a control. In addition, as the rate of expected deviation from a control increases, the auditor should increase the extent of testing of the control. However, the auditor should consider whether the rate of expected deviation indicates that obtaining audit evidence from the performance of tests of controls will not be sufficient to reduce the control risk of noncompliance for the assertions relevant to the compliance requirement. If the rate of expected deviation is expected to be high, the auditor may determine that tests of controls for a particular type of compliance requirement may be inappropriate. See chapter 11, "Audit Sampling Considerations of Circular A-133 Compliance Audits," of this guide for more information on audit sampling as it relates to a Circular A-133 compliance audit.

Existence of Ineffective Internal Control in Preventing or Detecting Noncompliance

9.27 While gaining an understanding of internal control over compliance, if the auditor determines that internal control over compliance for some or all of the types of compliance requirements for a major program have not been implemented or are likely to be ineffective in preventing or detecting noncompliance, the auditor is not required to plan and perform tests of internal control over compliance to support a low assessed level of control risk of noncompliance for the relevant assertions. (See also paragraphs 9.03, 9.22, and 9.32.) If internal control over compliance is deemed likely to be ineffective, Circular A-133 states that the auditor should assess control risk at the maximum[9] and consider whether any additional compliance tests are required because of ineffective internal control. The auditor also should report a significant deficiency or a material weakness in internal control over compliance as part of the audit findings. (Chapter 13 of this guide discusses the reporting of significant deficiencies and material weaknesses in internal control over compliance.)

9.28 The assessment of the effectiveness of internal control over compliance in preventing or detecting and correcting noncompliance is determined in relation to each individual type of compliance requirement or to an audit

---

[9] It is not acceptable to simply deem control risk to be "at the maximum." This assessment may be made in qualitative terms such as "high," "medium," and "low," or in quantitative terms such as percentages.

Consideration of Internal Control Over Compliance for Major Programs

objective identified in the *Compliance Supplement* for each major program. For example, controls over compliance with requirements for eligibility may be ineffective because of a lack of segregation of duties. In this case, the auditor would do the following:

- Report the lack of segregation of incompatible duties as it relates to eligibility as a significant deficiency or a material weakness in internal control over compliance.

- Assess the control risk of noncompliance related to requirements for eligibility at the maximum.

- Consider the lack of effective control when designing the nature, timing, and extent of procedures designed to test compliance with requirements for eligibility of the major program. In most cases, the extent of testing would need to be expanded.

9.29 In planning the tests of controls, consideration of the results of tests performed in prior years provides the auditor with important information. If the results of the prior year tests of controls prevented the auditor from assessing a low level of control risk of noncompliance, the auditor may consider expanded testing in the current audit period. Testing of any changes in internal control over compliance that were intended to eliminate deficiencies noted in the previous year also may provide relevant information. If, however, the auditor concluded in the prior year that internal control over compliance for one or more compliance requirements was ineffective and the auditee has made no changes to its internal control over compliance, the auditor may determine that controls are not likely to be effective and may choose not to plan and perform tests of controls. In this situation, the auditor should report a significant deficiency or a material weakness in internal control over compliance as discussed in paragraph 9.27.

Performing Tests to Evaluate the Effectiveness of Controls

9.30 As discussed in paragraph .A22 of AU-C section 330, testing the operating effectiveness of controls is different from obtaining an understanding of and evaluating the design and implementation of controls. However, the same types of audit procedures are used. The auditor may, therefore, decide it is efficient to test the operating effectiveness of controls at the same time the auditor is evaluating their design and determining that they have been implemented. This includes obtaining audit evidence about how controls were applied at relevant times during the period under audit, the consistency with which they were applied, and by whom or by what means they were applied.

9.31 As noted in paragraph 9.03, Circular A-133 states that auditors should perform tests of internal control over compliance as planned. (Paragraphs 9.27–.29 discuss an exception related to ineffective internal control over compliance.) In addition, paragraph .08 of AU-C section 330 states that the auditor should design and perform tests of controls when the auditor's risk assessment includes an expectation of the operating effectiveness of control. Testing of the operating effectiveness of controls ordinarily includes procedures such as (*a*) inquiries of appropriate entity personnel, including grant and contract managers; (*b*) the inspection of documents, reports, or electronic files indicating performance of the control; (*c*) the observation of the application of the specific controls; and (*d*) reperformance of the application of the control by the auditor. The auditor should perform such procedures regardless of whether he or she would otherwise choose to obtain evidence to support an assessment of control risk of noncompliance below the maximum level.

9.32 Furthermore, AU-C section 935 indicates that paragraphs .13–.14 and .31 of AU-C section 330 are not applicable to a compliance audit. Those paragraphs address the use of audit evidence obtained in prior audits related to testing the operating effectiveness of controls (and the rotation of such testing). Therefore, in a Circular A-133 compliance audit, controls that address the risks of noncompliance with direct and material types of compliance requirements for major programs should be tested every year.

9.33 Paragraph .A24 of AU-C section 330 provides guidance related to the testing of controls. When responding to the risk assessment, the auditor may design a test of controls to be performed concurrently with a test of details on the same transactions. Although the purpose of a test of controls is different from the purpose of a test of details, both may be accomplished concurrently by performing a test of controls and a test of details on the same transaction (a dual-purpose test). For example, the auditor may examine an invoice to determine whether it has been approved and whether it provides substantive evidence of a transaction. A dual purpose test is designed and evaluated by considering each purpose of the test separately. Also, when performing the tests, the auditor should consider how the outcome of the test of controls may affect the auditor's determination about the extent of substantive procedures to be performed. See chapter 11 of this guide for a discussion of the use of dual purpose samples in a compliance audit.

Emphasis Point

Quality control reviews of Circular A-133 compliance audits performed by federal agency staff have shown that in some cases auditors, when using dual purpose testing, have not clearly identified the procedures performed to test compliance versus internal control over compliance. It is important that the audit documentation relating to dual purpose tests separately identify the tests performed on internal control over compliance and the tests performed on compliance, along with the results of those tests. Documentation may be made through such mechanisms as narratives, tickmarks, attribute descriptions, or similar notations.

Evaluating the Results of Tests of Controls [10]

9.34 Based on the audit procedures performed related to controls, and the audit evidence obtained, the auditor should evaluate whether the assessment of the risk of material noncompliance of the relevant compliance requirements remain appropriate. An audit is a cumulative and iterative process. As the auditor performs planned audit procedures, the audit evidence obtained may cause the auditor to modify the nature, timing, or extent of other planned audit procedures. Information may come to the auditor's attention that differs significantly from the information on which the risk assessments were based.

---

[10] The discussion of audit sampling in a compliance audit, as found in chapter 11, will assist the auditor in evaluating the results of audit testing.

Consideration of Internal Control Over Compliance for Major Programs

Furthermore, the auditor should not assume that an instance of fraud or error is an isolated occurrence, and therefore should consider how the detection of such noncompliance affects the assessed risks of material noncompliance. Before the conclusion of the audit, the auditor should evaluate whether audit risk of noncompliance has been reduced to an appropriately low level and whether the nature, timing and extent of the audit procedures need to be reconsidered. The auditor should conclude whether sufficient appropriate audit evidence has been obtained to reduce to an appropriately low level the risks of material noncompliance with compliance requirements. In developing an opinion on compliance, the auditor should consider all relevant audit evidence, regardless of whether it appears to corroborate or to contradict the relevant assertions.

9.35 If, when evaluating the results of tests of controls, the auditor is not able to support a low assessed level of control risk of noncompliance for a direct and material compliance requirement for a major program, the auditor is not required to expand his or her testing of internal control over compliance for that compliance requirement. The auditor may choose not to perform further tests of controls. In that situation, the auditor would assess control risk of noncompliance at other than low, design tests of compliance accordingly, and consider the need to report an audit finding. In general, a significant deficiency or a material weakness in internal control over compliance will need to be reported. (See chapter 13 of this guide for further discussion on reporting audit findings.)

9.36 The concept of effectiveness of the operation of controls recognizes that some deviations in the way controls are applied by the entity may occur. When such deviations are detected during the performance of tests of controls, the auditor should make specific inquiries to understand these matters and their potential consequences. In addition, the auditor should consider whether any noncompliance detected from the performance of substantive procedures alter the auditor's judgment concerning the effectiveness of the related controls. The auditor should determine whether the tests of controls performed provide an appropriate basis for reliance on the controls, whether additional tests of controls are necessary, and how the remaining risks of noncompliance need to be addressed using substantive procedures.

9.37 The auditor may decide to expand the testing of internal control over compliance, but that decision would be based on whether the auditor considered expanded internal control testing to be more efficient than additional tests of compliance. Based on the testing performed, control risk of noncompliance might be assessed below the maximum and therefore reduce substantive tests of compliance. If it cannot be assessed below the maximum, it might be more appropriate to assess control risk of noncompliance at the maximum level. (See also paragraph 9.27.)

9.38 Regardless of the audit approach selected, the auditor should design and perform substantive procedures for all relevant assertions related to the direct and material compliance requirements for each major program. Because effective controls generally reduce, but do not eliminate, risks of material noncompliance, tests of controls reduce, but do not eliminate the need for substantive procedures.

9.39 When evaluating the operating effectiveness of internal control over compliance, instances of noncompliance detected by the auditor when performing compliance tests should be considered by the auditor. (For example, during a test of compliance for activities allowed or unallowed, it was noted that equipment was charged to a major program when the grant agreement does not allow program funds to be spent on equipment.) Detection of these instances of noncompliance is relevant, reliable audit evidence about the relative ineffectiveness of the related internal control over compliance. Noncompliance detected by the auditor that was not identified by the entity is evidence of a deficiency in internal control over compliance and may be an indicator of a significant deficiency or a material weakness in internal control over compliance.

9.40 In addition, the absence of noncompliance detected by a compliance test does not provide audit evidence that controls related to a compliance requirement are effective.

Significant Deficiencies and Material Weaknesses in Internal Control Over Compliance Related to Federal Programs

9.41 A deficiency in internal control over compliance exists when the design or operation of a control over compliance does not allow management or employees, in the normal course of performing their assigned functions, to prevent or detect and correct noncompliance with a type of compliance requirement of a federal program on a timely basis. See paragraph 9.53 for examples of circumstances that may be deficiencies, significant deficiencies, or material weaknesses in internal control over compliance.

9.42 AU-C section 935 defines *significant deficiency in internal control over compliance* and *material weakness in internal control over compliance* for the purposes of reporting on internal control over compliance. This guide further adapts the AU-C section 935 definitions for reporting on internal control over compliance in an audit under Circular A-133 as follows:

- A *significant deficiency in internal control over compliance* is a deficiency, or a combination of deficiencies, in internal control over compliance with a type of compliance requirement of a federal program that is less severe than a material weakness in internal control over compliance, yet important enough to merit attention by those charged with governance.

- A *material weakness in internal control over compliance* is a deficiency, or combination of deficiencies, in internal control over compliance such that there is a reasonable possibility that material noncompliance with a type of compliance requirement of a federal program will not be prevented or detected and corrected on a timely basis.[11]

9.43 In performing a Circular A-133 compliance audit, significant deficiencies and material weaknesses related to internal control over compliance and material noncompliance with provisions of laws, regulations, contract or grant agreements are to be considered as they relate to a type of compliance requirement for each major program or to an audit objective identified in the *Compliance Supplement*. Further, certain conditions may be significant

---

[11] A reasonable possibility exists when the likelihood of the event is either *reasonably possible* or *probable*, which are defined as follows:

reasonably possible. The chance of the future event or events occurring is more than remote but less than likely.

remote. The chance of the future event or events occurring is slight.

probable. The future event or events are likely to occur.

Consideration of Internal Control Over Compliance for Major Programs 225

deficiencies or material weaknesses for a major program and not be considered significant deficiencies or material weaknesses as they relate to the assertions of management in the financial statements.

9.44 AU-C section 265, *Communicating Internal Control Related Matters Identified in an Audit* (AICPA, *Professional Standards*), provides guidance related to evaluating the severity of deficiencies in internal control. The following paragraphs provide guidance to the auditor in adapting and applying this guidance to a Circular A-133 compliance audit.

9.45 In a Circular A-133 compliance audit, the auditor should evaluate the severity of each deficiency in internal control over compliance identified during the audit to determine whether the deficiency, individually or in combination, is a significant deficiency or material weakness in internal control over compliance. The severity of a deficiency depends on the magnitude of potential noncompliance resulting from the deficiency or deficiencies and whether there is a reasonable possibility that the entity's controls will fail to prevent or detect and correct noncompliance with a type of compliance requirement. In a Circular A-133 compliance audit, the significance of a deficiency in internal control over compliance depends on the potential for noncompliance, not on whether noncompliance actually has occurred. Accordingly, the absence of identified noncompliance does not provide evidence that identified deficiencies in internal control over compliance are not significant deficiencies or material weaknesses in internal control over compliance.

9.46 Risk factors affect whether there is a reasonable possibility that a deficiency, or combination of deficiencies, will result in noncompliance with a type of compliance requirement of a federal program. The factors include, but are not limited to,

- the nature of the type of compliance requirement involved. For example, a specific special test or provision may involve greater risk because it is unique to the program and may require unique controls.
- susceptibility of the program and related types of compliance requirements to fraud.
- subjectivity and complexity involved in meeting the compliance requirement, and the extent of judgment required in determining noncompliance.
- interaction or relationship of the control with other controls.
- interaction among the deficiencies.
- possible future consequences of the deficiency.

9.47 The evaluation of deficiencies in internal control over compliance includes the magnitude of potential noncompliance. Several factors affect the magnitude of potential noncompliance that could result from a deficiency or deficiencies in controls. The factors may include, but are not limited to

- program amounts or total of transactions exposed to the deficiency, in relation to the type of compliance requirement;
- volume of activity related to the compliance requirement exposed to the deficiency in the current period or expected in future periods; or
- adverse publicity or other qualitative factors.

9.48 Controls may be designed to operate individually, or in combination, to effectively prevent, or detect and correct, noncompliance. A deficiency in internal control over compliance on its own may not be sufficiently important to constitute a significant deficiency or a material weakness in internal control over compliance. However, a combination of deficiencies affecting the same type of compliance requirement or component of internal control over compliance may increase the risks of material noncompliance to such an extent to give rise to a significant deficiency or material weakness in internal control over compliance. This may be the case even though such deficiencies individually may be less severe. Therefore, the auditor should determine whether deficiencies that affect the same type of compliance requirement or component of internal control collectively result in a significant deficiency or material weakness in internal control over compliance.

9.49 The auditor may obtain evidence that a control does not operate effectively when performing compliance tests or tests of the operating effectiveness of controls, for example identifying an instance of noncompliance that was not prevented, or detected and corrected by the control. Management may inform the auditor, or the auditor may otherwise become aware, of the existence of compensating controls that, if effective, may limit the severity of the deficiency and prevent it from being a significant deficiency or material weakness in internal control over compliance. In these circumstances, although the auditor is not required to consider the effects of compensating controls, the auditor may consider the effects of compensating controls related to a deficiency in operation provided the auditor has tested the compensating controls for operating effectiveness. Compensating controls can limit the severity of the deficiency, but do not eliminate the deficiency.

9.50 The auditor may encounter deviations in the operating effectiveness of controls. A control that has an observed non-negligible deviation rate is at least a deficiency in internal control over compliance regardless of the reason for the deviation and could be, based upon further evaluation, a significant deficiency or material weakness in internal control over compliance. For example, if the auditor designs a test in which he or she selects a sample and expects no deviations, the finding of one deviation is a nonnegligible deviation rate because, based on the results of the auditor's test of the sample, the desired level of confidence was not obtained. See chapter 11 of this guide for more information on evaluating deviations in tests of controls.

9.51 If the auditor determines that a deficiency, or a combination of deficiencies, is not a material weakness in internal control over compliance, the auditor should consider whether prudent officials, having knowledge of the same facts and circumstances, would likely reach the same conclusion.

9.52 Indicators of material weaknesses in internal control over compliance include

- identification of fraud in the major program of any magnitude on the part of senior program management. For the purposes of evaluating and communicating deficiencies in internal control over compliance, the auditor should evaluate fraud of any magnitude of which he or she is aware on the part of senior program management, including fraud resulting in immaterial noncompliance.

- identification by the auditor of material noncompliance for the period under audit in circumstances that indicate that the noncompliance would not have been detected by the entity's internal control (for example, the noncompliance was not initially identified by the entity's internal control).

- ineffective oversight by management, or those charged with governance, over compliance with program requirements where the activity is subject to a type of compliance requirement (for example, lack of adequate review of federal financial reports prior to submission to the grantor).

9.53 Paragraph .A37 of AU-C section 265 contains examples of circumstances that may be deficiencies, significant deficiencies, or material weaknesses. Examples included relate to both deficiencies in the design of controls and deficiencies in the operation of controls. Some examples relevant to a Circular A-133 compliance audit are as follows:

- Deficiencies in the design of controls

    — Inadequate design of controls over activities subject to a type of compliance requirement

    — Inadequate design of controls over complex types of compliance requirements

    — Insufficient control consciousness within the entity; for example, the tone at the top and the control environment

    — Absent or inadequate segregation of duties over a type of compliance requirement

    — Inadequate design of IT controls relating to the activity subject to the type of compliance requirement

    — Employees or management who lack the qualifications and training to fulfill their assigned functions

    — Inadequate design of monitoring controls used to assess the design and operating effectiveness of the entity's internal control over compliance over time

    — The absence of an internal process to report deficiencies in internal control over compliance to management on a timely basis

- Deficiencies in the operation of controls

    — Failure in the operation of effectively designed controls over a type of compliance requirement

    — Failure of the information and communication component of internal control over compliance to provide complete and accurate output because of deficiencies in timeliness, completeness, or accuracy of information related to compliance

    — Misrepresentation by entity personnel to the auditor (an indicator of fraud)

    — Management override of controls

    — Failure of an application control caused by a deficiency in the design or operation of an IT general control

- An observed deviation rate that exceeds the number of deviations expected by the auditor in a test of the operating effectiveness of a control

Program Cluster Considerations

9.54 An entity may have separate controls related to federal programs that are treated as a cluster of programs in a Circular A-133 compliance audit, such as student financial assistance (SFA) and research and development (R&D). (Chapter 5, "Overview of the Single Audit Act, Circular A-133, and the *Compliance Supplement*," of this guide discusses clusters of programs.) In this case, when evaluating whether an identified deficiency is a significant deficiency or a material weakness in internal control over compliance, the significance of the deficiency in relation to the type of compliance requirement for the cluster of programs is an important factor. Following are some examples:

- Deficiencies in specific controls over the time cards of college work-study students would likely be considered significant deficiencies or material weaknesses in internal control over compliance when college work-study program expenditures are significant in relation to SFA programs.
- Deficiencies in controls over a single campus or department of a university where a significant amount of research was administered would likely be significant deficiencies or material weaknesses in internal control over compliance when considered in relation to the total expenditures of R&D programs.
- A deficiency in an SFA or R&D program that was clearly insignificant to the SFA or R&D program, respectively, as a whole would not necessarily be considered a significant deficiency or material weakness in internal control over compliance.

Documentation Requirements

9.55 As noted in paragraph .39 of AU-C section 935, the auditor should document the risk assessment procedures performed, including those related to gaining an understanding of internal control over compliance. Paragraph .40 of AU-C section 935 states that the auditor should document his or her responses to the assessed risks of material noncompliance, the procedures performed to test compliance with the applicable compliance requirements, and the results of those procedures, including any test of controls over compliance. Guidance related to this documentation is found in paragraph .33 of AU-C section 315, which notes that the auditor should document the following related to his or her understanding of internal control related to compliance requirements:

- The discussion among the audit team regarding the susceptibility of the entity's major programs to material noncompliance with direct and material compliance requirements, including how and when the discussion occurred, the subject matter discussed, the audit team members who participated, and significant decisions reached concerning planned responses to compliance requirements
- Key elements of the understanding obtained regarding each of the aspects of the entity and its environment, in this case as it relates to internal control over compliance, to assess the risks of

Consideration of Internal Control Over Compliance for Major Programs

material noncompliance, the sources of information from which the understanding was obtained; and the risk assessment procedures performed

- The identified and assessed risks of material noncompliance
- The risks identified and related controls about which the auditor has obtained an understanding as a result of the requirements found in paragraphs .28–.31 of AU-C section 315

9.56 Paragraph .30 of AU-C section 330 contains requirements regarding documentation of the testing of controls. Among the matters discussed of particular relevance to a Circular A-133 compliance audit is that the auditor should document the following:

- The overall responses to address the assessed risks of noncompliance as it relates to compliance requirements of major programs
- The nature, timing, and extent of further audit procedures
- The linkage of those procedures with the assessed risks
- The results of the audit procedures

9.57 As noted in chapter 3 of this guide, AU-C section 230, *Audit Documentation* (AICPA, *Professional Standards*), provides guidance on the form, content, extent, retention, and confidentiality of audit documentation as required by GAAS. Among other things, AU-C section 230 requires audit documentation to be sufficient to enable an experienced auditor, having no previous connection to the audit, to understand

- the nature, timing, and extent of auditing procedures performed to comply with GAAS, *Government Auditing Standards* and other applicable standards and requirements, such as Circular A-133 requirements;
- the results of the audit procedures performed and the audit evidence obtained; and
- significant findings or issues arising during the audit, the conclusions reached, and significant professional judgments made in reaching those conclusions.

AU-C section 230 contains guidance on documenting significant findings or issues; identifying the preparer and reviewer of audit documentation; documenting specific items tested; documenting departures from relevant Statements on Auditing Standards; revising audit documentation after the date of the auditor's report; and ownership and confidentiality of audit documentation. *Government Auditing Standards* includes an additional requirement that auditors should document, before the report release date, supervisory review of the evidence that supports the findings, conclusions, and recommendations contained in the auditor's report.

9.58 The form and extent of this documentation are influenced by the size and complexity of the auditee, as well as the nature of the auditee's internal control over compliance. For example, the documentation of the understanding of internal control over compliance of a large, complex entity may include flowcharts, questionnaires, or decision tables. For a small entity, however, the documentation may be less extensive. In general, the more complex internal control over compliance and the more extensive the procedures performed, the more extensive the auditor's documentation. (See chapter 11 of this guide for more information on documenting the testing of internal control.)

Transition Considerations Related to the Uniform Guidance

9.59 The A-102 Common Rule and OMB Circular A-110 (2 CFR Part 215) require that nonfederal entities receiving federal awards (that is, auditee management) establish and maintain internal control designed to reasonably ensure compliance with federal laws, regulations, and program compliance requirements. Similarly, the Uniform Guidance states that nonfederal entities must establish and maintain effective internal control over the federal award that provides reasonable assurance that the nonfederal entity is managing the federal award in compliance with federal statutes, regulations, and the terms and conditions of the federal award. The Uniform Guidance also goes on to identify the guidance in *Standards for Internal Control in the Federal Government* (known as the Green Book) issued by the Comptroller General of the United States and the "Internal Control Integrated Framework" (referred to as the COSO integrated framework) issued by the Committee of Sponsoring Organizations of the Treadway Commission (COSO), as best practices or recommended approaches for establishing and maintaining such internal control. Part 6 of the *Compliance Supplement* is the mechanism OMB has historically used to provide more detailed internal control guidance to both nonfederal entities and their auditors.

9.60 In light of the number of years that have passed since Part 6 was originally drafted, and as a result of the issuance of the Uniform Guidance, OMB has determined that Part 6 needs updating. OMB has also communicated that the update to Part 6 will not be made until the 2016 *Compliance Supplement*. In the meantime, OMB did not carry forward Part 6 to the 2015 *Compliance Supplement*. Instead, OMB is suggesting that nonfederal entities and their auditors look to the Green Book and the COSO integrated framework for guidance on internal control until such time that Part 6 is updated and reinserted back into the *Compliance Supplement*.

Chapter 10

Compliance Auditing Applicable to Major Programs (Circular A-133)

> **⊙ Update 10-1: Audits of Federal Awards**
>
> This chapter, and the remaining chapters of part II, *Circular A-133 Audits*, of this guide, should be used for performing a compliance audit of federal awards under Office of Management and Budget (OMB) Circular A-133, *Audits of States, Local Governments, and Non-Profit Organizations* (Circular A-133). Part III, *Uniform Guidance Audits*, of this guide should be used when performing a compliance audit under Title 2 U.S. *Code of Federal Regulations* (CFR) Part 200, *Uniform Administrative Requirements, Cost Principles, and Audit Requirements for Federal Awards* (Uniform Guidance). See the transitional guidance sections at the end of each chapter that highlight important matters for consideration.[1] Refer to the preface for additional information.
>
> **Important Uniform Guidance Effective Date Information**
>
> In December 2013, the OMB issued the Uniform Guidance, which is effective for nonfederal entities for all federal awards and certain funding increments provided on or after December 26, 2014. The requirements in Subpart F, "Audit Requirements," are effective for audits of fiscal years beginning on or after December 26, 2014, with no early implementation permitted. Therefore, auditees subject to a single audit with December 25, 2015, and later year ends (for example, December 31, 2015) will be required to undergo the audit under Subpart F of the Uniform Guidance. Note that audits of fiscal years ending prior to the effective date of the Uniform Guidance audit requirements are subject to an audit under Circular A-133.

10.01 This chapter discusses the auditor's consideration of compliance requirements applicable to major programs under OMB Circular A-133. (As discussed in chapter 14, "Program-Specific Audits (Circular A-133)," of this guide, much of the guidance in this chapter also would be applicable to a program-specific audit when a program-specific audit guide is not available.) Chapter 13, "Auditor Reporting Requirements and Other Communication Considerations in a Single Audit (Circular A-133)," of this guide discusses the related reporting requirements. Chapter 3, "Planning and Performing a Financial Statement Audit in Accordance With *Government Auditing Standards*," and chapter 4, "Auditor Reporting Requirements and Other Communication Considerations of *Government Auditing Standards*," of this guide discuss the auditor's consideration of and reporting on the auditee's compliance with laws, regulations, and provisions of contracts or grant agreements in a financial statement audit.

---

[1] See the information found at the end of certain chapters in part II, *Circular A-133 Audits*, of this guide for transition considerations when performing an audit under Office of Management and Budget (OMB) Circular A-133, *Audits of States, Local Governments, and Non-Profit Organizations* (Circular A-133), as it relates to the applicability of certain aspects of Title 2 U.S. *Code of Federal Regulations* Part 200, *Uniform Administrative Requirements, Cost Principles, and Audit Requirements for Federal Awards* (Uniform Guidance), to audits performed under Circular A-133. Transition considerations related to an audit performed under the Uniform Guidance can be found at the end of chapters in part III, *Uniform Guidance Audits*, of this guide in sections titled "Transition Considerations Related to the Uniform Guidance."

Compliance Objectives in a Circular A-133 Compliance Audit

10.02 AU-C section 935, *Compliance Audits* (AICPA, *Professional Standards*), states that the auditor's objectives in a compliance audit are to

- obtain sufficient appropriate audit evidence to form an opinion and report at the level specified in the governmental audit requirement on whether the entity complied in all material respects with the applicable compliance requirements,[2] which are the direct and material compliance requirements in a Circular A-133 compliance audit; and
- identify audit and reporting requirements specified in the governmental audit requirement that are supplemental to generally accepted auditing standards (GAAS) and *Government Auditing Standards*, if any, and perform procedures to address those requirements.

10.03 Circular A-133 (the governmental audit requirement covered in this guide) states that, in addition to performing a financial statement audit in accordance with GAAS and *Government Auditing Standards*, the auditor should determine whether the auditee has complied with laws, regulations, and the provisions of contracts or grant agreements that may have a direct and material effect on each of its major programs. A Circular A-133 compliance audit results in the auditor expressing an opinion on the auditee's compliance with those compliance requirements for each of its major programs. To express such an opinion, the auditor accumulates sufficient appropriate audit evidence by planning, performing risk assessment procedures, and performing tests of transactions and such other auditing procedures as are necessary in support of the auditee's compliance with direct and material compliance requirements, thereby limiting audit risk of noncompliance to an appropriately low level.

Responsibilities of Auditee

10.04 Following the guidance in AU-C section 935, the Circular A-133 compliance audit is based on the premise that management is responsible for the entity's compliance with compliance requirements. That responsibility includes the following:

- Identifying the entity's federal programs and understanding and complying with the types of compliance requirements
- Establishing and maintaining effective controls that provide reasonable assurance that the entity administers federal programs in compliance with the types of compliance requirements
- Evaluating and monitoring the entity's compliance with the types of compliance requirements

---

[2] AU-C section 935, *Compliance Audits* (AICPA, *Professional Standards*), defines *applicable compliance requirements* as the compliance requirements that are subject to the compliance audit. Paragraph .500(d) of OMB Circular A-133 states that the auditor should determine whether the auditee has complied with laws, regulations, and the provisions of contracts or grant agreements that may have a direct and material effect on each of its major programs. Therefore, in a Circular A-133 compliance audit, the direct and material compliance requirements are those that are subject to audit. Accordingly, for the purpose of adapting AU-C section 935 to a Circular A-133 compliance audit, the term *applicable compliance requirements* has been replaced by *direct and material compliance requirements* in this guide except when directly citing content from AU-C section 935.

Compliance Auditing Applicable to Major Programs (Circular A-133)

- Taking corrective action when instances of noncompliance are identified, including corrective action on audit findings of the compliance audit

Paragraphs 10.72–.74 discuss the auditor's responsibility to obtain management's written representations regarding its compliance and internal control responsibilities.

10.05 The form and extent of the documentation of management's compliance will vary depending on the nature of the compliance requirements and the size and complexity of the entity. The auditee may have documentation in the form of accounting or statistical data, case files, entity policy manuals, accounting manuals, narrative memorandums, procedural write-ups, flowcharts, completed questionnaires, or internal auditor's reports.

Use of Professional Judgment

10.06 The planning, conduct, and evaluation of the results of compliance testing in a Circular A-133 compliance audit require the auditor to exercise professional judgment. The auditor may consider the following factors in applying his or her professional judgment:

- The assessment of audit risk of noncompliance
- The assessment of materiality
- The evidence obtained from other auditing procedures
- The amount of expenditures for the program
- The diversity or homogeneity of expenditures for the program
- The length of time that the program has operated, or changes in its conditions
- The current and prior auditing experience with the program, particularly findings in previous audits and other evaluations (such as inspections, program reviews, or system reviews required by the Federal Acquisition Regulations found in Part 41 of the U.S. *Code of Federal Regulations*)
- The extent to which the program is carried out through subrecipients, as well as the related monitoring activities
- The extent to which the program contracts for goods or services
- The level to which the program already is subject to program reviews or other forms of independent oversight
- The expectation of noncompliance or compliance with the direct and material compliance requirements
- The extent to which computer processing is used to administer the program, as well as the complexity of the processing
- Whether the program has been identified as being higher risk by the OMB in the *OMB Compliance Supplement* (*Compliance Supplement*)

Audit Risk of Noncompliance Considerations

10.07 To express an opinion on compliance, the auditor accumulates sufficient appropriate audit evidence in support of compliance, thereby reducing audit risk of noncompliance to an appropriately low level. Requirements and guidance related to the auditor's consideration of audit risk and materiality are found in AU-C section 320, *Materiality in Planning and Performing an Audit* (AICPA, *Professional Standards*), and these requirements and guidance should be adapted and applied to the Circular A-133 compliance audit when planning and performing the audit. Audit risk of noncompliance and materiality, among other matters, need to be considered together for each major program being tested as well as for each direct and material compliance requirement in determining the nature, timing, and extent of auditing procedures and in evaluating the results of those procedures. See chapter 6, "Planning Considerations of Circular A-133," of this guide for a discussion of audit risk of noncompliance considerations, including a detailed description of the components of audit risk of noncompliance, performing risk assessment procedures, and assessing the risks of noncompliance.

Performing Further Audit Procedures in Response to Assessed Risks

10.08 The auditor should design and perform further audit procedures, including tests of details (which may include tests of transactions) to obtain sufficient appropriate audit evidence about the auditee's compliance with each of the direct and material compliance requirements in response to the assessed risks of material noncompliance. Risk assessment procedures, tests of controls, and analytical procedures alone are not sufficient to address a risk of material noncompliance.

10.09 Paragraph .18 of AU-C section 935 notes that if risks of material noncompliance are identified that are pervasive to the entity's compliance, the auditor should develop an overall response to such risks. AU-C section 330, *Performing Audit Procedures in Response to Assessed Risks and Evaluating the Audit Evidence Obtained* (AICPA, *Professional Standards*), provides guidance in developing an overall response to the risks of material noncompliance and this guidance should be adapted and applied to the Circular A-133 compliance audit.

Materiality Considerations

10.10 As discussed in chapter 6 of this guide, the auditor's consideration of materiality in a Circular A-133 compliance audit differs from that in an audit of the financial statements. Materiality is affected by (*a*) the nature of the compliance requirements, which may or may not be quantifiable in monetary terms; (*b*) the nature and frequency of noncompliance identified with an appropriate consideration of sampling risk; and (*c*) qualitative considerations, such as the needs and expectations of federal agencies and pass-through entities.

Materiality Judgments About Compliance Applied to Each Major Program

10.11 AU-C section 935 states that the auditor should establish and apply materiality levels for the compliance audit based on the governmental audit requirement. Therefore, in designing audit tests and developing an opinion on the auditee's compliance with direct and material compliance requirements in a Circular A-133 compliance audit, the auditor should apply the concept of materiality to each major program, rather than to all major programs combined.

Compliance Auditing Applicable to Major Programs (Circular A-133)

10.12 For purposes of evaluating the results of compliance testing, a material instance of noncompliance is defined as a failure to follow requirements, or a violation of prohibitions, established by law, regulation, contract, or grant agreement that results in an aggregation of noncompliance (that is, the auditor's best estimate of the overall noncompliance) that is material to the affected federal program. Instances of noncompliance that may not be individually material should be assessed to determine if, in the aggregate, they could have a material effect. Because the auditor expresses an opinion on each major program and not on all the major programs combined, reaching a conclusion about whether the instances of noncompliance (either individually or in the aggregate) are material to a major program requires consideration of the type and nature of the noncompliance, as well as the actual and projected effect on each major program in which the noncompliance was noted. Instances of noncompliance that are material to one major program may not be material to a major program of a different size or nature. In addition, the level of materiality relative to a particular major program can change from one audit to the next.

Effect of Material Noncompliance on the Financial Statements

10.13 If the tests of compliance reveal material noncompliance at the major program level, the auditor should consider its effect on the financial statements. The auditor also should consider the cumulative effect of all instances of noncompliance on the financial statements using the materiality level established for the financial statements.[3] (See also paragraph 10.55 and chapter 12, "Audit Considerations of Federal Pass-Through Awards (Circular A-133)," of this guide.)

Performing a Circular A-133 Compliance Audit[4, 5]

10.14 The auditor should exercise (*a*) due care in planning and performing the audit and in evaluating the results of his or her audit procedures, and (*b*) a proper degree of professional skepticism to achieve reasonable assurance that material noncompliance will be detected.

10.15 In a Circular A-133 compliance audit, the auditor should perform the following, as discussed in paragraphs 10.16–.69:

    a. Identify the auditee's major programs to be tested and reported on for compliance.

    b. Identify the compliance requirements applicable to each major program.

---

[3] As discussed in the Audit and Accounting Guide *State and Local Governments*, the auditor's consideration of materiality for purposes of planning, performing, evaluating the results of, and reporting on the audit of the financial statements of a state or local government is based on opinion units.

[4] *Government Auditing Standards* incorporates by reference AICPA Statements on Auditing Standards. Therefore, auditors performing financial statement audits and Circular A-133 compliance audits in accordance with *Government Auditing Standards* should comply with generally accepted auditing standards, the requirements found in chapters 1–3 of *Government Auditing Standards*, and the additional standards and related requirements for financial audits found in chapter 4, "Standards for Financial Audits," of *Government Auditing Standards*.

[5] The appendix, "AU-C Sections That Are Not Applicable to Compliance Audits," of AU-C section 935 provides a list of AU-C section requirements that are not applicable to a compliance audit. All other AU-C sections not identified in the appendix should be adapted and applied to a compliance audit.

c. Determine which of the compliance requirements identified in item *b* could have a direct and material effect on each major program.

d. Plan the engagement.

e. Consider relevant portions of the entity's internal control over compliance for each direct and material compliance requirement for each major program.

f. Obtain sufficient appropriate audit evidence, which involves testing internal control over compliance and compliance with direct and material compliance requirements for each major program.

g. Consider indications of abuse.

h. Consider subsequent events.

i. Form an opinion about whether the auditee complied with the direct and material compliance requirements.

j. Perform follow-up procedures on previously identified findings.

Identifying Major Programs to Be Tested

10.16 Circular A-133 states that the auditor should determine the major programs to be tested using a risk-based approach, applying a specific process established in the circular. Chapter 8, "Determination of Major Programs (Circular A-133)," of this guide discusses the application of the risk-based approach to determine major programs.

Identifying Direct and Material Compliance Requirements

10.17 As discussed in this section, the auditor should determine, after identifying the compliance requirements applicable to each major program, the direct and material compliance requirements to be tested and reported on in a Circular A-133 compliance audit. As further described in paragraph 10.20, Part 2 of the *Compliance Supplement* provides a matrix that is useful to the auditor in identifying whether particular types of compliance requirements may apply to federal programs. The auditor then assesses, based on the nature of the program and the transactions for the period under audit, those types of compliance requirements that may have a direct and material effect on each major program. The auditor should use professional judgment in making this determination.

Compliance Supplement[6]

10.18 The *Compliance Supplement* is based on the requirements of the Single Audit Act and Circular A-133, which provide for the issuance of a compliance supplement to assist auditors in performing the required audits. (Chapter 5, "Overview of the Single Audit Act, Circular A-133, and the *Compliance Supplement*," discusses the *Compliance Supplement* and how to obtain it.) The *Compliance Supplement* is a comprehensive source of information regarding

---

[6] Part 6, "Internal Control," of the 2015 *OMB Compliance Supplement* (*Compliance Supplement*) was scheduled to be updated for the revised *Standards for Internal Control in the Federal Government* (known as the Green Book) issued by the Comptroller General of the United States and the "Internal Control–Integrated Framework" issued by the Committee of Sponsoring Organizations of the Treadway Commission (COSO). It has been communicated that the update to Part 6 has been postponed until the 2016 *Compliance Supplement*, at which time it will be reinserted into the supplement.

Compliance Auditing Applicable to Major Programs (Circular A-133) 237

compliance. The various parts of the *Compliance Supplement* are interrelated and are intended to be used in conjunction with each other. Part 1 of the *Compliance Supplement* includes background, purpose, and applicability information, and Part 2 provides a matrix of types of compliance requirements that are applicable to the programs included in the supplement. Part 3[7] of the *Compliance Supplement* identifies 12 types of compliance requirements applicable to many federal programs, as listed in paragraph 10.19. Part 4 of the *Compliance Supplement* includes a discussion of the compliance requirements specific to certain of the largest federal programs and is to be used in conjunction with Part 3. The *Compliance Supplement* states that the auditor should look to Part 3 for a general description of the compliance requirements, audit objectives, and suggested audit procedures, and to Part 4 for information about the specific requirements for a program (see also paragraph 10.25). Part 5 of the *Compliance Supplement* contains information on clusters of programs. As further discussed in paragraph 10.28, Part 7 of the *Compliance Supplement* provides guidance to assist the auditor in identifying the types of compliance requirements for federal programs not included in the *Compliance Supplement*.

Twelve Types of Compliance Requirements

10.19 Part 3 of the *Compliance Supplement* lists and describes the 12 types of compliance requirements and the related audit objectives that the auditor should consider in every Circular A-133 compliance audit, with the exception of program-specific audits performed in accordance with a federal agency's program specific audit guide (see chapter 14). It also provides suggested audit procedures to assist the auditor in planning and performing tests of the auditee's compliance with the requirements of federal programs. The auditor's judgment will be necessary to determine whether the suggested audit procedures are sufficient to achieve the stated audit objectives and whether additional or alternative audit procedures are needed (see paragraph 10.43). The 12 types of compliance requirements are as follows:[8]

- A—Activities allowed or unallowed
- B—Allowable costs/cost principles
- C—Cash management
- D—Reserved
- E—Eligibility
- F—Equipment and real property management
- G—Matching, level of effort, earmarking
- H—Period of Availability of Federal Funds
- I—Procurement and suspension and debarment
- J—Program income
- K—Reserved

---

[7] The 2015 *Compliance Supplement* contains two sections of Part 3, *Compliance Requirements*. Part 3.1 applies to federal awards made prior to December 26, 2014. Part 3.2 applies to federal awards subject to the Uniform Guidance.

[8] Although "period of availability of federal funds" has been retained in Part 3.1 of the 2015 *Compliance Supplement*, the former compliance requirement H, "Period of Availability of Federal Funds," has been renamed "Period of Performance." In addition, two letters (D and K) associated with compliance requirements that have been removed ("Davis Bacon Act" and "Real Property Acquisition and Relocation Assistance") are listed as "Reserved."

- L—Reporting
- M—Subrecipient monitoring
- N—Special tests and provisions

10.20 The auditor should consider the applicability of these types of compliance requirements to the auditee's major programs. Part 2 of the *Compliance Supplement* provides a matrix that is useful to the auditor for this purpose; that matrix identifies whether particular types of compliance requirements may apply to the federal programs included in the *Compliance Supplement*. In making a determination not to test a type of compliance requirement identified as applicable to a particular program, the auditor should conclude, and document such conclusion, either that the requirement does not apply to the particular auditee or that noncompliance with the requirements could not have a direct and material effect on a major program. For example, a federal program may be designed such that subawards of federal funds may be made to subrecipients, and thus the matrix in Part 2 of the *Compliance Supplement* would identify the subrecipient monitoring type of compliance requirement as applicable. However, the auditee may not have made any, or made only an immaterial amount of, subawards of their federal program funds, and thus the auditor may determine that noncompliance with the subrecipient monitoring type of compliance requirement would not have a direct or material effect on the major program (even though it was identified as applicable in the Part 2 matrix). No testing would be required on types of compliance requirements not considered direct and material, but the auditor's conclusion relating to this determination should be documented.

Keeping Abreast of Changes in Compliance Requirements

10.21 Circular A-133 states that an audit of the compliance requirements related to federal programs contained in the *Compliance Supplement* will meet the requirements of the circular. However, it also states that when there have been changes to the compliance requirements and the changes are not reflected in the *Compliance Supplement*, the auditor should determine the current compliance requirements and modify the audit procedures accordingly.

10.22 Although Circular A-133 provides that federal agencies are responsible for informing the OMB annually of any updates needed to the *Compliance Supplement*, laws and regulations change periodically and delays will occur between such changes and revisions to the *Compliance Supplement*. Accordingly, the auditor should perform reasonable procedures to ensure that compliance requirements are current. Besides describing the types of compliance requirements, the *Compliance Supplement* includes references to the *Code of Federal Regulations* and other sources of information about the requirements. The auditor may refer to those other sources of information to identify significant changes to the requirements or perform other procedures, including the following:

- Hold discussions with appropriate individuals within the auditee organization (that is, the CFO, internal auditors, legal counsel, compliance officer, or grant or contract administrators)
- Review contracts or grant agreements, new guidance material issued by the granting agency or pass-through entity (for example, handbooks and operating procedures), and correspondence from the granting agency or pass-through entity

- Make inquiries of granting agency personnel (A listing of federal agency contacts, including addresses, phone numbers, and e-mail or Internet site addresses can be found in appendix 3 of the *Compliance Supplement*.)

Considering Additional Provisions of Contracts or Grant Agreements

10.23 The *Compliance Supplement* states that in addition to the compliance requirements identified in the supplement, auditors should consider whether there are any provisions of contracts or grant agreements that are unique to a particular entity. For example, the grant agreement may specify the matching percentage, or an entity may have agreed to additional requirements that are not required by law or regulation, perhaps as part of a resolution of prior audit findings.

10.24 Therefore, in using the *Compliance Supplement* to identify direct and material compliance requirements, the auditor should consider

    a. the applicability to the federal program of the 12 types of compliance requirements identified in Part 3 of the *Compliance Supplement*.

    b. additional compliance requirements specific to the federal program as identified in Part 4 of the *Compliance Supplement*.

    c. any provisions of contracts or grants that are unique to the particular entity.

Compliance Requirements Specific to Certain Federal Programs

10.25 Part 4 of the *Compliance Supplement* discusses program objectives, program procedures, and compliance requirements that are specific to each federal program included. With the exception of special tests and provisions, Part 3 of the *Compliance Supplement* identifies the audit objectives and suggested audit procedures that pertain to the compliance requirements associated with each program. Because special tests and provisions are unique to each program, Part 4 of the *Compliance Supplement* includes those compliance requirements and the related audit objectives and suggested audit procedures. (Part 4 of the *Compliance Supplement* is considered a supplement to Part 3 and is not a replacement for it.)

Compliance Requirements Specific to a Cluster of Programs

10.26 As discussed in chapter 5 of this guide, a cluster of programs is a grouping of closely related programs that have similar compliance requirements (for example, student financial assistance [SFA], research and development [R&D], and other clusters). Part 5 of the *Compliance Supplement* identifies those programs that the OMB considers clusters of programs. It also provides compliance requirements, audit objectives, and suggested audit procedures for the SFA and R&D clusters. (States also may designate clusters of programs for federal awards they provide to subrecipients when those awards are for groupings of closely related programs that have similar compliance requirements.)

Relationship of the Compliance Supplement to Federal Program Audit Guides

10.27 The *Compliance Supplement* states that when performing an audit in accordance with Circular A-133, the supplement replaces federal agency audit guides and other audit requirement documents for individual federal programs.[9] Accordingly, for a federal program included in the *Compliance Supplement* and having a separate federal program audit guide or other federal program audit requirement documents, the auditor needs to consider only those types of compliance requirements in the *Compliance Supplement* when performing a Circular A-133 compliance audit (versus a program-specific audit).

Federal Programs Not Included in the Compliance Supplement

10.28 The *Compliance Supplement* does not include all federal programs from which an auditee may receive federal awards. Circular A-133 states that for those federal programs not covered in the *Compliance Supplement*, the auditor should use the 12 types of compliance requirements (see paragraph 10.19) contained in the supplement as guidance for identifying the types of compliance requirements to test, and should determine the requirements governing the federal program by reviewing the provisions of contracts and grant agreements and the laws and regulations referred to in such contracts and grant agreements. The auditor should follow the guidance in Part 7 of the *Compliance Supplement* for identifying the direct and material compliance requirements to test and report on in a Circular A-133 compliance audit. That guidance outlines the following steps to determine which compliance requirements to test:

    a. Identify the compliance requirements that are applicable to the federal program.

    b. Determine which of the compliance requirements identified in item *a* could have a direct and material effect on the major program.

    c. Determine which of the compliance requirements identified in item *b* are susceptible to testing by the auditor.

    d. Determine which of the 12 types of compliance requirements the compliance requirements identified in item *c* fall into.

    e. For special tests and provisions, determine the applicable audit objectives and audit procedures.

Part 7 of the *Compliance Supplement* provides more detailed guidance on the steps to perform to identify direct and material compliance requirements.

---

[9] Some federal agencies have developed audit guides or supplements related to their programs. For programs not listed in the *Compliance Supplement*, the auditor may wish to consider that guidance in identifying the program objectives, program procedures, and compliance requirements, as suggested in Part 7 of the *Compliance Supplement*. That guidance, where available, may be obtained from the federal agency's Office of Inspector General. Auditors should consider whether such guidance is outdated with regard to compliance requirements or currently authoritative auditing standards and requirements. See the discussion regarding such situations in chapter 14, "Program-Specific Audits (Circular A-133)," of this guide.

Planning the Engagement

General Considerations

10.29 Planning a Circular A-133 compliance audit involves developing an overall strategy for the expected conduct and scope of the engagement. To develop such a strategy, auditors need to have sufficient knowledge to enable them to understand adequately the events, transactions, and practices that, in their judgment, have a significant effect on compliance. Also, it is important for auditors to gain an understanding of any additional audit requirements that are supplemental to GAAS and *Government Auditing Standards*. Proper planning and supervision contribute to the effectiveness of audit procedures. Proper planning directly influences the selection of appropriate procedures and the timeliness of their application, and proper supervision helps ensure that planned procedures are appropriately applied. (See also chapter 6 of this guide.)

10.30 Factors the auditor might consider in planning a Circular A-133 compliance audit include (*a*) the anticipated level of audit risk of noncompliance related to the direct and material compliance requirements on which the auditor will report (see paragraphs 10.07–.09), (*b*) preliminary judgments about materiality levels for audit purposes (see paragraphs 10.10–.13), and (*c*) conditions that may require the extension or modification of audit procedures.

10.31 The nature, timing, and extent of planning will vary with the nature and complexity of the compliance requirements and the auditor's prior experience with the auditee. Obtaining an understanding of an entity's major programs, the direct and material compliance requirements, and the entity's internal control over compliance establishes a frame of reference within which the auditor plans the compliance audit and exercises professional judgment about assessing risks of material noncompliance and responding to those risks throughout the compliance audit. As the Circular A-133 compliance audit progresses, changed conditions may make it necessary to modify planned procedures. Chapter 6 of this guide discusses additional planning considerations.

Multiple Organizational Unit Considerations

10.32 In a Circular A-133 compliance audit in which the auditee has operations in multiple organizational units (for example, operating units, locations or branches), the auditor may determine that it is not necessary to test compliance with requirements at every such unit. Making such a determination and selecting the units to be tested includes consideration of the following factors: (*a*) the degree to which the specified compliance requirements apply at the organizational unit; (*b*) judgments about materiality; (*c*) the degree of centralization of the records; (*d*) the effectiveness of controls, particularly those that affect management's direct control over the exercise of authority delegated to others, as well as its ability to supervise activities at various locations effectively; (*e*) the nature and extent of operations conducted at the various organizational units; and (*f*) the similarity of operations and controls over compliance for different organizational units. Chapter 8, chapter 9, "Consideration of Internal Control Over Compliance for Major Programs (Circular A-133)," and chapter 11, "Audit Sampling Considerations of Circular A-133 Compliance Audits," of this guide discuss other multiple organizational unit considerations.

Consideration of Internal Control Over Compliance for Major Programs

10.33 For each of the direct and material compliance requirements selected for testing for each major program, the auditor should perform risk assessment procedures to obtain a sufficient understanding of the direct and material compliance requirements and the entity's internal control over compliance with the direct and material compliance requirements. The auditor should use this knowledge to identify types of potential noncompliance, to consider factors that affect the risks of material noncompliance, and to design appropriate tests of compliance. Circular A-133 provides that the auditor should perform procedures to obtain an understanding of internal control over compliance for federal programs sufficient to plan the audit to support a low assessed level of control risk of noncompliance for major programs.[10] Circular A-133 also states that the auditor should perform testing of controls as planned. In some instances, the auditor may be able to perform compliance testing for major programs concurrently with tests of controls.[11] (Chapter 6 of this guide discusses how to develop an efficient audit approach.) Any significant deficiencies and material weaknesses in internal control over compliance for major programs that are noted should be reported as an audit finding. (Chapter 13 of this guide discusses the situations that Circular A-133 requires the auditor to report as audit findings.) Chapter 6 of this guide further discusses control risk of noncompliance, and chapter 9 of this guide discusses the auditor's consideration of internal control over compliance for major programs, including the final control risk of noncompliance assessment and the performance of tests of controls.

Performing Compliance Testing[12]

10.34 As described in chapter 9 of this guide, Circular A-133 specifically requires the auditor to perform procedures to obtain an understanding of internal control over compliance for federal programs sufficient to plan the audit to support a low assessed level of control risk for major programs. This includes performing procedures to evaluate the design and operating effectiveness of the internal control over compliance for each direct and material compliance requirement for each major program.

10.35 Circular A-133 states that compliance testing should include tests of transactions and such other auditing procedures as are necessary to provide the auditor with sufficient evidence to support an opinion on compliance for each major program. Such compliance testing may be performed (*a*) concurrently with tests of controls, (*b*) as separate substantive testing, or (*c*) as a combination of the two. In performing compliance testing, the auditor attempts to obtain reasonable assurance that the auditee complied, in all material respects, with the compliance requirements. In a Circular A-133 compliance audit this includes designing procedures to detect both intentional and unintentional noncompliance. The auditor can obtain reasonable, but not absolute, assurance about the entity's compliance because of factors such as the need for judgment,

---

[10] Although Circular A-133 uses the term *control risk*, this guide uses the term *control risk of noncompliance* in order to be consistent with the term as used and defined in AU-C section 935.

[11] However, see paragraph 6.56 for additional considerations.

[12] See chapter 11, "Audit Sampling Considerations of Circular A-133 Compliance Audits," for an in-depth discussion of audit sampling in a compliance audit, including a discussion of performing compliance testing for major programs concurrently with tests of controls (that is, dual purpose testing).

Compliance Auditing Applicable to Major Programs (Circular A-133) 243

the use of sampling, and the inherent limitations of internal control over compliance with direct and material compliance requirements and the fact that much of the evidence available to the auditor is persuasive rather than conclusive in nature. Also, procedures that are effective for detecting noncompliance that is unintentional may be ineffective for detecting noncompliance that is intentional and is concealed through collusion between the auditee's personnel and a third party or among the management or other employees of the entity. Therefore, the subsequent discovery that material noncompliance with direct and material compliance requirements exists does not, in and of itself, evidence inadequate planning, performance, or judgment on the part of the auditor.

10.36 In determining the nature, timing, and extent of tests to perform, the auditor should exercise professional judgment regarding the appropriate level of detection risk of noncompliance to accept.[13] (Paragraph 10.06 notes factors for the auditor to consider in applying professional judgment.) In determining the nature, timing, and extent of the testing of an auditee's compliance with compliance requirements, the auditor should consider both audit risk of noncompliance and materiality related to each major program as well as for each direct and material compliance requirement related to each major program. The auditor plans compliance tests to reduce detection risk of noncompliance to an acceptable level. The evidence provided by those tests, along with evidence regarding inherent risk of noncompliance and control risk of noncompliance, provides the basis for expressing an opinion on whether the auditee complied, in all material respects, with the direct and material compliance requirements for each major program.

10.37 In determining the nature of tests of compliance with requirements governing major programs, the consideration of the nature of those requirements will assist the auditor. For example, to test compliance with requirements applicable to the allowability of expenditures using program funds, the auditor should design audit procedures to provide sufficient appropriate audit evidence to evaluate how management expended the funds.

Sufficient Appropriate Audit Evidence

10.38 The auditor should apply procedures to provide reasonable assurance of detecting material noncompliance. The selection and application of procedures that will accumulate evidence that is sufficient and appropriate in the circumstances to provide a reasonable basis for expressing an opinion on compliance require the careful exercise of professional judgment. A broad array of available procedures may be applied in a Circular A-133 compliance audit. In establishing a proper combination of procedures to restrict audit risk of noncompliance appropriately, the auditor should consider the following generalizations, bearing in mind that they are not mutually exclusive and may be subject to important exceptions:

    a. Audit evidence is more reliable when it is obtained from knowledgeable independent sources outside the entity.

    b. Audit evidence that is generated internally is more reliable when the related controls imposed by the entity are effective.

    c. Audit evidence obtained directly by the auditor (for example, observation of the application of a control) is more reliable than audit

---

[13] See also chapter 11 of this guide for a discussion of audit sampling.

evidence obtained indirectly or by inference (for example, inquiry about the application of a control).

d. Audit evidence is more reliable when it exists in documentary form, whether paper, electronic, or other medium (for example, a contemporaneously written record of a meeting is more reliable than a subsequent oral representation of the matters discussed).

e. Audit evidence provided by original documents is more reliable than audit evidence provided by photocopies or facsimiles.

10.39 Thus, in the hierarchy of available audit procedures, those that involve search and verification (for example, inspection, confirmation, or observation)—particularly when independent sources outside the entity are used—generally are more effective in reducing audit risk of noncompliance than are those involving internal inquiries and comparisons of internal information (for example, analytical procedures and discussions with the individuals responsible for compliance).

10.40 In a Circular A-133 compliance audit, the auditor's objective is to accumulate sufficient appropriate audit evidence to limit audit risk of noncompliance to a level that is, in the auditor's professional judgment, appropriately low for the high level of assurance being provided. An auditor should select from all available procedures (that is, procedures that assess inherent and control risk of noncompliance and restrict detection risk of noncompliance) in any combination that can limit audit risk of noncompliance to such an appropriately low level.

10.41 For regulatory requirements, the auditor's procedures may include reviewing reports of significant examinations and related communications between regulatory agencies and the entity and, when appropriate, making inquiries of the regulatory agencies, including inquiries about examinations in progress.

Audit Objectives

10.42 As noted in paragraph 10.19, the *Compliance Supplement* contains the audit objectives for each type of compliance requirement that the auditor should consider in planning and performing tests of compliance requirements. The audit objectives are useful in understanding the specific objectives to be satisfied when the auditor performs audit tests and determines whether the noncompliance that is identified is material.

Suggested Audit Procedures

10.43 The *Compliance Supplement* contains suggested audit procedures for testing federal programs for compliance. Those suggested audit procedures represent procedures that may be used by the auditor in developing an audit plan. The suggested audit procedures also may be useful in testing the same types of compliance requirements for programs that are not included in the *Compliance Supplement*. The auditor should use professional judgment in determining the audit procedures to be performed to allow him or her to obtain sufficient appropriate audit evidence to form an opinion on the auditee's compliance with the compliance requirements that could have a direct and material effect on each major program.

Audit Sampling

10.44 The auditor generally uses audit sampling to obtain audit evidence. See chapter 11 of this guide for an in-depth discussion of audit sampling as it relates to compliance audits.

Consideration of Abuse

10.45 As discussed in chapter 3 of this guide, *Government Auditing Standards* provides requirements and guidance related to abuse.[14] Because the determination of abuse is subjective, auditors are not required to detect abuse. However, the requirements related to abuse in *Government Auditing Standards* apply to the entirety of the single audit, including the Circular A-133 compliance audit. Therefore, if in performing procedures on major programs, the auditor becomes aware of a situation or transaction that might constitute abuse, the auditor should extend procedures to determine whether it is indicative of abuse and potentially material to the financial statement amounts[15] or material in relation to a direct and material compliance requirement of a major program. (Chapter 3 of this guide further discusses procedures relating to and the evaluation of indications of abuse.) Because the OMB cost principles circulars require that costs charged to federal awards be reasonable and necessary for the performance and administration of the awards,[16] situations or transactions involving federal awards that might otherwise appear to constitute abuse instead generally are instances of noncompliance. (By definition, instances of noncompliance with provisions of laws, regulations, contracts, and grant agreements are not abuse.) However, there may be isolated situations or transactions involving federal awards that the auditor becomes aware of that do constitute abuse. Chapter 13 of this guide discusses the reporting of abuse involving federal awards.

Consideration of Subsequent Events

10.46 In a Circular A-133 compliance audit, two types of subsequent events may occur. The first type consists of events that provide additional evidence with respect to conditions that existed at the end of the reporting period that affect the auditee's compliance during the reporting period. The second type consists of events of noncompliance that did not exist at the end of the reporting period but arose subsequent to the reporting period.

10.47 The auditor should perform audit procedures up to the date of the auditor's report to obtain sufficient appropriate audit evidence that all subsequent events related to the auditee's compliance during the period covered by the auditor's report on compliance have been identified. The auditor should take into account the auditor's risk assessment in determining the nature and extent of such audit procedures. These procedures should include, but are not limited to, inquiring of management about and considering

---

[14] Paragraph 4.07 of *Government Auditing Standards* states that abuse "involves behavior that is deficient or improper when compared with behavior that a prudent person would consider reasonable and necessary business practice given the facts and circumstances." It goes on to state that abuse does not necessarily involve fraud or noncompliance with provisions of laws, regulations, contracts, or grant agreements.

[15] See footnote 3.

[16] This compliance requirement is explained in Part 3, "Compliance Requirements," of the *Compliance Supplement*, section B, "Allowable Costs/Cost Principles."

- relevant internal auditor's reports issued during the subsequent period,
- other auditor's reports identifying noncompliance that were issued during the subsequent period,
- reports from grantors and pass-through entities related to the auditee's noncompliance that were issued during the subsequent period, and
- information about the auditee's noncompliance obtained through other professional engagements performed for that entity.

10.48 The auditor has no obligation to perform any audit procedures related to the entity's compliance during the period subsequent to the period covered by the auditor's report. However, if before the report release date the auditor becomes aware of noncompliance in the period subsequent to the period covered by the auditor's report that is of such a nature and significance that its disclosure is needed to prevent report users from being misled, the auditor should discuss the matter with management and, if appropriate, those charged with governance and should include an other-matter paragraph in the auditor's report describing the nature of the noncompliance. An example of a matter of noncompliance that may occur subsequent to the period being audited but before the report release date that may warrant disclosure to prevent report users from being misled is the discovery of noncompliance in the subsequent period of such magnitude that it caused the grantor to stop funding the program.

Evaluation and Reporting of Noncompliance

Instances of Noncompliance (Findings)

10.49 The auditor's tests of compliance with compliance requirements may disclose instances of noncompliance. Circular A-133 refers to these instances of noncompliance, among other matters, as "findings." Such findings may be of a monetary nature and involve questioned costs or may be nonmonetary and not result in questioned costs. Both *Government Auditing Standards* and Circular A-133 specify how certain findings are to be reported.[17] Chapter 13 of this guide discusses the auditor's opinion on compliance and his or her responsibilities for reporting findings.

10.50 Furthermore, the auditor should not assume that an instance of fraud or error is an isolated occurrence, and therefore should consider how the detection of such noncompliance affects the assessed risks of material noncompliance. Before the conclusion of the audit, the auditor should evaluate whether audit risk of noncompliance has been reduced to an appropriately low level and whether the nature, timing, and extent of the audit procedures need to be reconsidered. The auditor should conclude whether sufficient appropriate audit evidence has been obtained to reduce to an appropriately low level the risks of material noncompliance with compliance requirements.

---

[17] Certain laws and regulations may require audit reports to be made publicly available; therefore, the auditor is cautioned not to include names, Social Security numbers, other personal identification, or other potentially sensitive information in the body of audit reports or any attached or referenced schedules or letters.

Compliance Opinion

10.51 The auditor should evaluate the sufficiency and appropriateness of the audit evidence obtained. Additionally, the auditor should consider all relevant audit evidence regardless of whether it appears to corroborate or to contradict the relevant assertions.

10.52 AU-C section 935 states that the auditor should form an opinion at the level specified by the governmental audit requirement. In a Circular A-133 compliance audit, the auditor should report on compliance, which includes an opinion (or disclaimer of opinion) regarding whether the auditee complied with laws, regulations, and the provisions of contracts or grant agreements that could have a direct and material effect on each major program. Note that Circular A-133 requires the auditor to prepare a schedule of findings and questioned costs. (Chapter 13 of this guide discusses that report and schedule.)

10.53 In determining whether the auditee complied with the direct and material compliance requirements in all material respects, the auditor may consider the following factors:

- The frequency of noncompliance with the direct and material compliance requirements identified during the compliance audit
- The nature of the noncompliance with the direct and material compliance requirements
- The adequacy of the entity's system for monitoring compliance with the direct and material compliance requirements and the possible effect of any noncompliance on the entity
- Whether any identified noncompliance with the direct and material compliance requirements resulted in likely questioned costs that are material to the federal program

The auditor's evaluation of whether the auditee materially complied with the direct and material compliance requirements includes consideration of noncompliance identified by the auditor, regardless of whether the entity corrected the noncompliance after the auditor brought it to management's attention.

10.54 Assessing materiality at the appropriate level is critical to the proper evaluation of findings. Paragraphs 10.10–.13 discuss materiality as it relates to expressing an opinion on the auditee's compliance. Paragraph 10.57 discusses the auditor's evaluation of the effect of questioned costs on the compliance opinion.

Financial Statement Effect

10.55 The auditor also has the responsibility of assessing the effect of the actual and likely error noted in the Circular A-133 compliance audit against the materiality level established for the basic financial statements (see paragraph 10.13). Consideration of the effect of the following items is part of this evaluation: (*a*) any contingent liability that may arise from the noncompliance in accordance with applicable FASB *Accounting Standards Codification* (ASC) 450, *Contingencies*, or GASB standards (for example, paragraphs .96–.113 of GASB Statement No. 62, *Codification of Accounting and Financial Reporting Guidance Contained in Pre-November 30, 1989 FASB and AICPA Pronouncements*), and (*b*) for nongovernmental entities, any uncertainty regarding the resolution of instances of noncompliance in accordance with FASB standards (for example, FASB ASC 275, *Risks and Uncertainties*).

Questioned Costs

10.56 Circular A-133 defines *questioned costs* to include costs that are questioned by the auditor because of an audit finding (*a*) that resulted from a violation or possible violation of a provision of a law, regulation contract, grant, cooperative agreement, or other agreement or document governing the use of federal funds, including funds used to match federal funds; (*b*) for which the costs, at the time of the audit, are not supported by adequate documentation; or (*c*) for which the costs incurred appear unreasonable and do not reflect the actions a prudent person would take in the circumstances.

Evaluating the Effect of Questioned Costs on the Compliance Opinion

10.57 In evaluating the effect of questioned costs on the opinion on compliance, the auditor considers the best estimate of the total costs questioned for each major program (likely questioned costs), not just the questioned costs specifically identified (known questioned costs). Likely questioned costs are developed by extrapolating from audit evidence obtained, for example, by projecting known questioned costs identified in an audit sample to the entire population from which the sample was drawn. There may be situations in which the known questioned costs are not considered material but the likely questioned costs are considered material. In those situations, the auditor should consider the noncompliance to be material (and report a finding) or may expand the scope of the Circular A-133 compliance audit and apply additional audit procedures to further establish the likely questioned costs. (See also paragraph 10.62 of this guide.)

Federal Agency Consideration of Findings and Questioned Costs

10.58 The auditor's designation of a cost as questioned does not necessarily mean that a federal grantor agency will disallow the cost. In most instances, the auditor is unable to determine whether a federal awarding agency or pass-through entity will ultimately disallow a questioned cost, because the agency or entity has considerable discretion in those matters.

10.59 Circular A-133 defines a *management decision* as the evaluation by the federal awarding agency or pass-through entity of the audit findings and corrective action plan and the issuance of a written decision about what corrective action is necessary. (Chapter 13 of this guide discusses the corrective action plan.) Circular A-133 allows a federal awarding agency or pass-through entity receiving an auditor's report indicating findings and questioned costs six months after receipt of the audit report to issue such a decision. The awarding agency or pass-through entity considers the nature of the questioned costs, as well as the amounts involved, in issuing a management decision and deciding whether to disallow them. In addition, most federal awarding agencies have established appeal and adjudication procedures for questioned costs. Because of the discretion allowed in resolving these matters, all questioned costs are subject to uncertainty regarding their resolution.

Reporting the Findings

10.60 As discussed in chapter 6 of this guide, Circular A-133 states that the auditor should consider a different level of materiality for the purposes of reporting audit findings. Circular A-133 states that the auditor, in addition to providing an opinion on compliance, should include the following, among other items, in the schedule of findings and questioned costs:

- Material noncompliance with the provisions of laws, regulations, contracts, or grant agreements related to a major program. The auditor's determination of whether noncompliance with the provisions of laws, regulations, contracts, or grant agreements is material for purpose of reporting an audit finding is in relation to a type of compliance requirement for a major program or an audit objective identified in the *Compliance Supplement*.

- Known questioned costs that are greater than $10,000 for a type of compliance requirement for a major program. (Paragraph 10.19 lists the 12 types of compliance requirements.) Known questioned costs are those specifically identified by the auditor.

- Known questioned costs when likely questioned costs are greater than $10,000 for a type of compliance requirement.

- Known questioned costs that are greater than $10,000 for a federal program that is not audited as a major program.

Chapter 13 of this guide discusses the reporting of audit findings and contains a complete listing of the items that Circular A-133 requires to be reported in the schedule of findings and questioned costs. That chapter also discusses the *Government Auditing Standards* requirement that the auditor communicate to the auditee in writing instances of noncompliance with provisions of contracts or grant agreements or abuse that are less than material but warrant the attention of those charged with governance.

Findings of Noncompliance That Cannot Be Quantified

10.61 The auditor may discover instances of noncompliance that cannot be quantified. The auditor's responsibility for reporting such findings can best be described through an example. Assume that the auditor encounters a pass-through entity that consistently fails to provide its subrecipients with federal award information. Circular A-133 requires the auditor to consider noncompliance findings in relation to a type of compliance requirement (in the example provided, subrecipient monitoring is the relevant type of compliance requirement) or an audit objective identified in the *Compliance Supplement*. The pertinent audit objective included in the *Compliance Supplement* and relating to the example provided here is for the auditor to "determine whether the pass-through entity identifies federal award information and compliance requirements to the subrecipient." Because the pass-through entity failed to provide federal award information to its subrecipients, this noncompliance would be material in relation to the audit objective and, therefore, should be reported as an audit finding. In addition, the auditor also should consider whether significant deficiencies or material weaknesses in internal control over compliance exist and require reporting with respect to subrecipient monitoring.

Reporting Based on Likely Questioned Costs

10.62 When evaluating the effect of questioned costs on the opinion on compliance, the auditor considers both known questioned costs and the best estimate of the total costs questioned (likely questioned costs). Known and likely questioned costs also need to be considered when audit findings are reported. In addition to reporting known questioned costs greater than $10,000 for a type of compliance requirement for a major program in the schedule of findings and questioned costs, the auditor also should report known questioned costs when likely questioned costs for a type of compliance requirement for a major program are greater than $10,000. For example, if the auditor specifically identifies $7,000 in questioned costs for a type of compliance requirement for a major program but, based on his or her evaluation of the effect of questioned costs for that compliance requirement estimates that the total questioned costs are in the $50,000 to $60,000 range, the auditor would report a finding that indicates the known questioned costs of $7,000. Chapter 13 of this guide further discusses reporting findings based on likely questioned costs.

Performing Follow-Up Procedures

Auditee Responsibilities for Audit Follow-Up and for the Summary Schedule of Prior Audit Findings[18]

10.63 Circular A-133 states that the auditee is responsible for follow-up and corrective action on all audit findings. Part of the follow-up required by Circular A-133 is that the auditee should prepare a summary schedule of prior audit findings. (Chapter 13 of this guide discusses the summary schedule of prior audit findings.) That schedule reports the status of all audit findings included in the prior audit's schedule of findings and questioned costs relative to federal awards. It also includes audit findings reported in the prior audit's summary schedule of prior audit findings that were not identified as either (*a*) fully corrected, (*b*) no longer valid, or (*c*) not warranting further actions. Circular A-133 states that a valid reason for considering an audit finding as not warranting further action is that *all* of the following have occurred:

- Two years have passed since the audit report in which the finding occurred was submitted to the federal clearinghouse.
- The federal agency or pass-through entity is not currently following up with the auditee on the audit finding.
- A management decision was not issued.

10.64 Circular A-133 also states the following with regard to the auditee's schedule of prior audit findings:

- When audit findings were fully corrected, the summary schedule need only list the audit findings and state that corrective action was taken.
- When audit findings were not fully corrected or were only partially corrected, the summary schedule should describe the planned corrective action as well as any partial corrective action taken.
- When the corrective action taken is significantly different from the corrective action previously reported in a corrective action plan or in the federal agency's or pass-through entity's management decision, the summary schedule should provide an explanation.
- When the auditee believes the audit findings are no longer valid or do not warrant further actions, the reasons for this position should be described in the summary schedule, as discussed in paragraph 10.63.

---

[18] Chapter 3, "Planning and Performing a Financial Statement Auditing in Accordance With *Government Auditing Standards*," of this guide discusses the auditee's responsibilities under *Government Auditing Standards* for audit follow-up.

Auditor Responsibilities for Follow-Up on Previously Reported Findings

10.65 Circular A-133 states that the auditor should follow up on prior audit findings, perform procedures to assess the reasonableness of the schedule of prior audit findings prepared by the auditee, and report, as a current-year audit finding, when the auditor concludes that the summary schedule of prior audit findings materially misrepresents the status of any prior audit finding. The auditor should perform audit follow-up procedures regardless of whether a prior audit finding relates to a major program in the current year. Chapter 13 of this guide further discusses the auditor's reporting responsibilities.

Auditor Follow-Up Procedures

10.66 To follow up on previous audit findings, the auditor should obtain the auditee's summary schedule of prior audit findings and perform appropriate procedures on that information. Although in many cases the procedures performed in the current audit will provide a basis for the auditor to assess the schedule, the auditor may find it necessary to perform procedures directed specifically at the status of prior audit findings. In these cases, consideration might include the following procedures:

- Make inquiries of auditee management and program personnel, including inquiries about the status of corrective actions and the estimated completion date for incomplete actions

- Review management decisions issued by federal awarding agencies or pass-through entities to the auditee (paragraph 10.59 discusses management decisions)

- Observe an activity that has been redesigned to address a prior-year finding

- Test similar current-year transactions

Audit Follow-Up for Findings Reported Under Government Auditing Standards

10.67 As discussed in chapter 3 of this guide, *Government Auditing Standards* establishes an additional requirement related to findings and recommendations in previous engagements that requires the auditor to evaluate whether the auditee has taken appropriate corrective action to address findings and recommendations from previous engagements that could have a material effect on the financial statements or other data significant to the audit objectives. The auditee's schedule of prior audit findings prepared as required by Circular A-133 includes only the status of certain prior-year findings relative to federal awards. *Government Auditing Standards* does not require the auditor to report the status of prior audit findings reported under *Government Auditing Standards* in a written report. However, there may be certain financial statement audit findings that were reported in the prior period under *Government Auditing Standards* that are also included in the summary schedule of prior audit findings (because they also relate to federal awards). Although not required, some auditees may decide to include the status of other financial statement audit findings (that is, those that are not related to federal awards) in the schedule.

Corrective Action Plan

10.68 Circular A-133 also requires that upon completion of the audit, the auditee should prepare a corrective action plan that identifies the contact person responsible for corrective action and indicates the corrective action planned for each audit finding (referred to by the auditor assigned reference number) and the anticipated completion date. If the auditee does not agree with a finding, the corrective action plan should contain an explanation and specific reasons why the auditee disagrees. The auditor may find the auditee's corrective action plan useful in performing audit follow-up (in addition to the auditee's summary schedule of prior audit findings) because it may provide a preliminary indication of the corrective steps planned by the auditee. (See also the discussions in chapters 4 and 13 concerning the *Government Auditing Standards* requirement that the auditor obtain and report the views of responsible officials concerning findings, conclusions, and recommendations, as well as planned corrective actions.)

Disputes or Unresolved Findings

10.69 There may be times when, as part of the follow-up on prior findings, the auditor determines that (*a*) a previous finding is the subject of a dispute between the auditee and the federal awarding agency or pass-through entity or (*b*) the federal awarding agency or pass-through entity has not addressed the finding by issuing a management decision. In these situations, if the finding relates to a current-year major program, this guide recommends that the auditor report similar transactions of the current year as findings and questioned costs until either the dispute is resolved or the initial finding no longer warrants further action under Circular A-133 as described in paragraph 10.63. However, if the auditor no longer believes that there is noncompliance because of additional evidence obtained in the current year, similar transactions need not be reported as findings.

Documentation Requirements

10.70 AU-C section 230, *Audit Documentation* (AICPA, *Professional Standards*), which establishes requirements and provides guidance on audit documentation, should be adapted and applied to the Circular A-133 compliance audit. Specific documentation requirements that should be adapted and applied to a Circular A-133 compliance audit may also be found in other AU-C sections, other standards, and supplementary audit requirements in laws and regulations applicable to the compliance audit.

10.71 AU-C section 935 contains requirements and guidance related to documentation of audit procedures performed in a compliance audit. In addition to those discussed in chapter 9 of this guide related to risk assessment and internal control, paragraphs .41–.42 of AU-C section 935 notes that the auditor should document:

- materiality levels and the basis on which they were determined.
- how the auditor complied with any specific government audit requirements that are supplementary to GAAS and *Government Auditing Standards*.

Paragraph .A38 of AU-C section 935 explains that the auditor is not expected to prepare specific documentation of how the auditor adapted and applied each of the applicable AU-C sections to the objectives of a compliance audit. The documentation of the audit strategy, audit plan, and work performed cumulatively demonstrate whether the auditor has complied with the requirements to apply and adapt AU-C sections to the compliance audit. (See chapter 6 for further discussion.)

> **Emphasis Point**
>
> Quality control reviews of Circular A-133 compliance audits performed by federal agency staff have found instances where audit documentation did not contain sufficient evidence that work was performed to support the auditor's opinion on compliance for one or more major program. In some cases they found that the audit documentation did not include evidence that the auditor tested certain compliance requirements applicable to a major program or, alternatively, did not explain why certain generally applicable compliance requirements identified in the *Compliance Supplement* were not applicable to a major program. Among the items the auditor should document when testing compliance requirements are the individual tests performed and the results of those tests.

Management Representations Related to Federal Awards

10.72 As part of a Circular A-133 compliance audit, the auditor should obtain written representations from management about matters related to federal awards. Therefore, in addition to the management representations obtained in connection with an audit of the financial statements as discussed in chapter 3 of this guide, the auditor should obtain written representations from management concerning the identification and completeness of federal award programs, representations concerning compliance with compliance requirements, and identification of known instances of noncompliance. Paragraph 10.73 contains a suggested listing of representations. Chapter 3 discusses the members of management and other officials from whom the auditor should consider obtaining representations. In a Circular A-133 audit, the auditor also should consider obtaining representations from officials responsible for managing federal awards.

Suggested Representations

10.73 AU-C section 935 states that the auditor should request from management written representations that are tailored to the entity and the governmental audit requirement. The auditor should consider obtaining the following written representations, which include those identified in AU-C section 935, as well as additional representations specific to Circular A-133:[19]

- Management is responsible for complying, and has complied, with the requirements of Circular A-133.

---

[19] The auditor should modify these representations, as appropriate, for different conditions, such as known noncompliance.

- Management is responsible for understanding and complying with the requirements of laws, regulations, and the provisions of contracts and grant agreements related to each of its federal programs.[20]
- Management is responsible for establishing and maintaining, and has established and maintained, effective internal control over compliance for federal programs that provides reasonable assurance that the auditee is managing federal awards in compliance with laws, regulations, and the provisions of contracts or grant agreements that could have a material effect on its federal programs.[21]
- Management has identified and disclosed to the auditor the requirements of laws, regulations, and the provisions of contracts and grant agreements that are considered to have a direct and material effect on each major program.
- Management has made available all contracts and grant agreements (including amendments, if any) and any other correspondence relevant to federal programs and related activities that have taken place with federal agencies or pass-through entities.
- Management has identified and disclosed to the auditor all amounts questioned and all known noncompliance with the direct and material compliance requirements of federal awards.
- Management believes that the auditee has complied with the direct and material compliance requirements (except for noncompliance it has disclosed to the auditor).
- Management has made available all documentation related to compliance with the direct and material compliance requirements, including information related to federal program financial reports and claims for advances and reimbursements.
- Management has provided to the auditor its interpretations of any compliance requirements that are subject to varying interpretations.
- Management has disclosed to the auditor any communications from grantors and pass-through entities concerning possible noncompliance with the direct and material compliance requirements, including communications received from the end of the period covered by the compliance audit to the date of the auditor's report.
- Management has disclosed to the auditor the findings received and related corrective actions taken for previous audits, attestation engagements, and internal or external monitoring that directly relate to the objectives of the compliance audit, including findings received and corrective actions taken from the end of the period covered by the compliance audit to the date of the auditor's report.

---

[20] AU-C section 935 notes that, in some cases, management may include qualifying language in the written representation to the effect that representations are made to the best of management's knowledge and belief. However, AU-C section 935 notes that qualifying language is not appropriate for this representation.

[21] See footnote 20.

Compliance Auditing Applicable to Major Programs (Circular A-133)

- Management is responsible for taking corrective action on audit findings of the compliance audit.[22]

- Management has provided the auditor with all information on the status of the follow-up on prior audit findings by federal awarding agencies and pass-through entities, including all management decisions.

- Management has disclosed the nature of any subsequent events that provide additional evidence with respect to conditions that existed at the end of the reporting period that affect noncompliance during the reporting period.

- Management has disclosed all known noncompliance with direct and material compliance requirements occurring subsequent to the period covered by the auditor's report or stating that there were no such known instances.

- Management has disclosed whether any changes in internal control over compliance or other factors that might significantly affect internal control, including any corrective action taken by management with regard to significant deficiencies and material weaknesses in internal control over compliance, have occurred subsequent to the date as of which compliance is audited.

- Federal program financial reports and claims for advances and reimbursements are supported by the books and records from which the basic financial statements have been prepared.

- The copies of federal program financial reports provided to the auditor are true copies of the reports submitted, or electronically transmitted, to the federal agency or pass-through entity, as applicable.

- If applicable, management has monitored subrecipients to determine that they have expended pass-through assistance in accordance with applicable laws and regulations and have met the requirements of Circular A-133.

- If applicable, management has issued management decisions timely after their receipt of subrecipients' auditor's reports that identified noncompliance with laws, regulations, or the provisions of contracts or grant agreements, and has ensured that subrecipients have taken the appropriate and timely corrective action on findings.

- If applicable, management has considered the results of subrecipient audits and has made any necessary adjustments to the auditee's own books and records.

- Management has charged costs to federal awards in accordance with applicable cost principles.

- Management is responsible for, and has accurately prepared, the summary schedule of prior audit findings to include all findings required to be included by Circular A-133.

---

[22] See footnote 20.

- Management has accurately completed the appropriate sections of the data collection form.[23]
- If applicable, management has disclosed all contracts or other agreements with service organizations.
- If applicable, management has disclosed to the auditor all communications from service organizations relating to noncompliance at those organizations.

The auditor may determine that additional representations related to the entity's compliance with the direct and material compliance requirements are necessary. If so, the auditor should request such additional representations. See chapter 7, "Schedule of Expenditures of Federal Awards (Circular A-133)," for representations the auditor should obtain when issuing an in-relation-to opinion on the schedule of expenditures of federal awards.[24]

Refusal to Furnish Written Representations

10.74 Management's refusal to furnish all written representations that the auditor considers necessary in the circumstances constitutes a limitation on the scope of the audit sufficient to require a qualified opinion or disclaimer of opinion on the auditee's compliance with major program requirements. The auditor also should consider the effects of management's refusal on his or her ability to rely on other management representations.

State and Local Government Compliance Auditing Considerations

10.75 An auditor also may be engaged to test and report on compliance with state and local laws and regulations in addition to the testing and reporting requirements imposed by *Government Auditing Standards* and Circular A-133. Although such auditing is outside the scope of this guide, such a requirement may specify compliance tests, similar to those in a single audit. When this is the case, auditors might consider consulting state or local government officials or other sources concerning the nature and scope of the required testing. It is important to distinguish state or local government funds from pass-through federal funds because pass-through federal funds are considered part of the federal awards received in an audit in accordance with Circular A-133.

Transition Considerations Related to the Uniform Guidance

10.76 As further discussed in the "Transition Considerations Related to the Uniform Guidance" section in chapter 6 of this guide, one of the challenges that auditors may face is that a major program may include expenditures from

---

[23] See chapter 13, "Auditor Reporting Requirements and Other Communication Considerations in a Single Audit (Circular A-133)," for information regarding revisions to the 2013–2015 data collection form and its submission to the Federal Audit Clearinghouse.

[24] Two separate management representation letters may be necessary when the required procedures on the schedule of expenditures of federal awards are completed after the date of the auditor's report on the financial statements. See chapters 7, "Schedule of Expenditures of Federal Awards (Circular A-133)," and 13 for more information.

both federal awards subject to the pre-Uniform Guidance requirements, as well as federal awards subject to the post-Uniform Guidance requirements. This situation could exist for several years until the pre-Uniform Guidance awards have been completely expended. When testing major program transactions, identification of the date of a federal award related to a particular expenditure is needed in order to determine the applicable criteria to use for the transaction being tested. It should be noted that a separate sample for pre-Uniform Guidance award transactions and post-Uniform Guidance award transactions within a major program would not typically be needed in this situation. However, this guide recommends that when testing major program transactions the audit documentation for testing compliance and internal control over compliance include an identification of the transactions tested that were subject to post-Uniform Guidance requirements. See the "Transition Considerations Related to the Uniform Guidance" section in chapter 11 for more information on sampling.

10.77 As set forth in the 2015 *Compliance Supplement*, the types of compliance requirements subject to audit have been reduced from 14 to 12. This change applies to both Circular A-133 compliance audits and Uniform Guidance compliance audits. The two requirements that have been removed are D, "Davis Bacon Act," and K, "Real Property Acquisition and Relocation Assistance." A listing of the remaining 12 types of compliance requirements is found in paragraph 10.19. The letters assigned to the types of compliance requirements that have been removed (D and K) are being held in reserve. Therefore, the letters assigned to the remaining 12 types of compliance requirements have not changed. Although the former type of compliance requirement D, "Davis Bacon Act," has been removed as a separate type of compliance requirement, it has been included in the "Special Tests and Provisions" type of compliance requirement for some programs. Finally, one type of compliance requirement has been renamed. The former type of compliance requirement H, "Period of Availability," has been renamed "Period of Performance" in the 2015 *Compliance Supplement*.

10.78 The 2015 *Compliance Supplement* also includes two versions of Part 3:

- Part 3.1 applies to testing federal awards that are not subject to the Uniform Guidance (that is, federal awards made prior to December 26, 2014).
- Part 3.2 applies to testing federal awards subject to the Uniform Guidance (that is, new federal awards made on or after December 26, 2014, and funding increments).

The former type of compliance requirement H, "Period of Availability of Federal Funds" has been renamed "Period of Performance" in Part 3.2 of the 2015 *Compliance Supplement*. "Period of Availability of Federal Funds" has been retained in Part 3.1 of the 2015 *Compliance Supplement*. See also paragraph 10.78.

10.79 A nonfederal entity may elect to continue to comply with the procurement standards in pre-Uniform Guidance requirements for one additional fiscal year after the Uniform Guidance goes into effect. This means a nonfederal entity may delay implementation of the Uniform Guidance procurement standards found in 2 CFR 200.317–.326 for the entity's first full fiscal year that begins on or after December 26, 2014. If a nonfederal entity makes this election, it must document whether it is in compliance with the old or new standard, and must meet the documented standard. For example, the first full fiscal year for an entity with a June 30 year end would be the year ending June 30, 2016. If the delayed implementation is elected, the entity is required to implement the Uniform Guidance procurement standards beginning July 1, 2016. Understanding whether a nonfederal entity has elected to delay implementation of the Uniform Guidance procurement standards is an important auditor consideration because it may impact the compliance testing performed in a Circular A-133 compliance audit.

Chapter 11

Audit Sampling Considerations of Circular A-133 Compliance Audits

> **⊘ Update 11-1: Audits of Federal Awards**
>
> This chapter, and the remaining chapters of part II, *Circular A-133 Audits*, of this guide, should be used for performing a compliance audit of federal awards under Office of Management and Budget (OMB) Circular A-133, *Audits of States, Local Governments, and Non-Profit Organizations* (Circular A-133). Part III, *Uniform Guidance Audits*, of this guide should be used when performing a compliance audit under Title 2 U.S. *Code of Federal Regulations* Part 200, *Uniform Administrative Requirements, Cost Principles, and Audit Requirements for Federal Awards* (Uniform Guidance). See the transitional guidance sections at the end of each chapter that highlight important matters for consideration.[1] Refer to the preface for additional information.
>
> **Important Uniform Guidance Effective Date Information**
>
> In December 2013, the OMB issued the Uniform Guidance, which is effective for nonfederal entities for all federal awards and certain funding increments provided on or after December 26, 2014. The requirements in Subpart F, "Audit Requirements," are effective for audits of fiscal years beginning on or after December 26, 2014, with no early implementation permitted. Therefore, auditees subject to a single audit with December 25, 2015, and later year ends (for example, December 31, 2015) will be required to undergo the audit under Subpart F of the Uniform Guidance. Note that audits of fiscal years ending prior to the effective date of the Uniform Guidance audit requirements are subject to an audit under Circular A-133.

Introduction

11.01 An auditor may decide to use audit sampling to obtain sufficient appropriate audit evidence in a compliance audit, as noted in paragraph .A21 of AU-C section 935, *Compliance Audits* (AICPA, *Professional Standards*). AU-C section 530, *Audit Sampling*[2] (AICPA, *Professional Standards*), addresses

---

[1] See the information found at the end of certain chapters in part II, *Circular A-133 Audits*, of this guide for transition considerations when performing an audit under Office of Management and Budget (OMB) Circular A-133, *Audits of States, Local Governments, and Non-Profit Organizations* (Circular A-133), as it relates to the applicability of certain aspects of Title 2 U.S. *Code of Federal Regulations* Part 200, *Uniform Administrative Requirements, Cost Principles, and Audit Requirements for Federal Awards* (Uniform Guidance), to audits performed under Circular A-133. Transition considerations related to an audit performed under the Uniform Guidance can be found at the end of chapters in part III, *Uniform Guidance Audits*, of this guide in sections titled "Transition Considerations Related to the Uniform Guidance."

[2] AICPA Audit Guide *Audit Sampling* is an interpretive publication, which assists practitioners in the application of the guidance found in AU-C section 530, *Audit Sampling* (AICPA, *Professional Standards*). Interpretive publications are recommendations on the application of auditing standards in specific circumstances and are issued under the authority of the Auditing Standards Board. An auditor should be aware of and consider interpretive publications applicable to his or her audit. If the auditor does not apply the auditing guidance included in an applicable interpretive publication, the auditor should be prepared to explain how he or she complied with the Statements on Auditing Standards provisions addressed by such auditing guidance. The Audit Guide *Audit Sampling* is available at www.cpa2biz.com.

the auditor's use of statistical and nonstatistical sampling when designing and selecting the audit sample, performing tests of controls and tests of details, and evaluating the results from the sample. It includes guidance related to sampling risk, sampling in substantive tests of details, and sampling in tests of controls. The guidance in AU-C section 530 primarily addresses sampling considerations when performing a financial statement audit, with an emphasis on testing account balances or classes of transactions that may contain misstatements as well as testing internal control over financial reporting. Sampling to accomplish compliance-related audit objectives in an OMB Circular A-133 compliance audit environment differs from sampling in a financial statement audit in that to meet the compliance-related objectives, the auditor gathers sufficient appropriate audit evidence on whether the auditee has complied with laws, regulations, and the provisions of contracts or grant agreements that could have a direct and material effect on each major program.

11.02 This chapter provides considerations in designing an audit approach that includes audit sampling to achieve both compliance and internal control over compliance related audit objectives in a Circular A-133 compliance audit or program-specific audit performed in accordance with Circular A-133. This chapter builds upon the general guidance set forth in AU-C section 530 (as discussed in the AICPA Audit Guide *Audit Sampling*) by providing specific, relevant sampling guidance for a Circular A-133 compliance audit or program-specific audit.

11.03 In addition to providing important considerations when applying sampling in a Circular A-133 compliance audit, this chapter provides suggested minimum sample sizes for tests of controls over compliance and tests of compliance based on certain engagement-specific inputs. Depending on the nature of the type of compliance requirement being tested, the results of other audit procedures performed during the audit, and the risks and complexities of the sampling population, there may be situations where auditors may determine, based on professional judgment, that it is appropriate to use larger sample sizes rather than the suggested minimum sample sizes.

11.04 This chapter does not include guidance on every possible valid method of selecting and evaluating audit samples in a Circular A-133 compliance audit. The AICPA Audit Guide *Audit Sampling* provides additional guidance and technical background, which forms the basis of the practical application of audit sampling to Circular A-133 compliance audits as outlined in this chapter.

Audit Sampling in a Circular A-133 Compliance Audit

11.05 Paragraph .05 of AU-C section 530 defines *audit sampling* as the selection and evaluation of less than 100 percent of the population of audit relevance such that the auditor expects the items selected (the sample) to be representative of the population and, thus, likely to provide a reasonable basis for conclusions about the population. In other words, audit sampling may provide the auditor an appropriate basis on which to conclude on a characteristic of a population based on examining evidence regarding that characteristic from a subset of the population. When using audit sampling, the auditor may choose between a statistical and a nonstatistical approach. Both methods are acceptable under AU-C section 530.

Purpose and Nature of Audit Sampling in a Circular A-133 Compliance Audit

11.06 The auditor's objectives in a Circular A-133 compliance audit include reporting on internal control over compliance (as discussed in chapter 9, "Consideration of Internal Control Over Compliance for Major Programs (Circular A-133)," of this guide) and expressing an opinion on whether the auditee has complied with laws, regulations, and the provisions of contracts or grant agreements pertaining to federal awards that may have a direct and material effect on each of its major programs (as discussed in chapter 10, "Compliance Auditing Applicable to Major Programs (Circular A-133)," of this guide). The auditor should obtain sufficient appropriate audit evidence to support the opinion on compliance for each major program, as well as to meet the requirements of Circular A-133 for testing and reporting on internal control over compliance. Such evidence may be obtained through a variety of procedures, including planning and performing risk assessment procedures, performing tests of controls, performing tests of details (including tests of transactions), and other auditing procedures as are necessary. Auditors frequently use audit sampling procedures to obtain such audit evidence.

11.07 When testing internal control over compliance, the auditor is primarily concerned about the rates of deviations from a prescribed control. Similarly, in tests of compliance, the auditor is concerned about whether or not there is evidence of compliance (that is the rate and likely magnitude of noncompliance). Therefore, *attributes sampling*, as defined in the AICPA Audit Guide *Audit Sampling*, is typically used for tests of controls over compliance and compliance testing in a Circular A-133 compliance audit. The underlying basis for the large population sample sizes provided in this chapter is attributes sampling.

11.08 Further, as noted in chapter 10 of this guide, Circular A-133 states that the auditor should report known questioned costs when likely questioned costs[3] for a type of compliance requirement for a major program are greater than $10,000. That is, the auditor should report known questioned costs but is not required to report the likely questioned costs. In evaluating the effect of questioned costs (found through sampling and other audit procedures) on the opinion on compliance, the auditor should consider the best estimate of the total costs questioned for each major program (likely questioned costs), not just the questioned costs specifically identified (known questioned costs).

11.09 When noncompliance is discovered related to monetary transactions of a major program, Circular A-133 does not require the auditor to report an exact amount or a statistical projection of likely questioned costs with related confidence bounds. Instead, as noted previously and further discussed in chapter 10 of this guide, the auditor should consider the effect of likely questioned costs on the opinion on compliance and should report an audit finding when the auditor's estimate of likely questioned costs is greater than $10,000.

---

[3] OMB Circular A-133 defines *likely questioned costs* as the auditor's best estimate of total costs questioned. *Known questioned costs* are questioned costs specifically identified by the auditor and a subset of likely questioned costs. As noted in the glossary of AU-C section 935, *Compliance Audits* (AICPA, *Professional Standards*), *likely questioned costs* are developed by extrapolating from audit evidence obtained, for example, by projecting known questioned costs identified in an audit sample to the entire population from which the sample was drawn.

Audit Sampling in the Context of Other Audit Procedures

11.10 It is important to note that sampling is one of many audit procedures designed to provide sufficient appropriate audit evidence to support the auditor's compliance opinion on each major program. An auditor often does not rely solely on the results of any single type of procedure to obtain sufficient appropriate audit evidence on each major program's compliance and internal control over compliance. Rather, audit conclusions may be based on evidence obtained from several sources and by applying a variety of audit procedures. Auditors should consider the combined evidence obtained from the various types of procedures to determine whether there is sufficient appropriate audit evidence to evaluate possible audit findings and to develop the auditor's report on internal control over compliance and the opinion on whether the auditee complied with laws, regulations, and the provisions of contracts or grants for each major program.

11.11 In a Circular A-133 compliance audit, just as in a financial statement audit, other audit procedures beyond sampling are performed. For instance, risk assessment procedures typically precede tests of controls. The following are specific examples of other audit procedures used in a Circular A-133 compliance audit that may be used in addition to audit sampling:

- Determining for each major program the direct and material types of compliance requirements to be tested and reported on in a Circular A-133 compliance audit (see chapter 10 of this guide for further discussion)
- Using the knowledge gained in the inherent risk of noncompliance assessment process (as described in chapter 6, "Planning Considerations of Circular A-133," of this guide) to identify types of potential noncompliance, to consider other factors that affect the risk of material noncompliance, and to design appropriate tests of compliance
- Performing analytical procedures to further understand the nature of a major program prior to performing compliance testing
- Identifying risks throughout the process of obtaining an understanding of the entity and its environment, including relevant controls that relate to the risks of noncompliance, evaluating the design of controls relevant to the Circular A-133 compliance audit, and determining whether they have been implemented
- Considering whether there are individually important items that may merit being specifically tested prior to selecting a sample and performing tests on such items (see paragraphs 11.21–.28)

Procedures That May Not Involve Audit Sampling

11.12 The following paragraphs discuss compliance and internal control over compliance audit procedures that generally do not involve audit sampling.

Inquiry and Observation

11.13 Inquiry, as discussed in paragraphs .A23–.A26 of AU-C section 500, *Audit Evidence* (AICPA, *Professional Standards*), consists of seeking information of knowledgeable persons, both financial and nonfinancial, within the entity or outside the entity. Observation, as discussed in paragraph .A17 of

Audit Sampling Considerations of Circular A-133 Compliance Audits

AU-C section 500 consists of looking at a process or procedure being performed by others. Inquiry and observation procedures commonly used in a Circular A-133 compliance audit include the following:

- Interviewing management and employees to obtain an understanding of internal control over compliance
- Observing the behavior of personnel and the functioning of business operations
- Observing cash handling activities
- Performing walkthrough procedures[4]
- Observing the existence of real property and equipment
- Obtaining written representations from management

In some cases, these procedures could be designed as sampling procedures, such as designing multiple observations of physical security controls; however, inquiry and observation generally do not involve audit sampling.

Analytical Procedures

11.14 Analytical procedures, as discussed in AU-C section 520, *Analytical Procedures* (AICPA, *Professional Standards*), consist of evaluations of information through analysis of plausible relationships among both financial and nonfinancial data. These procedures are not considered audit sampling because they do not result in the ability to project the results of testing a portion of the population to the total population.

11.15 As noted in paragraph .A23 of AU-C section 935, the use of analytical procedures to gather substantive evidence is generally less effective in a compliance audit than it is in a financial statement audit. However, substantive analytical procedures may contribute some evidence when performed in addition to tests of transactions and other auditing procedures necessary to provide the auditor with sufficient appropriate audit evidence.

11.16 An example of applying analytical procedures in a Circular A-133 compliance audit may include a test relating to the Activities Allowed or Unallowed type of compliance requirement for a school lunch program. An auditor may use analytical procedures to calculate an estimated total for nutritional expenditures and compare against actual expenditures to provide some audit evidence that could reduce compliance tests assuming the auditor is confident with the completeness and accuracy of the underlying data. Calculating estimated participation could be accomplished by multiplying the number of students enrolled in a school system by the percentage expected to participate in a school nutrition program. This percentage may be based on history, current economic trends and statistics in the area, or other factors. The calculated estimation then could be multiplied by an average daily cost of the nutrition program per student to estimate the total expenditures for the program. The auditor may then compare the estimation to the recorded expenditures to determine if there is a difference material to the program being tested.

11.17 Scanning is another common nonsampling analytical procedure. The following provide two examples of how scanning might be used in a Circular A-133 compliance audit:

---

[4] Walkthroughs may include an examination of evidence and reperformance, depending on their design and performance.

a. For a school district Circular A-133 compliance audit, auditors could scan a list of employees that charged time to a grant to determine that the type of employee and school appear reasonable (for example, when scanning a list of employees charged to vocational education programs, the auditor normally would not expect to see an elementary school teacher included).

b. For a social services grant or education training program that, by its nature, would not include equipment purchases, auditors could scan a list of program expenditures for captions that indicate a disbursement was made for equipment.

Procedures Applied to Every Item in a Population or Subpopulation in Compliance Testing

11.18 In some circumstances, an auditor might decide to examine every item in a population relating to a type of compliance requirement for a major program. In this situation, because the auditor is examining the entire population to reach a conclusion, rather than only a portion, this 100 percent examination is not a procedure that involves audit sampling.

11.19 When individually important items do not make up the entire population, after testing all individually important items, the auditor might apply audit sampling to the remaining items (see paragraphs 11.21–.28 for an additional discussion of individually important items).

11.20 Alternatively, after testing all individually important items, an auditor might either (*a*) apply other auditing procedures to the remaining items in the population (for example, scanning), or (*b*) apply no auditing procedures to remaining items because there is an acceptably low risk of material noncompliance in the remaining items. In these 2 scenarios, the auditor is not using sampling. Rather, the auditor has divided the entire population of items into 2 groups. One subpopulation is tested 100 percent, and the other subpopulation is either tested by other auditing procedures or is not tested.

Individually Important Items in Compliance Testing[5]

11.21 When planning compliance testing for each major program, the auditor may use judgment to determine what items, if any, represent individually important items that may be individually tested and separated from the remaining population. Items of individual importance may be large, risky, or unusual items or transactions that contain characteristics of a prior compliance finding. Individually important items are those that, standing alone, are significantly different from the remainder of the population, for example, spikes in activity around a certain time period, such as journal entries made at the beginning or the close of a grant (see paragraph 11.27 for additional examples).

11.22 Although the identification of individually important items is not required by Circular A-133, there are benefits to taking advantage of testing individually important transactions if they exist in a particular population. Specifically, the application of auditor judgment and experience in examining a population for risky or unusual transactions may be more effective at identifying noncompliance than a randomly or haphazardly selected sample (see

---

[5] AICPA Audit Guide *Audit Sampling* uses the term *individually significant*, whereas this guide uses *individually important*. Note that in the context of individually important, there is no requirement for auditors to consider or test, or both, such items.

paragraphs 11.94–.96 for further discussion of random and haphazard sample selection). Furthermore, testing individually important items may reduce detection risk of noncompliance in that the individually important items that the auditor decides to test are not part of the population subject to audit sampling. As such, testing individually important items may reduce the sample size for the items remaining in the sampling population, or it may eliminate having to sample altogether because it targets those items that have the largest effect on noncompliance. For example, if 80 percent of the total grant expenditures can be examined by testing the largest 10 expenditures, detection risk of noncompliance may be reduced such that the level of assurance needed from a sample of the remaining 20 percent of untested items will be lower.

11.23 It is important to note that the concept of identifying individually important items and focusing testing on a limited number of large or unusual items relates to compliance testing and not to testing internal control over compliance.

11.24 It is also important to clarify that a large number of transactions making up a significant percentage of the dollars expended or having a significant effect on compliance typically would not represent individually important items because individually important items are usually represented by only a relatively small number of items.

11.25 Identifying individually important items may involve discussions with auditees, analytical procedures such as scanning records (as described in paragraph 11.17), or using computer assisted auditing techniques. For example, in testing the Allowable Costs/Cost Principles type of compliance requirement, if there are a few very large expenditures, the auditor may deem these expenditures to be individually important.

11.26 Identifying individually important items may not be an efficient method when testing multiple types of compliance requirements at once because an individually important item with respect to a particular type of compliance requirement may not necessarily be an individually important item for another type of compliance requirement. For example, it would not likely be appropriate to identify a few individually important items to test the Activities Allowed or Unallowed type of compliance requirement, and then use the testing of those few items to support the auditor's conclusions relating to certain other direct and material compliance requirements.[6] It is likely that supplemental tests may be necessary to gather sufficient appropriate audit evidence related to compliance with other direct and material compliance requirements.

11.27 Additional examples of individually important items (and the relevant type of compliance requirement) might include the following:

- Transactions processed at the beginning or end of a grant award period (Activities Allowed or Unallowed, Period of Availability).

---

[6] AU-C section 935 defines *applicable compliance requirements* as the compliance requirements that are subject to the compliance audit. Paragraph .500(d) of Circular A-133 states that the auditor should determine whether the auditee has complied with laws, regulations, and the provisions of contracts or grant agreements that may have a direct and material effect on each of its major programs. Therefore, in a Circular A-133 compliance audit, the direct and material compliance requirements are those that are subject to audit. Accordingly, for the purpose of adapting AU-C section 935 to a Circular A-133 compliance audit, the term *applicable compliance requirements* has been replaced by *direct and material compliance requirements* in this guide except when directly citing content from AU-C section 935.

- Transactions processed at odd times in a cycle, such as new beneficiaries brought into a program in the spring when eligibility is usually granted only once a year during an enrollment period in the fall (Eligibility).
- Program beneficiaries that are near a qualifying age for benefits, or beneficiaries who have received multiple sources of funds (Eligibility).
- A grant close-out report, as compared to routine financial or progress reports (Reporting).
- Transactions related to subrecipients that are awarded unusually high dollar amounts of pass-through funds compared with prior periods or other subrecipients in the same program (Subrecipient Monitoring).
- Transactions related to subrecipients that are new to the grantee, especially newly formed entities that have a relatively immature infrastructure to support compliance (Subrecipient Monitoring).
- Transactions processed in foreign countries that may contain higher risks such as foreign currency risk or different payroll and human resources issues and laws in other countries that may affect allowable costs (Activities Allowed or Unallowed, Subrecipient Monitoring).
- Transactions that tests of internal control over compliance have indicated are either not subject to controls or are not being processed appropriately (multiple types of compliance requirements).
- Transactions related to a specific step within the *OMB Compliance Supplement* (Compliance Supplement). For example, large transfers of funds from program accounts which may have been used to fund unallowable activities (Activities Allowed or Unallowed).

11.28 The auditor should prepare appropriate documentation to support a clear understanding of the work performed on individually important items, which may include the rationale, selection criteria, results of testing, and effect on the planned testing of the remainder of the population.

Understanding and Testing the Operating Effectiveness of Controls Over Compliance

11.29 There are a variety of methods the auditor may use when performing risk assessment procedures, including inquiry, observation, inspection of documentary evidence, walkthrough, and reperformance of a process, that affect the auditor's understanding and testing of the operating effectiveness of controls. Although many procedures where documentary evidence is examined or where the auditor reperforms a control involve audit sampling, certain other methods may not involve sampling (for example, inspecting one or a few items to obtain an understanding of controls). Furthermore, paragraph .A29 of AU-C section 330, *Performing Audit Procedures in Response to Assessed Risks and Evaluating the Audit Evidence Obtained* (AICPA, *Professional Standards*), notes that the nature of the particular control influences the type of audit procedure necessary to obtain audit evidence about whether the control is operating effectively. For example, documentation of operation may not exist for some factors in the control environment, such as assignment of authority and responsibility. In such circumstances, audit evidence about operating effectiveness may be obtained through inquiry in combination with other audit procedures, such as observation.

11.30 Similarly, when testing internal control over compliance, the auditor does not use audit sampling when he or she applies an auditing procedure to one or a number of items relating to a control over a type of compliance requirement to clarify the auditor's understanding of the entity's internal control over compliance. For example, an auditor might trace several grant expenditure transactions through an auditee's accounting system to obtain an understanding of the design of the auditee's internal control over compliance with respect to the grant expenditures, such as approvals of the expenditures as an allowable activity, an allowable cost, or within the period of availability. In such cases, the auditor's intent is to gain a general understanding of the accounting system or other relevant parts of the internal control over compliance, rather than to evaluate a characteristic of all transactions processed. As a result, the auditor is not using audit sampling.

Planning Considerations for Sampling Related to Tests of Controls Over Compliance and Compliance Testing

Determining Audit Objectives

11.31 Paragraph 11.06 describes the audit objectives in a Circular A-133 compliance audit. Proper definition and documentation of the audit objective precedes sampling design and execution. When designing an audit sample, the auditor should consider the purpose of the audit procedure (for example, to determine whether a necessary control was performed effectively or determine whether an expenditure was charged to a grant allowable under the appropriate OMB Cost Circular).

11.32 The specific compliance audit objectives will differ for each type of compliance requirement. Part 3 of the *Compliance Supplement* lists and describes the 12 types of compliance requirements and the related audit objectives that the auditor should consider in Circular A-133 compliance audits.[7] Chapters 9–10 of this guide discuss the concepts involved in properly planning the testing of compliance and internal control over compliance.

Defining the Population and Considering Completeness

11.33 The population is defined in a manner consistent with the audit objective and the internal control and compliance attributes being tested. The auditor should determine that the sampling unit and the population from which units are selected for sampling is appropriate for the specific audit objective because sample results can be appropriately projected only to the population from which the sample was selected. For example, consider a situation where the auditor plans to test timesheets for proper authorization (that is, testing an internal control over the Activities Allowed or Unallowed type of compliance requirement) for a major program that involves multiple departments within an auditee. In defining the population, the auditor may first gain an understanding of how frequently timesheets are prepared and reviewed. Further,

---

[7] Chapter 14, "Program-Specific Audits (Circular A-133)," of this guide discusses program-specific audits and the use of federal program specific audit guides and other methods for determining compliance requirements and related audit objectives in a program-specific audit.

the auditor may also determine if the timesheets in the various departments within the auditee constitute one population or separate populations by considering whether the systems and controls for approval differ among the departments (for example, whether all supervisors approving timesheets attend a uniform training session), or other factors that would affect the definition of the control. There are also situations where a time period may define a sampling population (for example, for the Period of Availability type of compliance requirement, the *Compliance Supplement* defines certain time periods as a sampling population).

11.34 The sampling population includes the items constituting the transactions of interest for an audit objective related to a particular control or a type of compliance requirement after removing transactions tested with non-sampling techniques (for example, individually important items or a subset of items that are tested 100 percent). It is possible that the appropriate sampling population may only be a subset of the universe of transactions subject to a particular control or compliance requirement. For example, the universe of transactions within an expenditure pool may be defined by the auditor as multiple populations when transaction processing and the operation of related controls are decentralized.

11.35 The types of expenditures related to an audit objective are also an important factor in determining whether further division of the population may be necessary to achieve the stated objective. For example, the controls over the Allowable Costs/Cost Principles type of compliance requirement may vary depending on whether the expenditure is a direct (other than payroll), indirect, or payroll expenditure.

11.36 An auditee might change a specific control or compliance procedure during the period under audit. The auditor should obtain audit evidence about the nature and extent of any significant changes in internal control and may need to revise the audit plan. Chapter 3, "Nonstatistical and Statistical Audit Sampling in Test of Controls," of the AICPA Audit Guide *Audit Sampling* discusses additional considerations when there are changes in processes and procedures during the period under audit as well as important sampling considerations if testing is conducted at an interim date.

11.37 The auditor should select items for the sample in such a way that the auditor can reasonably expect the sample to be representative of the relevant population. If the physical or electronic representation (for example, a printout or electronic file purportedly containing all expenditures) and the desired population differ, the auditor might make erroneous conclusions about the population. To verify the completeness of a population, the auditor could, for example, reconcile the population to accounting or other relevant records or to the schedule of expenditures of federal awards, or perform other procedures to verify the population is complete. Populations relevant for a Circular A-133 compliance audit test may not consist of accounting records (for example, eligibility files for a particular major program do not directly relate to a financial statement amount). Regardless, the auditor should develop and perform audit procedures sufficient to conclude that the population includes all the transactions of interest for the specific audit objective.

11.38 If an initial sample does not include a particular attribute being tested, it may be an indication that the sampling population was not defined properly. For example, an initial sample may have been selected from a schedule of financial assistance that did not include a listing of students who were enrolled part-time or students enrolled in correspondence study. However, to meet the audit objective, the auditor would need to include such students in the testing. The auditor may consider maintaining the original sample and adding a selection of students who were enrolled part-time or students enrolled in correspondence study to the sample. The number of additional items to be added is a matter of professional judgment. In the previous example, the auditor may consider consistency of student financial assistance processing controls, number of students who were enrolled part-time or enrolled in correspondence study, and other considerations from the risk assessment process to determine whether to reevaluate the original population or add items with the needed attribute.

Sampling Unit

11.39 The sampling unit may be defined by any of the individual elements constituting the population. Each sampling unit constitutes one item in the population. In a Circular A-133 compliance audit, a sampling unit might be a cash disbursement, student file, refund paid, financial report due during a fiscal year, or a cost transfer made during the year.

11.40 The definition of the sampling unit depends on the audit objective and the nature of the audit procedures being applied. For example, a sampling unit for a test of controls related to the Activities Allowed or Unallowed type of compliance requirement may be a payment voucher, a journal entry, or another document that includes evidence of approval or review of the allowability of the expenditure. Note that each sampling unit may provide evidence of the application of more than one control. For example, a voucher package may provide support that the amounts were checked for accuracy, the vendor was checked for suspension and debarment, that the expenditure was for an allowable activity under the grant agreement and for an allowable cost under the relevant OMB Cost Circular, and that the expenditure was incurred and obligated within the period of availability of the grant period.

11.41 In order to properly define the sampling unit, it is also important that the auditor determine how the auditee maintains its records (for example, by participant, by program, by location). Based on the nature of the records, the auditor may then properly design a method to define the sampling unit and identify the sampling population.

Considering Multiple Major Programs

11.42 It is very common for auditees to have multiple major programs. Auditees may use the same controls for a particular type of compliance requirement (for example, Allowable Costs/Cost Principles) for more than 1 federal program. If the auditee's internal control for a type of compliance requirement is common to more than 1 major program, the transactions of those programs may be combined into 1 population for determining sample size and for making sample selections for internal control tests. If the initial sample (taken from a combined population) does not include items from each major program, the auditor typically will judgmentally add additional items from the program(s) not represented.[8] Alternatively, the auditor may plan the initial combined sample

---

[8] If an initial sample does not include a major program, it could also indicate that the physical representation (for example, a printout or electronic file purportedly containing all expenditures) of the population used to draw the sample was incomplete, see paragraphs 11.33–.38.

to draw items from each major program. For example, consider a situation where an auditee has common internal controls over the Allowable Costs/Cost Principles type of compliance requirement relating to 3 major programs. If in this example, the auditor decides to use a combined sample of 60 items and the programs are of similar size, the auditor may select 20 items from each of the 3 major programs. If the major programs are not of similar size, the sample may be allocated proportionately. In considering whether samples selected from across multiple programs can be designed for dual purposes, see paragraph 11.43 as well as a discussion of dual purpose testing at paragraphs 11.52–.57.

11.43 The auditor is required to obtain sufficient appropriate audit evidence to support an opinion on compliance for each major federal program. Experience has shown that it is preferable to select separate samples for compliance testing from each major program because the separate samples provide clear evidence of the compliance tests performed, the results of those tests, and the conclusions reached. Thus, unlike tests of controls over compliance, compliance testing is typically performed on samples selected with each major program considered a separate population. If an auditor believes a compliance sample can be selected from a population consisting of multiple major programs, an important aspect of the documentation includes how the results relate to separate programs and how that evidence, together with other audit evidence, is sufficient to support the auditor's opinion on compliance for each major program.

Considering Multiple Organizational Units

11.44 Auditors may have additional sampling considerations when the auditee has operations in multiple organizational units (for example, operating units, locations, or branches). Each organizational unit may maintain separate internal control over compliance that is relevant to the programs, or parts of programs, which the unit administers. In these situations, the auditor should consider the understanding of internal control over compliance to determine whether to define each organizational unit as a separate population (chapter 9 of this guide discusses internal control over compliance in multiple organizational units). For a discussion of multiple organizational unit considerations related to compliance, refer to chapter 10 of this guide.

11.45 If controls over compliance or compliance procedures at the various organizational units vary significantly, it may be necessary for each location to be considered a separate population. When transactions relating to types of compliance requirements are processed in organizational units using the same controls,[9] or compliance procedures are performed under common oversight and monitoring, it may be feasible for the auditor to obtain sufficient appropriate audit evidence about controls and compliance for major programs by selecting one overall sample across the organizational units (for example, selecting from centralized locations or visiting all organizational units). When it is not feasible to obtain the evidence centrally or to visit all the organizational

---

[9] When evaluating whether multiple organizational units use the same controls, *same* does not mean *identical*. The auditor may consider the important elements of the control such as the control activity, related monitoring, as well as the differences in experience and training of the individuals processing or monitoring the compliance transaction when determining if the controls are the *same*, or if there are significant variances.

units, and controls or compliance procedures, or both, are the same across organizational units, the auditor generally will select some organizational units from which to obtain audit evidence. In this case, the auditor may consider (a) testing the minimum sample size at each location of significance (or more than the minimum sample size depending on the results of risk assessment procedures preceding sampling), or (b) varying the selection of the less significant organizational units included in the testing from year to year. Appendix E, "Multilocation Sampling Considerations," of the AICPA Audit Guide *Audit Sampling* provides useful guidance in determining the appropriate organizational unit to visit, as well as implications on sample size.

Considering Clusters of Programs

11.46 The audit opinion on a cluster of programs is for the cluster as a whole and not each individual Catalog of Federal Domestic Assistance (CFDA) number, grant, award, and so forth that makes up the cluster. Chapter 5, "Overview of the Single Audit Act, Circular A-133, and the *Compliance Supplement*," of this guide further discusses clusters of programs. When sampling involves a cluster of programs, the auditor should consider whether, in the auditor's judgment, sufficient appropriate audit evidence has been gathered for the direct and material types of compliance requirements relating to the clustered programs as a whole. Random or haphazard selection (further discussed in paragraphs 11.94–.96) of sample items from the cluster generally would be expected to provide a representative sample.

11.47 There may be instances where the initial sample does not appear to be representative because it does not include items relating to certain direct and material types of compliance requirements for CFDA numbers, grants, awards, and so forth within the cluster. In this case, the auditor's determination of what additional evidence is needed requires professional judgment. Factors that may be considered by the auditor in determining whether to supplement the original sample include: the consistency of processing controls over the various programs within the cluster, the volume of transactions and the size of expenditures for a particular program as a component of the overall cluster being tested, the complexity of the compliance requirements, and the past history of compliance. As with other forms of audit testing, the auditor should document the objective of the cluster testing and the sample design.

11.48 An alternative approach to selecting sample items in a cluster, if auditee records permit, may be for the auditor to analyze the components of the cluster transactions (for example, expenses) and grants prior to selecting the sample and then to allocate the number of selections from the sample to the transactions or programs in proportion to the overall cluster. This alternative may be difficult to execute depending on how the auditee keeps their records.

Considering the Effect of Population Size

11.49 The size of the population has little or no effect on the determination of sample size, except in relatively small populations of 250 items or fewer. Some significant controls or compliance procedures the auditor may be testing operate infrequently. For example, controls over reporting may operate only 4, 12, 24, or 52 times a year. Paragraphs 11.86–.89 provide sample sizes for small populations.

Defining Control Deviation and Compliance Exception Conditions[10]

11.50 Based on the auditor's understanding of internal control over compliance and compliance requirements, an auditor generally will identify the characteristics that would indicate performance of the control or compliance with the compliance requirement to be tested. The auditor may then define the possible deviation or exception conditions. For tests of controls, a deviation is a departure from the expected performance of the prescribed control. For compliance testing, an exception is a departure from laws, regulations, and the provisions of contracts or grant agreements being tested. Defining a deviation or exception for each audit objective assists the auditor executing the procedures to properly identify deficiencies in internal control over compliance and instances of noncompliance.

11.51 In a Circular A-133 compliance audit, the auditor should consider the nature and cause of the internal control deviations and compliance exceptions identified in testing. The auditor should determine whether the deviation(s) or exception(s) constitutes a finding and whether the sampling evidence, in combination with other testing, might affect the auditor's opinion on compliance.

Dual Purpose Sample Considerations

11.52 In some circumstances, the auditor might design a test that uses a *dual purpose* sample. The most common dual purpose approach in a Circular A-133 compliance audit is testing the operating effectiveness of a control and testing whether the auditee complied with relevant laws, regulations, or provisions of contracts or grant agreements using the same sample. For example, subrecipient monitoring often can be tested with a dual purpose sample. If the sampling unit is a subrecipient reimbursement request, the documentation may contain evidence of review by the pass-through entity (for example, signature) and compliance with monitoring activities. When utilizing a dual purpose sample for internal control and compliance testing, it is important that the test objectives align to the same sampling unit and population (that is, the population being sampled is appropriate for the tests being applied to it). As stated in paragraph 11.33, an auditor should determine that the population from which the sample is selected is appropriate for the specific audit objectives being executed. The size of a sample designed for a dual purpose test will usually be the larger of the samples that would otherwise have been designed if the control and compliance samples were performed separately.

11.53 When testing both the operating effectiveness of a control and whether the auditee complied with a type of compliance requirement, the basis for the auditor's evaluation of the control is the operation of the control and not just whether the auditee complied. Further, a control that is not properly applied to a transaction may not necessarily lead to noncompliance. As such, the auditor may reach different conclusions on controls and compliance for the same sample item (for example, report a significant deficiency or material weakness in internal control over compliance but not a compliance related finding).

---

[10] In this chapter, the term *deviation* is associated with control testing, and the term *exception* is associated with compliance testing.

11.54 In evaluating the result of dual purpose tests, audit findings should be evaluated separately for the control attributes and the compliance attributes tested. In planning the tests of compliance, the auditor should use the knowledge obtained of the relevant portions of internal control over compliance to identify types of potential noncompliance, to consider factors that affect the risk of material noncompliance, and to design appropriate tests of compliance. Thus, deviations resulting from tests of controls, including when those control tests are part of a dual purpose sample, may result in a larger compliance sample than originally planned for the related type of compliance requirement due to the increased risk posed by the deficiency in internal control over compliance.

11.55 As described in chapter 10 of this guide, the auditor's documentation of internal control and compliance tests should be distinguished from one another so there is a clear distinction between the audit objectives and test results for each test so that separate conclusions may be reached on the internal control attributes and compliance attributes tested.

11.56 Another example of using a sample for multiple purposes is when auditors wish to use a single sample for testing for both Circular A-133 compliance audit objectives and financial statement audit objectives. Such an approach may present additional complexities to consider because often there are different characteristics, and even different appropriate populations, for single audit and financial statement audit tests. Although many auditees record grant transactions within their general ledgers, populations used for financial statement purposes often do not align well with sampling populations for testing in a Circular A-133 compliance audit. The same principles described previously for a dual purpose sample apply when a single sample is used to achieve both Circular A-133 compliance audit and financial statement audit objectives.

11.57 Although it is challenging to select samples that achieve both Circular A-133 compliance audit and financial statement objectives, they do occur. An example of a sample that achieves both Circular A-133 compliance audit and financial statement audit objectives is a sample of transactions inspected to determine the following:

- Indications of compliance with relevant laws, regulations, and compliance requirements over allowable costs and cost principles

- Indications of performance of internal controls over both allowable costs and cost principles and appropriateness of the expense for financial reporting

- Evidence that the recorded amount, account, and period are correct for financial reporting

Determining the Sample Size

11.58 This section discusses suggested minimum sample sizes as well as factors auditors may consider when using judgment to determine appropriate sample sizes. Because the objectives for tests of controls and tests of compliance are different, there are different factors to consider when determining sample sizes; thus, sample sizes should be considered separately for internal control testing and compliance testing. Audit documentation typically includes the inputs and assumptions for sample sizes to support each sample for every direct and material type of compliance requirement where sampling is used. Documentation is discussed in more depth in paragraphs 11.131–.135.

Control Testing Sample Size Table and Inputs

11.59 If the auditor determines that internal control over compliance is effectively designed and implemented (as discussed in chapter 9 of this guide), Circular A-133 requires that the auditor plan the audit to support a low level of assessed control risk of noncompliance.[11] This requires the auditor to plan to obtain a high level of assurance that controls operate as designed. Therefore, generally, samples for control tests are designed to achieve a 90 percent to 95 percent confidence level (see AICPA Audit Guide *Audit Sampling* for further discussion of confidence levels). Because there are typically few other procedures that provide evidence of the effectiveness of controls, the sample size table that follows is designed to provide a high level of assurance. The following table provides suggested minimum sample sizes for very and moderately significant controls with limited to higher inherent risk of material noncompliance in a major program (see discussions of these terms that follow as well as a discussion of inherent risk of noncompliance in chapter 6 of this guide).

Table 11-1

Control Testing Sample Size Table

Significance of Control and Inherent Risk of Compliance Requirement	Minimum Sample Size
(0 deviations expected)	
Very significant and higher inherent risk	60
Very significant and limited inherent risk *or* Moderately significant and higher inherent risk	40
Moderately significant and limited inherent risk	25

The previous sample size table is appropriate for sampling from populations of 250 items or greater. Small population testing guidance is discussed in paragraphs 11.86–.89.

11.60 The suggested minimum sample sizes are designed to provide sufficient appropriate audit evidence that controls are operating effectively in many Circular A-133 compliance audit testing situations. However, auditors may need to use professional judgment to determine if larger sample sizes are warranted in order to obtain sufficient appropriate audit evidence that controls are functioning in their particular circumstances. For example, there may be additional risks (for example, change in the design of the control or change in personnel operating the control), or the auditor may expect deviations (see discussion that follows). It is important to recognize that if controls are not deemed effective, further control testing may not be warranted. In such situations where internal control over some or all of the compliance requirements for a major program is not deemed effective, refer to chapter 9 of this guide for further guidance.

---

[11] Although Circular A-133 uses the term *control risk*, this guide uses the term *control risk of noncompliance* in order to be consistent with the term as used and defined in AU-C section 935.

Significance of Control Being Tested

11.61 The auditor may vary the type or amount of evidence obtained regarding the effectiveness of individual controls selected for testing based on the significance associated with the control. All controls that the auditor determines are to be tested to mitigate the risk of material noncompliance are significant controls, but a spectrum exists concerning the significance of each control. An important factor in determining the significance of a control is the potential magnitude of noncompliance (both qualitatively and quantitatively) if the particular control were to fail. The auditor should use the information gathered by performing the risk assessment procedures, including the audit evidence obtained in evaluating the design of controls and determining whether they have been implemented, as audit evidence to support the risk assessment. The risk assessment should be used to determine the nature, timing, and extent of further audit procedures to be performed for each control selected for testing as well as to assist the auditor in determining what controls are very significant or moderately significant because minimum sample sizes differ (due to different desired confidence levels and tolerable deviation rates).

11.62 The higher and more pervasive the risk relating to a given control objective (that is, "what could go wrong" risk), the greater the need for assurance on relevant preventive and detective controls to achieve a specific control objective, and the more likely it is that the auditor will assess greater significance to the related controls. Several factors may be considered in determining the significance level of a control including whether the program is identified as higher risk in the *Compliance Supplement* and the potential magnitude of noncompliance to the program. For example, with respect to the Allowable Costs/Cost Principles type of compliance requirement, if payroll is a large portion of the expenditures (in volume or dollars, or both) for the program, then the major control points related to payroll more likely would be considered very significant. However, for a program for which payroll is a smaller portion of the expenditures, these controls may be considered moderately significant or potentially not significant to the program.

11.63 A factor that may cause a control to be considered moderately significant is the existence of other complementary, compensating, or redundant controls. If the auditor plans the control testing level assuming reliance on complementary, compensating, or redundant controls, the auditor should obtain sufficient appropriate audit evidence on the effectiveness of the complementary, compensating, or redundant controls. This means that multiple controls necessary to achieve the control objective will be tested for operating effectiveness. In that case, each control may be tested as a moderately significant control.

11.64 If the auditor identifies that a tested control does not operate effectively, the auditor may subsequently become aware of the existence of complementary, compensating, or redundant controls that, if effective, may limit the severity of the deficiency of the original tested control and prevent it from being a significant deficiency or material weakness in internal control over compliance. In these circumstances, the auditor may consider the effects of complementary, compensating, or redundant controls provided the auditor obtains sufficient appropriate audit evidence that such controls are effective. This means that multiple controls would be tested for operating effectiveness.

Inherent Risk of Noncompliance Factors

11.65 Factors that may suggest higher inherent risk of noncompliance include the following (see also chapter 6 of this guide):

- New program with little history with compliance requirement
- Complex processing (for example, nonroutine versus routine, non-systematic versus systematic, manual versus programmed) or judgment
- Significant deficiencies or material weaknesses in internal control over compliance observed in the past
- Correspondence from program officials indicating potential problems
- Lack of adherence to applicable laws and regulations in prior years
- High employee turnover in a particular area
- Very high volume of activity
- Substantial change in the policies, processes, or personnel associated with the compliance requirement
- The program has been identified as higher risk by the OMB in the *Compliance Supplement*

It is important to note that the size of the program does not necessarily affect the potential for noncompliance. The presence of one or more of the factors listed previously may lead the auditor to determine that there is higher inherent risk of noncompliance; however, the auditor uses professional judgment to determine whether the number and combination of risk factors present higher or limited inherent risk of material noncompliance.

11.66 In order to properly apply the sampling tables illustrated in this chapter, it is useful to understand the inputs and assumptions underlying the suggested minimums (that is, confidence level, tolerable deviation rate, and expected deviation rate). These items are discussed in the following, and the AICPA Audit Guide *Audit Sampling* provides an extensive discussion of the concepts.

Confidence Level and Tolerable Deviation Rate

11.67 Although the sample sizes in the table in paragraph 11.59 are all designed to provide a high level of assurance, the inputs for the 3 sample sizes differ in terms of confidence level and tolerable deviation rate.[12] The tolerable deviation rate for control tests is the maximum rate of deviation from a prescribed control that auditors are willing to accept without altering the planned assessed level of control risk of noncompliance. Auditors seeking a high level of assurance related to controls (low control risk of noncompliance) from a test of control often set a risk of overreliance of 10 percent or less with a tolerable deviation rate of 10 percent or less. The more significant the control, the higher the required performance of the control (that is, the lower the tolerable deviation rate). A higher desired level of assurance (that is, higher desired

---

[12] The suggested minimum sample sizes are consistent with sample sizes provided in tables A-1 and A-2 of appendix A in the AICPA Audit Guide *Audit Sampling*. Although the sample sizes are consistent with statistically-based tables, the sample sizes provided in this chapter can be used for either statistical or nonstatistical sampling.

confidence level) results in a larger sample size to provide the appropriate assurance. In assessing the tolerable deviation rate, the auditor may consider that although deviations from pertinent controls increase the risks of material noncompliance, such deviations do not always result in noncompliance.

Expected Deviation Rate

11.68 For Circular A-133 compliance audits, the auditor often plans for zero deviations in the sample. The sample sizes in the previous table are based on an expectation of zero deviations in the sample and a high level of assurance. If testing discovers no deviations, then a high degree of assurance is achieved that the control is being performed at an acceptable level to be effective. When more deviations are encountered than were planned for, the auditor has not met the planned audit objective.

11.69 All deviations (whether expected or not) should be investigated to determine the potential effect on the program. Although not all deviations will lead to a finding, this guidance is written from the perspective of planning for zero deviations in the sample. Auditors may develop their own sample sizes with planned deviations. The AICPA Audit Guide *Audit Sampling* provides tables and guidance for auditors desiring to design audit samples when deviations are expected.[13] See paragraphs 11.100–.108 for discussion relating to when deviations are found in a sample.

Compliance Testing Sample Size Table and Inputs

11.70 The auditor typically performs a broad array of procedures to provide a reasonable basis for expressing an opinion on compliance for each major program. In a Circular A-133 compliance audit, just as in a financial statement audit, other audit procedures typically precede compliance audit sampling. For example, risk assessment procedures typically precede substantive procedures. Similarly, it is common for some controls-related procedures to be conducted prior to compliance testing (for example, understanding and testing the control environment). Before designing a compliance audit sample, it is also common for the auditor to consider whether there are individually important items that may be selected for testing prior to selecting a compliance sample (see paragraphs 11.21–.28). The auditor should consider other audit procedures when determining the appropriate sample size for compliance testing.

11.71 The risk of material noncompliance consists of inherent risk of noncompliance and control risk of noncompliance. The assurance required from a compliance sample and, therefore, the determination of the minimum compliance sample size, depends on the risk of material noncompliance remaining after other audit procedures (for example, risk assessment procedures, controls testing, substantive analytical procedures, tests of individually important items) have been executed. If the auditor gathers evidence that controls over

---

[13] If internal control over compliance is deemed likely to be ineffective, Circular A-133 states that the auditor should assess control risk at the maximum and consider whether any additional compliance tests are required because of ineffective internal control. The auditor could consider testing compensating or redundant controls as described in paragraphs 11.63–.64. If no compensating or redundant controls are operating effectively, the auditor also should report a significant deficiency or material weakness in internal control over compliance as part of the audit findings. (Chapter 13, "Auditor Reporting Requirements and Other Communication Considerations in a Single Audit (Circular A-133)," discusses the reporting of significant deficiencies and material weaknesses.)

compliance are effective through tests of controls, and other audit procedures do not identify instances of noncompliance or identify specific heightened risk factors, and the auditor determines that additional testing via audit sampling is warranted, it is likely the remaining risk of material noncompliance would be low or moderate. Conversely, if tests of controls identify control deficiencies in the controls over compliance, or other audit procedures identify instances of noncompliance or identify specific heightened risk factors, it may lead the auditor to assess the risk of material noncompliance as high or moderate.

11.72 The following table provides suggested minimum sample sizes associated with high, moderate, and low remaining risk of material noncompliance. The remaining risk of material noncompliance is an indicator of the desired level of assurance. A high remaining risk of material noncompliance indicates that a high level of assurance is desired to meet the audit objective. Desired level of assurance is discussed in more depth in paragraphs 11.76–.81.

Table 11-2

Compliance Testing Sample Size Table

Desired Level of Assurance (Remaining Risk of Material Noncompliance)	Minimum Sample Size
0 exceptions expected	
High	60
Moderate	40
Low	25

The previous sample size table is appropriate for sampling from populations of 250 items or greater. For smaller populations, see testing guidance in paragraphs 11.86–.89.

11.73 The minimum sample sizes in the previous table may be applied for each direct and material compliance requirement for each major program.[14] Although the minimum sample sizes suggested in the table often provide the appropriate extent of testing, auditors may use professional judgment to determine if larger sample sizes are warranted in order to obtain sufficient appropriate audit evidence in particular circumstances. Depending on the nature of the compliance requirement, the results of other procedures performed during the audit, and the risks and complexities of the sampling population, there may be situations when larger sample sizes would be more appropriate than the proposed minimum sample sizes. For example, if there were significant deficiencies or material weaknesses noted with the related controls, the auditor may expand testing to support the conclusion on compliance.

11.74 The sample sizes provided in the table are based on an expectation of zero exceptions and varying levels of assurance or confidence. A higher remaining risk of material noncompliance results in a need for a higher level of assurance (that is, a higher desired confidence level) and a larger sample size. Each type of compliance requirement tested should be evaluated separately for

---

[14] See footnote 12.

purposes of determining sample size. If the appropriate sample size is tested and no exceptions are discovered, then the planned degree of assurance has been obtained.

11.75 Many Circular A-133 compliance audits will include a spectrum of compliance testing sample sizes, meaning that some types of compliance requirements may present a high remaining risk of material noncompliance and would thus require a sample that provides high assurance, whereas other types of compliance requirements may present a low remaining risk of material noncompliance.

Desired Level of Assurance

11.76 When planning a particular sample, the auditor should consider the relationship of the sample to the audit objective. Thus, to the extent each compliance test has a different objective, samples should be separately considered. As noted in the compliance testing sample size table, the primary determinant of the appropriate minimum sample size for a particular compliance test is the risk of material noncompliance remaining after considering other audit procedures (for example, risk assessment, control testing, testing individually important items, substantive analytical procedures) and, therefore, the desired level of assurance.

11.77 The desired level of assurance or confidence from a compliance sample varies as the types of compliance requirements differ in importance and risk. There is also a broad array of audit procedures the auditor may use that contribute to the overall evidence of compliance. There is general consensus across audit sampling applications that high assurance is typically associated with 90 percent to 95 percent confidence levels. The confidence levels associated with moderate and low in the compliance table are considered appropriate in compliance testing associated with a Circular A-133 compliance audit.

11.78 As discussed previously, the basis for expressing an opinion on compliance for each major program often is based on multiple procedures. Although the combined totality of audit evidence gathered by the auditor should be sufficient to support a high level of assurance, an auditor may not need to design compliance samples to achieve high assurance when there are other sources of evidence beyond the compliance sample.

11.79 In evaluating the desired level of assurance, the auditor may consider the importance of the type of compliance requirement, inherent risk of noncompliance factors, the risk of fraud, and the results from tests of the operating effectiveness of controls for the type of compliance requirement. For example, if the auditor has obtained evidence that controls over compliance are properly designed and operating effectively to reduce the likelihood of material noncompliance, the auditor may assess the remaining risk of material noncompliance as moderate or low and similarly reduce the desired level of assurance from the compliance sample. A lower remaining risk of material noncompliance results in a need for a lower level of assurance from the sample and a smaller sample size. On the other hand, if tests of controls indicated that controls are not operating effectively and the auditor is not able to support a low assessed level of control risk of noncompliance for the major program, the auditor should assess control risk of noncompliance at the maximum. Maximum control risk of noncompliance may result in higher remaining risk of material noncompliance, and the desired level of assurance from the compliance test also increases to moderate or high to support an unmodified opinion on the auditee's compliance.[15]

11.80 As noted in the prior paragraph, the risk of material noncompliance is affected by the inherent risk of noncompliance for the particular type of compliance requirement. There are many factors that can affect inherent risk of noncompliance, for example, the regulatory environment, the significance of the particular requirement to the overall program, the complexity of relevant regulations, changes in regulations, or the experience the auditee has with the federal program. In assessing the remaining risk of material noncompliance, the engagement team may also consider the results of procedures performed in connection with the audit of the financial statements.

11.81 Auditors, in assessing inherent risk of noncompliance, typically assess risk factors associated with the types of compliance requirements being tested. Further, there are general risk factors which may suggest the need to obtain a higher level of assurance from an audit sample. Examples of such risk factors are discussed in paragraph 11.65. Audit risk of noncompliance considerations including inherent risk of noncompliance are also discussed in chapter 6 of this guide.

Tolerable Exception Rate

11.82 The tolerable exception rate for compliance tests is the maximum rate of compliance exceptions that auditors are willing to accept. The tolerable exception rate for all types of compliance requirements is related to program materiality. Materiality is considered in relation to each major program. The quantitative thresholds used to determine if an exception is an "audit finding" related to a major program is lower than the materiality used for planning the Circular A-133 compliance audit and expressing an opinion on the auditee's compliance (materiality is also discussed in chapter 6 and chapter 8, "Determination of Major Programs (Circular A-133)," of this guide).

11.83 The determination of major program materiality is a matter of professional judgment. The tolerable exception rate for a compliance sample testing nonmonetary compliance attributes (for example, Reporting type of compliance requirement) as well as monetary compliance attributes (for example, Allowable Costs/Cost Principles type of compliance requirement) is normally equal to or lower than the level of materiality for expressing an opinion on the auditee's compliance with requirements having a direct and material effect on each major program. For example, if program materiality is determined to be five percent of program expenditures, then the tolerable exception rate for a compliance sample testing monetary attributes would be five percent or less. Similarly, if a five percent exception rate for a nonmonetary compliance attribute is considered material, then the tolerable exception rate for compliance sample testing that nonmonetary attribute would be five percent or less. The compliance testing sample size table is based on a five percent tolerable exception rate for both nonmonetary and monetary attributes. If program materiality is set lower than five percent, then the tolerable exception rate would be lowered, and the minimum sample sizes may need to be adjusted upward. The AICPA Audit Guide *Audit Sampling* provides tables and guidance for auditors desiring to design audit samples for different tolerable exception rates.

---

[15] However, if during the testing of the compliance sample, the auditor finds sufficient evidence of noncompliance to support an opinion other than unmodified, the auditor is not required to test remaining or additional items.

Expected Population Exception Rate

11.84 The compliance testing sample size table is based on an expectation of no exceptions. If the auditor discovers no exceptions in the tests, then the desired level of assurance is obtained about compliance. When more exceptions are encountered than were planned for, the auditor has not met the planned audit objective. Auditors may develop their own sample sizes with planned exceptions. Appendix A of the AICPA Audit Guide *Audit Sampling* provides tables and guidance for auditors desiring to design audit samples when exceptions are expected.

11.85 All exceptions (whether planned or not) should be investigated to determine the potential effect on the program. Although not all exceptions will lead to a finding, the auditor should evaluate compliance exceptions (whether planned or not) for their nature and cause to determine the potential effect on the program.

Testing Small Populations

11.86 Some significant controls or instances of complying with a compliance requirement, or both, do not occur frequently (for example, submitting a required report). The following table provides suggested minimum sample sizes in testing small populations subject to controls and compliance requirements.[16] *Small populations*, for purposes of this chapter, are defined as populations of fewer than 250 items.

Table 11-3

Small Population Sample Size Table

Frequency and Population Size	Sample Size
Quarterly (4)	2
Monthly (12)	2–4
Semimonthly (24)	3–8
Weekly (52)	5–9

11.87 For populations between 52 and 250 items, a rule of thumb some auditors follow is to test a sample size of approximately 10 percent of the population, but the size is subject to professional judgment, which would include specific engagement risk assessment considerations.

11.88 For more significant controls discussed in paragraphs 11.61–.64, or for more significant types of compliance requirements, the auditor may determine the appropriate sample size is on the larger end of the ranges displayed in the small population sample size table.

11.89 The auditor may consider the size of the population by reference to the defined sampling unit. For example, in some cases, the auditor may need to consider the populations from several locations or organizational units; if there were weekly controls over the occurrence of expenses at each of 40 departments, the population of weekly expense test controls would be 2,080 (52 × 40), and this would not be a small population.

---

[16] The table is adapted from table 3-5, "Testing Operating Effectiveness of Small Population," in the AICPA Audit Guide *Audit Sampling*.

Selecting Sample Items for Testing

11.90 Once the population of transactions or items relevant for a control or type of compliance requirement is identified, the auditor may select items for testing from a physical or electronic representation of the population. For example, a physical representation might be a printout of expenditures for the period.

11.91 The auditor should select items for the sample in such a way that the auditor can reasonably expect the sample to be representative of the relevant population and likely to provide the auditor with a reasonable basis for conclusions about the population. The goal of sample selection, a representative sample, is the same for both nonstatistical and statistical sampling. For statistical sampling, it is necessary to use an appropriate random sampling method such as simple random sampling or systematic sampling. In nonstatistical sampling, the auditor uses a sample selection approach that approximates a random sampling approach.[17] Note that the *Compliance Supplement* provides specific guidance on sample selection for certain types of major programs.[18]

11.92 As noted previously in the discussion on determining the appropriate sampling population, it is common for control testing samples to be drawn from a population that contains multiple major programs (assuming common controls, policies, procedures, and competence of personnel). Experience has shown that it is preferable to select separate compliance samples from each major program because the separate samples provide clear evidence of the tests performed, the results of those tests, and the conclusions reached, which support the auditor's opinion on compliance for each major program.

11.93 An overview of selection methods follows. For nonstatistical sampling, the auditor may select the sample using any of the three techniques that follow. However, the haphazard selection technique is not appropriate for statistical sampling. The AICPA Audit Guide *Audit Sampling* contains additional guidance on applying the techniques discussed in the following paragraphs as well as additional sampling techniques such as block and sequential.

Random Selection

11.94 Random selection provides an equal chance of selection to each sampling item in the population. To perform this selection, the auditor may select a random sample by matching random numbers generated by a computer or selected from a random number table, or by generating random numbers with software such as Microsoft Excel or commercial audit software packages.

Haphazard Selection

11.95 The haphazard selection technique represents the auditor's best attempt at making a random selection judgmentally without the use of a structured selection technique (for example, random numbers or tables). It is the selection of sampling units without any intentional bias; that is, without any

---

[17] A properly designed nonstatistical sampling application that considers the same factors that would be considered in a properly designed statistical sample can provide results that are as effective as those from a properly designed statistical sampling application. See the AICPA Audit Guide *Audit Sampling* for further discussion of nonstatistical and statistical sampling.

[18] For example, the *OMB Compliance Supplement* (*Compliance Supplement*) provides guidance on how to select items in a research and development cluster that includes multiple federal agencies and award types.

special reasoning for including or omitting items from the sample. Haphazard selection does not consist of selecting sampling units in a careless manner. For example, when the physical representation of the population of all vouchers processed for the period under audit is a file cabinet drawer of vouchers, a haphazard sample might include any of the vouchers that the auditor haphazardly pulls from the drawer, regardless of each voucher's size, shape, location, or other physical features.

11.96 The auditor using haphazard selection is normally careful to avoid distorting the sample by selecting, for example, only large, only unusual, only convenient, or only physically small items or by omitting such items as the first or last in the physical representation of the population. The goal is to select a sample without bias. Although haphazard sampling is useful for nonstatistical sampling, it is not appropriate for statistical sampling because it does not allow the auditor to measure the probability of selecting a combination of sampling units.

Systematic Selection With a Random Start

11.97 Systematic selection with a random start determines a uniform interval by dividing the number of physical units in the population by the sample size. A starting point is randomly selected in the first interval, and 1 item is selected throughout the population at each of the uniform intervals from the starting point. For example, if the auditor wishes to select 60 items from a population of 12,000 items, the uniform interval is every 200th item. The auditor randomly selects the first item from within the first interval and then selects every 200th item from the random start.

11.98 If the deviation pattern is random, then systematic selection is equivalent to simple random selection. In the absence of a known pattern in the population, it is a practical and efficient alternative to simple random selection, particularly when items are being selected manually from a population.

Performing the Test Procedures

11.99 After the sampling plan has been designed, and the auditor has selected the sample, if the auditor is not able to apply the planned audit procedures or appropriate alternative procedures to selected items, the auditor should consider the reasons for this limitation and should ordinarily consider those selected items to be control deviations or compliance exceptions from the prescribed policy or procedure for the purpose of evaluating the sample. Additional guidance on performing the sampling plan, including how to handle sample items that are voided documents, unused or inapplicable documents, or documents that cannot be located, can be obtained in chapter 3 of the AICPA Audit Guide *Audit Sampling*.

Investigate and Understand the Nature and Cause of Control Deviations and Compliance Exceptions

11.100 In addition to providing an auditor's opinion on compliance for each major program, Circular A-133 requires the auditor to report on deficiencies in internal control over compliance which constitute significant deficiencies or material weaknesses in internal control over compliance. Circular A-133 also requires the auditor to report known questioned costs when the likely questioned costs are $10,000 or more.[19] Thus, whenever a control deviation or a compliance exception is identified, the auditor should evaluate the nature and cause of the deviation or exception. Understanding the potential effect on the program will assist the auditor in determining whether sufficient appropriate evidence has been obtained to support the auditor's opinion on compliance and whether to report an internal control finding, compliance finding, or both.

11.101 In evaluating deviations and exceptions, the auditor may consider factors such as the following:

- *Systematic nature of the deviation or exception.* If a control deviation or compliance exception is systematic in nature, it is more likely to lead to a finding than if the deviation or exception is contained to a subset of the population testing. Guidance regarding deviations or exceptions believed to be nonsystematic is provided in paragraphs 11.106–.130.

- *Intentional deviation or exception.* The discovery of fraud requires a broader consideration of the possible implications than does the discovery of a deviation or exception attributable to a mistake or lack of understanding.

- *Pattern relative to past history.* Control deviations or compliance exceptions observed in the current audit that are similar in nature to deviations or exceptions that led to a finding or material noncompliance in past audits typically increases the likelihood that a finding will be reported, or that there is material noncompliance in the current year. The nature of the pattern may lead the auditor to perform additional tests to determine the effect of the deviation or exception. Further, an auditee's failure to correct previously identified deficiencies in internal control over compliance or compliance exceptions is also a relevant factor in the evaluation consideration.

Determine If Additional Testing Is Warranted in Response to an Observed Deviation or Exception

11.102 If exceptions are found and the likely questioned cost is close to the audit materiality level for a major program or the audit finding reporting threshold of $10,000, the auditor may conduct additional tests to better substantiate the likely questioned costs. In addition, if findings occur in a particular risky area of a major program, additional testing may be warranted to substantiate the compliance opinion.

11.103 The sample sizes in the controls and compliance sample size tables are based on an expectation of zero deviations/exceptions. The auditor may encounter an unexpected deviation or exception rate in a sample from a population that was expected to be deviation/exception free or to have a low incidence of deviation/exception. In such cases, it is important for the auditor to recognize that the sample is expected to be representative only with respect to the occurrence rate or incidence of deviations or exceptions, not their nature or cause. An unexpected deviation or exception may be indicative of other deviations or exceptions in the population. Where the auditor, expecting a negligible or

---

[19] See footnote 3 in paragraph 11.08 for further discussion on *known questioned costs* and *likely questioned costs.*

zero deviation or exception rate, selected a small sample and found a deviation or exception rate slightly higher than expected, and the auditor believes the deviation or exception rate observed does not represent a reportable finding, it may be appropriate to extend the sample from that population, but the appropriate extension would not be small. More guidance on dealing with negligible exception rates is provided in the AICPA Audit Guide *Audit Sampling*.

11.104 In some instances, the auditor's understanding of the nature and cause of the deviation or exception may suggest the sample deviation/exception rate is not likely to be representative of the population (that is, it is not a systematic error). In such instances, the auditor may consider whether to pursue additional evidence to indicate that the sample deviation or exception rate is not representative of the entire population (that is, the error can be contained to a specific subpopulation). To conclude that a deviation or exception is nonsystemic typically requires the auditor to perform additional audit procedures to obtain sufficient appropriate audit evidence that the actual deviation or exception rate experienced in the sample is not representative of the deviation or exception rate in the population.

11.105 When the decision regarding reporting a finding is not straightforward, the auditor may consider reporting deviations and exceptions as findings and let the appropriate federal regulators investigate further.

Evaluating Sample Results

Evaluating Control Deviations

11.106 Whether the sample is statistical or nonstatistical, the auditor should investigate the nature and cause of such deviations and evaluate the possible effect on the purpose of the audit procedure and on other areas of the audit.

11.107 The controls sample size table in paragraph 11.59 is based on an expectation of zero deviations. When more deviations are encountered than were planned for, the auditor has not met the planned audit objective. In other words, although the auditor needs a *tolerance,* or tolerable deviation rate, in order to plan a sample, the observance of a deviation rate as high as the tolerable rate in a sample is not acceptable due to sampling risk (discussed in the following).

11.108 As previously discussed, when a control deviation is identified, the auditor should evaluate the nature and cause of the deviation. Control deviations should be evaluated to determine whether they are significant deficiencies or material weaknesses in internal control over compliance.

Calculating the Control Deviation Rate

11.109 Calculating the deviation rate in the control test sample involves dividing the number of observed deviations by the sample size. For example, if 3 deviations are observed in a sample of 60, the deviation rate is 5 percent (3/60). The deviation rate in the sample is the auditor's best estimate of the deviation rate in the population from which it was selected. Because the purpose of testing is generally to confirm the reliability of the control, it is common to assume that controls are effective when designing the audit plan. Thus, deviations observed in the sample are often important to the auditor's compliance testing strategy, depending on the deviation rate and reasons for the deviation.

Considering Sampling Risk Associated With Control Testing

11.110 When evaluating a sample for a test of controls, the auditor should give appropriate consideration to *sampling risk*—the risk that the auditor's conclusions based on a sample may be different from the conclusion if the entire population were subjected to the same audit procedure. If the estimate of the population deviation rate (the sample deviation rate) is less than the tolerable deviation rate for the population, the auditor should consider the risk that such a result might be obtained even if the true deviation rate for the population exceeds the tolerable rate for the population.

11.111 If an auditor performs a statistical sampling application, the auditor might use a table or computer program to assist in measuring the allowance for sampling risk. If the auditor performs a nonstatistical sampling application, sampling risk may not be directly measurable; however, it is generally appropriate for the auditor to conclude that the sample results do not support the planned assessed level of control risk of noncompliance if the rate of deviation identified in the sample exceeds the expected population deviation rate used in designing the sample (which is zero in the control testing sample size table in this guide).

11.112 The control sample size table is based on an expectation of zero deviations. When more deviations are encountered than were planned for, the auditor has not met the planned audit objective, and there is likely to be an unacceptably high risk that the true deviation rate in the population exceeds the tolerable rate due to sampling risk. In such a circumstance, after considering the reasons for the control deviation(s) and the number of deviations identified, the auditor may conclude it is appropriate to expand the test or perform other tests to include sufficient additional items to reduce control risk to an acceptable level.[20] Rather than testing additional items, however, it is often more efficient in a Circular A-133 compliance audit to report a deficiency in internal control over compliance and, when testing compliance, to increase the auditor's assessed level of risk of material noncompliance and increase the extent of compliance testing to reflect the change in the control risk of noncompliance assessment.

Assessing the Potential Magnitude of a Deficiency in Internal Control Over Compliance

11.113 If the auditor finds deviations, he or she determines whether they are deficiencies in internal control over compliance and, if so, whether those deficiencies are material weaknesses, significant deficiencies, or just deficiencies in internal control over compliance. AU-C section 265, *Communicating Internal Control Related Matters Identified in an Audit* (AICPA, *Professional Standards*), requires the auditor to consider the likelihood and magnitude of deficiencies, individually or in combination (see chapter 9 of this guide).[21]

---

[20] Additional guidance on expanding the sample is provided in chapter 3, "Nonstatistical and Statistical Audit Sampling in Tests of Controls," of the AICPA Audit Guide *Audit Sampling*.

[21] When the deficiency in internal control over compliance relates to monetary values, chapter 3 of the AICPA Audit Guide *Audit Sampling* provides an approach to quantifying the potential magnitude of monetary exposure to noncompliance.

Reaching an Overall Conclusion on Tests of Controls

11.114 The overall conclusion about the effect that the evaluation of the sample results will have on the assessed level of control risk of noncompliance, the risks of material noncompliance, and, thus, on the nature, timing, and extent of planned compliance tests requires professional judgment. If the sample results, along with other relevant audit evidence, support the planned low assessed level of control risk of noncompliance, the auditor may have no need to modify planned compliance tests. If a low assessed level of control risk of noncompliance is not supported, the auditor should consider either performing further tests of other controls that could result in supporting the planned level of control risk of noncompliance or increasing the assessed level of control risk of noncompliance and altering the nature, timing, or extent of the planned compliance tests accordingly.

11.115 Additional guidance regarding whether there is evidence of a finding, significant deficiency, or material weakness in internal control over compliance is found in chapters 9 and 13, "Auditor Reporting Requirements and Other Communication Considerations in a Single Audit (Circular A-133)," of this guide.

Evaluating Compliance Exceptions

11.116 Whether the sample is statistical or nonstatistical, the auditor should evaluate the nature and cause of the noncompliance to reach an overall conclusion on compliance with a particular type of compliance requirement.

Calculating the Compliance Exception Rate or Likely Questioned Costs

11.117 For nonmonetary compliance attributes, calculating the exception rate in the compliance test sample involves dividing the number of observed exceptions by the sample size. For example, if 3 exceptions are observed in a sample of 60, the exception rate is 5 percent (3/60). The exception rate in the sample generally is the auditor's best estimate of the exception rate in the population from which it was selected. Exceptions observed in the sample are important to the auditor's compliance testing strategy and should be evaluated to determine whether to report findings of material noncompliance. Further, compliance findings may affect the overall opinion regarding material compliance.

11.118 Although compliance testing in a Circular A-133 compliance audit often involves monetary amounts, the focus of the testing is on whether or not there is evidence of compliance to support the auditor's opinion on compliance. Additionally, when noncompliance is discovered related to monetary transactions of a program, Circular A-133 requires the auditor to determine both the known questioned costs and likely questioned costs associated with audit findings. The estimation of likely questioned costs may require the projection of sample results to determine the effect on the auditor's opinion on compliance and whether a finding is required to be reported in the Schedule of Findings and Questioned Costs.[22] The auditor is not required to expand his or her test work to definitively determine the total questioned costs because there is no requirement in Circular A-133 to report an exact amount or a statistical

---

[22] See footnote 3 in paragraph 11.08 for more information.

projection of likely questioned costs. Rather, Circular A-133 requires the auditor to consider the effect of likely questioned costs on the auditor's opinion on compliance and include an audit finding when the auditor's estimate of likely questioned costs is greater than $10,000.

11.119 As noted previously, the auditor should evaluate the finding to calculate an estimate of potential total questioned costs in order to determine whether likely questioned costs exceed $10,000. For example, if the auditor specifically identifies $7,000 in known questioned costs for a type of compliance requirement but, based on his or her projection of the exception to the population, develops an estimate that the total likely questioned costs are approximately $60,000, the auditor should report a finding that indicates only the known questioned costs of $7,000. Chapter 13 of this guide further discusses reporting findings based on likely questioned costs. If likely questioned costs exceed program materiality, the auditor may consider modifying the audit opinion on compliance for that program (chapter 6 of this guide further discusses materiality considerations as it relates to opining on major programs).

11.120 There are 2 approaches commonly used to project compliance results to a monetary population. First, if the monetary compliance exceptions are 100 percent errors (for example, the entire sampling unit contains all allowable or unallowable cost), from a population of similar sized transactions, the same exception rate technique discussed previously for nonmonetary compliance attributes can be applied to the population of dollars to estimate the likely questioned costs. For example, if 3 exceptions are observed in a sample of 60, the exception rate is 5 percent (3/60). Assuming the 3 exceptions were 100 percent errors, and the population is made up of homogeneous transactions, the 5 percent exception rate would be applied to the total population monetary value to estimate likely questioned costs. Continuing the example, if the total value of the sampling population were $1,000,000, then the likely questioned costs would be $50,000.

11.121 The second approach to projecting compliance sample results to the population applies the noncompliance or questioned cost rate of dollar noncompliance observed in the sample to the population. For example, an auditor might have selected a sample that sums to $10,000 and observed known questioned costs of $200, or 2 percent of the recorded amount of the expenditures tested. If the total recorded amount in the expenditures population is $1,000,000, then projected likely questioned cost is $20,000 ($1,000,000 × 2%). This approach is especially useful when a sampling unit is found to be only partially incorrect.

11.122 See the AIPCA Audit Guide *Audit Sampling* for additional methods to calculate the compliance exception rate or likely questioned costs.

Considering Sampling Risk Associated With Compliance Testing

11.123 When evaluating a sample for a test of compliance, the auditor should give appropriate consideration to sampling risk. If the estimate of the population exception rate (the sample exception rate) for nonmonetary attributes is less than the tolerable exception rate for the population, or if the estimate of likely questioned costs is less than tolerable error for a monetary population, the auditor might consider the risk that such a result might be obtained even if the true exception rate or questioned costs for the population exceeds the tolerable rate or tolerable error, respectively, for the population.

11.124 If an auditor performs a statistical sampling application, the auditor might use a table or computer program to assist in measuring the allowance for sampling risk. If the auditor performs a nonstatistical sampling application, sampling risk may not be directly measureable; however, it is generally appropriate for the auditor to conclude that the sample results do not support an acceptable level of compliance if the rate of exception or likely questioned costs identified in the sample exceeds the expected exception rate used in designing the sample (which is zero in the compliance testing sample size table in this guide).

11.125 The compliance sample size table in paragraph 11.72 is based on an expectation of zero exceptions. When more exceptions are encountered than were planned for, the auditor has not met the planned audit objective, and there is likely to be an unacceptably high risk that the true exception rate in the population exceeds the tolerable rate due to sampling risk. In such a circumstance, after considering the reasons for the compliance exception(s) and the number and magnitude of exception(s) identified, the auditor may conclude it is appropriate to expand testing or perform other tests to include sufficient additional items to reduce the risk of material noncompliance to an acceptable level.[23] Alternatively, rather than expand the scope of testing to improve the precision of the projected error, the auditor may consider it prudent to report the exceptions as a finding and evaluate the effect that the sample result has on the assessed level of risk of material noncompliance and the overall compliance opinion.

11.126 In evaluating whether an exception is a finding, it is particularly important to consider sampling risk when the projected likely cost is close to the reporting threshold of $10,000. The auditor would generally conclude that there is an unacceptable risk that the true questioned costs exceeds the reporting threshold. Even when the projected likely questioned costs are considerably less than the reporting threshold, the auditor should consider the risk that such a result might be obtained even though the true questioned costs for the population exceeds the reporting threshold (allowance for sampling risk). The smaller the sample, the greater the associated uncertainty or sampling risk associated with that sample.

Effect of Compliance Testing Results on Internal Control Results Reporting

11.127 The auditor should relate the evaluation of the compliance testing sample to other relevant audit evidence when forming a conclusion about compliance as well as internal control over compliance. If compliance testing results in exceptions, the auditor should relate this testing to the results of tests of internal controls. A compliance exception is an indicator of a potential deficiency in internal control over compliance.

Reaching an Overall Conclusion on Tests of Compliance

11.128 The overall conclusion about the effect that the evaluation of the sample results has on his or her assessed level of risk of material noncompliance and, thus, on the overall Circular A-133 compliance audit opinion, requires the auditor to use professional judgment. If the sample results, along with other

---

[23] Additional guidance on expanding the sample is provided in chapter 3 of the AICPA Audit Guide *Audit Sampling*.

relevant audit evidence, support other than an unmodified opinion, the auditor should modify the opinion accordingly.

11.129 For nonmonetary compliance attributes (for example, a report is submitted on a timely basis), the auditor should document noted exceptions and consider the guidance contained in Circular A-133 to determine if the finding should be included in the Schedule of Findings and Questioned Costs in the Circular A-133 compliance audit reporting package. For monetary attributes, the auditor should also document noted exceptions (and related questioned costs), and if the known or likely questioned cost exceeds $10,000, the auditor should report the finding.

11.130 When the auditor finds a compliance exception that, in itself, does not meet the criteria of a finding, the auditor would typically gain assurance that the exception may, indeed, be omitted from the Schedule of Findings and Questioned Costs. Although Circular A-133 does not require the auditor to expand his or her sample in the case of exceptions, there may be additional procedures performed to support the conclusion that the exception is not a finding, for example if the questioned costs are close to the reporting threshold of $10,000. In all cases where an initial exception is determined not to be a finding, the auditor should document the rationale for omitting the exception from the Schedule of Findings and Questioned Costs.

Documenting the Sampling Procedure

11.131 According to paragraph .40 of AU-C section 935, the auditor should document his or her responses to the assessed risks of material noncompliance, the procedures performed to test compliance with applicable compliance requirements,[24] and the results of those procedures, including any tests of controls over compliance. The following paragraphs provide information related to documenting sampling procedures and the results of such procedures as it applies to a compliance audit.

11.132 As noted in chapter 3, "Planning and Performing a Financial Statement Audit in Accordance With *Government Auditing Standards*," of this guide, AU-C section 230, *Audit Documentation* (AICPA, *Professional Standards*), provides requirements and guidance on the form, content, extent, retention, and confidentiality of audit documentation. AU-C section 230 contains guidance on documenting significant findings or issues; identifying the preparer and reviewer of audit documentation; documenting specific items tested; documenting departures from relevant Statements on Auditing Standards; revising audit documentation after the date of the auditor's report; and ownership and confidentiality of audit documentation. Among other things, AU-C section 230 states that an auditor should prepare audit documentation that is sufficient to enable an experienced auditor, having no previous connection to the audit, to understand the following:

- The nature, timing, and extent of auditing procedures performed to comply with generally accepted auditing standards and applicable legal and regulatory requirements (for example, *Government Auditing Standards* and Circular A-133)

---

[24] See footnote 6 in paragraph 11.26.

- The results of the audit procedures performed and the audit evidence obtained
- Significant findings or issues arising during the audit, the conclusions reached thereon, and significant professional judgments made in reaching those conclusions

11.133 In addition to the requirements found in AU-C section 230, *Government Auditing Standards* includes several additional audit documentation requirements that are described in chapter 3 of this guide.

11.134 The form and extent of documentation related to sampling are influenced by numerous factors, which may include the size and complexity of the auditee, the nature and complexity of the auditee's internal control over compliance, the nature and complexity of the compliance requirements, and the auditee's past experience relative to compliance.

11.135 Although AU-C section 230, AU-C section 530, and this guide do not contain a list of specific documentation requirements for audit sampling applications, examples of items that the auditor typically documents include the following:

- A description of the control or type of compliance requirement being tested
- A definition of the population and the sampling unit, including how the auditor considered the completeness of the population (discussed in paragraphs 11.33–.41)
- A definition of the deviation or exception condition (discussed in paragraphs 11.50–.51)
- The desired confidence or assurance level, the tolerable deviation or exception rate, and the expected population deviation or exception rate[25] (as discussed in paragraphs 11.58–.89)
- The chosen sample size[26]
- The sample selection method such as random, haphazard, or systematic selection (as discussed in paragraphs 11.90–.98)
- The selected sample items, which would include identifying characteristics of the specific items tested, clear documentation to support both controls and compliance testing when dual purpose testing is applied (as discussed in paragraphs 11.52–.57), and resolution of any documents that cannot be located (as discussed in paragraph 11.99). Paragraph .A14 of AU-C section 230 provides several alternatives regarding how an auditor can identify selected sample items in audit documentation
- An evaluation of the sample, including the following:

---

[25] Use of a sample size from the tables in this chapter provides adequate documentation of the underlying inputs to the table (that is, tolerable deviation/exception rate, confidence, and expected deviation/exception rate). However, the support for the sample size used within the range provided, which depends on factors such as the significance of the control tested or the remaining risk of material noncompliance, is based on auditor judgment and is not implicit in the tables and, thus, is important in documenting the sampling applications and procedures.

[26] See footnote 25. Similarly, if an auditor determines a sample size using other than the suggested minimums from the tables in this chapter (for example, some audit organizations may use their own internal guidance that results in a sample size that is slightly different from the tables in this chapter), the basis for that determination would also be important in documenting the sampling applications and procedures.

- The number of deviations or exceptions found in the sample
- Important qualitative aspects of the deviation(s) or exception(s)
- The projected population deviation or exception rate
- A determination of whether the sample results support the test objective
- The effect of the evaluation on other audit procedures (for example, if tests of controls do not allow the auditor to support a low assessed level of control risk of noncompliance for major programs, consideration of the effect on subsequent tests of compliance)
- The auditor's determination of known questioned costs and estimation of likely questioned costs
- A determination whether observed deviation(s) or exception(s) require a modification of the auditor's opinion on compliance or will result in a finding and, if not, how the auditor considered sampling risk (as discussed in paragraphs 11.106–.130)

- Any qualitative factors considered significant in making the sampling, selections, assessments, and judgments which may include multiple major programs, multiple organizational units, clusters, or other factors
- A summary of the overall conclusion (if not evident from the results)

Transition Considerations Related to the Uniform Guidance

11.136 The "Transition Considerations Related to the Uniform Guidance" sections in chapter 6 and chapter 10 of this guide contain important information about the effective date of the Uniform Guidance and how it will affect auditor planning and compliance testing in a Circular A-133 compliance audit. Refer to that guidance for more details. As noted in those sections, a major program may include expenditures from both federal awards subject to the pre-Uniform Guidance requirements, as well as federal awards subject to the post-Uniform Guidance requirements. This situation could exist for several years until the pre-Uniform Guidance awards have been completely expended. When testing major program transactions, identification of the date of a federal award related to a particular expenditure is needed in order to determine the applicable criteria to use for the transaction being tested. It should be noted that a separate sample for pre-Uniform Guidance award transactions and post-Uniform Guidance award transactions within a major program would not typically be needed in this situation. However, this guide recommends that when testing major program transactions the audit documentation for testing compliance and internal control over compliance include an identification of the transactions tested that were subject to post-Uniform Guidance requirements.

11.137 An example of how the effective date of the Uniform Guidance may impact sampling in the Circular A-133 compliance audit follows and is intended to assist the auditor in understanding the challenges in a compliance audit during the transition period. Assume a test for compliance with the Allowable Costs/Cost Principles type of compliance requirement indicates a sample size of 60 expenditure transactions. Some of the transactions in the sample may be subject to post-Uniform Guidance requirements, while others may be subject to pre-Uniform Guidance requirements. Identification of the date of a federal award related to a particular expenditure transaction is needed in order to determine the applicable criteria to use for the transaction being tested. Although, as noted previously, a separate sample would not typically be needed in this situation, the Allowable Costs/Cost Principles criteria for transactions subject to the post-Uniform Guidance requirements may be different from the criteria for transactions subject to the pre-Uniform Guidance requirements. In this example, the auditor would use both Part 3.1 and Part 3.2 of the *Compliance Supplement* to test this type of compliance requirement. See the "Transition Considerations Related to the Uniform Guidance" in chapter 10 for more information about changes to Part 3 of the *Compliance Supplement*.

Chapter 12

Audit Considerations of Federal Pass-Through Awards (Circular A-133)

> **© Update 12-1: Audits of Federal Awards**
>
> This chapter, and the remaining chapters of part II, *Circular A-133 Audits*, of this guide, should be used for performing a compliance audit of federal awards under Office of Management and Budget (OMB) Circular A-133, *Audits of States, Local Governments, and Non-Profit Organizations* (Circular A-133). Part III, *Uniform Guidance Audits*, of this guide should be used when performing a compliance audit under Title 2 U.S. *Code of Federal Regulations* Part 200, *Uniform Administrative Requirements, Cost Principles, and Audit Requirements for Federal Awards* (Uniform Guidance). See the transitional guidance sections at the end of each chapter that highlight important matters for consideration.[1] Refer to the preface for additional information.
>
> **Important Uniform Guidance Effective Date Information**
>
> In December 2013, the OMB issued the Uniform Guidance, which is effective for nonfederal entities for all federal awards and certain funding increments provided on or after December 26, 2014. The requirements in Subpart F, "Audit Requirements," are effective for audits of fiscal years beginning on or after December 26, 2014, with no early implementation permitted. Therefore, auditees subject to a single audit with December 25, 2015, and later year ends (for example, December 31, 2015) will be required to undergo the audit under Subpart F of the Uniform Guidance. Note that audits of fiscal years ending prior to the effective date of the Uniform Guidance audit requirements are subject to an audit under Circular A-133.

Introduction

12.01 Many nonfederal entities receiving federal awards make pass-through payments of federal awards to other entities that are considered subrecipients. The amount of those payments may be material to the pass-through entity's financial statements,[2] individual major programs, or both. This chapter discusses the auditor's consideration of pass-through federal awards in an audit of both pass-through entities and subrecipients of federal awards under OMB Circular A-133. It also discusses the auditee's and auditor's responsibilities with respect to activities carried out by vendors. An auditee with multiple

---

[1] See the information found at the end of certain chapters in part II, *Circular A-133 Audits*, of this guide for transition considerations when performing an audit under Office of Management and Budget (OMB) Circular A-133, *Audits of States, Local Governments, and Non-Profit Organizations* (Circular A-133), as it relates to the applicability of certain aspects of Title 2 U.S. *Code of Federal Regulations* Part 200, *Uniform Administrative Requirements, Cost Principles, and Audit Requirements for Federal Awards* (Uniform Guidance), to audits performed under Circular A-133. Transition considerations related to an audit performed under the Uniform Guidance can be found at the end of chapters in part III, *Uniform Guidance Audits*, of this guide in sections titled "Transition Considerations Related to the Uniform Guidance."

[2] As discussed in the AICPA Audit and Accounting Guide *State and Local Governments*, the auditor's consideration of materiality for purposes of planning, performing, evaluating the results of, and reporting on the audit of the financial statements of a state or local government is based on opinion units. See that guide for further guidance.

federal funding agreements may be a pass-through entity in regard to some awards, a subrecipient in regard to other awards, and a vendor with respect to other agreements.

Definitions

12.02 Circular A-133 includes the following definitions that are relevant to pass-through awards:

federal award. Federal financial assistance and federal cost-reimbursement contracts that nonfederal entities receive directly from federal awarding agencies or indirectly from pass-through entities. It does not include procurement contracts, under grants or contracts, used to buy goods or services from vendors.

nonfederal entity. A state, local government, or non-profit organization (not-for-profit entity or NFP).

recipient. A nonfederal entity that expends federal awards received directly from a federal awarding agency to carry out a federal program.

pass-through entity. A nonfederal entity that provides a federal award to a subrecipient to carry out a federal program.

subrecipient. A nonfederal entity that expends federal awards received from a pass-through entity to carry out a federal program but does not include an individual who is a beneficiary of such a program. A subrecipient may also be a recipient of other federal awards directly from a federal awarding agency.

vendor. A dealer, distributor, merchant, or other seller providing goods or services that are required for the conduct of a federal program. These goods or services may be for an organization's own use or for the use of beneficiaries of the federal program.

Applicability of Circular A-133

12.03 Circular A-133 applies to both recipients expending federal awards received directly from federal awarding agencies and subrecipients expending federal awards received from a pass-through entity. Accordingly, both recipients and subrecipients that expend $500,000 or more in federal awards should have a single or program-specific audit in accordance with Circular A-133. (Chapter 14, "Program-Specific Audits (Circular A-133)," of this guide discusses program-specific audits.)

12.04 The determination of when a federal award is expended is based on when the activity related to the award occurs. With respect to federal awards passed through to subrecipients, the activity that requires the pass-through entity to comply with laws, regulations, and the provisions of contracts or grant agreements is the disbursement of funds to subrecipients. The activity that requires subrecipients to comply with laws, regulations, and the provisions of contracts or grant agreements is the expenditure of the pass-through award.

12.05 Payments received by a vendor for goods or services provided in connection with a federal program are not considered federal awards. Furthermore, Medicaid payments to a subrecipient for providing patient care services to Medicaid-eligible individuals are not considered federal awards expended under Circular A-133 unless a state requires the funds to be treated as federal awards expended because reimbursement is on a cost-reimbursement basis.

12.06 If a pass-through entity provides federal awards to subrecipients, the pass-through entity should monitor the subrecipients' activities to provide reasonable assurance that the subrecipients administer federal awards in compliance with federal requirements. As part of the Circular A-133 compliance audit, the auditor of the pass-through entity should test and report on subrecipient monitoring (which is 1 of the 12 types of compliance requirements in the *OMB Compliance Supplement*, as discussed in chapter 10, "Compliance Auditing Applicable to Major Programs (Circular A-133)," of this guide) when federal awards passed through to subrecipients are material to a major program (see paragraphs 12.25–.36). If the federal awards provided are immaterial to a major program or relate to a program that is not considered major, the auditor of the pass-through entity has no additional compliance auditing responsibilities related to the funds passed through to subrecipients.

12.07 Most of this chapter focuses on compliance auditing considerations for auditors of pass-through entities. However, paragraphs 12.44–.48 provide additional considerations for auditors of subrecipients.

Pass-Through Entities, Subrecipients, and Vendors

Subrecipient Status Versus Vendor Status

12.08 The responsibilities for compliance with federal program requirements and the direct and material compliance requirements[3] to be tested by the auditor may be significantly different depending on whether the entity is a pass-through entity, subrecipient, or vendor. Section 210 of Circular A-133 provides guidance on distinguishing between a subrecipient and a vendor; paragraphs 12.09–.11 summarize that guidance.

Characteristics Indicative of a Federal Award Received by a Subrecipient

12.09 According to Circular A-133, characteristics indicative of a federal award received by a subrecipient are when the entity

- determines who is eligible to receive what federal financial assistance;
- has its performance measured against whether the objectives of the federal program are met;
- has responsibility for programmatic decision making;
- has responsibility for adherence to compliance requirements applicable to the federal program; and
- uses the federal funds to carry out a program of the entity as compared to providing goods or services for a program of the pass-through entity.

---

[3] AU-C section 935, *Compliance Audits* (AICPA, *Professional Standards*), defines *applicable compliance requirements* as the compliance requirements that are subject to the compliance audit. Paragraph .500(d) of OMB Circular A-133 states that the auditor should determine whether the auditee has complied with laws, regulations, and the provisions of contracts or grant agreements that may have a direct and material effect on each of its major programs. Therefore, in a Circular A-133 compliance audit, the direct and material compliance requirements are those that are subject to audit. Accordingly, for the purpose of adapting AU-C section 935 to a Circular A-133 compliance audit, the term *applicable compliance requirements* has been replaced by *direct and material compliance requirements* in this guide except when directly citing content from AU-C section 935.

Paragraph 12.12 provides examples of the relationship between pass-through entities and subrecipients.

Characteristics Indicative of a Payment for Goods or Services Received by a Vendor

12.10 According to Circular A-133, the characteristics indicative of a payment for goods or services received by a vendor are when the entity

- provides the goods and services within normal business operations;
- provides similar goods or services to many different purchasers;
- operates in a competitive environment;
- provides goods or services that are ancillary to the operation of the federal program; and
- is not subject to the compliance requirements of the federal program.

Paragraph 12.13 provides examples of the relationship between pass-through entities and vendors.

Use of Judgment in Determining Subrecipient or Vendor Status

12.11 Circular A-133 states that there may be unusual circumstances or exceptions to the characteristics listed in paragraphs 12.09–.10. In making the determination of whether a subrecipient or vendor relationship exists, the substance of the relationship is more important than the form of the agreement. It is not expected that all of the characteristics will be present, and judgment should be used in determining whether an entity is a subrecipient or vendor. In some cases, it may be difficult to determine whether the relationship with the entity is that of a subrecipient or of a vendor. The federal cognizant agency for audit, the oversight agency for audit, or the federal awarding agency may be of assistance in making those determinations.

Description of Relationships

Pass-Through Entity and Subrecipient

12.12 Following are examples of a typical relationship between a pass-through entity and a subrecipient:

- A state department of education (pass-through entity) receives a federal award and is responsible for administering and disbursing the federal award to local school districts (subrecipients) according to a formula or on some other basis.
- A regional planning commission (pass-through entity) receives a federal award for the feeding of elderly and low-income individuals, and the award is disbursed to NFPs (subrecipients) to support their feeding programs.
- A university (pass-through entity) receives a federal award, and the award is disbursed to a governmental hospital (subrecipient) to conduct research.
- A state arts commission (pass-through entity) receives a federal award, and the award is disbursed to an NFP theater group (subrecipient) to support a summer arts series.

Recipient and Vendor

12.13 Following are examples of a typical relationship between a recipient and a vendor:

- A local government (recipient) receives a federal award to provide mental health services in a designated area. Some of the funds are paid to a contractor (vendor) to repair a leaking roof.
- A county (recipient) receives a federal award to operate a Head Start program and pays an NFP (vendor) to provide temporary clerical services.
- An NFP (recipient) receives a federal award to run a preschool and pays a medical doctor (vendor) to perform health screening on a per-student basis.
- An NFP (recipient) receives a federal award to operate a child care center and pays a not-for-profit clinic (vendor) to perform physical exams.

Entity Is Both a Subrecipient and a Pass-Through Entity

12.14 Instances occur in which an entity can be both a subrecipient and a pass-through entity, as shown in the following examples:

- A local government receives a pass-through federal award from a state government agency (the local government is a subrecipient) and further passes through a portion of the federal award to an NFP (the local government also is a pass-through entity) to administer a federal program.
- An NFP area agency receives a pass-through federal award from a state (the NFP area agency is a subrecipient) and further passes through a portion of the federal award to a for-profit health care provider (the NFP area agency also is a pass-through entity). Paragraph 12.41 discusses a pass-through entity's responsibilities when the subrecipient is a for-profit entity.

Vendor Compliance Considerations

Auditee's Responsibilities

12.15 Circular A-133 states that in most cases, the auditee's compliance responsibility for a vendor is to ensure only that the procurement, receipt, and payment for goods and services comply with laws, regulations, and the provisions of contracts or grant agreements. A program's compliance requirements normally do not pass through to vendors. However, the auditee is responsible for ensuring compliance for vendor transactions which are structured such that the vendor is responsible for program compliance or the vendor's records must be reviewed to determine compliance.

Auditor's Responsibilities

12.16 When vendors are responsible for program compliance, the auditor should determine whether vendor transactions are in compliance with laws, regulations, and the provisions of contracts or grant agreements if such transactions are material to a major program of the auditee. In such a case, the auditor would normally evaluate a vendor's compliance by reviewing the auditee's records and the results of the auditee's procedures for ensuring compliance by the vendor. When the auditor cannot obtain sufficient assurance of compliance from reviewing the auditee's records and procedures, a deficiency in internal control over compliance exists. The auditor should evaluate the severity of each deficiency in internal control over compliance identified during the audit to determine whether the deficiency, individually or in combination, is a significant deficiency or material weakness in internal control over compliance. The auditor also should perform additional procedures to determine compliance. These procedures may include testing the vendor's records or obtaining reports on compliance procedures performed by the vendor's independent auditor.

12.17 Prior to performing a single or program-specific audit, it is important for the auditor to understand the nature of the auditee's vendor relationships, whether the vendors are responsible for program compliance, the auditee's procedures for ensuring vendor compliance, and whether it will be necessary for the auditor to test vendor records. Because the amount and type of work done by the auditor may be impacted by the nature of the auditee's relationships with its vendors, it may be appropriate to include in the communication used to agree upon the terms of the engagement with management information related to the auditee's vendors and the effect on the audit, particularly if vendors are responsible for program compliance. (Chapter 6, "Planning Considerations of Circular A-133," of this guide discusses agreeing upon the terms of the engagement with management.) If subsequent to undertaking a single or program-specific audit the auditor becomes aware of a significant vendor relationship that will require the auditor to perform additional procedures on vendor records, the auditor should inform the auditee that the requirements of Circular A-133 will not be met unless additional procedures are performed. If the auditee or vendor precludes the auditor from performing such additional procedures, the auditor should qualify his or her opinion or disclaim an opinion because of a scope limitation. (Chapter 13, "Auditor Reporting Requirements and Other Communication Considerations in a Single Audit (Circular A-133)," of this guide further discusses scope limitations.)

Single Audit Considerations of Pass-Through Entities

12.18 The following matters are relevant to planning and conducting a single audit of a pass-through entity, and discussed in the rest of this section:

- Pass-through entity responsibilities
- Audit planning considerations
- Consideration of internal control over compliance
- Subrecipient monitoring
- Reporting considerations
- For-profit subrecipients
- Non-U.S.-based entities
- A state's designation of a cluster of programs

Pass-Through Entity Responsibilities

12.19 A pass-through entity is responsible for ensuring that subrecipients expend awards in accordance with applicable laws, regulations, and provisions

Audit Considerations of Federal Pass-Through Awards (Circular A-133)

of contracts or grant agreements. Circular A-133 states that a pass-through entity should perform the following for the federal awards it provides to subrecipients:

- Identify the federal awards made by informing each subrecipient of the Catalog of Federal Domestic Assistance (CFDA) title and number, the award's name and number, the award year, whether the award is for research and development, and the name of the federal agency. When some of this information is not available, the pass-through entity should provide the best information available to describe the federal award.

- Advise subrecipients of the requirements imposed on them by federal laws, regulations, and the provisions of contracts or grant agreements, as well as any supplemental requirements imposed by the pass-through entity.

- Monitor the activities of subrecipients as necessary to ensure that federal awards are used for authorized purposes in compliance with laws, regulations, and the provisions of contracts or grant agreements and that performance goals are achieved.

- Ensure that subrecipients expending $500,000 or more in federal awards during the subrecipient's fiscal year have met the audit requirements of Circular A-133 for that fiscal year.

- Issue management decisions on audit findings within six months after receipt of subrecipients' audit reports, and ensure that subrecipients take appropriate and timely corrective action.

- Consider whether subrecipient audits necessitate the adjustment of the pass-through entity's own records.

- Require subrecipients to permit the pass-through entity and auditors to have access to the records and financial statements as necessary for the pass-through entity to comply with Circular A-133.

- Keep subrecipients' report submissions (or other written notification when the subrecipient is not required to submit a reporting package) on file for three years from the date of receipt. (See the further discussion in paragraph 12.48.)

12.20 In addition to auditee responsibilities under Circular A-133, the Federal Funding Accountability and Transparency Act of 2006 (FFATA) and subsequent 2008 amendments have imposed a federal award reporting requirement for certain prime grant recipients (direct recipients) and prime contractors for subawards made that are valued greater than or equal to $25,000. The reporting of required information about the subawards is made by these entities into the FFATA Subaward Reporting System (FSRS) at https://www.fsrs.gov, and the public can view the information entered into the FSRS at http://USASpending.gov. The FFATA reporting requirement, related suggested audit procedures, and references to other related OMB documents (which are relevant to certain pass-through entities) can be found in the "Reporting" section of Part 3 of the *Compliance Supplement*.

Audit Planning Considerations

Effect of Pass-Through Federal Awards on the Determination of Major Programs

12.21 As noted in paragraph 12.04, the determination of when a federal award is expended is based on when the activity related to the award occurs. With respect to federal awards provided by a pass-through entity to subrecipients, the federal awards are deemed to be expended by the pass-through entity when the funds are disbursed to subrecipients, regardless of when subrecipients expend the federal funds. Accordingly, the amount of federal funds disbursed to subrecipients should be included in the total expenditures of federal awards of the pass-through entity and in the determination of the pass-through entity's major programs. (Chapter 8, "Determination of Major Programs (Circular A-133)," of this guide discusses the determination of major programs.)

Pass-Through Entity Request for a Program to Be Audited as a Major Program

12.22 When a subrecipient expends $500,000 or more of federal awards, Circular A-133 permits the pass-through entity to request that the program be audited as a major program in lieu of the pass-through entity conducting or arranging for additional audits. If the pass-through entity makes such a request, it should pay the full incremental cost for such an audit. (Chapters 5, "Overview of the Single Audit Act, Circular A-133, and the *Compliance Supplement*," and 8 of this guide provide additional information.)

Materiality

12.23 The auditor's consideration of materiality is a matter of professional judgment and is influenced by the auditor's perception of the needs of a reasonable person who will rely upon the auditor's work. A comparison of the amount of federal funds passed through to subrecipients with the total amount of expenditures for each individual major program or cluster can assist the auditor in determining if the pass-through amount is material. When the amount of federal funds passed through to subrecipients is material either quantitatively or qualitatively, in relation to the major program being audited, the need is greater for the auditor to test the subrecipient monitoring requirements. Some federal programs are designed in such a manner that subrecipient expenditures are intended to be material to the pass-through entity's award. For example, the Community Services Block Grant requires a state to subgrant at least 90 percent of the state's award.

Consideration of Internal Control Over Compliance

12.24 As part of performing procedures to obtain an understanding of internal control over compliance for federal programs that is sufficient to plan the audit of the pass-through entity to support a low assessed level of control risk of noncompliance[4] for major programs, the auditor should consider the pass-through entity's internal control over compliance used to monitor subrecipients. (See chapter 9, "Consideration of Internal Control Over Compliance for Major Programs (Circular A-133)," of this guide.) Tests of internal control

---

[4] Although Circular A-133 uses the term *control risk*, this guide uses the term *control risk of noncompliance* in order to be consistent with the term as used and defined in AU-C section 935.

over compliance used to monitor subrecipients may include inquiry, observation and inspection of documentation, or a reperformance by the auditor of some or all of the monitoring procedures identified in paragraph 12.29. The nature and extent of the tests performed will vary depending on the auditor's assessment of inherent risk of noncompliance, understanding of the internal control over compliance, materiality, and professional judgment.[5] The results of the auditor's testing of internal control over compliance assist in determining the nature, timing, and extent of subrecipient monitoring compliance testing.

Subrecipient Monitoring

12.25 The Single Audit Act requires the pass-through entity to monitor subrecipients' use of federal awards through site visits, agreed-upon procedures engagements,[6] or other means. Because the pass-through entity is held accountable for federal awards administered by its subrecipients, the pass-through entity needs to establish an appropriate subrecipient monitoring process and to decide what, if any, additional monitoring procedures may be necessary to ensure the subrecipients' compliance. Generally, arrangements for subrecipient monitoring and clarification of the compliance requirements applicable to federal awards passed through are made by the pass-through entity in its agreements with subrecipients.

12.26 In a Circular A-133 compliance audit an auditor should consider subrecipient monitoring of an entity that disburses to subrecipients federal awards that are material to a major program. (Paragraph 12.23 discusses materiality.) The auditor should consider whether the pass-through entity monitors subrecipients and has established internal control over compliance that provides reasonable assurance that subrecipients are managing federal awards in compliance with laws, regulations, and the provisions of contracts or grant agreements that could have a direct and material effect on each of the pass-through entity's major programs.

Compliance Supplement *Guidance*

12.27 Subrecipient monitoring is 1 of the 12 types of compliance requirements included in the *Compliance Supplement*. The *Compliance Supplement* identifies several audit objectives for subrecipient monitoring. According to the *Compliance Supplement*, in a Circular A-133 compliance audit of a pass-through entity, the auditor should obtain an understanding of internal control, assess risk, and test internal control as required by the circular, and determine whether the pass-through entity

- properly identified federal award information and compliance requirements to the subrecipient, and approved only allowable activities in the award documents.
- monitored subrecipient activities to provide reasonable assurance that the subrecipient administers federal awards in compliance with federal requirements.

---

[5] In a compliance audit under Circular A-133, controls that address the risks of noncompliance with direct and material types of compliance requirements for major programs should be tested every year. See the section titled "Performing Tests to Evaluate the Effectiveness of Controls" in chapter 9, "Consideration of Internal Control Over Compliance for Major Programs (Circular A-133)," of this guide for more information.

[6] Circular A-133 uses the phrase "cost of limited-scope audits," but goes on to indicate that limited-scope audits only include agreed-upon procedures engagements.

- ensured that the required audits were performed, issued a management decision on audit findings within six months after receipt of the subrecipient's audit report, and ensured that the subrecipient took timely and appropriate corrective action on all audit findings.
- took appropriate action using sanctions in cases of continued inability or unwillingness of a subrecipient to have the required audits.
- evaluated the effect of subrecipient activities on the pass-through entity.

12.28 As discussed in chapter 10 of this guide, the *Compliance Supplement* also identifies the suggested audit procedures for testing the Circular A-133 compliance audit objectives for pass-through entities. The auditor may consider coordinating the subrecipient-related tests performed as part of *cash management* (tests of cash reports submitted by subrecipients), *eligibility* (tests that subawards were made only to eligible subrecipients), and *procurement* (tests of suspension and debarment certifications) with the tests of subrecipient monitoring.

Pass-Through Entity Monitoring Procedures

12.29 Part 3 of the *Compliance Supplement* discusses the pass-through entity's subrecipient monitoring responsibilities and activities. The monitoring procedures that a pass-through entity may use include on-site visits, reviews of financial and performance reports submitted by the subrecipient, regular contacts with subrecipients, appropriate inquiries concerning program activities, and agreed-upon procedures engagements. Agreed-upon procedures engagements are conducted in accordance with the AICPA attestation standards and are arranged and paid for by a pass-through entity. Such engagements generally only address one or more of the following types of compliance requirements: activities allowed or unallowed; allowable costs or cost principles; eligibility; matching, level of effort, and earmarking; and reporting. The following procedures are other monitoring activities that a pass-through entity may perform:

- Reviewing grant applications submitted by subrecipients to determine that
  - applications are filed and approved in a timely manner; and
  - each application contains the condition that the subrecipient comply with the federal requirements set by the federal agency.
- Establishing that internal control over compliance provides reasonable assurance that
  - funds are disbursed to subrecipients only on an as-needed basis;
  - funds are disbursed to subrecipients only on the basis of approved, properly completed reports submitted on a timely basis;
  - refunds that are due from subrecipients are billed and collected in a timely manner; and

— subrecipients and other entities and individuals receiving federal funds meet eligibility requirements.

- Reviewing financial and technical reports received from subrecipients on a timely basis and investigating unusual items.

- Reviewing subrecipient audit reports to evaluate them for completeness and for compliance with applicable laws and regulations.

- Evaluating audit findings; issuing appropriate management decisions, if necessary; and determining if an acceptable plan for corrective action has been prepared and implemented.

- Reviewing previously detected deficiencies and determining that corrective action was taken.

Monitoring When the Subrecipient Has a Single or Program-Specific Audit

12.30 As noted in paragraph 12.03, subrecipients that expend $500,000 or more in federal awards should have a single or program-specific audit in accordance with Circular A-133. This includes the submission of the reporting package and data collection form by the subrecipient to the Federal Audit Clearinghouse. If subrecipients have a single or program-specific audit, the pass-through entity's receipt and review of the results of that audit and its action on related findings may be sufficient to meet the subrecipient monitoring requirements of Circular A-133.[7] However, it is more likely that the receipt and review of such audit results is only 1 tool used by the pass-through entity as part of a comprehensive subrecipient-monitoring process. This is because a single audit is likely to provide varying degrees of assurance concerning a particular program. For example, a pass-through award may not have been tested as a major program as part of a subrecipient's audit. For this reason, the pass-through entity should consider the testing and results of the single audit of the subrecipient to determine what effect those results should have on other monitoring procedures employed by the pass-through entity.

12.31 In many cases, the pass-through entity will not have received all the subrecipient audit reports covering the time period being audited at the pass-through entity in time to incorporate the results into its own audit. The reports for the pass-through entity and the subrecipient are not required to be issued simultaneously, but the pass-through entity should have internal control over compliance in place to determine that (*a*) subrecipient audit reports have been received, and (*b*) corrective action is taken after the receipt of the subrecipient's audit. If the subrecipient's audit report is current, it need not cover the same period as the pass-through entity's audit. If the pass-through entity has an effective system for monitoring subrecipients, its auditor would be more likely

---

[7] As discussed in paragraph 12.48, a subrecipient is not required to submit its reporting package to the pass-through entity when it has no audit findings or the summary schedule of prior audit findings does not report the status of any audit findings. The *OMB Compliance Supplement* (*Compliance Supplement*) suggests that in these situations a pass-through entity may use the information in the Federal Audit Clearinghouse (FAC) database (available at the FAC website at http://harvester.census.gov/sac) as evidence to verify that the subrecipient had "no audit findings" and that the required audit was performed. In a case where the subrecipient is not required to submit its reporting package to the pass-through entity, the pass-through entity may request a copy of the reporting package from the subrecipient.

to rely on the subrecipient's audit cycle, even if it does not coincide with the pass-through entity's fiscal year.

Considering Risk Factors When Developing Monitoring Procedures

12.32 The *Compliance Supplement* states that the OMB expects pass-through entities to consider various risk factors (such as the relative size and complexity of the federal awards administered by subrecipients and other subrecipient risks identified by the entity based on its prior experience with each subrecipient) in developing the nature, timing, and extent of subrecipient monitoring procedures. Consider, for example, a pass-through entity that provides a large percentage of the only federal award it expends to 10 subrecipients that each expends less than $500,000 in federal awards annually. Careful consideration by the pass-through entity of the most effective method of monitoring these federal awards is needed. Perhaps a significant majority of this federal award is provided to 2 of the subrecipients. If so, the pass-through entity might consider conducting site visits at the 2 subrecipients that received a significant majority of the federal award and simply reviewing the documentation supporting requests for reimbursement from the other 8 subrecipients. Conversely, if a small percentage of a federal award is provided to subrecipients that each expends less than $500,000 in federal awards, the risk to the pass-through entity is most likely low and, therefore, the monitoring procedures could be minimal.

Unallowable Audit Costs

12.33 For subrecipients that expend less than $500,000 in federal awards annually, the cost of any audits or attestation engagements (other than the agreed-upon procedures engagements arranged and paid for by a pass-through entity as described in paragraph 12.29), are not allowable costs and, therefore, cannot be charged to any federal award. Accordingly, Circular A-133 would prohibit the cost of a financial statement audit conducted in accordance with generally accepted auditing standards or *Government Auditing Standards* from being charged (by either a pass-through entity or subrecipient) to federal awards for a subrecipient that expends less than $500,000 in federal awards annually. Chapter 5 of this guide discusses the allowability of audit costs in greater detail.

When the Subrecipient Monitoring System Is Not Sufficient

12.34 The auditor may determine that the pass-through entity's subrecipient-monitoring system is not sufficient to ensure the subrecipient's compliance with laws, regulations, and the provisions of grants and contracts. In this situation, the auditor should report a significant deficiency or material weakness in internal control over compliance and consider whether the insufficient monitoring system represents an instance of noncompliance that should be reported as a compliance finding (which is likely to be the case). The effect of the noncompliance on the opinion on compliance for major programs is primarily a function of the pervasiveness of the lack of monitoring and the materiality of subrecipient funding to a program. For example, if the pass-through entity did not perform subrecipient-monitoring procedures and 90 percent of the program was passed through to subrecipients, an opinion modification would likely be warranted. This would likely be the case even if the scope of the audit was expanded to include additional audit procedures to determine that the subrecipients actually complied with laws and regulations.

12.35 Instances may occur in which the pass-through entity asks the auditor to perform additional procedures to determine the compliance of a subrecipient with direct and material types of compliance requirements (such as conducting tests of records at the subrecipient's site). This would be considered an expansion of the scope of the audit. This expansion of the scope of the audit would not be sufficient to remedy the significant deficiency (or material weakness) and, if applicable, noncompliance of the pass-through entity's monitoring system. However, an expansion of the scope of the audit may remedy the noncompliance related to the type of compliance requirement being tested (for example, eligibility).

12.36 The auditor also should consider any implications of an insufficient subrecipient-monitoring system on the opinion on the financial statements. If amounts passed through to subrecipients are considered material to the financial statements of the pass-through entity, the auditor should determine whether the report on the financial statements should be modified. Factors to consider in making such a determination include any audit evidence available to the auditor (such as subrecipients' Circular A-133 audit reports and other financial reports that may have been submitted to the pass-through entity) that could indicate that the subrecipients administered the program in compliance with laws and regulations. Further, the auditor also should consider whether it is necessary to report an internal control or compliance finding in the report issued to meet the requirements of *Government Auditing Standards*.

Reporting Considerations[8]

Schedule of Expenditures of Federal Awards

12.37 Circular A-133 states that, to the extent practical, pass-through entities should identify in the schedule of expenditures of federal awards the total amount provided to subrecipients from each federal program. (Chapter 7, "Schedule of Expenditures of Federal Awards (Circular A-133)," of this guide discusses the schedule.) If a pass-through entity is unable to identify amounts provided to subrecipients, the auditor should consider whether a significant deficiency or material weakness in internal control over compliance should be reported. The auditor also should consider whether material noncompliance (for subrecipient monitoring) has occurred, which should be reported as an audit finding.

Evaluation of Audit Findings

12.38 Circular A-133 requires the auditor to consider a finding in relation to the type of compliance requirement (subrecipient monitoring, in this case) or an audit objective identified in the *Compliance Supplement*, whether or not the finding can be quantified. For example, the auditor may discover that a pass-through entity consistently failed to provide its subrecipients with federal award information, including the compliance requirements applicable to the federal program. The pertinent audit objective included in the *Compliance Supplement* and relating to this example is for the auditor to "determine

---

[8] Certain laws and regulations may require audit reports to be made publicly available, therefore the auditor is cautioned not to include names, Social Security numbers, other personal identification, or other potentially sensitive information in the body of audit reports or any attached or referenced schedules or letters.

whether the pass-through entity identifies federal award information and compliance requirements to the subrecipient." Because the pass-through entity failed to provide federal award information to its subrecipients, this noncompliance is material in relation to the audit objective and, therefore, should be reported as an audit finding. In addition, the auditor should consider whether significant deficiencies or material weaknesses in internal control over compliance exist and require reporting with respect to subrecipient monitoring.[9]

Effect of Subrecipients' Noncompliance on the Pass-Through Entity's Report

12.39 The instances of noncompliance reported in subrecipients' audit reports are not required to be included in the pass-through entity's audit report. However, as noted previously, the auditor of the pass-through entity should consider the effects of reported instances of subrecipient noncompliance or indications of weaknesses in the pass-through entity's subrecipient-monitoring system that could have a material effect on each of the pass-through entity's major programs.

Adjustment of Pass-Through Entity Financial Records and Reports

12.40 Questioned costs at the subrecipient level that are found to be unallowable by the pass-through entity may require the pass-through entity to adjust its financial records and its federal expenditure reports. The total of allowable program costs in excess of required expenditure levels and the requirements of individual programs regarding the timing of claims will affect whether the pass-through entity will need to reflect a liability to the awarding agency in its financial statements. As part of the finding-resolution process, the pass-through entity should estimate the total unallowable costs that are associated with each subrecipient finding and consider the need to adjust financial records and federal expenditure reports. The failure of the pass-through entity to make needed adjustments to its records and federal reports should be considered by the auditor in forming an opinion on compliance for major programs.

For-Profit Subrecipients

12.41 Because Circular A-133 does not apply to for-profit subrecipients, the pass-through entity is responsible for establishing requirements, as necessary, to ensure compliance by for-profit subrecipients. Circular A-133 states that the contract with the for-profit subrecipient should describe compliance requirements applicable to a federal program and the for-profit subrecipient's compliance responsibility. Methods to ensure compliance for federal awards made to for-profit subrecipients may include preaward audits, monitoring during the contract, and postaward audits. The auditor's responsibilities related to for-profit subrecipients are similar to those of not-for-profit subrecipients; see paragraphs 12.25–.36 (as applicable) for a further discussion of subrecipient monitoring.

---

[9] Chapters 4, "Auditor Reporting Requirements and Other Communication Considerations of *Government Auditing Standards*," and 13, "Auditor Reporting Requirements and Other Communication Considerations in a Single Audit (Circular A-133)," of this guide discuss the *Government Auditing Standards* requirement that the auditor communicate certain matters to the auditee in a written communication.

Non-U.S.-Based Entities

12.42 As discussed in chapter 5 of this guide, Circular A-133 does not apply to non-U.S.-based entities expending federal awards received either directly as a recipient or indirectly as a subrecipient. Therefore, the responsibilities that a pass-through entity and its auditor have for a non-U.S.-based entity are the same as those for a for-profit subrecipient (see paragraph 12.41).

State Designation of a Cluster of Programs

12.43 Circular A-133 includes a provision that allows a state to designate as a cluster a grouping of closely related programs that share common compliance requirements. When designating a cluster of programs, a state should identify the federal awards included in the cluster and advise subrecipients of the compliance requirements applicable to the cluster. (Chapter 5 of this guide discusses clusters of programs.)

Circular A-133 Audit Considerations of Subrecipients

12.44 Subrecipients may have additional audit considerations under Circular A-133 that their auditors may need to address. These considerations, as discussed in this section, concern (*a*) additional compliance requirements that may be established by the pass-through entity, (*b*) information included in the schedule of expenditures of federal awards, (*c*) audit findings, and (*d*) the submission of the report.

Additional Compliance Requirements Established by Pass-Through Entities

12.45 Federal awards normally are distributed to subrecipients only on the basis of properly completed and approved awards. These written agreements require subrecipients to comply with the requirements of the federal agency and, in some instances, additional requirements established by the pass-through entity. Hence, in addition to providing an audit satisfying the requirements of Circular A-133, the auditor may be engaged to test compliance with requirements specified by the pass-through entity.

Information Included in the Schedule of Expenditures of Federal Awards

12.46 For federal awards received as a subrecipient, Circular A-133 states that the schedule of expenditures of federal awards should include the name of the pass-through entity and identifying number assigned by the pass-through entity. Circular A-133 states that, to make the schedule easier to use, subrecipients may choose to provide information requested by federal awarding agencies and pass-through entities, although this information is not required. Chapter 7 of this guide discusses the schedule.

Audit Findings

12.47 Audit findings (for example, internal control findings, compliance findings, questioned costs, or fraud) that relate to the same issue should be presented as one audit finding. Circular A-133 states that where practical, audit findings should be organized by federal agency or pass-through entity. (Chapter 13 of this guide discusses audit findings.)

Submission of the Report

12.48 Section 320(e) of Circular A-133 has additional report-submission responsibilities for subrecipients. When a subrecipient is not required to submit a reporting package to the pass-through entity (because for the pass-through entity's programs the subrecipient has no audit findings and the summary schedule of prior audit findings does not report the status of any audit findings), the subrecipient should provide written notification of this to the pass-through entity. As an alternative, a reporting package may be submitted to the pass-through entity. Chapter 13 of this guide discusses the required contents of the written notification and the submission of the report by subrecipients.

Transition Considerations Related to the Uniform Guidance

12.49 Once the Uniform Guidance audit requirements become effective, a subrecipient is no longer required to submit its reporting package directly to a pass-through entity. In addition, the requirement that a pass-through entity retain a copy of the subrecipient reporting package is also being removed. Neither of these changes may be implemented by pass-through entities and subrecipients early (that is, they are not able to be implemented until such time that the subrecipient and pass-through entity become subject to an audit under the Uniform Guidance).

Chapter 13
Auditor Reporting Requirements and Other Communication Considerations in a Single Audit (Circular A-133)

> **⊙ Update 13-1: Audits of Federal Awards**
> This chapter, and the remaining chapters of part II, *Circular A-133 Audits*, of this guide, should be used for performing a compliance audit of federal awards under Office of Management and Budget (OMB) Circular A-133, *Audits of States, Local Governments, and Non-Profit Organizations* (Circular A-133). Part III, *Uniform Guidance Audits*, of this guide should be used when performing a compliance audit under Title 2 U.S. *Code of Federal Regulations* Part 200, *Uniform Administrative Requirements, Cost Principles, and Audit Requirements for Federal Awards* (Uniform Guidance). See the transitional guidance sections at the end of each chapter that highlight important matters for consideration.[1] Refer to the preface for additional information.
>
> **Important Uniform Guidance Effective Date Information**
>
> In December 2013, the OMB issued the Uniform Guidance, which is effective for nonfederal entities for all federal awards and certain funding increments provided on or after December 26, 2014. The requirements in Subpart F, "Audit Requirements," are effective for audits of fiscal years beginning on or after December 26, 2014, with no early implementation permitted. Therefore, auditees subject to a single audit with December 25, 2015, and later year ends (for example, December 31, 2015) will be required to undergo the audit under Subpart F of the Uniform Guidance. Note that audits of fiscal years ending prior to the effective date of the Uniform Guidance audit requirements are subject to an audit under Circular A-133.

Overview

13.01 This chapter discusses the auditor's reporting requirements and other communication considerations in a single audit under OMB Circular A-133. It also provides illustrative auditor's reports in the appendix, "Illustrative Auditor's Reports Under Circular A-133," of this chapter (paragraph 13.58). (Chapter 14, "Program-Specific Audits (Circular A-133)," discusses the auditor's reporting requirements and provides illustrative reports for a program-specific audit.)

13.02 The auditor's reporting responsibilities in a single audit are driven by three levels of auditing standards and requirements: generally accepted

---

[1] See the information found at the end of certain chapters in part II, *Circular A-133 Audits*, of this guide for transition considerations when performing an audit under Office of Management and Budget (OMB) Circular A-133, *Audits of States, Local Governments, and Non-Profit Organizations* (Circular A-133), as it relates to the applicability of certain aspects of Title 2 U.S. *Code of Federal Regulations* Part 200, *Uniform Administrative Requirements, Cost Principles, and Audit Requirements for Federal Awards* (Uniform Guidance), to audits performed under Circular A-133. Transition considerations related to an audit performed under the Uniform Guidance can be found at the end of chapters in part III, *Uniform Guidance Audits*, of this guide in sections titled "Transition Considerations Related to the Uniform Guidance."

auditing standards (GAAS), *Government Auditing Standards*, and Circular A-133. These standards and requirements expand the level of auditor responsibility from reporting on an auditee's financial statements to also reporting on internal control and on compliance. The auditor has additional reporting responsibilities for the audit of the financial statements in accordance with *Government Auditing Standards* (see chapter 4, "Auditor Reporting Requirements and Other Communication Considerations of *Government Auditing Standards*," of this guide), and for the Circular A-133 compliance audit applicable to major programs (see chapter 8, "Determination of Major Programs (Circular A-133)," chapter 9, "Consideration of Internal Control Over Compliance for Major Programs (Circular A-133)," and chapter 10, "Compliance Auditing Applicable to Major Programs (Circular A-133)," of this guide.) The auditor also has certain additional communication considerations under GAAS and *Government Auditing Standards* related to internal control, fraud, noncompliance with provisions of laws, regulations, contracts, and grant agreements, abuse, and other matters identified in the audit as discussed in this chapter and in chapter 4 of this guide.

Circular A-133 Requirements

Auditor's Reports

13.03 Circular A-133 states that the auditor's report(s) should include the following:

- An opinion (or disclaimer of opinion)[2] on whether the financial statements are presented fairly in all material respects in accordance with generally accepted accounting principles (GAAP) (paragraph 13.09 discusses basis of accounting) and an opinion (or a disclaimer of opinion) on whether the schedule of expenditures of federal awards is presented fairly in all material respects in relation to the financial statements as a whole.
- A report on the internal control related to the financial statements and on the internal control related to major programs. This report should describe the scope of testing of internal control and the results of the tests and, where applicable, refer to the separate schedule of findings and questioned costs.
- A report on compliance with laws, regulations, and the provisions of contracts and grant agreements (hereinafter referred to as *compliance requirements*), noncompliance that could have a material effect on the financial statements. This report should include an opinion (or a disclaimer of opinion) on whether the auditee complied with laws, regulations, and the provisions of contracts and grant agreements that could have a direct and material effect on each major program, and where applicable, refer to the separate schedule of findings and questioned costs.
- A schedule of findings and questioned costs.

---

[2] As explained in the AICPA Audit and Accounting Guide *State and Local Governments,* the auditor generally expresses or disclaims an opinion on a government's basic financial statements by providing an opinion or disclaimer of opinion on each opinion unit required to be presented in those financial statements. In addition, the auditor may provide opinions or disclaimers of opinions on additional opinion units if engaged to set the scope of the audit and assess materiality at a more detailed level than by the opinion units required for the basic financial statements. Throughout this guide, the use of the singular terms *opinion* and *disclaimer of opinion* encompasses the multiple opinions and disclaimers of opinion that generally will be provided on a government's basic financial statements.

Paragraphs 13.06–.08 describe the auditor's reports recommended in this guide.

Data Collection Form

13.04 Circular A-133 also states that the auditor should complete applicable sections of a data collection form that summarizes the auditor's results, findings, and questioned costs. The data collection form is required to be certified by the auditee and signed by the auditor prior to submission to the Federal Audit Clearinghouse (FAC) by the auditee. (See paragraphs 13.48–.54.)

Reporting Package

13.05 The auditee should submit a reporting package (as part of the data collection form submission) that includes the following:

- Financial statements and a supplementary schedule of expenditures of federal awards (see chapter 7, "Schedule of Expenditures of Federal Awards (Circular A-133)," of this guide)
- Auditor's reports (see paragraphs 13.06–.08)
- A summary schedule of prior audit findings (see paragraphs 13.45–.47)
- A corrective action plan (see paragraphs 13.45–.47)

Recommended Auditor's Reports

13.06 Reporting on a financial statement audit and on the compliance requirements that could have a direct and material[3] effect on each major program involves varying levels of materiality and different forms of reporting. Circular A-133 states that the auditor's report(s) may be in the form of either combined or separate reports and may be organized differently from the manner presented in the circular. Although not the only alternative, in an effort to make the reports understandable and to reduce the number of reports issued, this guide recommends that the following reports be issued:

    a. A report on the financial statements and on the supplementary schedule of expenditures of federal awards[4] (see chapter 4 and paragraphs 13.09–.20)

    b. A report on internal control over financial reporting[5] and on compliance and other matters based on an audit of financial statements performed in accordance with *Government Auditing Standards* (see chapter 4)

---

[3] AU-C section 935, *Compliance Audits* (AICPA, *Professional Standards*), defines *applicable compliance requirements* as the compliance requirements that are subject to the compliance audit. Section 500(d) of OMB Circular A-133 states that the auditor should determine whether the auditee has complied with laws, regulations, and the provisions of contracts and grant agreements that may have a direct and material effect on each of its major programs. Therefore, in a Circular A-133 compliance audit, the direct and material compliance requirements are those that are subject to audit. Accordingly, for the purpose of adapting AU-C section 935 to a Circular A-133 compliance audit in this chapter, the term *applicable* has been replaced by *direct and material* when referring to such compliance requirements, except when citing content from AU-C section 935.

[4] Note that in certain situations the auditor may report on the schedule of expenditures of federal awards in his or her report on compliance with requirements that could have a direct and material effect on each major program and on internal control over compliance in accordance with Circular A-133. See paragraphs 13.12 and 13.27 for a further discussion.

[5] Controls relevant to an audit of the financial statements are referred to collectively in this guide as "internal control over financial reporting" and are encompassed in the reporting on internal control required by *Government Auditing Standards*.

c. A report on compliance with requirements that could have a direct and material effect on each major federal program and on internal control over compliance[6] in accordance with Circular A-133 (see paragraphs 13.21–.28)

d. A schedule of findings and questioned costs (see paragraphs 13.33–.43)

13.07 The appendix of chapter 4 of this guide and the appendix (paragraph 13.58) in this chapter present illustrative auditor's reports for single audits. As noted previously, those reports combine reports on compliance and internal control at the financial statement audit level and at the major program compliance audit level. The reports in the appendix of this chapter are illustrative, therefore auditors may tailor the reporting based on the auditor's understanding of the intended purpose of the reports and the specific auditee facts and circumstances. Because the reports issued to comply with Circular A-133 involve varying levels of materiality and different forms of reporting, it is necessary to exercise care in issuing reports to ensure that they meet all of the varying reporting requirements of GAAS, *Government Auditing Standards*, and Circular A-133. Professional judgment may be exercised in any situation not specifically addressed in this guide.

13.08 Table 13-1 provides a matrix depicting the recommended auditor's reports in a single audit required by GAAS, *Government Auditing Standards*, and Circular A-133. The discussion which follows includes information on the recommended reports as it relates to single audit. See chapter 4 for information regarding the reporting required under *Government Auditing Standards*.

Table 13-1

Recommended Reporting in Single Audits

Report	GAAS	Government Auditing Standards	Circular A-133
		Required by	
Opinion (or disclaimer of opinion) on financial statements and supplementary schedule of expenditures of federal awards	X	X	X
Report on internal control over financial reporting and on compliance and other matters based on an audit of financial statements		X	X
Report on compliance and internal control over compliance applicable to *each* major federal program (this report includes separate opinions [or disclaimers of opinion] on each major program's compliance)			X
Schedule of findings and questioned costs			X

---

[6] Controls relevant to an audit of compliance with requirements applicable to major federal programs are referred to collectively in this guide as "internal control over compliance" and are encompassed in the reporting on internal control required by Circular A-133.

Reporting on the Financial Statements and Supplementary Schedule of Expenditures of Federal Awards in Accordance With GAAS and *Government Auditing Standards* in a Single Audit

Basis of Accounting

13.09 Circular A-133 does not prescribe the basis of accounting that an auditee uses to prepare its financial statements or the schedule of expenditures of federal awards. For example, a basis of accounting other than GAAP, referred to as a special purpose framework, may be used as the financial reporting framework.[7] However, auditees should clearly disclose the basis of accounting and the significant accounting policies used in preparing the financial statements and the schedule of expenditures of federal awards.[8] In addition, Circular A-133 states that the auditor should issue an opinion (or a disclaimer of opinion) on whether the financial statements are presented fairly in all material respects in accordance with GAAP and whether the schedule of expenditures of federal awards is fairly stated, in all material respects, in relation to the auditee's financial statements as a whole. Refer to chapter 7 for auditor considerations regarding issuing an in-relation-to opinion on the schedule of expenditures of federal awards when the schedule of expenditures of federal awards is prepared on a basis of accounting that is different from that of the financial statements.

Implementing Regulations of Federal Awarding Agencies May Define the Entity to Be Audited Differently Than Does GAAP

13.10 The regulations implementing Circular A-133 may define the entity to be audited for single audit purposes differently than the reporting entity would be defined in accordance with GAAP. For example, FASB *Accounting Standards Codification* 958–810 requires presentation of consolidated financial statements when one not-for-profit entity (NFP) (the parent) controls the voting majority of the board of and has an economic interest in another NFP. If the regulations of the federal agency that provides federal awards to the parent define the entity for single audit purposes to consist of only the parent, audited parent-only financial statements instead of consolidated financial statements

---

[7] AU-C section 800, *Special Consideration—Audits of Financial Statements Prepared in Accordance With Special Purpose Frameworks* (AICPA, *Professional Standards*), provides requirements and guidance for auditor reporting when the auditee prepares financial statements in accordance with a special purpose framework. AU-C section 800 defines a *special purpose framework* as a financial reporting framework other than generally accepted accounting principles and establishes requirements for reporting on those frameworks. Special purpose frameworks, such as the cash, tax, regulatory, and other bases of accounting, are sometimes referred to as *other comprehensive bases of accounting* (OCBOA). The term *OCBOA* is sometimes used when referring to this guidance in this guide.

[8] The AICPA Audit and Accounting Guide *State and Local Governments* discusses the application of AU-C section 800 to state and local governmental financial statements and also provides illustrative auditor's reports for financial statements prepared in accordance with a special purpose framework. In addition, the AICPA practice aid *Applying OCBOA in State and Local Governmental Financial Statements* (APAOCBO12P) provides nonauthoritative guidance on preparing and reporting on OCBOA financial statements of governmental entities. A second practice aid, *Accounting and Financial Reporting Guidelines for Cash- and Tax-Basis Financial Statements* (APACTB12P), provides nonauthoritative guidance for preparers regarding guidelines and best practices for the preparation of cash and tax basis financial statements. These publications are available at www.cpa2biz.com.

should be submitted to comply with these regulations. If the NFP's consolidated financial statements are not also prepared as required by GAAP, a modified opinion due to a material departure from GAAP on the parent-only financial statements may be required. AU-C section 705, *Modification to the Opinion in the Independent Auditor's Report* (AICPA, *Professional Standards*), and various AICPA Audit and Accounting Guides, including *Not-for-Profit Entities*, *State and Local Governments*, and *Health Care Entities*, provide guidance on reporting when there is a departure from GAAP.

Elements of the In-Relation-To Report on the Supplementary Schedule of Expenditures of Federal Awards[9]

13.11 In accordance with AU-C section 725, *Supplementary Information in Relation to the Financial Statements as a Whole* (AICPA, *Professional Standards*), when the entity presents the schedule of expenditures of federal awards with the financial statements, the auditor should report on the schedule in either (*a*) an other-matter paragraph in accordance with AU-C section 706, *Emphasis-of-Matter Paragraphs and Other-Matter Paragraphs in the Independent Auditor's Report* (AICPA, *Professional Standards*), or (*b*) in a separate report on the schedule of expenditures of federal awards. Reporting using an other-matter paragraph is applicable when the schedule of expenditures of federal awards is reported on in the auditor's report on the financial statements. Otherwise, the reporting on the schedule of expenditures of federal awards may be included in the report on compliance and on internal control over compliance required under Circular A-133, or in a separate report (for example, when the schedule of expenditures of federal awards is presented with the single audit reporting package). In any case, the following elements should be included in the report:

- A statement that the audit was conducted for the purpose of forming an opinion on the financial statements as a whole
- A statement that the schedule of expenditures of federal awards is presented for purposes of additional analysis and is not a required part of the financial statements
- A statement that the schedule of expenditures of federal awards is the responsibility of management and was derived from, and relates directly to, the underlying accounting and other records used to prepare the financial statements
- A statement that the schedule of expenditures of federal awards has been subjected to the auditing procedures applied in the audit of the financial statements and certain additional procedures,[10] including comparing and reconciling such information directly to the underlying accounting and other records used to prepare the

---

[9] It is important to note that under AU-C section 725, *Supplementary Information in Relation to the Financial Statements as a Whole* (AICPA, *Professional Standards*), an auditor may only provide an in-relation-to opinion on the schedule of expenditures of federal awards when the auditor audited the financial statements. If that is not the case, the auditor has not met all the requirements in paragraph .05 of AU-C section 725 necessary to opine on the schedule, and therefore may not provide an in-relation-to opinion. See chapter 7, "Schedule of Expenditures of Federal Awards (Circular A-133)," for additional information.

[10] See chapter 7 for information on procedures the auditor should perform in order to opine on supplementary information such as the schedule of expenditures of federal awards.

Auditor Reporting Requirements and Other Communication Considerations 317

financial statements or to the financial statements themselves and other additional procedures, in accordance with GAAS

- If the auditor issues an unmodified opinion[11] on the financial statements and the auditor has concluded that the schedule of expenditures of federal awards is fairly stated, in all material respects, in relation to the financial statements as a whole, a statement that, in the auditor's opinion, the schedule of expenditures of federal awards is fairly stated, in all material respects, in relation to the financial statements as a whole

- If the auditor issues a qualified opinion on the financial statements and the qualification has an effect on the schedule of expenditures of federal awards, a statement that, in the auditor's opinion, except for the effects on the schedule of expenditures of federal awards of (refer to the paragraph in the auditor's report explaining the qualification), such information is fairly stated, in all material respects, in relation to the financial statements as a whole

13.12 When the schedule of expenditures of federal awards is not presented with the financial statements and the auditor includes the in-relation-to reporting in either the report on compliance and on internal control over compliance required by Circular A-133 or in a separate report,[12] the following additional elements should be included (in addition to the report elements found in paragraph 13.11):

- A reference to the report on the financial statements
- The date of that report
- The nature of the opinion expressed on the financial statements
- Any report modifications

Furthermore, consistent with paragraph .A16 of AU-C section 725, when the auditor includes the in-relation-to reporting in either the report on compliance and on internal control over compliance required by Circular A-133 or in a separate report, the auditor may consider including an alert that restricts the use of the separate report solely to the appropriate specified parties. See AU-C section 905, *Alert That Restricts the Use of the Auditor's Written Communication* (AICPA, *Professional Standards*), for more information.

13.13 This guide recommends that, when possible, the auditor report on the schedule of expenditures of federal awards as supplementary information in the report on the financial statements. Chapter 4 of this guide describes the requirements of the auditor's standard report on the financial statements and

---

[11] AU-C section 700, *Forming an Opinion and Reporting on Financial Statements* (AICPA, *Professional Standards*), uses the term *unmodified opinion* to refer to an opinion expressed by the auditor when the auditor concludes that the financial statements are presented fairly, in all material respects, in accordance with the applicable financial reporting framework. Although Circular A-133 refers to this type of opinion as an unqualified opinion, this guide uses the term *unmodified opinion* when referring to such an opinion.

[12] As noted in chapter 7, there may be instances when the auditor is engaged to issue an opinion on the schedule of expenditures of federal awards under AU-C section 805, *Special Considerations—Audits of Single Financial Statements and Specific Elements, Accounts, or Items of a Financial Statement* (AICPA, *Professional Standards*), for example, when the auditor is engaged to perform only the compliance audit under Circular A-133. See paragraph 13.20 for information regarding the auditor reporting on the schedule of expenditures of federal awards in this circumstance.

on accompanying supplementary information—required supplementary information and supplementary information. The appendix in chapter 4 of this guide provides examples of the auditor's standard report on financial statements and illustrations of reporting on required supplementary information and supplementary information, including the schedule of expenditures of federal awards. (See paragraphs 13.19–.20 if the schedule of expenditures of federal awards does not accompany the financial statements.) The illustrative reports in the appendix of this chapter (paragraph 13.58), examples 13-1–13-6, provide illustrative wording for reporting on the schedule of expenditures of federal awards based on the requirements of AU-C section 725, and illustrate how to incorporate the reporting on the schedule of expenditures of federal awards into the report on compliance and on internal control over compliance required by Circular A-133.

Potential Report Modifications When Reporting on the Schedule of Expenditures of Federal Awards

13.14 Paragraph .13 of AU-C section 725 notes that if the auditor concludes, on the basis of the procedures performed, that the schedule of expenditures of federal awards is materially misstated in relation to the financial statements as a whole, the auditor should discuss the matter with management and propose an appropriate revision of the schedule. If management does not revise the schedule of expenditures of federal awards, the auditor should either (*a*) modify the auditor's opinion on the schedule and describe the misstatement in the auditor's report or, (*b*) if a separate report is being issued on the schedule, withhold the auditor's report on the schedule.

13.15 When reporting on supplementary information, the auditor should consider the effect of any modifications to the report on the financial statements. In applying paragraph .11 of AU-C section 725, when the auditor's report on the audited financial statements contains an adverse opinion or disclaimer of opinion and the auditor has been engaged to provide an in-relation-to opinion on the schedule of expenditures of federal awards, the auditor is precluded from expressing an in-relation-to opinion on the schedule of expenditures of federal awards. When permitted by law or regulation, the auditor may withdraw from the engagement to report on such supplementary information. Unless the auditor chooses to withdraw, the auditor's report on the schedule of expenditures of federal awards should state that because of the significance of the matter disclosed in the auditor's report, it is inappropriate to, and the auditor does not, express an opinion on the schedule of expenditures of federal awards. Paragraph .A17 of AU-C section 725 provides reporting examples, including reporting on supplementary information such as the schedule of expenditures of federal awards when the auditor's report on the financial statements contains an adverse or disclaimer of opinion.

Considerations When Dating the Report on the Schedule of Expenditures of Federal Awards

13.16 Paragraph .12 of AU-C section 725 states that the date of the auditor's report on supplementary information in relation to the financial statements as a whole should not be earlier than the date on which the auditor completed the procedures required in paragraph .07 of AU-C section 725. Therefore, the date of the auditor's report on the schedule of expenditures of federal awards may be the same date as the financial statement report or a later date.

In no case would the date of the in-relation-to opinion on the schedule of expenditures of federal awards be earlier than the date of the financial statement report.

Schedule of Expenditures of Federal Awards Presented With the Financial Statements

13.17 When the reporting on the schedule of expenditures of federal awards is included in the auditor's report on the financial statements, the date of the report on the schedule depends on when the auditor has completed the procedures relating to the schedule of expenditures of federal awards. When those procedures are performed concurrent with financial statement audit procedures, the date of the report on the schedule of expenditures of federal awards will be the same date as that of the auditor's report on the financial statements. However, in cases where the procedures related to the schedule of expenditures of federal awards are completed subsequent to the financial statement report date, the reporting on the schedule will carry a later date than the financial statement report, thus resulting in a dual dated report.

13.18 When the auditor has completed the procedures related to the schedule of expenditures of federal awards after the date of the auditor's report on the financial statements, Interpretation No. 1, "Dating the Auditor's Report on Supplementary Information," of AU-C section 725 (AICPA, *Professional Standards*, AU-C sec. 9725 par. .01–.04) provides guidance related to the use of an explanatory paragraph to make it clear that no additional procedures were performed on the audited financial statements subsequent to the date of the auditor's report on those financial statements. The interpretation, which also includes illustrative report wording, notes that, although not required, an auditor may

- when issuing a separate report on the supplementary information, include in the report a statement that the auditor has not performed any auditing procedures with respect to the audited financial statements subsequent to the date of the auditor's report on those financial statements.
- when reissuing a report on the audited financial statements to include an other-matter paragraph to report on the supplementary information, include two report dates to indicate that the date of reporting on the supplementary information is as of a later date.

Schedule of Expenditures of Federal Awards Presented With the Report Required Under Circular A-133

13.19 As noted previously, there may be circumstances in which the auditor includes the in-relation-to opinion on the schedule of expenditures of federal awards in the report on compliance and on internal control over compliance required by Circular A-133. In that situation, the date of the report on the schedule of expenditures of federal awards depends on the date the underlying audit procedures are completed. If using the same date is not possible because the procedures to satisfy Circular A-133 requirements are not completed as of the date the procedures related to the schedule of expenditures of federal awards are completed, the auditor has two options:

   a. The auditor can dual date the report on compliance and on internal control over compliance required by Circular A-133. The date related to the portion of the report pertaining to the in-relation-to opinion on the schedule of expenditures of federal awards would be when the audit procedures performed are completed. The date pertaining to the remainder of the report would be the date when the audit procedures performed to satisfy Circular A-133 requirements are completed. The appendix of this chapter (paragraph 13.58), example 13-1 provides illustrative wording.

b. The auditor can issue a separate report on the schedule of expenditures of federal awards. This report should be dated the date on which the auditor completed the procedures required under paragraph .07 of AU-C section 725.

Issuing an Opinion on the Schedule of Expenditures of Federal Awards Under AU-C Section 805 When the Auditor Is Engaged to Perform Only the Compliance Audit Under Circular A-133[13]

13.20 In some instances, the auditor may be engaged to issue a stand-alone opinion on the schedule of expenditures of federal awards, either as part of the report issued to meet the requirements of Circular A-133 or separately. It is important to note that when an auditor is engaged to perform only the compliance audit required under Circular A-133, and not the financial statement audit, an in-relation-to opinion may not be issued.[14] When this occurs, the auditee may consider engaging the auditor to issue an opinion on the schedule of expenditures of federal awards under AU-C section 805, *Special Considerations—Audits of Single Financial Statements and Specific Elements, Accounts, or Items of a Financial Statement* (AICPA, *Professional Standards*).[15] Although this engagement would be performed under *Government Auditing Standards*, because the schedule of expenditures of federal awards (the financial statement) presents only the activities of the federal programs, the auditor is not required to issue a separate report to meet the reporting requirements of *Government Auditing Standards*. See chapter 7 for additional information on the objectives and audit evidence needed in such an audit. See example 13-8 in paragraph 13.58 for an illustrative report on the schedule of expenditures of federal awards when the auditor issues an opinion under AU-C section 805.

Reporting on Compliance and Internal Control Over Compliance Applicable to Each Major Program

13.21 This section discusses the auditor's report and opinions that are issued based on a Circular A-133 compliance audit of major programs. The report on compliance with requirements applicable to major programs expresses the auditor's opinion on whether the auditee complied with the requirements that, if noncompliance occurred, could have a direct and material effect on a major program. AU-C section 935, *Compliance Audits* (AICPA, *Professional*

---

[13] An auditee may use a separate auditor to perform the compliance audit under Circular A-133 for various reasons. For example, a common reason is for an auditee to make positive efforts to use small business, minority-owned firms, and women's business enterprises in conjunction with the Circular A-133 audit.

[14] See footnote 9.

[15] An auditee may also consider engaging the auditor to examine the schedule of expenditures of federal awards or an assertion related to the schedule of expenditures of federal awards in accordance with AT section 101, *Attest Engagements* (AICPA, *Professional Standards*).

Auditor Reporting Requirements and Other Communication Considerations **321**

Standards), provides requirements and guidance when reporting on compliance and internal control over compliance. Also, AU-C section 700, *Forming an Opinion and Reporting on Financial Statements* (AICPA, *Professional Standards*), should be adapted and applied to a Circular A-133 compliance audit. When modification of the auditor's opinion on compliance is needed (for example, when the auditor's opinion is modified due to noncompliance or a scope restriction), the auditor should adapt and apply the requirements and guidance in AU-C section 705 to such report modifications.

Material Instances of Noncompliance

13.22 In accordance with AU-C section 705, when the audit of an auditee's compliance with requirements applicable to a major program detects material instances of noncompliance with those requirements, the auditor should express a qualified or adverse opinion on compliance in the report on compliance with requirements that could have a direct and material effect on each major program and on internal control over compliance. The auditor should state the basis for such an opinion in the report as shown in the appendix of this chapter (paragraph 13.58), examples 13-3–13-6. Chapter 10 of this guide discusses materiality considerations in evaluating the effect of instances of noncompliance on the opinion on compliance.

Scope Limitations

13.23 Testing an auditee's compliance with laws, regulations, and the provisions of contracts and grant agreements provides the evidence for the auditor to make a comply or noncomply decision about an auditee's adherence to those compliance requirements. The auditor is able to express an unmodified opinion only if he or she has been able to apply all the procedures the auditor considers necessary in the circumstances. Restrictions on the scope of the audit—whether imposed by the client or by circumstances such as the timing of the auditor's work, an inability to obtain sufficient appropriate audit evidence, or an inadequacy in the accounting records—may require the auditor to qualify his or her opinion or to disclaim an opinion.[16] In those instances, the auditor's report should describe the reasons for such a qualification or disclaimer of opinion. Furthermore, the auditor should consider the effects of those instances on his or her ability to express an unmodified opinion on the financial statements. The appendix of this chapter (paragraph 13.58), example 13-5, illustrates a qualified opinion on compliance due to a scope limitation.

13.24 The auditor's decision to qualify or disclaim an opinion because of a scope limitation depends on his or her assessment of the importance of the omitted procedure(s) to his or her ability to form an opinion on compliance with requirements governing each major program. This assessment will be affected by the nature and magnitude of the potential effects of the matters in question and by their significance to each major program. Restrictions imposed by the client that significantly limit the scope of the audit may require the auditor to disclaim an opinion on compliance.

---

[16] As noted in paragraph 13.38*e*, the auditor should report as a finding the circumstances concerning why the auditor's report on compliance for major programs is other than an unmodified opinion, unless such circumstances are otherwise reported as audit findings in the schedule of findings and questioned costs for federal awards (for example, a scope limitation that is not otherwise reported as a finding).

13.25 When disclaiming an opinion because of a scope limitation, the auditor should indicate in a separate basis for modification paragraph all of the substantive reasons for the disclaimer. The auditor should also state in a separate opinion paragraph that

    a. because of the significance of the matter(s) described in the basis for disclaimer of opinion paragraph, the auditor has not been able to obtain sufficient appropriate audit evidence to provide a basis for an audit opinion, and

    b. accordingly, the auditor does not express an opinion.

Report on Compliance for Each Major Program, Report on Internal Control Over Compliance, and Report on the Schedule of Expenditures of Federal Awards Required by Circular A-133

Report Requirements[17]

13.26 The basic elements of the auditor's standard report on compliance with requirements that could have a direct and material effect on each major program and on internal control over compliance[18] in accordance with Circular A-133 are in the following listing. The appendix of this chapter (paragraph 13.58) examples 13-1–13-6 illustrate that report:

    a. A title that includes the word *independent*.

    b. An addressee appropriate for the circumstances of the engagement.

    c. A section titled "Report on Compliance for Each Major Federal Program."

    d. An introductory paragraph that includes the following:

        i. A statement that the auditor has audited the auditee's compliance with the types of compliance requirements described in the *OMB Compliance Supplement* (*Compliance Supplement*) that could have a direct and material effect on each of its major federal programs.

        ii. Identification of the period covered by the report.

        iii. A statement that the auditee's major federal programs are identified in the summary of auditor's results section of the accompanying schedule of findings and questioned costs. (See paragraph 13.36)

    e. A subheading titled "Management's Responsibility" that includes a statement that compliance with the requirements of laws, regulations, contracts, and grants applicable to the auditee's federal programs is the responsibility of the auditee's management.

---

[17] The elements provided in this section are limited to the elements for situations when the auditor is expressing an unmodified opinion and/or qualified opinion on compliance. Additionally, the order of the elements (paragraph 13.26) of report requirements in this paragraph is not the proper order for all reporting circumstances. Refer to specific report illustrations in paragraph 13.58 for illustrations of other types of reporting (for example, an adverse opinion) and the typical ordering of the required elements in a particular reporting circumstance.

[18] In a particular single audit engagement, some controls may involve both internal control over financial reporting and internal control over compliance and thus be relevant to both the audit of the financial statements and the audit of compliance. When this occurs, those controls would be encompassed in both internal control reports. Section 505 of Circular A-133 provides guidance on reporting findings involving significant deficiencies and material weaknesses in internal control in such a circumstance as discussed in paragraph 13.34c.

Auditor Reporting Requirements and Other Communication Considerations

    f. A subheading titled "Auditor's Responsibility" that includes the following:

        i. A statement that the auditor's responsibility is to express an opinion on compliance for each of the entity's major federal programs based on the audit of the types of compliance requirements.

        ii. A statement that the compliance audit was conducted in accordance with auditing standards generally accepted in the United States of America,[19] the standards applicable to financial audits contained in *Government Auditing Standards* issued by the Comptroller General of the United States[20] and Circular A-133.

        iii. A statement that those standards and Circular A-133 require that the auditor plan and perform the audit to obtain reasonable assurance about whether noncompliance with the types of compliance requirements that could have a direct and material effect on a major federal program occurred.

        iv. A statement that an audit includes examining, on a test basis, evidence about the entity's compliance with those requirements and performing such other procedures as the auditor considered necessary in the circumstances.

        v. A statement that the auditor believes that the compliance audit provides a reasonable basis for the auditor's opinion.

        vi. A statement that the compliance audit does not provide a legal determination of the auditee's compliance with those requirements.

    g. When the auditor is expressing an unmodified opinion on all major programs, a subheading titled "Opinion on Each Major Federal Program" that contains a statement that in the auditor's opinion the entity complied, in all material respects, with the types of compliance requirements that could have a direct and material effect on each of its major federal programs for the year ended [*specify date*].

    h. If instances of noncompliance for a major program are noted that result in an opinion qualification, a subheading titled, "Basis for Qualified Opinion on [*Name of Major Federal Program*]" that includes the following (see item *i* for modifications needed for situations where one or more major programs receive a qualified opinion)

        i. A statement that, as described in the accompanying schedule of findings and questioned costs, the auditee did not comply with requirements regarding [*identify the major federal program and associated finding number(s) matched to the type(s) of compliance requirements*].

---

[19] See the discussion beginning in paragraph 13.23 for information on report modifications due to a scope limitation.

[20] The standards and guidance applicable to financial audits are found in chapters 1–4 of *Government Auditing Standards*.

Government Auditing Standards and Single Audits

      ii. a statement that compliance with such requirements is necessary, in the auditor's opinion, for the auditee to comply with the requirements applicable to the program(s).

  i. If instances of noncompliance are noted that result in an opinion qualification for one or more major programs, a subheading with an appropriate title (for example, "Qualified Opinion on [*Name of Major Federal Program*]") that includes the auditor's opinion on whether the auditee complied, in all material respects, with the types of compliance requirements that could have a direct and material effect on each of its major federal programs.

> [**Note:** *If instances of noncompliance are noted that result in an opinion qualification on one or more major programs, but there are other major programs receiving an unmodified opinion, the subheading to the opinion paragraph relating to the unmodified opinion(s) (see item g) may be modified to, "Unmodified Opinion on Each of the Other Major Federal Programs" to be more clear about the programs receiving an unmodified opinion.]*

  j. If other non-compliance is identified that does not result in a modified opinion but that is required to be reported in accordance with Circular A-133, a subheading titled "Other Matters" containing

      i. a reference to the schedule of findings and questioned costs in which the instances of non-compliance are described, including the reference number(s) of the finding(s).[21]

      ii. a statement that the auditor's opinion on each major federal program is not modified with respect to the matters.

      iii. a statement that the auditee's response to the noncompliance findings identified are described in the accompanying [insert name of document containing management's response to the auditor's findings, for example "schedule of findings and questioned costs" and/or "corrective action plan."]

      iv. a statement that the auditee's response was not subjected to the auditing procedures applied in the audit of compliance and, accordingly, the auditor expresses no opinion on the response.

  k. A section heading "Report on Internal Control Over Compliance" that includes the following statements and definitions:

      i. A statement that the auditee's management is responsible for establishing and maintaining effective internal control over compliance with the types of compliance requirements.

      ii. A statement that in planning and performing the compliance audit, the auditor considered the auditee's internal control over compliance with the types of requirements that could have a direct and material effect on each major federal program to determine the auditing procedures

---

[21] Paragraph 13.38 discusses the audit findings that are required to be reported under Circular A-133.

Auditor Reporting Requirements and Other Communication Considerations

that are appropriate in the circumstances for the purpose of expressing an opinion on compliance for each major federal program and to test and report on internal control over compliance in accordance with OMB Circular A-133, but not for the purpose of expressing an opinion on the effectiveness of internal control over compliance.

iii. A statement that the auditor is not expressing an opinion on the effectiveness of internal control over compliance.

iv. The definitions of *deficiency in internal control over compliance, material weakness in internal control over compliance,* and *significant deficiency in internal control over compliance.*

v. A statement that the auditor's consideration of internal control over compliance was for the limited purpose described in the first paragraph of the section and was not designed to identify all deficiencies in internal control over compliance that might be material weaknesses or significant deficiencies.

vi. If no material weaknesses in internal control over compliance were identified, a statement that the auditor did not identify any deficiencies in internal control over compliance that are considered to be material weaknesses.

vii. A statement that material weaknesses may exist that have not been identified. (For situations where significant deficiencies or material weaknesses are identified, this statement is revised to indicate that material weaknesses or significant deficiencies may exist that have not been identified.)

viii. If significant deficiencies in internal control over compliance were identified, a statement that no deficiencies in internal control over compliance were identified that are considered to be material weaknesses, however deficiencies in internal control over compliance were identified that are considered to be significant deficiencies, and a description of the significant deficiencies in internal control over compliance or a reference to the accompanying schedule of findings and questioned costs, including the reference number(s) of the finding(s).

ix. If material weaknesses in internal control over compliance were identified, a statement that deficiencies in internal control over compliance were identified that are considered to be material weaknesses and a description of the material weaknesses in internal control over compliance or a reference to the accompanying schedule of findings and questioned costs, including the reference number(s) of the finding(s).

x. If applicable, a statement that the auditee's written response to the findings identified in the audit are described in the accompanying schedule of findings and questioned costs, and that the auditee's written response was not subjected to the auditing procedures applied in the audit of compliance and, accordingly, the auditor expresses no opinion on it.

    xi. A separate paragraph at the end of the section stating that the purpose of the report on internal control over compliance is solely to describe the scope of our testing of internal control over compliance and the result of that testing based on the requirements of OMB Circular A-133. Accordingly, this report is not suitable for any other purpose.[22]

  l. The manual or printed signature of the auditor's firm.

  m. The city and state where the auditor practices.[23]

  n. The date of the auditor's report.

Further, as discussed in paragraph 13.39, the auditor may need to modify the report on compliance with requirements that could have a direct and material effect on each major program and on internal control over compliance in accordance with Circular A-133 for abuse findings reported in the federal awards section of the schedule of findings and questioned costs.

Option to Include Reporting on the Schedule of Expenditures of Federal Awards

13.27 As discussed in paragraph 13.06, this guide recommends reporting on the schedule of expenditures of federal awards in the report on the financial statements. However, in certain circumstances (for example, when the schedule of expenditures of federal awards is presented in a separate single audit reporting package), the auditor's report on the schedule may be incorporated into the report described in paragraph 13.21. Because of the added nuances when including the reporting on the schedule in the Circular A-133 report, examples 13-1–13-6 in the appendix of this chapter (paragraph 13.58) illustrate how to incorporate the reporting on the schedule into the Circular A-133 report. However, a footnote to example 13-1 provides information about how to report on the schedule using the recommended approach—that is, incorporating the reporting on the schedule in the report on the financial statements.

---

[22] This paragraph in the report conforms to paragraph .11 of AU-C section 905, *Alert That Restricts the Use of the Auditor's Written Communication* (AICPA, *Professional Standards*), which modifies the alert language used for compliance audits performed under *Government Auditing Standards*. This language should only be included in the internal control over compliance section of combined reports on the entity's compliance and internal control over compliance in light of the fact that it is the nature of the reporting on internal control over compliance that triggers the required use of alert language (see paragraph .06c of AU-C section 905). If the auditor issues separate reports on the entity's compliance and its internal control over compliance, this alert should be included in the report on internal control over compliance, but would not be included in the report on compliance.

[23] AU-C section 700 provides that the auditor's report should name the city and state where the auditor practices. City and state on a firm's letterhead typically is sufficient to meet this requirement. Technical Questions and Answers section 9100.08, "Audit Firm With Multiple Offices on Their Company Letterhead and Effect on Report" (AICPA, *Technical Questions and Answers*), notes that when a firm's letterhead contains multiple office locations the auditor would need to indicate the city and state where the auditor practices in the auditor's report.

Auditor Reporting Requirements and Other Communication Considerations

Dating the Report on Compliance With Requirements That Could Have a Direct and Material Effect on Each Major Federal Program and on Internal Control Over Compliance

13.28 The auditor's report on compliance and on internal control over compliance related to major federal programs required by Circular A-133 carries the same date as that of a financial statement report when the audit procedures performed to satisfy Circular A-133 requirements are completed along with the procedures performed on the financial statements. However, when some of the audit procedures performed to satisfy Circular A-133 requirements are completed subsequent to the procedures performed on the financial statements, the report required by Circular A-133 should be dated at a later date (that is, when the auditor has obtained sufficient appropriate audit evidence to support the report on the audit of compliance). The auditor should adapt and apply the applicable requirements and guidance from AU-C section 560, *Subsequent Events and Subsequently Discovered Facts* (AICPA, *Professional Standards*), for the purpose of performing subsequent events procedures from the date of the report on the financial statements to the date of the report on the Circular A-133 compliance audit.

Other Reporting Considerations

Reissuance of the Circular A-133 Report

13.29 If an auditor reissues the Circular A-133 report, the reissued report should include a paragraph within the other matters section of the report stating that the report is replacing a previously issued report, description of the reasons why the report is being reissued, and a listing of any changes from the previously issued report. Examples of situations in which the auditor may reissue the compliance report are (*a*) a quality control review performed by a governmental agency indicates that the auditor did not test a direct and material compliance requirement and (*b*) the discovery subsequent to the date of the compliance report that the entity had another major program that was required to be tested.

13.30 If additional procedures are performed to obtain sufficient appropriate audit evidence for all of the major programs being reported on, the auditor's report date should be updated to reflect the date the auditor obtained sufficient appropriate audit evidence regarding the events that caused the auditor to perform new procedures. If, however, additional procedures are performed to obtain sufficient appropriate audit evidence for only some of the major programs being reported on, the auditor should dual date the report with the updated report date reflecting the date the auditor obtained sufficient appropriate audit evidence regarding the major programs affected by the circumstances and referencing the major programs for which additional audit procedures have been performed. Reissuance of an auditor-prepared document required by Circular A-133 that is incorporated by reference into the auditor's report (for example, the schedule of findings and questioned costs) is considered to be a reissuance of the auditor's report.

Other Auditors

13.31 As noted in chapter 6, "Planning Considerations of Circular A-133," of this guide, when more than one independent auditor is involved in a single audit the auditor should use professional judgment to adapt and apply the guidance in AU-C section 600, *Special Considerations—Audits of Group Financial Statements (Including the Work of Component Auditors)* (AICPA, *Professional Standards*), with regard to determining whether to refer to the other auditors (that is, component auditors) in the auditor's report on compliance and on internal control over compliance.

When the Audit of Federal Awards Does Not Encompass the Entirety of the Auditee's Operations

13.32 If the audit of federal awards does not encompass the entirety of the auditee's operations expending federal awards, the operations that are not included should be identified in a separate paragraph following the first paragraph of the introductory section of the report on compliance for each major program. (See also the discussion in chapter 6 of this guide concerning the definition of the entity to be audited.) An example of such a paragraph follows:

> Example Entity's basic financial statements include the operations of the [*identify organizational unit, such as a governmental component unit, an operating unit, or a department*], which received [*include dollar amount*] in federal awards which is not included in the schedule during the year ended June 30, 20X1. Our audit, described below, did not include the operations of [*identify organizational unit*] because [*state the reason for the omission, such as the organizational unit engaged other auditors to perform an audit in accordance with OMB Circular A-133*].

Schedule of Findings and Questioned Costs [24]

13.33 Circular A-133 states that the auditor should prepare a schedule of findings and questioned costs, which should include the following three sections:

    a. A summary of the auditor's results

    b. Findings related to the financial statements that are required to be reported in accordance with *Government Auditing Standards*

    c. Findings and questioned costs for federal awards

The appendix of this chapter (paragraph 13.58) presents an illustrative schedule of findings and questioned costs in example 13-7.

What Should Be Reported

13.34 Specifically, Circular A-133 requires the schedule of findings and questioned costs to contain the following:

    a. A summary of the auditor's results, which should include the following:

        i. The type of report the auditor issued on the financial statements of the auditee (that is, unmodified opinion,

---

[24] There is no option for the auditor to report in a written communication (such as a communication sometimes referred to as a management letter), findings that *Government Auditing Standards* or Circular A-133 requires to be reported in the auditor's report or schedule of findings and questioned costs. See also paragraph 13.44.

Auditor Reporting Requirements and Other Communication Considerations **329**

           qualified opinion, adverse opinion, or disclaimer of opinion)[25]

    ii. Where applicable, a statement that significant deficiencies or material weaknesses in internal control were disclosed by the audit of the financial statements[26]

    iii. A statement on whether the audit disclosed any noncompliance that is material to the financial statements of the auditee

    iv. Where applicable, a statement that significant deficiencies or material weaknesses in the internal control over major programs were disclosed by the audit[27]

    v. The type of report the auditor issued on compliance for major programs (that is, unmodified opinion, qualified opinion, adverse opinion, or disclaimer of opinion)

    vi. A statement on whether the audit disclosed any audit findings that the auditor is required to report under Section 510(a) of Circular A-133 (see paragraph 13.38)[28]

    vii. An identification of major programs

    viii. The dollar threshold used to distinguish between type A and type B programs as described in Section 520(b) of Circular A-133 (see chapter 8 of this guide)

    ix. A statement on whether the auditee qualified as a low-risk auditee under Section 530 of Circular A-133 (see chapter 8 of this guide)

b. Findings related to the financial statements that are required to be reported in accordance with *Government Auditing Standards* (see paragraph 13.36).

c. Findings and questioned costs for federal awards, which should include audit findings as defined in Section 510(a) of Circular A-133 (see paragraph 13.38) and should include certain findings of abuse as required by *Government Auditing Standards* (see paragraph 13.39). Circular A-133 states that this section of the schedule should include the following:

    i. Audit findings (for example, internal control findings, compliance findings, questioned costs, or fraud) that relate to the same issue should be presented as one finding. Where

---

[25] As explained in the AICPA Audit and Accounting Guide *State and Local Governments,* the auditor generally expresses or disclaims an opinion on a government's basic financial statements by providing an opinion or disclaimer of opinion on each opinion unit required to be presented in those financial statements. (See footnote 2.) Therefore, the schedule of findings and questioned costs may need to indicate multiple types of opinions on a government's basic financial statements.

[26] AU-C section 265, *Communicating Internal Control Related Matters Identified in an Audit* (AICPA, *Professional Standards*), precludes an auditor from issuing a written report representing that no significant deficiencies were noted during an audit. Therefore, the illustrative schedule of findings and questioned costs in example 13-7 in the appendix of this chapter (paragraph 13.58) uses the term *none reported* to indicate that no significant deficiencies were included in the auditor's report (versus *none*, which would imply that there were no significant deficiencies).

[27] See footnote 26.

[28] As discussed in paragraph 13.39, the auditor may need to modify the summary of auditor's results for abuse findings reported in the federal awards section of the schedule of findings and questioned costs.

practical, audit findings should be organized by federal agency or pass-through entity.

ii. Audit findings that relate to both the financial statements and the federal awards should be reported in both sections of the schedule. However, the reporting in one section of the schedule may be in summary form, with a reference to a detailed reporting in the other section of the schedule. For example, a material weakness in internal control that affects the auditee as a whole, including its federal awards, would usually be reported in detail in the section of the schedule of findings and questioned costs that is related to the financial statements, with a summary identification and reference given in the section related to federal awards. Conversely, a finding of noncompliance with a federal program law that also is material to the financial statements would be reported in detail in the federal awards section of the schedule, with a summary identification and reference given in the financial statement section.

13.35 The following table summarizes the requirements found in Section 505(d)(2)–505(d)(3) of Circular A-133 for reporting findings in a Circular A-133 compliance audit report. More detailed information regarding findings required to be reported in accordance with *Government Auditing Standards* is located in chapter 4 of this guide.[29] See paragraphs 13.36–.39 for more information, including placement of the findings within the schedule of findings and questioned costs. Also included in this table are items that, although not required to be reported in the Circular A-133 compliance audit report, may be communicated under the guidance in AU-C section 260, *The Auditor's Communication With Those Charged With Governance*, and AU-C section 265, *Communicating Internal Control Related Matters Identified in an Audit* (AICPA, *Professional Standards*), as part of the compliance audit.

Table 13-2

Reporting Findings in a Circular A-133 Compliance Audit

	Schedule of Findings and Questioned Costs	Communicate in Writing or Orally
Findings related to the financial statements required to be reported in accordance with *Government Auditing Standards* (see table 4-1 in chapter 4 of this guide)	X	
Finding and questioned costs for federal awards required to be reported in accordance with Circular A-133:		

---

[29] Table 4-1, "*Government Auditing Standards* Requirements for Reporting Findings," in chapter 4, "Auditor Reporting Requirements and Other Communication Considerations of *Government Auditing Standards*," of this guide provides information regarding reporting financial statement related findings as part of the financial statement audit performed under *Government Auditing Standards*.

Auditor Reporting Requirements and Other Communication Considerations

	Schedule of Findings and Questioned Costs	Communicate in Writing or Orally
Deficiencies in internal control:		
Significant deficiencies in internal control over compliance	X	
Material weaknesses in internal control over compliance	X	
Other deficiencies in internal control over compliance that are not significant deficiencies or material weaknesses required to be reported but, in the auditor's judgment, are of sufficient importance to be communicated to management [1]		X
Noncompliance with provisions of laws, regulations, contracts, or grant agreements related to a federal program:		
That is material in relation to a type of compliance requirement for a major program or an audit objective identified in the *Compliance Supplement*	X	
That does not meet the criteria for reporting under Circular A-133 but, in the auditor's judgment, is of sufficient importance to communicate to management or those charged with governance [2]		X
Questioned Costs		
Known questioned costs that are greater than $10,000 for a type of compliance requirement for a major program	X	
Known questioned costs when likely questioned costs are greater than $10,000 for a type of compliance requirement for a major program	X	
Known questioned costs that are greater than $10,000 for programs that are not audited as major	X	
Fraud		
Known fraud affecting a federal award[3]	X	
Abuse [4]		
Involving federal awards that is material, either quantitatively or qualitatively, to a major program	X	

(continued)

Reporting Findings in a Circular A-133 Compliance Audit—*continued*

	Schedule of Findings and Questioned Costs	Communicate in Writing or Orally
That is less than material to a major program and not otherwise required to be reported but that, in the auditor's judgment, is of sufficient importance to communicate to management or those charged with governance		X
Other audit findings		
Circumstances concerning why the auditor's report on compliance for major programs is other than unmodified, unless such circumstances are otherwise reported in the schedule of findings and questioned costs.	X	
Instance in which the results of audit follow-up procedures disclosed that the summary schedule of prior audit findings materially misrepresents the status of any prior audit finding	X	
Other findings or issues arising from the compliance audit that are not otherwise required to be reported but are, in the auditor's professional judgment, significant and relevant to those charged with governance		X

[1] The threshold for reporting deficiencies in internal control over compliance for major programs is in relation to a type of compliance requirement for a major program or an audit objective identified in the *OMB Compliance Supplement (Compliance Supplement)* (that is, not in relation to financial statement materiality which is likely significantly higher). Even given this lower reporting threshold, there may be instances where the auditor deems it appropriate to communicate to management deficiencies in internal control over compliance for a major program or other federal program that are not required to be reported in the schedule of findings and questioned costs.

[2] The threshold for reporting noncompliance with provisions of laws, regulations, contracts, and grant agreements related to a federal program is one that is material in relation to a type of compliance requirement for a major program or an audit objective identified in the *Compliance Supplement* (that is, not in relation to financial statement materiality which is likely significantly higher). However, there may be instances where the auditor deems it appropriate to communicate to management noncompliance that is not required to be reported. Note that this type of communication may also be considered by the auditor for findings of abuse or other findings that are not otherwise required to be reported.

[3] See also paragraph 13.38*f*.

[4] As discussed in chapter 10, "Compliance Auditing Applicable to Major Programs (Circular A-133)," of this guide and in paragraph 13.39, situations or transactions involving federal awards that might otherwise appear to constitute abuse instead generally are instances of noncompliance. However, there may be isolated situations or transactions involving federal awards that the auditor becomes aware of that do constitute abuse.

Findings Related to the Financial Statements

13.36 As noted previously, Circular A-133 requires the schedule of findings and questioned costs to include a section that presents the detail of findings related to the financial statements. This section of the schedule includes all findings related to the audit of the financial statements that are required to be reported by GAAS and *Government Auditing Standards* in a Circular A-133 audit. See table 4-1, "*Government Auditing Standards* Requirements for Reporting Findings," in chapter 4 of this guide for information on what *Government Auditing Standards* requires to be reported in the audit of the financial statements under *Government Auditing Standards*.

13.37 Chapter 4 of this guide discusses the details that *Government Auditing Standards* requires be reported for findings. That chapter also discusses the requirement in paragraph 4.33 of *Government Auditing Standards* that the auditor obtain and report the views of responsible officials concerning the findings, conclusions, and recommendations, as well as his or her planned corrective actions. The auditor should present management views and planned corrective actions for findings related to the financial statement audit in the financial statement section of the schedule of findings and questioned costs. Alternatively, for audit findings that relate to both the financial statements and the federal awards and that are reported in both sections of the schedule of findings and questioned costs, depending on the status of the development of the corrective action plan at the time the auditor's reports are released, the auditor may be able to refer to the corrective action plan as the required presentation of the auditee's views and planned corrective actions.

Findings Related to Federal Awards[30]

13.38 Section 510(a) of Circular A-133, provides that the auditor should report as audit findings in the federal awards section of the schedule of findings and questioned costs

    a. significant deficiencies and material weaknesses in the internal control over major programs. The auditor's determination of whether a deficiency in internal control is a significant deficiency or material weakness for the purpose of reporting an audit finding is in relation to a type of compliance requirement for a major program or to an audit objective identified in the *Compliance Supplement*. (Chapter 9 of this guide discusses significant deficiencies and material weaknesses related to federal programs.)

    b. material noncompliance with the provisions of laws, regulations, contracts, and grant agreements related to a major program. The auditor's determination of whether noncompliance with the provisions of laws, regulations, contracts, and grant agreements is material for the purpose of reporting an audit finding is in relation to a type of compliance requirement for a major program or an audit objective identified in the *Compliance Supplement*. (Chapter 10 of this guide further discusses the evaluation and reporting of noncompliance.)

    c. known questioned costs that are greater than $10,000 for a type of compliance requirement for a major program. Known questioned

---

[30] See footnote 24.

costs are those specifically identified by the auditor. In evaluating the effect of questioned costs on the opinion on compliance, the auditor should consider the best estimate of the total costs questioned (likely questioned costs), not just the questioned costs specifically identified (known questioned costs). The auditor also should report (in the schedule of findings and questioned costs) known questioned costs when likely questioned costs are greater than $10,000 for a type of compliance requirement for a major program. For example, if the auditor specifically identifies $7,000 in questioned costs but, based on his or her evaluation of the effect of questioned costs on the opinion on compliance, estimates that the total questioned costs are in the $50,000 to $60,000 range, the auditor would report a finding that identifies the known questioned costs of $7,000. Although the auditor is not required to report his or her estimate of the total questioned costs, the auditor would include information to provide proper perspective for judging the prevalence and consequences of the questioned costs.

d. known questioned costs that are greater than $10,000 for programs that are not audited as major. Because (except for audit follow-up) the auditor is not required to perform audit procedures for federal programs that are not major, the auditor normally will not find questioned costs. However, if the auditor does become aware of questioned costs for a federal program that is not audited as a major program (for example, as part of audit follow-up or other audit procedures) and the known questioned costs are greater than $10,000, then the auditor should report this as an audit finding.

e. the circumstances concerning why the auditor's report on compliance for major federal programs is other than an unmodified opinion, unless such circumstances are otherwise reported as audit findings in the schedule of findings and questioned costs for federal awards (for example, a scope limitation that is not otherwise reported as a finding).

f. known fraud affecting a federal award, unless such fraud is otherwise reported as an audit finding in the schedule of findings and questioned costs for federal awards. Circular A-133 does not require the auditor to make an additional reporting when the auditor confirms that the fraud was reported outside of the auditor's reports under the direct reporting requirements of *Government Auditing Standards*. (Chapter 4 of this guide discusses the direct reporting requirements of *Government Auditing Standards*.)

g. instances in which the results of audit follow-up procedures disclosed that the summary schedule of prior audit findings prepared by the auditee in accordance with Section 315(b) of Circular A-133 materially misrepresents the status of any prior audit finding. (See paragraphs 13.45–.47.)

For those findings that are required to be reported in both the financial statement section and the federal awards section of the schedule of findings and questioned costs, reporting in one section may be in summary form with a reference to the detailed reporting in the other section of the schedule. See paragraph 13.34c and example 13-7 in the appendix of this chapter for additional information.

Findings of Abuse

13.39 Paragraph 4.25 of *Government Auditing Standards* states that auditors should report abuse that is either quantitatively or qualitatively material to the financial statements. That standard, like all of the standards applicable to financial audits in *Government Auditing Standards,* applies to the entirety of the single audit, including the Circular A-133 compliance audit. As discussed in Chapter 10 of this guide, situations or transactions involving federal awards that might otherwise appear to constitute abuse instead generally are instances of noncompliance. However, there may be isolated situations or transactions involving federal awards that the auditor becomes aware of that do constitute abuse. For abuse involving federal awards that is material to the financial statement amounts,[31] the auditor typically would present the finding in the financial statement section of the schedule of findings and questioned costs and refer to it from the *Government Auditing Standards* report. For abuse involving federal awards that is material to a major program, the auditor typically would present the finding in the federal awards section of the schedule of findings and questioned costs and refer to it from the Circular A-133 report. (Chapter 4 of this guide provides guidance for the placement of the reference from the *Government Auditing Standards* report to abuse findings based on the primary nature of the finding. That guidance also applies in referring to findings of abuse involving federal awards in the Circular A-133 report.) As discussed in paragraph 13.34c, the auditor should report abuse findings that relate to both the financial statements and the federal awards in both sections of the schedule. Those findings may be presented in detail in one section and in summary form in the other section, with a cross-reference to the detailed presentation. If abuse findings are reported in the federal awards section of the schedule of findings and questioned costs that do not otherwise meet the Circular A-133 requirements for reporting as findings as discussed in paragraph 13.38, modification of both (*a*) the report on compliance with requirements that could have a direct and material effect on each major program and on internal control over compliance and (*b*) the summary of the auditor's results section of the schedule of findings and questioned costs may be appropriate.

Detail of Audit Findings—Federal Awards

13.40 Section 510(b) of Circular A-133 states that audit findings should be presented in sufficient detail for the auditee to prepare a corrective action plan and take corrective action and for federal agencies and pass-through entities to arrive at a management decision. (However, as certain laws and regulations may require audit reports to be made publicly available, the auditor is cautioned not to include names, Social Security numbers, other personal identification, or other potentially sensitive information in the body of the audit reports or any attached or referenced schedules or letters.) The following specific information should be included according to Circular A-133 (as applicable):

    a. Identification of the federal program and specific federal award, including:

        i. The *Catalog of Federal Domestic Assistance* (CFDA) title and number.

---

[31] As discussed in the Audit and Accounting Guide *State and Local Governments*, the auditor's consideration of materiality for purposes of planning, performing, evaluating the results of, and reporting on the audit of the financial statements of a state or local government is based on opinion units.

ii. The federal award number and year.
   iii. The name of the federal agency.
   iv. The name of the applicable pass-through entity.

   When information such as the CFDA title and number or the federal award number is not available, the auditor should provide the best information available to describe the federal award. (Chapter 7 of this guide discusses an alternative for presentation if a CFDA number is not available.)

   b. The criteria or specific requirement upon which the audit finding is based, including the statutory, regulatory, or other citation.
   c. The condition found, including facts that support the deficiency identified in the audit finding.
   d. Identification of questioned costs and how they were computed.
   e. Information to provide a proper perspective for judging the prevalence and consequences of the audit findings (for example, whether the audit findings represent an isolated instance or a systemic problem). Where appropriate, the instances identified should be related to the universe and the number of cases examined and be quantified in terms of the dollar value.
   f. The possible asserted effect to provide sufficient information to the auditee and federal agency (or pass-through entity, in the case of a subrecipient) to permit them to determine the cause and effect, to facilitate prompt and proper corrective action.
   g. Recommendations to prevent future occurrences of the deficiency identified in the audit finding.

13.41 Audit findings related to federal awards also should meet the presentation requirements of *Government Auditing Standards*. Chapter 4 of this guide discusses the details that *Government Auditing Standards* requires be reported for findings. That chapter also discusses the requirement in paragraph 4.13 of *Government Auditing Standards* that the elements of a finding include the cause, as well as paragraphs 4.33–.39 of *Government Auditing Standards* that the auditor obtain and report the views of responsible officials concerning the findings, conclusions, and recommendations, including planned corrective actions.[32] Therefore, even though not specifically discussed in Circular A-133, the auditor should include as an element of each finding the cause of the finding. Further, the auditor should report management views and planned corrective actions for findings related to federal awards in the federal awards section of the schedule of findings and questioned costs. Alternatively, depending on the status of the development of the corrective action plan at the time the auditor's reports are released, the auditor may be able to refer to the corrective action plan as the required presentation of the auditee's views and planned corrective actions.

---

[32] Paragraph 4.38 of *Government Auditing Standards* states that if the auditee's comments are inconsistent or in conflict with the report's findings, conclusions, or recommendations, and are not, in the auditor's opinion, valid—or when the planned corrective actions do not adequately address the auditor's recommendations—the auditor should state reasons for disagreeing with the comments or planned corrective actions. That requirement subsumes the requirement in Section 510(b)(8) of Circular A-133 that audit findings include the views of responsible officials when there is disagreement with the audit findings, to the extent practical.

Other Preparation Guidance

13.42 Each audit finding in the schedule of findings and questioned costs should include a reference number to allow for easy referencing of the audit findings during follow-up. Going forward, the required format for assigning reference numbers is to use the fiscal year being audited as the beginning digits of each reference number, followed by a three digit numeric sequence.[33] For example, findings identified and reported in the audit of fiscal year 20X1 would be assigned reference numbers 20X1-001, 20X1-002, and so forth.

13.43 The auditor is required to issue a schedule of findings and questioned costs for every Circular A-133 audit, regardless of whether any findings or questioned costs are noted. That is because Circular A-133 requires that one section of the schedule summarize the audit results. (See paragraphs 13.33–.34.) In a situation in which there are no findings or questioned costs, the auditor should prepare the summary of auditor's results section of the schedule and either omit the other sections or include them, indicating that no matters were reported.

Communicating Other Findings to Management

13.44 The schedule of findings and questioned costs should include all audit findings required to be reported under Circular A-133. A separate written communication (such as a communication sometimes referred to as a management letter) may not be used to communicate such matters to the auditee in lieu of reporting them as audit findings in accordance with Circular A-133. See the discussion beginning at paragraph 13.33 for information on Circular A-133 requirements for the schedule of findings and questioned costs. If there are other matters that do not meet the Circular A-133 requirements for reporting but, in the auditor's judgment, warrant the attention of those charged with governance, they should be communicated in writing or orally. If such a communication is provided in writing to the auditee, there is no requirement for that communication to be referenced in the Circular A-133 report. See table 13-2 for more information.

Summary Schedule of Prior Audit Findings and Corrective Action Plan [34]

13.45 The auditee is responsible for follow-up and corrective action on all audit findings. As part of this responsibility, the auditee should prepare a summary schedule of prior audit findings. The auditee is not required to

---

[33] It is important to note that the audit finding reference numbers on the data collection form are required to match those on the schedule of findings and questioned costs and applicable auditor's reports. This numbering format (20XX-XXX) is the required format on the data collection form (and therefore on the schedule of findings and questioned costs).

[34] Section .315 of Circular A-133 requires the auditee to prepare a summary schedule of prior audit findings (summary schedule) and a corrective action plan. The summary schedule and corrective action plan are required to be included in the reporting package submitted to the Federal Audit Clearinghouse (FAC). Note that the inclusion of the summary schedule and corrective action plan in the reporting package is not considered to be "other information" under AU-C section 720, *Other Information in Documents Containing Audited Financial Statements* (AICPA, *Professional Standards*), or "supplementary information" under AU-C section 725, as it does not fit the criteria for such in either AU-C section.

prepare a summary schedule of prior audit findings if there are no matters reportable therein. The auditee also should prepare a corrective action plan that addresses each of the current-year audit findings.[35] The summary schedule of prior audit findings and the corrective action plan, both of which are part of the reporting package, should include the reference numbers the auditor assigns to audit findings in the schedule of findings and questioned costs. This numbering (or other identification) should include the fiscal year in which the finding initially occurred.

13.46 The auditor should follow up on prior audit findings, perform procedures to assess the reasonableness of the summary schedule of prior audit findings prepared by the auditee, and report, as a current-year audit finding, when the auditor concludes that the summary schedule of prior audit findings materially misrepresents the status of any prior audit finding in accordance with the requirements of Section 500(e) of Circular A-133. (Chapter 10 of this guide discusses follow-up procedures.)

13.47 The auditor has no responsibility for the corrective action plan; however, the auditor may be separately engaged by the auditee for assistance in developing appropriate corrective actions in response to audit findings. The auditor may find the auditee's corrective action plan useful in performing follow-up on prior audit findings (in addition to the schedule of prior audit findings) because it may provide an indication of the corrective steps planned by the auditee.

Data Collection Form

13.48 Circular A-133 states that the auditee should submit a data collection form (Form SF-SAC) that states whether the audit was completed in accordance with Circular A-133 and provides information about the auditee, its federal programs, and the results of the audit. This form is not part of the reporting package. The information required to be included in the form, however, represents a summary of the information contained in the reporting package, including the auditor's reports and the auditee's schedule of expenditures of federal awards. The auditee completes the data collection form online (through the FAC website at http://harvester.census.gov/sac/) and electronically certifies it (via an online signature) upon submission.

13.49 In addition, the auditor is required to complete certain sections of the data collection form online (for example, auditor contact information, and information on the results of the financial statement audit and the Circular A-133 compliance audit of federal programs) and electronically sign an auditor statement provided on the form. The auditor statement indicates, at a minimum, the source of the information included in the form, the auditor's responsibility for the information, that the form is not a substitute for the reporting package, and that the content of the form is limited to the data elements prescribed by the OMB. The date the auditor signs the statement indicates the completion date of the form as it relates to the auditor. The wording of the

---

[35] Paragraph 4.33 of *Government Auditing Standards* states that the auditor should obtain and report the views of responsible auditee officials concerning the findings, conclusions, and recommendations, as well as planned corrective actions. Paragraphs 13.37 and 13.41 discuss the interaction of that *Government Auditing Standards* requirement and the Circular A-133 requirement that the auditee prepare a corrective action plan.

auditor's statement section of the data collection form indicates that no additional procedures were performed since the date of the audit reports. This wording releases the auditor from any subsequent-event responsibility with regard to the timing of the completion of the form and the completion of the audit.

13.50 The data collection form and related instructions can be accessed from the FAC's website at http://harvester.census.gov/sac. The form number is SF-SAC.[36] The FAC requires electronic submission of the data collection form via an online Internet Data Entry System.

Submission of Reporting Package and Data Collection Form

13.51 The auditee is responsible for electronically submitting the data collection form and the reporting package, including the auditor's reports. After the data collection form is completed and the reporting package is uploaded to the FAC website (http://harvester.census.gov/sac/) by the auditee, certification by the auditee and a signature by the auditor on the auditor statement (described in paragraphs 13.48–.50) completes the submission. The auditee should submit the data collection form and the reporting package within the earlier of 30 days after the receipt of the auditor's reports or 9 months after the end of the audit period, unless a longer period is agreed to in advance by the cognizant or oversight agency for audit.[37]

Submission by Subrecipients

13.52 In addition to the submission requirements discussed in paragraph 13.51, auditees that also are subrecipients should submit to each pass-through entity one copy of the reporting package when the schedule of findings and questioned costs disclosed audit findings related to federal awards that the pass-through entity provided or when the summary schedule of prior audit findings reported the status of any audit findings related to federal awards that the pass-through entity provided. When a subrecipient is not required to submit a reporting package to a pass-through entity, the subrecipient instead should provide written notification to the pass-through entity that

- an audit of the subrecipient was conducted in accordance with Circular A-133 (including the period covered by the audit and the

---

[36] The OMB periodically revises the data collection form and its accompanying instructions. As of the date of this guide the latest version of the form available on the FAC website is the data collection form for 2013–2015 audits. Auditors are cautioned to make sure they complete the version of the form and instructions that applies to the fiscal year audited.

[37] Federal agencies are no longer granting extensions to due dates for single audit submissions. If circumstances will result in a late submission and the auditee or auditor wishes to inform the federal government that the required submission will be late, the suggested way to do so is to contact the federal oversight or cognizant agency for the audit (contact information is available at http://harvester.census.gov/fac/APPX3.htm).

Appendix 7 of the *OMB Compliance Supplement* clarifies that in order for an entity to meet the criteria for low-risk auditee status in the current year, the prior two years' audits must have met the requirements of Circular A-133, including report submission to the FAC by the due date. As stated in the *Compliance Supplement*, a report submission is considered late if the entity is not in compliance with the nine month due date rule or other revised due date in the case of a properly approved extension. Appendix 7 of the *Compliance Supplement* also includes suggested procedures to identify FAC submissions that do not meet the due date.

name, amount, and CFDA number of the federal awards provided by the pass-through entity).

- the schedule of findings and questioned costs disclosed no audit findings related to the federal awards that the pass-through entity provided.

- the summary schedule of prior audit findings did not report on the status of any audit findings related to the federal awards that the pass-through entity provided.

A subrecipient may submit a copy of the reporting package to a pass-through entity to comply with this notification requirement.

Distribution of Reporting Package to Federal Agencies

13.53 Once the reporting package is uploaded to the FAC, the FAC will distribute the reporting package to the appropriate federal agencies identified in the data collection form.

13.54 If the auditee or auditor revises a previous submission or other communication made to the FAC, such changes are done on the FAC website. See the FAC website for the most current information on the process for situations in which there are revisions to the form or other communication, including instructions for submitting those revisions to the FAC.

Freedom of Information Act and Similar Laws and Regulations

13.55 Often, federal, state, and local laws and regulations, such as the Freedom of Information Act (*Government Organization and Employees*, *U.S. Code* 5, Section 552), require governments to release certain documents, including audit reports and other required written communications of entities for which the government has oversight responsibilities, to members of the press and the general public. Other laws and regulations require that audit reports of governments be made publicly available. Accordingly, the auditor is cautioned not to include names, Social Security numbers, other personal identification, or other potentially sensitive matters in the body of audit reports or any attached or referenced schedules or letters.

Transition Considerations Related to the Uniform Guidance

13.56 Although, as noted in the "Transition Considerations Related to the Uniform Guidance" section in chapter 6, auditors may be required to test compliance in a Circular A-133 compliance audit using post-Uniform Guidance requirements, there is no related change needed to the auditor's report on compliance and on internal control over compliance related to major federal programs. This is because the report references the testing of types of compliance requirements described in the *Compliance Supplement*. This broad reference to the *Compliance Supplement* covers both testing performed using pre-Uniform Guidance requirements and post-Uniform Guidance requirements.

13.57 Once the Uniform Guidance audit requirements become effective, a subrecipient is no longer required to submit its reporting package directly to a pass-through entity. In addition, the requirement that a pass-through entity retain a copy of the subrecipient reporting package is also being removed. Neither of these changes may be implemented by pass-through entities and subrecipients early (that is, they are not able to be implemented until such time that the subrecipient and pass-through entity become subject to an audit under the Uniform Guidance).

13.58

Appendix—Illustrative Auditor's Reports Under Circular A-133

This appendix contains examples of the report on compliance with requirements that could have a direct and material effect on each major federal program and on internal control over compliance issued under Office of Management and Budget (OMB) Circular A-133, *Audits of States, Local Governments, and Non-Profit Organizations* (Circular A-133), in various circumstances for a Circular A-133 compliance audit as discussed in this chapter. The following table lists the illustrative reports. Auditors, using professional judgment, may adapt these examples to other situations not specifically addressed in this guide.

Example No.	Title
13-1	Report on Compliance for Each Major Federal Program; Report on Internal Control Over Compliance; and Report on Schedule of Expenditures of Federal Awards Required by OMB Circular A-133 (*Unmodified Opinion on Compliance for Each Major Federal Program; No Material Weaknesses or Significant Deficiencies in Internal Control Over Compliance Identified*)
13-2	Report on Compliance for Each Major Federal Program; Report on Internal Control Over Compliance; and Report on Schedule of Expenditures of Federal Awards Required by OMB Circular A-133 (*Unmodified Opinion on Compliance for Each Major Federal Program; Significant Deficiencies in Internal Control Over Compliance Identified*)
13-3	Report on Compliance for Each Major Federal Program; Report on Internal Control Over Compliance; and Report on Schedule of Expenditures of Federal Awards Required by OMB Circular A-133 (*Unmodified Opinion on Compliance for Each Major Federal Program; Material Weaknesses in Internal Control Over Compliance Identified; No Significant Deficiencies in Internal Control Over Compliance Identified*)
13-4	Report on Compliance for Each Major Federal Program; Report on Internal Control Over Compliance; and Report on Schedule of Expenditures of Federal Awards Required by OMB Circular A-133 (*Qualified Opinion on Compliance for One Major Federal Program; Unmodified Opinion on Compliance on Each of the Other Major Federal Programs; Material Weaknesses and Significant Deficiencies in Internal Control Over Compliance Identified*)

Auditor Reporting Requirements and Other Communication Considerations 343

Example No.	Title
13-5	Report on Compliance for Each Major Federal Program; Report on Internal Control Over Compliance; and Report on Schedule of Expenditures of Federal Awards Required by OMB Circular A-133 (*Qualified Opinion on Compliance—Scope Limitation for One Major Federal Program; Unmodified Opinion on Compliance on Each of the Other Major Federal Programs; Significant Deficiencies in Internal Control Over Compliance Identified*)
13-6	Report on Compliance for Each Major Federal Program; Report on Internal Control Over Compliance; and Report on Schedule of Expenditures of Federal Awards Required by OMB Circular A-133 (*Adverse Opinion on Compliance for One Major Federal Program; Unmodified Opinion on Compliance on Each of the Other Major Federal Programs; Material Weaknesses and Significant Deficiencies in Internal Control Over Compliance Identified*)
13-7	Schedule of Findings and Questioned Costs
13-8	Report on Schedule of Expenditures of Federal Awards When the Auditor Is Issuing a Stand-Alone Report Under AU-C Section 805, *Special Considerations—Audits of Single Financial Statements and Specific Elements, Accounts, or Items of a Financial Statement* (*Unmodified Opinion on Schedule of Expenditures of Federal Awards*)

In a single audit, auditors also are required to issue (*a*) an opinion (or disclaimer of opinion) on the financial statements and on the supplementary schedule of expenditures of federal awards and (*b*) a report on internal control over financial reporting and on compliance and other matters based on an audit of financial statements performed in accordance with *Government Auditing Standards*. The appendix in chapter 4, "Auditor Reporting Requirements and Other Communication Considerations of *Government Auditing Standards*," of this guide illustrates those reports. The appendix in chapter 14, "Program-Specific Audits (Circular A-133)," of this guide illustrates the reports issued for a program-specific audit.

Example 13-1

Report on Compliance for Each Major Federal Program; Report on Internal Control Over Compliance; and Report on Schedule of Expenditures of Federal Awards Required by OMB Circular A-133

(Unmodified Opinion on Compliance for Each Major Federal Program; No Material Weaknesses or Significant Deficiencies in Internal Control Over Compliance Identified)[1]

Independent Auditor's Report

[*Appropriate Addressee*]

Report on Compliance for Each Major Federal Program

We have audited Example Entity's compliance with the types of compliance requirements[2] described in the *OMB Compliance Supplement* that could have a direct and material effect[3] on each of Example Entity's major federal programs for the year ended June 30, 20X1. Example Entity's major federal programs are identified in the summary of auditor's results section of the accompanying schedule of findings and questioned costs.[4]

---

[1] Examples 13-1–13-6 are intended to provide illustrations for various situations. Auditors, using professional judgment, may adapt these examples to other situations not specifically addressed within the illustrations. For example, the compliance section of one example may be used along with the internal control section of another. See also paragraph 13.39 concerning the need to modify this report if the federal awards section of the schedule of findings and questioned costs includes abuse findings.

[2] Under Section 510(a) of Office of Management and Budget (OMB) Circular A-133, *Audits of States, Local Governments, and Non-Profit Organizations* (Circular A-133), the auditor's determination of whether a noncompliance with the provisions of laws, regulations, contracts, and grant agreements is material for the purpose of reporting an audit finding is in relation to a type of compliance requirement for a major program or an audit objective identified in the *OMB Compliance Supplement* (*Compliance Supplement*). Further, the auditor's determination of whether a deficiency in internal control over compliance is a significant deficiency or material weakness for the purpose of reporting an audit finding is also in relation to a type of compliance requirement for a major federal program or an audit objective identified in the *Compliance Supplement*. The reference to "type of compliance requirements" used here and elsewhere in this report illustration refers to the 12 types of compliance requirements (identified using specific letters from "A" through "N") described in Part 3 of the *Compliance Supplement*. For purposes of reporting audit findings, auditors are alerted that certain of the types of compliance requirements may include multiple compliance requirements with multiple audit objectives (for example, compliance requirement "G" covers three separate requirements [matching, level of effort, and earmarking], and "N" covers separate requirements specific to each individual special test and provision).

[3] AU-C section 935, *Compliance Audits* (AICPA, *Professional Standards*), defines *applicable compliance requirements* as the compliance requirements that are subject to the compliance audit. According to Section 505 of Circular A-133, the auditor's report on compliance with laws, regulations, and the provisions of contracts or grant agreements should include an opinion (or disclaimer of opinion) regarding whether the auditee complied with laws, regulations, and the provisions of contracts or grant agreements that could have a direct and material effect on each major program. Therefore, in a Circular A-133 compliance audit, the *applicable compliance* requirements, as the term is used in AU-C section 935, are those that could have a direct and material effect on a major federal program. Accordingly, for the purpose of adapting AU-C section 935 to a Circular A-133 compliance audit, the term *applicable* has been replaced by *direct and material* when referencing such compliance requirements in this report. See also footnote 2 of this appendix for a discussion related to the determination of material noncompliance.

[4] As discussed in paragraph 13.32 and in chapter 6, "Planning Considerations of Circular A-133," of this guide, there are situations in which the audit of federal awards may not encompass the entirety of the auditee's operations. In this case, the operations that are not included should be identified in a separate paragraph following the first paragraph of the report. An example of such a paragraph follows:

(continued)

Management's Responsibility

Management is responsible for compliance with the requirements of laws, regulations, contracts, and grants applicable to its federal programs.

Auditor's Responsibility

Our responsibility is to express an opinion on compliance for each of Example Entity's major federal programs based on our audit of the types of compliance requirements referred to above. We conducted our audit of compliance in accordance with auditing standards generally accepted in the United States of America; the standards applicable to financial audits contained in *Government Auditing Standards*, issued by the Comptroller General of the United States; and OMB Circular A-133, *Audits of States, Local Governments, and Non-Profit Organizations*. Those standards and OMB Circular A-133 require that we plan and perform the audit to obtain reasonable assurance about whether noncompliance with the types of compliance requirements referred to above that could have a direct and material effect on a major federal program occurred. An audit includes examining, on a test basis, evidence about Example Entity's compliance with those requirements and performing such other procedures as we considered necessary in the circumstances.

We believe that our audit provides a reasonable basis for our opinion on compliance for each major federal program. However, our audit does not provide a legal determination of Example Entity's compliance.

Opinion on Each Major Federal Program

In our opinion, Example Entity complied, in all material respects, with the types of compliance requirements referred to above that could have a direct and material effect on each of its major federal programs for the year ended June 30, 20X1.

Other Matters[5]

The results of our auditing procedures disclosed instances of noncompliance, which are required to be reported in accordance with OMB Circular A-133 and which are described in the accompanying schedule of findings and questioned costs as items [*list the reference numbers of the related findings, for example, 20X1-001 and 20X1-002*].[6] Our opinion on each major federal program is not modified with respect to these matters.

Example Entity's response to the noncompliance findings identified in our audit are described in the accompanying [*insert name of document containing*

(footnote continued)

Example Entity's basic financial statements include the operations of the [*identify organizational unit, such as a governmental component unit, an operating unit, or a department*], which received [*include dollar amount*] in federal awards which is not included in the schedule during the year ended June 30, 20X1. Our audit, described below, did not include the operations of [*identify organizational unit*] because [*state the reason for the omission, such as the organizational unit engaged other auditors to perform an audit in accordance with Circular A-133*].

[5] When there are no findings that are required to be reported, and thus, no management response to findings, this "Other Matters" section of the report would be omitted.

[6] The auditor may also consider adding a table to this section of the report, similar to the illustration provided in footnote 49, to more clearly communicate the other findings that are being reported and the programs and requirements to which they relate.

management's response to the auditor's findings; for example, schedule of findings and questioned costs and/or corrective action plan]. Example Entity's response was not subjected to the auditing procedures applied in the audit of compliance and, accordingly, we express no opinion on the response.[7]

Report on Internal Control Over Compliance[8]

Management of Example Entity is responsible for establishing and maintaining effective internal control over compliance with the types of compliance requirements referred to above. In planning and performing our audit of compliance, we considered Example Entity's internal control over compliance with the types of requirements that could have a direct and material effect on each major federal program to determine the auditing procedures that are appropriate in the circumstances for the purpose of expressing an opinion on compliance for each major federal program and to test and report on internal control over compliance in accordance with OMB Circular A-133, but not for the purpose of expressing an opinion on the effectiveness of internal control over compliance. Accordingly, we do not express an opinion on the effectiveness of Example Entity's internal control over compliance.

A *deficiency in internal control over compliance* exists when the design or operation of a control over compliance does not allow management or employees, in the normal course of performing their assigned functions, to prevent, or detect and correct, noncompliance with a type of compliance requirement of a federal program on a timely basis. A *material weakness in internal control over compliance* is a deficiency, or combination of deficiencies, in internal control over compliance, such that there is a reasonable possibility that material noncompliance with a type of compliance requirement of a federal program will not be prevented, or detected and corrected, on a timely basis. A *significant deficiency in internal control over compliance* is a deficiency, or a combination of deficiencies, in internal control over compliance with a type of compliance requirement of a federal program that is less severe than a material weakness in internal control over compliance, yet important enough to merit attention by those charged with governance.

Our consideration of internal control over compliance was for the limited purpose described in the first paragraph of this section and was not designed to identify all deficiencies in internal control over compliance that might be material weaknesses or significant deficiencies. We did not identify any deficiencies in internal control over compliance that we consider to be material weaknesses. However, material weaknesses may exist that have not been identified.

---

[7] Although the auditor does not audit management's response to identified findings, the auditor does have certain responsibilities related to reporting the views of responsible officials under *Government Auditing Standards*. As noted in paragraph 4.33 of *Government Auditing Standards*, auditors should obtain and report the views of responsible officials concerning the findings, conclusions, and recommendations, as well as planned corrective actions. See paragraphs 13.38g and 13.45 for further discussion.

[8] Examples 13-1–13-6 illustrate combined reports that also include the reporting on internal control over compliance. If an auditor prefers to issue a separate report on internal control over compliance this section would be omitted from the report. AU-C section 935 includes required elements for separate reporting on internal control over compliance.

Auditor Reporting Requirements and Other Communication Considerations

The purpose of this report on internal control over compliance is solely to describe the scope of our testing of internal control over compliance and the results of that testing based on the requirements of OMB Circular A-133. Accordingly, this report is not suitable for any other purpose.[9]

Report on Schedule of Expenditures of Federal Awards Required by OMB Circular A-133[10,11]

We have audited the financial statements of Example Entity as of and for the year ended June 30, 20X1, and have issued our report thereon dated August 15, 20X1, which contained an unmodified opinion on those financial statements. Our audit was conducted for the purpose of forming an opinion on the financial statements as a whole. The accompanying schedule of expenditures of federal awards is presented for purposes of additional analysis as required by OMB Circular A-133 and is not a required part of the financial statements. Such information is the responsibility of management and was derived from and relates directly to the underlying accounting and other records used to prepare the financial statements. The information has been subjected to the auditing procedures applied in the audit of the financial statements and certain additional procedures, including comparing and reconciling such information directly to the underlying accounting and other records used to prepare the financial statements or to the financial statements themselves, and other additional procedures in accordance with auditing standards generally accepted in the United States of America. In our opinion, the schedule of expenditure

---

[9] This paragraph has been adapted from AU-C section 905, *Alert That Restricts the Use of the Auditor's Written Communication* (AICPA, *Professional Standards*), to relate to the reporting on internal control over compliance that is required in an audit of compliance in accordance with Circular A-133.

[10] The wording of this report is based AU-C section 725, *Supplementary Information in Relation to the Financial Statements as a Whole* (AICPA, *Professional Standards*).

[11] As noted in paragraph 13.06, this guide recommends reporting on the schedule of expenditures of federal awards in the report on the financial statements. Chapter 4, "Auditor Reporting Requirements and Other Communication Considerations of *Government Auditing Standards*," illustrates the reporting on the schedule when such reporting is included in the financial statement report. However, as noted in paragraph 13.19, there may be certain circumstances when the auditor's report on the schedule is incorporated into the report issued to meet the requirements of OMB Circular A-133. Therefore, examples 13-1–13-6 illustrate the inclusion of the auditor's in-relation-to reporting on the schedule of expenditures of federal awards. Its inclusion in these examples is not intended to imply a best practice. If the in-relation-to reporting on the schedule is included in the report on the financial statements or in a separate report, this section would be omitted and the title of the report would be modified as follows: "Report on Compliance for Each Major Federal Program and Report on Internal Control Over Compliance Required by OMB Circular A-133."

of federal awards is fairly stated in all material respects in relation to the financial statements as a whole.[12]

[*Auditor's signature*]

[*Auditor's city and state*][13]

[*Date of the auditor's report*][14]

---

[12] The wording of this report on the schedule of expenditures of federal awards refers to the financial statements of a non-governmental entity. For audits of governmental entities, it would be replaced with the following:

Report on Schedule of Expenditures of Federal Awards Required by OMB Circular A-133

We have audited the financial statements of the governmental activities, the business-type activities, the aggregate discretely presented component units, each major fund, and the aggregate remaining fund information of Example Entity as of and for the year ended June 30, 20X1, and the related notes to the financial statements, which collectively comprise Example Entity's basic financial statements. We issued our report thereon dated August 15, 20X1, which contained unmodified opinions on those financial statements. Our audit was conducted for the purpose of forming opinions on the financial statements that collectively comprise the basic financial statements. The accompanying schedule of expenditures of federal awards is presented for purposes of additional analysis as required by OMB Circular A-133 and is not a required part of the basic financial statements. Such information is the responsibility of management and was derived from and relates directly to the underlying accounting and other records used to prepare the basic financial statements. The information has been subjected to the auditing procedures applied in the audit of the financial statements and certain additional procedures, including comparing and reconciling such information directly to the underlying accounting and other records used to prepare the basic financial statements or to the basic financial statements themselves, and other additional procedures in accordance with auditing standards generally accepted in the United States of America. In our opinion, the schedule of expenditure of federal awards is fairly stated in all material respects in relation to the basic financial statements as a whole.

[13] AU-C section 700, *Forming an Opinion and Reporting on Financial Statements* (AICPA, *Professional Standards*), provides that the auditor's report should name the city and state where the auditor practices. City and State on a firm's letterhead typically is sufficient to meet this requirement. Technical Questions and Answers section 9100.08, "Audit Firm With Multiple Offices on Their Company Letterhead and Effect on Report" (AICPA, *Technical Questions and Answers*), notes that when a firm's letterhead contains multiple office locations the auditor would need to indicate the city and state where the auditor practices in the auditor's report.

[14] As noted in footnote 11, examples 13-1–13-6 illustrate the inclusion of the in-relation-to opinion on the schedule of expenditures of federal awards. AU-C section 725 states that the date of the auditor's report on supplementary information (for example, the schedule of expenditures of federal awards in these illustrations) in-relation-to the financial statements as a whole should not be earlier than the date on which the auditor completed the procedures required by AU-C section 725. Therefore, when the required procedures in AU-C section 725 are completed on an earlier date than that of the auditor's "Report on Compliance for Each Major Federal Program," the auditor would dual-date this report. See the discussion beginning at paragraph 13.16 of this guide for further discussion of dating the in-relation-to reporting on the schedule of expenditures of federal awards. Illustrative wording when dual dating the report is as follows:

[Date], except for our report on the Schedule of Expenditures of Federal Awards, for which the date is [*Date the in-relation-to procedures completed*]

Example 13-2

Report on Compliance for Each Major Federal Program; Report on Internal Control Over Compliance; and Report on Schedule of Expenditures of Federal Awards Required by OMB Circular A-133

(Unmodified Opinion on Compliance for Each Major Federal Program; Significant Deficiencies in Internal Control Over Compliance Identified)[15]

<u>Independent Auditor's Report</u>

[*Appropriate Addressee*]

Report on Compliance for Each Major Federal Program

We have audited Example Entity's compliance with the types of compliance requirements[16] described in the *OMB Compliance Supplement* that could have a direct and material effect[17] on each of Example Entity's major federal programs for the year ended June 30, 20X1. Example Entity's major federal programs are identified in the summary of auditor's results section of the accompanying schedule of findings and questioned costs.[18]

Management's Responsibility

Management is responsible for compliance with the requirements of laws, regulations, contracts, and grants applicable to its federal programs.

Auditor's Responsibility

Our responsibility is to express an opinion on compliance for each of Example Entity's major federal programs based on our audit of the types of compliance requirements referred to above. We conducted our audit of compliance in accordance with auditing standards generally accepted in the United States of America; the standards applicable to financial audits contained in *Government Auditing Standards*, issued by the Comptroller General of the United States; and OMB Circular A-133, *Audits of States, Local Governments, and Non-Profit Organizations*. Those standards and OMB Circular A-133 require that we plan and perform the audit to obtain reasonable assurance about whether noncompliance with the types of compliance requirements referred to above that could have a direct and material effect on a major federal program occurred. An audit includes examining, on a test basis, evidence about Example Entity's compliance with those requirements and performing such other procedures as we considered necessary in the circumstances.

We believe that our audit provides a reasonable basis for our opinion on compliance for each major federal program. However, our audit does not provide a legal determination of Example Entity's compliance.

Opinion on Each Major Federal Program

In our opinion, Example Entity complied, in all material respects, with the types of compliance requirements referred to above that could have a direct and material effect on each of its major federal programs for the year ended June 30, 20X1.

---

[15] See footnote 1.
[16] See footnote 2.
[17] See footnote 3.
[18] See footnote 4.

Other Matters[19]

The results of our auditing procedures disclosed instances of noncompliance, which are required to be reported in accordance with OMB Circular A-133 and which are described in the accompanying schedule of findings and questioned costs as items [*list the reference numbers of the related findings, for example, 20X1-001 and 20X1-002*].[20] Our opinion on each major federal program is not modified with respect to these matters

Example Entity's response to the noncompliance findings identified in our audit are described in the accompanying [*insert name of document containing management's response to the auditor's findings; for example, schedule of findings and questioned costs and/or corrective action plan*]. Example Entity's response was not subjected to the auditing procedures applied in the audit of compliance and, accordingly, we express no opinion on the response.[21]

Report on Internal Control Over Compliance[22]

Management of Example Entity is responsible for establishing and maintaining effective internal control over compliance with the types of compliance requirements referred to above. In planning and performing our audit of compliance, we considered Example Entity's internal control over compliance with the types of requirements that could have a direct and material effect on each major federal program to determine the auditing procedures that are appropriate in the circumstances for the purpose of expressing an opinion on compliance for each major federal program and to test and report on internal control over compliance in accordance with OMB Circular A-133, but not for the purpose of expressing an opinion on the effectiveness of internal control over compliance. Accordingly, we do not express an opinion on the effectiveness of Example Entity's internal control over compliance.

A *deficiency in internal control over compliance* exists when the design or operation of a control over compliance does not allow management or employees, in the normal course of performing their assigned functions, to prevent, or detect and correct, noncompliance with a type of compliance requirement of a federal program on a timely basis. A *material weakness in internal control over compliance* is a deficiency, or combination of deficiencies, in internal control over compliance, such that there is a reasonable possibility that material noncompliance with a type of compliance requirement of a federal program will not be prevented, or detected and corrected, on a timely basis. A *significant deficiency in internal control over compliance* is a deficiency, or a combination of deficiencies, in internal control over compliance with a type of compliance requirement of a federal program that is less severe than a material weakness in internal control over compliance, yet important enough to merit attention by those charged with governance.

Our consideration of internal control over compliance was for the limited purpose described in the first paragraph of this section and was not designed to identify all deficiencies in internal control over compliance that might be material weaknesses or significant deficiencies and therefore, material weaknesses or significant deficiencies may exist that were not identified. We did not identify any deficiencies in internal control over compliance that we consider to be

---

[19] See footnote 5.
[20] See footnote 6.
[21] See footnote 7.
[22] See footnote 8.

material weaknesses. However, we identified certain deficiencies in internal control over compliance, as described in the accompanying schedule of findings and questioned costs as items [*list the reference numbers of the related findings, for example, 20X1-003, 20X1-004, and 20X1-005*],[23] that we consider to be significant deficiencies.

Example Entity's response to the internal control over compliance findings identified in our audit are described in the accompanying [*insert name of document containing management's response to the auditor's findings; for example, schedule of findings and questioned costs and/or corrective action plan*]. Example Entity's response was not subjected to the auditing procedures applied in the audit of compliance and, accordingly, we express no opinion on the response.

The purpose of this report on internal control over compliance is solely to describe the scope of our testing of internal control over compliance and the results of that testing based on the requirements of OMB Circular A-133. Accordingly, this report is not suitable for any other purpose.[24]

Report on Schedule of Expenditures of Federal Awards Required by OMB Circular A-133[25,26]

We have audited the financial statements of Example Entity as of and for the year ended June 30, 20X1, and have issued our report thereon dated August 15, 20X1, which contained an unmodified opinion on those financial statements. Our audit was conducted for the purpose of forming an opinion on the financial statements as a whole. The accompanying schedule of expenditures of federal awards is presented for purposes of additional analysis as required by OMB Circular A-133 and is not a required part of the financial statements. Such information is the responsibility of management and was derived from and relates directly to the underlying accounting and other records used to prepare the financial statements. The information has been subjected to the auditing procedures applied in the audit of the financial statements and certain additional procedures, including comparing and reconciling such information directly to the underlying accounting and other records used to prepare the financial statements or to the financial statements themselves, and other additional procedures in accordance with auditing standards generally accepted in the United States of America. In our opinion, the schedule of expenditure of federal awards is fairly stated in all material respects in relation to the financial statements as a whole.[27]

[*Auditor's signature*]

[*Auditor's city and state*][28]

[*Date of the auditor's report*][29]

---

[23] The auditor may also consider adding a table to this section of the report, similar to the illustration provided in footnote 49, to more clearly communicate any material weaknesses or significant deficiencies that were identified and the programs and requirements to which they relate.

[24] See footnote 9.

[25] See footnote 10.

[26] See footnote 11.

[27] See footnote 12.

[28] See footnote 13.

[29] See footnote 14.

Example 13-3

Report on Compliance for Each Major Federal Program; Report on Internal Control Over Compliance; and Report on Schedule of Expenditures of Federal Awards Required by OMB Circular A-133

(Unmodified Opinion on Compliance for Each Major Federal Program; Material Weaknesses in Internal Control Over Compliance Identified; No Significant Deficiencies in Internal Control Over Compliance Identified)[30]

Independent Auditor's Report

[*Appropriate Addressee*]

Report on Compliance for Each Major Federal Program

We have audited Example Entity's compliance with the types of compliance requirements[31] described in the *OMB Compliance Supplement* that could have a direct and material effect[32] on each of Example Entity's major federal programs for the year ended June 30, 20X1. Example Entity's major federal programs are identified in the summary of auditor's results section of the accompanying schedule of findings and questioned costs.[33]

Management's Responsibility

Management is responsible for compliance with the requirements of laws, regulations, contracts, and grants applicable to its federal programs.

Auditor's Responsibility

Our responsibility is to express an opinion on compliance for each of Example Entity's major federal programs based on our audit of the types of compliance requirements referred to above. We conducted our audit of compliance in accordance with auditing standards generally accepted in the United States of America; the standards applicable to financial audits contained in *Government Auditing Standards*, issued by the Comptroller General of the United States; and OMB Circular A-133, *Audits of States, Local Governments, and Non-Profit Organizations*. Those standards and OMB Circular A-133 require that we plan and perform the audit to obtain reasonable assurance about whether noncompliance with the types of compliance requirements referred to above that could have a direct and material effect on a major federal program occurred. An audit includes examining, on a test basis, evidence about Example Entity's compliance with those requirements and performing such other procedures as we considered necessary in the circumstances.

We believe that our audit provides a reasonable basis for our opinion on compliance for each major federal program. However, our audit does not provide a legal determination of Example Entity's compliance.

Opinion on Each Major Federal Program

In our opinion, Example Entity complied, in all material respects, with the types of compliance requirements referred to above that could have a direct and material effect on each of its major federal programs for the year ended June 30, 20X1.

---

[30] See footnote 1.
[31] See footnote 2.
[32] See footnote 3.
[33] See footnote 4.

Auditor Reporting Requirements and Other Communication Considerations **353**

Other Matters[34]

The results of our auditing procedures disclosed instances of noncompliance, which are required to be reported in accordance with OMB Circular A-133 and which are described in the accompanying schedule of findings and questioned costs as items [*list the reference numbers of the related findings, for example, 20X1-001 and 20X1-002*].[35] Our opinion on each major federal program is not modified with respect to these matters.

Example Entity's response to the noncompliance findings identified in our audit are described in the accompanying [*insert name of document containing management's response to the auditor's findings; for example, schedule of findings and questioned costs and/or corrective action plan*]. Example Entity's response was not subjected to the auditing procedures applied in the audit of compliance and, accordingly, we express no opinion on the response.[36]

Report on Internal Control Over Compliance[37]

Management of Example Entity is responsible for establishing and maintaining effective internal control over compliance with the types of compliance requirements referred to above. In planning and performing our audit of compliance, we considered Example Entity's internal control over compliance with the types of requirements that could have a direct and material effect on each major federal program to determine the auditing procedures that are appropriate in the circumstances for the purpose of expressing an opinion on compliance for each major federal program and to test and report on internal control over compliance in accordance with OMB Circular A-133, but not for the purpose of expressing an opinion on the effectiveness of internal control over compliance. Accordingly, we do not express an opinion on the effectiveness of Example Entity's internal control over compliance.

A *deficiency in internal control over compliance* exists when the design or operation of a control over compliance does not allow management or employees, in the normal course of performing their assigned functions, to prevent, or detect and correct, noncompliance with a type of compliance requirement of a federal program on a timely basis. A *material weakness in internal control over compliance* is a deficiency, or combination of deficiencies, in internal control over compliance, such that there is a reasonable possibility that material noncompliance with a type of compliance requirement of a federal program will not be prevented, or detected and corrected, on a timely basis. A *significant deficiency in internal control over compliance* is a deficiency, or a combination of deficiencies, in internal control over compliance with a type of compliance requirement of a federal program that is less severe than a material weakness in internal control over compliance, yet important enough to merit attention by those charged with governance.

Our consideration of internal control over compliance was for the limited purpose described in the first paragraph of this section and was not designed to identify all deficiencies in internal control over compliance that might be material weaknesses or significant deficiencies and therefore, material weaknesses or significant deficiencies may exist that were not identified. We identified certain deficiencies in internal control over compliance, as described in the

---

[34] See footnote 5.
[35] See footnote 6.
[36] See footnote 7.
[37] See footnote 8.

accompanying schedule of findings and questioned costs as items [*list the reference numbers of the related findings, for example, 20X1-003, 20X1-004, and 20X1-005*], that we consider to be material weaknesses.

Example Entity's response to the internal control over compliance findings identified in our audit are described in the accompanying [*insert name of document containing management's response to the auditor's findings; for example, schedule of findings and questioned costs and / or corrective action plan*]. Example Entity's response was not subjected to the auditing procedures applied in the audit of compliance and, accordingly, we express no opinion on the response.

The purpose of this report on internal control over compliance is solely to describe the scope of our testing of internal control over compliance and the results of that testing based on the requirements of OMB Circular A-133. Accordingly, this report is not suitable for any other purpose.[38]

Report on Schedule of Expenditures of Federal Awards Required by OMB Circular A-133[39,40]

We have audited the financial statements of Example Entity as of and for the year ended June 30, 20X1, and have issued our report thereon dated August 15, 20X1, which contained an unmodified opinion on those financial statements. Our audit was conducted for the purpose of forming an opinion on the financial statements as a whole. The accompanying schedule of expenditures of federal awards is presented for purposes of additional analysis as required by OMB Circular A-133 and is not a required part of the financial statements. Such information is the responsibility of management and was derived from and relates directly to the underlying accounting and other records used to prepare the financial statements. The information has been subjected to the auditing procedures applied in the audit of the financial statements and certain additional procedures, including comparing and reconciling such information directly to the underlying accounting and other records used to prepare the financial statements or to the financial statements themselves, and other additional procedures in accordance with auditing standards generally accepted in the United States of America. In our opinion, the schedule of expenditure of federal awards is fairly stated in all material respects in relation to the financial statements as a whole.[41]

[*Auditor's signature*]

[*Auditor's city and state*][42]

[*Date of the auditor's report*][43]

---

[38] See footnote 9.
[39] See footnote 10.
[40] See footnote 11.
[41] See footnote 12.
[42] See footnote 13.
[43] See footnote 14.

Example 13-4

Report on Compliance for Each Major Federal Program; Report on Internal Control Over Compliance; and Report on Schedule of Expenditures of Federal Awards Required by OMB Circular A-133

(Qualified Opinion on Compliance for One Major Federal Program; Unmodified Opinion on Compliance on Each of the Other Major Federal Programs; Material Weaknesses and Significant Deficiencies in Internal Control Over Compliance Identified)[44]

Independent Auditor's Report

[*Appropriate Addressee*]

Report on Compliance for Each Major Federal Program

We have audited Example Entity's compliance with the types of compliance requirements[45] described in the *OMB Compliance Supplement* that could have a direct and material effect[46] on each of Example Entity's major federal programs for the year ended June 30, 20X1. Example Entity's major federal programs are identified in the summary of auditor's results section of the accompanying schedule of findings and questioned costs.[47]

Management's Responsibility

Management is responsible for compliance with the requirements of laws, regulations, contracts, and grants applicable to its federal programs.

Auditor's Responsibility

Our responsibility is to express an opinion on compliance for each of Example Entity's major federal programs based on our audit of the types of compliance requirements referred to above. We conducted our audit of compliance in accordance with auditing standards generally accepted in the United States of America; the standards applicable to financial audits contained in *Government Auditing Standards*, issued by the Comptroller General of the United States; and OMB Circular A-133, *Audits of States, Local Governments, and Non-Profit Organizations*. Those standards and OMB Circular A-133 require that we plan and perform the audit to obtain reasonable assurance about whether noncompliance with the types of compliance requirements referred to above that could have a direct and material effect on a major federal program occurred. An audit includes examining, on a test basis, evidence about Example Entity's compliance with those requirements and performing such other procedures as we considered necessary in the circumstances.

We believe that our audit provides a reasonable basis for our opinion on compliance for each major federal program. However, our audit does not provide a legal determination of Example Entity's compliance.

---

[44] See footnote 1.
[45] See footnote 2.
[46] See footnote 3.
[47] See footnote 4.

Basis for Qualified Opinion on [Identify Major Federal Program][48,49]

As described in the accompanying schedule of findings and questioned costs, Example Entity did not comply with requirements regarding [*identify the major federal program and associated finding number(s) matched to the type(s) of compliance requirements; for example, CFDA 93.600 Head Start as described in finding numbers 20X1-001 for Eligibility and 20X1-002 for Reporting*]. Compliance with such requirements is necessary, in our opinion, for Example Entity to comply with the requirements applicable to that program.

Qualified Opinion on [Identify Major Federal Program]

In our opinion, except for the noncompliance described in the Basis for Qualified Opinion paragraph, Example Entity complied, in all material respects, with the types of compliance requirements referred to above that could have a direct and material effect on [*identify the major federal program*] for the year ended June 30, 20X1.

Unmodified Opinion on Each of the Other Major Federal Programs[50]

In our opinion, Example Entity complied, in all material respects, with the types of compliance requirements referred to above that could have a direct and material effect on each of its other major federal programs identified in the summary of auditor's results section of the accompanying schedule of findings and questioned costs for the year ended June 30, 20X1.

Other Matters[51]

The results of our auditing procedures disclosed other instances of noncompliance, which are required to be reported in accordance with OMB Circular A-133 and which are described in the accompanying schedule of findings and questioned costs as items [*list the reference numbers of the related findings, for example, 20X1-003 and 20X1-004*].[52] Our opinion on each major federal program is not modified with respect to these matters.

Example Entity's response to the noncompliance findings identified in our audit are described in the accompanying [*insert name of document containing*

---

[48] The heading to this section, and the qualified opinion paragraph that follows, illustrates identifying the specific major federal programs being referred to in each heading.

[49] The auditor may also consider adding a table to more clearly communicate the basis for the qualified opinion such as the following:

As described in Findings 20X1-001 and 20X1-002 in the accompanying schedule of findings and questioned costs, Example Entity did not comply with requirements regarding the following:

Finding #	CFDA #	Program (or Cluster) Name	Compliance Requirement
20X1-001	93.600	Head Start	Eligibility
20X1-002	93.600	Head Start	Reporting

Compliance with such requirements is necessary, in our opinion, for Example Entity to comply with the requirements applicable to that program.

[50] There is nothing to preclude an auditor from including the name(s) of the federal programs for which the auditor is providing an unmodified opinion in this heading or in the opinion paragraph itself. This example illustrates referencing the other major federal programs more generally in the unmodified opinion heading and in the opinion paragraph, along with a reference to the summary of auditor's results section of the schedule of findings and questioned costs where the other major federal programs are specifically identified.

[51] See footnote 5.

[52] See footnote 6.

management's response to the auditor's findings; for example, schedule of findings and questioned costs and/or corrective action plan]. Example Entity's response was not subjected to the auditing procedures applied in the audit of compliance and, accordingly, we express no opinion on the response.[53]

Report on Internal Control Over Compliance[54]

Management of Example Entity is responsible for establishing and maintaining effective internal control over compliance with the types of compliance requirements referred to above. In planning and performing our audit of compliance, we considered Example Entity's internal control over compliance with the types of requirements that could have a direct and material effect on each major federal program to determine the auditing procedures that are appropriate in the circumstances for the purpose of expressing an opinion on compliance for each major federal program and to test and report on internal control over compliance in accordance with OMB Circular A-133, but not for the purpose of expressing an opinion on the effectiveness of internal control over compliance. Accordingly, we do not express an opinion on the effectiveness of Example Entity's internal control over compliance.

Our consideration of internal control over compliance was for the limited purpose described in the preceding paragraph and was not designed to identify all deficiencies in internal control over compliance that might be material weaknesses or significant deficiencies and therefore, material weaknesses or significant deficiencies may exist that were not identified. However, as discussed below, we identified certain deficiencies in internal control over compliance that we consider to be material weaknesses and significant deficiencies.

A *deficiency in internal control over compliance* exists when the design or operation of a control over compliance does not allow management or employees, in the normal course of performing their assigned functions, to prevent, or detect and correct, noncompliance with a type of compliance requirement of a federal program on a timely basis. A *material weakness in internal control over compliance* is a deficiency, or combination of deficiencies, in internal control over compliance, such that there is reasonable possibility that material noncompliance with a type of compliance requirement of a federal program will not be prevented, or detected and corrected, on a timely basis. We consider the deficiencies in internal control over compliance described in the accompanying schedule of findings and questioned costs as items [*list the reference numbers of the related findings, for example 20X1-005 and 20X1-006*][55] to be material weaknesses.

A *significant deficiency in internal control over compliance* is a deficiency, or a combination of deficiencies, in internal control over compliance with a type of compliance requirement of a federal program that is less severe than a material weakness in internal control over compliance, yet important enough to merit attention by those charged with governance. We consider the deficiencies in internal control over compliance described in the accompanying schedule of findings and questioned costs as items [*list the reference numbers

---

[53] See footnote 7.
[54] See footnote 8.
[55] See footnote 23.

of the related findings, for example 20X1-007 and 20X1-008][56] to be significant deficiencies.

Example Entity's response to the internal control over compliance findings identified in our audit are described in the accompanying [*insert name of document containing management's response to the auditor's findings; for example, schedule of findings and questioned costs and / or corrective action plan*]. Example Entity's response was not subjected to the auditing procedures applied in the audit of compliance and, accordingly, we express no opinion on the response.

The purpose of this report on internal control over compliance is solely to describe the scope of our testing of internal control over compliance and the results of that testing based on the requirements of OMB Circular A-133. Accordingly, this report is not suitable for any other purpose.[57]

Report on Schedule of Expenditures of Federal Awards Required by OMB Circular A-133[58,59]

We have audited the financial statements of Example Entity as of and for the year ended June 30, 20X1, and have issued our report thereon dated August 15, 20X1, which contained an unmodified opinion on those financial statements. Our audit was conducted for the purpose of forming an opinion on the financial statements as a whole. The accompanying schedule of expenditures of federal awards is presented for purposes of additional analysis as required by OMB Circular A-133 and is not a required part of the financial statements. Such information is the responsibility of management and was derived from and relates directly to the underlying accounting and other records used to prepare the financial statements. The information has been subjected to the auditing procedures applied in the audit of the financial statements and certain additional procedures, including comparing and reconciling such information directly to the underlying accounting and other records used to prepare the financial statements or to the financial statements themselves, and other additional procedures in accordance with auditing standards generally accepted in the United States of America. In our opinion, the schedule of expenditure of federal awards is fairly stated in all material respects in relation to the financial statements as a whole.[60]

[*Auditor's signature*]

[*Auditor's city and state*][61]

[*Date of the auditor's report*][62]

---

[56] See footnote 23.
[57] See footnote 9.
[58] See footnote 10.
[59] See footnote 11.
[60] See footnote 12.
[61] See footnote 13.
[62] See footnote 14.

Auditor Reporting Requirements and Other Communication Considerations **359**

Example 13-5

Report on Compliance for Each Major Federal Program; Report on Internal Control Over Compliance; and Report on Schedule of Expenditures of Federal Awards Required by OMB Circular A-133

(Qualified Opinion on Compliance—Scope Limitation for One Major Federal Program; Unmodified Opinion on Compliance on Each of the Other Major Federal Programs; Significant Deficiencies in Internal Control Over Compliance Identified)[63]

Independent Auditor's Report

[*Appropriate Addressee*]

Report on Compliance for Each Major Federal Program

We have audited Example Entity's compliance with the types of compliance requirements[64] described in the *OMB Compliance Supplement* that could have a direct and material effect[65] on each of Example Entity's major federal programs for the year ended June 30, 20X1. Example Entity's major federal programs are identified in the summary of auditor's results section of the accompanying schedule of findings and questioned costs.[66]

Management's Responsibility

Management is responsible for compliance with the requirements of laws, regulations, contracts, and grants applicable to its federal programs.

Auditor's Responsibility

Our responsibility is to express an opinion on compliance for each of Example Entity's major federal programs based on our audit of the types of compliance requirements referred to above. We conducted our audit of compliance in accordance with auditing standards generally accepted in the United States of America; the standards applicable to financial audits contained in *Government Auditing Standards*, issued by the Comptroller General of the United States; and OMB Circular A-133, *Audits of States, Local Governments, and Non-Profit Organizations*. Those standards and OMB Circular A-133 require that we plan and perform the audit to obtain reasonable assurance about whether noncompliance with the types of compliance requirements referred to above that could have a direct and material effect on a major federal program occurred. An audit includes examining, on a test basis, evidence about Example Entity's compliance with those requirements and performing such other procedures as we considered necessary in the circumstances.

We believe that our audit provides a reasonable basis for our opinion on compliance for each major federal program. However, our audit does not provide a legal determination of Example Entity's compliance.

---

[63] See footnote 1.
[64] See footnote 2.
[65] See footnote 3.
[66] See footnote 4.

Basis for Qualified Opinion on [Identify Major Federal Program][67,68]

As described in the accompanying schedule of findings and questioned costs, we were unable to obtain sufficient appropriate audit evidence supporting the compliance of Example Entity with [*identify the major federal program and associated finding number(s) matched to the type(s) of compliance requirements; for example, CFDA 93.600 Head Start as described in finding numbers 20X1-001 for Eligibility and 20X1-002 for Reporting*], consequently we were unable to determine whether Example Entity complied with those requirements applicable to that program.

Qualified Opinion on [Identify Major Federal Program]

In our opinion, except for the possible effects of the matter described in the Basis for Qualified Opinion paragraph, Example Entity complied, in all material respects, with the types of compliance requirements referred to above that could have a direct and material effect on [*identify the major federal program*] for the year ended June 30, 20X1.

Unmodified Opinion on Each of the Other Major Federal Programs[69]

In our opinion, Example Entity complied, in all material respects, with the types of compliance requirements referred to above that could have a direct and material effect on each of its other major federal programs identified in the summary of auditor's results section of the accompanying schedule of findings and questioned costs for the year ended June 30, 20X1.

Other Matters[70]

The results of our auditing procedures disclosed other instances of noncompliance, which are required to be reported in accordance with OMB Circular A-133 and which are described in the accompanying schedule of findings and questioned costs as items [*list the reference numbers of the related findings, for example, 20X1-003 and 20X1-004*].[71] Our opinion on each major federal program is not modified with respect to these matters.

Example Entity's response to the noncompliance findings identified in our audit are described in the accompanying [*insert name of document containing management's response to the auditor's findings; for example, schedule of findings and questioned costs and / or corrective action plan*]. Example Entity's response was not subjected to the auditing procedures applied in the audit of compliance and, accordingly, we express no opinion on the response.[72]

Report on Internal Control Over Compliance[73]

Management of Example Entity is responsible for establishing and maintaining effective internal control over compliance with the types of compliance

---

[67] See footnote 48.
[68] See footnote 49.
[69] See footnote 50.
[70] See footnote 5.
[71] See footnote 6.
[72] See footnote 7.
[73] See footnote 8.

requirements referred to above. In planning and performing our audit of compliance, we considered Example Entity's internal control over compliance with the types of requirements that could have a direct and material effect on each major federal program to determine the auditing procedures that are appropriate in the circumstances for the purpose of expressing an opinion on compliance for each major federal program and to test and report on internal control over compliance in accordance with OMB Circular A-133, but not for the purpose of expressing an opinion on the effectiveness of internal control over compliance. Accordingly, we do not express an opinion on the effectiveness of Example Entity's internal control over compliance.

A *deficiency in internal control over compliance* exists when the design or operation of a control over compliance does not allow management or employees, in the normal course of performing their assigned functions, to prevent, or detect and correct, noncompliance with a type of compliance requirement of a federal program on a timely basis. A *material weakness in internal control over compliance* is a deficiency, or combination of deficiencies, in internal control over compliance, such that there is a reasonable possibility that material noncompliance with a type of compliance requirement of a federal program will not be prevented, or detected and corrected, on a timely basis. A *significant deficiency in internal control over compliance* is a deficiency, or a combination of deficiencies, in internal control over compliance with a type of compliance requirement of a federal program that is less severe than a material weakness in internal control over compliance, yet important enough to merit attention by those charged with governance.

Our consideration of internal control over compliance was for the limited purpose described in the first paragraph of this section and was not designed to identify all deficiencies in internal control over compliance that might be material weaknesses or significant deficiencies and therefore, material weaknesses or significant deficiencies may exist that were not identified. We did not identify any deficiencies in internal control over compliance that we consider to be material weaknesses. However, we identified certain deficiencies in internal control over compliance, as described in the accompanying schedule of findings and questioned costs as items [*list the reference numbers of the related findings, for example, 20X1-005, 20X1-006, and 20X1-007*],[74] that we consider to be significant deficiencies.

Example Entity's response to the internal control over compliance findings identified in our audit are described in the accompanying [*insert name of document containing management's response to the auditor's findings; for example, schedule of findings and questioned costs and/or corrective action plan*]. Example Entity's response was not subjected to the auditing procedures applied in the audit of compliance and, accordingly, we express no opinion on the response.

The purpose of this report on internal control over compliance is solely to describe the scope of our testing of internal control over compliance and the results of that testing based on the requirements of OMB Circular A-133. Accordingly, this report is not suitable for any other purpose.[75]

---

[74] See footnote 23.
[75] See footnote 9.

Report on Schedule of Expenditures of Federal Awards Required by OMB Circular A-133[76,77]

We have audited the financial statements of Example Entity as of and for the year ended June 30, 20X1, and have issued our report thereon dated August 15, 20X1, which contained an unmodified opinion on those financial statements. Our audit was conducted for the purpose of forming an opinion on the financial statements as a whole. The accompanying schedule of expenditures of federal awards is presented for purposes of additional analysis as required by OMB Circular A-133 and is not a required part of the financial statements. Such information is the responsibility of management and was derived from and relates directly to the underlying accounting and other records used to prepare the financial statements. The information has been subjected to the auditing procedures applied in the audit of the financial statements and certain additional procedures, including comparing and reconciling such information directly to the underlying accounting and other records used to prepare the financial statements or to the financial statements themselves, and other additional procedures in accordance with auditing standards generally accepted in the United States of America. In our opinion, the schedule of expenditure of federal awards is fairly stated in all material respects in relation to the financial statements as a whole.[78]

[*Auditor's signature*]

[*Auditor's city and state*][79]

[*Date of the auditor's report*][80]

---

[76] See footnote 10.
[77] See footnote 11.
[78] See footnote 12.
[79] See footnote 13.
[80] See footnote 14.

Example 13-6

Report on Compliance for Each Major Federal Program; Report on Internal Control Over Compliance; and Report on Schedule of Expenditures of Federal Awards Required by OMB Circular A-133

(Adverse Opinion on Compliance for One Major Federal Program; Unmodified Opinion on Compliance on Each of the Other Major Federal Programs; Material Weaknesses and Significant Deficiencies in Internal Control Over Compliance Identified)[81]

<u>Independent Auditor's Report</u>

[*Appropriate Addressee*]

Report on Compliance for Each Major Federal Program

We have audited Example Entity's compliance with the types of compliance requirements[82] described in the *OMB Compliance Supplement* that could have a direct and material effect[83] on each of Example Entity's major federal programs for the year ended June 30, 20X1. Example Entity's major federal programs are identified in the summary of auditor's results section of the accompanying schedule of findings and questioned costs.[84]

Management's Responsibility

Management is responsible for compliance with the requirements of laws, regulations, contracts, and grants applicable to its federal programs.

Auditor's Responsibility

Our responsibility is to express an opinion on compliance for each of Example Entity's major federal programs based on our audit of the types of compliance requirements referred to above. We conducted our audit of compliance in accordance with auditing standards generally accepted in the United States of America; the standards applicable to financial audits contained in *Government Auditing Standards*, issued by the Comptroller General of the United States; and OMB Circular A-133, *Audits of States, Local Governments, and Non-Profit Organizations*. Those standards and OMB Circular A-133 require that we plan and perform the audit to obtain reasonable assurance about whether noncompliance with the types of compliance requirements referred to above that could have a direct and material effect on a major federal program occurred. An audit includes examining, on a test basis, evidence about Example Entity's compliance with those requirements and performing such other procedures as we considered necessary in the circumstances.

We believe that our audit provides a reasonable basis for our opinion on compliance for each major federal program. However, our audit does not provide a legal determination of Example Entity's compliance.

***Basis for Adverse Opinion on [Identify Major Federal Program]*[85,86]**

As described in the accompanying schedule of findings and questioned costs, Example Entity did not comply with requirements regarding [*identify the*

---

[81] See footnote 1.
[82] See footnote 2.
[83] See footnote 3.
[84] See footnote 4.
[85] See footnote 48.
[86] See footnote 49.

major federal program and associated finding number(s) matched to the type(s) of compliance requirements; for example, CFDA 93.600 Head Start as described in finding numbers 20X1-001 for Eligibility and 20X1-002 for Reporting]. Compliance with such requirements is necessary, in our opinion, for Example Entity to comply with the requirements applicable to that program.

Adverse Opinion on [Identify Major Federal Program]

In our opinion, because of the significance of the matter discussed in the Basis for Adverse Opinion paragraph, Example Entity did not comply in all material respects, with the types of compliance requirements referred to above that could have a direct and material effect on [identify the major federal program] for the year ended June 30, 20X1.

Unmodified Opinion on Each of the Other Major Federal Programs[87]

In our opinion, Example Entity complied, in all material respects, with the types of compliance requirements referred to above that could have a direct and material effect on each of its other major federal programs identified in the summary of auditor's results section of the accompanying schedule of findings and questioned costs for the year ended June 30, 20X1.

Other Matters[88]

The results of our auditing procedures disclosed other instances of noncompliance, which are required to be reported in accordance with OMB Circular A-133 and which are described in the accompanying schedule of findings and questioned costs as items [list the reference numbers of the related findings, for example, 20X1-003 and 20X1-004].[89] Our opinion on each major federal program is not modified with respect to these matters.

Example Entity's response to the noncompliance findings identified in our audit are described in the accompanying [insert name of document containing management's response to the auditor's findings; for example, schedule of findings and questioned costs and/or corrective action plan]. Example Entity's response was not subjected to the auditing procedures applied in the audit of compliance and, accordingly, we express no opinion on the response.[90]

Report on Internal Control Over Compliance[91]

Management of Example Entity is responsible for establishing and maintaining effective internal control over compliance with the types of compliance requirements referred to above. In planning and performing our audit of compliance, we considered Example Entity's internal control over compliance with the types of requirements that could have a direct and material effect on each major federal program to determine the auditing procedures that are appropriate in the circumstances for the purpose of expressing an opinion on compliance for each major federal program and to test and report on internal control over compliance in accordance with OMB Circular A-133, but not for the purpose of expressing an opinion on the effectiveness of internal control over compliance. Accordingly, we do not express an opinion on the effectiveness of Example Entity's internal control over compliance.

---

[87] See footnote 50.
[88] See footnote 5.
[89] See footnote 6.
[90] See footnote 7.
[91] See footnote 8.

Our consideration of internal control over compliance was for the limited purpose described in the preceding paragraph and was not designed to identify all deficiencies in internal control over compliance that might be material weaknesses or significant deficiencies and therefore, material weaknesses or significant deficiencies may exist that were not identified. However, as discussed below, we identified certain deficiencies in internal control over compliance that we consider to be material weaknesses and significant deficiencies.

A *deficiency in internal control over compliance* exists when the design or operation of a control over compliance does not allow management or employees, in the normal course of performing their assigned functions, to prevent, or detect and correct, noncompliance with a type of compliance requirement of a federal program on a timely basis. A *material weakness in internal control over compliance* is a deficiency, or combination of deficiencies, in internal control over compliance, such that there is reasonable possibility that material noncompliance with a type of compliance requirement of a federal program will not be prevented, or detected and corrected, on a timely basis. We consider the deficiencies in internal control over compliance described in the accompanying schedule of findings and questioned costs as items [*list the reference numbers of the related findings, for example 20X1-005 and 20X1-006*][92] to be material weaknesses.

A *significant deficiency in internal control over compliance* is a deficiency, or a combination of deficiencies, in internal control over compliance with a type of compliance requirement of a federal program that is less severe than a material weakness in internal control over compliance, yet important enough to merit attention by those charged with governance. We consider the deficiencies in internal control over compliance described in the accompanying schedule of findings and questioned costs as items [*list the reference numbers of the related findings, for example 20X1-007 and 20X1-008*][93] to be significant deficiencies.

Example Entity's response to the internal control over compliance findings identified in our audit are described in the accompanying [*insert name of document containing management's response to the auditor's findings; for example, schedule of findings and questioned costs and / or corrective action plan*]. Example Entity's response was not subjected to the auditing procedures applied in the audit of compliance and, accordingly, we express no opinion on the response.

The purpose of this report on internal control over compliance is solely to describe the scope of our testing of internal control over compliance and the results of that testing based on the requirements of OMB Circular A-133. Accordingly, this report is not suitable for any other purpose.[94]

Report on Schedule of Expenditures of Federal Awards Required by OMB Circular A-133[95,96]

We have audited the financial statements of Example Entity as of and for the year ended June 30, 20X1, and have issued our report thereon dated August 15, 20X1, which contained an unmodified opinion on those financial statements. Our audit was conducted for the purpose of forming an opinion on the financial statements as a whole. The accompanying schedule of expenditures of federal

---

[92] See footnote 23.
[93] See footnote 23.
[94] See footnote 9.
[95] See footnote 10.
[96] See footnote 11.

awards is presented for purposes of additional analysis as required by OMB Circular A-133 and is not a required part of the financial statements. Such information is the responsibility of management and was derived from and relates directly to the underlying accounting and other records used to prepare the financial statements. The information has been subjected to the auditing procedures applied in the audit of the financial statements and certain additional procedures, including comparing and reconciling such information directly to the underlying accounting and other records used to prepare the financial statements or to the financial statements themselves, and other additional procedures in accordance with auditing standards generally accepted in the United States of America. In our opinion, the schedule of expenditure of federal awards is fairly stated in all material respects in relation to the financial statements as a whole.[97]

[Auditor's signature]

[Auditor's city and state][98]

[Date of the auditor's report][99]

Example 13-7

Schedule of Findings and Questioned Costs
Section I—Summary of Auditor's Results

Financial Statements		
Type of auditor's report issued [unmodified, qualified, adverse, or disclaimer]:[100]		
Internal control over financial reporting:		
• Material weakness(es) identified?	____ yes	____ no
• Significant deficiency(ies) identified?	____ yes	____ none reported
Noncompliance material to financial statements noted?	____ yes	____ no
Federal Awards		
Internal control over major federal programs:		
• Material weakness(es) identified?	____ yes	____ no
• Significant deficiency(ies) identified?	____ yes	____ none reported

---

[97] See footnote 12.
[98] See footnote 13.
[99] See footnote 14.

[100] As explained in the AICPA Audit and Accounting Guide *State and Local Governments*, the auditor generally expresses or disclaims an opinion on a government's basic financial statements by providing an opinion or disclaimer of opinion on each opinion unit required to be presented in those financial statements. Therefore, there could be multiple responses to this question for audits of a government's basic financial statements.

Type of auditor's report issued on compliance for major federal programs [*unmodified, qualified, adverse, or disclaimer*]:[101]		
Any audit findings disclosed that are required to be reported in accordance with Section 510(a) of OMB Circular A-133?	_____ yes	_____ no
Identification of major federal programs:[102]		
CFDA Number(s)[103]		Name of Federal Program or Cluster[104]
Dollar threshold used to distinguish between type A and type B programs:	$_____	
Auditee qualified as low-risk auditee?	_____ yes	

Section II—Financial Statement Findings

This section should identify the significant deficiencies, material weaknesses, fraud, noncompliance with provisions of laws, regulations, contracts, and grant agreements, and abuse related to the financial statements for which Government Auditing Standards *requires reporting in a Circular A-133 audit. (See paragraph 13.36.) Auditors may refer to chapter 4 of this guide for a discussion of the* Government Auditing Standards *requirements for presenting findings.*

Audit findings that relate to both the financial statements and federal awards should be reported in both section II and section III. However, the reporting in one section may be in summary form with a reference to a detailed reporting in the other section of the schedule. For example, a material weakness in internal control that affects an entity as a whole, including its federal awards, generally would be reported in detail in this section. Section III would then include a summary identification of the finding and a reference back to the specific finding in this section.

---

[101] If the audit report for one or more major federal programs is other than unmodified, indicate the type of report issued for each program. For example, if the audit report on major federal program compliance for an auditee having five major federal programs includes an unmodified opinion for three of the programs, a qualified opinion for one program, and a disclaimer of opinion for one program, the response to this question could be as follows: "Unmodified for all major federal programs except for [*name of program*], which was qualified and [*name of program*], which was a disclaimer."

[102] Major federal programs generally would be identified in the same order as reported on the schedule of expenditures of federal awards.

[103] When the *Catalog of Federal Domestic Assistance* (CFDA) number is not available, include other identifying number, if applicable. The contract or grant number typically is used in lieu of a CFDA number, or, if no grant or contract number is available, "Unknown."

[104] The name of the federal program or cluster should be the same as that listed in the schedule of expenditures of federal awards. For clusters, auditors are required only to list the name of the cluster and not each individual award or program within the cluster.

Identify each finding with a reference number.[105] *If there are no findings, this section could state that no matters were reported. Alternatively, this section could be omitted without confusing the schedule's users because the summary of auditor's results section would indicate that there are no findings. Each finding should be presented in the level of detail shown in the following listing, as applicable. Auditors also may refer to chapter 4 of this guide for a discussion of the* Government Auditing Standards *requirements for presenting findings:*

- *Criteria or specific requirement*
- *Condition*
- *Context*[106]
- *Effect*
- *Cause*
- *Recommendation*
- *Views of responsible officials and planned corrective actions*[107]

Section III—Federal Award Findings and Questioned Costs

This section should identify the audit findings required to be reported by Section 510(a) of Circular A-133 (for example, significant deficiencies, material weaknesses, and material instances of noncompliance, including questioned costs—see paragraph 13.38) as well as any abuse findings involving federal awards that is material to a major federal program (see paragraph 13.39). Where practical, findings should be organized by federal agency or pass-through entity.

Audit findings that relate to both the financial statements and federal awards should be reported in both section II and section III. However, the reporting in one section may be in summary form with a reference to a detailed reporting in the other section of the schedule. For example, a finding of noncompliance with a federal program law that is also material to the financial statements generally would be reported in detail in this section. Section II would then include a summary identification of the finding and a reference back to the specific finding in this section.

Identify each finding with a reference number.[108] *If there are no findings, this section could state that no matters were reported. Alternatively, this section could be omitted without confusing the schedule's users because the summary of auditor's results section would indicate that there are no findings. Each finding should be presented in the level of detail shown in the following listing,*

---

[105] Reference numbers on the data collection form should match those reported in the schedule of findings and questioned costs and applicable auditor's reports. The required format for reference numbers is the four digits of the fiscal year followed by a numerical sequence of three digit numbers. For example, findings identified and reported in the fiscal year 20X1 audit would be numbered 20X1-001, 20X1-002, and so forth. This standardized numbering format follows the Federal Audit Clearinghouse numbering format that is required on the data collection form.

[106] Describe the work performed that resulted in the finding, and provide sufficient information for judging the prevalence and consequences of the finding, such as the relation to the population or universe of costs or the number of cases examined as well as quantification of audit findings in dollars.

[107] Paragraphs 13.37 and 13.41 and chapter 4 of this guide provide guidance on reporting views of responsible officials and planned corrective action.

[108] See footnote 105.

Auditor Reporting Requirements and Other Communication Considerations **369**

as applicable. Auditors also may refer to chapter 4 of this guide for a discussion of the Government Auditing Standards requirements for presenting findings:

- Information on the federal program[109,110]
- Criteria or specific requirement (including statutory, regulatory, or other citation)
- Condition[111]
- Questioned costs[112]
- Context[113]
- Effect
- Cause
- Recommendation
- Views of responsible officials and planned corrective actions[114]

Example 13-8

Report on Schedule of Expenditures of Federal Awards When the Auditor Is Issuing a Stand-Alone Report Under AU-C Section 805, Special Considerations—Audits of Single Financial Statements and Specific Elements, Accounts, or Items of a Financial Statement[115]

(Unmodified Opinion on Schedule of Expenditures of Federal Awards)

Independent Auditor's Report

[Appropriate Addressee]

Report on Schedule of Expenditures of Federal Awards

We have audited the accompanying schedule of expenditures of federal awards of the City of Example for the year ended June 30, 20X1, and the related notes (the financial statement).

Management's Responsibility

Management is responsible for the preparation and fair presentation of this financial statement in accordance with accounting principles generally accepted

---

[109] Provide the federal program (CFDA number and title) and agency, the federal award's number and year, and the name of the pass-through entity, if applicable. When this information is not available, provide the best information available to describe the federal award.

[110] For findings related to American Recovery and Reinvestment Act of 2009 (Recovery Act) funds, the auditor should include in the audit findings detail of the schedule of findings and questioned costs explicit identification of applicable Recovery Act programs. This requirement of separate identification of findings related to Recovery Act funds can be found in Appendix 7 of the *Compliance Supplement*. See paragraphs 13.56–.57 for more information on considerations related to Recovery Act funds.

[111] Include facts that support the deficiency identified in the audit finding.

[112] Identify questioned costs as required by Sections 510(a)(3) and 510(a)(4) of Circular A-133.

[113] See footnote 106.

[114] See footnote 107.

[115] This illustration assumes that the auditor is engaged to issue a stand-alone opinion on the schedule of expenditures of federal awards using the guidance in AU-C section 805, *Special Considerations—Audits of Single Financial Statements and Specific Elements, Accounts, or Items of a Financial Statement* (AICPA, *Professional Standards*). See paragraph 13.20 of this guide for more information about this reporting and chapter 7, "Schedule of Expenditures of Federal Awards (Circular A-133)," of this guide for a discussion of when this may occur and information on the objectives and audit evidence needed in such an audit.

©2015, AICPA AAG-GAS 13.58

in the United States of America; this includes the design, implementation, and maintenance of internal control relevant to the preparation and fair presentation of a financial statement that is free from material misstatement, whether due to fraud or error.

Auditors' Responsibility

Our responsibility is to express an opinion on this financial statement based on our audit. We conducted our audit in accordance with auditing standards generally accepted in the United States of America; the standards applicable to financial audits contained in *Government Auditing Standards*, issued by the Comptroller General of the United States;[116] and OMB Circular A-133, *Audits of States, Local Governments, and Non-Profit Organizations*. Those standards and OMB Circular A-133 require that we plan and perform the audit to obtain reasonable assurance about whether the financial statement is free from material misstatement.

An audit involves performing procedures to obtain audit evidence about the amounts and disclosures in the financial statement. The procedures selected depend on the auditor's judgment, including the assessment of the risks of material misstatement of the financial statement, whether due to fraud or error. In making those risk assessments, the auditor considers internal control relevant to the entity's preparation and fair presentation of the financial statement in order to design audit procedures that are appropriate in the circumstances, but not for the purpose of expressing an opinion on the effectiveness of the entity's internal control. Accordingly, we express no such opinion. An audit also includes evaluating the appropriateness of accounting policies used and the reasonableness of significant accounting estimates made by management, as well as evaluating the overall presentation of the financial statement.

We believe that the audit evidence we have obtained is sufficient and appropriate to provide a basis for our audit opinion.

Opinion

In our opinion, the financial statement referred to above presents fairly, in all material respects, the expenditures of federal awards of the City of Example for the year ended June 30, 20X1 in accordance with accounting principles generally accepted in the United States of America.[117]

[Auditor's signature]

[Auditor's city and state][118]

[Date of the auditor's report]

---

[116] The standards and guidance applicable to financial audits are found in chapters 1–4 of *Government Auditing Standards*.

[117] AU-C section 800, *Special Considerations—Audits of Financial Statements Prepared in Accordance With Special Purpose Frameworks* (AICPA, *Professional Standards*), provides requirements and guidance for auditor reporting when the auditee prepares financial statements in accordance with a special purpose framework. AU-C section 800 defines a *special purpose framework* as a financial reporting framework other than generally accepted accounting principles and establishes requirements for reporting on those frameworks. Special purpose frameworks, such as the cash, tax, regulatory, and other bases of accounting, are sometimes referred to as an *other comprehensive bases of accounting* (OCBOA). The term *OCBOA* is sometimes used when referring to this guidance in this guide.

[118] See footnote 13.

Chapter 14

Program-Specific Audits (Circular A-133)

> **⊚ Update 14-1: Audits of Federal Awards**
>
> This chapter, and the remaining chapters of part II, *Circular A-133 Audits*, of this guide, should be used for performing a compliance audit of federal awards under Office of Management and Budget (OMB) Circular A-133, *Audits of States, Local Governments, and Non-Profit Organizations* (Circular A-133). Part III, *Uniform Guidance Audits*, of this guide should be used when performing a compliance audit under Title 2 U.S. *Code of Federal Regulations* Part 200, *Uniform Administrative Requirements, Cost Principles, and Audit Requirements for Federal Awards* (Uniform Guidance). See the transitional guidance sections at the end of each chapter that highlight important matters for consideration.[1] Refer to the preface for additional information.
>
> **Important Uniform Guidance Effective Date Information**
>
> In December 2013, the OMB issued the Uniform Guidance, which is effective for nonfederal entities for all federal awards and certain funding increments provided on or after December 26, 2014. The requirements in Subpart F, "Audit Requirements," are effective for audits of fiscal years beginning on or after December 26, 2014, with no early implementation permitted. Therefore, auditees subject to a single audit with December 25, 2015, and later year-ends (for example, December 31, 2015) will be required to undergo the audit under Subpart F of the Uniform Guidance. Note that audits of fiscal years ending prior to the effective date of the Uniform Guidance audit requirements are subject to an audit under Circular A-133.

14.01 A program-specific audit[2] is an audit of an entity's compliance with direct and material[3] compliance requirements as they relate to an individual federal program (rather than a single audit, which includes an audit of an

---

[1] See the information found at the end of certain chapters in part II, *Circular A-133 Audits*, of this guide for transition considerations when performing an audit under Office of Management and Budget (OMB) Circular A-133, *Audits of States, Local Governments, and Non-Profit Organizations* (Circular A-133), as it relates to the applicability of certain aspects of Title 2 U.S. *Code of Federal Regulations* Part 200, *Uniform Administrative Requirements, Cost Principles, and Audit Requirements for Federal Awards* (Uniform Guidance), to audits performed under Circular A-133. Transition considerations related to an audit performed under the Uniform Guidance can be found at the end of chapters in part III, *Uniform Guidance Audits*, of this guide in sections titled "Transition Considerations Related to the Uniform Guidance."

[2] AU-C section 935, *Compliance Audits* (AICPA, *Professional Standards*), is applicable when performing a program-specific compliance audit under OMB Circular A-133. See the other chapters in part II of this guide for guidance found in AU-C section 935 that applies to all compliance audits, including program-specific audits.

[3] AU-C section 935 defines *applicable compliance requirements* as the compliance requirements that are subject to the compliance audit. Section 500(d) of Circular A-133 states that the auditor should determine whether the auditee has complied with laws, regulations, and the provisions of contracts and grant agreements that may have a direct and material effect on each of its major programs. Therefore, in a Circular A-133 compliance audit, the direct and material compliance requirements are those that are subject to audit. Accordingly, for the purpose of adapting AU-C section 935 to a Circular A-133 compliance audit in this chapter, the term *applicable* has been replaced by *direct and material* when referring to such compliance requirements, except when citing content from AU-C section 935.

entity's financial statements and federal programs). Section 235 of OMB Circular A-133 provides guidance on program-specific audits.

Use of a Program-Specific Audit to Satisfy Circular A-133 Audit Requirements

14.02 Section 200 of Circular A-133 states that when an auditee expends federal awards under only one federal program (excluding research and development) and the federal program's laws, regulations, or grant agreements do not require a financial statement audit of the auditee, the auditee may elect to have a program-specific audit performed in accordance with Section 235 of the circular.[4] Therefore, the auditor should determine whether there is a financial statement audit requirement before performing a program-specific audit. A program-specific audit may not be elected for research and development unless all federal awards expended were received from the same federal agency (or the same federal agency and the same pass-through entity) and that federal agency (or pass-through entity, in the case of a subrecipient) approves a program-specific audit in advance.

Program-Specific Audit Requirements

14.03 Circular A-133 states that program-specific audits are subject to the following sections of Circular A-133 as they may apply to program-specific audits, unless contrary to the provisions of Section 235 of Circular A-133, a federal program-specific audit guide, or the program's laws and regulations:

- Purpose, definitions, audit requirements, basis for determining the federal awards expended, subrecipient and vendor determinations, and relation to other audit requirements (Sections 100–215[b])
- Frequency of audits, sanctions, and audit costs (Sections 220–230)
- Auditee responsibilities and auditor selection (Sections 300–305)
- Follow-up on audit findings (Section 315)
- Submission of report (Sections 320[f]–320[j])
- Responsibilities of federal agencies and pass-through entities and management decisions (Sections 400–405)
- Audit findings and audit working papers (Sections 510–515)

Program-specific audits also are subject to other provisions, referred to in Section 235 of Circular A-133.

Availability of Program-Specific Audit Guides

14.04 In many cases, a federal agency's Office of the Inspector General (OIG) will have issued a program-specific audit guide that provides guidance

---

[4] An example of a situation where a program-specific audit would not be allowed would be a not-for-profit college that receives student financial assistance (SFA) (and no other federal awards). That is because the Higher Education Act of 1965, as amended, requires institutions that receive SFA to undergo an annual financial statement audit.

on internal control, compliance requirements, suggested audit procedures, and audit reporting requirements for a particular federal program. The auditor should contact the OIG of the federal agency to determine whether such a guide is available and current. When a current program-specific audit guide is available, the auditor should follow *Government Auditing Standards* and the guide when performing a program-specific audit. However, if significant changes have been made to a program's compliance requirements and the related program-specific audit guide has not been updated with regard to the changes, the auditor should follow Section 235 of Circular A-133 and the *OMB Compliance Supplement* (*Compliance Supplement*) in lieu of an outdated guide. In addition, paragraph .22 of AU-C section 935, *Compliance Audits* (AICPA, *Professional Standards*), notes that in instances in which audit guidance provided by a governmental agency for the performance of compliance audits has not been updated for, or otherwise conflicts with, current generally accepted auditing standards (GAAS) or *Government Auditing Standards*, the auditor should comply with the most current applicable professional standards and guidance instead of the outdated or conflicting guidance.

14.05 When a program-specific audit guide is not available, the auditee and the auditor have basically the same responsibilities for the federal program as they have for an audit of a major program in a Circular A-133 compliance audit as discussed in chapters 9, "Consideration of Internal Control Over Compliance for Major Programs (Circular A-133)," and 10, "Compliance Auditing Applicable to Major Programs (Circular A-133)," of this guide. (See also paragraph 14.07 for more information.)

Auditee's Responsibilities When a Program-Specific Audit Guide Is Not Available

14.06 In addition to the responsibilities included in the sections of Circular A-133 as described in paragraph 14.03, Circular A-133 states that when a program-specific audit guide is not available, auditees have the responsibility to prepare the following:

- The financial statements for the federal program, which include, at a minimum, a schedule of expenditures of federal awards for the program and notes that describe the significant accounting policies used in preparing the schedule (Chapter 7, "Schedule of Expenditures of Federal Awards (Circular A-133)," of this guide discusses the schedule.)

- A summary schedule of prior audit findings consistent with the requirements of Section 315(b) of Circular A-133 (See chapter 13, "Auditor Reporting Requirements and Other Communication Considerations in a Single Audit (Circular A-133)," of this guide.)

- If applicable, a corrective action plan consistent with the requirements of Section 315(c) of Circular A-133 (See chapter 13 of this guide.)

Auditor's Responsibilities When a Program-Specific Audit Guide Is Not Available

Audit Scope and Requirements

14.07 When a program-specific audit guide is not available, Circular A-133 states that the auditor should do the following:

- Perform an audit of the financial statement(s) for the federal program in accordance with *Government Auditing Standards*. (Chapters 3, "Planning and Performing a Financial Statement Audit in Accordance With *Government Auditing Standards*," and 4, "Auditor Reporting Requirements and Other Communication Considerations of *Government Auditing Standards*," of this guide provide guidance on financial statement audits.) Paragraph 14.11 further discusses the *Government Auditing Standards* report.

- Obtain an understanding of the internal control over compliance and perform tests of the internal control over compliance for the federal program, so that they are consistent with the requirements of Section 500(c) of Circular A-133 for a major program. (Chapter 9 of this guide provides guidance on the internal control considerations for major programs.)

- Perform procedures to determine whether the auditee has complied with laws, regulations, and the provisions of contracts and grant agreements that could have a direct and material effect on the federal program consistent with the requirements of Section 500(d) of Circular A-133 for a major program. (Chapter 10 of this guide provides guidance on the compliance-auditing considerations for major programs.)

- Follow up on prior audit findings, perform procedures to assess the reasonableness of the summary schedule of prior audit findings that has been prepared by the auditee, and when the auditor concludes that the summary schedule of prior audit findings materially misrepresents the status of any prior audit finding, report this as a current-year audit finding, in accordance with the requirements of Section 500(e) of Circular A-133. (See chapter 13 of this guide.)

Auditor Procedures

14.08 Paragraph .A11 of AU-C section 935 lists procedures the auditor may perform to identify and obtain an understanding of the applicable compliance requirements if the *Compliance Supplement* or a program-specific audit guide is not applicable:

- Reading the laws, regulations, rules, and provisions of contracts and grant agreements that pertain to the program

- Making inquiries of management and other knowledgeable entity personnel

- Making inquiries of appropriate individuals outside the entity, such as (*a*) the office of the federal, state, or local program official or auditor or other appropriate audit oversight organizations or

regulators, about the laws and regulations applicable to entities within their jurisdiction, including statutes and uniform reporting requirements or (b) a third party specialist, such as an attorney
- Reading the minutes of meetings of the governing board of the entity being audited
- Reading audit documentation about the applicable compliance requirements prepared during prior years' audits or other engagements
- Discussing applicable compliance requirements with auditors who performed prior years' audits or other engagements

The procedures in the preceding list also may assist the auditor in obtaining a further understanding of the applicable compliance requirements for those engagements when the *Compliance Supplement* or program-specific audit guide is available.

Auditor's Reports[5]

Circular A-133 Requirements[6]

14.09 Circular A-133 states that the auditor's reports may be in the form of either combined or separate reports and may be organized differently from the manner described in Circular A-133 and as listed in this paragraph. The auditor's reports should state that the audit was conducted in accordance with Circular A-133. Because the audit is also subject to GAAS reporting requirements and *Government Auditing Standards*, the report should also include a reference to auditing standards generally accepted in the United States of America and *Government Auditing Standards*. The auditor's reports should include the following:

- An opinion (or disclaimer of opinion) on whether the financial statement(s) of the federal program are presented fairly in all material respects in accordance with the stated accounting policies
- A report on the internal control related to the federal program, which should describe the scope of the testing of the internal control and the results of the tests
- A report on compliance, which includes an opinion (or a disclaimer of opinion) on whether the auditee complied with laws, regulations, and the provisions of contracts and grant agreements that could have a direct and material effect on the federal program
- A schedule of findings and questioned costs for the federal program that includes a summary of the auditor's results relative to the audit of the federal program in a format consistent with

---

[5] See also chapter 13, "Auditor Reporting Requirements and Other Communication Considerations in a Single Audit (Circular A-133)," for a discussion of the basic elements of the auditor's reports.

[6] AU-C section 700, *Forming an Opinion and Reporting on Financial Statements* (AICPA, *Professional Standards*), uses the term *unmodified opinion* to refer to an opinion expressed by the auditor when the auditor concludes that the financial statements are presented fairly, in all material respects, in accordance with the applicable financial reporting framework. Although Circular A-133 refers to this type of opinion as an *unqualified opinion*, this guide uses the term *unmodified opinion* when referring to such an opinion.

the requirements for the summary of auditor's results in Section 505(d)(1) of Circular A-133, as well as findings and questioned costs for federal awards consistent with the requirements of Section 505(d)(3) of the circular (See chapter 13 of this guide.)[7]

Recommended Auditor's Reports

14.10 In an effort to make program-specific audit reporting understandable and to reduce the number of reports issued, this guide recommends that the following reports be issued for a program-specific audit: (*a*) an opinion (or disclaimer of opinion) on the financial statement(s) of the federal program, and (*b*) a report on compliance with requirements that could have a direct and material effect on the federal program and on the internal control over compliance in accordance with the program-specific audit option under Circular A-133. Paragraph 14.11 discusses the possible issuance of a third report to meet the reporting requirements of *Government Auditing Standards*. The appendix, "Illustrative Auditor's Reports for Program-Specific Audits," of this chapter (paragraph 14.17) illustrates program-specific audit reports. Chapters 4 and 13 of this guide discuss the *Government Auditing Standards* requirement that the auditor communicate certain matters to officials of the audited entity in writing.

Reporting in Accordance With Government Auditing Standards

14.11 If the financial statement(s) of the program present only the activity of the federal program, the auditor is not required to issue a separate report to meet the reporting requirements of *Government Auditing Standards*. This is because, in many cases, by definition, the financial statements of the program consist only of the schedule of expenditures of federal awards. In this situation, the program-specific audit reports in the appendix of this chapter (paragraph 14.17) would meet the financial, compliance, and internal control over compliance reporting requirements of both *Government Auditing Standards* and Circular A-133. However, the auditor always has the option of issuing a separate *Government Auditing Standards* report (in addition to the two reports described in paragraph 14.10). In situations when the auditor is engaged to perform a separate engagement, in addition to the program-specific audit (for example, a financial statement audit in accordance with *Government Auditing Standards*), the appropriate audit reports should be issued including a separate *Government Auditing Standards* report. Chapter 4 in this guide discusses the *Government Auditing Standards* report and the appendix in chapter 4 illustrates the *Government Auditing Standards* report.

Evaluating and Reporting Abuse

14.12 Chapters 9–10 and 13 of this guide discuss the *Government Auditing Standards* requirements for evaluating and reporting abuse in an audit in accordance with Circular A-133. Auditors who report abuse findings should consider the need to modify the auditor's reports to refer to those findings.

---

[7] As discussed in chapter 13 of this guide, the schedule of findings and questioned costs also should meet the presentation requirements of *Government Auditing Standards* and report the views of responsible officials concerning the findings, conclusions, and recommendations, as well as planned corrective actions.

Submission of Report

Timing of Submission

14.13 Circular A-133 states that the audit should be completed and the reporting required by Sections 235(c)(2) and 235(c)(3) of the circular be submitted within the earlier of 30 days after the receipt of the auditor's reports or 9 months after the end of the audit period, unless a longer period is agreed to in advance by the federal agency that provided the funding or unless a different period is specified in a program-specific audit guide.[8] Circular A-133 also states that unless restricted by law or regulation, the auditee should make copies of the report available for public inspection.

Submission When a Program-Specific Audit Guide Is Available

14.14 When a program-specific audit guide is available, the auditee should submit to the Federal Audit Clearinghouse (FAC) the data collection form prepared in accordance with Section 320(b) of the circular, as applicable for a program-specific audit, and also submit the reporting that is required by the program-specific audit guide. (Chapter 13 of this guide provides guidance on the FAC and the completion and submission of the data collection form.) The auditee also should submit any reporting required by the program-specific audit guide to the federal awarding agency or pass-through entity. (See also paragraph 14.16).

Submission When a Program-Specific Audit Guide Is Not Available

14.15 When a program-specific audit guide is not available, the reporting package for a program-specific audit consists of the following:

- The financial statement(s) of the federal program
- A summary schedule of prior audit findings, if applicable (See chapter 13 of this guide.)
- A corrective action plan, if applicable (See chapter 13 of this guide.)
- The auditor's report(s) described in paragraphs 14.09–.11

14.16 Circular A-133 states that the auditee should submit the data collection form, as applicable to a program-specific audit, and the reporting package to the FAC, as discussed in chapter 13 of this guide. When a subrecipient is not required to submit a reporting package to the pass-through entity, the subrecipient should provide written notification to the pass-through entity, consistent with the requirements of Section 320(e)(2) of Circular A-133, as discussed in chapter 13 of this guide. A subrecipient may submit a copy of the reporting package to the pass-through entity to comply with the notification requirement.

---

[8] If the auditee or auditor wishes to inform to the federal government that the required submission will be late, the suggested way to do so is to contact the federal oversight or cognizant agency for the audit (contact information is available on the "Resources" tab at http://harvester.census.gov/fac/APPX3.htm).

14.17

Appendix—Illustrative Auditor's Reports for Program-Specific Audits (Circular A-133)

The illustrative reports in this appendix are examples of the reports issued under Office of Management and Budget (OMB) Circular A-133, *Audits of States, Local Governments, and Non-Profit Organizations*, for a program-specific audit. These reports have been updated for the guidance in AU-C section 805, *Special Considerations—Audits of Single Financial Statements and Specific Elements, Accounts, or Items of a Financial Statement* (AICPA, *Professional Standards*), and AU-C section 935, *Compliance Audits* (AICPA, *Professional Standards*). The following table lists the illustrative reports. Auditors using professional judgment, may adapt these examples in any situation not specifically addressed in these illustrations. (As discussed in paragraph 14.11, the auditor should, in certain circumstances, issue these program-specific audit reports as well as a separate *Government Auditing Standards* report. The appendix in chapter 4, "Auditor Reporting Requirements and Other Communication Considerations of Government Auditing Standards," of this guide illustrates the *Government Auditing Standards* report.)

Example No.	Title
14-1	Unmodified Opinion on the Financial Statement of a Federal Program When Using the Program-Specific Audit Option to Satisfy OMB Circular A-133 Requirements
14-2	Report on Compliance for a Federal Program and Report on Internal Control Over Compliance When Using the Program-Specific Audit Option to Satisfy OMB Circular A-133 Requirements *(Unmodified Opinion on Compliance; No Material Weaknesses or Significant Deficiencies in Internal Control Over Compliance Identified)*

Example 14-1

Unmodified Opinion on the Financial Statement of a Federal Program When Using the Program-Specific Audit Option to Satisfy OMB Circular A-133 Requirements

Independent Auditor's Report

[*Appropriate Addressee*]

Report on the Schedule of Expenditures of Federal Awards

We have audited the accompanying schedule of expenditures of federal awards for the [*identify the federal program*] of Example Entity for the year ended June 30, 20X1, and the related notes (the financial statement).

Management's Responsibility for the Schedule of Expenditures of Federal Awards

Management is responsible for the preparation and fair presentation of this financial statement in accordance with accounting principles generally accepted in the United States of America; this includes the design, implementation, and maintenance of internal control relevant to the preparation and fair presentation of a financial statement that is free from material misstatement, whether due to fraud or error.

Auditor's Responsibility

Our responsibility is to express an opinion on this financial statement based on our audit.[1]

We conducted our audit in accordance with auditing standards generally accepted in the United States of America; the standards applicable to financial audits contained in *Government Auditing Standards*,[2] issued by the Comptroller General of the United States; and OMB Circular A-133, *Audits of States, Local Governments, and Non-Profit Organizations*. Those standards and OMB Circular A-133 require that we plan and perform the audit to obtain reasonable assurance about whether the financial statement is free from material misstatement.

An audit involves performing procedures to obtain audit evidence about the amounts and disclosures in the financial statement. The procedures selected depend on the auditor's judgment, including the assessment of the risks of material misstatement of the financial statement, whether due to fraud or error. In making those risk assessments, the auditor considers internal control relevant to the entity's preparation and fair presentation of the financial statement in order to design audit procedures that are appropriate in the circumstances, but not for the purpose of expressing an opinion on the effectiveness of the entity's internal control. Accordingly, we express no such opinion. An audit also includes evaluating the appropriateness of accounting policies used and the reasonableness of significant accounting estimates made by management, as well as evaluating the overall presentation of the financial statement.

We believe that the audit evidence we have obtained is sufficient and appropriate to provide a basis for our audit opinion.

---

[1] In many cases, the financial statement of the program consists only of the schedule of expenditures of federal awards (and the related notes), which is the minimum financial statement presentation required by Section 235 of the Office of Management and Budget (OMB) Circular A-133, *Audits of States, Local Governments, and Non-Profit Organizations* (Circular A-133). If the auditee issues financial statements that consist of more than the schedule, this paragraph would be modified to describe the financial statements.

[2] The standards and guidance applicable to financial audits are found in chapters 1–4 of *Government Auditing Standards*.

Opinion

In our opinion, the financial statement referred to above presents fairly, in all material respects, the expenditures of federal awards[3] for the [*identify the federal program*] of Example Entity for the year ended June 30, 20X1, in accordance with accounting principles generally accepted in the United States of America.[4,5]

[*Auditor's signature*]

[*Auditor's city and state*][6]

[*Date of the auditor's report*]

---

[3] If the auditee issues financial statements that consist of more than the schedule, this sentence should be modified to identify the results displayed in the financial presentation.

[4] AU-C section 800, *Special Consideration—Audits of Financial Statements Prepared in Accordance With Special Purpose Frameworks* (AICPA, *Professional Standards*), provides requirements and guidance for auditor reporting when the auditee prepares financial statements in accordance with a special purpose framework. AU-C section 800 defines a *special purpose framework* as a financial reporting framework other than generally accepted accounting principles and establishes requirements for reporting on those frameworks. Special purpose frame-works, such as the cash, tax, regulatory, and other bases of accounting, are sometimes referred to as an *other comprehensive bases of accounting* (OCBOA). The term *OCBOA* is sometimes used when referring to this guidance in this guide.

[5] If a separate report is issued to meet the reporting requirements of *Government Auditing Standards* (see paragraph 14.11), an additional section with the heading "Other Reporting Required by *Government Auditing Standards*," would be added after the opinion paragraph as follows:

> In accordance with *Government Auditing Standards*, we have also issued our report dated [*date of report*] on our consideration of Example Entity's internal control over financial reporting and on our tests of its compliance with certain provisions of laws, regulations, contracts, and grant agreements and other matters. The purpose of that report is to describe the scope of our testing of internal control over financial reporting and compliance and the results of that testing, and not to provide an opinion on internal control over financial reporting or on compliance. That report is an integral part of an audit performed in accordance with *Government Auditing Standards* in considering Example Entity's internal control over financial reporting and compliance.

See chapter 4, "Auditor Reporting Requirements and Other Communication Considerations of *Government Auditing Standards*," of this guide for information regarding modifying report wording when issuing reports required by *Government Auditing Standards*.

[6] AU-C section 700, *Forming an Opinion and Reporting on Financial Statements* (AICPA, *Professional Standards*), provides that the auditor's report should name the city and state where the auditor practices. City and state on a firm's letterhead typically is sufficient to meet this requirement. Technical Questions and Answers section 9100.08, "Audit Firm With Multiple Offices on Their Company Letterhead and Effect on Report" (AICPA, *Technical Questions and Answers*), notes that when a firm's letterhead contains multiple office locations the auditor would need to indicate the city and state where the auditor practices in the auditor's report.

Example 14-2

Report on Compliance for a Federal Program and Report on Internal Control Over Compliance When Using the Program-Specific Audit Option to Satisfy OMB Circular A-133 Requirements[7]

(Unmodified Opinion on Compliance; No Material Weaknesses or Significant Deficiencies In Internal Control Over Compliance Identified) [8]

Independent Auditor's Report

[*Appropriate Addressee*]

Report on Compliance for [*identify the federal program*][9]

We have audited Example Entity's compliance with the types of compliance requirements[10] described in the *OMB Compliance Supplement* that could have a direct and material[11] effect on its [*identify the federal program*] for the year ended June 30, 20X1.

---

[7] This is an example of a report on a program-specific audit under Circular A-133 when no federal audit guide applicable to the program being audited is available. When a federal audit guide applicable to the program is available, Circular A-133 requires that the auditor follow the reporting requirement of that federal audit guide. (Paragraph 14.04 discusses the auditor's responsibility when a program-specific audit guide is not current.)

[8] Auditors, using professional judgment, may adapt this example to other situations not specifically addressed in the illustration. For example, if issuing a qualified or adverse opinion on compliance, the auditor may modify the compliance opinion section of this report. Additionally, if reporting significant deficiencies or material weaknesses, the auditor also may modify the internal control section of this report. The portions of examples 13-2–13-6 in the appendix of chapter 13, "Auditor Reporting Requirements and Other Communication Considerations in a Single Audit (Circular A-133)," of this guide that apply to a specific auditee situation in a single audit may be useful in modifying this report. See also paragraph 14.12 concerning the need to modify this report if the schedule of finding and questioned costs includes abuse findings.

[9] This report sequences the reporting on compliance before the reporting on internal control over compliance. However, the *Government Auditing Standards* reports in the appendix of chapter 4 of this guide sequence the reporting on internal control over financial reporting before the reporting on compliance and other matters. Auditors may present the internal control over compliance and compliance sections of Circular A-133 and *Government Auditing Standards* reports in whichever sequence better meets their needs.

[10] Under Section 510(a) of Circular A-133, the auditor's determination of whether noncompliance with the provisions of laws, regulations, contracts, or grant agreements is material for the purpose of reporting an audit finding is in relation to a type of compliance requirement for a major program or an audit objective identified in the *OMB Compliance Supplement (Compliance Supplement)*. Further, the auditor's determination of whether a deficiency in internal control over compliance is a material weakness or significant deficiency for the purpose of reporting an audit finding is also in relation to a type of compliance requirement for a major program or an audit objective identified in the *Compliance Supplement*. This reference to *type of compliance requirements* used here and elsewhere in this report illustration refers to the 12 types of compliance requirements (identified using specific letters from "A" through "N") described in Part 3 of the 2015 *Compliance Supplement*. For purposes of reporting audit findings, auditors are alerted that certain of the types of compliance requirements may include multiple compliance requirements with multiple audit objectives (for example, compliance requirement "G" covers three separate requirements—matching, level of effort, and earmarking; and "N" covers separate requirements specific to each individual special test and provision).

[11] AU-C section 935, *Compliance Audits* (AICPA, *Professional Standards*), defines *applicable compliance requirements as the compliance requirements* that are subject to the compliance audit. Paragraph .500(d) of Circular A-133 states that the auditor should determine whether the auditee has complied with laws, regulations, and the provisions of contracts or grant agreements that may have a direct and material effect on each of its major programs. Therefore, in a Circular A-133 compliance audit (including a program-specific audit), the direct and material compliance requirements are those that are subject to audit. Accordingly, for the purpose of adapting AU-C section 935 to a Circular A-133 program-specific audit the term *applicable compliance requirements* has been replaced by *direct and material compliance requirements* in this guide except when directly citing content from AU-C section 935. See also footnote 10 of this appendix for a discussion related to the determination of material noncompliance.

Management's Responsibility

Management is responsible for compliance with the requirements of laws, regulations, contracts, and grants applicable to [*identify the federal program*].

Auditor's Responsibility

Our responsibility is to express an opinion on compliance for Example Entity's [*identify the federal program*] based on our audit of the types of compliance requirements referred to above.

We conducted our audit of compliance in accordance with auditing standards generally accepted in the United States of America; the standards applicable to financial audits contained in *Government Auditing Standards*,[12] issued by the Comptroller General of the United States; and OMB Circular A-133, *Audits of States, Local Governments, and Non-Profit Organizations.* Those standards and OMB Circular A-133 require that we plan and perform the audit to obtain reasonable assurance about whether noncompliance with the types of compliance requirements referred to above that could have a direct and material effect on [*identify the federal program*] occurred. An audit includes examining, on a test basis, evidence about Example Entity's compliance with those requirements and performing such other procedures as we considered necessary in the circumstances.

We believe that our audit provides a reasonable basis for our opinion on compliance for Example Entity's [*identify the federal program*]. However our audit does not provide a legal determination of Example Entity's compliance.

Opinion on Compliance for [identify the federal program]

In our opinion, Example Entity complied, in all material respects, with the compliance requirements referred to above that could have a direct and material effect on its [*identify the federal program*] for the year ended June 30, 20X1.

Other Matters[13]

The results of our auditing procedures disclosed instances of noncompliance, which are required to be reported in accordance with OMB Circular A-133 and which are described in the accompanying schedule of findings and questioned costs as items [*list the reference numbers of the related findings, for example, 20X1-001 and 20X1-002*].[14,15] Our opinion on Example Entity's [*identify the federal program*] is not modified with respect to these matters.

---

[12] See footnote 2.

[13] When there are no noncompliance findings that are required to be reported, and therefore no management response to findings, this "Other Matters" section of the report would be omitted.

[14] Because the auditor's reporting may include findings from multiple years, this numbering should include the fiscal year in which the finding initially occurred. The required format for reference numbers is the four digits of the fiscal year followed by a numerical sequence of three digit numbers. This is the reference number format for audit findings required for data collection form submissions to the Federal Audit Clearinghouse.

[15] The auditor may also consider adding a table to this section of the report to more clearly communicate the other findings that are being reported and the requirements to which they relate. See example 13-4 in the appendix of chapter 13 for an example of a table approach that could be modified for this purpose.

Example Entity's response to the noncompliance findings identified in our audit are described in the accompanying schedule of findings and questioned costs. Example Entity's response was not subjected to the auditing procedures applied in the audit of compliance and, accordingly, we express no opinion on the response.[16]

Report on Internal Control Over Compliance[17]

Management of Example Entity is responsible for establishing and maintaining effective internal control over compliance with the types of compliance requirements referred to above. In planning and performing our audit of compliance, we considered Example Entity's internal control over compliance with the types of requirements that could have a direct and material effect on its [*identify the federal program*] to determine the auditing procedures that are appropriate in the circumstances for the purpose of expressing an opinion on compliance for its [*identify the federal program*] and to test and report on internal control over compliance in accordance with OMB Circular A-133, but not for the purpose of expressing an opinion on the effectiveness of internal control over compliance. Accordingly, we do not express an opinion on the effectiveness of Example Entity's internal control over compliance.

A *deficiency in internal control over compliance* exists when the design or operation of a control over compliance does not allow management or employees, in the normal course of performing their assigned functions, to prevent, or detect and correct, noncompliance with a type of compliance requirement of a federal program on a timely basis. A *material weakness in internal control over compliance* is a deficiency, or combination of deficiencies, in internal control over compliance, such that there is a reasonable possibility that material noncompliance with a type of compliance requirement of a federal program will not be prevented, or detected and corrected, on a timely basis. A *significant deficiency in internal control over compliance* is a deficiency, or a combination of deficiencies, in internal control over compliance with a type of compliance requirement of a federal program that is less severe than a material weakness in internal control over compliance, yet important enough to merit attention by those charged with governance.

Our consideration of internal control over compliance was for the limited purpose described in the first paragraph of this section and was not designed to identify all deficiencies in internal control over compliance that might be material weaknesses or significant deficiencies. We did not identify any deficiencies in internal control over compliance that we consider to be material weaknesses. However, material weaknesses may exist that have not been identified.

The purpose of this report on internal control over compliance is solely to describe the scope of our testing of internal control over compliance and the

---

[16] Although the auditor does not audit management's responses to identified findings, the auditor does have certain responsibilities related to reporting the views of responsible officials under *Government Auditing Standards*. As noted in paragraph 4.33 of *Government Auditing Standards*, auditors should obtain and report the views of responsible officials concerning the findings, conclusions, and recommendations, as well as planned corrective actions. See paragraph 13.41 for further information.

[17] This example illustrates a combined report that also includes the reporting on internal control over compliance. If an auditor prefers to issue a separate report on internal control over compliance this section would be omitted from the report. AU-C section 935 includes required elements for separate reporting on internal control over compliance.

results of that testing based on the requirements of OMB Circular A-133. Accordingly, this report is not suitable for any other purpose.[18]

[*Auditor's signature*]

[*Auditor's city and state*][19]

[*Date of the auditor's report*]

---

[18] This paragraph has been adapted from AU-C section 905, *Alert That Restricts the Use of the Auditor's Written Communication* (AICPA, *Professional Standards*), to relate to the reporting on internal control over compliance that is required in an audit of compliance in accordance with Circular A-133.

[19] See footnote 6.

Part III
Uniform Guidance Audits

Chapter 15

Overview of the Single Audit Act, the Uniform Guidance Audit Requirements, and the Compliance Supplement

> **⊙ Update 15-1: Audits of Federal Awards**
>
> This chapter, and the remaining chapters of part III, *Uniform Guidance Audits*, of this guide, should be used for performing a compliance audit of federal awards under the audit requirements of Title 2 U.S. *Code of Federal Regulations* (CFR) Part 200, Uniform Administrative Requirements, Cost Principles, and Audit Requirements for Federal Awards (Uniform Guidance).[1] Part II, *Circular A-133 Audits*, of this guide should be used for performing a compliance audit under Office of Management and Budget (OMB) Circular A-133, *Audits of States, Local Governments, and Non-Profit Organizations* (Circular A-133). See the transitional guidance sections at the end of each chapter that highlight important matters for consideration. Additionally, refer to the preface of this guide for more information.
>
> **Important Effective Date Information**
>
> In December 2013, the OMB issued the Uniform Guidance, which is effective for nonfederal entities for all federal awards and certain funding increments provided on or after December 26, 2014. The requirements in Subpart F, "Audit Requirements," are effective for audits of fiscal years beginning on or after December 26, 2014, with no early implementation permitted. Therefore, auditees subject to a single audit with December 25, 2015, and later year ends (for example, December 31, 2015) will be required to undergo the audit under Subpart F of the Uniform Guidance. Note that audits of fiscal years ending prior to the effective date of the Uniform Guidance audit requirements are subject to an audit under Circular A-133.

Introduction [2]

15.01 This chapter provides an overview of the significant requirements and guidance in the Single Audit Act; the Uniform Guidance;[3] and the *OMB*

---

[1] See the information found at the end of this chapter (paragraph 15.50), and other part III, *Uniform Guidance Audits*, chapters of this guide, for transition considerations when performing an audit under Title 2 U.S. *Code of Federal Regulations* (CFR) Part 200, *Uniform Administrative Requirements, Cost Principles, and Audit Requirements for Federal Awards* (Uniform Guidance). Transition considerations can also be found at the end of certain part II, *Circular A-133 Audits*, chapters as it relates to an audit performed under Office of Management and Budget (OMB) Circular A-133, *Audits of States, Local Governments, and Non-Profit Organizations* (Circular A-133).

[2] In part III, the use of the terms *single audit* or *audit in accordance with the Uniform Guidance* includes both the financial statement audit and the compliance audit that is performed under the Uniform Guidance. The use of the term *Uniform Guidance compliance audit* includes only the compliance audit that is performed under the Uniform Guidance.

[3] Because the Uniform Guidance implements the requirements of the Single Audit Act, the requirements of the Uniform Guidance and the act often are discussed together as one in this guide. Accordingly, references to the Uniform Guidance also include the requirements of the Single Audit Act.

©2015, AICPA　　　　　　　　　　　　　　　　　　　　　　　　　　AAG-GAS 15.01

Compliance Supplement (*Compliance Supplement*). As discussed in paragraph 15.09, the Single Audit Act and the Uniform Guidance requires a nonfederal entity[4] that expends $750,000 or more of federal awards in a fiscal year to have a single or program-specific audit. Refer to the Single Audit Act, the Uniform Guidance, and the *Compliance Supplement* for a complete understanding of the requirements. Supplement A, "Single Audit Act Amendments of 1996," of this guide reprints the Single Audit Act. Footnote 24 in paragraph 15.48 provides instructions for obtaining the *Compliance Supplement*.

15.02 The Single Audit Act was enacted to streamline and improve the effectiveness of audits of federal awards and to reduce the audit burden on nonfederal entities. The Single Audit Act and the Uniform Guidance require auditors to perform single and program-specific audits of federal awards in accordance with *Government Auditing Standards*, which incorporates by reference the AICPA Statements on Auditing Standards (SASs).[5] The Single Audit Act requires the audits to be conducted by an independent auditor.[6] The Single Audit Act gives the Director of the OMB the authority to develop government-wide guidelines and policy on performing audits to comply with the act. The OMB's Uniform Guidance establishes such audit requirements and, in addition, guidelines and policies on all aspects of managing federal awards. Individual federal departments and agencies have adopted the Uniform Guidance in regulation.[7] This provides a uniform system for auditing nonfederal entities that expend federal awards.

Uniform Guidance

15.03 The Uniform Guidance is contained in six subparts of 2 CFR Part 200:[8]

- Subpart A, "Acronyms and Definitions," contains acronyms and definitions used throughout the Uniform Guidance.
- Subpart B, "General Provisions," discusses general provisions including the purpose of the Uniform Guidance, its applicability, and effective date.

---

[4] Subpart A, "Acronyms and Definitions," of the Uniform Guidance defines a *nonfederal entity* as a state, local government, Indian tribe, institution of higher education, or nonprofit organization that carries out a federal award as a recipient or subrecipient. The term *nonfederal entity* is used throughout part III of this guide as that term is used in the Uniform Guidance.

[5] *Government Auditing Standards* incorporates by reference AICPA Statements on Auditing Standards (SASs). Therefore, auditors performing financial statement audits and Uniform Guidance compliance audits in accordance with *Government Auditing Standards* should comply with generally accepted auditing standards (GAAS), the requirements found in chapters 1–3 of *Government Auditing Standards*, and the additional standards and related requirements for financial audits found in chapter 4, "Standards for Financial Audits," of *Government Auditing Standards*.

[6] The Single Audit Act defines *independent auditor* as (a) an external state or local government auditor who meets the independence standards included in *Government Auditing Standards* or (b) a public accountant who meets such independence standards. Chapter 2, "*Government Auditing Standards*—Ethical Principles and General Standards," of this guide discusses the independence requirements of *Government Auditing Standards*.

[7] The Uniform Guidance was issued in December 2013. A joint interim final rule was issued on December 19, 2014, which included implementing regulations for the Uniform Guidance for all federal grant-making agencies. Technical corrections to the Uniform Guidance were also included in the joint interim final rule. Those technical corrections are available at https://cfo.gov/cofar/. See the preface of this guide for more information on the joint interim final rule.

[8] 2 CFR 200.101 of Subpart B, "General Provisions," the Uniform Guidance provides a table that lists which subparts are applicable to particular types of federal awards. The audit requirements found in Subpart F are applicable to audits of all types of federal awards.

Overview of the Single Audit Act 389

- Subpart C, "Pre-Federal Award Requirements and Contents of Federal Awards," covers administrative requirements directed primarily at federal agencies including pre-award activities and requirements for the contents of federal awards.
- Subpart D, "Post Federal Award Requirements," covers administrative requirements including procurement, internal control, and subrecipient monitoring.
- Subpart E, "Cost Principles," includes uniform cost principles for federal awards.
- Subpart F, "Audit Requirements," includes the single audit requirements.

Single Audit Act and Uniform Guidance Audit Requirements

Objectives of a Single Audit

15.04 In a single audit, the auditor has the following objectives, each of which results in the issuance of certain auditor reports (as discussed in chapter 23, "Auditor Reporting Requirements and Other Communication Considerations in a Single Audit (Uniform Guidance)," and chapter 24, "Program-Specific Audits (Uniform Guidance)," of this guide):

- Audit of the entity's financial statements and reporting on the supplementary schedule of expenditures of federal awards
    — Determine whether the financial statements of the auditee are presented fairly, in all material respects, in accordance with generally accepted accounting principles (GAAP). (Note that the Uniform Guidance does not prescribe the basis of accounting for financial statement preparation. See further discussion in chapter 16, "Auditor Planning Considerations Under the Uniform Guidance," of this guide.)
    — Determine whether the schedule of expenditures of federal awards is stated fairly in all material respects in relation to the auditee's financial statements as a whole. (See also chapter 17, "Schedule of Expenditures of Federal Awards (Uniform Guidance).")
- Compliance audit of federal awards[9]
    — Obtain an understanding of internal control over federal programs sufficient to plan the audit to support a low

---

[9] AU-C section 935, *Compliance Audits* (AICPA, *Professional Standards*), defines *applicable compliance requirements* as the compliance requirements that are subject to the compliance audit. 2 CFR 200.514(d)(1) states that the auditor must determine whether the auditee has complied with the federal statutes, regulations, and the terms and conditions of the federal awards that may have a direct and material effect on each of its major programs. Therefore, in a Uniform Guidance compliance audit, the direct and material compliance requirements are those that are subject to audit. Accordingly, for the purpose of adapting AU-C section 935 to a Uniform Guidance compliance audit, the term *applicable compliance requirements* has been replaced by *direct and material compliance requirements* in this guide except when directly citing content from AU-C section 935.

©2015, AICPA AAG-GAS 15.04

assessed level of control risk of noncompliance for major programs; plan the testing of internal control over compliance for major programs to support a low assessed level of control risk for the assertions relevant to the compliance requirements for each major program; and perform testing of internal control as planned. (See also chapter 19, "Consideration of Internal Control Over Compliance for Major Programs (Uniform Guidance).")

— Determine whether the auditee has complied with federal statutes, regulations, and the terms and conditions of federal awards[10] that may have a direct and material effect on each of its major programs (hereinafter referred to as *compliance requirements*). (See also chapter 20, "Compliance Auditing Applicable to Major Programs (Uniform Guidance).")

Audit of an Entity's Financial Statements and Reporting on the Schedule of Expenditures of Federal Awards

15.05 The financial statement audit required by the Uniform Guidance is performed in accordance with generally accepted auditing standards (GAAS) and the standards applicable to financial audits contained in *Government Auditing Standards*.[11] That audit results in the auditor reporting on the entity's financial statements and on the scope of the auditor's testing of compliance and internal control over financial reporting and the results of those tests. The auditor also should report certain fraud and abuse. The primary sources of guidance and standards regarding financial statement audits are the AICPA SASs;[12] *Government Auditing Standards*; and the AICPA Audit and Accounting Guides, including *Not-for-Profit Entities*, *State and Local Governments*, and *Health Care Entities*. Chapter 16 of this guide discusses financial statement audit considerations under the Uniform Guidance.

15.06 In an audit in accordance with the Uniform Guidance, the auditee is responsible for the preparation of the schedule of expenditures of federal awards. The auditor is then required to determine and report on whether the schedule of expenditures of federal awards is stated fairly in all material respects in relation to the financial statements as a whole. AU-C section 725, *Supplementary Information in Relation to the Financial Statements as a Whole* (AICPA, *Professional Standards*), provides guidance on such reporting. Chapter 17 of this guide discusses the schedule of expenditures of federal awards, and chapter 23 of this guide discusses the auditor's reporting on the schedule.

---

[10] The Uniform Guidance uses the terminology "federal statutes, regulations, and the terms and conditions of federal awards," which is equivalent to "provisions of laws, regulations, contracts, and grant agreements," as found in *Government Auditing Standards*.

[11] In performing audits in accordance with the standards applicable to financial audits contained in *Government Auditing Standards,* the auditor assumes certain responsibilities beyond those of audits performed in accordance with GAAS. Chapters 2, 3, "Planning and Performing a Financial Statement Audit in Accordance With *Government Auditing Standards*," and 4, "Auditor Reporting Requirements and Other Communication Considerations of *Government Auditing Standards*," of this guide discuss those responsibilities.

[12] SASs are codified in AICPA *Professional Standards*. See the "References to Professional Standards" section in the preface of this guide for further explanation.

Uniform Guidance Compliance Audit

15.07 Under the Single Audit Act and the Uniform Guidance, the auditor has additional testing and reporting responsibilities for compliance, as well as internal control over compliance, beyond a financial statement audit performed in accordance with GAAS and *Government Auditing Standards*. AU-C section 935, *Compliance Audits* (AICPA, *Professional Standards*), applies when an auditor is engaged, or required by law or regulation, to perform a compliance audit in accordance with all of the following: (*a*) GAAS, (*b*) the standards for financial audits under *Government Auditing Standards*, and (*c*) a governmental audit requirement[13] that requires an auditor to express or disclaim an opinion on compliance. It is the primary source of guidance and standards regarding compliance audits. The guidance clarifies that AU-C section 935 does not apply to the financial statement audit component of a compliance audit. The Uniform Guidance compliance audit of federal awards expended during the fiscal year provides a basis for issuing an additional report on compliance and on internal control over compliance related to major programs. Table 15-1 in paragraph 15.08 presents the additional compliance testing and internal control requirements relating to the Uniform Guidance compliance audit of federal awards expended. The Uniform Guidance defines *major programs*; chapter 18, "Determination of Major Programs (Uniform Guidance)," of this guide discusses that definition. Chapters 19–21 of this guide discuss auditing considerations applicable to compliance and internal control over compliance related to major programs.

15.08 The additional compliance testing and internal control responsibilities related to a Uniform Guidance compliance audit are presented in the following table.

Table 15-1

Additional Compliance Testing and Internal Control Responsibilities

	Obtaining Sufficient Appropriate Audit Evidence	*Reporting Responsibilities*
Compliance Testing Responsibilities	The auditor must determine whether the auditee has complied with federal statutes, regulations, and the terms and conditions of federal awards that may have a direct and material effect on each of its major programs.	The auditor must report on compliance for each major program and express or disclaim an opinion about whether the auditee complied with federal statutes, regulations, and the terms and conditions of federal awards that could have a direct and material effect on each major program and, where applicable, refer to the separate schedule of findings and questioned costs.

(continued)

---

[13] AU-C section 935 defines a *governmental audit requirement* as a government requirement established by law, regulation, rule, or provision of contracts or grant agreements requiring that an entity undergo an audit of its compliance with applicable compliance requirements related to one or more government programs that the entity administers. An example of a governmental audit requirement is the Uniform Guidance.

Additional Compliance Testing and Internal Control Responsibilities—*continued*

	Obtaining Sufficient Appropriate Audit Evidence	*Reporting Responsibilities*
Internal Control Responsibilities	With regard to internal control over compliance, the auditor must (1) perform procedures to obtain an understanding of internal control over federal programs that is sufficient to plan the audit to support a low assessed level of control risk of noncompliance for major programs, (2) plan the testing of internal control over major programs to support a low assessed level of control risk for the assertions relevant to the compliance requirements for each major program,[1] and (3) perform tests of internal control as planned (unless the internal control over some or all of the compliance requirements for a major program are likely to be ineffective in preventing or detecting noncompliance). The auditor uses evidence gained from the tests of controls relevant to compliance requirements to determine the nature, timing, and extent of the testing required to express an opinion on compliance with requirements that have a direct and material effect on each of its major federal programs.	The auditor must provide a written report on internal control over compliance describing the scope of testing internal control and the results of the tests and, where applicable, refer to a separate schedule of findings and questioned costs.

[1] Title 2 U.S. Code of Federal Regulations Part 200, *Uniform Administrative Requirements, Cost Principles, and Audit Requirements for Federal Awards*, requires the auditor to plan the audit to support a low assessed level of control risk for the assertions relevant to the compliance requirements for each major program; however, it does not actually require the auditor to achieve a low assessed level of control risk of noncompliance. Chapter 19, "Consideration of Internal Control Over Compliance for Major Programs (Uniform Guidance)," of this guide further discusses that Uniform Guidance provision.

General Audit Requirements

> **Emphasis Point**
>
> The use of the term *must* in the Uniform Guidance indicates a requirement. This is consistent with the use of the term *must* in GAAS and *Government Auditing Standards*. The use of the term *should* in the Uniform Guidance indicates a best practice or recommended approach. However, GAAS and *Government Auditing Standards* use the term *should* to indicate a presumptively mandatory requirement. An auditor must comply with a presumptively mandatory requirement in all cases in which such a requirement is relevant, except in rare circumstances. In this guide, the term ***should***, when italicized and bolded, indicates a best practice or recommended approach in the Uniform Guidance. This is intended to differentiate it from the term "should" used throughout the guide to refer to presumptively mandatory requirements in GAAS and *Government Auditing Standards*. See chapter 1, "Introduction and Overview of *Government Auditing Standards*," of this guide for more information regarding presumptively mandatory requirements.

Audit Threshold

15.09 The Uniform Guidance states that nonfederal entities that expend $750,000 or more of federal awards in a fiscal year must have a single or program-specific audit. Entities expending federal awards under only one program (excluding the research and development cluster [R&D]) may elect to have a program-specific audit if the program's statutes, regulations, or the terms and conditions of the federal award do not require a financial statement audit. A program-specific audit may not be elected for R&D unless (*a*) all expenditures are for awards received from the same federal agency or from the same federal agency and the same pass-through entity, and (*b*) advance approval is obtained from the federal agency, or pass-through entity in the case of a subrecipient. (Chapter 24 provides additional guidance on program-specific audits.) Entities that expend less than $750,000 in a fiscal year in federal awards are exempt from federal audit requirements for that year. However, those entities are not exempt from other federal requirements (including those to maintain records) concerning federal awards provided to the entity. Further, 2 CFR 200.501(d) states that records must be available for review or audit by appropriate officials of a federal agency, pass-through entity, and the U.S. Government Accountability Office (GAO).

> **Emphasis Point**
>
> Auditors are reminded that early implementation of the Uniform Guidance audit requirements is not permitted. The first time the Uniform Guidance is to be applied from an audit perspective is generally for December 31, 2015, year-end audits and later. Accordingly, the $750,000 threshold referred to previously is not to be applied earlier.

Types of Federal Awards and Payment Methods

Definition of Federal Awards

15.10 Included in the definition of a *federal award* under the Uniform Guidance are

    a. federal financial assistance that a nonfederal entity receives directly from a federal awarding agency or indirectly from a pass-through entity. Nonfederal entities receive or administer federal financial assistance in the form of grants, cooperative agreements, noncash contributions or donations of property (including donated surplus property), direct appropriations, food commodities, and other financial assistance. For purposes of applying the audit requirements of the Uniform Guidance, federal financial assistance also includes assistance received or administered in the form of loans, loan guarantees, interest subsidies, and insurance.

    b. a cost-reimbursement contract under the Federal Acquisition Regulations that a nonfederal entity receives directly from a federal awarding agency or indirectly from a pass-through entity. These are contracts with nonfederal entities to provide goods or services to the federal government.

    c. the instrument setting forth the terms and conditions which is the grant agreement, cooperative agreement, other agreement for assistance, or the cost-reimbursement contract.

A federal award does not include other contracts that a federal agency uses to buy goods or services from a contractor or a contract to operate a federal government owned, contractor operated facility.

Federal Financial Assistance—Classification and Types

15.11 Federal financial assistance is classified into program categories in the *Catalog of Federal Domestic Assistance* (CFDA), published by the Government Printing Office. (An electronic searchable version of the CFDA is available at www.cfda.gov.) The Uniform Guidance defines a *federal program* as all federal awards assigned a single CFDA number. When no CFDA number is assigned, all federal awards to nonfederal entities from the same agency made for the same purpose must be combined and considered one program. Federal programs also include clusters of programs. See paragraph 15.31 for a discussion of clusters of programs.

15.12 Sometimes, state governments combine funding from different federal awards in providing assistance to their subrecipients when the awards are closely related programs and share common compliance requirements. An other cluster may be designated by a state in these situations as long as it meets the definition of a cluster of programs as found in the Uniform Guidance. See also paragraph 15.31.

15.13 There are more than 2,000 individual grant programs. Many of these programs are described in the CFDA; however, certain programs may not be included. For example, cost-reimbursement contracts under the FAR may not be listed in the CFDA. As noted in paragraph 15.11, when no CFDA number is assigned, all federal awards to nonfederal entities from the same agency made for the same purpose must be combined and considered one program.

Overview of the Single Audit Act

This results in those programs being treated as one program for major program determination purposes.

15.14 Programs in the CFDA are classified into 15 types of assistance. Benefits and services are provided through 7 financial and 8 nonfinancial types of assistance.[14] The following list describes the 8 most prevalent types of assistance that are available:

- *Formula grants.* Allocations of money to states or their subdivisions are made in accordance with a distribution formula prescribed by law or administrative regulation for activities of a continuing nature not confined to a specific project. One example is the Department of Agriculture's award to land-grant universities for cooperative extension services. Another example is the Department of Justice's award to state and local governments for drug control and systems improvement.

- *Project grants.* These involve the funding, for fixed or known periods, of specific projects. Project grants can include fellowships, scholarships, research grants, training grants, traineeships, experimental and demonstration grants, evaluation grants, planning grants, technical assistance grants, survey grants, and construction grants.

- *Direct payments for specific use.* Financial assistance is provided by the federal government directly to individuals, private firms, and other private institutions to encourage or subsidize a particular activity by conditioning the receipt of the assistance on a particular performance by the recipient. This does not include solicited contracts for the procurement of goods and services for the federal government.

- *Direct payments with unrestricted use.* Financial assistance is provided by the federal government directly to beneficiaries who satisfy federal eligibility requirements with no restrictions imposed on how the money is spent. Included are payments under retirement, pension, and compensation programs.

- *Direct loans.* Financial assistance is provided through the lending of federal monies for a specific period of time, with a reasonable expectation of repayment. Such loans may or may not require the payment of interest.

- *Guaranteed/insured loans.* Programs in which the federal government makes an arrangement to indemnify a lender against part or all of any defaults by those responsible for the repayment of loans.

- *Insurance.* Financial assistance is provided to assure reimbursement for losses sustained under specified conditions. Coverage may be provided directly by the federal government or through a private carrier and may or may not involve the payment of premiums.

- *Sale, exchange, or donation of property and goods.* These programs provide for the sale, exchange, or donation of federal real property,

---

[14] The Catalog of Federal Domestic Assistance website at www.cfda.gov provides information on all types of assistance.

personal property, commodities, and other goods, including land, buildings, equipment, food, and drugs. This does not include the loan of, use of, or access to federal facilities or property.

Payment Methods

15.15 There are several distinct types of federal award payment methods. Awards may be provided to entities through reimbursement arrangements in which recipients bill grantors for costs as incurred. Some programs provide for advance payments or installment payments. Other programs permit entities to draw cash as grant expenditures are incurred.

Defining the Entity to Be Audited

15.16 As discussed in chapter 16 of this guide, the single audit must cover the entire operations of the auditee or, at the option of the auditee, the audit must include a series of audits that cover departments, agencies, and other organizational units that expended or otherwise administered federal awards during the audit period, provided that each audit must encompass the financial statements and the schedule of expenditures of federal awards for each such department, agency, and other organizational unit which must be considered to be a nonfederal entity. The financial statements and schedule of expenditures of federal awards must be for the same audit period.

Relationship to Other Audit Requirements

15.17 An audit in accordance with the Uniform Guidance must be in lieu of any financial audit of federal awards that a nonfederal entity is required to undergo under any other federal statute or regulation. However, a federal agency, including a federal agency's Inspectors General or the GAO, may conduct or arrange for additional audits[15] that are necessary to carry out its responsibilities under federal statute or regulation. In that case, the federal agency carrying out or arranging for such additional audit must plan the audit to not be duplicative of other audits of federal awards. Prior to commencing such an audit, the federal agency or pass-through entity must review the Federal Audit Clearinghouse (FAC) for recent audits submitted by the nonfederal entity, and to the extent such audits meet a federal agency or pass-through entity's needs, the federal agency or pass-through entity must rely upon and use such audits. Any additional audits must be planned and performed in such a way as to build upon work performed, including the audit documentation, sampling, and testing already performed, by other auditors. The Uniform Guidance requires a federal agency that conducts or arranges for additional audits to arrange for funding the full cost of such additional audits. Paragraph 15.32 discusses the federal agency or pass-through entity option to request certain programs to be audited as major programs.

15.18 The Uniform Guidance states that the audit must be performed in accordance with *Government Auditing Standards*. Consequently, *Government Auditing Standards* applies not only to the audit of the financial statements but also to the Uniform Guidance compliance audit. Therefore, the requirements and guidance found in chapters 1–4 of *Government Auditing Standards* are applicable to the Uniform Guidance compliance audit. Those standards

---

[15] The use of the term *audit* in this context includes other types of engagements, such as agreed-upon procedures engagements, that may be requested to be performed.

Overview of the Single Audit Act

are discussed in chapters 1–4 of this guide. Areas that may require particular attention in the Uniform Guidance compliance audit are auditor communication, procedures and reporting on abuse, the reporting of findings and related management views and planned corrective actions, and the reporting of certain matters in writing to officials of the auditee. For example

- auditors should communicate pertinent information that, in the auditor's professional judgment, needs to be communicated to individuals contracting for or requesting the audit and to cognizant legislative committees when auditors perform the audit pursuant to a law or regulation, or they conduct the work for the legislative committee that has oversight of the auditee. (This requirement does not apply if the law or regulation requiring an audit of the financial statements does not specifically identify the entities to be audited, such as audits required by the Single Audit Act Amendments of 1996.)

- auditors have no responsibility to design the audit to detect abuse.[16] However, if auditors become aware of abuse that could be quantitatively or qualitatively material to the financial statements or one or more major programs, auditors should apply audit procedures specifically directed to ascertain the potential effect on the financial statements or major program(s). Chapter 3, "Planning and Performing a Financial Statement Audit in Accordance With *Government Auditing Standards*," of this guide discusses procedures relating to the evaluation of indications of abuse, and chapter 20 of this guide discusses the nature of abuse as it relates to federal awards. Chapter 23 of this guide discusses the reporting of abuse involving federal awards.

- auditors should obtain and report the views of responsible officials concerning findings, conclusions, and recommendations, as well as their planned corrective actions. As discussed in chapter 23 of this guide, the auditor may be able to refer to the auditee's corrective action plan in the finding to satisfy the Uniform Guidance requirement for the views of responsible officials. However, the corrective action plan must be in a separate document from the auditor's findings. In addition, all findings, including federal award-related audit findings, are subject to the presentation requirements of *Government Auditing Standards*, as discussed in chapters 4, "Auditor Reporting Requirements and Other Communication Considerations of *Government Auditing Standards*," and 23 of this guide.

- *Government Auditing Standards* states that the auditor should communicate to officials of the auditee, in writing instances of noncompliance with provisions of contracts or grant agreements or abuse that have an effect on the financial statements or other financial data significant to the audit objectives that are less than material but warrant the attention of those charged with governance. As discussed in chapter 23 of this guide, in an audit in

---

[16] *Government Auditing Standards* describes *abuse* by stating that it does not necessarily involve fraud or noncompliance with provisions of laws, regulations, contracts, or grant agreements. Abuse, it states, "involves behavior that is deficient or improper when compared with behavior that a prudent person would consider reasonable and necessary business practice given the facts and circumstances."

accordance with the Uniform Guidance, the auditor should evaluate such matters involving federal awards for the purpose of that communication based only on their consequence to the financial statements.

Frequency of Audits[17]

15.19 The Uniform Guidance states that audits must be performed annually unless an auditee meets one of the following criteria that would allow it to have biennial audits (biennial audits must cover both years within the biennial period):

- A state or local government, or Indian tribe, that is required by constitution or statute (in effect on January 1, 1987) to undergo audits less frequently than annually is permitted to have an audit in accordance with the Uniform Guidance biennially. This requirement must still be in effect for the biennial period.

- Any NFP that had biennial audits for all biennial periods ending between July 1, 1992, and January 1, 1995, is permitted to have an audit in accordance with the Uniform Guidance biennially.

For-Profit and Foreign Entities

15.20 2 CFR 200.101 of Subpart B of the Uniform Guidance states that federal agencies may apply Subparts A through E to for-profit entities, foreign public entities, or foreign organizations, except where the federal awarding agency determines that the application of these subparts would be inconsistent with the international obligations of the United States or the statute or regulations of a foreign government. In this guidance, there is no mention of the audit requirements in Subpart F being applicable to these entities. However, as it relates to for-profit entities, some federal agencies have made provisions for audits of for-profit entities within their implementing regulations for the Uniform Guidance (for example, the U.S. Department of Health and Human Services). These agency-specific audit requirements for for-profit entities are outside the scope of this guide. With regard to foreign entities, the audit requirements in the Uniform Guidance do not apply to foreign public entities or foreign organizations expending federal awards received either directly as a recipient or indirectly as a subrecipient.

Reporting Matters

Audit Reports

15.21 2 CFR 200.515 includes specific auditor reporting requirements. It states that the auditor's reporting must include

    a. an opinion (or disclaimer of opinion) as to whether the financial statements are presented fairly in all material respects in accordance with GAAP and an opinion (or disclaimer of opinion) as to whether the schedule of expenditures of federal awards is fairly stated in all material respects in relation to the financial statements as a whole;

---

[17] See chapter 16, "Auditor Planning Considerations Under the Uniform Guidance," for information regarding a stub period audit.

Overview of the Single Audit Act

b. a report on internal control over financial reporting and compliance with provisions of laws, regulations, contracts, and award agreements, noncompliance with which could have a material effect on the financial statements.

c. a report on compliance for each major program and a report on internal control over compliance; and

d. a schedule of findings and questioned costs.[18]

Chapters 23–24 of this guide discuss auditor reporting requirements for single and program-specific audits and include appendixes that illustrate schedules of findings and questioned costs and auditor's reports.

Timing of the Submission of the Report

15.22 Upon the completion of the single audit, the reporting package (described in paragraph 15.38), including the auditor's reports, and the data collection form (described in paragraph 15.39) must be electronically submitted by the auditee to the FAC. That submission must be completed within the earlier of 30 calendar days after receipt of the auditor's reports or 9 months after the end of the audit period.[19] Chapter 23 of this guide further describes the report submission requirements of the Uniform Guidance.

Audit Follow-Up

15.23 The Uniform Guidance provides requirements related to audit follow-up stating that the auditor must follow up on prior audit findings, perform procedures to assess the reasonableness of the summary schedule of prior audit findings prepared by the auditee, and report a current-year audit finding when the auditor concludes that the summary schedule of prior audit findings materially misrepresents the status of any prior audit finding. Chapter 16 of this guide further discusses the auditor's responsibility for audit follow-up.

Auditor Selection and Audit Costs

Procurement of Audit Services and Restriction on Auditors Who Prepare Indirect Cost Proposals

15.24 In procuring audit services, the auditee must follow the procurement standards prescribed in Subpart D of the Uniform Guidance. 2 CFR 200.509 states that when procuring audit services, the objective is to obtain high-quality audits. In requesting proposals for audit services, the objectives and scope of the audit must be made clear, and the nonfederal entity must request a copy of the audit organization's peer review report that the auditor is required to provide under *Government Auditing Standards*. 2 CFR 200.509 also includes factors for the auditee to consider in evaluating each proposal for audit

---

[18] Chapter 4 of this guide further discusses the auditor's reports under GAAS and *Government Auditing Standards* (that is, an opinion [or disclaimer of opinion] concerning whether the financial statements are presented fairly, in all material respects, in accordance with the applicable financial reporting framework [for example, generally accepted accounting principles] and a report on internal control over financial reporting and compliance with laws, regulations, and provisions of contracts or grant agreements) and includes an appendix that illustrates those reports.

[19] If the auditee or auditor wishes to inform the federal government that the required submission will be late, the suggested way to do so is to contact the federal oversight or cognizant agency for the audit (contact information is available on the "Resources" tab at http://harvester.census.gov/fac/APPX3.htm). See the discussion beginning at paragraph 15.42 for information on cognizant agency for audit and oversight agency for audit.

services. In addition, that section provides auditee guidance regarding the selection of auditors who also prepare the indirect cost proposal or cost allocation plan. As further discussed in chapter 16 of this guide, auditors who prepare the indirect cost proposal or cost allocation plan may not also be selected to perform the audit in accordance with the Uniform Guidance when the indirect costs recovered by the auditee during the prior year exceeded $1 million.

> **Emphasis Point**
>
> The preparation of an entity's indirect cost proposal or cost allocation plan is considered to be a nonaudit service under *Government Auditing Standards*. Nonaudit services may create threats to an auditor's independence. When an auditor has prepared the entity's indirect cost proposal or cost allocation plan and is not otherwise precluded from performing the audit under the Uniform Guidance, evaluation is needed as to whether independence is impaired. This evaluation is done using the conceptual framework in chapter 3.
>
> See chapter 2, "*Government Auditing Standards*—Ethical Principles and General Standards," of this guide for more information on the requirements related to independence found in *Government Auditing Standards*, and for information regarding the AICPA "2011 Yellow Book Independence—Non-Audit Services Documentation Practice Aid."

Audit Costs

15.25 2 CFR 200.425 of Subpart E of the Uniform Guidance provides guidance on charging audit services to federal awards stating that a reasonably proportionate share of the costs of audits required by, and performed in accordance with, the Single Audit Act and the Uniform Guidance are allowable. However, any costs of audits that are not conducted under the Uniform Guidance or have been conducted but not in accordance with the Uniform Guidance are not allowable. Additionally, audit costs associated with an audit in accordance with the Uniform Guidance of entities that expend less than $750,000 per year in federal awards are unallowable. This provision does not prohibit pass-through entities from charging federal awards for the costs of agreed-upon procedures engagements to monitor its subrecipients. Chapter 22, "Audit Considerations of Federal Pass-Through Awards (Uniform Guidance)," of this guide further discusses the allowability of audit costs associated with agreed-upon procedures engagements to monitor its subrecipients. With regard to the amount of audit cost that can be charged to a federal award, the Single Audit Act states that in the absence of documentation demonstrating a higher actual cost, the percentage of the cost of single audits charged to federal awards by an entity may not exceed the ratio of total federal awards expended to the entity's total expenditures for the fiscal year.

Basis for Determining When Federal Awards Are Expended

15.26 The determination of when a federal award is expended must be based on when the activity related to the award occurs. In general, the activity pertains to events that require the auditee to comply with federal statutes, regulations, and the terms and conditions of federal awards. Such events include the following:

Overview of the Single Audit Act

- Expenditure or expense transactions associated with awards, including grants, cost reimbursement contracts under the FAR, compacts with Indian tribes, cooperative agreements, and direct appropriations
- The disbursement of funds to subrecipients
- The use of loan proceeds under loan and loan-guarantee programs
- The receipt of property, including surplus property
- The receipt or use of program income
- The distribution or use of food commodities
- The disbursement of amounts entitling the nonfederal entity to an interest subsidy
- The period when insurance is in force

15.27 As further discussed in chapter 17 of this guide, the Uniform Guidance provides specific guidance on the basis for determining federal awards expended or the valuation for the following noncash items:

- Loans and loan guarantees, including those at institutions of higher education
- Prior loans and loan guarantees
- Endowment funds
- Free rent
- Noncash assistance, such as free rent, food commodities, and donated property, including donated surplus property

The Uniform Guidance does not consider Medicare payments made to a nonfederal entity for providing patient care services to Medicare-eligible individuals to be federal awards expended. It also does not consider Medicaid payments to a subrecipient for providing patient care services to Medicaid-eligible individuals to be federal awards expended unless a state requires the funds to be treated as federal awards expended because reimbursement is on a cost-reimbursement basis. Finally, loans made from the National Credit Union Share Insurance Fund and the Central Liquidity Facility that are funded by contributions from insured nonfederal entities are not considered federal awards expended.

Subrecipient and Contractor Determinations

15.28 An auditee may simultaneously be a recipient, a subrecipient, and a contractor depending on the substance of its agreements with federal awarding agencies and pass-through entities. Federal awards expended as a recipient or a subrecipient are subject to audit under the Uniform Guidance. 2 CFR 200.501(f) states that payments received for goods and services provided as a contractor are not federal awards. Therefore, such payments would not be subject to an audit in accordance with the Uniform Guidance. See chapter 22 of this guide for further discussion.

Major Program Determination

Risk-Based Approach

15.29 The Uniform Guidance states that the auditor must use a risk-based approach to determine which federal programs are major programs. This determination is important because it affects the scope of the audit. The Uniform Guidance places the responsibility for identifying major programs on the auditor, and prescribes requirements for the auditor to use in applying a risk-based approach. Chapter 18 of this guide discusses that risk-based approach and the determination of major programs.

Low-Risk Auditee

15.30 The Uniform Guidance states that an auditee that meets certain conditions listed in 2 CFR 200.520 for each of the two preceding audit periods must qualify as a low-risk auditee and be eligible for reduced audit coverage. *Low-risk auditee* is a term defined in the Uniform Guidance for the purpose of applying the percentage-of-coverage rule in the risk-based approach. (Chapter 18 of this guide discusses the low-risk auditee criteria and the percentage-of-coverage rule.) The term *low-risk auditee* is not directly related to the assessment of risk in the audit; it does not imply or require the auditor to assess audit risk of noncompliance as low for an entity that meets the definition of a low-risk auditee.

Cluster of Programs

15.31 The Uniform Guidance defines a *cluster of programs* as a grouping of closely related federal programs that share common compliance requirements. The types of clusters of programs are R&D, Student Financial Assistance, and other clusters. *Other clusters* are defined by the OMB in the *Compliance Supplement* or are designated as such by a state for the federal awards the state provides to its subrecipients that meet the definition of a cluster of programs. An auditee or auditor may not create its own cluster of programs based on programs that share common compliance requirements. Similarly, an auditee or auditor may not de-cluster a cluster of programs that is defined by the OMB or designated by a state. When a state designates federal awards as an other cluster, it must identify the federal awards included in the cluster and advise the subrecipients of the compliance requirements applicable to the cluster consistent with 2 CFR 331(a) of Subpart D of the Uniform Guidance. Chapter 22 of this guide describes in more detail the requirements in 2 CFR 331(a). A cluster of programs must be considered as one program for determining major programs and (with the exception of R&D) whether a program-specific audit may be elected.

Federal Agency Selection of Additional Major Programs

15.32 2 CFR 200.503(e) permits a federal awarding agency to request an auditee to have a particular federal program audited as a major program in lieu of the federal agency conducting or arranging for additional audits. To allow for planning, such requests ***should*** be made at least 180 days prior to the end of the fiscal year to be audited. After consultation with its auditor, the auditee ***should*** promptly respond to such a request by informing the federal awarding agency whether the program would otherwise be audited as a major program using the risk-based approach and, if not, the estimated incremental cost. The federal awarding agency must then promptly confirm to the auditee whether it wants the program audited as a major program. If the program is to be audited as a major program based upon the federal awarding agency's request, and the federal awarding agency agrees to pay the full incremental costs, then the auditee must have the program audited as a major program. This approach also may be used by pass-through entities for a subrecipient.[20]

Auditee Responsibilities

Financial Statements and Schedule of Expenditures of Federal Awards

15.33 As discussed in chapter 16 of this guide, the Uniform Guidance states that auditees must prepare financial statements that reflect their financial position, the results of operations or changes in net assets, and, where appropriate, cash flows for the fiscal year audited. The financial statements must be for the same organizational unit and fiscal year that is chosen to meet the requirements of the Uniform Guidance. However, entity-wide financial statements also may include departments, agencies, and other organizational units that have separate audits in accordance with the Uniform Guidance and prepare separate financial statements. The Uniform Guidance also states that auditees must prepare a schedule of expenditures of federal awards for the period covered by the financial statements. See chapter 17 for information on the preparation of the schedule of expenditures of federal awards.

Summary Schedule of Prior Audit Findings

15.34 In accordance with the Uniform Guidance, the auditee must prepare a summary schedule of prior audit findings. The schedule must report the status of all audit findings included in the prior audit's summary schedule of findings and questioned costs, including findings relating to the financial statements which are required to be reported in accordance with *Government Auditing Standards*. It also must include audit findings reported in the prior audit's summary schedule of prior audit findings, except audit findings that have been corrected or are no longer valid. Chapter 23 of this guide further discusses that schedule.

Other Responsibilities

15.35 The Uniform Guidance establishes certain other responsibilities for auditees as it relates to a single audit. The auditee must

- identify in its accounts all federal awards received and expended and the federal programs under which they were received, including, as applicable, the CFDA title and number, the federal award identification number and year, the name of the federal agency, and the name of the pass-through entity, if any.
- comply with federal statutes, regulations, and the terms and conditions of federal awards
- establish and maintain effective internal control over federal awards that provides reasonable assurance that the auditee is managing federal awards in compliance with federal statutes, regulations, and the terms and conditions of federal awards.

---

[20] In addition, 2 CFR 200.518(c)(2) permits a federal awarding agency to request OMB approval that a type A program for certain recipients not be considered low risk so that it would be audited as a major program. Further, 2 CFR 200.519(c)(2) states that federal agencies, with the concurrence of the OMB, may identify federal programs that are higher risk. That identification is provided by the OMB in the *OMB Compliance Supplement* (*Compliance Supplement*). See the further discussion of those provisions and the definition of type A programs in chapter 18, "Determination of Major Programs (Uniform Guidance)," of this guide.

- procure or otherwise arrange for the required audit under the Uniform Guidance and ensure it is properly performed and submitted when due.

- evaluate and monitor noncompliance with federal statutes, regulations, and the terms and conditions of federal awards.

- take prompt action when instances of noncompliance are identified including noncompliance identified in audit findings

- promptly follow up and take corrective action on audit findings, including preparation of a summary schedule of prior audit findings (see paragraph 15.34) and a separate corrective action plan.

- take reasonable measures to safeguard protected personally identifiable information and other information the federal awarding agency or pass-through entity designates as sensitive or the nonfederal entity considers sensitive consistent with applicable federal, state, and local laws regarding privacy and obligations of confidentially.

- provide the auditor with access to personnel, accounts, books, records, supporting documentation, and other information as needed for the auditor to perform the audit required by the Uniform Guidance.

Responsibility for Compliance at the Financial Statement Level and for Internal Control Over Financial Reporting

15.36 The auditee is responsible for complying with the requirements of all laws and regulations (including federal statutes) and the provisions of contracts and grant agreements (including award agreements) to which it is subject, for establishing and maintaining effective internal control over financial reporting, and for implementing systems designed to achieve compliance with applicable laws and regulations.

Corrective Action Plan

15.37 At the completion of the audit, the auditee must prepare a corrective action plan to address each audit finding included in the current year's auditor's reports. This includes findings relating to the financial statements that are required to be reported under *Government Auditing Standards*. The corrective action plan must be in a document separate from the auditor's findings. Chapter 23 of this guide further discusses the corrective action plan.

Reporting Package

15.38 The auditee must submit to the FAC a reporting package that includes the previously discussed financial statements and schedule of expenditures of federal awards, summary schedule of prior audit findings, auditor's reports, and corrective action plan. The auditee must submit the reporting package with the data collection form described in paragraph 15.39. These items are submitted electronically via the FAC's Internet Data Entry System. Chapter 23 of this guide describes the report submission process and related requirements of the Uniform Guidance.

Data Collection Form

15.39 The auditee is required to submit a data collection form (SF-SAC) that provides information about the auditee, its federal programs, and the results of the audit. The auditor also is required to complete certain sections of the form and electronically sign an auditor statement provided on the form. Chapter 23 of this guide further discusses the data collection form and the submission process.

Federal Awarding Agency Responsibilities

15.40 The Uniform Guidance establishes certain responsibilities for federal agencies that provide federal awards directly to nonfederal entities (that is, a federal awarding agency). A federal awarding agency must perform the following for the federal awards it makes:[21]

- Ensure that audits are completed and reports are received in a timely manner and in accordance with the requirements of the Uniform Guidance.

- Provide technical advice and counsel to auditees and auditors as requested.

- Follow up on audit findings to ensure that the recipient takes appropriate and timely corrective action. This includes issuing management decisions, monitoring the recipient taking appropriate and timely corrective action, using cooperative audit resolution mechanisms, and developing a baseline, metrics, and targets to track, over time, the effectiveness of the federal agency's process to follow-up on audit findings and on the effectiveness of single audits.

- Provide the OMB annual updates to the *Compliance Supplement* and work with the OMB to ensure that the *Compliance Supplement* focuses the auditor to test the compliance requirements most likely to cause improper payments, fraud, waste, abuse or generate audit findings for which the federal awarding agency will take actions.

- Provide the OMB with the name of a single audit accountable official from among the senior policy officials of the federal awarding agency and the name of the key management single audit liaison. Responsibilities for both of these individuals are described in the Uniform Guidance.

Pass-Through Entity Responsibilities

15.41 Pass-through entities have many responsibilities that are similar to those of federal awarding agencies. Chapter 22 of this guide describes the responsibilities of pass-through entities.

---

[21] 2 CFR 200.210 of Subpart C, "Pre-federal Award Requirements and Contents of Federal Awards," of the Uniform Guidance provides requirements regarding the information that must be included in a federal award.

Cognizant Agency for Audit

Definition

15.42 Subpart A of the Uniform Guidance defines the *cognizant agency for audit* as the federal agency designated to carry out the responsibilities described in 2 CFR 200.513(a). A nonfederal entity expending more than $50 million a year in federal awards must have a cognizant agency for audit. The designated cognizant agency for audit must be the federal awarding agency that provides the predominant amount of direct funding to a nonfederal entity unless the OMB designates a specific cognizant agency for audit. The determination of the predominant amount of direct funding must be based on the direct federal awards expended in the nonfederal entity's fiscal years ending in 2009, 2014, 2019, and every fifth year thereafter.[22] For example, audit cognizance for periods ending in 2016–2020 will be determined based on the federal awards expended in 2014. A federal awarding agency with cognizance for an auditee may reassign cognizance to another federal awarding agency that provides substantial funding and agrees to be the cognizant agency for audit. Within 30 calendar days after any reassignment both the old and the new cognizant agency for audit must provide notice of the change to the FAC, the auditee, and, if known, the auditor. The cognizant agency for audit is not necessarily the same as the cognizant agency for indirect costs (as defined in 2 CFR 200.19 of Subpart A of the Uniform Guidance). Therefore, a nonfederal entity may have one federal agency responsible for audit cognizance and another federal agency responsible for the negotiation of indirect costs.

Responsibilities

15.43 The Uniform Guidance provides that a cognizant agency for audit must

- provide technical audit advice and liaison assistance to auditees and auditors.

- obtain or conduct quality control reviews on selected audits made by nonfederal auditors and provide the results to other interested organizations.[23]

- cooperate and provide support to the federal agency designated by OMB to lead a government-wide project to determine the quality of single audits (see paragraph 15.47).

- promptly inform other affected federal agencies and appropriate federal law enforcement officials of any direct reporting by the auditee or its auditor required by *Government Auditing Standards* or statutes and regulations.

---

[22] See footnote 19 for a link to the "Federal Cognizant Agent List" as found on the Federal Audit Clearinghouse website.

[23] Cognizant and oversight agencies use various checklists and tools to perform quality control reviews and desk reviews. One source of information regarding these reviews is the Council of Inspectors General on Integrity and Efficiency (CIGIE) website at www.ignet.gov/. Guides and manuals published by CIGIE that are used in quality control reviews and desk reviews of Circular A-133 compliance audits are available at www.ignet.gov/content/manuals-guides. However, it is noted that these tools have not yet been updated for the Uniform Guidance, and therefore should not be used for a review of a Uniform Guidance compliance audit.

- advise the community of independent auditors of any noteworthy or important factual trends related to the quality of audits stemming from quality control reviews. Significant problems or quality issues consistently identified through quality control reviews of audit reports must be referred to appropriate state licensing agencies and professional bodies.

- advise the auditor, federal awarding agencies, and, where appropriate, the auditee of any deficiencies found in the audits when the deficiencies require corrective action by the auditor. When advised of deficiencies, the auditee must work with the auditor to take corrective action. If corrective action is not taken, the cognizant agency for audit must notify the auditor, the auditee, and applicable federal awarding agencies and pass-through entities of the facts and make recommendations for follow-up action. Major inadequacies or repetitive substandard performance by auditors must be referred to appropriate state licensing agencies and professional bodies for disciplinary action.

- coordinate, to the extent practical, audits or reviews made by or for federal agencies that are in addition to audits made under the Uniform Guidance, so that the additional audits or reviews build upon, rather than duplicate, audits performed under the Uniform Guidance.

- coordinate a management decision for cross-cutting audit findings (as defined in 2 CFR 200.30) that affect the federal programs of more than one agency when requested by any federal awarding agency whose awards are included in the audit finding of the auditee.

- coordinate the audit work and reporting responsibilities among auditors to achieve the most cost-effective audit.

- provide advice to auditees as to how to handle changes in fiscal years.

Oversight Agency for Audit

Definition

15.44 An auditee that does not have a designated cognizant agency for audit (that is, one that expends $50 million or less in federal awards) will have an oversight agency for audit. Subpart A of the Uniform Guidance defines the *oversight agency for audit* as a federal awarding agency that provides the predominant amount of funding directly to a nonfederal entity not assigned a cognizant agency for audit. When there is no direct funding, the federal awarding agency which is the predominant source of pass-through funding must assume the oversight responsibilities. An oversight agency for audit may reassign oversight to another federal agency that agrees to be the oversight agency for audit. Within 30 calendar days after any reassignment, both the old and the new oversight agency for audit must provide notice of the change to the FAC, the auditee, and, if known, the auditor.

Responsibilities

15.45 The Uniform Guidance describes the duties of oversight agencies for audit. Although an oversight agency must provide technical advice to auditees and auditors as requested, in general, the responsibilities of an oversight agency for audit are not as broad as those of a cognizant agency for audit. However, an oversight agency may assume all or some of the responsibilities normally performed by a cognizant agency for audit.

Program-Specific Audits

15.46 The Uniform Guidance provides general guidance on performing program-specific audits. In some cases, a program-specific audit guide will be available. A listing of current program-specific audit guides can be found in the *Compliance Supplement* including the federal awarding agency contact information and a website where a copy of the guide can be obtained. The audit guide will provide specific guidance to the auditor with respect to internal control, compliance requirements, suggested audit procedures, and audit reporting requirements. When a current program-specific audit guide is available, the auditor must follow *Government Auditing Standards* and the guide when performing a program-specific audit. When a current program-specific audit guide is not available, the auditee and auditor have basically the same responsibilities for the federal program as they would have for an audit of a major program in a single audit. Chapter 24 of this guide further discusses program-specific audits.

Required Government-wide Evaluation of Single Audit Quality

15.47 The Uniform Guidance provides that a government-wide audit quality project must be performed once every six years beginning in 2018 or at such other interval as determined by OMB, and the results must be public. This project will be led by a federal agency designated by OMB, along with cooperation and support of cognizant agencies for audit. The project will determine the quality of single audits by providing a statistically reliable estimate of the extent that single audits conform to applicable requirements, standards, and procedures. Recommendations will be made to address noted quality issues, including recommendations for any changes to applicable requirements, standards, and procedures indicated by the results of the project.

Emphasis Point

Auditors should ensure that staff is competent to perform single audits and that they are appropriately trained on the Uniform Guidance audit requirements. Internal quality control systems should also emphasize single audits. Keep in mind that engagements selected for review by federal agencies could include audits for periods in 2017, 2018, or both depending on the timing of the federal project.

OMB Compliance Supplement

15.48 As part of the Uniform Guidance compliance audit, the auditor must determine whether the auditee has complied with federal statutes, regulations, and the terms and conditions of federal awards (compliance requirements) that may have a direct and material effect on each of its major programs.

Overview of the Single Audit Act

The principal tool for this purpose is the *Compliance Supplement,* which is updated annually.[24] Under the Uniform Guidance, the *Compliance Supplement* is located in Appendix XI to 2 CFR 200. Chapter 20 of this guide further discusses compliance requirements and the *Compliance Supplement.*

15.49 The *Compliance Supplement* is based on the requirements of the Single Audit Act and the Uniform Guidance, which provide for the issuance of a compliance supplement to assist auditors in performing the required audits. The Uniform Guidance states that federal agencies must provide to OMB annual updates to the *Compliance Supplement* and work with OMB to ensure that the *Compliance Supplement* focuses the auditor to test the compliance requirements most likely to cause improper payments, fraud, waste, abuse, or generate audit findings for which the federal awarding agency will take sanctions. The requirements and guidance found in the separate parts of the *Compliance Supplement* are interrelated, and should be used in conjunction with each other. One purpose of the *Compliance Supplement* is to identify existing compliance requirements that the federal government expects to be considered as part of an audit in accordance with the Single Audit Act and the Uniform Guidance:

- For the programs it includes, the *Compliance Supplement* provides a source of information for auditors to understand the federal program's objectives, procedures, and types of compliance requirements relevant to the audit, as well as the audit objectives and suggested audit procedures for determining compliance with these requirements.

- For programs not listed in the *Compliance Supplement,* the auditor must determine the current compliance requirements and modify the audit procedures accordingly. The auditor must follow *Compliance Supplement* Part 7, "Guidance for Auditing Programs Not Included in This Compliance Supplement." Part 7 instructs the auditor to use the types of compliance requirements (for example, cash management, reporting, allowable costs/cost principles, activities allowed or unallowed, eligibility, and matching, level of effort, and earmarking) contained in the *Compliance Supplement* as guidance for identifying the types of compliance requirements to test, and to determine the requirements governing the federal program by reviewing the provisions of contracts and grant agreements and the laws and regulations referred to in such contracts and grant agreements.

Transition Considerations Related to the Uniform Guidance

15.50 Nonfederal entities are required to implement the Uniform Guidance administrative requirements and cost principles beginning December 26, 2014, for all new federal awards and funding increments (additional funding to existing federal awards) with modified award terms and conditions that are awarded on or after that date. Typically, the terms and conditions of the federal award should identify whether the funding increment is subject to the Uniform Guidance requirements, or whether it will continue to be governed

---

[24] The *Compliance Supplement* can be accessed on the OMB website at www.whitehouse.gov/omb/circulars default/.

by the original terms and conditions of the federal award (that is, subject to the pre-Uniform Guidance requirements). Note that the effective date of the Uniform Guidance as it relates to a subaward is the same as the effective date of the federal award from which the subaward is made.

15.51 The audit requirements of the Uniform Guidance are effective for audits of fiscal years beginning on or after December 26, 2014. Therefore, auditees subject to a single audit with December 25, 2015, and later year ends will be required to undergo the single audit under the Uniform Guidance. Early implementation of the audit requirements is not permitted.

15.52 The audit requirements applicable to an auditee that undergoes biennial audits is dependent on the beginning date of the biennial audit period. For example, for a nonfederal entity that has a biennial audit period of July 1, 2014 to June 30, 2016, the audit will be performed under Circular A-133. Furthermore, for those biennial audits performed under Circular A-133, the audit reports will not be publicly available on the FAC website and the auditee will need to provide the reports to any pass-through entities. The Uniform Guidance audit requirements apply to any biennial period beginning on or after the effective date of the Uniform Guidance.

15.53 The effective dates within the Uniform Guidance may present a challenge to auditees as they will be affected immediately upon the receipt of a new federal award or certain funding increments (see paragraph 15.50) received on or after December 26, 2014. One of the challenges that auditees may face is that they may incur expenditures from both federal awards subject to the pre-Uniform Guidance requirements, as well as federal awards subject to the post-Uniform Guidance requirements. This situation could exist for several years until the pre-Uniform Guidance awards have been completely expended. It is important that auditees identify the requirements that apply to each federal award or funding increment, document that identification, and develop a system to properly apply the appropriate compliance requirements to the award. Council on Financial Assistance Reform (COFAR) FAQ 110.13 addresses this situation and states that nonfederal entities may have federal awards subject to differing administrative requirements (for example, payroll or procurement systems) due to the effective date of the Uniform Guidance. It goes on to state that nonfederal entities that make system-wide changes to comply with the Uniform Guidance will not be penalized for applying these changes to funding not subject to the Uniform Guidance. See paragraph 15.56 for more information on the COFAR FAQs.

15.54 On December 19, 2014, a joint interim final rule was issued containing the implementing regulations of all federal awarding agencies. Those regulations are effective on December 26, 2014. As part of each department or agency's adoption or implementation of the OMB guidance in 2 CFR Part 200, the department or agency was able to request needed exceptions. Most departments and agencies requested such exceptions. Some of the exceptions could affect auditee compliance requirements, as well as the Uniform Guidance compliance audit. Auditees and auditors can find a listing and the text of the exceptions in a document titled, "Uniform Guidance Crosswalk for Federal Agency Exceptions and Additions," at https://cfo.gov/wp-content/uploads/2014/12/Agency-Exceptions.pdf. Appendix VII, "Other Audit Advisories," of the 2015 *Compliance Supplement* also includes a summarized listing, by organization, of the affected sections. Although the interim final regulations are binding upon issuance, Part 3, *Compliance Requirements*, of the 2015 *Compliance Supplement* states that federal awarding agencies will be considering all comments and are expected to issue final regulations during 2015, which may include changes to their interim final regulations. Both auditees and auditors should watch for developments in this area.

15.55 The joint interim final rule also included technical corrections made to the Uniform Guidance. The technical corrections include revisions due to errors, unclear language, or in cases where the language in the final guidance did not match the intent of the guidance. Some technical correction items of note are as follows:

- In various places throughout the Uniform Guidance the use of *should* was changed to *must*,
- The effective/applicability date was revised to allow a grace period of one fiscal year for nonfederal entities to implement changes to their procurement policies and procedures in accordance with the revised procurement standards.

Auditees and auditors can find the most up-to-date version of the Uniform Guidance, which includes technical corrections using the website in paragraph 15.57.

Frequently Asked Questions

15.56 Frequently Asked Questions (FAQ) documents have been released by COFAR that provide information regarding specific sections of the Uniform Guidance. The most up-to-date version of the FAQs are available at https://cfo.gov/cofar/#RUUG. Part 3 of the 2015 *Compliance Supplement* refers to COFAR FAQs in several places. It states that the FAQs provide additional information about the implementation of 2 CFR Part 200 and that auditors should consider the FAQs in conjunction with 2 CFR Part 200, Subpart E, when evaluating compliance. The cover of the FAQs also state that in case of any discrepancy, the actual guidance at 2 CFR 200 governs.

Reference Materials

15.57 The most current version of the Uniform Guidance, including technical corrections, is available on the electronic CFR (eCFR) system at Part 200. Other information, including the original version of the Uniform Guidance and crosswalk documents from the circulars to the Uniform Guidance, is available on the COFAR website at https://cfo.gov/cofar/#RUUG.

Chapter 16

Auditor Planning Considerations Under the Uniform Guidance

> **© Update 16-1: Audits of Federal Awards**
>
> This chapter, and the remaining chapters of part III, *Uniform Guidance Audits*, of this guide should be used for performing a compliance audit of federal awards under the audit requirements of Title 2 U.S. *Code of Federal Regulations* Part 200, *Uniform Administrative Requirements, Cost Principles, and Audit Requirements for Federal Awards* (Uniform Guidance).[1] Part II, *Circular A-133 Audits*, of this guide should be used for performing a compliance audit under Office of Management and Budget (OMB) Circular A-133, *Audits of States, Local Governments, and Non-Profit Organizations* (Circular A-133). See the transitional guidance sections at the end of each chapter that highlight important matters for consideration. Additionally, refer to the preface of this guide for more information.
>
> **Important Effective Date Information**
>
> In December 2013, the OMB issued the Uniform Guidance, which is effective for nonfederal entities for all federal awards and certain funding increments provided on or after December 26, 2014. The requirements in Subpart F, "Audit Requirements," are effective for audits of fiscal years beginning on or after December 26, 2014, with no early implementation permitted. Therefore, auditees subject to a single audit with December 25, 2015, and later year ends (for example, December 31, 2015) will be required to undergo the audit under Subpart F of the Uniform Guidance. Note that audits of fiscal years ending prior to the effective date of the Uniform Guidance audit requirements are subject to an audit under Circular A-133.

Introduction

16.01 In planning an audit to meet the requirements of the Uniform Guidance the auditor needs to consider a number of matters in addition to those ordinarily associated with an audit of financial statements in accordance with generally accepted auditing standards (GAAS) and *Government Auditing Standards*. This chapter discusses additional planning considerations in a single audit conducted in accordance with the Uniform Guidance. Many of these planning considerations also are applicable in program-specific audits, which are discussed in chapter 24, "Program-Specific Audits (Uniform Guidance)," of this guide.

16.02 Chapter 3, "Planning and Performing a Financial Statement Audit in Accordance With *Government Auditing Standards*," of this guide discusses

---

[1] See the information found at the end of this chapter (paragraph 16.74) and other part III, *Uniform Guidance Audits*, chapters of this guide, for transition considerations when performing an audit under Title 2 U.S. *Code of Federal Regulations* (CFR) Part 200, *Uniform Administrative Requirements, Cost Principles, and Audit Requirements for Federal Awards* (Uniform Guidance). Transition considerations can also be found at the end of certain part II, *Circular A-133 Audits*, chapters as it relates to an audit performed under Office of Management and Budget Circular A-133, *Audits of States, Local Governments, and Non-Profit Organizations* (Circular A-133).

matters that are relevant to the planning of a financial statement audit. The rest of this chapter discusses the following additional or expanded matters relevant to the planning of a single audit:

- Adapting and applying applicable auditing standards to a Uniform Guidance compliance audit
- Identifying supplementary audit requirements
- Agreeing upon the terms of the engagement with management
- Financial statement audit considerations
- Developing an efficient audit approach
- Defining the entity to be audited
- Determining the audit period
- Initial-year audit considerations
- Timing of the completion of the audit and report submission deadlines
- Determining the major programs to be audited
- Identifying direct and material compliance requirements
- Audit risk of noncompliance considerations
- Assessing the risks of material noncompliance
- Audit materiality considerations
- Audit documentation
- Audit documentation access and audit follow-up
- Group audit considerations in a Uniform Guidance compliance audit
- Existence of an internal audit function
- Communications with the cognizant or oversight agency for audit and others
- State and local compliance requirements
- Desk reviews and on-site reviews
- Restriction on the auditor's preparation of indirect cost proposals

Adapting and Applying Applicable Auditing Standards to a Uniform Guidance Compliance Audit

16.03 Single audits are required to be performed in accordance with *Government Auditing Standards*, which incorporates by reference the AICPA Statements on Auditing Standards. AU-C section 935, *Compliance Audits* (AICPA, *Professional Standards*), addresses a compliance audit, which is one part of a single audit. It is applicable when an auditor is engaged, or required by law or regulation, to perform a compliance audit in accordance with all of the following:

- GAAS
- The standards for financial audits under *Government Auditing Standards*
- A governmental audit requirement that requires the auditor to express an opinion on compliance

16.04 AU-C section 935 defines a *governmental audit requirement* as a government requirement established by law, regulation, rule, or provision of contracts or grant agreements requiring that an entity undergo an audit of its compliance with applicable compliance requirements[2] related to one or more government programs that the entity administers. Therefore, AU-C section 935 is applicable to and provides requirements and guidance for auditors conducting an audit in accordance with the Uniform Guidance. Chapters 19, "Consideration of Internal Control Over Compliance for Major Programs (Uniform Guidance)," and 20, "Compliance Auditing Applicable to Major Programs (Uniform Guidance)," of this guide provide additional information and guidance related to AU-C section 935. Part I of this guide provides information and guidance for a financial statement audit performed under *Government Auditing Standards*.

16.05 AU-C sections 200–800 address audits of financial statements, as well as other kinds of engagements. AU-C section 935 notes that when performing a compliance audit, the auditor, using professional judgment, should adapt and apply the AU-C sections to the objectives of a compliance audit except for those AU-C sections, or portions thereof, that are identified as not applicable to a compliance audit in the appendix, "AU-C Sections That Are Not Applicable to Compliance Audits," to AU-C section 935.[3] For those AU-C sections that are applicable to a compliance audit, AU-C section 935 states that the auditor is not required, in planning and performing a compliance audit, to make a literal translation of each procedure that might be performed in a financial statement audit but rather to obtain sufficient appropriate audit evidence to support the auditor's opinion on compliance.

16.06 Paragraph .06 of AU-C section 935 notes that some AU-C sections can be adapted and applied to a compliance audit with relative ease, for example, by replacing the word *misstatement* with *noncompliance*. However, other AU-C sections are more difficult to adapt and apply without additional modification. For that reason, AU-C section 935 provides more specific guidance on how to adapt certain AU-C sections to a compliance audit. This guide also provides information on how an auditor may adapt certain AU-C sections to a Uniform Guidance compliance audit.

Identifying Supplementary Audit Requirements

16.07 In a Uniform Guidance compliance audit, the auditor should determine the additional audit requirements that are supplementary to GAAS and *Government Auditing Standards* and perform procedures to address those requirements. Part III of this guide provides information to assist the auditor

---

[2] AU-C section 935, *Compliance Audits* (AICPA, *Professional Standards*), defines *applicable compliance requirements* as the compliance requirements that are subject to the compliance audit. 2 CFR 200.514(d)(1) states that the auditor must determine whether the auditee has complied with the federal statutes, regulations, and the terms and conditions of the federal awards that may have a direct and material effect on each of its major programs. Therefore, in a Uniform Guidance compliance audit, the direct and material compliance requirements are those that are subject to audit. Accordingly, for the purpose of adapting AU-C section 935 to a Uniform Guidance compliance audit, the term *applicable compliance requirements* has been replaced by *direct and material compliance requirements* in this guide except when directly citing content from AU-C section 935.

[3] The appendix, "AU-C Sections That Are Not Applicable to Compliance Audits," of AU-C section 935 provides a list of AU-C section requirements that are not applicable to a compliance audit. All other AU-C sections not identified in the appendix should be adapted and applied to a compliance audit.

in addressing the supplementary audit requirements of the Uniform Guidance. In instances in which the audit guidance provided by a governmental agency for the performance of a compliance audit has not been updated, or otherwise conflicts with current standards and requirements, the auditor should comply with the most current applicable GAAS and *Government Auditing Standards* instead of the outdated guidance.

Agreeing Upon the Terms of the Engagement With Management

16.08 As discussed in chapter 3 of this guide, AU-C section 210, *Terms of Engagement* (AICPA, *Professional Standards*), provides guidance related to the auditor's responsibilities in agreeing upon the terms of an audit engagement with management or, when appropriate, those charged with governance. AU-C section 210 introduces certain preconditions that should be present before the auditor accepts the engagement. See chapter 3 of this guide for more information.

16.09 The terms of the engagement generally include the information found in paragraph .10 of AU-C section 210 and should be documented in an audit engagement letter or other suitable form of written agreement. In addition to the matters communicated as part of the financial statement audit performed in accordance with *Government Auditing Standards* (as further described in chapter 3), the communication should include the planned work and level of assurance related to internal control over compliance and compliance with federal statutes, regulations, and the terms and conditions of federal awards necessary for an audit in accordance with the Uniform Guidance. Examples of the type of information that might be included in the communication when performing an audit in accordance with the Uniform Guidance are as follows:

- A statement that the supplementary schedule(s) to be considered in the audit include the schedule of expenditures of federal awards
- The objective of an audit in accordance with the Uniform Guidance
- A description of the additional reports required by the Uniform Guidance that the auditor is expected to prepare and issue, including any limitation on their use
- A description of management's responsibility for (*a*) identifying all federal awards received; (*b*) preparing the schedule of expenditures of federal awards (including notes and noncash assistance received) in accordance with Uniform Guidance requirements;[4] (*c*) internal control over compliance; (*d*) compliance with federal statutes, regulations, and the terms and conditions of federal awards; (*e*) following up and taking corrective action on audit findings, including the preparation of a summary schedule of prior audit findings and a corrective action plan; and (*f*) submitting the reporting package and data collection form

---

[4] AU-C section 725, *Supplementary Information in Relation to the Financial Statements as a Whole* (AICPA, *Professional Standards*), sets forth specific requirements related to management's responsibility when the auditor is engaged to report on whether supplementary information (for example, the schedule of expenditures of federal awards) is fairly stated, in all material respects, in relation to the financial statements as a whole. See chapter 17, "Schedule of Expenditures of Federal Awards (Uniform Guidance)," of this guide for more information.

Auditor Planning Considerations Under the Uniform Guidance

- A statement that management will make the auditor aware of significant contractor relationships in which the contractor is responsible for program compliance (so that the auditor can determine if additional procedures on contractor records will be necessary—see chapter 22, "Audit Considerations of Federal Pass-Through Awards (Uniform Guidance)," of this guide)
- A description of the auditor's responsibility in a compliance audit of major programs under the Uniform Guidance, including the determination of major programs, the consideration of internal control over compliance, and reporting responsibilities
- A statement that the parties to whom audit documentation will be made available upon request include federal agencies and the U.S. Government Accountability Office (GAO)

In addition, paragraph .37 of AU-C section 935 states that the auditor should communicate to those charged with governance the auditor's responsibilities under GAAS, *Government Auditing Standards*, and the governmental audit requirement (for example, the Uniform Guidance), an overview of the planned scope and timing of the compliance audit, and significant findings from the compliance audit.

Financial Statement Audit Considerations

Emphasis Point

The use of the term *must* in the Uniform Guidance indicates a requirement. This is consistent with the use of the term *must* in GAAS and *Government Auditing Standards*. The use of the term *should* in the Uniform Guidance indicates a best practice or recommended approach. However, GAAS and *Government Auditing Standards* use the term *should* to indicate a presumptively mandatory requirement. An auditor must comply with a presumptively mandatory requirement in all cases in which such a requirement is relevant, except in rare circumstances. In this guide, the term ***should***, when italicized and bolded, indicates a best practice or recommended approach in the Uniform Guidance. This is intended to differentiate it from the term "should" used throughout the guide to refer to presumptively mandatory requirements in GAAS and *Government Auditing Standards*. See chapter 1, "Introduction and Overview of *Government Auditing Standards*," of this guide for more information regarding presumptively mandatory requirements.

16.10 The Uniform Guidance states that auditees must prepare financial statements that reflect their financial position, results of operations or changes in net assets, and, where appropriate, cash flows for the fiscal year audited. The financial statements must be for the same organizational unit and fiscal year that is chosen to meet the requirements of the Uniform Guidance. However, entity-wide financial statements may include departments, agencies, and other organizational units that have separate audits in accordance with the Uniform Guidance and prepare separate financial statements (see paragraph 16.15). The Uniform Guidance states that the auditee must prepare a schedule of expenditures of federal awards for the period covered by the auditee's financial statements.[5] Chapter 17, "Schedule of Expenditures of Federal Awards (Uniform Guidance)," of this guide discusses the schedule of expenditures of federal awards.

16.11 The Uniform Guidance does not prescribe the basis of accounting that auditees use to prepare their financial statements. However, auditees should disclose the basis of accounting and significant accounting policies used in preparing the financial statements. The Uniform Guidance states that auditees must be able to identify in their accounts all federal awards received and expended and the federal programs under which they were received. Such identification must include, as applicable, the Catalog of Federal Domestic Assistance (CFDA) title and number, federal award identification number and year, name of the federal agency, and name of the pass-through entity, if any. Generally, auditees further evidence the ability to identify federal awards expended by preparing a reconciliation of amounts presented in the financial statements to the amounts and programs in the schedule of expenditures of federal awards.

16.12 Under the Uniform Guidance, the auditor must issue an opinion (or a disclaimer of opinion) about whether the financial statements are presented fairly in all material respects in accordance with generally accepted accounting principles (GAAP).[6] (Chapters 4, "Auditor Reporting Requirements and Other Communication Considerations of *Government Auditing Standards*," and 23, "Auditor Reporting Requirements and Other Communication Considerations in a Single Audit (Uniform Guidance)," of this guide provide guidance on reporting on the auditee's financial statements.)

16.13 If the auditee prepares its financial statements in accordance with a special purpose framework,[7] the auditor still is required to express or disclaim an opinion on the special purpose financial statements. The auditor's report on special purpose financial statements should include an emphasis-of-matter paragraph that, among other things, states that the special purpose framework

---

[5] When comparative financial statements are presented by the auditee, the schedule of expenditures of federal awards includes information on the current period only.

[6] As explained in the AICPA Audit and Accounting Guide *State and Local Governments*, the auditor generally expresses or disclaims an opinion on a government's basic financial statements by providing an opinion or disclaimer of opinion on each opinion unit required to be presented in those financial statements. In addition, the auditor may provide opinions or disclaimers of opinion on additional opinion units if engaged to set the scope of the audit and assess materiality at a more detailed level than by the opinion units required for the basic financial statements. Throughout this guide, the use of the singular terms *opinion* and *disclaimer of opinion* encompasses the multiple opinions and disclaimers of opinion that generally will be provided on a government's basic financial statements.

[7] AU-C section 800, *Special Considerations—Audits of Financial Statements Prepared in Accordance With Special Purpose Frameworks* (AICPA, *Professional Standards*), defines a *special purpose framework* as a financial reporting framework other than generally accepted accounting principles and establishes requirements for reporting on those frameworks. Special purpose frameworks, such as the cash, tax, regulatory, and other bases of accounting, are sometimes referred to as an *other comprehensive bases of accounting* (OCBOA). The term *OCBOA* is sometimes used when referring to this guidance in this guide.

The AICPA Audit and Accounting Guide *State and Local Governments* discusses the application of AU-C section 800 to state and local governmental financial statements and also provides illustrative auditor's reports for financial statements prepared in accordance with a special purpose framework. In addition, the AICPA practice aid *Applying OCBOA in State and Local Governmental Financial Statements* (APAOCBO12P) provides nonauthoritative guidance on preparing and reporting on OCBOA financial statements of governmental entities. A second practice aid, *Accounting and Financial Reporting Guidelines for Cash- and Tax-Basis Financial Statements* (APACTB12P), provides nonauthoritative guidance for preparers regarding guidelines and best practices for the preparation of cash and tax basis financial statements. These publications are available at www.cpa2biz.com.

is a basis of accounting other than GAAP. However, if the special purpose financial statements are prepared in accordance with a regulatory basis of accounting and the special purpose financial statements together with the auditor's report are intended for general use, the auditor's report should not include such an emphasis-of-matter paragraph. Instead, the auditor should express an opinion about whether the financial statements are presented fairly, in all material respects, in accordance with GAAP and include in a separate paragraph an opinion about whether the financial statements are prepared in accordance with the special purpose framework. AU-C section 800, *Special Considerations—Audits of Financial Statements Prepared in Accordance With Special Purpose Frameworks* (AICPA, *Professional Standards*), contains relevant requirements and guidance.

Emphasis Point

As per paragraph .A5 of AU-C section 800, if a regulator permits, but not requires, a cash basis of accounting, it would not be considered a regulatory basis of accounting, but rather a cash basis of accounting. Therefore, in this situation, an emphasis-of-matter paragraph would be used in the auditor's report to indicate that the special purpose framework is a basis of accounting other than GAAP (versus the regulatory basis of accounting reporting which would include an opinion on whether the financial statements are prepared fairly, in all material respects, in accordance with GAAP).

Developing an Efficient Audit Approach

16.14 Consideration of ways to achieve maximum audit efficiency may be useful in the planning stage of the audit. Examples of ways to achieve audit efficiency follow:

- The financial statement audit and the Uniform Guidance compliance audit could be planned at the same time.

- If the auditee's internal control for a compliance requirement is common to more than one major program, the transactions of those programs could be combined into one population for selecting sample sizes for internal control tests. Although this approach may be efficient for internal control tests, experience has shown that it is preferable to select separate samples for compliance testing from each major program because the separate samples provide clear evidence of the compliance tests performed, the results of those tests, and the conclusions reached. It also assists the auditor in ensuring sufficient testing is performed to meet the audit objectives required for each major program. (See chapter 21, "Audit Sampling Considerations of Uniform Guidance Compliance Audits," of this guide for information related to audit sampling in a compliance audit.)

- The Uniform Guidance requires the auditor to plan the testing of internal control over compliance and perform such testing to support a low assessed level of control risk of noncompliance for major programs. Therefore, when a low assessed level of control risk is achieved, the auditor may be able to take advantage of that low assessed level of control risk of noncompliance for major programs when performing the testing of compliance.

- Helpful quality control materials (such as planning checklists and reporting checklists) could be used.[8]

Defining the Entity to Be Audited

16.15 One of the initial tasks during the planning process of a single audit is determining whether management has properly defined the entity to be audited. The Uniform Guidance states that the audit must cover the entire operations of the auditee, or, at the option of the auditee, such audit must include a series of audits that cover an auditee's departments, agencies, and other organizational units that expended or otherwise administered federal awards during the audit period. If an auditee elects this option, each audit must encompass the financial statements and the schedule of expenditures of federal awards for each such department, agency, or other organizational unit, which must be considered a nonfederal entity.[9] The financial statements and schedule of expenditures of federal awards must be for the same audit period. In these circumstances, the nonfederal entity-wide financial statements may also include the departments, agencies, or other organizational units that have separate audits and prepare separate financial statements. For example, if a local government has its school districts audited separately, it would be acceptable for the local government's financial statements to include the school districts, even though the school districts were not included in the local government's Uniform Guidance compliance audit (and, consequently, the schedule of expenditures of federal awards for the local government did not include the school districts' federal awards) because a separate Uniform Guidance compliance audit was conducted on the school districts. However, if separate financial statements were not prepared for the school districts, it would be unacceptable for a separate Uniform Guidance compliance audit to be conducted on the school districts (that is, the local government's entity-wide financial statements could not be used as a substitute for separate financial statements for the school districts). Chapter 23 of this guide discusses auditor reporting in situations in which (*a*) the implementation regulations of federal awarding agencies[10] define the entity to be audited differently than does GAAP and (*b*) the audit of federal awards does not encompass the entirety of the auditee's operations expending federal awards.

Determining the Audit Period

Fiscal Year and Program Period May Differ

16.16 An audit performed in accordance with the Uniform Guidance should cover the auditee's financial transactions (including transactions

---

[8] Once they are updated for the Uniform Guidance, the AICPA peer review checklists are a good resource. Once updated, these checklists will be available at www.aicpa.org, and a number of the checklists related to single audits will also be accessible via the Governmental Audit Quality Center website. To access these checklists, go to the Resources page of the GAQC website at www.aicpa.org/gaqc. See also footnote 22 at paragraph 16.72.

[9] Subpart A, "Acronyms and Definitions," of the Uniform Guidance defines a *nonfederal entity* as a state, local government, Indian tribe, institution of higher education, or nonprofit organization that carries out a federal award as a recipient or subrecipient. The term *nonfederal entity* is used throughout part III of this guide as that term is used in the Uniform Guidance.

[10] Certain federal agencies, such as the U.S. Department of Housing and Urban Development, have specifically defined the level of the entity subject to audit.

related to federal awards) for its fiscal year (or a two-year period, if allowed by the Uniform Guidance), which is not necessarily the same as the period of the program being funded. (Chapter 15, "Overview of the Single Audit Act, the Uniform Guidance Audit Requirements, and the *Compliance Supplement*," of this guide discusses the allowability of biennial audits). Thus, the audit might include only a part of the transactions of a federal award because some transactions may not occur within the period covered by the audit.

Stub Periods

16.17 Stub periods may occur when an auditee converts from a program-specific audit to a single audit or changes audit periods. An example would be a community college with a September 30 year end that previously had a program-specific audit and is now converting to a single audit. The prior program-specific audits were performed based on a June 30 award year. The first single audit will be for the year ending September 30. This would leave the community college with an unaudited stub period of July 1 to September 30. The audit requirements of the Uniform Guidance still apply to federal expenditures during the stub period and are generally met through a separate audit of the stub period or by including the expenditures of the stub period in the scope of the following period's single audit. Either way, the threshold for audit requirement is still $750,000 in federal expenditures for the period. Auditees or their auditors can contact the cognizant or oversight agency for audit or the pass-through entity for advice on how stub periods can be addressed.

Initial-Year Audit Considerations

Preceding Period Audited by Another Auditor

16.18 AU-C section 210 provides guidance when an auditor is considering accepting an engagement in which the federal awards of the preceding period were audited by another auditor. Paragraph .11 of AU-C section 210 notes that before accepting an engagement for an initial audit, including a re-audit engagement, the auditor should request management to authorize the predecessor auditor to respond fully to the auditor's inquiries regarding matters that will assist the auditor in determining whether to accept the engagement.[11] If management refuses to authorize the predecessor auditor to respond, or limits the response, the auditor should inquire about the reasons and consider the implications of that refusal in deciding whether to accept the engagement.

Factors to Consider Under the Risk-Based Approach[12]

16.19 An auditor accepting, or contemplating accepting, a Uniform Guidance compliance audit engagement might consider gathering certain information to assist in the major program determination process. Information that will assist the auditor includes the following:

---

[11] As noted in chapter 3, "Planning and Performing a Financial Statement Audit in Accordance With *Government Auditing Standards*," of this guide, an auditor may be required by law or regulation to audit the entity. However, inquiries of the predecessor auditor may still be relevant for the purpose of obtaining information that is used by the auditor in planning and performing the audit.

[12] See the discussion in chapter 18, "Determination of Major Programs (Uniform Guidance)," of this guide for more information on the risk-based approach to selecting major programs.

- Federal awards expended by federal programs
- Prior-period findings and questioned costs (including the corrective action plan and management decision related to the findings and summary schedule of prior audit findings)
- Correspondence from program officials indicating potential problems
- New programs
- Changes to programs
- Amount of funding passed through to subrecipients by individual federal programs
- Federal programs audited as a major program for the last two years

Timing of the Completion of the Audit and Report Submission Deadlines

16.20 When planning the timing of the single audit, an important consideration is the Uniform Guidance requirement that the audit be completed and the data collection form and reporting package be submitted to the Federal Audit Clearinghouse within a certain time period.[13] Chapters 15 and 23 of this guide discuss the reporting package and the timing requirements for submission.

Determining the Major Programs to Be Audited

16.21 As discussed in chapter 15 of this guide, the Uniform Guidance states that the auditor must use a risk-based approach to determine which federal programs are major programs. This determination will affect the scope of the Uniform Guidance compliance audit and the compliance requirements to be tested. Chapter 18, "Determination of Major Programs (Uniform Guidance)," of this guide discusses the determination of major programs.

Identifying Direct and Material Compliance Requirements[14]

16.22 As noted in AU-C section 935, a compliance audit is based on the premise that management is responsible for identifying the entity's government programs and understanding and complying with the compliance requirements. As part of the compliance audit, the auditor should determine which of those government programs and compliance requirements to test in accordance with the Uniform Guidance.

16.23 AU-C section 935 defines *applicable compliance requirements* as compliance requirements that are subject to a compliance audit. Some governmental audit requirements specifically identify the applicable compliance

---

[13] If the auditee or auditor wishes to inform the federal government that the required submission will be late, the suggested way to do so is to contact the federal oversight or cognizant agency for the audit (contact information is available on the "Resources" tab at http://harvester.census.gov/fac/APPX3.htm).

[14] See footnote 2.

requirements. Paragraph .A9 of AU-C section 935 notes that other governmental audit requirements provide a framework for the auditor to determine the applicable compliance requirements and cites the *OMB Compliance Supplement (Compliance Supplement)* as such a framework. In a Uniform Guidance compliance audit, the applicable compliance requirements are those that may have a direct and material effect on each major program (direct and material compliance requirements).

16.24 The *Compliance Supplement* is the primary source for identifying compliance requirements for federal programs in a Uniform Guidance compliance audit, and the auditor, using professional judgment, determines which of the 12 types of compliance requirements may have a direct and material effect on each major program. These direct and material compliance requirements are tested as part of the compliance audit. A program-specific audit guide issued by a grantor agency may be another source for identifying applicable compliance requirements. For programs not included in the *Compliance Supplement*, the Uniform Guidance states that the auditor must follow the compliance supplement's guidance for programs not included in the supplement. Among other things, that guidance, included in Part 7 of the *Compliance Supplement*, indicates the auditor should review the federal award document and referenced laws and regulations applicable to the program and the CFDA. Chapter 20 of this guide further discusses the use of the *Compliance Supplement* to identify direct and material compliance requirements.

Audit Risk of Noncompliance Considerations

16.25 The requirements and guidance related to the auditor's consideration of audit risk of noncompliance and materiality when planning and performing a single audit is found in AU-C section 935 and AU-C section 320, *Materiality in Planning and Performing an Audit* (AICPA, *Professional Standards*). Audit risk of noncompliance and materiality, among other matters, need to be considered together for each major program being audited as well as for each direct and material compliance requirement in determining the nature, timing, and extent of audit procedures and in evaluating the results of those procedures.

16.26 Furthermore, the Uniform Guidance states that the auditor must determine whether the auditee has complied with federal statutes, regulations, and the terms and conditions of federal awards that may have a direct and material effect on each of its major programs. Therefore, in developing an audit plan for a single audit, the auditor should assess not only the risk that noncompliance may have a material effect on the financial statements, but also the risk that noncompliance may have a material effect on each major program.

Components of Audit Risk of Noncompliance

16.27 *Audit risk of noncompliance* is the risk that the auditor expresses an inappropriate audit opinion on the entity's compliance when material noncompliance exists. It is a function of the risks of material noncompliance and detection risk of noncompliance.

Risk of Material Noncompliance

16.28 The risk of material noncompliance is the risk that material noncompliance exists before the audit. It consists of inherent risk of noncompliance and control risk of noncompliance. For the purposes of a single audit and the auditor's opinion on compliance, these risk components are defined as follows:[15]

> **inherent risk of noncompliance.** The susceptibility of a major program's compliance requirements to noncompliance that could be material, either individually or when aggregated with other instances of noncompliance, before consideration of any related controls over compliance.

> **control risk of noncompliance.** The risk that noncompliance with a compliance requirement that could occur and that could be material to a major program, either individually or when aggregated with other instances of noncompliance, will not be prevented, or detected and corrected, on a timely basis by the entity's internal control over compliance.

Detection Risk of Noncompliance

16.29 Detection risk of noncompliance is managed by the auditor's response to the risks of material noncompliance. It is defined as follows:

> **detection risk of noncompliance.** The risk that the procedures performed by the auditor to reduce audit risk of noncompliance to an acceptably low level will not detect noncompliance that exists and that could be material to a major program, either individually or when aggregated with other instances of noncompliance.

Performing Risk Assessment Procedures

16.30 For each of the major programs and direct and material compliance requirements selected for testing, the auditor should perform risk assessment procedures to obtain a sufficient understanding of the direct and material compliance requirements and the entity's internal control over compliance with those compliance requirements. Obtaining an understanding of the major program, the direct and material compliance requirements, and the entity's internal control over compliance establishes a frame of reference within which the auditor plans the compliance audit and exercises professional judgment about assessing risks of material noncompliance and responding to those risks throughout the compliance audit.

16.31 The nature and extent of the risk assessment procedures performed may vary from entity to entity and are influenced by the following factors:

- The newness and complexity of the direct and material compliance requirements
- The auditor's knowledge of the entity's internal control over compliance with the direct and material compliance requirements obtained in previous audits or other professional engagements
- The nature of the compliance requirement
- The services provided by the entity and how they are affected by external factors

---

[15] The definitions of *inherent risk of noncompliance*, *control risk of noncompliance*, and *detection risk of noncompliance* have been modified from the definition found in AU-C section 935 to reflect terminology used in a Uniform Guidance compliance audit.

Auditor Planning Considerations Under the Uniform Guidance 425

- The level of oversight by the grantor or pass-through entity
- How management addresses findings

16.32 As noted in paragraph .A14 of AU-C section 935, performing risk assessment procedures to obtain an understanding of the entity's internal control over compliance includes an evaluation of the design of controls and whether the controls have been implemented. Internal control consists of the following five interrelated components: control environment, the entity's risk assessment, information and communication systems, control activities, and monitoring. The Uniform Guidance requires the auditor to plan the testing of internal control over compliance for major programs to support a low assessed level of control risk of noncompliance for the assertions relevant to the compliance requirements for each major program. The Uniform Guidance does not, however, actually require the auditor to achieve a low assessed level of control risk of noncompliance. The assessment of control risk of noncompliance contributes to the auditor's evaluation of the risk that material noncompliance exists in a major program. See chapter 19 of this guide for more information.

16.33 The process of assessing inherent risk of noncompliance and control risk of noncompliance provides audit evidence about the risk that material noncompliance may exist. The auditor uses this audit evidence as part of the basis for the opinion on compliance. It is important to note that paragraph .19 of AU-C section 935 states that risk assessment procedures, tests of controls, and analytical procedures alone are not sufficient to address a risk of material noncompliance. Chapter 19 of this guide discusses the auditor's consideration of internal control over compliance for major programs, including a further discussion of the assessment of control risk of noncompliance.

16.34 In determining an acceptable level of detection risk of noncompliance, the auditor considers his or her assessments of inherent risk of noncompliance and control risk of noncompliance and the extent to which he or she seeks to restrict the audit risk of noncompliance related to the major program. As assessed inherent risk of noncompliance or control risk of noncompliance decreases, the acceptable level of detection risk of noncompliance increases. Accordingly, the auditor may alter the nature, timing, and extent of the compliance tests performed based on the assessments of inherent risk of noncompliance and control risk of noncompliance. The Uniform Guidance requires compliance testing to include tests of transactions and such other auditing procedures necessary to provide the auditor with sufficient evidence to support an opinion on compliance. Such compliance testing serves to limit detection risk of noncompliance. Chapter 21 of this guide discusses audit sampling as it relates to a compliance audit.

16.35 In performing risk assessment procedures, the auditor should inquire of management about whether there are findings and recommendations in reports or other written communications resulting from previous audits, attestation engagements, and internal or external monitoring[16] that directly relate to the objectives of the compliance audit. The auditor should gain an understanding of management's response to findings and recommendations that could have a material effect on the entity's compliance with direct and material compliance requirements (for example, taking corrective action). This

---

[16] Examples of external monitoring include regulatory reviews and program reviews by government agencies or pass-through entities. Examples of internal monitoring include reports prepared by the internal audit function and internal quality assessments.

information should be used to assess risk and determine the nature, timing, and extent of the audit procedures for the compliance audit, including determining the extent to which testing the implementation of any corrective actions is applicable to the audit objectives. These procedures are performed to assist the auditor in understanding whether management responded appropriately to such findings.

Assessing the Risks of Material Noncompliance

16.36 AU-C section 935 states that the auditor should assess the risks of material noncompliance whether due to fraud or error for each applicable compliance requirement[17] and should consider whether any of those risks are pervasive to the entity's compliance. If the risks are pervasive, they may affect the entity's compliance with many compliance requirements. Examples of situations in which there may be a risk of material noncompliance that is pervasive to the entity's noncompliance are (*a*) an entity that is experiencing financial difficulty and for which there is an increased risk that grant funds will be diverted for unauthorized purposes and (*b*) an entity that has a history of poor recordkeeping for its federal programs.

16.37 As part of the audit of the financial statements, members of the audit team, including the auditor with final responsibility for the audit, should discuss the susceptibility of the entity's financial statements to material misstatement as part of the risk assessment process. Similarly, the auditor should hold a discussion of the susceptibility of the entity's major programs to material noncompliance with compliance requirements in the planning meeting of the financial statement audit. This discussion may also be held separately from the general planning meeting if the planning of the Uniform Guidance compliance audit is done at a later date.

16.38 In assessing the risks of material noncompliance, the auditor may evaluate inherent risk of noncompliance and control risk of noncompliance individually or in combination. See chapter 20 for information on performing further audit procedures in response to assessed risks.

16.39 In a Uniform Guidance compliance audit, the factors an auditor may consider in assessing the risks of material noncompliance are as follows:

- The complexity of the direct and material compliance requirements
- The susceptibility of the direct and material compliance requirements to noncompliance
- The length of time the entity has been subject to the direct and material compliance requirements
- The auditor's observations about how the entity has complied with the direct and material compliance requirements in prior years
- The potential effect on the entity of noncompliance with the direct and material compliance requirements
- The degree of judgment involved in adhering to the direct and material compliance requirements

---

[17] See footnote 2.

Auditor Planning Considerations Under the Uniform Guidance

- The auditor's assessment of the risks of material misstatement in the financial statement audit

16.40 In assessing the risks of material noncompliance, the auditor should

- identify risks throughout the process of obtaining an understanding of the entity and its environment, including relevant controls that relate to the risks;
- relate the identified risks to what can go wrong at the relevant compliance level;
- consider whether the risks are of a magnitude that could result in noncompliance with requirements that have a direct and material effect on one or more of the entity's major programs; and
- consider the likelihood that the risks could result in noncompliance with requirements that have a direct and material effect on one or more of the entity's major programs.

Assessing the Risks of Material Noncompliance Due to Fraud

16.41 As part of the risk assessment process, the auditor should specifically assess the risks of material noncompliance with a major program's compliance requirements occurring due to fraud (fraud risk). The auditor should consider that assessment in designing the audit procedures to be performed. The assessment of fraud risk should be ongoing throughout the audit.

16.42 AU-C section 240, *Consideration of Fraud in a Financial Statement Audit* (AICPA, *Professional Standards*), addresses the auditor's responsibility to plan and perform the audit to obtain reasonable assurance about whether the financial statements are free of material misstatement due to fraud. AU-C section 240 also applies to a compliance audit. In a Uniform Guidance compliance audit, the assessment of fraud risk relates to fraudulent acts[18] that may result in material noncompliance with a major federal program's compliance requirements or the misappropriation of federal funds.

16.43 When performing the Uniform Guidance compliance audit, the auditor, using professional judgment, should adapt AU-C section 240 to the objectives of a compliance audit. As part of that adaptation, the auditor may consider performing the following procedures for each major program. Auditor judgment regarding specific situations found with respect to the auditee may indicate alternative procedures. This list of procedures is not intended to be an all-inclusive list of procedures. These procedures include

- conducting a meeting of audit team members to discuss the risks of material noncompliance due to fraud. Depending on the number of major programs and the size of the overall audit team, it may be most effective to hold a separate meeting for each major program or groups of major programs audited by an individual segment of the overall audit team. For smaller engagements, holding one meeting covering all major programs may be sufficient.
- gathering information necessary to assess fraud risk factors for major programs prior to the audit team meeting. This may include

---

[18] The auditor's assessment of fraud risk focuses on fraud that originates within the entity. It does not include fraud perpetrated by persons outside the entity.

considering the results of the financial statement fraud risk assessment to determine the applicability to the compliance audit's fraud risk assessment procedures. When identifying fraud risk factors, the auditor assesses whether those risk factors, individually or in combination, present a risk of material noncompliance with compliance requirements that could have a direct and material effect on a major federal program.

- documenting entity-wide programs and controls in place to prevent, detect, and deter fraud; auditor identification and evaluation of the suitability of the design; and whether such programs and controls have been implemented. Many of these programs and controls may have been considered and documented as part of the fraud risk assessment related to the financial statement audit.
- inquiring of management (including those involved with grants management), those charged with governance, internal audit, and others about the risks of fraud related to major programs. The auditor inquires about instances of possible or actual noncompliance or abuses of broad programs and controls that have come to their attention occurring during the period under audit or the period subsequent to that date. The inquiries may cover more than one major program.

16.44 Based on the information gathered, analyses, and communication among the audit team members, the auditor identifies and documents specific fraud risks, including the risk of management override of controls, that may result in material noncompliance with a major program's compliance requirements due to fraud. Consideration of any programs and controls in place to mitigate the risk of such fraud assists the auditor in the assessment of control risk of noncompliance of the related direct and material compliance requirement. Based on the specific fraud risks identified and the results of tests of design and implementation of controls, the auditor determines the planned audit response (including consideration of testing major program journal entries).

16.45 Upon the completion of Uniform Guidance compliance audit procedures, the auditor considers whether the results of audit procedures performed and other conditions affect the assessment of fraud risk made when planning the audit. This evaluation may provide further insight about the risks of material noncompliance due to fraud and whether there is a need to perform additional or alternative audit procedures.

16.46 Table 16-1 contains examples of fraud risk factors specific to a compliance audit. The risk factors are classified based on the three conditions generally present when material noncompliance due to fraud occurs:

1. Incentives or pressures
2. Opportunities
3. Attitudes or rationalizations

Although the risk factors cover a broad range of situations, they are examples only; accordingly, the auditor may consider additional or different risk factors. Also, the order of the examples of risk factors provided is not intended to reflect their relative importance or frequency of occurrence.

Table 16-1

Fraud Risk Factors

Incentives or Pressures

- Substantial political pressure on management creates an undue concern about federal award program accomplishments.
- Imminent or anticipated adverse changes in program legislation or regulations that could impair the financial stability or profitability of the entity.
- High degree of competition for federal awards, especially when accompanied by declining availability of federal awards nationally or regionally.
- A stagnant tax or revenue base or declining federal funding, enrollments, or eligible participants.
- Complex or frequently revised compliance requirements or participant requirements (such as cost sharing or matching requirements) that create incentives to shift costs or incorrectly value transactions.
- A significant portion of program management's compensation or performance appraisal is linked to federal award budgetary or program accomplishments or other incentives, the value or results of which are contingent upon the entity achieving unduly aggressive targets for budgetary or programmatic results.
- Unrealistically aggressive budget or program goals.
- A mix of fixed price and cost reimbursable program types that create incentives to shift costs or otherwise manipulate accounting transactions.
- Financial pressure due to declining revenues or increasing expenses, creating incentive to apply non-program costs to federal awards.
- Significant pressure to obtain additional funding necessary to stay viable and maintain levels of service considering the financial or budgetary position of the entity or of specific federal award programs, including need for funds to finance major research and development or capital expenditures.
- Threat of imminent program termination or significant reduction in scope, the effect of which could have a material financial impact on the entity.

Opportunities

- The nature of the entity's operations provide opportunities to engage in fraud.
- An organizational structure that is unstable or unnecessarily complex.
- Rapid growth due to significant increases in funds without the organizational structure to support it.

(continued)

Fraud Risk Factors—*continued*

- Inadequate internal control due to outdated or ineffective accounting or information systems.
- Inadequate oversight by those charged with governance over the financial reporting process and management activities.
- Inadequate monitoring by management for compliance with policies, laws, and regulations.
- Lack of appropriate segregation of duties or independent checks, especially in areas such as eligibility determination and benefit awards.
- Lack of appropriate system of authorization and approval of transactions, such as purchasing, contracting, benefit determinations, and eligibility, due to either poorly designed or outdated controls.
- Lack of timely and appropriate documentation for transactions, such as eligibility and benefit determinations.
- Lack of asset accountability or safeguarding procedures.
- Rapid changes in federal award programs, such as significant centralization or decentralization initiatives, funding shifts from federal to state or local levels, increases or decreases in participant populations, high vulnerability to significant changes in compliance requirements, or pending program elimination.
- High turnover rates or employment of accounting, internal audit, or IT staff.

Attitudes or Rationalizations

- An ineffective or nonexistent means of communicating and supporting the entity's values or ethics, especially regarding such matters as acceptable business practices, conflicts of interests, and codes of conduct.
- Significant subrecipient or subcontract relationships for which there appears to be no clear programmatic or business justification (for example, a subrecipient providing services it does not appear qualified to provide or a contractor geographically distant from the entity when nearby contractors are available).
- Management displaying or conveying an attitude of disinterest regarding strict adherence to federal award rules and regulations such as those related to participant eligibility, benefit determinations, or eligibility.
- An individual or individuals with no apparent executive position(s) within the entity appearing to exercise substantial influence over its affairs or over individual federal award programs (for example, a major donor, fund-raiser, or politician).
- An attitude among program personnel that given their position they, or parties related to them, are due benefits from the program, such as expenses reimbursed by the federal award or participation in the program, to which they would otherwise not be entitled, resulting in questioned costs.

Audit Materiality Considerations

16.47 Paragraph .13 of AU-C section 935 states that the auditor should establish and apply materiality levels for the compliance audit based on the governmental audit requirement. In a Uniform Guidance compliance audit, there are multiple materiality considerations as discussed in the following paragraphs. As noted in paragraph .A8 of AU-C section 935, in a compliance audit, the auditor's judgment about matters that are material to users of the auditor's report is based on consideration of the needs of users as a group, including grantors.

Materiality Differences Between the Financial Statement Audit and the Uniform Guidance Compliance Audit

16.48 In auditing compliance with requirements governing major programs in a Uniform Guidance compliance audit, the auditor's consideration of materiality differs from that in an audit of financial statements in accordance with GAAS and *Government Auditing Standards*. In an audit of financial statements, materiality is considered in relation to the financial statements being audited.[19] However, in designing audit tests and developing an opinion on an auditee's compliance with requirements having a direct and material effect on each major program, paragraph .A7 of AU-C section 935 states that the auditor generally considers materiality in relation to each major program. Chapter 20 of this guide further discusses materiality considerations in a Uniform Guidance compliance audit. Chapter 21 of this guide further discusses audit sampling in a compliance audit.

16.49 In a compliance audit, the auditor's purpose for establishing materiality levels is to

- determine the nature and extent of risk assessment procedures.
- identify and assess the risks of material noncompliance.
- determine the nature, timing, and extent of further audit procedures.
- evaluate whether the entity complied with the direct and material compliance requirements.
- report findings of noncompliance and other matters required to be reported by the governmental audit requirement.

Although the auditor's consideration of materiality for the purposes identified in this paragraph is generally in relation to the government program as a whole, the governmental audit requirement may specify a different level of materiality for one or more of these purposes. For example, for purposes of reporting findings, the Uniform Guidance establishes a specific materiality requirement as discussed in paragraph 16.50.

Materiality for Purposes of Reporting Audit Findings

16.50 The Uniform Guidance requires the auditor to consider a lower level of materiality for purposes of reporting audit findings in the schedule of

---

[19] Because an audit of a government's financial statements under the provisions of the AICPA Audit and Accounting Guide *State and Local Governments* is based on opinion units (see footnote 6), auditors make separate materiality determinations for purposes of planning, performing, evaluating the results of, and reporting for each opinion unit.

findings and questioned costs than for other purposes. The materiality for an "audit finding" under the Uniform Guidance is different (and generally lower) than (*a*) the materiality used for planning and performing the single audit, (*b*) the materiality used for planning, performing, evaluating the results of, and reporting on the financial statement audit, or (*c*) expressing an opinion on the auditee's compliance with requirements having a direct and material effect on each major program.

16.51 Among other findings to be reported, the Uniform Guidance states that the auditor must report in the schedule of findings and questioned costs material noncompliance with the federal statutes, regulations, and the terms and conditions of federal awards related to a major program. (Chapter 23 of this guide describes other findings that the Uniform Guidance requires to be reported.) The auditor's determination of whether an instance of noncompliance with federal statutes, regulations, and the terms and conditions of federal awards is material for the purpose of reporting an audit finding is in relation to a type of compliance requirement identified in the *Compliance Supplement* (for example, activities allowed or unallowed, cash management, eligibility, or reporting) for a major program.

16.52 If, for example, when the auditor discovers one or more instances of noncompliance involving the reporting type of compliance requirement for a particular major program, certain materiality determinations should be made using professional judgment. First, the auditor should decide whether the noncompliance is material to the reporting type of compliance requirement for the particular major program. If the auditor determines the noncompliance is material to the reporting type of compliance requirement, the noncompliance would be reported as a finding in the schedule of findings and questioned costs. Second, the auditor should decide whether the discovered noncompliance is material, either individually or when aggregated with other noncompliance findings, in relation to the particular major program as a whole. If the auditor determines the noncompliance is material to the major program as a whole, the auditor would express a qualified or adverse opinion on compliance with respect to the particular major program.

Audit Documentation

16.53 As discussed in chapter 3 of this guide, audit documentation requirements and guidance are found in AU-C section 230, *Audit Documentation* (AICPA, *Professional Standards*). Audit documentation is important because it provides the principal support that the audit was performed in accordance with GAAS, *Government Auditing Standards*, and the Uniform Guidance and provides the principal support for each of the opinions issued. Furthermore, *Government Auditing Standards* contains additional documentation requirements that are applicable to a Uniform Guidance compliance audit. See chapter 20 for more information regarding documentation requirements in a Uniform Guidance compliance audit.

Audit Documentation Access and Audit Follow-Up [20]

Audit Documentation Access and Retention

16.54 The Uniform Guidance also provides requirements regarding audit documentation access. It states that audit documentation must be made available upon request to the cognizant or oversight agency for audit or its designee, cognizant agency for indirect cost, a federal agency, or GAO at the completion of the audit, as part of a quality review to resolve audit findings or to carry out oversight responsibilities. It also states that access to the audit documentation includes the right of federal agencies to obtain copies, as is reasonable and necessary. The Senate Committee report that accompanied the Single Audit Act Amendments of 1996 stated that federal agencies should be judicious in the exercise of this authority and that it was the committee's intent that the federal agencies recognize that audit documentation may contain trade secrets and confidential commercial and financial information and should treat such information as confidential under the Freedom of Information Act (*Government Organization and Employees, U.S. Code* Title 5, Section 552). Interpretation No. 1, "Providing Access to or Copies of Audit Documentation to a Regulator," of AU-C section 230 (AICPA, *Professional Standards*, AU-C sec. 9230 par. .01–.15), contains guidance for when a regulator requests access to audit documentation pursuant to law, regulation, or audit contract.

16.55 The Uniform Guidance states that auditors must retain audit documentation and reports for a minimum of three years after the date of issuance of the auditor's report to the auditee, unless the auditor is notified in writing by certain parties (including the cognizant agency for audit, cognizant agency for indirect costs, oversight agency for audit, or pass-through entity) to extend the retention period. Paragraph .17 of AU-C section 230 states that the audit documentation retention period should not be shorter than five years from the report release date; statutes, regulations, or an audit firm's quality control policies may dictate a longer period.[21] The AU-C section 230 documentation retention guidance should be followed for a compliance audit because the five-year retention period is longer than the three-year period defined in the Uniform Guidance. When the auditor is aware that the federal awarding agency, pass-through entity, or auditee is contesting an audit finding, the auditor should contact the parties contesting the audit finding for guidance before the destruction of the audit documentation and reports.

Audit Follow-Up

16.56 The Uniform Guidance states that the auditor must follow up on prior audit findings, perform procedures to assess the reasonableness of the summary schedule of prior audit findings prepared by the auditee, and report, as a current-year audit finding, when the auditor concludes that the summary schedule of prior audit findings materially misrepresents the status of any prior audit finding. Chapters 20 and 23 of this guide further discuss the auditor's responsibility for audit follow-up.

---

[20] Chapter 3 of this guide discusses the *Government Auditing Standards* audit documentation access and follow-up requirements.

[21] Some state boards of accountancy prescribe longer document retention periods. Documents should be retained for the longest retention period of any required documentation retention periods that may apply.

Group Audit Considerations in a Uniform Guidance Compliance Audit

16.57 The requirements of AU-C section 600, *Special Considerations—Audits of Group Financial Statements (Including the Work of Component Auditors)* (AICPA, *Professional Standards*), address special considerations that apply to group audits of financial statements that include the financial information of more than one component (that is, group financial statements). AU-C section 600 is, in part, intended to address the audit risk that results from the aggregation of component financial information (referred to here as *aggregation risk*). It also establishes requirements for when it is appropriate to make reference to a component auditor in the auditor's report on the financial statements. In accordance with AU-C section 935, the auditor should use professional judgment to adapt and apply the provisions in the AU-C sections to meet the objective of a compliance audit. Therefore, it will be necessary for the auditor to use professional judgment in adapting and applying the provisions of AU-C section 600 to a Uniform Guidance compliance audit because of the differing nature and objectives of such an engagement. The following paragraphs are intended to provide guidance to auditors in adapting and applying the provisions of AU-C section 600 to a Uniform Guidance compliance audit.

16.58 The concept of aggregation risk in AU-C section 600 is not directly applicable to Uniform Guidance compliance audits because each major program is being opined on separately. Unlike a financial statement audit, there is no entity-wide opinion on compliance in a Uniform Guidance compliance audit. Additionally, even when a major program is administered by multiple organizational units, locations, or branches within a major program because the focus of the Uniform Guidance compliance audit is attribute-based (that is, there is either compliance or noncompliance), the concepts of aggregation risk and component materiality as contemplated in AU-C section 600 would not be relevant. Instead, the auditor may have additional sampling considerations in such situations. See the guidance in chapter 21 of this guide for guidance on the effect of such a structure on the sampling considerations for the major program. Therefore, as a result of the unique nature of a Uniform Guidance compliance audit, the concept of a component in AU-C section 600 generally should only be applied when other auditors have been separately engaged to perform a portion of a Uniform Guidance compliance audit. In those cases, the auditor should follow the guidance in AU-C section 600 as it relates to other auditors (that is, component auditors), including considerations of whether to make reference to the other auditors in the auditor's report on compliance and on internal control over compliance. See chapter 23 of this guide for more information on referring to other auditors.

16.59 Governmental entities and entities that receive governmental assistance may engage independent accounting firms on a joint venture or subcontract basis. This sometimes occurs due to legal or contractual requirements to make positive efforts to use small business, minority-owned firms, and women-owned business enterprises. Making reference to other auditors in these circumstances is usually not appropriate. In the case of a joint audit, each of the auditors participating in the audit will sign the audit reports. The guidance in AU-C section 600 is appropriate only when each auditor or firm has complied with GAAS and *Government Auditing Standards* and is in a position that would justify being the only signatory of the report. In the case of a subcontract relationship, the subcontracting auditor often does not issue a separate report.

Therefore, without a separate report, it would also not be appropriate to make reference to the subcontracting auditor.

Existence of an Internal Audit Function

16.60 Internal auditors may monitor not only compliance requirements that affect the financial statement audit, but also those that affect major programs. AU-C section 610, *Using the Work of Internal Auditors* (AICPA, *Professional Standards*), provides requirements and guidance related to the external auditor's (auditor) responsibilities if using the work of internal auditors. Using the work of internal auditors includes both (*a*) using the work of the internal audit function in obtaining audit evidence and (*b*) using internal auditors to provide direct assistance under the direction, supervision, and review of the external auditor. AU-C section 610 does not apply when the activities of the internal audit function are not relevant to the audit, the external auditor does not expect to use the work of the internal audit function, or the external auditor does not plan to use an entity's internal auditors to provide direct assistance in the audit.

16.61 Paragraph .09 of AU-C section 610 states that the external auditor has sole responsibility for the audit opinion expressed and that responsibility is not reduced by the external auditor's use of the work of the internal audit function. The objectives of the external auditor, when the entity has an internal audit function and the auditor expects to use the work of internal auditors to modify the nature or timing, or reduce the extent, of audit procedures to be performed directly by the external auditor are as follows

- to determine whether to use the work of the internal audit function in obtaining audit evidence or to use internal auditors to provide direct assistance, and if so, in which areas and to what extent,
- if using the work of the internal audit function in obtaining audit evidence, to determine whether that work is adequate for purposes of the audit,
- if using internal auditors to provide direct assistance, to appropriately direct, supervise, and review their work.

Considerations Related to the Internal Audit Function

16.62 When gaining an understanding of internal control, the auditor should obtain an understanding of the internal audit function sufficient to identify internal audit activities that are relevant to planning the audit. The work of internal auditors may affect the nature, timing, and extent of the procedures the auditor performs (*a*) to obtain an understanding of the entity and its environment, including its internal control over compliance, (*b*) to assess risk, and (*c*) in response to the assessed risk. In obtaining an understanding of the internal audit function as it relates to compliance requirements in a Uniform Guidance compliance audit, the following procedures may be helpful in assessing the relevance of internal audit activities:

- Consideration of knowledge from prior year audits
- Reviewing how the internal auditors allocate their audit resources to compliance activities

- Reading internal audit reports to obtain detailed information about the scope of internal audit activities as it relates to compliance with direct and material compliance requirements

Using the Work of the Internal Auditor in Obtaining Audit Evidence

16.63 The external auditor may be able to use the work of the internal audit function in obtaining audit evidence depending on

- the level of competency of the internal audit function,
- whether the internal audit function's organizational status and relevant policies and procedures adequately support the objectivity of the internal auditors, and
- whether the function applies a systematic and disciplined approach, including quality control.

16.64 In making judgments about the extent of the effect of the internal auditor's work on the auditor's procedures over direct and material compliance requirements, the auditor considers both the risks of material noncompliance (consisting of both inherent risk of noncompliance and control risk of noncompliance) and the degree of subjectivity involved in the evaluation of the audit evidence gathered in support of compliance with direct and material compliance requirements. As either the degree of risk of material noncompliance rises or the degree of subjectivity increases, the need for the auditor to perform his or her own tests increase.

16.65 In the case in which the work of internal auditors significantly affects the nature, timing, and extent of the auditor's procedures, the auditor should perform procedures to evaluate the quality and effectiveness of the internal auditor's work. In making the evaluation, the auditor should test some of the internal auditor's work relating to each direct and material compliance requirement. These tests may be accomplished by either (*a*) examining some of the controls or transactions examined or compliance requirements tested by the internal auditor or (*b*) examining similar controls or transactions not actually examined or compliance requirements not actually tested by the internal auditor. Such testing will assist the auditor in determining the nature, timing, and extent of further audit procedures. In reaching conclusions about the internal auditor's work, the results of the auditor's tests should be compared with the results of the internal auditor's work.

16.66 As noted in paragraph .A35 of AU-C section 610, and as it relates to a compliance audit, the more judgment involved, the higher the assessed risk of material noncompliance, the less the internal audit function's organization status and relevant policies and procedures adequately support the objectivity of the internal auditors, or the lower the level of competence of the internal audit function, the more audit procedures are needed to be performed by the external auditor on the overall body of work of the internal audit function to support the decision to use the work of the function in obtaining sufficient appropriate audit evidence on which to base the opinion.

16.67 When using the work of the internal audit function, the external auditor should make all significant judgments in the audit engagement. The auditor should evaluate whether, in aggregate, using the work of the internal audit function in obtaining audit evidence to the extent planned, together with any planned use of internal auditors to provide direct assistance, would result in the auditor still being sufficiently involved in the audit, given the auditor's sole responsibility for the audit opinion expressed.

Using Internal Auditors to Provide Direct Assistance to the Auditor

16.68 In performing the single audit, the auditor may request direct assistance from the internal auditors. Direct assistance relates to the use of internal auditors to perform procedures under the direction, supervision, and review of the external auditor. For example, internal auditors may assist the auditor in obtaining an understanding of internal control over compliance or performing tests of controls or tests of compliance. Prior to using internal auditors to provide direct assistance, the auditor should obtain written acknowledgment from management or those charged with governance, as appropriate, that internal auditors providing direct assistance will be allowed to follow the auditor's instructions and that the entity will not intervene in the work the internal auditors are providing to the auditor. The auditor should direct, supervise, and review the work performed by internal auditors on the engagement in accordance with AU-C section 220, *Quality Control for an Engagements Conducted in Accordance with Generally Accepted Auditing Standards* (AICPA, *Professional Standards*). Paragraphs .33–.35 of AU-C section 610 provide requirements regarding documentation when using the work of the internal audit function or using internal auditors to provide direct assistance on the audit.

16.69 Paragraphs .A42–.A43 of AU-C section 610 provide information on determining the nature and extent of work that can be assigned to internal auditors providing direct assistance. When direct assistance is provided, the auditor should assess the internal auditor's competence and objectivity and supervise, review, evaluate, and test the work performed by internal auditors to the extent appropriate in the circumstances. The auditor should inform the internal auditors of their responsibilities, the objectives of the procedures they are to perform, and matters that may affect the nature, timing, and extent of audit procedures, such as possible compliance and auditing issues. The auditor should also inform the internal auditors that all significant compliance and auditing issues identified during the audit should be brought to the auditor's attention.

Communications With the Cognizant or Oversight Agency for Audit and Others

16.70 Chapter 3 of this guide discusses planning the financial statement audit and the areas that may be considered. In a single audit, the auditor may communicate with the cognizant agency for audit or the oversight agency for audit. If a planning meeting is held with that agency, the following matters may be discussed:

- The scope of the compliance testing of federal programs
- The intended use of the *Compliance Supplement*
- The identification of federal awards, including those that are considered to be major programs
- The form and content of the supplementary schedule of expenditures of federal awards
- The testing of the monitoring of subrecipients

- The scope of the review and testing of internal control over compliance
- The testing of compliance requirements
- The status of prior audit findings and questioned costs
- Federal agency or pass-through entity management decisions on prior audit findings
- Compliance requirements and any changes to those requirements

State and Local Compliance Requirements

16.71 In addition to testing and reporting on the compliance requirements as provided by *Government Auditing Standards* and the Uniform Guidance, there may be state-imposed requirements on state funds provided to political subdivisions or not-for-profit entities (in this example, the state is not a pass-through entity). Even though such nonfederal awards are not considered part of the total federal awards expended by the auditee and are not subject to audit in accordance with the Uniform Guidance, auditors would still need to consider such laws and regulations under GAAS and *Government Auditing Standards*. Therefore, in connection with the financial statement audit, auditors should obtain an understanding of applicable state and local compliance and reporting requirements that have a direct and material effect on the financial statements being audited. Chapter 3 of this guide discusses possible audit procedures to assess the completeness of management's identification of compliance requirements in connection with the financial statement audit. Chapter 17 of this guide discusses auditee reporting considerations.

Desk Reviews and On-Site Reviews

16.72 In addition to the quality control requirements set forth in *Government Auditing Standards* as discussed in chapter 2, "*Government Auditing Standards*—Ethical Principles and General Standards," of this guide, cognizant agencies for audit have implemented procedures for evaluating the quality of audits. These procedures include both desk reviews and on-site reviews (note that the oversight agencies for audit also may perform these reviews).[22] As a part of the cognizant agencies' evaluation of the completed reports of such engagements, and, as required by the Uniform Guidance, the supporting audit documentation must be made available upon request by the representative of the federal agency. Audit documentation typically is reviewed at a location agreed upon by the cognizant agency for audit and the independent auditor. (Paragraph 16.54 and chapter 3 of this guide further discuss access to audit documentation.)

16.73 Whenever a review of the audit report or audit documentation discloses an inadequacy, the audit firm is contacted for corrective action. When major inadequacies are identified and the representative of the cognizant agency

---

[22] Cognizant and oversight agencies use various checklists and tools to perform quality control reviews and desk reviews. One source of information regarding these reviews is the Council of Inspectors General on Integrity and Efficiency (CIGIE) website at www.ignet.gov/. Guides and manuals are published by CIGIE that are used in quality control reviews and desk reviews of Circular A-133 compliance audits. Note that these tools have not yet been updated for the Uniform Guidance, and therefore should not be used for a review of a Uniform Guidance compliance audit until such time they are updated.

for audit determines that the audit report and the audit documentation are substandard, cognizant agencies may take further steps. In those instances in which the audit is determined to be substandard by the federal agency, the matter may be submitted to state boards of accountancy or the AICPA's Professional Ethics Division.

Restriction on the Auditor's Preparation of Indirect Cost Proposals

16.74 The Uniform Guidance precludes the auditor who prepares the indirect cost proposal or cost allocation plan from performing the single audit when indirect costs recovered by the auditee during the prior year exceeded $1 million.[23] This restriction applies to the base year used in the preparation of the indirect proposal or cost allocation plan and to any subsequent years in which the resulting indirect cost agreement or cost allocation plan is used to recover costs. For example, an auditor who prepares an indirect cost proposal or cost allocation plan that is used as the basis for charging indirect costs in the fiscal year ending June 30, 20X1, is not permitted to perform the 20X1 single audit (assuming that the indirect costs recovered during the prior year exceeded $1 million).

Transition Considerations Related to the Uniform Guidance

16.75 Auditors should consider the effective date provisions of the Uniform Guidance when planning the compliance audit. This is because the administrative requirements and cost principles included in the Uniform Guidance are required to be implemented by nonfederal entities beginning December 26, 2014, for all new federal awards and funding increments (additional funding to existing federal awards) with modified award terms and conditions that are awarded on or after that date. Typically, the terms and conditions of the federal award should identify whether the funding increment is subject to the Uniform Guidance requirements, or whether it will continue to be governed by the original terms and conditions of the federal award (that is, subject to the pre-Uniform Guidance requirements).

16.76 In light of the Uniform Guidance effective date provisions, as part of the audit planning process auditors should determine the applicable criteria that will be used in performing the compliance audit (that is, whether an award is subject to pre-Uniform Guidance requirements versus post-Uniform Guidance requirements). Federal awarding documents will be important tools for making this determination. Nonfederal entities and auditors that have questions regarding the applicable criteria for federal awards may consult with agency single audit coordinators or program officials. Contact information for

---

[23] The preparation of an entity's indirect cost proposal or cost allocation plan is considered to be a nonaudit service under *Government Auditing Standards*. Nonaudit services may create threats to an auditor's independence. When an auditor has prepared the entity's indirect cost proposal or cost allocation plan and is not otherwise precluded from performing the audit under the Uniform Guidance, evaluation is needed regarding whether independence is impaired. This evaluation is done using the conceptual framework in chapter 3, "General Standards," of *Government Auditing Standards*. See chapter 2, "*Government Auditing Standards*—Ethical Principles and General Standards," of this guide for more information on the requirements related to independence found in *Government Auditing Standards*.

these agency representatives can be found in Appendix 3, "Federal Agency Single Audit and Program Contacts" of the 2015 *Compliance Supplement*.

16.77 One of the challenges that auditors may face is that a major program may include expenditures from both federal awards subject to the pre-Uniform Guidance requirements, as well as federal awards subject to the post-Uniform Guidance requirements. This situation could exist for several years until the pre-Uniform Guidance awards have been completely expended. When testing major program transactions, identification of the date of a federal award related to a particular expenditure is needed in order to determine the applicable criteria to use for the transaction being tested. It should be noted that a separate sample for pre-Uniform Guidance award transactions and post-Uniform Guidance award transactions within a major program would not typically be needed in this situation. However, this guide recommends that when testing major program transactions that the audit documentation for testing compliance and internal control over compliance include an identification of the transactions tested that were subject to post-Uniform Guidance requirements.

16.78 It is important to note that some federal agencies received OMB approval to make exceptions to the Uniform Guidance regulations as part of the agency implementing regulations. It may be challenging, particularly in the first year of implementation, for nonfederal entities and their auditors to determine such agency exceptions and the effect of any such exceptions on the audit. Appendix 7, "Other Audit Advisories," of the 2015 *Compliance Supplement* includes a summary, by federal agency, of the sections of the Uniform Guidance where agencies have made exceptions. Appendix 7 refers to a document titled, "Uniform Guidance Crosswalk for Federal Agency Exceptions and Additions," posted on COFAR's website (https://cfo.gov/cofar/) that contains a complete listing and text of the exceptions. Nonfederal entities and auditors that have questions about the nature of agency exceptions and the effect of such exceptions on the audit, may consult with agency single audit coordinators or programs officials using the contact information in Appendix 3 of the 2015 *Compliance Supplement*.

Chapter 17

Schedule of Expenditures of Federal Awards (Uniform Guidance)

> **Update 17-1: Audits of Federal Awards**
>
> This chapter, and the remaining chapters of part III, *Uniform Guidance Audits*, of this guide, should be used for performing a compliance audit of federal awards under the audit requirements of Title 2 U.S. *Code of Federal Regulations* (CFR) Part 200, *Uniform Administrative Requirements, Cost Principles, and Audit Requirements for Federal Awards* (Uniform Guidance).[1] Part II, *Circular A-133 Audits*, of this guide should be used for performing a compliance audit under Office of Management and Budget (OMB) Circular A-133, *Audits of States, Local Governments, and Non-Profit Organizations* (Circular A-133). See the transitional guidance sections at the end of each chapter that highlight important matters for consideration. Additionally, refer to the preface of this guide for more information.
>
> **Important Effective Date Information**
>
> In December 2013, the OMB issued the Uniform Guidance, which is effective for nonfederal entities for all federal awards and certain funding increments provided on or after December 26, 2014. The requirements in Subpart F, "Audit Requirements," are effective for audits of fiscal years beginning on or after December 26, 2014, with no early implementation permitted. Therefore, auditees subject to a single audit with December 25, 2015, and later year ends (for example, December 31, 2015) will be required to undergo the audit under Subpart F of the Uniform Guidance. Note that audits of fiscal years ending prior to the effective date of the Uniform Guidance audit requirements are subject to an audit under Circular A-133.

Introduction

17.01 The Uniform Guidance requires the auditee to prepare a schedule of expenditures of federal awards for the period covered by the auditee's financial statements that includes certain required elements (as described further in paragraph 17.21), including total federal awards expended for each individual federal program. The Uniform Guidance requires the auditor to determine whether the auditee's schedule of expenditures of federal awards is fairly stated, in all material respects, in relation to the auditee's financial statements as a whole. In addition, the Uniform Guidance places the responsibility for identifying major programs on the auditor (see chapter 18, "Determination of Major Programs (Uniform Guidance)," of this guide), and the schedule of

---

[1] See the information found at paragraph 17.39, and other part III, *Uniform Guidance Audits*, chapters of this guide, for transition considerations when performing an audit under Title 2 U.S. *Code of Federal Regulations* Part 200, *Uniform Administrative Requirements, Cost Principles, and Audit Requirements for Federal Awards* (Uniform Guidance). Transition considerations can also be found at the end of certain part II, *Circular A-133 Audits*, chapters as it relates to an audit performed under Office of Management and Budget (OMB) Circular A-133, *Audits of States, Local Governments, and Non-Profit Organizations* (Circular A-133).

expenditures of federal awards serves as the primary basis for the auditor's major program determination. Therefore, appropriate major program determination by the auditor is dependent on the accuracy and completeness of the information in the schedule of expenditures of federal awards.

17.02 This chapter describes the federal agency, pass-through entity, and auditee requirements relating to the identification of federal awards, and the general presentation requirements governing the schedule of expenditures of federal awards, pass-through awards, and noncash awards. This chapter also discusses the auditor's responsibilities related to issuing an in-relation-to opinion and the additional auditor considerations for the schedule of expenditures of federal awards relating to compliance audit objectives. Chapter 23, "Auditor Reporting Requirements and Other Communication Considerations in a Single Audit (Uniform Guidance)," of this guide discusses the auditor's reporting on the schedule of expenditures of federal awards. The appendix, "Illustrative Schedules of Expenditures of Federal Awards" of this chapter (paragraph 17.43), presents illustrative schedules of expenditures of federal awards.

Identification of Federal Awards

Federal Agency and Pass-Through Entity Requirements

17.03 Federal awarding agencies have certain responsibilities related to the federal awards they make. 2 CFR 200.210 of Subpart C, "Pre-federal Award Requirements and Contents of Federal Awards," provides the federal award information that must be provided to each recipient in the federal award. The general award information required to be included is as follows:

1. Recipient name (which must match the name associated with its unique entity identifier as defined in 2 CFR 25.315)
2. Recipient's unique entity identifier
3. Unique federal award identification number
4. Federal award date
5. Period of performance start and end date
6. Amount of federal funds obligated by this action
7. Total amount of federal funds obligated
8. Total amount of the federal award
9. Budget approved by the federal awarding agency
10. Total approved cost sharing or matching, where applicable
11. Federal award project description (to comply with statutory requirements, for example, the Federal Funding Accountability and Transparency Act)
12. Name of federal awarding agency and contact information for awarding official
13. CFDA number and name
14. Identification of whether the award is Research and Development (R&D)
15. Indirect cost rate for the federal award (including if the de minimis rate is charged per 2 CFR 200.414)

Schedule of Expenditures of Federal Awards (Uniform Guidance)

> **Emphasis Point**
>
> The use of the term *must* in the Uniform Guidance indicates a requirement. This is consistent with the use of the term *must* in generally accepted auditing standards (GAAS) and *Government Auditing Standards*. The use of the term *should* in the Uniform Guidance indicates a best practice or recommended approach. However, GAAS and *Government Auditing Standards* use the term *should* to indicate a presumptively mandatory requirement. An auditor must comply with a presumptively mandatory requirement in all cases in which such a requirement is relevant, except in rare circumstances. In this guide, the term ***should***, when italicized and bolded, indicates a best practice or recommended approach in the Uniform Guidance. This is intended to differentiate it from the term "should" used throughout the guide to refer to presumptively mandatory requirements in GAAS and *Government Auditing Standards*. See chapter 1, "Introduction and Overview of *Government Auditing Standards*," of this guide for more information regarding presumptively mandatory requirements.

17.04 2 CFR 200.331 of Subpart D, "Post Federal Award Requirements," of the Uniform Guidance requires pass-through entities to ensure that every subaward is clearly identified to the subrecipient as a subward and that the pass-through entity include certain information at the time of the subaward. When some of the required information is not available, the pass-through entity must provide the best information available to describe the federal award and subaward. The required information to be provided is similar to the information listed in the previous paragraph, as modified for a subaward. However, items 9 and 10 in paragraph 17.03 are not required to be provided by a pass-through entity. The required subaward information to be provided also includes the following:

- All requirements imposed by the pass-through entity on the subrecipient so that the federal award is used in accordance with federal statutes, regulations and the terms and conditions of the federal award

- Any additional requirements that the pass-through entity imposes on the subrecipient in order for the pass-through entity to meet its own responsibility to the federal awarding agency including identification of any required financial and performance reports

- An approved federally recognized indirect cost rate negotiated between the subrecipient and the federal government, or, if no such rate exists, either a rate negotiated between the pass-through entity and the subrecipient or a de minimis indirect cost rate

- A requirement that the subrecipient permit the pass-through entity and auditors to have access to the subrecipient's records and financial statements as necessary for the pass-through entity to meet the applicable requirements

- Appropriate terms and conditions concerning the closeout of the award

Auditee Requirements

17.05 The Uniform Guidance states that the nonfederal entity[2] must identify in its accounts all federal awards received and expended, as well as the federal programs under which they were received. Federal program and award identification must include, as applicable, the CFDA title and number, the federal award identification number and year, the name of the federal agency, and the name of the pass-through entity, if any. This information enables the auditee to reconcile amounts presented in the financial statements to related amounts in the schedule of expenditures of federal awards.

Audit Considerations Related to the Schedule of Expenditures of Federal Awards[3]

Conditions for and Procedures Related to Issuing the In-Relation-To Opinion

17.06 AU-C section 725, *Supplementary Information in Relation to the Financial Statements as a Whole* (AICPA, *Professional Standards*), includes requirements and guidance on reporting on supplementary information, such as the schedule of expenditures of federal awards, when engaged to report on whether supplementary information[4] is fairly stated, in all material respects, in relation to the financial statements as a whole.[5] When issuing an in-relation-to opinion on the schedule of expenditures of federal awards, the auditor need not apply procedures as extensive as would be necessary to express an opinion on the schedule of expenditures of federal awards on a stand-alone basis. The following paragraphs describe the requirements and guidance in AU-C section 725 as they apply to the schedule of expenditures of federal awards.

17.07 In order to opine on whether the schedule of expenditures of federal awards is fairly stated, in all material respects, in relation to the financial statements as a whole, the auditor should determine that all the following conditions are met:

---

[2] Subpart A, "Acronyms and Definitions," of the Uniform Guidance defines a *nonfederal entity* as a state, local government, Indian tribe, institution of higher education, or nonprofit organization that carries out a federal award as a recipient or subrecipient. The term *nonfederal entity* is used throughout part III of this guide as that term is used in the Uniform Guidance.

[3] *Government Auditing Standards* incorporates by reference AICPA Statements on Auditing Standards. Therefore, auditors performing financial statement audits and Uniform Guidance compliance audits in accordance with *Government Auditing Standards* should comply with generally accepted auditing standards, the requirements found in chapters 1–3 of *Government Auditing Standards*, and the additional standards and related requirements for financial audits found in chapter 4, "Standards for Financial Audits," of *Government Auditing Standards*.

[4] Paragraph .04 of AU-C section 725, *Supplementary Information in Relation to the Financial Statements as a Whole* (AICPA, *Professional Standards*), defines *supplementary information* as information presented outside the basic financial statements, excluding required supplementary information, that is not considered necessary for the financial statements to be fairly presented in accordance with the applicable financial reporting framework. The reporting related to the schedule of expenditures of federal awards required by the Uniform Guidance is supplementary information subject to the requirements of AU-C section 725. In this chapter, the terms *supplementary information* and *schedule of expenditures of federal awards* are both used to indicate supplementary information when discussing the guidance in AU-C section 725.

[5] In certain circumstances the auditor may not meet the requirements to issue an in-relation-to opinion on the schedule of expenditures of federal awards. See the discussion beginning at paragraph 17.36 for more information.

Schedule of Expenditures of Federal Awards (Uniform Guidance)

- The information contained in the schedule of expenditures of federal awards was derived from, and relates directly to, the underlying accounting and other records used to prepare the financial statements.
- The information contained in the schedule of expenditures of federal awards relates to the same period as the financial statements.
- The financial statements were audited, and the auditor reporting on the schedule of expenditures of federal awards audited those financial statements.
- Neither an adverse opinion nor a disclaimer of opinion was issued on the financial statements (see chapter 23).
- The schedule of expenditures of federal awards will accompany the entity's audited financial statements, or such financial statements will be made readily available.[6]

17.08 The auditor should obtain the agreement of management that it acknowledges and understands its responsibility related to the schedule of expenditures of federal awards:

- For the preparation of the schedule of expenditures of federal awards in accordance with the Uniform Guidance
- To provide the auditor with certain written representations (see paragraph 17.17)
- To include the auditor's report on the schedule of expenditures of federal awards in any document that contains the schedule and that indicates that the auditor has reported on such information
- To present the schedule of expenditures of federal awards with the audited financial statements, or if the schedule will not be presented with the audited financial statements, to make the audited financial statements readily available[7] to the intended users of the schedule no later than the date of issuance of the schedule and the auditor's report thereon

Management's acknowledgement and understanding related to the schedule of expenditures of federal awards may be obtained as part of the engagement letter.

17.09 In order to opine on whether the schedule of expenditures of federal awards is fairly stated, in all material respects, in relation to the financial statements as a whole, the auditor should perform certain procedures that are in addition to the procedures performed during the audit of the financial statements. Using the same materiality level used in the audit of the financial statements, the auditor should[8]

---

[6] Paragraph .A9 of AU-C section 725 notes that audited financial statements are deemed to be readily available if a third party user can obtain the financial statements without any further action by the audited entity. Financial statements posted on an entity's website may be considered readily available. However, being available by request is not considered readily available.

[7] See footnote 6.

[8] As noted in paragraph .A15 of AU-C section 725, for most state and local governments, the auditor's report on the financial statements includes multiple opinions to address individual reporting units or aggregation of reporting units of the governmental entity. Accordingly, materiality is considered by the auditor for each opinion unit. However, in the context of AU-C section 725, the auditor's opinion on the schedule of expenditures of federal awards is in relation to the financial statements as a whole. Accordingly, in this situation, materiality is considered at a level that represents the entire governmental entity.

- inquire of management about the criteria used by management to prepare the schedule of expenditures of federal awards.
- determine whether the form and content of the schedule of expenditures of federal awards complies with the Uniform Guidance.
- obtain an understanding about the methods of preparing the schedule of expenditures of federal awards and determine whether the methods have changed from those used in the prior period and, if those methods of preparing the schedule have changed, the reasons for such changes.
- compare and reconcile the schedule of expenditures of federal awards to the underlying accounting and other records used in preparing the financial statements or to the financial statements themselves.
- inquire of management about any significant assumptions or interpretations underlying the measurement or presentation of the schedule of expenditures of federal awards.
- evaluate the appropriateness and completeness of the information contained in the schedule of expenditures of federal awards, considering the results of the procedures performed and other knowledge obtained during the audit of the financial statements.
- obtain certain written representations from management (see paragraph 17.17).

17.10 Materiality[9] may be considered when determining which information to compare and reconcile to the underlying accounting and other records or to the financial statements. In addition, when evaluating the appropriateness and completeness of supplementary information, the auditor may consider testing accounting or other records through observation or examination of source documents or other procedures ordinarily performed in an audit of the financial statements.

17.11 As noted in paragraph 17.20, the Uniform Guidance does not specifically prescribe the basis of accounting to be used by the auditee to prepare the schedule of expenditures of federal awards. Therefore, it is not unusual for the schedule of expenditures of federal awards to be prepared on a basis of accounting that is different from that of the financial statements. For example, the schedule of expenditures of federal awards may be prepared on the cash basis, whereas the financial statements are prepared on an accrual basis in accordance with generally accepted accounting principles. Q&A section 9160.27, "Providing Opinion on a Schedule of Expenditures of Federal Awards in Relation to an Entity's Financial Statements as a Whole When the Schedule of Expenditures of Federal Awards Is on a Different Basis of Accounting Than the Financial Statements" (AICPA, *Technical Questions and Answers*), clarifies that the auditor may provide an in-relation-to opinion on the schedule of expenditures of federal awards in this situation as long as the schedule can be reconciled back to the underlying accounting and other records used in preparing the financial statements or to the financial statements themselves and as long as the other conditions and requirements of AU-C section 725 are met.

17.12 If the auditor concludes, on the basis of the procedures performed, that the schedule of expenditures of federal awards is materially misstated in

---

[9] See footnote 8.

Schedule of Expenditures of Federal Awards (Uniform Guidance) **447**

relation to the financial statements as a whole, the auditor should discuss the matter with management and propose appropriate revision of the schedule. Chapter 23 discusses the effect on the auditor's report on the schedule of expenditures of federal awards when management does not revise the schedule in this circumstance.

Additional Auditor Requirements Relating to Compliance Audit Objectives and Internal Control Over Compliance

17.13 As mentioned previously, it is important to note that the schedule of expenditures of federal awards is unlike other types of supplementary information included in documents containing audited financial statements in that it serves as the primary basis for the auditor's major program determination. Therefore, compliance audit procedures should be performed to obtain sufficient appropriate audit evidence supporting the accuracy and completeness of the schedule of expenditures of federal awards, including the identification of federal programs in the schedule. In testing the accuracy and completeness of the schedule of expenditures of federal awards, the auditor may use evidence obtained from audit procedures performed during the audit of the financial statements and the Uniform Guidance compliance audit regarding the accuracy, completeness, and classification of recorded revenues and expenditures. Additionally, the auditor may consider reviewing an auditee-prepared reconciliation of amounts reported in the schedule of expenditures of federal awards and the related notes to corresponding amounts reported in the financial statements or other underlying records used to prepare the schedule (for example, the general ledger, reimbursement requests, loan agreements, or other supporting documentation). The auditor may also consider sending confirmations to federal awarding agencies or pass-through entities in an audit of a subrecipient. Finally, because the Uniform Guidance requires the auditee to include certain elements in the schedule of expenditures of federal awards, the procedures should also include a review of the auditee's schedule for the required elements set forth in 2 CFR 200.510(b) and described in paragraph 17.21.

17.14 Although AU-C section 725 does not require the auditor to obtain a separate understanding of the entity's internal control or to assess fraud risk with respect to supplementary information, the auditor has additional responsibilities regarding internal control related to the schedule of expenditures of federal awards in a Uniform Guidance compliance audit. For example, as part of the Uniform Guidance compliance audit, the auditor has a responsibility to consider internal control over compliance, including a consideration of internal control over the accuracy and completeness of the expenditure amounts reported on the schedule of expenditures of federal awards.

17.15 Chapter 19, "Consideration of Internal Control Over Compliance for Major Programs (Uniform Guidance)," of this guide further discusses the auditor's responsibility for considering internal control over compliance, including obtaining an understanding of the five components of internal control over compliance sufficient to assess the risks of material noncompliance. This understanding, coupled with the auditor's understanding of internal control over financial reporting required for the financial statement audit, should include the auditee's controls over the accuracy and completeness of the program information and expenditure amounts reported on the schedule of expenditures of federal awards, including controls over the accuracy of the CFDA numbers. Procedures may include inquiring of entity personnel, observing the application of specific controls, and inspecting documents and reports used in the preparation of the schedule of expenditures of federal awards. The understanding obtained should be sufficient for the auditor to assess the risks of material misstatement of the schedule of expenditures of federal awards and to design the nature, timing, and extent of further compliance audit procedures to test the accuracy and completeness of the schedule.[10]

17.16 When the auditor identifies deficiencies in internal control that relate to the auditee's preparation of a complete and accurate schedule of expenditures of federal awards, the auditor should evaluate the severity of each deficiency in internal control identified to determine whether the deficiency, individually or in combination, is a significant deficiency or material weakness in internal control over financial reporting, internal control over compliance, or both. Chapters 3, "Planning and Performing a Financial Statement Audit in Accordance With *Government Auditing Standards*," and 19 of this guide include a discussion of internal control and provide guidance to assist auditors in making an assessment of deficiencies in internal control. If a deficiency in internal control is determined to be a significant deficiency or material weakness, the auditor should report a finding in the schedule of findings and questioned costs. Chapter 23 of this guide further discusses the reporting of findings and the schedule of findings and questioned costs.

Management Representations Relating to the Schedule of Expenditures of Federal Awards

17.17 In addition to the written representations typically obtained in the financial statement audit and the Uniform Guidance compliance audit, auditors should obtain certain additional representations related to the schedule of expenditures of federal awards. Representations should be obtained from management with regard to the schedule of expenditures of federal awards

- that management acknowledges and understands its responsibility for the presentation of the schedule of expenditures of federal awards in accordance with the Uniform Guidance;
- that management believes the schedule of expenditures of federal awards, including its form and content, is fairly presented in accordance with the Uniform Guidance;
- that the methods of measurement or presentation have not changed from those used in the prior period, or if the methods of measurement or presentation have changed, the reasons for such changes;
- about any significant assumptions or interpretations underlying the measurement or presentation of the schedule of expenditures of federal awards; and
- that when the schedule of expenditures of federal awards is not presented with the audited financial statements, management will make the audited financial statements readily available to the intended users of the schedule no later than the issuance date by the entity of the schedule of expenditures of federal awards and the auditor's report thereon.[11]

---

[10] The auditor's risk assessment may also be used in deciding what additional procedures, if any, should be performed in order to render an in-relation-to opinion.

[11] See footnote 6.

Paragraph .20 of AU-C section 580, *Written Representations* (AICPA, *Professional Standards*), notes that representations should be made as of the date of the auditor's report on the financial statements. Therefore, two separate management representation letters may be necessary when the financial statement opinion and schedule of expenditures of federal awards in-relation-to opinion contain different dates. This would occur when the audit procedures related to the schedule of expenditures of federal awards are completed subsequent to the financial statement report date. See chapter 23 for more information.

Subsequent Events

17.18 AU-C section 725 states that the auditor has no responsibility for the consideration of subsequent events with respect to the supplementary information. However, the relevant requirements of AU-C section 560, *Subsequent Events and Subsequently Discovered Facts* (AICPA, *Professional Standards*), should be applied if information comes to the auditor's attention

- prior to the release of the auditor's report on the financial statements regarding subsequent events that affect the financial statements, or

- subsequent to the release of the auditor's report on the financial statements regarding facts that, had they been known to the auditor at the date of the auditor's report, may have caused the auditor to revise the auditor's report.

Although AU-C section 725 does not impose a subsequent event requirement with respect to supplementary information, there are additional subsequent event considerations relating to the compliance audit. See chapter 20, "Compliance Auditing Applicable to Major Programs (Uniform Guidance)," of this guide for further information.

Reporting on the Schedule of Expenditures of Federal Awards

17.19 The auditor should include the required AU-C section 725 in-relation-to reporting on the schedule of expenditures of federal awards in either (*a*) an other-matter paragraph in accordance with AU-C section 706, *Emphasis-of-Matter Paragraphs and Other-Matter Paragraphs in the Independent Auditor's Report* (AICPA, *Professional Standards*), or (*b*) in a separate report on the schedule of expenditures of federal awards. Chapter 23 provides additional information on the auditor's reporting on the schedule of expenditures of federal awards and other considerations, such as dating the report and certain modifications to the report that are needed if the schedule of expenditures of federal awards is materially misstated.

General Presentation Requirements

Basis of Accounting

17.20 The Uniform Guidance does not specifically prescribe the basis of accounting to be used by the auditee to prepare the schedule of expenditures of federal awards. For example, the basis of accounting used may be an other comprehensive basis of accounting.[12] However, it does state that the determination of when an award is expended must be based on when the activity related to the federal award occurs. The Uniform Guidance provides the guidance shown in table 17-1. (The Uniform Guidance also specifies the values that should be presented on the schedule of expenditures of federal awards for certain types of awards; see table 17-2 in paragraph 17.33). A schedule of expenditures of federal awards, or certain awards in the schedule, may be presented on a basis of accounting that differs from that used in the financial statements.[13] In any case, the auditee must clearly disclose the significant accounting policies used in preparing the schedule of expenditures of federal awards in the notes to the schedule. As noted previously, the auditee should also be able to reconcile amounts presented in the financial statements to related amounts in the schedule of expenditures of federal awards.

Table 17-1

Basis for Determining When Federal Awards Are Expended

Federal Awards	Basis for Determining When Expended
Grants, cost reimbursement contracts, compacts with Indian tribes, cooperative agreements under the Federal Acquisition Regulations (FAR), and direct appropriations	When the expenditure or expense transactions occur
Amounts passed through to subrecipients	When the disbursement is made to the subrecipient
Loan and loan guarantees	When the loan proceeds are used by the nonfederal entity (See the further discussion on loans and loan guarantees in table 17-2 and paragraph 17.34.)
Donated property, including donated surplus property	When the property is received
Food commodities	When the food commodities are distributed or consumed

---

[12] AU-C section 800, *Special Considerations—Audits of Financial Statements Prepared in Accordance With Special Purpose Frameworks* (AICPA, *Professional Standards*), provides requirements and guidance for auditor reporting when the auditee prepares financial statements in accordance with a special purpose framework. AU-C section 800 defines a *special purpose framework* as a financial reporting framework other than generally accepted accounting principles and establishes requirements for reporting on those frameworks. Special purpose frameworks, such as the cash, tax, regulatory, and other bases of accounting, are sometimes referred to as *other comprehensive bases of accounting* (OCBOA). The term *OCBOA* is sometimes used when referring to this guidance in this guide.

The AICPA Audit and Accounting Guide *State and Local Governments* discusses the application of AU-C section 800 to state and local governmental financial statements and also provides illustrative auditor's reports for financial statements prepared in accordance with a special purpose framework. In addition, the AICPA practice aid *Applying OCBOA in State and Local Governmental Financial Statements* (APAOCBO12P) provides nonauthoritative guidance on preparing and reporting on OCBOA financial statements of governmental entities. A second practice aid, *Accounting and Financial Reporting Guidelines for Cash- and Tax-Basis Financial Statements* (APACTB12P), provides nonauthoritative guidance for preparers regarding guidelines and best practices for the preparation of cash- and tax-basis financial statements. These publications are available at www.cpa2biz.com.

[13] See also paragraph 17.11.

Federal Awards	Basis for Determining When Expended
Interest subsidies	When amounts are disbursed entitling the entity to the subsidy
Insurance	When the insurance is in force
Endowments	When federally restricted amounts are held
Program income	When received or used

Required Content for the Schedule of Expenditures of Federal Awards

17.21 The Uniform Guidance states that the auditee must prepare a schedule of expenditures of federal awards for the period covered by the auditee's financial statements, which must include the total federal awards expended as determined by 2 CFR 200.502. (See table 17-1). The Uniform Guidance specifies what must go on the face of the schedule and what must go in the notes to the schedule. At a minimum, the face of the schedule of expenditures of federal awards must

- list individual federal programs by federal agency. For a cluster of programs, provide the cluster name, list individual federal programs within the cluster of programs, and provide the applicable federal agency name. (Chapter 15, "Overview of the Single Audit Act, the Uniform Guidance Audit Requirements, and the *Compliance Supplement*," of this guide discusses clusters of programs.) For R&D, total federal awards expended must be shown either by individual award or by federal agency and major subdivision within the federal agency. For example, the National Institutes of Health is a major subdivision in the Department of Health and Human Services (the federal agency).

- for federal awards received as a subrecipient, include the name of the pass-through entity and the identifying number assigned by the pass-through entity.

- provide the total federal awards expended for each individual federal program and the CFDA number or other identifying number when the CFDA information is not available. For a cluster of programs, also provide the total for the cluster. Note that under the Uniform Guidance all noncash awards must go on the face of the schedule. See the discussion beginning at paragraph 17.31 for information on noncash awards.

- include the total amount of federal awards expended for loan or loan guarantee programs. (See paragraph 17.34 and table 17-2 for additional information.)

- include the total amount provided to subrecipients from each federal program. (Chapter 22, "Audit Considerations of Federal Pass-Through Awards (Uniform Guidance)," of this guide further discusses the audit considerations of federal pass-through awards.)

17.22 The Uniform Guidance provides that the following must be included in the notes to the schedule

- the balances of loan and loan guarantee programs (loans) outstanding at the end of the audit period for those loans described in 2 CFR 200.502(b).[14]
- the significant accounting policies used in preparing the schedule and note whether or not the auditee elected to use the 10-percent de minimis indirect cost rate

> **Emphasis Point**
>
> Under the Uniform Guidance the total amount of federal expenditures on the schedule of expenditures of federal awards will typically be the same as the total used to calculate the type A threshold for determining major programs. (A final type A threshold calculation may be impacted by the requirements in 2 CFR 200.518(b)(3) for large loan and loan guarantees.)

17.23 Note that the auditor's opinion on the schedule of expenditures of federal awards may be affected when required information is not included in the schedule. See paragraph 17.09 for more information. The appendix (paragraph 17.43) of this chapter presents example schedules of expenditures of federal awards.

Providing Additional Information

17.24 Although not required, the auditee may choose to provide other information (in addition to the foregoing requirements) that is requested by federal awarding agencies and pass-through entities to make the schedule of expenditures of federal awards easier to use. For example, when a federal program has multiple award years, the auditee may list the amount of federal awards expended for each award year separately.

Schedule May Not Agree With Other Federal Award Reporting

17.25 The information included in the schedule of expenditures of federal awards may not fully agree with other federal award reports that the auditee submits directly to federal awarding agencies or pass-through entities. AU-C section 725 requires the information in the schedule of expenditures of federal awards to relate to the same period as the financial statements. However, federal award reports submitted directly to an awarding agency (*a*) may be prepared for a different fiscal period and, (*b*) may include cumulative (from prior years) data rather than data for the current year only.

Inclusion of Nonfederal Awards

17.26 The Uniform Guidance does not require nonfederal awards (for example, state awards) to be presented in the schedule of expenditures of federal awards. However, to meet state or other requirements, auditees may decide to

---

[14] Loan information is not included in the notes to the schedule for loan and loan guarantees at institutions of higher education (IHE) when the loans are made to students but the IHE does not make the loans. Furthermore, prior loan and loan guarantee balances for which there are no continuing compliance requirements other than to repay the loans are not required to be included in the notes to the schedule. See table 17-2 and paragraph 17.33 for additional information.

include such awards in the schedule. See paragraph 17.27 for information on modifications to the schedule of expenditures of federal awards when including nonfederal awards in that schedule.

Considerations Relating to State Awards

17.27 Several state governments have auditing and reporting requirements for state awards that are similar to those for federal awards under the Uniform Guidance. In these states, auditors may be engaged to test and report on compliance with the state compliance requirements as provided in the state award(s) and under applicable state laws or regulation. Some states require a separate compliance audit with a separate schedule of expenditures of state awards. However, others accept a combined schedule of federal and state awards along with additional testing of the state expenditures. If state (or other nonfederal) awards are included in the schedule of expenditures of federal awards they are required to be segregated and clearly designated as nonfederal.[15] The title of the schedule should also be modified to indicate that nonfederal awards are included, and the reference to the schedule in the auditor's reporting on the schedule should reference the correct title.

CFDA Number Not Available

17.28 The auditee may be unable to obtain the CFDA number, which is sometimes the case for new federal programs and R&D programs. In addition, cost-type contracts under the FAR normally will not have a CFDA number. When the CFDA number is not available, the auditee has alternatives for presenting that information. The auditee could indicate that the CFDA number is not available and include, if available, another identifying number, such as a contract or grant number. The auditee also could apply the guidance presented in the Federal Audit Clearinghouse's data collection form instructions for when a federal program does not have a CFDA number. Specifically, if the program has a contract or grant number, the number shown as the CFDA number could be the awarding agency's 2-digit prefix listed for the agency in an appendix to the form's instructions (or 99 if the agency is not listed) followed by the contract or grant number. If the program does not have a contract or grant number, the number shown as the CFDA number could be the awarding agency's 2-digit prefix (or 99) followed by "UNKNOWN."

Pass-Through Awards

Treatment of Pass-Through Awards

17.29 The Uniform Guidance defines a *subrecipient* as a nonfederal entity that receives a subaward from a pass-through entity to carry out part of a federal program, but does not include an individual that is a beneficiary of such program. A subrecipient may also be a recipient of other federal awards directly from a federal awarding agency. State or local government redistributions of federal awards to subrecipients, known as *pass-through awards*, should be treated by the subrecipient as though they were received directly from the federal government. That is, federal awards expended as a subrecipient are

---

[15] Totals for federal awards must be shown separately, and exclude nonfederal amounts, to meet the Uniform Guidance requirement that the schedule provide the total federal awards expended for each individual federal program.

subject to a single audit on the same basis as that of federal awards that are received directly. Chapter 22 of this guide further discusses the audit considerations of federal pass-through awards. As noted in paragraph 17.21, in addition to the other general presentation requirements, the Uniform Guidance states that the schedule of expenditures of federal awards must include the name of the pass-through entity and the identifying number assigned by the pass-through entity for federal awards received as a subrecipient.

Commingled Assistance

17.30 Even though the Uniform Guidance requires federal awarding agencies and pass-through entities to identify the federal funding at the time of each award and subward, or modification thereof, (as described in subsequent paragraphs 17.03–.04), the individual sources (that is, federal, state, and local) of federal awards may not be separately identifiable because of commingled assistance from different levels of government. If the commingled portion cannot be separated to specifically identify the individual funding sources, the total amount should be included in the schedule of expenditures of federal awards, with a note to the schedule describing the commingled nature of the funds. When federal awards are not clearly identified, the auditor should consider whether the auditee has deficiencies in the financial management system required by 2 CFR 200.300.

Noncash Awards

Treatment of Noncash Awards

17.31 Most federal awards are in the form of cash awards. However, a number of federal programs do not involve cash transactions. These programs may include loans and loan guarantees (including interest subsidies), insurance, endowments, free rent, food commodities, and donated property (including donated surplus property). The value of federal awards expended in the form of noncash assistance must be reported on the face of the schedule of expenditures of federal awards. Paragraph 17.20, table 17-1, and chapter 15 of this guide discuss the determination of when awards, including noncash awards, are considered to be expended.

17.32 Under 2 CFR 200.502(h)-(j) the following are not considered to be federal awards expended under the Uniform Guidance:

- Medicare payments to a nonfederal entity for providing patient care services to Medicare-eligible individuals

- Medicaid payments to a subrecipient for providing patient care services to Medicaid-eligible individuals, unless a state requires the funds to be treated as federal awards expended because reimbursement is made on a cost-reimbursement basis

- Certain loans provided by the National Credit Union Administration. Loans made from the National Credit Union Share Insurance Fund and the Central Liquidity Facility that are funded by contributions from insured non-federal entities are not considered federal awards expended.

Determining the Value of the Noncash Awards Expended

17.33 Table 17-2 shows the bases generally used to determine the value of noncash awards expended. (See 2 CFR 200.502 for additional details.)

Table 17-2

Determining the Value of Noncash Awards Expended

Types of Noncash Awards	Basis Used to Determine the Value of Noncash Awards Expended
Loans and loan guarantees (loans), including interest subsidies	Amount expended equals the value of new loans made or received during the audit period plus the beginning of the audit period balance of loans from previous years for which the federal government imposes continuing compliance requirements (see paragraph 17.34), plus any interest subsidy, cash, or administrative cost allowance received. (The proceeds of loans that were received and expended in prior years are not considered federal awards expended under the Uniform Guidance when the federal statutes, regulations, and the terms and conditions of federal awards pertaining to such loans impose no continuing compliance requirements other than to repay the loans.)
Loans at institutions of higher education (IHE)	Amount expended is the same as for loans and loan guarantees (loans), including interest subsidies, mentioned previously, except that when loans are made to students of an IHE but the IHE does not make the loans, then only the value of loans made during the audit period must be considered federal awards expended in that audit period. The balance of loans for previous audit periods is not included as federal awards expended because the lender accounts for the prior balances.
Insurance	Amount expended equals the fair value of the insurance contract at the time of receipt or the assessed value provided by the federal agency.
Endowments	Amount expended equals the cumulative balance of federal awards for endowment funds that are federally restricted in each audit period in which the funds are still restricted.
Free rent	Amount expended equals the fair value at the time of receipt or the assessed value provided by the federal agency. Free rent is not considered an award expended unless it is received as part of an award to carry out a federal program.
Food commodities and donated property (including donated surplus property)	Amount expended equals the fair value at the time of receipt or the assessed value provided by the federal agency.

Loan and Loan Guarantee Continuing Compliance Requirements

17.34 As noted previously, in determining the value of total federal awards expended for loans and loan guarantees, auditees must include the balances of loans from previous years in the schedule of expenditures of federal awards if the federal government imposes continuing compliance requirements. The Uniform Guidance does not specifically define the term *continuing compliance requirements*, although some federal agencies indicate (for example, in the *Compliance Supplement*) that their loans have continuing compliance requirements, such as the U.S. Department of Housing and Urban Development (HUD) with regard to their insured, direct, and HUD-held loans. Auditors may use professional judgment in evaluating the auditee's determination of whether continuing compliance requirements are significant enough to require inclusion of prior-year loan or loan guarantee balances. For example, if in a prior year an auditee expended the proceeds of a federal loan to construct a building, and the current-year activity consists only of loan repayments and a requirement by the federal lender for the auditee to submit a report that details only loan payment information, it may not be necessary to include the prior year's loan balance in determining the total amount of loans expended. However, if the federal lender requires the auditee to ensure on an ongoing basis that a certain percentage of the building is rented to low-income residents, it would likely be necessary to include the prior year's loan balance in determining the total amount of loans expended. Communication with the federal agency's Office of Inspector General or other such program contact listed in Appendix III of the *Compliance Supplement* may be appropriate if there is any question about an auditee's determination of whether continuing compliance requirements are significant enough to require inclusion of the balances of prior loans or loan guarantees.

Documentation Requirements

17.35 The audit procedures performed on the schedule of expenditures of federal awards support the basis for the auditor's major program determination, as well as the auditor's in-relation-to opinion on the schedule. The audit work performed on the schedule to support these engagement objectives should be documented in accordance with AU-C section 230, *Audit Documentation* (AICPA, *Professional Standards*). Documenting the audit work performed on the schedule in an audit plan is an effective way to record the audit procedures performed, relevant audit evidence obtained, conclusions reached, and significant findings relating to the schedule, if any.

Issuing an Opinion on the Schedule of Expenditures of Federal Awards Under AU-C Section 805 When the Auditor Is Engaged to Perform Only the Compliance Audit Under the Uniform Guidance

17.36 One of the required conditions in AU-C section 725 for an auditor to provide an in-relation-to opinion on supplementary information is that the financial statements were audited by the auditor. When this is not the case, the auditor is precluded from issuing an in-relation-to opinion on the supplementary information. See paragraph 17.09 and chapter 23 for additional information.

17.37 Sometimes, an auditor is engaged to perform only the compliance audit required under the Uniform Guidance and not the financial statement audit.[16] When this occurs, the auditor is precluded from issuing an in-relation-to opinion on the schedule of expenditures of federal awards. Instead, to meet the reporting requirements of the Uniform Guidance, the auditee may consider engaging the auditor to issue an opinion on the schedule of expenditures of federal awards under AU-C section 805, *Special Considerations—Audits of Single Financial Statements and Specific Elements, Accounts, or Items of a Financial Statement* (AICPA, *Professional Standards*).[17] See the appendix to chapter 23 for an illustration of reporting on the schedule of expenditures of federal awards under AU-C section 805.

17.38 When performing the audit of the schedule of expenditures of federal awards under AU-C section 805, the objective of the auditor is to obtain sufficient appropriate audit evidence to enable the auditor to express an opinion on the schedule. Such an audit is designed to provide the auditor with reasonable assurance that the schedule is not misstated by an amount that would be material to the information contained in the schedule.

Transition Considerations Related to the Uniform Guidance

17.39 OMB Circular A-133 required nonfederal entities to present certain items on the face of the schedule of expenditures of federal awards, but also provided an alternative for those items to be included in the notes to the schedule. The Uniform Guidance removes the previous flexibility and now requires the following to be presented only on the face of the schedule of expenditures of federal awards:

- total amounts provided to subrecipients from each federal program,
- the total federal awards expended for loan or loan guarantee programs,[18] and
- noncash awards (for example, free rent, food commodities, and donated property and the value of insurance in effect).

17.40 As noted in paragraph 17.03, the Uniform Guidance requires that federal agencies include specific information in federal awards made to each recipient including information such as CFDA number and name, identification of whether the award is R&D, and the indirect cost rate for the federal award. This federal award information will assist nonfederal entities in complying with the Uniform Guidance requirements for what is to be included on the

---

[16] An auditee may use a separate auditor to perform the compliance audit under the Uniform Guidance for various reasons. For example, a common reason is for an auditee to make positive efforts to use small business, minority-owned firms, and women's business enterprises in conjunction with the compliance audit.

[17] An auditee may also consider engaging the auditor to examine the schedule of expenditures of federal awards or an assertion related to the schedule of expenditures of federal awards in accordance with AT section 101, *Attest Engagements* (AICPA, *Professional Standards*).

[18] See table 17-2 for determining the value of "total federal awards expended" for loan and loan guarantee programs. In addition to presenting the total federal awards expended for loan and loan guarantee programs on the face of the schedule of expenditures of federal awards, certain related information is also required in the notes to the schedule. See paragraph 17.22.

schedule of expenditures of federal awards as it relates to the identification and source of federal awards.

17.41 Other specific changes to the schedule of expenditures of federal awards introduced by the implementation of the Uniform Guidance are

- the schedule of expenditure of federal awards must now include a total for each cluster of programs.
- the notes to the schedule must include whether or not the auditee elected to use the 10-percent de minimis indirect cost rate.

17.42 The administrative requirements and cost principles included in the Uniform Guidance are required to be implemented by nonfederal entities beginning December 26, 2014, for all new federal awards and funding increments (additional funding to existing federal awards) with modified award terms and conditions that are awarded on or after that date. See the "Transition Considerations Related to the Uniform Guidance" section in chapter 16, "Auditor Planning Considerations Under the Uniform Guidance," for more information on the effective date and funding increments. As a result, in a Uniform Guidance compliance audit, a nonfederal entity may present both federal awards subject to the Uniform Guidance requirements, as well as other federal awards that continue to be subject to the pre-Uniform Guidance requirements, in the schedule of expenditures of federal awards. When this occurs, the illustrative note to the schedule of expenditures of federal awards related to significant accounting policies may be revised to also reflect that expenditures subject to the pre-Uniform Guidance requirements are recognized following the guidance contained in the pre-Uniform Guidance cost principles. See footnote 7 in the appendix of this chapter (paragraph 17.43) for more information.

17.43

Appendix—Illustrative Schedules of Expenditures of Federal Awards

Example Entity
Schedule of Expenditures of Federal Awards[1]
for the Year Ended June 30, 20X1

Federal Grantor/Pass-Through Grantor/Program or Cluster Title	Federal CFDA Number[2]	Pass-Through Entity Identifying Number[3]	Passed Through to Subrecipients	Total Federal Expenditures
Department of Agriculture Direct Programs				
Commodity Supplemental Food Program[4]	10.565			$ 134,268
Total Department of Agriculture Direct Programs				$ 134,268
Department of Housing and Urban Development Direct Programs				
Community Development Block Grants—Entitlement Grants	14.218		$423,965	$1,235,632
Section 8 Housing Choice Vouchers	14.871			800,534
Total Department of Housing and Urban Development Direct Programs			$423,965	$2,036,166
Department of Education Direct Programs				
Impact Aid	84.041			$ 372,555
Arts in Education	84.351			28,655
Subtotal Department of Education Direct Programs				$ 401,210
Department of Education Pass-Through Programs From:				
State Department of Education—Title I Grants to Local Educational Agencies	84.010	23-8345-7612		$1,239,398
Total Department of Education				$1,640,608
Total Expenditures of Federal Awards			$423,965	$3,811,042

The accompanying notes are an integral part of this schedule.

---

[1] To meet state or other requirements, auditees may decide to include certain nonfederal awards (for example, state awards) in this schedule. If such nonfederal awards are presented, they should be segregated and clearly designated as nonfederal. The title of the schedule also should be modified to indicate that nonfederal awards are included. See paragraphs 17.26–.27.

[2] When the Catalog of Federal Domestic Assistance number is not available, the auditee has alternatives for presenting that information. See paragraph 17.28.

[3] When awards are received as a subrecipient, the schedule must include the identifying number assigned by the pass-through entity.

[4] Under the Uniform Guidance all noncash awards must go on the face of the schedule.

Example Entity
Notes to the Schedule of Expenditures of Federal Awards
for the Year Ended June 30, 20X1

Note 1. Basis of Presentation[5]

The accompanying schedule of expenditures of federal awards (the "Schedule") includes the federal award activity of Example Entity under programs of the federal government for the year ended June 30, 20X1. The information in this Schedule is presented in accordance with the requirements of Title 2 U.S. Code of Federal Regulations Part 200, *Uniform Administrative Requirements, Cost Principles, and Audit Requirements for Federal Awards* (Uniform Guidance). Because the Schedule presents only a selected portion of the operations of Example Entity, it is not intended to and does not present the financial position, changes in net assets, or cash flows of Example Entity.

Note 2. Summary of Significant Accounting Policies[6]

Expenditures reported on the Schedule are reported on the *(identify basis of accounting)* basis of accounting. Such expenditures are recognized following the cost principles contained in the Uniform Guidance,[7] wherein certain types of expenditures are not allowable or are limited as to reimbursement. Negative amounts shown on the Schedule represent adjustments or credits made in the normal course of business to amounts reported as expenditures in prior years. Example Entity has elected to use the 10-percent de minimis indirect cost rate as allowed under the Uniform Guidance.

---

[5] This note is included to meet the Uniform Guidance requirement that the schedule include notes that describe the significant accounting policies used in preparing the schedule.

[6] See footnote 5.

[7] As noted in paragraph 17.42, there may be situations where federal expenditures presented in the schedule of expenditures of federal awards also include expenditures subject to pre-Uniform Guidance requirements. In this situation, the second sentence of this illustrative note may be modified as appropriate for the type of entity being audited. For a not-for-profit entity an example follows:

> Such expenditures are recognized following, as applicable, either the cost principles in OMB Circular A-122, *Cost Principles for Non-Profit Organizations*, or the cost principles contained in Title 2 U.S. Code of Federal Regulations Part 200, *Uniform Administrative Requirements, Cost Principles, and Audit Requirements for Federal Awards*, wherein certain types of expenditures are not allowable or are limited as to reimbursement.

Example Entity University
Schedule of Expenditures of Federal Awards[8]
for the Year Ended June 30, 20X1

Federal Grantor / Pass-Through Grantor / Program or Cluster Title	Federal CFDA Number[9]	Pass-Through Entity Identifying Number[10]	Passed Through to Subrecipients	Total Federal Expenditures[11]
Student Financial Assistance—Cluster				
Department of Education Direct Programs[12]				
Federal Pell Grant Program	84.063			$ 4,757,853
Federal Direct Student Loans	84.268			2,143,587
Federal Supplemental Educational Opportunity Grants	84.007			974,873
Federal Work-Study Program	84.033			575,417
Teacher Education Assistance for College and Higher Education Grants (TEACH)	84.379			230,584
Postsecondary Education Scholarships for Veterans' Dependents	84.408			239,438
Federal Perkins Loan Program (note 3)	84.038			4,384,978
Total Department of Education Direct Programs				$13,306,730
Department of Health and Human Services Direct Programs				
Nursing Student Loans (note 3)	93.364			$ 2,159,823
Health Professions Student Loans (note 3)	93.342			2,897,021
Total Department of Health and Human Services Direct Programs				$5,056,844
Total Student Financial Assistance Cluster				$18,363,574

(continued)

---

[8] See footnote 1.

[9] See footnote 2.

[10] See footnote 3.

[11] Material construction projects funded by a federal program are often capitalized in the financial statements of an auditee. However, for purposes of the schedule of expenditures of federal awards, they would be considered an expenditure.

[12] (Institutions of higher education often participate in certain loan and loan guarantee programs (for example, the Federal Family Education Loan Program and the Federal Direct Loan Program), as shown here. The Uniform Guidance requires that when loans are made to students but the institution of higher education does not make the loans, the value of the loans made during the year is considered federal awards expended. Under the Uniform Guidance, those loans and loan guarantees are required to be reported on the face of the schedule.

Federal Grantor / Pass-Through Grantor / Program or Cluster Title	Federal CFDA Number	Pass-Through Entity Identifying Number	Passed Through to Subre- cipients	Total Federal Expenditures
Research and Development—Cluster[13]				
Department of Defense Direct Programs				
Department of Army				
Collaborative Research and Development	12.114		$55,195	$87,403
Military Medical Research and Development	12.420		65,837	73,107
Subtotal Department of Defense Direct Programs			$121,032	$160,510
Department of Defense Pass-Through Programs From:				
XYZ Labs—Effects of Ice on Radar Images	12.UNKNOWN	4532		11,987
Total Department of Defense			$121,032	$172,497
National Science Foundation Direct Programs				
Geosciences	47.050		$280,374	$358,245
Biological Sciences	47.074		63,000	96,543
Subtotal National Science Foundation Direct Programs			$343,374	$454,788
National Science Foundation Pass-Through Programs From:				
ABC University—Atmospheric Effects of Volcano Eruptions	47.ABC-852	ABC-852		25,987
Total National Science Foundation			$343,374	$480,775
Department of Health and Human Services:				
National Institutes of Health Direct Programs				
Mental Health Research Grants	93.242		$92,685	$110,499
Drug Abuse and Addiction Research Programs	93.279		61,000	89,075
National Institutes of Health Pass-Through Programs From:				
ABC Hospital—Heart Research	93.UNKNOWN	5489-5		230,433
Centers for Disease Control and Prevention Direct Programs				
Chronic Diseases: Research, Control, and Prevention	93.068		97,413	112,446
Total Department of Health and Human Services			$251,098	$542,453

---

[13] For research and development, the Uniform Guidance states that total federal awards expended must be shown either by individual award or by federal agency and major subdivision within the federal agency. This example illustrates the individual award option.

Schedule of Expenditures of Federal Awards (Uniform Guidance)

Federal Grantor / Pass-Through Grantor / Program or Cluster Title	Federal CFDA Number	Pass-Through Entity Identifying Number	Passed Through to Subre-cipients	Total Federal Expenditures
Total Research and Development Cluster			$715,504	$1,195,725
Trio Cluster				
Department of Education Direct Programs				
TRIO—Talent Search	84.044			$308,465
TRIO—Upward Bound	84.047			78,654
Total TRIO Cluster				$387,119
Other Programs				
Department of State Direct Programs				
Academic Exchange Programs—Scholars	19.401			$17,823
Total Department of State Direct Programs				$17,823
Department of Education Direct Programs				
Safe and Drug-Free Schools and Communities—National Programs	84.184			$59,723
Undergraduate International Studies and Foreign Language Programs	84.016			34,688
Subtotal Department of Education Direct Programs				$94,411
Department of Education Pass-Through Programs From:				
State Department of Education—Career and Technical Education—Basic Grants to States	84.048	874-90-5473		$3,115
State Department of Education—Adult Education—Basic Grants to States	84.002	25-8594-2167		176,885
Subtotal Department of Education Pass-Through Programs				$180,000
Total Department of Education				$274,411
Total Expenditures of Federal Awards			$715,504	$20,220,829

The accompanying notes are an integral part of this schedule.

Example Entity University
Notes to the Schedule of Expenditures of Federal Awards
for the Year Ended June 30, 20X1

Note 1. Basis of Presentation [14]

The accompanying schedule of expenditures of federal awards (the "Schedule") includes the federal award activity of Example Entity University under programs of the federal government for the year ended June 30, 20X1. The information in this Schedule is presented in accordance with the requirements of Title 2 U.S. Code of Federal Regulations Part 200, *Uniform Administrative Requirements, Cost Principles, and Audit Requirements for Federal Awards* (Uniform Guidance). Because the Schedule presents only a selected portion of the operations of Example Entity University, it is not intended to and does not present the financial position, changes in net assets, or cash flows of Example Entity University.

Note 2. Summary of Significant Accounting Policies [15]

Expenditures reported on the Schedule are reported on the *(identify basis of accounting)* basis of accounting. Such expenditures are recognized following the cost principles contained in the Uniform Guidance,[16] wherein certain types of expenditures are not allowable or are limited as to reimbursement. Negative amounts shown on the Schedule represent adjustments or credits made in the normal course of business to amounts reported as expenditures in prior years. Example Entity has elected not to use the 10-percent de minimis indirect cost rate allowed under the Uniform Guidance.

Note 3. Federal Student Loan Programs [17]

The federal student loan programs listed subsequently are administered directly by Example Entity University, and balances and transactions relating to these programs are included in Example Entity University's basic financial statements. Loans outstanding at the beginning of the year and loans made during the year are included in the federal expenditures presented in the Schedule. The balance of loans outstanding at June 30, 20X1 consists of:

---

[14] See footnote 5.

[15] See footnote 5.

[16] See footnote 7.

[17] This note is intended to meet the Uniform Guidance requirement that the balances of loan or loan guarantees outstanding at year end be included in the notes to the schedule. The total federal awards expended for loan or loan guarantee programs must be included on the face of the schedule of expenditures of federal awards. The basis used to determine loan or loan guarantees expended is the amount of new loans made or received during the fiscal year plus the balance of loans from previous years for which the federal government imposes continuing compliance requirements, plus any interest subsidy, cash, or administrative cost allowance received. This note reflects an institution of higher education (IHE) that makes loans to its students. When loans are made to students of an IHE, but the IHE does not make the loans, the basis used to determine loans or loan guarantees expended is the amount of new loans made during the fiscal year. The balance for loans for previous periods is not included as federal awards expended because the lender accounts for the prior balances. Therefore, an IHE that does not make the loans will not have loan balances to disclose in the notes to the schedule because the lender accounts for the prior balances. See table 17-2 and paragraph 17.34 for more discussion of loans and loan guarantees.

Schedule of Expenditures of Federal Awards (Uniform Guidance)

CFDA Number	Program Name	Outstanding Balance at June 30, 20X1
84.038	Federal Perkins Loan	$4,341,180
93.364	Nursing Student Loans	$ 2,115,635
93.342	Health Professions Student Loans	$2,853,248

Chapter 18

Determination of Major Programs (Uniform Guidance)

> **⊕ Update 18-1: Audits of Federal Awards**
>
> This chapter, and the remaining chapters of part III, *Uniform Guidance Audits*, of this guide, should be used for performing a compliance audit of federal awards under the audit requirements of Title 2 U.S. I (CFR) Part 200, *Uniform Administrative Requirements, Cost Principles, and Audit Requirements for Federal Awards* (Uniform Guidance).[1] Part II, *Circular A-133 Audits*, of this guide should be used for performing a compliance audit under Office of Management and Budget (OMB) Circular A-133, *Audits of States, Local Governments, and Non-Profit Organizations* (Circular A-133). See the transitional guidance sections at the end of each chapter that highlight important matters for consideration. Additionally, refer to the preface of this guide for more information.
>
> **Important Effective Date Information**
>
> In December 2013, the OMB issued the Uniform Guidance, which is effective for nonfederal entities for all federal awards and certain funding increments provided on or after December 26, 2014. The requirements in Subpart F, "Audit Requirements," are effective for audits of fiscal years beginning on or after December 26, 2014, with no early implementation permitted. Therefore, auditees subject to a single audit with December 25, 2015, and later year ends (for example, December 31, 2015) will be required to undergo the audit under Subpart F of the Uniform Guidance. Note that audits of fiscal years ending prior to the effective date of the Uniform Guidance audit requirements are subject to an audit under Circular A-133.

Introduction[2, 3]

18.01 The Uniform Guidance states that the auditee must identify in its accounts all federal awards received and expended and the federal programs

---

[1] See the information found at the end of this chapter (paragraph 18.33) and other part III, *Uniform Guidance Audits*, chapters of this guide for transition considerations when performing an audit under Title 2 U.S. *Code of Federal Regulations* (CFR) Part 200, *Uniform Administrative Requirements, Cost Principles, and Audit Requirements for Federal Awards* (Uniform Guidance). Transition considerations can also be found at the end of certain part II, *Circular A-133 Audits*, chapters as it relates to an audit performed under Office of Management and Budget (OMB) Circular A-133, *Audits of States, Local Governments, and Non-Profit Organizations* (Circular A-133).

[2] *Government Auditing Standards* incorporates by reference AICPA Statements on Auditing Standards. Therefore, auditors performing financial statement audits and Uniform Guidance compliance audits in accordance with *Government Auditing Standards* should comply with generally accepted auditing standards (GAAS), the requirements found in chapters 1–3 of *Government Auditing Standards*, and the additional standards and related requirements for financial audits found in chapter 4, "Standards for Financial Audits," of *Government Auditing Standards*.

[3] As noted in AU-C section 935, *Compliance Audits* (AICPA, *Professional Standards*), the auditor should determine whether audit requirements are specified in a governmental audit requirement that are supplementary to GAAS and *Government Auditing Standards* and perform procedures to address those requirements, if any. An example of supplementary audit requirements are the procedures performed to identify major programs in a Uniform Guidance compliance audit.

under which they were received. The auditee must also prepare a schedule of expenditures of federal awards for the period covered by its financial statements. (Chapter 17, "Schedule of Expenditures of Federal Awards (Uniform Guidance)," of this guide discusses the requirements related to that schedule.) However, the Uniform Guidance places the responsibility for identifying major programs on the auditor, and it provides the criteria to be used in that determination. The auditor's determination of the programs to be audited is based on the guidance found in 2 CFR 200.518. That guidance states that the auditor must use a risk-based approach to determine which federal programs are major programs.

> **Emphasis Point**
>
> The use of the term *must* in the Uniform Guidance indicates a requirement. This is consistent with the use of the term *must* in generally accepted auditing standards (GAAS) and *Government Auditing Standards*. The use of the term *should* in the Uniform Guidance indicates a best practice or recommended approach. However, GAAS and *Government Auditing Standards* use the term *should* to indicate a presumptively mandatory requirement. An auditor must comply with a presumptively mandatory requirement in all cases in which such a requirement is relevant, except in rare circumstances. In this guide, the term ***should***, when italicized and bolded, indicates a best practice or recommended approach in the Uniform Guidance. This is intended to differentiate it from the term *should* used throughout the guide to refer to presumptively mandatory requirements in GAAS and *Government Auditing Standards*. See chapter 1, "Introduction and Overview of *Government Auditing Standards*," of this guide for more information regarding presumptively mandatory requirements.

Determining Major Programs Under the Uniform Guidance

18.02 The guidance on determining major programs is organized here as provided in the Uniform Guidance and consists of the steps in the following listing. Exhibit 18-1 is a flowchart illustrating the application of the risk-based approach for determining major programs:

- Step 1—Determination of type A and type B programs (paragraphs 18.03–.08)
- Step 2—Identification of low-risk type A programs (paragraphs 18.09–.13)
- Step 3—Identification of high-risk type B programs (paragraphs 18.14–.15)
- Step 4—Determination of programs to be audited as major (paragraph 18.16)

Exhibit 18-1

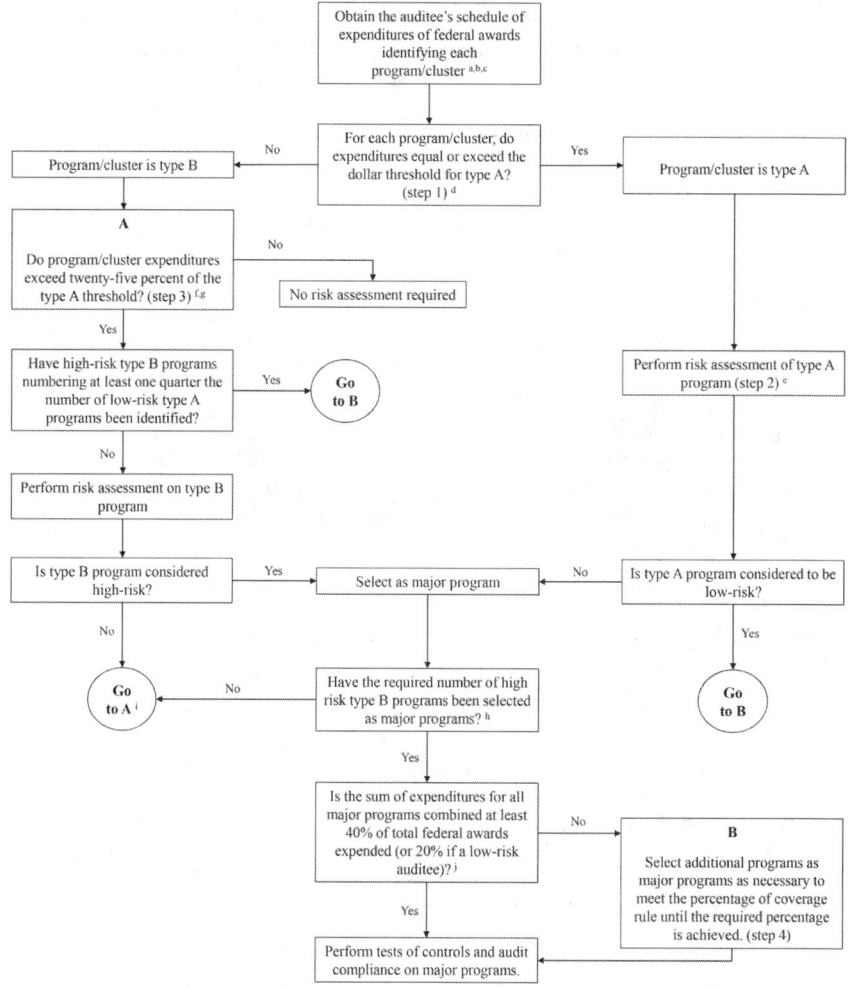

a   The use of the term *program* in this flowchart includes both programs and clusters.

b   Chapter 15, "Overview of the Single Audit Act, the Uniform Guidance Audit Requirements, and the *Compliance Supplement*," of this guide defines federal programs, including clusters.

c   Stop if the SEFA shows less than $750,000 of federal expenditures. A Uniform Guidance compliance audit is not required.

d   Paragraphs 18.03–.08 discuss step 1.

e   Paragraphs 18.09–.13 discuss step 2.

f   Paragraphs 18.14–.15 discuss step 3.

g   See paragraph 18.14.

 h Once the required number of high-risk type B programs are identified, that is, at least one quarter the number of low-risk type A programs, no further risk assessment of type B programs is needed.

 i The process beginning at box A is repeated until the required number of high-risk type B programs have been identified or there are no more type B programs subject to risk assessment (that is, type B programs exceeding twenty-five percent of the type A threshold).

 j The additional programs selected (box B on the flowchart) to meet the percentage-of-coverage rule are audited as major programs in addition to type A and type B programs identified in steps 1–4. Paragraph 18.17 discusses the percentage-of-coverage rule.

Emphasis Point

Under the Uniform Guidance, the minimum threshold for identifying type A programs is $750,000 (as noted in table 18-1, "Criteria for Identifying Type A Programs"). This is the same dollar amount as the $750,000 threshold for determining whether a single audit is required (audit threshold).

Step 1—Determination of Type A and Type B Programs

 18.03 The schedule of expenditures of federal awards, prepared by the auditee, is the basis of the auditor's identification of type A and type B programs. Using the schedule of expenditures of federal awards, the auditor identifies each federal program and cluster. After the type A threshold amount is determined, the auditor identifies the federal programs as being either type A or type B, as defined in the Uniform Guidance. In general, type A programs are larger federal programs, and type B programs are smaller federal programs. Federal awards expended for purposes of determining type A and type B programs are the amount of cash and noncash awards, after all adjustments are made, in the *final* current-year schedule of expenditures of federal awards. An auditor who uses the prior-year schedule or preliminary current-year estimates to plan the audit should recalculate the threshold for type A programs based on the final amounts to ensure that federal awards are properly classified as type A or B. (For purposes of determining major programs, federal programs with the same Catalog of Federal Domestic Assistance number are considered as one program. In addition, a cluster of programs must be considered as one program. Chapter 15, "Overview of the Single Audit Act, the Uniform Guidance Audit Requirements, and the *Compliance Supplement*," of this guide discusses clusters of programs.)

Type A Program Criteria

 18.04 The larger federal programs are labeled as type A. Table 18-1 presents the criteria that the Uniform Guidance establishes for identifying type A programs.

Table 18-1
Criteria for Identifying Type A Programs

Total Federal Awards Expended[1]	Type A Threshold
Equal to or exceed $750,000 but less than or equal to $25 million	$750,000
Exceed $25 million but less than or equal to $100 million	Total federal awards expended times 0.03
Exceed $100 million but less than or equal to $1 billion	$3 million
Exceed $1 billion but less than or equal to $10 billion	Total federal awards expended times 0.003
Exceed $10 billion but less than or equal to $20 billion	$30 million
Exceed $20 billion	Total federal awards expended times 0.0015

[1] Includes both cash and noncash awards.

Type B Program Criteria

18.05 Federal programs that do not meet the type A criteria are labeled type B programs.

Effect of Large Loans and Loan Guarantees on Identification of Type A Programs

18.06 Chapter 17 of this guide discusses the various types of federal awards, including loans and loan guarantees, and when they are recognized as expended and how they are valued for purposes of the Uniform Guidance compliance audit. The Uniform Guidance states that when the auditor applies the dollar criteria shown in table 18-1 to identify type A programs, the inclusion of large loans and loan guarantees must not result in the exclusion of other federal programs as type A programs. This requirement relates only to loans and loan guarantees and not to any other large noncash federal awards. The effect of large loan and loan guarantees on the identification of the type A threshold is summarized as follows:

- For the purpose of this calculation, a program is considered to be a federal program providing loans if the value of federal awards expended[4] for loans within the program comprises 50 percent or more of the total federal awards for the program. (Note that a cluster of programs is treated as one program.)
- When a federal program providing loans or loan guarantees exceeds four times the largest non-loan program, it is considered a "large loan program," and the auditor must consider this federal program as a type A program and exclude its value in determining the type A threshold.

---

[4] The value of federal awards expended is determined using the guidance in 2 CFR 200.502. See chapter 17, "Schedule of Expenditures of Federal Awards (Uniform Guidance)," for more information.

- The type A threshold is then calculated after removing the total of all large loan programs.[5]

18.07 Paragraph 18.08 demonstrates the effect of loans and loan guarantees on major program determination using the example programs in table 18-2 and after applying the guidance regarding large loan and loan guarantee programs found in the Uniform Guidance.

Table 18-2

Identification of Type A Programs and the Effect of Loans and Loan Guarantees[1]

Program / Federal Grantor	*Federal Awards Expended*
Cash program A—U.S. Department of Labor	$1,335,000
Cash program B—U.S. Department of Health and Human Services	8,000,000
Cash program C-1—U.S. Department of Education	175,000
Cash program C-2—U.S. Department of Education	280,000
Cash program D—U.S. Department of Housing and Urban Development (a pass-through grant from a local government)	310,000
Subtotal—Cash federal awards expended	$10,100,000
Commodities program E—U.S. Department of Agriculture (a pass-through grant from a state)	2,000,000
Subtotal—Cash and commodities federal awards expended (non-loan programs)	$12,100,000
Loan program F—U.S. Department of Housing and Urban Development	30,500,000[2]
Subtotal—federal awards expended— non-loan programs and a loan program that does not exceed the criteria for exclusion from type A threshold determination (see paragraph 18.08)	$42,600,000
Loan guarantee program G—U.S. Department of Agriculture	55,000,000[3]
Total federal awards expended	$97,600,000

---

[1] In accordance with Title 2 U.S. *Code of Federal Regulations* Part 200, *Uniform Administrative Requirements, Cost Principles, and Audit Requirements for Federal Awards*, loans and loan guarantees include new loans made during the year, plus prior-year loans for which the federal government imposes continuing compliance requirements, plus any interest subsidy, cash, or administrative cost allowance received. Chapter 17, "Schedule of Expenditures of Federal Awards (Uniform Guidance)," of this guide provides additional information.

[2] This loan guarantee program does not meet the criteria to be designated as a large loan or loan guarantee program because it does not exceed the threshold of $32,000,000 [4 times the amount of the largest non-loan program (4 × $8,000,000 = $32,000,000)]. (See paragraph 18.06 for information regarding determining whether the program is considered a loan program for the purpose of this calculation.)

[3] This loan guarantee program meets the criteria to be designated as a large loan or loan guarantee program because it exceeds the threshold of $32,000,000 [4 times the amount of the largest non-loan program (4 × $8,000,000 = $32,000,000)].

---

[5] In the event the removal of large loan balances causes the adjusted expenditures to fall below $750,000, the type A threshold would be considered to be $750,000.

Determination of Major Programs (Uniform Guidance)

18.08 Table 18-2 shows that the auditee has $97,600,000 in total federal awards expended, including both loan and non-loan programs. Using the guidance in 2 CFR 200.518(b)(3), before calculating the type A threshold for major program determination purposes, there is one large loan guarantee program that must be excluded from the base of $97,600,000, that is, the $55,000,000 loan guarantee program G (see note 3 at table 18-2). After removing loan guarantee program G, the revised base becomes $42,600,000 ($97,600,000 − $55,000,000), which results in a type A threshold of $1,278,000 (3 percent of $42,600,000). Therefore, in addition to the loan guarantee program G, programs A, B, E, and F would also be type A programs.

Step 2—Identification of Low-Risk Type A Programs

18.09 After completing step 1, the auditor must identify type A programs that are low risk using the criteria in 2 CFR 200.518(c), as described in the following paragraph.

General Conditions for Low-Risk Type A Programs

18.10 In making the determination about whether a type A program is low risk, the auditor must consider whether there is an indication of significantly increased risk based on the following criteria for federal program risk that would preclude the program from being low risk:[6]

- Oversight exercised by federal agencies and pass-through entities as described in 200.519(c) (for example, results of recent monitoring or other reviews or indication in the *OMB Compliance Supplement* (*Compliance Supplement*) that a federal agency has identified a federal program as higher risk
- The results of audit follow-up; or
- Any changes in personnel or systems affecting the program

Note that these are the only criteria that the Uniform Guidance permits the auditor to consider in evaluating whether there is significantly increased risk for a type A program (that is, the auditor is not permitted to use judgment based on the inherent risk of a type A program).

18.11 In addition, for a type A program to be considered low risk it must

    a. have been audited as a major program in at least one of the two most recent audit periods (in the most recent audit period in the case of a biennial audit) and

    b. in the most recent audit period, the program must not have had

        i. internal control deficiencies which were identified as material weaknesses in the auditor's report on internal control for major programs,

        ii. a modified opinion on the program in the auditor's report on major programs, or

        iii. known or likely questioned costs that exceed five percent of the total federal awards expended for the program.

---

[6] See paragraph 18.22 for information on assessing risk when determining low-risk type A and high-risk type B programs.

18.12 It is important for auditors to note that every type A program that was not audited in one of the two prior years is required to be audited as a major program. If a type A program is new to an entity in the current year (for example, because the entity did not previously participate in the program or because it is a new federal program or because a new program was added to another cluster as defined in Part 5 of the *Compliance Supplement*), it must be audited as a major program in the current year because it was not audited in one of the prior two years. If a program that previously was a type B program is a type A program in the current year (for example, because the funding level increased), and the program was not audited as a major program in one of the two prior years, it must be audited as a major program in the current year.

> **Emphasis Point**
>
> Consider the following example. An auditor is going through the process of determining which type A programs are low risk. Using the criteria in paragraph 18.11, one of the programs that is deemed to be low-risk is Student Financial Assistance (SFA). That is, SFA was audited as major program in one of the prior two audit periods and had no material weaknesses, no modified opinion, and no known or likely questioned costs that exceeded five percent of the total federal awards expended for the program. Additionally when the auditor considered the criteria in paragraph 18.10 (that is, oversight exercised by federal agencies and pass-through entities; the results of audit follow-up; and any changes in personnel or systems affecting the program), the auditor concluded that there was no indication of significantly increased risk that would preclude the program from being low-risk.
>
> **Question**: Can the auditor, using judgment, override the low-risk type A conclusion on SFA in this example based on the inherent risk of SFA?
>
> **Answer**: The auditor is not able to use judgment to override the low-risk type A conclusion based on the inherent risk of a federal program. In this example, the auditor is required to consider SFA a low-risk type A program.
>
> This answer is based on a revision to Step 2 of the risk-based approach for determining major programs made by the Uniform Guidance – which removed the consideration of the inherent risk of the program (as described in 2 CFR 200.519(d)) from the type A program risk assessment determination. This change may result in a type A program which the auditor previously audited as a major program solely based on the inherent risk of the program, to be a low-risk type A program in the current year. An increase in the number of low-risk type A programs may also increase the number of high-risk type B programs required to be selected as major programs.

Type A Program Not Considered Low Risk at Request of Federal Awarding Agency

18.13 The Uniform Guidance permits a federal awarding agency to request that a type A program for certain recipients not be considered low risk so that it would be audited as a major program. For example, it may be necessary for a large type A program to be audited as major each year for particular recipients to allow the federal agency to comply with the Government Management Reform Act of 1994. In this instance, the Uniform Guidance requires the federal awarding agency to obtain approval from OMB. (OMB has not yet made any such approvals.) Furthermore, the federal awarding agency should notify the recipient and, if known, the auditor, at least 180 days before the end of the fiscal year end to be audited. (Paragraph 18.31 discusses the federal agency option to identify federal programs as higher risk in the *Compliance Supplement*.)

Step 3—Identification of High-Risk Type B Programs

18.14 After completing steps 1–2, the auditor must identify type B programs that are high risk, using professional judgment and the criteria for federal program risk described in paragraphs 18.23–.32. However, the auditor is not required to identify more high-risk type B programs than at least one fourth the number of type A programs identified as low risk under step 2. Except for known material weaknesses in internal control or compliance problems as discussed in 2 CFR 200.519(b)(1), (b)(2), and (c)(1) (that is, weaknesses in internal control, prior audit findings, and oversight exercised by federal agencies and pass-through entities), a single risk criterion would seldom cause a type B program to be considered high risk. The Uniform Guidance encourages the auditor to use an approach that provides an opportunity for different high-risk type B programs to be audited as major over a period of time.

Criteria for Performing Risk Assessments on Type B Programs

18.15 An auditor is not expected to perform risk assessments on relatively small federal programs. Therefore, the auditor is only required to perform risk assessments on type B programs that exceed 25 percent (0.25) of the type A threshold determined in step 1 (paragraph 18.04). For example, at the minimum type A threshold of $750,000, the auditor would not be required to risk assess small type B programs with federal awards expended of $187,500 or less (25 percent of $750,000). When the type A threshold calculation includes adjustment for large loan or loan guarantee programs under 2 CFR 200.518(b)(3), the type A threshold used for this 25 percent calculation for relatively small type B programs is the same as this adjusted type A threshold which is required to be reported in the summary of the auditor's results in the schedule of findings and questioned costs.

Step 4—Determination of Programs to Be Audited as Major

Criteria for Major Programs

18.16 After completing steps 1–3, the auditor identifies the major programs. The Uniform Guidance states that, at a minimum, the auditor must audit all of the following as major programs:

- All type A programs not identified as low risk under step 2 (paragraphs 18.09–.13)
- All type B programs identified as high risk under step 3 (paragraphs 18.14–.15)
- Programs to be audited as major based on a federal agency or pass-through entity request (in lieu of the federal agency or pass-through entity conducting or arranging for additional audits or other procedures; paragraph 18.20 provides further information)

- Additional programs, if any, that are necessary to meet the percentage of coverage rule described in paragraph 18.17

The Uniform Guidance notes that these requirements may require the auditor to audit more programs as major programs than the number of type A programs.

Percentage of Coverage Rule

18.17 In addition to the federal programs required to be audited as major programs under steps 1–3, the auditor must audit additional federal programs as major programs such that the total federal awards expended in the major programs, in the aggregate, encompass at least 40 percent of the total federal awards expended. However, if the auditee meets the criteria for a low-risk auditee (see paragraph 18.21), the auditor is required to audit as major programs federal programs with federal awards expended that, in the aggregate, encompass at least 20 percent of the total federal awards expended. A computation of the total federal awards expended for the major programs audited, determined under step 4, as a percentage of the total federal awards expended will indicate the percentage of coverage. If the total does not equal or exceed 40 percent (or 20 percent in the case of a low-risk auditee) of the total federal awards expended, the auditor must select additional programs (either type A or type B) to equal or exceed 40 percent (or 20 percent in the case of a low-risk auditee) and audit them as major programs. When selecting additional programs to meet the percentage-of-coverage rule, the auditor may select programs without regard to risk assessment. If loans or loan guarantees are major programs, these programs may be used for purposes of meeting the percentage of coverage rule. Furthermore, when a federal agency or pass-through entity requests and pays for a program to be audited as major (see paragraph 18.20), that program may also be used for purposes of meeting the percentage of coverage rule.

Emphasis Point

It is important to note that the percentage of coverage rule represents the minimum coverage to be achieved and is calculated after the determination of programs to be audited is made in step 4 (described in paragraph 18.16). Once the initial determination of major programs to be audited is made, the percentage of coverage rules determine if additional programs are required to be selected for audit.

Note that the percentage of coverage calculation is based on final total federal expenditures in the schedule of expenditures of federal awards. Auditors may begin the audit prior to the availability of the final year-end expenditure amounts. In this case, once final total federal expenditures are known, both the type A program threshold and percentage of coverage dollar amounts will need to be rechecked to ensure that the proper major programs have been selected and that the percentage of coverage rule has been met.

Documentation of Risk Assessment

18.18 The Uniform Guidance states that the auditor must include in the audit documentation the risk analysis process used in determining major programs. It is, therefore, necessary for the auditor to develop adequate audit documentation, as required by GAAS and *Government Auditing*

Determination of Major Programs (Uniform Guidance)

Standards, which includes documentation supporting the determination of major programs. (Chapter 3, "Planning and Performing a Financial Statement Audit in Accordance With *Government Auditing Standards*," and chapter 16, "Auditor Planning Considerations Under the Uniform Guidance," of this guide discuss the audit documentation requirements of GAAS and *Government Auditing Standards*.)

Auditor Judgment in the Risk Assessment Process

18.19 The Uniform Guidance states that when the determination of major programs is performed and documented by the auditor in accordance with the Uniform Guidance, the auditor's judgment in applying the risk-based approach to determine major programs must be presumed correct. Challenges by federal agencies and pass-through entities must only be for clearly improper use of the requirements in Subpart F of the Uniform Guidance. However, federal agencies and pass-through entities may provide the auditor with guidance about the risk of a particular federal program, and the auditor must consider this guidance in determining major programs not yet completed.

Other Considerations Regarding the Determination of Major Programs

Federal Agency and Pass-Through Entity Requests for Additional Major Programs

18.20 2 CFR 200.503(e) permits a federal agency to request an auditee to have a particular federal program audited as a major program in lieu of the federal awarding agency conducting or arranging for additional audits. To allow for planning, such requests should be made at least 180 days before the end of the fiscal year to be audited. After consultation with its auditor, the auditee should promptly respond to such a request by informing the federal agency whether the program would otherwise be audited as a major program using the risk-based approach and, if not, the estimated incremental cost. The federal awarding agency must then promptly confirm to the auditee whether it wants the program audited as a major program. If the program is to be audited as a major program based on the federal agency's request, and the federal agency agrees to pay the full incremental costs, then the auditee must have the program audited as a major program. This approach also may be used by pass-through entities for a subrecipient.

Low-Risk Auditee Criteria

18.21 The Uniform Guidance establishes certain criteria for determining whether an auditee is low risk. An auditee that meets all of the following conditions for each of the preceding two audit periods[7] must qualify as a low-risk auditee and be eligible for the reduced audit coverage discussed in paragraph 18.17:

- Single audits were performed on an annual basis in accordance with the Uniform Guidance, including submitting the data

---

[7] An auditor may not use professional judgment to override these required conditions for low-risk auditee status. For example, it would not be appropriate for an auditor to make a determination that a material weakness under the requirements of *Government Auditing Standards* that was reported in one of the preceding two audit periods would not be important enough to cause an entity to lose its low-risk auditee status.

collection form and reporting package to the Federal Audit Clearinghouse (FAC) within the earlier of 30 calendar days after the receipt of the auditor's report or 9 months after the end of the audit period. An auditee that has biennial audits does not qualify as a low-risk auditee.

- The auditor's opinion on whether the financial statements[8] were prepared in accordance with U.S. generally accepted accounting principles (GAAP), or a basis of accounting required by state law, was unmodified.

- The auditor's in-relation-to opinion on the schedule of expenditures of federal awards was unmodified.

- There were no deficiencies in internal control over financial reporting that were identified as material weaknesses under the requirements of *Government Auditing Standards*.

- The auditor did not report a substantial doubt about the auditee's ability to continue as a going concern.

- None of the federal programs had audit findings from any of the following in either of the preceding two audit periods in which they were classified as type A programs:

    — Internal control deficiencies that were identified as material weaknesses in the auditor's report on internal control for major programs

    — A modified opinion on a major program in the auditor's report on major programs

    — Known or likely questioned costs that exceed five percent of the total federal awards expended for a type A program during the audit period

Assessing Risk When Determining Major Programs

18.22 The Uniform Guidance specifies the criteria to be used when assessing type A and type B programs for risk. Note that the risk criteria used in the determination of low-risk type A programs is different than the risk criteria used in the determination of high-risk type B programs. A discussion of the risk criteria used in determining high-risk type B programs follows in paragraphs 18.23–.32. As noted in paragraphs 18.10–.12, the criteria to be used in determining type A programs is limited (*a*) to oversight exercised by federal agencies and pass-through entities, (*b*) the results of audit follow-up, and (*c*) any changes in personnel or systems affecting the program.

Criteria for Federal Program Risk

18.23 The auditor's determination of federal program risk ***should*** be based on an overall evaluation of the risk of noncompliance occurring that

---

[8] As explained in the AICPA Audit and Accounting Guide *State and Local Governments*, the auditor generally expresses or disclaims an opinion on a government's basic financial statements by providing an opinion or disclaimer of opinion on each opinion unit required to be presented in those financial statements. For purposes of determining low-risk auditee status for governmental entities, the auditor's opinion on each opinion unit should be unmodified.

could be material to the federal program being evaluated. That risk assessment must consider certain criteria as set forth in the Uniform Guidance. As a part of the risk assessment, the auditor may also wish to discuss a particular federal program with auditee management and with the federal agency or pass-through entity. The discussion that follows is used in the identification of type B programs that are high risk. See paragraph 18.13 for additional considerations.

Current and Prior Audit Experience

18.24 As part of determining federal program risk, the auditor must consider current and prior audit experience, which includes consideration of the following:

- Weaknesses in internal control over federal programs
- Prior audit findings
- Federal programs not recently audited as major

Weaknesses in Internal Control Over Federal Programs

18.25 In assessing program risk under the Uniform Guidance, weaknesses in internal control over compliance for federal programs would be an indication of higher risk. Consideration should be given to the control environment over federal programs and such factors as the expectation of management's adherence to federal statutes, regulations, and the terms and conditions of federal awards and the competence and experience of the personnel who administer the federal programs. For example, an indication of higher risk would exist in instances in which the staff are new or do not have experience with a program.

18.26 Federal programs administered under multiple internal control structures may have higher risk. This occurs when multiple organizational units (for example, locations or branches) are involved in the administration of federal programs. An example of this would be a university that has several campuses administering a federal program. When assessing risk, the auditor must consider whether weaknesses in internal control are isolated in a single operating unit (that is, one college campus) or are pervasive throughout the entity.

18.27 The extent to which federal programs are passed through to subrecipients may affect federal program risk. When significant parts of a federal program are passed through to subrecipients, a weak system for monitoring subrecipients would indicate higher risk. Alternatively, if the auditee passes a significant portion of programs to subrecipients and the auditee has an effective system in place to monitor the subrecipients, this might be indicative of a lower level of risk to the program.

Prior Audit Findings

18.28 As a part of assessing program risk, the Uniform Guidance states that the auditor must consider prior audit findings. This information should be used in assessing risk and determining the nature, timing, and extent of current audit work. An indication of higher risk would exist for prior audit findings that could have a significant impact on a federal program or have not been corrected. These findings may be the result, for example, of previous single audits by independent auditors or of compliance or financial audits performed by internal auditors or government auditors in conjunction with the federal awarding agency's monitoring activities.

Federal Programs Not Recently Audited as Major

18.29 Federal programs that have not recently been audited as major programs may be of higher risk than federal programs recently audited as major without audit findings. For example, some of the auditee's type B programs may never have been audited as major programs in the past. A higher level of risk would likely be assessed on such programs than on those programs that have been consistently audited as major programs without audit findings.

Oversight Exercised by Federal Agencies and Pass-Through Entities

18.30 2 CFR 200.519(c)(1) states that the oversight exercised by federal agencies or pass-through entities could be used to assess risk. One factor in assessing this risk could be the results of recent audits performed by federal agencies or pass-through entities. For example, recent monitoring or other reviews that were performed by an oversight entity and that disclosed no significant problems would indicate lower risk, whereas monitoring that disclosed significant problems would indicate higher risk. However, reviews performed by federal agencies or pass-through entities vary widely with coverage and intensity. Therefore, consideration of the scope of reviews performed may assist the auditor in evaluating whether the oversight activities increase, decrease, or have no impact on risk.

18.31 The Uniform Guidance provides that federal agencies, with the concurrence of OMB, may identify federal programs that are higher risk. That identification is provided by OMB in the *Compliance Supplement*. For example, the U.S. Department of Health and Human Services has identified the Medicaid Assistance Program as a program of higher risk in the *Compliance Supplement*. Although such an identification by a federal agency does not preclude an auditor from determining that a program is low risk (for example, because prior audits have shown strong internal control and compliance), the consideration of this identification of higher risk is part of the risk assessment process.

Inherent Risk of Noncompliance of the Federal Programs

18.32 Programs with higher inherent risk of noncompliance may be of a higher risk for the purpose of determining whether a type B program is high risk. The Uniform Guidance provides the following examples of program characteristics with potentially higher inherent risk of noncompliance:

- The nature of the federal program may indicate risk. Consideration *should* be given to the complexity of the program, and the extent to which a program contracts for goods and services. For example, federal programs that disburse funds through third-party contracts or have eligibility criteria may be of higher risk. Federal programs primarily involving staff payroll costs may have a high risk for time-and-effort reporting but may otherwise be low risk.

- The phase of a federal program's life cycle at the federal agency may indicate risk. For example, a new program with new or interim regulations may have a higher risk than an established program with time-tested regulations. Also, significant changes in federal programs, statutes, regulations, or in the terms or conditions of federal awards may increase risk.

- The phase of a program's life cycle at the auditee may indicate risk. For example, during the first and last years in which an auditee participates in a program, the risk may be higher because of the start-up or closeout of the program's activities and staff.
- Type B programs with larger federal awards expended would be of higher risk than would programs with substantially smaller federal awards expended.

Transition Considerations Related to the Uniform Guidance

18.33 Under the Uniform Guidance, both the minimum threshold for identifying type A programs and the threshold used to determine whether a single audit is required (audit threshold) is $750,000. Under Circular A-133, the minimum threshold for identifying type A programs is $300,000, and the single audit threshold is $500,000.

18.34 The Uniform Guidance specifically addresses the effect of large loan and loan guarantees on the identification of the type A program threshold (see paragraph 18.06). Under Circular A-133, guidance on the effect of large loan and loan guarantees was only provided in Appendix VII, "Other OMB Circular A-133 Advisories," of the *Compliance Supplement*. In incorporating this topic, the Uniform Guidance slightly changed the previous guidance on this topic by stating that for the purpose of the threshold calculation, a program is considered to be a federal program providing loans if the value of federal awards expended for loans within the program comprises 50 percent or more of the total federal awards for the program.

18.35 Under the Uniform Guidance, the percentage of coverage rule specifies at least 40 percent of total federal expenditures (at least 20 percent for low-risk auditees) be audited as major programs. This is a change from the percentage of coverage rule under Circular A-133, which specified that at least 50 percent of total federal expenditures (at least 25 percent for low-risk auditees) be audited as major programs. It is important to note that the percentage of coverage rule represents the minimum coverage to be achieved and is calculated after the determination of programs to be audited is made in step 4 (described in paragraph 18.16).

18.36 The criteria and process used to identify low-risk type A programs and high-risk type B programs has been revised. The Uniform Guidance simplified step 2 (see paragraphs 18.09–.13) for determining low-risk type A programs to focus more on fact-based criteria and higher risk audit findings. As a result, under the Uniform Guidance, the determination of type A low risk programs is less dependent on auditor judgment than is the case under Circular A-133. A significant change in this regard is that, in determining whether a type A program is low risk under the Uniform Guidance, the inherent risk of the program is no longer a consideration. The Emphasis Point in paragraph 18.12 illustrates how this change affects the auditor's risk assessment. In addition, under Circular A-133, auditor judgment could be used to conclude that certain types of prior findings did not preclude a type A program from being low risk. That provision is not found in the Uniform Guidance. Instead, the Uniform Guidance is very specific regarding the types of findings the auditor must consider in the type A program risk assessment process.

18.37 With regard to the type B program risk assessment process, there is no longer an option 1 and option 2 when determining how many type B programs need to be risk assessed (see chapter 8, "Determination of Major Programs (Circular A-133)," for a more detailed description of option 1 and option 2 under Circular A-133). Under the Uniform Guidance, the auditor is not required to identify (and, therefore, risk assess) more high-risk type B programs than at least one-fourth the number of low-risk type A programs. See the discussion beginning at paragraph 18.14. In addition, the criteria for determining whether a type B program is considered a relatively small program, and, therefore, not required to be risk assessed, has been revised. See paragraph 18.15.

18.38 The Uniform Guidance did not retain the provision found in Circular A-133 related to the deviation from risk criteria in a first year audit. Therefore, in a Uniform Guidance compliance audit, an auditor is not permitted to audit as major all type A programs plus any type B programs as necessary to meet the percentage of coverage rule.

18.39 The requirements for low-risk auditee status have also been revised. First, the Uniform Guidance clarifies what had been a confusing point under Circular A-133. That is, under the Uniform Guidance, the low-risk auditee criteria explicitly state that the data collection form and the reporting package must have been submitted to the FAC within the time frame specified in 2 CFR 200.512 in each of the two preceding periods for the entity to qualify as a low-risk auditee. Also, a new low-risk auditee criterion states that if the auditor reported a substantial doubt about the auditee's ability to continue as a going concern for either of the two prior periods, the auditee is precluded from being a low-risk auditee. Furthermore, low-risk auditee criteria now requires that the auditor's opinion on whether the financial statements were prepared in accordance with GAAP, or a basis of accounting required by state law, must be unmodified for each of the two prior periods in order for the entity to qualify as a low-risk auditee. Therefore, unless required by state law, an auditee that prepares its financial statements on a non-GAAP basis of accounting, such as the cash or modified cash basis, cannot be considered a low-risk auditee. See paragraph 18.21 for additional low-risk auditee requirements under the Uniform Guidance.

Chapter 19

Consideration of Internal Control Over Compliance for Major Programs (Uniform Guidance)

> **© Update 19-1: Audits of Federal Awards**
>
> This chapter, and the remaining chapters of part III, *Uniform Guidance Audits*, of this guide, should be used for performing a compliance audit of federal awards under the audit requirements of Title 2 U.S. *Code of Federal Regulations* (CFR) Part 200, *Uniform Administrative Requirements, Cost Principles, and Audit Requirements for Federal Awards* (Uniform Guidance).[1] Part II, *Circular A-133 Audits*, of this guide should be used for performing a compliance audit under Office of Management and Budget (OMB) Circular A-133, *Audits of States, Local Governments, and Non-Profit Organizations* (Circular A-133). See the transitional guidance sections at the end of each chapter that highlight important matters for consideration. Additionally, refer to the preface of this guide for more information.
>
> **Important Effective Date Information**
>
> In December 2013, the OMB issued the Uniform Guidance, which is effective for nonfederal entities for all federal awards and certain funding increments provided on or after December 26, 2014. The requirements in Subpart F, "Audit Requirements," are effective for audits of fiscal years beginning on or after December 26, 2014, with no early implementation permitted. Therefore, auditees subject to a single audit with December 25, 2015, and later year ends (for example, December 31, 2015) will be required to undergo the audit under Subpart F of the Uniform Guidance. Note that audits of fiscal years ending prior to the effective date of the Uniform Guidance audit requirements are subject to an audit under Circular A-133.

19.01 The Uniform Guidance establishes requirements for additional audit procedures and reporting relative to the auditor's consideration of internal control over compliance for major programs. The requirements are beyond those of a financial statement audit conducted in accordance with generally accepted auditing standards (GAAS) and *Government Auditing Standards*.[2] Chapter 3, "Planning and Performing a Financial Statement Audit in Accordance With

---

[1] See the information found at the end of this chapter (paragraph 19.62), and other part III, *Uniform Guidance Audits*, chapters of this guide, for transition considerations when performing an audit under Title 2 U.S. *Code of Federal Regulations* (CFR) Part 200, *Uniform Administrative Requirements, Cost Principles, and Audit Requirements for Federal Awards* (Uniform Guidance). Transition considerations can also be found at the end of certain part II, *Circular A-133 Audits*, chapters as it relates to an audit performed under Office of Management and Budget (OMB) Circular A-133, *Audits of States, Local Governments, and Non-Profit Organizations*.

[2] *Government Auditing Standards* incorporates by reference AICPA Statements on Auditing Standards. Therefore, auditors performing financial statement audits and Uniform Guidance compliance audits in accordance with *Government Auditing Standards* should comply with generally accepted auditing standards, the requirements found in chapters 1–3 of *Government Auditing Standards*, and the additional standards and related requirements for financial audits found in chapter 4, "Standards for Financial Audits," of *Government Auditing Standards*.

Government Auditing Standards," of this guide discusses the auditor's consideration of internal control over financial reporting in a financial statement audit. (As discussed in chapter 16, "Auditor Planning Considerations Under the Uniform Guidance," of this guide, the Uniform Guidance does not impose on the financial statement audit any additional audit requirements beyond *Government Auditing Standards*.) This chapter discusses the additional considerations of internal control over compliance for major programs and adapts GAAS guidance to a Uniform Guidance compliance audit as applicable. Paragraph 19.07 and chapter 23, "Auditor Reporting Requirements and Other Communication Considerations in a Single Audit (Uniform Guidance)," of this guide discuss the reporting on internal control over compliance for major programs.

Uniform Guidance—Definitions

19.02 The Uniform Guidance defines *internal control* as a process, implemented by a nonfederal entity,[3] designed to provide reasonable assurance regarding the achievement of objectives in the following categories:

   a. Effectiveness and efficiency of operations
   b. Reliability of reporting for internal and external use
   c. Compliance with applicable laws and regulations

19.03 The Uniform Guidance defines internal control over compliance requirements for federal awards as the following:

> Internal control over compliance requirements for federal awards means a process implemented by a nonfederal entity designed to provide reasonable assurance regarding the achievement of the following objectives for federal awards:
>
> 1. Transactions are properly recorded and accounted for, in order to:
>   *a.* Permit the preparation of reliable financial statements and federal reports;
>   *b.* Maintain accountability over assets; and
>   *c.* Demonstrate compliance with federal statutes, regulations, and the terms and conditions of federal awards;
> 2. Transactions are executed in compliance with:
>   *a.* Federal statutes, regulations, and the terms and conditions of the federal award that could have a direct and material effect on a federal program; and
>   *b.* Any other federal statutes and regulations that are identified in the *OMB Compliance Supplement (Compliance Supplement)*; and
> 3. Funds, property, and other assets are safeguarded against loss from unauthorized use or disposition.

---

[3] Subpart A, "Acronyms and Definitions," of the Uniform Guidance defines a *nonfederal entity* as a state, local government, Indian tribe, institution of higher education, or nonprofit organization that carries out a federal award as a recipient or subrecipient. The term *nonfederal entity* is used throughout part III of this guide as that term is used in the Uniform Guidance.

Internal Control Over Compliance for Federal Awards

Auditee Responsibilities

19.04 The Uniform Guidance provides requirements regarding the auditee's responsibility related to internal control in 2 CFR 200.303 of Subpart D, "Post Federal Award Requirements Standards for Financial and Program Management," of the Uniform Guidance. As noted in that section, the nonfederal entity must

- establish and maintain effective internal control over federal awards (see paragraph 19.05),
- comply with federal statutes, regulations, and the terms and conditions of the federal awards,
- evaluate and monitor the entity's compliance with statutes, regulations, and the terms and conditions of federal awards,
- take prompt action when instances of noncompliance are identified, including noncompliance identified in audit findings,
- take reasonable measures to safeguard protected personally identifiable and other sensitive information (see paragraph 19.06)

19.05 The nonfederal entity must establish and maintain effective internal control over the federal award that provides reasonable assurance that the entity is managing the federal award in compliance with federal statutes, regulations, and the terms and conditions of the federal award. The internal controls established *should* be in compliance with guidance in *Standards for Internal Control in the Federal Government* (known as the Green Book), issued by the Comptroller General of the United States, or the *Internal Control—Integrated Framework*, issued by the Committee of Sponsoring Organizations of the Treadway Commission (COSO).[4]

Emphasis Point

The use of the term *must* in the Uniform Guidance indicates a requirement. This is consistent with the use of the term *must* in GAAS and *Government Auditing Standards*. The use of the term *should* in the Uniform Guidance indicates a best practice or recommended approach. However, GAAS and *Government Auditing Standards* use the term *should* to indicate a presumptively mandatory requirement. An auditor must comply with a presumptively mandatory requirement in all cases in which such a requirement is relevant, except in rare circumstances. In this guide, the term ***should***, when italicized and bolded, indicates a best practice or recommended approach in the Uniform Guidance. This is intended to differentiate it from the term *should* used throughout the guide to refer to presumptively mandatory requirements in GAAS and *Government Auditing Standards*. See chapter 1, "Introduction and Overview of *Government Auditing Standards*," of this guide for more information regarding presumptively mandatory requirements.

---

[4] The publication *Internal Control—Integrated Framework* is available for purchase on the COSO website at www.coso.org. *Standards for Internal Control in the Federal Government* (Green Book), issued by the Comptroller General of the United States, is publicly available on the GAO website at www.gao.gov/greenbook/overview.

Protected Personally Identifiable Information

19.06 As part of establishing the system of internal control the nonfederal entity must take reasonable measures to safeguard protected personally identifiable information (protected PII)[5] and other information the federal awarding agency or pass-through entity designates as sensitive or the nonfederal entity considers sensitive consistent with applicable federal, state, and local laws regarding privacy and obligations of confidentiality.

Requirements Related to Internal Control in the Uniform Guidance Compliance Audit

Auditor Responsibilities

19.07 As it relates to internal control, in addition to the requirements of GAAS and *Government Auditing Standards*, the Uniform Guidance provides that the auditor must

- perform procedures to obtain an understanding of internal control over federal programs sufficient to plan the audit to support a low assessed level of control risk of noncompliance for major programs.

  plan the testing of internal control over compliance for major programs to support a low assessed level of control risk of noncompliance for the assertions relevant to the compliance requirements for each major program.[6]

- perform testing of internal control over compliance as planned.

- report on internal control over compliance describing the scope of the testing of internal control and the results of the tests and, where applicable, referring to the separate schedule of findings and questioned costs. This schedule includes, where applicable, a statement that significant deficiencies and material weaknesses in internal control over compliance for major programs were identified in the audit. See chapter 23 for information regarding reporting on internal control over compliance.

Auditor Responsibility for Internal Control Over Compliance for Programs That Are Not Major

19.08 The auditor has no responsibility under the Uniform Guidance to obtain an understanding of internal control over compliance for programs that are not considered major or to plan or perform any related testing of internal control over compliance for those programs except for any procedures the auditor may choose to perform as part of the risk assessment process in

---

[5] Protected personally identifiable information means an individual's first name or first initial and last name in combination with any one or more other types of information, including, but not limited to, social security number, passport number, credit card numbers, clearances, bank numbers, biometrics, date and place of birth, mother's maiden name, criminal, medical and financial records, and educational transcripts. This does not include personally identifiable information (as defined in 2 CFR 200.79) that is required by law to be disclosed.

[6] See paragraphs 19.26–.29 for a discussion of planning tests of internal control over compliance to support a low assessed level of control risk of noncompliance. See paragraphs 19.30–.32 for situations when internal control over some or all of the compliance requirements for a major program is likely to be ineffective.

determining major programs. (Chapter 18, "Determination of Major Programs (Uniform Guidance)," of this guide discusses the risk assessment process.) However, a program that is not considered major could still be material to the financial statements.[7] In that situation, in conjunction with the financial statement audit, the auditor may need to obtain an understanding of that program's internal control over financial reporting.

Control Objectives and the Components of Internal Control

19.09 AU-C section 315, *Understanding the Entity and Its Environment and Assessing the Risks of Material Misstatement* (AICPA, *Professional Standards*), states that there are three objectives of internal control: reliability of the entity's financial reporting, effectiveness and efficiency of its operations, and compliance with applicable laws and regulations. There is a direct relationship between an entity's objectives and the controls it implements to provide reasonable assurance about their achievement. For purposes of this guide, controls relevant to the audit of the financial statements are referred to as *internal control over financial reporting* and are encompassed in the report on internal control over financial reporting that is required by *Government Auditing Standards*. (See chapters 3–4 of this guide.) Controls relevant to an audit of compliance with requirements applicable to major federal programs are referred to collectively in this guide as *internal control over compliance* and are encompassed in the report on internal control over compliance required by the Uniform Guidance. In a particular single audit engagement, some controls may be relevant to both the audit of the financial statements and the audit of compliance. When this occurs, those controls would be encompassed in both internal control reports. Chapter 23 of this guide provides guidance on reporting findings involving significant deficiencies and material weaknesses in internal control in such a circumstance.

19.10 Paragraph .A50 of AU-C section 315 states that the division of internal control into five interrelated components,[8] for purposes of GAAS, provides a useful framework for auditors when considering how different aspects of an entity's internal control may affect the audit. The five components, as adapted to a Uniform Guidance compliance audit, follow:

- **control environment.** Sets the tone of the entity, influencing the control consciousness of its people. It is the foundation for all other components of internal control over compliance, providing discipline and structure.
- **risk assessment.** The entity's identification, analysis, and management of risks relevant to the objectives of the Uniform Guidance compliance audit. If the risk assessment process is appropriate to the circumstances, including the nature, size, and complexity of the entity, it assists the auditor in identifying risks of material noncompliance.

---

[7] As discussed in the AICPA Audit and Accounting Guide *State and Local Governments*, the auditor's consideration of materiality for purposes of planning, performing, evaluating the results of, and reporting on the audit of the financial statements of a state or local government is based on opinion units. See that guide for further guidance.

[8] These five components are the same as those found in both the Green Book and the COSO integrated framework.

information and communication systems. Includes the business processes relevant to compliance with the applicable compliance requirements. It consists of procedures and records designed and established to support the identification, capture, and exchange of information related to compliance in a form and time frame that enable people to carry out their responsibilities.

control activities. The policies and procedures that help ensure that management directives are carried out.

monitoring. A process to assess the effectiveness of internal control over compliance performance over time.

These components assist the auditor in considering how the different aspects of an entity's internal control over compliance may affect the audit. When considering internal control over compliance for major programs, the auditor's focus is on the internal control objective related to compliance with federal statutes, regulations, and the terms and conditions of the federal award.

Auditor's Consideration of Internal Control Over Compliance for Each Major Program

19.11 The auditor's consideration of internal control over compliance for each major program is similar to the consideration of internal control over financial reporting in a financial statement audit as described in AU-C section 315. The same concepts apply for understanding internal control over compliance, assessing risk, and the testing of controls. However, as noted in paragraph 19.07, the Uniform Guidance adds requirements to plan the audit to support a low assessed level of control risk of noncompliance for major programs, to perform related procedures and testing, and to report on internal control over compliance. (See paragraph 19.30 when internal control is not likely to be effective.) An important aspect of the consideration of internal control over compliance in an audit under the Uniform Guidance is that instead of the objective being reliability of financial reporting, it is compliance with federal statutes, regulations, and the terms and conditions of federal awards.

19.12 When considering internal control over compliance, the auditor should obtain an understanding of the five components of internal control sufficient to assess the risks of material noncompliance with each direct and material compliance requirement[9] for each major program. The auditor should obtain a sufficient understanding by performing risk assessment procedures to evaluate the design of controls relevant to the compliance audit and to determine whether they have been implemented. The auditor should use the information gathered by performing the risk assessment procedures, including the audit evidence obtained in evaluating the design of controls and

---

[9] AU-C section 935, *Compliance Audits* (AICPA, *Professional Standards*), defines *applicable compliance requirements* as the compliance requirements that are subject to the compliance audit. 2 CFR 200.514(d)(1) states that the auditor must determine whether the auditee has complied with federal statutes, regulations, and the terms and conditions of the federal awards that may have a direct and material effect on each of its major programs. Therefore, in a Uniform Guidance compliance audit, the direct and material compliance requirements are those that are subject to audit. Accordingly, for the purpose of adapting AU-C section 935 to a Uniform Guidance compliance audit, the term *applicable compliance requirements* has been replaced by *direct and material compliance requirements* in this guide except when directly citing content from AU-C section 935.

Consideration of Internal Control Over Compliance for Major Programs **489**

determining whether they have been implemented, as audit evidence to support the risk assessment. The risk assessment should be used to determine the nature, timing, and extent of further audit procedures to be performed.

19.13 As noted in paragraph .20 of AU-C section 935, *Compliance Audits* (AICPA, *Professional Standards*), the auditor should design and perform further audit procedures in response to the assessed risks of material noncompliance. These procedures should include performing tests of controls over compliance if

- the auditor's risk assessment includes an expectation of the operating effectiveness of controls over compliance related to the direct and material compliance requirements;
- substantive procedures alone do not provide sufficient appropriate audit evidence; or
- such tests of controls over compliance are required by the governmental audit requirement.

As further described in paragraph 19.07, the Uniform Guidance requires testing of internal control over compliance, therefore, there are additional considerations related to testing controls in a Uniform Guidance compliance audit.

19.14 Procedures for gaining an understanding of internal control over compliance and an assessment of the risks of noncompliance may be performed concurrently in an audit. Similarly, based on the assessed level of control risk of noncompliance that the auditor expects to support and audit efficiency considerations, the auditor may perform some tests of controls concurrently with obtaining an understanding of controls. See the discussion beginning at paragraph 19.33 for information on the testing of controls.

Obtaining an Understanding of Internal Control Over Direct and Material Compliance Requirements for Major Programs

Understanding Direct and Material Compliance Requirements and Identifying Relevant Controls

19.15 As noted in paragraph 19.07, the auditor should perform procedures to obtain an understanding of internal control over compliance for federal programs that is sufficient to plan the audit to support a low assessed level of control risk of noncompliance for major programs. (Chapter 18 of this guide discusses the determination of major programs.) In order to do this, an understanding is needed of which of the 12 types of compliance requirements identified in the *Compliance Supplement* have a direct and material effect on each major program.[10] Once the auditor has identified the compliance requirements that have a direct and material effect on each major program,

---

[10] See chapter 20, "Compliance Auditing Applicable to Major Programs (Uniform Guidance)," for information on identifying the types of compliance requirements applicable to the program and related documentation requirements.

an understanding of the direct and material compliance requirements will determine the types of controls the auditor needs to consider in a Uniform Guidance compliance audit.

19.16 In order to identify the controls relevant to the direct and material compliance requirements, the auditor should obtain an understanding of the five components of internal control in relation to the direct and material compliance requirements for each major program. In obtaining an understanding of internal control, paragraphs .13–.25 of AU-C section 315 provide requirements and guidance. Obtaining an understanding of internal control involves evaluating the design of a control and determining whether it has been implemented. Evaluating the design of a control involves consideration of whether the control, individually or in combination with other controls, is capable of effectively preventing or detecting and correcting instances of noncompliance. Implementation of a control means that the control exists and the entity is using it. The auditor should consider the design of the control in determining whether to consider its implementation. (See paragraph 19.30 for a discussion of ineffective internal control.)

19.17 For each of the programs and direct and material compliance requirements selected for testing, the auditor should perform risk assessment procedures to obtain a sufficient understanding of the direct and material compliance requirements and the entity's internal control over compliance with those compliance requirements. The objective of these procedures is to obtain audit evidence about the design and implementation of relevant controls over compliance, and may include procedures such as inquiry of entity personnel, observing the application of a specific control, and inspecting documents and reports. Paragraph .A69 of AU-C section 315 states that inquiry alone is not sufficient to evaluate the design of a control and to determine whether it has been implemented. (See chapter 16 for a discussion of risk assessment.)

19.18 In understanding the entity's control activities as it relates to a Uniform Guidance compliance audit, the auditor should obtain an understanding of how the entity has responded to risks arising from IT, particularly in that the information systems and programs may include controls related to direct and material compliance requirements. An entity's use of IT may affect any of the five components of internal control relevant to the achievement of the entity's financial reporting, operations, or compliance objectives and its operating units or business functions. For example, an entity may use IT as part of discrete systems that support only particular business activities. Alternatively, an entity may have complex, highly integrated systems that share data and that are used to support all aspects of the entity's financial reporting, operations, and compliance objectives. As noted in paragraph .A98 of AU-C section 315, the use of IT affects the way that control activities are implemented. From the auditor's perspective, controls over the IT system(s) are effective when they maintain the integrity of information and the security of the data such systems process and when they include effective IT general and application controls. (See paragraphs .A98–.A101 of AU-C section 315 for more guidance on the effect IT has on the auditor's risk assessment process.)

19.19 Obtaining an understanding of an entity's controls ordinarily does not provide sufficient evidence about their operating effectiveness. Further, simply testing compliance in accordance with the Uniform Guidance does not provide evidence that controls are appropriately designed or operating effectively. Testing compliance gives indirect evidence on the effectiveness of controls, but cannot serve as the basis for assessing controls as operating effectively. Generally, testing controls assists the auditor in determining the nature, timing, and extent of substantive audit procedures to perform in order to gather evidence related to the opinion on compliance.

19.20 Entities may use the same controls for more than one federal program and for similar transactions (for example, cash disbursements). Accordingly, those controls will often provide assurance regarding the achievement of the compliance objectives related to some or all federal program transactions and assets. However, the use of the same controls does not negate the need to gain an understanding of internal control over compliance for each major program.

Compliance Supplement Internal Control Guidance

19.21 Part 6, "Internal Control," of the 2015 *Compliance Supplement* consists of references and links to both the Green Book and the COSO integrated framework.[11]

Multiple Organizational Unit Considerations

19.22 Federal programs often are administered by multiple organizational units (for example, operating units, locations, or branches) within an auditee. Each organizational unit may maintain separate internal control over compliance that is relevant to programs, or parts of programs, that the unit administers. In these situations, the auditor should perform procedures to obtain an understanding of internal control over compliance that is separately maintained by organizational units and that is relevant to each material part of a major program, and should plan and perform testing of those controls as discussed in this guide. (Chapters 18, 20, "Compliance Auditing Applicable to Major Programs (Uniform Guidance)," and 21, "Audit Sampling Considerations of Uniform Guidance Compliance Audits," of this guide discuss other multiple organizational unit considerations.)

Subrecipient Considerations

19.23 Many entities that are pass-through entities for federal awards make subcontract or subgrant awards and disburse their own funds, as well as federal funds, to subrecipients. The auditor of the pass-through entity has certain responsibilities related to the entity's internal control over the monitoring of subrecipients. If significant pass-through funds are awarded, subrecipient considerations could have a major impact on the risk assessment and internal control procedures performed. Chapter 22, "Audit Considerations of Federal Pass-Through Awards (Uniform Guidance)," of this guide discusses the audit considerations of federal pass-through awards.

---

[11] Part 6, "Internal Control," has been removed from the 2015 *Compliance Supplement*. See paragraphs 19.62-63 for additional information.

Planning and Performing the Test of Operating Effectiveness of Internal Control Over Direct and Material Compliance Requirements for Each Major Program[12]

Assessing Control Risk of Noncompliance

19.24 *Control risk of noncompliance* is the risk that noncompliance with a compliance requirement that could occur and that could be material, either individually or when aggregated with other instances of noncompliance, will not be prevented, or detected and corrected, on a timely basis by the entity's internal control over compliance. After obtaining an understanding of internal control over compliance for major programs, the auditor makes a preliminary assessment of control risk of noncompliance related to the direct and material compliance requirements for each major program. This information is used to determine whether the auditor can support a low assessed level of control risk of noncompliance. When the auditor believes, based on the understanding of internal control, that controls are capable of effectively preventing, or detecting and correcting, material noncompliance, the auditor may initially assess control risk of noncompliance at less than the maximum during the risk assessment phase of the audit. (See also chapter 16 of this guide, which discusses audit risk of noncompliance considerations in a Uniform Guidance compliance audit, including control risk of noncompliance.)

19.25 The assessment of control risk of noncompliance is the process of evaluating preliminarily the effectiveness of an entity's internal control over compliance in preventing, or detecting and correcting, material noncompliance with the compliance requirements for each major program. Paragraphs 19.26–.29 discuss the Uniform Guidance requirement to plan the testing of internal control over compliance to support a low assessed level of control risk of noncompliance for major programs. Paragraphs 19.30–.32 discuss the auditor's responsibilities when internal control over compliance is ineffective in preventing, or detecting and correcting, noncompliance. The auditor's basis for judgment of the assessed level of control risk of noncompliance should be documented to support the decisions made. See paragraph 19.58 for a further discussion of audit documentation as it relates to internal control over compliance. The auditor should consider the results of his or her assessment of control risk of noncompliance and any additional controls or tests of operating effectiveness in designing the nature, extent, and timing of substantive tests of compliance.

Planning the Test of Operating Effectiveness of Internal Control Over Compliance for Each Major Program to Support a Low Assessed Level of Control Risk of Noncompliance

19.26 The Uniform Guidance states that the auditor must plan the test of internal control over compliance for major programs to support a low assessed level of control risk for the assertions relevant to the compliance requirements for each major program except in the circumstances described in paragraph

---

[12] See also chapter 21, "Audit Sampling Considerations of Uniform Guidance Compliance Audits," for more information related to understanding, planning, and performing tests related to internal control over compliance.

Consideration of Internal Control Over Compliance for Major Programs 493

19.30 regarding ineffective controls. Professional standards do not define or quantify a low assessed level of control risk of noncompliance. Therefore, professional judgment is needed in determining the extent of control testing necessary to obtain a low level of control risk of noncompliance. In exercising professional judgment, one factor to consider is that this requirement is intended to address federal agencies' desire to know if conditions indicate that auditees have not implemented adequate internal control over compliance for federal programs to ensure compliance with federal statutes, regulations, and the terms and conditions of federal awards.

19.27 The auditor should obtain sufficient appropriate audit evidence to support that assessed level of control risk of noncompliance. The type of audit evidence, its source, its timeliness, and the existence of other audit evidence related to the conclusions to which it leads all bear on the degree of assurance the audit evidence provides.

19.28 The guidance in AU-C section 330, *Performing Audit Procedures in Response to Assessed Risks and Evaluating the Audit Evidence Obtained* (AICPA, *Professional Standards*), addresses the auditor's responsibility to design and implement responses to the risks of material misstatement identified and assessed by the auditor. In a compliance audit, this responsibility relates to the risk of material noncompliance identified and assessed by the auditor. Paragraph .11 of AU-C section 330 states that the auditor should test controls for the particular time or throughout the period for which the auditor intends to rely on those controls in order to provide an appropriate basis for the auditor's intended reliance. If the auditor intends to rely on a control over a period, audit evidence pertaining only to a point in time may be insufficient, and the auditor should supplement those tests with other tests of controls that are capable of providing audit evidence that the control operated effectively at relevant times during the period under audit. This guidance, along with the Uniform Guidance requirement to perform the testing of internal control to support a low assessed level of control risk of noncompliance, supports the testing of internal control over compliance every year. (See paragraph 19.35 for related information.)

19.29 Paragraphs .08–.10 of AU-C section 330 contain guidance related to the extent of tests of controls. As it relates to a Uniform Guidance compliance audit, and assuming an understanding that controls are effective, the auditor should design and perform tests of controls to obtain sufficient appropriate audit evidence that the controls are operating effectively for each direct and material compliance requirement for each major program throughout the period of reliance. Several factors are listed that auditors may consider in determining the extent of the tests of controls:

- The frequency of the performance of the control by the entity during the period
- The length of time during the audit period that the auditor is relying on the operating effectiveness of the control
- The expected deviation from the control
- The relevance and reliability of the audit evidence to be obtained in supporting that the control prevents, or detects and corrects, material noncompliance with respect to the type of compliance requirement being considered
- The extent to which audit evidence is obtained from tests of other controls related to the type of compliance requirement

In designing and performing tests of controls, the auditor should obtain more persuasive audit evidence when the auditor plans to place greater reliance on the effectiveness of a control. In addition, as the rate of expected deviation from a control increases, the auditor should increase the extent of testing of the control. However, the auditor should consider whether the rate of expected deviation indicates that obtaining audit evidence from the performance of tests of controls will not be sufficient to reduce the control risk of noncompliance for the assertions relevant to the compliance requirement. If the rate of expected deviation is expected to be high, the auditor may determine that tests of controls for a particular type of compliance requirement may be inappropriate. See chapter 21 of this guide for more information on audit sampling as it relates to a Uniform Guidance compliance audit.

Existence of Ineffective Internal Control in Preventing or Detecting Noncompliance

19.30 Under the Uniform Guidance, when the auditor determines that internal control over some or all of the compliance requirements for a major program are likely to be ineffective in preventing or detecting noncompliance, the auditor is not required to plan and perform tests of internal control over compliance for those compliance requirements. (See also paragraphs 19.07, 19.25, and 19.35.) However, the auditor must report a significant deficiency or a material weakness in internal control over compliance as part of the audit findings. In addition, the auditor must assess control risk at the maximum[13] and consider whether any additional compliance tests are required because of ineffective internal control. (Chapter 23 of this guide discusses the reporting of significant deficiencies and material weaknesses in internal control over compliance.)

19.31 The assessment of the effectiveness of internal control over compliance in preventing, detecting, and correcting noncompliance is determined in relation to each individual type of compliance requirement for each major program. For example, controls over compliance with requirements for eligibility may be ineffective because of a lack of segregation of duties. In this case, the auditor would do the following:

- Report the lack of segregation of incompatible duties as it relates to eligibility as a significant deficiency or a material weakness in internal control over compliance.

- Assess the control risk of noncompliance related to requirements for eligibility at the maximum.

- Consider the lack of effective control when designing the nature, timing, and extent of procedures designed to test compliance with requirements for eligibility of the major program. In most cases, the extent of testing would need to be expanded.

19.32 In planning the tests of controls, consideration of the results of tests performed in prior years provides the auditor with important information. If

---

[13] The Uniform Guidance states that control risk must be assessed "at the maximum" in this situation. In making this assessment, it is not acceptable for the auditor to simply deem control risk to be "at the maximum" without a basis for determining why internal control over compliance is likely to be ineffective. This assessment may be made in qualitative terms such as *high*, *medium*, and *low*, or in quantitative terms such as percentages.

the results of the prior year tests of controls prevented the auditor from assessing a low level of control risk of noncompliance, the auditor may consider expanded testing in the current audit period. Testing of any changes in internal control over compliance that were intended to eliminate deficiencies noted in the previous year also may provide relevant information. If, however, the auditor concluded in the prior year that internal control over compliance for one or more compliance requirements was ineffective and the auditee has made no changes to its internal control over compliance, the auditor may determine that controls are not likely to be effective and may choose not to plan and perform tests of controls. In this situation, the auditor must report a significant deficiency or a material weakness in internal control over compliance as discussed in paragraph 19.30.

Performing Tests to Evaluate the Effectiveness of Controls

19.33 As discussed in paragraph .A22 of AU-C section 330, testing the operating effectiveness of controls is different from obtaining an understanding of and evaluating the design and implementation of controls. However, the same types of audit procedures are used. The auditor may, therefore, decide it is efficient to test the operating effectiveness of controls at the same time the auditor is evaluating their design and determining that they have been implemented. This includes obtaining audit evidence about how controls were applied at relevant times during the period under audit, the consistency with which they were applied, and by whom or by what means they were applied.

19.34 As noted in paragraph 19.07, the Uniform Guidance states that the auditors must perform tests of internal control over compliance as planned. (Paragraphs 19.30–.32 discuss an exception related to ineffective internal control over compliance.) In addition, paragraph .08 of AU-C section 330 states that the auditor should design and perform tests of controls when the auditor's risk assessment includes an expectation of the operating effectiveness of control. Testing of the operating effectiveness of controls ordinarily includes procedures such as (*a*) inquiries of appropriate entity personnel, including grant and contract managers; (*b*) the inspection of documents, reports, or electronic files indicating performance of the control; (*c*) the observation of the application of the specific controls; and (*d*) reperformance of the application of the control by the auditor. The auditor should perform such procedures regardless of whether he or she would otherwise choose to obtain evidence to support an assessment of control risk of noncompliance below the maximum level.

19.35 Furthermore, AU-C section 935 indicates that paragraphs .13–.14 and .31 of AU-C section 330 are not applicable to a compliance audit. Those paragraphs address the use of audit evidence obtained in prior audits related to testing the operating effectiveness of controls (and the rotation of such testing). Therefore, in a Uniform Guidance compliance audit, controls that address the risks of noncompliance with direct and material types of compliance requirements for major programs should be tested every year.

19.36 Paragraph .A24 of AU-C section 330 provides guidance related to the testing of controls. When responding to the risk assessment, the auditor may design a test of controls to be performed concurrently with a test of details on the same transactions. Although the purpose of a test of controls is different from the purpose of a test of details, both may be accomplished concurrently by performing a test of controls and a test of details on the same transaction (a dual purpose test). For example, the auditor may examine an invoice to determine whether it has been approved and whether it provides substantive evidence of a transaction. A dual purpose test is designed and evaluated by considering each purpose of the test separately. Also, when performing the tests, the auditor should consider how the outcome of the test of controls may affect the auditor's determination about the extent of substantive procedures to be performed. See chapter 21 of this guide for a discussion of the use of dual purpose samples in a compliance audit.

> **Emphasis Point**
>
> Quality control reviews performed by federal agency staff have shown that in some cases auditors, when using dual purpose testing, have not clearly identified the procedures performed to test the operating effectiveness of internal control over compliance versus compliance. It is important that the audit documentation relating to dual purpose tests separately identify the tests performed on internal control over compliance and the tests performed on compliance, along with the results of those tests. Documentation may be made through such mechanisms as narratives, tick marks, attribute descriptions, or similar notations.

Evaluating the Results of Tests of Controls [14]

19.37 Based on the audit procedures performed related to controls, and the audit evidence obtained, the auditor should evaluate whether the assessment of the risk of material noncompliance of the relevant compliance requirements remain appropriate. An audit is a cumulative and iterative process. As the auditor performs planned audit procedures, the audit evidence obtained may cause the auditor to modify the nature, timing, or extent of other planned audit procedures. Information may come to the auditor's attention that differs significantly from the information on which the risk assessments were based. Furthermore, the auditor should not assume that an instance of fraud or error is an isolated occurrence, and, therefore, should consider how the detection of such noncompliance affects the assessed risks of material noncompliance. Before the conclusion of the audit, the auditor should evaluate whether audit risk of noncompliance has been reduced to an appropriately low level and whether the nature, timing, and extent of the audit procedures need to be reconsidered. The auditor should conclude whether sufficient appropriate audit evidence has been obtained to reduce to an appropriately low level the risks of material noncompliance with compliance requirements. In developing an opinion on compliance, the auditor should consider all relevant audit evidence, regardless of whether it appears to corroborate or to contradict the relevant assertions.

19.38 If, when evaluating the results of tests of controls, the auditor is not able to support a low assessed level of control risk of noncompliance for a direct and material compliance requirement for a major program, the auditor is not required to expand his or her testing of internal control over compliance for that compliance requirement. The auditor may choose not to perform further tests of controls. In that situation, the auditor would assess control risk of noncompliance at other than low, design tests of compliance accordingly, and

---

[14] The discussion of audit sampling in a compliance audit, as found in chapter 21, will assist the auditor in evaluating the results of audit testing.

consider the need to report an audit finding. In general, a significant deficiency or a material weakness in internal control over compliance will need to be reported. (See chapter 23 of this guide for further discussion on reporting audit findings.)

19.39 The concept of effectiveness of the operation of controls recognizes that some deviations in the way controls are applied by the entity may occur. When such deviations are detected during the performance of tests of controls, the auditor should make specific inquiries to understand these matters and their potential consequences. In addition, the auditor should consider whether any noncompliance detected from the performance of substantive procedures alter the auditor's judgment concerning the effectiveness of the related controls. The auditor should determine whether the tests of controls performed provide an appropriate basis for reliance on the controls, whether additional tests of controls are necessary, and how the remaining risks of noncompliance need to be addressed using substantive procedures.

19.40 The auditor may decide to expand the testing of internal control over compliance, but that decision would be based on whether the auditor considered expanded internal control testing to be more efficient than additional tests of compliance. Based on the testing performed, control risk of noncompliance might be assessed below the maximum and, therefore, reduce substantive tests of compliance. If it cannot be assessed below the maximum, it might be more appropriate to assess control risk of noncompliance at the maximum level. (See also paragraph 19.30.)

19.41 Regardless of the audit approach selected, the auditor should design and perform substantive procedures for all relevant assertions related to the direct and material compliance requirements for each major program. Because effective controls generally reduce, but do not eliminate, risks of material noncompliance, tests of controls reduce, but do not eliminate, the need for substantive procedures.

19.42 When evaluating the operating effectiveness of internal control over compliance, instances of noncompliance detected by the auditor when performing compliance tests should be considered by the auditor. (For example, during a test of compliance for activities allowed or unallowed, it was noted that equipment was charged to a major program when the grant agreement does not allow program funds to be spent on equipment.) Detection of these instances of noncompliance is relevant, reliable audit evidence about the relative ineffectiveness of the related internal control over compliance. Noncompliance detected by the auditor that was not identified by the entity is evidence of a deficiency in internal control over compliance and may be an indicator of a significant deficiency or a material weakness in internal control over compliance.

19.43 However, the absence of noncompliance detected by a compliance test does not provide audit evidence that controls related to a compliance requirement are effective.

Significant Deficiencies and Material Weaknesses in Internal Control Over Compliance Related to Federal Programs

19.44 A deficiency in internal control over compliance exists when the design or operation of a control over compliance does not allow management or employees, in the normal course of performing their assigned functions, to prevent, or detect and correct, noncompliance with a type of compliance requirement of a federal program on a timely basis. See paragraph 19.56 for examples of circumstances that may be deficiencies, significant deficiencies, or material weaknesses in internal control over compliance.

19.45 AU-C section 935 defines *significant deficiency in internal control over compliance* and *material weakness in internal control over compliance* for the purposes of reporting on internal control over compliance. This guide further adapts the AU-C section 935 definitions for reporting on internal control over compliance in an audit under the Uniform Guidance as follows:

- A *significant deficiency in internal control over compliance* is a deficiency, or a combination of deficiencies, in internal control over compliance with a type of compliance requirement of a federal program that is less severe than a material weakness in internal control over compliance, yet important enough to merit attention by those charged with governance.

- A *material weakness in internal control over compliance* is a deficiency, or combination of deficiencies, in internal control over compliance such that there is a reasonable possibility that material noncompliance with a type of compliance requirement of a federal program will not be prevented, or detected and corrected, on a timely basis.[15]

19.46 In performing a Uniform Guidance compliance audit, the auditor's determination of whether a deficiency in internal control over compliance is a significant deficiency or material weakness for the purpose of reporting an audit finding is in relation to a type of compliance requirement for a major program identified in the *Compliance Supplement*. Further, certain conditions may be significant deficiencies or material weaknesses in internal control over compliance for a major program and not be considered significant deficiencies or material weaknesses in internal control over financial reporting.

19.47 AU-C section 265, *Communicating Internal Control Related Matters Identified in an Audit* (AICPA, *Professional Standards*), provides guidance related to evaluating the severity of deficiencies in internal control. The following paragraphs provide guidance to the auditor in adapting and applying this guidance to a Uniform Guidance compliance audit.

19.48 In a Uniform Guidance compliance audit, the auditor should evaluate the severity of each deficiency in internal control over compliance identified during the audit to determine whether the deficiency, individually or in combination, is a significant deficiency or material weakness in internal control over compliance. The severity of a deficiency depends on the magnitude of potential noncompliance resulting from the deficiency or deficiencies and whether there is a reasonable possibility that the entity's controls will fail to prevent, or detect and correct, noncompliance with a type of compliance requirement. In a Uniform Guidance compliance audit, the significance of a deficiency in internal control over compliance depends on the potential for noncompliance, not

---

[15] A reasonable possibility exists when the likelihood of the event is either *reasonably possible* or *probable*, which are defined as follows:

    reasonably possible. The chance of the future event or events occurring is more than remote but less than likely.
    remote. The chance of the future event or events occurring is slight.
    probable. The future event or events are likely to occur.

Consideration of Internal Control Over Compliance for Major Programs 499

on whether noncompliance actually has occurred. Accordingly, the absence of identified noncompliance does not provide evidence that identified deficiencies in internal control over compliance are not significant deficiencies or material weaknesses in internal control over compliance.

19.49 Risk factors affect whether there is a reasonable possibility that a deficiency, or combination of deficiencies, will result in noncompliance with a type of compliance requirement of a federal program. The factors include, but are not limited to

- the nature of the type of compliance requirement involved. For example, a specific special test or provision may involve greater risk because it is unique to the program and may require unique controls.
- susceptibility of the program and related types of compliance requirements to fraud.
- subjectivity and complexity involved in meeting the compliance requirement and the extent of judgment required in determining noncompliance.
- interaction or relationship of the control with other controls.
- interaction among the deficiencies.
- possible future consequences of the deficiency.

19.50 The evaluation of deficiencies in internal control over compliance includes the magnitude of potential noncompliance. Several factors affect the magnitude of potential noncompliance that could result from a deficiency or deficiencies in controls. The factors may include, but are not limited to

- program amounts or total of transactions exposed to the deficiency in relation to the type of compliance requirement;
- volume of activity related to the compliance requirement exposed to the deficiency in the current period or expected in future periods; or
- adverse publicity or other qualitative factors.

19.51 Controls may be designed to operate individually, or in combination, to effectively prevent, or detect and correct, noncompliance. A deficiency in internal control over compliance on its own may not be sufficiently important to constitute a significant deficiency or a material weakness in internal control over compliance. However, a combination of deficiencies affecting the same type of compliance requirement or component of internal control over compliance may increase the risks of material noncompliance to such an extent to give rise to a significant deficiency or material weakness in internal control over compliance. This may be the case even though such deficiencies individually may be less severe. Therefore, the auditor should determine whether deficiencies that affect the same type of compliance requirement or component of internal control collectively result in a significant deficiency or material weakness in internal control over compliance.

19.52 The auditor may obtain evidence that a control does not operate effectively when performing compliance tests or tests of the operating effectiveness of controls, for example, identifying an instance of noncompliance that was not prevented, or detected and corrected, by the control. Management may inform the auditor, or the auditor may otherwise become aware, of the existence of compensating controls that, if effective, may limit the severity of the deficiency and prevent it from being a significant deficiency or material weakness in internal control over compliance. In these circumstances, although the auditor is not required to consider the effects of compensating controls, the auditor may consider the effects of compensating controls related to a deficiency in operation provided the auditor has tested the compensating controls for operating effectiveness. Compensating controls can limit the severity of the deficiency, but do not eliminate the deficiency.

19.53 The auditor may encounter deviations in the operating effectiveness of controls. A control that has an observed non-negligible deviation rate is at least a deficiency in internal control over compliance regardless of the reason for the deviation and could be, based upon further evaluation, a significant deficiency or material weakness in internal control over compliance. For example, if the auditor designs a test in which he or she selects a sample and expects no deviations, the finding of one deviation is a non-negligible deviation rate because, based on the results of the auditor's test of the sample, the desired level of confidence was not obtained. See chapter 21 of this guide for more information on evaluating deviations in tests of controls.

19.54 If the auditor determines that a deficiency, or a combination of deficiencies, is not a material weakness in internal control over compliance, the auditor should consider whether prudent officials, having knowledge of the same facts and circumstances, would likely reach the same conclusion.

19.55 Indicators of material weaknesses in internal control over compliance include

- identification of fraud in the major program of any magnitude on the part of senior program management. For the purposes of evaluating and communicating deficiencies in internal control over compliance, the auditor should evaluate fraud of any magnitude of which he or she is aware on the part of senior program management, including fraud resulting in immaterial noncompliance.
- identification by the auditor of material noncompliance for the period under audit in circumstances that indicate that the noncompliance would not have been detected by the entity's internal control (for example, the noncompliance was not initially identified by the entity's internal control).
- ineffective oversight by management, or those charged with governance, over compliance with program requirements where the activity is subject to a type of compliance requirement (for example, lack of adequate review of federal financial reports prior to submission to the grantor).

19.56 Paragraph .A37 of AU-C section 265 contains examples of circumstances that may be deficiencies, significant deficiencies, or material weaknesses. Examples included relate to both deficiencies in the design of controls and deficiencies in the operations of controls. Some examples relevant to a Uniform Guidance compliance audit are as follows:

- Deficiencies in the design of controls
    - Inadequate design of controls over activities subject to a type of compliance requirement

Consideration of Internal Control Over Compliance for Major Programs

- Inadequate design of controls over complex types of compliance requirements
- Insufficient control consciousness within the entity, for example, the tone at the top and the control environment
- Absent or inadequate segregation of duties over a type of compliance requirement
- Inadequate design of IT controls relating to the activity subject to the type of compliance requirement
- Employees or management who lack the qualifications and training to fulfill their assigned functions
- Inadequate design of monitoring controls used to assess the design and operating effectiveness of the entity's internal control over compliance over time
- The absence of an internal process to report deficiencies in internal control over compliance to management on a timely basis

- Deficiencies in the operation of controls
  - Failure in the operation of effectively designed controls over a type of compliance requirement
  - Failure of the information and communication component of internal control over compliance to provide complete and accurate output because of deficiencies in timeliness, completeness, or accuracy of information related to compliance
  - Misrepresentation by entity personnel to the auditor (an indicator of fraud)
  - Management override of controls
  - Failure of an application control caused by a deficiency in the design or operation of an IT general control
  - An observed deviation rate that exceeds the number of deviations expected by the auditor in a test of the operating effectiveness of a control

Program Cluster Considerations

19.57 An entity may have separate controls related to federal programs that are treated as a cluster of programs in a Uniform Guidance compliance audit, such as student financial assistance (SFA) and research and development (R&D). (Chapter 15, "Overview of the Single Audit Act, the Uniform Guidance Audit Requirements, and the *Compliance Supplement*," of this guide discusses clusters of programs.) In this case, when evaluating whether an identified deficiency is a significant deficiency or a material weakness in internal control over compliance, the significance of the deficiency in relation to the type of compliance requirement for the cluster of programs is an important factor. Following are some examples:

- Deficiencies in specific controls over the time cards of college work-study students would likely be considered significant deficiencies or material weaknesses in internal control over compliance when college work-study program expenditures are significant in relation to SFA programs.

- Deficiencies in controls over a single campus or department of a university where a significant amount of research was administered would likely be significant deficiencies or material weaknesses in internal control over compliance when considered in relation to the total expenditures of R&D programs.

- A deficiency in an SFA or R&D program that was clearly insignificant to the SFA or R&D program, respectively, as a whole would not necessarily be considered a significant deficiency or material weakness in internal control over compliance.

Documentation Requirements

19.58 As noted in paragraph .39 of AU-C section 935, the auditor should document the risk assessment procedures performed, including those related to gaining an understanding of internal control over compliance. Paragraph .40 of AU-C section 935 states that the auditor should document his or her responses to the assessed risks of material noncompliance, the procedures performed to test compliance with the applicable compliance requirements, and the results of those procedures, including any test of controls over compliance. Guidance related to this documentation is found in paragraph .33 of AU-C section 315, which notes that the auditor should document the following related to his or her understanding of internal control related to compliance requirements:

- The discussion among the audit team regarding the susceptibility of the entity's major programs to material noncompliance with direct and material compliance requirements, including how and when the discussion occurred, the subject matter discussed, the audit team members who participated, and significant decisions reached concerning planned responses to compliance requirements

- Key elements of the understanding obtained regarding each of the aspects of the entity and its environment, in this case, as it relates to internal control over compliance, to assess the risks of material noncompliance, the sources of information from which the understanding was obtained; and the risk assessment procedures performed

- The identified and assessed risks of material noncompliance

- The risks identified and related controls about which the auditor has obtained an understanding as a result of the requirements found in paragraphs .28–.31 of AU-C section 315

19.59 Paragraph .30 of AU-C section 330 contains requirements regarding documentation of the testing of controls. Among the matters discussed of particular relevance to a Uniform Guidance compliance audit is that the auditor should document the following:

- The overall responses to address the assessed risks of noncompliance as it relates to compliance requirements of major programs

- The nature, timing, and extent of further audit procedures

Consideration of Internal Control Over Compliance for Major Programs 503

- The linkage of those procedures with the assessed risks
- The results of the audit procedures

19.60 As noted in chapter 3 of this guide, AU-C section 230, *Audit Documentation* (AICPA, *Professional Standards*), provides guidance on the form, content, extent, retention, and confidentiality of audit documentation as required by GAAS. Among other things, AU-C section 230 requires audit documentation to be sufficient to enable an experienced auditor, having no previous connection to the audit, to understand

- the nature, timing, and extent of auditing procedures performed to comply with GAAS, *Government Auditing Standards* and other applicable standards and requirements, such as the Uniform Guidance;
- the results of the audit procedures performed and the audit evidence obtained; and
- significant findings or issues arising during the audit, the conclusions reached, and significant professional judgments made in reaching those conclusions.

AU-C section 230 contains guidance on documenting significant findings or issues; identifying the preparer and reviewer of audit documentation; documenting specific items tested; documenting departures from relevant Statements on Auditing Standards; revising audit documentation after the date of the auditor's report; and ownership and confidentiality of audit documentation. *Government Auditing Standards* includes an additional requirement that auditors should document, before the report release date, supervisory review of the evidence that supports the findings, conclusions, and recommendations contained in the auditor's report.

19.61 The form and extent of this documentation are influenced by the size and complexity of the auditee, as well as the nature of the auditee's internal control over compliance. For example, the documentation of the understanding of internal control over compliance of a large, complex entity may include flowcharts, questionnaires, or decision tables. For a small entity, however, the documentation may be less extensive. In general, the more complex internal control over compliance and the more extensive the procedures performed, the more extensive the auditor's documentation. (See chapter 21 of this guide for more information on documenting the testing of internal control.)

Transition Considerations Related to the Uniform Guidance

19.62 The Uniform Guidance states that nonfederal entities must establish and maintain effective internal control over the federal award that provides reasonable assurance that the nonfederal entity is managing the federal award in compliance with federal statutes, regulations, and the terms and conditions of the federal award. The Uniform Guidance also goes on to identify the guidance the Green Book and the COSO integrated framework as best practices or recommended approaches for establishing and maintaining such internal control. Part 6 of the *Compliance Supplement* is the mechanism OMB has historically used to provide more detailed internal control guidance to both nonfederal entities and their auditors.

19.63 In light of the number of years that have passed since Part 6 was originally drafted, and as a result of the issuance of the Uniform Guidance, OMB has determined that Part 6 needs updating. OMB has also communicated that the update to Part 6 will not be made until the 2016 *Compliance Supplement*. In the meantime, OMB did not carry forward Part 6 to the 2015 *Compliance Supplement*. Instead, OMB is suggesting that nonfederal entities and their auditors look to the Green Book and the COSO integrated framework for guidance on internal control until such time that Part 6 is updated and reinserted back into the *Compliance Supplement*.

19.64 As found on the COFAR website (https://cfo.gov/cofar/), the Frequently Asked Question document FAQ .303-3 notes that, although nonfederal entities must have effective internal control, there is no expectation or requirement that the nonfederal entity document or evaluate internal controls prescriptively in accordance with the Green Book or the COSO integrated framework or that the nonfederal entity or auditor reconcile technical differences between them. It states that nonfederal entities and their auditors will need to exercise judgment in determining the most appropriate and cost effective internal control in a given environment or circumstance to provide reasonable assurance for compliance with federal program requirements.

19.65 As a result of implementing the requirements of the Uniform Guidance, auditees may have changed or updated their internal control over compliance, even more so than in a typical year. Therefore, auditors should consider such changes when gaining an understanding of internal control over compliance, assessing risk, and testing controls. Furthermore, when controls have changed, the results of internal control testing in prior years may have no bearing when planning the testing of internal control in the current year.

Chapter 20

Compliance Auditing Applicable to Major Programs (Uniform Guidance)

> **Update 20-1: Audits of Federal Awards**
>
> This chapter, and the remaining chapters of part III, *Uniform Guidance Audits*, of this guide, should be used for performing a compliance audit of federal awards under the audit requirements of Title 2 U.S. *Code of Federal Regulations* (CFR) Part 200, *Uniform Administrative Requirements, Cost Principles, and Audit Requirements for Federal Awards* (Uniform Guidance).[1] Part II, *Circular A-133 Audits*, of this guide should be used for performing a compliance audit under Office of Management and Budget (OMB) Circular A-133, *Audits of States, Local Governments, and Non-Profit Organizations* (Circular A-133). See the transitional guidance sections at the end of each chapter that highlight important matters for consideration. Additionally, refer to the preface of this guide for more information.
>
> **Important Effective Date Information**
>
> In December 2013, the OMB issued the Uniform Guidance, which is effective for nonfederal entities for all federal awards and certain funding increments provided on or after December 26, 2014. The requirements in Subpart F, "Audit Requirements," are effective for audits of fiscal years beginning on or after December 26, 2014, with no early implementation permitted. Therefore, auditees subject to a single audit with December 25, 2015, and later year ends (for example, December 31, 2015) will be required to undergo the audit under Subpart F of the Uniform Guidance. Note that audits of fiscal years ending prior to the effective date of the Uniform Guidance audit requirements are subject to an audit under Circular A-133.

20.01 This chapter discusses the auditor's consideration of compliance requirements applicable to major programs under the Uniform Guidance. (As discussed in chapter 24, "Program-Specific Audits (Uniform Guidance)," of this guide, much of the guidance in this chapter also would be applicable to a program-specific audit when a program-specific audit guide is not available.) Chapter 23, "Auditor Reporting Requirements and Other Communication Considerations in a Single Audit (Uniform Guidance)," of this guide discusses the related reporting requirements. Chapter 3, "Planning and Performing a Financial Statement Audit in Accordance With *Government Auditing Standards*,"

---

[1] See the information found at the end of this chapter (paragraph 20.75), and other part III, *Uniform Guidance Audits*, chapters of this guide, for transition considerations when performing an audit under Title 2 U.S. *Code of Federal Regulations* (CFR) Part 200, *Uniform Administrative Requirements, Cost Principles, and Audit Requirements for Federal Awards* (Uniform Guidance). Transition considerations can also be found at the end of certain part II, *Circular A-133 Audits*, chapters as it relates to an audit performed under Office of Management and Budget (OMB) Circular A-133, *Audits of States, Local Governments, and Non-Profit Organizations*.

and chapter 4, "Auditor Reporting Requirements and Other Communication Considerations of *Government Auditing Standards*," of this guide discuss the auditor's consideration of and reporting on the auditee's compliance with laws, regulations, and provisions of contracts or grant agreements[2] in a financial statement audit.

Compliance Objectives in a Uniform Guidance Compliance Audit

20.02 AU-C section 935, *Compliance Audits* (AICPA, *Professional Standards*), states that the auditor's objectives in a compliance audit are to

- obtain sufficient appropriate audit evidence to form an opinion and report at the level specified in the governmental audit requirement on whether the entity complied, in all material respects, with the applicable compliance requirements,[3] which are the direct and material compliance requirements in a Uniform Guidance compliance audit and

- identify audit and reporting requirements specified in the governmental audit requirement that are supplemental to generally accepted auditing standards (GAAS) and *Government Auditing Standards*, if any, and perform procedures to address those requirements.

20.03 The Uniform Guidance (the governmental audit requirement covered in this part) states that, in addition to performing a financial statement audit in accordance with *Government Auditing Standards* (and, therefore, GAAS), the auditor must determine whether the auditee has complied with federal statutes, regulations, and the terms and conditions of federal awards that may have a direct and material effect on each of its major programs. A Uniform Guidance compliance audit results in the auditor expressing an opinion on the auditee's compliance with those compliance requirements for each of its major programs. To express such an opinion, the auditor accumulates sufficient appropriate audit evidence by planning, performing risk assessment procedures, and performing tests of transactions and such other auditing procedures as are necessary in support of the auditee's compliance with direct and material compliance requirements, thereby limiting audit risk of noncompliance to an appropriately low level.

---

[2] The Uniform Guidance uses the terminology "federal statutes, regulations, and the terms and conditions of federal awards," which is equivalent to "provisions of laws, regulations, contracts, and grant agreements," as found in *Government Auditing Standards*.

[3] AU-C section 935, *Compliance Audits* (AICPA, *Professional Standards*), defines *applicable compliance requirements* as the compliance requirements that are subject to the compliance audit. 2 CFR 200.514(d)(1) states that the auditor must determine whether the auditee has complied with the federal statutes, regulations, and the terms and conditions of the federal awards that may have a direct and material effect on each of its major programs. Therefore, in a Uniform Guidance compliance audit, the direct and material compliance requirements are those that are subject to audit. Accordingly, for the purpose of adapting AU-C section 935 to a Uniform Guidance compliance audit, the term *applicable compliance requirements* has been replaced by *direct and material compliance requirements* in this guide except when directly citing content from AU-C section 935.

Compliance Auditing Applicable to Major Programs (Uniform Guidance) 507

> **Emphasis Point**
>
> The use of the term *must* in the Uniform Guidance indicates a requirement. This is consistent with the use of the term *must* in generally accepted auditing standards (GAAS) and *Government Auditing Standards*. The use of the term *should* in the Uniform Guidance indicates a best practice or recommended approach. However, GAAS and *Government Auditing Standards* use the term *should* to indicate a presumptively mandatory requirement. An auditor must comply with a presumptively mandatory requirement in all cases in which such a requirement is relevant, except in rare circumstances. In this guide, the term ***should***, when italicized and bolded, indicates a best practice or recommended approach in the Uniform Guidance. This is intended to differentiate it from the term "should" used throughout the guide to refer to presumptively mandatory requirements in GAAS and *Government Auditing Standards*. See chapter 1, "Introduction and Overview of *Government Auditing Standards*," of this guide for more information regarding presumptively mandatory requirements.

Responsibilities of Auditee

20.04 Following the guidance in AU-C section 935, the Uniform Guidance compliance audit is based on the premise that management is responsible for the entity's compliance with compliance requirements. As per AU-C section 935, that responsibility includes the following:

- Identifying the entity's federal programs and understanding and complying with the types of compliance requirements
- Establishing and maintaining effective controls that provide reasonable assurance that the entity administers federal programs in compliance with the types of compliance requirements
- Evaluating and monitoring the entity's compliance with the types of compliance requirements
- Taking corrective action when instances of noncompliance are identified, including corrective action on audit findings of the compliance audit

Paragraphs 20.71–.73 discuss the auditor's responsibility to obtain management's written representations regarding its compliance and internal control responsibilities.

20.05 The form and extent of the documentation of management's compliance will vary depending on the nature of the compliance requirements and the size and complexity of the entity. The auditee may have documentation in the form of accounting or statistical data, case files, entity policy manuals, accounting manuals, narrative memorandums, procedural write-ups, flowcharts, completed questionnaires, or internal auditor's reports.

Use of Professional Judgment

20.06 The planning, conduct, and evaluation of the results of compliance testing in a Uniform Guidance compliance audit require the auditor to exercise professional judgment. The auditor may consider the following factors in applying his or her professional judgment:

- The assessment of audit risk of noncompliance
- The assessment of materiality
- The evidence obtained from other auditing procedures
- The amount of expenditures for the program
- The diversity or homogeneity of expenditures for the program
- The length of time that the program has operated or changes in its conditions
- The current and prior auditing experience with the program, particularly findings in previous audits and other evaluations (such as inspections, program reviews, or system reviews required by the Federal Acquisition Regulations found in Part 41 of the U.S. *Code of Federal Regulations*)
- The extent to which the program is carried out through subrecipients as well as the related monitoring activities
- The extent to which the program contracts for goods or services
- The level to which the program already is subject to program reviews or other forms of independent oversight
- The expectation of noncompliance or compliance with the direct and material compliance requirements
- The extent to which computer processing is used to administer the program as well as the complexity of the processing
- Whether the program has been identified as being higher risk by the OMB in the *OMB Compliance Supplement (Compliance Supplement)*

Audit Risk of Noncompliance Considerations

20.07 To express an opinion on compliance, the auditor accumulates sufficient appropriate audit evidence in support of compliance, thereby reducing audit risk of noncompliance to an appropriately low level. Requirements and guidance related to the auditor's consideration of audit risk and materiality are found in AU-C section 320, *Materiality in Planning and Performing an Audit* (AICPA, *Professional Standards*), and these requirements and guidance should be adapted and applied to the Uniform Guidance compliance audit when planning and performing the audit. Audit risk of noncompliance and materiality, among other matters, need to be considered together for each major program being tested as well as for each direct and material compliance requirement in determining the nature, timing, and extent of auditing procedures and in evaluating the results of those procedures. See chapter 16, "Auditor Planning Considerations Under the Uniform Guidance," of this guide for a discussion of audit risk of noncompliance considerations, including a detailed description of the components of audit risk of noncompliance, performing risk assessment procedures, and assessing the risks of noncompliance.

Compliance Auditing Applicable to Major Programs (Uniform Guidance)

Performing Further Audit Procedures in Response to Assessed Risks

20.08 The auditor should design and perform further audit procedures, including tests of details (which may include tests of transactions) to obtain sufficient appropriate audit evidence about the auditee's compliance with each of the direct and material compliance requirements in response to the assessed risks of material noncompliance. Risk assessment procedures, tests of controls, and analytical procedures alone are not sufficient to address a risk of material noncompliance.

20.09 Paragraph .18 of AU-C section 935 notes that if risks of material noncompliance are identified that are pervasive to the entity's compliance, the auditor should develop an overall response to such risks. AU-C section 330, *Performing Audit Procedures in Response to Assessed Risks and Evaluating the Audit Evidence Obtained* (AICPA, *Professional Standards*), provides guidance in developing an overall response to the risks of material noncompliance, and this guidance should be adapted and applied to the Uniform Guidance compliance audit.

Materiality Considerations

20.10 As discussed in chapter 16 of this guide, the auditor's consideration of materiality in a Uniform Guidance compliance audit differs from that in an audit of the financial statements. Materiality is affected by (*a*) the nature of the compliance requirements, which may or may not be quantifiable in monetary terms; (*b*) the nature and frequency of noncompliance identified with an appropriate consideration of sampling risk; and (*c*) qualitative considerations, such as the needs and expectations of federal agencies and pass-through entities.

Materiality Judgments About Compliance Applied to Each Major Program

20.11 AU-C section 935 states that the auditor should establish and apply materiality levels for the compliance audit based on the governmental audit requirement. Therefore, in designing audit tests and developing an opinion on the auditee's compliance with direct and material compliance requirements in a Uniform Guidance compliance audit, the auditor should apply the concept of materiality to each major program, rather than to all major programs combined.

20.12 For purposes of evaluating the results of compliance testing, a *material instance of noncompliance* is a failure to comply with federal statutes, regulations, and the terms and conditions of the federal award that results in an aggregation of noncompliance (that is, the auditor's best estimate of the overall noncompliance) that is material to the affected federal program. Instances of noncompliance that may not be individually material should be assessed to determine if, in the aggregate, they could have a material effect. Because the auditor expresses an opinion on each major program and not on all the major programs combined, reaching a conclusion about whether the instances of noncompliance (either individually or in the aggregate) are material to a major program requires consideration of the type and nature of the noncompliance as well as the actual and projected effect on each major program in which the noncompliance was noted. Instances of noncompliance that are material to one major program may not be material to a major program of a different size or nature. In addition, the level of materiality relative to a particular major program can change from one audit to the next.

Effect of Material Noncompliance on the Financial Statements

20.13 If the tests of compliance reveal material noncompliance at the major program level, the auditor should consider its effect on the financial statements. The auditor also should consider the cumulative effect of all instances of noncompliance on the financial statements using the materiality level established for the financial statements.[4] (See also paragraph 20.54 and chapter 22, "Audit Considerations of Federal Pass-Through Awards (Uniform Guidance)," of this guide.)

Performing a Uniform Guidance Compliance Audit[5,6]

20.14 The auditor should exercise (*a*) due care in planning and performing the audit and evaluating the results of his or her audit procedures and (*b*) a proper degree of professional skepticism to achieve reasonable assurance that material noncompliance will be detected.

20.15 In a Uniform Guidance compliance audit, the auditor should perform the following, as discussed in paragraphs 20.16–.68:

   a. Identify the auditee's major programs to be tested and reported on for compliance.
   b. Identify the compliance requirements applicable to each major program.
   c. Determine which of the compliance requirements identified in item *b* could have a direct and material effect on each major program.
   d. Plan the engagement.
   e. Consider relevant portions of the entity's internal control over compliance for each direct and material compliance requirement for each major program.
   f. Obtain sufficient appropriate audit evidence, which involves testing internal control over compliance and compliance with direct and material compliance requirements for each major program.
   g. Consider indications of abuse.
   h. Consider subsequent events.

---

[4] As discussed in the Audit and Accounting Guide *State and Local Governments*, the auditor's consideration of materiality for purposes of planning, performing, evaluating the results of, and reporting on the audit of the financial statements of a state or local government is based on opinion units.

[5] *Government Auditing Standards* incorporates by reference AICPA Statements on Auditing Standards. Therefore, auditors performing financial statement audits and Uniform Guidance compliance audits in accordance with *Government Auditing Standards* should comply with GAAS, the requirements found in chapters 1–3 of *Government Auditing Standards*, and the additional standards and related requirements for financial audits found in chapter 4, "Standards for Financial Audits," of *Government Auditing Standards*.

[6] The appendix, "AU-C Sections That Are Not Applicable to Compliance Audits," of AU-C section 935 provides a list of AU-C section requirements that are not applicable to a compliance audit. All other AU-C sections not identified in the appendix should be adapted and applied to a compliance audit.

i. Form an opinion about whether the auditee complied with the direct and material compliance requirements.

j. Perform follow-up procedures on previously identified findings.

Identifying Major Programs to Be Tested

20.16 The Uniform Guidance sets forth a specific process, referred to as the risk-based approach, to be used in identifying major programs to be tested. Chapter 18, "Determination of Major Programs (Uniform Guidance)," of this guide discusses the application of the risk-based approach to determine major programs.

Identifying Direct and Material Compliance Requirements

20.17 As discussed in this section, the auditor should determine, after identifying the compliance requirements applicable to each major program, the direct and material compliance requirements to be tested and reported on in the Uniform Guidance compliance audit. As further described in paragraph 20.20, Part 2 of the *Compliance Supplement* provides a matrix that identifies the compliance requirements that are applicable to the programs included in the supplement. The auditor then determines, based on the nature of the program and the transactions for the period under audit, those types of compliance requirements that may have a direct and material effect on each major program. The auditor should use professional judgment in making this determination.

Compliance Supplement

20.18 The *Compliance Supplement* is based on the requirements of the Single Audit Act and the Uniform Guidance, which provide for the issuance of a compliance supplement to assist auditors in performing the required audits. (Chapter 15, "Overview of the Single Audit Act, the Uniform Guidance Audit Requirements, and the *Compliance Supplement*," discusses the *Compliance Supplement* and how to obtain it.) The *Compliance Supplement* is a comprehensive source of information regarding compliance. The various parts of the *Compliance Supplement* are interrelated and are intended to be used in conjunction with each other. Part 1 of the *Compliance Supplement* includes background, purpose, and applicability information, and Part 2 provides a matrix of types of compliance requirements that are applicable to the programs included in the supplement. Part 3 of the *Compliance Supplement* identifies 12 types of compliance requirements applicable to many federal programs, as listed in paragraph 20.19. Part 4 of the *Compliance Supplement* includes a discussion of the compliance requirements specific to certain of the largest federal programs and is to be used in conjunction with Part 3. The *Compliance Supplement* states that the auditor should look to Part 3 for a general description of the compliance requirements, audit objectives, and suggested audit procedures,[7] and to Part 4 for information about the specific requirements for a program (see also paragraph 20.25). Part 5 of the *Compliance Supplement* contains information on clusters of programs. As further discussed in paragraph 20.28, Part 7 of the

---

[7] See the discussion beginning at paragraph 20.75 for information regarding how the 2015 *OMB Compliance Supplement (Compliance Supplement)* has been revised to address the Uniform Guidance, including the addition of a new section of Part 3 to specifically address the testing of federal awards subject to the Uniform Guidance. Note that Part 6, "Internal Control," has been removed from the 2015 *Compliance Supplement*. An updated Part 6 is expected for the 2016 *Compliance Supplement*.

Compliance Supplement provides guidance to assist the auditor in identifying the types of compliance requirements for federal programs not included in the *Compliance Supplement*.

Twelve Types of Compliance Requirements

20.19 Part 3 of the *Compliance Supplement* lists and describes the 12 types of compliance requirements and the related audit objectives that the auditor should consider in every Uniform Guidance compliance audit, with the exception of program-specific audits performed in accordance with a federal agency's program specific audit guide (see chapter 24). It also provides suggested audit procedures to assist the auditor in planning and performing tests of the auditee's compliance with the requirements of federal programs. The auditor's judgment will be necessary to determine whether the suggested audit procedures are sufficient to achieve the stated audit objectives and whether additional or alternative audit procedures are needed (see paragraph 20.42). The 12 types of compliance requirements are as follows:[8]

- A—Activities allowed or unallowed
- B—Allowable costs/cost principles
- C—Cash management
- D—Reserved
- E—Eligibility
- F—Equipment and real property management
- G—Matching, level of effort, earmarking
- H—Period of performance
- I—Procurement and suspension and debarment
- J—Program income
- K—Reserved
- L—Reporting
- M—Subrecipient monitoring
- N—Special tests and provisions

20.20 The auditor should consider the applicability of these types of compliance requirements to each of the auditee's major programs. As noted previously, Part 2 of the *Compliance Supplement* provides a matrix that the auditor uses for this purpose. In making a determination not to test a type of compliance requirement identified as applicable to a particular program, the auditor should conclude, and document such conclusion, either that the requirement does not apply to the particular auditee or that noncompliance with the requirements could not have a direct and material effect on a major program. For example, a federal program may be designed such that subawards may be made to subrecipients, and, thus, the matrix in Part 2 of the *Compliance Supplement* would identify the subrecipient monitoring type of compliance requirement as applicable. However, the auditee may not have made any, or made only an immaterial amount of, subawards from the federal program, thus the auditor may determine that noncompliance with the subrecipient monitoring type of compliance requirement would not have a direct or material effect on the major

---

[8] The letters "D" and "K" are listed as reserved in the 2015 *Compliance Supplement*. See paragraph 20.76 for more information.

program (even though it was identified as applicable in the Part 2 matrix). No testing would be required on types of compliance requirements not considered direct and material, but the auditor's conclusion relating to this determination should be documented.

Keeping Abreast of Changes in Compliance Requirements

20.21 The Uniform Guidance states that an audit of the compliance requirements related to federal programs contained in the *Compliance Supplement* will meet the requirements of the Uniform Guidance. However, it also states that where there have been changes to the compliance requirements and the changes are not reflected in the *Compliance Supplement*, the auditor must determine the current compliance requirements and modify the audit procedures accordingly. For those federal programs not covered in the *Compliance Supplement*, the auditor must follow the *Compliance Supplement*'s guidance as found in Part 7 of the supplement.

20.22 The Uniform Guidance states that federal agencies must provide to OMB annual updates to the *Compliance Supplement* and work with OMB to ensure that the *Compliance Supplement* focuses the auditor to test the compliance requirements most likely to cause improper payments, fraud, waste, abuse, or generate audit findings for which the federal awarding agency will take sanctions. However, delays may occur between such changes and revisions to the *Compliance Supplement*. Accordingly, the auditor is required to perform reasonable procedures to ensure that compliance requirements are current. Besides describing the types of compliance requirements, the *Compliance Supplement* includes references to federal statutes, the *Code of Federal Regulations* and other sources of information about the requirements. The auditor may refer to those other sources of information to identify significant changes to the requirements or perform other procedures, including the following:

- Hold discussions with appropriate individuals within the auditee organization (that is, the CFO, internal auditors, legal counsel, compliance officer, or grant or contract administrators)
- Review federal awards, new guidance material issued by the federal awarding agency or pass-through entity (for example, handbooks and operating procedures), and correspondence from the federal awarding agency or pass-through entity
- Make inquiries of federal awarding agency personnel (a listing of federal agency contacts, including addresses, phone numbers, and email or Internet site addresses can be found in Appendix 3 of the *Compliance Supplement*.)

Considering Additional Terms and Conditions of Federal Awards

20.23 The *Compliance Supplement* states that in addition to the compliance requirements identified in the supplement, auditors should consider whether there are any terms and conditions of federal awards that are unique to a particular entity. For example, the federal award may specify the matching percentage, or an entity may have agreed to additional requirements that are not required by federal statute or regulation, perhaps as part of a resolution of prior audit findings.

20.24 Therefore, in using the *Compliance Supplement* to identify direct and material compliance requirements, the auditor should consider

a. the applicability to the federal program of the types of compliance requirements identified in Part 3 of the *Compliance Supplement.*
   b. additional compliance requirements specific to the federal program as identified in Part 4 (or Part 5 in the case of clusters of programs) of the *Compliance Supplement.*
   c. any terms and conditions of federal awards that are unique to the particular entity.

Compliance Requirements Specific to Certain Federal Programs

20.25 Part 4 of the *Compliance Supplement* discusses program objectives, program procedures, and compliance requirements that are specific to each federal program included. With the exception of special tests and provisions, Part 3 of the *Compliance Supplement* identifies the audit objectives and suggested audit procedures that pertain to the compliance requirements associated with each program. Because special tests and provisions are unique to each program, Part 4 of the *Compliance Supplement* includes those compliance requirements and the related audit objectives and suggested audit procedures. (Part 4 of the *Compliance Supplement* is considered a supplement to Part 3 and is not a replacement for it.)

Compliance Requirements Specific to a Cluster of Programs

20.26 As discussed in chapter 15 of this guide, a *cluster of programs* is a grouping of closely related programs that have similar compliance requirements (for example, student financial assistance [SFA], research and development [R&D], and other clusters). Part 5 of the *Compliance Supplement* identifies those programs that the OMB considers clusters of programs. It also provides compliance requirements, audit objectives, and suggested audit procedures for the SFA and R&D clusters. (States also may designate clusters of programs for federal awards they provide to subrecipients that meet the definition of a cluster of programs (for example, when those awards are for groupings of closely related programs that have similar compliance requirements.)

Relationship of the Compliance Supplement to Federal Program Audit Guides

20.27 The *Compliance Supplement* states that when performing an audit in accordance with the Uniform Guidance, the supplement replaces federal agency audit guides and other audit requirement documents for individual federal programs.[9] Accordingly, for a federal program included in the *Compliance Supplement* and having a separate federal program audit guide or other federal program audit requirement documents, the auditor needs to consider only those types of compliance requirements in the *Compliance Supplement* when performing a Uniform Guidance compliance audit (versus a program-specific audit).

---

[9] Some federal agencies have developed audit guides or supplements related to their programs. For programs not listed in the *Compliance Supplement*, the auditor may wish to consider that guidance in identifying the program objectives, program procedures, and compliance requirements. That guidance, where available, may be obtained from the federal agency's Office of Inspector General. Auditors should consider whether such guidance is outdated with regard to compliance requirements or currently authoritative auditing standards and requirements. See the discussion regarding such situations in chapter 24, "Program-Specific Audits (Uniform Guidance)," of this guide.

Federal Programs Not Included in the Compliance Supplement

20.28 The *Compliance Supplement* does not include all federal programs from which an auditee may receive federal awards. The Uniform Guidance states that for those federal programs not covered in the *Compliance Supplement*, the auditor must follow the *Compliance Supplement's* guidance for programs not included in the *Compliance Supplement*. That guidance is found in Part 7 of the *Compliance Supplement*, which explains that the auditor uses the types of compliance requirements in Part 3 (see paragraph 20.19) as guidance for identifying the compliance requirements to test and report on. A review of the terms and conditions of federal awards and the federal statutes and regulations referred to in such awards will also assist the auditor in determining compliance requirements to test. Part 7 also outlines the following steps to determine which compliance requirements to test:

a. Identify the compliance requirements that are applicable to the federal program.

b. Determine which of the compliance requirements identified in item *a* could have a direct and material effect on the major program.

c. Determine which of the compliance requirements identified in item *b* are susceptible to testing by the auditor.

d. Determine into which of the 12 types of compliance requirements the compliance requirements identified in item *c* fall.

e. For special tests and provisions, determine the applicable audit objectives and audit procedures.

Part 7 of the *Compliance Supplement* provides more detailed guidance on the steps to perform to identify direct and material compliance requirements.

Planning the Engagement

General Considerations

20.29 Planning a Uniform Guidance compliance audit involves developing an overall strategy for the expected conduct and scope of the engagement. To develop such a strategy, auditors need to have sufficient knowledge to enable them to understand adequately the events, transactions, and practices that, in their judgment, have a significant effect on compliance. Also, it is important for auditors to gain an understanding of any additional audit requirements that are supplemental to GAAS and *Government Auditing Standards*. Proper planning and supervision contribute to the effectiveness of audit procedures. Proper planning directly influences the selection of appropriate procedures and the timeliness of their application, and proper supervision helps ensure that planned procedures are appropriately applied. (See also chapter 16 of this guide.)

20.30 Factors the auditor might consider in planning a Uniform Guidance compliance audit include (*a*) the anticipated level of audit risk of noncompliance related to the direct and material compliance requirements on which the auditor will report (see paragraphs 20.07–.09), (*b*) preliminary judgments about materiality levels for audit purposes (see paragraphs 20.10–.13), and (*c*) conditions that may require the extension or modification of audit procedures.

20.31 The nature, timing, and extent of planning will vary with the nature and complexity of the compliance requirements and the auditor's prior experience with the auditee. Obtaining an understanding of an entity's major programs, the direct and material compliance requirements, and the entity's internal control over compliance establishes a frame of reference within which the auditor plans the compliance audit and exercises professional judgment about assessing risks of material noncompliance and responding to those risks throughout the compliance audit. As the Uniform Guidance compliance audit progresses, changed conditions may make it necessary to modify planned procedures. Chapter 16 of this guide discusses additional planning considerations.

Multiple Organizational Unit Considerations

20.32 In a Uniform Guidance compliance audit in which the auditee has operations in multiple organizational units (for example, operating units, locations, or branches), the auditor may determine that it is not necessary to test compliance with requirements at every such unit. Making such a determination and selecting the units to be tested includes consideration of the following factors: (*a*) the degree to which the specified compliance requirements apply at the organizational unit; (*b*) judgments about materiality; (*c*) the degree of centralization of the records; (*d*) the effectiveness of controls, particularly those that affect management's direct control over the exercise of authority delegated to others, as well as its ability to supervise activities at various locations effectively; (*e*) the nature and extent of operations conducted at the various organizational units; and (*f*) the similarity of operations and controls over compliance for different organizational units. Chapters 18, 19, "Consideration of Internal Control Over Compliance for Major Programs (Uniform Guidance)," and 21, "Audit Sampling Considerations of Uniform Guidance Compliance Audits," of this guide discuss other multiple organizational unit considerations.

Consideration of Internal Control Over Compliance for Major Programs

20.33 For each of the direct and material compliance requirements selected for testing for each major program, the auditor should perform risk assessment procedures to obtain a sufficient understanding of the direct and material compliance requirements and the entity's internal control over compliance with the direct and material compliance requirements. The auditor should use this knowledge to identify types of potential noncompliance, consider factors that affect the risks of material noncompliance, and design appropriate tests of compliance. The Uniform Guidance states that, in addition to the requirements of *Government Auditing Standards*, the auditor must perform procedures to obtain an understanding of internal control over compliance for federal programs sufficient to plan the audit to support a low assessed level of control risk of noncompliance for major programs. The Uniform Guidance also states that the auditor must plan the testing of internal control over compliance for major programs to support a low assessed level of control risk for the assertions relevant to the compliance requirements for each major program, and to perform the tests as planned. This includes performing procedures to evaluate the design and operating effectiveness of the internal control over compliance for each direct and material compliance requirement for each major program. In some instances, the auditor may be able to perform compliance testing for major programs concurrently with tests of controls. (Chapter 16 of this guide discusses how to develop an efficient audit approach.) Any significant deficiencies and material weaknesses in internal control over compliance for major programs that are identified must be reported as an audit finding. (Chapter 23 of this guide discusses the situations that the Uniform Guidance requires the auditor to report as audit findings.) Chapter 16 of this guide further discusses control risk of noncompliance, and chapter 19 of this guide discusses the auditor's consideration of internal control over compliance for major programs, including the final control risk of noncompliance assessment and the performance of tests of controls.

Performing Compliance Testing [10]

20.34 The Uniform Guidance states that compliance testing must include tests of transactions and such other auditing procedures necessary to provide the auditor sufficient appropriate audit evidence to support an opinion on compliance for each major program. Such compliance testing may be performed (*a*) concurrently with tests of controls, (*b*) as separate substantive testing, or (*c*) as a combination of the two. In performing compliance testing, the auditor attempts to obtain reasonable assurance that the auditee complied, in all material respects, with the compliance requirements. In a Uniform Guidance compliance audit, this includes designing procedures to detect both intentional and unintentional noncompliance. The auditor can obtain reasonable, but not absolute, assurance about the entity's compliance because of factors such as the need for judgment, the use of sampling, and the inherent limitations of internal control over compliance with direct and material compliance requirements and the fact that much of the evidence available to the auditor is persuasive rather than conclusive in nature. Also, procedures that are effective for detecting noncompliance that is unintentional may be ineffective for detecting noncompliance that is intentional and is concealed through collusion between the auditee's personnel and a third party or among the management or other employees of the entity. Therefore, the subsequent discovery that material noncompliance with direct and material compliance requirements exists does not, in and of itself, evidence inadequate planning, performance, or judgment on the part of the auditor.

20.35 In determining the nature, timing, and extent of tests to perform, the auditor should exercise professional judgment regarding the appropriate level of detection risk of noncompliance to accept.[11] (Paragraph 20.06 notes factors for the auditor to consider in applying professional judgment.) In determining the nature, timing, and extent of the testing of an auditee's compliance with compliance requirements, the auditor should consider both audit risk of noncompliance and materiality related to each major program as well as for each direct and material compliance requirement related to each major program. The auditor plans compliance tests to reduce detection risk of noncompliance to an acceptable level. The evidence provided by those tests, along with evidence regarding inherent risk of noncompliance and control risk of noncompliance, provides the basis for expressing an opinion on whether the auditee complied, in all material respects, with the direct and material compliance requirements for each major program.

---

[10] See chapter 21, "Audit Sampling Considerations of Uniform Guidance Compliance Audits," for an in-depth discussion of audit sampling in a compliance audit, including a discussion of performing compliance testing for major programs concurrently with tests of controls (that is, dual purpose testing).

[11] See also chapter 21 of this guide for a discussion of audit sampling.

20.36 In determining the nature of tests of compliance with requirements governing major programs, the consideration of the nature of those requirements will assist the auditor. For example, to test compliance with requirements applicable to the allowability of expenditures using program funds, the auditor should design audit procedures to provide sufficient appropriate audit evidence to evaluate how management expended the funds.

Sufficient Appropriate Audit Evidence

20.37 The auditor should apply procedures to provide reasonable assurance of detecting material noncompliance. The selection and application of procedures that will accumulate evidence that is sufficient and appropriate in the circumstances to provide a reasonable basis for expressing an opinion on compliance require the careful exercise of professional judgment. A broad array of available procedures may be applied in a Uniform Guidance compliance audit. In establishing a proper combination of procedures to restrict audit risk of noncompliance appropriately, the auditor should consider the following generalizations, bearing in mind that they are not mutually exclusive and may be subject to important exceptions:

    a. Audit evidence is more reliable when it is obtained from knowledgeable independent sources outside the entity.

    b. Audit evidence that is generated internally is more reliable when the related controls imposed by the entity are effective.

    c. Audit evidence obtained directly by the auditor (for example, observation of the application of a control) is more reliable than audit evidence obtained indirectly or by inference (for example, inquiry about the application of a control).

    d. Audit evidence is more reliable when it exists in documentary form, whether paper, electronic, or other medium (for example, a contemporaneously written record of a meeting is more reliable than a subsequent oral representation of the matters discussed).

    e. Audit evidence provided by original documents is more reliable than audit evidence provided by photocopies or facsimiles.

20.38 Thus, in the hierarchy of available audit procedures, those that involve search and verification (for example, inspection, confirmation, or observation)—particularly when independent sources outside the entity are used—generally are more effective in reducing audit risk of noncompliance than are those involving internal inquiries and comparisons of internal information (for example, analytical procedures and discussions with the individuals responsible for compliance).

20.39 In a Uniform Guidance compliance audit, the auditor's objective is to accumulate sufficient appropriate audit evidence to limit audit risk of noncompliance to a level that is, in the auditor's professional judgment, appropriately low for the high level of assurance being provided. An auditor should select from all available procedures (that is, procedures that assess inherent and control risk of noncompliance and restrict detection risk of noncompliance) in any combination that can limit audit risk of noncompliance to such an appropriately low level.

20.40 For regulatory requirements, the auditor's procedures may include reviewing reports of significant examinations and related communications between regulatory agencies and the entity and, when appropriate, making inquiries of the regulatory agencies, including inquiries about examinations in progress.

Audit Objectives

20.41 As noted in paragraph 20.19, the *Compliance Supplement* contains the audit objectives for each type of compliance requirement that the auditor should consider in planning and performing tests of compliance requirements. The audit objectives are useful in understanding the specific objectives to be satisfied when the auditor performs audit tests and determines whether the noncompliance that is identified is material.

Suggested Audit Procedures

20.42 The *Compliance Supplement* contains suggested audit procedures for testing federal programs for compliance. Those suggested audit procedures represent procedures that may be used by the auditor in developing an audit plan. The suggested audit procedures also may be useful in testing the same types of compliance requirements for programs that are not included in the *Compliance Supplement*. The auditor should use professional judgment in determining the audit procedures to be performed to allow him or her to obtain sufficient appropriate audit evidence to form an opinion on the auditee's compliance with the compliance requirements that could have a direct and material effect on each major program.

Audit Sampling

20.43 The auditor generally uses audit sampling to obtain audit evidence. See chapter 21 of this guide for an in-depth discussion of audit sampling as it relates to compliance audits.

Consideration of Abuse

20.44 As discussed in chapter 3 of this guide, *Government Auditing Standards* provides requirements and guidance related to abuse.[12] Because the determination of abuse is subjective, auditors are not required to detect abuse. However, the requirements related to abuse in *Government Auditing Standards* apply to the entirety of the single audit, including the Uniform Guidance compliance audit. The Uniform Guidance also requires the auditor to report as an audit finding significant instances of abuse relating to major programs. Therefore, if in performing procedures on major programs, the auditor becomes aware of a situation or transaction that might constitute abuse, the auditor should extend procedures to determine whether it is indicative of abuse and potentially material to the financial statement amounts[13] or material in relation to a direct and material compliance requirement of a major program. (Chapter 3 of this guide further discusses procedures relating to, and the evaluation of, indications of abuse.) Because the cost principles found in Subpart E, "Cost Principles," of the Uniform Guidance require that costs charged to federal awards be reasonable and necessary for the performance and administration

---

[12] Paragraph 4.07 of *Government Auditing Standards* states that abuse "involves behavior that is deficient or improper when compared with behavior that a prudent person would consider reasonable and necessary business practice given the facts and circumstances." It goes on to state that abuse does not necessarily involve fraud or noncompliance with provisions of laws, regulations, contracts, or grant agreements.

[13] See footnote 4.

of the awards,[14] situations or transactions involving federal awards that might otherwise appear to constitute abuse instead generally are instances of noncompliance. (By definition, instances of noncompliance with federal statutes, regulations, or terms and conditions of federal awards are not abuse.) However, there may be isolated situations or transactions involving federal awards that the auditor becomes aware of that do constitute abuse. Chapter 23 of this guide discusses the reporting of abuse involving federal awards.

Consideration of Subsequent Events

20.45 In a Uniform Guidance compliance audit, two types of subsequent events may occur. The first type consists of events that provide additional evidence with respect to conditions that existed at the end of the reporting period that affect the auditee's compliance during the reporting period. The second type consists of events of noncompliance that did not exist at the end of the reporting period but arose subsequent to the reporting period.

20.46 The auditor should perform audit procedures up to the date of the auditor's report to obtain sufficient appropriate audit evidence that all subsequent events related to the auditee's compliance during the period covered by the auditor's report on compliance have been identified. The auditor should take into account the auditor's risk assessment in determining the nature and extent of such audit procedures. These procedures should include, but are not limited to, inquiring of management about and considering

- relevant internal auditor's reports issued during the subsequent period,
- other auditor's reports identifying noncompliance that were issued during the subsequent period,
- reports from federal awarding agencies and pass-through entities related to the auditee's noncompliance that were issued during the subsequent period, and
- information about the auditee's noncompliance obtained through other professional engagements performed for that entity.

20.47 The auditor has no obligation to perform any audit procedures related to the entity's compliance during the period subsequent to the period covered by the auditor's report. However, if before the report release date the auditor becomes aware of noncompliance in the period subsequent to the period covered by the auditor's report that is of such a nature and significance that its disclosure is needed to prevent report users from being misled, the auditor should discuss the matter with management and, if appropriate, those charged with governance and should include an other-matter paragraph in the auditor's report describing the nature of the noncompliance. An example of a matter of noncompliance that may occur subsequent to the period being audited but before the report release date that may warrant disclosure to prevent report users from being misled is the discovery of noncompliance in the subsequent period of such magnitude that it caused the federal awarding agency to stop funding the program.

---

[14] This compliance requirement is explained in Part 3, "Compliance Requirements," of the *Compliance Supplement*, section B, "Allowable Costs/Cost Principles."

Compliance Auditing Applicable to Major Programs (Uniform Guidance) **521**

Evaluation and Reporting of Noncompliance

Instances of Noncompliance (Findings)

20.48 The auditor's tests of compliance with compliance requirements may disclose instances of noncompliance. The Uniform Guidance refers to these instances of noncompliance, among other matters, as audit findings. Such findings may be of a monetary nature and involve questioned costs or may be nonmonetary and not result in questioned costs. Both *Government Auditing Standards* and the Uniform Guidance specify how certain findings are to be reported.[15] Chapter 23 of this guide discusses the auditor's opinion on compliance and his or her responsibilities for reporting findings.

20.49 Furthermore, the auditor should not assume that an instance of fraud or error is an isolated occurrence and, therefore, should consider how the detection of such noncompliance affects the assessed risks of material noncompliance. Before the conclusion of the audit, the auditor should evaluate whether audit risk of noncompliance has been reduced to an appropriately low level and whether the nature, timing, and extent of the audit procedures need to be reconsidered. The auditor should conclude whether sufficient appropriate audit evidence has been obtained to reduce to an appropriately low level the risks of material noncompliance with compliance requirements.

Compliance Opinion

20.50 The auditor should evaluate the sufficiency and appropriateness of the audit evidence obtained. Additionally, the auditor should consider all relevant audit evidence regardless of whether it appears to corroborate or contradict the relevant assertions.

20.51 AU-C section 935 states that the auditor should form an opinion at the level specified by the governmental audit requirement. In a Uniform Guidance compliance audit, the auditor must report on compliance for each major program, which includes an opinion or modified opinion (or disclaimer of opinion) about whether the auditee complied with federal statutes, regulations, and the terms and conditions of federal awards that could have a direct and material effect on each major program. Note that the Uniform Guidance requires the auditor to prepare a schedule of findings and questioned costs. (Chapter 23 of this guide discusses that report and schedule.)

20.52 In determining whether the auditee complied with the direct and material compliance requirements in all material respects, the auditor may consider the following factors:

- The frequency of noncompliance with the direct and material compliance requirements identified during the compliance audit

---

[15] In accordance with 2 CFR 200.512, unless restricted by federal statutes or regulations, the auditee must make copies of reports available for public inspection. Auditees and auditors must ensure that their respective part of the reporting package does not include protected personally identifiable information, and in the report submission to the Federal Audit Clearinghouse (FAC) a senior level representative of the auditee must sign a statement that the reporting package does not include protected personally identifiable information. See chapter 23, "Auditor Reporting Requirements and Other Communication Considerations (Uniform Guidance)," for more information. Note that the Uniform Guidance does have a provision that an Indian tribe or tribal organization (as defined in the Indian Self-Determination Act (ISDEAA), 25 U.S.C. 450(b)(1)) may opt not to authorize the FAC to make the reporting package publicly available on the website.

- The nature of the noncompliance with the direct and material compliance requirements
- The adequacy of the entity's system for monitoring compliance with the direct and material compliance requirements and the possible effect of any noncompliance on the entity
- Whether any identified noncompliance with the direct and material compliance requirements resulted in likely questioned costs that are material to the federal program

The auditor's evaluation of whether the auditee materially complied with the direct and material compliance requirements includes consideration of noncompliance identified by the auditor, regardless of whether the entity corrected the noncompliance after the auditor brought it to management's attention.

20.53 Assessing materiality at the appropriate level is critical to the proper evaluation of findings. Paragraphs 20.10–.13 discuss materiality as it relates to expressing an opinion on the auditee's compliance. Paragraph 20.56 discusses the auditor's evaluation of the effect of questioned costs on the compliance opinion.

Financial Statement Effect

20.54 The auditor also has the responsibility of assessing the effect of the actual and likely error noted in the Uniform Guidance compliance audit against the materiality level established for the basic financial statements (see paragraph 20.13). Consideration of the effect of the following items is part of this evaluation: (*a*) any contingent liability that may arise from the noncompliance in accordance with applicable FASB *Accounting Standards Codification* (ASC) 450, *Contingencies*, or GASB standards (for example, paragraphs .96–.113 of GASB Statement No. 62, *Codification of Accounting and Financial Reporting Guidance Contained in Pre-November 30, 1989 FASB and AICPA Pronouncements*), and (*b*) for nongovernmental entities, any uncertainty regarding the resolution of instances of noncompliance in accordance with FASB standards (for example, FASB ASC 275, *Risks and Uncertainties*).

Questioned Costs

20.55 The Uniform Guidance defines *questioned costs* as costs that are questioned by the auditor because of an audit finding (*a*) which resulted from a violation or possible violation of a statute, regulation, or the terms and conditions of a federal award, including funds used to match federal funds; (*b*) where the costs, at the time of the audit, are not supported by adequate documentation; or (*c*) where the costs incurred appear unreasonable and do not reflect the actions a prudent person would take in the circumstances.

Evaluating the Effect of Questioned Costs on the Compliance Opinion

20.56 In evaluating the effect of questioned costs on the opinion on compliance, the auditor considers the best estimate of the total costs questioned for each major program (likely questioned costs), not just the questioned costs specifically identified (known questioned costs). Likely questioned costs are developed by extrapolating from audit evidence obtained, for example, by projecting known questioned costs identified in an audit sample to the entire population from which the sample was drawn. There may be situations in which the known questioned costs are not considered material, but the likely questioned costs are considered material. In those situations, the auditor should consider the noncompliance to be material (and report a finding) or may expand the scope of the Uniform Guidance compliance audit and apply additional audit procedures to further establish the likely questioned costs. (See also paragraph 20.61 of this guide.)

Federal Agency Consideration of Findings and Questioned Costs

20.57 The auditor's designation of a cost as questioned does not necessarily mean that a federal awarding agency will disallow the cost. In most instances, the auditor is unable to determine whether a federal awarding agency or pass-through entity will ultimately disallow a questioned cost because the agency or entity has considerable discretion in those matters.

20.58 The Uniform Guidance defines a *management decision* as the evaluation by the federal awarding agency or pass-through entity of the audit findings[16] and corrective action plan and the issuance of a written decision to the auditee as to what corrective action is necessary. (Chapter 23 of this guide discusses the corrective action plan.) The Uniform Guidance states that a federal awarding agency or pass-through entity responsible for issuing a management decision must do so within six months of acceptance of the audit report by the Federal Audit Clearinghouse. Management decisions must include the reference numbers the auditor assigned to each audit finding. The federal awarding agency or pass-through entity considers the nature of the questioned costs, as well as the amounts involved, in issuing a management decision and deciding whether to disallow them. In addition, most federal awarding agencies have established appeal and adjudication procedures for questioned costs. Because of the discretion allowed in resolving these matters, all questioned costs are subject to uncertainty regarding their resolution.

Reporting the Findings

20.59 As discussed in chapter 16 of this guide, under the Uniform Guidance the auditor considers a different level of materiality for the purposes of reporting audit findings. The Uniform Guidance states that the auditor, in addition to providing an opinion on compliance, must include the following as audit findings, among other items, in the schedule of findings and questioned costs:

- Material noncompliance with provisions of federal statutes, regulations, or the terms and conditions of federal awards related to a major program. The auditor's determination of whether noncompliance with the provisions of federal statutes, regulations, or the terms and conditions of federal awards is material for purposes of reporting an audit finding is in relation to a type of compliance requirement for a major program identified in the *Compliance Supplement*.

- Known questioned costs that are greater than $25,000 for a type of compliance requirement for a major program. (Paragraph 20.19 lists the types of compliance requirements.) Known questioned costs are those specifically identified by the auditor.

---

[16] A management decision contains an evaluation of only those findings found in 2 CFR 200.516, which are the audit findings identified as part of the Uniform Guidance compliance audit of federal awards.

- Known questioned costs when likely questioned costs are greater than $25,000 for a type of compliance requirement for a major program.

- Known questioned costs that are greater than $25,000 for a federal program that is not audited as a major program.

Chapter 23 of this guide discusses the reporting of audit findings and contains a complete listing of the items that the Uniform Guidance requires to be reported in the schedule of findings and questioned costs. That chapter also discusses the *Government Auditing Standards* requirement that the auditor communicate to the auditee in writing instances of noncompliance with provisions of contracts or grant agreements or abuse that are less than material but warrant the attention of those charged with governance.

Findings of Noncompliance That Cannot Be Quantified

20.60 The auditor may discover instances of noncompliance that cannot be quantified. The auditor's responsibility for reporting such findings can best be described through an example. Assume that the auditor is auditing a pass-through entity that consistently fails to monitor the activities of its subrecipients as necessary to ensure that the subaward is used for authorized purposes. The Uniform Guidance requires the auditor to consider material noncompliance findings in relation to a type of compliance requirement identified in the *Compliance Supplement*. In this example, subrecipient monitoring is the relevant type of compliance requirement. Because the pass-through entity failed to monitor the activity of its subrecipients, this noncompliance would likely be material in relation to the compliance requirement of subrecipient monitoring and, therefore, should be reported as an audit finding. This would be the case even if it is found that the subrecipient actually complied with the terms and conditions of the subaward and achieved performance goals. In addition, the auditor also should consider whether significant deficiencies or material weaknesses in internal control over compliance exist that require reporting with respect to subrecipient monitoring. In the example provided, when there is a consistent failure to monitor subrecipients that would likely be the case.

Reporting Based on Likely Questioned Costs

20.61 When evaluating the effect of questioned costs on the opinion on compliance, the auditor considers both known questioned costs and the best estimate of the total costs questioned (likely questioned costs). Known and likely questioned costs also need to be considered when audit findings are reported. In addition to reporting known questioned costs greater than $25,000 for a type of compliance requirement for a major program in the schedule of findings and questioned costs, the auditor also must report known questioned costs when likely questioned costs are greater than $25,000 for a type of compliance requirement for a major program. For example, if the auditor specifically identifies $7,000 in questioned costs for a type of compliance requirement for a major program but, based on his or her evaluation of the effect of questioned costs for that compliance requirement estimates that the total questioned costs are in the $50,000 to $60,000 range, the auditor would report a finding that indicates the known questioned costs of $7,000. Chapter 23 of this guide further discusses reporting findings based on likely questioned costs.

Performing Follow-Up Procedures

Auditee Responsibilities for Audit Follow-Up and for the Summary Schedule of Prior Audit Findings[17]

20.62 The Uniform Guidance states that the auditee must promptly follow up and take corrective action on audit findings. As part of the follow-up required by the Uniform Guidance, the auditee must prepare a summary schedule of prior audit findings. (Chapter 23 of this guide discusses the summary schedule of prior audit findings.) That schedule reports the status of all audit findings included in the prior audit's schedule of findings and questioned costs. It also includes audit findings reported in the prior audit's summary schedule of prior audit findings that were not identified as either (*a*) fully corrected, (*b*) no longer valid, or (*c*) not warranting further actions. The Uniform Guidance states that a valid reason for considering an audit finding as not warranting further action is that *all* of the following have occurred:

- Two years have passed since the audit report in which the finding occurred was submitted to the FAC.
- The federal agency or pass-through entity is not currently following up with the auditee on the audit finding.
- A management decision was not issued.

20.63 The Uniform Guidance also states the following with regard to the auditee's summary schedule of prior audit findings:

- When audit findings were fully corrected, the summary schedule need only list the audit findings and state that corrective action was taken.
- When audit findings were not corrected or were only partially corrected, the summary schedule must describe the reasons for the finding's recurrence and planned corrective action as well as any partial corrective action taken.
- When the corrective action taken is significantly different from the corrective action previously reported in a corrective action plan or in the federal agency's or pass-through entity's management decision, the summary schedule must provide an explanation.
- When the auditee believes the audit findings are no longer valid or do not warrant further actions, the reasons for this position must be described in the summary schedule, as discussed in paragraph 20.62
- The summary schedule must include findings related to the financial statements which are required to be reported in accordance with *Government Auditing Standards*.

Auditor Responsibilities for Follow-Up on Previously Reported Audit Findings

20.64 The Uniform Guidance states that the auditor must follow up on prior audit findings, perform procedures to assess the reasonableness of the

---

[17] Chapter 3, "Planning and Performing a Financial Statement Auditing in Accordance With *Government Auditing Standards*," of this guide discusses the auditee's responsibilities under *Government Auditing Standards* for audit follow-up.

summary schedule of prior audit findings prepared by the auditee, and report, as a current-year audit finding, when the auditor concludes that the summary schedule of prior audit findings materially misrepresents the status of any prior audit finding. The auditor must perform audit follow-up procedures regardless of whether a prior audit finding relates to a major program in the current year. Chapter 23 of this guide further discusses the auditor's reporting responsibilities.

Auditor Follow-Up Procedures

20.65 To follow up on previous audit findings, the auditor should obtain the auditee's summary schedule of prior audit findings and perform appropriate procedures to determine the status of the audit findings included in the summary schedule that were reported in accordance with 2 CFR 200.516. Although, in many cases, the procedures performed in the current audit will provide a basis for the auditor to assess the schedule, the auditor may find it necessary to perform procedures directed specifically at the status of prior audit findings. In these cases, consideration might include the following procedures:

- Make inquiries of auditee management and program personnel, including inquiries about the status of corrective actions and the estimated completion date for incomplete actions
- Review management decisions issued by federal awarding agencies or pass-through entities to the auditee (paragraph 20.58 discusses management decisions)
- Observe an activity that has been redesigned to address a prior-year finding
- Test similar current-year transactions

Audit Follow-Up for Findings Reported Under Government Auditing Standards

20.66 Although the auditee's summary schedule of prior audit findings prepared as required by the Uniform Guidance must include the status of all findings (which encompass audit findings described in 2 CFR 200.516(a) and findings related to the financial statements) included in the prior audit's schedule of findings and questioned costs, the Uniform Guidance limits the auditor's follow-up responsibility to audit findings in 2 CFR 200.516(a). However, *Government Auditing Standards* includes a requirement, (discussed in chapter 3 of this guide), that requires the auditor to evaluate whether the auditee has taken appropriate corrective action to address findings and recommendations from previous engagements that could have a material effect on the financial statements or other data significant to the audit objectives. Therefore, performing the follow-up procedures described in paragraph 20.65 on findings relating to the financial statements would be an effective way for an auditor to meet the follow-up responsibilities under *Government Auditing Standards*.

Corrective Action Plan

20.67 2 CFR 200.511(c) of the Uniform Guidance requires that upon completion of the audit the auditee must prepare, in a document separate from the schedule of findings and questioned costs, a corrective action plan to address each audit finding included in the current year auditor's report. 2 CFR 511(a) requires the corrective action plan to include findings relating to the financial statements required to be reported in accordance with *Government Auditing*

Standards. The corrective action plan must provide the name(s) of the contact person(s) responsible for corrective action, the corrective action planned for each audit finding (referred to by the auditor-assigned reference number), and the anticipated completion date. If the auditee does not agree with the audit findings, or believes corrective action is not required, the corrective action plan must contain an explanation and specific reasons why the auditee disagrees. The auditor may find the auditee's prior year corrective action plan useful in performing audit follow-up (in addition to the auditee's summary schedule of prior audit findings) because it may provide a preliminary indication of the corrective steps planned by the auditee. (See also the discussions in chapters 4 and 23 concerning the *Government Auditing Standards* requirement that the auditor obtain and report the views of responsible officials concerning findings, conclusions, and recommendations, as well as planned corrective actions.)

Disputes or Unresolved Findings

20.68 There may be times when, as part of the follow-up on prior findings, the auditor determines that (*a*) a previous finding is the subject of a dispute between the auditee and the federal awarding agency or pass-through entity or (*b*) the federal awarding agency or pass-through entity has not addressed the finding by issuing a management decision. In these situations, if the finding relates to a current-year major program, this guide recommends that the auditor report similar transactions of the current year as findings and questioned costs until either the dispute is resolved or the initial finding no longer warrants further action under the Uniform Guidance as described in paragraph 20.62. However, if the auditor no longer believes that there is noncompliance because of additional evidence obtained in the current year, similar transactions need not be reported as findings.

Documentation Requirements

20.69 AU-C section 230, *Audit Documentation* (AICPA, *Professional Standards*), which establishes requirements and provides guidance on audit documentation, should be adapted and applied to the Uniform Guidance compliance audit. Specific documentation requirements that should be adapted and applied to a Uniform Guidance compliance audit may also be found in other AU-C sections, other standards, and supplementary audit requirements in laws and regulations applicable to the compliance audit.

20.70 AU-C section 935 contains requirements and guidance related to documentation of audit procedures performed in a compliance audit. In addition to those discussed in chapter 19 of this guide related to risk assessment and internal control, paragraphs .41–.42 of AU-C section 935 notes that the auditor should document:

- materiality levels and the basis on which they were determined.
- how the auditor complied with any specific governmental audit requirements that are supplementary to GAAS and *Government Auditing Standards*.

Paragraph .A38 of AU-C section 935 explains that the auditor is not expected to prepare specific documentation of how the auditor adapted and applied each of the applicable AU-C sections to the objectives of a compliance audit. The documentation of the audit strategy, audit plan, and work performed cumulatively demonstrate whether the auditor has complied with the requirements to apply and adapt AU-C sections to the compliance audit. (See chapter 16 for further discussion.)

> **Emphasis Point**
>
> Quality control reviews performed by federal agency staff have found instances when audit documentation did not contain sufficient evidence that work was performed to support the auditor's opinion on compliance for one or more major program. In some cases, they found that the audit documentation did not include evidence that the auditor tested certain compliance requirements applicable to a major program or, alternatively, did not explain why certain generally applicable compliance requirements identified in the *Compliance Supplement* were not applicable to a major program. Among the items the auditor should document when testing compliance requirements are the individual tests performed and the results of those tests.

Management Representations Related to Federal Awards

20.71 As part of a Uniform Guidance compliance audit, the auditor should obtain written representations from management about matters related to federal awards. Therefore, in addition to the management representations obtained in connection with an audit of the financial statements as discussed in chapter 3 of this guide, the auditor should obtain written representations from management concerning the identification and completeness of federal award programs, representations concerning compliance with compliance requirements, and identification of known instances of noncompliance. Paragraph 20.72 contains a suggested listing of representations. Chapter 3 discusses the members of management and other officials from whom the auditor should consider obtaining representations. In a compliance audit, the auditor also should consider obtaining representations from officials responsible for managing federal awards.

Suggested Representations

20.72 AU-C section 935 states that the auditor should request from management written representations that are tailored to the entity and the governmental audit requirement. The auditor should consider obtaining the following written representations, which include those identified in AU-C section 935, as well as additional representations specific to the Uniform Guidance:[18]

- Management is responsible for complying, and has complied, with the requirements of the Uniform Guidance.
- Management is responsible for understanding and complying with the requirements of federal statutes, regulations, and the terms and conditions of federal awards related to each of its federal programs.[19]

---

[18] The auditor should modify these representations, as appropriate, for different conditions, such as known noncompliance.

[19] AU-C section 935 notes that, in some cases, management may include qualifying language in the written representation to the effect that representations are made to the best of management's knowledge and belief. However, AU-C section 935 notes that qualifying language is not appropriate for this representation.

Compliance Auditing Applicable to Major Programs (Uniform Guidance) 529

- Management is responsible for establishing and maintaining, and has established and maintained, effective internal control over compliance for federal programs that provides reasonable assurance that the auditee is managing federal awards in compliance with federal statutes, regulations, and the terms and conditions of the federal award that could have a material effect on its federal programs.[20]

- Management has identified and disclosed all of its government programs and related activities subject to the Uniform Guidance compliance audit.

- Management has identified and disclosed to the auditor the requirements of federal statutes, regulations, and the terms and conditions of federal awards that are considered to have a direct and material effect on each major program.

- Management has made available all federal awards (including amendments, if any) and any other correspondence relevant to federal programs and related activities that have taken place with federal agencies or pass-through entities.

- Management has identified and disclosed to the auditor all amounts questioned and all known noncompliance with the direct and material compliance requirements of federal awards or stated that there was no such noncompliance.

- Management believes that the auditee has complied with the direct and material compliance requirements (except for noncompliance it has disclosed to the auditor).

- Management has made available all documentation related to compliance with the direct and material compliance requirements, including information related to federal program financial reports and claims for advances and reimbursements.

- Management has provided to the auditor its interpretations of any compliance requirements that are subject to varying interpretations.

- Management has disclosed to the auditor any communications from federal awarding agencies and pass-through entities concerning possible noncompliance with the direct and material compliance requirements, including communications received from the end of the period covered by the compliance audit to the date of the auditor's report.

- Management has disclosed to the auditor the findings received and related corrective actions taken for previous audits, attestation engagements, and internal or external monitoring that directly relate to the objectives of the compliance audit, including findings received and corrective actions taken from the end of the period covered by the compliance audit to the date of the auditor's report.

---

[20] See footnote 19.

- Management is responsible for taking corrective action on audit findings of the compliance audit and has developed a corrective action plan that meets the requirements of the Uniform Guidance.[21]
- Management has provided the auditor with all information on the status of the follow-up on prior audit findings by federal awarding agencies and pass-through entities, including all management decisions.
- Management has disclosed the nature of any subsequent events that provide additional evidence with respect to conditions that existed at the end of the reporting period that affect noncompliance during the reporting period.
- Management has disclosed all known noncompliance with direct and material compliance requirements occurring subsequent to the period covered by the auditor's report or stating that there were no such known instances.
- Management has disclosed whether any changes in internal control over compliance or other factors that might significantly affect internal control, including any corrective action taken by management with regard to significant deficiencies and material weaknesses in internal control over compliance, have occurred subsequent to the period covered by the auditor's report.
- Federal program financial reports and claims for advances and reimbursements are supported by the books and records from which the basic financial statements have been prepared.
- The copies of federal program financial reports provided to the auditor are true copies of the reports submitted, or electronically transmitted, to the federal agency or pass-through entity, as applicable.
- If applicable, management has monitored subrecipients, as necessary, to determine that they have expended subawards in compliance with federal statutes, regulations, and the terms and conditions of the subaward and have met the other pass-through entity requirements of the Uniform Guidance.
- If applicable, management has issued management decisions for audit findings that relate to federal awards it makes to subrecipients and that such management decisions are issued within six months of acceptance of the audit report by the FAC. Additionally, management has followed-up ensuring that the subrecipient takes timely and appropriate action on all deficiencies detected through audits, on-site reviews, and other means that pertain to the federal award provided to the subrecipient from the pass-through entity.
- If applicable, management has considered the results of subrecipient audits and has made any necessary adjustments to management's own books and records.
- Management has charged costs to federal awards in accordance with applicable cost principles.

---

[21] See footnote 19.

- Management is responsible for, and has accurately prepared, the summary schedule of prior audit findings to include all findings required to be included by the Uniform Guidance.

- The reporting package does not contain protected personally identifiable information.

- Management has accurately completed the appropriate sections of the data collection form.[22]

- If applicable, management has disclosed all contracts or other agreements with service organizations.

- If applicable, management has disclosed to the auditor all communications from service organizations relating to noncompliance at those organizations.

The auditor may determine that additional representations related to the entity's compliance with the direct and material compliance requirements are necessary. If so, the auditor should request such additional representations. See chapter 17, "Schedule of Expenditures of Federal Awards (Uniform Guidance)," for representations the auditor should obtain when issuing an in-relation-to opinion on the schedule of expenditures of federal awards.[23]

Refusal to Furnish Written Representations

20.73 Management's refusal to furnish all written representations that the auditor considers necessary in the circumstances constitutes a limitation on the scope of the audit sufficient to require a qualified opinion or disclaimer of opinion on the auditee's compliance with major program requirements. The auditor also should consider the effects of management's refusal on his or her ability to rely on other management representations.

State and Local Government Compliance Auditing Considerations

20.74 An auditor also may be engaged to test and report on compliance with state and local laws and regulations in addition to the testing and reporting requirements imposed by *Government Auditing Standards* and the Uniform Guidance. Although such auditing is outside the scope of this guide, such a requirement may specify compliance tests, similar to those in a single audit. When this is the case, auditors might consider consulting state or local government officials or other sources concerning the nature and scope of the required testing. It is important to distinguish state or local government funds from pass-through federal funds because pass-through federal funds are considered part of the federal awards received in an audit in accordance with the Uniform Guidance.

---

[22] See chapter 23 for information regarding revisions to the 2013–2015 data collection form and its submission to the FAC.

[23] Two separate management representation letters may be necessary when the required procedures on the schedule of expenditures of federal awards are completed after the date of the auditor's report on the financial statements. See chapters 17, "Schedule of Expenditures of Federal Awards (Uniform Guidance)," and 23 for more information.

Transition Considerations Related to the Uniform Guidance

20.75 As further discussed in the "Transition Considerations Related to the Uniform Guidance" in chapter 16 of this guide, one of the challenges that auditors may face is that a major program may include expenditures from both federal awards subject to the pre-Uniform Guidance requirements, as well as federal awards subject to the post-Uniform Guidance requirements. This situation could exist for several years until the pre-Uniform Guidance awards have been completely expended. When testing major program transactions, identification of the date of a federal award related to a particular expenditure is needed in order to determine the applicable criteria to use for the transaction being tested. It should be noted that a separate sample for pre-Uniform Guidance award transactions and post-Uniform Guidance award transactions within a major program would not typically be needed in this situation. However, this guide recommends that when testing major program transactions that the audit documentation for testing compliance and internal control over compliance include an identification of the transactions tested that were subject to post-Uniform Guidance requirements. See the "Transition Considerations Related to the Uniform Guidance" in chapter 21 for more information on sampling.

20.76 As set forth in the 2015 *Compliance Supplement*, the types of compliance requirements subject to audit have been reduced from 14 to 12. This change applies to both Circular A-133 compliance audits and Uniform Guidance compliance audits. The two requirements that have been removed are D, "Davis Bacon" and K, "Real Property Acquisition and Relocation Assistance." A listing of the remaining 12 types of compliance requirements is found in paragraph 20.19. The letters assigned to the types of compliance requirements that have been removed (D and K) are being held in reserve. Therefore, the letters assigned to the remaining 12 types of compliance requirements have not changed. While the former type of compliance requirement D, "Davis Bacon," has been removed as a separate type of compliance requirement, it has been included in the "Special Tests and Provisions" type of compliance requirement for some programs. Finally, one type of compliance requirement has been renamed. The former type of compliance requirement H, "Period of Availability of Federal Funds" has been renamed "Period of Performance" in Part 3.2 of the 2015 *Compliance Supplement*. Part 3.1 of the *Compliance Supplement* continues to refer to this type of compliance requirement as "Period of Availability of Federal Funds." See the following paragraph for more information on Part 3 of the *Compliance Supplement*.

20.77 The 2015 *Compliance Supplement* includes two versions of Part 3:

- Part 3.1 applies to testing federal awards that are not subject to the Uniform Guidance (that is, federal awards made prior to December 26, 2014)
- Part 3.2 applies to testing federal awards subject to the Uniform Guidance (that is, new federal awards and funding increments with modified award terms and conditions made on or after December 26, 2014)

As noted previously, a major program may include expenditures from both federal awards subject to pre-Uniform Guidance requirements, as well as federal awards subject to post-Uniform Guidance requirements. In these situations, the auditor will use both Part 3.1 and 3.2 to perform compliance testing.

20.78 A nonfederal entity may elect to continue to comply with the procurement standards in pre-Uniform Guidance requirements for one additional fiscal year after the Uniform Guidance goes into effect. This means a nonfederal entity may delay implementation of the Uniform Guidance procurement standards found in 2 CFR 200.317 - .326 for the entity's first full fiscal year that begins on or after December 26, 2014. If a nonfederal entity makes this election it must document whether it is in compliance with the old or new standard, and must meet the documented standard. For example, the first full fiscal year for an entity with a June 30 year end would be the year ending June 30, 2016. If the delayed implementation is elected, the entity is required to implement the Uniform Guidance procurement standards beginning July 1, 2016. Understanding whether a nonfederal entity has elected to delay implementation of the Uniform Guidance procurement standards is an important auditor consideration since it may impact the compliance testing performed in a Uniform Guidance compliance audit.

Chapter 21

Audit Sampling Considerations of Uniform Guidance Compliance Audits

> **⊛ Update 21-1: Audits of Federal Awards**
>
> This chapter, and the remaining chapters of part III, *Uniform Guidance Audits*, of this guide, should be used for performing a compliance audit of federal awards under the audit requirements of Title 2 U.S. *Code of Federal Regulations* Part 200, *Uniform Administrative Requirements, Cost Principles, and Audit Requirements for Federal Awards* (Uniform Guidance).[1] Part II, *Circular A-133 Audits*, of this guide should be used for performing a compliance audit under Office of Management and Budget (OMB) Circular A-133, *Audits of States, Local Governments, and Non-Profit Organizations* (Circular A-133). See the transitional guidance sections at the end of each chapter that highlight important matters for consideration. Additionally, refer to the preface of this guide for more information.
>
> **Important Effective Date Information**
>
> In December 2013, the OMB issued the Uniform Guidance, which is effective for nonfederal entities for all federal awards and certain funding increments provided on or after December 26, 2014. The requirements in Subpart F, "Audit Requirements," are effective for audits of fiscal years beginning on or after December 26, 2014, with no early implementation permitted. Therefore, auditees subject to a single audit with December 25, 2015, and later year ends (for example, December 31, 2015) will be required to undergo the audit under Subpart F of the Uniform Guidance. Note that audits of fiscal years ending prior to the effective date of the Uniform Guidance audit requirements are subject to an audit under Circular A-133.

Introduction

21.01 An auditor may decide to use audit sampling to obtain sufficient appropriate audit evidence in a compliance audit, as noted in paragraph .A21 of AU-C section 935, *Compliance Audits* (AICPA, *Professional Standards*). AU-C section 530, *Audit Sampling* (AICPA, *Professional Standards*),[2] addresses

---

[1] See the information found at the end of this chapter (paragraph 21.136), and other part III, *Uniform Guidance Audits*, chapters of this guide, for transition considerations when performing an audit under Title 2 U.S. *Code of Federal Regulations* (CFR) Part 200, *Uniform Administrative Requirements, Cost Principles, and Audit Requirements for Federal Awards* (Uniform Guidance). Transition considerations can also be found at the end of certain part II, *Circular A-133 Audits*, chapters as it relates to an audit performed under Office of Management and Budget (OMB) Circular A-133, *Audits of States, Local Governments, and Non-Profit Organizations*.

[2] The AICPA Audit Guide *Audit Sampling* is an interpretive publication, which assists practitioners in the application of the guidance found in AU-C section 530, *Audit Sampling* (AICPA, *Professional Standards*). Interpretive publications are recommendations on the application of auditing standards in specific circumstances and are issued under the authority of the Auditing Standards Board. An auditor should be aware of and consider interpretive publications applicable to his or her audit. If the auditor does not apply the auditing guidance included in an applicable interpretive publication, the auditor should be prepared to explain how he or she complied with the Statements on Auditing Standards provisions addressed by such auditing guidance. The Audit Guide *Audit Sampling* is available at www.cpa2biz.com.

the auditor's use of statistical and nonstatistical sampling when designing and selecting the audit sample, performing tests of controls and tests of details, and evaluating the results from the sample. It includes guidance related to sampling risk, sampling in substantive tests of details, and sampling in tests of controls. The guidance in AU-C section 530 primarily addresses sampling considerations when performing a financial statement audit, with an emphasis on testing account balances or classes of transactions that may contain misstatements as well as testing internal control over financial reporting. Sampling to accomplish compliance-related audit objectives in a Uniform Guidance compliance audit environment differs from sampling in a financial statement audit in that to meet the compliance-related objectives, the auditor gathers sufficient appropriate audit evidence on whether the auditee has complied with federal statutes, regulations, and the terms and conditions of federal awards that could have a direct and material effect on each major program.

21.02 This chapter provides considerations in designing an audit approach that includes audit sampling to achieve both compliance and internal control over compliance related audit objectives in a compliance audit or program-specific audit performed in accordance with the Uniform Guidance. This chapter builds upon the general guidance set forth in AU-C section 530 (as discussed in the AICPA Audit Guide *Audit Sampling*) by providing specific, relevant sampling guidance for a single audit or program-specific audit.

21.03 In addition to providing important considerations when applying sampling in a Uniform Guidance compliance audit, this chapter provides suggested minimum sample sizes for tests of controls over compliance and tests of compliance based on certain engagement-specific inputs. Depending on the nature of the type of compliance requirement being tested, the results of other audit procedures performed during the audit, and the risks and complexities of the sampling population, there may be situations when auditors may determine, based on professional judgment, that it is appropriate to use larger sample sizes rather than the suggested minimum sample sizes.

21.04 This chapter does not include guidance on every possible valid method of selecting and evaluating audit samples in a Uniform Guidance compliance audit. The AICPA Audit Guide *Audit Sampling* provides additional guidance and technical background, which forms the basis of the practical application of audit sampling to Uniform Guidance compliance audits as outlined in this chapter.

Audit Sampling in a Uniform Guidance Compliance Audit

21.05 Paragraph .05 of AU-C section 530 defines *audit sampling* as the selection and evaluation of less than 100 percent of the population of audit relevance such that the auditor expects the items selected (the sample) to be representative of the population and, thus, likely to provide a reasonable basis for conclusions about the population. In other words, audit sampling may provide the auditor an appropriate basis on which to conclude on a characteristic of a population based on examining evidence regarding that characteristic from a subset of the population. When using audit sampling, the auditor may choose between a statistical and a nonstatistical approach. Both methods are acceptable under AU-C section 530.

Purpose and Nature of Audit Sampling in a Uniform Guidance Compliance Audit

21.06 The auditor's objectives in a Uniform Guidance compliance audit include reporting on internal control over compliance (as discussed in chapter 19, "Consideration of Internal Control Over Compliance for Major Programs (Uniform Guidance)," of this guide) and expressing an opinion on whether the auditee has complied with federal statutes, regulations, and the terms and conditions of federal awards that may have a direct and material effect on each of its major programs (as discussed in chapter 20, "Compliance Auditing Applicable to Major Programs (Uniform Guidance)," of this guide). The auditor's compliance testing must include tests of transactions and such other auditing procedures necessary to provide the auditor with sufficient appropriate audit evidence to support the opinion on compliance for each major program. The auditor also must meet the requirements of the Uniform Guidance for testing and reporting on internal control over compliance. Sufficient appropriate audit evidence may be obtained through a variety of procedures, including planning and performing risk assessment procedures, performing tests of controls, performing tests of details (including tests of transactions), and other auditing procedures as are necessary. Auditors frequently use audit sampling procedures to obtain such audit evidence.

21.07 When testing internal control over compliance, the auditor is primarily concerned about the rates of deviations from a prescribed control. Similarly, in tests of compliance, the auditor is concerned about whether or not there is evidence of compliance (that is, the rate and likely magnitude of noncompliance). Therefore, *attributes sampling*, as defined in the AICPA Audit Guide *Audit Sampling*, is typically used for tests of controls over compliance and compliance testing in a Uniform Guidance compliance audit. The underlying basis for the large population sample sizes provided in this chapter is attributes sampling.

21.08 Further, as noted in chapter 20 of this guide, the Uniform Guidance states that the auditor must report known questioned costs when likely questioned costs[3] are greater than $25,000 for a type of compliance requirement for a major program. That is, the auditor must report known questioned costs but is not required to report the likely questioned costs. In evaluating the effect of questioned costs (found through sampling and other audit procedures) on the opinion on compliance, the auditor considers the best estimate of the total costs questioned for each major program (likely questioned costs), not just the questioned costs specifically identified (known questioned costs).

21.09 When noncompliance is discovered related to monetary transactions of a major program, the Uniform Guidance does not require the auditor to report an exact amount or a statistical projection of likely questioned costs with related confidence bounds. Instead, as noted previously and further discussed in chapter 20 of this guide, the auditor considers the effect of likely questioned costs on the opinion on compliance and must report an audit finding when the auditor's estimate of likely questioned costs is greater than $25,000.

---

[3] The Uniform Guidance defines *likely questioned costs* as the auditor's best estimate of total costs questioned. *Known questioned costs* are questioned costs specifically identified by the auditor and a subset of likely questioned costs. As noted in the "Definitions" section of AU-C section 935, *Compliance Audits* (AICPA, *Professional Standards*), *likely questioned costs* are developed by extrapolating from audit evidence obtained, for example, by projecting known questioned costs identified in an audit sample to the entire population from which the sample was drawn.

> **Emphasis Point**
>
> The use of the term *must* in the Uniform Guidance indicates a requirement. This is consistent with the use of the term *must* in generally accepted auditing standards (GAAS) and *Government Auditing Standards*. The use of the term *should* in the Uniform Guidance indicates a best practice or recommended approach. However, GAAS and *Government Auditing Standards* use the term *should* to indicate a presumptively mandatory requirement. An auditor must comply with a presumptively mandatory requirement in all cases in which such a requirement is relevant, except in rare circumstances. In this guide, the term ***should***, when italicized and bolded, indicates a best practice or recommended approach in the Uniform Guidance. This is intended to differentiate it from the term *should* used throughout the guide to refer to presumptively mandatory requirements in GAAS and *Government Auditing Standards*. See chapter 1, "Introduction and Overview of *Government Auditing Standards*," of this guide for more information regarding presumptively mandatory requirements.

Audit Sampling in the Context of Other Audit Procedures

21.10 It is important to note that sampling is one of many audit procedures designed to provide sufficient appropriate audit evidence to support the auditor's compliance opinion on each major program. An auditor often does not rely solely on the results of any single type of procedure to obtain sufficient appropriate audit evidence on each major program's compliance and internal control over compliance. Rather, audit conclusions may be based on evidence obtained from several sources and by applying a variety of audit procedures. Auditors should consider the combined evidence obtained from the various types of procedures to determine whether there is sufficient appropriate audit evidence to evaluate possible audit findings and to develop the auditor's report on internal control over compliance and the opinion on whether the auditee complied with federal statutes, regulations, and the terms and conditions of federal awards for each major program.

21.11 In a Uniform Guidance compliance audit, just as in a financial statement audit, other audit procedures beyond sampling are performed. For instance, risk assessment procedures typically precede tests of controls. The following are specific examples of other audit procedures used in a Uniform Guidance compliance audit that may be used in addition to audit sampling:

- Determining for each major program the direct and material types of compliance requirements to be tested and reported on in a Uniform Guidance compliance audit (See chapter 20 of this guide for further discussion.)
- Using the knowledge gained in the inherent risk of noncompliance assessment process (as described in chapter 16, "Auditor Planning Considerations Under the Uniform Guidance," of this guide) to identify types of potential noncompliance, to consider other factors that affect the risk of material noncompliance, and to design appropriate tests of compliance
- Performing analytical procedures to further understand the nature of a major program prior to performing compliance testing

Audit Sampling Considerations of Uniform Guidance Compliance Audits

- Identifying risks throughout the process of obtaining an understanding of the entity and its environment, including relevant controls that relate to the risks of noncompliance, evaluating the design of controls relevant to the Uniform Guidance compliance audit, and determining whether they have been implemented
- Considering whether there are individually important items that may merit being specifically tested prior to selecting a sample and performing tests on such items (See paragraphs 21.21–.28.)

Procedures That May Not Involve Audit Sampling

21.12 The following paragraphs discuss compliance and internal control over compliance audit procedures that generally do not involve audit sampling.

Inquiry and Observation

21.13 Inquiry, as discussed in paragraphs .A23–.A26 of AU-C section 500, *Audit Evidence* (AICPA, *Professional Standards*), consists of seeking information, both financial and nonfinancial, of knowledgeable persons within the entity or outside the entity. Observation, as discussed in paragraph .A17 of AU-C section 500 consists of looking at a process or procedure being performed by others. Inquiry and observation procedures commonly used in a Uniform Guidance compliance audit include the following:

- Interviewing management and employees to obtain an understanding of internal control over compliance
- Observing the behavior of personnel and the functioning of business operations
- Observing cash handling activities
- Performing walkthrough procedures[4]
- Observing the existence of real property and equipment
- Obtaining written representations from management

In some cases, these procedures could be designed as sampling procedures, such as designing multiple observations of physical security controls; however, inquiry and observation generally do not involve audit sampling.

Analytical Procedures

21.14 Analytical procedures, as discussed in AU-C section 520, *Analytical Procedures* (AICPA, *Professional Standards*), consist of evaluations of information through analysis of plausible relationships among both financial and nonfinancial data. These procedures are not considered audit sampling because they do not result in the ability to project the results of testing a portion of the population to the total population.

21.15 As noted in paragraph .A23 of AU-C section 935, the use of analytical procedures to gather substantive evidence is generally less effective in a compliance audit than it is in a financial statement audit. However, substantive analytical procedures may contribute some evidence when performed in

---

[4] Walkthroughs may include an examination of evidence and reperformance, depending on their design and performance.

addition to tests of transactions and other auditing procedures necessary to provide the auditor with sufficient appropriate audit evidence.

21.16 An example of applying analytical procedures in a Uniform Guidance compliance audit may include a test relating to the Activities Allowed or Unallowed type of compliance requirement for a school lunch program. An auditor may use analytical procedures to calculate an estimated total for nutritional expenditures and compare against actual expenditures to provide some audit evidence that could reduce compliance tests, assuming the auditor is confident with the completeness and accuracy of the underlying data. Calculating estimated participation could be accomplished by multiplying the number of students enrolled in a school system by the percentage expected to participate in a school nutrition program. This percentage may be based on history, current economic trends and statistics in the area, or other factors. The calculated estimation then could be multiplied by an average daily cost of the nutrition program per student to estimate the total expenditures for the program. The auditor may then compare the estimation to the recorded expenditures to determine if there is a difference material to the program being tested.

21.17 Scanning is another common non-sampling analytical procedure. The following are two examples of how scanning might be used in a Uniform Guidance compliance audit:

a. For a school district, auditors could scan a list of employees that charged time to a federal award to determine that the type of employee and school appear reasonable (for example, when scanning a list of employees charged to vocational education programs, the auditor normally would not expect to see an elementary school teacher included).

b. For a social services federal award or education training program that, by its nature, would not include equipment purchases, auditors could scan a list of program expenditures for captions that indicate a disbursement was made for equipment.

Procedures Applied to Every Item in a Population or Subpopulation in Compliance Testing

21.18 In some circumstances, an auditor might decide to examine every item in a population relating to a type of compliance requirement for a major program. In this situation, because the auditor is examining the entire population to reach a conclusion, rather than only a portion, this 100 percent examination is not a procedure that involves audit sampling.

21.19 When individually important items do not make up the entire population, after testing all individually important items, the auditor might apply audit sampling to the remaining items. (See paragraphs 21.21–.28 for an additional discussion of individually important items.)

21.20 Alternatively, after testing all individually important items, an auditor might either (*a*) apply other auditing procedures to the remaining items in the population (for example, scanning) or (*b*) apply no auditing procedures to remaining items because there is an acceptably low risk of material noncompliance in the remaining items. In these two scenarios, the auditor is not using sampling. Rather, the auditor has divided the entire population of items into two groups. One subpopulation is tested 100 percent, and the other subpopulation is either tested by other auditing procedures or is not tested.

Individually Important Items in Compliance Testing[5]

21.21 When planning compliance testing for each major program, the auditor may use judgment to determine what items, if any, represent individually important items that may be individually tested and separated from the remaining population. Items of individual importance may be large, risky, or unusual items or transactions that contain characteristics of a prior compliance finding. Individually important items are those that, standing alone, are significantly different from the remainder of the population, for example, spikes in activity around a certain time period, such as journal entries made at the beginning or the close of a federal award. (See paragraph 21.27 for additional examples.)

21.22 Although the identification of individually important items is not required by the Uniform Guidance, there are benefits to taking advantage of testing individually important transactions if they exist in a particular population. Specifically, the application of auditor judgment and experience in examining a population for risky or unusual transactions may be more effective at identifying noncompliance than a randomly or haphazardly selected sample (see paragraphs 21.94–.96 for further discussion of random and haphazard sample selection). Furthermore, testing individually important items may reduce detection risk of noncompliance in that the individually important items that the auditor decides to test are not part of the population subject to audit sampling. As such, testing individually important items may reduce the sample size for the items remaining in the sampling population, or it may eliminate having to sample altogether because it targets those items that have the largest effect on noncompliance. For example, if 80 percent of the total federal award expenditures can be examined by testing the largest 10 expenditures, detection risk of noncompliance may be reduced such that the level of assurance needed from a sample of the remaining 20 percent of untested items will be lower.

21.23 It is important to note that the concept of identifying individually important items and focusing testing on a limited number of large or unusual items relates to compliance testing and not to testing internal control over compliance.

21.24 It is also important to clarify that a large number of transactions making up a significant percentage of the dollars expended or having a significant effect on compliance typically would not represent individually important items because individually important items are usually represented by only a relatively small number of items.

21.25 Identifying individually important items may involve discussions with auditees, analytical procedures such as scanning records (as described in paragraph 21.17), or using computer assisted auditing techniques. For example, in testing the Allowable Costs/Cost Principles type of compliance requirement, if there are a few very large expenditures, the auditor may deem these expenditures to be individually important.

21.26 Identifying individually important items may not be an efficient method when testing multiple types of compliance requirements at once

---

[5] The AICPA Audit Guide *Audit Sampling* uses the term *individually significant*, whereas this guide uses *individually important*. Note that in the context of individually important, there is no requirement for auditors to consider or test, or both, such items.

because an individually important item with respect to a particular type of compliance requirement may not necessarily be an individually important item for another type of compliance requirement. For example, it would not likely be appropriate to identify a few individually important items to test the Activities Allowed or Unallowed type of compliance requirement and then use the testing of those few items to support the auditor's conclusions relating to certain other direct and material compliance requirements.[6] It is likely that supplemental tests may be necessary to gather sufficient appropriate audit evidence related to compliance with other direct and material compliance requirements.

21.27 Additional examples of individually important items (and the relevant type of compliance requirement) might include the following:

- Transactions processed at the beginning or end of a federal award period (Activities Allowed or Unallowed, Period of Performance).
- Transactions processed at odd times in a cycle, such as new beneficiaries brought into a program in the spring when eligibility is usually granted only once a year during an enrollment period in the fall (Eligibility).
- Program beneficiaries that are near a qualifying age for benefits, or beneficiaries who have received multiple sources of funds (Eligibility).
- A federal award close-out report, as compared to routine financial or progress reports (Reporting).
- Transactions related to subrecipients that are awarded unusually high dollar amounts of pass-through funds compared with prior periods or other subrecipients in the same program (Subrecipient Monitoring).
- Transactions related to subrecipients that are new to the grantee, especially newly formed entities that have a relatively immature infrastructure to support compliance (Subrecipient Monitoring).
- Transactions processed in foreign countries that may contain higher risks, such as foreign currency risk or different payroll and human resources issues and laws in other countries that may affect allowable costs (Activities Allowed or Unallowed, Subrecipient Monitoring).
- Transactions that tests of internal control over compliance have indicated are either not subject to controls or are not being processed appropriately (multiple types of compliance requirements).
- A type of transaction for which there have been findings in the past.
- Transactions related to a specific step within the *OMB Compliance Supplement* (*Compliance Supplement*). For example, large

---

[6] AU-C section 935 defines *applicable compliance requirements* as the compliance requirements that are subject to the compliance audit. 2 CFR 200.514(d)(1) states that the auditor must determine whether the auditee has complied with federal statutes, regulations, and the terms and conditions of federal awards that may have a direct and material effect on each of its major programs. Therefore, in a Uniform Guidance compliance audit, the direct and material compliance requirements are those that are subject to audit. Accordingly, for the purpose of adapting AU-C section 935 to a Uniform Guidance compliance audit, the term *applicable compliance requirements* has been replaced by *direct and material compliance requirements* in this guide, except when directly citing content from AU-C section 935.

transfers of funds from program accounts which may have been used to fund unallowable activities (Activities Allowed or Unallowed).

21.28 The auditor should prepare appropriate documentation to support a clear understanding of the work performed on individually important items, which may include the rationale, selection criteria, results of testing, and effect on the planned testing of the remainder of the population.

Understanding and Testing the Operating Effectiveness of Controls Over Compliance

21.29 There are a variety of methods the auditor may use when performing risk assessment procedures, including inquiry, observation, inspection of documentary evidence, walkthrough, and reperformance of a process, that affect the auditor's understanding and testing of the operating effectiveness of controls. Although many procedures in which documentary evidence is examined or the auditor reperforms a control involve audit sampling, certain other methods may not involve sampling (for example, inspecting one or a few items to obtain an understanding of controls). Furthermore, paragraph .A29 of AU-C section 330, *Performing Audit Procedures in Response to Assessed Risks and Evaluating the Audit Evidence Obtained* (AICPA, *Professional Standards*), notes that the nature of the particular control influences the type of audit procedure necessary to obtain audit evidence about whether the control is operating effectively. For example, documentation of operation may not exist for some factors in the control environment, such as assignment of authority and responsibility. In such circumstances, audit evidence about operating effectiveness may be obtained through inquiry in combination with other audit procedures, such as observation.

21.30 Similarly, when testing internal control over compliance, the auditor does not use audit sampling when he or she applies an auditing procedure to one or a number of items relating to a control over a type of compliance requirement to clarify the auditor's understanding of the entity's internal control over compliance. For example, an auditor might trace several federal award expenditure transactions through an auditee's accounting system to obtain an understanding of the design of the auditee's internal control over compliance with respect to the federal award expenditures, such as approvals of the expenditures as an allowable activity, an allowable cost, or within the period of performance. In such cases, the auditor's intent is to gain a general understanding of the accounting system or other relevant parts of the internal control over compliance, rather than to evaluate a characteristic of all transactions processed. As a result, the auditor is not using audit sampling.

Planning Considerations for Sampling Related to Tests of Controls Over Compliance and Compliance Testing

Determining Audit Objectives

21.31 Paragraph 21.06 describes the audit objectives in a Uniform Guidance compliance audit. Proper definition and documentation of the audit objective precedes sampling design and execution. When designing an audit sample, the auditor should consider the purpose of the audit procedure (for example, to determine whether a necessary control was performed effectively or determine whether an expenditure charged to a federal award was allowable under the applicable cost principles).

21.32 The specific compliance audit objectives will differ for each type of compliance requirement. Part 3 of the *Compliance Supplement* lists and describes the 12 types of compliance requirements and the related audit objectives that the auditor should consider in a Uniform Guidance compliance audit.[7] Chapters 19–20 of this guide discuss the concepts involved in properly planning the testing of compliance and internal control over compliance.

Defining the Population and Considering Completeness

21.33 The population is defined in a manner consistent with the audit objective and the internal control and compliance attributes being tested. The auditor should determine that the sampling unit and the population from which units are selected for sampling is appropriate for the specific audit objective because sample results can be appropriately projected only to the population from which the sample was selected. For example, consider a situation when the auditor plans to test timesheets for proper authorization (that is, testing an internal control over the Activities Allowed or Unallowed type of compliance requirement) for a major program that involves multiple departments within an auditee. In defining the population, the auditor may first gain an understanding of how frequently timesheets are prepared and reviewed. Further, the auditor may also determine if the timesheets in the various departments within the auditee constitute one population or separate populations by considering whether the systems and controls for approval differ among the departments (for example, whether all supervisors approving timesheets attend a uniform training session) or other factors that would affect the definition of the control. There are also situations when a time period may define a sampling population (for example, for the Period of Performance type of compliance requirement, the *Compliance Supplement* defines certain time periods as a sampling population).

21.34 The sampling population includes the items constituting the transactions of interest for an audit objective related to a particular control or a type of compliance requirement after removing transactions tested with nonsampling techniques (for example, individually important items or a subset of items that are tested 100 percent). It is possible that the appropriate sampling population may only be a subset of the universe of transactions subject to a particular control or compliance requirement. For example, the universe of transactions within an expenditure pool may be defined by the auditor as multiple populations when transaction processing and the operation of related controls are decentralized.

21.35 The types of expenditures related to an audit objective are also an important factor in determining whether further division of the population may be necessary to achieve the stated objective. For example, the controls over the Allowable Costs/Cost Principles type of compliance requirement may vary depending on whether the expenditure is a direct (other than payroll), indirect, or payroll expenditure.

---

[7] Chapter 24, "Program-Specific Audits (Uniform Guidance)," of this guide discusses program-specific audits and the use of federal program specific audit guides and other methods for determining compliance requirements and related audit objectives in a program-specific audit.

Audit Sampling Considerations of Uniform Guidance Compliance Audits

21.36 An auditee might change a specific control or compliance procedure during the period under audit. The auditor should obtain audit evidence about the nature and extent of any significant changes in internal control and may need to revise the audit plan. Chapter 3, "Nonstatistical and Statistical Audit Sampling in Test of Controls," of the AICPA Audit Guide *Audit Sampling* discusses additional considerations when there are changes in processes and procedures during the period under audit as well as important sampling considerations if testing is conducted at an interim date.

21.37 The auditor should select items for the sample in such a way that the auditor can reasonably expect the sample to be representative of the relevant population. If the physical or electronic representation (for example, a printout or electronic file purportedly containing all expenditures) and the desired population differ, the auditor might make erroneous conclusions about the population. To verify the completeness of a population, the auditor could, for example, reconcile the population to accounting or other relevant records or to the schedule of expenditures of federal awards, or perform other procedures to verify the population is complete. Populations relevant for a Uniform Guidance compliance audit test may not consist of accounting records (for example, eligibility files for a particular major program do not directly relate to a financial statement amount). Regardless, the auditor should develop and perform audit procedures sufficient to conclude that the population includes all the transactions of interest for the specific audit objective.

21.38 If an initial sample does not include a particular attribute being tested, it may be an indication that the sampling population was not defined properly. For example, an initial sample may have been selected from a schedule of financial assistance that did not include a listing of students who were enrolled part-time or students enrolled in correspondence study. However, to meet the audit objective, the auditor would need to include such students in the testing. The auditor may consider maintaining the original sample and adding a selection of students who were enrolled part-time or in correspondence study to the sample. The number of additional items to be added is a matter of professional judgment. In the previous example, the auditor may consider consistency of student financial assistance processing controls, number of students who were enrolled part-time or enrolled in correspondence study, and other considerations from the risk assessment process to determine whether to reevaluate the original population or add items with the needed attribute.

Sampling Unit

21.39 The sampling unit may be defined by any of the individual elements constituting the population. Each sampling unit constitutes one item in the population. In a Uniform Guidance compliance audit, a sampling unit might be a cash disbursement, student file, refund paid, financial report due during a fiscal year, or a cost transfer made during the year.

21.40 The definition of the sampling unit depends on the audit objective and the nature of the audit procedures being applied. For example, a sampling unit for a test of controls related to the Activities Allowed or Unallowed type of compliance requirement may be a payment voucher, a journal entry, or another document that includes evidence of approval or review of the allowability of the expenditure. Note that each sampling unit may provide evidence of the application of more than one control. For example, a voucher package may provide support that the amounts were checked for accuracy; the contractor was checked for suspension and debarment; the expenditure was for an allowable activity under the federal award and for an allowable cost under the Uniform Guidance; and the expenditure was incurred and obligated within the period of performance of the federal award.

21.41 In order to properly define the sampling unit, it is also important that the auditor determine how the auditee maintains its records (for example, by participant, by program, by location). Based on the nature of the records, the auditor may then properly design a method to define the sampling unit and identify the sampling population.

Considering Multiple Major Programs

21.42 It is very common for auditees to have multiple major programs. Auditees may use the same controls for a particular type of compliance requirement (for example, Allowable Costs/Cost Principles) for more than 1 federal program. If the auditee's internal control for a type of compliance requirement is common to more than 1 major program, the transactions of those programs may be combined into 1 population for determining sample size and making sample selections for internal control tests. If the initial sample (taken from a combined population) does not include items from each major program, the auditor typically will judgmentally add additional items from the program(s) from which items were not selected.[8] Alternatively, the auditor may plan the initial combined sample to draw items from each major program. For example, consider a situation in which an auditee has common internal controls over the Allowable Costs/Cost Principles type of compliance requirement relating to 3 major programs. If, in this example, the auditor decides to use a combined sample of 60 items and the programs are of similar size, the auditor may select 20 items from each of the 3 major programs. If the major programs are not of similar size, the sample may be allocated proportionately. In considering whether samples selected from across multiple programs can be designed for dual purposes, see paragraph 21.43, as well as a discussion of dual purpose testing at paragraphs 21.52–.57.

21.43 The auditor is required to obtain sufficient appropriate audit evidence to support an opinion on compliance for each major federal program. Experience has shown that it is preferable to select separate samples for compliance testing from each major program because the separate samples provide clear evidence of the compliance tests performed, the results of those tests, and the conclusions reached. Thus, unlike tests of controls over compliance, compliance testing is typically performed on samples selected with each major program considered a separate population. If an auditor believes a compliance sample can be selected from a population consisting of multiple major programs, an important aspect of the documentation includes how the results relate to separate programs and how that evidence, together with other audit evidence, is sufficient to support the auditor's opinion on compliance for each major program.

Considering Multiple Organizational Units

21.44 Auditors may have additional sampling considerations when the auditee has operations in multiple organizational units (for example, operating

---

[8] If an initial sample does not include a major program, it could also indicate that the physical representation (for example, a printout or electronic file purportedly containing all expenditures) of the population used to draw the sample was incomplete, see paragraphs 21.33–.38.

units, locations, or branches). Each organizational unit may maintain separate internal control over compliance that is relevant to the programs, or parts of programs, which the unit administers. In these situations, the auditor should consider the understanding of internal control over compliance to determine whether to define each organizational unit as a separate population. (Chapter 19 of this guide discusses internal control over compliance in multiple organizational units.) For a discussion of multiple organizational unit considerations related to compliance, please refer to chapter 20 of this guide.

21.45 If controls over compliance or compliance procedures at the various organizational units vary significantly, it may be necessary for each location to be considered a separate population. When transactions relating to types of compliance requirements are processed in organizational units using the same controls[9] or compliance procedures are performed under common oversight and monitoring, it may be feasible for the auditor to obtain sufficient appropriate audit evidence about controls and compliance for major programs by selecting one overall sample across the organizational units (for example, selecting from centralized locations or visiting all organizational units). When it is not feasible to obtain the evidence centrally or to visit all the organizational units, and controls or compliance procedures, or both, are the same across organizational units, the auditor generally will select some organizational units from which to obtain audit evidence. In this case, the auditor may consider (*a*) testing the minimum sample size at each location of significance (or more than the minimum sample size depending on the results of risk assessment procedures preceding sampling) or (*b*) varying the selection of the less significant organizational units included in the testing from year to year. Appendix E, "Multilocation Sampling Considerations," of the AICPA Audit Guide *Audit Sampling* provides useful guidance in determining the appropriate organizational unit to visit, as well as implications on sample size.

Considering Clusters of Programs

21.46 The audit opinion on a cluster of programs is for the cluster as a whole and not each individual Catalog of Federal Domestic Assistance (CFDA) number, award, and so forth that makes up the cluster. Chapter 15, "Overview of the Single Audit Act, the Uniform Guidance Audit Requirements, and the *Compliance Supplement*," of this guide further discusses clusters of programs. When sampling involves a cluster of programs, the auditor should consider whether, in the auditor's judgment, sufficient appropriate audit evidence has been gathered for the direct and material types of compliance requirements relating to the clustered programs as a whole. Random or haphazard selection (further discussed in paragraphs 21.94–.96) of sample items from the cluster generally would be expected to provide a representative sample.

21.47 There may be instances when the initial sample does not appear to be representative because it does not include items relating to certain direct and material types of compliance requirements for CFDA numbers, awards, and so forth within the cluster. In this case, the auditor's determination of what additional evidence is needed requires professional judgment. Factors

---

[9] When evaluating whether multiple organizational units use the same controls, *same* does not mean *identical*. The auditor may consider the important elements of the control, such as the control activity and related monitoring, as well as the differences in experience and training of the individuals processing or monitoring the compliance transaction when determining if the controls are the *same* or if there are significant variances.

that may be considered by the auditor in determining whether to supplement the original sample include the consistency of processing controls over the various programs within the cluster, the volume of transactions and the size of expenditures for a particular program as a component of the overall cluster being tested, the complexity of the compliance requirements, and the past history of compliance. As with other forms of audit testing, the auditor should document the objective of the cluster testing and the sample design.

21.48 An alternative approach to selecting sample items in a cluster, if auditee records permit, may be for the auditor to analyze the components of the cluster transactions (for example, expenses) and federal awards prior to selecting the sample and then to allocate the number of selections from the sample to the transactions or programs in proportion to the overall cluster. This alternative may be difficult to execute depending on how the auditee keeps their records.

Considering the Effect of Population Size

21.49 The size of the population has little or no effect on the determination of sample size, except in relatively small populations of 250 items or fewer. Some significant controls, or instances of complying with a compliance requirement, occur infrequently. For example, controls over reporting may operate only 4, 12, 24, or 52 times a year. Paragraphs 21.86–.89 provide sample sizes for small populations.

Defining Control Deviation and Compliance Exception Conditions[10]

21.50 Based on the auditor's understanding of internal control over compliance and compliance requirements, an auditor generally will identify the characteristics that would indicate performance of the control or compliance with the compliance requirement to be tested. The auditor may then define the possible deviation or exception conditions. For tests of controls, a deviation is a departure from the expected performance of the prescribed control. For compliance testing, an exception is a departure from federal statutes, regulations, and the terms and conditions of federal awards being tested. Defining a deviation or exception for each audit objective assists the auditor executing the procedures to properly identify deficiencies in internal control over compliance and instances of noncompliance.

21.51 In a Uniform Guidance compliance audit, the auditor should consider the nature and cause of the internal control deviations and compliance exceptions identified in testing. The auditor should determine whether the deviation(s) or exception(s) constitutes a finding and whether the sampling evidence, in combination with other testing, might affect the auditor's opinion on compliance. See the discussion regarding evaluation of sample results beginning at paragraph 21.106 for more information.

Dual Purpose Sample Considerations

21.52 In some circumstances, the auditor might design a test that uses a *dual purpose* sample. The most common dual purpose approach in a Uniform

---

[10] In this chapter, the term *deviation* is associated with control testing, and the term *exception* is associated with compliance testing.

Guidance compliance audit is testing the operating effectiveness of a control and testing whether the auditee complied with relevant federal statutes, regulations, or terms and conditions of federal awards using the same sample. For example, subrecipient monitoring often can be tested with a dual purpose sample. If the sampling unit is a subrecipient reimbursement request, the documentation may contain evidence of review by the pass-through entity (for example, signature) and compliance with monitoring activities. When utilizing a dual purpose sample for internal control and compliance testing, it is important that the test objectives align to the same sampling unit and population (that is, the population being sampled is appropriate for the tests being applied to it). As stated in paragraph 21.33, an auditor should determine that the population from which the sample is selected is appropriate for the specific audit objectives being executed. The size of a sample designed for a dual purpose test will usually be the larger of the samples that would otherwise have been designed if the control and compliance samples were performed separately.

21.53 When testing both the operating effectiveness of a control and whether the auditee complied with a type of compliance requirement, the basis for the auditor's evaluation of the control is the operation of the control and not just whether the auditee complied. Further, a control that is not properly applied to a transaction may not necessarily lead to noncompliance. As such, the auditor may reach different conclusions on controls and compliance for the same sample item (for example, report a significant deficiency or material weakness in internal control over compliance but not a compliance-related finding).

21.54 In evaluating the result of dual purpose tests, audit findings should be evaluated separately for the control attributes and the compliance attributes tested. In planning the tests of compliance, the auditor should use the knowledge obtained of the relevant portions of internal control over compliance to identify types of potential noncompliance, to consider factors that affect the risk of material noncompliance, and to design appropriate tests of compliance. Thus, deviations resulting from tests of controls, including when those control tests are part of a dual purpose sample, may result in a larger compliance sample than originally planned for the related type of compliance requirement due to the increased risk posed by the deficiency in internal control over compliance.

21.55 As described in chapter 20 of this guide, the auditor's documentation of internal control and compliance tests should be distinguished from one another so there is a clear distinction between the audit objectives and test results for each test so that separate conclusions may be reached on the internal control attributes and compliance attributes tested.

21.56 Another example of using a sample for multiple purposes is when auditors wish to use a single sample for testing for both Uniform Guidance compliance audit objectives and financial statement audit objectives. Such an approach may present additional complexities to consider because often there are different characteristics, and even different appropriate populations, for single audit and financial statement audit tests. Although many auditees record federal award transactions within their general ledgers, populations used for financial statement purposes often do not align well with sampling populations for testing in a Uniform Guidance compliance audit. The same principles described previously for a dual purpose sample apply when a single sample is used to achieve both Uniform Guidance compliance audit and financial statement audit objectives.

21.57 Although it is challenging to select samples that achieve both Uniform Guidance compliance audit and financial statement objectives, they do occur. An example of a sample that achieves both Uniform Guidance compliance audit and financial statement audit objectives is a sample of transactions inspected to determine the following:

- Indications of compliance with relevant federal statutes, regulations, and compliance requirements over allowable costs and cost principles
- Indications of performance of internal controls over both allowable costs and cost principles and appropriateness of the expense for financial reporting
- Evidence that the recorded amount, account, and period are correct for financial reporting

Determining the Sample Size

21.58 This section discusses suggested minimum sample sizes as well as factors auditors may consider when using judgment to determine appropriate sample sizes. Because the objectives for tests of controls and tests of compliance are different, there are different factors to consider when determining sample sizes; thus, sample sizes should be considered separately for internal control testing and compliance testing. Audit documentation typically includes the inputs and assumptions for sample sizes to support each sample for every direct and material type of compliance requirement in which sampling is used. Documentation is discussed in more depth in paragraphs 21.131–.135.

Control Testing Sample Size Table and Inputs

21.59 If the auditor determines that internal control over compliance is effectively designed and implemented (as discussed in chapter 19 of this guide), the Uniform Guidance requires that the auditor plan the audit to support a low assessed level of control risk for the assertions relevant to the compliance requirements for each major program. This requires the auditor to plan to obtain a high level of assurance that controls operate as designed. Therefore, generally, samples for control tests are designed to achieve a 90 percent to 95 percent confidence level. (See AICPA Audit Guide *Audit Sampling* for further discussion of confidence levels.) Because there are typically few other procedures that provide evidence of the effectiveness of controls, the sample size table that follows is designed to provide a high level of assurance. Table 21-1 provides suggested minimum sample sizes for very and moderately significant controls with limited to higher inherent risk of material noncompliance in a major program (see discussions of these terms that follow as well as a discussion of inherent risk of noncompliance in chapter 16 of this guide).

Table 21-1

Control Testing Sample Size Table

Significance of Control and Inherent Risk of Compliance Requirement	Minimum Sample Size
0 deviations expected	
Very significant and higher inherent risk	60
Very significant and limited inherent risk or Moderately significant and higher inherent risk	40
Moderately significant and limited inherent risk	25

The previous sample size table is appropriate for sampling from populations of 250 items or greater. Small population testing guidance is discussed in paragraphs 21.86–.89.

21.60 The suggested minimum sample sizes are designed to provide sufficient appropriate audit evidence that controls are operating effectively in many Uniform Guidance compliance audit testing situations. However, auditors may need to use professional judgment to determine if larger sample sizes are warranted in order to obtain sufficient appropriate audit evidence that controls are functioning in their particular circumstances. For example, there may be additional risks (for example, change in the design of the control or change in personnel operating the control), or the auditor may expect deviations (see discussion that follows). It is important to recognize that if controls are not deemed effective, further control testing may not be warranted. In such situations when internal control over some or all of the compliance requirements for a major program is not deemed effective, refer to chapter 19 of this guide for further guidance.

Significance of Control Being Tested

21.61 The auditor may vary the type or amount of evidence obtained regarding the effectiveness of individual controls selected for testing based on the significance associated with the control. All controls that the auditor determines are to be tested to mitigate the risk of material noncompliance are significant controls, but a spectrum exists concerning the significance of each control. An important factor in determining the significance of a control is the potential magnitude of noncompliance (both qualitatively and quantitatively) if the particular control were to fail. The auditor should use the information gathered by performing the risk assessment procedures, including the audit evidence obtained in evaluating the design of controls and determining whether they have been implemented as audit evidence to support the risk assessment. The risk assessment should be used to determine the nature, timing, and extent of further audit procedures to be performed for each control selected for testing as well as to assist the auditor in determining what controls are very significant or moderately significant because minimum sample sizes differ (due to different desired confidence levels and tolerable deviation rates).

21.62 The higher and more pervasive the risk relating to a given control objective (that is, "what could go wrong" risk), the greater the need for assurance on relevant preventive and detective controls to achieve a specific control objective, and the more likely it is that the auditor will assess greater significance to the related controls. Several factors may be considered in determining the significance level of a control, including whether the program is identified as higher risk in the *Compliance Supplement* and the potential magnitude of noncompliance to the program. For example, with respect to the Allowable Costs/Cost Principles type of compliance requirement, if payroll is a large portion of the expenditures (in volume or dollars, or both) for the program, then the major control points related to payroll more likely would be considered very significant. However, for a program for which payroll is a smaller portion of the expenditures, these controls may be considered moderately significant or potentially not significant to the program.

21.63 A factor that may cause a control to be considered moderately significant is the existence of other complementary, compensating, or redundant controls. If the auditor plans the control testing level assuming reliance on complementary, compensating, or redundant controls, the auditor should obtain sufficient appropriate audit evidence on the effectiveness of the complementary, compensating, or redundant controls. This means that multiple controls necessary to achieve the control objective will be tested for operating effectiveness. In that case, each control may be tested as a moderately significant control.

21.64 If the auditor identifies that a tested control does not operate effectively, the auditor may subsequently become aware of the existence of complementary, compensating, or redundant controls that, if effective, may limit the severity of the deficiency of the original tested control and prevent it from being a significant deficiency or material weakness in internal control over compliance. In these circumstances, the auditor may consider the effects of complementary, compensating, or redundant controls provided the auditor obtains sufficient appropriate audit evidence that such controls are effective. This means that multiple controls would be tested for operating effectiveness.

Inherent Risk of Noncompliance Factors

21.65 Factors that may suggest higher inherent risk of noncompliance include the following (See also chapter 16 of this guide.):

- New program with little history with compliance requirement
- The phase of the program in its life cycle at the auditee (for example during the first and last years the risk may be higher due to start-up or closeout of program activities and staff)
- The phase of the program in its life cycle at the federal agency (for example, a new federal program with new or interim regulations may have a higher risk than an established program)
- The complexity of the program
- Complex processing (for example, nonroutine versus routine, nonsystematic versus systematic, manual versus programmed) or judgment
- The extent to which the auditee contracts with outside parties for goods and services related to compliance (for example, a third party disburses funds or applies eligibility criteria)
- Significant deficiencies or material weaknesses in internal control over compliance observed in the past

Audit Sampling Considerations of Uniform Guidance Compliance Audits

- Correspondence from program officials indicating potential problems
- Lack of adherence to applicable federal statutes and regulations or the terms and conditions of the federal award in prior years
- High employee turnover in a particular area
- Very high volume of activity
- Substantial change in the policies, processes, or personnel associated with the compliance requirement
- Significant changes in federal statutes, regulations, or the terms and conditions of federal awards
- The program has been identified as higher risk by the OMB in the *Compliance Supplement*

It is important to note that the size of the program does not necessarily affect the potential for noncompliance. The presence of one or more of the factors listed previously may lead the auditor to determine that there is higher inherent risk of noncompliance; however, the auditor uses professional judgment to determine whether the number and combination of risk factors present higher or limited inherent risk of material noncompliance.

21.66 In order to properly apply the sampling tables illustrated in this chapter, it is useful to understand the inputs and assumptions underlying the suggested minimums (that is, confidence level, tolerable deviation rate, and expected deviation rate). These items are discussed in the following section, and the AICPA Audit Guide *Audit Sampling* provides an extensive discussion of the concepts.

Confidence Level and Tolerable Deviation Rate

21.67 Although the sample sizes in table 21-1 are all designed to provide a high level of assurance, the inputs for the three sample sizes differ in terms of confidence level and tolerable deviation rate.[11] The *tolerable deviation rate* for control tests is the maximum rate of deviation from a prescribed control that auditors are willing to accept without altering the planned assessed level of control risk of noncompliance. Auditors seeking a high level of assurance related to controls (low control risk of noncompliance) from a test of control often set a risk of overreliance of 10 percent or less with a tolerable deviation rate of 10 percent or less. The more significant the control, the higher the required performance of the control (that is, the lower the tolerable deviation rate). A higher desired level of assurance (that is, higher desired confidence level) results in a larger sample size to provide the appropriate assurance. In assessing the tolerable deviation rate, the auditor may consider that although deviations from pertinent controls increase the risks of material noncompliance, such deviations do not always result in noncompliance.

Expected Deviation Rate

21.68 For Uniform Guidance compliance audits, the auditor often plans for zero deviations in the sample. The sample sizes in the previous table are

---

[11] The suggested minimum sample sizes are consistent with sample sizes provided in tables A-1 and A-2 of appendix A in the AICPA Audit Guide *Audit Sampling*. Although the sample sizes are consistent with statistically-based tables, the sample sizes provided in this chapter can be used for either statistical or nonstatistical sampling.

based on an expectation of zero deviations in the sample and a high level of assurance. If testing discovers no deviations, then a high degree of assurance is achieved that the control is being performed at an acceptable level to be effective. When more deviations are encountered than were planned for, the auditor has not met the planned audit objective.

21.69 All deviations (whether expected or not) should be investigated to determine the potential effect on the program. Although not all deviations will lead to a finding, this guidance is written from the perspective of planning for zero deviations in the sample. Auditors may develop their own sample sizes with planned deviations. The AICPA Audit Guide *Audit Sampling* provides tables and guidance for auditors desiring to design audit samples when deviations are expected.[12] See paragraphs 21.100–.108 for discussion relating to when deviations are found in a sample.

Compliance Testing Sample Size Table and Inputs

21.70 The auditor typically performs a broad array of procedures to provide a reasonable basis for expressing an opinion on compliance for each major program. In a Uniform Guidance compliance audit, just as in a financial statement audit, other audit procedures typically precede compliance audit sampling. For example, risk assessment procedures typically precede substantive procedures. Similarly, it is common for some controls-related procedures to be conducted prior to compliance testing (for example, understanding and testing the control environment). Before designing a compliance audit sample, it is also common for the auditor to consider whether there are individually important items that may be selected for testing prior to selecting a compliance sample. (See paragraphs 21.21–.28.) The auditor should consider other audit procedures (for example, analytical procedure discussed in paragraphs 21.14–.17) when determining the appropriate sample size for compliance testing.

21.71 The risk of material noncompliance consists of inherent risk of noncompliance and control risk of noncompliance. The assurance required from a compliance sample and, therefore, the determination of the minimum compliance sample size, depends on the risk of material noncompliance remaining after other audit procedures (for example, risk assessment procedures, controls testing, substantive analytical procedures, tests of individually important items) have been executed. If the auditor gathers evidence that controls over compliance are effective through tests of controls, and other audit procedures do not identify instances of noncompliance or identify specific heightened risk factors, and the auditor determines that additional testing via audit sampling is warranted, it is likely the remaining risk of material noncompliance would be low or moderate. Conversely, if tests of controls identify control deficiencies in the controls over compliance or other audit procedures identify instances of noncompliance or identify specific heightened risk factors, it may lead the auditor to assess the remaining risk of material noncompliance as high or moderate.

---

[12] If internal control over compliance is deemed likely to be ineffective, the Uniform Guidance states that the auditor should assess control risk at the maximum and consider whether any additional compliance tests are required because of ineffective internal control. See paragraphs 21.63–.64 regarding the consideration of compensating or redundant controls. If no compensating or redundant controls are operating effectively, the auditor also should report a significant deficiency or material weakness in internal control over compliance as part of the audit findings. (Chapter 23, "Auditor Reporting Requirements and Other Communication Considerations in a Single Audit (Uniform Guidance)," discusses the reporting of significant deficiencies and material weaknesses.)

21.72 Table 21-2 provides suggested minimum sample sizes associated with high, moderate, and low remaining risk of material noncompliance. The remaining risk of material noncompliance is an indicator of the desired level of assurance. A high remaining risk of material noncompliance indicates that a high level of assurance is desired to meet the audit objective. Desired level of assurance is discussed in more depth in paragraphs 21.76–.81.

Table 21-2

Compliance Testing Sample Size Table

Desired Level of Assurance (Remaining Risk of Material Noncompliance)	Minimum Sample Size
0 exceptions expected	
High	60
Moderate	40
Low	25

The previous sample size table is appropriate for sampling from populations of 250 items or greater. For smaller populations, see testing guidance in paragraphs 21.86–.89.

21.73 The minimum sample sizes in the previous table may be applied for each direct and material compliance requirement for each major program.[13] Although the minimum sample sizes suggested in the table often provide the appropriate extent of testing, auditors may use professional judgment to determine if larger sample sizes are warranted in order to obtain sufficient appropriate audit evidence in particular circumstances. Depending on the nature of the compliance requirement, the results of other procedures performed during the audit, and the risks and complexities of the sampling population, there may be situations when larger sample sizes would be more appropriate than the proposed minimum sample sizes. For example, if there were significant deficiencies or material weaknesses noted with the related controls, the auditor may expand testing to support the conclusion on compliance.

21.74 The sample sizes provided in the table are based on an expectation of zero exceptions and varying levels of assurance or confidence. A higher remaining risk of material noncompliance results in a need for a higher level of assurance (that is, a higher desired confidence level) and a larger sample size. Each type of compliance requirement tested should be evaluated separately for purposes of determining sample size. If the appropriate sample size is tested and no exceptions are discovered, then the planned degree of assurance has been obtained.

21.75 Many Uniform Guidance compliance audits will include a spectrum of compliance testing sample sizes, meaning that some types of compliance requirements may present a high remaining risk of material noncompliance and, thus, would require a sample that provides high assurance, whereas other types of compliance requirements may present a low remaining risk of material noncompliance.

---

[13] See footnote 11.

Desired Level of Assurance

21.76 When planning a particular sample, the auditor should consider the relationship of the sample to the audit objective. Thus, to the extent each compliance test has a different objective, samples should be separately considered. As noted in the compliance testing sample size table, the primary determinant of the appropriate minimum sample size for a particular compliance test is the risk of material noncompliance remaining after considering other audit procedures (for example, risk assessment, control testing, testing individually important items, substantive analytical procedures) and, therefore, the desired level of assurance.

21.77 The desired level of assurance or confidence from a compliance sample varies as the types of compliance requirements differ in importance and risk. There is also a broad array of audit procedures the auditor may use that contribute to the overall evidence of compliance. There is general consensus across audit sampling applications that high assurance is typically associated with 90 percent to 95 percent confidence levels. The confidence levels associated with moderate and low in the compliance table are considered appropriate in compliance testing associated with a Uniform Guidance compliance audit.

21.78 As discussed previously, the basis for expressing an opinion on compliance for each major program often is based on multiple procedures. Although the combined totality of audit evidence gathered by the auditor should be sufficient to support a high level of assurance, an auditor may not need to design compliance samples to achieve high assurance when there are other sources of evidence beyond the compliance sample.

21.79 In evaluating the desired level of assurance, the auditor may consider the importance of the type of compliance requirement, inherent risk of noncompliance factors, the risk of fraud, and the results from tests of the operating effectiveness of controls for the type of compliance requirement. For example, if the auditor has obtained evidence that controls over compliance are properly designed and operating effectively to reduce the likelihood of material noncompliance, the auditor may assess the remaining risk of material noncompliance as moderate or low and similarly reduce the desired level of assurance from the compliance sample. A lower remaining risk of material noncompliance results in a need for a lower level of assurance from the sample and a smaller sample size. On the other hand, if tests of controls indicated that controls are not operating effectively and the auditor is not able to support a low assessed level of control risk of noncompliance for the major program, the auditor must assess control risk of noncompliance at the maximum. Maximum control risk of noncompliance may result in higher remaining risk of material noncompliance, and the desired level of assurance from the compliance test also increases to moderate or high to support an unmodified opinion on the auditee's compliance.[14]

21.80 As noted in the prior paragraph, the risk of material noncompliance is affected by the inherent risk of noncompliance for the particular type of compliance requirement. There are many factors that can affect inherent risk of noncompliance, for example, the regulatory environment, the significance of

---

[14] However, if during the testing of the compliance sample, the auditor finds sufficient evidence of noncompliance to support an opinion other than unmodified, the auditor is not required to test remaining or additional items.

the particular requirement to the overall program, the complexity of relevant regulations, changes in regulations, or the experience the auditee has with the federal program. In assessing the remaining risk of material noncompliance, the engagement team may also consider the results of procedures performed in connection with the audit of the financial statements.

21.81 Auditors, in assessing inherent risk of noncompliance, typically assess risk factors associated with the types of compliance requirements being tested. Further, there are general risk factors which may suggest the need to obtain a higher level of assurance from an audit sample. Examples of such risk factors are discussed in paragraph 21.65. Audit risk of noncompliance considerations, including inherent risk of noncompliance, are also discussed in chapter 16 of this guide.

Tolerable Exception Rate

21.82 The tolerable exception rate for compliance tests is the maximum rate of compliance exceptions that auditors are willing to accept. The tolerable exception rate for all types of compliance requirements is related to program materiality. Materiality is considered in relation to each major program. The quantitative thresholds used to determine if an exception is an "audit finding" related to a major program is lower than the materiality used for planning the Uniform Guidance compliance audit and expressing an opinion on the auditee's compliance. (Materiality is also discussed in chapters 16 and 18, "Determination of Major Programs (Uniform Guidance)," of this guide.)

21.83 The determination of major program materiality is a matter of professional judgment. The tolerable exception rate for a compliance sample testing nonmonetary compliance attributes (for example, Reporting type of compliance requirement) as well as monetary compliance attributes (for example, Allowable Costs/Cost Principles type of compliance requirement) is normally equal to or lower than the level of materiality for expressing an opinion on the auditee's compliance with requirements having a direct and material effect on each major program. For example, if program materiality is determined to be 5 percent of program expenditures, then the tolerable exception rate for a compliance sample testing monetary attributes would be 5 percent or less. Similarly, if a 5 percent exception rate for a nonmonetary compliance attribute is considered material, then the tolerable exception rate for compliance sample testing that nonmonetary attribute would be 5 percent or less. The compliance testing sample size table is based on a 5 percent tolerable exception rate for both nonmonetary and monetary attributes. If program materiality is set lower than 5 percent, then the tolerable exception rate would be lowered, and the minimum sample sizes may need to be adjusted upward. The AICPA Audit Guide *Audit Sampling* provides tables and guidance for auditors desiring to design audit samples for different tolerable exception rates.

Expected Population Exception Rate

21.84 The compliance testing sample size table is based on an expectation of no exceptions. If no exceptions are discovered in testing, then the desired level of assurance is obtained about compliance. When more exceptions are encountered than were planned for, the auditor has not met the planned audit objective. Auditors may develop their own sample sizes with planned exceptions. Appendix A of the AICPA Audit Guide *Audit Sampling* provides tables and guidance for auditors desiring to design audit samples when exceptions are expected.

21.85 All exceptions (whether planned or not) should be investigated to determine the potential effect on the program. Although not all exceptions will lead to a finding, the auditor should evaluate compliance exceptions (whether planned or not) for their nature and cause to determine the potential effect on the program.

Testing Small Populations

21.86 Some significant controls, or instances of complying with a compliance requirement, occur infrequently (for example, submitting a required report). Table 21-3 provides suggested minimum sample sizes in testing small populations subject to controls and compliance requirements.[15] *Small populations*, for purposes of this chapter, are defined as populations of fewer than 250 items.

Table 21-3

Small Population Sample Size Table

Frequency and Population Size	Sample Size
Quarterly (4)	2
Monthly (12)	2–4
Semimonthly (24)	3–8
Weekly (52)	5–9

21.87 For populations between 52 and 250 items, a rule of thumb some auditors follow is to test a sample size of approximately 10 percent of the population, but the size is subject to professional judgment, which would include specific engagement risk assessment considerations.

21.88 For more significant controls discussed in paragraphs 21.61–.64, or for more significant types of compliance requirements, the auditor may determine the appropriate sample size is on the larger end of the ranges displayed in the small population sample size table.

21.89 The auditor may consider the size of the population by reference to the defined sampling unit. For example, in some cases, the auditor may need to consider the populations from several locations or organizational units; if there were weekly controls over the occurrence of expenses at each of 40 departments, the population of weekly expense test controls would be 2,080 (52 × 40), and this would not be a small population.

Selecting Sample Items for Testing

21.90 Once the population of transactions or items relevant for a control or type of compliance requirement is identified, the auditor may select items

---

[15] The table is adapted from table 3-5, "Testing Operating Effectiveness of Small Population," in the AICPA Audit Guide *Audit Sampling*.

Audit Sampling Considerations of Uniform Guidance Compliance Audits 559

for testing from a physical or electronic representation of the population. For example, a physical representation might be a printout of expenditures for the period.

21.91 The auditor should select items for the sample in such a way that the auditor can reasonably expect the sample to be representative of the relevant population and likely provide the auditor with a reasonable basis for conclusions about the population. The goal of sample selection, a representative sample, is the same for both nonstatistical and statistical sampling. For statistical sampling, it is necessary to use an appropriate random sampling method, such as simple random sampling or systematic sampling. In nonstatistical sampling, the auditor uses a sample selection approach that approximates a random sampling approach.[16] Please note that the *Compliance Supplement* provides specific guidance on sample selection for certain types of major programs.[17]

21.92 As noted previously in the discussion on determining the appropriate sampling population, it is common for control testing samples to be drawn from a population that contains multiple major programs (assuming common controls, policies, procedures, and competence of personnel). Experience has shown that it is preferable to select separate compliance samples from each major program because the separate samples provide clear evidence of the tests performed, the results of those tests, and the conclusions reached, which support the auditor's opinion on compliance for each major program.

21.93 An overview of selection methods follows. For nonstatistical sampling, the auditor may select the sample using any of the three techniques that follow. However, the haphazard selection technique is not appropriate for statistical sampling. The AICPA Audit Guide *Audit Sampling* contains additional guidance on applying the techniques discussed in the following paragraphs as well as additional sampling techniques, such as block and sequential.

Random Selection

21.94 Random selection provides an equal chance of selection to each sampling item in the population. To perform this selection, the auditor may select a random sample by matching random numbers generated by a computer or selected from a random number table or by generating random numbers with software such as Microsoft Excel or commercial audit software packages.

Haphazard Selection

21.95 The haphazard selection technique represents the auditor's best attempt at making a random selection judgmentally without the use of a structured selection technique (for example, random numbers or tables). It is the selection of sampling units without any intentional bias, that is, without any special reasoning for including or omitting items from the sample. Haphazard selection does not consist of selecting sampling units in a careless manner. For example, when the physical representation of the population of all vouchers

---

[16] A properly designed nonstatistical sampling application that considers the same factors that would be considered in a properly designed statistical sample can provide results that are as effective as those from a properly designed statistical sampling application. Please see the AICPA Audit Guide *Audit Sampling* for further discussion of nonstatistical and statistical sampling.

[17] For example, the *OMB Compliance Supplement* provides guidance on how to select items in a research and development cluster that includes multiple federal agencies and award types.

processed for the period under audit is a file cabinet drawer of vouchers, a haphazard sample might include any of the vouchers that the auditor haphazardly pulls from the drawer, regardless of each voucher's size, shape, location, or other physical features.

21.96 The auditor using haphazard selection is normally careful to avoid distorting the sample by selecting, for example, only large, only unusual, only convenient, or only physically small items or by omitting such items as the first or last in the physical representation of the population. The goal is to select a sample without bias. Although haphazard sampling is useful for nonstatistical sampling, it is not appropriate for statistical sampling because it does not allow the auditor to measure the probability of selecting a combination of sampling units.

Systematic Selection With a Random Start

21.97 Systematic selection with a random start determines a uniform interval by dividing the number of physical units in the population by the sample size. A starting point is randomly selected in the first interval, and 1 item is selected throughout the population at each of the uniform intervals from the starting point. For example, if the auditor wishes to select 60 items from a population of 12,000 items, the uniform interval is every 200th item. The auditor randomly selects the first item from within the first interval and then selects every 200th item from the random start.

21.98 If the deviation pattern is random, then systematic selection is equivalent to simple random selection. In the absence of a known pattern in the population, it is a practical and efficient alternative to simple random selection, particularly when items are being selected manually from a population.

Performing the Test Procedures

21.99 After the sampling plan has been designed, and the auditor has selected the sample, if the auditor is not able to apply the planned audit procedures or appropriate alternative procedures to selected items, the auditor should consider the reasons for this limitation and should ordinarily consider those selected items to be control deviations or compliance exceptions from the prescribed policy or procedure for the purpose of evaluating the sample. Additional guidance on performing the sampling plan, including how to handle sample items that are voided documents, unused or inapplicable documents, or documents that cannot be located, can be obtained in chapter 3 of the AICPA Audit Guide *Audit Sampling*.

Investigate and Understand the Nature and Cause of Control Deviations and Compliance Exceptions

21.100 In addition to providing an auditor's opinion on compliance for each major program, the Uniform Guidance requires the auditor to report on deficiencies in internal control over compliance which constitute significant deficiencies or material weaknesses in internal control over compliance. The Uniform Guidance also requires the auditor to report known questioned costs when the likely questioned costs are $25,000 or more.[18] Thus, whenever

---

[18] See footnote 3 in paragraph 21.08 for further discussion on *known questioned costs* and *likely questioned costs*.

a control deviation or a compliance exception is identified, the auditor should evaluate the nature and cause of the deviation or exception. Understanding the potential effect on the program will assist the auditor in determining whether sufficient appropriate evidence has been obtained to support the auditor's opinion on compliance and whether to report an internal control finding, compliance finding, or both.

21.101 In evaluating deviations and exceptions, the auditor may consider factors such as the following:

- *Systematic nature of the deviation or exception.* If a control deviation or compliance exception is systematic in nature, it is more likely to lead to a finding than if the deviation or exception is contained to a subset of the population testing. Guidance regarding deviations or exceptions believed to be nonsystematic is provided in paragraphs 21.106–.130.

- *Intentional deviation or exception.* The discovery of fraud requires a broader consideration of the possible implications than does the discovery of a deviation or exception attributable to a mistake or lack of understanding.

- *Pattern relative to past history.* Control deviations or compliance exceptions observed in the current audit that are similar in nature to deviations or exceptions that led to a finding or material noncompliance in past audits typically increases the likelihood that a finding will be reported, or that there is material noncompliance in the current year. The nature of the pattern may lead the auditor to perform additional tests to determine the effect of the deviation or exception. Further, an auditee's failure to correct previously identified deficiencies in internal control over compliance or compliance exceptions is also a relevant factor in the evaluation consideration.

Determine If Additional Testing Is Warranted in Response to an Observed Deviation or Exception

21.102 If exceptions are found and the likely questioned cost is close to the audit materiality level for a major program or the audit finding reporting threshold of $25,000, the auditor may conduct additional tests to better substantiate the likely questioned costs. In addition, if findings occur in a particular risky area of a major program, additional testing may be warranted to substantiate the compliance opinion.

21.103 The sample sizes in the controls and compliance sample size tables are based on an expectation of zero deviations or exceptions. The auditor may encounter an unexpected deviation or exception rate in a sample from a population that was expected to be deviation- or exception-free or to have a low incidence of deviation or exception. In such cases, it is important for the auditor to recognize that the sample is expected to be representative only with respect to the occurrence rate or incidence of deviations or exceptions, not their nature or cause. An unexpected deviation or exception may be indicative of other deviations or exceptions in the population. When the auditor, expecting a negligible or zero deviation or exception rate, selected a small sample and found a deviation or exception rate slightly higher than expected, and the auditor believes the deviation or exception rate observed does not represent a reportable finding, it may be appropriate to extend the sample from that population, but the appropriate extension would not be small. More guidance on dealing with negligible exception rates is provided in the AICPA Audit Guide *Audit Sampling*.

21.104 In some instances, the auditor's understanding of the nature and cause of the deviation or exception may suggest the sample deviation or exception rate is not likely to be representative of the population (that is, it is not a systematic error). In such instances, the auditor may consider whether to pursue additional evidence to indicate that the sample deviation or exception rate is not representative of the entire population (that is, the error can be contained to a specific subpopulation). To conclude that a deviation or exception is nonsystemic typically requires the auditor to perform additional audit procedures to obtain sufficient appropriate audit evidence that the actual deviation or exception rate experienced in the sample is not representative of the deviation or exception rate in the population.

21.105 When the decision regarding reporting a finding is not straightforward, the auditor may consider reporting deviations and exceptions as findings and letting the appropriate officials of the federal awarding agency or pass-through entity investigate further.

Evaluating Sample Results

Evaluating Control Deviations

21.106 Whether the sample is statistical or nonstatistical, the auditor should investigate the nature and cause of such deviations and evaluate the possible effect on the purpose of the audit procedure and on other areas of the audit.

21.107 The controls sample size table in paragraph 21.59 is based on an expectation of zero deviations. When more deviations are encountered than were planned for, the auditor has not met the planned audit objective. In other words, although the auditor needs a *tolerance*, or tolerable deviation rate, in order to plan a sample, the observance of a deviation rate as high as the tolerable rate in a sample is not acceptable due to sampling risk (discussed in the following).

21.108 As previously discussed, when a control deviation is identified, the auditor should evaluate the nature and cause of the deviation. Control deviations should be evaluated to determine whether they are significant deficiencies or material weaknesses in internal control over compliance.

Calculating the Control Deviation Rate

21.109 Calculating the deviation rate in the control test sample involves dividing the number of observed deviations by the sample size. For example, if 3 deviations are observed in a sample of 60, the deviation rate is 5 percent (3/60). The deviation rate in the sample is the auditor's best estimate of the deviation rate in the population from which it was selected. Because the purpose of testing is generally to confirm the reliability of the control, it is common to assume that controls are effective when designing the audit plan. Thus, deviations observed in the sample are often important to the auditor's compliance testing strategy, depending on the deviation rate and reasons for the deviation.

Audit Sampling Considerations of Uniform Guidance Compliance Audits

Considering Sampling Risk Associated With Control Testing

21.110 When evaluating a sample for a test of controls, the auditor should give appropriate consideration to *sampling risk*—the risk that the auditor's conclusions based on a sample may be different from the conclusion if the entire population were subjected to the same audit procedure. If the estimate of the population deviation rate (the sample deviation rate) is less than the tolerable deviation rate for the population, the auditor should consider the risk that such a result might be obtained even if the true deviation rate for the population exceeds the tolerable rate for the population.

21.111 If an auditor performs a statistical sampling application, the auditor might use a table or computer program to assist in measuring the allowance for sampling risk. If the auditor performs a nonstatistical sampling application, sampling risk may not be directly measurable; however, it is generally appropriate for the auditor to conclude that the sample results do not support the planned assessed level of control risk of noncompliance if the rate of deviation identified in the sample exceeds the expected population deviation rate used in designing the sample (which is zero in the control testing sample size table in this guide).

21.112 The control sample size table is based on an expectation of zero deviations. When more deviations are encountered than were planned for, the auditor has not met the planned audit objective, and there is likely to be an unacceptably high risk that the true deviation rate in the population exceeds the tolerable rate due to sampling risk. In such a circumstance, after considering the reasons for the control deviation(s) and the number of deviations identified, the auditor may conclude it is appropriate to expand the test or perform other tests to include sufficient additional items to reduce control risk to an acceptable level.[19] Rather than testing additional items, however, it is often more efficient in a Uniform Guidance compliance audit to report a deficiency in internal control over compliance and, when testing compliance, to increase the auditor's assessed level of remaining risk of material noncompliance and increase the extent of compliance testing to reflect the change in the control risk of noncompliance assessment.

Assessing the Potential Magnitude of a Deficiency in Internal Control Over Compliance

21.113 If the auditor finds deviations, he or she determines whether they are deficiencies in internal control over compliance and, if so, whether those deficiencies are material weaknesses, significant deficiencies, or just deficiencies in internal control over compliance. AU-C section 265, *Communicating Internal Control Related Matters Identified in an Audit* (AICPA, *Professional Standards*), requires the auditor to consider the likelihood and magnitude of deficiencies, individually or in combination. (See chapter 19 of this guide.)[20]

---

[19] Additional guidance on expanding the sample is provided in chapter 3, "Nonstatistical and Statistical Audit Sampling in Tests of Controls," of the AICPA Audit Guide *Audit Sampling*.

[20] When the deficiency in internal control over compliance relates to monetary values, chapter 3 of the AICPA Audit Guide *Audit Sampling* provides an approach to quantifying the potential magnitude of monetary exposure to noncompliance.

Reaching an Overall Conclusion on Tests of Controls

21.114 The overall conclusion about the effect that the evaluation of the sample results will have on the assessed level of control risk of noncompliance, the risks of material noncompliance, and, thus, on the nature, timing, and extent of planned compliance tests requires professional judgment. If the sample results, along with other relevant audit evidence, support the planned low assessed level of control risk of noncompliance, the auditor may have no need to modify planned compliance tests. If a low assessed level of control risk of noncompliance is not supported, the auditor should consider either performing further tests of other controls that could result in supporting the planned level of control risk of noncompliance or increasing the assessed level of control risk of noncompliance and altering the nature, timing, or extent of the planned compliance tests accordingly.

21.115 Additional guidance regarding whether there is evidence of a finding, significant deficiency, or material weakness in internal control over compliance is found in chapters 19 and 23, "Auditor Reporting Requirements and Other Communication Considerations in a Single Audit (Uniform Guidance)," of this guide.

Evaluating Compliance Exceptions

21.116 Exceptions observed in a sample are important to the auditor's compliance testing strategy and should be evaluated to determine whether to report findings of material noncompliance. Further, compliance findings may affect the opinion on the auditee's compliance with the compliance requirements that could have a direct and material effect on major programs. Whether the sample is statistical or nonstatistical, the auditor should evaluate the nature and cause of the noncompliance to reach an overall conclusion on compliance with a particular type of compliance requirement.

Calculating the Compliance Exception Rate or Likely Questioned Costs

21.117 For nonmonetary compliance attributes, calculating the exception rate in the compliance test sample involves dividing the number of observed exceptions by the sample size. For example, if 3 exceptions are observed in a sample of 60, the exception rate is 5 percent (3/60). The exception rate in the sample generally is the auditor's best estimate of the exception rate in the population from which it was selected.

21.118 Although compliance testing in a Uniform Guidance compliance audit often involves monetary amounts, the focus of the testing is on whether or not there is evidence of compliance to support the auditor's opinion on compliance. Additionally, when noncompliance is discovered related to monetary transactions of a program, the Uniform Guidance requires the auditor to determine both known questioned costs and likely questioned costs associated with the audit finding. The estimation of likely questioned costs may require the projection of sample results to determine the effect on the auditor's opinion on compliance and whether an audit finding is required to be reported in the Schedule of Findings and Questioned Costs.[21] The auditor is not required to expand his or her test work to definitively determine the total questioned costs because there is no requirement in the Uniform Guidance to report an exact

---

[21] See footnote 3 in paragraph 21.08 for more information.

Audit Sampling Considerations of Uniform Guidance Compliance Audits

amount or a statistical projection of likely questioned costs. Rather, the Uniform Guidance requires the auditor to consider the effect of likely questioned costs on the auditor's opinion on compliance and include an audit finding when the auditor's estimate of likely questioned costs is greater than $25,000.

21.119 As noted previously, the auditor should evaluate the finding to calculate an estimate of likely questioned costs in order to determine whether likely questioned costs exceed $25,000. For example, the auditor specifically identifies $7,000 in known questioned costs for a type of compliance requirement but, based on his or her projection of the exception to the population, develops an estimate that the total likely questioned costs are approximately $60,000. In that case, based on the $60,000 of likely questioned costs, the auditor must report an audit finding that identifies the known questioned costs of $7,000. Chapter 23 of this guide further discusses reporting findings based on likely questioned costs. If likely questioned costs exceed program materiality, the auditor may consider modifying the audit opinion on compliance for that program (chapter 16 of this guide further discusses materiality considerations as it relates to opining on major programs).

21.120 There are two approaches commonly used to project compliance results to a monetary population. First, if the monetary compliance exceptions are 100 percent errors (for example, the entire sampling unit contains all allowable or unallowable cost), from a population of similar sized transactions, the same exception rate technique discussed previously for nonmonetary compliance attributes can be applied to the population of dollars to estimate the likely questioned costs. For example, if 3 exceptions are observed in a sample of 60, the exception rate is 5 percent (3/60). Assuming the 3 exceptions were 100 percent errors, and the population is made up of homogeneous transactions, the 5 percent exception rate would be applied to the total population monetary value to estimate likely questioned costs. Continuing the example, if the total value of the sampling population was $1,000,000, then the likely questioned costs would be $50,000.

21.121 The second approach to projecting compliance sample results to the population applies the noncompliance or questioned cost rate of dollar noncompliance observed in the sample to the population. For example, an auditor might have selected a sample that sums to $15,000 and observed known questioned costs of $450, or 3 percent of the recorded amount of the expenditures tested. If the total recorded amount in the expenditures population is $1,000,000, then projected likely questioned cost is $30,000 ($1,000,000 × 3%). This approach is especially useful when a sampling unit is found to be only partially incorrect.

21.122 See the AICPA Audit Guide *Audit Sampling* for additional methods to calculate the compliance exception rate or likely questioned costs.

Considering Sampling Risk Associated With Compliance Testing

21.123 When evaluating a sample for a test of compliance, the auditor should give appropriate consideration to sampling risk. If the estimate of the population exception rate (the sample exception rate) for nonmonetary attributes is less than the tolerable exception rate for the population, or if the estimate of likely questioned costs is less than tolerable error for a monetary population, the auditor might consider the risk that such a result might be obtained even if the true exception rate or questioned costs for the population exceeds the tolerable rate or tolerable error, respectively, for the population.

21.124 If an auditor performs a statistical sampling application, the auditor might use a table or computer program to assist in measuring the allowance for sampling risk. If the auditor performs a nonstatistical sampling application, sampling risk may not be directly measurable; however, it is generally appropriate for the auditor to conclude that the sample results do not support an acceptable level of compliance if the rate of exception or likely questioned costs identified in the sample exceeds the expected exception rate used in designing the sample (which is zero in the compliance testing sample size table in this guide).

21.125 The compliance sample size table in paragraph 21.72 is based on an expectation of zero exceptions. When more exceptions are encountered than were planned for, the auditor has not met the planned audit objective, and there is likely to be an unacceptably high risk that the true exception rate in the population exceeds the tolerable rate due to sampling risk. In such a circumstance, after considering the reasons for the compliance exception(s) and the number and magnitude of exception(s) identified, the auditor may conclude it is appropriate to expand testing or perform other tests to include sufficient additional items to reduce the risk of material noncompliance to an acceptable level.[22] Alternatively, rather than expand the scope of testing to improve the precision of the projected error, the auditor may consider it prudent to report the exceptions as a finding and evaluate the effect that the sample result has on the assessed level of risk of material noncompliance and the overall compliance opinion.

21.126 In evaluating whether an exception is a finding, it is particularly important to consider sampling risk when the projected likely cost is close to the reporting threshold of $25,000. The auditor would generally conclude that there is an unacceptable risk that the true questioned costs exceeds the reporting threshold. Even when the projected likely questioned costs are considerably less than the reporting threshold, the auditor should consider the risk that such a result might be obtained even though the true questioned costs for the population exceeds the reporting threshold (allowance for sampling risk). The smaller the sample, the greater the associated uncertainty or sampling risk associated with that sample.

Effect of Compliance Testing Results on Internal Control Results Reporting

21.127 The auditor should relate the evaluation of the compliance testing sample to other relevant audit evidence when forming a conclusion about compliance as well as internal control over compliance. If compliance testing results in exceptions, the auditor should relate this testing to the results of tests of internal control. A compliance exception is an indicator of a potential deficiency in internal control over compliance.

Reaching an Overall Conclusion on Tests of Compliance

21.128 The overall conclusion about the effect that the evaluation of the sample results has on his or her assessed level of risk of material noncompliance and, thus, on the overall Uniform Guidance compliance audit opinion, requires the auditor to use professional judgment. If the sample results, along with

---

[22] Additional guidance on expanding the sample is provided in chapter 3 of the AICPA Audit Guide *Audit Sampling*.

Audit Sampling Considerations of Uniform Guidance Compliance Audits

other relevant audit evidence, support other than an unmodified opinion, the auditor should modify the opinion accordingly.

21.129 For nonmonetary compliance attributes (for example, a report is submitted on a timely basis), the auditor should document noted exceptions and consider the guidance contained in the Uniform Guidance to determine if the finding should be included in the Schedule of Findings and Questioned Costs in the Uniform Guidance compliance audit reporting package. For monetary attributes, the auditor should also document noted exceptions (and any related questioned costs), and if the known or likely questioned cost exceeds $25,000, the auditor must report the finding.

21.130 When the auditor finds a compliance exception that, in itself, does not meet the criteria of a finding, the auditor would typically gain assurance that the exception may, indeed, be omitted from the Schedule of Findings and Questioned Costs. Although the Uniform Guidance does not require the auditor to expand his or her sample in the case of exceptions, there may be additional procedures performed to support the conclusion that the exception is not a finding, for example if the questioned costs are close to the reporting threshold of $25,000. In all cases when an initial exception is determined not to be a finding, the auditor should document the rationale for omitting the exception from the Schedule of Findings and Questioned Costs.

Documenting the Sampling Procedure

21.131 According to paragraph .40 of AU-C section 935, the auditor should document his or her responses to the assessed risks of material noncompliance, the procedures performed to test compliance with applicable compliance requirements,[23] and the results of those procedures, including any tests of controls over compliance. The following paragraphs provide information related to documenting sampling procedures and the results of such procedures as it applies to a compliance audit.

21.132 As noted in chapter 3, "Planning and Performing a Financial Statement Audit in Accordance With *Government Auditing Standards*," of this guide, AU-C section 230, *Audit Documentation* (AICPA, *Professional Standards*), provides requirements and guidance on the form, content, extent, retention, and confidentiality of audit documentation. AU-C section 230 contains guidance on documenting significant findings or issues; identifying the preparer and reviewer of audit documentation; documenting specific items tested; documenting departures from relevant Statements on Auditing Standards; revising audit documentation after the date of the auditor's report; and ownership and confidentiality of audit documentation. Among other things, AU-C section 230 states that an auditor should prepare audit documentation that is sufficient to enable an experienced auditor, having no previous connection to the audit, to understand the following:

- The nature, timing, and extent of auditing procedures performed to comply with generally accepted auditing standards and applicable legal and regulatory requirements (for example, *Government Auditing Standards* and the Uniform Guidance)

---

[23] See footnote 6 in paragraph 21.26.

- The results of the audit procedures performed and the audit evidence obtained
- Significant findings or issues arising during the audit, the conclusions reached thereon, and significant professional judgments made in reaching those conclusions

21.133 In addition to the requirements found in AU-C section 230, *Government Auditing Standards* includes several additional audit documentation requirements that are described in chapter 3 of this guide.

21.134 The form and extent of documentation related to sampling are influenced by numerous factors, which may include the size and complexity of the auditee, the nature and complexity of the auditee's internal control over compliance, the nature and complexity of the compliance requirements, and the auditee's past experience relative to compliance.

21.135 Although AU-C section 230, AU-C section 530, and this guide do not contain a list of specific documentation requirements for audit sampling applications, examples of items that the auditor typically documents include the following:

- A description of the control or type of compliance requirement being tested
- A definition of the population and the sampling unit, including how the auditor considered the completeness of the population (discussed in paragraphs 21.33–.41)
- A definition of the deviation or exception condition (discussed in paragraphs 21.50–.51)
- The desired confidence or assurance level, the tolerable deviation or exception rate, and the expected population deviation or exception rate[24] (as discussed in paragraphs 21.58–.89)
- The chosen sample size[25]
- The sample selection method such as random, haphazard, or systematic selection (as discussed in paragraphs 21.90–.98)
- The selected sample items, which would include identifying characteristics of the specific items tested, clear documentation to support both controls and compliance testing when dual purpose testing is applied (as discussed in paragraphs 21.52–.57), and resolution of any documents that cannot be located (as discussed in paragraph 21.99). Paragraph .A14 of AU-C section 230 provides several alternatives regarding how an auditor can identify selected sample items in audit documentation
- An evaluation of the sample, including the following:

---

[24] Use of a sample size from the tables in this chapter provides adequate documentation of the underlying inputs to the table (that is, tolerable deviation or exception rate, confidence, and expected deviation or exception rate). However, the support for the sample size used within the range provided, which depends on factors such as the significance of the control tested or the remaining risk of material noncompliance, is based on auditor judgment and is not implicit in the tables and, thus, is important in documenting the sampling applications and procedures.

[25] See footnote 24. Similarly, if an auditor determines a sample size using other than the suggested minimums from the tables in this chapter (for example, some audit organizations may use their own internal guidance that results in a sample size that is slightly different from the tables in this chapter), the basis for that determination would also be important in documenting the sampling applications and procedures.

- The number of deviations or exceptions found in the sample
- Important qualitative aspects of the deviation(s) or exception(s)
- The projected population deviation or exception rate
- A determination of whether the sample results support the test objective
- The effect of the evaluation on other audit procedures (for example, if tests of controls do not allow the auditor to support a low assessed level of control risk of noncompliance for major programs, consideration of the effect on subsequent tests of compliance)
- The auditor's determination of known questioned costs and estimation of likely questioned costs
- A determination whether observed deviation(s) or exception(s) require a modification of the auditor's opinion on compliance or will result in a finding and, if not, how the auditor considered sampling risk (as discussed in paragraphs 21.106–.130)

- Any qualitative factors considered significant in making the sampling, selections, assessments, and judgments, which may include multiple major programs, multiple organizational units, clusters, or other factors
- A summary of the overall conclusion (if not evident from the results)

Transition Considerations Related to the Uniform Guidance

21.136 The "Transition Considerations Related to the Uniform Guidance" in chapters 16 and 20 of this guide contain important information about the effective date of the Uniform Guidance and how it will affect auditor planning and compliance testing in a Uniform Guidance compliance audit. Refer to that guidance for more details. As noted in those sections, a major program may include expenditures from both federal awards subject to the pre-Uniform Guidance requirements, as well as federal awards subject to the post-Uniform Guidance requirements. This situation could exist for several years until the pre-Uniform Guidance awards have been completely expended. When testing major program transactions, identification of the date of a federal award related to a particular expenditure is needed in order to determine the applicable criteria to use for the transaction being tested. It should be noted that a separate sample for pre-Uniform Guidance award transactions and post-Uniform Guidance award transactions within a major program would not typically be needed in this situation. However, this guide recommends that when testing major program transactions that the audit documentation for testing compliance and internal control over compliance include an identification of the transactions tested that were subject to post-Uniform Guidance requirements.

21.137 An example of how the effective date of the Uniform Guidance may impact sampling in the Uniform Guidance compliance audit follows and is intended to assist the auditor in understanding the challenges in a compliance audit during the transition period. Assume a test for compliance with the Allowable Costs/Cost Principles type of compliance requirement indicates a sample size of 60 expenditure transactions. Some of the transactions in the sample may be subject to post-Uniform Guidance requirements, while others may be subject to pre-Uniform Guidance requirements. Identification of the date of a federal award related to a particular expenditure transaction is needed in order to determine the applicable criteria to use for the transaction being tested. Although, as noted previously, a separate sample would not typically be needed in this situation, the Allowable Costs/Cost Principles criteria for transactions subject to the post-Uniform Guidance requirements may be different from the criteria for transactions subject to the pre-Uniform Guidance requirements. In this example, the auditor would use both Part 3.1 and Part 3.2 of the *Compliance Supplement* to test this type of compliance requirement. See the "Transition Considerations Related to the Uniform Guidance" section in chapter 20 of this guide for more information about changes to Part 3 of the *Compliance Supplement*.

Chapter 22

Audit Considerations of Federal Pass-Through Awards (Uniform Guidance)

> **Update 22-1: Audits of Federal Awards**
>
> This chapter, and the remaining chapters of part III, *Uniform Guidance Audits*, of this guide, should be used for performing a compliance audit of federal awards under the audit requirements of Title 2 U.S. *Code of Federal Regulations* (CFR) Part 200, *Uniform Administrative Requirements, Cost Principles, and Audit Requirements for Federal Awards* (Uniform Guidance).[1] Part II, *Circular A-133 Audits*, of this guide should be used for performing a compliance audit under Office of Management and Budget (OMB) Circular A-133, *Audits of States, Local Governments, and Non-Profit Organizations* (Circular A-133). See the transitional guidance sections at the end of each chapter that highlight important matters for consideration. Additionally, refer to the preface of this guide for more information.
>
> **Important Effective Date Information**
>
> In December 2013, the OMB issued the Uniform Guidance, which is effective for nonfederal entities for all federal awards and certain funding increments provided on or after December 26, 2014. The requirements in Subpart F, "Audit Requirements," are effective for audits of fiscal years beginning on or after December 26, 2014, with no early implementation permitted. Therefore, auditees subject to a single audit with December 25, 2015, and later year ends (for example, December 31, 2015) will be required to undergo the audit under Subpart F of the Uniform Guidance. Note that audits of fiscal years ending prior to the effective date of the Uniform Guidance audit requirements are subject to an audit under Circular A-133.

Introduction

22.01 Many nonfederal entities receiving federal awards make pass-through payments of federal awards to other entities that are considered subrecipients. The amount of those payments may be material to the pass-through entity's financial statements,[2] individual major programs, or both. This chapter discusses the auditor's consideration of pass-through federal awards in an audit of federal awards under the Uniform Guidance as it relates to both pass-through entities and subrecipients. It also discusses the auditee's and auditor's responsibilities with respect to activities carried out by contractors. An auditee

---

[1] See the information found at the end of this chapter (paragraph 22.50), and other part III, *Uniform Guidance Audits*, chapters of this guide, for transition considerations when performing an audit under Title 2 U.S. *Code of Federal Regulations* (CFR) Part 200, *Uniform Administrative Requirements, Cost Principles, and Audit Requirements for Federal Awards* (Uniform Guidance). Transition considerations can also be found at the end of certain part II, *Circular A-133 Audits*, chapters as it relates to an audit performed under Office of Management and Budget (OMB) Circular A-133, *Audits of States, Local Governments, and Non-Profit Organizations*.

[2] As discussed in the AICPA Audit and Accounting Guide *State and Local Governments*, the auditor's consideration of materiality for purposes of planning, performing, evaluating the results of, and reporting on the audit of the financial statements of a state or local government is based on opinion units. See that guide for further guidance.

with multiple federal funding agreements may be a pass-through entity in regard to some awards, a subrecipient in regard to other awards, and a contractor with respect to other agreements.

Definitions

22.02 The Uniform Guidance includes the following definitions that are relevant to pass-through awards:

- **federal award.** Federal financial assistance that a nonfederal entity receives directly from a federal awarding agency or indirectly from a pass-through entity, or a federal cost-reimbursement contract under the Federal Acquisition Regulations that a nonfederal entity receives directly from a federal awarding agency or indirectly from a pass-through entity. The term may also refer to the instrument setting forth the terms and conditions which is the grant agreement, cooperative agreement, federal financial assistance, or cost-reimbursement contract. It does not include other contracts that a federal agency uses to buy goods or services from a contractor or a contract to operate federal government owned, contractor operated facilities.
- **subaward.** An award provided by a pass-through entity to a subrecipient for the subrecipient to carry out part of a federal award received by the pass-through entity. It does not include payments to a contractor or payments to an individual that is a beneficiary of a federal program. A subaward may be provided through any form of legal agreement, including an agreement that the pass-through entity considers a contract.
- **nonfederal entity.** A state, local government, Indian tribe, institution of higher education, or non-profit organization (not-for-profit entity or NFP) that carries out a federal award as a recipient or subrecipient.
- **recipient.** A nonfederal entity that receives a federal award directly from a federal awarding agency to carry out an activity under a federal program. This term does not include subrecipients.
- **pass-through entity.** A nonfederal entity that provides a subaward to a subrecipient to carry out part of a federal program.
- **subrecipient.** A nonfederal entity that receives a subaward from a pass-through entity to carry out part of a federal program but does not include an individual who is a beneficiary of such program. A subrecipient may also be a recipient of other federal awards directly from a federal awarding agency.
- **contract.** A legal instrument by which a nonfederal entity purchases property or services needed to carry out the project or program under a federal award. It does not include a legal instrument, even if the nonfederal entity considers it a contract, where the substance of the transaction meets the definition of a federal award or subaward.
- **contractor.** An entity that receives a contract.

Applicability of the Uniform Guidance for Federal Awards

22.03 The Uniform Guidance applies to both recipients expending federal awards received directly from federal awarding agencies and subrecipients

Audit Considerations of Federal Pass-Through Awards (Uniform Guidance)

expending federal awards received from a pass-through entity. Accordingly, both recipients and subrecipients that expend $750,000 or more in federal awards are required to have a single or program-specific audit in accordance with the Uniform Guidance. (Chapter 24, "Program-Specific Audits (Uniform Guidance)," of this guide discusses program-specific audits.)

22.04 The determination of when a federal award is expended must be based on when the activity related to the award occurs. Generally, the activity pertains to events that require the nonfederal entity to comply with federal statutes, regulations, and the terms and conditions of federal awards. With respect to federal awards passed through to subrecipients, the activity that requires pass-through entities to comply with federal statutes, regulations, and the terms and conditions of federal awards is the disbursement of funds to subrecipients. The activity that requires subrecipients to comply with federal statutes, regulations, and the terms and conditions of federal awards is the expenditure of a subaward.

22.05 Payments received by a contractor for goods or services provided in connection with a federal program are not considered federal awards. Furthermore, Medicaid payments to a subrecipient for providing patient care services to Medicaid-eligible individuals are not considered federal awards expended under the Uniform Guidance unless a state requires the funds to be treated as federal awards expended because reimbursement is on a cost-reimbursement basis.

22.06 When a pass-through entity provides a federal award to a subrecipient, the pass-through entity must monitor the activities of the subrecipient as necessary to ensure that the subaward is used for authorized purposes, in compliance with federal statutes, regulations, and the terms and conditions of the subaward. As part of the Uniform Guidance compliance audit, the auditor of the pass-through entity should test and report on subrecipient monitoring (which is 1 of the 12 types of compliance requirements in the *OMB Compliance Supplement (Compliance Supplement)*, as discussed in chapter 20, "Compliance Auditing Applicable to Major Programs (Uniform Guidance)," of this guide) when federal awards passed through to subrecipients are material to a major program (see paragraphs 22.26–.38). If the federal awards provided are immaterial to a major program or relate to a program that is not considered major, the auditor of the pass-through entity has no additional compliance auditing responsibilities related to the funds passed through to subrecipients.

22.07 Most of this chapter focuses on Uniform Guidance compliance auditing considerations for auditors of pass-through entities. However, paragraphs 22.46–.49 provide additional considerations for auditors of subrecipients.

Emphasis Point

The use of the term *must* in the Uniform Guidance indicates a requirement. This is consistent with the use of the term *must* in generally accepted auditing standards (GAAS) and *Government Auditing Standards*. The use of the term *should* in the Uniform Guidance indicates a best practice or recommended approach. However, GAAS and *Government Auditing Standards* use the term *should* to indicate a presumptively mandatory requirement. An auditor must comply with a presumptively mandatory requirement in all cases in which such a

(continued)

> requirement is relevant, except in rare circumstances. In this guide, the term ***should***, when italicized and bolded, indicates a best practice or recommended approach in the Uniform Guidance. This is intended to differentiate it from the term *should* used throughout the guide to refer to presumptively mandatory requirements in GAAS and *Government Auditing Standards*. See chapter 1, "Introduction and Overview of *Government Auditing Standards*," of this guide for more information regarding presumptively mandatory requirements.

Pass-Through Entities, Subrecipients, and Contractors

Subrecipient Status Versus Contractor Status

22.08 A nonfederal entity may concurrently receive federal funds as a recipient, subrecipient, and contractor, depending on the substance of its agreements with federal awarding agencies and pass-through entities. Therefore, a pass-through entity must make case-by-case determinations whether each agreement it makes for the disbursement of federal program funds casts the party receiving the funds as a subrecipient or a contractor. In addition, the federal awarding agency may supply, and require recipients to comply with, additional guidance to support these determinations provided that guidance does not conflict with the Uniform Guidance. The responsibilities for compliance with federal program requirements and the direct and material compliance requirements[3] to be tested by the auditor may be significantly different depending on whether the entity is a pass-through entity, subrecipient, or contractor. 2 CFR 200.330 of Subpart D, "Post Federal Award Requirements Standards for Financial and Program Management," provides guidance on distinguishing between a subrecipient and a contractor; paragraphs 22.09–.11 summarize that guidance.

Characteristics Indicative of a Subrecipient

22.09 According to the Uniform Guidance, characteristics that support the classification of the nonfederal entity as a subrecipient include when the nonfederal entity

- determines who is eligible to receive what federal assistance;
- has its performance measured in relation to whether objectives of a federal program were met;
- has responsibility for programmatic decision making;
- is responsible for adherence to applicable federal program requirements specified in the federal award; and
- in accordance with its agreement, uses the federal funds to carry out a program for a public purpose specified in authorizing

---

[3] AU-C section 935, *Compliance Audits* (AICPA, *Professional Standards*), defines *applicable compliance requirements* as the compliance requirements that are subject to the compliance audit. 2 CFR 200.514(d) states that the auditor must determine whether the auditee has complied with federal statutes, regulations, and the terms and conditions of federal awards that may have a direct and material effect on each of its major programs. Therefore, in a Uniform Guidance compliance audit, the direct and material compliance requirements are those that are subject to audit. Accordingly, for the purpose of adapting AU-C section 935 to a Uniform Guidance compliance audit, the term *applicable compliance requirements* has been replaced by *direct and material compliance requirements* in this guide except when directly citing content from AU-C section 935.

Audit Considerations of Federal Pass-Through Awards (Uniform Guidance)

statutes, as opposed to providing goods or services for the benefit of the pass-through entity.

Paragraph 22.12 provides examples of the relationship between pass-through entities and subrecipients.

Characteristics Indicative of a Contractor

22.10 According to the Uniform Guidance, the characteristics indicative of a procurement relationship between the nonfederal entity and a contractor are when the nonfederal entity receiving the federal funds

- provides the goods and services within normal business operations;
- provides similar goods or services to many different purchasers;
- normally operates in a competitive environment;
- provides goods or services that are ancillary to the operation of the federal program; and
- is not subject to the compliance requirements of the federal program as the result of the agreement, though similar requirements may apply for other reasons.

Paragraph 22.13 provides examples of the relationship between recipient and contractors.

Use of Judgment in Determining Subrecipient or Contractor Status

22.11 The Uniform Guidance states that in determining whether an agreement between a pass-through entity and another nonfederal entity casts the latter as a subrecipient or a contractor, the substance of the relationship is more important than the form of the agreement. All of the characteristics listed in paragraphs 22.09–.10 may not be present in all cases, and the pass-through entity must use judgment in classifying each agreement as a subaward or a procurement contract. In some cases, it may be difficult for the pass-through entity to determine whether the relationship with the entity is that of a subrecipient or a contractor. The federal cognizant agency for audit, the oversight agency for audit, or the federal awarding agency may be of assistance to the pass-through entity in making those determinations.

Description of Relationships

Pass-Through Entity and Subrecipient

22.12 Following are examples of a typical relationship between a pass-through entity and a subrecipient:

- A state department of education (pass-through entity) receives a federal award and is responsible for administering and disbursing the federal award to local school districts (subrecipients) according to a formula or on some other basis.
- A regional planning commission (pass-through entity) receives a federal award for the feeding of elderly and low-income individuals, and the award is disbursed to NFPs (subrecipients) to support their feeding programs.

- A university (pass-through entity) receives a federal award, and the award is disbursed to a governmental hospital (subrecipient) to conduct research.
- A state arts commission (pass-through entity) receives a federal award, and the award is disbursed to an NFP theater group (subrecipient) to support a summer arts series.

Recipient and Contractor

22.13 Following are examples of a typical relationship between a recipient and a contractor:

- A local government (recipient) receives a federal award to provide mental health services in a designated area. Some of the funds are paid to a construction company (contractor) to repair a leaking roof.
- A county (recipient) receives a federal award to operate a Head Start program and pays an NFP (contractor) to provide temporary clerical services.
- An NFP (recipient) receives a federal award to run a preschool and pays a medical doctor (contractor) to perform health screening on a per-student basis.
- An NFP (recipient) receives a federal award to operate a child care center and pays an NFP clinic (contractor) to perform physical exams.

Entity Is Both a Subrecipient and a Pass-Through Entity

22.14 Instances occur in which an entity can be both a subrecipient and a pass-through entity, as shown in the following examples:

- A local government receives a pass-through federal award from a state government agency (the local government is a subrecipient) and further passes through a portion of the federal award to an NFP (the local government also is a pass-through entity) to administer a federal program.
- An NFP area agency receives a pass-through federal award from a state (the NFP area agency is a subrecipient) and further passes through a portion of the federal award to a for-profit health care provider (the NFP area agency also is a pass-through entity). Paragraph 22.43 discusses a pass-through entity's responsibilities when the subrecipient is a for-profit entity.

Contractor Compliance Considerations

Auditee's Responsibilities

22.15 The Uniform Guidance provides that in most cases, the auditee's compliance responsibility for contractors is only to ensure that the procurement, receipt, and payment for goods and services comply with federal statutes, regulations, and the terms and conditions of federal awards. Federal award compliance requirements normally do not pass through to a contractor. However, the auditee is responsible for ensuring compliance for procurement transactions that are structured such that the contractor is responsible for program compliance or the contractor's records must be reviewed to determine program compliance.

22.16 Furthermore, when an auditee engages a contractor to perform work related to compliance with federal awards, the auditee may assign tasks related to compliance to the contractor. For example, an auditee may engage a contractor to collect information the auditee uses to make eligibility determinations and maintain a system to support eligibility determinations and store related data. Using the contractor for this purpose does not relieve the auditee of its responsibility for ensuring compliance for eligibility related to federal awards.

Auditor's Responsibilities

22.17 The Uniform Guidance provides that when contractors are responsible for program compliance, and the procurement transactions relate to a major program, the scope of the audit must include determining whether contractor transactions are in compliance with federal statutes, regulations, and the terms and conditions of federal awards if such transactions are material to a major program of the auditee. In such a case, the auditor would normally evaluate a contractor's compliance by reviewing the auditee's records and the results of the auditee's procedures for ensuring compliance by the contractor. When the auditor cannot obtain sufficient assurance of compliance from reviewing the auditee's records and procedures, a deficiency in internal control over compliance exists. The auditor should evaluate the severity of each deficiency in internal control over compliance identified during the audit to determine whether the deficiency, individually or in combination, is a significant deficiency or material weakness in internal control over compliance. The auditor also should perform additional procedures to determine compliance. These procedures may include testing the contractor's records or obtaining reports on compliance procedures performed by the contractor's independent auditor.

22.18 Prior to performing a single or program-specific audit, it is important for the auditor to understand the nature of the auditee's contractor relationships, whether the contractors are responsible for program compliance, the auditee's procedures for ensuring contractor compliance, and whether it will be necessary for the auditor to test contractor records. Because the amount and type of work done by the auditor may be affected by the nature of the auditee's relationships with its contractors, it may be appropriate to include in the communication used to agree upon the terms of the engagement with management information related to the auditee's contractors and the effect on the audit, particularly if contractors are responsible for program compliance. (Chapter 16, "Auditor Planning Considerations Under the Uniform Guidance," of this guide discusses agreeing upon the terms of the engagement with management.) If subsequent to undertaking a single or program-specific audit the auditor becomes aware of a significant contractor relationship that will require the auditor to perform additional procedures on contractor records, the auditor should inform the auditee that the requirements of the Uniform Guidance will not be met unless additional procedures are performed. If the auditee or contractor precludes the auditor from performing such additional procedures, the auditor should qualify his or her opinion or disclaim an opinion because of a scope limitation. (Chapter 23, "Auditor Reporting Requirements and Other Communication Considerations in a Single Audit (Uniform Guidance)," of this guide further discusses scope limitations.)

Single Audit Considerations of Pass-Through Entities

22.19 The following matters are relevant to planning and conducting a single audit of a pass-through entity and discussed in the rest of this section:

- Pass-through entity responsibilities
- Audit planning considerations
- Consideration of internal control over compliance
- Subrecipient monitoring
- Reporting considerations
- For-profit subrecipients
- Foreign public entities and foreign organizations
- A state's designation of a cluster of programs

Pass-Through Entity Responsibilities

22.20 A pass-through entity is responsible for ensuring that subrecipients expend awards in accordance with applicable federal statutes, regulations, and the terms and conditions of federal awards. 2 CFR 200.331 provides that a pass-through entity must

- ensure that every subaward is clearly identified to the subrecipient as a subaward and includes certain information set forth in 2 CFR 200.331(a) at the time of the subaward. If any of these data elements change, include the changes in subsequent subaward notifications. When some of the information is not available, the pass-through entity must provide the best information available to describe the federal award and subaward. (See chapter 17, "Schedule of Expenditures of Federal Awards (Uniform Guidance)," for a listing of required subaward information.)
- evaluate each subrecipient's risk of noncompliance with federal statutes, regulations, and the terms and conditions of the subaward for the purpose of determining the appropriate subrecipient monitoring.
- consider imposing specific subaward conditions, if appropriate.
- monitor the activities of the subrecipient as necessary to ensure that the federal subaward is used for authorized purposes, in compliance with federal statutes, regulations, and the terms and conditions of the subaward, and that subaward performance goals are achieved.
- depending upon the pass-through entity's assessment of risk posed by the subrecipient, consider certain monitoring tools to ensure proper accountability and compliance with program requirements and achievement of performance goals.
- verify that every subrecipient is audited as required by the Uniform Guidance when it is expected that the subrecipient's federal awards expended during the respective fiscal year equaled or exceeded the threshold for audit.
- consider whether the results of subrecipient audits, on-site reviews, or other monitoring indicate conditions that necessitate adjustments to the pass-through entity's own records.

- consider taking enforcement action against noncompliant subrecipients as described in 2 CFR 200.338 and in program regulations.

Audit Planning Considerations

Effect of Pass-Through Federal Awards on the Determination of Major Programs

22.21 As noted in paragraph 22.04, the determination of when a federal award is expended must be based on when the activity related to the award occurs. With respect to federal awards provided by a pass-through entity to subrecipients, the federal awards are deemed to be expended by the pass-through entity when the funds are disbursed to subrecipients, regardless of when subrecipients expend the federal funds. Accordingly, the amount of federal funds disbursed to subrecipients must be included in the total expenditures of federal awards of the pass-through entity and in the determination of the pass-through entity's major programs. (Chapter 18, "Determination of Major Programs (Uniform Guidance)," of this guide discusses the determination of major programs.)

Subrecipient or Contractor Determination

22.22 As part of the Uniform Guidance compliance audit the pass-through entity auditor considers whether the subrecipient and contractor determinations made by the auditee are in compliance with the Uniform Guidance when testing subrecipient monitoring and the amounts passed through to subrecipients on the schedule of expenditures of federal awards.

Pass-Through Entity Request for a Program to Be Audited as a Major Program

22.23 When a subrecipient expends $750,000 or more of federal awards, the Uniform Guidance permits the pass-through entity to request that a subrecipient's program be audited as a major program in lieu of the pass-through entity conducting or arranging for additional audits. If the pass-through entity makes such a request, it must pay the full incremental cost for such an audit. (Chapters 15, "Overview of the Single Audit Act, the Uniform Guidance Audit Requirements, and the *Compliance Supplement*," and 18 of this guide provide additional information.)

Materiality

22.24 The auditor's consideration of materiality is a matter of professional judgment and is influenced by the auditor's perception of the needs of a reasonable person who will rely upon the auditor's work. A comparison of the amount of federal funds passed through to subrecipients with the total amount of expenditures for each individual major program or cluster can assist the auditor in determining if the pass-through amount is material. When the amount of federal funds passed through to subrecipients is material either quantitatively or qualitatively, in relation to the major program being audited, the auditor is required to test subrecipient monitoring for the program. Some federal programs are designed in such a manner that subrecipient expenditures are intended to be material to the pass-through entity's award. For example, the Community Services Block Grant requires a state to subaward at least 90 percent of the state's award.

Auditor Consideration of Internal Control Over Compliance

22.25 Under the Uniform Guidance, the auditor must perform procedures to obtain an understanding of internal control over compliance for federal programs that is sufficient to plan the audit of the pass-through entity to support a low assessed level of control risk of noncompliance for major programs. As part of this, the auditor should consider the pass-through entity's internal control over compliance used to monitor subrecipients and plan the testing of internal control to support a low assessed level of control risk for subrecipient monitoring. (See chapter 19, "Consideration of Internal Control Over Compliance for Major Programs (Uniform Guidance)," of this guide.) Tests of internal control over compliance related to subrecipient monitoring may include inquiry, observation and inspection of documentation, or a reperformance by the auditor of some or all of the pass-through entity's monitoring activities. The nature and extent of the tests performed will vary depending on the auditor's assessment of inherent risk of noncompliance, understanding of the internal control over compliance, materiality, and professional judgment.[4,5] The results of the auditor's testing of internal control over compliance assist in determining the nature, timing, and extent of subrecipient monitoring compliance testing.

Subrecipient Monitoring

22.26 The Single Audit Act requires the pass-through entity to monitor subrecipients' use of federal awards. Because the pass-through entity is held accountable for federal awards administered by its subrecipients, the pass-through entity should establish an appropriate subrecipient monitoring process and to evaluate what, if any, additional monitoring activities may be necessary to ensure the subrecipients' compliance. Generally, arrangements for subrecipient monitoring and clarification of the compliance requirements applicable to federal awards passed through are made by the pass-through entity in its agreements with subrecipients.

22.27 In a Uniform Guidance compliance audit, an auditor considers the subrecipient monitoring process of an entity that disburses to subrecipients federal awards that are material to a major program. (Paragraph 22.24 discusses materiality.) The auditor evaluates whether the pass-through entity monitors subrecipients in compliance with the Uniform Guidance, including whether the pass-through entity has established internal control over compliance that provides reasonable assurance that subrecipients are managing federal awards in compliance with federal statutes, regulations, and the terms and conditions of federal awards that could have a direct and material effect on each of the pass-through entity's major programs.

---

[4] In a compliance audit under the Uniform Guidance, controls that address the risks of noncompliance with direct and material types of compliance requirements for major programs should be tested every year. See the "Performing Tests to Evaluate the Effectiveness of Controls" section in chapter 19, "Consideration of Internal Control Over Compliance for Major Programs (Uniform Guidance)," of this guide for more information.

[5] Part 6 of the *OMB Compliance Supplement (Compliance Supplement)* is the mechanism OMB has historically used to provide more detailed internal control guidance to both nonfederal entities and their auditors, including describing (among other things) certain characteristics of internal control over compliance that, when present and operating effectively, may ensure compliance with program requirements for subrecipient monitoring. Part 6 has been removed from the 2015 *Compliance Supplement*. An updated Part 6 is expected for the 2016 *Compliance Supplement*. See the "Transition Considerations Related to the Uniform Guidance" section in chapter 19 of this guide for more information.

Subrecipient Monitoring Considerations in a Single or Program-Specific Audit

22.28 As noted in paragraph 22.03, subrecipients that expend $750,000 or more in federal awards are required to have a single or program-specific audit in accordance with the Uniform Guidance. This includes the submission of the reporting package and data collection form by the subrecipient to the Federal Audit Clearinghouse. The review of such audit results is only one tool used by the pass-through entity as part of a comprehensive subrecipient-monitoring process.

22.29 In many cases, the pass-through entity will not have access to all the subrecipient audit reports covering the time period being audited at the pass-through entity in time to evaluate the results. The reports for the pass-through entity and the subrecipient are not required to be issued simultaneously, but the pass-through entity should have internal control over compliance in place to determine that (*a*) subrecipient audit reports have been obtained, and (*b*) corrective action is taken after the receipt of the subrecipient's audit. If the subrecipient's audit report is current, it need not cover the same period as the pass-through entity's audit. If the pass-through entity has an effective system for monitoring subrecipients, its auditor would be more likely to rely on the subrecipient's audit cycle, even if it does not coincide with the pass-through entity's fiscal year.

22.30 Subrecipient monitoring is 1 of the 12 types of compliance requirements included in the *Compliance Supplement*. An understanding of the pass-through entity requirements found in the *Compliance Supplement* will assist the auditor in designing appropriate tests of the pass-through entity's monitoring of subrecipients. As found in the *Compliance Supplement*, the pass-through entity must

- clearly identify to the subrecipient
    - the award as a subaward at the time of subaward by providing the information described in 2 CFR 200.331(a)(1);
    - all requirements imposed by the pass-through entity on the subrecipient so that the federal award is used in accordance with federal statutes, regulations, and the terms and conditions of the award; and
    - any additional requirements that the pass-through entity imposes on the subrecipient in order for the pass-through entity to meet its own responsibility for the federal award (for example, financial, performance, and special reports).
- evaluate each subrecipient's risk of noncompliance for purposes of determining the appropriate subrecipient monitoring related to the subaward. This evaluation of risk may include consideration of such factors as the following:
    - The subrecipient's prior experience with the same or similar subawards;
    - The results of previous audits including whether or not the subrecipient receives a single audit in accordance with the Uniform Guidance audit requirements, and the

- extent to which the same or similar subaward has been audited as a major program;
- Whether the subrecipient has new personnel or new or substantially changed systems; and
- The extent and results of federal awarding agency monitoring (for example, if the subrecipient also receives federal awards directly from a federal awarding agency).

- monitor the activities of the subrecipient as necessary to ensure that the subaward is used for authorized purposes, complies with the terms and conditions of the subaward and achieves performance goals. In addition to procedures identified as necessary based upon the evaluation of subrecipient risk or specifically required by the program's federal statutes or regulations, subaward monitoring must include the following:
  - Reviewing financial and programmatic (performance and special) reports required by the pass-through entity.
  - Following-up and ensuring that the subrecipient takes timely and appropriate action on all deficiencies pertaining to the federal award provided to the subrecipient from the pass-through entity detected through audits, on-site reviews, and other means.
  - Issuing a management decision for audit findings pertaining to the federal award provided to the subrecipient from the pass-through entity as required by 2 CFR 200.521.

- ensure accountability of for-profit subrecipients. Some federal awards may be passed through to for-profit entities. For-profit subrecipients are accountable to the pass-through entity for the use of the federal funds provided. Because the Uniform Guidance audit requirements are not applicable to for-profit subrecipients, the pass-through entity is responsible for establishing requirements, as necessary, to ensure compliance by for-profit subrecipients for the subaward. The agreement with the for-profit subrecipient should describe applicable compliance requirements and the for-profit subrecipient's compliance responsibility. Methods to ensure compliance for federal awards made to for-profit subrecipients may include pre-award audits, monitoring during the agreement, and post-award audits.

22.31 The *Compliance Supplement* also identifies the audit objectives and suggested audit procedures for testing the subrecipient monitoring type of compliance requirement for pass-through entities. The auditor may consider coordinating the subrecipient-related tests performed as part of *cash management* (tests of cash reports submitted by subrecipients), *eligibility* (tests that subawards were made only to eligible subrecipients), and *procurement* (tests of suspension and debarment certifications) with the tests of subrecipient monitoring.

22.32 Monitoring procedures that a pass-through entity may use include on-site visits, reviews of financial and performance reports submitted by the subrecipient, regular contacts with subrecipients, appropriate inquiries concerning program activities, and agreed-upon procedures engagements.

Agreed-upon procedures engagements are conducted in accordance with the AICPA attestation standards and are arranged and paid for by a pass-through entity. Such engagements generally only address one or more of the following types of compliance requirements: activities allowed or unallowed; allowable costs or cost principles; eligibility; matching, level of effort, earmarking; and reporting.

22.33 The following are examples of subrecipient monitoring activities that a pass-through entity may perform:

- Reviewing grant applications submitted by subrecipients to determine that applications are filed and approved in a timely manner
- Reviewing subaward transactions to obtain assurance that
    — funds are disbursed to subrecipients only on an as-needed basis;
    — funds are disbursed to subrecipients only on the basis of approved, properly completed reports submitted on a timely basis;
    — refunds that are due from subrecipients are billed and collected in a timely manner; and
    — subrecipients and other entities and individuals receiving federal funds meet eligibility requirements.
- Reviewing financial, performance, and technical reports received from subrecipients on a timely basis and investigating unusual items.
- Reviewing subrecipient audit reports to evaluate them for completeness and for compliance with federal statutes, regulations, and the terms and conditions of the subaward.
- Evaluating audit findings; issuing appropriate management decisions, if necessary; and determining if an acceptable plan for corrective action has been prepared and implemented.
- Reviewing previously detected deficiencies and determining that corrective action was taken.

Subrecipient's Risk of Noncompliance

22.34 Under the Uniform Guidance, a pass-through entity must evaluate each subrecipient's risk of noncompliance with federal statutes, regulations, and the terms and conditions of the subaward for purposes of determining the appropriate subrecipient monitoring. As part of the evaluation of a subrecipient's risk of noncompliance, a pass-through entity may consider various risk factors (such as the relative size and complexity of the federal awards administered by a subrecipient and other subrecipient risks identified by the pass-through entity based on its prior experience with each subrecipient) in developing the nature, timing, and extent of subrecipient monitoring activities. Consider, for example, a pass-through entity that provides a large percentage of the only federal award it expends to 10 subrecipients that each expends less than $750,000 in federal awards annually. Careful consideration by the pass-through entity of the most effective method of monitoring these federal awards is needed. Perhaps a significant majority of this federal award is provided to 2 of the subrecipients. If so, the pass-through entity might consider conducting site visits at the 2 subrecipients that received a significant majority of the federal award and simply reviewing the documentation supporting requests for reimbursement from the other 8 subrecipients. Conversely, if a small percentage of a federal award is provided to subrecipients that each expends less than $750,000 in federal awards, the risk to the pass-through entity is most likely low and, therefore, fewer monitoring activities would typically be required.

Unallowable Audit Costs

22.35 For subrecipients that expend less than $750,000 in federal awards annually, the cost of any audits or attestation engagements (other than the agreed-upon procedures engagements arranged and paid for by a pass-through entity as described in paragraph 22.32), are not allowable costs and, therefore, cannot be charged to any federal award. Accordingly, the Uniform Guidance would prohibit the cost of a financial statement audit conducted in accordance with generally accepted auditing standards or *Government Auditing Standards* from being charged (by either a pass-through entity or subrecipient) to federal awards for a subrecipient that expends less than $750,000 in federal awards annually. Chapter 15 of this guide discusses the allowability of audit costs in greater detail.

When the Subrecipient Monitoring System Is Not Sufficient

22.36 The auditor may determine that the pass-through entity's subrecipient-monitoring system is not sufficient to ensure the subrecipient's compliance with federal statutes, regulations, and terms and conditions of federal awards. In this situation, the auditor should report a significant deficiency or material weakness in internal control over compliance and consider whether the insufficient monitoring system represents an instance of noncompliance that should be reported as a compliance finding (which is likely to be the case). See paragraph 22.40 for information on evaluating the compliance finding. The effect of the noncompliance on the opinion on compliance for major programs is primarily a function of the pervasiveness of the lack of monitoring and the materiality of subrecipient funding to a program. For example, if the pass-through entity did not perform subrecipient-monitoring procedures and 90 percent of the program was passed through to subrecipients, an opinion modification would likely be warranted. This would likely be the case even if the scope of the audit was expanded to include additional audit procedures to determine that the subrecipients actually complied with laws and regulations.

22.37 The pass-through entity may ask the auditor to perform additional procedures beyond the scope of the Uniform Guidance compliance audit to determine whether the subrecipient is in compliance with one or more compliance requirements (such as conducting tests of records for eligibility at the subrecipient's site). Such additional procedures would generally be performed as a separate engagement. Such additional procedures generally would not be sufficient to remedy an internal control deficiency or noncompliance of the pass-through entity's subrecipient monitoring system. However, such additional procedures may provide evidence about whether subrecipient noncompliance could affect the pass-through entity's own records and, if they disclosed material noncompliance (for example, with eligibility), may strengthen the effect in a finding of noncompliance of the pass-through entity's monitoring system.

22.38 The auditor also should consider any implications of an insufficient subrecipient monitoring system on the opinion on the financial statements.

If amounts passed through to subrecipients are considered material to the financial statements of the pass-through entity, the auditor should determine whether the report on the financial statements should be modified. Factors to consider in making such a determination include any audit evidence available to the auditor (such as subrecipients' Uniform Guidance compliance audit reports and other financial reports that may have been submitted to the pass-through entity) that could indicate that the subrecipients administered the program in compliance with laws and regulations. Further, the auditor also should consider whether it is necessary to report an internal control or compliance finding in the report issued to meet the requirements of *Government Auditing Standards*.

Reporting Considerations[6]

Schedule of Expenditures of Federal Awards

22.39 The Uniform Guidance requires pass-through entities to identify in the schedule of expenditures of federal awards the total amount provided to subrecipients from each federal program. (Chapter 17 of this guide discusses the schedule.) If a pass-through entity is unable to identify amounts provided to subrecipients, the auditor should consider whether a significant deficiency or material weakness in internal control over compliance should be reported. The auditor also should consider whether material noncompliance (for subrecipient monitoring) has occurred, which should be reported as an audit finding.

Evaluation of Audit Findings

22.40 The Uniform Guidance requires the auditor to consider a finding in relation to the type of compliance requirement (subrecipient monitoring, in this case) identified in the *Compliance Supplement*, regardless of whether the finding can be quantified. The auditor's responsibility for reporting such findings can best be described through an example. Assume that the auditor is auditing a pass-through entity that consistently fails to monitor the activities of its subrecipients as necessary to ensure that the subaward is used for authorized purposes. In this example, subrecipient monitoring is the relevant type of compliance requirement. Because the pass-through entity failed to monitor the activity of its subrecipients, this noncompliance would likely be material in relation to the compliance requirement of subrecipient monitoring and, therefore, should be reported as an audit finding. This would be the case even if it is found that the subrecipient actually complied with the terms and conditions of the subaward and achieved performance goals. In addition, the auditor also should consider whether significant deficiencies or material weaknesses in internal control over compliance exist that require reporting with respect to subrecipient monitoring. In the example provided, when there is a consistent failure to monitor subrecipients that would likely be the case.[7]

---

[6] In accordance with 2 CFR 200.512, unless restricted by federal statutes or regulations, the auditee must make copies of reports available for public inspection. Auditees and auditors must ensure that their respective part of the reporting package does not include protected personally identifiable information. See chapter 23, "Auditor Reporting Requirements and Other Communication Considerations in a Single Audit (Uniform Guidance)," for more information.

[7] Chapters 4, "Auditor Reporting Requirements and Other Communication Considerations of *Government Auditing Standards*," and 23 of this guide discuss the requirement that the auditor communicate certain matters to the auditee in a written communication.

Effect of Subrecipients' Noncompliance on the Pass-Through Entity's Report

22.41 The instances of noncompliance reported in subrecipients' audit reports are not required to be included in the pass-through entity's audit report. However, as noted previously, the auditor of the pass-through entity should consider the effects of reported instances of subrecipient noncompliance. This may be an indication of weaknesses in the pass-through entity's subrecipient monitoring system that may need to be reported. See also paragraph 22.42 for further considerations.

Adjustment of Pass-Through Entity Financial Records and Reports

22.42 Questioned costs at the subrecipient level that are found to be unallowable by the pass-through entity may require the pass-through entity to adjust its financial records and its federal expenditure reports. The total of allowable program costs in excess of required expenditure levels and the requirements of individual programs regarding the timing of claims will affect whether the pass-through entity will need to reflect a liability to the awarding agency in its financial statements. As part of the finding-resolution process, the pass-through entity should estimate the total unallowable costs that are associated with each subrecipient finding and consider the need to adjust financial records and federal expenditure reports. The failure of the pass-through entity to make needed adjustments to its records and federal reports should be considered by the auditor in forming an opinion on the financial statements and on compliance for major programs.

For-Profit Subrecipients

22.43 The auditor's responsibilities related to for-profit subrecipients are similar to those of not-for-profit subrecipients; see the discussion beginning at paragraph 22.26 for a further discussion of subrecipient monitoring. Because the Uniform Guidance does not require for-profit subrecipients to have an audit, the risk of noncompliance is different from that of a subrecipient that is required to have an audit under the Uniform Guidance.

Foreign Public Entities and Foreign Organizations

22.44 As discussed in chapter 15 of this guide, the audit requirements found in Subpart F of the Uniform Guidance do not apply to foreign public entities or foreign organizations expending federal awards received either directly as a recipient or indirectly as a subrecipient. Therefore, the responsibilities that a pass-through entity and its auditor have for a foreign public entity or foreign organization are the same as those for a for-profit subrecipient (see paragraph 22.43).

State Designation of a Cluster of Programs

22.45 The Uniform Guidance includes a provision that allows a state to designate as a cluster a grouping of closely related programs that share common compliance requirements. When designating a cluster of programs, a state must identify the federal awards included in the cluster and advise subrecipients of the compliance requirements applicable to the cluster. (Chapter 15 of this guide discusses clusters of programs.)

Audit Considerations of Subrecipients

22.46 Subrecipients may have additional audit considerations under the Uniform Guidance that their auditors may need to address. These considerations, as discussed in this section, concern (*a*) additional compliance requirements that may be established by the pass-through entity, (*b*) information related to the schedule of expenditures of federal awards, (*c*) audit findings, and (*d*) the submission of the report.

Additional Compliance Requirements Established by Pass-Through Entities

22.47 Federal awards normally are distributed to subrecipients only on the basis of properly completed and approved awards. These written agreements (subawards) require subrecipients to comply with the requirements of the federal agency and may contain additional requirements established by the pass-through entity. Hence, as part of the audit under the Uniform Guidance, the auditor may be engaged to test compliance with the requirements specified by the pass-through entity in the subaward.

Information Related to the Schedule of Expenditures of Federal Awards

22.48 For federal awards received as a subrecipient, the Uniform Guidance states that the schedule of expenditures of federal awards must include the name of the pass-through entity and identifying number assigned by the pass-through entity. The Uniform Guidance also provides that, although not required, the auditee (subrecipient) may choose to provide information requested by federal awarding agencies and pass-through entities to make the schedule easier to use. For example, when a federal program has multiple federal award years, the auditee may list the amount of federal awards expended for each federal award year separately. Chapter 17 of this guide discusses the schedule of expenditures of federal awards.

Audit Findings

22.49 Audit findings (for example, internal control findings, compliance findings, questioned costs, or fraud) that relate to the same issue must be presented as a single audit finding. The Uniform Guidance states that when practical, audit findings ***should*** be organized by federal agency or pass-through entity. (Chapter 23 of this guide discusses audit findings).

Transition Considerations Related to the Uniform Guidance

22.50 Subpart D of the Uniform Guidance contains guidance related to subrecipient monitoring and management. 2 CFR 200.330 contains guidance on subrecipient and contractor determinations, while 2 CFR 200.331 sets forth the requirements for pass-through entities. Prior to the Uniform Guidance, requirements and guidance regarding subrecipient monitoring was housed in both Circular A-133 and the *Compliance Supplement*.

22.51 The Uniform Guidance no longer uses the term *vendor*. That term has been replaced by the term *contractor*. When determining whether a relationship is one of contractor or subrecipient, the substance of the relationship, not the form of the arrangement, is the determining factor. A pass-through entity may provide a subaward to a subrecipient in a document called a *contract*. Conversely, the agreement with a contractor may be called a *subaward*.

22.52 A listing of the specific information required to be included in a subaward document is included in the Uniform Guidance at 2 CFR 200.331(a). That guidance notes that when some of the information is not available, the pass-through entity must provide the best information available to describe the federal award and subaward. If any data elements of the subaward change, those changes are to be included in a subaward modification.

22.53 Under the Uniform Guidance, a pass-through entity must evaluate each subrecipient's risk of noncompliance with federal statutes, regulations, and the terms and conditions of the subaward for purposes of determining appropriate subrecipient monitoring. This was not an explicit requirement in previous OMB guidance related to a compliance audit of federal awards.

22.54 Once the Uniform Guidance audit requirements become effective, a subrecipient is no longer required to submit its reporting package directly to a pass-through entity. In addition, the requirement that a pass-through entity retain a copy of the subrecipient reporting package is also being removed. Neither of these changes may be implemented by pass-through entities and subrecipients early (that is, they are not able to be implemented until such time that the subrecipient and pass-through entity become subject to an audit under the Uniform Guidance).

22.55 2 CFR 200.414 of Subpart E, "Cost Principles," of the Uniform Guidance states that pass-through entities are subject to the requirements found in 200.331(a)(4) of Subpart D. This section requires a pass-through entity to include a subrecipient's negotiated indirect cost rate in a pass-through award, unless certain exceptions apply. If the subrecipient has never received a negotiated indirect cost rate, the indirect cost rate will be either a rate negotiated between the pass-through entity and the subrecipient or a de minimis rate of 10 percent of modified total direct costs. As noted in 2 CFR 200.414, an exception may apply when a federal awarding agency uses a different rate for a class of federal awards, when a federal statute or regulation requires a different rate for that award, or when a deviation is approved by the federal awarding agency head.

Chapter 23

Auditor Reporting Requirements and Other Communication Considerations in a Single Audit (Uniform Guidance)

> **© Update 23-1: Audits of Federal Awards**
>
> This chapter, and the remaining chapters of part III, *Uniform Guidance Audits*, of this guide, should be used for performing a compliance audit of federal awards under the audit requirements of Title 2 U.S. *Code of Federal Regulations* (CFR) Part 200, *Uniform Administrative Requirements, Cost Principles, and Audit Requirements for Federal Awards* (Uniform Guidance).[1] Part II, *Circular A-133 Audits*, of this guide should be used for performing a compliance audit under Office of Management and Budget (OMB) Circular A-133, *Audits of States, Local Governments, and Non-Profit Organizations* (Circular A-133). See the transitional guidance sections at the end of each chapter that highlight important matters for consideration. Additionally, refer to the preface of this guide for more information.
>
> **Important Effective Date Information**
>
> In December 2013, the OMB issued the Uniform Guidance, which is effective for nonfederal entities for all federal awards and certain funding increments provided on or after December 26, 2014. The requirements in Subpart F, "Audit Requirements," are effective for audits of fiscal years beginning on or after December 26, 2014, with no early implementation permitted. Therefore, auditees subject to a single audit with December 25, 2015, and later year ends (for example, December 31, 2015) will be required to undergo the audit under Subpart F of the Uniform Guidance. Note that audits of fiscal years ending prior to the effective date of the Uniform Guidance audit requirements are subject to an audit under Circular A-133.

Overview

23.01 This chapter discusses the auditor's reporting requirements and other communication considerations in a single audit under the Uniform Guidance. It also provides illustrative auditor's reports in the appendix, "Illustrative Auditor's Reports Under the Uniform Guidance for Federal Awards," of this chapter (paragraph 23.67). (Chapter 24, "Program-Specific Audits (Uniform Guidance)," discusses the auditor's reporting requirements and provides illustrative reports for a program-specific audit.)

23.02 The auditor's reporting responsibilities in a single audit are driven by three levels of auditing standards and requirements: generally accepted

---

[1] See the information found at the end of this chapter (paragraph 23.60), and other part III, *Uniform Guidance Audits*, chapters of this guide, for transition considerations when performing an audit under Title 2 U.S. *Code of Federal Regulations* (CFR) Part 200, *Uniform Administrative Requirements, Cost Principles, and Audit Requirements for Federal Awards* (Uniform Guidance). Transition considerations can also be found at the end of certain part II, *Circular A-133 Audits*, chapters as it relates to an audit performed under Office of Management and Budget (OMB) Circular A-133, *Audits of States, Local Governments, and Non-Profit Organizations*.

auditing standards (GAAS), *Government Auditing Standards*, and the Uniform Guidance. These standards and requirements expand the level of auditor responsibility from reporting on an auditee's financial statements to also reporting on internal control and on compliance. The auditor has additional reporting responsibilities for the audit of the financial statements in accordance with *Government Auditing Standards*. (See chapter 4, "Auditor Reporting Requirements and Other Communication Considerations of *Government Auditing Standards*," of this guide.) In addition to the reporting responsibilities, the auditor also has certain additional communication considerations under GAAS and *Government Auditing Standards* related to internal control, fraud, noncompliance with provisions of laws, regulations, contracts, and grant agreements, abuse, and other matters identified in the audit as discussed in this chapter and in chapter 4 of this guide. Furthermore, the auditor has additional reporting responsibilities under the Uniform Guidance for the compliance audit applicable to major programs. See chapter 18, "Determination of Major Programs (Uniform Guidance)," chapter 19, "Consideration of Internal Control Over Compliance for Major Programs (Uniform Guidance)," and chapter 20, "Compliance Auditing Applicable to Major Programs (Uniform Guidance)," of this guide.

Requirements Under the Uniform Guidance for Federal Awards

Auditor Reporting

23.03 Under the Uniform Guidance, the auditor's report(s) must include the following:

- An opinion (or disclaimer of opinion)[2] as to whether the financial statements are presented fairly in all material respects in accordance with generally accepted accounting principles (GAAP) (paragraph 23.09 discusses basis of accounting) and an opinion (or a disclaimer of opinion) as to whether the schedule of expenditures of federal awards is presented fairly in all material respects in relation to the financial statements as a whole.

- A report on internal control over financial reporting and compliance with provisions of laws, regulations, contracts, and award agreements, noncompliance with which could have a material effect on the financial statements. This report must describe the scope of testing of internal control and compliance and the results of the tests and, where applicable, refer to the separate schedule of findings and questioned costs.

- A report on compliance for each major program and report on internal control over compliance. This report must describe the scope of testing of internal control over compliance, include an

---

[2] As explained in the AICPA Audit and Accounting Guide *State and Local Governments*, the auditor generally expresses or disclaims an opinion on a government's basic financial statements by providing an opinion or disclaimer of opinion on each opinion unit required to be presented in those financial statements. In addition, the auditor may provide opinions or disclaimers of opinions on additional opinion units if engaged to set the scope of the audit and assess materiality at a more detailed level than by the opinion units required for the basic financial statements. Throughout this guide, the use of the singular terms *opinion* and *disclaimer of opinion* encompasses the multiple opinions and disclaimers of opinion that generally will be provided on a government's basic financial statements.

opinion (or disclaimer of opinion) as to whether the auditee complied with federal statutes, regulations, and the terms and conditions of federal awards[3] which could have a direct and material effect on each major program, and refer to the separate schedule of findings and questioned costs.

- A schedule of findings and questioned costs.

Paragraphs 23.06–.08 describe the auditor's reports that are illustrated in this guide.

Data Collection Form

23.04 The Uniform Guidance states that the auditor must complete applicable data elements of the data collection form. In addition, the auditor must sign a statement to be included as part of the data collection form submission to the Federal Audit Clearinghouse (FAC) by the auditee. (See paragraphs 23.51–.58.)

Emphasis Point

The use of the term *must* in the Uniform Guidance indicates a requirement. This is consistent with the use of the term *must* in GAAS and *Government Auditing Standards*. The use of the term *should* in the Uniform Guidance indicates a best practice or recommended approach. However, GAAS and *Government Auditing Standards* use the term *should* to indicate a presumptively mandatory requirement. An auditor must comply with a presumptively mandatory requirement in all cases in which such a requirement is relevant, except in rare circumstances. In this guide, the term ***should***, when italicized and bolded, indicates a best practice or recommended approach in the Uniform Guidance. This is intended to differentiate it from the term *should* used throughout the guide to refer to presumptively mandatory requirements in GAAS and *Government Auditing Standards*. See chapter 1, "Introduction and Overview of *Government Auditing Standards*," of this guide for more information regarding presumptively mandatory requirements.

Reporting Package

23.05 The electronic submission to the FAC includes the data collection form and the reporting package. The reporting package must include the following:

- Financial statements and a supplementary schedule of expenditures of federal awards (See chapter 17, "Schedule of Expenditures of Federal Awards (Uniform Guidance)," of this guide.)
- Auditor's reports (See paragraphs 23.06–.08.)
- A summary schedule of prior audit findings (See paragraphs 23.46–.50.)
- A corrective action plan (See paragraphs 23.46–.50.)

---

[3] Although *Government Auditing Standards* uses "provisions of laws, regulations, contracts, and grant agreements," the Uniform Guidance uses the terminology "federal statutes, regulations, and the terms and conditions of federal awards." In general, the meaning of both phrases is consistent.

Illustrative Auditor's Reports

23.06 Reporting on a financial statement audit and on the compliance requirements that could have a direct and material[4] effect on each major program involves varying levels of materiality and different forms of reporting. The Uniform Guidance states that the auditor's report(s) may be in the form of either combined or separate reports and may be organized differently from the manner presented. The sections that follow present a discussion of the reports required under 2 CFR 200.515, illustrations of which are included in the appendix to chapter 4 and this chapter's appendix (paragraph 23.67). These illustrative reports include the following:

    a. A report on the financial statements and on the supplementary schedule of expenditures of federal awards[5] (See chapter 4 and paragraphs 23.09–.20.)

    b. A report on internal control over financial reporting[6] and on compliance and other matters based on an audit of financial statements performed in accordance with *Government Auditing Standards* (See chapter 4.)

    c. A report on compliance with requirements that could have a direct and material effect on each major federal program and on internal control over compliance[7] in accordance with the Uniform Guidance (See paragraphs 23.21–.28.)

    d. A schedule of findings and questioned costs (See paragraphs 23.33–.44.)

23.07 The reports in chapter 4 and the appendix of this chapter (paragraph 23.67) are illustrative. Therefore, auditors may tailor the reporting based on the auditor's understanding of the intended purpose of the reports and the specific auditee facts and circumstances. Care is needed by auditors when issuing reports to ensure that they meet all the varying reporting requirements of GAAS, *Government Auditing Standards*, and the Uniform Guidance.

---

[4] AU-C section 935, *Compliance Audits* (AICPA, *Professional Standards*), defines *applicable compliance requirements* as the compliance requirements that are subject to the compliance audit. 2 CFR 200.514(d)(1) states that the auditor must determine whether the auditee has complied with the federal statutes, regulations, and the terms and conditions of federal awards that may have a direct and material effect on each of its major programs. Therefore, in a Uniform Guidance compliance audit, the direct and material compliance requirements are those that are subject to audit. Accordingly, for the purpose of adapting AU-C section 935 to a Uniform Guidance compliance audit in this chapter, the term *applicable* has been replaced by *direct and material* when referring to such compliance requirements, except when citing content from AU-C section 935.

[5] Note that in certain situations the auditor may include the reporting on the schedule of expenditures of federal awards in the report on compliance with requirements that could have a direct and material effect on each major federal program and on internal control over compliance in accordance with the Uniform Guidance. See paragraphs 23.12 and 23.27 for further discussion. As noted in paragraph 23.12, an auditor may be engaged to report on the schedule of expenditures of federal awards in a stand-alone report. See paragraph 23.20 for a further discussion.

[6] Controls relevant to an audit of the financial statements are referred to collectively in this guide as *internal control over financial reporting* and are encompassed in the reporting on internal control required by *Government Auditing Standards*.

[7] Controls relevant to an audit of compliance with requirements applicable to major federal programs are referred to collectively in this guide as *internal control over compliance* and are encompassed in the reporting on internal control required by the Uniform Guidance. The Uniform Guidance uses the terms *internal control over compliance*, *internal control over major programs*, and *internal control over federal programs* interchangeably.

Professional judgment may be exercised in any situation not specifically addressed in this guide.

23.08 Table 23-1 provides a matrix depicting the auditor's reports in a single audit required by GAAS, *Government Auditing Standards*, and the Uniform Guidance. The discussion that follows includes information on the reports as it relates to a single audit. See chapter 4 for information regarding the reporting required under *Government Auditing Standards*.

Table 23-1

Reporting in Single Audits

Report	Required by		
	GAAS	Government Auditing Standards	Uniform Guidance
Opinion (or disclaimer of opinion) on financial statements and supplementary schedule of expenditures of federal awards	X	X	X
Report on internal control over financial reporting and on compliance and other matters based on an audit of financial statements		X	X
Report on compliance and internal control over compliance applicable to *each* major federal program (this report includes separate opinions [or disclaimers of opinion] on each major program's compliance)			X
Schedule of findings and questioned costs			X

Reporting on the Financial Statements and Supplementary Schedule of Expenditures of Federal Awards in Accordance With GAAS and *Government Auditing Standards* in a Single Audit

Basis of Accounting

23.09 The Uniform Guidance does not prescribe the basis of accounting that an auditee uses to prepare its financial statements or the schedule of expenditures of federal awards. For example, a basis of accounting other than GAAP, referred to as a *special purpose framework*, may be used as the financial reporting framework.[8,9] However, auditees should clearly disclose the basis of accounting and the significant accounting policies used in preparing the financial statements and the schedule of expenditures of federal awards.[10,11] The Uniform Guidance states that the auditor must include a note that describes the significant accounting policies used in preparing the schedule of expenditures of federal awards. In addition, the Uniform Guidance states that the auditor must issue an opinion (or a disclaimer of opinion) as to whether the financial statements are presented fairly in all material respects in accordance with GAAP and whether the schedule of expenditures of federal awards is fairly stated, in all material respects, in relation to the auditee's financial statements as a whole. Refer to chapter 17 for auditor considerations regarding issuing an in-relation-to opinion on the schedule of expenditures of federal awards when the schedule of expenditures of federal awards is prepared on a basis of accounting that is different from that of the financial statements.

Implementing Regulations of Federal Awarding Agencies May Define the Entity to Be Audited Differently Than Does GAAP

23.10 The regulations implementing the Uniform Guidance may define the entity to be audited for single audit purposes differently than the reporting entity would be defined in accordance with GAAP. For example, FASB *Accounting Standards Codification* 958–810 requires presentation of consolidated financial statements when one not-for-profit entity (NFP) (the parent) controls the voting majority of the board of and has an economic interest in another NFP. If the regulations of the federal agency that provides federal awards to the parent define the entity for single audit purposes to consist of only the parent, audited parent-only financial statements, instead of consolidated financial statements, should be submitted to comply with these regulations. If the NFP's consolidated financial statements are not also prepared as required by GAAP, a modified opinion due to a material departure from GAAP on the parent-only financial statements may be required. AU-C section 705, *Modification to the Opinion in the Independent Auditor's Report* (AICPA, *Professional*

---

[8] AU-C section 800, *Special Consideration—Audits of Financial Statements Prepared in Accordance With Special Purpose Frameworks* (AICPA, *Professional Standards*), provides requirements and guidance for auditor reporting when the auditee prepares financial statements in accordance with a special purpose framework. AU-C section 800 defines a *special purpose framework* as a financial reporting framework other than generally accepted accounting principles and establishes requirements for reporting on those frameworks. Special purpose frameworks, such as the cash, tax, regulatory, and other bases of accounting, are sometimes referred to as *other comprehensive bases of accounting* (OCBOA). The term *OCBOA* is sometimes used when referring to this guidance in this guide.

[9] Under the Uniform Guidance, an auditee cannot be considered a low-risk auditee unless, among other things, the financial statements were prepared in accordance with generally accepted accounting principles or a basis of accounting required by state law. Therefore, unless required by state law, an auditee that prepares its financial statements using a special purpose framework cannot be considered a low-risk auditee. See chapter 18, "Determination of Major Programs (Uniform Guidance)," for more information on low-risk auditee status.

[10] See chapter 17, "Schedule of Expenditures of Federal Awards (Uniform Guidance)," for more information.

[11] The AICPA Audit and Accounting Guide *State and Local Governments* discusses the application of AU-C section 800 to state and local governmental financial statements and also provides illustrative auditor's reports for financial statements prepared in accordance with a special purpose framework. In addition, the AICPA practice aid *Applying OCBOA in State and Local Governmental Financial Statements* (APAOCBO12P) provides nonauthoritative guidance on preparing and reporting on OCBOA financial statements of governmental entities. A second practice aid, *Accounting and Financial Reporting Guidelines for Cash- and Tax-Basis Financial Statements* (APACTB12P), provides nonauthoritative guidance for preparers regarding guidelines and best practices for the preparation of cash- and tax-basis financial statements. These publications are available at www.cpa2biz.com.

Standards), and various AICPA Audit and Accounting Guides, including *Not-for-Profit Entities*, *State and Local Governments*, and *Health Care Entities*, provide guidance on reporting when there is a departure from GAAP.

Elements of the In-Relation-To Report on the Supplementary Schedule of Expenditures of Federal Awards[12]

23.11 In accordance with AU-C section 725, *Supplementary Information in Relation to the Financial Statements as a Whole* (AICPA, *Professional Standards*), when the entity presents the schedule of expenditures of federal awards with the financial statements, the auditor should report on the schedule in either (*a*) an other-matter paragraph in accordance with AU-C section 706, *Emphasis-of-Matter Paragraphs and Other-Matter Paragraphs in the Independent Auditor's Report* (AICPA, *Professional Standards*), or (*b*) in a separate report on the schedule of expenditures of federal awards. Reporting using an other-matter paragraph is applicable when the schedule of expenditures of federal awards is reported on in the auditor's report on the financial statements. Otherwise, the reporting on the schedule of expenditures of federal awards may be included in the report on compliance and on internal control over compliance required under the Uniform Guidance or in a separate report. In any case, the following elements should be included in the report:

- A statement that the audit was conducted for the purpose of forming an opinion on the financial statements as a whole
- A statement that the schedule of expenditures of federal awards is presented for purposes of additional analysis and is not a required part of the financial statements
- A statement that the schedule of expenditures of federal awards is the responsibility of management and was derived from, and relates directly to, the underlying accounting and other records used to prepare the financial statements
- A statement that the schedule of expenditures of federal awards has been subjected to the auditing procedures applied in the audit of the financial statements and certain additional procedures,[13] including comparing and reconciling such information directly to the underlying accounting and other records used to prepare the financial statements or to the financial statements themselves and other additional procedures, in accordance with GAAS
- If the auditor issues an unmodified opinion on the financial statements and the auditor has concluded that the schedule of expenditures of federal awards is fairly stated, in all material respects, in relation to the financial statements as a whole, a statement that, in the auditor's opinion, the schedule of expenditures of federal

---

[12] It is important to note that under AU-C section 725, *Supplementary Information in Relation to the Financial Statements as a Whole* (AICPA, *Professional Standards*), an auditor may only provide an in-relation-to opinion on the schedule of expenditures of federal awards when the auditor audited the financial statements. If that is not the case, the auditor has not met all the requirements in paragraph .05 of AU-C section 725 necessary to opine on the schedule and, therefore, may not provide an in-relation-to opinion. See chapter 17 for additional information. An option in this circumstance would be for the auditee to engage the auditor to report on the schedule of expenditures of federal awards in a stand-alone report. See paragraph 23.20 for a further discussion.

[13] See chapter 17 for information on procedures the auditor should perform in order to opine on supplementary information such as the schedule of expenditures of federal awards.

awards is fairly stated, in all material respects, in relation to the financial statements as a whole

- If the auditor issues a qualified opinion on the financial statements and the qualification has an effect on the schedule of expenditures of federal awards, a statement that, in the auditor's opinion, except for the effects on the schedule of expenditures of federal awards of (refer to the paragraph in the auditor's report explaining the qualification), such information is fairly stated, in all material respects, in relation to the financial statements as a whole

23.12 When the schedule of expenditures of federal awards is not presented with the financial statements and the auditor includes the in-relation-to reporting in either the report on compliance and on internal control over compliance required by the Uniform Guidance or in a separate report,[14] the following additional elements should be included (in addition to the report elements found in paragraph 23.11):

- A reference to the report on the financial statements
- The date of that report
- The nature of the opinion expressed on the financial statements
- Any report modifications

Furthermore, consistent with paragraph .A16 of AU-C section 725, when the auditor includes the in-relation-to reporting in either the report on compliance and on internal control over compliance required by the Uniform Guidance or in a separate report, the auditor may consider including an alert that restricts the use of the separate report solely to the appropriate specified parties. See AU-C section 905, *Alert That Restricts the Use of the Auditor's Written Communication* (AICPA, *Professional Standards*), for more information.

23.13 This guide recommends that, when possible, the auditor report on the schedule of expenditures of federal awards as supplementary information in the report on the financial statements. Chapter 4 of this guide describes the requirements of the auditor's standard report on the financial statements and on accompanying supplementary information—required supplementary information and supplementary information. The appendix in chapter 4 of this guide provides examples of the auditor's standard report on financial statements and illustrations of reporting on required supplementary information and supplementary information, including the schedule of expenditures of federal awards. (See paragraphs 23.19–.20 if the schedule of expenditures of federal awards does not accompany the financial statements.) The illustrative reports in examples 23-1–23-6 in the appendix of this chapter (paragraph 23.67) provide illustrative wording for reporting on the schedule of expenditures of federal awards based on the requirements of AU-C section 725, and illustrate how to incorporate the reporting on the schedule of expenditures of federal awards into the report on compliance and on internal control over compliance required by the Uniform Guidance.

---

[14] As noted in chapter 17, there may be instances when the auditor is engaged to issue an opinion on the schedule of expenditures of federal awards under AU-C section 805, *Special Considerations—Audits of Single Financial Statements and Specific Elements, Accounts, or Items of a Financial Statement* (AICPA, *Professional Standards*), for example, when the auditor is engaged to perform only the compliance audit under the Uniform Guidance. See paragraph 23.20 for information regarding the auditor reporting on the schedule of expenditures of federal awards in this circumstance.

Potential Report Modifications When Reporting on the Schedule of Expenditures of Federal Awards

23.14 Paragraph .13 of AU-C section 725 notes that if the auditor concludes, on the basis of the procedures performed, that the schedule of expenditures of federal awards is materially misstated in relation to the financial statements as a whole, the auditor should discuss the matter with management and propose an appropriate revision of the schedule. If management does not revise the schedule of expenditures of federal awards, the auditor should either (*a*) modify the auditor's opinion on the schedule and describe the misstatement in the auditor's report or, (*b*) if a separate report is being issued on the schedule, withhold the auditor's report on the schedule.

23.15 When reporting on supplementary information, the auditor should consider the effect of any modifications to the report on the financial statements. In applying paragraph .11 of AU-C section 725, when the auditor's report on the audited financial statements contains an adverse opinion or disclaimer of opinion and the auditor has been engaged to provide an in-relation-to opinion on the schedule of expenditures of federal awards, the auditor is precluded from expressing an in-relation-to opinion on the schedule of expenditures of federal awards. When permitted by law or regulation, the auditor may withdraw from the engagement to report on such supplementary information. Unless the auditor chooses to withdraw, the auditor's report on the schedule of expenditures of federal awards should state that because of the significance of the matter disclosed in the auditor's report, it is inappropriate to, and the auditor does not, express an opinion on the schedule of expenditures of federal awards. Paragraph .A17 of AU-C section 725 provides reporting examples, including reporting on supplementary information such as the schedule of expenditures of federal awards when the auditor's report on the financial statements contains an adverse or disclaimer of opinion.

Considerations When Dating the Report on the Schedule of Expenditures of Federal Awards

23.16 Paragraph .12 of AU-C section 725 states that the date of the auditor's report on supplementary information in relation to the financial statements as a whole should not be earlier than the date on which the auditor completed the procedures required in paragraph .07 of AU-C section 725. Therefore, the date of the auditor's report on the schedule of expenditures of federal awards may be the same date as the financial statement report or a later date. In no case would the date of the in-relation-to opinion on the schedule of expenditures of federal awards be earlier than the date of the financial statement report.

Schedule of Expenditures of Federal Awards Presented With the Financial Statements

23.17 When the reporting on the schedule of expenditures of federal awards is included in the auditor's report on the financial statements, the date of the report on the schedule depends on when the auditor has completed the procedures relating to the schedule of expenditures of federal awards. When those procedures are performed concurrent with financial statement audit procedures, the date of the report on the schedule of expenditures of federal awards will be the same date as that of the auditor's report on the financial statements.

However, in cases when the procedures related to the schedule of expenditures of federal awards are completed subsequent to the financial statement report date, the reporting on the schedule will carry a later date than the financial statement report, thus, resulting in a dual dated report.

23.18 When the auditor has completed the procedures related to the schedule of expenditures of federal awards after the date of the auditor's report on the financial statements, Interpretation No. 1, "Dating the Auditor's Report on Supplementary Information," of AU-C section 725 (AICPA, *Professional Standards*, AU-C sec. 9725 par. .01–.04), provides guidance related to the use of an explanatory paragraph to make it clear that no additional procedures were performed on the audited financial statements subsequent to the date of the auditor's report on those financial statements. The interpretation, which also includes illustrative report wording, notes that, although not required, an auditor may

- when issuing a separate report on the supplementary information, include in the report a statement that the auditor has not performed any auditing procedures with respect to the audited financial statements subsequent to the date of the auditor's report on those financial statements.

- when reissuing a report on the audited financial statements to include an other-matter paragraph to report on the supplementary information, include two report dates to indicate that the date of reporting on the supplementary information is as of a later date.

Schedule of Expenditures of Federal Awards Presented With the Report Required Under the Uniform Guidance

23.19 As noted previously, there may be circumstances in which the auditor includes the in-relation-to opinion on the schedule of expenditures of federal awards in the report on compliance and on internal control over compliance required by the Uniform Guidance. In that situation, the date of the report on the schedule of expenditures of federal awards depends on the date the underlying audit procedures are completed. If using the same date is not possible because the procedures to satisfy the Uniform Guidance requirements are not completed as of the date the procedures related to the schedule of expenditures of federal awards are completed, the auditor has two options:

   a. The auditor can dual date the report on compliance and on internal control over compliance required by the Uniform Guidance. The date related to the portion of the report pertaining to the in-relation-to opinion on the schedule of expenditures of federal awards would be when the audit procedures performed are completed. The date pertaining to the remainder of the report would be the date when the audit procedures performed to satisfy the Uniform Guidance requirements are completed. Example 23-1 in the appendix of this chapter (paragraph 23.67) provides illustrative wording.

   b. The auditor can issue a separate report on the schedule of expenditures of federal awards. This report should be dated the date on which the auditor completed the procedures required under paragraph .07 of AU-C section 725.

Issuing an Opinion on the Schedule of Expenditures of Federal Awards Under AU-C Section 805 When the Auditor Is Engaged to Perform Only the Compliance Audit Under the Uniform Guidance[15]

23.20 In some instances, the auditor may be engaged to issue a stand-alone opinion on the schedule of expenditures of federal awards, either as part of the report issued to meet the requirements of the Uniform Guidance or separately. It is important to note that when an auditor is engaged to perform only the compliance audit required under the Uniform Guidance, and not the financial statement audit, an in-relation-to opinion may not be issued.[16] When this occurs, the auditee may consider engaging the auditor to issue an opinion on the schedule of expenditures of federal awards under AU-C section 805, *Special Considerations—Audits of Single Financial Statements and Specific Elements, Accounts, or Items of a Financial Statement* (AICPA, *Professional Standards*).[17] Although this engagement would be performed under *Government Auditing Standards*, because the schedule of expenditures of federal awards (the financial statement) presents only the activities of the federal programs, the auditor is not required to issue a separate report on internal control over financial reporting and on compliance with provisions of laws, regulations, contracts, and grant agreements to meet the reporting requirements of *Government Auditing Standards*. See chapter 17 for additional information on the objectives and audit evidence needed in such an audit. See example 23-7 in the appendix of this chapter (paragraph 23.67) for an illustrative report on the schedule of expenditures of federal awards when the auditor issues an opinion under AU-C section 805.

Reporting on Compliance and Internal Control Over Compliance Applicable to Each Major Program

23.21 This section discusses the auditor's report and opinions that are issued based on a compliance audit of major programs performed under the Uniform Guidance. The report on compliance with requirements applicable to major programs expresses the auditor's opinion on whether the auditee complied with the requirements that, if noncompliance occurred, could have a direct and material effect on a major program. AU-C section 935, *Compliance Audits* (AICPA, *Professional Standards*), provides requirements and guidance when reporting on compliance and internal control over compliance. Also, AU-C section 700, *Forming an Opinion and Reporting on Financial Statements* (AICPA, *Professional Standards*), should be adapted and applied to a Uniform Guidance compliance audit. When modification of the auditor's opinion on compliance is needed (for example, when the auditor's opinion is modified due to noncompliance or a scope restriction), the auditor should adapt and apply the requirements and guidance in AU-C section 705 to such report modifications.

---

[15] An auditee may use a separate auditor to perform the Uniform Guidance compliance audit for various reasons. For example, a common reason is for an auditee to make positive efforts to use small business, minority-owned firms, and women's business enterprises in conjunction with the Uniform Guidance compliance audit.

[16] See footnote 15.

[17] An auditee may also consider engaging the auditor to examine the schedule of expenditures of federal awards or an assertion related to the schedule of expenditures of federal awards in accordance with AT section 101, *Attest Engagements* (AICPA, *Professional Standards*).

Material Instances of Noncompliance

23.22 In accordance with AU-C section 705, when the audit of an auditee's compliance with requirements applicable to a major program detects material instances of noncompliance with those requirements, the auditor should express a qualified or adverse opinion on compliance in the report on compliance with requirements that could have a direct and material effect on each major program and on internal control over compliance. The auditor should state the basis for such an opinion in the report as shown in examples 23-4–23-6 in the appendix of this chapter (paragraph 23.67). Chapter 20 of this guide discusses materiality considerations in evaluating the effect of instances of noncompliance on the opinion on compliance.

Scope Limitations

23.23 Testing an auditee's compliance with federal statutes, regulations, and the terms and conditions of federal awards provides the evidence for the auditor to make a comply or non-comply decision about an auditee's adherence to those compliance requirements. The auditor is able to express an unmodified opinion only if he or she has been able to apply all the procedures the auditor considers necessary in the circumstances. Restrictions on the scope of the audit—whether imposed by the client or by circumstances such as the timing of the auditor's work, an inability to obtain sufficient appropriate audit evidence or an inadequacy in the accounting records—may require the auditor to qualify his or her opinion or to disclaim an opinion.[18] In those instances, the auditor's report should describe the reasons for such a qualification or disclaimer of opinion. Furthermore, the auditor should consider the effects of those instances on his or her ability to express an unmodified opinion on the financial statements. Example 23-5 in appendix of this chapter (paragraph 23.67) illustrates a qualified opinion on compliance due to a scope limitation.

23.24 The auditor's decision to qualify or disclaim an opinion because of a scope limitation depends on his or her assessment of the importance of the omitted procedure(s) to his or her ability to form an opinion on compliance with requirements governing each major program. This assessment will be affected by the nature and magnitude of the potential effects of the matters in question and by their significance to each major program. Restrictions imposed by the client that significantly limit the scope of the audit may require the auditor to disclaim an opinion on compliance.

23.25 When disclaiming an opinion because of a scope limitation, the auditor should indicate in a separate basis for modification paragraph all of the substantive reasons for the disclaimer. The auditor should also state in a separate opinion paragraph that

    a. because of the significance of the matter(s) described in the basis for disclaimer of opinion paragraph, the auditor has not been able to obtain sufficient appropriate audit evidence to provide a basis for an audit opinion, and

    b. accordingly, the auditor does not express an opinion.

---

[18] As noted in paragraph 23.38g, the auditor must report as a finding the circumstances concerning why the auditor's report on compliance for each major program is other than an unmodified opinion, unless such circumstances are otherwise reported as an audit finding in the schedule of findings and questioned costs for federal awards (for example, a scope limitation that is not otherwise reported as a finding).

Report on Compliance for Each Major Program, Report on Internal Control Over Compliance and Report on the Schedule of Expenditures of Federal Awards Required by the Uniform Guidance for Federal Awards

Report Requirements[19]

23.26 The basic elements of the auditor's standard report on compliance with requirements that could have a direct and material effect on each major program and on internal control over compliance[20] in accordance with the Uniform Guidance are in the following listing. Examples 23-1–23-6 in the appendix of this chapter (paragraph 23.67) illustrate that report:

    a. A title that includes the word *independent*

    b. An addressee appropriate for the circumstances of the engagement

    c. A section titled "Report on Compliance for Each Major Federal Program"

    d. An introductory paragraph that includes the following:

        i. A statement that the auditor has audited the auditee's compliance with the types of compliance requirements described in the *OMB Compliance Supplement (Compliance Supplement)* that could have a direct and material effect on each of its major federal programs

        ii. Identification of the period covered by the report

        iii. A statement that the auditee's major federal programs are identified in the summary of auditor's results section of the accompanying schedule of findings and questioned costs. (See paragraph 23.34.)

    e. A subheading titled "Management's Responsibility" that includes a statement that compliance with the requirements of federal statutes, regulations, and the terms and conditions of federal awards is the responsibility of the auditee's management.

    f. A subheading titled "Auditor's Responsibility" that includes the following:

        i. A statement that the auditor's responsibility is to express an opinion on compliance for each of the entity's major federal programs based on the audit of the types of compliance requirements.

---

[19] The elements provided in this section are limited to the elements for situations when the auditor is expressing an unmodified opinion or qualified opinion on compliance, or both. Additionally, the order of the elements (paragraph 23.26) of report requirements in this paragraph is not the proper order for all reporting circumstances. Refer to specific report illustrations in the appendix of this chapter (paragraph 23.67) for illustrations of other types of reporting (for example, an adverse opinion) and the typical ordering of the required elements in a particular reporting circumstance.

[20] In a particular single audit engagement, some controls may involve both internal control over financial reporting and internal control over compliance and, thus, be relevant to both the audit of the financial statements and the audit of compliance. When this occurs, those controls would be encompassed in both internal control reports. 2 CFR 200.515 provides guidance on reporting findings involving significant deficiencies and material weaknesses in internal control in such a circumstance as discussed in paragraph 23.34c.

　　　　　ii. A statement that the compliance audit was conducted in accordance with auditing standards generally accepted in the United States of America,[21] the standards applicable to financial audits contained in *Government Auditing Standards* issued by the Comptroller General of the United States[22] and the audit requirements of Title 2 U.S. *Code of Federal Regulations* Part 200, *Uniform Administrative Requirements, Cost Principles, and Audit Requirements for Federal Awards*.

　　　　　iii. A statement that those standards and the Uniform Guidance require that the auditor plan and perform the audit to obtain reasonable assurance about whether noncompliance with the types of compliance requirements that could have a direct and material effect on a major federal program occurred.

　　　　　iv. A statement that an audit includes examining, on a test basis, evidence about the entity's compliance with those requirements and performing such other procedures as the auditor considered necessary in the circumstances.

　　　　　v. A statement that the auditor believes that the compliance audit provides a reasonable basis for the auditor's opinion.

　　　　　vi. A statement that the compliance audit does not provide a legal determination of the auditee's compliance with those requirements.

　　g. When the auditor is expressing an unmodified opinion on all major programs, a subheading titled "Opinion on Each Major Federal Program" that contains a statement that in the auditor's opinion the entity complied, in all material respects, with the types of compliance requirements that could have a direct and material effect on each of its major federal programs for the year ended [*specify date*].

　　h. If instances of noncompliance for a major program are noted that result in an opinion qualification, a subheading titled, "Basis for Qualified Opinion on [*Name of Major Federal Program*]" that includes the following (see item *i* for modifications needed for situations when one or more major programs receive a qualified opinion)

　　　　　i. A statement that, as described in the accompanying schedule of findings and questioned costs, the auditee did not comply with requirements regarding [*identify the major federal program and associated finding number(s) matched to the type(s) of compliance requirements*].

　　　　　ii. a statement that compliance with such requirements is necessary, in the auditor's opinion, for the auditee to comply with the requirements applicable to the program(s).

　　i. If instances of noncompliance are noted that result in an opinion qualification for one or more major programs, a subheading with

---

[21] See the discussion beginning in paragraph 23.23 for information on report modifications due to a scope limitation.

[22] The standards and guidance applicable to financial audits are found in chapters 1–4 of *Government Auditing Standards*.

an appropriate title (for example, "Qualified Opinion on [*Name of Major Federal Program*]") that includes the auditor's opinion on whether the auditee complied, in all material respects, with the types of compliance requirements that could have a direct and material effect on each of its major federal programs.

> [**Note:** *If instances of noncompliance are noted that result in an opinion qualification on one or more major programs, but there are other major programs receiving an unmodified opinion, the subheading to the opinion paragraph relating to the unmodified opinion(s) (see item g) may be modified to "Unmodified Opinion on Each of the Other Major Federal Programs" to be more clear about the programs receiving an unmodified opinion.]*

j. If other noncompliance is identified that does not result in a modified opinion but that is required to be reported in accordance with the Uniform Guidance, a subheading titled "Other Matters" containing

   i. a reference to the schedule of findings and questioned costs in which the instances of noncompliance are described, including the reference number(s) of the finding(s).[23]

   ii. a statement that the auditor's opinion on each major federal program is not modified with respect to the matters.

   iii. a statement that the auditee's response to the noncompliance findings identified are described in the accompanying [*insert name of document containing management's response to the auditor's findings, for example "schedule of findings and questioned costs and/or corrective action plan."*]

   iv. a statement that the auditee's response was not subjected to the auditing procedures applied in the audit of compliance and, accordingly, the auditor expresses no opinion on the response.

k. A section heading "Report on Internal Control Over Compliance" that includes the following statements and definitions:

   i. A statement that the auditee's management is responsible for establishing and maintaining effective internal control over compliance with the types of compliance requirements.

   ii. A statement that in planning and performing the compliance audit, the auditor considered the auditee's internal control over compliance with the types of requirements that could have a direct and material effect on each major federal program to determine the auditing procedures that are appropriate in the circumstances for the purpose of expressing an opinion on compliance for each major federal program and to test and report on internal control over compliance in accordance with the Uniform Guidance, but

---

[23] Paragraph 23.38 discusses the audit findings that are required to be reported under the Uniform Guidance.

not for the purpose of expressing an opinion on the effectiveness of internal control over compliance.

iii. A statement that the auditor is not expressing an opinion on the effectiveness of internal control over compliance.

iv. The definitions of *deficiency in internal control over compliance*, *material weakness in internal control over compliance*, and *significant deficiency in internal control over compliance*.

v. A statement that the auditor's consideration of internal control over compliance was for the limited purpose described in the first paragraph of the section and was not designed to identify all deficiencies in internal control over compliance that might be material weaknesses or significant deficiencies.

vi. If no material weaknesses in internal control over compliance were identified, a statement that the auditor did not identify any deficiencies in internal control over compliance that are considered to be material weaknesses.

vii. A statement that material weaknesses may exist that have not been identified. (For situations when significant deficiencies or material weaknesses are identified, this statement is revised to indicate that material weaknesses or significant deficiencies may exist that have not been identified.)

viii. If significant deficiencies in internal control over compliance were identified, a statement that no deficiencies in internal control over compliance were identified that are considered to be material weaknesses, however deficiencies in internal control over compliance were identified that are considered to be significant deficiencies, and a description of the significant deficiencies in internal control over compliance or a reference to the accompanying schedule of findings and questioned costs, including the reference number(s) of the finding(s).

ix. If material weaknesses in internal control over compliance were identified, a statement that deficiencies in internal control over compliance were identified that are considered to be material weaknesses and a description of the material weaknesses in internal control over compliance or a reference to the accompanying schedule of findings and questioned costs, including the reference number(s) of the finding(s).

x. If applicable, a statement that the auditee's written response to the internal control findings identified in the audit are described in the accompanying schedule of findings and questioned costs, and that the auditee's written response was not subjected to the auditing procedures applied in the audit of compliance and, accordingly, the auditor expresses no opinion on it.

xi. A separate paragraph at the end of the section stating that the purpose of the report on internal control over

Auditor Reporting Requirements and Other Communication

compliance is solely to describe the scope of our testing of internal control over compliance and the result of that testing based on the requirements of the Uniform Guidance. Accordingly, this report is not suitable for any other purpose.[24]

    l. The manual or printed signature of the auditor's firm.

    m. The city and state where the auditor practices.[25]

    n. The date of the auditor's report.

Further, as discussed in paragraph 23.40, the auditor may need to modify the report on compliance with requirements that could have a direct and material effect on each major program and on internal control over compliance in accordance with the Uniform Guidance for abuse findings reported in the federal awards section of the schedule of findings and questioned costs.

Option to Include Reporting on the Schedule of Expenditures of Federal Awards

23.27 As discussed in paragraph 23.13, this guide recommends reporting on the schedule of expenditures of federal awards in the report on the financial statements. However, in certain circumstances (for example, when the schedule of expenditures of federal awards is presented in a separate single audit reporting package), the auditor's report on the schedule may be incorporated into the report described in paragraph 23.19. Because of the added nuances when including the reporting on the schedule in the Uniform Guidance compliance report, examples 23-1–23-6 in the appendix of this chapter (paragraph 23.67) illustrate how to incorporate the reporting on the schedule into the Uniform Guidance compliance report. However, a footnote to example 23-1 provides information about how to report on the schedule using the recommended approach—that is, incorporating the reporting on the schedule in the report on the financial statements.

Dating the Report on Compliance With Requirements That Could Have a Direct and Material Effect on Each Major Program and on Internal Control Over Compliance

23.28 The auditor's report on compliance and on internal control over compliance related to major programs required by the Uniform Guidance carries the same date as that of a financial statement report when the audit procedures performed to satisfy Uniform Guidance requirements are completed along with

---

[24] This paragraph in the report conforms to paragraph .11 of AU-C section 905, *Alert That Restricts the Use of the Auditor's Written Communication* (AICPA, *Professional Standards*), which modifies the alert language used for compliance audits performed under *Government Auditing Standards*. This language should only be included in the internal control over compliance section of combined reports on the entity's compliance and internal control over compliance in light of the fact that it is the nature of the reporting on internal control over compliance that triggers the required use of alert language (see paragraph .06c of AU-C section 905). If the auditor issues separate reports on the entity's compliance and its internal control over compliance, this alert should be included in the report on internal control over compliance, but would not be included in the report on compliance.

[25] AU-C section 700, *Forming an Opinion and Reporting on Financial Statements* (AICPA, *Professional Standards*), provides that the auditor's report should name the city and state where the auditor practices. City and state on a firm's letterhead typically is sufficient to meet this requirement. Technical Questions and Answers section 9100.08, "Audit Firm With Multiple Offices on Their Company Letterhead and Effect on Report" (AICPA, *Technical Questions and Answers*), notes that when a firm's letterhead contains multiple office locations the auditor would need to indicate the city and state where the auditor practices in the auditor's report.

the procedures performed on the financial statements. However, when some of the audit procedures performed to satisfy Uniform Guidance requirements are completed subsequent to the procedures performed on the financial statements, the report on compliance for each major program and report on internal control over compliance required by the Uniform Guidance should be dated at a later date (that is, when the auditor has obtained sufficient appropriate audit evidence to support the report on the audit of compliance). The auditor should adapt and apply the applicable requirements and guidance from AU-C section 560, *Subsequent Events and Subsequently Discovered Facts* (AICPA, *Professional Standards*), for the purpose of performing subsequent events procedures from the date of the report on the financial statements to the date of the report on the Uniform Guidance compliance audit.

Other Reporting Considerations

Reissuance of the Uniform Guidance Compliance Report

23.29 If an auditor reissues the Uniform Guidance compliance report, the reissued report should include a paragraph within the other matters section of the report stating that the report is replacing a previously issued report, description of the reasons why the report is being reissued, and a listing of any changes from the previously issued report. Examples of situations in which the auditor may reissue the Uniform Guidance compliance report are (*a*) a quality control review performed by a governmental agency indicates that the auditor did not test a direct and material compliance requirement and (*b*) the discovery subsequent to the date of the compliance report that the entity had another major program that was required to be tested.

23.30 If additional procedures are performed to obtain sufficient appropriate audit evidence for all of the major programs being reported on, the auditor's report date should be updated to reflect the date the auditor obtained sufficient appropriate audit evidence regarding the events that caused the auditor to perform new procedures. If, however, additional procedures are performed to obtain sufficient appropriate audit evidence for only some of the major programs being reported on, the auditor should dual date the report with the updated report date reflecting the date the auditor obtained sufficient appropriate audit evidence regarding the major programs affected by the circumstances and referencing the major programs for which additional audit procedures have been performed. Reissuance of an auditor-prepared document required by the Uniform Guidance that is incorporated by reference into the auditor's report (for example, the schedule of findings and questioned costs) is considered to be a reissuance of the auditor's report.

Other Auditors

23.31 As noted in chapter 16, "Auditor Planning Considerations Under the Uniform Guidance," of this guide, when more than one independent auditor is involved in a single audit, the auditor should use professional judgment to adapt and apply the guidance in AU-C section 600, *Special Considerations—Audits of Group Financial Statements (Including the Work of Component Auditors)* (AICPA, *Professional Standards*), with regard to determining whether to refer to the other auditors (that is, component auditors) in the auditor's report on compliance and on internal control over compliance.

When the Audit of Federal Awards Does Not Encompass the Entirety of the Auditee's Operations

23.32 If the audit of federal awards does not encompass the entirety of the auditee's operations expending federal awards, the operations that are not included should be identified in a separate paragraph following the first paragraph of the introductory section of the report on compliance for each major program. (See also the discussion in chapter 16 of this guide concerning the definition of the entity to be audited.) An example of such a paragraph follows:

> Example Entity's basic financial statements include the operations of the [*identify organizational unit, such as a governmental component unit, an operating unit, or a department*], which received [*include dollar amount*] in federal awards which is not included in Example Entity's schedule of expenditures of federal awards during the year ended June 30, 20X1. Our audit, described below, did not include the operations of [*identify organizational unit*] because [*state the reason for the omission, such as the organizational unit engaged other auditors to perform an audit of compliance*].

Schedule of Findings and Questioned Costs [26]

23.33 The Uniform Guidance states that the auditor must prepare a schedule of findings and questioned costs, which must include the following three components:

a. A summary of the auditor's results

b. Findings relating to the financial statements that are required to be reported in accordance with *Government Auditing Standards*

c. Findings and questioned costs for federal awards

Example 23-7 in the appendix of this chapter (paragraph 23.67) presents an illustrative schedule of findings and questioned costs.

What Is Required to Be Reported

23.34 Specifically, the Uniform Guidance requires the schedule of findings and questioned costs to contain the following:

a. A summary of the auditor's results, which must include the following:

   i. The type of report the auditor issued on whether the financial statements audited were prepared in accordance with GAAP (that is, unmodified opinion, qualified opinion, adverse opinion, or disclaimer of opinion)[27]

---

[26] There is no option for the auditor to report in a written communication (such as a communication sometimes referred to as a *management letter*), findings that *Government Auditing Standards* or the Uniform Guidance requires to be reported in the auditor's report or schedule of findings and questioned costs. See also paragraph 23.45.

[27] As explained in the AICPA Audit and Accounting Guide *State and Local Governments*, the auditor generally expresses or disclaims an opinion on a government's basic financial statements by providing an opinion or disclaimer of opinion on each opinion unit required to be presented in those financial statements. (See footnote 2.) Therefore, the schedule of findings and questioned costs may need to indicate multiple types of opinions on a government's basic financial statements.

ii. Where applicable, a statement that significant deficiencies or material weaknesses in internal control were disclosed by the audit of the financial statements[28]
iii. A statement on whether the audit disclosed any noncompliance that is material to the financial statements of the auditee
iv. Where applicable, a statement that significant deficiencies or material weaknesses in the internal control over major programs were disclosed by the audit[29]
v. The type of report the auditor issued on compliance for major programs (that is, unmodified opinion, qualified opinion, adverse opinion, or disclaimer of opinion)
vi. A statement on whether the audit disclosed any audit findings that the auditor is required to report (See paragraph 23.38.)[30]
vii. An identification of major programs (in the case of a cluster of programs, only the cluster name as shown on the schedule of expenditures of federal awards is required)
viii. The dollar threshold used to distinguish between type A and type B programs (See chapter 18 of this guide.)
ix. A statement on whether the auditee qualified as a low-risk auditee (See chapter 18 of this guide.)

b. Findings relating to the financial statements that are required to be reported in accordance with *Government Auditing Standards*. (See paragraph 23.36.)

c. Findings and questioned costs for federal awards, which must include audit findings as defined in 2 CFR 200.516(a). (See paragraph 23.38.) Under the Uniform Guidance, this section of the schedule should include the following:

i. Audit findings (for example, internal control findings, compliance findings, questioned costs, fraud, or abuse) that relate to the same issue must be presented as one finding. When practical, audit findings **should** be organized by federal agency or pass-through entity.

ii. Audit findings that relate to both the financial statements and the federal awards must be reported in both sections of the schedule. However, the reporting in one section of the schedule may be in summary form, with a reference to a detailed reporting in the other section of the schedule. For example, a material weakness in internal control

---

[28] AU-C section 265, *Communicating Internal Control Related Matters Identified in an Audit* (AICPA, *Professional Standards*), precludes an auditor from issuing a written report representing that no significant deficiencies were noted during an audit. Therefore, the illustrative schedule of findings and questioned costs in example 23-7 in the appendix of this chapter (paragraph 23.67) uses the term *none reported* to indicate that no significant deficiencies were included in the auditor's report (versus *none*, which would imply that there were no significant deficiencies).

[29] See footnote 28.

[30] As discussed in paragraph 23.40, the auditor may need to modify the summary of auditor's results for abuse findings reported in the federal awards section of the schedule of findings and questioned costs.

that affects the auditee as a whole, including its federal awards, would usually be reported in detail in the section of the schedule of findings and questioned costs that is related to the financial statements, with a summary identification and reference given in the section related to federal awards. Conversely, a finding of noncompliance with a federal program law that also is material to the financial statements would be reported in detail in the federal awards section of the schedule, with a summary identification and reference given in the financial statement section.

23.35 The following table summarizes the requirements related to reporting findings in a Uniform Guidance compliance audit report. More detailed information regarding findings required to be reported in accordance with *Government Auditing Standards* is located in chapter 4 of this guide.[31] See paragraphs 23.36–.40 for more information, including the placement of findings within the schedule of findings and questioned costs. Also included in this table are items that, although not required to be reported under the Uniform Guidance, may be communicated under the guidance in AU-C section 260, *The Auditor's Communication With Those Charged With Governance*, and AU-C section 265, *Communicating Internal Control Related Matters Identified in an Audit* (AICPA, *Professional Standards*), as part of the compliance audit.

Table 23-2

Reporting in a Uniform Guidance Compliance Audit

	Schedule of Findings and Questioned Costs	Communicate in Writing or Orally
Findings related to the financial statements required to be reported in accordance with *Government Auditing Standards* (see table 4-1 in chapter 4 of this guide)	X	
Matters reported in a Uniform Guidance audit:		
Deficiencies in internal control:		
Significant deficiencies in internal control over compliance with a type of compliance requirement for a major program	X	

(continued)

---

[31] Table 4-1, "*Government Auditing Standards* Requirements for Reporting Findings," in chapter 4, "Auditor Reporting Requirements and Other Communication Considerations of *Government Auditing Standards*," of this guide provides information regarding reporting financial statement related findings as part of the financial statement audit performed under *Government Auditing Standards*.

Reporting in a Uniform Guidance Compliance Audit—*continued*

	Schedule of Findings and Questioned Costs	Communicate in Writing or Orally
Material weaknesses in internal control over compliance with a type of compliance requirement for a major program	X	
Other deficiencies in internal control over compliance that are not significant deficiencies or material weaknesses required to be reported but, in the auditor's judgment, are of sufficient importance to be communicated to management [1]		X
Noncompliance with federal statutes, regulations, or the terms and conditions of federal awards related to a major program:		
That is material in relation to a type of compliance requirement for a major program identified in the *Compliance Supplement*	X	
That does not meet the criteria for reporting under the Uniform Guidance but, in the auditor's judgment, is of sufficient importance to communicate to management or those charged with governance [2]		X
Questioned Costs		
Known questioned costs that are greater than $25,000 for a type of compliance requirement for a major program	X	
Known questioned costs when likely questioned costs are greater than $25,000 for a type of compliance requirement for a major program	X	
Known questioned costs that are greater than $25,000 for a program that is not audited as a major program	X	
Fraud		
Known or likely fraud affecting a federal award [3]	X	

Reporting in a Uniform Guidance Compliance Audit—*continued*

	Schedule of Findings and Questioned Costs	Communicate in Writing or Orally
Abuse[4]		
Significant instances of abuse relating to major programs, that is, abuse that is either quantitatively or qualitatively material to a major program	X	
Abuse that is less than material to a major program and not otherwise required to be reported but that, in the auditor's judgment, is of sufficient importance to communicate to management and those charged with governance		X
Other audit findings		
Circumstances concerning why the auditor's report on compliance for each major program is other than unmodified, unless such circumstances are otherwise reported as an audit finding in the schedule of findings and questioned costs.	X	
Instance when the results of audit follow-up procedures disclosed that the summary schedule of prior audit findings materially misrepresents the status of any prior audit finding	X	
Other findings or issues arising from the compliance audit that are not otherwise required to be reported but are, in the auditor's professional judgment, significant and relevant to those charged with governance		X

[1] The threshold for reporting deficiencies in internal control over compliance for major programs is in relation to a type of compliance requirement for a major program identified in the *OMB Compliance Supplement (Compliance Supplement)* (that is, not in relation to financial statement materiality or major program materiality, which is likely significantly higher). Even given this lower reporting threshold, there may be instances when the auditor deems it appropriate to communicate to management deficiencies in internal control over compliance for a major program or other federal program that are not required to be reported in the schedule of findings and questioned costs.

(continued)

Reporting in a Uniform Guidance Compliance Audit—*continued*

> ² The threshold for reporting noncompliance with federal statutes, regulations, and the terms and conditions of federal awards related to a federal program is one that is material in relation to a type of compliance requirement for a major program identified in the *Compliance Supplement* (that is, not in relation to financial statement materiality or major program materiality, which is likely significantly higher). However, there may be instances when the auditor deems it appropriate to communicate to management noncompliance that is not required to be reported. Note that this type of communication may also be considered by the auditor for findings of abuse or other findings that are not otherwise required to be reported.
> ³ See also paragraph 23.38*e*.
> ⁴ As discussed in chapter 20, "Compliance Auditing Applicable to Major Programs (Uniform Guidance)," of this guide and in paragraph 23.40, situations or transactions involving federal awards that might otherwise appear to constitute abuse, instead, generally are instances of noncompliance. However, there may be isolated situations or transactions involving federal awards that the auditor becomes aware of that do constitute abuse.

Findings Related to the Financial Statements

23.36 As noted previously, the Uniform Guidance requires the schedule of findings and questioned costs to include a section that presents the detail of findings related to the financial statements. This section of the schedule includes all findings related to the audit of the financial statements that are required to be reported by GAAS and *Government Auditing Standards*. See table 4-1, "*Government Auditing Standards* Requirements for Reporting Findings," in chapter 4 of this guide for information on what *Government Auditing Standards* requires to be reported in the audit of the financial statements under *Government Auditing Standards*.

23.37 Chapter 4 of this guide discusses the details that *Government Auditing Standards* requires be reported for findings. That chapter also discusses the requirement in paragraph 4.33 of *Government Auditing Standards* that the auditor obtain and report the views of responsible officials concerning the findings, conclusions, and recommendations, as well as his or her planned corrective actions. The auditor should present management's views and planned corrective actions for findings related to the financial statement audit in the financial statement section of the schedule of findings and questioned costs. Alternatively, for audit findings that relate to both the financial statements and the federal awards and that are required to be reported in both sections of the schedule of findings and questioned costs, depending on the status of the development of the corrective action plan at the time the auditor's reports are released, the auditor may be able to refer to management's corrective action plan as the required presentation of the auditee's views and planned corrective actions.

Audit Findings Related to Federal Awards[32]

23.38 2 CFR 200.516(a) provides that the auditor must report as audit findings in the federal awards section of the schedule of findings and questioned costs

    a. significant deficiencies and material weaknesses in internal control over major programs. The auditor's determination of whether a deficiency in internal control is a significant deficiency or material weakness for the purpose of reporting an audit finding is in relation to a type of compliance requirement for a major program identified in the *Compliance Supplement*. (Chapter 19 of this guide discusses significant deficiencies and material weaknesses related to federal programs.)

    b. material noncompliance with federal statutes, regulations, or the terms and conditions of federal awards related to a major program. The auditor's determination of whether an instance of noncompliance with federal statutes, regulations, or the terms and conditions of the federal awards is material for the purpose of reporting an audit finding is in relation to a type of compliance requirement for a major program identified in the *Compliance Supplement*. (Chapter 20 of this guide further discusses the evaluation and reporting of noncompliance.)

    c. known questioned costs that are greater than $25,000 for a type of compliance requirement for a major program. Known questioned costs are those specifically identified by the auditor. In evaluating the effect of questioned costs on the opinion on compliance, the auditor considers the best estimate of the total costs questioned (likely questioned costs), not just the questioned costs specifically identified (known questioned costs). The auditor also must report (in the schedule of findings and questioned costs) known questioned costs when likely questioned costs are greater than $25,000 for a type of compliance requirement for a major program. For example, if the auditor specifically identifies $7,000 in questioned costs but, based on his or her evaluation of the effect of questioned costs on the opinion on compliance, estimates that the total questioned costs are in the $50,000 to $60,000 range, the auditor would report a finding that identifies the known questioned costs of $7,000. Although the auditor is not required to report his or her estimate of the total questioned costs, the auditor must include information to provide proper perspective for judging the prevalence and consequences of the questioned costs.

    d. known questioned costs that are greater than $25,000 for a program that is not audited as a major program. Except for audit follow-up, the auditor is not required to perform audit procedures for such federal programs. Therefore, the auditor will normally not find questioned costs for a program that is not audited as a major program. However, if the auditor does become aware of questioned costs for a federal program that is not audited as a major program (for example, as part of audit follow-up or other audit procedures)

---

[32] See footnote 26.

and the known questioned costs are greater than $25,000, then the auditor must report this as an audit finding.

e. known or likely fraud affecting a federal award, unless such fraud is otherwise reported as an audit finding in the schedule of findings and questioned costs for federal awards. The Uniform Guidance does not require the auditor to report publicly information that could compromise investigative or legal proceedings or to make an additional reporting when the auditor confirms that the fraud was reported outside of the auditor's reports under the direct reporting requirements of *Government Auditing Standards*. (Chapter 4 of this guide discusses the direct reporting requirements of *Government Auditing Standards*.)

f. significant instances of abuse relating to major programs (see paragraph 23.40).

g. the circumstances concerning why the opinion in the auditor's report on compliance for each major program is other than an unmodified opinion, unless such circumstances are otherwise reported as audit findings in the schedule of findings and questioned costs for federal awards (for example, a scope limitation that is not otherwise reported as a finding).

h. instances in which the results of audit follow-up procedures disclosed that the summary schedule of prior audit findings prepared by the auditee in accordance with the Uniform Guidance materially misrepresents the status of any prior audit finding. (See paragraphs 23.46–.50.)

23.39 For those findings that are required to be reported in both the financial statement section and the federal awards section of the schedule of findings and questioned costs, reporting in one section may be in summary form with a reference to the detailed reporting in the other section of the schedule. See paragraph 23.34c and example 23-7 in the appendix of this chapter for additional information.

Findings of Abuse

23.40 As discussed in chapter 20 of this guide, situations or transactions involving federal awards that might otherwise appear to constitute abuse instead generally are instances of noncompliance. However, there may be isolated situations or transactions involving federal awards that the auditor becomes aware of that do constitute abuse. For abuse involving federal awards that is material to the financial statement amounts,[33] the auditor should report the finding in the report required by *Government Auditing Standards* and must present it in the financial statement section of the schedule of findings and questioned costs. For significant instances of abuse relating to a major program, the auditor must report an audit finding in the federal awards section of the schedule of findings and questioned costs. As discussed in paragraph 23.34c, the auditor must report abuse findings that relate to both the financial statements and the federal awards in both sections of the schedule. Those

---

[33] As discussed in the Audit and Accounting Guide *State and Local Governments*, the auditor's consideration of materiality for purposes of planning, performing, evaluating the results of, and reporting on the audit of the financial statements of a state or local government is based on opinion units.

findings may be presented in detail in one section and in summary form in the other section, with a cross-reference to the detailed presentation.

Detail of Audit Findings—Federal Awards

23.41 2 CFR 200.516(b) states that audit findings must be presented in sufficient detail for the auditee to prepare a corrective action plan and take corrective action and for federal agencies and pass-through entities to arrive at a management decision. (However, auditors [and auditees] must ensure that their part of the reporting package does not include protected personally identifiable information [protected PII]).[34] The following specific information must be included, as applicable, in audit findings:

- a. Identification of the federal program and specific federal award, including
    - i. the *Catalog of Federal Domestic Assistance* (CFDA) title and number.
    - ii. the federal award identification number and year.
    - iii. the name of the federal agency.
    - iv. the name of the applicable pass-through entity.

    When information such as the CFDA title and number or the federal award identification number is not available, the auditor must provide the best information available to describe the federal award. (Chapter 17 of this guide discusses an alternative for presentation if a CFDA number is not available.)

- b. The criteria or specific requirement upon which the audit finding is based, including the federal statutes, regulations, or the terms and conditions of the federal awards.

- c. The condition found, including facts that support the deficiency identified in the audit finding.

- d. A statement of cause that identifies the reason or explanation for the condition or the factors responsible for the difference between the situation that exists (condition) and the required or desired state (criteria), which may also serve as a basis for recommendations for corrective action.

- e. The possible asserted effect to provide sufficient information to the auditee and federal agency, or pass-through entity in the case of a subrecipient, to permit them to determine the cause and effect to facilitate prompt and proper corrective action. A statement of the effect or potential effect **should** provide a clear, logical link to establish the impact or potential impact of the difference between the condition and the criteria.

- f. Identification of questioned costs and how they were computed. Known questioned costs must be identified by applicable CFDA number(s) and applicable federal award identification number(s).

---

[34] Protected personally identifiable information means an individual's first name or first initial and last name in combination with any one or more other types of information, including, but not limited to, social security number, passport number, credit card numbers, clearances, bank numbers, biometrics, date and place of birth, mother's maiden name, criminal, medical and financial records, and educational transcripts. This does not include personally identifiable information (as defined in 2 CFR 200.79) that is required by law to be disclosed.

  g. Information to provide a proper perspective for judging the prevalence and consequences of the audit findings (for example, whether the audit findings represent an isolated instance or a systemic problem). When appropriate, the instances identified must be related to the universe and the number of cases examined and be quantified in terms of the dollar value. The auditor ***should*** report whether the sampling was a statistically valid sample.

  h. Identification of whether the audit finding was a repeat of a finding in the immediately prior audit and, if so, any applicable prior year audit finding numbers.

  i. Recommendations to prevent future occurrences of the deficiency identified in the audit finding.

  j. Views of responsible officials of the auditee.

23.42 Audit findings related to federal awards also should meet the presentation requirements of *Government Auditing Standards*. Chapter 4 of this guide discusses the details that *Government Auditing Standards* requires be reported for findings. That chapter also discusses the requirements in paragraphs 4.33–.39 of *Government Auditing Standards* that the auditor obtain and report the views of responsible officials concerning the findings, conclusions, and recommendations, including planned corrective actions.[35]

Other Preparation Guidance

23.43 Each audit finding in the schedule of findings and questioned costs must include a reference number in the format meeting the requirements of the data collection form submission to allow for easy referencing of the audit findings during follow-up. That format is the fiscal year being audited (or the fiscal year in which the finding initially occurred) as the beginning digits of each reference number, followed by a three-digit numeric sequence. For example, findings identified and reported in the audit of fiscal year 20X1 would be assigned reference numbers 20X1-001, 20X1-002, and so forth.

23.44 The auditor is required to issue a schedule of findings and questioned costs for every Uniform Guidance compliance audit, regardless of whether any findings or questioned costs are noted. That is because the Uniform Guidance requires that one section of the schedule summarize the audit results. (See paragraphs 23.33–.34.) In a situation in which there are no findings or questioned costs, the auditor is required to prepare the summary of auditor's results section of the schedule and either omit the other sections or include them, indicating that no matters were reported.

Communicating Other Findings to Management

23.45 The schedule of findings and questioned costs must include all audit findings required to be reported under the Uniform Guidance. A separate written communication (such as a communication sometimes referred to as a

---

[35] Paragraph 4.38 of *Government Auditing Standards* states that when the auditee's comments are inconsistent or in conflict with the report's findings, conclusions, or recommendations, and are not, in the auditor's opinion, valid—or when the planned corrective actions do not adequately address the auditor's recommendations—the auditor should state reasons for disagreeing with the comments or planned corrective actions. Conversely, the auditor should modify their report as necessary if they find the comments valid and supported with sufficient, appropriate evidence.

management letter)[36] may not be used to communicate such matters to the auditee in lieu of reporting them as audit findings in accordance with the Uniform Guidance. See the discussion beginning at paragraph 23.33 for information on Uniform Guidance requirements for the schedule of findings and questioned costs. If there are other matters that do not meet the Uniform Guidance requirements for reporting but, in the auditor's judgment, warrant the attention of those charged with governance, they should be communicated in writing or orally. If such a communication is provided in writing to the auditee, there is no requirement for that communication to be referenced in the Uniform Guidance compliance report. See table 23-2 for more information.

Summary Schedule of Prior Audit Findings and Corrective Action Plan [37]

23.46 The auditee is responsible for follow-up and corrective action on findings relating to federal awards and the financial statements. As part of this responsibility, the auditee must prepare a summary schedule of prior audit findings. The auditee is not required to prepare a summary schedule of prior audit findings if there are no matters reportable therein. The auditee also must prepare a separate corrective action plan that addresses each of the current-year audit findings.[38] (See chapter 20 for additional information on the corrective action plan.) The summary schedule of prior audit findings and the corrective action plan, both of which are part of the reporting package, must include the reference numbers the auditor assigns to audit findings in the schedule of findings and questioned costs. Because the summary schedule of prior audit findings may include audit findings from multiple years, it must include the fiscal year in which the finding initially occurred.[39]

23.47 The summary schedule of prior audit findings must report the status of all audit findings (which encompass those defined in 2 CFR 200.516(a)) included in the prior audit's schedule of findings and questioned costs. See paragraph 23.38 for a listing of audit findings required to be reported. The schedule must also include audit findings reported in the prior audit's summary schedule of prior audit findings unless those audit findings were listed as corrected, no longer valid, or not warranting further action.[40] When audit

---

[36] In response to requests by a federal agency or pass-through entity, an auditee must submit a copy of any management letters issued by the auditor.

[37] The Uniform Guidance requires the auditee to prepare a summary schedule of prior audit findings (summary schedule) and a corrective action plan. These two documents are required to be included in the reporting package submitted to the Federal Audit Clearinghouse (FAC). Note that the inclusion of the summary schedule and corrective action plan in the reporting package is not considered to be "other information" under AU-C section 720, *Other Information in Documents Containing Audited Financial Statements* (AICPA, *Professional Standards*), or "supplementary information" under AU-C section 725, as it does not fit the criteria for such in either AU-C section.

[38] Paragraph 4.33 of *Government Auditing Standards* states that the auditor should obtain and report the views of responsible auditee officials concerning the findings, conclusions, and recommendations, as well as planned corrective actions. Paragraphs 23.37 and 23.42 discuss the interaction of that *Government Auditing Standards* requirement and the Uniform Guidance requirement that the auditee prepare a corrective action plan.

[39] This may be accomplished by way of using the required finding reference numbering format as discussed in paragraph 23.43.

[40] See chapter 20, "Compliance Auditing Applicable to Major Programs (Uniform Guidance)," for additional information regarding this requirement.

findings were fully corrected, the schedule need only list the audit findings and state that corrective action was taken. When audit findings were not corrected, or were only partially corrected, the schedule must describe the reasons for the audit finding's recurrence and planned corrective action and any partial corrective action taken. When corrective action taken is significantly different from corrective action previously reported in a corrective action plan or in the federal agency's or pass-through entity's management decision, the schedule must provide an explanation.

23.48 The auditor must follow up on prior audit findings, perform procedures to assess the reasonableness of the summary schedule of prior audit findings prepared by the auditee in accordance with the Uniform Guidance, and report, as a current-year audit finding, when the auditor concludes that the summary schedule of prior audit findings materially misrepresents the status of any prior audit finding. The auditor must perform audit follow-up regardless of whether a prior audit finding relates to a major program in the current year. (Chapter 20 of this guide discusses follow-up procedures.)

23.49 In accordance with 2 CFR 200.511, the summary schedule of prior audit findings must also include findings relating to the financial statements which are required to be reported in accordance with *Government Auditing Standards*. Although the Uniform Guidance technically limits the auditor's follow-up responsibility to audit findings in 2 CFR 200.516(a), *Government Auditing Standards* includes a requirement, (discussed in chapter 3, "Planning and Performing a Financial Statement Audit in Accordance with *Government Auditing Standards*," of this guide), that the auditor evaluate whether the auditee has taken appropriate corrective action to address findings and recommendations from previous engagements that could have a material effect on the financial statements or other data significant to the audit objectives. Therefore, performing the auditor follow-up procedures described in paragraph 23.48 on findings relating to the financial statements would be an effective way to meet the follow-up responsibilities under *Government Auditing Standards*.

23.50 The auditor has no responsibility for the preparation of the corrective action plan; however, the auditor may be separately engaged by the auditee for assistance in developing appropriate corrective actions in response to audit findings. The auditor may find the auditee's prior year corrective action plan useful in performing follow-up on prior audit findings (in addition to the summary schedule of prior audit findings) because it may provide an indication of the corrective action planned by the auditee.

Data Collection Form

23.51 The Uniform Guidance states that the auditee must submit a data collection form (Form SF-SAC) that states whether the audit was completed in accordance with the Uniform Guidance and provides information about the auditee, its federal programs, and the results of the audit. The data collection form must include information available from the audit that is necessary for federal agencies to use the audit to ensure integrity for federal programs. This form is not an element of the reporting package; instead, the required information on the form represents a summary of the information contained in the reporting package. (See paragraph 23.05 for the elements of a reporting package.) The auditee completes the data collection form online (through the

FAC website at http://harvester.census.gov/sac/) and electronically certifies it (via an online signature) upon submission.

23.52 In addition, the auditor must complete the applicable data elements of the data collection form online (for example, auditor contact information and information on the results of the financial statement audit and the compliance audit of federal programs under the Uniform Guidance) and electronically sign an auditor statement provided on the form. The auditor statement indicates, at a minimum, the source of the information included in the form, the auditor's responsibility for the information, that the form is not a substitute for the reporting package, and that the content of the form is limited to the collection of information prescribed by the OMB. The date the auditor signs the statement indicates the completion date of the form as it relates to the auditor. The wording of the auditor's statement section of the data collection form indicates that no additional procedures were performed since the date of the audit reports. This wording releases the auditor from any subsequent-event responsibility with regard to the timing of the completion of the form and the completion of the audit.

23.53 Under the Uniform Guidance, unless restricted by federal statutes or regulations, the auditee must make copies of the reporting package available for public inspection. The data collection form and reporting package are available for public inspection through the FAC.[41] Auditees and auditors must ensure that their respective parts of the reporting package do not include protected PII.[42]

23.54 The data collection form and related instructions can be accessed from the FAC's website at http://harvester.census.gov/sac. The form number is SF-SAC.[43] The FAC requires electronic submission of the data collection form via an online Internet Data Entry System.

Submission of Reporting Package and Data Collection Form

23.55 The auditee must electronically submit to the FAC the data collection form and the reporting package, including the auditor's reports. After the data collection form is completed and the reporting package is uploaded to the FAC website (http://harvester.census.gov/sac/) by the auditee, certification by the auditee and a signature by the auditor on the auditor statement (described in paragraphs 23.51–.54) completes the submission. The auditee must submit the data collection form and the reporting package within the earlier of 30 days

---

[41] The Uniform Guidance does provide an exception for Indian tribes and tribal organizations. An auditee that is an Indian tribe or tribal organization may opt not to authorize the FAC to make the reporting package publicly available on a website by excluding the authorization allowing the FAC to make the reporting package and form publicly available from the required statement.

[42] The auditor must ensure that protected PII is not included in the body of audit reports or any attached or referenced schedules or letters. The auditor is also cautioned not to include other potentially sensitive information. See also footnote 34 at paragraph 23.41.

[43] The OMB periodically revises the data collection form and its accompanying instructions. As of the date of this guide, the latest version of the form available on the FAC website is the data collection form for 2013–2015 audits. However, this form will be updated to accommodate nonfederal entities with December 25, 2015, year ends that are required to be audited in accordance with the Uniform Guidance. Auditors are cautioned to make sure they complete the version of the form and instructions that apply to the required compliance auditing standards and the fiscal year audited.

after the receipt of the auditor's reports or 9 months after the end of the audit period.[44,45]

Federal Audit Clearinghouse Responsibilities

23.56 The FAC must make available to the public the reporting packages received.[46] It must maintain a data base of completed audits, provide appropriate information to federal agencies, and follow up with known auditees that have not submitted the required data collection forms and reporting packages.

23.57 The FAC is the repository of record for the data collection forms and reporting packages. All federal agencies, pass-through entities, and others interested in a reporting package and data collection form must obtain it by accessing the FAC.

23.58 If the auditee or auditor revises a previous submission or other communication made to the FAC, such changes are done on the FAC website. See the FAC website for the most current information on the process for situations in which there are revisions to the form or other communication, including instructions for submitting those revisions to the FAC.

Freedom of Information Act and Similar Laws and Regulations

23.59 Often, federal, state, and local laws and regulations, such as the Freedom of Information Act (*Government Organization and Employees*, *U.S. Code* 5, Section 552), require governments to release certain documents, including audit reports and other required written communications of entities for which the government has oversight responsibilities, to members of the press and the general public. Other laws and regulations require that audit reports of governments be made publicly available.

Transition Considerations Related to the Uniform Guidance

23.60 The following are some overall areas of note in compliance audit reporting under the Uniform Guidance:

- The requirements regarding findings and the content of the schedule of findings and questioned costs has been revised.
- The threshold for reporting questioned costs has been revised.
- Some terminology has changed. Under the Uniform Guidance management is responsible for compliance with "federal statutes, regulations, and the terms and conditions of federal awards." (In

---

[44] If the auditee or auditor wishes to report to the federal government that the required submission will be late, the suggested way to do so is to contact the federal oversight or cognizant agency for the audit (contact information is available on the "Resources" tab at http://harvester.census.gov/fac/APPX3.htm).

[45] 2 CFR 200.520 provides that one of the conditions necessary for an entity to meet the criteria for low-risk auditee status in the current year is that the prior 2 years' audits must have been performed on an annual basis in accordance with the Uniform Guidance, including report submission to the FAC by the due date.

[46] See footnote 42.

Auditor Reporting Requirements and Other Communication

a Circular A-133 report the equivalent language is that management is responsible for compliance with "the requirements of laws, regulations, contracts and grants applicable to its federal programs.")

- The concept of abuse appears in the Uniform Guidance. Abuse was not mentioned in Circular A-133.

23.61 Several revisions found in the Uniform Guidance relate to findings and the schedule of findings and questioned costs. Under the Uniform Guidance, the following are changes to those requirements from those previously found in Circular A-133, along with some related considerations:

- The threshold for reporting known questioned costs was increased to $25,000 (from $10,000). Known questioned cost must also be reported when likely questioned costs are greater than $25,000 for a type of compliance requirement for a major program. Known questioned costs must be identified by applicable CFDA and federal award identification number(s).
- Both known and likely fraud affecting federal awards are required to be reported in the schedule of findings and questioned costs, not just known fraud. Prior to the Uniform Guidance, this requirement was found only in *Government Auditing Standards*.
- Audit findings required to be reported in the schedule of findings and questioned costs under the Uniform Guidance includes significant instances of abuse relating to major programs. Prior to the Uniform Guidance, guidance regarding abuse was found only in *Government Auditing Standards*.
- The elements of a finding presented in the schedule of findings and questioned costs must include a statement of cause that identifies the reason or explanation for the conditions or the factors responsible for the finding. Prior to the Uniform Guidance, this requirement was found only in *Government Auditing Standards*. In addition, identification of whether the audit finding was a repeat of a finding in the immediately prior year, and the related finding number, is a new required element.
- The schedule of findings and questioned costs must include the views of responsible officials for all findings, not only those where there is a disagreement.
- Audit finding reference numbers are required to be in a format that meets the requirements of the data collection form submission, that is, 201X-XXX.
- Audit findings detail ***should*** include a statement about whether the sample was a statistically valid sample.

23.62 Under the Uniform Guidance, findings related to the financial statements that are required to be reported in accordance with *Government Auditing Standards* are required to be included in the summary schedule of prior audit findings.

23.63 Beginning with audits performed under the Uniform Guidance, unless restricted by federal statutes or regulations, the auditee must make copies of the data collection form and reporting package available for public inspection. The FAC will be the repository of record for data collection forms and reporting packages, and federal agencies and pass-through entities must obtain the reporting package by accessing the FAC website. That means under the Uniform Guidance a subrecipient is only required to submit the reporting package to the FAC and is no longer required to submit a copy to a pass-through entity. In addition, the requirement that a pass-through entity retain a copy of the subrecipient reporting package was removed because it will now be publicly available on the Internet. Note that Indian tribes and tribal organizations may opt to not authorize the FAC to make the reporting package publicly available. See 2 CFR 200.512(b)(2) for additional information. One item of note is that some state laws may still require submission of subrecipient reports to the pass-through entity or have other subreicpient submission requirements that go beyond what the Uniform Guidance requires.

23.64 The FAC will be revising the data collection form and submission processes to accommodate audits that are performed under Subpart F of the Uniform Guidance. The FAC has stated that it plans to be ready to collect data collection forms and reporting packages for audits performed under the Uniform Guidance no earlier than March 2016.

23.65 As noted in the "Transition Considerations Related to the Uniform Guidance" section in chapter 20 of this guide, the auditor may be required to test federal award transactions using both the pre-Uniform Guidance requirements and post-Uniform Guidance requirements. In that case, there is no related change needed to the auditor's report on compliance and on internal control over compliance related to major federal programs. This is because the report references the testing of types of compliance requirements described in the *Compliance Supplement*. This broad reference to the *Compliance Supplement* covers both testing performed using pre-Uniform Guidance requirements and post-Uniform Guidance requirements.

23.66 The Uniform Guidance states that the auditor and auditee must ensure that their respective parts of the reporting package do not include protected personally identifiable information. For auditors, this would include ensuring that the findings described in the schedule of findings and questioned costs and the auditor's reports do not include protected personally identifiable information. Protected personally identifiable information means an individual's first name or first initial and last name in combination with any one or more other types of information, including, but not limited to, social security number, passport number, credit card numbers, clearances, bank numbers, biometrics, date and place of birth, mother's maiden name, criminal, medical and financial records, and educational transcripts. This does not include personally identifiable information (as defined in 2 CFR 200.79) that is required by law to be disclosed.

23.67

Appendix—Illustrative Auditor's Reports Under the Uniform Guidance for Federal Awards

This appendix contains examples of the report on compliance with requirements that could have a direct and material effect on each major federal program and on internal control over compliance issued under the audit requirements of Title 2 U.S. *Code of Federal Regulations* (CFR) Part 200, *Uniform Administrative Requirements, Cost Principles, and Audit Requirements for Federal Awards* (Uniform Guidance), in various circumstances as discussed in this chapter. The following table lists the illustrative reports. Auditors, using professional judgment, may adapt these examples to other situations not specifically addressed in this guide.

Example No.	Title
23-1	Report on Compliance for Each Major Federal Program; Report on Internal Control Over Compliance; and Report on Schedule of Expenditures of Federal Awards Required by the Uniform Guidance (*Unmodified Opinion on Compliance for Each Major Federal Program; No Material Weaknesses or Significant Deficiencies in Internal Control Over Compliance Identified*)
23-2	Report on Compliance for Each Major Federal Program; Report on Internal Control Over Compliance; and Report on Schedule of Expenditures of Federal Awards Required by the Uniform Guidance (*Unmodified Opinion on Compliance for Each Major Federal Program; Significant Deficiencies in Internal Control Over Compliance Identified*)
23-3	Report on Compliance for Each Major Federal Program; Report on Internal Control Over Compliance; and Report on Schedule of Expenditures of Federal Awards Required by the Uniform Guidance (*Unmodified Opinion on Compliance for Each Major Federal Program; Material Weaknesses in Internal Control Over Compliance Identified; No Significant Deficiencies in Internal Control Over Compliance Identified*)
23-4	Report on Compliance for Each Major Federal Program; Report on Internal Control Over Compliance; and Report on Schedule of Expenditures of Federal Awards Required by the Uniform Guidance (*Qualified Opinion on Compliance for One Major Federal Program; Unmodified Opinion on Compliance on Each of the Other Major Federal Programs; Material Weaknesses and Significant Deficiencies in Internal Control Over Compliance Identified*)

(continued)

Example No.	Title
23-5	Report on Compliance for Each Major Federal Program; Report on Internal Control Over Compliance; and Report on Schedule of Expenditures of Federal Awards Required by the Uniform Guidance (*Qualified Opinion on Compliance—Scope Limitation for One Major Federal Program; Unmodified Opinion on Compliance on Each of the Other Major Federal Programs; Significant Deficiencies in Internal Control Over Compliance Identified*)
23-6	Report on Compliance for Each Major Federal Program; Report on Internal Control Over Compliance; and Report on Schedule of Expenditures of Federal Awards Required by the Uniform Guidance (*Adverse Opinion on Compliance for One Major Federal Program; Unmodified Opinion on Compliance on Each of the Other Major Federal Programs; Material Weaknesses and Significant Deficiencies in Internal Control Over Compliance Identified*)
23-7	Schedule of Findings and Questioned Costs
23-8	Report on Schedule of Expenditures of Federal Awards When the Auditor Is Issuing a Stand-Alone Report Under AU-C Section 805, *Special Considerations—Audits of Single Financial Statements and Specific Elements, Accounts, or Items of a Financial Statement* (*Unmodified Opinion on Schedule of Expenditures of Federal Awards*)

In a single audit, auditors also are required to issue (*a*) an opinion (or disclaimer of opinion) on the financial statements and on the supplementary schedule of expenditures of federal awards and (*b*) a report on internal control over financial reporting and on compliance and other matters based on an audit of financial statements performed in accordance with *Government Auditing Standards*. The appendix in chapter 4, "Auditor Reporting Requirements and Other Communication Considerations of *Government Auditing Standards*," of this guide illustrates those reports. The appendix in chapter 24, "Program-Specific Audits (Uniform Guidance)," of this guide illustrates the reports issued for a program-specific audit.

Auditor Reporting Requirements and Other Communication   **625**

Example 23-1

Report on Compliance for Each Major Federal Program; Report on Internal Control Over Compliance; and Report on Schedule of Expenditures of Federal Awards Required by the Uniform Guidance

(Unmodified Opinion on Compliance for Each Major Federal Program; No Material Weaknesses or Significant Deficiencies in Internal Control Over Compliance Identified)[1]

<u>Independent Auditor's Report</u>

[*Appropriate Addressee*]

Report on Compliance for Each Major Federal Program

We have audited Example Entity's compliance with the types of compliance requirements[2] described in the *OMB Compliance Supplement* that could have a direct and material effect[3] on each of Example Entity's major federal programs for the year ended June 30, 20X1. Example Entity's major federal programs are identified in the summary of auditor's results section of the accompanying schedule of findings and questioned costs.[4]

---

[1] Examples 23-1–23-6 are intended to provide illustrations for various situations. Auditors, using professional judgment, may adapt these examples to other situations not specifically addressed within the illustrations. For example, the compliance section of one example may be used along with the internal control section of another.

[2] Under 2 CFR 200.516(a) the auditor's determination of whether a noncompliance with federal statutes, regulations, or the terms and conditions of federal awards is material for the purpose of reporting an audit finding is in relation to a type of compliance requirement for a major program identified in the *OMB Compliance Supplement (Compliance Supplement)*. Further, the auditor's determination of whether a deficiency in internal control over compliance is a significant deficiency or material weakness for the purpose of reporting an audit finding is also in relation to a type of compliance requirement for a major federal program identified in the *Compliance Supplement*. The reference to "type of compliance requirements" used here and elsewhere in this report illustration refers to the 12 types of compliance requirements described in Part 3 of the 2015 *Compliance Supplement*.

[3] AU-C section 935, *Compliance Audits* (AICPA, *Professional Standards*), defines *applicable compliance requirements* as the compliance requirements that are subject to the compliance audit. According to 2 CFR 200.515, the auditor's report on compliance with federal statutes, regulations, and the terms and conditions of federal awards must include an opinion (or disclaimer of opinion) regarding whether the auditee complied with federal statutes, regulations, and the terms and conditions of federal awards that could have a direct and material effect on each major program. Therefore, in a Uniform Guidance compliance audit, the *applicable compliance* requirements are those that are subject to audit. Accordingly, for the purpose of adapting AU-C section 935 to a Uniform Guidance compliance audit, the term *applicable* has been replaced by *direct and material* when referencing such compliance requirements in this report. See also footnote 2 of this appendix for a discussion related to the determination of material noncompliance.

[4] As discussed in paragraph 23.32 and in chapter 16, "Planning Considerations Under the Uniform Guidance," of this guide, there are situations in which the audit of federal awards may not encompass the entirety of the auditee's operations. In this case, the operations that are not included should be identified in a separate paragraph following the first paragraph of the report. An example of such a paragraph follows:

> Example Entity's basic financial statements include the operations of the [*identify organizational unit, such as a governmental component unit, an operating unit, or a department*], which received [*include dollar amount*] in federal awards which is not included in Example Entity's schedule of expenditures of federal awards during the year ended June 30, 20X1. Our audit, described below, did not include the operations of [*identify organizational unit*] because [*state the reason for the omission, such as the organizational unit engaged other auditors to perform an audit of compliance*].

©2015, AICPA   AAG-GAS 23.67

Management's Responsibility

Management is responsible for compliance with federal statutes, regulations, and the terms and conditions of its federal awards applicable to its federal programs.

Auditor's Responsibility

Our responsibility is to express an opinion on compliance for each of Example Entity's major federal programs based on our audit of the types of compliance requirements referred to above. We conducted our audit of compliance in accordance with auditing standards generally accepted in the United States of America; the standards applicable to financial audits contained in *Government Auditing Standards*, issued by the Comptroller General of the United States; and the audit requirements of Title 2 U.S. *Code of Federal Regulations* Part 200, *Uniform Administrative Requirements, Cost Principles, and Audit Requirements for Federal Awards* (Uniform Guidance). Those standards and the Uniform Guidance require that we plan and perform the audit to obtain reasonable assurance about whether noncompliance with the types of compliance requirements referred to above that could have a direct and material effect on a major federal program occurred. An audit includes examining, on a test basis, evidence about Example Entity's compliance with those requirements and performing such other procedures as we considered necessary in the circumstances.

We believe that our audit provides a reasonable basis for our opinion on compliance for each major federal program. However, our audit does not provide a legal determination of Example Entity's compliance.

Opinion on Each Major Federal Program

In our opinion, Example Entity complied, in all material respects, with the types of compliance requirements referred to above that could have a direct and material effect on each of its major federal programs for the year ended June 30, 20X1.

Other Matters [5]

The results of our auditing procedures disclosed instances of noncompliance, which are required to be reported in accordance with the Uniform Guidance and which are described in the accompanying schedule of findings and questioned costs as items [*list the reference numbers of the related findings, for example, 20X1-001 and 20X1-002*].[6] Our opinion on each major federal program is not modified with respect to these matters.

Example Entity's response to the noncompliance findings identified in our audit are described in the accompanying [*insert name of document containing management's response to the auditor's findings; for example, schedule of findings and questioned costs and/or corrective action plan*]. Example Entity's response

---

[5] When there are no findings that are required to be reported and, thus, no management response to findings, this "Other Matters" section of the report would be omitted.

[6] The auditor may also consider adding a table to this section of the report, similar to the illustration provided in footnote 50, to more clearly communicate the other findings that are being reported and the programs and requirements to which they relate.

was not subjected to the auditing procedures applied in the audit of compliance and, accordingly, we express no opinion on the response.[7]

Report on Internal Control Over Compliance[8]

Management of Example Entity is responsible for establishing and maintaining effective internal control over compliance with the types of compliance requirements referred to above. In planning and performing our audit of compliance, we considered Example Entity's internal control over compliance with the types of requirements that could have a direct and material effect on each major federal program to determine the auditing procedures that are appropriate in the circumstances for the purpose of expressing an opinion on compliance for each major federal program and to test and report on internal control over compliance in accordance with the Uniform Guidance, but not for the purpose of expressing an opinion on the effectiveness of internal control over compliance. Accordingly, we do not express an opinion on the effectiveness of Example Entity's internal control over compliance.

A *deficiency in internal control over compliance* exists when the design or operation of a control over compliance does not allow management or employees, in the normal course of performing their assigned functions, to prevent, or detect and correct, noncompliance with a type of compliance requirement of a federal program on a timely basis. A *material weakness in internal control over compliance* is a deficiency, or combination of deficiencies, in internal control over compliance, such that there is a reasonable possibility that material noncompliance with a type of compliance requirement of a federal program will not be prevented, or detected and corrected, on a timely basis. A *significant deficiency in internal control over compliance* is a deficiency, or a combination of deficiencies, in internal control over compliance with a type of compliance requirement of a federal program that is less severe than a material weakness in internal control over compliance, yet important enough to merit attention by those charged with governance.

Our consideration of internal control over compliance was for the limited purpose described in the first paragraph of this section and was not designed to identify all deficiencies in internal control over compliance that might be material weaknesses or significant deficiencies. We did not identify any deficiencies in internal control over compliance that we consider to be material weaknesses. However, material weaknesses may exist that have not been identified.

---

[7] Although the auditor does not audit management's response to identified findings, the auditor does have certain responsibilities related to reporting the views of responsible officials under the Uniform Guidance and *Government Auditing Standards*. See paragraphs 23.38*h* and 23.46 or further discussion.

[8] Examples 23-1–23-6 illustrate combined reports that also include the reporting on internal control over compliance. If an auditor prefers to issue a separate report on internal control over compliance, this section would be omitted from the report. AU-C section 935 includes required elements for separate reporting on internal control over compliance.

The purpose of this report on internal control over compliance is solely to describe the scope of our testing of internal control over compliance and the results of that testing based on the requirements of the Uniform Guidance. Accordingly, this report is not suitable for any other purpose.[9]

Report on Schedule of Expenditures of Federal Awards Required by the Uniform Guidance[10,11]

We have audited the financial statements of Example Entity as of and for the year ended June 30, 20X1, and have issued our report thereon dated August 15, 20X1, which contained an unmodified opinion on those financial statements. Our audit was conducted for the purpose of forming an opinion on the financial statements as a whole. The accompanying schedule of expenditures of federal awards is presented for purposes of additional analysis as required by the Uniform Guidance and is not a required part of the financial statements. Such information is the responsibility of management and was derived from and relates directly to the underlying accounting and other records used to prepare the financial statements. The information has been subjected to the auditing procedures applied in the audit of the financial statements and certain additional procedures, including comparing and reconciling such information directly to the underlying accounting and other records used to prepare the financial statements or to the financial statements themselves, and other additional procedures in accordance with auditing standards generally accepted in the United States of America. In our opinion, the schedule of expenditure

---

[9] This paragraph has been adapted from AU-C section 905, *Alert That Restricts the Use of the Auditor's Written Communication* (AICPA, *Professional Standards*), to relate to the reporting on internal control over compliance that is required in an audit of compliance in accordance with the Uniform Guidance.

[10] The wording of this report is based AU-C section 725, *Supplementary Information in Relation to the Financial Statements as a Whole* (AICPA, *Professional Standards*).

[11] As noted in paragraph 23.06, this guide recommends reporting on the schedule of expenditures of federal awards in the report on the financial statements. Chapter 4, "Auditor Reporting Requirements and Other Communication Considerations of *Government Auditing Standards*," of this guide illustrates the reporting on the schedule when such reporting is included in the financial statement report. However, as noted in paragraph 23.19, there may be certain circumstances when the auditor's report on the schedule is incorporated into the report issued to meet the requirements of the Uniform Guidance. Therefore, examples 23-1–23-6 illustrate the inclusion of the auditor's in-relation-to reporting on the schedule of expenditures of federal awards. Its inclusion in these examples is not intended to imply a best practice. If the in-relation-to reporting on the schedule is included in the report on the financial statements or in a separate report, this section would be omitted, and the title of the report would be modified as follows:

"Report on Compliance for Each Major Federal Program and Report on Internal Control Over Compliance Required by the Uniform Guidance."

of federal awards is fairly stated in all material respects in relation to the financial statements as a whole.[12]

[*Auditor's signature*]

[*Auditor's city and state*][13]

[*Date of the auditor's report*][14]

---

[12] The wording of this report on the schedule of expenditures of federal awards refers to the financial statements of a nongovernmental entity. For audits of governmental entities, it would be replaced with the following:

Report on Schedule of Expenditures of Federal Awards Required by the Uniform Guidance

We have audited the financial statements of the governmental activities, the business-type activities, the aggregate discretely presented component units, each major fund, and the aggregate remaining fund information of Example Entity as of and for the year ended June 30, 20X1, and the related notes to the financial statements, which collectively comprise Example Entity's basic financial statements. We issued our report thereon dated August 15, 20X1, which contained unmodified opinions on those financial statements. Our audit was conducted for the purpose of forming opinions on the financial statements that collectively comprise the basic financial statements. The accompanying schedule of expenditures of federal awards is presented for purposes of additional analysis as required by the Uniform Guidance and is not a required part of the basic financial statements. Such information is the responsibility of management and was derived from and relates directly to the underlying accounting and other records used to prepare the basic financial statements. The information has been subjected to the auditing procedures applied in the audit of the financial statements and certain additional procedures, including comparing and reconciling such information directly to the underlying accounting and other records used to prepare the basic financial statements or to the basic financial statements themselves, and other additional procedures in accordance with auditing standards generally accepted in the United States of America. In our opinion, the schedule of expenditure of federal awards is fairly stated in all material respects in relation to the basic financial statements as a whole.

[13] AU-C section 700, *Forming an Opinion and Reporting on Financial Statements* (AICPA, *Professional Standards*), provides that the auditor's report should name the city and state where the auditor practices. City and State on a firm's letterhead typically is sufficient to meet this requirement. Technical Questions and Answers section 9100.08, "Audit Firm With Multiple Offices on Their Company Letterhead and Effect on Report" (AICPA, *Technical Questions and Answers*), notes that when a firm's letterhead contains multiple office locations, the auditor would need to indicate the city and state where the auditor practices in the auditor's report.

[14] As noted in footnote 11, examples 23-1–23-6 illustrate the inclusion of the in-relation-to opinion on the schedule of expenditures of federal awards. AU-C section 725 states that the date of the auditor's report on supplementary information (for example, the schedule of expenditures of federal awards in these illustrations) in relation to the financial statements as a whole should not be earlier than the date on which the auditor completed the procedures required by AU-C section 725. Therefore, when the required procedures in AU-C section 725 are completed on an earlier date than that of the auditor's "Report on Compliance for Each Major Federal Program," the auditor would dual-date this report. See the discussion beginning at paragraph 23.16 of this guide for further discussion of dating the in-relation-to reporting on the schedule of expenditures of federal awards. Illustrative wording when dual dating the report is as follows:

[Date], except for our report on the Schedule of Expenditures of Federal Awards, for which the date is [*Date the in-relation-to procedures completed*]

Example 23-2

Report on Compliance for Each Major Federal Program; Report on Internal Control Over Compliance; and Report on Schedule of Expenditures of Federal Awards Required by the Uniform Guidance

(Unmodified Opinion on Compliance for Each Major Federal Program; Significant Deficiencies in Internal Control Over Compliance Identified) [15]

Independent Auditor's Report

[*Appropriate Addressee*]

Report on Compliance for Each Major Federal Program

We have audited Example Entity's compliance with the types of compliance requirements[16] described in the *OMB Compliance Supplement* that could have a direct and material effect[17] on each of Example Entity's major federal programs for the year ended June 30, 20X1. Example Entity's major federal programs are identified in the summary of auditor's results section of the accompanying schedule of findings and questioned costs.[18]

Management's Responsibility

Management is responsible for compliance with federal statutes, regulations, and the terms and conditions of its federal awards applicable to its federal programs.

Auditor's Responsibility

Our responsibility is to express an opinion on compliance for each of Example Entity's major federal programs based on our audit of the types of compliance requirements referred to above. We conducted our audit of compliance in accordance with auditing standards generally accepted in the United States of America; the standards applicable to financial audits contained in *Government Auditing Standards*, issued by the Comptroller General of the United States; and the audit requirements of Title 2 U.S. *Code of Federal Regulations* Part 200, *Uniform Administrative Requirements, Cost Principles, and Audit Requirements for Federal Awards* (Uniform Guidance). Those standards and the Uniform Guidance require that we plan and perform the audit to obtain reasonable assurance about whether noncompliance with the types of compliance requirements referred to above that could have a direct and material effect on a major federal program occurred. An audit includes examining, on a test basis, evidence about Example Entity's compliance with those requirements and performing such other procedures as we considered necessary in the circumstances.

We believe that our audit provides a reasonable basis for our opinion on compliance for each major federal program. However, our audit does not provide a legal determination of Example Entity's compliance.

Opinion on Each Major Federal Program

In our opinion, Example Entity complied, in all material respects, with the types of compliance requirements referred to above that could have a direct

---

[15] See footnote 1.
[16] See footnote 2.
[17] See footnote 3.
[18] See footnote 4.

Auditor Reporting Requirements and Other Communication

and material effect on each of its major federal programs for the year ended June 30, 20X1.

Other Matters[19]

The results of our auditing procedures disclosed instances of noncompliance, which are required to be reported in accordance with the Uniform Guidance and which are described in the accompanying schedule of findings and questioned costs as items [*list the reference numbers of the related findings, for example, 20X1-001 and 20X1-002*].[20] Our opinion on each major federal program is not modified with respect to these matters.

Example Entity's response to the noncompliance findings identified in our audit are described in the accompanying [*insert name of document containing management's response to the auditor's findings; for example, schedule of findings and questioned costs and/or corrective action plan*]. Example Entity's response was not subjected to the auditing procedures applied in the audit of compliance and, accordingly, we express no opinion on the response.[21]

Report on Internal Control Over Compliance[22]

Management of Example Entity is responsible for establishing and maintaining effective internal control over compliance with the types of compliance requirements referred to above. In planning and performing our audit of compliance, we considered Example Entity's internal control over compliance with the types of requirements that could have a direct and material effect on each major federal program to determine the auditing procedures that are appropriate in the circumstances for the purpose of expressing an opinion on compliance for each major federal program and to test and report on internal control over compliance in accordance with the Uniform Guidance, but not for the purpose of expressing an opinion on the effectiveness of internal control over compliance. Accordingly, we do not express an opinion on the effectiveness of Example Entity's internal control over compliance.

A *deficiency in internal control over compliance* exists when the design or operation of a control over compliance does not allow management or employees, in the normal course of performing their assigned functions, to prevent, or detect and correct, noncompliance with a type of compliance requirement of a federal program on a timely basis. A *material weakness in internal control over compliance* is a deficiency, or combination of deficiencies, in internal control over compliance, such that there is a reasonable possibility that material noncompliance with a type of compliance requirement of a federal program will not be prevented, or detected and corrected, on a timely basis. A *significant deficiency in internal control over compliance* is a deficiency, or a combination of deficiencies, in internal control over compliance with a type of compliance requirement of a federal program that is less severe than a material weakness in internal control over compliance, yet important enough to merit attention by those charged with governance.

Our consideration of internal control over compliance was for the limited purpose described in the first paragraph of this section and was not designed to identify all deficiencies in internal control over compliance that might be material weaknesses or significant deficiencies and therefore, material weaknesses

---

[19] See footnote 5.
[20] See footnote 6.
[21] See footnote 7.
[22] See footnote 8.

or significant deficiencies may exist that were not identified. We did not identify any deficiencies in internal control over compliance that we consider to be material weaknesses. However, we identified certain deficiencies in internal control over compliance, as described in the accompanying schedule of findings and questioned costs as items [*list the reference numbers of the related findings, for example, 20X1-003, 20X1-004, and 20X1-005*],[23] that we consider to be significant deficiencies.

Example Entity's response to the internal control over compliance findings identified in our audit are described in the accompanying [*insert name of document containing management's response to the auditor's findings; for example, schedule of findings and questioned costs and/or corrective action plan*]. Example Entity's response was not subjected to the auditing procedures applied in the audit of compliance and, accordingly, we express no opinion on the response.

The purpose of this report on internal control over compliance is solely to describe the scope of our testing of internal control over compliance and the results of that testing based on the requirements of the Uniform Guidance. Accordingly, this report is not suitable for any other purpose.[24]

Report on Schedule of Expenditures of Federal Awards Required by the Uniform Guidance[25,26]

We have audited the financial statements of Example Entity as of and for the year ended June 30, 20X1, and have issued our report thereon dated August 15, 20X1, which contained an unmodified opinion on those financial statements. Our audit was conducted for the purpose of forming an opinion on the financial statements as a whole. The accompanying schedule of expenditures of federal awards is presented for purposes of additional analysis as required by the Uniform Guidance and is not a required part of the financial statements. Such information is the responsibility of management and was derived from and relates directly to the underlying accounting and other records used to prepare the financial statements. The information has been subjected to the auditing procedures applied in the audit of the financial statements and certain additional procedures, including comparing and reconciling such information directly to the underlying accounting and other records used to prepare the financial statements or to the financial statements themselves, and other additional procedures in accordance with auditing standards generally accepted in the United States of America. In our opinion, the schedule of expenditure of federal awards is fairly stated in all material respects in relation to the financial statements as a whole.[27]

[*Auditor's signature*]

[*Auditor's city and state*][28]

[*Date of the auditor's report*][29]

---

[23] The auditor may also consider adding a table to this section of the report, similar to the illustration provided in footnote 50, to more clearly communicate any material weaknesses or significant deficiencies that were identified and the programs and requirements to which they relate.

[24] See footnote 9.

[25] See footnote 10.

[26] See footnote 11.

[27] See footnote 12.

[28] See footnote 13.

[29] See footnote 14.

Example 23-3

Report on Compliance for Each Major Federal Program; Report on Internal Control Over Compliance; and Report on Schedule of Expenditures of Federal Awards Required by the Uniform Guidance

(Unmodified Opinion on Compliance for Each Major Federal Program; Material Weaknesses in Internal Control Over Compliance Identified; No Significant Deficiencies in Internal Control Over Compliance Identified)[30]

Independent Auditor's Report

[*Appropriate Addressee*]

Report on Compliance for Each Major Federal Program

We have audited Example Entity's compliance with the types of compliance requirements[31] described in the *OMB Compliance Supplement* that could have a direct and material effect[32] on each of Example Entity's major federal programs for the year ended June 30, 20X1. Example Entity's major federal programs are identified in the summary of auditor's results section of the accompanying schedule of findings and questioned costs.[33]

Management's Responsibility

Management is responsible for compliance with the requirements of laws, regulations, contracts, and grants applicable to its federal programs.

Auditor's Responsibility

Our responsibility is to express an opinion on compliance for each of Example Entity's major federal programs based on our audit of the types of compliance requirements referred to above. We conducted our audit of compliance in accordance with auditing standards generally accepted in the United States of America; the standards applicable to financial audits contained in *Government Auditing Standards*, issued by the Comptroller General of the United States; and the audit requirements of Title 2 U.S. *Code of Federal Regulations* Part 200, *Uniform Administrative Requirements, Cost Principles, and Audit Requirements for Federal Awards* (Uniform Guidance). Those standards and the Uniform Guidance require that we plan and perform the audit to obtain reasonable assurance about whether noncompliance with the types of compliance requirements referred to above that could have a direct and material effect on a major federal program occurred. An audit includes examining, on a test basis, evidence about Example Entity's compliance with those requirements and performing such other procedures as we considered necessary in the circumstances.

We believe that our audit provides a reasonable basis for our opinion on compliance for each major federal program. However, our audit does not provide a legal determination of Example Entity's compliance.

Opinion on Each Major Federal Program

In our opinion, Example Entity complied, in all material respects, with the types of compliance requirements referred to above that could have a direct

---

[30] See footnote 1.
[31] See footnote 2.
[32] See footnote 3.
[33] See footnote 4.

and material effect on each of its major federal programs for the year ended June 30, 20X1.

Other Matters[34]

The results of our auditing procedures disclosed instances of noncompliance, which are required to be reported in accordance with the Uniform Guidance and which are described in the accompanying schedule of findings and questioned costs as items [*list the reference numbers of the related findings, for example, 20X1-001 and 20X1-002*].[35] Our opinion on each major federal program is not modified with respect to these matters.

Example Entity's response to the noncompliance findings identified in our audit are described in the accompanying [*insert name of document containing management's response to the auditor's findings; for example, schedule of findings and questioned costs and / or corrective action plan*]. Example Entity's response was not subjected to the auditing procedures applied in the audit of compliance and, accordingly, we express no opinion on the response.[36]

Report on Internal Control Over Compliance[37]

Management of Example Entity is responsible for establishing and maintaining effective internal control over compliance with the types of compliance requirements referred to above. In planning and performing our audit of compliance, we considered Example Entity's internal control over compliance with the types of requirements that could have a direct and material effect on each major federal program to determine the auditing procedures that are appropriate in the circumstances for the purpose of expressing an opinion on compliance for each major federal program and to test and report on internal control over compliance in accordance with the Uniform Guidance, but not for the purpose of expressing an opinion on the effectiveness of internal control over compliance. Accordingly, we do not express an opinion on the effectiveness of Example Entity's internal control over compliance.

A *deficiency in internal control over compliance* exists when the design or operation of a control over compliance does not allow management or employees, in the normal course of performing their assigned functions, to prevent, or detect and correct, noncompliance with a type of compliance requirement of a federal program on a timely basis. A *material weakness in internal control over compliance* is a deficiency, or combination of deficiencies, in internal control over compliance, such that there is a reasonable possibility that material noncompliance with a type of compliance requirement of a federal program will not be prevented, or detected and corrected, on a timely basis. A *significant deficiency in internal control over compliance* is a deficiency, or a combination of deficiencies, in internal control over compliance with a type of compliance requirement of a federal program that is less severe than a material weakness in internal control over compliance, yet important enough to merit attention by those charged with governance.

Our consideration of internal control over compliance was for the limited purpose described in the first paragraph of this section and was not designed to

---

[34] See footnote 5.
[35] See footnote 6.
[36] See footnote 7.
[37] See footnote 8.

identify all deficiencies in internal control over compliance that might be material weaknesses or significant deficiencies and therefore, material weaknesses or significant deficiencies may exist that were not identified. We identified certain deficiencies in internal control over compliance, as described in the accompanying schedule of findings and questioned costs as items [*list the reference numbers of the related findings, for example, 20X1-003, 20X1-004, and 20X1-005*],[38] that we consider to be material weaknesses.

Example Entity's response to the internal control over compliance findings identified in our audit are described in the accompanying [*insert name of document containing management's response to the auditor's findings; for example, schedule of findings and questioned costs and/or corrective action plan*]. Example Entity's response was not subjected to the auditing procedures applied in the audit of compliance and, accordingly, we express no opinion on the response.

The purpose of this report on internal control over compliance is solely to describe the scope of our testing of internal control over compliance and the results of that testing based on the requirements of the Uniform Guidance. Accordingly, this report is not suitable for any other purpose.[39]

Report on Schedule of Expenditures of Federal Awards Required by the Uniform Guidance[40,41]

We have audited the financial statements of Example Entity as of and for the year ended June 30, 20X1, and have issued our report thereon dated August 15, 20X1, which contained an unmodified opinion on those financial statements. Our audit was conducted for the purpose of forming an opinion on the financial statements as a whole. The accompanying schedule of expenditures of federal awards is presented for purposes of additional analysis as required by the Uniform Guidance and is not a required part of the financial statements. Such information is the responsibility of management and was derived from and relates directly to the underlying accounting and other records used to prepare the financial statements. The information has been subjected to the auditing procedures applied in the audit of the financial statements and certain additional procedures, including comparing and reconciling such information directly to the underlying accounting and other records used to prepare the financial statements or to the financial statements themselves, and other additional procedures in accordance with auditing standards generally accepted in the United States of America. In our opinion, the schedule of expenditure of federal awards is fairly stated in all material respects in relation to the financial statements as a whole.[42]

[*Auditor's signature*]

[*Auditor's city and state*][43]

[*Date of the auditor's report*][44]

---

[38] See footnote 23.
[39] See footnote 9.
[40] See footnote 10.
[41] See footnote 11.
[42] See footnote 12.
[43] See footnote 13.
[44] See footnote 14.

Example 23-4

Report on Compliance for Each Major Federal Program; Report on Internal Control Over Compliance; and Report on Schedule of Expenditures of Federal Awards Required by the Uniform Guidance

(Qualified Opinion on Compliance for One Major Federal Program; Unmodified Opinion on Compliance on Each of the Other Major Federal Programs; Material Weaknesses and Significant Deficiencies in Internal Control Over Compliance Identified)[45]

Independent Auditor's Report

[*Appropriate Addressee*]

Report on Compliance for Each Major Federal Program

We have audited Example Entity's compliance with the types of compliance requirements[46] described in the *OMB Compliance Supplement* that could have a direct and material effect[47] on each of Example Entity's major federal programs for the year ended June 30, 20X1. Example Entity's major federal programs are identified in the summary of auditor's results section of the accompanying schedule of findings and questioned costs.[48]

Management's Responsibility

Management is responsible for compliance with federal statutes, regulations, and the terms and conditions of its federal awards applicable to its federal programs.

Auditor's Responsibility

Our responsibility is to express an opinion on compliance for each of Example Entity's major federal programs based on our audit of the types of compliance requirements referred to above. We conducted our audit of compliance in accordance with auditing standards generally accepted in the United States of America; the standards applicable to financial audits contained in *Government Auditing Standards*, issued by the Comptroller General of the United States; and the audit requirements of Title 2 U.S. *Code of Federal Regulations* Part 200, *Uniform Administrative Requirements, Cost Principles, and Audit Requirements for Federal Awards* (Uniform Guidance). Those standards and the Uniform Guidance require that we plan and perform the audit to obtain reasonable assurance about whether noncompliance with the types of compliance requirements referred to above that could have a direct and material effect on a major federal program occurred. An audit includes examining, on a test basis, evidence about Example Entity's compliance with those requirements and performing such other procedures as we considered necessary in the circumstances.

We believe that our audit provides a reasonable basis for our opinion on compliance for each major federal program. However, our audit does not provide a legal determination of Example Entity's compliance.

---

[45] See footnote 1.
[46] See footnote 2.
[47] See footnote 3.
[48] See footnote 4.

Basis for Qualified Opinion on [Identify Major Federal Program][49,50]

As described in the accompanying schedule of findings and questioned costs, Example Entity did not comply with requirements regarding [*identify the major federal program and associated finding number(s) matched to the type(s) of compliance requirements; for example, CFDA 93.600 Head Start as described in finding numbers 20X1-001 for Eligibility and 20X1-002 for Reporting*]. Compliance with such requirements is necessary, in our opinion, for Example Entity to comply with the requirements applicable to that program.

Qualified Opinion on [Identify Major Federal Program]

In our opinion, except for the noncompliance described in the Basis for Qualified Opinion paragraph, Example Entity complied, in all material respects, with the types of compliance requirements referred to above that could have a direct and material effect on [*identify the major federal program*] for the year ended June 30, 20X1.

Unmodified Opinion on Each of the Other Major Federal Programs[51]

In our opinion, Example Entity complied, in all material respects, with the types of compliance requirements referred to above that could have a direct and material effect on each of its other major federal programs identified in the summary of auditor's results section of the accompanying schedule of findings and questioned costs for the year ended June 30, 20X1.

Other Matters[52]

The results of our auditing procedures disclosed other instances of noncompliance, which are required to be reported in accordance with the Uniform Guidance and which are described in the accompanying schedule of findings and questioned costs as items [*list the reference numbers of the related findings, for example, 20X1-003 and 20X1-004*].[53] Our opinion on each major federal program is not modified with respect to these matters.

Example Entity's response to the noncompliance findings identified in our audit are described in the accompanying [*insert name of document containing*

---

[49] The heading to this section, and the qualified opinion paragraph that follows, illustrates identifying the specific major federal programs being referred to in each heading.

[50] The auditor may also consider adding a table to more clearly communicate the basis for the qualified opinion such as the following:

As described in Findings 20X1-001 and 20X1-002 in the accompanying schedule of findings and questioned costs, Example Entity did not comply with requirements regarding the following:

Finding #	CFDA #	Program (or Cluster) Name	Compliance Requirement
20X1-001	93.600	Head Start	Eligibility
20X1-002	93.600	Head Start	Reporting

Compliance with such requirements is necessary, in our opinion, for Example Entity to comply with the requirements applicable to that program.

[51] There is nothing to preclude an auditor from including the name(s) of the federal programs for which the auditor is providing an unmodified opinion in this heading or in the opinion paragraph itself. This example illustrates referencing the other major federal programs more generally in the unmodified opinion heading and in the opinion paragraph, along with a reference to the summary of auditor's results section of the schedule of findings and questioned costs where the other major federal programs are specifically identified.

[52] See footnote 5.

[53] See footnote 6.

management's response to the auditor's findings; for example, schedule of findings and questioned costs and/or corrective action plan]. Example Entity's response was not subjected to the auditing procedures applied in the audit of compliance and, accordingly, we express no opinion on the response.[54]

Report on Internal Control Over Compliance[55]

Management of Example Entity is responsible for establishing and maintaining effective internal control over compliance with the types of compliance requirements referred to above. In planning and performing our audit of compliance, we considered Example Entity's internal control over compliance with the types of requirements that could have a direct and material effect on each major federal program to determine the auditing procedures that are appropriate in the circumstances for the purpose of expressing an opinion on compliance for each major federal program and to test and report on internal control over compliance in accordance with the Uniform Guidance, but not for the purpose of expressing an opinion on the effectiveness of internal control over compliance. Accordingly, we do not express an opinion on the effectiveness of Example Entity's internal control over compliance.

Our consideration of internal control over compliance was for the limited purpose described in the preceding paragraph and was not designed to identify all deficiencies in internal control over compliance that might be material weaknesses or significant deficiencies and therefore, material weaknesses or significant deficiencies may exist that were not identified. However, as discussed below, we identified certain deficiencies in internal control over compliance that we consider to be material weaknesses and significant deficiencies.

A *deficiency in internal control over compliance* exists when the design or operation of a control over compliance does not allow management or employees, in the normal course of performing their assigned functions, to prevent, or detect and correct, noncompliance with a type of compliance requirement of a federal program on a timely basis. A *material weakness in internal control over compliance* is a deficiency, or combination of deficiencies, in internal control over compliance, such that there is reasonable possibility that material noncompliance with a type of compliance requirement of a federal program will not be prevented, or detected and corrected, on a timely basis. We consider the deficiencies in internal control over compliance described in the accompanying schedule of findings and questioned costs as items [*list the reference numbers of the related findings, for example 20X1-005 and 20X1-006*][56] to be material weaknesses.

A *significant deficiency in internal control over compliance* is a deficiency, or a combination of deficiencies, in internal control over compliance with a type of compliance requirement of a federal program that is less severe than a material weakness in internal control over compliance, yet important enough to merit attention by those charged with governance. We consider the deficiencies in internal control over compliance described in the accompanying schedule of findings and questioned costs as items [*list the reference numbers of the related findings, for example 20X1-007 and 20X1-008*][57] to be significant deficiencies.

---

[54] See footnote 7.
[55] See footnote 8.
[56] See footnote 23.
[57] See footnote 23.

Example Entity's response to the internal control over compliance findings identified in our audit are described in the accompanying [*insert name of document containing management's response to the auditor's findings; for example, schedule of findings and questioned costs and/or corrective action plan*]. Example Entity's response was not subjected to the auditing procedures applied in the audit of compliance and, accordingly, we express no opinion on the response.

The purpose of this report on internal control over compliance is solely to describe the scope of our testing of internal control over compliance and the results of that testing based on the requirements of the Uniform Guidance. Accordingly, this report is not suitable for any other purpose.[58]

Report on Schedule of Expenditures of Federal Awards Required by the Uniform Guidance[59,60]

We have audited the financial statements of Example Entity as of and for the year ended June 30, 20X1, and have issued our report thereon dated August 15, 20X1, which contained an unmodified opinion on those financial statements. Our audit was conducted for the purpose of forming an opinion on the financial statements as a whole. The accompanying schedule of expenditures of federal awards is presented for purposes of additional analysis as required by the Uniform Guidance and is not a required part of the financial statements. Such information is the responsibility of management and was derived from and relates directly to the underlying accounting and other records used to prepare the financial statements. The information has been subjected to the auditing procedures applied in the audit of the financial statements and certain additional procedures, including comparing and reconciling such information directly to the underlying accounting and other records used to prepare the financial statements or to the financial statements themselves, and other additional procedures in accordance with auditing standards generally accepted in the United States of America. In our opinion, the schedule of expenditure of federal awards is fairly stated in all material respects in relation to the financial statements as a whole.[61]

[*Auditor's signature*]

[*Auditor's city and state*][62]

[*Date of the auditor's report*][63]

---

[58] See footnote 9.
[59] See footnote 10.
[60] See footnote 11.
[61] See footnote 12.
[62] See footnote 13.
[63] See footnote 14.

Example 23-5

Report on Compliance for Each Major Federal Program; Report on Internal Control Over Compliance; and Report on Schedule of Expenditures of Federal Awards Required by the Uniform Guidance

(Qualified Opinion on Compliance—Scope Limitation for One Major Federal Program; Unmodified Opinion on Compliance on Each of the Other Major Federal Programs; Significant Deficiencies in Internal Control Over Compliance Identified)[64]

Independent Auditor's Report

[*Appropriate Addressee*]

Report on Compliance for Each Major Federal Program

We have audited Example Entity's compliance with the types of compliance requirements[65] described in the *OMB Compliance Supplement* that could have a direct and material effect[66] on each of Example Entity's major federal programs for the year ended June 30, 20X1. Example Entity's major federal programs are identified in the summary of auditor's results section of the accompanying schedule of findings and questioned costs.[67]

Management's Responsibility

Management is responsible for compliance with federal statutes, regulations, and the terms and conditions of its federal awards applicable to its federal programs.

Auditor's Responsibility

Our responsibility is to express an opinion on compliance for each of Example Entity's major federal programs based on our audit of the types of compliance requirements referred to above. We conducted our audit of compliance in accordance with auditing standards generally accepted in the United States of America; the standards applicable to financial audits contained in *Government Auditing Standards*, issued by the Comptroller General of the United States; and the audit requirements of Title 2 U.S. *Code of Federal Regulations* Part 200, *Uniform Administrative Requirements, Cost Principles, and Audit Requirements for Federal Awards* (Uniform Guidance). Those standards and the Uniform Guidance require that we plan and perform the audit to obtain reasonable assurance about whether noncompliance with the types of compliance requirements referred to above that could have a direct and material effect on a major federal program occurred. An audit includes examining, on a test basis, evidence about Example Entity's compliance with those requirements and performing such other procedures as we considered necessary in the circumstances.

We believe that our audit provides a reasonable basis for our opinion on compliance for each major federal program. However, our audit does not provide a legal determination of Example Entity's compliance.

---

[64] See footnote 1.
[65] See footnote 2.
[66] See footnote 3.
[67] See footnote 4.

Basis for Qualified Opinion on [Identify Major Federal Program][68,69]

As described in the accompanying schedule of findings and questioned costs, we were unable to obtain sufficient appropriate audit evidence supporting the compliance of Example Entity with [*identify the major federal program and associated finding number(s) matched to the type(s) of compliance requirements; for example, CFDA 93.600 Head Start as described in finding numbers 20X1-001 for Eligibility and 20X1-002 for Reporting*], consequently we were unable to determine whether Example Entity complied with those requirements applicable to that program.

Qualified Opinion on [Identify Major Federal Program]

In our opinion, except for the possible effects of the matter described in the Basis for Qualified Opinion paragraph, Example Entity complied, in all material respects, with the types of compliance requirements referred to above that could have a direct and material effect on [*identify the major federal program*] for the year ended June 30, 20X1.

Unmodified Opinion on Each of the Other Major Federal Programs[70]

In our opinion, Example Entity complied, in all material respects, with the types of compliance requirements referred to above that could have a direct and material effect on each of its other major federal programs identified in the summary of auditor's results section of the accompanying schedule of findings and questioned costs for the year ended June 30, 20X1.

Other Matters[71]

The results of our auditing procedures disclosed other instances of noncompliance, which are required to be reported in accordance with the Uniform Guidance and which are described in the accompanying schedule of findings and questioned costs as items [*list the reference numbers of the related findings, for example, 20X1-003 and 20X1-004*].[72] Our opinion on each major federal program is not modified with respect to these matters.

Example Entity's response to the noncompliance findings identified in our audit are described in the accompanying [*insert name of document containing management's response to the auditor's findings; for example, schedule of findings and questioned costs and/or corrective action plan*]. Example Entity's response was not subjected to the auditing procedures applied in the audit of compliance and, accordingly, we express no opinion on the response.[73]

Report on Internal Control Over Compliance[74]

Management of Example Entity is responsible for establishing and maintaining effective internal control over compliance with the types of compliance requirements referred to above. In planning and performing our audit of compliance, we considered Example Entity's internal control over compliance with the types of requirements that could have a direct and material effect on each major federal program to determine the auditing procedures that are appropriate in the circumstances for the purpose of expressing an opinion on compliance

---

[68] See footnote 49.
[69] See footnote 50.
[70] See footnote 51.
[71] See footnote 5.
[72] See footnote 6.
[73] See footnote 7.
[74] See footnote 8.

for each major federal program and to test and report on internal control over compliance in accordance with the Uniform Guidance, but not for the purpose of expressing an opinion on the effectiveness of internal control over compliance. Accordingly, we do not express an opinion on the effectiveness of Example Entity's internal control over compliance.

A *deficiency in internal control over compliance* exists when the design or operation of a control over compliance does not allow management or employees, in the normal course of performing their assigned functions, to prevent, or detect and correct, noncompliance with a type of compliance requirement of a federal program on a timely basis. A *material weakness in internal control over compliance* is a deficiency, or combination of deficiencies, in internal control over compliance, such that there is a reasonable possibility that material noncompliance with a type of compliance requirement of a federal program will not be prevented, or detected and corrected, on a timely basis. A *significant deficiency in internal control over compliance* is a deficiency, or a combination of deficiencies, in internal control over compliance with a type of compliance requirement of a federal program that is less severe than a material weakness in internal control over compliance, yet important enough to merit attention by those charged with governance.

Our consideration of internal control over compliance was for the limited purpose described in the first paragraph of this section and was not designed to identify all deficiencies in internal control over compliance that might be material weaknesses or significant deficiencies and therefore, material weaknesses or significant deficiencies may exist that were not identified. We did not identify any deficiencies in internal control over compliance that we consider to be material weaknesses. However, we identified certain deficiencies in internal control over compliance, as described in the accompanying schedule of findings and questioned costs as items [*list the reference numbers of the related findings, for example, 20X1-005, 20X1-006, and 20X1-007*][75] that we consider to be significant deficiencies.

Example Entity's response to the internal control over compliance findings identified in our audit are described in the accompanying [*insert name of document containing management's response to the auditor's findings; for example, schedule of findings and questioned costs and / or corrective action plan*]. Example Entity's response was not subjected to the auditing procedures applied in the audit of compliance and, accordingly, we express no opinion on the response.

The purpose of this report on internal control over compliance is solely to describe the scope of our testing of internal control over compliance and the results of that testing based on the requirements of the Uniform Guidance. Accordingly, this report is not suitable for any other purpose.[76]

Report on Schedule of Expenditures of Federal Awards Required by the Uniform Guidance[77,78]

We have audited the financial statements of Example Entity as of and for the year ended June 30, 20X1, and have issued our report thereon dated August 15, 20X1, which contained an unmodified opinion on those financial statements.

---

[75] See footnote 23.
[76] See footnote 9.
[77] See footnote 10.
[78] See footnote 11.

Our audit was conducted for the purpose of forming an opinion on the financial statements as a whole. The accompanying schedule of expenditures of federal awards is presented for purposes of additional analysis as required by the Uniform Guidance and is not a required part of the financial statements. Such information is the responsibility of management and was derived from and relates directly to the underlying accounting and other records used to prepare the financial statements. The information has been subjected to the auditing procedures applied in the audit of the financial statements and certain additional procedures, including comparing and reconciling such information directly to the underlying accounting and other records used to prepare the financial statements or to the financial statements themselves, and other additional procedures in accordance with auditing standards generally accepted in the United States of America. In our opinion, the schedule of expenditure of federal awards is fairly stated in all material respects in relation to the financial statements as a whole.[79]

[Auditor's signature]

[Auditor's city and state][80]

[Date of the auditor's report][81]

Example 23-6

Report on Compliance for Each Major Federal Program; Report on Internal Control Over Compliance; and Report on Schedule of Expenditures of Federal Awards Required by the Uniform Guidance

(Adverse Opinion on Compliance for One Major Federal Program; Unmodified Opinion on Compliance on Each of the Other Major Federal Programs; Material Weaknesses and Significant Deficiencies in Internal Control Over Compliance Identified)[82]

Independent Auditor's Report

[Appropriate Addressee]

Report on Compliance for Each Major Federal Program

We have audited Example Entity's compliance with the types of compliance requirements[83] described in the *OMB Compliance Supplement* that could have a direct and material effect[84] on each of Example Entity's major federal programs for the year ended June 30, 20X1. Example Entity's major federal programs are identified in the summary of auditor's results section of the accompanying schedule of findings and questioned costs.[85]

Management's Responsibility

Management is responsible for compliance with federal statutes, regulations, and the terms and conditions of its federal awards applicable to its federal programs.

---

[79] See footnote 12.
[80] See footnote 13.
[81] See footnote 14.
[82] See footnote 1.
[83] See footnote 2.
[84] See footnote 3.
[85] See footnote 4.

Auditor's Responsibility

Our responsibility is to express an opinion on compliance for each of Example Entity's major federal programs based on our audit of the types of compliance requirements referred to above. We conducted our audit of compliance in accordance with auditing standards generally accepted in the United States of America; the standards applicable to financial audits contained in *Government Auditing Standards*, issued by the Comptroller General of the United States; and the audit requirements of Title 2 U.S. *Code of Federal Regulations* Part 200, *Uniform Administrative Requirements, Cost Principles, and Audit Requirements for Federal Awards* (Uniform Guidance). Those standards and the Uniform Guidance require that we plan and perform the audit to obtain reasonable assurance about whether noncompliance with the types of compliance requirements referred to above that could have a direct and material effect on a major federal program occurred. An audit includes examining, on a test basis, evidence about Example Entity's compliance with those requirements and performing such other procedures as we considered necessary in the circumstances.

We believe that our audit provides a reasonable basis for our opinion on compliance for each major federal program. However, our audit does not provide a legal determination of Example Entity's compliance.

Basis for Adverse Opinion on [Identify Major Federal Program][86],[87]

As described in the accompanying schedule of findings and questioned costs, Example Entity did not comply with requirements regarding [*identify the major federal program and associated finding number(s) matched to the type(s) of compliance requirements; for example, CFDA 93.600 Head Start as described in finding numbers 20X1-001 for Eligibility and 20X1-002 for Reporting*]. Compliance with such requirements is necessary, in our opinion, for Example Entity to comply with the requirements applicable to that program.

Adverse Opinion on [Identify Major Federal Program]

In our opinion, because of the significance of the matter discussed in the Basis for Adverse Opinion paragraph, Example Entity did not comply in all material respects, with the types of compliance requirements referred to above that could have a direct and material effect on [*identify the major federal program*] for the year ended June 30, 20X1.

Unmodified Opinion on Each of the Other Major Federal Programs[88]

In our opinion, Example Entity complied, in all material respects, with the types of compliance requirements referred to above that could have a direct and material effect on each of its other major federal programs identified in the summary of auditor's results section of the accompanying schedule of findings and questioned costs for the year ended June 30, 20X1.

Other Matters[89]

The results of our auditing procedures disclosed other instances of noncompliance, which are required to be reported in accordance with the Uniform Guidance and which are described in the accompanying schedule of findings

---

[86] See footnote 49.
[87] See footnote 50.
[88] See footnote 51.
[89] See footnote 5.

and questioned costs as items [*list the reference numbers of the related findings, for example, 20X1-003 and 20X1-004*].[90] Our opinion on each major federal program is not modified with respect to these matters.

Example Entity's response to the noncompliance findings identified in our audit are described in the accompanying [*insert name of document containing management's response to the auditor's findings; for example, schedule of findings and questioned costs and/or corrective action plan*]. Example Entity's response was not subjected to the auditing procedures applied in the audit of compliance and, accordingly, we express no opinion on the response.[91]

Report on Internal Control Over Compliance[92]

Management of Example Entity is responsible for establishing and maintaining effective internal control over compliance with the types of compliance requirements referred to above. In planning and performing our audit of compliance, we considered Example Entity's internal control over compliance with the types of requirements that could have a direct and material effect on each major federal program to determine the auditing procedures that are appropriate in the circumstances for the purpose of expressing an opinion on compliance for each major federal program and to test and report on internal control over compliance in accordance with the Uniform Guidance, but not for the purpose of expressing an opinion on the effectiveness of internal control over compliance. Accordingly, we do not express an opinion on the effectiveness of Example Entity's internal control over compliance.

Our consideration of internal control over compliance was for the limited purpose described in the preceding paragraph and was not designed to identify all deficiencies in internal control over compliance that might be material weaknesses or significant deficiencies and therefore, material weaknesses or significant deficiencies may exist that were not identified. However, as discussed below, we identified certain deficiencies in internal control over compliance that we consider to be material weaknesses and significant deficiencies.

A *deficiency in internal control over compliance* exists when the design or operation of a control over compliance does not allow management or employees, in the normal course of performing their assigned functions, to prevent, or detect and correct, noncompliance with a type of compliance requirement of a federal program on a timely basis. A *material weakness in internal control over compliance* is a deficiency, or combination of deficiencies, in internal control over compliance, such that there is reasonable possibility that material noncompliance with a type of compliance requirement of a federal program will not be prevented, or detected and corrected, on a timely basis. We consider the deficiencies in internal control over compliance described in the accompanying schedule of findings and questioned costs as items [*list the reference numbers of the related findings, for example 20X1-005 and 20X1-006*][93] to be material weaknesses.

A *significant deficiency in internal control over compliance* is a deficiency, or a combination of deficiencies, in internal control over compliance with a type of compliance requirement of a federal program that is less severe than a material weakness in internal control over compliance, yet important enough to merit

---

[90] See footnote 6.
[91] See footnote 7.
[92] See footnote 8.
[93] See footnote 23.

attention by those charged with governance. We consider the deficiencies in internal control over compliance described in the accompanying schedule of findings and questioned costs as items [*list the reference numbers of the related findings, for example 20X1-007 and 20X1-008*][94] to be significant deficiencies.

Example Entity's response to the internal control over compliance findings identified in our audit are described in the accompanying [*insert name of document containing management's response to the auditor's findings; for example, schedule of findings and questioned costs and/or corrective action plan*]. Example Entity's response was not subjected to the auditing procedures applied in the audit of compliance and, accordingly, we express no opinion on the response.

The purpose of this report on internal control over compliance is solely to describe the scope of our testing of internal control over compliance and the results of that testing based on the requirements of the Uniform Guidance. Accordingly, this report is not suitable for any other purpose.[95]

Report on Schedule of Expenditures of Federal Awards Required by the Uniform Guidance[96,97]

We have audited the financial statements of Example Entity as of and for the year ended June 30, 20X1, and have issued our report thereon dated August 15, 20X1, which contained an unmodified opinion on those financial statements. Our audit was conducted for the purpose of forming an opinion on the financial statements as a whole. The accompanying schedule of expenditures of federal awards is presented for purposes of additional analysis as required by the Uniform Guidance and is not a required part of the financial statements. Such information is the responsibility of management and was derived from and relates directly to the underlying accounting and other records used to prepare the financial statements. The information has been subjected to the auditing procedures applied in the audit of the financial statements and certain additional procedures, including comparing and reconciling such information directly to the underlying accounting and other records used to prepare the financial statements or to the financial statements themselves, and other additional procedures in accordance with auditing standards generally accepted in the United States of America. In our opinion, the schedule of expenditure of federal awards is fairly stated in all material respects in relation to the financial statements as a whole.[98]

[*Auditor's signature*]

[*Auditor's city and state*][99]

[*Date of the auditor's report*][100]

---

[94] See footnote 23.
[95] See footnote 9.
[96] See footnote 10.
[97] See footnote 11.
[98] See footnote 12.
[99] See footnote 13.
[100] See footnote 14.

Example 23-7

Schedule of Findings and Questioned Costs
Section I—Summary of Auditor's Results

Financial Statements		
Type of report the auditor issued on whether the financial statements audited were prepared in accordance with GAAP [*unmodified, qualified, adverse, or disclaimer*]:[101]		
Internal control over financial reporting:		
• Material weakness(es) identified?	____ yes	____ no
• Significant deficiency(ies) identified?	____ yes	____ none reported
Noncompliance material to financial statements noted?	____ yes	____ no
Federal Awards		
Internal control over major federal programs:		
• Material weakness(es) identified?	____ yes	____ no
• Significant deficiency(ies) identified?	____ yes	____ none reported
Type of auditor's report issued on compliance for major federal programs [*unmodified, qualified, adverse, or disclaimer*]:[102]		
Any audit findings disclosed that are required to be reported in accordance with 2 CFR 200.516(a)?	____ yes	____ no
Identification of major federal programs:[103]		

---

[101] As explained in the AICPA Audit and Accounting Guide *State and Local Governments*, the auditor generally expresses or disclaims an opinion on a government's basic financial statements by providing an opinion or disclaimer of opinion on each opinion unit required to be presented in those financial statements. Therefore, there could be multiple responses to this question for audits of a government's basic financial statements.

[102] If the audit report for one or more major federal programs is other than unmodified, indicate the type of report issued for each program. For example, if the audit report on major federal program compliance for an auditee having five major federal programs includes an unmodified opinion for three of the programs, a qualified opinion for one program, and a disclaimer of opinion for one program, the response to this question could be as follows:

"Unmodified for all major federal programs except for [*name of program*], which was qualified and [*name of program*], which was a disclaimer."

[103] Major federal programs generally would be identified in the same order as reported on the schedule of expenditures of federal awards. In the case of a cluster of programs, only the cluster name as shown on the schedule of expenditures of federal awards is required.

CFDA Number(s)[104]		Name of Federal Program or Cluster[105]	
Dollar threshold used to distinguish between type A and type B programs:		$_____	
Auditee qualified as low-risk auditee?		_____ yes	_____ no

Section II—Financial Statement Findings

This section should identify the significant deficiencies, material weaknesses, fraud, noncompliance with provisions of laws, regulations, contracts, and grant agreements, and abuse related to the financial statements for which Government Auditing Standards *requires reporting. (See paragraph 23.36.) Auditors may refer to chapter 4 of this guide for a discussion of the* Government Auditing Standards *requirements for presenting findings.*

Audit findings that relate to both the financial statements and federal awards must[106] *be reported in both section II and section III. However, the reporting in one section may be in summary form with a reference to a detailed reporting in the other section of the schedule. For example, a material weakness in internal control that affects an entity as a whole, including its federal awards, generally would be reported in detail in this section. Section III would then include a summary identification of the finding and a reference back to the specific finding in this section.*

Identify each finding with a reference number.[107] *If there are no findings, this section could state that no matters were reported. Alternatively, this section could be omitted without confusing the schedule's users because the summary of auditor's results section would indicate that there are no findings. Each*

---

[104] When the *Catalog of Federal Domestic Assistance* (CFDA) number is not available, include other identifying number, if applicable. The contract or grant number typically is used in lieu of a CFDA number, or, if no grant or contract number is available, "Unknown."

[105] The name of the federal program or cluster should be the same as that listed in the schedule of expenditures of federal awards. For clusters, auditors are required only to list the name of the cluster and not each individual award or program within the cluster.

[106] The use of the term *must* in the Uniform Guidance indicates a requirement. This is consistent with the use of the term *must* in generally accepted auditing standards (GAAS) and *Government Auditing Standards*. The use of the term *should* in the Uniform Guidance indicates a best practice or recommended approach. However, GAAS and *Government Auditing Standards* use the term *should* to indicate a presumptively mandatory requirement. An auditor must comply with a presumptively mandatory requirement in all cases in which such a requirement is relevant, except in rare circumstances. In this guide, the term ***should***, when italicized and bolded, indicates a best practice or recommended approach in the Uniform Guidance. This is intended to differentiate it from the term *should* used throughout the guide to refer to presumptively mandatory requirements in GAAS and *Government Auditing Standards*. See chapter 1, "Introduction and Overview of *Government Auditing Standards*," of this guide for more information regarding presumptively mandatory requirements.

[107] Finding reference numbers must follow the format meeting the requirements of the data collection form submission. See paragraph 23.43.

Auditor Reporting Requirements and Other Communication 649

finding should be presented in the level of detail shown in the following listing, as applicable. Auditors also may refer to chapter 4 of this guide for a discussion of the Government Auditing Standards *requirements for presenting findings:*

- *Criteria or specific requirement*
- *Condition*
- *Context*[108]
- *Effect*
- *Cause*
- *Recommendation*
- *Views of responsible officials and planned corrective actions*[109]

Section III—Federal Award Findings and Questioned Costs

This section should identify the audit findings required to be reported by the 2 CFR 200.516(a) (for example, significant deficiencies, material weaknesses, material instances of noncompliance, including questioned costs, and material abuse—see paragraph 23.38). Where practical, findings should be organized by federal agency or pass-through entity.

Audit findings that relate to both the financial statements and federal awards must be reported in both section II and section III. However, the reporting in one section may be in summary form with a reference to a detailed reporting in the other section of the schedule. For example, a finding of noncompliance with a federal program statute that is also material to the financial statements generally would be reported in detail in this section. Section II would then include a summary identification of the finding and a reference back to the specific finding in this section.

Identify each finding with a reference number.[110] *If there are no findings, this section could state that no matters were reported. Alternatively, this section could be omitted without confusing the schedule's users because the summary of auditor's results section would indicate that there are no findings. Each finding should be presented in the level of detail shown in the following listing, as applicable. Auditors also may refer to chapter 4 of this guide for a discussion of the* Government Auditing Standards *requirements for presenting findings:*

- *Information on the federal program*[111]
- *Criteria or specific requirement (including statutory, regulatory, or other citation)*
- *Condition*[112]

---

[108] Describe the work performed that resulted in the finding, and provide sufficient information for judging the prevalence and consequences of the finding, such as the relation to the population or universe of costs or the number of cases examined as well as quantification of audit findings in dollars. The auditor should report whether the sampling was a statistically valid sample.

[109] Paragraphs 23.37 and 23.42 and chapter 4 of this guide provide guidance on reporting views of responsible officials and planned corrective action.

[110] See footnote 107.

[111] Provide the federal program (CFDA number and title) and agency, the federal award identification number and year, and the name of the pass-through entity, if applicable. When this information is not available, provide the best information available to describe the federal award.

[112] Include facts that support the deficiency identified in the audit finding.

- Questioned costs[113]
- Context[114]
- Effect
- Cause
- Identification as a repeat finding, if applicable
- Recommendation
- Views of responsible officials and planned corrective actions[115]

Example 23-8

Report on Schedule of Expenditures of Federal Awards When the Auditor Is Issuing a Stand-Alone Report Under AU-C Section 805, Special Considerations—Audits of Single Financial Statements and Specific Elements, Accounts, or Items of a Financial Statement[116]

(Unmodified Opinion on Schedule of Expenditures of Federal Awards)

<u>Independent Auditor's Report</u>

[Appropriate Addressee]

Report on Schedule of Expenditures of Federal Awards

We have audited the accompanying schedule of expenditures of federal awards of the City of Example for the year ended June 30, 20X1, and the related notes (the financial statement).

Management's Responsibility

Management is responsible for the preparation and fair presentation of this financial statement in accordance with accounting principles generally accepted in the United States of America; this includes the design, implementation, and maintenance of internal control relevant to the preparation and fair presentation of a financial statement that is free from material misstatement, whether due to fraud or error.

Auditor's Responsibility

Our responsibility is to express an opinion on this financial statement based on our audit. We conducted our audit in accordance with auditing standards generally accepted in the United States of America; the standards applicable to financial audits contained in *Government Auditing Standards*, issued by the Comptroller General of the United States;[117] and the audit requirements of Title 2 U.S. *Code of Federal Regulations* Part 200, *Uniform Administrative Requirements, Cost Principles, and Audit Requirements for Federal* Awards

---

[113] Identify questioned costs and how they were computed. Known questioned costs must be identified by applicable CFDA number(s) and applicable federal award identification number(s).

[114] See footnote 108.

[115] See footnote 109.

[116] This illustration assumes that the auditor is engaged to issue a stand-alone opinion on the schedule of expenditures of federal awards using the guidance in AU-C section 805, *Special Considerations—Audits of Single Financial Statements and Specific Elements, Accounts, or Items of a Financial Statement* (AICPA, *Professional Standards*). See paragraph 23.20 of this guide for more information about this reporting and chapter 17, "Schedule of Expenditures of Federal Awards (Uniform Guidance)" of this guide for a discussion of when this may occur and information on the objectives and audit evidence needed in such an audit.

[117] The standards and guidance applicable to financial audits are found in chapters 1–4 of *Government Auditing Standards*.

(Uniform Guidance). Those standards and the Uniform Guidance require that we plan and perform the audit to obtain reasonable assurance about whether the financial statement is free from material misstatement.

An audit involves performing procedures to obtain audit evidence about the amounts and disclosures in the financial statement. The procedures selected depend on the auditor's judgment, including the assessment of the risks of material misstatement of the financial statement, whether due to fraud or error. In making those risk assessments, the auditor considers internal control relevant to the entity's preparation and fair presentation of the financial statement in order to design audit procedures that are appropriate in the circumstances, but not for the purpose of expressing an opinion on the effectiveness of the entity's internal control. Accordingly, we express no such opinion. An audit also includes evaluating the appropriateness of accounting policies used and the reasonableness of significant accounting estimates made by management, as well as evaluating the overall presentation of the financial statement.

We believe that the audit evidence we have obtained is sufficient and appropriate to provide a basis for our audit opinion.

Opinion

In our opinion, the financial statement referred to above presents fairly, in all material respects, the expenditures of federal awards of the City of Example for the year ended June 30, 20X1, in accordance with accounting principles generally accepted in the United States of America.[118]

[*Auditor's signature*]

[*Auditor's city and state*][119]

[*Date of the auditor's report*]

---

[118] AU-C section 800, *Special Considerations—Audits of Financial Statements Prepared in Accordance With Special Purpose Frameworks* (AICPA, *Professional Standards*), provides requirements and guidance for auditor reporting when the auditee prepares financial statements in accordance with a special purpose framework. AU-C section 800 defines a *special purpose framework* as a financial reporting framework other than generally accepted accounting principles and establishes requirements for reporting on those frameworks. Special purpose frameworks, such as the cash, tax, regulatory, and other bases of accounting, are sometimes referred to as an *other comprehensive bases of accounting* (OCBOA). The term *OCBOA* is sometimes used when referring to this guidance in this guide.

[119] See footnote 13.

Chapter 24
Program-Specific Audits (Uniform Guidance)

> **Ⓤ Update 24-1: Audits of Federal Awards**
>
> This chapter, and the other chapters of part III, *Uniform Guidance Audits*, of this guide, should be used for performing a compliance audit of federal awards under the audit requirements of Title 2 U.S. *Code of Federal Regulations* (CFR) Part 200, *Uniform Administrative Requirements, Cost Principles, and Audit Requirements for Federal Awards* (Uniform Guidance).[1] Part II, *Circular A-133 Audits*, of this guide should be used for performing a compliance audit under Office of Management and Budget (OMB) Circular A-133, *Audits of States, Local Governments, and Non-Profit Organizations* (Circular A-133). See the transitional guidance sections at the end of each chapter that highlight important matters for consideration. Additionally, refer to the preface of this guide for more information.
>
> **Important Effective Date Information**
>
> In December 2013, the OMB issued the Uniform Guidance, which is effective for nonfederal entities for all federal awards and certain funding increments provided on or after December 26, 2014. The requirements in Subpart F, "Audit Requirements," are effective for audits of fiscal years beginning on or after December 26, 2014, with no early implementation permitted. Therefore, auditees subject to a single audit with December 25, 2015, and later year ends (for example, December 31, 2015) will be required to undergo the audit under Subpart F of the Uniform Guidance. Note that audits of fiscal years ending prior to the effective date of the Uniform Guidance audit requirements are subject to an audit under Circular A-133.

24.01 A program-specific audit[2] is an audit of an entity's compliance with direct and material[3] compliance requirements as they relate to an individual federal program (rather than a single audit, which includes an audit of an entity's financial statements and federal programs). 2 CFR 200.507 provides guidance on program-specific audits.

---

[1] See the information found in other part III, *Uniform Guidance Audits*, chapters of this guide for transition considerations when performing an audit under Title 2 U.S. *Code of Federal Regulations* (CFR) Part 200, *Uniform Administrative Requirements, Cost Principles, and Audit Requirements for Federal Awards* (Uniform Guidance). Transition considerations can also be found at the end of certain part II, *Circular A-133 Audits*, chapters as it relates to an audit performed under Office of Management and Budget Circular A-133, *Audits of States, Local Governments, and Non-Profit Organizations*.

[2] AU-C section 935, *Compliance Audits* (AICPA, *Professional Standards*), is applicable when performing a program-specific compliance audit under the Uniform Guidance. See the other chapters in part III of this guide for guidance found in AU-C section 935 that applies to all compliance audits, including program-specific audits.

[3] AU-C section 935 defines *applicable compliance requirements* as the compliance requirements that are subject to the compliance audit. 2 CFR 200.514(d)(1) states that the auditor must determine whether the auditee has complied with federal statutes, regulations, and the terms and conditions of the federal awards that may have a direct and material effect on each of its major programs. Therefore, in a Uniform Guidance program-specific audit, the direct and material compliance requirements are those that are subject to audit. Accordingly, for the purpose of adapting AU-C section 935 to a program-specific audit in this chapter, the term *applicable* has been replaced by *direct and material* when referring to such compliance requirements, except when citing content from AU-C section 935.

Use of a Program-Specific Audit to Satisfy Uniform Guidance Audit Requirements

24.02 The Uniform Guidance provides that when an auditee expends federal awards under only one federal program (excluding research and development) and statutes, regulations, or the terms and conditions of the federal award[4] do not require a financial statement audit of the auditee, the auditee may elect to have a program-specific audit performed in accordance with 2 CFR 200.507.[5] Therefore, the auditee should determine whether there is a financial statement audit requirement prior to arranging for a program-specific audit. In addition, a program-specific audit may not be elected for research and development unless all federal awards expended were received from the same federal agency (or the same federal agency and the same pass-through entity) and that federal agency (or pass-through entity, in the case of a subrecipient) approves a program-specific audit in advance.

Program-Specific Audit Requirements

24.03 The Uniform Guidance states that program-specific audits are subject to the following sections of the Uniform Guidance as they may apply to program-specific audits:

- Purpose, audit requirements, basis for determining federal awards expended and relation to other audit requirements (2 CFR 200.500-.503[d])
- Frequency of audits, sanctions, and audit costs (2 CFR 200.504-.506)
- Auditee responsibilities and auditor selection (2 CFR 200.508-.509)
- Audit findings follow-up (2 CFR 200.511)
- Report submission (2 CFR 200.512[e]–.512[h])
- Responsibilities (Federal Agencies) (2 CFR 200.513)
- Audit findings and audit documentation (2 CFR 200.516-.517)
- Management decision (2 CFR 200.521)
- Other referenced provisions of 2 CFR 200.507, unless contrary to the provisions of that section, a program-specific audit guide, or program statutes and regulations

Availability of Program-Specific Audit Guide

24.04 For some programs, a federal agency's Office of the Inspector General will have issued a program-specific audit guide that provides guidance on internal control, compliance requirements, suggested audit procedures, and audit reporting requirements for a particular federal program. A listing of current

---

[4] Although *Government Auditing Standards* uses "provisions of laws, regulations, contracts, and grant agreements," the Uniform Guidance uses the terminology *federal statutes, regulations, and the terms and conditions of federal awards.*

[5] An example of a situation when a program-specific audit would not be allowed would be a not-for-profit college that receives student financial assistance (SFA) (and no other federal awards). That is because the Higher Education Act of 1965, as amended, requires institutions that receive SFA to undergo an annual financial statement audit.

audit guides can be found in Appendix VI of the *OMB Compliance Supplement* (*Compliance Supplement*), including the federal awarding agency contact information and a website where a copy of the guide can be obtained. When a current program-specific audit guide is available, the auditor must follow *Government Auditing Standards* and the guide when performing a program-specific audit. However, if significant changes have been made to a program's compliance requirements and the related program-specific audit guide has not been updated with regard to the changes, the auditor should follow 2 CFR 200.507(b) and the *Compliance Supplement* in lieu of an outdated guide. In addition, paragraph .22 of AU-C section 935, *Compliance Audits* (AICPA, *Professional Standards*), notes that in instances in which audit guidance provided by a governmental agency for the performance of compliance audits has not been updated for, or otherwise conflicts with, current generally accepted auditing standards (GAAS) or *Government Auditing Standards*, the auditor should comply with the most current applicable professional standards and guidance instead of the outdated or conflicting guidance.

24.05 When a current program-specific audit guide is not available, the auditee and the auditor must have basically the same responsibilities for the federal program as they have for an audit of a major program in a single audit as discussed in chapters 19, "Consideration of Internal Control Over Compliance for Major Programs (Uniform Guidance)," and 20, "Compliance Auditing Applicable to Major Programs (Uniform Guidance)," of this guide. (See also paragraphs 24.06–.07 for more information.)

Emphasis Point

The use of the term *must* in the Uniform Guidance indicates a requirement. This is consistent with the use of the term *must* in GAAS and *Government Auditing Standards*. The use of the term *should* in the Uniform Guidance indicates a best practice or recommended approach. However, GAAS and *Government Auditing Standards* use the term *should* to indicate a presumptively mandatory requirement. An auditor must comply with a presumptively mandatory requirement in all cases in which such a requirement is relevant, except in rare circumstances. In this guide, the term ***should***, when italicized and bolded, indicates a best practice or recommended approach in the Uniform Guidance. This is intended to differentiate it from the term *should* used throughout the guide to refer to presumptively mandatory requirements in GAAS and *Government Auditing Standards*. See chapter 1, "Introduction and Overview of *Government Auditing Standards*," of this guide for more information regarding presumptively mandatory requirements.

Auditee's Responsibilities When a Program-Specific Audit Guide Is Not Available

24.06 In addition to the responsibilities included in the sections of the Uniform Guidance as described in paragraph 24.03, the Uniform Guidance states that when a program-specific audit guide is not available, auditees must prepare the following:

- The financial statement(s) for the federal program that includes, at a minimum, a schedule of expenditures of federal awards for the program and notes that describe the significant accounting policies used in preparing the schedule (Chapter 17, "Schedule of Expenditures of Federal Awards (Uniform Guidance)," of this guide discusses the schedule.)
- A summary schedule of prior audit findings consistent with the requirements of 2 CFR 200.511(b) (See chapter 23, "Auditor Reporting Requirements and Other Communication Considerations in a Single Audit (Uniform Guidance)," of this guide.)
- If applicable, a corrective action plan consistent with the requirements of 2 CFR 200.507(c) (See chapter 23 of this guide.)

Auditor's Responsibilities When a Program-Specific Audit Guide Is Not Available

Audit Scope and Requirements

24.07 When a program-specific audit guide is not available, the Uniform Guidance states that the auditor must

- perform an audit of the financial statement(s) for the federal program in accordance with *Government Auditing Standards*. (Chapters 3, "Planning and Performing a Financial Statement Audit in Accordance With *Government Auditing Standards*," and 4, "Auditor Reporting Requirements and Other Communication Considerations of *Government Auditing Standards*," of this guide provide guidance on financial statement audits.) Paragraph 24.11 further discusses the *Government Auditing Standards* report.
- obtain an understanding of the internal control over compliance and perform tests of the internal control over compliance for the federal program consistent with the requirements of 2 CFR 200.514(c) for a major program. (Chapter 19 of this guide provides guidance on the internal control considerations for major programs.)
- perform procedures to determine whether the auditee has complied with federal statutes, regulations, and the terms and conditions of federal awards that could have a direct and material effect on the federal program consistent with the requirements of 2 CFR 200.514(d) for a major program. (Chapter 20 of this guide provides guidance on the compliance auditing considerations for major programs.)
- follow up on prior audit findings, perform procedures to assess the reasonableness of the summary schedule of prior audit findings that has been prepared by the auditee in accordance with 2 CFR 200.511, and report, as a current year audit finding, when the auditor concludes that the summary schedule of prior audit findings materially misrepresents the status of any prior audit finding. (See chapter 23 of this guide.)
- report any audit findings consistent with the requirements of 2 CFR 200.516. (See chapter 23 of this guide.)

Program-Specific Audits (Uniform Guidance)

Auditor Procedures

24.08 Paragraph .A11 of AU-C section 935 lists procedures the auditor may perform to identify and obtain an understanding of the applicable compliance requirements if the *Compliance Supplement* or a program-specific audit guide is not applicable:

- Reading the federal statutes, regulations, and the terms and conditions of the federal award that pertain to the program
- Making inquiries of management and other knowledgeable entity personnel
- Making inquiries of appropriate individuals outside the entity, such as (*a*) the office of the federal, state, or local program official or auditor or other appropriate audit oversight organizations or regulators, about the laws and regulations applicable to entities within their jurisdiction, including statutes and uniform (that is, common) reporting requirements or (*b*) a third-party specialist, such as an attorney
- Reading the minutes of meetings of the governing board of the entity being audited
- Reading audit documentation about the applicable compliance requirements prepared during prior years' audits or other engagements
- Discussing applicable compliance requirements with auditors who performed prior years' audits or other engagements

The procedures in the preceding list also may assist the auditor in obtaining a further understanding of the applicable compliance requirements for those engagements when the *Compliance Supplement* or program-specific audit guide is available.

Auditor's Reports[6]

Uniform Guidance Requirements

24.09 The Uniform Guidance states that the auditor's reports may be in the form of either combined or separate reports and may be organized differently from the manner described in the Uniform Guidance and as listed in this paragraph. The auditor's reports must state that the audit was conducted in accordance with the Uniform Guidance. Because the audit is also subject to GAAS reporting requirements and *Government Auditing Standards*, the report should also include a reference to auditing standards generally accepted in the United States of America and *Government Auditing Standards*. The auditor's reports must include the following:

- An opinion (or disclaimer of opinion) on whether the financial statement(s) of the federal program are presented fairly in all material respects in accordance with the stated accounting policies

---

[6] See also chapter 23, "Auditor Reporting Requirements and Other Communication Considerations in a Single Audit (Uniform Guidance)," for a discussion of the basic elements of the auditor's reports.

- A report on the internal control related to the federal program, which must describe the scope of the testing of the internal control and the results of the tests
- A report on compliance, which includes an opinion (or a disclaimer of opinion) on whether the auditee complied with federal statutes, regulations, and the terms and conditions of federal awards that could have a direct and material effect on the federal program
- A schedule of findings and questioned costs for the federal program that includes a summary of the auditor's results relative to the federal program in a format consistent with 2 CFR 200.515(d)(1) and findings and questioned costs for federal awards consistent with the requirements of 2 CFR 200.515(d)(3) (See chapter 23 of this guide.)[7]

Recommended Auditor's Reports

24.10 In an effort to make program-specific audit reporting understandable and reduce the number of reports issued, this guide recommends that the following reports be issued for a program-specific audit: (*a*) an opinion (or disclaimer of opinion) on the financial statement(s) of the federal program and (*b*) a report on compliance with requirements that could have a direct and material effect on the federal program and on the internal control over compliance in accordance with the program-specific audit option under the Uniform Guidance. Paragraph 24.11 discusses the possible issuance of a third report to meet the reporting requirements of *Government Auditing Standards*. The appendix, "Illustrative Auditor's Reports for Program-Specific Audits (Uniform Guidance)," of this chapter (paragraph 24.16) illustrates program-specific audit reports. Chapters 4 and 23 of this guide discuss the *Government Auditing Standards* requirement that the auditor communicate certain matters to officials of the audited entity in writing.

Reporting in Accordance With Government Auditing Standards

24.11 When the financial statement(s) of the program present only the activity of the federal program, the auditor is not required to issue a separate report to meet the reporting requirements of *Government Auditing Standards*. This is because, in many cases, by definition, the financial statement(s) of the program consist only of the schedule of expenditures of federal awards. In this situation, the program-specific audit reports in the appendix of this chapter (paragraph 24.16) would meet the financial, compliance, and internal control over compliance reporting requirements of both *Government Auditing Standards* and the Uniform Guidance. However, the auditor always has the option of issuing a separate *Government Auditing Standards* report (in addition to the two reports described in paragraph 24.10). In situations when the auditor is engaged to perform a separate engagement in addition to the program-specific audit (for example, an entity-wide financial statement audit in accordance with *Government Auditing Standards*), the appropriate audit reports

---

[7] Note that under the Uniform Guidance, more detailed information is required related to findings in the schedule of findings and questioned costs. (See chapter 23 of this guide for more information.) The findings in the schedule of findings and questioned costs also should meet the presentation requirements of *Government Auditing Standards*. See chapter 4, "Auditor Reporting Requirements and Other Communication Considerations of *Government Auditing Standards*," of this guide for more information.

should be issued, including a separate *Government Auditing Standards* report. Chapter 4 in this guide discusses the *Government Auditing Standards* report, and the appendix in chapter 4 illustrates the *Government Auditing Standards* report.

Submission of Report

Timing of Submission

24.12 The audit must be completed and the auditee must submit the reporting required by the Uniform Guidance within the earlier of 30 days after the receipt of the auditor's reports or 9 months after the end of the audit period, unless a different period is specified in a program-specific audit guide.[8] The Uniform Guidance also states that unless restricted by federal law or regulation, the auditee must make copies of the report available for public inspection. Auditees and auditors must ensure that their respective parts of the reporting package do not include protected personally identifiable information.

Submission When a Program-Specific Audit Guide Is Available

24.13 When a program-specific audit guide is available, the auditee must electronically submit to the Federal Audit Clearinghouse (FAC) the data collection form prepared in accordance with 2 CFR 200.512(b), as applicable for a program-specific audit, and the reporting required by the program-specific audit guide. (Chapter 23 of this guide provides guidance on the FAC and the completion and submission of the data collection form.)

Submission When a Program-Specific Audit Guide Is Not Available

24.14 When a program-specific audit guide is not available, the reporting package for a program-specific audit must consist of the following:

- The financial statement(s) of the federal program
- A summary schedule of prior audit findings (See chapter 23 of this guide.)
- A corrective action plan (See chapter 23 of this guide.)
- The auditor's report(s) (which includes the schedule of findings and questioned costs) described in paragraphs 24.09–.11

24.15 In addition, the auditee must electronically submit the data collection form, as applicable to a program-specific audit, and the reporting package to the FAC, as discussed in chapter 23 of this guide.

---

[8] If the auditee or auditor wishes to report to the federal government that the required submission will be late, the suggested way to do so is to contact the federal oversight or cognizant agency for the audit (contact information is available on the "Resources" tab at http://harvester.census.gov/fac/APPX3.htm).

24.16

Appendix—Illustrative Auditor's Reports for Program-Specific Audits (Uniform Guidance)

The illustrative reports in this appendix are examples of the reports issued under the audit requirements of Title 2 U.S. *Code of Federal Regulations* (CFR) Part 200, *Uniform Administrative Requirements, Cost Principles, and Audit Requirements for Federal Awards* (Uniform Guidance), for a program-specific audit. The following table lists the illustrative reports. Auditors, using professional judgment, may adapt these examples in any situation not specifically addressed in these illustrations. (As discussed in paragraph 24.11, the auditor should, in certain circumstances, issue these program-specific audit reports as well as a separate *Government Auditing Standards* report. The appendix in chapter 4, "Auditor Reporting Requirements and Other Communication Considerations of Government Auditing Standards," of this guide illustrates the *Government Auditing Standards* report.)

Example No.	Title
24-1	Unmodified Opinion on the Financial Statement of a Federal Program When Using the Program-Specific Audit Option to Satisfy the Uniform Guidance Audit Requirements
24-2	Report on Compliance for a Federal Program and Report on Internal Control Over Compliance When Using the Program-Specific Audit Option to Satisfy the Uniform Guidance Audit Requirements *(Unmodified Opinion on Compliance; No Material Weaknesses or Significant Deficiencies in Internal Control Over Compliance Identified)*

Example 24-1

Unmodified Opinion on the Financial Statement of a Federal Program When Using the Program-Specific Audit Option to Satisfy the Uniform Guidance Audit Requirements[1]

Independent Auditor's Report

[*Appropriate Addressee*]

Report on the Schedule of Expenditures of Federal Awards

We have audited the accompanying schedule of expenditures of federal awards for the [*identify the federal program*] of Example Entity for the year ended June 30, 20X1, and the related notes (the financial statement).

Management's Responsibility for the Schedule of Expenditures of Federal Awards

Management is responsible for the preparation and fair presentation of this financial statement in accordance with accounting principles generally accepted in the United States of America; this includes the design, implementation, and maintenance of internal control relevant to the preparation and fair presentation of a financial statement that is free from material misstatement, whether due to fraud or error.

Auditor's Responsibility

Our responsibility is to express an opinion on this financial statement based on our audit.[2]

We conducted our audit in accordance with auditing standards generally accepted in the United States of America; the standards applicable to financial audits contained in *Government Auditing Standards*,[3] issued by the Comptroller General of the United States; and the audit requirements of Title 2 U.S. Code of Federal Regulations (CFR) Part 200, *Uniform Administrative Requirements, Cost Principles, and Audit Requirements for Federal Awards* (Uniform Guidance). Those standards and the Uniform Guidance require that we plan and perform the audit to obtain reasonable assurance about whether the financial statement is free from material misstatement.

An audit involves performing procedures to obtain audit evidence about the amounts and disclosures in the financial statement. The procedures selected depend on the auditor's judgment, including the assessment of the risks of material misstatement of the financial statement, whether due to fraud or error. In making those risk assessments, the auditor considers internal control relevant to the entity's preparation and fair presentation of the financial statement in order to design audit procedures that are appropriate in the circumstances, but not for the purpose of expressing an opinion on the effectiveness of the

---

[1] This report example is based on the guidance found in AU-C section 805, *Special Considerations—Audits of Single Financial Statements and Specific Element, Accounts, or Items of a Financial Statement* (AICPA, *Professional Standards*). See AU-C section 805 for additional information, for example, if report modifications are needed.

[2] In many cases, the financial statement of the program consists only of the schedule of expenditures of federal awards (and the related notes), which is the minimum financial statement presentation required by 2 CFR 200.507. If the auditee issues financial statements that consist of more than the schedule, this paragraph would be modified to describe the financial statements.

[3] The standards and guidance applicable to financial audits are found in chapters 1–4 of *Government Auditing Standards*.

entity's internal control. Accordingly, we express no such opinion. An audit also includes evaluating the appropriateness of accounting policies used and the reasonableness of significant accounting estimates made by management, as well as evaluating the overall presentation of the financial statement.

We believe that the audit evidence we have obtained is sufficient and appropriate to provide a basis for our audit opinion.

Opinion

In our opinion, the financial statement referred to above presents fairly, in all material respects, the expenditures of federal awards[4] for the [*identify the federal program*] of Example Entity for the year ended June 30, 20X1, in accordance with accounting principles generally accepted in the United States of America.[5,6]

[*Auditor's signature*]

[*Auditor's city and state*][7]

[*Date of the auditor's report*]

---

[4] If the auditee issues financial statements that consist of more than the schedule, this sentence should be modified to identify the results displayed in the financial presentation.

[5] AU-C section 800, *Special Consideration—Audits of Financial Statements Prepared in Accordance With Special Purpose Frameworks* (AICPA, *Professional Standards*), provides requirements and guidance for auditor reporting when the auditee prepares financial statements in accordance with a special purpose framework. AU-C section 800 defines a *special purpose framework* as a financial reporting framework other than generally accepted accounting principles and establishes requirements for reporting on those frameworks. Special purpose frameworks, such as the cash, tax, regulatory, and other bases of accounting, are sometimes referred to as an *other comprehensive bases of accounting* (OCBOA). The term *OCBOA* is sometimes used when referring to this guidance in this guide.

[6] If a separate report is issued to meet the reporting requirements of *Government Auditing Standards* (see paragraph 24.11), an additional section with the heading "Other Reporting Required by *Government Auditing Standards*," would be added after the opinion paragraph as follows:

> In accordance with *Government Auditing Standards*, we have also issued our report dated [*date of report*] on our consideration of Example Entity's internal control over financial reporting and on our tests of its compliance with certain provisions of laws, regulations, contracts, and grant agreements and other matters. The purpose of that report is to describe the scope of our testing of internal control over financial reporting and compliance and the results of that testing, and not to provide an opinion on internal control over financial reporting or on compliance. That report is an integral part of an audit performed in accordance with *Government Auditing Standards* in considering Example Entity's internal control over financial reporting and compliance.

See chapter 4, "Auditor Reporting Requirements and Other Communication Considerations of *Government Auditing Standards*," of this guide for information regarding modifying report wording when issuing reports required by *Government Auditing Standards*.

[7] AU-C section 700, *Forming an Opinion and Reporting on Financial Statements* (AICPA, *Professional Standards*), provides that the auditor's report should name the city and state where the auditor practices. City and state on a firm's letterhead typically is sufficient to meet this requirement. Technical Questions and Answers section 9100.08, "Audit Firm With Multiple Offices on Their Company Letterhead and Effect on Report" (AICPA, *Technical Questions and Answers*), notes that when a firm's letterhead contains multiple office locations, the auditor would need to indicate the city and state where the auditor practices in the auditor's report.

Example 24-2
Report on Compliance for a Federal Program and Report on Internal Control Over Compliance When Using the Program-Specific Audit Option to Satisfy the Uniform Guidance Audit Requirements[8]
(Unmodified Opinion on Compliance; No Material Weaknesses or Significant Deficiencies in Internal Control Over Compliance Identified)[9]

Independent Auditor's Report

[Appropriate Addressee]

Report on Compliance for [*identify the federal program*][10]

We have audited Example Entity's compliance with the types of compliance requirements[11] described in the *OMB Compliance Supplement* that could have a direct and material[12] effect on its [*identify the federal program*] for the year ended June 30, 20X1.

---

[8] This is an example of a report on a program-specific audit under the Uniform Guidance audit requirements when no current federal audit guide applicable to the program being audited is available. When a current federal audit guide applicable to the program is available the auditor must follow the reporting requirement of that federal audit guide. (Paragraph 24.04 discusses the auditor's responsibility when a program-specific audit guide is not current.)

[9] Auditors, using professional judgment, may adapt this example to other situations not specifically addressed in the illustration. For example, if issuing a qualified or adverse opinion on compliance, the auditor may modify the compliance opinion section of this report. Additionally, if reporting significant deficiencies or material weaknesses, the auditor also may modify the internal control section of this report. The portions of examples 23-2–23-6 in the appendix of chapter 23, "Auditor Reporting Requirements and Other Communication Considerations in a Single Audit (Uniform Guidance)," of this guide that apply to a specific auditee situation in a single audit may be useful in modifying this report.

[10] This report sequences the reporting on compliance before the reporting on internal control over compliance. However, the *Government Auditing Standards* reports in the appendix of chapter 4 of this guide sequence the reporting on internal control over financial reporting before the reporting on compliance and other matters. Auditors may present the internal control over compliance and compliance sections of Uniform Guidance and *Government Auditing Standards* reports in whichever sequence better meets their needs.

[11] Under 2 CFR 200.516, the auditor's determination of whether noncompliance with federal statutes, regulations, and the terms and conditions of federal awards is material for the purpose of reporting an audit finding is in relation to a type of compliance requirement for a major program identified in the *OMB Compliance Supplement* (*Compliance Supplement*). Further, the auditor's determination of whether a deficiency in internal control over compliance is a material weakness or significant deficiency for the purpose of reporting an audit finding is also in relation to a type of compliance requirement for a major program identified in the *Compliance Supplement*. This reference to *type of compliance requirements* used here and elsewhere in this report illustration refers to the 12 types of compliance requirements described in Part 3 of the 2015 *Compliance Supplement*.

[12] AU-C section 935, *Compliance Audits* (AICPA, *Professional Standards*), defines *applicable compliance requirements* as the compliance requirements that are subject to the compliance audit. According to 2 CFR 200.515, the auditor's report on compliance with federal statutes, regulations, and the terms and conditions of federal awards must include an opinion (or disclaimer of opinion) regarding whether the auditee complied with federal statutes, regulations, and the terms and conditions of federal awards that could have a direct and material effect on each of its major programs. Therefore, in a Uniform Guidance compliance audit (including a program-specific audit), the direct and material compliance requirements are those that are subject to audit. Accordingly, for the purpose of adapting AU-C section 935 to a program-specific audit under the Uniform Guidance the term *applicable compliance requirements* has been replaced by *direct and material compliance requirements* in this guide except when directly citing content from AU-C section 935. See also footnote 11 of this appendix for a discussion related to the determination of material noncompliance.

Management's Responsibility

Management is responsible for compliance with federal statutes, regulations, and the terms and conditions of federal awards applicable to [*identify the federal program*].

Auditor's Responsibility

Our responsibility is to express an opinion on compliance for Example Entity's [*identify the federal program*] based on our audit of the types of compliance requirements referred to above.

We conducted our audit of compliance in accordance with auditing standards generally accepted in the United States of America; the standards applicable to financial audits contained in *Government Auditing Standards*,[13] issued by the Comptroller General of the United States; and the audit requirements of Title 2 U.S. *Code of Federal Regulations* (CFR) Part 200, *Uniform Administrative Requirements, Cost Principles, and Audit Requirements for Federal Award* (Uniform Guidance). Those standards and the Uniform Guidance require that we plan and perform the audit to obtain reasonable assurance about whether noncompliance with the types of compliance requirements referred to above that could have a direct and material effect on [*identify the federal program*] occurred. An audit includes examining, on a test basis, evidence about Example Entity's compliance with those requirements and performing such other procedures as we considered necessary in the circumstances.

We believe that our audit provides a reasonable basis for our opinion on compliance for Example Entity's [*identify the federal program*]. However, our audit does not provide a legal determination of Example Entity's compliance.

Opinion on Compliance for [*identify the federal program*]

In our opinion, Example Entity complied, in all material respects, with the compliance requirements referred to above that could have a direct and material effect on its [*identify the federal program*] for the year ended June 30, 20X1.

Other Matters[14]

The results of our auditing procedures disclosed instances of noncompliance, which are required to be reported in accordance with the Uniform Guidance and which are described in the accompanying schedule of findings and questioned costs as items [*list the reference numbers of the related findings, for example, 20X1-001 and 20X1-002*].[15,16] Our opinion on Example Entity's [*identify the federal program*] is not modified with respect to these matters.

---

[13] See footnote 3.

[14] When there are no findings that are required to be reported, and thus, no management response to findings, this "Other Matters" section of the report would be omitted.

[15] Finding reference numbers must follow the format meeting the requirements of the data collection form submission, that is, the four digits of the fiscal year followed by a numerical sequence of three digit numbers (201X-xxx).

[16] The auditor may also consider adding a table to this section of the report to more clearly communicate the other findings that are being reported and the requirements to which they relate. See example 23-4 in the appendix of chapter 23 for an example of a table approach that could be modified for this purpose.

Example Entity's response to the noncompliance findings identified in our audit are described in the accompanying schedule of findings and questioned costs. Example Entity's response was not subjected to the auditing procedures applied in the audit of compliance and, accordingly, we express no opinion on the response.[17]

Report on Internal Control Over Compliance[18]

Management of Example Entity is responsible for establishing and maintaining effective internal control over compliance with the types of compliance requirements referred to above. In planning and performing our audit of compliance, we considered Example Entity's internal control over compliance with the types of requirements that could have a direct and material effect on its [*identify the federal program*] to determine the auditing procedures that are appropriate in the circumstances for the purpose of expressing an opinion on compliance for its [*identify the federal program*] and to test and report on internal control over compliance in accordance with the Uniform Guidance, but not for the purpose of expressing an opinion on the effectiveness of internal control over compliance. Accordingly, we do not express an opinion on the effectiveness of Example Entity's internal control over compliance.

A *deficiency in internal control over compliance* exists when the design or operation of a control over compliance does not allow management or employees, in the normal course of performing their assigned functions, to prevent, or detect and correct, noncompliance with a type of compliance requirement of a federal program on a timely basis. A *material weakness in internal control over compliance* is a deficiency, or combination of deficiencies, in internal control over compliance, such that there is a reasonable possibility that material noncompliance with a type of compliance requirement of a federal program will not be prevented, or detected and corrected, on a timely basis. A *significant deficiency in internal control over compliance* is a deficiency, or a combination of deficiencies, in internal control over compliance with a type of compliance requirement of a federal program that is less severe than a material weakness in internal control over compliance, yet important enough to merit attention by those charged with governance.

Our consideration of internal control over compliance was for the limited purpose described in the first paragraph of this section and was not designed to identify all deficiencies in internal control over compliance that might be material weaknesses or significant deficiencies. We did not identify any deficiencies in internal control over compliance that we consider to be material weaknesses. However, material weaknesses may exist that have not been identified.

The purpose of this report on internal control over compliance is solely to describe the scope of our testing of internal control over compliance and the

---

[17] Although the auditor does not audit management's responses to identified findings, the auditor is required to report the views of responsible officials under the Uniform Guidance.

[18] This example illustrates a combined report that also includes the reporting on internal control over compliance. If an auditor prefers to issue a separate report on internal control over compliance, this section would be omitted from the report. AU-C section 935 includes required elements for separate reporting on internal control over compliance.

results of that testing based on the requirements of the Uniform Guidance. Accordingly, this report is not suitable for any other purpose.[19]

[*Auditor's signature*]

[*Auditor's city and state*][20]

[*Date of the auditor's report*]

---

[19] This paragraph has been adapted from AU-C section 905, *Alert That Restricts the Use of the Auditor's Written Communication* (AICPA, *Professional Standards*), to relate to the reporting on internal control over compliance that is required in an audit of compliance in accordance with the Uniform Guidance.

[20] See footnote 7.

Supplement A
Single Audit Act Amendments of 1996
This supplement contains authoritative material.

Public Law 104-156
104th Congress

July 5, 1996
[S. 1579]

Single Audit Act Amendments of 1996.
31 USC 7501 note.

An Act

To streamline and improve the effectiveness of chapter 75 of title 31, United States Code (commonly referred to as the "Single Audit Act").

Be it enacted by the Senate and House of Representatives of the United States of America in Congress assembled,

SECTION 1. SHORT TITLE; PURPOSES.

(a) Short Title—This Act may be cited as the ASingle Audit Act Amendments of 1996".

(b) Purposes—The purposes of this Act are to—

(1) promote sound financial management, including effective internal controls, with respect to Federal awards administered by non-Federal entities;

(2) establish uniform requirements for audits of Federal awards administered by non-Federal entities;

(3) promote the efficient and effective use of audit resources;

(4) reduce burdens on State and local governments, Indian tribes, and nonprofit organizations; and

(5) ensure that Federal departments and agencies, to the maximum extent practicable, rely upon and use audit work done pursuant to chapter 75 of title 31, United States Code (as amended by this Act).

SEC. 2 . AMENDMENT TO TITLE 31, UNITED STATES CODE.

Chapter 75 of title 31, United States Code, is amended to read as follows:

"CHAPTER 75—REQUIREMENTS FOR SINGLE AUDITS

"Sec.
"7501. Definitions.
"7502. Audit requirements; exemptions.
"7503. Relation to other audit requirements.
"7504. Federal agency responsibilities and relations with non-Federal entities.
"7505. Regulations.
"7506. Monitoring responsibilities of the Comptroller General.
"7507. Effective date.

"**§ 7501. Definitions**

"(a) As used in this chapter, the term—

"(1) 'Comptroller General' means the Comptroller General of the United States;

"(2) 'Director' means the Director of the Office of Management and Budget;

"(3) 'Federal agency' has the same meaning as the term 'agency' in section 551(1) of title 5;

"(4) 'Federal awards' means Federal financial assistance and Federal cost-reimbursement contracts that non-Federal entities receive directly from Federal awarding agencies or indirectly from pass-through entities;

"(5) 'Federal financial assistance' means assistance that non-Federal entities receive or administer in the form of grants, loans, loan guarantees, property, cooperative agreements, interest subsidies, insurance, food commodities, direct appropriations, or other assistance, but does not include amounts received as reimbursement for services rendered to individuals in accordance with guidance issued by the Director;

"(6) 'Federal program' means all Federal awards to a non-Federal entity assigned a single number in the Catalog of Federal Domestic Assistance or encompassed in a group of numbers or other category as defined by the Director;

"(7) 'generally accepted government auditing standards' means the government auditing standards issued by the Comptroller General;

"(8) 'independent auditor' means—

"(A) an external State or local government auditor who meets the independence standards included in generally accepted government auditing standards; or

"(B) a public accountant who meets such independence standards;

"(9) 'Indian tribe' means any Indian tribe, band, nation, or other organized group or community, including any Alaskan Native village or regional or village corporation (as defined in, or established under, the Alaskan Native Claims Settlement Act) that is recognized by the United States as eligible for the special programs and services provided by the United States to Indians because of their status as Indians;

"(10) 'internal controls' means a process, effected by an entity's management and other personnel, designed to provide reasonable assurance regarding the achievement of objectives in the following categories:

"(A) Effectiveness and efficiency of operations.

"(B) Reliability of financial reporting.

"(C) Compliance with applicable laws and regulations;

"(11) 'local government' means any unit of local government within a State, including a county, borough, municipality, city, town, township, parish, local public authority, special district, school district, intrastate district, council of governments, any other instrumentality of local government and, in accordance with guidelines issued by the Director, a group of local governments;

"(12) 'major program' means a Federal program identified in accordance with risk-based criteria prescribed by the Director under this chapter, subject to the limitations described under subsection (b);

"(13) 'non-Federal entity' means a State, local government, or nonprofit organization;

"(14) 'nonprofit organization' means any corporation, trust, association, cooperative, or other organization that—

"(A) is operated primarily for scientific, educational, service, charitable, or similar purposes in the public interest;

"(B) is not organized primarily for profit; and

"(C) uses net proceeds to maintain, improve, or expand the operations of the organization;

"(15) 'pass-through entity' means a non-Federal entity that provides Federal awards to a subrecipient to carry out a Federal program;

"(16) 'program-specific audit' means an audit of one Federal program;

"(17) 'recipient' means a non-Federal entity that receives awards directly from a Federal agency to carry out a Federal program;

"(18) 'single audit' means an audit, as described under section 7502(d), of a non-Federal entity that includes the entity's financial statements and Federal awards;

"(19) 'State' means any State of the United States, the District of Columbia, the Commonwealth of Puerto Rico, the Virgin Islands, Guam, American Samoa, the Commonwealth of the Northern Mariana Islands, and the Trust Territory of the Pacific Islands, any instrumentality thereof, any multi-State, regional, or interstate entity which has governmental functions, and any Indian tribe; and

"(20) 'subrecipient' means a non-Federal entity that receives Federal awards through another non-Federal entity to carry out a Federal program, but does not include an individual who receives financial assistance through such awards.

"(b) In prescribing risk-based program selection criteria for major programs, the Director shall not require more programs to be identified as major for a particular non-Federal entity, except as prescribed under subsection (c) or as provided under subsection (d), than would be identified if the major programs were defined as any program for which total expenditures of Federal awards by the non-Federal entity during the applicable year exceed—

"(1) the larger of $30,000,000 or 0.15 percent of the non-Federal entity's total Federal expenditures, in the case of a non-Federal entity for which such total expenditures for all programs exceed $10,000,000,000;

"(2) the larger of $3,000,000, or 0.30 percent of the non-Federal entity's total Federal expenditures, in the case of a non-Federal entity for which such total expenditures for all programs exceed $100,000,000 but are less than or equal to $10,000,000,000; or

"(3) the larger of $300,000, or 3 percent of such total Federal expenditures for all programs, in the case of a non-Federal entity for which such total expenditures for all programs equal or exceed $300,000 but are less than or equal to $100,000,000.

"(c) When the total expenditures of a non-Federal entity's major programs are less than 50 percent of the non-Federal entity's total expenditures of all Federal awards (or such lower percentage as specified by the Director), the auditor shall select and test additional programs as major programs as necessary to achieve audit coverage of at least 50 percent of Federal expenditures by the non-Federal entity (or such lower percentage as specified by the Director), in accordance with guidance issued by the Director.

"(d) Loan or loan guarantee programs, as specified by the Director, shall not be subject to the application of subsection (b).

"**§ 7502. Audit requirements; exemptions**

"(a)(1)(A) Each non-Federal entity that expends a total amount of Federal awards equal to or in excess of $300,000 or such other amount specified by the Director under subsection (a)(3) in any fiscal year of such non-Federal entity shall have either a single audit or a program-specific audit made for such fiscal year in accordance with the requirements of this chapter.

(B) Each such non-Federal entity that expends Federal awards under more than one Federal program shall undergo a single audit in accordance with the requirements of subsections (b) through (i) of this section and guidance issued by the Director under section 7505.

"(C) Each such non-Federal entity that expends awards under only one Federal program and is not subject to laws, regulations, or Federal award agreements that require a financial statement audit of the non-Federal entity, may elect to have a program-specific audit conducted in accordance with applicable provisions of this section and guidance issued by the Director under section 7505.

(2)(A) Each non-Federal entity that expends a total amount of Federal awards of less than $300,000 or such other amount specified by the Director under subsection (a)(3) in any fiscal year of such entity, shall be exempt for such fiscal year from compliance with

(i) the audit requirements of this chapter; and

(ii) any applicable requirements concerning financial audits contained in Federal statutes and regulations governing programs under which such Federal awards are provided to that non-Federal entity.

"(B) The provisions of subparagraph (A)(ii) of this paragraph shall not exempt a non-Federal entity from compliance with any provision of a Federal statute or regulation that requires such non-Federal entity to maintain records concerning Federal awards provided to such non-Federal entity or that permits a Federal agency, pass-through entity, or the Comptroller General access to such records.

"(3) Every 2 years, the Director shall review the amount for requiring audits prescribed under paragraph (1)(A) and may adjust such dollar amount consistent with the purposes of this chapter, provided the Director does not make such adjustments below $300,000.

Single Audit Act Amendments of 1996

"(b)(1) Except as provided in paragraphs (2) and (3), audits conducted pursuant to this chapter shall be conducted annually.

"(2) A State or local government that is required by constitution or statute, in effect on January 1, 1987, to undergo its audits less frequently than annually, is permitted to undergo its audits pursuant to this chapter biennially. Audits conducted biennially under the provisions of this paragraph shall cover both years within the biennial period.

"(3) Any nonprofit organization that had biennial audits for all biennial periods ending between July 1, 1992, and January 1, 1995, is permitted to undergo its audits pursuant to this chapter biennially. Audits conducted biennially under the provisions of this paragraph shall cover both years within the biennial period.

"(c) Each audit conducted pursuant to subsection (a) shall be conducted by an independent auditor in accordance with generally accepted government auditing standards, except that, for the purposes of this chapter, performance audits shall not be required except as authorized by the Director.

"(d) Each single audit conducted pursuant to subsection (a) for any fiscal year shall

"(1) cover the operations of the entire non-Federal entity; or

"(2) at the option of such non-Federal entity such audit shall include a series of audits that cover departments, agencies, and other organizational units which expended or otherwise administered Federal awards during such fiscal year provided that each such audit shall encompass the financial statements and schedule of expenditures of Federal awards for each such department, agency, and organizational unit, which shall be considered to be a non-Federal entity.

"(e) The auditor shall—

"(1) determine whether the financial statements are presented fairly in all material respects in conformity with generally accepted accounting principles;

"(2) determine whether the schedule of expenditures of Federal awards is presented fairly in all material respects in relation to the financial statements taken as a whole;

"(3) with respect to internal controls pertaining to the compliance requirements for each major program—

"(A) obtain an understanding of such internal controls;

"(B) assess control risk; and

"(C) perform tests of controls unless the controls are deemed to be ineffective; and

"(4) determine whether the non-Federal entity has complied with the provisions of laws, regulations, and contracts or grants pertaining to Federal awards that have a direct and material effect on each major program.

"(f)(1) Each Federal agency which provides Federal awards to a recipient shall—

"(A) provide such recipient the program names (and any identifying numbers) from which such awards are derived, and the Federal requirements which govern the use of such awards and the requirements of this chapter; and

"(B) review the audit of a recipient as necessary to determine whether prompt and appropriate corrective action has been taken with respect to audit findings, as defined by the Director, pertaining to Federal awards provided to the recipient by the Federal agency.

"(2) Each pass-through entity shall—

"(A) provide such subrecipient the program names (and any identifying numbers) from which such assistance is derived, and the Federal requirements which govern the use of such awards and the requirements of this chapter;

"(B) monitor the subrecipient's use of Federal awards through site visits, limited scope audits, or other means;

"(C) review the audit of a subrecipient as necessary to determine whether prompt and appropriate corrective action has been taken with respect to audit findings, as defined by the Director, pertaining to Federal awards provided to the subrecipient by the pass-through entity; and

"(D) require each of its subrecipients of Federal awards to permit, as a condition of receiving Federal awards, the independent auditor of the pass-through entity to have such access to the subrecipient's records and financial statements as may be necessary for the pass-through entity to comply with this chapter.

"(g)(1) The auditor shall report on the results of any audit conducted pursuant to this section, in accordance with guidance issued by the Director.

"(2) When reporting on any single audit, the auditor shall include a summary of the auditor's results regarding the non-Federal entity's financial statements, internal controls, and compliance with laws and regulations.

"(h) The non-Federal entity shall transmit the reporting package, which shall include the non-Federal entity's financial statements, schedule of expenditures of Federal awards, corrective action plan defined under subsection (i), and auditor's reports developed pursuant to this section, to a Federal clearinghouse designated by the Director, and make it available for public inspection within the earlier of

"(1) 30 days after receipt of the auditor's report; or

"(2)(A) for a transition period of at least 2 years after the effective date of the Single Audit Act Amendments of 1996, as established by the Director, 13 months after the end of the period audited; or

(B) for fiscal years beginning after the period specified in subparagraph (A), 9 months after the end of the period audited, or within a longer time frame authorized by the Federal agency, determined under criteria issued under section 7504, when the 9-month time frame would place an undue burden on the non-Federal entity.

Single Audit Act Amendments of 1996

"(i) If an audit conducted pursuant to this section discloses any audit findings, as defined by the Director, including material noncompliance with individual compliance requirements for a major program by, or reportable conditions in the internal controls of, the non-Federal entity with respect to the matters described in subsection (e), the non-Federal entity shall submit to Federal officials designated by the Director, a plan for corrective action to eliminate such audit findings or reportable conditions or a statement describing the reasons that corrective action is not necessary. Such plan shall be consistent with the audit resolution standard promulgated by the Comptroller General (as part of the standards for internal controls in the Federal Government) pursuant to section 3512(c).

"(j) The Director may authorize pilot projects to test alternative methods of achieving the purposes of this chapter. Such pilot projects may begin only after consultation with the Chair and Ranking Minority Member of the Committee on Governmental Affairs of the Senate and the Chair and Ranking Minority Member of the Committee on Government Reform and Oversight of the House of Representatives.

"§ 7503. Relation to other audit requirements

"(a) An audit conducted in accordance with this chapter shall be in lieu of any financial audit of Federal awards which a non-Federal entity is required to undergo under any other Federal law or regulation. To the extent that such audit provides a Federal agency with the information it requires to carry out its responsibilities under Federal law or regulation, a Federal agency shall rely upon and use that information.

"(b) Notwithstanding subsection (a), a Federal agency may conduct or arrange for additional audits which are necessary to carry out its responsibilities under Federal law or regulation. The provisions of this chapter do not authorize any non-Federal entity (or subrecipient thereof) to constrain, in any manner, such agency from carrying out or arranging for such additional audits, except that the Federal agency shall plan such audits to not be duplicative of other audits of Federal awards.

"(c) The provisions of this chapter do not limit the authority of Federal agencies to conduct, or arrange for the conduct of, audits and evaluations of Federal awards, nor limit the authority of any Federal agency Inspector General or other Federal official.

"(d) Subsection (a) shall apply to a non-Federal entity which undergoes an audit in accordance with this chapter even though it is not required by section 7502(a) to have such an audit.

"(e) A Federal agency that provides Federal awards and conducts or arranges for audits of non-Federal entities receiving such awards that are in addition to the audits of non-Federal entities conducted pursuant to this chapter shall, consistent with other applicable law, arrange for funding the full cost of such additional audits. Any such additional audits shall be coordinated with the Federal agency determined under criteria issued under section 7504 to preclude duplication of the audits conducted pursuant to this chapter or other additional audits.

"(f) Upon request by a Federal agency or the Comptroller General, any independent auditor conducting an audit pursuant to this chapter shall make the auditor's working papers available to the Federal agency or the Comptroller General as part of a quality review, to resolve audit findings, or to carry out oversight responsibilities consistent with the purposes of this chapter. Such access to auditor's working papers shall include the right to obtain copies.

"§ 7504. Federal agency responsibilities and relations with non-Federal entities

"(a) Each Federal agency shall, in accordance with guidance issued by the Director under section 7505, with regard to Federal awards provided by the agency—

"(1) monitor non-Federal entity use of Federal awards, and

"(2) assess the quality of audits conducted under this chapter for audits of entities for which the agency is the single Federal agency determined under subsection (b).

"(b) Each non-Federal entity shall have a single Federal agency, determined in accordance with criteria established by the Director, to provide the non-Federal entity with technical assistance and assist with implementation of this chapter.

"(c) The Director shall designate a Federal clearinghouse to—

"(1) receive copies of all reporting packages developed in accordance with this chapter;

"(2) identify recipients that expend $300,000 or more in Federal awards or such other amount specified by the Director under section 7502(a)(3) during the recipient's fiscal year but did not undergo an audit in accordance with this chapter; and

"(3) perform analyses to assist the Director in carrying out responsibilities under this chapter.

"§ 7505. Regulations

"(a) The Director, after consultation with the Comptroller General, and appropriate officials from Federal, State, and local governments and nonprofit organizations shall prescribe guidance to implement this chapter. Each Federal agency shall promulgate such amendments to its regulations as may be necessary to conform such regulations to the requirements of this chapter and of such guidance.

"(b)(1) The guidance prescribed pursuant to subsection (a) shall include criteria for determining the appropriate charges to Federal awards for the cost of audits. Such criteria shall prohibit a non-Federal entity from charging to any Federal awards—

"(A) the cost of any audit which is—

"(i) not conducted in accordance with this chapter; or

"(ii) conducted in accordance with this chapter when expenditures of Federal awards are less than amounts cited in section 7502(a)(1)(A) or specified by the Director under section 7502(a)(3), except that the Director may allow the cost of limited scope audits to monitor subrecipients in accordance with section 7502(f)(2)(B); and

"(B) more than a reasonably proportionate share of the cost of any such audit that is conducted in accordance with this chapter.

"(2) The criteria prescribed pursuant to paragraph (1) shall not, in the absence of documentation demonstrating a higher actual cost, permit the percentage of the cost of audits performed pursuant to this chapter charged to Federal awards, to exceed the ratio of total Federal awards expended by such non-Federal entity during the applicable fiscal year or years, to such non-Federal entity's total expenditures during such fiscal year or years.

"(c) Such guidance shall include such provisions as may be necessary to ensure that small business concerns and business concerns owned and controlled by socially and economically disadvantaged individuals will have the opportunity to participate in the performance of contracts awarded to fulfill the audit requirements of this chapter.

"**§ 7506. Monitoring responsibilities of the Comptroller General**

"(a) The Comptroller General shall review provisions requiring financial audits of non-Federal entities that receive Federal awards that are contained in bills and resolutions reported by the committees of the Senate and the House of Representatives.

"(b) If the Comptroller General determines that a bill or resolution contains provisions that are inconsistent with the requirements of this chapter, the Comptroller General shall, at the earliest practicable date, notify in writing—

"(1) the committee that reported such bill or resolution; and

"(2)(A) the Committee on Governmental Affairs of the Senate (in the case of a bill or resolution reported by a committee of the Senate); or

"(B) the Committee on Government Reform and Oversight of the House of Representatives (in the case of a bill or resolution reported by a committee of the House of Representatives).

31 USC 7501 note.

"**§ 7507. Effective date**

"This chapter shall apply to any non-Federal entity with respect to any of its fiscal years which begin after June 30, 1996.".

SEC. 3. TRANSITIONAL APPLICATION

Subject to section 7507 of title 31, United States Code (as amended by section 2 of this Act) the provisions of chapter 75 of such title (before amendment by section 2 of this Act) shall continue to apply to any State or local government with respect to any of its fiscal years beginning before July 1, 1996.

Approved July 5, 1996.

LEGISLATIVE HISTORY—S. 1579 (H.R. 3184)

HOUSE REPORTS: No. 104—607 accompanying H.R. 3184 (Comm. on Government Reform and Oversight).

SENATE REPORTS: No. 104—266 (Comm. On Governmental Affairs).

CONGRESSIONAL RECORD, Vol. 142 (1996):

June 14, considered and passed Senate.

June 18, considered and passed House.

WEEKLY COMPILATION OF PRESIDENTIAL DOCUMENTS, Vol. 32 (1996):

July 5, Presidential statement.

Supplement B

OMB Circular A-133, Audits of States, Local Governments, and Non-Profit Organizations

This supplement contains authoritative Office of Management and Budget material.

Circular No. A-133, revised to show changes published in the Federal Register *June 27, 2003 and June 26, 2007*

Audits of States, Local Governments, and Non-Profit Organizations

Accompanying *Federal Register* Materials:

- Audits of States, Local Governments, and Non-Profit Organizations June 30, 1997

    — Revision published June 27, 2003. This revision (1) increased the dollar threshold for the audit requirement; and (2) made changes regarding determination of cognizant and oversight agencies for audit.

    — Revision published June 26, 2007. This revision (1) replaced the term *reportable conditions* with *significant deficiencies* to conform with current auditing standards; and (2) updated report submission requirements. Definition of *significant deficiencies* and *material weaknesses* are as defined in generally accepted auditing standards issued by the American Institute of Certified Public Accountants (AICPA) and *Government Auditing Standards* issued by the Government Accountability Office.

Note: The June 27, 2003 revisions (1) increased the dollar threshold for the audit requirement, and (2) made changes regarding determination of cognizant and oversight agencies for audit. The June 26, 2007 revisions make changes to (1) to replace the terms *reportable conditions* with *significant deficiencies* to conform with changes in auditing standards; and (2) reporting submission requirements.

In several places, the Circular includes guidelines for the reporting of *significant deficiencies* and *material weaknesses*. These terms are to be used as defined in generally accepted auditing standards issued by the American Institute of Certified Public Accountants (AICPA), and *Government Auditing Standards* issued by the Government Accountability Office.

To the Heads of Executive Departments and Establishments

SUBJECT: Audits of States, Local Governments, and Non-Profit Organizations

1. *Purpose.* This Circular is issued pursuant to the Single Audit Act of 1984, P.L. 98-502, and the Single Audit Act Amendments of 1996, P.L. 104-156. It sets forth standards for obtaining consistency and uniformity among Federal agencies for the audit of States, local governments, and non-profit organizations expending Federal awards.

2. *Authority.* Circular A-133 is issued under the authority of sections 503, 1111, and 7501 et seq. of title 31, United States Code, and Executive Orders 8248 and 11541.

3. *Rescission and Supersession.* This Circular rescinds Circular A-128, "Audits of State and Local Governments," issued April 12, 1985, and supersedes the prior Circular A-133, "Audits of Institutions of Higher Education and Other Non-Profit Institutions," issued April 22, 1996. For effective dates, see paragraph 10.

4. *Policy.* Except as provided herein, the standards set forth in this Circular shall be applied by all Federal agencies. If any statute specifically prescribes policies or specific requirements that differ from the standards provided herein, the provisions of the subsequent statute shall govern.

Federal agencies shall apply the provisions of the sections of this Circular to non-Federal entities, whether they are recipients expending Federal awards received directly from Federal awarding agencies, or are subrecipients expending Federal awards received from a pass-through entity (a recipient or another subrecipient).

This Circular does not apply to non-U.S. based entities expending Federal awards received either directly as a recipient or indirectly as a subrecipient.

5. *Definitions.* The definitions of key terms used in this Circular are contained in §__.105 in the Attachment to this Circular.

6. *Required Action.* The specific requirements and responsibilities of Federal agencies and non-Federal entities are set forth in the Attachment to this Circular. Federal agencies making awards to non-Federal entities, either directly or indirectly, shall adopt the language in the Circular in codified regulations as provided in Section 10 (below), unless different provisions are required by Federal statute or are approved by the Office of Management and Budget (OMB).

7. *OMB Responsibilities.* OMB will review Federal agency regulations and implementation of this Circular, and will provide interpretations of policy requirements and assistance to ensure uniform, effective and efficient implementation.

8. *Information Contact.* Further information concerning Circular A-133 may be obtained by contacting the Financial Standards and Reporting Branch, Office of Federal Financial Management, Office of Management and Budget, Washington, DC 20503, telephone (202) 395-3993.

9. *Review Date.* This Circular will have a policy review three years from the date of issuance.

10. *Effective Dates.* The standards set forth in §__.400 of the Attachment to this Circular, which apply directly to Federal agencies, shall be effective July 1, 1996, and shall apply to audits of fiscal years beginning after June 30, 1996, except as otherwise specified in §__.400(a).

The standards set forth in this Circular that Federal agencies shall apply to non-Federal entities shall be adopted by Federal agencies in codified regulations not later than 60 days after publication of this final revision in the **Federal Register**, so that they will apply to audits of fiscal years beginning after June 30, 1996, with the exception that §__.305(b) of the Attachment applies to audits of fiscal years beginning after June 30, 1998. The requirements of Circular A-128, although the Circular is rescinded, and the 1990 version of Circular A-133 remain in effect for audits of fiscal years beginning on or before June 30, 1996.

The revisions published in the Federal Register June 27, 2003, are effective for fiscal years ending after December 31, 2003, and early implementation is not permitted with the exception of the definition of oversight agency for audit which is effective July 28, 2003.

Augustine T. Smythe,
Acting Director

The revisions published in the Federal Register June 26, 2007, are effective for fiscal years ending on or after December 15, 2006.

Rob Portman
Director

Attachment

PART—AUDITS OF STATES, LOCAL GOVERNMENTS, AND NON-PROFIT ORGANIZATIONS

Subpart A—General

Sec.

__.100 Purpose.

__.105 Definitions.

Subpart B—Audits

__.200 Audit requirements.

__.205 Basis for determining Federal awards expended.

__.210 Subrecipient and vendor determinations.

__.215 Relation to other audit requirements.

__.220 Frequency of audits.

__.225 Sanctions.

__.230 Audit costs.

__.235 Program-specific audits.

Subpart C—Auditees

__.300 Auditee responsibilities.

__.305 Auditor selection.

__.310 Financial statements.

__.315 Audit findings follow-up.

__.320 Report submission.

Subpart D—Federal Agencies and Pass-Through Entities

__.400 Responsibilities.

__.405 Management decision.

Subpart E—Auditors

__.500 Scope of audit.

__.505 Audit reporting.

__.510 Audit findings.

__.515 Audit working papers.

__.520 Major program determination.

__.525 Criteria for Federal program risk.

__.530 Criteria for a low-risk auditee.

Appendix A to Part—Data Collection Form (Form SF-SAC).

Appendix B to Part—Circular A-133 Compliance Supplement.

Subpart A—General

§__.100 Purpose.

This part sets forth standards for obtaining consistency and uniformity among Federal agencies for the audit of non-Federal entities expending Federal awards.

§__.105 Definitions.

Auditee means any non-Federal entity that expends Federal awards which must be audited under this part.

Auditor means an auditor, that is a public accountant or a Federal, State or local government audit organization, which meets the general standards specified in generally accepted government auditing standards (GAGAS). The term auditor does not include internal auditors of non-profit organizations.

Audit finding means deficiencies which the auditor is required by §__.510(a) to report in the schedule of findings and questioned costs.

CFDA number means the number assigned to a Federal program in the Catalog of Federal Domestic Assistance (CFDA).

Cluster of programs means a grouping of closely related programs that share common compliance requirements. The types of clusters of programs are research and development (R&D), student financial aid (SFA), and other clusters. "Other clusters" are as defined by the Office of Management and Budget (OMB) in the compliance supplement or as designated by a State for Federal awards the State provides to its subrecipients that meet the definition of a cluster of programs. When designating an "other cluster," a State shall identify the Federal awards included in the cluster and advise the subrecipients of compliance requirements applicable to the cluster, consistent with §__.400(d)(1) and §__.400(d)(2), respectively. A cluster of programs shall be considered as one program for determining major programs, as described in §__.520, and, with the exception of R&D as described in §__.200(c), whether a program-specific audit may be elected.

Cognizant agency for audit means the Federal agency designated to carry out the responsibilities described in §__.400(a).

Compliance supplement refers to the Circular A-133 Compliance Supplement, included as Appendix B to Circular A-133, or such documents as OMB or its designee may issue to replace it. This document is available from the Government Printing Office, Superintendent of Documents, Washington, DC 20402-9325.

Corrective action means action taken by the auditee that:

   (1) Corrects identified deficiencies;

   (2) Produces recommended improvements; or

   (3) Demonstrates that audit findings are either invalid or do not warrant auditee action.

Federal agency has the same meaning as the term agency in Section 551(1) of title 5, United States Code.

Federal award means Federal financial assistance and Federal cost-reimbursement contracts that non-Federal entities receive directly from Federal awarding agencies or indirectly from pass-through entities. It does not include procurement contracts, under grants or contracts, used to buy goods or services from vendors. Any audits of such vendors shall be covered by the terms and conditions of the contract. Contracts to operate Federal Government owned, contractor operated facilities (GOCOs) are excluded from the requirements of this part.

Federal awarding agency means the Federal agency that provides an award directly to the recipient.

Federal financial assistance means assistance that non-Federal entities receive or administer in the form of grants, loans, loan guarantees, property (including donated surplus property), cooperative agreements, interest subsidies, insurance, food commodities, direct appropriations, and other assistance, but does not include amounts received as reimbursement for services rendered to individuals as described in §__.205(h) and §__.205(i).

Federal program means:

(1) All Federal awards to a non-Federal entity assigned a single number in the CFDA.

(2) When no CFDA number is assigned, all Federal awards from the same agency made for the same purpose should be combined and considered one program.

(3) Notwithstanding paragraphs (1) and (2) of this definition, a cluster of programs. The types of clusters of programs are:

(i) Research and development (R&D);

(ii) Student financial aid (SFA); and

(iii) "Other clusters," as described in the definition of *cluster of programs* in this section.

GAGAS means generally accepted government auditing standards issued by the Comptroller General of the United States, which are applicable to financial audits.

Generally accepted accounting principles has the meaning specified in generally accepted auditing standards issued by the American Institute of Certified Public Accountants (AICPA).

Indian tribe means any Indian tribe, band, nation, or other organized group or community, including any Alaskan Native village or regional or village corporation (as defined in, or established under, the Alaskan Native Claims Settlement Act) that is recognized by the United States as eligible for the special programs and services provided by the United States to Indians because of their status as Indians.

Internal control means a process, effected by an entity's management and other personnel, designed to provide reasonable assurance regarding the achievement of objectives in the following categories:

(1) Effectiveness and efficiency of operations;

(2) Reliability of financial reporting; and

(3) Compliance with applicable laws and regulations.

Internal control pertaining to the compliance requirements for Federal programs (Internal control over Federal programs) means a process—effected by an entity's management and other personnel—designed to provide reasonable assurance regarding the achievement of the following objectives for Federal programs:

(1) Transactions are properly recorded and accounted for to:

(i) Permit the preparation of reliable financial statements and Federal reports;

(ii) Maintain accountability over assets; and

(iii) Demonstrate compliance with laws, regulations, and other compliance requirements;

(2) Transactions are executed in compliance with:

(i) Laws, regulations, and the provisions of contracts or grant agreements that could have a direct and material effect on a Federal program; and

(ii) Any other laws and regulations that are identified in the compliance supplement; and

(3) Funds, property, and other assets are safeguarded against loss from unauthorized use or disposition.

Loan means a Federal loan or loan guarantee received or administered by a non-Federal entity.

Local government means any unit of local government within a State, including a county, borough, municipality, city, town, township, parish, local public authority, special district, school district, intrastate district, council of governments, and any other instrumentality of local government.

Major program means a Federal program determined by the auditor to be a major program in accordance with §__.520 or a program identified as a major program by a Federal agency or pass-through entity in accordance with §__.215(c).

Management decision means the evaluation by the Federal awarding agency or pass-through entity of the audit findings and corrective action plan and the issuance of a written decision as to what corrective action is necessary.

Non-Federal entity means a State, local government, or non-profit organization.

Non-profit organization means:

(1) any corporation, trust, association, cooperative, or other organization that:

(i) Is operated primarily for scientific, educational, service, charitable, or similar purposes in the public interest;

(ii) Is not organized primarily for profit; and

(iii) Uses its net proceeds to maintain, improve, or expand its operations; and

(2) The term non-profit organization includes non-profit institutions of higher education and hospitals.

OMB means the Executive Office of the President, Office of Management and Budget.

Oversight agency for audit means the Federal awarding agency that provides the predominant amount of direct funding to a recipient not assigned a cognizant agency for audit. When there is no direct funding, the Federal agency with the predominant indirect funding shall assume the oversight responsibilities. The duties of the oversight agency for audit are described in §__.400(b).

Effective July 28, 2003, the following is added to this definition:

A Federal agency with oversight for an auditee may reassign oversight to another Federal agency which provides substantial funding and agrees to be the oversight agency for audit. Within 30 days after any reassignment, both the old and the new oversight agency for audit shall notify the auditee, and, if known, the auditor of the reassignment.

Pass-through entity means a non-Federal entity that provides a Federal award to a subrecipient to carry out a Federal program.

Program-specific audit means an audit of one Federal program as provided for in §__.200(c) and §__.235.

Questioned cost means a cost that is questioned by the auditor because of an audit finding:

(1) Which resulted from a violation or possible violation of a provision of a law, regulation, contract, grant, cooperative agreement, or other agreement or document governing the use of Federal funds, including funds used to match Federal funds;

(2) Where the costs, at the time of the audit, are not supported by adequate documentation; or

(3) Where the costs incurred appear unreasonable and do not reflect the actions a prudent person would take in the circumstances.

Recipient means a non-Federal entity that expends Federal awards received directly from a Federal awarding agency to carry out a Federal program.

Research and development (R&D) means all research activities, both basic and applied, and all development activities that are performed by a non-Federal entity. Research is defined as a systematic study directed toward fuller scientific knowledge or understanding of the subject studied. The term research also includes activities involving the training of individuals in research techniques where such activities utilize the same facilities as other research and development activities and where such activities are not included in the instruction function. Development is the systematic use of knowledge and understanding gained from research directed toward the production of useful materials, devices, systems, or methods, including design and development of prototypes and processes.

Single audit means an audit which includes both the entity's financial statements and the Federal awards as described in §__.500.

State means any State of the United States, the District of Columbia, the Commonwealth of Puerto Rico, the Virgin Islands, Guam, American Samoa, the Commonwealth of the Northern Mariana Islands, and the Trust Territory of the Pacific Islands, any instrumentality thereof, any multi-State, regional, or interstate entity which has governmental functions, and any Indian tribe as defined in this section.

Student Financial Aid (SFA) includes those programs of general student assistance, such as those authorized by Title IV of the Higher Education Act of 1965, as amended, (20 U.S.C. 1070 *et seq.*) which is administered by the U.S. Department of Education, and similar programs provided by other Federal agencies. It does not include programs which provide fellowships or similar

Federal awards to students on a competitive basis, or for specified studies or research.

Subrecipient means a non-Federal entity that expends Federal awards received from a pass-through entity to carry out a Federal program, but does not include an individual that is a beneficiary of such a program. A subrecipient may also be a recipient of other Federal awards directly from a Federal awarding agency. Guidance on distinguishing between a subrecipient and a vendor is provided in §__.210.

Types of compliance requirements refers to the types of compliance requirements listed in the compliance supplement. Examples include: activities allowed or unallowed; allowable costs/cost principles; cash management; eligibility; matching, level of effort, earmarking; and, reporting.

Vendor means a dealer, distributor, merchant, or other seller providing goods or services that are required for the conduct of a Federal program. These goods or services may be for an organization's own use or for the use of beneficiaries of the Federal program. Additional guidance on distinguishing between a subrecipient and a vendor is provided in §__.210.

Subpart B—Audits

§__.200 Audit requirements.

(a) *Audit required.* Non-Federal entities that expend $300,000 *($500,000 for fiscal years ending after December 31, 2003)* or more in a year in Federal awards shall have a single or program-specific audit conducted for that year in accordance with the provisions of this part. Guidance on determining Federal awards expended is provided in §__.205.

(b) *Single audit.* Non-Federal entities that expend $300,000 *($500,000 for fiscal years ending after December 31, 2003)* or more in a year in Federal awards shall have a single audit conducted in accordance with §__.500 except when they elect to have a program-specific audit conducted in accordance with paragraph (c) of this section.

(c) *Program-specific audit election.* When an auditee expends Federal awards under only one Federal program (excluding R&D) and the Federal program's laws, regulations, or grant agreements do not require a financial statement audit of the auditee, the auditee may elect to have a program-specific audit conducted in accordance with §__.235. A program-specific audit may not be elected for R&D unless all of the Federal awards expended were received from the same Federal agency, or the same Federal agency and the same pass-through entity, and that Federal agency, or pass-through entity in the case of a subrecipient, approves in advance a program-specific audit.

(d) *Exemption when Federal awards expended are less than $300,000 ($500,000 for fiscal years ending after December 31, 2003).* Non-Federal entities that expend less than $300,000 ($500,000 for fiscal years ending after December 31, 2003) a year in Federal awards are exempt from Federal audit requirements for that year, except as noted in §__.215(a), but records must be available for review or audit by appropriate officials of the Federal agency, pass-through entity, and General Accounting Office (GAO).

(e) *Federally Funded Research and Development Centers* (FFRDC). Management of an auditee that owns or operates a FFRDC may elect to treat the FFRDC as a separate entity for purposes of this part.

§__.205 Basis for determining Federal awards expended.

(a) *Determining Federal awards expended.* The determination of when an award is expended should be based on when the activity related to the award occurs. Generally, the activity pertains to events that require the non-Federal entity to comply with laws, regulations, and the provisions of contracts or grant agreements, such as: expenditure/expense transactions associated with grants, cost-reimbursement contracts, cooperative agreements, and direct appropriations; the disbursement of funds passed through to subrecipients; the use of loan proceeds under loan and loan guarantee programs; the receipt of property; the receipt of surplus property; the receipt or use of program income; the distribution or consumption of food commodities; the disbursement of amounts entitling the non-Federal entity to an interest subsidy; and, the period when insurance is in force.

(b) *Loan and loan guarantees* (loans). Since the Federal Government is at risk for loans until the debt is repaid, the following guidelines shall be used to calculate the value of Federal awards expended under loan programs, except as noted in paragraphs (c) and (d) of this section:

(1) Value of new loans made or received during the fiscal year; plus

(2) Balance of loans from previous years for which the Federal Government imposes continuing compliance requirements; plus

(3) Any interest subsidy, cash, or administrative cost allowance received.

(c) *Loan and loan guarantees (loans) at institutions of higher education.* When loans are made to students of an institution of higher education but the institution does not make the loans, then only the value of loans made during the year shall be considered Federal awards expended in that year. The balance of loans for previous years is not included as Federal awards expended because the lender accounts for the prior balances.

(d) *Prior loan and loan guarantees* (loans). Loans, the proceeds of which were received and expended in prior-years, are not considered Federal awards expended under this part when the laws, regulations, and the provisions of contracts or grant agreements pertaining to such loans impose no continuing compliance requirements other than to repay the loans.

(e) *Endowment funds.* The cumulative balance of Federal awards for endowment funds which are federally restricted are considered awards expended in each year in which the funds are still restricted.

(f) *Free rent.* Free rent received by itself is not considered a Federal award expended under this part. However, free rent received as part of an award to carry out a Federal program shall be included in determining Federal awards expended and subject to audit under this part.

(g) *Valuing non-cash assistance.* Federal non-cash assistance, such as free rent, food stamps, food commodities, donated property, or donated surplus property, shall be valued at fair market value at the time of receipt or the assessed value provided by the Federal agency.

(h) *Medicare.* Medicare payments to a non-Federal entity for providing patient care services to Medicare eligible individuals are not considered Federal awards expended under this part.

(i) *Medicaid.* Medicaid payments to a subrecipient for providing patient care services to Medicaid eligible individuals are not considered Federal awards expended under this part unless a State requires the funds to be treated as Federal awards expended because reimbursement is on a cost-reimbursement basis.

(j) *Certain loans provided by the National Credit Union Administration.* For purposes of this part, loans made from the National Credit Union Share Insurance Fund and the Central Liquidity Facility that are funded by contributions from insured institutions are not considered Federal awards expended.

§__.210 Subrecipient and vendor determinations.

(a) *General.* An auditee may be a recipient, a subrecipient, and a vendor. Federal awards expended as a recipient or a subrecipient would be subject to audit under this part. The payments received for goods or services provided as a vendor would not be considered Federal awards. The guidance in paragraphs (b) and (c) of this section should be considered in determining whether payments constitute a Federal award or a payment for goods and services.

(b) *Federal award.* Characteristics indicative of a Federal award received by a subrecipient are when the organization:

(1) Determines who is eligible to receive what Federal financial assistance;

(2) Has its performance measured against whether the objectives of the Federal program are met;

(3) Has responsibility for programmatic decision making;

(4) Has responsibility for adherence to applicable Federal program compliance requirements; and

(5) Uses the Federal funds to carry out a program of the organization as compared to providing goods or services for a program of the pass-through entity.

(c) *Payment for goods and services.* Characteristics indicative of a payment for goods and services received by a vendor are when the organization:

(1) Provides the goods and services within normal business operations;

(2) Provides similar goods or services to many different purchasers;

(3) Operates in a competitive environment;

(4) Provides goods or services that are ancillary to the operation of the Federal program; and

(5) Is not subject to compliance requirements of the Federal program.

(d) *Use of judgment in making determination.* There may be unusual circumstances or exceptions to the listed characteristics. In making the determination of whether a subrecipient or vendor relationship exists, the substance of the relationship is more important than the form of the agreement. It is not expected that all of the characteristics will be present and judgment should be used in determining whether an entity is a subrecipient or vendor.

(e) *For-profit subrecipient.* Since this part does not apply to for-profit subrecipients, the pass-through entity is responsible for establishing requirements, as necessary, to ensure compliance by for-profit subrecipients. The contract with the for-profit subrecipient should describe applicable compliance requirements and the for-profit subrecipient's compliance responsibility. Methods to ensure compliance for Federal awards made to for-profit subrecipients may include pre-award audits, monitoring during the contract, and post-award audits.

(f) *Compliance responsibility for vendors.* In most cases, the auditee's compliance responsibility for vendors is only to ensure that the procurement, receipt, and payment for goods and services comply with laws, regulations, and the provisions of contracts or grant agreements. Program compliance requirements normally do not pass through to vendors. However, the auditee is responsible for ensuring compliance for vendor transactions which are structured such that the vendor is responsible for program compliance or the vendor's records must be reviewed to determine program compliance. Also, when these vendor transactions relate to a major program, the scope of the audit shall include determining whether these transactions are in compliance with laws, regulations, and the provisions of contracts or grant agreements.

§__.215 Relation to other audit requirements.

(a) *Audit under this part in lieu of other audits.* An audit made in accordance with this part shall be in lieu of any financial audit required under individual Federal awards. To the extent this audit meets a Federal agency's needs, it shall rely upon and use such audits. The provisions of this part neither limit the authority of Federal agencies, including their Inspectors General, or GAO to conduct or arrange for additional audits (e.g., financial audits, performance audits, evaluations, inspections, or reviews) nor authorize any auditee to constrain Federal agencies from carrying out additional audits. Any additional audits shall be planned and performed in such a way as to build upon work performed by other auditors.

(b) *Federal agency to pay for additional audits.* A Federal agency that conducts or contracts for additional audits shall, consistent with other applicable laws and regulations, arrange for funding the full cost of such additional audits.

(c) *Request for a program to be audited as a major program.* A Federal agency may request an auditee to have a particular Federal program audited as a major program in lieu of the Federal agency conducting or arranging for the additional audits. To allow for planning, such requests should be made at least 180 days prior to the end of the fiscal year to be audited. The auditee, after consultation with its auditor, should promptly respond to such request by informing the Federal agency whether the program would otherwise be audited as a major program using the risk-based audit approach described in §__.520 and, if not, the estimated incremental cost. The Federal agency shall then promptly confirm to the auditee whether it wants the program audited as a major program. If the program is to be audited as a major program based upon this Federal agency request, and the Federal agency agrees to pay the full incremental costs, then the auditee shall have the program audited as a major program. A pass-through entity may use the provisions of this paragraph for a subrecipient.

§__.220 Frequency of audits.

Except for the provisions for biennial audits provided in paragraphs (a) and (b) of this section, audits required by this part shall be performed annually. Any biennial audit shall cover both years within the biennial period.

(a) A State or local government that is required by constitution or statute, in effect on January 1, 1987, to undergo its audits less frequently than annually, is permitted to undergo its audits pursuant to this part biennially. This requirement must still be in effect for the biennial period.

(b) Any non-profit organization that had biennial audits for all biennial periods ending between July 1, 1992, and January 1, 1995, is permitted to undergo its audits pursuant to this part biennially.

§__.225 Sanctions.

No audit costs may be charged to Federal awards when audits required by this part have not been made or have been made but not in accordance with this part. In cases of continued inability or unwillingness to have an audit conducted in accordance with this part, Federal agencies and pass-through entities shall take appropriate action using sanctions such as:

(a) Withholding a percentage of Federal awards until the audit is completed satisfactorily;

(b) Withholding or disallowing overhead costs;

(c) Suspending Federal awards until the audit is conducted; or

(d) Terminating the Federal award.

§__.230 Audit costs.

(a) *Allowable costs.* Unless prohibited by law, the cost of audits made in accordance with the provisions of this part are allowable charges to Federal awards. The charges may be considered a direct cost or an allocated indirect cost, as determined in accordance with the provisions of applicable OMB cost principles circulars, the Federal Acquisition Regulation (FAR) (48 CFR parts 30 and 31), or other applicable cost principles or regulations.

(b) *Unallowable costs.* A non-Federal entity shall not charge the following to a Federal award:

(1) The cost of any audit under the Single Audit Act Amendments of 1996 (31 U.S.C. 7501 et seq.) not conducted in accordance with this part.

(2) The cost of auditing a non-Federal entity which has Federal awards expended of less than $300,000 ($500,000 for fiscal years ending after December 31, 2003) per year and is thereby exempted under §__.200(d) from having an audit conducted under this part. However, this does not prohibit a pass-through entity from charging Federal awards for the cost of limited scope audits to monitor its subrecipients in accordance with §__.400(d)(3),provided the subrecipient does not have a single audit. For purposes of this part, limited scope audits only include agreed-upon procedures engagements conducted in accordance with either the AICPA's generally accepted auditing standards or attestation standards, that are paid for and arranged by a pass-through entity and address only one or more of the following types of compliance requirements: activities allowed or unallowed; allowable costs/cost principles; eligibility; matching, level of effort, earmarking; and, reporting.

§__.235 Program-specific audits.

(a) *Program-specific audit guide available.* In many cases, a program-specific audit guide will be available to provide specific guidance to the auditor with respect to internal control, compliance requirements, suggested audit procedures, and audit reporting requirements. The auditor should contact the Office of Inspector General of the Federal agency to determine whether such a guide

OMB Circular A-133

is available. When a current program-specific audit guide is available, the auditor shall follow GAGAS and the guide when performing a program-specific audit.

(b) *Program-specific audit guide not available.* (1) When a program-specific audit guide is not available, the auditee and auditor shall have basically the same responsibilities for the Federal program as they would have for an audit of a major program in a single audit.

    (2) The auditee shall prepare the financial statement(s) for the Federal program that includes, at a minimum, a schedule of expenditures of Federal awards for the program and notes that describe the significant accounting policies used in preparing the schedule, a summary schedule of prior audit findings consistent with the requirements of §__.315(b), and a corrective action plan consistent with the requirements of §__.315(c).

    (3) The auditor shall:

        (i) Perform an audit of the financial statement(s) for the Federal program in accordance with GAGAS;

        (ii) Obtain an understanding of internal control and perform tests of internal control over the Federal program consistent with the requirements of §__.500(c) for a major program;

        (iii) Perform procedures to determine whether the auditee has complied with laws, regulations, and the provisions of contracts or grant agreements that could have a direct and material effect on the Federal program consistent with the requirements of §__.500(d) for a major program; and

        (iv) Follow up on prior audit findings, perform procedures to assess the reasonableness of the summary schedule of prior audit findings prepared by the auditee, and report, as a current year audit finding, when the auditor concludes that the summary schedule of prior audit findings materially misrepresents the status of any prior audit finding in accordance with the requirements of §__.500(e).

    (4) The auditor's report(s) may be in the form of either combined or separate reports and may be organized differently from the manner presented in this section. The auditor's report(s) shall state that the audit was conducted in accordance with this part and include the following:

        (i) An opinion (or disclaimer of opinion) as to whether the financial statement(s) of the Federal program is presented fairly in all material respects in conformity with the stated accounting policies;

        (ii) A report on internal control related to the Federal program, which shall describe the scope of testing of internal control and the results of the tests;

        (iii) A report on compliance which includes an opinion (or disclaimer of opinion) as to whether the auditee complied with laws, regulations, and the provisions of contracts or grant agreements which could have a direct and material effect on the Federal program; and

(iv) A schedule of findings and questioned costs for the Federal program that includes a summary of the auditor's results relative to the Federal program in a format consistent with §__.505(d)(1) and findings and questioned costs consistent with the requirements of §__.505(d)(3).

(c) *Report submission for program-specific audits.*

(1) The audit shall be completed and the reporting required by paragraph (c)(2)or (c)(3) of this section submitted within the earlier of 30 days after receipt of the auditor's report(s), or nine months after the end of the audit period, unless a longer period is agreed to in advance by the Federal agency that provided the funding or a different period is specified in a program-specific audit guide. (However, for fiscal years beginning on or before June 30, 1998, the audit shall be completed and the required reporting shall be submitted within the earlier of 30 days after receipt of the auditor's report(s), or 13 months after the end of the audit period, unless a different period is specified in a program-specific audit guide.) Unless restricted bylaw or regulation, the auditee shall make report copies available for public inspection.

(2) When a program-specific audit guide is available, the auditee shall submit to the Federal clearinghouse designated by OMB the data collection form prepared in accordance with §__.320(b), as applicable to a program-specific audit, and the reporting required by the program-specific audit guide to be retained as an archival copy. Also, the auditee shall submit to the Federal awarding agency or pass-through entity the reporting required by the program-specific audit guide.

(3) When a program-specific audit guide is not available, the reporting package for a program-specific audit shall consist of the financial statement(s) of the Federal program, a summary schedule of prior audit findings, and a corrective action plan as described in paragraph (b)(2) of this section, and the auditor's report(s) described in paragraph (b)(4) of this section. The data collection form prepared in accordance with §__.320(b), as applicable to a program-specific audit, and one copy of this reporting package shall be submitted to the Federal clearinghouse designated by OMB to be retained as an archival copy. Also, when the schedule of findings and questioned costs disclosed audit findings or the summary schedule of prior audit findings reported the status of any audit findings, the auditee shall submit one copy of the reporting package to the Federal clearinghouse on behalf of the Federal awarding agency, or directly to the pass-through entity in the case of a subrecipient. Instead of submitting the reporting package to the pass-through entity, when a subrecipient is not required to submit a reporting package to the pass-through entity, the subrecipient shall provide written notification to the pass-through entity, consistent with the requirements of §__.320(e)(2). A subrecipient may submit a copy of the reporting package to the pass-through entity to comply with this notification requirement.

(d) *Other sections of this part may apply.* Program-specific audits are subject to §__.100 through §__.215(b), §__.220 through §__.230, §__.300 through §__.305, §__.315, §__.320(f) through §__.320(j), §__.400through §__.405, §__.510 through

§__.515, and other referenced provisions of this part unless contrary to the provisions of this section, a program-specific audit guide, or program laws and regulations.

Subpart C—Auditees

§__.300 Auditee responsibilities.

The auditee shall:

(a) Identify, in its accounts, all Federal awards received and expended and the Federal programs under which they were received. Federal program and award identification shall include, as applicable, the CFDA title and number, award number and year, name of the Federal agency, and name of the pass-through entity.

(b) Maintain internal control over Federal programs that provides reasonable assurance that the auditee is managing Federal awards in compliance with laws, regulations, and the provisions of contracts or grant agreements that could have a material effect on each of its Federal programs.

(c) Comply with laws, regulations, and the provisions of contracts or grant agreements related to each of its Federal programs.

(d) Prepare appropriate financial statements, including the schedule of expenditures of Federal awards in accordance with §__.310.

(e) Ensure that the audits required by this part are properly performed and submitted when due. When extensions to the report submission due date required by §__.320(a) are granted by the cognizant or oversight agency for audit, promptly notify the Federal clearinghouse designated by OMB and each pass-through entity providing Federal awards of the extension.

(f) Follow up and take corrective action on audit findings, including preparation of a summary schedule of prior audit findings and a corrective action plan in accordance with §__.315(b) and §__.315(c), respectively.

§__.305 Auditor selection.

(a) *Auditor procurement.* In procuring audit services, auditees shall follow the procurement standards prescribed by the Grants Management Common Rule (hereinafter referred to as the "A-102 Common Rule") published March 11, 1988 and amended April 19, 1995 [insert appropriate CFR citation], Circular A-110, "Uniform Administrative Requirements for Grants and Agreements with Institutions of Higher Education, Hospitals and Other Non-Profit Organizations," or the FAR (48 CFR part 42), as applicable (OMB Circulars are available from the Office of Administration, Publications Office, room 2200, New Executive Office Building, Washington, DC 20503). Whenever possible, auditees shall make positive efforts to utilize small businesses, minority-owned firms, and women's business enterprises, in procuring audit services as stated in the A-102 Common Rule, OMB Circular A-110, or the FAR (48 CFR part 42), as applicable. In requesting proposals for audit services, the objectives and scope of the audit should be made clear. Factors to be considered in evaluating each proposal for audit services include the responsiveness to the request for proposal, relevant experience, availability of staff with professional qualifications and technical abilities, the results of external quality control reviews, and price.

(b) *Restriction on auditor preparing indirect cost proposals.* An auditor who prepares the indirect cost proposal or cost allocation plan may not also be selected to perform the audit required by this part when the indirect costs recovered by the auditee during the prior year exceeded $1 million. This restriction applies to the base year used in the preparation of the indirect cost proposal or cost allocation plan and any subsequent years in which the resulting indirect cost agreement or cost allocation plan is used to recover costs. To minimize any disruption in existing contracts for audit services, this paragraph applies to audits of fiscal years beginning after June 30, 1998.

(c) *Use of Federal auditors.* Federal auditors may perform all or part of the work required under this part if they comply fully with the requirements of this part.

§__.310 Financial statements.

(a) *Financial statements.* The auditee shall prepare financial statements that reflect its financial position, results of operations or changes in net assets, and, where appropriate, cash flows for the fiscal year audited. The financial statements shall be for the same organizational unit and fiscal year that is chosen to meet the requirements of this part. However, organization-wide financial statements may also include departments, agencies, and other organizational units that have separate audits in accordance with §__.500(a) and prepare separate financial statements.

(b) *Schedule of expenditures of Federal awards.* The auditee shall also prepare a schedule of expenditures of Federal awards for the period covered by the auditee's financial statements. While not required, the auditee may choose to provide information requested by Federal awarding agencies and pass-through entities to make the schedule easier to use. For example, when a Federal program has multiple award years, the auditee may list the amount of Federal awards expended for each award year separately. At a minimum, the schedule shall:

 (1) List individual Federal programs by Federal agency. For Federal programs included in a cluster of programs, list individual Federal programs within a cluster of programs. For R&D, total Federal awards expended shall be shown either by individual award or by Federal agency and major subdivision within the Federal agency. For example, the National Institutes of Health is a major subdivision in the Department of Health and Human Services.

 (2) For Federal awards received as a subrecipient, the name of the pass-through entity and identifying number assigned by the pass-through entity shall be included.

 (3) Provide total Federal awards expended for each individual Federal program and the CFDA number or other identifying number when the CFDA information is not available.

 (4) Include notes that describe the significant accounting policies used in preparing the schedule.

 (5) To the extent practical, pass-through entities should identify in the schedule the total amount provided to subrecipients from each Federal program.

 (6) Include, in either the schedule or a note to the schedule, the value of the Federal awards expended in the form of non-cash assistance, the amount of insurance in effect during the year, and loans or

loan guarantees outstanding at year end. While not required, it is preferable to present this information in the schedule.

§__.315 Audit findings follow-up.

(a) *General.* The auditee is responsible for follow-up and corrective action on all audit findings. As part of this responsibility, the auditee shall prepare a summary schedule of prior audit findings. The auditee shall also prepare a corrective action plan for current year audit findings. The summary schedule of prior audit findings and the corrective action plan shall include the reference numbers the auditor assigns to audit findings under §__.510(c). Since the summary schedule may include audit findings from multiple years, it shall include the fiscal year in which the finding initially occurred.

(b) *Summary schedule of prior audit findings.* The summary schedule of prior audit findings shall report the status of all audit findings included in the prior audit's schedule of findings and questioned costs relative to Federal awards. The summary schedule shall also include audit findings reported in the prior audit's summary schedule of prior audit findings except audit findings listed as corrected in accordance with paragraph (b)(1) of this section, or no longer valid or not warranting further action in accordance with paragraph (b)(4) of this section.

> (1) When audit findings were fully corrected, the summary schedule need only list the audit findings and state that corrective action was taken.
>
> (2) When audit findings were not corrected or were only partially corrected, the summary schedule shall describe the planned corrective action as well as any partial corrective action taken.
>
> (3) When corrective action taken is significantly different from corrective action previously reported in a corrective action plan or in the Federal agency's or pass-through entity's management decision, the summary schedule shall provide an explanation.
>
> (4) When the auditee believes the audit findings are no longer valid or do not warrant further action, the reasons for this position shall be described in the summary schedule. A valid reason for considering an audit finding as not warranting further action is that all of the following have occurred:
>
>> (i) Two years have passed since the audit report in which the finding occurred was submitted to the Federal clearinghouse;
>>
>> (ii) The Federal agency or pass-through entity is not currently following up with the auditee on the audit finding; and
>>
>> (iii) A management decision was not issued.

(c) *Corrective action plan.* At the completion of the audit, the auditee shall prepare a corrective action plan to address each audit finding included in the current year auditor's reports. The corrective action plan shall provide the name(s) of the contact person(s) responsible for corrective action, the corrective action planned, and the anticipated completion date. If the auditee does not agree with the audit findings or believes corrective action is not required, then the corrective action plan shall include an explanation and specific reasons.

§__.320 Report submission.

(a) *General.* The audit shall be completed and the data collection form described in paragraph (b) of this section and reporting package described in paragraph (c) of this section shall be submitted within the earlier of 30 days after receipt of the auditor's report(s), or nine months after the end of the audit period, unless a longer period is agreed to in advance by the cognizant or oversight agency for audit. (However, for fiscal years beginning on or before June 30, 1998, the audit shall be completed and the data collection form and reporting package shall be submitted within the earlier of 30 days after receipt of the auditor's report(s), or 13 months after the end of the audit period.) Unless restricted by law or regulation, the auditee shall make copies available for public inspection.

(b) *Data Collection.* (1) The auditee shall submit a data collection form which states whether the audit was completed in accordance with this part and provides information about the auditee, its Federal programs, and the results of the audit. The form shall be approved by OMB, available from the Federal clearinghouse designated by OMB, and include data elements similar to those presented in this paragraph. A senior level representative of the auditee (e.g., State controller, director of finance, chief executive officer, or chief financial officer) shall sign a statement to be included as part of the form certifying that: the auditee complied with the requirements of this part, the form was prepared in accordance with this part (and the instructions accompanying the form), and the information included in the form, in its entirety, are accurate and complete.

(2) The data collection form shall include the following data elements:

(i) The type of report the auditor issued on the financial statements of the auditee (i.e., unqualified opinion, qualified opinion, adverse opinion, or disclaimer of opinion).

(ii) Where applicable, a statement that significant deficiencies in internal control were disclosed by the audit of the financial statements and whether any such conditions were material weaknesses.

(iii) A statement as to whether the audit disclosed any noncompliance which is material to the financial statements of the auditee.

(iv) Where applicable, a statement that significant deficiencies in internal control over major programs were disclosed by the audit and whether any such conditions were material weaknesses.

(v) The type of report the auditor issues on compliance for major programs (i.e., unqualified opinion, qualified opinion, adverse opinion, or disclaimer of opinion).

(vi) A list of the Federal awarding agencies which will receive a copy of the reporting package pursuant to §__.320(d)(2) of OMB Circular A-133.

(vii) A yes or no statement as to whether the auditee qualified as a low-risk auditee under §__.530 of OMB Circular A-133.

(viii) The dollar threshold used to distinguish between Type A and Type B programs as defined in §__.520(b) of OMB Circular A-133.

OMB Circular A-133

(ix) The *Catalog of Federal Domestic Assistance* (CFDA) number for each Federal program, as applicable.

(x) The name of each Federal program and identification of each major program. Individual programs within a cluster of program should be listed in the same level of detail as they are listed in the schedule of expenditures of Federal awards.

(xi) The amount of expenditures in the schedule of expenditures of Federal awards associated with each Federal program.

(xii) For each Federal program, a yes or no statement as to whether there are audit findings in each of the following types of compliance requirements and the total amount of any questioned costs:

    (A) Activities allowed or unallowed.
    (B) Allowable costs/cost principles.
    (C) Cash management.
    (D) Davis-Bacon Act.
    (E) Eligibility.
    (F) Equipment and real property management.
    (G) Matching, level of effort, earmarking.
    (H) Period of availability of Federal funds.
    (I) Procurement and suspension and debarment.
    (J) Program income.
    (K) Real property acquisition and relocation assistance.
    (L) Reporting.
    (M) Subrecipient monitoring.
    (N) Special tests and provisions.

(xiii) Auditee Name, Employer Identification Number(s), Name and Title of Certifying Official, Telephone Number, Signature, and Date.

(xiv) Auditor Name, Name and Title of Contact Person, Auditor Address, Auditor Telephone Number, Signature, and Date.

(xv) Whether the auditee has either a cognizant or oversight agency for audit.

(xvi) The name of the cognizant or oversight agency for audit determined in accordance with §__.400(a) and §__.400(b), respectively.

(3) Using the information included in the reporting package described in paragraph (c) of this section, the auditor shall complete the applicable sections of the form. The auditor shall sign a statement to be included as part of the data collection form that indicates, at a minimum, the source of the information included in the form, the auditor's responsibility for the information, that the form is not a substitute for the reporting package described in paragraph (c) of

this section, and that the content of the form is limited to the data elements prescribed by OMB.

(c) *Reporting package.* The reporting package shall include the:

    (1) Financial statements and schedule of expenditures of Federal awards discussed in §__.310(a) and §__.310(b), respectively;

    (2) Summary schedule of prior audit findings discussed in §__.315(b);

    (3) Auditor's report(s) discussed in §__.505; and

    (4) Corrective action plan discussed in §__.315(c).

(d) *Submission to clearinghouse.* All auditees shall submit to the Federal clearinghouse designated by OMB a single copy of the data collection form described in paragraph (b) of this section and the reporting package described in paragraph (c) of this section.

(e) *Additional submission by subrecipients.* (1) In addition to the requirements discussed in paragraph (d) of this section, auditees that are also subrecipients shall submit to each pass-through entity one copy of the reporting package described in paragraph (c) of this section for each pass-through entity when the schedule of findings and questioned costs disclosed audit findings relating to Federal awards that the pass-through entity provided or the summary schedule of prior audit findings reported the status of any audit findings relating to Federal awards that the pass-through entity provided.

    (2) Instead of submitting the reporting package to a pass-through entity, when a subrecipient is not required to submit a reporting package to a pass-through entity pursuant to paragraph (e)(1) of this section, the subrecipient shall provide written notification to the pass-through entity that: an audit of the subrecipient was conducted in accordance with this part (including the period covered by the audit and the name, amount, and CFDA number of the Federal award(s) provided by the pass-through entity); the schedule of findings and questioned costs disclosed no audit findings relating to the Federal award(s) that the pass-through entity provided; and, the summary schedule of prior audit findings did not report on the status of any audit findings relating to the Federal award(s) that the pass-through entity provided. A subrecipient may submit a copy of the reporting package described in paragraph (c) of this section to a pass-through entity to comply with this notification requirement.

(f) *Requests for report copies.* In response to requests by a Federal agency or pass-through entity, auditees shall submit the appropriate copies of the reporting package described in paragraph (c) of this section and, if requested, a copy of any management letters issued by the auditor.

(g) *Report retention requirements.* Auditees shall keep one copy of the data collection form described in paragraph (b) of this section and one copy of the reporting package described in paragraph (c) of this section on file for three years from the date of submission to the Federal clearinghouse designated by OMB. Pass-through entities shall keep subrecipients' submissions on file for three years from date of receipt.

(h) *Clearinghouse responsibilities.* The Federal clearinghouse designated by OMB shall distribute the reporting packages received in accordance with paragraph (d)(2) of this section and §__.235(c)(3) to applicable Federal awarding agencies, maintain a data base of completed audits, provide appropriate information to Federal agencies, and follow up with known auditees which have not submitted the required data collection forms and reporting packages.

(i) *Clearinghouse address.* The address of the Federal clearinghouse currently designated by OMB is Federal Audit Clearinghouse, Bureau of the Census, 1201 E. 10th Street, Jeffersonville, IN 47132.

(j) *Electronic filing.* Nothing in this part shall preclude electronic submissions to the Federal clearinghouse in such manner as may be approved by OMB. With OMB approval, the Federal clearinghouse may pilot test methods of electronic submissions.

Subpart D—Federal Agencies and Pass-Through Entities
§__.400 **Responsibilities.**

(a) *Cognizant agency for audit responsibilities.* Recipients expending more than $25 million (*$50 million for fiscal years ending after December 31, 2003*) a year in Federal awards shall have a cognizant agency for audit. The designated cognizant agency for audit shall be the Federal awarding agency that provides the predominant amount of direct funding to a recipient unless OMB makes a specific cognizant agency for audit assignment.

Following is effective for fiscal years ending on or before December 31, 2003:

To provide for continuity of cognizance, the determination of the predominant amount of direct funding shall be based upon direct Federal awards expended in the recipient's fiscal years ending in 1995, 2000, 2005, and every fifth year thereafter. For example, audit cognizance for periods ending in 1997 through 2000 will be determined based on Federal awards expended in 1995. (However, for States and local governments that expend more than $25 million a year in Federal awards and have previously assigned cognizant agencies for audit, the requirements of this paragraph are not effective until fiscal years beginning after June 30, 2000.)

Following is effective for fiscal years ending after December 31, 2003:

The determination of the predominant amount of direct funding shall be based upon direct Federal awards expended in the recipient's fiscal years ending in 2004, 2009, 2014, and every fifth year thereafter. For example, audit cognizance for periods ending in 2006 through 2010 will be determined based on Federal awards expended in 2004. (However, for 2001 through 2005, the cognizant agency for audit is determined based on the predominant amount of direct Federal awards expended in the recipient's fiscal year ending in 2000).

Notwithstanding the manner in which audit cognizance is determined, a Federal awarding agency with cognizance for an auditee may reassign cognizance to another Federal awarding agency which provides substantial direct funding and agrees to be the cognizant agency for audit. Within 30 days after any reassignment, both the old and the new cognizant agency for audit shall notify the auditee, and, if known, the auditor of the reassignment. The cognizant agency for audit shall:

   (1) Provide technical audit advice and liaison to auditees and auditors.

   (2) Consider auditee requests for extensions to the report submission due date required by §__.320(a). The cognizant agency for audit may grant extensions for good cause.

(3) Obtain or conduct quality control reviews of selected audits made by non-Federal auditors, and provide the results, when appropriate, to other interested organizations.

(4) Promptly inform other affected Federal agencies and appropriate Federal law enforcement officials of any direct reporting by the auditee or its auditor of irregularities or illegal acts, as required by GAGAS or laws and regulations.

(5) Advise the auditor and, where appropriate, the auditee of any deficiencies found in the audits when the deficiencies require corrective action by the auditor. When advised of deficiencies, the auditee shall work with the auditor to take corrective action. If corrective action is not taken, the cognizant agency for audit shall notify the auditor, the auditee, and applicable Federal awarding agencies and pass-through entities of the facts and make recommendations for follow-up action. Major inadequacies or repetitive substandard performance by auditors shall be referred to appropriate State licensing agencies and professional bodies for disciplinary action.

(6) Coordinate, to the extent practical, audits or reviews made by or for Federal agencies that are in addition to the audits made pursuant to this part, so that the additional audits or reviews build upon audits performed in accordance with this part.

(7) Coordinate a management decision for audit findings that affect the Federal programs of more than one agency.

(8) Coordinate the audit work and reporting responsibilities among auditors to achieve the most cost-effective audit.

(9) For biennial audits permitted under §__.220, consider auditee requests to qualify as a low-risk auditee under §__.530(a).

(b) *Oversight agency for audit responsibilities.* An auditee which does not have a designated cognizant agency for audit will be under the general oversight of the Federal agency determined in accordance with §__.105. The oversight agency for audit:

(1) Shall provide technical advice to auditees and auditors as requested.

(2) May assume all or some of the responsibilities normally performed by a cognizant agency for audit.

(c) *Federal awarding agency responsibilities.* The Federal awarding agency shall perform the following for the Federal awards it makes:

(1) Identify Federal awards made by informing each recipient of the CFDA title and number, award name and number, award year, and if the award is for R&D. When some of this information is not available, the Federal agency shall provide information necessary to clearly describe the Federal award.

(2) Advise recipients of requirements imposed on them by Federal laws, regulations, and the provisions of contracts or grant agreements.

(3) Ensure that audits are completed and reports are received in a timely manner and in accordance with the requirements of this part.

(4) Provide technical advice and counsel to auditees and auditors as requested.

(5) Issue a management decision on audit findings within six months after receipt of the audit report and ensure that the recipient takes appropriate and timely corrective action.

(6) Assign a person responsible for providing annual updates of the compliance supplement to OMB.

(d) *Pass-through entity responsibilities.* A pass-through entity shall perform the following for the Federal awards it makes:

(1) Identify Federal awards made by informing each subrecipient of CFDA title and number, award name and number, award year, if the award is R&D, and name of Federal agency. When some of this information is not available, the pass-through entity shall provide the best information available to describe the Federal award.

(2) Advise subrecipients of requirements imposed on them by Federal laws, regulations, and the provisions of contracts or grant agreements as well as any supplemental requirements imposed by the pass-through entity.

(3) Monitor the activities of subrecipients as necessary to ensure that Federal awards are used for authorized purposes in compliance with laws, regulations, and the provisions of contracts or grant agreements and that performance goals are achieved.

(4) Ensure that subrecipients expending $300,000 ($500,000 for fiscal years ending after December 31, 2003) or more in Federal awards during the subrecipient's fiscal year have met the audit requirements of this part for that fiscal year.

(5) Issue a management decision on audit findings within six months after receipt of the subrecipient's audit report and ensure that the subrecipient takes appropriate and timely corrective action.

(6) Consider whether subrecipient audits necessitate adjustment of the pass-through entity's own records.

(7) Require each subrecipient to permit the pass-through entity and auditors to have access to the records and financial statements as necessary for the pass-through entity to comply with this part.

§__.405 Management decision.

(a) *General.* The management decision shall clearly state whether or not the audit finding is sustained, the reasons for the decision, and the expected auditee action to repay disallowed costs, make financial adjustments, or take other action. If the auditee has not completed corrective action, a timetable for follow-up should be given. Prior to issuing the management decision, the Federal agency or pass-through entity may request additional information or documentation from the auditee, including a request for auditor assurance related to the documentation, as a way of mitigating disallowed costs. The management decision should describe any appeal process available to the auditee.

(b) *Federal agency.* As provided in §__.400(a)(7), the cognizant agency for audit shall be responsible for coordinating a management decision for audit findings that affect the programs of more than one Federal agency. As provided in §__.400(c)(5), a Federal awarding agency is responsible for issuing a management decision for findings that relate to Federal awards it makes to recipients.

Alternate arrangements may be made on a case-by-case basis by agreement among the Federal agencies concerned.

(c) *Pass-through entity.* As provided in §__.400(d)(5), the pass-through entity shall be responsible for making the management decision for audit findings that relate to Federal awards it makes to subrecipients.

(d) *Time requirements.* The entity responsible for making the management decision shall do so within six months of receipt of the audit report. Corrective action should be initiated within six months after receipt of the audit report and proceed as rapidly as possible.

(e) *Reference numbers.* Management decisions shall include the reference numbers the auditor assigned to each audit finding in accordance with §__.510(c).

Subpart E—Auditors

§__.500 Scope of audit.

(a) *General.* The audit shall be conducted in accordance with GAGAS. The audit shall cover the entire operations of the auditee; or, at the option of the auditee, such audit shall include a series of audits that cover departments, agencies, and other organizational units which expended or otherwise administered Federal awards during such fiscal year, provided that each such audit shall encompass the financial statements and schedule of expenditures of Federal awards for each such department, agency, and other organizational unit, which shall be considered to be a non-Federal entity. The financial statements and schedule of expenditures of Federal awards shall be for the same fiscal year.

(b) *Financial statements.* The auditor shall determine whether the financial statements of the auditee are presented fairly in all material respects in conformity with generally accepted accounting principles. The auditor shall also determine whether the schedule of expenditures of Federal awards is presented fairly in all material respects in relation to the auditee's financial statements taken as a whole.

(c) *Internal control.* (1) In addition to the requirements of GAGAS, the auditor shall perform procedures to obtain an understanding of internal control over Federal programs sufficient to plan the audit to support a low assessed level of control risk for major programs.

    (2) Except as provided in paragraph (c)(3) of this section, the auditor shall:

        (i) Plan the testing of internal control over major programs to support a low assessed level of control risk for the assertions relevant to the compliance requirements for each major program; and

        (ii) Perform testing of internal control as planned in paragraph (c)(2)(i) of this section.

    (3) When internal control over some or all of the compliance requirements for a major program are likely to be ineffective in preventing or detecting noncompliance, the planning and performing of testing described in paragraph (c)(2) of this section are not required for those compliance requirements. However, the auditor shall report a significant deficiency (including whether any such condition is a material weakness) in accordance with §__.510, assess the related control risk at the maximum, and consider whether additional compliance tests are required because of ineffective internal control.

(d) *Compliance.* (1) In addition to the requirements of GAGAS, the auditor shall determine whether the auditee has complied with laws, regulations, and the provisions of contracts or grant agreements that may have a direct and material effect on each of its major programs.

 (2) The principal compliance requirements applicable to most Federal programs and the compliance requirements of the largest Federal programs are included in the compliance supplement.

 (3) For the compliance requirements related to Federal programs contained in the compliance supplement, an audit of these compliance requirements will meet the requirements of this part. Where there have been changes to the compliance requirements and the changes are not reflected in the compliance supplement, the auditor shall determine the current compliance requirements and modify the audit procedures accordingly. For those Federal programs not covered in the compliance supplement, the auditor should use the types of compliance requirements contained in the compliance supplement as guidance for identifying the types of compliance requirements to test, and determine the requirements governing the Federal program by reviewing the provisions of contracts and grant agreements and the laws and regulations referred to in such contracts and grant agreements.

 (4) The compliance testing shall include tests of transactions and such other auditing procedures necessary to provide the auditor sufficient evidence to support an opinion on compliance.

(e) *Audit follow-up.* The auditor shall follow-up on prior audit findings, perform procedures to assess the reasonableness of the summary schedule of prior audit findings prepared by the auditee in accordance with §__.315(b), and report, as a current year audit finding, when the auditor concludes that the summary schedule of prior audit findings materially misrepresents the status of any prior audit finding. The auditor shall perform audit follow-up procedures regardless of whether a prior audit finding relates to a major program in the current year.

(f) *Data Collection Form.* As required in §__.320(b)(3), the auditor shall complete and sign specified sections of the data collection form.

§__.505 Audit reporting.

The auditor's report(s) may be in the form of either combined or separate reports and may be organized differently from the manner presented in this section. The auditor's report(s) shall state that the audit was conducted in accordance with this part and include the following:

(a) An opinion (or disclaimer of opinion) as to whether the financial statements are presented fairly in all material respects in conformity with generally accepted accounting principles and an opinion (or disclaimer of opinion) as to whether the schedule of expenditures of Federal awards is presented fairly in all material respects in relation to the financial statements taken as a whole.

(b) A report on internal control related to the financial statements and major programs. This report shall describe the scope of testing of internal control and the results of the tests, and, where applicable, refer to the separate schedule of findings and questioned costs described in paragraph (d) of this section.

(c) A report on compliance with laws, regulations, and the provisions of contracts or grant agreements, noncompliance with which could have a material effect on the financial statements. This report shall also include an opinion (or disclaimer of opinion) as to whether the auditee complied with laws, regulations, and the provisions of contracts or grant agreements which could have a direct and material effect on each major program, and, where applicable, refer to the separate schedule of findings and questioned costs described in paragraph (d) of this section.

(d) A schedule of findings and questioned costs which shall include the following three components:

(1) A summary of the auditor's results which shall include:

  (i) The type of report the auditor issued on the financial statements of the auditee (i.e., unqualified opinion, qualified opinion, adverse opinion, or disclaimer of opinion);

  (ii) Where applicable, a statement that significant deficiencies in internal control were disclosed by the audit of the financial statements and whether any such conditions were material weaknesses;

  (iii) A statement as to whether the audit disclosed any noncompliance which is material to the financial statements of the auditee;

  (iv) Where applicable, a statement that significant deficiencies in internal control over major programs were disclosed by the audit and whether any such conditions were material weaknesses;

  (v) The type of report the auditor issued on compliance for major programs (i.e., unqualified opinion, qualified opinion, adverse opinion, or disclaimer of opinion);

  (vi) A statement as to whether the audit disclosed any audit findings which the auditor is required to report under §__.510(a);

  (vii) An identification of major programs;

  (viii) The dollar threshold used to distinguish between Type A and Type B programs, as described in §__.520(b); and

  (ix) A statement as to whether the auditee qualified as a low-risk auditee under §__.530.

(2) Findings relating to the financial statements which are required to be reported in accordance with GAGAS.

(3) Findings and questioned costs for Federal awards which shall include audit findings as defined in §__.510(a).

  (i) Audit findings (e.g., internal control findings, compliance findings, questioned costs, or fraud) which relate to the same issue should be presented as a single audit finding. Where practical, audit findings should be organized by Federal agency or pass-through entity.

  (ii) Audit findings which relate to both the financial statements and Federal awards, as reported under paragraphs (d)(2) and (d)(3) of this section, respectively, should be reported in both sections of the schedule. However, the reporting in one section of the schedule may be in summary form with a reference to a detailed reporting in the other section of the schedule.

§__.510 Audit findings.

(a) *Audit findings reported.* The auditor shall report the following as audit findings in a schedule of findings and questioned costs:

(1) Significant deficiencies in internal control over major programs. The auditor's determination of whether a deficiency in internal control is a significant deficiency for the purpose of reporting an audit finding is in relation to a type of compliance requirement for a major program or an audit objective identified in the compliance supplement. The auditor shall identify significant deficiencies which are individually or cumulatively material weaknesses.

(2) Material noncompliance with the provisions of laws, regulations, contracts, or grant agreements related to a major program. The auditor's determination of whether a noncompliance with the provisions of laws, regulations, contracts, or grant agreements is material for the purpose of reporting an audit finding is in relation to a type of compliance requirement for a major program or an audit objective identified in the compliance supplement.

(3) Known questioned costs which are greater than $10,000 for a type of compliance requirement for a major program. Known questioned costs are those specifically identified by the auditor. In evaluating the effect of questioned costs on the opinion on compliance, the auditor considers the best estimate of total costs questioned (likely questioned costs), not just the questioned costs specifically identified (known questioned costs). The auditor shall also report known questioned costs when likely questioned costs are greater than $10,000 for a type of compliance requirement for a major program. In reporting questioned costs, the auditor shall include information to provide proper perspective for judging the prevalence and consequences of the questioned costs.

(4) Known questioned costs which are greater than $10,000 for a Federal program which is not audited as a major program. Except for audit follow-up, the auditor is not required under this part to perform audit procedures for such a Federal program; therefore, the auditor will normally not find questioned costs for a program which is not audited as a major program. However, if the auditor does become aware of questioned costs for a Federal program which is not audited as a major program (e.g., as part of audit follow-up or other audit procedures) and the known questioned costs are greater than $10,000, then the auditor shall report this as an audit finding.

(5) The circumstances concerning why the auditor's report on compliance for major programs is other than an unqualified opinion, unless such circumstances are otherwise reported as audit findings in the schedule of findings and questioned costs for Federal awards.

(6) Known fraud affecting a Federal award, unless such fraud is otherwise reported as an audit finding in the schedule of findings and questioned costs for Federal awards. This paragraph does not require the auditor to make an additional reporting when the auditor confirms that the fraud was reported outside of the auditor's reports under the direct reporting requirements of GAGAS.

(7) Instances where the results of audit follow-up procedures disclosed that the summary schedule of prior audit findings prepared by the

auditee in accordance with §__.315(b) materially misrepresents the status of any prior audit finding.

(b) *Audit finding detail.* Audit findings shall be presented in sufficient detail for the auditee to prepare a corrective action plan and take corrective action and for Federal agencies and pass-through entities to arrive at a management decision. The following specific information shall be included, as applicable, in audit findings:

(1) Federal program and specific Federal award identification including the CFDA title and number, Federal award number and year, name of Federal agency, and name of the applicable pass-through entity. When information, such as the CFDA title and number or Federal award number, is not available, the auditor shall provide the best information available to describe the Federal award.

(2) The criteria or specific requirement upon which the audit finding is based, including statutory, regulatory, or other citation.

(3) The condition found, including facts that support the deficiency identified in the audit finding.

(4) Identification of questioned costs and how they were computed.

(5) Information to provide proper perspective for judging the prevalence and consequences of the audit findings, such as whether the audit findings represent an isolated instance or a systemic problem. Where appropriate, instances identified shall be related to the universe and the number of cases examined and be quantified in terms of dollar value.

(6) The possible asserted effect to provide sufficient information to the auditee and Federal agency, or pass-through entity in the case of a subrecipient, to permit them to determine the cause and effect to facilitate prompt and proper corrective action.

(7) Recommendations to prevent future occurrences of the deficiency identified in the audit finding.

(8) Views of responsible officials of the auditee when there is disagreement with the audit findings, to the extent practical.

(c) *Reference numbers.* Each audit finding in the schedule of findings and questioned costs shall include a reference number to allow for easy referencing of the audit findings during follow-up.

§__.515 Audit working papers.

(a) *Retention of working papers.* The auditor shall retain working papers and reports for a minimum of three years after the date of issuance of the auditor's report(s) to the auditee, unless the auditor is notified in writing by the cognizant agency for audit, oversight agency for audit, or pass-through entity to extend the retention period. When the auditor is aware that the Federal awarding agency, pass-through entity, or auditee is contesting an audit finding, the auditor shall contact the parties contesting the audit finding for guidance prior to destruction of the working papers and reports.

(b) *Access to working papers.* Audit working papers shall be made available upon request to the cognizant or oversight agency for audit or its designee, a Federal agency providing direct or indirect funding, or GAO at the completion of the audit, as part of a quality review, to resolve audit findings, or to carry out oversight responsibilities consistent with the purposes of this part. Access

OMB Circular A-133 **705**

to working papers includes the right of Federal agencies to obtain copies of working papers, as is reasonable and necessary.

§__.520 Major program determination.

(a) *General.* The auditor shall use a risk-based approach to determine which Federal programs are major programs. This risk-based approach shall include consideration of: Current and prior audit experience, oversight by Federal agencies and pass-through entities, and the inherent risk of the Federal program. The process in paragraphs (b) through (i) of this section shall be followed.

(b) *Step 1.* (1) The auditor shall identify the larger Federal programs, which shall be labeled Type A programs. Type A programs are defined as Federal programs with Federal awards expended during the audit period exceeding the larger of:

    (i) $300,000 or three percent (.03) of total Federal awards expended in the case of an auditee for which total Federal awards expended equal or exceed $300,000 but are less than or equal to $100 million.

    (ii) $3 million or three-tenths of one percent (.003) of total Federal awards expended in the case of an auditee for which total Federal awards expended exceed $100 million but are less than or equal to $10 billion.

    (iii) $30 million or 15 hundredths of one percent (.0015) of total Federal awards expended in the case of an auditee for which total Federal awards expended exceed $10 billion.

  (2) Federal programs not labeled Type A under paragraph (b)(1) of this section shall be labeled Type B programs.

  (3) The inclusion of large loan and loan guarantees (loans) should not result in the exclusion of other programs as Type A programs. When a Federal program providing loans significantly affects the number or size of Type A programs, the auditor shall consider this Federal program as a Type A program and exclude its values in determining other Type A programs.

  (4) For biennial audits permitted under §__.220, the determination of Type A and Type B programs shall be based upon the Federal awards expended during the two-year period.

(c) *Step 2.* (1) The auditor shall identify Type A programs which are low-risk. For a Type A program to be considered low-risk, it shall have been audited as a major program in at least one of the two most recent audit periods (in the most recent audit period in the case of a biennial audit), and, in the most recent audit period, it shall have had no audit findings under §__.510(a). However, the auditor may use judgment and consider that audit findings from questioned costs under §__.510(a)(3) and §__.510(a)(4), fraud under §__.510(a)(6), and audit follow-up for the summary schedule of prior audit findings under §__.510(a)(7) do not preclude the Type A program from being low-risk. The auditor shall consider: the criteria in §__.525(c), §__.525(d)(1), §__.525(d)(2), and §__.525(d)(3); the results of audit follow-up; whether any changes in personnel or systems affecting a Type A program have significantly increased risk; and apply professional judgment in determining whether a Type A program is low-risk.

  (2) Notwithstanding paragraph (c)(1) of this section, OMB may approve a Federal awarding agency's request that a Type A program

at certain recipients may not be considered low-risk. For example, it may be necessary for a large Type A program to be audited as major each year at particular recipients to allow the Federal agency to comply with the Government Management Reform Act of 1994 (31 U.S.C. 3515). The Federal agency shall notify the recipient and, if known, the auditor at least 180 days prior to the end of the fiscal year to be audited of OMB's approval.

(d) *Step 3.* (1) The auditor shall identify Type B programs which are high-risk using professional judgment and the criteria in §__.525. However, should the auditor select Option 2 under Step 4 (paragraph (e)(2)(i)(B) of this section), the auditor is not required to identify more high-risk Type B programs than the number of low-risk Type A programs. Except for known significant deficiencies in internal control or compliance problems as discussed in §__.525(b)(1), §__.525(b)(2), and §__.525(c)(1), a single criteria in §__.525 would seldom cause a Type B program to be considered high-risk.

(2) The auditor is not expected to perform risk assessments on relatively small Federal programs. Therefore, the auditor is only required to perform risk assessments on Type B programs that exceed the larger of:

(i) $100,000 or three-tenths of one percent (.003) of total Federal awards expended when the auditee has less than or equal to $100 million in total Federal awards expended.

(ii) $300,000 or three-hundredths of one percent (.0003) of total Federal awards expended when the auditee has more than $100 million in total Federal awards expended.

(e) *Step 4.* At a minimum, the auditor shall audit all of the following as major programs:

(1) All Type A programs, except the auditor may exclude any Type A programs identified as low-risk under Step 2 (paragraph (c)(1) of this section).

(2) (i) High-risk Type B programs as identified under either of the following two options:

(A) Option 1. At least one half of the Type B programs identified as high-risk under Step 3 (paragraph (d) of this section), except this paragraph (e)(2)(i)(A) does not require the auditor to audit more high-risk Type B programs than the number of low-risk Type A programs identified as low-risk under Step 2.

(B) Option 2. One high-risk Type B program for each Type A program identified as low-risk under Step 2.

(ii) When identifying which high-risk Type B programs to audit as major under either Option 1 or 2 in paragraph (e)(2)(i)(A) or (B), the auditor is encouraged to use an approach which provides an opportunity for different high-risk Type B programs to be audited as major over a period of time.

(3) Such additional programs as may be necessary to comply with the percentage of coverage rule discussed in paragraph (f) of this

section. This paragraph (e)(3) may require the auditor to audit more programs as major than the number of Type A programs.

(f) *Percentage of coverage rule.* The auditor shall audit as major programs Federal programs with Federal awards expended that, in the aggregate, encompass at least 50 percent of total Federal awards expended. If the auditee meets the criteria in §__.530 for a low-risk auditee, the auditor need only audit as major programs Federal programs with Federal awards expended that, in the aggregate, encompass at least 25 percent of total Federal awards expended.

(g) *Documentation of risk.* The auditor shall document in the working papers the risk analysis process used in determining major programs.

(h) *Auditor's judgment.* When the major program determination was performed and documented in accordance with this part, the auditor's judgment in applying the risk-based approach to determine major programs shall be presumed correct. Challenges by Federal agencies and pass-through entities shall only be for clearly improper use of the guidance in this part. However, Federal agencies and pass-through entities may provide auditors guidance about the risk of a particular Federal program and the auditor shall consider this guidance in determining major programs in audits not yet completed.

(i) *Deviation from use of risk criteria.* For first-year audits, the auditor may elect to determine major programs as all Type A programs plus any Type B programs as necessary to meet the percentage of coverage rule discussed in paragraph (f) of this section. Under this option, the auditor would not be required to perform the procedures discussed in paragraphs (c), (d), and (e) of this section.

> (1) A first-year audit is the first year the entity is audited under this part or the first year of a change of auditors.
>
> (2) To ensure that a frequent change of auditors would not preclude audit of high-risk Type B programs, this election for first-year audits may not be used by an auditee more than once in every three years.

§__.525 Criteria for Federal program risk.

(a) *General.* The auditor's determination should be based on an overall evaluation of the risk of noncompliance occurring which could be material to the Federal program. The auditor shall use auditor judgment and consider criteria, such as described in paragraphs (b), (c), and (d) of this section, to identify risk in Federal programs. Also, as part of the risk analysis, the auditor may wish to discuss a particular Federal program with auditee management and the Federal agency or pass-through entity.

(b) *Current and prior audit experience.* (1) Weaknesses in internal control over Federal programs would indicate higher risk. Consideration should be given to the control environment over Federal programs and such factors as the expectation of management's adherence to applicable laws and regulations and the provisions of contracts and grant agreements and the competence and experience of personnel who administer the Federal programs.

> (i) A Federal program administered under multiple internal control structures may have higher risk. When assessing risk in a large single audit, the auditor shall consider whether weaknesses are isolated in a single operating unit (e.g., one college campus) or pervasive throughout the entity.

(ii) When significant parts of a Federal program are passed through to subrecipients, a weak system for monitoring subrecipients would indicate higher risk.
  (iii) The extent to which computer processing is used to administer Federal programs, as well as the complexity of that processing, should be considered by the auditor in assessing risk. New and recently modified computer systems may also indicate risk.
 (2) Prior audit findings would indicate higher risk, particularly when the situations identified in the audit findings could have a significant impact on a Federal program or have not been corrected.
 (3) Federal programs not recently audited as major programs may be of higher risk than Federal programs recently audited as major programs without audit findings.

(c) *Oversight exercised by Federal agencies and pass-through entities.* (1) Oversight exercised by Federal agencies or pass-through entities could indicate risk. For example, recent monitoring or other reviews performed by an oversight entity which disclosed no significant problems would indicate lower risk. However, monitoring which disclosed significant problems would indicate higher risk.

 (2) Federal agencies, with the concurrence of OMB, may identify Federal programs which are higher risk. OMB plans to provide this identification in the compliance supplement.

(d) *Inherent risk of the Federal program.* (1) The nature of a Federal program may indicate risk. Consideration should be given to the complexity of the program and the extent to which the Federal program contracts for goods and services. For example, Federal programs that disburse funds through third party contracts or have eligibility criteria may be of higher risk. Federal programs primarily involving staff payroll costs may have a high-risk for time and effort reporting, but otherwise be at low-risk.

 (2) The phase of a Federal program in its life cycle at the Federal agency may indicate risk. For example, a new Federal program with new or interim regulations may have higher risk than an established program with time-tested regulations. Also, significant changes in Federal programs, laws, regulations, or the provisions of contracts or grant agreements may increase risk.

 (3) The phase of a Federal program in its life cycle at the auditee may indicate risk. For example, during the first and last years that an auditee participates in a Federal program, the risk may be higher due to start-up or closeout of program activities and staff.

 (4) Type B programs with larger Federal awards expended would be of higher risk than programs with substantially smaller Federal awards expended.

§__.530 Criteria for a low-risk auditee.

An auditee which meets all of the following conditions for each of the preceding two years (or, in the case of biennial audits, preceding two audit periods) shall qualify as a low-risk auditee and be eligible for reduced audit coverage in accordance with §__.520:

(a) Single audits were performed on an annual basis in accordance with the provisions of this part. A non-Federal entity that has biennial audits does not qualify as a low-risk auditee, unless agreed to in advance by the cognizant or oversight agency for audit.

(b) The auditor's opinions on the financial statements and the schedule of expenditures of Federal awards were unqualified. However, the cognizant or oversight agency for audit may judge that an opinion qualification does not affect the management of Federal awards and provide a waiver.

(c) There were no deficiencies in internal control which were identified as material weaknesses under the requirements of GAGAS. However, the cognizant or oversight agency for audit may judge that any identified material weaknesses do not affect the management of Federal awards and provide a waiver.

(d) None of the Federal programs had audit findings from any of the following in either of the preceding two years (or, in the case of biennial audits, preceding two audit periods) in which they were classified as Type A programs:

   (1) Internal control deficiencies which were identified as material weaknesses;

   (2) Noncompliance with the provisions of laws, regulations, contracts, or grant agreements which have a material effect on the Type A program; or

   (3) Known or likely questioned costs that exceed five percent of the total Federal awards expended for a Type A program during the year.

Appendix A to Part—Data Collection Form (Form SF-SAC)

[insert SF-SAC after finalized]

Appendix B to Part—Circular A-133 Compliance Supplement

Note: Provisional OMB Circular A-133 Compliance Supplement is available from the Office of Administration, Publications Office, room 2200, New Executive Office Building, Washington, DC 20503.

Appendix A

Overview of Statements on Quality Control Standards

This appendix is nonauthoritative and is included for informational purposes only.

This appendix is a partial reproduction of chapter 1 of the AICPA practice aid *Establishing and Maintaining a System of Quality Control for a CPA Firm's Accounting and Auditing Practice,* available at www.aicpa.org/interestareas/frc/pages/enhancingauditqualitypracticeaid.aspx.

1.01 The objectives of a system of quality control are to provide a CPA firm with reasonable assurance[1] that the firm and its personnel comply with professional standards and applicable regulatory and legal requirements, and that the firm or engagement partners issue reports that are appropriate in the circumstances. QC section 10, *A Firm's System of Quality Control* (AICPA, *Professional Standards*), addresses a CPA firm's responsibilities for its system of quality control for its accounting and auditing practice. That section is to be read in conjunction with the AICPA Code of Professional Conduct and other relevant ethical requirements.

1.02 A system of quality control consists of policies designed to achieve the objectives of the system and the procedures necessary to implement and monitor compliance with those policies. The nature, extent, and formality of a firm's quality control policies and procedures will depend on various factors such as the firm's size; the number and operating characteristics of its offices; the degree of authority allowed to, and the knowledge and experience possessed by, firm personnel; and the nature and complexity of the firm's practice.

Communication of Quality Control Policies and Procedures

1.03 The firm should communicate its quality control policies and procedures to its personnel. Most firms will find it appropriate to communicate their policies and procedures in writing and distribute them, or make them available electronically, to all professional personnel. Effective communication includes the following:

- A description of quality control policies and procedures and the objectives they are designed to achieve
- The message that each individual has a personal responsibility for quality
- A requirement for each individual to be familiar with and to comply with these policies and procedures

---

[1] The term *reasonable assurance*, which is defined as a high, but not absolute, level of assurance, is used because absolute assurance cannot be attained. Paragraph .53 of QC section 10, *A Firm's System of Quality Control* (AICPA, *Professional Standards*), states, "Any system of quality control has inherent limitations that can reduce its effectiveness."

Effective communication also includes procedures for personnel to communicate their views or concerns on quality control matters to the firm's management.

Elements of a System of Quality Control

1.04 A firm must establish and maintain a system of quality control. The firm's system of quality control should include policies and procedures that address each of the following elements of quality control identified in paragraph .17 of QC section 10:

- Leadership responsibilities for quality within the firm (the "tone at the top")
- Relevant ethical requirements
- Acceptance and continuance of client relationships and specific engagements
- Human resources
- Engagement performance
- Monitoring

1.05 The elements of quality control are interrelated. For example, a firm continually assesses client relationships to comply with relevant ethical requirements, including independence, integrity, and objectivity, and policies and procedures related to the acceptance and continuance of client relationships and specific engagements. Similarly, the human resources element of quality control encompasses criteria related to professional development, hiring, advancement, and assignment of firm personnel to engagements, all of which affect policies and procedures related to engagement performance. In addition, policies and procedures related to the monitoring element of quality control enable a firm to evaluate whether its policies and procedures for each of the other five elements of quality control are suitably designed and effectively applied.

1.06 Policies and procedures established by the firm related to each element are designed to achieve reasonable assurance with respect to the purpose of that element. Deficiencies in policies and procedures for an element may result in not achieving reasonable assurance with respect to the purpose of that element; however, the system of quality control, as a whole, may still be effective in providing the firm with reasonable assurance that the firm and its personnel comply with professional standards and applicable regulatory and legal requirements and that the firm or engagement partners issue reports that are appropriate in the circumstances.

1.07 If a firm merges, acquires, sells, or otherwise changes a portion of its practice, the surviving firm evaluates and, as necessary, revises, implements, and maintains firm-wide quality control policies and procedures that are appropriate for the changed circumstances.

Leadership Responsibilities for Quality Within the Firm (the "Tone at the Top")

1.08 The purpose of the leadership responsibilities element of a system of quality control is to promote an internal culture based on the recognition that quality is essential in performing engagements. The firm should establish and maintain the following policies and procedures to achieve this purpose:

- Require the firm's leadership (managing partner, board of managing partners, CEO, or equivalent) to assume ultimate responsibility for the firm's system of quality control.

- Provide the firm with reasonable assurance that personnel assigned operational responsibility for the firm's quality control system have sufficient and appropriate experience and ability to identify and understand quality control issues and develop appropriate policies and procedures, as well as the necessary authority to implement those policies and procedures.

1.09 Establishing and maintaining the following policies and procedures assists firms in recognizing that the firm's business strategy is subject to the overarching requirement for the firm to achieve the objectives of the system of quality control in all the engagements that the firm performs:

- Assign management responsibilities so that commercial considerations do not override the quality of the work performed.

- Design policies and procedures addressing performance evaluation, compensation, and advancement (including incentive systems) with regard to personnel to demonstrate the firm's overarching commitment to the objectives of the system of quality control.

- Devote sufficient and appropriate resources for the development, communication, and support of its quality control policies and procedures.

Relevant Ethical Requirements

1.10 The purpose of the relevant ethical requirements element of a system of quality control is to provide the firm with reasonable assurance that the firm and its personnel comply with relevant ethical requirements when discharging professional responsibilities. Relevant ethical requirements include independence, integrity, and objectivity. Establishing and maintaining policies such as the following assist the firm in obtaining this assurance:

- Require that personnel adhere to relevant ethical requirements such as those in regulations, interpretations, and rules of the AICPA, state CPA societies, state boards of accountancy, state statutes, the U.S. Government Accountability Office, and any other applicable regulators.

- Establish procedures to communicate independence requirements to firm personnel and, where applicable, others subject to them.

- Establish procedures to identify and evaluate possible threats to independence and objectivity, including the familiarity threat that may be created by using the same senior personnel on an audit or attest engagement over a long period of time, and to take appropriate action to eliminate those threats or reduce them to an acceptable level by applying safeguards.

- Require that the firm withdraw from the engagement if effective safeguards to reduce threats to independence to an acceptable level cannot be applied.
- Require written confirmation, at least annually, of compliance with the firm's policies and procedures on independence from all firm personnel required to be independent by relevant requirements.
- Establish procedures for confirming the independence of another firm or firm personnel in associated member firms who perform part of the engagement. This would apply to national firm personnel, foreign firm personnel, and foreign-associated firms.[2]
- Require the rotation of personnel for audit or attest engagements where regulatory or other authorities require such rotation after a specified period.

Acceptance and Continuance of Client Relationships and Specific Engagements

1.11 The purpose of the quality control element that addresses acceptance and continuance of client relationships and specific engagements is to establish criteria for deciding whether to accept or continue a client relationship and whether to perform a specific engagement for a client. A firm's client acceptance and continuance policies represent a key element in mitigating litigation and business risk. Accordingly, it is important that a firm be aware that the integrity and reputation of a client's management could reflect the reliability of the client's accounting records and financial representations and, therefore, affect the firm's reputation or involvement in litigation. A firm's policies and procedures related to the acceptance and continuance of client relationships and specific engagements should provide the firm with reasonable assurance that it will undertake or continue relationships and engagements only where it

- is competent to perform the engagement and has the capabilities, including the time and resources, to do so;
- can comply with legal and relevant ethical requirements;
- has considered the client's integrity and does not have information that would lead it to conclude that the client lacks integrity; and
- has reached an understanding with the client regarding the services to be performed.

1.12 This assurance should be obtained before accepting an engagement with a new client, when deciding whether to continue an existing engagement, and when considering acceptance of a new engagement with an existing client. Establishing and maintaining policies such as the following assist the firm in obtaining this assurance:

---

[2] A *foreign-associated firm* is a firm domiciled outside of the United States and its territories that is a member of, correspondent with, or similarly associated with an international firm or international association of firms.

Overview of Statements on Quality Control Standards

- Evaluate factors that have a bearing on management's integrity and consider the risk associated with providing professional services in particular circumstances.[3]
- Evaluate whether the engagement can be completed with professional competence; undertake only those engagements for which the firm has the capabilities, resources, and professional competence to complete; and evaluate, at the end of specific periods or upon occurrence of certain events, whether the relationship should be continued.
- Obtain an understanding, preferably in writing, with the client regarding the services to be performed.
- Establish procedures on continuing an engagement and the client relationship, including procedures for dealing with information that would have caused the firm to decline an engagement if the information had been available earlier.
- Require documentation of how issues relating to acceptance or continuance of client relationships and specific engagements were resolved.

Human Resources

1.13 The purpose of the human resources element of a system of quality control is to provide the firm with reasonable assurance that it has sufficient personnel with the capabilities, competence, and commitment to ethical principles necessary (a) to perform its engagements in accordance with professional standards and regulatory and legal requirements, and (b) to enable the firm to issue reports that are appropriate in the circumstances. Establishing and maintaining policies such as the following assist the firm in obtaining this assurance:

- Recruit and hire personnel of integrity who possess the characteristics that enable them to perform competently.
- Determine capabilities and competencies required for an engagement, especially for the engagement partner, based on the characteristics of the particular client, industry, and kind of service being performed. Specific competencies necessary for an engagement partner are discussed in paragraph .A27 of QC section 10.
- Determine the capabilities and competencies possessed by personnel.
- Assign the responsibility for each engagement to an engagement partner.

---

[3] Such considerations would include the risk of providing professional services to significant clients or to other clients for which the practitioner's objectivity or the appearance of independence may be impaired. In broad terms, the significance of a client to a member or a firm refers to relationships that could diminish a practitioner's objectivity and independence in performing attest services. Examples of factors to consider in determining the significance of a client to an engagement partner, office, or practice unit include (a) the amount of time the partner, office, or practice unit devotes to the engagement, (b) the effect on the partner's stature within the firm as a result of his or her service to the client, (c) the manner in which the partner, office, or practice unit is compensated, or (d) the effect that losing the client would have on the partner, office, or practice unit.

- Assign personnel based on the knowledge, skills, and abilities required in the circumstances and the nature and extent of supervision needed.
- Have personnel participate in general and industry-specific continuing professional education and professional development activities that enable them to accomplish assigned responsibilities and satisfy applicable continuing professional education requirements of the AICPA, state boards of accountancy, and other regulators.
- Select for advancement only those individuals who have the qualifications necessary to fulfill the responsibilities they will be called on to assume.

Engagement Performance

1.14 The purpose of the engagement performance element of quality control is to provide the firm with reasonable assurance (*a*) that engagements are consistently performed in accordance with applicable professional standards and regulatory and legal requirements, and (*b*) that the firm or the engagement partner issues reports that are appropriate in the circumstances. Policies and procedures for engagement performance should address all phases of the design and execution of the engagement, including engagement performance, supervision responsibilities, and review responsibilities. Policies and procedures also should require that consultation takes place when appropriate. In addition, a policy should establish criteria against which all engagements are to be evaluated to determine whether an engagement quality control review should be performed.

1.15 Establishing and maintaining policies such as the following assist the firm in obtaining the assurance required relating to the engagement performance element of quality control:

- Plan all engagements to meet professional, regulatory, and the firm's requirements.
- Perform work and issue reports and other communications that meet professional, regulatory, and the firm's requirements.
- Require that work performed by other team members be reviewed by qualified engagement team members, which may include the engagement partner, on a timely basis.
- Require the engagement team to complete the assembly of final engagement files on a timely basis.
- Establish procedures to maintain the confidentiality, safe custody, integrity, accessibility, and retrievability of engagement documentation.
- Require the retention of engagement documentation for a period of time sufficient to meet the needs of the firm, professional standards, laws, and regulations.
- Require that
    — consultation take place when appropriate (for example, when dealing with complex, unusual, unfamiliar, difficult, or contentious issues);

Overview of Statements on Quality Control Standards

- sufficient and appropriate resources be available to enable appropriate consultation to take place;
- all the relevant facts known to the engagement team be provided to those consulted;
- the nature, scope, and conclusions of such consultations be documented; and
- the conclusions resulting from such consultations be implemented.

• Require that

- differences of opinion be dealt with and resolved;
- conclusions reached are documented and implemented; and
- the report not be released until the matter is resolved.

• Require that

- all engagements be evaluated against the criteria for determining whether an engagement quality control review should be performed;
- an engagement quality control review be performed for all engagements that meet the criteria; and
- the review be completed before the report is released.

• Establish procedures addressing the nature, timing, extent, and documentation of the engagement quality control review.
• Establish criteria for the eligibility of engagement quality control reviewers.

Monitoring

1.16 The purpose of the monitoring element of a system of quality control is to provide the firm and its engagement partners with reasonable assurance that the policies and procedures related to the system of quality control are relevant, adequate, operating effectively, and complied with in practice. Monitoring involves an ongoing consideration and evaluation of the appropriateness of the design, the effectiveness of the operation of a firm's quality control system, and a firm's compliance with its quality control policies and procedures. The purpose of monitoring compliance with quality control policies and procedures is to provide an evaluation of the following:

- Adherence to professional standards and regulatory and legal requirements
- Whether the quality control system has been appropriately designed and effectively implemented
- Whether the firm's quality control policies and procedures have been operating effectively so that reports issued by the firm are appropriate in the circumstances

1.17 Establishing and maintaining policies such as the following assist the firm in obtaining the assurance required relating to the monitoring element of quality control:

- Assign responsibility for the monitoring process to a partner or partners or other persons with sufficient and appropriate experience and authority in the firm to assume that responsibility.
- Assign performance of the monitoring process to competent individuals.
- Require the performance of monitoring procedures that are sufficiently comprehensive to enable the firm to assess compliance with all applicable professional standards and the firm's quality control policies and procedures. Monitoring procedures consist of the following:
    — Review of selected administrative and personnel records pertaining to the quality control elements.
    — Review of engagement documentation, reports, and clients' financial statements.
    — Summarization of the findings from the monitoring procedures, at least annually, and consideration of the systemic causes of findings that indicate that improvements are needed.
    — Determination of any corrective actions to be taken or improvements to be made with respect to the specific engagements reviewed or the firm's quality control policies and procedures.
    — Communication of the identified findings to appropriate firm management personnel.
    — Consideration of findings by appropriate firm management personnel who should also determine that any actions necessary, including necessary modifications to the quality control system, are taken on a timely basis.
    — Assessment of
        - the appropriateness of the firm's guidance materials and any practice aids;
        - new developments in professional standards and regulatory and legal requirements and how they are reflected in the firm's policies and procedures where appropriate;
        - compliance with policies and procedures on independence;
        - the effectiveness of continuing professional development, including training;
        - decisions related to acceptance and continuance of client relationships and specific engagements; and
        - firm personnel's understanding of the firm's quality control policies and procedures and implementation thereof.
- Communicate at least annually, to relevant engagement partners and other appropriate personnel, deficiencies noted as a result

Overview of Statements on Quality Control Standards

of the monitoring process and recommendations for appropriate remedial action.
- Communicate the results of the monitoring of its quality control system process to relevant firm personnel at least annually.
- Establish procedures designed to provide the firm with reasonable assurance that it deals appropriately with the following:
  — Complaints and allegations that the work performed by the firm fails to comply with professional standards and regulatory and legal requirements.
  — Allegations of noncompliance with the firm's system of quality control.
  — Deficiencies in the design or operation of the firm's quality control policies and procedures, or noncompliance with the firm's system of quality control by an individual or individuals, as identified during the investigations into complaints and allegations.

  This includes establishing clearly defined channels for firm personnel to raise any concerns in a manner that enables them to come forward without fear of reprisal and documenting complaints and allegations and the responses to them.
- Require appropriate documentation to provide evidence of the operation of each element of its system of quality control. The form and content of documentation evidencing the operation of each of the elements of the system of quality control is a matter of judgment and depends on a number of factors, including the following, for example:
  — The size of the firm and the number of offices.
  — The nature and complexity of the firm's practice and organization.
- Require retention of documentation providing evidence of the operation of the system of quality control for a period of time sufficient to permit those performing monitoring procedures and peer review to evaluate the firm's compliance with its system of quality control, or for a longer period if required by law or regulation.

1.18 Some of the monitoring procedures discussed in the previous list may be accomplished through the performance of the following:

- Engagement quality control review
- Review of engagement documentation, reports, and clients' financial statements for selected engagements after the report release date
- Inspection[4] procedures

---

[4] *Inspection* is a retrospective evaluation of the adequacy of the firm's quality control policies and procedures, its personnel's understanding of those policies and procedures, and the extent of the firm's compliance with them. Although monitoring procedures are meant to be ongoing, they may include inspection procedures performed at a fixed point in time. Monitoring is a broad concept; inspection is one specific type of monitoring procedure.

Documentation of Quality Control Policies and Procedures

1.19 The firm should document each element of its system of quality control. The extent of the documentation will depend on the size, structure, and nature of the firm's practice. Documentation may be as simple as a checklist of the firm's policies and procedures or as extensive as practice manuals.

Appendix B

Schedule of Changes Made to the Text From the Previous Edition

This appendix is nonauthoritative and is included for informational purposes only.

As of February 1, 2015

This schedule of changes identifies areas in the text and footnotes of this guide that have changed since the previous edition. Entries in the table of this appendix reflect current numbering, lettering (including that in appendix names), and character designations that resulted from the renumbering or reordering that occurred in the updating of this guide.

Reference	Change
General	Information regarding Title 2 U.S. *Code of Federal Regulations* Part 200, *Uniform Administrative Requirements, Cost Principles, and Audit Requirements for Federal Awards* (Uniform Guidance) has been added to part I, Government Auditing Standards *Audits*, and part II, *Circular A-133 Audits*, as appropriate.
General	Part III, *Uniform Guidance Audits*, has been added to this edition of the guide. Part III chapters consist of part II chapters fully updated for the Uniform Guidance and related changes as found in the *OMB Compliance Supplement*.
General	Information related to the Uniform Guidance effective date has been placed in a text box located under the title to all chapters.
General	A section titled "Transition Considerations Related to the Uniform Guidance" has been added to appropriate chapters of parts II and III.
General	"Emphasis Point" boxes have been added to highlight certain information related to chapter content.
General	Information related to the American Recovery and Reinvestment Act has been removed.
General	Editorial changes, including rephrasing, may have been made in this guide to improve readability where necessary.

(continued)

Reference	Change
Preface	Updated.
Footnote 4 in paragraph 2.18	Added for the revised AICPA Code of Professional Conduct.
Footnotes to heading before paragraph 2.28	Former footnote 4 deleted due to the revised AICPA Code of Professional Conduct. Footnote 5 revised for the AICPA Code of Professional Conduct.
Paragraph 2.28	Revised for the revised AICPA Code of Professional Conduct.
Former footnotes 6–7 and former paragraphs 2.30–.31	Deleted for the revised AICPA Code of Professional Conduct.
Footnote 22 in paragraph 3.25	Added for the issuance of the revised Green Book.
Paragraph 4.17	Revised for clarification.
Paragraph 4.88	Added example 4-7, "Report on Internal Control Over Financial Reporting and on Compliance and Other Matters Based on an Audit of Financial Statements Performed in Accordance With Government Auditing Standards (for a Governmental Entity) (Material Weaknesses Identified; No Significant Deficiencies Identified; Reportable Instances of Noncompliance and Other Matters Identified)."
Paragraphs 5.22 and 5.27 and footnote 15	Revised for the passage of time.
Paragraph 5.43	Revised for clarification; former footnote 19 deleted.
Paragraph 6.17 and footnote 8	Added for clarification.
Paragraph 6.27	Revised to reflect revisions to the *Compliance Supplement*.
Paragraphs 6.60–.69	Revised for Statement on Auditing Standards No. 128, *Using the Work of Internal Auditors* (AICPA, *Professional Standards*, AU-C sec. 610).
Footnote 22 at paragraph 6.72; paragraphs 7.36 and 8.27 and footnote 7	Revised for the passage of time.
Paragraph 9.18	Revised to reflect revisions to the *Compliance Supplement*.
Footnote 6 to heading before paragraph 10.18	Added to reflect revisions to the *Compliance Supplement*.

Schedule of Changes Made to the Text From the Previous Edition

Reference	Change
Paragraph 10.18	Revised to reflect revisions to the *Compliance Supplement*; footnote 7 added to reflect revisions to the *Compliance Supplement*.
Paragraph 10.19	Revised to reflect revisions to the *Compliance Supplement*; footnote 8 added to reflect revisions to the *Compliance Supplement*.
Paragraph 10.20	Revised for the passage of time.
Paragraphs 10.24 and 10.28	Revised to reflect revisions to the *Compliance Supplement*.
Paragraph 10.55	Revised for the passage of time; former footnote 14 deleted for the passage of time.
Paragraph 10.60	Revised to reflect revisions to the *Compliance Supplement*.
Paragraphs 11.27, 11.30, 11.32–.33, 11.40, 12.06, 12.24, and 12.27	Revised to reflect revisions to the *Compliance Supplement*.
Footnote 33 at paragraph 13.42	Revised for the passage of time.
Paragraph 13.58	Added example 13-3, "Report on Compliance for Each Major Federal Program; Report on Internal Control Over Compliance; and Report on Schedule of Expenditures of Federal Awards Required by OMB Circular A-133 (Unmodified Opinion on Compliance for Each Major Federal Program; Material Weaknesses in Internal Control Over Compliance Identified; No Significant Deficiencies in Internal Control Over Compliance Identified);" footnote 2 revised to reflect revisions to the *Compliance Supplement*.
Footnote 10 at paragraph 14.17	Revised to reflect revisions to the *Compliance Supplement*.
Chapters 15–24	Added.
Former appendix A	Deleted.
Appendix A	Added.
Index of Pronouncements and Other Technical Guidance	Updated.
Subject Index	Updated.

Index of Pronouncements and Other Technical Guidance

A

Title	Paragraphs
AT section 101, *Attest Engagement*	4.87
AU-C section	
200, *Overall Objectives of the Independent Auditor and the Conduct of an Audit in Accordance With Generally Accepted Auditing Standards*	1.05, 2.07, 2.31, 2.34, 6.68
210, *Terms of Engagement*	3.04–.07, 6.08–.09, 6.21, 16.08–.09, 16.18
220, *Quality Control for an Engagement Conducted in Accordance With Generally Accepted Auditing Standards*	16.68
230, *Audit Documentation*	3.19–.20, 6.11–.12, 7.31, 9.57, 10.70, 11.132–.133, 11.135, 20.69, 21.132–.133, 21.135
Interpretation No. 1, "Providing Access to or Copies of Audit Documentation to a Regulator"	16.54–.55, 17.35, 19.60
240, *Consideration of Fraud in a Financial Statement Audit*	3.36–.38, 3.40–.42, 4.25–.29, 6.45–.46, 16.42–.43
250, *Consideration of Laws and Regulations in an Audit of Financial Statements*	3.43–.44, 3.52, 4.31–.32, 4.35
260, *The Auditor's Communication With Those Charged With Governance*	3.14, 3.61–.65, 13.35, Table 13-2, 23.35
265, *Communicating Internal Control Related Matters Identified in an Audit*	3.66, 4.14–.22, Appendix at 4.88, 9.44, 9.53, 11.113, 13.35, Table 13-2, 19.47, 19.56, 21.113, 23.35
300, *Planning an Audit*	3.08–.09
315, *Understanding the Entity and Its Environment and Assessing the Risks of Material Misstatement*	3.23, 3.26–.27, 3.30–.32, 8.33, 9.06–.08, 9.13–.15, 9.55, 19.09–.11, 19.16–.18, 19.58

Title	Paragraphs
320, *Materiality in Planning and Performance of an Audit*	3.17, 6.28, 10.07, 16.25, 20.07
330, *Performing Audit Procedures in Response to Assessed Risks and Evaluation the Audit Evidence Obtained*	3.30, 3.35, 9.25–.26, 9.30–.33, 9.56, 10.09, 11.29, 19.28–.29, 19.33–.36, 19.59, 20.09, 21.29
450, *Evaluation of Misstatements Identified During the Audit*	3.59
500, *Audit Evidence*	8.33, 11.13, 21.13
520, *Analytical Procedures*	11.14, 21.14
530, *Audit Sampling*	11.01–.02, 11.05, 11.135, 21.01–.02, 21.05, 21.135
560, *Subsequent Events and Subsequently Discovered Facts*	13.28, 17.18, 23.28
580, *Written Representations*	3.50, 3.67, 7.16, 17.17
600, *Special Considerations—Audits of Group Financial Statements*	3.16, 4.77, 6.57–.59, 13.31, 16.57–.59, 23.31
610, *The Auditor's Consideration of the Internal Audit Function in an Audit of Financial Statements*	3.13, 6.60–.61, 6.66, 6.68–.69, 16.60, 16.66
700, *Forming an Opinion and Reporting on Financial Statements*	4.02–.04, 4.46–.48, Appendix at 4.88, 13.21, 23.21
705, *Modifications to the Opinion in the Independent Auditor's Report*	4.47, 13.10, 13.21–.22, 23.10, 23.21–.22
706, *Emphasis-of-Matter Paragraphs and Other-Matter Paragraphs in the Independent Auditor's Report*	4.47, 7.18, 13.11, 17.19, 23.11
720, *Other Information in Documents Containing Audited Financial Statements*	4.03
725, *Supplementary Information in Relation to the Financial Statements as a Whole*	4.03, 5.05, 7.05, 7.10, 7.13, 7.17–.18, 7.22, 7.32, 13.11–.16, 13.19, 15.06, 17.06, 17.11, 17.14, 17.18–.19, 17.25, 17.36, 23.11–.16, 23.19
Interpretation No. 1, "Dating the Auditor's Report on Supplementary Information"	13.18, 23.18
730, *Required Supplementary Information*	4.03

Index of Pronouncements and Other Technical Guidance

Title	Paragraphs
800, *Special Considerations—Audits of Financial Statements Prepared in Accordance With Special Purpose Frameworks*	6.17, 16.13
805, *Special Considerations—Audits of Single Financial Statements and Specific Elements, Accounts, or Items of a Financial Statement*	7.32–.34, 13.20, 14.17, 17.36–.38, 23.20
905, *Alert That Restricts the Use of the Auditor's Written Communication*	3.61, 13.12, 23.12
935, *Compliance Audits*	1.09, 1.11, 5.06, 6.03–.06, 6.09, 6.25–.26, 6.28, 6.35–.36, 6.39, 6.50–.51, 6.57, 9.10, 9.55, 10.02, 10.09, 10.11, 10.52, 10.71, 10.73, 11.01, 11.15, 11.131, 13.21, 14.04, 14.08, 14.17, 15.07, 16.03–.06, 16.09, 16.22–.23, 16.25, 16.32–.33, 16.36, 16.47–.48, 16.57, 19.13, 19.35, 19.45, 19.58, 20.02, 20.04, 20.09, 20.11, 20.51, 20.70, 20.72, 21.01, 21.15, 21.131, 23.21, 24.04, 24.08
Audit and Accounting Guides	
Depository and Lending Institutions	1.04, 3.38, 4.03
Employee Benefit Plans	1.04
Gaming	1.04
Health Care Entities	1.04, 3.16–.17, 3.38, 4.03, 4.78, 5.04, 13.10
Not-For-Profit Entities	1.04, 3.16–.17, 3.38, 4.03, 4.78, 5.04, 13.10
State and Local Governments	1.04, 3.16–.17, 3.38, 4.03, 4.78, 5.04, 13.10
Audit Guide *Audit Sampling*	11.07, 11.36, 11.45, 11.59, 11.66, 11.69, 11.84, 11.93, 11.99, 11.103, 11.122, 21.04, 21.66, 21.84, 21.93, 21.99, 21.103, 21.122

C

Title	Paragraphs
CFR Title	
2 CFR 200, *Uniform Administrative Requirements, Cost Principles, and Audit Requirements for Federal Awards*	15.03, 15.20, 15.50–.53, 16.78, 18.39, 22.44, 23.64
Code of Professional Conduct	2.07, 2.28–.29
Committee of Sponsoring Organizations of the Treadway Commission	
Internal Control Integrated Framework	9.59
Standards for Internal Control in the Federal Government (Green Book)	9.59

F

Title	Paragraphs
FASB *Accounting Standards Codification*	
275, *Risks and Uncertainties*	20.54
450, *Contingencies*	10.55, 20.54
958, *Not-For-Profit Entities*	
958-810	13.10, 23.10

G

Title	Paragraphs
GASB Statement No.	
14, *The Financial Reporting Entity*	4.74
62, *Codification of Accounting and Financial Reporting Guidance Contained In Pre-November 30, 1989 FASB and AICPA Pronouncements*	20.54

O

Title	Paragraphs
OMB Circular A-110, *Uniform Administrative Requirements for Grants and Other Agreements With Institutions of Higher Education, Hospitals and Other Non-Profit Organizations*	9.59
OMB Circular A-133, *Audits of States, Local Governments, and Non-Profit Organizations*	
Section 200	14.02
Section 210	12.08
Section 215	8.25
Section 235	14.01–.04, 14.13
Section 315	14.03, 14.06
Section 320	14.03, 14.14, 14.16
Section 500	14.07
Section 505	13.35, Table 13-2, 14.09
Section 520	8.02, 8.14, 8.19, 8.24
Section 525	8.02, 8.37
Section 530	8.02
Sections 100-215	14.03
Sections 220-230	14.03
Sections 300-305	14.03
Sections 400-405	14.03
Sections 510-515	14.03
OMB Uniform Guidance (Title 2 CFR Part 200, *Uniform Administrative Requirements, Cost Principles, And Audit Requirements For Federal Awards*)	15.03, 15.20, 15.50–.53, 16.78, 18.39, 22.44, 23.64,

P

Title	Paragraphs
Practice Aid *Establishing and Maintaining a System of Quality Control for a CPA Firm's Accounting and Auditing Practice*	Appendix A

Q

Title	Paragraphs
QC section 10, *A Firm's System of Quality Control*	2.43, Appendix A

T

Title	Paragraphs
TIS section 9160.27, "Providing Opinion on a Schedule of Expenditures of Federal Awards in Relation to an Entity's Financial Statements as a Whole When the Schedule of Expenditures of Federal Awards Is on a Different Basis of Accounting Than the Financial Statements"	7.10

U

Title	Paragraphs
U.S. Department of Energy *Audit Guidance for For-Profit Recipients*	1.09

Subject Index

A

ABUSE
- Auditor responsibilities 3.07, 5.18, 15.18
- Compliance audits 10.45, 20.44
- Decision tree for evaluation and reporting .... Exhibit 3-1 at 3.58
- Determination of 3.56
- Evaluation 3.57–.58
- Financial statement audits 3.53–.56
- Government Auditing Standards .... 3.53–.56, ... 4.07, 4.36–.38, 4.40–.45, 4.55–.62, ... Table 4-3 at 4.82, 4.83
- Program-specific audits 14.12
- Qualitative factors 3.57
- Reporting .... 4.07, 13.34, 13.39, ... 23.38, 23.40

ACCESS TO DOCUMENTS **6.11, 16.54**

ACTIVITIES ALLOWED OR UNALLOWED .... **11.16, 11.26–.27, ... 21.16, 21.26–.27**

ADVERSE OPINION .... **4.03, 13.22, ... 23.15, 23.22**

AGGREGATION RISK **6.58, 16.58**

AGREED-UPON PROCEDURES ENGAGEMENTS ..... **5.25, 12.25, 12.29, ... 12.33, 15.25, 22.32, 22.35**

ANALYTICAL PROCEDURES ...... **11.14–.17, ... 11.25, 21.13–.17**

APPLICABLE COMPLIANCE REQUIREMENTS, DEFINED **6.26, 16.23**

ASSURANCE TO REGULATORS AND OVERSIGHT AGENCIES, GOVERNMENT AUDITING STANDARDS REPORTING **4.86–.87**

ATTITUDES, FRAUD RISK FACTORS .... **Table 16-1 at 16.46**

ATTRIBUTES SAMPLING, DEFINED .... **11.07, ... 21.07**

AUDIT COSTS. *See also* **questioned costs** .... **5.24–.25, 6.74, 12.33, ... 15.24–.25, 22.35**

AUDIT DOCUMENTATION. *See* **documentation**

AUDIT EVIDENCE
- Audit planning 6.63–.67
- Audit sampling as method to gather ... 11.06, ... 21.06
- Detecting sufficient appropriate 20.37–.41
- Evaluation, financial statement audits 3.32–.35
- Evaluation for sufficiency and appropriateness 20.50
- Performing risk assessment procedures 16.33–.34

AUDIT EVIDENCE—continued
- Responsibility to collect in single audit .... Table 15-1 at 15.08
- Schedule of expenditures of federal awards 17.13, 17.38
- Tests of compliance 10.38–.41
- Using work of internal auditor to obtain 16.63

AUDIT FINDINGS
- Accounting for sampling risk in determining 21.126
- Communication with management ..... 13.44, ... 23.45
- Compliance exceptions 11.105
- Control deviations 11.105
- Disputes 10.69, 20.68
- Federal awards, details of 13.40–.41
- Financial statement audits 3.60
- Follow-up. *See* follow-up procedures
- Government Auditing Standards .... 3.60, ... 4.55–.62, 10.37, 20.66
- Material weaknesses 19.44–.57
- Materiality evaluation .... 10.54, 10.60, ... 16.50–.52
- Noncompliance .... 4.55–.62, 10.49–.62, ... 10.69, 16.51, 20.48–.49, 20.57–.61, ... 23.22, 23.38
- Pass-through entities ...... 12.38, 22.40–.42, ... 22.49
- Prior audit findings. *See* prior audit findings; schedule of findings and questioned costs
- Reporting .... 4.55–.62, 6.53–.55, ... 10.60–.62, 11.105, 20.59–.61, ... 23.33–.46, Table 23-2 at 23.35
- Schedule of 23.33–.44
- Significant deficiencies 19.44–.57
- Subrecipients 10.61, 12.47, 22.40
- Transition considerations related to the Uniform Guidance 23.61–.62
- Unresolved findings 10.69, 20.68

AUDIT OBJECTIVES
- Audit sampling 11.31–.32, 21.31–.32
- Compliance audits .... 10.02–.03, 10.42, ... 15.04–.08, Table 15-1 at 15.08, ... 20.02–.03, 20.41
- Financial statement audits 4.02
- Schedule of expenditures of federal awards 17.13

AUDIT PERIOD DETERMINATION ... **6.19–.20, ... 16.16–.17**

AUDIT PLANNING ...... **6.01–.78, 16.01–.78, ... 21.31–.89**
- Audit follow-up 6.13, 16.56
- Audit period 6.19–.20, 16.16–.17
- Audit risk of noncompliance .... 6.28–.49, ... 16.25–.46

AUDIT PLANNING—continued
- Circular A-133 audits 6.01–.78
- Communication with cognizant or oversight agency 6.70, 16.70
- Compliance audits .... 6.03–.07, 6.25–.27, ... 6.56, 10.29–.32, 16.03–.06, ... 16.22–.24, 20.29–.32
- Desk reviews 6.72–.73, 16.72–.73
- Determining objectives 21.31–.32
- Documentation 6.10–.12, 16.53–.56
- Efficient approach 6.56, 16.14
- Entity to be audited 6.18, 16.15
- Financial statement audits .... 3.08–.15, ... 6.14–.17, 6.56, 16.10–.13
- Generally 6.01–.02, 16.01–.02
- Government Auditing Standards .. 2.01–.51, ... 3.08–.15, 6.01–.02
- Group audits 6.57–.59, 16.57–.59
- Identification of supplementary audit requirements 6.07, 16.07
- Indirect cost proposal restriction 6.74, 16.74
- Initial-year audits 6.21–.22, 16.18–.19
- Internal audit function .. 6.60–.69, 16.60–.69
- Major programs 6.24, 16.21
- Materiality considerations .... 6.50–.55, ... 16.47–.52
- On-site reviews 6.72–.73, 16.72–.73
- Pass-through entities .... 12.21–.23, ... 22.21–.24
- Report submission deadlines 6.23, 16.20
- Sampling 11.31–.89, 21.31–.89
- State and local compliance requirements 16.71
- Terms of engagement .... 6.08–.09, ... 16.08–.09
- Timing of completion 6.23, 16.20
- Transition considerations related to the Uniform Guidance 6.75–.78, 16.75–.78

AUDIT REVIEWS **6.72–.73, 16.72–.73**

AUDIT RISK OF NONCOMPLIANCE .... **6.28–.49, ... 16.25–.46**
- Compliance audits ..... 6.28–.49, 10.07–.09, ... 20.07–.09
- Components 16.27–.29
- Control risk assessment 9.21–.22
- Control risk of noncompliance. *See* control risk of noncompliance
- Criteria for major program identification 18.23
- Defined 6.30, 16.27
- Detection risk of noncompliance ... 6.32, 6.37, 16.29, 16.34
- Elements 6.30–.32
- Evaluation and reporting of noncompliance 20.48–.61
- Federal program risk 8.38
- Generally 6.28–.29
- Inherent risk of noncompliance. *See* inherent risk of noncompliance

AUDIT RISK OF NONCOMPLIANCE—continued
- Material noncompliance. *See* material noncompliance
- Performing risk assessment procedures 16.30–.35
- Risk assessment 6.33–.49, 9.11
- Subrecipients of pass-through entities 22.34, 22.53
- Tests of controls 9.23–.26, 20.35–.40

AUDIT SAMPLING .... **11.01–.137, ... 21.01–.137**
- Audit objectives 11.31–.32, 21.31–.32
- Clusters of programs .... 11.46–.48, ... 21.46–.48
- Compliance audits 10.44–.45
- Compliance exception conditions 11.50–.51, 21.50–.51
- Context 11.10–.11, 21.10–.11
- Control deviation 11.50–.51, 21.50–.51
- Defined 11.05, 21.05
- Defining population 11.33–.38, 21.33–.38
- Documentation .... 11.28, 11.131–.135, ... 21.131–.135
- Dual purpose samples .... 11.52–.57, ... 21.52–.57
- Evaluating results 11.106–.130
- Evaluation of results 21.106–.130
- Generally 11.01–.04, 21.01–.04
- Multiple major programs .... 11.42–.43, ... 21.42–.43, 21.92
- Multiple organizational units .... 11.44–.45, ... 21.44–.45
- Planning considerations .... 11.31–.89, ... 21.31–.89
- Population size effects 11.49, 21.49
- Procedures not involving .... 11.12–.30, ... 21.12–.30
- Purpose and nature of .... 11.06–.09, ... 21.06–.09
- Related to tests of controls .... 11.29–.30, ... 11.59–.69, 11.110–.112, 21.29–.30, ... 21.52–.57, 21.110–.112
- Sample item selection .... 11.90–.98, ... 21.90–.98
- Sample size determination .... 11.58–.89, ... 21.58–.89
- Sampling unit 11.39–.41, 21.38
- Test procedures 11.99–.105, 21.99–.105
- Tests of compliance related to .... 11.18–.28, ... 11.70–.89, 11.106–.130, 20.43, ... Table 21-3 at 21.86, 21.86–.89
- Transition considerations related to the Uniform Guidance 11.136–.137, 21.136–.137

AUDIT SCOPE .... **4.75–.76, 13.23–.25, ... 14.07, 15.29, 23.23–.25, 24.07**

AUDIT STRATEGY **3.08–.09**

AUDIT TEAM DISCUSSION **16.37, 16.43**

AUDIT THRESHOLD **5.08, 15.09, 18.33**

Subject Index

AUDITEE RESPONSIBILITIES
- Circular A-133 audits 5.33–.39
- Compliance audits 10.04–.05, 15.33–.39,
  .... 20.04–.05
- Contractor compliance 22.15–.16
- Corrective action plan. *See* corrective action
- Data collection form 15.39, 23.51–.55
- Defining entity to be audited 15.16
- Federal awards identification 7.04, 17.05
- Financial statements 15.33, 15.36, 16.10
- Follow-up 10.63–.64, 20.62–.63
- Internal control over compliance for federal awards 5.35, 9.02, 15.36, 19.04–.06
- Internal control over financial reporting ... 5.36
- Low-risk auditees 5.30, 8.21, 8.26–.27,
  .... 15.30, 18.21, 18.39
- Major program determination 8.01, 18.01
- Program-specific audits 14.06, 24.03, 24.06
- Prohibition on clusters of program changes 15.31
- Reporting federal awards 16.11
- Reporting package 5.38–.39, 13.05,
  .... 15.38–.39, 23.05
- Schedule of expenditures of federal awards 5.05, 5.33, 15.06, 15.33,
  .... 16.10, 17.13
- Schedule of findings and questioned costs 10.63
- Summary schedule of prior audit findings 10.63–.64, 13.45, 15.34,
  .... 20.62–.63, 23.46–.50
- Uniform Guidance for federal awards, impact of 15.53
- Vendor compliance 12.15

AUDITOR RESPONSIBILITIES
- Abuse considerations 3.07, 5.18, 15.18
- Auditor's assumption of management responsibilities 2.20
- Cognizant agency for audit's relationship to 15.43
- Communication by. *See* communication
- Competence 2.06, 2.34–.42, 2.37
- Component auditors 4.77–.83, 16.57–.58
- Contractor compliance audit responsibilities 22.17–.18
- Corrective action plans 5.18, 13.47,
  .... 15.18, 23.47
- External auditor over internal auditors 3.13
- Follow-up 10.65–.66, 20.64
- Government auditors 2.16
- Independence 2.07–.30, 15.02
- Indirect cost proposal restriction 15.24
- Internal auditors 6.60–.69, 16.60–.69
- Internal control over compliance for federal awards 9.03–.04, 19.07–.08
- Internal control over financial reporting ... 9.04
- Issuing an opinion on schedule of expenditures of federal awards 7.32–.34
- Judgment. *See* professional judgment
- Major program determination role ... 8.01–.02

AUDITOR RESPONSIBILITIES—continued
- Opinion. *See* opinion
- Other auditors, working with 23.31
- Program-specific audits 14.07–.12,
  .... 24.07–.15
- Prohibition on clusters of program changes 15.31
- Reports. *See* auditor's reports
- Selection 5.24, 15.24
- Single compliance audits 15.07–.08,
  .... Table 15-1 at 15.08, 16.05–.06,
  .... 20.14–.15
- Team discussion 16.37, 16.43
- Terms of engagement 16.08–.09
- Vendor compliance responsibilities 12.16–.17

AUDITOR'S REPORTS. *See also* **reporting**
- Compliance for each major program ... 13.06,
  .... 13.21–.28
- Dating 4.48, 13.16–.19, 13.28
- Direct and material compliance requirements 13.03, 13.06, 13.22,
  .... 13.26, 13.28, 23.03, 23.06,
  .... 23.21–.22, 23.26, 23.28
- Elements 5.21, 13.03, 13.06–.08,
  .... Table 13-1 at 13.08
- Examples .... Appendix at 4.88, 14.17
- Financial statements and supplementary schedule of expenditures 13.06,
  .... 13.09–.20
- Government Auditing Standards 4.48–.51,
  .... Appendix at 4.88
- Internal control over compliance for federal programs ...... 13.03, 13.06, Table 13-1 at
  .... 13.08, 13.21–.28
- Internal control over financial reporting 13.03, 13.06,
  .... Table 13-1 at 13.08
- Opinion on financial statements 4.47
- Other auditors 13.31
- Program-specific audits 14.09–.11, 14.17
- Reissuance 13.29–.30
- Schedule of expenditures of federal awards 5.21, 7.18, 13.11–.20, 13.28
- Schedule of findings and questioned costs .... 13.06, Table 13-1 at 13.08,
  .... 13.33–.43
- When audit does not encompass entirety of auditee's operations 13.32

B

BASIS OF ACCOUNTING
- Auditor's reports 13.09
- Federal award compliance audit 16.11, 16.22
- Reporting 23.09
- Schedule of expenditures of federal awards 7.10, 7.19, 7.20, 17.20,
  .... Table 17-1 at 17.20
- Special purpose framework 16.13

BIENNIAL AUDITS 5.19, 5.43, 16.16
BY-PRODUCT REPORTS 3.62

C

CASH MANAGEMENT, DEFINED 22.31
CASH MANAGEMENT TESTS 12.28
CASH TO ACCRUAL CONVERSIONS 2.18,
.... 2.30
CATALOG OF FEDERAL DOMESTIC
ASSISTANCE (CFDA)
- Auditees' access to information 7.03
- Clusters of programs 11.46
- Identification of federal
  awards 12.19, 16.11
- Program categories 5.10–.14
- Schedule of findings and questioned
  costs 13.40
- Unavailability of numbers 7.25, 17.21

CFDA. *See* Catalog of Federal Domestic
Assistance

CHANGES IN COMPLIANCE
REQUIREMENTS 10.21–.22

CHANGES TO TEXT FROM PREVIOUS
EDITION, SCHEDULE OF ..... Appendix B

CIRCULAR A-133, AUDITS OF STATES,
LOCAL GOVERNMENTS, AND
NON-PROFIT ORGANIZATIONS. *See also*
Compliance Supplement (OMB)
- Audit costs 5.24–.25
- Audit sampling 11.01–.137
- Audit threshold 5.08
- Auditee responsibilities 5.33–.39
- Auditor selection 5.24
- Cognizant agency for audit 5.42–.43
- Compliance audits 10.01–.79
- Determination of when award is
  expended ...... 5.26–.27, Table 7-1 at 7.19
- Entity to be audited 5.16
- Federal award types and payment
  methods 5.09–.15
- Federal awarding agency
  responsibilities 5.40
- Frequency of audits 5.19
- Generally 5.01–.02, 11.01
- Internal control over compliance 9.01–.60
- Major program determination 8.01–.41,
  .... 18.36–.38
- Non-U.S.-based entities 5.20
- Objectives .... 5.03–.07, Table 5-1 at 5.07
- Oversight agency for audit 5.44–.45
- Pass-through awards 12.01–.49
- Planning considerations 6.01–.78
- Program-specific audits 14.01–.17
- Relationship to other audit
  requirements 5.17–.18
- Reporting matters 13.01–.58,
  .... Appendix at 14.17

CIRCULAR A-133, AUDITS OF STATES,
LOCAL GOVERNMENTS, AND NON-
PROFIT ORGANIZATIONS—continued
- Reprinted .... Supplement B
- Schedule of expenditures of federal
  awards 7.01–.35
- Subrecipient determinations 5.28
- Transition considerations related to the
  Uniform Guidance 5.49, 6.75–.78, 7.35,
  .... 8.39, 9.59–.60, 10.76–.79,
  .... 11.136–.137, 12.49, 13.56–.57,
  .... 15.52, 17.39, 20.76, 23.61
- Vendor determinations 5.28

CIRCULAR A-133 AUDIT
REPORTING 13.01–.58
- Audit findings 4.55–.62, 6.53–.55,
  .... 10.60–.62, 11.105
- Communicating other findings to
  management 13.44
- Data collection form 5.39, 13.04,
  .... 13.48–.50, 14.14, 14.16
- Federal Funding Accountability and
  Transparency Act requirements 12.20
- Freedom of Information Act
  considerations 13.55
- Generally ...... 13.01–.02, Appendix at 14.17
- Illustrative .... 13.54, Appendix at 13.57,
  .... Appendix at 14.17
- Materiality 6.53–.55
- Pass-through entities 12.37–.40
- Program-specific audits 14.06–.16
- Report on compliance and internal control over
  compliance applicable to each major
  program 13.21–.28
- Report submission deadlines 6.23
- Reporting package 5.22, 5.38–.39,
  .... 13.05, 13.48–.50, 14.13–.16
- State and local governments 7.23–.24
- Subrecipient submissions 12.48, 13.52
- Subrecipients 12.39
- Summary schedule of prior audit
  findings 13.45–.47
- Transition considerations related to the
  Uniform Guidance 5.49, 6.75–.78, 7.35,
  .... 8.39, 9.59–.60, 10.76–.79,
  .... 11.136–.137, 12.49, 13.56–.57

CLOSING CONFERENCES 3.69–.70

CLUSTERS OF PROGRAMS
- Audit sampling 11.46–.48, 21.46–.48
- Compliance requirements specific to ... 20.26
- Defined 15.31
- Designation, state and local
  governments 12.43, 22.45
- Direct and material compliance
  requirements 20.26
- Major program determination 5.31
- Material weakness in internal control over
  compliance 9.54, 19.57
- Schedule of expenditures of federal
  awards 17.21

Subject Index

CLUSTERS OF PROGRAMS—continued
- Special programs 10.26
- By state governments 22.45
- Tests of controls 19.57

COFAR. *See* **Council on Financial Assistance Reform**

COGNIZANT AGENCY FOR AUDIT
- Audit reviews 6.72–.73, 16.72–.73
- Circular A-133 .... 5.42–.43
- Communications with cognizant or oversight agency 6.70, 16.70
- Defined 15.42–.43
- Responsibilities 15.43

COMMINGLED ASSISTANCE **7.27, 17.29**

COMMITTEE OF SPONSORING ORGANIZATIONS OF THE TREADWAY COMMISSION (COSO) **19.05**

COMMUNICATION
- Audit findings 13.44, 23.45
- Auditor responsibilities 15.18
- Cognizant agencies 6.70, 16.70
- Compliance documentation 10.05
- Data collection form from auditee ..... 15.39, ... 23.51–.55
- Fraud 3.42, 4.26–.29, 4.72–.73
- Internal control matters ...... 3.66, 4.14–.21, ... 19.47, 19.56, 21.113, 23.35
- Legal and regulatory compliance .... 3.03, ... 3.46–.47, 3.49, 4.32
- With management. *See* management, communication with
- Noncompliance 4.72–.73, 5.18, 10.60
- With other entities in financial statement audits 3.15
- Oversight agencies 6.70, 16.70
- Terms of engagement .... 1.15, 3.04–.07, ... 6.08–.09, 16.08–.09, ... 20.29–.32, 22.37
- Written. *See* written communication

COMMUNICATION AND INFORMATION SYSTEMS ...... **3.27, 9.07, 9.15, 19.10,** **19.18**

COMPENSATING CONTROLS **9.49, 19.52**

COMPETENCE **2.06, 2.34–.42**

COMPLIANCE AUDITS. *See also* **single audit** **10.01–.79, 20.01–.78**
- Abuse consideration 10.45, 20.44
- Audit findings. *See* audit findings
- Audit planning ..... 6.03–.07, 6.25–.27, 6.56, ... 10.29–.32
- Audit risk of noncompliance .... 6.28–.49, ... 10.07–.09, 20.07–.09
- Auditee responsibilities .... 10.04–.06, ... 20.04–.05
- Auditor responsibilities 20.14–.15
- Basis for 16.22
- Compliance Supplement 15.48–.49
- Defining entity to be audited 15.16

COMPLIANCE AUDITS—continued
- Direct and material compliance requirements .... 6.25–.27, 10.17–.28, ... 16.22–.24, 20.17–.28
- Documentation. *See* documentation
- Engagement planning .... 10.29–.32, ... 20.29–.32
- Follow-up procedures .... 10.63–.69, ... 20.62–.68
- For-profit entities 15.20
- Foreign entities 15.20
- Frequency of audits 15.19
- Generally .... 5.03, 5.06–.07, 10.01, ... 15.01–.03
- Government Auditing Standards ... 5.18, 6.03
- Group audits 6.57–.59, 16.57–.59
- Internal control over compliance 17.14–.16, 20.33
- Internal control over compliance for federal programs 10.33, 13.21–.28
- Issuing opinion on schedule of expenditures of federal awards during 23.20
- Major programs for testing identification 10.16, 20.16
- Management representations ..... 10.72–.74, ... 20.71–.73
- Materiality considerations .... 6.50–.55, ... 10.10–.13, 10.54–.55, 20.10–.13
- Noncompliance evaluation .... 10.49–.59, ... 20.48–.61
- Objectives .... 10.02–.03, 15.04, 17.13, ... 20.02–.03, 20.41
- Procedures 10.14–.69, 20.14–.68
- Professional judgment 10.06, 20.06
- Program-specific audits .... 14.07, 15.01, ... 15.46, 20.01
- Quality control reviews 10.71
- Reporting .... 10.60–.62, 13.21–.28, ... Table 13-2 at 13.35, 23.03, ... 23.26, 23.28
- Sampling 21.01–.137
- Sampling in 11.01–.137
- State and local governments 20.74
- Subrecipient monitoring 12.26
- Subsequent events 10.46–.48, 20.45–.47
- Terms of engagement 6.09
- Testing procedures 20.34–.43
- Transition considerations related to the Uniform Guidance ... 10.76–.79, 15.50–.57, ... 20.75–.78
- Types of compliance requirements 10.19–.20, 20.19–.20
- Uniform Guidance relationship to other audit requirements 15.17–.18

COMPLIANCE EXCEPTIONS ...... **11.50–.51,** ..... **11.100–.105, 11.116–.127, 15.54,** ..... **19.10–.15, 21.50–.51, 21.82–.83,** **21.116–.122**

COMPLIANCE OPINION .... **10.51–.54,** .... **10.56–.57, 13.23, 20.03,** **20.50–.53, 20.56**

COMPLIANCE REQUIREMENTS, DEFINED.
See also **direct and material compliance requirements** 13.03, 15.04

COMPLIANCE SUPPLEMENT (OMB)
- Audit findings 12.38
- Audit objectives 10.42, 11.32, 20.41
- Audit procedures 10.43
- Audit sampling .... 11.27, 11.32, 11.46, ... 11.137
- Auditor reports 13.56
- Clusters of programs 11.46, 15.31
- Compliance audits .... 10.17–.28, 10.42–.43, ... 10.61, 10.77–.79
- As compliance requirement resource 16.23–.24
- Compliance requirements ... 6.27, 10.17–.28
- Exceptions to Uniform Guidance regulations 16.78
- Federal awarding agencies 5.40, 15.40
- Federal program risk 8.37
- Generally 5.01, 5.47–.48
- High-risk major program determination 18.31
- Internal control guidance 19.21, 19.63
- Internal control over compliance for federal programs 9.12, 9.28
- Internal control section, removal and update 9.18
- Loan and loan guarantees 8.08, 17.34
- Low-risk auditee criteria 8.26–.27
- Noncompliance findings that can't be quantified 10.61
- Overview of contents 20.17–.28
- Pass-through awards 12.49
- Program-specific audits .... 14.04, 15.46, ... 24.04
- Purpose 15.48
- Reporting findings 10.60
- Requirements for update and content ... 15.49
- Significant deficiencies and material weaknesses 9.43
- Subrecipient monitoring ... 12.06, 12.27–.36, ... 22.30–.31
- Transition considerations related to the Uniform Guidance 20.76–.77, 23.65
- Types of compliance requirements ... 19.15, ... 20.19–.20, 20.76

COMPLIANCE TESTING. *See* **tests of compliance**

COMPONENT AUDITORS .... 4.77–.83, ... 16.57–.58

COMPUTER ASSISTED AUDITING TECHNIQUES 11.25, 21.25

COMPUTER PROCESSING 8.33

CONFIDENCE LEVEL .... 11.67, 21.67, ... 21.76–.81

CONFIDENTIAL AND SENSITIVE INFORMATION 4.29, 4.68–.71

CONSOLIDATED FINANCIAL STATEMENTS 4.74, 13.10, 23.10

CONTINGENT LIABILITY 3.51–.52

CONTINUING COMPLIANCE REQUIREMENTS 7.30, 17.34

CONTINUING PROFESSIONAL EDUCATION (CPE) 2.38–.42

CONTRACT, DEFINED 22.02, 22.51

CONTRACTORS. *See also* **vendors**
- Compliance considerations 22.15–.18
- Defined 22.02, 22.51
- Pass-through award relationships 22.06
- Status determinations ..... 15.28, 22.10–.11, ... 22.22
- Status of disbursements to 22.05

CONTRACTS AND GRANT AGREEMENTS
- Compliance audits 10.03, 20.01
- Compliance opinions 10.52
- Compliance requirements .... 10.22–.24, ... 10.28, 20.22
- Management representations ... 10.73, 20.72
- Noncompliance with provisions ..... 4.35–.38, ... 4.40–.45, 4.55–.62, 10.60, 20.59
- Pass-through entity subrecipient monitoring 12.29
- Reporting 10.60, 13.23, 20.59, 23.20

CONTROL ACTIVITIES 9.07, 19.10

CONTROL DEVIATIONS .... 11.50–.51, ... 11.100–.113, 19.53, 19.10–.13, ... 21.50–.51

CONTROL ENVIRONMENT .... 3.27, 9.07, ... 19.10

CONTROL RISK OF NONCOMPLIANCE
- Assessing 19.24–.25
- Audit planning 6.31, 6.36
- Audit sampling 11.71, 11.79
- Defined 16.28, 19.24
- Evaluating test results 19.37–.43
- Internal control identification 19.15–.20
- Internal controls 9.03, 9.21–.27, 9.35
- Low assessed level of .... 9.23–.27, 9.35, ... 19.11, 19.15, 19.24–.26, 19.28, 19.38
- Pass-through award auditing 22.25
- Performing risk assessment procedures 16.34, 16.38
- Sampling .... 21.67, 21.71, 21.79, ... 21.111–.114
- Tests of controls .... 9.21–.26, 16.33, 19.07, ... 19.24–.32

CONTROL TESTS. *See* **tests of controls**

CORRECTIVE ACTION
- Auditee responsibilities .... 5.35, 5.37, 10.63, ... 10.68, 13.47, 14.06, 15.37, 24.06
- Auditor responsibilities .... 5.18, 13.47, ... 15.18, 23.47
- Cognizant agency contact with audit firm for 16.73

Subject Index

CORRECTIVE ACTION—continued
- Compliance audits 10.68
- Desk or on-site reviews 6.73
- Exit conferences 3.69
- Federal program risk 8.34
- Follow-up procedures 20.67
- Government Auditing Standards reporting 4.63–.66
- Plan summary 23.46, 23.50
- Program-specific audits 14.06, 24.06
- Reporting 4.63–.66
- Schedule of findings and questioned costs 23.37
- Summary schedule of prior audit findings 20.63

COSO. *See* **Committee of Sponsoring Organizations of the Treadway Commission**

COSO INTEGRATED FRAMEWORK 19.62

COST ALLOCATION PLAN 16.74

COST-REIMBURSEMENT CONTRACTS ..... 5.09, 5.13–.14, 15.10, ... 15.27

COSTS. *See also* **questioned costs**
- Audit costs ..... 5.24–.25, 6.74, 12.33, ... 15.24–.25, 22.35
- Indirect costs ..... 5.24, 6.74, 15.24, 16.74, ... 22.55

COUNCIL ON FINANCIAL ASSISTANCE REFORM (COFAR) 15.53

CPE. *See* **continuing professional education**

D

DATA COLLECTION FORM
- Auditee responsibilities ..... 15.39, ... 23.51–.55
- Circular A-133 audit reporting ..... 5.39, 13.04, ... 13.48–.50, 14.14, 14.16
- Program-specific audits 24.13, 24.15
- Requirement for 23.04–.05
- Transition considerations related to the Uniform Guidance 23.64

DATING OF REPORTS
- Auditor's reports 13.16–.19, 13.28
- Compliance and internal control over compliance for each major program 23.28
- Reissuance of compliance report 23.30
- Schedule of expenditures of federal awards 23.16–.19

DEFICIENCIES IN INTERNAL CONTROL OVER COMPLIANCE. *See also* **significant deficiency in internal control over compliance**
- Assessing magnitude 19.50, 21.113
- For federal programs ..... Appendix at 3.71, ... 9.41, 11.113

DEFICIENCIES IN INTERNAL CONTROL OVER COMPLIANCE—continued
- Reporting on 21.100
- Testing of controls 19.44–.57

DESIRED LEVEL OF ASSURANCE 11.76–.81, 21.76–.81

DESK REVIEWS 6.72–.73, 16.72–.73

DETECTION RISK OF NONCOMPLIANCE ..... 6.32, 6.37, ... 16.29, 16.34

DEVIATION RATES ..... 11.67–.69, 11.107, ... 21.67–.69, 21.107

DEVIATIONS IN TESTS OF CONTROLS ..... 19.53, 19.10–.13, ... 21.50–.51

DIRECT AND MATERIAL COMPLIANCE REQUIREMENTS. *See also* **program-specific audits** ..... 9.12–.54, ... 19.15–.57
- Additional terms and conditions of federal awards 20.23–.24
- Auditor's reports ..... 13.03, 13.06, 13.22, ... 13.26, 13.28, 23.03, 23.06, ... 23.21–.22, 23.26, 23.28
- Compliance opinion 10.53, 20.52
- Compliance Supplement 20.18, 20.27
- Identification 6.22–.24, 6.25–.27
- Keeping abreast of changes 20.21–.22
- By major program 10.17–.28, 20.17–.28
- Multiple organizational units 9.19, 19.22
- Risk assessment procedures 16.30, 20.33
- Subrecipient considerations 9.20, 19.23
- Test of operating effectiveness of internal control over 9.21–.54, 19.24–.57
- Testing during audit 20.34–.43
- Types of compliance requirements 20.19–.20
- Understanding 9.12–.20, 19.15–.21

DIRECT LOANS 5.13, 15.14

DIRECT PAYMENTS 5.13, 15.14

DISBURSEMENT OF FUNDS TO SUBRECIPIENTS 12.04, 22.04

DISCLAIMER OF OPINION
- Circular A-133 audit reporting ..... 13.03, ... Table 13-1 at 13.08, 13.23–.25
- Government Auditing Standards reporting 4.03
- Illustrative reports ..... Table 23-1 at 23.08
- Program-specific audits 14.09
- Reporting requirement 23.03, 24.09
- Scope of audit limitations ..... 23.15, ... 23.23–.25

DISCLOSURE OF CONFIDENTIAL AND SENSITIVE INFORMATION 4.68–.71

DISPUTES, AUDIT FINDINGS 10.69, 20.68

DISTRIBUTION OF REPORTS, UNDER GOVERNMENT AUDITING STANDARDS 4.67

©2015, AICPA

AAG-GAS DIS

DOCUMENTATION
- Access and retention 6.12, 16.54–.55
- Audit sampling .... 11.28, 11.131–.135, ... 21.28, 21.131–.135
- Compliance audits .... 5.18, 6.10, 6.12, ... 9.56, 10.05, 10.70–.71, ... 16.43–.44, 20.69–.70
- Financial statement audits 3.19–.22
- Of independence 2.27
- Internal control over compliance .... 9.55–.58, ... 19.58–.61
- Major program determination risk assessment 8.22–.23, 18.18
- Management nonaudit service skills 2.30
- Planning 6.10–.12, 16.53–.56
- Risk assessment 9.55
- Schedule of expenditures of federal awards 7.31, 17.33
- Terms of engagement 16.09
- Tests of controls 9.56, 19.59

DUAL PURPOSE SAMPLES .... 11.52–.57, ... 21.52–.57

DUAL PURPOSE TESTS 9.33, 19.36

E

EFFECTIVE DATE PROVISIONS 16.76–.78

ELIGIBILITY PROGRAM 11.27, 21.27

ELIGIBILITY TESTING 12.28, 22.31

EMPHASIS-OF-MATTER PARAGRAPHS 4.03

ENGAGEMENT, TERMS OF .... 1.15, ... 3.04–.07, 6.08–.09, 16.08–.09, ... 20.29–.32, 22.37

ENGAGEMENT LETTERS 3.07

ENTITY TO BE AUDITED .... 5.16, 6.18, ... 15.16, 16.15

ETHICAL PRINCIPLES, GOVERNMENT AUDITING STANDARDS 2.02–.05

EXCEPTION RATES ... 11.82–.85, 21.82–.85

EXCEPTIONS, COMPLIANCE .... 15.54, ... 19.10–.15, 21.50–.51, 21.82–.83, ... 21.116–.122

EXIT CONFERENCES 3.69–.70

EXPECTED DEVIATION RATE ..... 11.68–.69, ... 21.68–.69

EXPECTED POPULATION EXCEPTION RATE 11.84, 21.84–.85

EXPENDITURES
- Determination of federal awards .... 5.26–.27, ... 5.35, 15.26–.27
- Pass-through awards .... 7.26–.27, 12.04, ... 12.37, 12.46, 12.49, 17.29–.30, ... 22.39, 22.48
- Schedule of, for federal awards. *See* schedule of expenditures of federal awards

EXTERNAL PEER REVIEW 2.46–.50

F

FAC. *See* **Federal Audit Clearinghouse**

FAIL, EXTERNAL PEER REVIEW REPORT 2.47

FEDERAL ACQUISITION REGULATIONS .... 5.14, 5.25, 5.38, ... 10.06, 15.10, 20.06

FEDERAL AGENCIES
- Additional audit requirements 5.17
- Additional major program audit requests 8.25, 18.20
- Audit guides 1.09, 10.27
- Circular A-133 audit responsibilities 5.40
- Federal award identification .... 7.03, ... 17.03–.04
- List by program in schedule of expenditures of federal awards 17.21
- Major program determination 5.32, 15.32
- Management decision 20.58
- Noncompliance evaluation and reporting 20.57–.58
- Oversight and federal program risk 8.36–.37
- Reporting package distribution .... 13.53–.54, ... 23.56–.57
- Type A program not considered low risk at request of 18.13
- Uniform Guidance requirements 15.40
- Updates to Compliance Supplement 20.22

FEDERAL AUDIT CLEARINGHOUSE (FAC)
- Circular A-133 reporting .... 5.22, ... 13.04, 13.53–.54
- Data collection form 14.14, 23.64
- Program-specific audit report submission 24.13, 24.15
- Responsibilities 23.56–.58, 23.63
- Reviewing for recent audits 15.17
- Submission of reporting package and data collection form to 23.04–.05, 23.55
- Subrecipients 8.27

FEDERAL AWARDS
- Auditee responsibility to report 16.11
- Compliance audits of major programs. *See* compliance audits
- Defined ... 5.09, 12.02, 12.05, 15.10, 22.02
- Determining when expended .... 7.29, ... Table 7-2 at 7.29
- Expenditure determination .... 5.26–.27, 5.35, ... 15.26–.27
- Internal control in meeting objectives of 19.03
- Low-risk type A federal award programs 8.03, 8.11–.14
- Major programs. *See* major programs
- Noncash awards 7.28–.31, 8.03
- Pass-through. *See* pass-through awards

Subject Index 739

FEDERAL AWARDS—continued
- Payment methods 5.15, 15.15
- Schedule of expenditures. *See* Schedule of Expenditures of Federal Awards
- Types 5.10–.14
- Types and classifications of assistance 15.10–.14

FEDERAL COST-REIMBURSEMENT CONTRACTS **5.09, 5.14**

FEDERAL FINANCIAL ASSISTANCE **5.09, 5.10–.13, 15.10–.14**

FEDERAL FUNDING ACCOUNTABILITY AND TRANSPARENCY ACT (2006) (FFATA) **12.20**

FEDERAL PASS-THROUGH AWARDS. *See* pass-through awards

FFATA. *See* Federal Funding Accountability and Transparency Act

FFATA SUBAWARD REPORTING SYSTEM (FSRS) **12.20**

FINANCIAL STATEMENTS
- Auditor preparation 2.18, 2.30
- Audits of. *See* financial statements, audits of
- Basis of accounting 13.09
- Circular A-133 auditee responsibilities ... 5.33
- Consolidated 23.10
- Material noncompliance risk effect 20.13
- Noncompliance evaluation and reporting 20.54
- Program-specific audits 14.06, 24.10–.11
- Schedule of expenditures of federal awards .... 13.17–.18, 15.06, 23.11, ... 23.15, 23.17–.18
- Supplementary information 13.13

FINANCIAL STATEMENTS, AUDITS OF
- Abuse considerations 3.53–.56
- Audit documentation 3.19–.22
- Audit evidence evaluation 3.32–.35
- Audit findings reporting requirements 23.36, 23.39
- Audit planning ..... 3.08–.15, 6.14–.17, 6.56, ... 16.10–.13
- Audit procedures 3.32–.35
- Audit sampling 11.56–.57
- Auditee responsibilities .... 15.33, 15.36, ... 16.10
- Auditor competence 2.37
- Communication about internal control matters identified in audit 3.66
- Communication with other entities 3.15
- Communication with those charged with governance 3.61–.65
- Entity to be audited definition 13.10
- Exit conferences 3.69–.70
- Federal awards audit 15.05–.06
- Findings 3.60
- Fraud considerations 3.36–.42, 3.56
- GAAS requirements 3.01, 4.01

FINANCIAL STATEMENTS, AUDITS OF—continued
- Generally 3.01–.03
- Government Auditing Standards .... 3.01–.71, ... 4.02–.06, 4.46–.52
- Group audits 3.16, 16.57–.59
- Laws and regulations 3.43–.52
- Materiality 3.17–.18, 6.51, 16.48–.49
- Misstatement identification 3.59
- Objectives 4.02, 15.04
- Program-specific audits 14.07
- Reporting 4.02–.06, 4.46–.52
- Single audits 5.03–.05
- Terms of engagement 3.04–.07
- Understanding entity and its environment 16.30–.32
- Understanding entity and its environment and assessing risk of material misstatement 3.23–.31
- Written representations 3.67–.68

FINDINGS, AUDIT. *See* audit findings

FIRST-YEAR AUDIT **8.24, 18.38**

FISCAL YEAR AUDIT PERIODS ...**6.19, 16.16**

FOLLOW-UP PROCEDURES **15.23**
- Audit planning 6.13
- Auditee responsibilities 20.62–.63
- Auditor responsibilities 20.64
- Circular A-133 requirements 5.23
- Compliance audits 10.63–.69, 20.62–.68
- Corrective action plan 20.67
- Disputes or unresolved findings 20.68
- Findings reported under GAS 20.66
- Prior audit findings 10.64–.67, 13.46–.47
- Procedures 20.65
- Program-specific audits 14.07
- Reporting audit findings 23.38, 23.49
- Uniform Guidance requirements .... 15.23, ... 16.56

FOR-PROFIT ENTITIES .... **15.20, 22.30, ... 22.43**

FOR-PROFIT SUBRECIPIENTS, PASS-THROUGH AWARDS **12.41**

FOREIGN ENTITIES **15.20**

FOREIGN PUBLIC ENTITIES AND FOREIGN ORGANIZATIONS **22.44**

FORMULA GRANTS **5.13, 15.14**

FRAUD
- Abuse having potential for 3.53–.55
- Communication 3.42, 4.26–.29, 4.72–.73
- Financial statement audit considerations 3.36–.42, 3.56
- Government Auditing Standards .... 4.07, ... 4.24–.30, Exhibit 4-1 at 4.39, ... 4.39–.45, 4.55–.62
- Management, communication with 3.42, 4.26–.29, 4.72–.73
- Management inquiry about fraud risk ... 16.43

FRAUD—continued
- Material misstatement due to ....3.23–.24, ... 3.36–.42
- Material noncompliance due to ....6.39, ... 6.44–.49, Table 6-1 at 6.49, ... 10.50, 16.41–.46, Table 16-1 at 16.46, 20.49
- Reporting .... 4.07, 4.24–.30, ... Exhibit 4-1 at 4.39, 4.39–.45, 23.38
- Risk factors .... Table 16-1 at 16.46
- Those charged with governance, communication with 3.42, 4.27–.29
- Transition considerations related to the Uniform Guidance 23.61

FREEDOM OF INFORMATION ACT 4.84–.85, 6.11, 13.55, 23.59

FREQUENCY, OF CIRCULAR A-133 AUDITS 5.19

FREQUENTLY ASKED QUESTIONS (FAQS), UNIFORM GUIDANCE 15.46

FSRS. *See* FFATA Subaward Reporting System

FURTHER AUDIT PROCEDURES ....9.10, ... 10.08–.09, 20.08–.09

G

GAAP. *See* generally accepted accounting principles

GAAS. *See* generally accepted auditing standards

GAO. *See* Government Accountability Office

GAS. *See* Government Auditing Standards

GENERALLY ACCEPTED ACCOUNTING PRINCIPLES (GAAP) .... 4.74, 6.17, ... 13.02, 13.10, 16.13, 16.15, ... 23.09–.10

GENERALLY ACCEPTED AUDITING STANDARDS (GAAS)
- Audit planning 6.01
- Auditor's responsibility to ascertain audit and reporting requirements 20.02–.03
- Circular A-133 audits 5.04
- Documentation 16.53, 18.18, 19.60
- Federal award audit .... 15.05, 15.07, 16.01, ... 16.03, 16.07
- Financial statement audits 3.01, 4.01
- Financial statements 4.02–.03, 13.09–.10
- Fraud considerations 3.36
- Government Auditing Standards and 1.04
- Group audit considerations 16.59
- Internal control components 19.10
- Materiality consideration in audit 16.48
- Program-specific audits 14.04, 24.09
- Reporting requirements .... 4.06, 13.02, ... Table 13-1 at 13.08, 23.02, 23.07, ... 23.08, 23.36, 24.09, ... Table 23-1 at 23.08

GENERALLY ACCEPTED AUDITING STANDARDS (GAAS)—continued
- Schedule of findings and questioned costs 13.36
- State and local compliance requirements 16.71
- Supplementary schedule of expenditures of federal awards 13.11–.20
- Terms of engagement 16.09
- Use of must compared to should 15.10
- Written representations 3.67

GOVERNMENT ACCOUNTABILITY OFFICE (GAO) 1.01, 1.05, 5.08, 15.09

GOVERNMENT ACCOUNTING STANDARDS BOARD (GASB) 10.55, 20.54

GOVERNMENT AUDIT REQUIREMENT, DEFINED 6.04, 16.04

GOVERNMENT AUDITING STANDARDS (GAS)
- Abuse considerations .... 3.53–.56, ... Exhibit 3-1 at 3.58, 10.45, 13.39, 20.44
- Additional requirements 1.14–.15
- Applicability 1.12–.13
- Audit evidence evaluation 3.32–.35
- Audit findings ....3.60, 4.55–.62, 10.37, ... 20.66
- Audit planning ....2.01–.51, 3.08–.15, ... 6.01–.02
- Audit procedures 3.32–.35
- Circular A-133 audits 5.04, 5.18
- Cognizant agency responsibilities 5.43
- Communication about internal control matters identified in audit 3.66
- Communication with those charged with governance 3.61–.65
- Competence 2.34–.42
- Compliance audits .... 10.01–.03, 20.02–.03, ... 20.66
- Conceptual framework for independence .... Exhibit at 2.51
- Corrective action plan 20.67
- Deficiencies in internal control Appendix at 3.71
- Documentation 3.19–.22, 16.53, 18.18
- Ethical principles 2.02–.05
- Exit conferences 3.69–.70
- External peer review 2.46–.50
- Federal program risk 8.34
- Financial statement audits ....3.01–.71, ... 4.02–.06, 4.46–.52
- Follow-up findings 20.66
- Fraud considerations ....3.36–.42, 3.56, ... 4.24–.30, Exhibit 4-1 at 4.39, 4.39–.45
- General standards 2.01, 2.06–.50
- Generally 1.01–.19
- Group audit considerations 16.59
- Guidance on GAGAS Requirements for Continuing Professional Education 2.40
- Independence 2.07–.30
- Insufficient subrecipient monitoring 22.38
- Internal control over compliance for federal programs 9.01, 9.57

Subject Index

GOVERNMENT AUDITING STANDARDS (GAS)—continued
- Laws and regulations 3.43–.52
- Materiality 3.17–.18, 16.48
- Misstatement identification 3.59
- Peer review report for auditor services 15.24
- Professional judgment 2.31–.32
- Program-specific audits .... 14.04, 15.46, ... 24.04, 24.09
- Quality control and assurance 2.43–.45
- Reporting. *See* Government Auditing Standards reporting
- Schedule of expenditures of federal awards 13.11–.20
- Schedule of findings and questioned costs .... 13.34, 13.38, ... 13.40–.41
- Single Audit Act 5.02, 15.02
- State and local compliance requirements 16.71
- Summary schedule of prior audit findings 20.63
- Terminology 1.11, 1.16–.19
- Terms of engagement .... 1.15, 3.04–.07, ... 6.09, 16.09
- Understanding entity and its environment and assessing risks of material misstatement 3.23–.31
- Uniform Guidance audit compliance with .... 15.18, 16.01, 16.03, ... 16.07
- Written representations 3.67–.68

GOVERNMENT AUDITING STANDARDS REPORTING 4.01–.88
- Abuse considerations 4.07
- Assurance to regulators and oversight agencies 4.86–.87
- Audit findings 4.55–.62, 10.67
- Audit follow-up for findings reported under 10.67
- Audited financial statements .... 4.02–.06, ... 4.46–.52
- Auditor's reports examples .... Appendix at 4.88
- Confidential and sensitive information ... 4.29, ... 4.68–.71
- Corrective actions 4.63–.66
- Distribution 4.67
- Fraud considerations .... 4.07, 4.24–.30, ... Exhibit 4-1 at 4.39, 4.39–.45
- Freedom of Information Act considerations 4.84–.85
- GAAS 4.06, 13.02, 13.09–.10
- Generally 4.01–.04
- Group audits 4.77–.83
- Internal control over compliance, for federal programs .... 9.01, 9.57, Table 13-1 .... at 13.08
- Internal control over compliance, material weakness in 4.13–.21, 4.54

GOVERNMENT AUDITING STANDARDS REPORTING—continued
- Internal control over compliance, significant deficiency in .... 4.07, 4.13–.21, ... Table 4-2 at 4.22, 4.54
- Internal control over financial reporting ...... Table 4-1 at 4.12, 4.13–.23, ... Table 4-2 at 4.22
- Internal control over financial reporting and on compliance .... 4.07–.12, Table 4-1 at 4.12, ... 4.13, 4.17, 4.21, 4.23, 4.25, 4.52–.54, ... 4.58, 4.74, 4.76, 4.80
- Internal control over financial reporting and on compliance and other matters .... 4.11, ... Table 4-1 at 4.12, 4.13, 4.17, 4.21, 4.23, ... 4.25, 4.52–.54, 4.58, 4.74, 4.76, 4.80
- Noncompliance .... 4.24, 4.31–.45, ... Exhibit 4-1 at 4.39, 4.55–.62, ... Table 4-3 at 4.82, 4.83
- Portions of entity not audited in accordance with 4.74–.76
- Program-specific audits 14.09–.11
- Requirements ......23.02, 23.35–.37, 23.42, ... 23.61–.62, 24.09–.11
- Tests of controls 4.08
- Views of responsible officials 4.63–.66
- Written communication 4.72–.73

GOVERNMENT AUDITORS **2.16**

GOVERNMENT OWNED, CONTRACTOR OPERATED FACILITY (GOCOS) **15.10**

GOVERNMENT-WIDE EVALUATION OF SINGLE AUDIT QUALITY **15.47**

GOVERNMENTAL AUDIT REQUIREMENT, DEFINED **16.04**

GRANTS. *See* **contracts and grant agreements**

GREEN BOOK. *See* **Standards for Internal Control in the Federal Government**

GROUP AUDITS .... **3.16, 4.77–.83,** **6.57–.59, 13.31, 16.57–.59**

GUARANTEED/INSURED LOANS **15.14**

H

HAPHAZARD SELECTION .... **11.95–.96,** **21.93, 21.95–.96**

HIGH-RISK TYPE B MAJOR PROGRAMS .**8.03, 8.15–.20, 18.14–.15,** **18.23–.32, 18.36–.37**

HOUSING AND URBAN DEVELOPMENT (HUD), U.S. DEPARTMENT OF **7.30, 17.34**

I

IN-RELATION-TO OPINION ...**7.05–.11, 7.32,** ...... **13.15–.16, 13.19–.20, 17.06–.12,** **17.19, 17.36, 23.19**

IN-RELATION-TO REPORTING .... **13.12,** **23.11–.13**

INCENTIVES OR PRESSURES, FRAUD RISK FACTORS .... Table 16-1 at 16.46

INCLUSION OPTION, COMPONENT AUDITOR REFERENCES .... 4.78–.82, ... Table 4-3 at 4.82

INDEPENDENCE 2.07–.30
- AICPA compared to Government Auditing Standards 2.28–.30
- Conceptual framework .... 2.09, 2.12–.16, ... 2.29, Exhibit at 2.51
- Documentation of 2.27
- Generally 2.06–.11
- Nonaudit services 2.17–.26, 2.30
- Threats to 2.09–.11

INDEPENDENT ACCOUNTING FIRMS, ENGAGEMENT OF 6.59, 16.59

INDIAN TRIBE .... 15.01, 15.19, 15.26, ... 23.53, 23.63

INDIRECT COSTS
- Proposals .... 5.24, 6.74, 15.24, ... 16.74
- Rates for pass-through entity 22.55

INDIVIDUALLY IMPORTANT ITEMS IN COMPLIANCE TESTING ...... 11.21–.28, ... 21.21–.28

INFORMATION AND COMMUNICATION SYSTEMS .... 3.27, 9.07, 9.15, ... 19.10, 19.18

INFORMATION TECHNOLOGY (IT) .... 9.15, ... 19.18

INHERENT RISK OF NONCOMPLIANCE
- Audit planning 6.31, 6.36
- Audit sampling .... 11.65–.66, 11.71, ... 11.80–.81, 21.71
- Defined 16.28
- Factors suggesting 21.65
- Major program determination 8.38, 18.32
- Risk assessment procedures .... 16.34, ... 16.38
- Risk criteria for major program determination 18.32
- Tests 16.33

INITIAL-YEAR AUDITS .... 6.21–.22, ... 16.18–.19

INQUIRY, IN COMPLIANCE AUDITS ... 11.13, ... 21.13

INSTRUMENTS SETTING FORTH TERMS AND CONDITIONS FOR FEDERAL AWARD 15.10

INSURANCE 15.14

INTENTIONAL DEVIATIONS OR EXCEPTIONS 11.101, 21.101

INTERNAL AUDIT FUNCTION 16.60–.69

INTERNAL AUDITORS 6.60–.69

INTERNAL CONTROL
- Communication about 3.66
- Defined 19.02
- Government Auditing Standards 4.55–.62
- Over compliance. *See* internal control over compliance
- Over compliance for federal programs. *See* internal control over compliance for federal programs
- Over financial reporting. *See* internal control over financial reporting
- Over financial reporting and on compliance and other matters, GAS .... 4.11, Table 4-1 ..... at 4.12, 4.13, 4.17, 4.21, 4.23, 4.25, ... 4.52–.54, 4.58, 4.74, 4.76, 4.80
- Pass-through entity subrecipient monitoring 12.29
- Understanding 3.25–.28

INTERNAL CONTROL OVER COMPLIANCE 19.01–.65
- Audit sampling. *See* audit sampling
- Auditee responsibilities 15.36, 19.04–.06
- Auditor responsibilities 19.07–.08
- Auditor's examination for each major program 19.11–.14
- Compliance audits 20.33
- Components of control 19.10, 19.16
- Definitions 19.02–.03, 19.09
- Direct and material compliance requirements 19.15–.57
- Documentation 19.58–.61
- Efficient approach to testing 16.14
- For federal programs 9.01–.60
- Generally 19.01
- Material weakness 4.13–.21, 4.54
- Multiple organizational units 19.22
- Objectives of control 19.09
- Pass-through awards 19.23, 22.25
- Report on. *See* internal control over financial reporting and on compliance, report on
- Risk assessment procedures ..... 16.30–.32, ... 16.33
- Risk criteria for major program determination 18.25–.27
- Schedule of expenditures of federal awards 17.14–.16
- Significant deficiency in. *See* significant deficiency in internal control over compliance
- Test of operating effectiveness 19.24–.57
- Transition considerations related to the Uniform Guidance 19.62–.65
- Uniform Guidance audits .... Table 15-1 at 15.08

INTERNAL CONTROL OVER COMPLIANCE FOR FEDERAL PROGRAMS 9.01–.60
- Audit approach 6.56
- Auditee responsibilities 5.35, 9.02
- Auditor responsibilities 9.03–.04
- Auditor's consideration for each major program 9.08–.11

Subject Index

INTERNAL CONTROL OVER COMPLIANCE FOR FEDERAL PROGRAMS—continued
- Auditor's reports .... 13.03, 13.06, ... Table 13-1 at 13.08, 13.21–.28
- Circular A-133 audits .... 5.06–.07, ... Table 5-1 at 5.07
- Compliance audits 10.33, 13.21–.28
- Compliance testing results relationship 11.127
- Deficiency in. *See also* significant deficiency in internal control over compliance .... Appendix at 3.71, 9.41, ... 11.113
- Defined 9.05–.06
- Direct and material compliance requirements 9.12–.54
- Documentation 9.55–.58
- Elements 9.07
- Federal program risk 8.30–.31
- Generally 9.01
- Government Auditing Standards ... 9.01, 9.57, ... Table 13-1 at 13.08
- By major program 13.21–.28
- Objectives 9.06
- Pass-through awards 12.24
- Quality control reviews 9.33
- Reporting .... Table 13-1 at 13.08
- Risk assessment procedures 6.35
- Schedule of expenditures of federal awards 7.12–.15
- Test of operating effectiveness 9.21–.54
- Transition considerations related to the Uniform Guidance 9.59–.60
- Understanding of 9.12–.20, 9.27, 14.07

INTERNAL CONTROL OVER FINANCIAL REPORTING
- Auditee responsibilities 5.36, 15.36
- Auditor responsibilities .... 9.04, 19.01, ... 19.08
- Auditor's reports .... 13.03, 13.06, ... Table 13-1 at 13.08, 23.03, 23.06, ... Table 23-1 at 23.08
- Circular A-133 auditee responsibilities ... 5.36
- Deficiencies or material weaknesses ... 19.46
- Defined 9.06, 19.09
- Elements 9.07
- Government Auditing Standards ..... Table 4-1 at 4.12, 4.13–.23, ... Table 4-2 at 4.22
- Objectives 9.06, 19.09
- Report on. *See* internal control over financial reporting and on compliance, report on

INTERNAL CONTROL OVER FINANCIAL REPORTING AND ON COMPLIANCE, REPORT ON
- Audit findings 4.58
- Auditor's report reference 4.52
- Dating reports 23.28
- Elements 4.53–.54
- Fraud 4.30

INTERNAL CONTROL OVER FINANCIAL REPORTING AND ON COMPLIANCE, REPORT ON—continued
- Government Auditing Standards .... 4.07–.12, ... Table 4-1 at 4.12, 4.13, 4.17, 4.21, ... 4.23, 4.25, 4.52–.54, 4.58, 4.74, ... 4.76, 4.80
- Group audits 4.78–.82
- Material weakness in .... 4.13–.21, 4.54, ... 23.26, 23.34, 23.38
- Noncompliance with laws and regulations 4.34
- Opinion .... 15.21, 23.03, ... Table 23-1 at 23.08
- Separate reports 4.11

INTERNAL SPECIALISTS 2.41–.42

INTERNATIONAL AUDITING AND ASSURANCE STANDARDS BOARD 1.03

INVESTIGATIONS 4.42

IT. *See* information technology

J

JOINT VENTURES 6.59

JUDGMENT. *See* professional judgment

L

LAWS AND REGULATIONS, COMPLIANCE WITH .... 3.43–.52, 4.31–.34, ... 4.40–.45, 4.55–.62

LEGISLATIVE COMMITTEES 3.63, 3.65

LETTERS
- Engagement letters 3.07
- Management letters 4.72–.73, 23.45

LOANS AND LOAN GUARANTEES
- Effects on type A program determination .... 8.07–.09, ... Table 8-2 at 8.09
- Major program threshold 18.34
- Schedule of expenditures of federal awards 7.30, 17.21, 17.22
- Treatment of noncash awards 17.31–.32
- Type A major programs .... 8.07–.09, ... Table 8-2 at 8.09, 18.06–.08, ... Table 18-2 at 18.07
- Value of noncash awards .... 17.33–.34, ... Table 17-2 at 17.33

LOCAL GOVERNMENTS. *See* state and local governments

LOW ASSESSED LEVEL OF CONTROL RISK OF NONCOMPLIANCE ... 9.23–.27, 9.35, ... 19.11, 19.15, 19.24–.26, ... 19.28, 19.38

LOW-RISK AUDITEES .... 5.30, 8.21, ... 8.26–.27, 15.30, 18.21, ... 18.39

**LOW-RISK TYPE A FEDERAL AWARD
PROGRAMS** 8.03, 8.11–.14,
.... 18.09–.12, 18.36

M

**MAGNITUDE OF POTENTIAL
NONCOMPLIANCE** 19.50, 21.113

MAJOR PROGRAMS
- Audit planning 16.21
- Audit sampling 21.42–.43, 21.92
- Auditee responsibilities 16.21, 20.04–.05
- Defined 15.07
- Determination of 8.01–.41, 18.01–.39
- Determining auditee compliance 15.04
- Expenditure reporting, Uniform Guidance transition considerations 16.77
- Internal audit function 16.60
- Materiality 16.52, 19.46
- Pass-through entity requests for additional 18.20
- Reporting on internal control over compliance for each 13.21–.28, 23.21–.28
- Risk assessment procedures .... 16.30, ... 16.33–.34
- Subsequent events 20.45–.47
- Testing procedures 20.34–.43
- Transition considerations related to the Uniform Guidance .... 8.39, 16.77, ... 18.33–.39, 20.75–.78

**MAJOR PROGRAMS, DETERMINATION
OF** 8.01–.41, 18.01–.39
- Audit planning 6.24, 16.21
- Auditee's role 8.01, 18.01
- Auditor's role 8.01–.02, 18.01–.02, 18.19
- Cluster of programs 5.31
- Criteria 18.16
- Federal agency and pass-through entity requests 18.20
- Federal agency selection of additional programs 5.32
- Generally 8.01–.02, 18.01–.02
- Pass-through awards ...... 12.21–.22, 22.21, ... 22.23
- Percentage of coverage rule ... 18.17, 18.35, ... 18.38
- Risk-based approach. See risk-based approach, major program determination
- Single audit 15.29–.32, 20.16
- Type A and type B programs ...... 18.03–.08, ... Table 18-1 at 18.04, Table 18-2 at 18.07

MANAGEMENT
- Auditor's assumption of responsibilities 2.20
- Communication with. See management, communication with
- Compliance audit responsibilities ...... 17.08, ... 20.04–.05
- Inquiries of 3.24
- Nonaudit service skills documentation ... 2.30

MANAGEMENT—continued
- Override of controls risk 16.44
- Terms of engagement 16.08–.09, 22.37

MANAGEMENT, COMMUNICATION WITH
- Audit findings 13.44, 23.45
- Audit planning 16.35
- Compliance documentation 10.05
- Follow-up procedures 20.65
- Fraud 3.42, 4.26–.29, 4.72–.73
- Inquiry about fraud risk 16.43
- Internal control deficiencies 4.15–.21
- Internal control matters 23.35
- Legal and regulatory compliance .... 3.03, ... 3.46–.47, 3.49
- Noncompliance 4.72–.73
- Schedule of findings and questioned costs 23.45
- Terms of engagement .... 1.15, 3.04–.07, ... 6.08–.09, 16.08–.09

MANAGEMENT DECISION 10.59, 20.58

MANAGEMENT LETTERS ... 4.72–.73, 23.45

MANAGEMENT REPRESENTATIONS. See
written representations

**MATERIAL AND DIRECT COMPLIANCE
REQUIREMENTS.** See direct and material
compliance requirements

**MATERIAL INSTANCE OF NONCOMPLIANCE,
DEFINED** ... 10.12, 13.22, 20.12, 23.22

MATERIAL MISSTATEMENTS
- Assessing risks of. See risk assessment
- Due to fraud 3.23–.24, 3.36–.42
- Due to noncompliance with laws and regulations 3.43–.52
- Further audit procedures 3.32
- Schedule of expenditures of federal awards 7.11, 13.14, 17.12

MATERIAL NONCOMPLIANCE
- Audit risk of noncompliance 16.28
- Audit sampling considerations ..... 21.71–.81, ... Table 21-2 at 21.72
- Desired level of assurance 21.79–.80
- Detection of risk of material noncompliance 16.29
- Due to fraud .... 6.39, 6.44–.49, ... Table 6-1 at 6.49, 10.50, 16.41–.46, ... Table 16-1 at 16.46, 20.49
- Evaluating internal control tests 19.37–.38
- Financial statement effects ..... 10.13, 10.55, ... 20.13
- Internal audit function's capabilities 16.64–.67
- Reporting 10.50, 16.51, 23.22, 23.38
- Risk assessment .... 6.39–.49, 10.08–.09, ... 16.36–.46, Table 16-1 at 16.46, ... 19.12–.14
- Risk components 11.71
- Schedule of findings and questioned costs 13.38

Subject Index

MATERIAL WEAKNESS IN INTERNAL CONTROL OVER COMPLIANCE 9.41–.54, 19.44–.57
- Assessing severity of deficiencies leading to 19.47–.48
- Clusters of programs 9.54, 19.57
- Combination effect in assessing 19.51
- Compensating controls 9.49
- Compliance audits 9.43–.45
- Component auditor references 4.82–.83
- Conditions for 19.44, 19.54–.56
- Defined 9.42, 19.45
- Detecting ineffective control ...... 19.30–.32, ... 19.52–.54
- Deviations in operating effectiveness of controls 9.50
- Evaluation 9.47
- Examples 9.53
- Generally 9.27, 9.29, 9.35
- Government Auditing Standards reporting 4.13–.21, 4.54
- Indicators 9.52
- Magnitude of potential noncompliance 19.50, 21.113
- Multiple deficiencies 9.48
- Professional judgment 9.51
- Reporting .... 4.13–.21, 4.54, 23.26, ... 23.34, 23.38
- Risk factors 9.46, 19.49
- Schedule of findings and questioned costs 13.38, 23.38
- Subrecipient monitoring .... 12.34–.36, ... 22.36
- Types of major programs 19.46

MATERIALITY
- Audit finding evaluation 10.54, 10.60
- Audit findings reporting 16.50–.52
- Audit planning considerations .... 6.50–.55, ... 16.47–.52
- Audit risk of noncompliance 16.25–.26
- Compliance audits ..... 6.50–.55, 10.10–.13, ... 10.54–.55, 16.49, 20.10–.13
- Financial statement audits .... 3.17–.18, 6.51, ... 16.48–.49
- Financial statement effects 10.55
- Pass-through awards 12.23, 22.24
- Schedule of expenditures of federal awards 7.05–.09, 17.09–.10
- Tolerable exception rate for compliance tests 11.82–.83, 21.83

MEDICAID .... 8.37, 12.05, 15.27, ... 17.32, 22.05

MEDICAID PAYMENTS 5.27

MEDICARE 15.27, 17.32

MEDICARE PAYMENTS 5.27

MISSTATEMENT. See noncompliance

MISSTATEMENTS. See also material misstatements 3.17, 3.35, 3.59

MODIFIED OPINION 4.03

MONITORING
- Control component 3.27
- Defined 9.07
- As internal control component 19.10
- Subrecipients .... 8.32, 11.27, 11.52, ... 12.06, 12.25–.36

MULTIPLE MAJOR PROGRAMS, AUDIT SAMPLING .... 11.42–.43, 11.92, ... 21.42–.43, 21.92

MULTIPLE ORGANIZATIONAL UNITS .... 9.19, ... 10.32, 11.44–.45, 19.22, 20.32, ... 21.44–.45

MULTIPLE TYPES OF COMPLIANCE REQUIREMENTS 11.26–.27

N

NATIONAL CREDIT UNION ADMINISTRATION 17.32

NATIONAL CREDIT UNION SHARE INSURANCE FUND 5.27, 15.27

NFP. See not-for-profit entities

NON-U.S.-BASED ENTITIES 5.20, 12.42

NONAUDIT SERVICE, DEFINTED 15.24

NONAUDIT SERVICES 2.17–.26, 2.30

NONCASH AWARDS 7.28–.31, 17.31–.35

NONCOMPLIANCE
- Audit risk of. See audit risk of noncompliance
- Communication about .... 4.72–.73, ... 5.18, 10.60
- Compliance audits 10.49–.62, 20.48–.61
- Compliance opinion 20.50–.53, 20.56
- Contracts and grant agreement provisions .... 4.35–.38, 4.40–.45, ... 4.55–.62, 10.60
- Control risk of. See control risk of noncompliance
- Detection risk of ... 6.32, 6.37, 16.29, 16.34
- Federal agency consideration of findings 20.57–.58
- Financial statement effect 20.54
- Government Auditing Standards reporting ..... 4.24, 4.31–.45, Exhibit 4-1 at ... 4.39, 4.55–.62, Table 4-3 at 4.82, 4.83
- Inherent risk of. See inherent risk of noncompliance
- Instances of noncompliance 20.48–.49
- With laws and regulations .... 3.43–.52, ... 4.31–.34
- Material. See material noncompliance
- Questioned costs 20.55–.58, 20.61
- Reporting .... 4.24, 4.31–.45, Exhibit 4-1 .... at 4.39, 4.55–.62, Table 4-3 .... at 4.82, 4.83
- Reporting of findings ... 4.55–.62, 10.49–.62, ... 10.69, 20.59–.61

NONCOMPLIANCE—continued
- Subrecipients .... 10.61, 12.39, 20.34, ... 22.36, 22.41
- Test of controls detection 9.39–.40

NONFEDERAL AWARDS, INCLUSION OF 7.23

NONFEDERAL ENTITY, DEFINED. *See also* pass-through awards ..... 12.02, 16.15, ... 22.02

NONSTATISTICAL SAMPLING .... 11.91, ... 11.93, 21.93

NOT-FOR-PROFIT ENTITIES (NFP) ...... 1.01, ... 1.11, 13.10, 23.10

NOTES TO SCHEDULE OF EXPENDITURES OF FEDERAL AWARDS, REQUIRED INFORMATION 17.22

O

OBJECTIVES, AUDIT. *See* audit objectives

OBSERVATION, IN COMPLIANCE AUDITS 11.13, 21.13

OFFICE OF MANAGEMENT AND BUDGET (OMB) COMPLIANCE SUPPLEMENT. *See* Compliance Supplement

OFFICE OF MANAGEMENT AND BUDGET (OMB) DIRECTOR, AUTHORITY 5.02

OFFICE OF MANAGEMENT AND BUDGET (OMB) UNIFORM GUIDANCE. *See* Uniform Guidance

ON-SITE REVIEWS 6.72–.73, 16.72–.73

OPERATING EFFECTIVENESS OF INTERNAL CONTROL, TESTS OF. *See* tests of controls

OPINION
- Adverse .... 4.03, 13.22, 23.15, ... 23.22
- Compliance audits .... 20.03, 20.50–.53, ... 20.56
- Disclaimer of. *See* disclaimer of opinion
- Federal award audit report 15.21
- Financial statement audits 4.46–.47
- In-relation-to .... 17.06–.12, 17.19, 17.36, ... 23.19
- Insufficient subrecipient monitoring system 22.36, 22.38
- Issuing an opinion on schedule of expenditures of federal awards 7.32–.34
- Issuing an opinion under AU-C Section 805 .... 17.36–.38
- Modified 4.03
- Qualified .... 4.03, 13.11, 13.22–.24, ... 23.11, 23.22–.25
- Reporting audit findings 16.12, 23.38
- Requirement for 23.03
- Schedule of expenditures of federal awards 23.11, 23.20

OPINION—continued
- Scope of audit limitations 23.23–.25
- As sole responsibility of external auditor 16.61

OPPORTUNITIES, FRAUD RISK FACTORS .... Table 16-1 at 16.46

OTHER CLUSTERS, FEDERAL PROGRAMS 5.31, 15.31

OTHER-MATTER PARAGRAPHS .... 4.03, ... 7.18, 13.11, 17.19, 23.29

OVERSIGHT AGENCIES .... 4.86–.87, ... 5.44–.45, 6.70, 15.44–.45, 16.70

OVERSIGHT EXERCISED BY FEDERAL AGENCIES AND PASS-THROUGH ENTITIES 18.10, 18.30–.31

P

PASS, EXTERNAL PEER REVIEW REPORT 2.47

PASS-THROUGH AWARDS 22.01–.55
- Applicability of federal awards to subrecipients 22.03–.07
- Compliance audits 22.19–.45
- Contractor compliance 22.15–.18
- Contractor status characteristics 22.10–.11
- Defined 17.29, 22.02
- Expenditures .... 7.26–.27, 12.04, 12.37, ... 12.46, 12.49, 17.29–.30, 22.39, 22.48
- Generally 22.01
- Pass-through entity and subrecipient relationship 22.12
- Pass-through entity and subrecipient status together 22.14
- Recipient and contractor relationship ... 22.13
- Schedule of expenditures of federal awards .... 7.26–.27, 12.04, 12.37, 12.46, ... 12.49, 17.29–.30, 22.39, 22.48
- Subrecipient audit considerations 22.46–.49
- Subrecipient status characteristics .... 22.09, ... 22.11
- Transition considerations related to the Uniform Guidance 22.50–.55

PASS-THROUGH AWARDS, AUDIT CONSIDERATIONS 12.01–.49
- Circular A-133 applicability 12.03–.07
- Definitions 12.02
- For-profit subrecipients 12.41
- Generally 12.01
- Non-U.S.-based entities 12.42
- Pass-through entity audit considerations 12.18–.43
- Relationships of parties 12.12–.14
- State designation of cluster of programs 12.43
- Subrecipient audit considerations 12.44–.48

Subject Index

PASS-THROUGH AWARDS, AUDIT CONSIDERATIONS—continued
- Subrecipient distinguished from vendor status 12.08–.11
- Transition considerations related to the Uniform Guidance 12.49
- Vendor compliance considerations 12.15–.17

PASS-THROUGH ENTITIES. *See also* **contractors; subrecipients**
- Additional major program audit requests 8.25, 18.20
- Defined 12.02, 22.02
- Federal awards identification .... 7.03, ... 17.03–.04
- For-profit subrecipient contracts 12.41
- Management decision responsibility 20.58
- Non-U.S.-based entities 12.42
- Oversight and federal program risk 8.36–.37
- Relationship to contractor 22.13
- Relationship to subrecipients ...... 12.12–.14, ... 22.12
- Reporting 12.37–.40
- Single audit considerations ...... 12.18–.36, ... 15.25, 15.41, 22.19–.45
- Subaward identification 17.04
- Subrecipient compliance requirements 12.45
- Subrecipient monitoring procedures ..... 8.32, ... 11.27, 11.52, 12.06, 12.25–.36

PASS WITH DEFICIENCIES, EXTERNAL PEER REVIEW REPORT 2.47

PATTERN OF CONTROL DEVIATION AND COMPLIANCE EXCEPTIONS 11.101

PAYMENT METHODS FOR FEDERAL AWARDS 15.15

PAYMENTS, RECEIVED BY VENDOR FOR GOODS OR SERVICES 12.05, 12.10

PCAOB. *See* **Public Company Accounting Oversight Board**

PEER REVIEW, EXTERNAL 2.46–.50

PERCENTAGE-OF-COVERAGE RULE .... 8.16, ... 8.18, 8.21, 18.17, 18.35, 18.38

POPULATION, DEFINING 11.33–.38

POPULATION FOR COMPLIANCE TESTING
- Defining 21.33–.38
- Expected population exception rate 21.84–.85
- Procedures applied to every item 21.18–.20
- Size compared to sample size 21.49
- Testing of small populations ..... Table 21-3 at 21.86, 21.86–.89

POPULATION SIZE, SAMPLE SIZE EFFECTS 11.49

PORTIONS OF ENTITY NOT AUDITED 4.74–.76

PRECEDING PERIOD AUDITED BY ANOTHER AUDITOR 16.18

PRIOR AUDIT FINDINGS. *See also* **summary schedule of prior audit findings**
- Auditee responsibilities .... 15.34, 20.62–.63, ... 23.46–.50
- Auditor follow-up 15.23, 20.64–.67
- Auditor responsibilities 20.64
- Federal program risk criteria 18.28
- Reporting 23.46–.50
- Tests to evaluate effectiveness of controls 19.35

PRIOR AUDITS, MAJOR PROGRAM DETERMINATION. *See also* **summary schedule of prior audit findings 8.29–.35, 18.12**

PROCUREMENT OF AUDIT SERVICES 15.24

PROCUREMENT TESTS 12.28, 22.31

PROFESSIONAL JUDGMENT
- Assessing material noncompliance due to fraud 16.43
- Audit sampling 11.114, 21.03, 21.38
- Clusters of programs 21.46–.47
- Communications with other entities 3.15
- Compliance audits ...... 10.06, 15.18, 16.05, ... 20.06, 20.14
- Component auditor references 4.83
- Government Auditing Standards .... 1.08, ... 2.06, 2.31–.32
- Group audit considerations 16.57
- In identifying individually important items 21.22
- Loan and loan guarantee continuing compliance requirements 17.34
- Low assessed level of control risk of noncompliance 9.23, 19.25
- Major program determination ..... 8.13, 8.23, ... 8.28, 18.14, 18.19
- Materiality 12.23
- Pass-through awards 12.11, 22.11
- Population size 11.87
- Reporting findings under GAS .... Table 4-1 .... at 4.12
- Significant deficiency or material weakness in internal control over compliance 9.51
- Test of operating effectiveness of internal control over compliance 19.26, 19.39
- Working with other auditors 23.31

PROFESSIONAL SKEPTICISM 2.32, 3.38

PROGRAM CLUSTERS. *See* **clusters of programs**

PROGRAM PERIOD 6.19–.20

PROGRAM-SPECIFIC AUDITS ..... 14.01–.17, ... 24.01–.16
- Abuse considerations 14.12
- Audit guide availability 14.04–.05, 24.04
- Auditee responsibilities 14.06, 24.06

PROGRAM-SPECIFIC AUDITS—continued
- Auditor responsibilities 14.07–.12, 24.07
- Auditor's illustrative reports 14.17
- Auditor's reports 14.09–.11
- Circular A-133 requirements 14.02–.03
- Compliance audits .... 14.07, 15.01, ... 15.46, 20.01
- Compliance Supplement as resource for 16.24
- Data collection form 24.13, 24.15
- Defined 24.01
- Examples .... Appendix at 24.16
- Financial statements 24.10–.11
- Generally 5.46, 14.01, 24.01
- Illustrative auditor's reports .... Appendix at 24.16
- Reporting 24.09–.15
- Requirements when audit guide not available 24.05–.08, 24.14
- Uniform Guidance requirements applicable to 24.03
- Using to satisfy Uniform Guidance requirements 24.02

PROJECT GRANTS 5.13, 15.14

PROPERTY AND GOODS, SALE, EXCHANGE, OR DONATION OF 5.13

PROTECTED PERSONALLY IDENTIFIABLE INFORMATION (PROTECTED PII) 19.06, 23.66

PUBLIC COMPANY ACCOUNTING OVERSIGHT BOARD (PCAOB) 1.03

Q

QUALIFIED OPINION .... 4.03, 13.11, ... 13.22–.24, 23.11, 23.22–.25

QUALITY CONTROL AND ASSURANCE, GOVERNMENT AUDITING STANDARDS 2.06, 2.43–.45

QUALITY CONTROL STANDARDS, OVERVIEW OF STATEMENTS .... Appendix A

QUESTIONED COSTS. *See also* **schedule of findings and questioned costs**
- Analyzing observed deviations or exceptions 21.102
- Audit findings decision 21.126
- Calculating likely 21.118–.122
- Compliance opinion effects 10.57
- In conclusion on tests of compliance 21.129–.130
- Defined 10.56
- Federal agency consideration 10.58–.59
- Likely questioned costs .... 10.62, ... 11.117–.122, 11.126, 13.38
- Noncompliance evaluation and reporting 20.55–.58, 20.61
- Pass-through awards 12.40
- Reporting 10.62, 11.08–.09
- Reporting audit findings 23.38

QUESTIONED COSTS—continued
- Reporting requirement 21.08–.09
- Schedule of. *See* Schedule of Findings and Questioned Costs
- Subrecipient level 22.42
- Transition considerations related to the Uniform Guidance 23.61

R

RANDOM SELECTION 11.94, 21.94

RATIONALIZATIONS, FRAUD RISK FACTORS .... Table 16-1 at 16.46

R&D. *See* **research and development**

R&D CLUSTER, FEDERAL PROGRAMS 15.31

REASONABLE CARE 2.32

RECIPIENT OF FEDERAL AWARD, DEFINED 12.02

RECIPIENTS
- Defined 22.02
- Eligibility for compliance audit 22.03
- Multiple status 22.08

RECONCILIATIONS, DEFINED AS NONAUDIT SERVICES 2.18

REFERENCE MATERIALS, UNIFORM GUIDANCE 15.57

REFERENCE NUMBERS .... 4.62, 13.32, ... 23.43

REFERENCE OPTION, COMPONENT AUDITOR REFERENCES 4.78–.82

REGULATIONS AND LAWS, COMPLIANCE WITH .... 3.43–.52, 4.31–.34, ... 4.40–.45, 4.55–.62

REISSUED REPORTS .... 13.29–.30, ... 23.29–.30

REPORTING 23.01–.67, 24.01–.16
- By auditors. *See* auditor's reports
- Basis of accounting 23.09
- Circular A-133 audits. *See also* Circular A-133 audit reporting .... 13.01–.58, ... Appendix at 14.17
- Corrective action plan summary 23.46, 23.50
- Deviation from GAAP by federal awarding agency regulation 23.10
- Examples .... Appendix at 23.67, ... Appendix at 24.16
- Follow-up 15.23
- Fraud .... 4.07, 4.24–.30, ... Exhibit 4-1 at 4.39, 4.39–.45, 23.38
- GAAS ...... 4.06, 13.02, Table 13-1 at 13.08
- Government Auditing Standards. *See* Government Auditing Standards reporting
- Illustrative reports .... 23.06–.07, 23.67, ... Appendix at 23.67, Appendix at 24.16

Subject Index

REPORTING—continued
- Internal control over compliance. *See also* internal control over financial reporting and on compliance, report on .... 13.21–.28, ... 23.21–.28
- Materiality level for audit findings ... 16.50–.52
- Noncompliance .... 4.24, 4.31–.45, ... Exhibit 4-1 at 4.39, 4.55–.62, ... Table 4-3 at 4.82, 4.83
- Other auditors 23.31
- Overview .... 23.01–.08, 23.03–.08, ... Table 23-1 at 23.08
- Partial nature of audit 23.32
- Pass-through awards 22.39–.42
- Prior audit findings 23.46–.50
- Program-specific audits 24.01–.16
- Reissuance of Uniform Guidance compliance report 23.29–.30
- Schedule of expenditures of federal awards .... 5.21, 7.18, 13.11–.20, ... 13.27–.28, 17.18–.19, ... 23.11–.20, 23.27
- Schedule of findings and questioned costs 23.33–.44, 23.61
- Significant deficiency in internal control over compliance ...... 4.07, 4.13–.21, Table 4-2 .... at 4.22, 4.54, 23.38
- Single compliance audit .... Table 15-1 .... at 15.08, 15.21–.23
- Submission of auditee's report. *See* reporting package
- Subrecipients 12.39, 12.48, 13.52, 22.54
- Tests of controls 4.08
- Timing for compliance audit 15.22
- Transition considerations related to the Uniform Guidance 23.60–.66
- Uniform Guidance 23.01–.67
- When audit does not encompass entirety of auditee's operations 23.32

REPORTING PACKAGE
- Auditee responsibilities ..... 5.38–.39, 13.05, ... 15.38–.39, 23.05
- Circular A-133 audit reporting .... 5.22, ... 5.38–.39, 13.05, 13.48–.50, 14.13–.16
- Distribution to federal agencies ... 13.53–.54, ... 23.56–.57
- Program-specific audit 24.13–.15
- Schedule of expenditures of federal awards 5.38
- Submission of 23.05, 23.54–.55
- Timing of completion 16.20
- Transition considerations related to the Uniform Guidance 23.66

REPRESENTATIONS. *See* written representations

REPRESENTATIVE SAMPLE GOAL FOR COMPLIANCE TESTING 21.91

RESEARCH AND DEVELOPMENT (R&D) .... 5.10, 5.40, 9.54, ... 10.26, 15.31

RESPONSIBLE OFFICIALS, VIEWS OF 4.63–.66

RETENTION OF DOCUMENTS .... 6.12, ... 16.54–.55

REVIEWS, DESK OR ON-SITE ...... 6.72–.73, ... 16.72–.73

RISK. *See also* **audit risk of noncompliance**
- Aggregation 6.58, 16.58
- Assessing. *See* risk assessment
- Criteria for federal program 18.23–.32
- Major program determination. *See* risk-based approach, major program determination
- Sampling .... 11.110–.112, 11.123–.126, ... 21.110–.112, 21.123–.126
- Significant 3.31

RISK ASSESSMENT
- Audit planning 6.33–.49
- Component of internal control .... 19.10, ... 19.12–.13
- Defined 9.07
- Direct and material compliance requirements 16.30, 20.33
- Documentation 9.55, 18.18
- Financial statement audits 3.23–.31
- Internal control over compliance .... 9.14, ... 16.30–.32, 16.33
- Major program determination .... 8.16–.17, ... Table 8-3 at 8.17, 8.22–.23, ... 8.28–.38
- Major programs 16.30, 16.33–.34
- Material noncompliance .... 16.36–.46, ... Table 16-1 at 16.46, 19.12–.14
- Methods 11.29
- Objectives 9.09
- Subrecipient monitoring procedures 12.32
- Testing sample size table and inputs ... 21.70
- Timing 11.11, 11.70

RISK-BASED APPROACH, MAJOR PROGRAM DETERMINATION .... 8.03–.27, ... 18.03–.39
- Application flowchart ...... Exhibit 8-1 at 8.03, ... Exhibit 18-1 at 18.02
- Audit planning 6.24, 16.21
- Current audit experience 18.24–.27
- Deviation from risk criteria use 8.24
- Documentation of risk assessment 18.18
- Factors 6.22
- Federal programs not recently audited as major 18.29
- First-year audit exception 8.24
- Generally 5.29, 8.03
- High-risk type B programs .... 8.03, 8.15–.20, ... 18.14–.15, 18.23–.32, 18.36–.37
- Inherent risk of noncompliance 18.32
- Initial-year audits 16.19
- Loan and loan guarantee effects on type A program determination .... 8.07–.09, ... Table 8-2 at 8.09
- Low-risk auditees 5.30, 8.26–.27, 18.21

RISK-BASED APPROACH, MAJOR PROGRAM DETERMINATION—continued
- Low-risk type A programs .... 8.03, 8.11–.14, ... 18.09–.12, 18.36
- Major program criteria 8.18
- Major program determination .... 15.29, ... 16.19, 16.21, Exhibit 18-1 at 18.02
- Oversight by federal agencies and pass-through entities 18.30–.31
- Percentage-of-coverage rule ...... 8.16, 8.18, ... 8.21, 18.17, 18.35, 18.38
- Prior audit experience 18.28
- Requests for additional major programs 8.25
- Risk assessment criteria and documentation .... 8.16–.17, Table 8-3 .... at 8.17, 8.22–.23
- Risk criteria 8.24, 8.28–.38, 18.22–.32
- Transition considerations related to the Uniform Guidance 18.33–.39
- Type A and type B programs .... 8.03–.10, ... Table 8-1 at 8.05, 18.03–.08, ... Table 18-1 at 18.04, Table 18-2 .... at 18.07, 18.10–.12, 18.22
- Type A low-risk programs .... 8.03, 8.11–.14, ... 18.09–.12, 18.36
- Type A program not considered low risk at request of federal awarding agency ... 18.13
- Type B high-risk programs ... 8.03, 8.15–.20, ... 18.14–.15, 18.23–.32, 18.36–.37

S

SAFE HARBORS 8.08
SAFEGUARDS 2.11
SALE, EXCHANGE, OR DONATION OF PROPERTY AND GOODS 5.13, 15.14
SAMPLE SIZE DETERMINATION ... 11.58–.89
- For audit 21.58–.89
- Compliance testing .... 11.70–.89, ... Table 11-2 at 11.72
- Control testing .... Table 11-1 at 11.59, ... 11.59–.69
- Generally 11.58

SAMPLE SIZE FOR AUDIT 21.58–.89
- Compared to population size 21.49
- Determining ....21.58–.69, ... Table 21-1 at 21.59
- Generally 21.58
- Testing small populations .... Table 21-3 .... at 21.86, 21.86–.89
- Testing table and inputs .... 21.70–.85, ... Table 21-2 at 21.72

SAMPLING, GENERALLY. *See* audit sampling
SAMPLING RISK .... 11.110–.112, ... 11.123–.126, 21.110–.112, ... 21.123–.126
SAMPLING UNIT 11.39–.41, 21.39–.41
SCANNING 11.17, 11.25

SCHEDULE OF CHANGES MADE TO TEXT FROM PREVIOUS EDITION ... Appendix B
SCHEDULE OF EXPENDITURES OF FEDERAL AWARDS 7.01–.35, 17.01–.43
- Additional information 17.24
- Audit considerations 7.05–.18
- Audit requirements 15.06, 17.13–.16
- Auditee responsibilities .... 5.05, 5.33, 15.06, ... 15.33, 16.10, 17.13
- Basis of accounting .... 17.20, ... Table 17-1 at 17.20
- CFDA number as not available 17.28
- Dating of report on 13.16–.19
- Generally 7.01–.02, 17.01–.02
- Identification of federal awards 7.03–.05
- Illustrative example 7.36, 17.43
- In-relation-to opinion .... 17.06–.12, 17.19, ... 17.36, 23.19
- Inclusion of nonfederal awards 17.26
- Internal control over compliance ... 17.15–.16
- Issuing an opinion on 7.32–.34
- Issuing an opinion under AU-C Section 805 .... 17.36–.38
- Lack of agreement with other federal award reporting 17.25
- Major program determination 8.04
- Management representations 17.17
- Modifications when reporting on ... 13.14–.15
- Noncash awards 7.28–.31, 17.31–.35
- Objectives of single audit 15.04
- Overview 15.05–.06
- Pass-through awards .... 7.26–.27, 12.04, ... 12.37, 12.46, 12.49, 17.29–.30, ... 22.39, 22.48
- Presentation 7.19–.25
- Program-specific audits 14.06
- Providing additional information 17.24
- Reporting .... 5.21, 7.18, 13.11–.20, ... 13.27–.28, 17.18–.19, 23.11–.20, ... 23.27
- Reporting package 5.38
- Required content 17.21–.23
- Single audit objectives 5.03–.05
- In single audit report 23.11–.20
- State award considerations 17.27
- Subsequent events 17.18
- Timing of expenditure 22.04
- Transition considerations related to the Uniform Guidance 7.35, 17.39–.42
- Type A and B major program determination 18.03

SCHEDULE OF FINDINGS AND QUESTIONED COSTS 23.33–.44
- Abuse considerations 23.40
- Abuse findings 13.39
- Audit findings 13.38, 13.40–.41
- Auditee responsibilities 10.63, 20.62
- Auditor's reports .... 13.06, Table 13-1 at 13.08, 13.33–.43
- Communicating to management 23.45

Subject Index

SCHEDULE OF FINDINGS AND QUESTIONED COSTS—continued
- Compliance opinion 10.52
- Corrective action plan 20.67
- Detail of findings 23.41–.42
- Elements 10.60, 13.34
- Financial statement findings 23.36–.37
- Findings related to federal awards ..... 13.38, ... 23.38–.39
- Findings related to financial statements 13.36
- Follow-up on prior audit findings .... 20.66, ... 23.46–.47
- Generally 13.43, 23.33
- Likeliness of questioned costs 10.62
- Program-specific audits 14.09
- Reference numbers 13.32, 23.43
- Reporting .... 13.35, Table 13-2 at 13.35, ... 23.03, 23.06, 23.26, 23.34–.35, ... Table 23-2 at 23.35, 23.44
- Situations without findings or questioned costs 13.43
- Transition considerations related to the Uniform Guidance 23.60–.61, 23.66

SCHEDULE OF PRIOR AUDIT FINDINGS. *See* summary schedule of prior audit findings

SCOPE OF AUDIT ...... 4.75–.76, 13.23–.25, ... 14.07

SELECTING SAMPLE ITEMS FOR TESTING IN COMPLIANCE AUDIT 21.90–.98

SENSITIVE AND CONFIDENTIAL INFORMATION 4.29, 4.68–.71

SF-SAC. *See* data collection form

SFA. *See* Student Financial Assistance

SI. *See* supplementary information

SIGNFICANT CONTROLS, DETERMINING FOR TESTING 21.61–.63

SIGNIFICANCES LEVEL OF CONTROL 11.61–.64

SIGNIFICANT DEFICIENCY IN INTERNAL CONTROL OVER COMPLIANCE
- Assessing severity 19.47–.49
- Audit sampling to test for 21.63–.64
- Clusters of programs 9.54, 19.57
- Combination effect in assessing significance 19.51
- Compensating controls 9.49, 19.52
- Compliance audits 9.43–.45
- Component auditor references 4.82–.83
- Conditions for 19.44
- Defined 9.42, 19.45
- Design of controls 19.56
- Deviation rate 19.43
- Deviations in operating effectiveness of controls 9.50
- Evaluation 9.47
- Examples .... Appendix at 3.71, 9.53

SIGNIFICANT DEFICIENCY IN INTERNAL CONTROL OVER COMPLIANCE—continued
- Government Auditing Standards reporting .... 4.07, 4.13–.21, ... Table 4-2 at 4.22, 4.54
- Magnitude of potential noncompliance factor 19.50, 21.113
- Multiple deficiencies 9.48
- Operation of controls 19.56
- Reporting .... 4.07, 4.13–.21, Table 4-2 .... at 4.22, 4.54, 23.38
- Risk factors 9.46
- Schedule of findings and questioned costs 13.38
- Subrecipient monitoring 12.34–.36
- Tests of controls .... 9.27, 9.29, 9.35, ... 9.41–.54, 19.44–.57
- Type of major program 19.46

SIGNIFICANT RISK 3.31

SINGLE AUDIT. *See also* Circular A-133; compliance audits; Uniform Guidance 15.04–.48
- Applicability to Uniform Guidance compliance audit 16.03
- Audit costs 15.25
- Audit risk of noncompliance 16.26
- Auditee responsibilities 15.33–.39
- Auditor selection 15.24
- Basis for determining when federal awards are expended 15.26–.27, 17.11
- Cognizant agency for audit 15.42–.43
- Contractor determination 15.28
- Federal awarding agency responsibilities 15.40
- General audit requirements 15.09–.20
- Generally 15.01–.02
- Government-wide evaluation of single audit quality 15.47
- Internal auditors' assistance with ... 16.68–.69
- Major program determination 15.29–.32
- Objectives of Single Audit .... 15.04–.08, ... Table 15-1 at 15.08
- Oversight agency for audit 15.44–.45
- Pass-through entities 15.41, 22.19–.45
- Program-specific audits 15.46
- Purpose 15.02
- Reporting matters 15.21–.23
- Subrecipient determination 15.28
- Threshold for requirement of 18.33

SINGLE AUDIT ACT (1984). *See also* specific topics
- Audit cost charged to federal award 5.25
- Audit documentation access and retention 6.11
- Audit threshold 5.08
- Compliance 5.06
- Compliance Supplement based on 5.48
- Generally 5.01–.02
- Subrecipient monitoring 12.25

SINGLE AUDIT ACT (1984)—continued
- Terminology in guide comparable to 1.11
- Transition considerations related to the Uniform Guidance 5.49

SINGLE AUDIT ACT AMENDMENTS (1996) **1.01**

SMALL POPULATIONS .... **Table 11-3** .... **at 11.86, 11.86–.89, Table 21-3** .... **at 21.86, 21.86–.89**

SPECIAL PURPOSE FRAMEWORK ...... **6.17,** **16.13, 23.09**

SPECIALISTS **2.41–.42**

STAND-ALONE OPINIONS **13.20**

STANDARDS FOR INTERNAL CONTROL IN THE FEDERAL GOVERNMENT ..... **19.05,** **19.63–.64**

STATE AND LOCAL GOVERNMENTS
- Additional audit requirements 1.10
- Cluster of programs designation .... 12.43, ... 22.45
- Combining of federal awards 15.12
- Compliance audits 10.75, 20.74
- Compliance requirements 6.71, 16.71
- Frequency of federal award audit 15.19
- Government Auditing Standards 1.01
- Inclusion in schedule of expenditures of federal awards 17.26
- Medicare or Medicaid arrangements as federal expenditure 15.27
- Portions of entity not audited 4.76
- Reporting requirements for awards 7.23–.24

STATISTICAL SAMPLING ...... **11.91, 11.93,** **21.93**

STRATEGY, AUDIT **3.08–.09**

STUB PERIODS **6.20, 16.17**

STUDENT FINANCIAL ASSISTANCE (SFA) .... **5.10, 8.08, 9.54, 10.26,** **15.31, 18.12, 20.26**

SUBAWARDS
- Defined 22.02, 22.51
- Monitoring subrecipients 22.30
- Required information for document 22.52
- Schedule of expenditures of federal awards 17.04
- Uniform Guidance applicability to 15.50

SUBCONTRACTING **6.59**

SUBRECIPIENTS. See also pass-through awards
- Additional audit considerations 22.46
- Additional compliance requirements ... 12.45, ... 22.47
- Audit findings 10.61, 12.47, 22.40
- Characteristics indicative of federal award received by 12.09
- Circular A-133 audit considerations 12.44–.48

SUBRECIPIENTS—continued
- Combined with pass-through entity 22.14
- Defined 7.26, 12.02, 17.29, 22.02
- Determination of 17.04, 17.21
- Determining status versus contractor ...22.22
- Eligibility for compliance audit 22.03
- Federal program risk 18.27
- Internal control over compliance .... 9.20, ... 19.23
- Major program designation 22.23
- Monitoring of pass-through award 22.40
- Monitoring systems ...... 8.32, 11.27, 11.52, ... 12.06, 12.25–.36
- Noncompliance 10.61, 12.39
- Pass-through entities' responsibilities to 12.19
- Relationship to pass-through entities ... 12.12, ... 12.14, 22.04, 22.06, 22.12
- Reporting 12.39, 12.48, 13.52, 22.54
- Schedule of expenditures of federal awards 12.46
- Status characteristics for pass-through awards 22.09, 22.11
- Status determinations ...... 5.28, 12.08–.11, ... 15.28, 22.08–.11
- Transition considerations related to the Uniform Guidance 23.63

SUBSEQUENT EVENTS ..... **7.17, 10.46–.48,** **13.28, 17.18, 20.45–.47, 23.28**

SUBSTANTIVE PROCEDURES .... **9.36, 9.38,** **11.70**

SUGGESTED AUDIT PROCEDURES, COMPLIANCE AUDIT APPLICABLE TO MAJOR PROGRAMS **20.42**

SUMMARY SCHEDULE OF PRIOR AUDIT FINDINGS. See also prior audit findings
- Auditee responsibilities .... 10.63–.64, 13.45, ... 15.34, 20.62–.63, 23.46–.50
- Auditor follow-up ...... 10.64–.67, 13.46–.47, ... 15.23, 20.64–.67, 23.46–.50
- Generally 5.34, 15.34
- Management representations 10.73
- Program-specific audits .... 14.06, 14.07, ... 24.07
- Reporting 23.46–.50
- Reporting package inclusion 5.38

SUPPLEMENTARY AUDIT REQUIREMENTS, IDENTIFYING **16.07**

SUPPLEMENTARY INFORMATION (SI). See also schedule of expenditures of federal awards **13.13, 23.13–.18**

SYSTEMATIC SELECTION WITH RANDOM START **21.97–.98**

SYSTEMIC DEVIATIONS OR EXCEPTIONS **11.101, 21.101**

SYSTEMIC SELECTION WITH RANDOM START **11.97–.98**

Subject Index

T

TECHNICAL KNOWLEDGE, SKILLS, AND EXPERIENCE 2.36

TERMINOLOGY USE, GOVERNMENT AUDITING STANDARDS ....1.11, ... 1.16–.19

TERMS OF ENGAGEMENT ....1.15, ... 3.04–.07, 6.08–.09, 16.08–.09, ... 20.29–.32, 22.37

TESTS OF COMPLIANCE .... 10.33–.44, ... 20.34–.44
- Abuse consideration 20.44
- Audit objectives 20.41
- Audit sampling related to .... 11.18–.28, ... 11.70–.89, 11.106–.130, 20.43, ... Table 21-3 at 21.86, 21.86–.89
- Circular A-133 audits .... 5.06–.07, ... Table 5-1 at 5.07
- Generally 10.33, 20.34–.36
- Government Auditing Standards 4.39
- Individually important items in ..... 11.21–.28, ... 21.21–.28
- Material noncompliance at major program level 10.13
- Objectives 11.07
- Procedures 10.34–.44
- Purpose 11.07
- Reaching a conclusion on 11.128–.130
- Single Audit Act 5.06
- Sufficient audit evidence 20.37–.40
- Suggested procedures 20.42

TESTS OF CONTROLS .... 9.21–.54, ... 19.24–.57
- Audit sampling related to .... 11.29–.30, ... 11.59–.69, 11.110–.112, 21.29–.30, ... 21.52–.57, 21.110–.112
- Cluster program considerations 19.57
- Compared to understanding controls ... 19.19
- Control risk of noncompliance .... 9.21–.22, ... 9.23–.36, 19.07, 19.24–.32
- Documentation 9.56, 19.59
- Evaluating results 9.35–.40, 19.37–.43
- Financial statement audits 3.34–.35
- Government Auditing Standards reporting 4.08
- Ineffective internal control in preventing or detecting noncompliance 9.27–.29
- Limitations 9.16
- Material weakness findings 19.44–.57
- Overall conclusion on 21.114–.115
- Performing tests 19.33–.36
- Procedures and timing 9.30–.33
- Program-specific audits 14.07
- Purpose 11.07, 21.07
- Reporting 4.08
- Significant deficiencies and material weaknesses ... 9.27, 9.29, 9.35, 9.41–.54, ... 19.44–.57
- Timing 11.11, 21.11

THOSE CHARGED WITH GOVERNANCE, COMMUNICATION WITH
- Auditor responsibilities 3.61–.65
- Fraud 3.42, 4.27–.29
- Internal control deficiencies 4.14–.21
- Legal and regulatory compliance .. 3.49, 4.32
- Noncompliance 10.60

THOSE CHARGED WITH GOVERNANCE, DEFINED 3.63

THREATS TO INDEPENDENCE 2.09–.11

THRESHOLD, AUDIT 5.08, 15.09, 18.33

TIMING OF AUDIT COMPLETION AND REPORT SUBMISSION DEADLINES .... 6.23, 14.13, 15.22, ... 16.20, 24.12

TOLERABLE DEVIATION RATE ....11.67, ... 11.107, 21.67, 21.107

TOLERABLE EXCEPTION RATE ... 11.82–.83, ... 21.82–.83

TRANSITION CONSIDERATIONS. *See* **Uniform Guidance, transition considerations related to**

TYPE A MAJOR PROGRAMS
- Criteria ....Table 18-1 at 18.04
- Determination of ......18.03–.04, 18.06–.13, ... Table 18-2 at 18.07, 18.22
- Loan and loan guarantee effects ....8.07–.09, ... Table 8-2 at 8.09, 18.06–.07, ... Table 18-2 at 18.07
- Low-risk ...8.03, 8.11–.14, 18.09–.12, 18.36
- Major program determination ....8.03–.10, ... Table 8-1 at 8.05
- Not considered low risk at request of federal agency 18.13
- Percentage of coverage rule 18.17
- Transition consideration related to the Uniform Guidance 18.33

TYPE B MAJOR PROGRAMS
- Determination of 18.03, 18.05
- High-risk ....8.03, 8.15–.20, 18.14–.15, ... 18.23–.32, 18.36–.37
- Major program determination 8.04–.10
- Percentage of coverage rule 18.17
- Risk assessment criteria and documentation ....Table 8-3 at 8.17
- Transition consideration related to the Uniform Guidance 18.36–.37

U

UNALLOWABLE AUDIT COSTS FOR SUBRECIPIENTS 22.35

UNDERSTANDING ENTITY AND ITS ENVIRONMENT, FINANCIAL STATEMENT AUDITS 3.23–.31, 16.30–.32

UNDERSTANDING OF INTERNAL CONTROL OVER COMPLIANCE .... 9.12–.20, ... 9.27, 19.11–.23

...NCE (TITLE 2 CFR PART ...RM ADMINISTRATIVE ...NTS, COST PRINCIPLES, ...REQUIREMENTS ...RAL—*continued*
  · ....Appendix at 24.16
  · Audit pla....ng 16.01–.78
  · Audit sampling 21.01–.137
  · Compliance audits 20.01–.78
  · Internal control over compliance 19.01–.65
  · Major program determination 18.01–.39
  · Pass-through awards 22.01–.55
  · Program-specific audits 24.01–.16
  · Reporting 23.01–.67
  · Schedule of expenditures of federal awards 17.01–.43
  · Timing of audit requirements 15.50–.53
  · Transition considerations. *See* Uniform Guidance, transition considerations related to

UNIFORM GUIDANCE, TRANSITION CONSIDERATIONS RELATED TO
  · Audit findings 23.61–.62
  · Audit planning 6.75–.78, 16.75–.78
  · Audit sampling ... 11.136–.137, 21.136–.137
  · Circular A-133 and ..... 5.49, 6.75–.78, 7.35, ... 8.39, 9.59–.60, 10.76–.79, ... 11.136–.137, 12.49, 13.56–.137, ... 15.52, 17.39, 20.76, 23.61
  · Compliance audits .... 10.76–.79, 15.50–.57, ... 20.75–.78
  · Data collection form 23.64
  · Fraud 23.61
  · Generally 15.50–.57
  · Internal control over compliance .... 9.59–.60, ... 19.62–.65
  · Major programs .... 8.39, ... 16.77, 18.33–.39, 20.75–.78
  · OMB Compliance Supplement ..... 20.76–.77, ... 23.65
  · Pass-through awards 12.49, 22.50–.55
  · Questioned costs 23.61
  · Reporting 23.60–.66
  · Risk-based approach, major program determination 18.33–.39
  · Schedule of expenditures of federal awards 7.35, 17.39–.42
  · Schedule of findings and questioned costs 23.60–.61, 23.66

UNIFORM GUIDANCE, TRANSITION CONSIDERATIONS RELATED TO—*continued*
  · Single Audit Act (1984) 5.49
  · Subrecipients 23.63

UNMODIFIED OPINION 13.11, 13.23

UNRESOLVED AUDIT FINDINGS .... **10.69,** **20.68**

V

VENDORS
  · Characteristics indicative of a payment for goods or services received by 12.09
  · Compliance considerations 12.15–.17
  · Defined 12.02
  · Pass-through award relationships ...... 12.01, ... 12.11, 12.13
  · Payments received by 12.05
  · Removal of term from Uniform Guidance. *See also* contractors 22.51
  · Status determinations 5.28, 12.08–.11

W

WALKTHROUGH PROCEDURES **11.13, 21.13**

WRITTEN COMMUNICATION
  · Alerts restricting use 3.62, 23.12
  · Component auditor's reported matters .... Table 4-3 at 4.82
  · Engagement letters 3.07
  · Government Auditing Standards, reporting under 4.72–.73
  · Management letters 4.72–.73

WRITTEN REPRESENTATIONS
  · Compliance audits .... 10.72–.74, 11.13, ... 20.71–.73
  · Financial statement audits 3.50, 3.67–.68
  · Legal and regulatory compliance 3.50
  · Refusal to provide 10.74, 20.73
  · Related to federal awards 20.71–.73
  · Schedule of expenditures of federal awards 7.16, 17.17

Y

YELLOW BOOK. *See* **Government Auditing Standards**